NEW DICTIONARY OF AMERICAN SLANG

NEW DICTIONARY OF AMERICAN SLANG

EDITED BY
ROBERT L. CHAPMAN, PH.D.

HARPER & ROW, PUBLISHERS, New York
Grand Rapids, Philadelphia, St. Louis, San Francisco
London, Singapore, Sydney, Tokyo, Toronto

1817

This work is based on the *Dictionary of American Slang* by Harold Wentworth and Stuart Berg Flexner.

Designed by Sidney Feinberg

Library of Congress Cataloging-in-Publication Data

Chapman, Robert L.
  New dictionary of American slang.

  Rev. ed. of: Dictionary of American slang / compiled
and edited by Harold Wentworth and Stuart Berg Flexner.
2nd supplemented ed. 1975.
  1. English language—United States—Slang—
Dictionaries. 2. English language—Slang—
Dictionaries. 3. Americanisms—Dictionaries.
I. Wentworth, Harold, 1904–   Dictionary of
American slang. II. Title.
PE2846.C46 1986   427'.973   86-45086
ISBN 0-06-181157-2

  95 96 RRD 10 9

Contents

> . . . banish plump Jack, and banish all the world.
>
> *Henry IV*, Part 1

> Considering Language then as some mighty potentate, into the majestic audience-hall of the monarch ever enters a personage like one of Shakespere's clowns, and takes position there, and plays a part even in the stateliest ceremonies. Such is Slang, or indirection, an attempt of common humanity to escape from bald literalism, and express itself illimitably.
>
> Walt Whitman, "Slang in America"

Preface

The editor of a new dictionary of slang owes explanations to people at large and to those who use the book. To the public he should explain *why* such a book is made and deserves to be made. To the users he must explain *how* the book was made and how to use it. Finally, to all these and to himself, he must attempt to explain *what* slang is, anyway. (For a brief working answer to this last question, the reader may look up *slang* in this dictionary; for a more considered account, see below.)

Why This Book Was Made   The question will be: Why does a serious scholar devote himself to this uncouth sort of language, and why does he connive, worse yet, in foisting it on us and our innocent youth? Even though to a lexicographer that question is not very relevant, it is far from trivial. Dictionaries are popularly thought to have strong influence. They are thought to give validity and authority to their entries, and therefore to have social and moral impact. A dictionary like this, which specializes in terms not to be lightly used in polite society, is therefore thought of as teaching and advocating these terms, and hence akin to pornography.

The question may be answered in two veins, the theoretical and the historical. Theoretically, in linguistics any corpus or body of vocabulary is worth recording, and all are equally worthy. Linguistics, lexicography, is like a science in that its values have to do with accuracy, completeness, and demonstrability rather than with moral or social good. As a lexicographer I collect and record slang because it is there, and I take as much professional delight in a faithful transcript of all this nasty talk as I do in capturing and recording for our descendants the differing elegancies of standard language.

So, as a lexicographer I answer that I will collect every slang term I can get my hands on, will treat these as carefully and responsibly as I am able, and will leave their use up to others, who will have been warned against the undeliberate wielding of these powerful and provocative words. Yes, children will sneak off into corners with this book, and find the dirty words, and have dirty thoughts. If I believed that our whole culture could be made the least bit more decent, more respectful, more harmonious, happier, and mentally healthier by *not* making a slang dictionary, I might refrain. But I do not believe that and have not refrained.

This line of justification is nicely summed up in a story I heard Elie Wiesel tell: A magisterial historian was challenged with the question, "Why does a scholar like you occupy himself with a silly and contemptible subject like X?" To which the savant replied, "X is, as you say, silly and contemptible; but the *history* of X is scholarship!"

History of Slang Lexicography

In historical justification, this book joins itself to an Anglo-American tradition going back just over two hundred years, and of which the high spots may be mentioned.

Credit as founder of general slang lexicography, as distinct from those who dealt in specialized lexicons, goes to the distinguished British antiquarian Francis Grose, who published *A Classical Dictionary of the Vulgar Tongue* in 1785. After two further editions, the book became the basis of an 1811 updating and expansion called *Lexicon Balatronicum: A Dictionary of Buckish Slang, University Wit, and Pickpocket Eloquence,* of about 260 pages, with nearly five thousand defined entries. A half-dozen or so earlier compilations exist from as early as the 1560s, but they deal only in the special vocabularies of thieves and tramps. Grose's book and its successor include the slang of the so-called *balatrones*—"jesters, buffoons, contemptible persons; literally, babblers," who are urban dandies or men-about-town—and of the learned humorists of and from the universities, as well as of thieves.

Grose's work held the field until 1859, when it was superseded by John C. Hotten's *A Dictionary of Modern Slang, Cant, and Vulgar Words*, which had new editions in 1860, 1864, and 1874. The attribution to Hotten is not certain, since the book was anonymous, but it is generally accepted. Henry Bradley of the *Oxford English Dictionary* judged it "a work of considerable merit" and praised its scholarly authority.

In 1887 Albert M. V. Barrere, Professor of French at the Royal Military Academy in Woolwich, published at his own expense *Argot and Slang: A New French and English Dictionary.* Two years later the Ballantyne Press brought out for subscribers only *A Dictionary of Slang, Jargon & Cant*, in two volumes totaling 956 pages. Barrere had as collaborator Charles Godfrey Leland, an American. Leland had been a Philadelphia lawyer, a journalist and editor, a three-day barricades veteran of the 1848 Revolution in Paris, on the whole a rather Hemingwayish character, and was the first American to figure prominently in general slang lexicography. He had made a particular study of British gypsies and their language, and was the first to describe Shelta, a jargon of certain Irish and Welsh gypsies. The dictionary embraces "English, American, and Anglo-Indian slang, Pidgin English, tinkers' jargon and other irregular phraseology."

One year later the first volume of John Stephen Farmer and William Ernest Henley's *Slang and Its Analogues* was published, without Henley's name on the title page. Henley let his name be used on Volume 2 in 1891 and on the subsequent five volumes through 1904. He was a poet and editor, now undervalued as a poet though popularly known for the stirring *Invictus*, set to music as a virile baritone solo and ending "I am the master of my fate; I am the captain of my soul." Contemporary brief biographies of Henley refrain from mentioning the slang dictionary, and indeed his part in it is not well understood. Farmer, probably the originator and major author, was a prodigious scholar and editor, especially of Tudor drama and other texts of that epoch. His production comes to more than twenty volumes in that field alone. He also collected and edited six volumes of songs, especially of the "merry" sort. He wrote three books on spiritualism, a late Victorian craze. More to the point here, in 1888 he published *Americanisms Old and New*, "by J. S. F.," surely written as a preliminary by-product of his work on the seven-volume slang dictionary. An American authority on our national English, Richard H. Thornton, discovered that nine-tenths of the examples in Farmer's 564-page book came from material published in 1888. This indicates very great efficiency and/or a white-hot pace of work. When the Farmer and Henley work was completed in 1904, it amounted to 2736 pages.

A less useful contribution to general slang lexicography was James Maitland's 308-page *The American Slang Dictionary* of 1891. This book is not a jewel in the tradition, perhaps for the reasons that caused an anonymous reviewer in the *Nation* to observe that most of the entries were not American and not slang, and that the philological grounding of the editor was meager indeed. The review concluded, in cruelly measured words that make any slang lexicographer cringe in a nightmare, " . . . it must be said of the present work that it not only has no reason to show for its existence, but furnishes a good many reasons to suggest the desirability of its non-existence."

After Farmer and Henley, good general slang lexicography was not resumed until 1937, when Eric Partridge brought out the first edition of his masterwork, *A Dictionary of Slang and Unconventional English,* which was updated and enlarged in seven editions and numerous reprintings by Partridge himself through 1980 and has recently been posthumously revised and published in an eighth. Eric Partridge—New Zealander, Australian, Englishman, soldier, scholar, university teacher, essayist, novelist—is the lofty star at whose work and book all other slang lexicographers must hopelessly aim. He is also, for the twentieth century, the one who made slang lexicography more or less respectable and enabled us to cease lurking behind pseudonyms or anonyms or initials, or being privately and furtively printed.

The first full-scale dictionary of American slang had to wait until 1960, when Harold Wentworth and Stuart Berg Flexner's *Dictionary of American Slang* was published by Thomas Y. Crowell (a company now incorporated into Harper & Row). Professor Wentworth had previously written an *American Dialect Dictionary*, portions of which were adapted for the slang dictionary. Mr. Flexner added thousands of slang definitions from other sources and wrote the invaluable preface, our best treatment of the sociolinguistics of slang. The preface to that edition is reprinted in this book. He also did the immense analytical work reflected in the appendix, which treats the processes of word-formation in slang with unequaled authority and exhaustiveness. Flexner was responsible for final defining and editing of all the entries in the seven-hundred-page volume, which at once became the standard work in its field. Wentworth and Flexner, as it is usually called, was enlarged and updated in 1967 and 1975 and is the basis of the present book.

These are the theoretical and historical justifications of this book, to which a practical note must be added. First, obviously the book has a primary utility for people who find slang terms in their reading, or who overhear them, and need help with their meaning. Finally, it means to serve people who just plain enjoy slang and are curious about it and where it came from.

How This Book Was Made   This dictionary came into being in a five-stage process that may be quickly explained but was only slowly carried out.

1. Policies were determined and a "style manual" made that embodied these decisions on the format of the entries, their typefaces, their punctuation, the ordering of information, etc. The basic policies of the book are that it means to be a general dictionary of current American slang, rather than a collection of special vocabularies, a scholarly historical treatment, or a book with regional or other bias.
2. The Wentworth and Flexner *Dictionary of American Slang* was "recycled" and its wealth of material retained, altered, or discarded according to the new policies.
3. A corps of collectors was recruited for the accumulation of new material. At its most numerous this group consisted of fifty or more collectors, these dwindling as the years passed to an indefatigable hard core who are still submitting material as this preface is written. The collectors are listed, gratefully, at the end of the preface.
4. The definitions were written, rewritten, and then were edited and reedited by gimlet-eyed faultfinders whose crucial work is also acknowledged, gratefully, below.
5. Computers were used throughout in many ways. Citations were stored and sorted in computers. Entries were coded and typed directly onto discs, making editing and checking more easy, fast, and reliable. And, the typesetting was computer-generated.

Working by these stages and with this copious help, and having the advantage of standing on the strong shoulders of predecessors, making a dictionary is not the momentous and Olympian task it is popularly thought to be. It is simply an affair of knowing it can be done and knowing the practical steps to take. And working and worrying.

The style and apparatus of this dictionary are explained in the section called "Guide to the Dictionary."

What Is Slang?   In linguistics, where definitions at best are often imprecise and leaky, that of slang is especially notorious. The problem is one of complexity, such that a definition satisfying to one person or authority would seem inadequate to another because the prime focus is different. Like the proverbial blind men describing an elephant, all correctly, none sufficiently, we tend to stress one aspect or another of slang. My own stress will be on the individual psychology of slang speakers.

Sociolinguistic Aspects of Slang   The external and quantitative aspects of slang, its sociolinguistics, have been very satisfactorily treated, nowhere more so than in Stuart Berg Flexner's masterful preface to the *Dictionary of American Slang,* included in this book. Readers may also consult Eric Partridge's 1954 book *Slang To-Day and Yesterday,* in particular parts III and IV.

Updating Flexner's discussion of the social milieux from which American slang emerges would involve no real correction of his findings, but only an account of the historical shifts that twenty-five years have brought.

Recorded slang emerged, as the sketch of dictionaries has shown, from the special languages of subcultures, or perhaps we should call the more despised of them "undercultures." The group studied longest and most persistently has been the criminal underworld itself, including the prison population, whose "cant" or "argot" still provides a respectable number of unrespectable terms. Other undercultures contributing heavily are those of hoboes, of gypsies, of soldiers and sailors, of the police, of narcotics users, of gamblers, of cowboys, of all sorts of students, of show-business workers, of jazz musicians and devotees, of athletes and their fans, of railroad and other transportation workers, and of immigrant or ethnic populations cutting across these other subcultures.

In the 1980s, we must note that some of these traditional spawning grounds for slang have lost their productivity, and that other subcultures have emerged to replace them. For example, general adoption of terms from hoboes, from railroad workers, from gypsies, and from cowboys has very nearly ceased, although the contributions of all these persist in the substrata of current slang. Criminals and police (cops and robbers) still make their often identical contributions, and gamblers continue to give us zesty coinages. Teenagers and students can still be counted on for innovation and effrontery. Show business workers, although they have largely shed the raffish image of their roving and carnival past, are still a fertile source of slang. But several centers of gravity have shifted greatly during the past fifty or so years, as reflected in the entries of this book.

For example, the adoption of military, naval, and merchant marine slang has slowed to a relative trickle, not surprisingly. World Wars 1 and 2 probably gave us more general slang than any other events in history but they are now history, and the Korean and Vietnam wars have had in comparison a meager effect. Railroad slang has been replaced, though on a lesser scale, by the usage of airline workers and truck drivers. The jazz world, formerly so richly involved with drug use, prostitution, booze, and gutter life, is no longer so contributory, nor has rock and roll quite made up the loss, but taken as a whole, popular music—rock, blues, funk, rap, reggae, etc.—are making inroads.

Terms from "the drug scene" have multiplied astronomically, and a specialized book this size could easily be made from them alone. The "counterculture" helped disseminate many drug terms that might otherwise have remained part of a special vocabulary. Sports also make a much larger contribution, with football and even basketball not challenging but beginning to match baseball as prime producers. Among the immigrant-ethnic bestowals, the influx from Yiddish continues strong in spite of the sociological shifting of the Jewish population. The old Dutch and German sources have dried up. The Italian carries on in modest proportion. The Hispanic has been surprisingly uninfluential, although a heavier contribution is surely predictable. All these are far outstripped by increased borrowing from black America, and this from the urban ghetto rather than the old Southern heartland. Close analysis would probably show that, what with the prominence of black people in the armed forces, in music, in the entertainment world, and in street and ghetto life, the black influence on American slang has been more pervasive in recent times than that of any other ethnic group in history. This can be conjectured, of course, without any implication that black Americans constitute a homogeneous culture.

Some sources of the slang in this book will be entirely or relatively new. Examples of this are the computer milieu and the hospital-medical-nursing complex. In the first case an exciting technological inundation is at the base, and in the other, as in so many other trends of our era, the reason is television.

In the matter of sex, our period has witnessed a great increase in the number of terms taken over from homosexuals, expecially male homosexuals. And it would be wrong to restrict the range of their contribution to sex terms alone, since the gay population merges with so many others that are educated, witty, observant, acerbic, and modish.

The "growth sector" hardest to characterize just now is in linear descent from the people old Captain Francis Grose, and Ben Jonson and others before him, called "university wits." Today, trying to mark off this most fecund assemblage, I need a clumsy compound like "the Washington-Los Angeles-Houston-Wall Street-Madison Avenue nexus." Our culture occupies these centers, and they occupy the culture through pervasive and unifying communications media. They give us the slang of the brass, of the execs, of middle management, of dwellers in bureaucracies, of yuppies, and of the talk shows and the "people" sort of columns and magazines. Bright, expressive, sophisticated people, moving and prospering with our lively popular culture, and not entirely buying it. They are the trend-setters and source of the slang that seems to come from everywhere and not to be susceptible of labeling. We will need more historical perspective before we can be usefully analytic about them, but they, whoever they are, clearly make up the wave of the present.

This new emphasis in the fortunes of American slang, by the way, points to one of its important distinctions, that between what I call "primary" and "secondary" slang. Primary slang is the pristine speech of subculture members, so very natural to its speakers that it seems they might be mute without it. Of course they would not be, since we know that slang is by definition always an alternative idiom, to be chosen rather than required. Much of teenage talk, and the speech of urban street gangs, would be examples of primary slang. Secondary slang is chosen not so much to fix one in a group as to express one's attitudes and resourcefulness by *pretending*, momentarily, in a little shtick of personal guerilla theater, to be a member of a street gang, or a criminal, or a gambler, or a drug user, or a professional football player, and so forth—and hence to express one's contempt, superiority, and cleverness by borrowing someone else's verbal dress. Secondary slang is a matter of stylistic choice rather than true identification. The increasing currency of the "Washington-Los Angeles-Houston, etc.," sort of slang may mean that in the future secondary or acquired slang will be our major variety. That is, the old disreputable groups will blend gradually into the mass, and slang will become more a matter of individual wit and self-advertisement, with its sources no more apparent than those of, say, a dirty joke. In fact it may be conjectured that even now the strong influence of black slang and gay slang has less to do with those subcultures per se than with the fact that both put a very high premium on verbal skill. Blacks, for example, are particularly given to rhyme and other prosodic features that seem to be increasingly prominent in slang.

Individual Psychology of Slang   Obviously an individual in one of the groups or subcultures mentioned above, or any of many others, resorts to slang as a means of attesting membership in the group and of dividing him- or herself off from the mainstream culture. He or she merges both verbally and psychologically into the subculture that preens itself on being different from, in conflict with, and superior to the mainstream culture, and in particular to its assured rectitude and its pomp. Slang is thus an act of bracketing a smaller social group that can be comfortably joined and understood and be a shelter for the self. It is simultaneously an act of featuring and obtruding the self within the subculture—by cleverness, by control, by up-to-dateness, by insolence, by virtuosities of audacious and usually satirical wit, by aggression (phallic, if you wish). All this happens at fairly shallow levels in the psyche and can be readily understood. It explains most of what we know and feel about slang.

But what explains "it"? If, as the authorities agree, slang is a universal human trait and as old as the race itself, and if it came into being in the same human society where language itself was born, can we not seek deeper and more generalized explanations? Authorities also agree, as it happens, that the roots of slang must be sought in the deepest parts of the mind, in the unconscious itself. Although that territory is perilous ground for a working lexicographer, a few conjectures and a few relationships can be proposed for consideration.

It seems to me that the deeper psychodynamics of slang have to do with two things: (1) defense of the ego against the superego, and (2) our simultaneous eagerness and reluctance to be human.

Surely wounded egos are the most common human nonanatomic possession. Slang might be seen as a remedy for them, as a self-administered therapy old as the first family that spoke. The family, like society, entails a hierarchy of power and of right, against which the healthy growing self of the child needs measures to compensate for its weakness and sinfulness. Slang as a remedy denies the weakness and brags about the sinfulness.

In this view, it would not be too much to claim that therapeutic slang is necessary for the development of the self; that society would be impossible without slang. It is curious that a linguistic phenomenon that seems so fleeting and so frivolous, as slang undeniably does, should at the same time be so deep and so vital to human growth and order. This is only one of the paradoxes of slang.

This aspect of slang is "deeper" than the matters mentioned above, like group identification and so on, only because it existed before groups, and it persists as groups themselves chop and change in the flux of history. In this aspect slang is similar to, and perhaps the same as, profanity. Like profanity slang is a surrogate for destructive physical action. Freud once remarked that the founder of civilization was the first man who hurled a curse rather than a rock or spear at his enemy. Slang also has this usefulness, and I suspect that profanity is a subcategory of slang, the more elemental phenomenon.

Hence, slang is language that has little to do with the main aim of language, the connection of sounds with ideas in order to communicate ideas, but is rather an attitude, a feeling, and an act. To pose another paradox: Slang is the most nonlinguistic sort of language.

"Our simultaneous eagerness and reluctance to be human"—what can that have to do with slang? My notion here is that when you try to consider it deeply slang seems to join itself with several other phenomena: with Freud's "dream-work," with comedy, with elements of myth.

It seems to me that slang (I mean the slang impulse of the psyche) shares with all these the salvational and therapeutic function of both divorcing us from and maintaining our connection with genetic animality. Dream-work relieves us of the need to be reasonable and discharges the tension of the great burden with which our angelic rationality charges us. Although we are uncomfortable with paradox in ordinary language, we easily tolerate it in slang, where it seems as much at home as it is in the study of logic.

Slang links itself with comedy in the respect that it exploits and even celebrates human weakness, animality, without working to extirpate it. It makes room for our vileness, but only so much room. The great comic figures of our culture usually come in pairs, each member having its legitimacy, and each limiting the other: Sancho Panza and Don Quixote; Falstaff and Prince Hal; Huck Finn and who?—Tom Sawyer, Aunt Polly, even Jim. To these we may add the Wife of Bath, whose counterfigure was a part of herself, making her more like most of us than Sancho or Falstaff or Huck are. We may add, without too much strain, the comic figure Dante Alighieri over against Beatrice and the lightweight devil Mephistopheles over against Faust. What we seem to have in the comic heroes and in our own slang impulse is a reaching for or clinging to the primal earth, a *nostalgie de la boue*, which helps make tolerable the hard aspiration to be civilized and decent.

As to myth, Sancho, Alice of Bath, and Falstaff are modern myths themselves. For ancient myth we might think of Antaeus, whose strength was valid only while he had his feet on the earth, and of Silenus and the satyrs, and even of the Devil himself, who must, when he is not quoting scripture, speak a great deal of slang. We may also attend to the intriguing "trickster" figure who is so prevalent in world mythology. C. G. Jung reminds me of the slang impulse when he asserts, for example, ". . . [the trickster's] fondness for sly jokes and malicious pranks, his powers as a shape-shifter, his dual nature, half animal, half divine, his exposure to all kinds of tortures, and—last but not least—his approximation to the figure of a saviour." In the same essay, "On the Psychology of the Trickster-Figure," Jung relates the trickster to the medieval Feast of Fools and other manifestations of the comic and slang spirit, especially those that deflate pomp, that prick presumption, that trip up our high horses. Jung believed that the civilizing process began within the framework of the trickster myth, which is a race memory of the human achievement of self-consciousness.

As the literary scholar Wylie Sypher said, ". . . man is not man without being somehow uneasy about the 'nastiness' of his body, [and] obscenity . . . is a threshold over which man enters into the human condition." For *obscenity* we might read *slang*, and observe that we are not so far beyond the threshold that we cannot always reach it with our foot, which is of clay.

Slang is also the idiom of the life force. That is, it has roots somewhere near those of sexuality, and it regularly defies death. What I have in mind is partly the "dirty" and taboo constituent of slang, but even more its tendency to kid about being hanged, electrocuted, murdered, or otherwise annihilated. Gallows humor is, from this point of view, more central to slang than may have been thought.

One changing pattern that has obvious connections with both socio- and psycholinguistics is the relation of slang to gender. In these times, and partly because of the feminist movement, women are more and more using the taboo and vulgar slang formerly accounted a male preserve. Sociologically this shows the determination of some women to enter the power structure by taking on this badge, among others, that denotes "maleness," and simultaneously to shed the restrictions of the "ladylike" persona. Psychologically the implications are not that clear, but it may be that some women are determined to replicate at the core of their psyches the aggressive and ordering nature we have usually identified as a part of profound maleness, or else to show that these masculine traits do not lie as deep as we thought.

Apologies   Our aim has been to make a dictionary of current general American slang, but even a cursory look will show that we have retained from the *Dictionary of American Slang* many entries that are only dubiously current and not very general. We have done so for two reasons: (1) we felt that these would be helpful to readers baffled by slang found in earlier writings or writings that use earlier slang, and (2) some of these obsolete terms are aids in understanding the derivation of current terms.

In the absence of a litmus test for slang and nonslang we must ask some indulgence. Slang shares misty boundaries with a relaxed register usually called "informal" or "colloquial," and we have inevitably strayed across the boundary. Eric Partridge spared himself the embarrassment of this apology by calling his book the dictionary of "slang and unconventional English." This book should probably have the same title.

Slang also shares a boundary with a stylistic register we might call "figurative idiom," in which inventive and poetic terms, especially metaphors, are used for novelty and spice, and incidentally for self-advertisement and cheekiness, in relief of a standard language that is accurate and clear but not personal and kinetic. Here again we beg the indulgence of those who disagree with our choices, as we would hope to be indulgent of theirs.

We are interested in getting the book right, and would be grateful for corrections and suggestions. These can be addressed to the publisher.

—ROBERT L. CHAPMAN
May 1986

Preface to the
Dictionary of American Slang

by Stuart Berg Flexner

American slang, as used in the title of this dictionary, is the body of words and expressions frequently used by or intelligible to a rather large portion of the general American public, but not accepted as good, formal usage by the majority. No word can be called slang simply because of its etymological history; its source, its spelling, and its meaning in a larger sense do *not* make it slang. Slang is best defined by a dictionary that points out who uses slang and what "flavor" it conveys.

I have called all slang used in the United States "American," regardless of its country of origin or use in other countries.

In this preface I shall discuss the human element in the formation of slang (what American slang is, and how and why slang is created and used).

The English language has several levels of vocabulary:

Standard usage comprises those words and expressions used, understood, and accepted by a majority of our citizens under any circumstances or degree of formality. Such words are well defined and their most accepted spellings and pronunciations are given in our standard dictionaries. In standard speech one might say: *Sir, you speak English well.*

Colloquialisms are familiar words and idioms used in informal speech and writing, but not considered explicit or formal enough for polite conversation or business correspondence. Unlike slang, however, colloquialisms are used and understood by nearly everyone in the United States. The use of slang conveys the suggestion that the speaker and the listener enjoy a special "fraternity," but the use of colloquialisms emphasizes only the informality and familiarity of a general social situation. Almost all idiomatic expressions, for example, could be labeled colloquial. Colloquially, one might say: *Friend, you talk plain and hit the nail right on the head.*

Dialects are the words, idioms, pronunciations, and speech habits peculiar to specific geographical locations. A dialecticism is a regionalism or localism. In popular use "dialect" has come to mean the words, foreign accents, or speech patterns associated with any ethnic group. In Southern dialect one might say: *Cousin, y'all talk mighty fine.* In ethnic-immigrant "dialects" one might say: *Paisano, you speak good the English,* or *Landsman, your English is plenty all right already.*

Cant, jargon, and *argot* are the words and expressions peculiar to special segments of the population. *Cant* is the conversational, familiar idiom used and generally understood only by members of a specific occupation, trade, profession, sect, class, age group, interest group, or other sub-group of our culture. *Jargon* is the technical or even secret vocabulary of such a sub-group; jargon is "shop talk." *Argot* is both the cant and the jargon of any professional criminal group. In such usages one might say, respectively: *CQ-CQ-CQ . . . the tone of your transmission is good; You are free of anxieties related to interpersonal communication;* or *Duchess, let's have a bowl of chalk.*

Slang[1] is generally defined above. In slang one might say: *Buster, your line is the cat's pajamas,* or *Doll, you come on with the straight jazz, real cool like.*

Each of these levels of language, save standard usage, is more common in speech than in writing, and slang as a whole is no exception. Thus, very few slang words and expressions (hence very few of the entries in this dictionary) appear in standard dictionaries.

American slang tries for a quick, easy, personal mode of speech. It comes mostly from cant, jargon, and argot words and expressions whose popularity has increased until a large number of the general public uses or understands them. Much of this slang retains a basic characteristic of its origin: it is *fully* intelligible only to initiates.

Slang may be represented pictorially as the more popular portion of the cant, jargon, and argot from many sub-groups (only a few of the sub-groups are shown below). The shaded areas represent only general overlapping between groups:

1. For the evolution of the word "slang," see F. Klaeber, "Concerning the Etymology of Slang," *American Speech,* April 1926.

Eventually, some slang passes into standard speech; other slang flourishes for a time with varying popularity and then is forgotten; finally, some slang is never fully accepted nor completely forgotten. *O.K., jazz* (music), and *A-bomb* were recently considered slang, but they are now standard usages. *Bluebelly, Lucifer,* and *the bee's knees* have faded from popular use. *Bones* (dice) and *beat it* seem destined to remain slang forever: Chaucer used the first and Shakespeare used the second.

It is impossible for any living vocabulary to be static. Most new slang words and usages evolve quite naturally: they result from specific situations. New objects, ideas, or happenings, for example, require new words to describe them. Each generation also seems to need some new words to describe the same old things.

Railroaders (who were probably the first American sub-group to have a nationwide cant and jargon) thought *jerk water town* was ideally descriptive of a community that others called a *one-horse town*. The changes from *one-horse town* and *don't spare the horses* to a *wide place in the road* and *step on it* were natural and necessary when the automobile replaced the horse. The automobile also produced such new words and new meanings (some of them highly specialized) as *gas buggy, jalopy, bent eight, Chevvie, convertible,* and *lube*. Like most major innovations, the automobile affected our social history and introduced or encouraged *dusters, hitch hikers, road hogs, joint hopping, necking, chicken* (the game), *car coats,* and *suburbia*.

The automobile is only one obvious example. Language always responds to new concepts and developments with new words.

Consider the following:

wars: *redcoats, minutemen, bluebelly, over there, doughboy, gold brick, jeep.*
mass immigrations: *Bohunk, greenhorn, shillalagh, voodoo, pizzeria.*
science and technology: *'gin, side-wheeler, wash-and-wear, fringe area, fallout.*
turbulent eras: *Redskin, maverick, speak, Chicago pineapple, free love, fink, breadline.*
evolution in the styles of eating: *applesauce, clambake, luncheonette, hot dog, coffee and.*
dress: *Mother Hubbard, bustle, shimmy, sailor, Long Johns, zoot suit, Ivy League.*
housing: *lean-to, bundling board, chuckhouse, W.C., railroad flat, split-level, sectional.*
music: *cakewalk, bandwagon, fish music, long hair, rock.*
personality: *Yankee, alligator, flapper, sheik, hepcat, B.M.O.C., beetle, beat.*
new modes of transportation: *stage, pinto, jitney, kayducer, hot shot, jet jockey.*
new modes of entertainment: *barnstormer, two-a-day, clown alley, talkies, d.j., Spectacular.*
changing attitudes toward sex: *painted woman, fast, broad, wolf, jailbait, sixty-nine.*
human motivations: *boy crazy, gold-digger, money-mad, Momism, Oedipus complex, do-gooder, sick.*
personal relationships: *bunky, kids, old lady, steady, ex, gruesome twosome, John.*
work and workers: *clod buster, scab, pencil pusher, white collar, graveyard shift, company man.*
politics: *Tory, do-nothing, mug-wump, third party, brain trust, fellow traveler, Veep.*
and even hair styles: *bun, rat, peroxide blonde, Italian cut, pony tail, D.A.*

Those social groups that first confront a new object, cope with a new situation, or work with a new concept devise and use new words long before the population at large does. The larger, more imaginative, and useful a group's vocabulary, the more likely it is to contribute slang. To generate slang, a group must either be very large and in constant contact with the dominant culture or be small, closely knit, and removed enough from the dominant culture to evolve an extensive, highly personal, and vivid vocabulary. Teenagers are an example of a large subgroup contributing many words. Criminals, carnival workers, and hoboes are examples of the smaller groups. The smaller groups, because their vocabulary is personal and vivid, contribute to our general slang out of proportion to their size.

Whether the United States has more slang words than any other country (in proportion to number of people, area, or the number of words in the standard vocabulary) I do not know.[2] Certainly the French and the Spanish enjoy extremely large slang vocabularies. Americans, however, do use their general slang more than any other people.

American slang reflects the kind of people who create and use it. Its diversity and popularity are in part due to the imagination, self-confidence, and optimism of our people. Its vitality is in further part due to our guarantee of free speech and to our lack of a national academy of language or of any "official" attempt to purify our speech. Americans are restless and frequently move from region to region and from job to job. This hopeful wanderlust, from the time of the pioneers through our westward expansion to modern mobility, has helped spread regional and group terms until they have become general slang. Such restlessness has created constantly new situations which provoke new words. Except for a few Eastern industrial areas and some rural regions in the South and West, America just doesn't look or sound "lived in."

---

2. The vocabulary of the average American, most of which he knows but never uses, is usually estimated at 10,000–20,000 words. Of this quantity I estimate conservatively that 2,000 words are slang. Slang, which thus forms about 10 percent of the words known by the average American, belongs to the part of his vocabulary most frequently *used*.

The English language is now estimated to have at least 600,000 words; this is over four times the 140,000 recorded words of the Elizabethan period. Thus over 450,000 *new words or meanings* have been added since Shakespeare's day, without counting the replacement words or those that have been forgotten between then and now. There are now approximately 10,000 slang words in American English, and about 35,000 cant, jargon, and argot words.

Despite this quantity, 25 percent of all communication is composed of just nine words. According to McKnight's study, another 25 percent of all speech is composed of an additional 34 words (or: 43 words comprise 50 percent of all speech). Scholars do differ, however, on just which nine words are the most popular. Three major studies are: G. H. McKnight, *English Words and Their Background*, Appleton-Century-Crofts, Inc., 1923 (for spoken words only); Godfrey Dewey, "Relative Frequency of English Speech Sounds," *Harvard Studies in Education*, vol. IV, 1923 (for written words only); and Norman R. French, Charles W. Carter, and Walter Koenig, Jr., "Words and Sounds of Telephone Conversations," *Bell System Technical Journal*, April 1930 (telephone speech only). Their lists of the most common nine words are:

McKnight's speech	Dewey's written	Bell Telephone conversations
	a	a
and	and	
be		
have		
	in	
		I
	is	is
it	it	it
		on
of	of	
	that	that
the	the	the
to	to	to
will		
you		you

We often act and speak as if we were simply visiting and observing. What should be an ordinary experience seems new, unique, or colorful to us, worthy of words and forceful speech. People do not "settle down" in their jobs, towns, or vocabularies.

Nor do we "settle down" intellectually, spiritually, or emotionally. We have few religious, regional, family, class, psychological, or philosophical roots. We don't believe in roots, we believe in teamwork. Our strong loyalties, then, are directed to those social groups—or sub-groups as they are often called—with which we are momentarily identified. This ever-changing "membership" helps to promote and spread slang.

But even within each sub-group only a few new words are generally accepted. Most cant and jargon are local and temporary. What persists are the exceptionally apt and useful cant and jargon terms. These become part of the permanent, personal vocabulary of the group members, giving prestige to the users by providing their acceptance and status in the group. Group members then spread some of this more honored cant and jargon in the dominant culture. If the word is also useful to non-group members, it is on its way to becoming slang. Once new words are introduced into the dominant culture, via television, radio, movies or newspapers, the rapid movement of individuals and rapid communication between individuals and groups spread the new word very quickly.

For example, consider the son of an Italian immigrant living in New York City. He speaks Italian at home. Among neighborhood youths of similar background he uses many Italian expressions because he finds them always on the tip of his tongue and because they give him a sense of solidarity with his group. He may join a street gang, and after school and during vacations work in a factory. After leaving high school, he joins the navy; then he works for a year seeing the country as a carnival worker. He returns to New York, becomes a longshore-man, marries a girl with a German background, and becomes a boxing fan. He uses Italian and German borrowings, some teenage street-gang terms, a few factory terms, slang with a navy origin, and carnival, dockworker's, and boxing words. He spreads words from each group to all other groups he belongs to. His Italian parents will learn and use a few street-gang, factory, navy, carnival, dockworker's, and boxing terms; his German in-laws will learn some Italian words from his parents; his navy friends will begin to use some of his Italian expressions; his carnival friends a few navy words; his co-workers on the docks some carnival terms, in addition to all the rest; and his social friends, with whom he may usually talk boxing and dock work, will be interested in and learn some of his Italian and carnival terms. His speech may be considered very "slangy" and picturesque because he has belonged to unusual, colorful sub-groups.

On the other hand, a man born into a Midwestern, middle-class, Protestant family whose ancestors came to the United States in the eighteenth century might carry with him popular high-school terms. At high school he had an interest in hot rods and rock and roll. He may have served two years in the army, then gone to an Ivy League college where he became an adept bridge player and an enthusiast of cool music. He may then have become a sales execu-tive and developed a liking for golf. This second man, no more usual or unusual than the first, will know cant and jargon terms of teenage high-school use, hot rods, rock and roll, Ivy League schools, cool jazz, army life, and some golf player's and bridge player's terms. He knows fur-ther a few slang expressions from his parents (members of the Jazz Age of the 1920s), from listening to television programs, seeing both American and British movies, reading popular literature, and from frequent meetings with people having completely different backgrounds. When he uses cool terms on the golf course, college expressions at home, business words at the bridge table, when he refers to whiskey or drunkenness by a few words he learned from his parents, curses his next-door neighbor in a few choice army terms—then he too is popularizing slang.

It is, then, clear that three cultural conditions especially contribute to the creation of a large slang vocabulary: (1) hospitality to or acceptance of new objects, situations, and concepts; (2) existence of a large number of diversified sub-groups; (3) democratic mingling between these sub-groups and the dominant culture. Primitive peoples have little if any slang because their life is restricted by ritual; they develop few new concepts; and there are no sub-groups that mingle with the dominant culture. (Primitive sub-groups, such as medicine men or magic men, have their own vocabularies; but such groups do not mix with the dominant culture and their jargon can never become slang because it is secret or sacred.)

But what, after all, are the advantages that slang possesses which make it useful? Though our choice of any specific word may usually be made from habit, we sometimes consciously select a slang word because we believe that it communicates more quickly and easily, and more personally, than does a standard word. Sometimes we resort to slang because there is no one standard word to use. In the 1940s, *WAC, cold war,* and *cool* (music) could not be expressed quickly by any standard synonyms. Such words often become standard quickly, as have the first two. We also use slang because it often is more forceful, vivid, and expressive than are standard usages. Slang usually avoids the sentimentality and formality that older words often assume. Taking a girl to a *dance* may seem sentimental, may convey a degree of formal, emotional interest in the girl, and has overtones of fancy balls, fox trots, best suits, and corsages. At times it is more fun to go to a *hop*. To be *busted* or without a *hog* in one's *jeans* is not only more vivid and forceful than being penniless or without funds, it is also a more optimistic state. A *mouthpiece* (or *legal beagle*), *pencil pusher, sawbones, boneyard, bottle washer,* or a course in *biochem* is more vivid and forceful than a lawyer, clerk, doctor, cemetery, laboratory assistant, or a course in biochemistry—and is much more real and less formidable than a legal counsel, junior executive, surgeon, necropolis (or memorial park), laboratory technician, or a course in biological chemistry.

Although standard English is exceedingly hospitable to polysyllabicity and even sesquipedalianism, slang is not. Slang is sometimes used not only because it is concise but just because its brevity makes it forceful. As this dictionary demonstrates, slang seems to prefer short words, especially monosyllables, and, best of all, words beginning with an explosive or an aspirate.[3]

We often use slang *fad* words as a bad habit because they are close to the tip of our tongue. Most of us apply several favorite but vague words to any of several somewhat similar

3. Many such formations are among our most frequently used slang words. As listed in this dictionary, *bug* has 30 noun meanings, *shot* 14 noun and 4 adjective meanings, *can* 11 noun and 6 verb, *bust* 9 verb and 6 noun, *hook* 8 noun and 5 verb, *fish* 14 noun, and *sack* 8 noun, 1 adjective, and 1 verb meaning. Monosyllabic words also had by far the most citations found in our source reading of popular literature. Of the 40 words for which we found the most quotations, 29 were monosyllabic. Before condensing, *fink* had citations from 70 different sources, *hot* 67, *bug* 62, *blow* and *dog* 60 each, *joint* 59, *stiff* 56, *punk* 53, *bum* and *egg* 50 each, *guy* 43, *make* 41, *bull* and *mug* 37 each, *bird* 34, *fish* and *hit* 30 each, *ham* 25, *yak* 23, *sharp* 14, and *cinch* 10. (Many of these words, of course, have several slang meanings; many of the words also appeared scores of times in the same book or article.)

situations; this saves us the time and effort of thinking and speaking precisely. At other times we purposely choose a word because it is vague, because it does not commit us too strongly to what we are saying. For example, if a friend has been praising a woman, we can reply "she's *the bee's knees*" or "she's a real *chick*," which can mean that we consider her very modern, intelligent, pert, and understanding—or can mean that we think she is one of many nondescript, somewhat confused, followers of popular fads. We can also tell our friend that a book we both have recently read is *the cat's pajamas* or *the greatest*. These expressions imply that we liked the book for exactly the same reasons that our friend did, without having to state what these reasons were and thus taking the chance of ruining our rapport.

In our language we are constantly recreating our image in our own minds and in the minds of others. Part of this image, as mentioned above, is created by using sub-group cant and jargon in the dominant society; part of it is created by our choice of both standard and slang words. A sub-group vocabulary shows that we have a group to which we "belong" and in which we are "somebody"—outsiders had better respect us. Slang is used to show others (and to remind ourselves of) our biographical, mental, and psychological background; to show our social, economic, geographical, national, racial, religious, educational, occupational, and group interests, memberships, and patriotisms. One of the easiest and quickest ways to do this is by using counterwords. These are automatic, often one-word responses of like or dislike, of acceptance or rejection. They are used to counter the remarks, or even the presence, of others. Many of our fad words and many student and quasi-intellectual slang words are counterwords. For liking: *beat, the cat's pajamas, drooly, gas, George, the greatest, keen, nice, reet, smooth, super, way out,* etc. For rejection of an outsider (implying incompetence to belong to our group): *boob, creep, dope, drip, droop, goof, jerk, kookie, sap, simp, square, weird,* etc. Such automatic counters are overused, almost meaningless, and are a substitute for thought. But they achieve one of the main purposes of speech: quickly and automatically they express our own sub-group and personal criteria. Counterwords are often fad words creating a common bond of self-defense. All the rejecting counters listed above could refer to a moron, an extreme introvert, a birdwatcher, or a genius. The counters merely say that the person is rejected—he does not belong to the group. In uttering the counter we don't care what the person is; we are pledging our own group loyalty, affirming our identity, and expressing our satisfaction at being accepted.

In like manner, at various periods in history, our slang has abounded in words reflecting the fear, distrust, and dislike of people unlike ourselves. This intolerance is shown by the many derogatory slang words for different immigrant, religious, and racial groups: *Chink, greaser, Heinie, hunkie, mick, mockie, nigger, spik.* Many counters and derogatory words try to identify our own group status, to dare others to question our group's, and therefore our own, superiority.

Sometimes slang is used to escape the dull familiarity of standard words, to suggest an escape from the established routine of everyday life. When slang is used, our life seems a little fresher and a little more personal. Also, as at all levels of speech, slang is sometimes used for the pure joy of making sounds, or even for a need to attract attention by making noise. The sheer newness and informality of certain slang words produces a pleasure.

But more important than this expression of a more or less hidden esthetic motive on the part of the speaker is slang's reflection of the personality, the outward, clearly visible characteristics of the speaker. By and large, the man who uses slang is a forceful, pleasing, acceptable personality. Morality and intellect (too frequently not considered virtues in the modern American man) are overlooked in slang, and this has led to a type of reverse morality: many words, once standing for morally good things, are now critical. No one, for example, though these words were once considered complimentary, wants to be called a *prude* or *Puritan*. Even in standard usage they are mildly derisive.

Moreover, few of the many slang synonyms for drunk are derogatory or critical. To call a person a standard drunk may imply a superior but unsophisticated attitude toward drinking. Thus we use slang and say someone is *boozed up, gassed, high, potted, stinking, has a glow on,* etc., in a verbal attempt to convey our understanding and awareness. These slang words show that we too are human and know the effects of excessive drinking.

In the same spirit we refer to people sexually as *big ass man, fast, John, sex pot, shack job, wolf,* etc., all of which accept unsanctioned sexual intercourse as a matter of fact. These words are often used in a complimentary way and in admiration or envy. They always show acceptance of the person as a "regular guy." They are never used to express a moral judgment. Slang has few complimentary or even purely descriptive words for "virgin," "good girl," or "gentleman." Slang has *bag, bat, ex, gold digger, jerk, money mad, n.g., old lady, square,* etc.; but how many words are there for a good wife and mother, an attractive and chaste woman, an honest, hard-working man who is kind to his family, or even a respected elderly person? Slang —and it is frequently true for all language levels—always tends toward degradation rather than elevation. As slang shows, we would rather share or accept vices than be excluded from a social group. For this reason, for self-defense, and to create an aura (but not the fact) of modernity and individuality, much of our slang purposely expresses amorality, cynicism, and "toughness."

Reverse morality also affects slang in other ways. Many use slang just because it is not standard or polite. Many use slang to show their rebellion against *boobs, fuddy-duddies, marks,* and *squares.* Intellectuals and politicians often use slang to create the "common touch" and others use slang to express either their anti-intellectualism or avant-garde leanings. Thus, for teenagers, entertainers, college students, beatniks, jazz fans, intellectuals, and other large groups, slang is often used in preference to standard words and expressions. Slang is the "official" modern language of certain vociferous groups in our population.

In my work on this dictionary, I was constantly aware that most American slang is created and used by males. Many types of slang words—including the taboo and strongly derogatory ones, those referring to sex, women, work, money, whiskey,[4] politics, transportation, sports, and the like—refer primarily to male endeavor and interest. The majority of entries in this dictionary could be labeled "primarily masculine use." Men belong to more sub-groups than do women; men create and use occupational cant and jargon; in business, men have acquaintances who belong to many different sub-groups. Women, on the other hand, still tend to be

---

4. It would appear that the word having the most slang synonyms is *drunk*.

restricted to family and neighborhood friends. Women have very little of their own slang.[5] The new words applied to women's clothing, hair styles, homes, kitchen utensils and gadgets are usually created by men. Except when she accompanies her boy friend or husband to _his_ recreation (baseball, hunting, etc.) a woman seldom mingles with other groups. When women do mingle outside of their own neighborhood and family circles, they do not often talk of the outside world of business, politics, or other fields of general interest where new feminine names for objects, concepts, and viewpoints could evolve.

Men also tend to avoid words that sound feminine or weak. Thus there are sexual differences in even the standard vocabularies of men and women. A woman may ask her husband to set the table for dinner, asking him to put out the _silver, crystal,_ and _china_—while the man will set the table with _knives, forks, spoons, glasses,_ and _dishes._ His wife might think the _table linen_ attractive, the husband might think the _tablecloth_ and _napkins_ pretty. A man will buy a _pocketbook_ as a gift for his wife, who will receive a _bag._ The couple will live under the same roof, the wife in her _home,_ the man in his _house._ Once outside of their domesticity the man will begin to use slang quicker than the woman. She'll get into the _car_ while he'll get into the _jalopy_ or _Chevvie._ And so they go: she will learn much of her general slang from him; for any word she associates with the home, her personal belongings, or any female concept, he will continue to use a less descriptive, less personal one.

Males also use slang to shock. The rapid tempo of life, combined with the sometimes low boiling point of males, can evoke emotions—admiration, joy, contempt, anger—stronger than our old standard vocabulary can convey. In the stress of the moment a man is not just in a standard "untenable position," he is _up the creek._ Under strong anger a man does not feel that another is a mere "incompetent"—he is a _jerk_ or a _fuck-off._

Men also seem to relish hyperbole in slang. Under many situations, men do not see or care to express fine shades of meaning: a girl is either a _knockout_ or a _dog,_ liquor either _good stuff_ or _panther piss,_ a person either has _guts_ or is _chicken,_ a book is either _great_ or nothing but _crap._ Men also like slang and colloquial wording because they express action or even violence: we _draw pay, pull a boner, make a score, grab some sleep, feed our face, kill time_—in every instance we tend to use the transitive verb, making ourselves the active doer.

The relation between a sub-group's psychology and its cant and jargon is interesting, and the relation between an individual's vocabulary and psychological personality is even more so. Slang can be one of the most revealing things about a person, because our own personal slang vocabulary contains many words used by choice, words which we use to create our own image, words which we find personally appealing and evocative—as opposed to our frequent use of standard words merely from early teaching and habit. Whether a man calls his wife _baby, doll, honey, the little woman, the Mrs.,_ or _my old lady_ certainly reveals much about him. What words one uses to refer to a mother (_Mom, old lady_), friend (_buddy, bunkie, old man_), the bathroom (_can, John, little boy's room_), parts of the body and sex acts (_boobies, gigi, hard, laid, score_),

---

5. Women who do work usually replace men at men's jobs, are less involved in business life than men, and have a shorter business career (often but an interim between school and marriage). The major female sub-groups contributing to American slang are: airline stewardesses, beauty-parlor operators, chorus girls, nurses, prostitutes, and waitresses.

being tired (*all in, beat*), being drunk (*clobbered, high, lit up like a Christmas tree, paralyzed*), and the like, reveal much about a person and his motivations.[6]

The basic metaphors, at any rate, for all levels of language depend on the five senses. Thus *rough, smooth, touch; prune, sour puss, sweet; fishy, p.u., rotten egg; blow, loud; blue, red, square*. In slang, many metaphors refer to touch (including the sense of heat and cold) and to taste.

Food is probably our most popular slang image. Food from the farm, kitchen, or table, and its shape, color, and taste suggest many slang metaphors. This is because food can appeal to taste, smell, sight, and touch, four of our five senses; because food is a major, universal image to all people, all sub-groups; because men work to provide it and women devote much time to buying and preparing it; because food is before our eyes three times every day.

Many standard food words mean money in nonstandard use: *cabbage, kale, lettuce*. Many apply to parts of the body: *cabbage head, cauliflower ear, meat hooks, nuts, plates of meat*. Many food words refer to people: *apple, cold fish, Frog, fruitcake, honey, sweetie pie*. Others refer to general situations and attitudes: to *brew* a plot, to receive a *chewing out*, to find oneself *in a pickle* or something *not kosher*, to be unable to *swallow* another's story, to ask *what's cooking?* Many drunk words also have food images: *boiled, fried, pickled;* and so do many words for nonsense: *applesauce, banana oil, spinach*. Many standard food words also have sexual meanings in slang. The many food words for money, parts of the body, people, and sex reveal that food means much more to us than mere nourishment. When a *good egg brings home the bacon* to his *honey,* or when a *string bean* of a *sugar daddy* takes his *piece* of *barbecue* out to get *fried* with his hard-earned *kale*, food images have gone a long way from the farm, kitchen, and table.

Sex has contributed comparatively few words to modern slang,[7] but these are among our most frequently used. The use of sex words to refer to sex in polite society and as metaphors in other fields is increasing. Sex metaphors are common for the same conscious reasons that food metaphors are. Sex appeals to, and can be used to apply to, most of the five senses. It is common to all persons in all sub-groups, and so we are aware of it continually.

Slang words for sexual attraction and for a variety of sexual acts, positions, and relationships are more common than standard words. Standard nontaboo words referring to sex are so scarce or remote and scientific that slang is often used in referring to the most romantic, the most obscene, and the most humorous sexual situations. Slang is so universally used in sexual communication that when "a man meets a maid" it is best for all concerned that they know slang.[8] Slang words for sex carry little emotional connotation; they express naked desire or mechanical acts, devices, and positions. They are often blunt, cynical and "tough."

The subconscious relating of sex and food is also apparent from reading this dictionary. Many words with primary, standard meanings of food have sexual slang meanings. The body,

6. For just the last example, *clobbered* may indicate that a drinker is punishing himself, *high* that he is escaping, *lit up like a Christmas tree* that he is seeking attention and a more dominant personality, and *paralyzed* that he seeks punishment, escape or death.

7. Many so-called bedroom words are not technically slang at all, but are sometimes associated with slang only because standard speech has rejected them as taboo. However, many of these taboo words do have further metaphorical meanings in slang: *fucked, jerk, screw you*, etc.

8. On the other hand, Madame de Staël is reported to have complimented one of her favorite lovers with "speech is not his language."

parts of the body, and descriptions of each, often call food items into use: _banana, bread, cheese cake, cherry, jelly roll, meat,_ etc. Beloved, or simply sexually attractive, people are also often called by food names: _cookie, cup of tea, honey, peach, quail, tomato,_ etc. This primary relation between sex and food depends on the fact that they are man's two major sensuous experiences. They are shared by all personalities and all sub-groups and they appeal to the same senses—thus there is bound to be some overlapping in words and imagery. However, there are too many standard food words having sexual meanings in slang for these conscious reasons to suffice. Sex and food seem to be related in our subconscious.

Also of special interest is the number of slang expressions relating sex and cheating. Used metaphorically, many sex words have secondary meanings of being cheated, deceived, swindled, or taken advantage of, and several words whose primary meaning is cheating or deceiving have further specific sexual meanings: _cheating, fucked, make, royal screwing, score, turn a trick,_ etc. As expressed in slang, sex is a trick somehow, a deception, a way to cheat and deceive us. To curse someone we can say _fuck you_ or _screw you,_ which expresses a wish to deprive him of his good luck, his success, perhaps even his potency as a man.[9] Sex is also associated with confusion, exhausting tasks, and disaster: _ball buster, screwed up, snafu,_ etc. It seems clear, therefore, that, in slang, success and sexual energy are related or, to put it more accurately, that thwarted sexual energy will somehow result in personal disaster.

Language is a social symbol. The rise of the middle class coincided with the period of great dictionary makers, theoretical grammarians, and the "correct usage" dogma. The new middle class gave authority to the dictionaries and grammarians in return for "correct usage" rules that helped solidify their social position. Today, newspaper ads still implore us to take mail-order courses in order to "learn to speak like a college graduate," and some misguided English instructors still give a good speaking ability as the primary reason for higher education.

The gap between "correct usage" and modern practice widens each day. Are there valid theoretical rules for speaking good English, or should "observed usage" be the main consideration? Standard words do not necessarily make for precise, forceful, or useful speech. On the other hand, "observed usage" can never promise logic and clarity. Today, we have come to depend on "observed usage," just as eighteenth- and nineteenth-century social climbers depended on "correct usage," for social acceptance.

Because it is not standard, formal, or acceptable under all conditions, slang is usually considered vulgar, impolite, or boorish. As this dictionary shows, however, the vast majority of slang words and expressions are neither taboo, vulgar, derogatory, nor offensive in meaning, sound, or image. There is no reason to avoid any useful, explicit word merely because it is labeled "slang." Our present language has not decayed from some past and perfect "King's English," Latin, Greek, or pre-Tower of Babel tongue. All languages and all words have been, are, and can only be but conventions mutually agreed upon for the sake of communicating.

9. See F. P. Wood, "The Vocabulary of Failure," _Better English,_ Nov. 1938, p. 34. The vocabulary of failure is itself very revealing. Failure in one's personality, school, job, business, or an attempted love affair are all expressed by the same vocabulary. One gets the _brush off,_ the _gate,_ a _kiss off,_ or _walking papers_ in both business and personal relationships. As the previous discussion of counterwords demonstrates, slang allows no distinction or degree among individual failures. Incompetence does not apply to just one job or facet of life—either one belongs or is considered unworthy. This unworthiness applies to the entire personality, there are no alternate avenues for success or happiness. One is not merely of limited intelligence, not merely an introvert, not merely ugly, unknowing, or lacking in aggression—but one is a failure in all these things, a complete _drip, jerk,_ or _square._ The basic failure is that of personality, the person is not a mere failure—he is an outcast, an untouchable; he is taboo.

Slang came to America on the Mayflower. In general, it is not vulgar, new, or even peculiarly American: an obvious illustration of this is the polite, old French word *tête*, which was originally slang from a Latin word *testa*—cooking pot.

Cant and jargon in no way refer only to the peculiar words of undesirable or underworld groups. Slang does not necessarily come from the underworld, dope addicts, degenerates, hoboes, and the like. Any cultural sub-group develops its own personal cant and jargon which can later become general slang. All of us belong to several of these specific sub-groups using our own cant and jargon. Teenagers, steel workers, soldiers, Southerners, narcotic addicts, churchgoers, truck drivers, advertising men, jazz musicians, pickpockets, retail salesmen in every field, golf players, immigrants from every country, college professors, baseball fans—all belong to typical sub-groups from which slang originates. Some of these sub-groups are colorful; most are composed of prosaic, average people.

Many people erroneously believe that a fundamental of slang is that it is intentionally picturesque, strained in metaphor, or jocular. Picturesque metaphor (and metonymy, hyperbole, and irony) does or should occur frequently in all levels of speech. Picturesque metaphor is a frequent characteristic of slang, but it does not define slang or exist as an inherent part of it. The picturesque or metaphorical aspect of slang is often due to its direct honesty or to its newness. Many standard usages are just as picturesque, but we have forgotten their original metaphor through habitual use. Thus slang's *jerk* and *windbag* are no more picturesque than the standard *incompetent* and *fool*. *Incompetent* is from the Latin *competens* plus the negating prefix *in-* and = "unable or unwilling to compete"; *fool* is Old French, from the Latin *follis* which actually = "bellows or wind bag"; slang's *windbag* and the standard *fool* actually have the same metaphor.

As for picturesque sounds, I find very few in slang. Onomatopoeia, reduplications, harsh sounds and pleasing sounds, even rhyming terms, exist on all levels of speech. Readers of this dictionary will find no more picturesque or unusual sounds here than in a similar length dictionary of standard words. Many slang words are homonyms for standard words.

As has been frequently pointed out, many slang words have the same meaning. There seems to be an unnecessary abundance of counterwords, synonyms for "drunk," hundreds of fad words with almost the same meaning, etc. This is because slang introduces word after word year after year from many, many sub-groups. But slang is a scatter-gun process; many new words come at the general public; most are ignored; a few stick in the popular mind.

Remember that "slang" actually does not exist as an entity except in the minds of those of us who study the language. People express themselves and are seldom aware that they are using the artificial divisions of "slang" or "standard." First and forever, language is language, an attempt at communication and self-expression. The fact that some words or expressions are labeled "slang" while others are labeled "jargon" or said to be "from the Anglo-Saxon" is of little value except to scholars. Thus this dictionary is a legitimate addition to standard dictionaries, defining many words just as meaningful as and often more succinct, useful, and popular than many words in standard dictionaries.

Acknowledgments

Grateful acknowledgment is first made to the collectors who over the years have provided most of the new material in the book, and many examples of previously entered terms. The collectors are listed in three groups. The first have been so faithful, productive, and acute as to have become genuine colleagues. The second group have made very substantial contributions, and the third group important but lesser ones.

Palmer Price (Mrs. William Carl) Clark of Fairfax, Virginia
Bernard Kane of Ridley Park, Pennsylvania
Joseph Oleszycki of Philadelphia, Pennsylvania

Bernard Arkules of Scottsdale, Arizona
Jean Billman of Macon, Georgia
Brian A. Court of Vandalia, Ohio
Kendra Crossen of Somerville, Massachusetts
Porter J. Crow of West Palm Beach, Florida
Julie Downs of North Bend, Oregon
Maria Erskine of Pickering, Ontario, Canada
Elizabeth Glick of Whittier, California
Jeanne Goessling of Evanston, Illinois
William J. Griffin of Nashville, Tennessee
Paul Kocak of Dover, New Jersey
Stanley L. Korwin of San Francisco, California
Esther Lafair of Philadelphia, Pennsylvania
Virginia Langlois of Rutland, Vermont
Arlene Larson of Casper, Wyoming
Joyce Mahan of Tuscaloosa, Alabama
Altha Patten of Linden, New Jersey
Robert F. Perkins of Fort Atkinson, Wisconsin
Jane Sarnoff of New York, New York
John Shunny of Albuquerque, New Mexico
Judy Tucker of Elkins Park, Pennsylvania

Leslie R. Axelrod of Highland Park, Illinois
Dorothy M. Barrett of Elyria, Ohio

Nancy Burkhalter of Columbus, Ohio
John Campbell of Columbus, Georgia
Jane Closson of Winnemucca, Nevada
Jane Coil Cole of Madison, New Jersey
Keith Denning of Brooklyn, New York
David De Witt of Glenview, Illinois
Marjorie Glazer of Worcester, Massachusetts
Barry Goldstein of Newton Centre, Massachusetts
Stanley Gutin of Wilkes-Barre, Pennsylvania
Batya Harlow of Leonia, New Jersey
David L. Kent of Austin, Texas
Ruth McGrew of St. Paul, Minnesota
John T. Metcalf of Lake Forest, Illinois
Katherine Noordsij of Madison, New Jersey
Angela Palmisono of Ridgefield, New Jersey
Dorothy Powell of Huntington Beach, California
Lawrence C. Scholz of West Orange, New Jersey
Michael Silvia of Acushnet, Massachusetts
Betti Slack of Boulder, Colorado
Susan Welsh of Highland Park, New Jersey
Laura Winters of Totowa, New Jersey

Additional acknowledgment is gratefully made to those below for particular help and advice:

Robert S. Claiborne of New York City for collegial and very sage counsel
    and miscellaneous contributions
Captain Jack Gill for Army terms
Captain Jack B. Moser of Orlando for airline terms
Norman Roberts of Pearl City, Hawaii, for Hawaiian slang
Eva Witte

I must credit my dear wife Sarah for long-suffering support as this book, through thick and thin, gradually took shape. If dictionaries were dedicated, I would dedicate it to her.

Both the publishers and I have been enormously lucky to have Carol Cohen in keen and effective charge of the project.

—ROBERT L. CHAPMAN

A reference book would not be possible without the work of many people. The work on this book began at least six years ago in the office of Pat Barrett, reference editor of Thomas Y. Crowell. The citation collectors, listed above, were recruited and more editors became involved. Special thanks are due to Paul Heacock for his editorial and copyediting work as well as his many valuable editorial additions and suggestions that improved the dictionary. Thanks are due to Helen Moore and to Lucy Adelman O'Brien for their contributions to the editorial process. Copyediting was under the capable direction of Coral Tysliava. Computers were introduced to this dictionary very early when it was decided to store the collected citations, write the entries, edit, and do the necessary checking using computers. Dealing with the dictionary in this form became the responsibility of Roz Barrow, Harper & Row's director of production, who very ably directed the production of the handsome book you now hold in your hands. The complex computer work would not have been possible without Fred Alexander and Dan Kirklin of Alexander Typesetting, and special thanks are due to Gene Clarke for his understanding and support throughout this project. We are grateful to Jean Palmer, Debby Carpenter, and Portia Levine, who keyboarded and corrected the discs, and to Beena Kamlani, Scott Prentzas, Gail Gavert, Eric Wirth, and Brenda Woodward for proofreading and dealing with mountains of computer printouts.

—CAROL COHEN
Editorial Director, Trade Reference

Guide to the Dictionary

The editors have tried to make the apparatus of this book clear and self-explanatory, but a few guidelines may help the reader. These are given more or less in the order of the elements in the definition block itself.

The Main Entry   The main entry sometimes contains portions that do not appear in boldface and are not taken into account in alphabetization. These include the articles *a, an,* and *the,* when they appear at the beginning of an entry, and the variable pronoun in a phrase, indicated by *someone, someone's, something, one's,* etc. Variant forms following *or* and variants found within parentheses appear in boldface but do not affect alphabetization.

Impact Symbols   Main entries considered to have strong social or emotional impact are indicated by delta symbols bracketing the entry itself or the separate definition numbers if the impact symbol does not apply to all senses of the term. The symbols are assigned on a two-level principle, corresponding to what have usually been called "taboo" and "vulgar" levels. Taboo terms are *never* to be used, and vulgar terms are to be used only when one is aware of and desires their strong effect. In this book terms of contempt and derision for racial or other groups have been included among the taboo terms.

Terms of strongest impact are marked with the symbols ◄ ► and those of lesser impact with the symbols ◁ ▷. The assignment of these is a matter of editorial judgment, and not everyone will agree with us. In some places it was difficult to assign impact symbols to terms that are acceptable within a group but are considered offensive when used by those outside the group. We have taken account of recent changes in the currency and acceptability of terms previously unspeakable, and some may feel we have gone too far with the trend.

Pronunciations   Words are respelled for pronunciation only when "normal" pronunciation cannot be readily ascertained or when pronunciation is crucial to the meaning of the term. The system of respelling is designedly very simple, depending on what we regard as a majority pronunciation of the respelled syllable and showing stressed syllables in capital letters.

Part-of-Speech Labels   Parts of speech and a few other grammatical particulars are indicated by rather self-explanatory abbreviations or labels:

n	noun
v	verb
pron	pronoun
adj	adjective
adv	adverb
affirmation	
negation	
conj	conjunction
prep	preposition
interj	interjection
modifier	
infix	
phr	phrase
sentence	
pres part	present participle
past part	past participle
prefix	
suffix	
combining form	
combining word	

Variant Forms   Variation is shown in three ways:

1. In the main entry itself, up to three variants are shown, separated by *or.*
2. Where there are more than three variants, or they apply to various parts of the main entry, they are shown in parentheses with the label *Variations.*
3. Where variant forms apply to particular numbered definitions, this is shown by printing the form or forms at the beginning of the numbered sense, introduced by *also.*

Dating Labels   Even though this is not meant to be a full-fledged historical dictionary, the time of origin and/or special currency of the terms is shown by a dating phrase. These usually designate the early, middle, or late part of a century, or in more recent times they indicate decades of origin when known. All labels are based upon evidence found in published scholarship or lexicography, and most are of course subject to correction where better evidence is found.

When an entry does not carry a dating label, the inference is either that the date was undiscoverable or that the term is relatively recent and would have to be labeled *1970s* or *1980s.*

Provenience Labels   When the social group or milieu from which a term emerged is known, it is indicated by a labeling that is often intermixed with the dating labels; for example, *fr late 1800s cowboys,* or *esp 1960s teenagers.* Two abbreviations are used in provenience labels: *fr* for *from* and *esp* for *especially.* Some attempt at precision has been made in these labels, but they are regrettably sometimes rather vague and general. Nevertheless, no label has been applied without evidence.

Definitions   Definitions were written in what most users will accept as a normal form. A few explanations need to be made, however:

1. The usual distinction between transitive and intransitive verbs has not been used, in the belief that the definitions and the examples will make that distinction clear when useful.
2. After the label *sentence,* another sentence has been provided that translates the main entry sentence.
3. Interjections, prefixes and suffixes, and combining forms and words have been explained "objectively," with no attempt made to provide a strictly substitutable version of the form.
4. When a word is defined in one part of speech but is often used in others, it may be "defined by example" in this book. The most common case is the one where a noun is often used as an attributive modifier, which in this book is shown by the label *modifier* followed by a colon and by an example of the use. Definitions by example apply strictly only to part-of-speech shifts from the definition immediately preceding them.
5. Definitions are not always given in chronological order, even when that is known. The order is rather a logical-semantic one that attempts to show how senses have grown from previous senses. Sometimes the order can hardly be anything but arbitrary.

Slang Synonyms   Often slang synonyms will be provided at the ends of definitions, after an equal sign. This is meant to be an aid in definition rather than a serious comprehensive collection of synonyms.

Slang synonyms are also used as quick definitions when a full definition is given elsewhere, at a synonymous entry, usually at a more current or frequently used or interesting term. Slang synonyms are not used as cross-references to variant terms, although sometimes this distinction may not be a sharp one.

Editorial Notes   When certain information seems useful but does not fit into the normal format of the definition block, it is included as an editorial note. These are introduced by a large black dot.

Examples   In this book usage examples are given either when they have been collected from the media or when an invented example seems to help in definition or in showing context and structure. Examples thus have a double function: to illustrate usage and to validate usage and the inclusion of the term.

Examples are attributed to authors, especially when these are well known; when newspapers or magazines are cited, authors are generally not named, even though the articles may have had bylines. Attributions are to be taken essentially as evidence that the material quoted did in fact appear in the place or under the name cited. They are not, of course, to be taken as characterizing the typical style of the source.

Derivations   Derivations are given in square brackets at the end of the definition block proper, before the cross-references.

Slang etymology is less certain and precise than standard etymology, for two chief reasons: (1) because of the moral and social dubiousness of slang, relatively little of it was printed over the centuries, yielding less evidence than one needs; and (2) it is an etymology of meaning rather than form, and semantic connections are seldom as public, positive, and knowable as are formal relations. Hence slang etymology must be to an uncomfortable degree a matter of assessing probabilities.

Derivations are not given here when they are deemed to be obvious. When they are accepted and demonstrable, they are stated as fact. When probability, or even possibility, proposes them, they are stated tentatively. The ruling criterion has been common sense and occasionally another sense that in German is called *Sprachgefühl,* a sort of personal linguistic intuition.

In cases where a derivation seems patently necessary, but none can be discovered or surmised, the notation *origin unknown* is used. This must not be taken absolutely, but only to mean that the derivation is not now known to the editor.

A part of the fun of making a slang dictionary is the exercise of ingenuity and insight for derivations, especially those that have not apparently been proposed before. The editor does not apologize for his attempts, although he asks to be enlightened if ignorant and corrected if perverse.

Cross-References   An extraordinary attempt has been made to help the user find the term in question by cross-referencing nearly every important term in every phrase (prepositions, particles, articles, and the like are, of course, not cross-referenced). Since this book defines a very great number of phrasal entries, much space has been given to this purpose, and we hope these merely utilitarian features will not get in the way.

NEW DICTIONARY OF AMERICAN SLANG

A

A *narcotics* **1** *n* Amphetamine **2** *n* LSD; = ACID

See FROM A TO Z, Q AND A

AA (pronounced as separate letters) *armed forces fr WW1* **1** *n* An antiaircraft weapon, or antiaircraft fire; = ACK-ACK, FLAK **2** *modifier: an AA barrage/ AA battery*

abbot *n narcotics* Nembutal (a trade name), a barbiturate; = DOWNER [fr the name of the pharmaceutical company that produces it]

Abe's cabe *n phr jive talk fr 1930s & rock and roll fr 1950s* A five-dollar bill [fr the portrait of Lincoln on the bill, and perhaps fr a shortening and repronouncing of "cabbage"]

◀**Abie**▶ **1** *n* Any Jewish male **2** *n* A tailor

A-bomb **1** *n* An atomic bomb **2** *n hot rodders* A car especially modified for quick acceleration and speed; = HOT ROD **3** *n narcotics* A combination of drugs, typically marijuana or hashish plus opium

abortion *n* Something of very poor quality; a messy failure; = DISASTER: *That show is a real abortion*

about that See SORRY ABOUT THAT

about town See MAN-ABOUT-TOWN

above one's **head** See IN OVER one's HEAD

academy See LAUGHING ACADEMY

Acapulco gold *n phr narcotics* Marijuana of high quality grown near Acapulco, Mexico, and having leaves with a golden hue

accidentally on purpose *adv phr* As if by accident, but really by intention: *She missed the meeting accidentally on purpose*

accommodation collar *n phr police* An arrest made to fulfill a quota, usu in response to pressure for strong police action against crime

account See NO-ACCOUNT

accounting See CREATIVE ACCOUNTING

AC-DC (Variations: **AC/DC** or **ac-dc** or **ac/dc**) **1** *adj* Practicing both heterosexual and homosexual sex; bisexual **2** *adv: I think she does it AC-DC* [fr the abbreviations for the two types of electrical current, alternating and direct; an appliance that can operate with either type is marked *AC-DC*]

ace **1** *n* A person of extraordinary skill, usu in a specified activity: *poker ace/ the ace of headwaiters* **2** *modifier: an ace mechanic/ the ace professor* **3** *adv: He did it ace every time*—Richard Merkin **4** *n fr WW1* A combat pilot who has shot down five or more enemy aircraft **5** *n* An unusually

pleasant, generous, and decent person, esp a male; = PRINCE **6** *n black & street gang* A very close friend; = BUDDY, PAL **7** *n black* A man who favors flamboyant, up-to-the-minute dress; = DUDE **8** *n narcotics* A marijuana cigarette; = JOINT **9** *n* A dollar bill **10** *n golf* A hole scored in one stroke **11** *n racquet games* An unreturnable serve that scores a quick point **12** *v sports* To score by an ace: *He aced the fifth hole/ She aced him six times in one set* **13** *v* (also **ace out**) *college students* To make a perfect or nearly perfect score: *My sister aced the chemistry exam/ Ace the test and you go on to the next subject*—Flying **14** *n restaurant* A table for one; also, a single customer **15** *n lunch counter* A grilled cheese sandwich [fr the name of the unitary playing card]

See CASE ACE, CHINESE ACE, COME WITHIN AN ACE, COOL AS A CHRISTIAN WITH ACES WIRED

◁**ace boon coon**▷ or **ace boon** or **ace buddy** *n phr black* A very good friend; best friend

ace-deuce *n* Three, esp a three of playing cards

ace-high *adj* Of the best; first rate: *His reputation is ace-high*

ace in **1** *v phr* To use strategy in getting oneself into a good or profitable position **2** *v phr* To understand; = DIG

ace in the hole *n phr* Something held privately in reserve until needed, esp for a winning stroke; a hidden reserve or advantage [fr poker term *in the hole* for a card dealt face down in a stud game]

ace of spades ◀**1**▶ *n phr* A black person, esp a very dark one ◁**2**▷ *n phr* The female genitals [fr the color and shape of the playing-card symbol]

ace out See ACE

aces *adj* Of the very best quality; superior; finest: *I said it in this very sincere voice. "You're aces...."* —JD Salinger

aces wired See COOL AS A CHRISTIAN WITH ACES WIRED

ace up one's **sleeve** *n phr* A hidden advantage, esp a tricky one [fr a common technique of magicians and cardsharps]

acey-deucey **1** *adj* Of mixed quality; having both good and bad, high and low; ambiguous: *an acey-deucey proposition* **2** *adj* So vague, generalized, or inclusive as to offend no one; satisfactory; mediocre; = SO-SO [fr card games in which the *ace* is the highest and the *deuce* the lowest card in value]

1

acid *narcotics* **1** *n* The hallucinogen LSD, which is chemically an acid; =A **2** *modifier: an acid party*
See AUGUSTUS OWSLEY, BATTERY ACID

acid freak or **acidhead** *n phr* or *n narcotics* A person who uses LSD, esp one who uses the drug heavily or habitually: *He has suggested that some of our recent Presidents were acidheads*—Saul Bellow

acid pad *n phr narcotics* A place, esp someone's home or apartment, where LSD is taken

acid rock **1** *n phr* A form of very loud rock music featuring electronic sound effects and often accompanied by stroboscopic and other extraordinary lighting to suggest the hallucinatory impact of LSD **2** *modifier: an acid rock disk/ acid-rock guitar*

acid test *narcotics* **1** *n phr* A party at which LSD is added to food and drink **2** *v phr* To provide special effects at a party, usu of a psychedelic sort: *He acid tested his place with colored strobe lights* [a punning adaptation of the standard phrase, "a final and decisive test"]

ack-ack *armed forces fr WW1* **1** *n* Antiaircraft gun or guns; antiaircraft fire; =AA, FLAK **2** *modifier: ack-ack positions*

across the board **1** *adj phr horse-racing* Designating a bet in which the same amount of money is wagered on the horse to win, place, or show **2** *adv phr: Marcus bet $2 across the board on Duck Giggle in the fifth* **3** *adj phr* Designating an equal alteration to each member of a related set, esp an equal raising or lowering of related wages or salaries: *They got an across-the-board increase of 80 cents an hour* **4** *adv phr: The fees were lowered across the board* [fr the *totalizator board* that shows the odds at horse-racing tracks]

act **1** *n* A display of pretended feeling; an affected pretense: *His elaborate grief was just an act* **2** *n* A dramatic mimicking; =SHTICK, TAKEOFF: *You oughta see my Brando act*
See a CLASS ACT, CLEAN UP one's ACT, DO THE DUTCH, DUMB ACT, GO INTO one's ACT, SISTER ACT, TANK FIGHT

acting jack *n phr Army* An acting sergeant; soldier wearing the insignia of and having the authority of a sergeant but without the official rank

action **1** *n* Gambling activity; a crap game or other game of chance: *Most people now go to Atlantic City for the action* **2** *n* Activity or entertainment: *looking for the local action* **3** *n* The, or a, sex act: *He was ogling the girls, looking for a little action*
See a PIECE OF THE ACTION, WHERE THE ACTION IS

◁**act like** one's **shit doesn't stink**▷ *v phr* To behave with self-assured haughtiness; show a sense of superiority

actor *n sports* An athlete who is good at pretending he has been hurt or fouled; *esp*, a baseball player who very convincingly mimes the pain of being hit by a pitch
See BAD ACTOR

Ada from Decatur *See* EIGHTER FROM DECATUR

Adam *See* NOT KNOW someone FROM ADAM

add one's **two cents in** *See* PUT one's TWO CENTS IN

ad lib **1** *v phr* To speak, play, dance, or otherwise perform a passage not in one's prescribed plan, often with an original and spontaneous effect: *The Senator ad libbed for ten minutes waiting for the President to show* **2** *n phr* A passage or comment, etc, given spontaneously: *He forgot his lines and did a stupid ad lib* **3** *modifier: an ad-lib gag/ a quick ad-lib put-down* **4** *adv: They danced ad lib until the conductor found his place again* [fr Latin *ad libitum* "as one wishes"]

◁**adobe dollar**▷ *n phr* A Mexican peso

advantage *See* HOME-COURT ADVANTAGE

African black *n phr narcotics* A grade of marijuana grown in Africa

◀**African dominoes**▶ **1** *n phr* Dice **2** *n phr* The game of craps; =AFRICAN GOLF [fr the racist presumption that the game of craps is a specialty and a special weakness of blacks]

◀**African golf**▶ *n phr* The game of craps

Afro **1** *n* A hair style worn by many blacks and some whites, usu with an exaggerated bouffant style of tightly curled hair **2** *n* A black person **3** *modifier: an Afro social club*

◁**Afro-Saxon**▷ *n black* A black person who has assumed the behavior and values of the dominant white society; =OREO, TOM

against the wall *See* UP AGAINST THE WALL

agate *See* SHOOT THE AGATE

age out *v phr narcotics* To reach an age, usu in the 30s or 40s, when drugs no longer have the desired effect, whereupon the user gradually withdraws from them voluntarily

ager *See* GOLDEN-AGER

a-go-go *esp 1960s & 70s* **1** *n* A discotheque or other venue for rock-and-roll dancing **2** *modifier: a couple of a-go-go patrons/ a-go-go music* **3** *adj* Rapid and dizzying tempo: *our crazy a-go-go pace of life* **4** *adj* In the newest style; faddish; =TRENDY: *his a-go-go opinions about sexual freedom* [fr French *à gogo* "galore," used in the name of a Parisian club, *Whisky à Gogo*]
See GO-GO

agreement *See* SWEETHEART CONTRACT

ah *See* OOH AND AH

ahead *See* COME OUT AHEAD, STRAIGHT-AHEAD

A-head *narcotics* **1** *n* A frequent user of amphetamines **2** *n* =ACIDHEAD

ahead of the game *adv phr* In a winning or advantageous position: *Hard as I try, I can't seem to get ahead of the game*

-aholic *suffix used to form nouns and adjectives* Addicted to and overengaging in what is indicated: *fuckaholic/ sleepaholic/ workaholic*

something or **someone ain't** *negation* Something or someone emphatically is not ● Said as a wry and intensive negator in a comparative statement: *My joint? Buckingham palace it ain't/ Well, she sings OK, but Joan Sutherland she ain't* [perhaps fr a Yiddish syntactic pattern]

ain't hay *See* THAT AIN'T HAY

air *v* To broadcast by radio or television: *to air a new miniseries*
See A BEAR IN THE AIR, DANCE ON AIR, FLOATING ON AIR, FULL OF HOT AIR, GET THE AIR, GIVE someone THE AIR, GO UP IN THE AIR, GRAB A HANDFUL OF AIR, HOT AIR, OFF THE AIR, SUCK AIR, UP IN THE AIR

air one's **belly** *v phr* To vomit

air one's **dirty linen** *See* WASH one's DIRTY LINEN

airhead or **airbrain** *n* A stupid or silly person; vapid nincompoop; = BUBBLEHEAD, DITZ: *The steel-bellied airheads were in Lonnie's suite*—Dan Jenkins

airheaded or **airbrained** *adj* Stupid; silly; vapid; = BUBBLEHEADED, DITZY: *the delightfully airbrained Mickie*—Village Voice

airmail *n* Garbage thrown out of a window

air out *black* **1** *v phr* To stroll; saunter **2** *v phr* To leave; = SCRAM, SPLIT

airplane *n narcotics* A tweezerlike clip for holding a marijuana cigarette stub; = ROACH CLIP

airplay *n* The playing of a phonograph record on the radio: *after 18 months of spotty airplay and gigging*—Aquarian

airs *See* PUT ON AIRS

aisles *See* LAY THEM IN THE AISLES

◁**AK** or **ak**▷ (pronounced as separate letters) **1** *n* = ALTER KOCKER **2** *n* = ASS-KISSER

aka (pronounced as separate letters) *prep phr* Also known as; alias: *He's an asshole, aka a big deal*

Al or **Alfred** *n shoeshop* The shoe width A

Albert *n outdated pawnshop & underworld* A watch chain, esp a gold one [probably fr the common portraits of Albert, the Prince Consort of Queen Victoria of Great Britain, where he is shown wearing a conspicuous gold watch chain]
See FAT ALBERT

Alibi Ike *n phr* A person who habitually offers excuses and plausible explanations for dubious actions

alike *See* LOOK-ALIKE

alkied or **alkeyed** (AL keed) *adj* Drunk

alky or **alki** (AL kee) **1** *n* Alcohol **2** *n esp 1920s* Inferior or bootleg whiskey **3** *n* A chronic alcoholic, esp one who is a homeless drifter or street denizen; = BUM

all bases *See* TOUCH ALL BASES

all by one's **lonesome** *adv phr* Alone; solo: *She did it all by her lonesome*

all ears *adj phr* Very eager to hear; keenly attentive: *Something juicy's coming, and they're all ears*

alley *See* BACK ALLEY

Alley *See* TIN PAN ALLEY

alley apple **1** *n phr* (also **road apple**) A piece of horse manure **2** *n phr* A rock put into a stocking and used as an impromptu blackjack; = GROUND BISCUIT

alley cat **1** *n phr* A homeless cat; stray cat **2** *n phr* A sexually promiscuous person, esp a woman

all-fired *fr early 1800s* **1** *adv* To an extreme or extravagant degree: *Don't be so all-fired stupid* **2** *adj*: *He's got an all-fired lot of nerve* [a euphemism for *hell-fired*]

all fired up *See* FIRED UP

all fours *See* DOWN ON ALL FOURS

all get out or **all get up** *n phr fr late 1800s* The extreme or absolute case of what is indicated: *overwhelmingly white, and affluent as all get-out*—Ebony

all hanging out *See* HAVE IT ALL HANGING OUT

all hang out *See* LET IT ALL HANG OUT

all hell broke loose *sentence* Things became very turbulent, dangerous, noisy, etc: *All Hell Breaking Loose*—Time

all hollow *See* BEAT ALL HOLLOW

alligator **1** *n black* An assertively masculine, flashily dressed, and up-to-the-minute male; = DUDE, SPORT **2** *n esp 1930s jive talk* An active devotee of swing and jive music, dancing, and speech ● The salutation "See you later, alligator" was commonly heard **3** *n black jazz musicians* A white jazz musician or jazz enthusiast

◁**alligator bait**▷ *n phr black* A black person, esp one from Florida or Louisiana

alligators *See* UP TO one's ASS IN something

all in *adj phr fr early 1900s* Tired; exhausted; = BEAT, POOPED

all in one piece or **in one piece** *adv phr* Intact; unharmed: *brought us kids through it all in one piece*—Playboy/ *She came out of it in one piece*

all (or **all stuff**) **like that there** *n phr* Other such things; etcetera: *They sold boots and shoes and all like that there*

all-nighter *See* PULL AN ALL-NIGHTER

all of a doodah *adj phr fr early 1900s British* Upset; nervous; confused

all-originals scene *n phr black* A party or other occasion where only blacks are present: *I dig you holding this all-originals scene at the track*—Malcolm X

all-out **1** *adj* Holding nothing back; sparing nothing: *an all-out effort* **2** *adv*: *He ran all-out for ten minutes*

all over *See* HAVE IT ALL OVER someone or something

all over someone **1** *adj phr* Very affectionate; eagerly amorous: *When they found out I was single they were all over me*/ *The wife went to get some popcorn and the husband was all over me*—Playgirl **2** *adj phr* Aggressively smothering or battering; assaulting: *They broke through the line and were all over the quarterback*

all over the lot (or **the ballpark**) *adv phr* Very unfocused and inconsistent; confused: *His answers are all over the lot*/ *But otherwise...you were all over the ballpark*—Philadelphia

all-pro *adj* Of first quality; blue-ribbon; stellar: *an all-pro team of Washington super-lobbyists*—Washingtonian [fr the annual designation of certain professional football players to the putative team of the best]

all quiet on the Western front *adj phr fr WW1* Calm; peaceful; uneventful [fr the title of a WW1 novel by Erich Maria Remarque reflecting the stagnation and stability of trench warfare]

all reet (or **reat** or **root**) *interj esp 1930s jive talk* An exclamation of approval: *"All reat"...is the rug-cutters' way of saying "all right"*—New Yorker

all (or **aw**) **right** (aw RĪT) **1** *interj* An exclamation of strong approval, esp of something well done or successful; = WAY TO GO **2** *affirmation* Yes; I agree: *All right, I'll go when you want*

all-right *adj* Good; commendable; of the proper sort ● Most often used of persons: *all-right guys trying to make a living*—James M Cain

all right already *interj* A comment protesting that one has heard or had enough or a bit too much [fr Yiddish idiom patterns, and translating Yiddish *genuk shoyn*]

all righty *affirmation* (Variations: **rightie** or **rightee** or **rightey** may replace **righty**) A humorous or deliberately cute and childish way of saying "all right"

all she wrote *See* THAT'S ALL SHE WROTE

all shook up or **all shook** *See* SHOOK UP

all six *See* HIT ON ALL SIX

all stuff like that there *See* ALL LIKE THAT THERE

all one's **switches** *See* NOT HAVE ALL one's SWITCHES ON

all that jazz *n phr* Other such things; etcetera: *baseball, apple pie, Chevrolet, and all that jazz*

◁**all that kind of crap**▷ *n phr* (Variations: **shit** or **stuff** or **bull** may replace **crap**) Other such stupid and boring things; the depressing remainder: *what my lousy childhood was like, and how my parents were occupied before they had me, and all that kind of crap*—JD Salinger

all that meat and no potatoes *interj* An exclamation of pleasure and appreciation, by a man, on seeing a well-built woman ● Has the sense of a wolf-whistle; regarded by many women as offensive

all the answers *See* KNOW ALL THE ANSWERS

all the marbles *See* GO FOR BROKE

all the moves *See* HAVE ALL THE MOVES

all there *adj phr* Intelligent; = TOGETHER: *At least Prudence is all there*
See NOT ALL THERE

all the way *adv phr* Without reservation; to the end: *I'll back her all the way*
See GO ALL THE WAY

all the way live *adj phr* high school students Exciting; vibrant and animated: *That party was all the way live* [fr the sense of immediacy and tension of *live* in its television use]

all thumbs *adj phr* Very awkward; inept: *I'm all thumbs when it comes to drawing*

all together *See* GET IT TOGETHER, HAVE IT ALL TOGETHER

all to hell *See* EXCUSE ME ALL TO HELL, PARDON ME ALL TO HELL

all washed up *See* WASHED UP

all wet *adj phr fr 1920s* Incorrect; wrong: *Your idea is all wet, I'm afraid*

the **almost** *n phr 1950s beat & cool talk* Nearly the best or greatest person or thing: *He's not top line, but he's sure the almost*

alone *See* GO IT ALONE

along for the ride *See* GO ALONG FOR THE RIDE

Alps *See* JEWISH ALPS

already 1 *adv* Without further ado; such being the case: *Let's go already* **2** *adv* Right now; at once: *Shut up already* **3** *adv* Very specifically; precisely: *Drop dead already* ● The full semantic range of **already** is broad and the distinctions are subtle. It is used chiefly for a humorous exasperated effect and to suggest Yiddish speech patterns

also-ran *n* A person, competitive product, etc, that does not succeed; a person of mediocre talents; = LOSER [fr the term for a race-horse who runs fourth or worse]

◁**alter kocker** (or **cocker**)▷ (AL tə KAH kər) *n phr* An old man, esp a disgusting and querulous one; = AK: *You young bloods have got it all over us alter cockers*—Bernard Malamud

the **altogether** *See* IN THE ALTOGETHER

alum (ə LUM) *n* An alumnus or alumna

alvin or **Alvin** *n carnival, circus & underworld* A person who can be fooled or defrauded easily; = MARK, PATSY, SUCKER

alyo *underworld & sports* **1** *n* Any routine task **2** *n* A person not easily disconcerted; = COOL HAND **3** *n* A condition of calm or safety **4** *n* An arrangement between criminals and the police giving the former immunity from arrest or harassment; = the FIX [possibly fr Italian *aglio* "garlic," in the idiom *mangiare aglio*, literally "to eat garlic," meaning to be outwardly calm and placid although perhaps inwardly angry; perhaps related to the folk belief that garlic averts evil]

am *See* PRO-AM

-ama *See* -RAMA

amateur night 1 *n phr* Any occasion on which professionals do a bad or mediocre job: *After the third inning it was strictly amateur night* **2** *n phr* A casual sex act done with a person who is not a prostitute [fr the special occasions or evenings when *amateurs* perform at theaters or on television or radio programs]

ambidextrous *adj* Bisexual; = AC-DC

ambish (am BISH) *n esp theater* Ambition; aggressiveness

ambulance chaser 1 *n phr fr late 1800s* Any unethical lawyer, or one who is too aggressive in getting clients; = SHYSTER **2** *n phr fr early 1900s* A lawyer or lawyer's helper who urges accident victims to sue for damages, negligence, etc

ammo (AM oh) **1** *n fr around 1930* Ammunition: *The platoon is out of ammo* **2** *modifier: The fat ammo barge rocked up and down*—This Week **3** *n* Information and other material that may be used in a debate, campaign, exposé, etc: *Your shabby personal life gives lots of ammo to the opposition*

amp 1 *n* An ampere, the electrical unit of measurement **2** *n* An audio amplifier, esp one used for electronic musical instruments **3** *n narcotics* An ampoule of a narcotic

amscray *v* To leave at once; = BEAT IT, SCRAM [pig Latin for *scram*]

◁**Amy-John**▷ *n homosexuals* A lesbian, esp one who plays the dominant role; = BUTCH, DIESEL-DYKE [origin uncertain; perhaps fr French *ami Jean* "friend John," or fr a corruption of *Amazon* "female warrior"]

anchor *See* SWALLOW THE ANCHOR

anchor man 1 *n phr* *college students fr 1920s* The student having the lowest academic standing in the class **2** *n phr* (also **anchor, anchor person**) A television news broadcaster who has the principal and coordinating role in the program

and *n lunch counter* The second of two items that normally go together ● "Coffee and" means "coffee and doughnuts," "ham and" means "ham and eggs," etc

and how *interj fr early 1900s* An exclamation of emphatic agreement or confirmation: *Are we happy? And how!*

angel 1 *n fr about 1920* A person who contributes to a politician's campaign fund **2** *n fr theater fr 1920s* A financial contributor to any enterprise, esp a stage production; = BUTTER-AND-EGG MAN **3** *v: My doctor angeled one of Hansberry's plays* **4** *n underworld* A thief's or confidence man's victim; = MARK, PATSY **5** *n homosexuals fr 1930s* A homosexual male **6** *n* A vague and illusory image on a radar screen, often due to bird flights, rare atmospheric conditions, or electronic defects **7** *n Vietnam War Navy* A helicopter that hovers near an aircraft carrier to rescue air crew who crash into the water

angel dust *narcotics* **1** *n phr* The powdered form of PCP, a tranquilizer used in veterinary medicine, which as a narcotic is either sniffed or smoked in a tightly rolled cigarette **2** *n phr* A synthetic heroin

angel food *n phr hoboes* Mission-house preaching

Angelino or **Angeleno** (an jə LEE noh) *n* A resident or native of Los Angeles

◁**angel teat** (or **tit**)▷ **1** *n phr* A mellow whiskey with a rich aroma: *Distillery workers smacked their lips over angel teat*—Labor's Special Language **2** *n phr* Any pleasant or easy task

angle *n* Something one does for profit or advantage, esp a devious action disguised as altruism: *That guy never does anything unless there's an angle*

◁**Anglo**▷ *n Hispanics* A white person; = PATTY

animal *n fr Army & students fr 1940s* A brutal or aggressive person, esp one given to excessive sexuality or violence

ankle *v* To walk: *I ankled over to the bar* [perhaps in part from *angle*, cited fr 1890s in sense of "to walk"]

See BEATEN DOWN TO THE ANKLES

Ann *See* MARY ANN

Annie *See* BASEBALL ANNIE

Annie Oakley or **Annie** *n phr* or *n fr early 1900s sports & show business* A free ticket or pass to a game or entertainment [fr the name of a 19th-century trick-shot artist who could riddle a playing card tossed into the air so that it looked like an often-punched ticket]

another country (or **county** or **precinct**) **heard from** *sentence* Still another voice makes itself heard ● Usu an irritated and contemptuous response to a new or unwanted contribution of opinion

another pretty face *See* JUST ANOTHER PRETTY FACE

answers *See* KNOW ALL THE ANSWERS

ante *See* PENNY ANTE, UP THE ANTE

ante up *v phr fr middle 1800s* To contribute money one is responsible for or is expected to give: *On April 15 we all ante up to Uncle Sam* [fr the poker term for an initial contribution to the pot as a game begins]

anti (AN tī) *n* A person opposed to a particular plan, position, action, etc: *The vote showed three pros and six antis*

antifreeze *n narcotics* Heroin

antinuke 1 *adj* Antinuclear; opposed to nuclear energy and nuclear armaments **2** *n: The antinukes assaulted Wall Street, holding hands, singing, and sitting in*—New York Daily News

ants or **ants in** one's **pants 1** *n* or *n phr* An unrelaxed, disturbed condition; anxiety; acute restlessness: *After two days at sea she began to get ants* **2** *n* or *n phr* Sexual excitement; = the HOTS

antsy 1 *adj* In an anxious, disturbed state; nervous; jittery: *But when things are quiet, I get antsy* —Jackie Friedrich/ *"Maybe we're antsy," he acknowledged*—Lawrence Sanders **2** *adj* Sexually aroused; lustful; = HOT

A-number-1 or **A-number-one** *adj* Of the highest or best quality; first class; excellent

anyhoo (EN ee hoō) *adv* Anyhow ● Mispronunciation used for presumed humorous effect

any old *adj phr* Having only ordinary or mediocre quality; of no special distinction: *Any old car will do me*

A-OK or **A-Okay** or **A O-K** *fr astronautics fr 1960s* **1** *adj* Proceeding or functioning properly; giving no cause for worry; = COPACETIC, GO: *Your X rays are A-OK* **2** *adv: The plan's going A-OK*

A-1 or **A-one** *adj* = A-NUMBER-1

ape ◀**1**▶ *n* A black person **2** *n beat talk & rock and roll* The best or greatest; the ultimate: *Her paintings are truly ape* **3** *adj* (also **ape-shit**) Stupid and destructive; irrational; berserk: *You acted like you were ape, pounding the wall* **4** *adj* (also **ape-shit**) Very enthusiastic; highly excited; = BANANAS: *He's ape about my new symphony* **5** *n* An especially strong and pugnacious hoodlum; a strong-arm man or muscle man; = GOON, GORILLA

See BRUSH APE, DRAPE APE, GO APE, HOUSE APE, RUG APE

the **ape** *adv phr beat talk & rock and roll* Very well; best: *Maybe we could dig each other the ape*—S Boal

aped *adj early 1900s* Drunk

ape hangers *n phr motorcyclists* High swooping motorcycle handlebars

◁**ape-shit**▷ *See* APE, GO APE

apparatchik *n* An aide, staff member, etc, esp of a bureaucratic sort; flunky; = RUNNING DOG: *the politicians and their technocratic apparatchiki on both sides*—Philadelphia [fr Russian, "member of the Communist party, or *apparat*"]

apple 1 *n* A man; fellow; = ARTICLE, GUY ● Always preceded by an adjective: *He's a real slick*

apple **2** *n* A ball, esp a baseball **3** *n* *esp 1930s jazz musicians* A street or district where excitement may be found **4** *n* *esp 1930s jazz musicians* Any large town or city ◁**5**▷ *n* *Native American* A Native American who has taken on the values and behavior of the white community; =UNCLE TOMAHAWK

See ALLEY APPLE, the BIG APPLE, GROUND APPLE, HEN-APPLE, HORSE APPLES, POLISH APPLES, SAD APPLE, SMART APPLE, SURE AS GOD MADE LITTLE GREEN APPLES, SWALLOW THE APPLE, WISE GUY

the Apple *See* the BIG APPLE

applehead *n* A stupid person; idiot: *You, sir...are an applehead*—Arthur Daley

applejack cap *n phr* *black* A round, usu knitted and bright-colored cap with a wide peak and a pom-pom; =BOP CAP

◁**apple-knocker**▷ **1** *n* Any fruit picker, esp a migratory orchard worker **2** *n* A rural person; unsophisticated rustic; =HICK [fr the practice of *knocking apples* out of trees]

apple-pie-and-motherhood *modifier* Having obvious and unexceptionable virtue: *They'll always vote yes on an apple-pie-and-motherhood issue*

apple-pie order *n phr* A condition of neatness, correctness, and propriety: *MacFarlane finds in this "apple-pie order of oppositeness"...a singular problem*—Toronto Life

apple-polish *v* To flatter and pamper in order to gain personal advantage; curry favor; =BROWN-NOSE, SUCK UP TO someone: *He started apple-polishing the Skipper as soon as he got on board*

apple-polisher *n* A person who apple-polishes [fr the traditional figure of the pupil who brings the teacher a shiny red apple]

apples *See* HOW DO YOU LIKE THEM APPLES

applesauce *n* *fr early 1900s* Nonsense; pretentious talk; =BULLSHIT, BUNK: *"Ideologies"...freely translated into American means "applesauce"*—Max Eastman [fr the fact that relatively cheap, hence worthless, *applesauce* would be copiously served instead of choicer food in boarding houses]

appropriate *v* *esp WW2 Army* =LIBERATE

AR (pronounced as separate letters) *n* *police* Armed robbery

-arama *See* -RAMA

arcadenik (ar KAYD nik) *n* A habitué of video-game arcades: *video-game mags...which...are a surprise hit with arcadeniks*—Washington Post

Archie Bunker **1** *n phr* A bigoted lower-middle-class American; =HARDHAT, REDNECK **2** *modifier*: *He has the support of the traditional Republican establishment, and is adding the Archie Bunker vote*—James M Reston [fr the name of the leading character of a television comedy series "All in the Family," who exhibited the traits indicated]

argle-bargle *n* *middle 1800s* *fr Scottish* Silly debate, esp specious objections; trivial arguing: *turn questions of sense into mere argle-bargle*—Newsweek [fr a Scottish phrase, "to bandy words"]

-arino *See* -ERINO

arithmetic *See* HARDER THAN CHINESE ARITHMETIC

Arkansas lizard *n phr* *hoboes* A louse

Arky or **Arkie** **1** *n* A migratory worker, esp one from Arkansas **2** *n* Any poor Southern farmer, esp a white sharecropper **3** *modifier*: *the Arky drawl of the CB radio user* **4** *n* =OKIE

arm **1** *v* *cabdrivers* =HIGHFLAG **2** *n* A police officer [police sense fr *arm of the law*]

See AS LONG AS YOUR ARM, BROKEN ARMS, CROOKED ARM, GLASS ARM, HOOK ARM, ONE-ARM BANDIT, ONE-ARM JOINT, RIDE THE ARM, SHORT-ARM INSPECTION, STIFF, TWIST someone's ARM

the arm *See* PUT THE ARM ON someone, RIDE THE ARM, a SHOT IN THE ARM

an arm and a leg *n phr* An exorbitantly high price: *The trip cost an arm and a leg*

armchair general (or **strategist**) *n phr* A person who speaks authoritatively but not convincingly on matters where that person lacks practical experience; =BLOWHARD, KNOW-IT-ALL

arm it *v phr* *cabdrivers* To convey a customer and collect the fare without using the meter; =HIGH-FLAG, RIDE THE ARM [fr the vertical *arm* of the taxi meter, turned horizontal to start the meter]

armored cow (or **heifer**) *n phr* *esp armed forces fr WW2* Canned milk

armpit *n* A very undesirable place; geographical nadir; =ASSHOLE: *My home town is the armpit of the universe*

See PULL TEETH THROUGH THE ARMPIT

Armstrong[1] or **armstrong** *n* A high note or run played on the trumpet [fr Louis *Armstrong*, who was among the first to exploit the high register of the trumpet in jazz]

Armstrong[2] or **armstrong** *n* *railroad* A locomotive fired by hand [fr the *strong arms* required for such work]

Armstrong heater *n phr* The encircling arms of one's girl- or boyfriend

Armstrong mower *n phr* A scythe

Armstrong starter *n phr* A crank for starting an engine

arm-waver *n* An excitable or emphatic person

army chicken *n phr* *WW2 Army* Beans and frankfurters

the (or **the old**) **army game** *n phr* Any swindle or confidence game; a dishonest gambling game; =FLIMFLAM: *It's nothing but...the army game*—James M Cain

army strawberries *n phr* *WW2 Army* Prunes

-aroo *See* -EROO

-arooney or **-erooney** *suffix used to form nouns* A suffix added to the term indicated to imply familiarity or humor: *This little cararooney's got only 10,000 miles on her*

around the axle *See* WRAPPED AROUND THE AXLE

around the bend **1** *adv phr* With most or the hardest part done; =OVER THE HILL: *Two more days and we'll be around the bend on this project* **2** *adj phr* *chiefly British* Insane; =BONKERS: *The Free Islamic Revolutionary Movement and all its around-the-bend comrades*—New Yorker/ *It's a wonder Vanderbilt...isn't totally around the bend herself*—Washington Post

around the bush *See* BEAT AROUND THE BUSH

around (or **round**) **the horn 1** *adv phr underworld fr 1930s* Legally detained on a minor charge but suspected and not yet charged for a more serious crime **2** *adj phr baseball* Of throws from third base to second base to first base: *a brilliant round-the-horn double play* [fr the length and circuitousness of a voyage around Cape Horn at the southern tip of South America]

around the world *See* GO AROUND THE WORLD

arrow *See* STRAIGHT ARROW

art *n police* A photograph or photographs of criminals, esp wanted criminals; =MUG SHOT: *Information began to appear under art of Karpis on post office bulletin boards*—A Hynd

See STATE OF THE ART, TIT ART

article *n* A person, esp one considered to be clever, cute, or resourceful; =NUMBER ● Always preceded by an adjective, or by the locution "Quite an": *He is some slick article/Your little sister's quite an article*

artillery 1 *n underworld fr early 1900s* A weapon or weapons, esp a handgun carried by a criminal; =HEATER **2** *n narcotics* A drug user's hypodermic syringe

See HEAVY ARTILLERY

artist *See* BULLSHIT ARTIST, BUNCO ARTIST, BURN ARTIST, CLIP-ARTIST, DIT-DA ARTIST, GYP, HEAT ARTIST, MAKE-OUT ARTIST, OFF ARTIST, PUFF ARTIST, PUT-ON, RIPOFF, SACK ARTIST, SHORT-CHANGE ARTIST

artsy-craftsy or **artsy** or **arty** *adj fr 1940s* Pretentiously and self-consciously artistic; straining for esthetic effect: *an artsy-craftsy little boutique on Nantucket*

artsy-fartsy or **artsy-smartsy** *adj* Pompously or blatantly esthetical ● The superlative degree of **artsy-craftsy**: *The...pianist veers toward the artsy-fartsy*—Village Voice

asap or **ASAP** (pronounced either as separate letters or as an acronym AY sap) *adv armed forces* Right away; immediately: *Our job is simple—to liberate US POWs from Asia, ASAP*—Washington Post [fr *as soon as possible*]

ash can *n phr Navy fr WW1* An antisubmarine depth charge

See KNOCK someone FOR A LOOP

ash cat *n phr railroad* An engine stoker

ashes *See* GET one's ASHES HAULED

◁**Asiatic**▷ *adj Navy & Marine Corps fr before WW2* Crazy; wild; violent: *He could wind up some tapped-out old Asiatic rumdum*—Earl Thompson [fr presumed unstable character of those who had served too long in *Asiatic* posts]

ask for it *v phr fr early 1900s* To behave in a way that invites and deserves trouble; provoke: *I'm sorry you had that wreck, but with no brakes you were asking for it*

asleep at the switch *adj phr fr railroad* Not attending to one's duty or safety; unvigilant; inattentive

as long as your arm *adj phr* Very extensive; remarkably long: *The guy's a jailbird, a record as long as your arm*—WT Tyler

as per usual *adv phr* As usual

◁**ass**▷ **1** *n* The buttocks; posterior; =BUTT: *a kick in the ass* **2** *n* The anus; =ASSHOLE: *You can take it and shove it up your ass* **3** *n* A person regarded solely as a sex partner or target; =TAIL: *She looks like good ass* **4** *n* Sexual activity; sexual gratification: *He was out looking for ass* **5** *n* The whole self; the person ● Used for emphasis and euphony: *Get your ass out of here pronto/ I'm out in Kansas for the first time...eighteen or nineteen, my ass drafted*—WT Tyler

See one's ASS IS DRAGGING, someone's ASS IS ON THE LINE, BAG ASS, BARREL ASS, BET YOUR BOOTS, BURN someone's ASS, BUST one's ASS, CANDY ASS, CANDY-ASSED, CHEW someone's ASS, COLD AS HELL, COVER one's ASS, DEADASS, DRAG ASS, DRAG one's TAIL, DUMB-ASS, FALL ON one's ASS, FLAT-ASS, FLAT ON one's ASS, GET one's ASS IN GEAR, GET one's HEAD OUT OF one's ASS, GET OFF one's ASS, GET THE LEAD OUT, GET THE RED ASS, GIVE someone A PAIN, GO POUND SALT, GRIPE one's ASS, one HAS HAD IT, HAUL ASS, HAVE A BUG UP one's ASS, HAVE someone's ASS, HAVE one's ASS IN A SLING, HAVE one's HEAD PULLED, HAVE LEAD IN one's PANTS, one's HEAD IS UP one's ASS, HORSE'S ASS, IN A PIG'S ASS, IS A FROG'S ASS WATERPROOF, IT WILL BE someone's ASS, JUMP THROUGH one's ASS, KICK ASS, a KICK IN THE ASS, KISS MY ASS, MAN WITH A PAPER ASS, MY ASS, NO SKIN OFF MY ASS, NOT HAVE A HAIR ON one's ASS, NOT KNOW one's ASS FROM one's ELBOW, ON one's ASS, OUT ON one's ASS, a PAIN IN THE ASS, PIECE OF ASS, PISSY, PULL something OUT OF one's ASS, PUT one's ASS ON THE LINE, RAGGEDY-ASS, a RAT'S ASS, RATTY, SHAG ASS, SHIT-ASS, a SHOT IN THE ASS, SIT ON one's ASS, SIT THERE WITH one's FINGER UP one's ASS, SMART-ASS, SOFT-ASS, SORRY-ASS, STACK ASSES, STAND AROUND WITH one's FINGER UP one's ASS, STICK IT, SUCK ASS, TEAR OFF A PIECE, THROW someone OUT ON someone's ASS, TIRED-ASS, UP THE ASS, UP TO one's ASS IN something, WHAT'S-HIS-NAME, WILD-ASS, WORK one's ASS OFF

◁**-ass** or **-assed**▷ **1** *suffix used to form adjectives* Having buttocks of the specified sort: *big-ass/ fat-assed* **2** *suffix used to form adjectives and nouns* Having a specified character or nature to a high degree: *badass/ wildassed/ silly-ass*

◁**ass backwards**▷ **1** *adv phr* In a reversed position or confused manner: *You installed it ass backwards/ She had it all ass backwards* **2** *adj phr*: *The whole plan is ass backwards*

◁**assbite**▷ *n* A strong rebuke; reprimand: *I took the assbite without looking at him*—Joseph Wambaugh

◁**assed**▷ *See* HALF-ASSED, PUCKER-ASSED, RED-ASSED

◀**assfuck**▶ **1** *v* To do anal intercourse; =BUGGER, BUNGHOLE **2** *n* An act of anal intercourse

◁**as shit**▷ *See* SURE AS SHIT

◁**asshole** or **butthole**▷ **1** *n* The anus; rectum **2** *n* A fool; idiot: *Oh, Christ, what ass-holes be Americans*—Norman Mailer/ *Better not, you butthole*—Cameron Crowe/ *He was that kind of guy, an asshole, a jerk*—WT Tyler **3** *n* =ASSHOLE BUDDY **4** *n* The most despised and loathsome part; =ARMPIT: *This town's the asshole of the North*

See BLOW IT OUT, BREAK OUT INTO ASSHOLES, FLAMER, TANGLE ASSHOLES

◁ **asshole** (or **buttfuck**) **buddy**▷ *n phr* A very close friend; best friend; = PAL ● Usu with only a humorous connotation of homosexuality: *The big cheese who teaches you butt-fuck buddies how to blow a few of the Baptists away*—Richard Merkin/ *Agnelli discussed his "asshole buddy David Rockefeller"*—Village Voice

◁ **asshole deep**▷ *See* UP TO one's ASS IN something

◁ **ass in a sling**▷ *See* HAVE one's ASS IN A SLING

◁ one's **ass is dragging**▷ *sentence* The subject is very tired; one is exhausted, and hence sluggish

◁ one's **ass is getting light**▷ *sentence* Army The subject has been repeatedly and thoroughly rebuked; one has been severely chastened [fr the concept that when one is thoroughly rebuked one's anus is chewed or reamed out]

◁ one's **ass is grass**▷ *sentence fr 1940s* The subject is in trouble; one will be ruined, undone, etc: *Give me a title, in short, or your ass is grass*—Boston Magazine

◁ someone's **ass is on the line**▷ *sentence* Someone is at risk; someone has taken a perilous responsibility: *A friend's ass is on the line and I promised I'd talk to you*—Lawrence Sanders/ *I better be right this time, because my ass is on the line* [fr the notion of a *line* separating hostile persons, such that encroaching on it is a challenge and a risk]

◁ **asskicker**▷ *fr Army* **1** *n* An energetic person, esp an officer who harasses subordinates **2** *n* Something that functions very well: *That little motor's a real asskicker* **3** *n* An exhausting experience

◁ **asskicking**▷ *adj Army* Functioning or performing well: *That's an asskicking little heater*

◁ **ass-kisser**▷ *n* (Variations: **licker** or **sucker** may replace **kisser**) A person who flatters and serves obsequiously to gain favor with a superior; sycophant; = AK, BROWN-NOSE, YES-MAN

◁ **ass-kissing**▷ *n* Flattery; currying favor with superiors; = BROWN-NOSING: *It's a short step from lip service to ass-kissing*—Saul Bellow

◁ **ass man**▷ **1** *n phr* A man with an extraordinary and consuming interest in doing the sex act; lecher; satyr; = COCKSMAN **2** *n phr* A man whose favorite part of female anatomy is the buttocks

◁ one's **ass** (or **buns** or **tail**) **off**▷ *adv phr* Very hard; one's best; to one's utmost: *I worked my ass off for that ungrateful jerk/ listen to Oscar Peterson play his buns off*—Down Beat

◁ **ass over tincups** (or **teacups** or **teakettle**)▷ *adv phr* In or into helplessness; head over heels: *She's so beautiful she'll knock you ass over tincups* [a variant of the early-20th-century British *arse over tip* "head over heels"]

◁ **ass peddler**▷ *n phr* A prostitute, of either sex

◁ **ass-wipe** or **ass-wiper**▷ **1** *n* Toilet paper or something similarly used **2** *n* Idiot; fool; = ASSHOLE

◁ **assy**▷ *adj homosexuals* Malicious; nasty; mean; = BITCHY

-ateria *suffix used to form nouns* (Variations: **-teria** or **-eria** or **-eteria**) Place or establishment where the indicated thing is done or sold: *bookateria/ caviarteria*

Atkins *See* TOMMY ATKINS

at liberty *adv phr* Unemployed

-atorium or **-torium** or **-orium** *suffix used to form nouns* Place where an indicated thing is done: *drinkatorium/ lubritorium/ printorium*

attaboy or **attagirl** *interj* An exclamation of approval or encouragement; = WAY TO GO [fr *that's the boy*]

at the double *See* ON THE DOUBLE

at the switch *See* ASLEEP AT THE SWITCH

attitude *n fr black & prison* A resentful and hostile manner; pugnacity
See HAVE AN ATTITUDE

attrit **1** *v* To dispose of or dispense with gradually; subject to attrition: *Workers never retire, resign, or die...they are attritted*—New York Times **2** *v* To kill: *Well, if we can attrit the population base of the Vietcong, it'll accelerate the process of degrading the VC*—Frances FitzGerald **3** *n* Air Force An expected rate of loss or attrition: *Attrit...is now sometimes seen in Air Force publications to refer to an expected rate of loss or attrition*—American Speech

auction *See* JAM AUCTION

audible **1** *n football* A play or formation announced at the line of scrimmage and different from the one called in the huddle **2** *n* Any sudden or impromptu change of instructions, esp when issued orally: *The boss said if anything went wrong he'd give us an audible*

Augustus Owsley *n phr narcotics* A high-grade form of LSD; = OWSLEY ACID [fr the name of the man who first produced this high-grade variety]

aunt or **Aunt** **1** *n* The madame of a brothel **2** *n homosexuals* An elderly male homosexual

auntie[1] *n fr early 1800s* Any elderly black woman

auntie[2] *n Air Force* An antimissile missile [fr humorous mispronunciation of *anti*]

Aunt Tom *n phr* A woman who does not support or sympathize with the women's liberation movement [fr the analogy with *Uncle Tom*]

ausgespielt (OUS kee speelt) *adj* Thoroughly exhausted; enervated; = FRAZZLED, PLAYED OUT [fr German, "played out"]

Aussie **1** *n* An Australian **2** *adj: the Aussie movie industry*

Aussie steak *n phr* Mutton

avoirdupois (AV ər də poyz) *n* Body weight; fat or fatness: *too much avoirdupois, so I'm dieting*

aw *interj* An exclamation of entreaty, disappointment, disbelief, regret, and various other uncomfortable feelings ● Used either alone or before certain fixed expressions like "come on," "hell," "man," "shit," or "shoot"

awash **1** *adj* Full of a liquid; full to surfeit: *Dr Johnson was awash in tea, drinking thirty cups each day* **2** *adj* Overwhelmed with; drowning in: *The dean was awash in niggling student complaints*
See DECKS AWASH

away 1 *adv* *baseball* Out: *Two away in the top of the eighth* **2** *adv* *underworld* In prison

awesome *teenagers* *adj* Excellent; wonderful; outstanding; = COOL, NEAT

awful 1 *adj* Extremely unpleasant or objectionable **2** *adv* Very; intensely: *I feel awful bad about that*
See GOD-AWFUL

awfully *adv* Very; very much: *It's awfully dark here*

AWOL or **awol** (pronounced either as separate letters or as an acronym AY wawl) *armed forces fr WW1* **1** *adj* Absent without leave **2** *n* A person who is absent without leave

aw right *See* ALL RIGHT

aw shucks 1 *interj* An exclamation of embarrassment, self-abnegation, regret, and various other mildly uncomfortable feelings ● Usu used in imitation of rural or extremely naive, boyish males **2** *v phr*: *good-ole-boy aw shucksing*—Time

awshucksness *n phr* Modesty; self-abnegating embarrassment: *Young Crosby displayed all the easygoing awshucksness of his late father*—Time

ax or **axe 1** *v* To dismiss someone from a job, a team, a school, a relationship, etc; = CAN, FIRE: *who suggested to Reagan that Deaver be axed*—Washingtonian **2** *v* To eliminate; cut: *They axed a lot of useless stuff from the budget* **3** *n* *jazz musicians fr 1950s* Any musical instrument, esp the saxophone: *The piano player noodled on his ax* **4** *n* *rock and roll* A guitar [sense three originally fr the resemblance in shape between a saxophone and an ax, and possibly fr the rhyme with *sax*; also related to the transferred idea of *chops*, originally related to a musician's embouchure, then thought of as blows with an ax]
See MEAT-AX

the ax *See* GET THE AX, GIVE someone THE AX

axle *See* WRAPPED AROUND THE AXLE

axle grease *n phr* Butter

Aztec two-step *n phr* Diarrhea; = MONTEZUMA'S REVENGE, TURISTA

azul (ah zōōl) **1** *n* A police officer; = COP **2** *n* The police; = FUZZ

B

b *See* SON OF A BITCH

B *narcotics* **1** *n* Benzedrine (a trade name); =BENNY **2** *n* =BEE

ba (pronounced as separate letters) *adj* =BARE-ASSED

bab (pronounced as separate letters) *n* A beach where one swims nude [fr *bare-ass beach*]

babe *n* A girl or woman, esp a sexually desirable one; =CHICK, DOLL ● Used almost entirely by men, and considered offensive by many women

baby **1** *n* A wife, girlfriend, or other cherished woman; also, less frequently, a husband, boyfriend, or cherished man: *My baby don't love me no more* **2** *n* Any cherished or putatively cherished person ● This expanded use apparently began in and is characteristic of show business **3** *n* A mean and dangerous man; =TOUGH GUY: *I knew there'd be trouble when those babies walked in* **4** *n* Anything regarded with special affection, admiration, pride, or awe: *Those babies'll turn on a dime/ What we had heard was the firing of those big babies a mile and a half from shore*—Time
See BAWL BABY, BOTTLE BABY, HOT BABY

baby blues *n phr* Blue eyes: *gazing into her baby blues*

babycakes or **honeycakes** *n* A sweetheart or other cherished person ● A term of endearment: *I know it's early, Babycakes*—Armistead Maupin/ *"Ain't that right, baby?" "Sure is, honeycakes"*—New Yorker

baby doll **1** *n phr* A pretty woman, esp one cherished by a man as his own **2** *n phr* A notably pretty and shapely woman, esp a girlish sort of blue-eyed blonde: *Judy played those ditsy baby dolls on the screen* **3** *n phr* Any nice, pleasant, amiable person; =DOLL: *He thought his boss was a real baby doll*

baby-kisser *n* A politician, esp one campaigning for office

baby-lifter *n railroad* A brakeman on a passenger train [possibly fr the extraordinary care needed in this job]

baby-sit **1** *v* To attend and care for anyone or anything: *He baby-sat his weeping pal/ I had to baby-sit the new printer for the computer, feeding it more paper all day* **2** *v narcotics* To be a guide and companion to someone undergoing a psychedelic drug experience [fr the practice of employing someone to stay with and care for a child or children while the parents are not at home]

baby-sitter *n Navy fr Vietnam War* A destroyer that guards an aircraft carrier

bach or **batch** *n* A bachelor

bachelor girl **1** *n phr* An unmarried young woman, usu with a career or a profession; =CAREER GIRL **2** *modifier: a bachelor-girl apartment*

bachelor mother **1** *n phr* A woman who is, by choice, both unmarried and a mother **2** *n phr* A mother who, although previously married, raises her children alone

bach (or **batch**) **it** *v phr* To live alone as an unmarried man, esp to do so for a brief and often slovenly period while one's wife is away: *He had to bach it a while when his wife went to her mother's*

back **1** *v* To give one's support to some effort or person: *I'll back your application* **2** *v* To bet on: *He backed Green Goo in the eighth* **3** *v* To contribute money for; =BANKROLL: *My cousin backed the rock show in the park*
See BIRDYBACK, FISHYBACK, GET one's or someone's BACK UP, GET OFF someone's BACK, GET THE MONKEY OFF, GIVE someone THE SHIRT OFF one's BACK, JACK BENNY, KNOCK BACK, LAID-BACK, MELLOW-BACK, MOSS-BACK, ON someone's BACK, PIGGYBACK, PIN someone's EARS BACK, RAZORBACK, SCRATCH someone's BACK, YOU SCRATCH MY BACK, I SCRATCH YOURS

back alley **1** *n phr* An alley or street in a mean and disreputable neighborhood; slum street or area **2** *modifier: a back-alley saloon/ back-alley language* **3** *n phr jazz musicians* A slow, accented type of jazz that imitates a strip-tease act or the sex act itself

backasswards *adv* =ASS BACKWARDS

back-breaker *n* A very difficult job or task; =BALL-BUSTER, BITCH, PISSER

the back burner *n phr* The location of an idea, project, suggestion, etc, when it is kept in ready reserve for the time being: *Sounds great, but let's put it on the back burner for a few weeks*
See ON THE BACK BURNER

back-burner **1** *v* To put a project, idea, suggestion, etc, in reserve: *Shall we just back-burner that one?* **2** *modifier: a back-burner crisis*—Elizabeth Drew

back door **1** *n phr citizens band* The rear of a car or truck **2** *n phr citizens band* The last truck of a convoy ◁**3**▷ *n phr* The anus; =ASSHOLE

back-door *adj* Dishonest; dubious: *a sleazy little back-door business*

11

backdoor man *n phr black* A married woman's lover

back down *v phr fr middle 1800s* To retreat from one's position; surrender; retract: *He wouldn't back down even when they beat him up*

backgate (or **backdoor**) **parole** *n phr prison* The death of a prisoner from natural causes

backhouse *n* An outdoor toilet house without plumbing; outhouse; =FIRELESS COOKER, PRIVY

back number *n phr fr late 1800s* Someone or something out of date; =HAS-BEEN: *Mr Stale is a back number*—H McHugh

back off 1 *v phr* To stop annoying or harassing someone ● Often a command or threat **2** *v phr* To soften or moderate; relent: *The president backed off a little from his hardnosed line* **3** *v phr* To slow down; go easier: *Hey, back off a little, I don't get you*

back someone **off** *v phr* To order someone to leave; eject someone: *The bouncer backed him off real quick*

back out *v phr fr middle 1800s* To cancel or renege on an arrangement; =CRAWFISH, FINK OUT: *We can't back out just because we're scared*

backroom *adj* Having to do with political expediency; from the inner circles of party affairs: *a backroom decision/ backroom motives*

backscratch *n* A helping or accommodating of one by another: *It's got to be a mutual backscratch*—American Libraries
See YOU SCRATCH MY BACK, I SCRATCH YOURS

back seat *See* TAKE A BACK SEAT

backseat driver *n phr* A person who gives unwanted and officious advice; =KIBITZER

back talk *n phr* Impudent response; impertinent comment; =SASS

one's **back teeth are floating** *sentence* One needs very urgently to urinate

back time *n phr prison* The pending part of a prison sentence which a parole violator must serve if sent back to prison

back to square one *adv phr* Returned to the starting point, usu having wasted a great deal of effort; no farther ahead: *sends the search back to square one*—Village Voice

back to the salt mines *adv phr* Returned to hard work and unremitting discomfort, after a period of relative ease and pleasure: *I had a week off, then back to the salt mines* [fr the tradition of Russian penal servitude in Siberian *salt mines*]

back-track *See* BOOT

backup 1 *n* A replacement, substitute or something or someone in reserve: *We can't afford to lose her because we've got no backup* **2** *modifier:* a *backup system/ backup wide receiver* ◁**3**▷ *n* An occasion when several males do the sex act serially with one woman; =GANG BANG

back up 1 *v phr* To support or confirm, esp to verify the statement of: *You explain it, and I'll back up your version* **2** *v phr* To refer to some earlier place: *They couldn't understand, so he backed up and told 'em once more*

back someone **up 1** *v phr* To confirm what someone says; support what someone does: *If you want to go in to complain, I'll back you up* **2** *v phr* To be ready to substitute for someone; be in reserve: *We've got three other drivers to back him up* **3** *v phr baseball* To play behind a fielder to retrieve balls that might be missed

the **back yard** *n phr circus* The performers as distinguished from the management

bacon *See* BRING HOME THE BACON

bad *adj esp teenagers fr jazz musicians & black fr early 1950s* Good; excellent; admirable: *real bad licks/ bad nigger* ● The use is attested from slavery times, when this sense was marked by a lengthened vowel and a falling tone in pronunciation
See NOT BAD FOR A COUNTRY BOY, SO BAD one CAN TASTE IT

bad actor 1 *n phr* A vicious animal **2** *n phr* A malicious or deceitful person **3** *n phr* A habitual criminal

◁**badass**▷ *fr black* **1** *n* A belligerent and worthless person; =BAD ACTOR, BUM: *It's the badasses who don't want him back*—Philadelphia Journal/ *He still burned with a desire to show us Mad Dogs what a badass we'd passed up*—Easyriders **2** *adj:* sounds as bad-ass as John Denver singing "Macho Man"—Aquarian

bad books *See* IN someone's BAD BOOKS

bad cop *See* GOOD COP BAD COP

bad count 1 *n phr* Dishonest treatment; an unfair decision: *I expected a bad count from that bastard* **2** *n phr* A quantity of illicit drugs that is smaller than paid for [fr the *count* of ten before a fighter is declared defeated]

baddie 1 *n* Someone or something that is bad, esp a movie, television, or sports villain **2** *n* A criminal or other habitually reprehensible person; =BAD MAN

bad egg *n phr fr middle 1800s* A villain, criminal, or other deplorable person; =BAD ACTOR, BADDIE

not **bad for a country boy** *See* NOT BAD FOR A COUNTRY BOY

badge *n 1920s underworld* A police officer
See SCARE BADGE

badge bandit *n phr hot rodders* A police officer

badger game 1 *n phr* A method of extortion in which a woman entices the victim into a sexually compromising situation, whereupon a male accomplice appears and demands payment for keeping the situation quiet **2** *n phr* Any means of blackmail, extortion, or intimidation

bad man (or **guy**) *n phr fr late 1800s cowboys* A villain, esp a killer, rustler, etc, in a cowboy movie

bad-mouth *fr black* **1** *v phr* To disparage; denigrate: *I won't bad-mouth him, but I don't like him* **2** *n phr:* If you can't say anything good, at least *don't be a bad mouth* **3** *n phr* A person who speaks in a belligerent, provocative way

bad news 1 *n phr* An unpleasant or depressing person, esp a persistently annoying one: *Isn't she bad news since her old man left her?* **2** *n phr* A dangerous person; a menace: *Their big new linebacker is bad news* **3** *n phr* Any unfortunate or regrettable situation or event: *That meeting was strictly bad news* **4** *n phr* The bill for goods or services, esp a restaurant check; = BEEF

bad nigger *black* **1** *n phr* A black person, usu a male, who wins the respect of his own people by resisting the dominant white society: *A bad nigger was a nigger who "didn't take no shit from nobody"* —Claude Brown ◁**2**▷ *n phr* A belligerent black male, esp one who mistreats women

bad paper *n phr* Worthless or counterfeit money, checks, etc: *They passed some bad paper*

bad pay *n phr* A person who does not pay his debts or pays them dilatorily

bad rap 1 *n phr* *underworld* An erroneous conviction or sentence; wrongful punishment; = BUM RAP **2** *n phr* Any unjustified condemnation: *Mobil has taken a bad rap from Congress*—Newsweek

bad scene *n phr fr black & 1960s counterculture* Something unpleasant, esp a displeasing and depressing experience or situation

◁**bad shit**▷ **1** *n phr* Something menacing and nasty: *A lot of bad shit goes down at the track, man* —Harry Crews **2** *n phr* Bad luck: *Breaking my leg was just bad shit*

bad talk *n phr black* Gloomy comments

bad time *n phr armed forces fr WW2* Time spent in the guardhouse and therefore not a part of one's required period of service

bad (or **bum** or **down**) **trip 1** *n phr narcotics* A frightening or depressing drug experience, esp a nightmarish time with LSD **2** *n phr fr 1960s counterculture* Any unpleasant occasion or experience; = BUMMER, DOWNER: *The party was a real bad trip*

bafflegab *n* The pompous and opaque prose style affected by bureaucrats and certain scholars

bag ◁**1**▷ *n* The scrotum ◁**2**▷ *n* A condom **3** *n baseball* The cushionlike marker that serves as a base **4** *n narcotics* A portion of narcotics, often wrapped in a paper or glassine envelope: *They found three nickel bags of marijuana on him* ◁**5**▷ *n* A woman's breast **6** *v* To get or capture: *to bag a gold medal/ They bagged the mugger in the next block* **7** *v* To arrest: *You don't have to bag nuns*—Philadelphia Journal **8** *n* An unattractive girl or woman; ugly woman **9** *n* An old woman, esp a repulsive old shrew; = OLD BAT **10** *n esp 1960s counterculture* That which one prefers or is doing currently; = KICK, THING **11** *n* An environment; milieu: *That fox comes out of a very intellectual bag*—WM Kelley **12** *v* To discharge; = CAN, FIRE: *Just say the author was willing to bag an old friend*—Philadelphia Journal **13** *v* To suppress; get rid of; discard: *Let's bag the whole notion, okay?* **14** *v esp students* To avoid; = SKIP: *We can bag gym class*—William Goldman/ *Like bag this movie, for sure*—Newsweek **15** *v* (also **bag it**) *esp students* To abandon; cease; give up: *I had to bag it...I had to give up all that stuff*—New York Magazine **16** *v* To include; categorize; group with: *We're always bagged in England with bands like Iron Maiden*—Rolling Stone

See BEAN BAG, BROWN-BAG, DIME BAG, DITTY BAG, DOGGY BAG, DOUCHE BAG, FAG BAG, FLEABAG, GRAB-BAG, GROUCH-BAG, HAIR BAG, HALF IN THE BAG, HAVE A BAG ON, HOLD THE BAG, IN THE BAG, JIFFY BAG, LET THE CAT OUT OF THE BAG, NICKEL BAG, POWDER-BAG, RUM BAG, SANDBAG, SLEAZEBAG, SLIMEBAG, STASH BAG, TIE A BAG ON, TOTE BAG, WINDBAG

◁**bag ass**▷ *v phr* To leave quickly; get out; hurry; = HAUL ASS

baggage *See* BLIND BAGGAGE, EXCESS BAGGAGE

baggage smasher *n phr fr middle 1800s* A baggage-handler at a railroad station, airport, etc

bagged *adj* Drunk
See HALF-BAGGED

bagged-out *adj* Wearing old or unstylish clothing

bagger *See* BROWN BAGGER, DOUBLE-BAGGER, FOUR-BAGGER, ONE-BAGGER, THREE-BAGGER, TWO-BAGGER

baggies 1 *n* A pair of loose-cut boxer-type men's bathing trunks: *girls in bikinis and boys in "baggies"* —New York Times **2** *n* A pair of full trousers, resembling those of the 1930s: *Then comes a pair of "baggies," very baggy trousers*—New Yorker

bag job *n phr* A theft or burglary: *Someone had done a bag job on his precious files*—C McCrystal/ *The spectators...sure know a bag job when they see one*—Sports Illustrated

bag lady or **shopping-bag lady** or **bag woman 1** *n phr* A woman who goes about the streets collecting discarded objects and taking them home in shopping bags: *a bag lady whose tiny room was crammed with garbage*—New York Post **2** *n phr* A homeless woman, often elderly, who lives in public places and carries her possessions in shopping bags: *bag ladies, the Big Apple's discarded, homeless women*—New York Post

bagman 1 *n underworld* A person who collects money for bribers, extortionists, mobsters, etc: *The defendant was described...as the "bagman" or collector*—New York Times **2** *n narcotics* A person who peddles drugs; = PUSHER

bag (or **load**) **of wind** *n phr* = WINDBAG

bag of worms *See* CAN OF WORMS

bag opener *n phr* A thief who opens and robs purses: *jostling when a bag opener attempts to take a woman's handbag but gets caught in the act*—New York Times

bag-play or **bagging** *n* An attempt to gain favor with one's superior; currying favor; = BROWN-NOSING

bags 1 *n* Trousers ◁**2**▷ *n* A woman's breasts; = TITS **3** *n* A great quantity: *He's got bags of money*
See MONEYBAGS

bag some rays *v phr* To sunbathe

bag your face *sentence high school students* Conceal your face; you are repulsive ● A generalized insult

bag Zs *See* COP ZS

bail 1 *v outdated railroad* To shovel coal into a firebox **2** *v college students* To leave; = CUT OUT, SPLIT
See JUMP BAIL

bail out *v phr* To abandon an effort, project, relationship, etc, in order to minimize losses: *Peters decided to bail out of the business deal* [fr the aviation use, "to parachute from an aircraft"]

bail someone out *v phr* To get someone out of a difficult plight; relieve someone of debt, embarrassment, etc: *I'll bail you out this time, but next time bring enough money*

bait *n homosexuals* A man used as a police decoy to entrap homosexuals

baked *See* HALF-BAKED

baked wind *n phr* = HOT AIR

bakehead *n outdated railroad* A locomotive engineer or fireman

the baker *n phr underworld* The electric chair

Baker flying *See* HAVE THE RAG ON

bald *adj hoboes* Not wrapped, usu said of a handout meal

bald face *n phr fr middle 1800s* Unaged or inferior whiskey; homemade or bootleg whiskey

bald-headed row **1** *n phr* The front row in a burlesque or other theater **2** *n phr* Any group of men, esp old men, who ogle women

baldy or **baldie** **1** *n* A bald man **2** *n* A worn automobile tire

ball ◁**1**▷ *n* A testicle; = NUT ◁**2**▷ *v* To do the sex act; copulate with; = SCREW **3** *v narcotics* To introduce a narcotic, like cocaine, into the body through the genitals **4** *n early 1900s underworld* A dollar, esp a silver dollar **5** *n early 1900s underworld* A prisoner's allowance for making small purchases **6** *n lunch counter* A single scoop of ice cream **7** *n narcotics* A pill or portion of marijuana or some other narcotic **8** *v* To have an especially good time; enjoy oneself in a relaxed and uninhibited way: *A good-time town, where everybody comes to ball*—New York Daily News *See* BALL UP, BEANBALL, BILLYBALL, BUTTERFLY BALL, CANNONBALL, CARRY THE LOAD, EMERY BALL, FIREBALL, FLY COP, FORKBALL, FOUL BALL, GET ON THE BALL, GO FOR THE LONG BALL, GOLF BALL, GOOFBALL, GOPHER BALL, GREASEBALL, GREEDBALL, HAVE A BALL, JUNK-BALL, KEEP one's EYE ON THE BALL, MADBALL, MEATBALL, NOT GET one's BALLS IN AN UPROAR, NUTBALL, ODDBALL, ON THE BALL, PLAY BALL, PLAY CATCH-UP, RED BALL, SLEAZEBAG, SLIMEBAG, SLUDGEBALL, SMOKEBALL, SOFTBALL, SOURBALL, THAT'S THE WAY THE BALL BOUNCES

-ball **1** *combining word* A person who is obnoxious or strange because of what is indicated: *oddball/ goofball/ dirtball/ sleazeball* **2** *combining word* Baseball of a specified sort: *Billyball/ greedball*

a ball *n phr* An especially good time; an occasion of extraordinary pleasure: *The concert was a ball/ Man, we had us a ball*

ball-and-chain *n* One's wife; = OLD WOMAN

◁**ball-bearing hostess**▷ *n phr airline* A male cabin attendant on an aircraft

◁**ball-buster**▷ (Variations: **breaker** or **wracker** may replace **buster**) **1** *n* Something that is very difficult to accomplish; a Herculean task; = KILLER **2** *n* Someone who assigns and monitors extremely difficult tasks: *a real ball-buster of a skipper* **3** *n* A woman who saps or negates a man's masculinity; castrating female

◁**ball-busting**▷ **1** *n* The sapping or destruction of masculinity; = NUT-CRUNCHING **2** *adj:* *his lily-black reputation with that ball-busting wife of his* —Charles Beardsley

balled up *adj phr* In a thoroughly confused and futile condition; erroneous and useless because of perverse incompetence; = FUCKED UP, SCREWED UP: *Things were totally balled up when the alarm went* [origin uncertain; perhaps, as euphemistically explained, fr the helplessness of a horse on a slippery street when its shoes have accumulated *balls* of ice; somehow the term has come to be associated with the testicles, as the related term *bollixed up* shows]

ball game **1** *n phr* A given set of conditions; complex of circumstances; situation: *What we do and what they do isn't the same ball game* **2** *n phr* A competition; rivalry: *It's NBC ahead in the network ratings ball game, NBC says*—R Doan/ *Goodbye, ball game, he said*—R Grossbach **3** *n phr* The decisive element or event, esp in a competition or encounter; = the NAME OF THE GAME: *The third ward vote is the ball game in this town* *See* LOSE THE BALL GAME, THAT'S THE BALL GAME, a WHOLE NEW BALL GAME, a WHOLE 'NOTHER THING

balling *n black fr 1930s* Fun, esp of an uninhibited sort

the ball is in someone's **court** *sentence* The next action, decision, response, etc, belongs to the person or persons indicated: *That's my offer. The ball is in your court* [fr tennis]

ball of fire **1** *n phr* A dazzling performer; spectacularly successful striver; overachiever; = GO-GETTER, HOT SHOT **2** *n phr railroad* A very fast train

ball of wax *See* the WHOLE BALL OF WAX

balloon **1** *n hoboes* A hobo's bedroll; = BINDLE **2** *n narcotics* A toy rubber balloon used to hold heroin **3** *n* A condom **4** *v theater* To lose one's lines completely during a performance; = BLOW UP **5** *n* A dollar bill; one dollar: *It'll cost you six balloons* **6** *n Army* A platoon **7** *n* The floating blob with a line to a speaker's mouth, used to show speech in comic strips *See* LEAD BALLOON, TRIAL BALLOON, WHEN THE BALLOON GOES UP

balloonhead *n* A stupid person; = AIRHEAD

balloonheaded *adj* Stupid; oafish: *Listen, you balloon-headed fool*—Jerome Weidman

balloon room *n phr 1960s narcotics* A room where marijuana is smoked; = BEAT PAD

ballot box *See* STUFF THE BALLOT BOX

ballpark *See* ALL OVER THE LOT, IN THE BALLPARK

ballpark figure (or **estimate**) *n phr* A rough numerical approximation: *I'd say forty, but that's a ballpark figure*

balls ◁**1**▷ *n* The testicles ◁**2**▷ *n* Courage; nerve; = GUTS: *They have balls but not soul*—Richard Goldstein/ *I admire a woman with the balls to bare her breasts*—Playboy **3** *interj* An exclamation of incredulity, disappointment, or disgust **4** *n*

British Nonsense; =POPPYCOCK: *That story is just such patent balls that I've written a letter*—Interview/ *He was talking high-minded balls. Twaddle!* —Saul Bellow

See BLUE BALLS, BUST one's ASS, the CAT'S MEOW, DOES HOWDY DOODY HAVE WOODEN BALLS, FREEZE THE BALLS OFF A BRASS MONKEY, GRIPE one's ASS, HAVE BRASS (or CAST-IRON) BALLS, HAVE someone BY THE BALLS, HAVE THE WORLD BY THE BALLS, NOT GET one's BALLS IN AN UPROAR, PUT BALLS ON, TIGHT AS KELSEY'S NUTS

◁**ballsiness** or **balliness**▷ *n* Courage; =BALLS, GUTS: *a dangerous ethic of ballsiness in international affairs*—Newsweek

balls-out *adj car-racing & motorcyclists* Very great; extreme; total: *the balls-out go-power of modern snowmobiles*—Car and Driver

balls to the wall *fr Air Force* **1** *adv phr* At or to the extreme; at full speed; =ALL-OUT, FLAT OUT: *driving balls to the wall* **2** *adj phr*: *They are not the cigar-chomping "balls to the wall" warmongers of popular perceptions*—Newsweek [fr the thrusting of an aircraft throttle, topped by a ball, to the bulkhead of the cockpit to attain full speed]

balls-up *n fr British* A confused and inept blunder; =FUCK-UP: *an expensive, embarrassing balls-up* —Village Voice

◁**ballsy**▷ *adj* Courageous; spunky; =GUTSY: *Valerie Green's a very ballsy lady*—Anne Bernays

ball the jack **1** *v phr* To move or work very rapidly **2** *v phr* To gamble or risk everything on one stroke or try [fr railroad term meaning "to go full speed"; related to the railroad sense of *highball* and of *jack*]

ball up **1** *v phr* To confuse; mix up; lead astray: *This guy has balled me up totally* **2** *v phr* To wreck or ruin by incompetence; botch; =BOLLIX UP, FUCK UP, SCREW UP: *I managed to ball up the whole project* **3** *n*: *The second concert was a thorough ball-up*

ball-wracker *See* BALL-BUSTER

bally *n and v* =BALLYHOO

ballyhoo **1** *n circus & carnival* A short sample of a sideshow, presented with a barker's spiel **2** *n* Advertising or publicity, esp of a raucous and colorful sort; =FLACK, HYPE: *to peddle a product with sheer ballyhoo* **3** *modifier*: *the ballyhoo department/ a ballyhoo expert* **4** *v*: *They ballyhooed him right into office* [origin unknown]

bally show *n phr carnival & circus* A sideshow

bally stand *n phr carnival & circus* The platform in front of a sideshow where the barker presents the ballyhoo

baloney or **balony** or **boloney** **1** *n* Nonsense; pretentious talk; bold and deceitful absurdities; =APPLESAUCE, BULLSHIT, HOOEY: *No matter how you slice it, it's still baloney*—Carl Sandburg **2** *v*: *And don't try to baloney me, either* **3** *n* A stupid person: *You dumb baloney*—Jerome Weidman **4** *n electricians* Insulated cable

bam[1] **1** *v* To strike or hit: *Heads may be biffed or bammed*—M Doolittle **2** *interj* An exclamation imitating a hard blow

See WHAM-BAM THANK YOU MA'AM

bam[2] *n narcotics* A mixture of a depressant with a stimulant drug, esp of a barbiturate with an amphetamine [fr *barbiturate* + *amphetamine*]

bam[3] *n fr WW2* A woman Marine [fr *broad-assed Marine*]

bamboo *adj Navy* Crazy; erratic

bamboo curtain *n phr* The barrier of secrecy and exclusion that cut the People's Republic of China and other Asian Communist countries off from the rest of the world [modeled on *iron curtain*]

bamboozle *fr early 1700s* *v* To hoax; trick; swindle; =FLIMFLAM: *My worthy opponent thrives by bamboozling the public*

bamboula (bam Bō̄ lə) **1** *n* A traditional, often erotic dance of New Orleans Creoles **2** *n jazz musicians fr early 1900s* A drum [fr an African name for a type of drum]

banana **1** *n show business* A comedian, esp in a burlesque show ● These performers were ranked as "top banana," "second banana," etc **2** *n black* A sexually attractive light-skinned black woman ● Considered offensive by the women to whom this term is applied **3** *n* The nose, esp a big or hooked nose ◁**4**▷ *n* The penis ◁**5**▷ *n* An Oriental sympathetic with and part of the white majority society ● Because white on the inside though yellow on the outside **6** *n* An automobile bumper-guard **7** *n hospital* A patient with jaundice

See HAVE one's BANANA PEELED, TOP BANANA

bananahead *n* A stupid person

banana oil *n fr 1920s* Nonsense, esp when used to flatter and mislead; =BUNK [perhaps fr the oily smoothness and fruity odor of amyl acetate; when used to tighten the fabric of airplane wings, amyl acetate was called *dope*, perhaps lending the suggestion of a soothing intoxicant]

◁**banana republic**▷ *n phr* A small country, esp Central American, dominated by foreign companies [fr the fact that such places were typically under the control of the United Fruit Company, and grew bananas]

bananas **1** *adj* Crazy; =NUTS: *Others were simply unprincipled and crooked, he was in addition bananas*—Saul Bellow **2** *adj* Very enthusiastic; highly excited; =APE **3** *adj underworld* Homosexual **4** *interj* =BANANA OIL

See GO BANANAS

banana stick *n phr baseball* A baseball bat made of inferior wood

band *See* BIG BAND, TO BEAT THE BAND

Band-Aid **1** *n* A temporary or stop-gap remedy: *All they did to rectify the problem was to put a Band-Aid on it*—Wall Street Journal **2** *modifier*: *a Band-Aid expedient* [fr *Band-Aid*, trade name for a brand of small adhesive bandages]

bandbox *n prison* A small or rural jail, esp one that seems easy to escape from [fr the lightly built *box* formerly used by ladies to carry bits of finery]

B and D *n phr* Bondage and discipline; sadomasochistic sexual practice

bandit 1 *n armed forces fr WW2* An enemy aircraft **2** *n prison* An aggressive homosexual who often resorts to violence

See BADGE BANDIT, LIKE A BANDIT, MAKE OUT LIKE A BANDIT, ONE-ARM BANDIT, SPACE BANDIT

B and T *See* BT

bandwagon *n railroad* A car from which railroad workers are paid

the bandwagon 1 *n phr* The strong current popularity and impetus of a person, idea, party, etc: *the Reagan bandwagon/ the antinuke bandwagon* **2** *modifier: the bandwagon phenomenon*

See GET ON THE BANDWAGON

bang 1 *n* A very pleasurable sensation; surge of joy; thrill: *This'll give you a big bang* **2** *n narcotics* An injection of a narcotic, esp an intravenous shot of heroin **3** *v: They banged some horse and got high* ◁**4**▷ *v* To do the sex act with or to; copulate with: *He banged her twice and left happy* ◁**5**▷ *n* The sex act: *The wedding night, you idiot. The first bang. How was it?*—Lawrence Sanders **6** *n underworld* A criminal charge or prison sentence; = RAP **7** *adv* Precisely; exactly: *bang on the hour* **8** *n computer* An exclamation point; = SHRIEK

See BIG BANG, GANG BANG, GET A BANG OUT OF someone or something, GO OVER WITH A BANG, WHIZBANG, WITH A BANG

bang-bang 1 *n* A gun **2** *n* A Western movie; = HORSE OPERA, OATER

banger 1 *n hot rodders* A cylinder in an automobile engine: *a souped-up four-banger* **2** *n* A car: *this wonderful banger*—Sports Illustrated **3** *n* A boxer who hits hard: *He's a great banger*—Time

See BIBLE-BANGER, BIT BANGER, EAR-BANGER, FOUR-BANGER, WALL BANGER

bang for the buck *n phr* Value for what one pays: *You get the best bang for the buck right here*—Chicago Magazine/ *Yet the bang we are getting for our buck is worth whimpering about*—Philadelphia [fr a frivolous way of referring to the national defense budget and the destructive power it produces]

bang pipes *v phr* To get practical work experience; work in the field rather than in a cloistered office: *We insist that people bang pipes for a while and go out in the field and talk to customers*—Morris County Daily Record

bangtail *n fr middle 1800s* A racehorse [fr the manner of cropping and tying the *tail* of a racehorse as if it were chopped squarely off with a *bang*]

bang the hostess *v phr airline* To ring for the cabin attendant

bang to rights *See* DEAD TO RIGHTS

bang-up *adj fr early 1800s* Excellent; superior: *I have some bang-up gin*—Gene Fowler/ *You've done a bang-up job on that report, Smythe*

banjax *v fr Irish fr early 1900s* To defeat utterly; = CLOBBER: *She upped and banjaxed the old man*—New Yorker

banjo *n* (also **Irish banjo**) *fr hoboes & railroad fr early 1900s* A shovel

banjo hit *n phr baseball* A hit between the infield and outfield; = TEXAS LEAGUER

banjo hitter *n phr* A player who generally gets banjo hits: *Two banjo hitters came through like bongo drummers as they walloped homers*—Herm Weiskopf

bankable *adj* Having a reputation or influence that insures the success of a project: *after a decade when bankable stars have all but monopolized movies*—New York/ *She had established herself as the most bankable female actress in Hollywood*—Philadelphia

bank on *v phr* Depend or rely on: *You can bank on his word*

bankroll *v* To finance; put up the money for, esp for a theatrical production; = ANGEL: *Whoever bankrolled this turkey will go broke*

See PHILADELPHIA BANKROLL

banner *See* CARRY THE BANNER

bantam *n black* A woman or girl; = CHICK

bar *See* HERSHEY BAR, NUTBALL, SIDEBAR, SISSY BAR

barbecue 1 *n outdated black* A sexually attractive young woman **2** *n* A gathering; meeting; = CLAMBAKE: *What's the point of this barbecue?*

barber 1 *n baseball* A talkative baseball player **2** *v* To converse; chat: *I shouldn't ought to barber with you*—Raymond Chandler **3** *n baseball* A pitcher who forces the batter back from the plate by throwing at his head [pitching sense fr association with a close shave, meaning a near miss]

barber chair *n phr astronautics* The adjustable seat used by an astronaut in a space craft

barber-shop 1 *n* Close-harmony singing, esp by a quartet **2** *modifier: a barber-shop quartet/ barber-shop harmony* [fr the presumed and archetypal male-quartet singing that occurred in *barber shops*]

barbershop quartet *n phr* The trick or torment of holding someone's head and rubbing very hard and painfully at a small area of scalp with the fist; = DUTCH RUB, NOOGIE [because a *quartet* of fingers is working on the hair, as it were]

Barbie Doll 1 *n phr* A mindless man or woman; a person lacking any but typical, bland, and neatly attractive traits: *a Barbie Doll...programmed to sing, dance, and fall in love*—Time **2** *modifier: Our Barbie Doll president with his Barbie Doll wife*—Hunter S Thompson [fr the trade name of a very popular blue-eyed blonde teenaged doll for young children]

barbs *n narcotics* Barbiturates

barbwire garter *See* WIN THE PORCELAIN HAIRNET

◁**bare-ass** or **bare-assed**▷ *adj* Naked; = BA, BUCK NAKED

bareback 1 *adv* Without using a condom **2** *adj: a bareback lay*

bareback rider *n phr* A man who does the sex act without using a condom

bare-bones *adj* Unadorned; spare; austere: *a bare-bones prose style*

barefaced or **bareface** *adj* Bold; shameless; unscrupulous: *a barefaced lie/ bareface liar*

bare face hanging out *See* STAND THERE WITH
ONE'S BARE FACE HANGING OUT

barefoot *adj railroad* Having no brakes: *a barefoot
caboose*

barf **1** *v chiefly students* To vomit [probably
echoic] **2** *v computer* To respond strangely or
with an error warning after unacceptable input: *The
machine barfed when I put in the wrong password*

Barf City *adj phr chiefly students* Disgusting; loathsome; = YUCKY

bar-fly *n* A heavy drinker; = LUSH, SOUSE

barf me out *interj high school students* An exclamation of disgust; = YUCK

bargain *See* NO BARGAIN

bargaining chip *n phr* Something to be offered,
conceded, threatened, etc, in negotiations; a "card
that one plays" in bargaining: *The prime minister
went to the summit meeting without very many
strong bargaining chips/ He is using his information
like a bargaining chip*—New York Times

barge in **1** *v phr* To enter a place without hesitation or ceremony, esp when not invited: *You can't
just barge into the Yale Club* **2** *v phr* To interrupt; esp, to intrude with unwanted counsel; = BUTT
IN, KIBITZ

bar-girl *n* = B-GIRL

bargle *See* ARGLE-BARGLE

barhop *v* (also **bar crawl** or **pub crawl**) To go
drinking from bar to bar; = JOINT HOP

barker **1** *n carnival & circus fr middle 1800s* A
person who attracts customers to a sideshow with a
spiel and a sample **2** *n armed forces & underworld* A pistol **3** *n baseball* A first-base coach

barking dogs *n phr* Tired or sore feet

barn **1** *n* Any very large house or room, esp one
which is rather too large and bare for comfort **2** *n*
A summer theater in a rural district
See someone CAN'T HIT THE SIDE OF A BARN, GO
AROUND ROBIN HOOD'S BARN

barn-burner *n* Anything sensational or exciting:
*whether they have a barn burner of a natural gas
well or a dry hole*—Newsweek/ *George's Bank has
proved to be, in the words of one oil-company executive, "no barn-burner"*—Boston Globe

barney *n* A prize fight or race whose outcome has
been prearranged, a fixed fight or race: *looked like
a barney, as if there were some collusion*—AJ
Liebling

barnstorm **1** *v fr early 1900s* To travel as an
entertainer, making short or one-night appearances
in small towns **2** *v fr 1920s* To travel about in an
airplane or with an air show, doing aerobatics, giving rides, etc, esp in rural places

barnstormer **1** *n* A person who barnstorms **2**
n An inferior actor

barnyard golf *n phr* The game of horseshoe pitching

barracks bag *See* BLOW IT OUT

barracks lawyer *See* LATRINE LAWYER

barrel or **barrel along** *v* or *v phr* To speed, esp
to drive a car very fast; career

See CIDER BARREL, CRACKER-BARREL, IN THE BARREL,
LIKE SHOOTING FISH IN A BARREL, OVER A BARREL,
SCRAPE THE BOTTOM OF THE BARREL

◁**barrel ass**▷ *v phr* To barrel: *We're barrel-assing
toward Van Nuys*—Esquire

barrelhouse **1** *n fr late 1800s* A cheap saloon,
esp one in combination with a brothel: *barrelhouse
kings, with feet unstable*—Vachel Lindsay **2** *n* A
jazz style marked by strong beat and ensemble
improvisation; also, music in this style **3** *modifier: barrelhouse jazz/ barrelhouse beat*

barrelhouse bum *n phr* = SKID ROW BUM

bar the door *See* KATIE BAR THE DOOR

base *See* GET TO FIRST BASE, OFF BASE, OFF ONE'S
BASE, TOUCH BASE WITH someone

baseball *See* OLDER THAN GOD

baseball Annie *n phr* A young female baseball
fan: *The baseball Annies...are a fairly comely lot*
—Wall Street Journal/ *the groupies (known as
Baseball Annies) who hang around the players'
hotels*—New York Times

bases *See* TOUCH ALL BASES

bash **1** *v* To hit; = CLOBBER, SOCK **2** *n* A party,
esp a good, exciting one: *Her little soiree turned
into a real bash* **3** *n* An attempt; = CRACK,
WHACK ● Chiefly British: *Let's have a bash at moving this thing*

-basher *combining word* A person who harasses or
beats the person or item indicated: *car-basher/ fag-
basher*

-bashing *combining word* Hating and attacking
what or who is indicated: *author-bashing/ faggot-
bashing/ gringo-bashing/ Paki-bashing*

basket **1** *n* The pit of the stomach; = BREADBAS-
KET: *a blow flush in the basket*—Joseph Auslander
2 *n homosexuals* The male genitals, esp when
prominently displayed in tight pants: *Steep enthusiastic eyes, Flicker after tits and baskets*—WH Auden

basket case **1** *n phr* A helpless, hopeless, distraught person: *If I worried after a decision...I'd be a
basket case*—Time **2** *n phr* Anything ruined and
hopeless: *Those are only the best-known corporate
basket cases*—Toronto Life/ *the reconstitution of
the East Wing as an autonomous...nation and international basket case*—Time

Basra belly *n phr* Diarrhea [fr *Basra*, Iraq]

◁**bassackward** or **bassackwards**▷ **1** *adj*
Backwards; reverse; = ASS BACKWARDS: *sort of bassackward hydraulic gimcrackery*—Car and Driver **2**
adv: He got it all bassackwards

◁**bastard**▷ **1** *n* A man one dislikes or disapproves
of, esp a mean, dishonest, self-serving man;
= PRICK, SON OF A BITCH **2** *n* Anything unpleasant
or arduous; = BITCH: *Ain't it a bastard the way it
keeps raining*

basted *adj* Drunk

bastille (ba STEEL) *n* A jail or prison [fr the former
French royal prison]

bat **1** *n fr early 1600s* A prostitute **2** *n* = OLD
BAT **3** *n fr middle 1800s* A spree; carousal;
= BINGE **4** *n horse-racing* A jockey's whip

See GO TO BAT AGAINST, GO TO BAT FOR, HAVE BATS IN one's BELFRY, LIKE A BAT OUT OF HELL, RIGHT OFF THE BAT, TAKE OFF LIKE A BIGASS BIRD

not **bat an eye** *See* NOT BAT AN EYE

bat around[1] **1** *v phr* To do nothing in particular; go about in idle pursuit of pleasure: *I want the kids home instead o' battin' around the street*—Elmer Rice **2** *v phr* To discuss the pros and cons of an idea, project, etc: *We batted around the notion of a sick-out*

bat around[2] *v phr* To have every batter on a baseball team's starting lineup come to bat in a single inning

bat carrier *n phr underworld fr 1920s* A police informer; = STOOL PIGEON

batch *See* BACH, BACH IT, LAY A BATCH

batch out *v phr hot rodders* To start and accelerate a car from a standstill

bat cleanup *v phr baseball* To be the fourth hitter in a team's batting order [see the *cleanup spot*]

bat one's **gums** *v phr* (Variations: **beat** or **hump** or **flap** may replace **bat**; **chops** or **jaw** or **jowls** or **lip** may replace **gums**) To talk, esp idly or frivolously: *He didn't mean it, he was just batting his gums/ Well, you weren't just flapping your lip that time*—Peter De Vries

bath *See* TAKE A BATH

bathtub **1** *n* A motorcycle sidecar **2** *n* A small ship
See WIN THE PORCELAIN HAIRNET

bathtub gin *n phr esp 1920s* Gin made at home by mixing alcohol with flavoring, often literally in a bathtub

bat out *v phr* To write something more quickly than one ought; = WHOMP UP: *He kept batting out scenes*—Budd Schulberg/ *Bat me out a memo, please*

bats or **batty** *adj* Crazy; = NUTS: *He was grinning like he was bats/ funnier than you'd expect, fairly batty*—Village Voice
See HAVE BATS IN one's BELFRY

batter *v hoboes* To beg; = PANHANDLE

battered *adj* Drunk

battery acid *n phr WW2 armed forces* Coffee

bat the breeze *v phr* To chat; converse, esp easily and idly; = RAP, SHOOT THE BREEZE: *a couple of cops batting the breeze*

battle-ax *n* An ill-tempered woman, esp a mean old woman; virago

Battle of the Bulge *n phr* The constant struggle to keep slim [fr the name of the Ardennes campaign of late 1944 in World War 2]

battleship *n railroad* The heaviest type of locomotive or passenger car

battlewagon **1** *n Navy* A battleship **2** *n hoboes & railroad* An iron railroad coal-car **3** *n 1920s underworld* A police patrol wagon

batty *See* BATS

bawl baby *n phr* = CRYBABY

bawl someone **out** *v phr* To reprimand severely; rebuke; = CHEW someone OUT

bayou blue *n phr* Inferior or bootleg whiskey

bay window *n phr* A protuberant stomach; paunch; = POTBELLY: *He's lean and mean, no bay window and no patience*

bazillion *n* A very large number; a zillion: *he'd have a bazillion goals*—Village Voice

◁**bazongas** or **bazoongies**▷ (bə ZAHN gəz, bə ZŌŌN geez) *n* A woman's breasts; = BAZOOM, JUGS

bazoo (bə ZŌŌ) *n fr middle 1800s* The mouth, esp regarded as a speech organ: *if you would close that big bazoo*—Walt Kelly [fr Dutch *bazuin* "trumpet"]
See SHOOT OFF one's MOUTH

bazooka (bə ZŌŌ kə) *n fr WW2 Army* A small anti-tank rocket launcher [fr its resemblance to a tubular musical instrument played by the 1940s comedian Bob Burns]

◁**bazoom**▷ (bə ZŌŌM) *n* A woman's breast or breasts: *Whatever Julie Andrews wants to do with her bazooms is OK with me*—Susan Rausch [fr comic mispronunciation of *bosom*, and association with the excitement of *zoom*]

B-bag *See* BLOW IT OUT

beach blanket bingo *n phr* Sexual activity on the beach; the love game pursued semi-nude amidst sun and sand

beach bum *n phr* A man who frequents beaches, esp one who is a surfer, who conspicuously shows his muscles, etc

beach bunny *n phr* A girl who, whether or not a surfer, spends time with surfers; = GREMLIN

bead *See* DREAM BEADS, DROP BEADS, GET A BEAD ON something or someone

the **beads** *n phr* Fate; destiny: *fate, or whatever else you called it: "the beads"*—John Rechy

beady eye *See* GIVE someone THE FISH-EYE

beagle *n outdated underworld* A lawyer or judge
See LEGAL EAGLE

beak[1] **1** *n* A mayor, magistrate, or trial judge ● Outdated in US use, though still current in British slang **2** *n* A lawyer [fr Celtic *beachd* "judgment, judge"]

beak[2] *n* The nose: *The beak-buster in the opening round was the first punch Moore had thrown*—Associated Press
See EAGLE-BEAK

beak-hunting *n hoboes* Poultry-stealing

the **beam** *See* OFF THE BEAM, ON THE BEAM

bean **1** *n outdated underworld* A five-dollar gold piece **2** *n* A dollar: *without a coat on his back or a bean in his pocket*—J Lilienthal **3** *n gambling* A poker chip **4** *n* The head, esp the human head and brain: *Whistling at a crook is not near as effective as to crack him on the bean with a hickory stick*—Will Rogers **5** *v* To strike someone on the head, esp to hit a baseball batter on the head with a pitch: *The Landmark itself can make a reader feel beaned*—Time ◀**6**▶ *n* (also **beaner**) A person of Spanish-American background, esp a Chicano
See FULL OF BEANS, JELLYBEAN, LOOSE IN THE BEAN, MEAN BEAN, ON THE BEAN, SPILL THE BEANS, USE one's HEAD

bean bag *n phr police* A rifle projectile consisting of a small canvas bag full of birdshot or similar material and used for repelling rioters

beanball *n* A baseball pitch that hits or nearly hits the batter's head and is sometimes used to intimidate the batter: *Mr Bender places much reliance on the bean ball*—C Dryden

bean counter *n phr* A statistician or arithmetical clerk in government or business; = GNOME, NUMBER CRUNCHER: *Even in Britain, the bean counters couldn't tolerate a negative cash flow forever*—Car and Driver

bean-counting *modifier* Having to do with bureaucratic statistics and calculations: *We have our bean-counting ways, they, Russians, Cubans, etc, have their bean-counting ways*—National Public Radio/ *This bean-counting approach is an easy way to score debating points*—New York Times

bean-eater 1 *n* A resident of Boston ◄**2**► *n* A person of Spanish-American background, esp a Chicano; = BEAN

◄**beaner**► *See* BEAN

beanery 1 *n* A restaurant or diner, esp a cheap one: *a beanery in Hell's Kitchen*—John McCarten **2** *n* underworld A jail

beanhead *n* A stupid person

beanie *n* A skull cap, esp one worn by schoolboys and college freshmen

beanpole *n* A tall, thin person; = HATRACK: *She was tall, but no beanpole*—Raymond Chandler

bean rag *n phr* Navy A red pennant flown from a ship to show that a minimum crew is on duty because it is mealtime

beans 1 *n* *fr middle 1800s* Nothing; a minimal amount; = DIDDLY ● Semantically very similar to **bubkes**: *I wouldn't give you beans for that idea/ She would get all of her famous friends to appear and pay them beans*—Time **2** *interj* An exclamation of disbelief or contempt

See FULL OF BEANS, a HILL OF BEANS, KNOW one's ONIONS

bean-shooter *n* A small-caliber pistol

bean stripe *n phr* Marine Corps = HASH MARK

Bean Town *n phr* Boston, Massachusetts

bean wagon *n phr* A small restaurant or diner, esp a cheap one [perhaps fr the mid-19th-century inception of prepared food selling from *wagons*, noted, for example, in Providence, Rhode Island]

bear 1 *n* narcotics A capsule containing a narcotic **2** *n* students A difficult school or college course **3** *n* Anything arduous or very disagreeable; = BITCH **4** *n* = BEARCAT **5** *n* A large, gruff man

See DOES A BEAR SHIT IN THE WOODS

Bear *See* SMOKEY BEAR

bearcat 1 *n* A durable and determined person; tough fighter or worker: *a bearcat for jobs like this* **2** *n* Something remarkable, wonderful, superior, etc; = BEAUT, HUMDINGER

beard 1 *n* *1950s beat & cool talk* An up-to-the-minute, alert person; = HIPSTER **2** *n* fr gambling A person used as an agent, to conceal the principal's identity: *Use him as a beard, is what Donny thought he'd do*—Dan Jenkins/ *He's the beard. That's what they call the other man who pretends to be the lover*—Lawrence Sanders **3** *n* A bearded man, esp someone of apparent dignity and authority: *I can't believe the sainted beards would bang me with a manufactured case*—Paul Sann **4** *n* The pubic hair; = BUSH

See GRAYBEARD

◄**bearded clam**► *n phr* The vulva

a **bear in the air** *n phr* A police officer in a helicopter [fr *Smokey Bear*]

bearish *adj* Showing a negative and unhopeful attitude; disheartening ● Often used with "on" or "about": *He's quite bearish on our chances/ She's not entirely discouraging but rather bearish* [fr the stock market term *bear market* "market in which price, sales, etc, tend to decrease"]

bear trap *n phr* citizens band A police radar trap for speeders [related to *Smokey Bear* "policeman"]

◄**be** someone's **ass**► *See* IT WILL BE someone's ASS

beast 1 *n* A cheap prostitute **2** *n* (also **beastie, beasty**) An especially unattractive woman **3** *n* Any woman whatever, but esp a young attractive one **4** *n* Any new or complicated machine, esp a very fast vehicle, that strikes one as dangerous and fickle: *Let's see if we can get this beast off the ground*

beat 1 *n* *fr middle 1800s* A loafer; drifter; = DEADBEAT, MOOCHER **2** *v* hoboes To avoid paying train fares and other bills **3** *v* fr underworld To avoid a fine or conviction: *to beat a burglary rap* **4** *n* news media News printed or broadcast first, before one's competitors; = SCOOP: *The News scored an important beat* **5** *n* fr police & news media The area or subject matter which one is assigned to handle: *cop on his beat/ a reporter on the courthouse beat* **6** *adj* Looking as if battered; disheveled; damaged; = BEAT UP **7** *adj* Very tired; = ALL IN, POOPED **8** *n* The basic meter of a piece of music, esp the insistent percussive rhythm of some jazz styles and rock and roll **9** *adj* 1950s beat talk Alienated from the general society, and expressing this by a wandering life, the avoidance of work, the advocacy of sexual freedom, the use of narcotics, a distinctive style of dress and grooming, and the adoption of certain aspects of Far Eastern religions: *the beat generation/ beat poets* **10** *n* = BEATNIK **11** *v* To be robbed or shortchanged, esp in an illegal exchange: *I sure got beat when I bought marijuana in the park* **12** *adj* Inferior: *This is beat stuff. I smoked it all day and all I got is a headache*

See DOWNBEAT, OFFBEAT, UPBEAT

beat a dead horse *v phr* To continue arguing, discussing, or broaching a matter which is settled or proved unavailing

beat all *v phr* To surprise one; be a wonder: *Doesn't it beat all how Fred is always first in line?*

beat all hollow *v phr* fr middle 1800s To defeat easily; surpass completely: *The Cubs beat'em all hollow/ His story beats mine all hollow*

beat around *v phr* To loaf or idle; = GOOF AROUND

beat around (or **about**) **the bush** *v phr* To avoid speaking directly and precisely; evade; tergiversate

beat one's **brains out 1** *v phr* To labor strenuously with the mind, often with a sense of having failed: *I beat my brains out getting ready for it, but flunked anyway* **2** *v phr* To threaten with bodily harm: *If you don't come through, I'll beat your brains out*

beaten down to the ankles *adj phr* Totally exhausted; =BEAT, POOPED

beaten-up *See* BEAT-UP

beater *n* A car, esp an old and used one: *when he's stolen the beater off the streets*—Ann Rule *See* EGGBEATER, GUM-BEATER, WORLD-BEATER

beat one's **gums** *See* BAT one's GUMS

beating *See* GUM-BEATING, TAKE A BEATING

beat it *v phr* To go away; depart; =SCRAM ● Often a command: *When the cop told us to beat it we didn't waste any time*

◁**beat** one's **meat**▷ *v phr* (Variations: **flog** or **pound** may replace **beat**; **dummy** or **log** may replace **meat**) To masturbate

beatnik *n fr 1950s* A person who is beat in the sense of alienation from society, etc [See *beat* and *-nik*; coined by San Francisco newspaper columnist Herb Caen in 1958]

◁**beat off**▷ *v* To masturbate

beat-out *adj fr 1870s* Tired; exhausted; =BEAT, POOPED

beat someone **out** *v phr* To surpass or best someone, esp by a narrow margin: *She just beat me out for the job, probably because she had more schooling*

beat pad *n phr 1960s narcotics* A place where marijuana may be bought and smoked, esp inferior marijuana; =BALLOON ROOM

beats me 1 *interj* An exclamation or acknowledgement of ignorance; =SEARCH ME **2** *sentence* I don't know; I don't understand: *Why was he hired? Beats me*

be at square one *See* GO BACK TO SQUARE ONE

beat the bushes *v phr* To search diligently; seek ardently: *They're beating the bushes for a new president*

beat the drum *v phr* To recommend emphatically and constantly; insistently feature: *He's beating the drum for that pet idea*

beat the gong *v phr outdated narcotics* To smoke opium

◁**beat the hog**▷ *v phr* To masturbate

beat the rap *v phr underworld* To go unpunished; be acquitted: *Every time they arrest him he beats the rap*

◁**beat the shit out of** someone or something▷ *v phr* (Variations: **bejesus** or **daylights** or **hell** or **kishkes** or **living daylights** or **living shit** or **stuffing** or **tar** may replace **shit**; **kick** or **knock** or another term denoting assault or punishment may replace **beat**) To defeat or thrash thoroughly; trounce; =CLOBBER: *The two joggers caught up with him and beat the shit out of him/ He told us that the cops kicked the bejesus out of his old man/ If he tries that again I'd knock the living shit out of him/ "I'll sue the shit out of her," vowed Professor Gold*—Joseph Heller

beat the socks off someone *v phr* To defeat decisively; trounce; =CLOBBER: *In a surprising upset, Hart beat the socks off Mondale*

beat someone's **time** *v phr* To win out over a rival, esp to take someone's girlfriend or boyfriend away

beat someone **to the draw** (or **to the punch**) *v phr* To act sooner or quicker than someone else; forestall: *The President beat Congress to the punch with that recommendation, which several representatives planned to present tomorrow*

beat to the ground *adj phr* Totally exhausted; =POOPED: *Frankie Machine, looking beat to the ground, brushed past*—Nelson Algren

beat-up *adj* Battered and damaged, esp by age and use: *He drove a beat-up Volvo/ an old beat-up dog*

beat up on *v phr* To attack and damage; criticize harshly; trounce; =CLOBBER: *a message to people who beat up on the public programs*—New York Times

beat one's **way** *v phr fr hoboes* To travel without paying; travel in the cheapest possible way

beaut (BYOOT) *n* A person or thing that is remarkable or extraordinary; =HUMDINGER, LOLLAPALOOZA: *While the president doesn't go off on these tangents often, when he does, they are beauts*—Drew Pearson/ *That black eye was a beaut*

beautiful *interj* An exclamation of approval and gratification

the **beautiful people** *n phr* People who are fashionable, wealthy, admired for style and opulence, etc; =the JET SET

beauty *adj Canadian* Excellent; superior; =GREAT: *I thought the guy was beauty*

beauty contest *n phr* A canvass or occasion that reveals preference, without the force of an election: *the mini-convention billed as a beauty contest for those seeking the presidential nomination*—Village Voice/ *Today's primary is considered a beauty contest because no delegates to the convention will actually be chosen*—National Public Radio

beaver 1 *n* A full beard **2** *n* A bearded man ◁**3**▷ *n* The female genitals, esp with a display of pubic hair ◁**4**▷ *n* Pornography: *The editor...lovingly runs his beaver one column over from his furious tirade*—New York Times ◁**5**▷ *n* A pornographic film; =SKIN FLICK ◁**6**▷ *n citizens band* A woman **7** *n* A person who works hard and diligently *See* SPLIT BEAVER

◁**beaver loop**▷ *n phr* A pornographic film strip in a coin-operated viewing machine

◁**beaver-shooter**▷ *n* A man obsessed with peering at female genitals: *A beaver shooter is, at bottom, a Peeping Tom*—Jim Bouton

◁**beaver shot**▷ *n phr* A photograph showing the female genitals prominently, esp one focusing on the vulva

bebop *See* BOP

not **be caught dead** *See* NOT BE CAUGHT DEAD

bed *See* GO TO BED, GO TO BED WITH someone, HOT-BED, MUSICAL BEDS, one SHOULD HAVE STOOD IN BED

bedbug *n railroad* A Pullman porter

See CRAZY AS A LOON

bed house **1** *n phr* *railroad* A caboose **2** *n phr* A brothel

bedpan commando *n phr* *WW2 armed forces* A medical orderly

bedposts *See* the DEVIL'S BEDPOSTS

bedrock **1** *n* The basic facts; the crucial elements **2** *modifier: a bedrock discussion/ bedrock decision*

bee **1** *n* = BEE IN one's BONNET **2** *n* *narcotics* Enough narcotic to fill a penny match box, a unit used in selling drugs; = B
See PUT THE BEE ON someone, PUT THE BITE ON someone

bee-bee *n* *WW2 armed forces* A machine-gun bullet

beef **1** *n* *fr middle 1900s underworld* A complaint; grievance: *Her mother called up to register a beef* —Billy Rose **2** *v: The hospital beefed when the city announced plans*—Philadelphia Bulletin **3** *n* A quarrel; argument: *I've got no beef with you, buddy* **4** *n* A customer's bill or check; = BAD NEWS **5** *n* Muscle; strength; huskiness ◁**6**▷ *n* The penis
See CUT A BEEF, SQUARE THE BEEF, WHERE'S THE BEEF

beefcake *n* A photograph or photographs of a muscular male body with little or no clothing: *The actor has no objections to male cheesecake, or beefcake as it is called in Hollywood*—Bob Thomas

beefcakery *n* Photography showing the nude or nearly nude male body

beefeater *n* An Englishman; = LIMEY [fr the preeminence of beef, esp roast beef, in the traditional English diet]

beefer *hoboes & underworld* **1** *n* A complainer; malcontent **2** *n* A police informer; = STOOL PIGEON

beef squad *n phr* A group of fighters or hoodlums, esp as used in labor disputes; = GOON SQUAD

beefsteak *v* *outdated cowboy* To manage a horse so badly that its back becomes raw and sore

the **Beefsteak and Onions** *n phr* *hoboes* The Baltimore and Ohio railroad

beef trust *n phr* Any group of stout or fat people, esp a chorus line of hefty women [fr the muckraker term for those who controlled the meat business]

beef up *v phr* To strengthen; reinforce: *The Patriots beefed up their defense by adding an all-star lineman*

bee in one's **bonnet** *n phr* A particular idea or notion, esp a fantastic or eccentric one; obsession: *He's got a bee in his bonnet about wheat germ curing all the world's ills*

beekie *n* *labor union* A company spy: *The "beekies" must go*—Michael Quill [probably fr beak]

beely bopper *See* DEELY BOPPER

beep **1** *v* To sound the horn of a car **2** *n: The car gave a few hearty beeps* **3** *v* A usu high-pitched short burst of sound used as a signal in an electronic device, on the telephone, etc: *Please give your message when you hear the beep*

beeper *n* A tiny radio receiver that gives a coded signal to a person being notified of a telephone call or other summons: *Beepers proliferate, tolling for many besides the doctor*—Wall Street Journal

beer *See* CRY IN one's BEER, DRINK one's BEER, SLING BEER, SMALL POTATOES

beer belly **1** *n* A protuberant paunch **2** *n* A man with a prominent paunch

beer bust (or **blast**) *n phr* *chiefly college students* A party where beer is the featured drink; = BREW-OUT: *It was supposed to be a party, a beerbust* —James Jones

beer jerker *n phr* *fr middle 1800s* A person whose work is drawing draught beer and serving it: *waiter girls, popularly known as "beer-jerkers"*—H Asbury

beer joint *n phr* A tavern or bar serving primarily beer

beerslinger *n* *fr late 1800s* A bartender

Beertown *n* Milwaukee, Wisconsin: *tiny minimum-security prisons right in the midst of Beertown*—Milwaukee Journal

beer up *v phr* To drink a lot of beer, esp enough to get drunk: *the mechanics, beering up with the guys and driving off to Detroit*—John Clellon Holmes

bees *See* the BIRDS AND THE BEES

beeswax *n* Business; concern: *What I do at home is none of his beeswax*

beetle **1** *n* *esp 1920s* A girl; young woman: *We could find plenty of nice beetles to rub ourselves against*—James T Farrell **2** *n* *horse-racing* A racehorse; = ROACH: *some beetle whose neck will feel the caress of a floral horseshoe*—S McLemore **3** *n* An early model of Volkswagen car, with a squat body curving down at front and rear

beeveedees *n* = BVDS

beewy (BEE wee) *n* *Navy* Money, esp coins [fr BWI "British West Indies" a term widely used in the Caribbean to mean "money"]

beezer **1** *n* *fr hoboes and prizefight* The nose **2** *n* The face

beggar's velvet *n phr* = HOUSE MOSS

be good *interj* A parting salutation

behind *n* The buttocks; rump; = ASS: *her broad, plain Slavic face, absence of waistline, and enormously broad behind*—Vogue

behind the cork *adj phr* Drunk

behind the ears *See* NOT DRY BEHIND THE EARS

behind the eight ball *adv phr* In a losing or endangered position: *He was sick and broke, right behind the eight ball* [fr the position of a pool player behind the black eight ball, which he must not hit]

behind the stick *See* WORK BEHIND THE STICK

beige **1** *n* *black* A black person with a light complexion **2** *adj* *high school students* Boring; insipid; = HO-HUM

be-in *n* *esp 1960s counterculture* A large, peaceable gathering of young people, esp of hippies, where they don't do anything in particular: *a San Francisco "Be-in" attracted more than 100,000 persons*—New York Times/ *with buttons and beards and Be-Ins* —WH Auden [modeled on *sit-in*]

the **bejesus** *See* BEAT THE SHIT OUT OF someone or something

belch **1** *n* *circus, hoboes & underworld* A complaint; = BEEF **2** *v: All she did was belch about* *how bad he treats her* **3** *v* To inform; =SQUEAL: *I feel good that I didn't belch on my friend*

belfry *See* HAVE BATS IN one's BELFRY

believe *See* YOU BETTER BELIEVE something

believer *See* MAKE A BELIEVER OUT OF someone

bell *See* DUMBBELL, HELL'S BELLS, MA BELL, RING A BELL, RING someone's BELL, RING THE BELL, SAVED BY THE BELL, WITH BELLS ON

bellhop *See* SEAGOING BELLHOP

bellied *See* YELLOW-BELLIED

bell-ringer **1** *n* A door-to-door salesman or canvasser **2** *n* A local politician **3** *n* A fact or event that causes one to recall something **4** *n* A tobacco chewer, who causes the cuspidor to chime when hit **5** *n* railroad A fire stoker **6** *n* A noteworthy occasion or celebration

bells **1** *n* In non-nautical use, equivalent to "o'clock": *It's ten bells already* **2** *n* cool musicians A vibraphone, esp as a jazz instrument: *Lionel Hampton the Leonardo of the bells* **3** *n* Bell-bottom trousers

See HELL'S BELLS, WITH BELLS ON

bells and whistles **1** *n phr* Unessential elements, esp when impressive and decorative; frills: *the latest "bells and whistles," as high-tech frills are called*—Time/ *you strip away the technological bells and whistles and...*—New York Times **2** *n phr* Accessories and accoutrements esp of the flashier sort; refinements; adornments; finishing touches: *Maserati...with all the bells and whistles*—Wall Street Journal **3** *modifier: If you are a bells and whistles guy, you will probably find these cars to be of more value*—New York Times

belly **1** *n* The stomach; abdomen; paunch; =GUT: *That's not my belly, my chest just sagged a little south* **2** *n* =BELLY LAUGH

See AIR one's BELLY, BASRA BELLY, BEER BELLY, JELLY-BELLY, LOW-BELLY STRIPPERS, MELON-BELLY, POSSUM BELLY, POTBELLY, POTBELLY STOVE, RICE-BELLY, SOURBALL, SOW-BELLY, YELLOW-BELLY

bellyache **1** *v* fr early 1900s To complain, esp to do so habitually; =BITCH: *always bellyaching about me*—James T Farrell **2** *n* A complaint; =BEEF

belly brass *n phr* outdated college students Various ornaments worn on a chain across one's vest

belly-buster *See* BELLY-WHOPPER

belly button *n phr* The navel

belly fiddle *n phr* jazz talk A guitar

belly flop *n phr* A dive in which one strikes the water stomach first; =BELLY-WHOPPER

belly-flopper *See* BELLY-WHOPPER

bellyful *n* The limit of what one can stand; an overplus; surfeit: *I've had a bellyful of your bellyaching*

belly gun *n phr* A short-barreled pistol inaccurate at any long range, but quite effective at very close range: *about .32 caliber, a belly gun, with practically no barrel*—Raymond Chandler

belly laugh *n phr* An especially loud, vigorous, and appreciative laugh; =BELLY, BOFFOLA

belly-robber or **belly-burglar** *n armed forces fr WW1* A cook or a mess sergeant

belly-rub *n* outdated college students A dance, esp at a public dance hall where one pays for each dance

belly-smacker *See* BELLY-WHOPPER

belly stove *See* POTBELLY STOVE

belly telly *n phr* A small television set, such as might be perched on one's stomach for viewing as one lies flat

belly up **1** *v phr* fr cowboys To die; be down and out; collapse; =GO BELLY UP: *were the schools to belly up tomorrow*—Philadelphia **2** *adj phr: The whole project's belly up*

See GO BELLY UP

belly up to *v phr* fr cowboys To push or come up close to, esp to a bar for a drink: *Sammy Davis, Jr bellied up to the bar*—People Weekly/ *Meat Loaf bellies up to Billy Joel at a softball showdown*—Rolling Stone

belly-wash *n* Any drink one holds in contempt; =SWILL

belly-whopper (Variations: **-buster** or **-flopper** or **-smacker** may replace **-whopper**) **1** *n* A sled ride begun by running with the sled held at one's side, then leaping onto it stomach down **2** *n* =BELLY FLOP

below the belt **1** *adv phr* Not according to decent and usual practice; unconscionably irregular: *to hit below the belt/ aim below the belt* **2** *adj phr* Nasty; malicious; =DIRTY: *That remark was below the belt/ his below-the-belt tricks* [fr boxing where blows to the lower part of the body are forbidden]

belt **1** *v* To hit; strike; =SOCK: *Ed belts him in the kisser/ He belted the ball a mile* **2** *n* A blow; stroke; =WHACK: *She gave it a good belt* **3** *n* A thrill; transport of pleasure; =KICK: *You'll get a belt out of this one* **4** *n* narcotics A marijuana cigarette; =JOINT **5** *v* To drink, esp vigorously and often: *He's belting down the booze again* **6** *n* A drink; swig; swallow: *He handed me the bottle and I took a belt at it*—H Allen Smith

See BORSCHT BELT, TIGHTEN one's BELT

belt around *v phr* To travel or move fast, esp in a fast car

belt out *v phr* To sing in a loud and vigorous style

be my guest *sentence* Do as you please ● Often an ironical acquiescence to something ill-advised: *You want to tell the cop he's wrong? Be my guest*

bench warmer *n phr* A person not among the most active and important members of an enterprise; esp, a substitute athlete who seldom plays

bend **1** *v* To violate or contravene to some degree: *to bend one's principles a bit* **2** *v* jazz musicians To slur a note: *they alter pitch...they call it "bending"*—Stephen Longstreet **3** *n* =BENDER

See AROUND THE BEND

bend someone's **ear** *v phr* To talk to someone insistently and at length: *He was bending my ear about his new car*

bender **1** *n* fr middle 1800s A spree, esp a drinking spree; =BAT, BINGE: *That three-day bender left Jim hurting all over/ a carrot-juice bender* **2** *n* underworld A stolen car [first sense fr *hell-bender* "alligator," of obscure origin, which came to mean "anything spectacular and superior" and was applied to a great spree in the middle 19th century] **See** BONE-BENDER, EAR-BENDER, ELBOW-BENDER, FENDER-BENDER, KNEE-BENDER, MIND-BLOWER, PRETZEL-BENDER

bending *See* ELBOW-BENDING, MIND-BLOWING

bend someone's **mind** *v phr* To have a very strong and usu disturbing mental effect; impress powerfully: *This one really bends her mind; she starts philosophizing*—Washington Post

bend over backwards *v phr* To make every effort; strive mightily; = GO OUT OF ONE'S WAY: *I bent over backwards trying to be fair*

the **bends** *n phr* Caisson disease, a painful result of rapid decompression after a deep dive

bend the (or one's) **elbow** (Variations: **crook** or **tip** may replace **bend**; **his** or **her** or **an** may replace **the**) *fr early 1800s* **1** *v phr* To drink frequently and heavily, esp whiskey: *They cautioned him that maybe he was bending the elbow a little too often* **2** *v phr* To have a drink: *We'll tip the elbow over at my place*

bend the throttle *v phr Air Force fr WW2 & teenagers* To drive or fly very fast

benny or **bennie** **1** *n narcotics* Any amphetamine pill, esp Benzedrine (a trade name) **2** *modifier: The kid was a benny addict* **3** *n* = BENNY²

Benny¹ *n shoeshop* The shoe size B

Benny² or **Benjamin** *n fr hoboes fr British underworld* A man's overcoat

Benny³ *See* JACK BENNY

bent 1 *adj* Intoxicated, either from alcohol or narcotics **2** *adj* Having very little money: *I'm not quite broke, but quite bent* **3** *adj* Homosexual **4** *adj* Sexually aberrant; = KINKY: *Charley got bent bad over women...he was kinky when it came to ladies*—Harry Crews **5** *adj* Dishonest; shady; = CROOKED: *look a little bent...look like you were up for a little whoremongering and black-marketing and smuggling*—Richard Merkin **6** *adj underworld fr early 1900s* Stolen, said esp of car **7** *adj fr Air Force* Angry; upset

bent-eight *See* FORKED-EIGHT

bentnose *n* A drug-addicted criminal: *this bentnose in their town, a crud with a long drug sheet*—Lawrence Saunders

bent out of shape 1 *adj phr* Intoxicated; drunk; = STONED **2** *adj fr Air Force* Very angry; extremely upset: *He is so far bent out of shape by the press reaction*—Washington Post/ *Why are you bent out of shape?*—Armistead Maupin

Bernice or **burnese** *n outdated narcotics* Cocaine crystals inhaled by users [perhaps from a random code name]

berries *n Army* Wine

the **berries** *n phr esp 1920s & 1930s* The best; = the MOST [fr early-20th-century college slang *berry* "something easy and pleasant, a good thing"]

berry *n fr early 1900s* A dollar [perhaps fr the notion of a small unit of something good, and alliterating with *buck*; see the *berries*]
See OYSTER-BERRY

Bertha *See* BIG BERTHA

beside oneself *adj phr* Undergoing a surge or transport of emotion, esp of anger: *She was beside herself when she found out he was cheating/ He was beside himself with despair*

best *See* someone's LEVEL BEST

best bib and tucker *n phr fr early 1800s* One's best clothes; = GLAD RAGS

best fellow *n phr* = MAIN MAN

best girl *n phr* = MAIN SQUEEZE

best shot *See* GIVE something one's BEST SHOT

the **best** (or **greatest**) **thing since sliced bread** *n phr* A person or thing that is superlative; a paragon; = WINNER: *I thought she was the best thing since sliced bread*—Washington Post

bet *See* IF BET

bet one's **bottom dollar** *v phr* To be absolutely sure of something; be totally convinced; = BET THE FARM: *I'll bet my bottom dollar she'll be back*

Bete *See* PHI BETE

betsy or **Betsy** or **Betsey** *n* A firearm of any sort: *I got a lot of votes in ol' Betsey here*—Walt Kelly
See IRON BETSY

better *See* GO something or someone ONE BETTER, NO BETTER THAN SHE OUGHT TO BE, YOU BETTER BELIEVE something

better half *n phr* One's wife; occasionally, one's husband

bet the farm (or **the ranch**) *v phr* Bet everything one has; = GO FOR BROKE, BET one's BOTTOM DOLLAR: *I wouldn't have bet the farm...but I'd sure bet the back forty*—Washingtonian/ *I wouldn't bet the ranch that he'll be reappointed*—National Public Radio

bet the rent *v phr* To be so sure of something that one would bet one's most necessary money; be very confident of something: *You can bet the rent the Jacksons will go where the big money is*—Washington Post

between a (or **the**) **rock and a** (or **the**) **hard place** *adv phr fr cowboys* In a dilemma: *So a writer is caught between the rock and the hard place*—New York Times/ *informants, caught between the rock of prison and the hard place of the snitch*—Washington Post

between the lily whites *See* SLIP IN BETWEEN THE LILY WHITES

bet your boots *v phr* (Variations: **ass** or **sweet ass** or **bibby** or **bippy** or **bottom dollar** or **life** or **shirt** or **whiskers** may replace **boots**) To be absolutely assured; count on it: *You can bet your boots I'll be there/ You bet your sweet ass it was easier at the museum*—Leslie Hollander

bevels *n gambling* A pair of dishonest dice with some edges beveled to affect the roll

bewitched *adj* Drunk

bfd or **BFD** (pronounced as separate letters) *n* Something or someone of importance ● Usually used sarcastically [fr *big fucking deal*]

B-girl *n fr 1940s* A promiscuous girl or woman, esp one who works in a bar as a sort of hostess to stimulate the sale of drinks; = BAR-GIRL

bi (BĪ) **1** *adj* Bisexual; =AC-DC **2** *n: I think maybe Vi is a bi*

bib *n lunch counter* A napkin
See BEST BIB AND TUCKER

bibby *See* BIPPY

bibful *n* A great deal of talk, esp on personal gossipy matters

bible **1** *n* Any indispensable and authoritative book or text **2** *n circus* A platform that holds the reserved seats, and can be folded like a book
See CALIFORNIA PRAYER BOOK

Bible *See* SWALLOW THE BIBLE, SWEAR ON A STACK OF BIBLES, TIJUANA BIBLE

Bible-banger or **Bible-thumper** *n* A strict religionist, esp a Protestant fundamentalist: *to ensure it doesn't offend some Bible-banger in Mississippi* —Playboy

◁**bicho**▷ (BEE choh) *n* The penis [fr Spanish]

bicoastal *adj* Active on both the Atlantic and Pacific coasts: *a pair of bicoastal type A males* —Time

bicycle *See* GET ON one's BICYCLE

biddle *See* BINDLE

biddy **1** *n* A woman, esp an old shrewish woman ● Nearly always with "old": *Charley had met an old biddy named Zoe Winthrop*—W Fuller **2** *n* =CHICK [diminutive of the name *Bridget*]

biff **1** *n fr late 1800s* A blow with the fist; =SOCK **2** *v: He wouldn't quit, so she biffed him* **3** *n musicians* A missed high note on a brass instrument ◁**4**▷ *n* =BIFFER

◁**biffer**▷ *n black* A homely woman who compensates by being promiscuous

biff-guy *n underworld* A hoodlum; thug

biffy *n chiefly Canadian* A toilet; bathroom

big **1** *adj* Important; powerful: *the big names in this business/ the big guy* **2** *adj* Popular; successful: *If I do say so, we were very big*—Bing Crosby/ *The book's big in Chicago* **3** *adv* Successfully; outstandingly well: *to hit it big*
See BIG WITH someone, GO OVER BIG, MAKE IT BIG, TAKE IT HARD, TALK BIG

Big *adj* Good; decent; admirable ● Used as an epithet for an admired person: *Hey, what's up, Big Eddy?*
See MISTER BIG

the **Big Apple** or the **Apple** **1** *n phr* New York City: *New York is the Big Apple*—Stephen Longstreet/ *young musicians storming into the Apple* —Village Voice **2** *n phr* A jitterbug dance of the late 1930s [fr jazz musicians' term *apple* for a city, esp a city in the North]

◁**bigass**▷ **1** *adj* Pretentiously large: *Abraham opened the door of his bigass Cadillac*—Hugh Selby, Jr **2** *adj* Pretentious; self-important: *Don't act bigass with me*

◁**bigass bird**▷ *See* TAKE OFF LIKE A BIGASS BIRD

big band **1** *n phr* A large band of dance or swing musicians, like the Benny Goodman or Tommy Dorsey bands of the 1930s **2** *modifier: the big-band sound/ big-band era*

big bang **1** *n phr* The primordial explosion by which the universe was hypothetically created **2**

modifier: the big-bang theory/ big-bang cosmology

Big Bertha **1** *n phr* A large or fat woman **2** *n phr fr WW1* Any very large cannon [the artillery sense is said to be fr *Frau Bertha Krupp*, a member of the German armaments-making family]

big boy **1** *n phr* You there; man; =MAC ● A term of address variously used with the intention to challenge, flatter, attract, etc: *Want a little fun, big boy?* **2** *n phr* An important man; =BIGGIE, BIG SHOT: *He tried to shake down one of the big boys* —Raymond Chandler **3** *n phr* An adult male; grown-up man ● Most often used in rebuke: *Cut that out, you're a big boy now*

Big Brother or **big brother** **1** *n phr* The faceless and ruthless power of the totalitarian or bureaucratic state personified **2** *n phr airline* The tracking radar used by ground controllers [fr its use by George Orwell in his novel *Nineteen Eighty-Four*]

big brown eyes *n phr* A woman's breasts; =HEADLIGHTS

big bucks *n phr* A large amount of money; great sums of money; =MEGABUCKS: *That car would cost you big bucks today*

big bug *n phr* An important person; =BIG SHOT: *even among the big bugs of his own Cabinet* —Robert Lynd

big butter-and-egg man *See* BUTTER-AND-EGG MAN

big buzz *n phr* Loudest current rumor: *the big buzz around Broadway is the announcement*—Aquarian

Big C *n phr* Cancer

the **big cage** *n phr underworld* A state or federal prison or reformatory; =the BIG HOUSE

big cheese **1** *n phr* =BIG BUG, BIG SHOT **2** *n phr* A stupid or rude man; lout [for first sense, see the *cheese*]

big D *n phr* LSD

Big D **1** *n phr* Detroit, Michigan **2** *n phr* Dallas, Texas

Big Daddy or **big daddy** **1** *n phr* You there; man; =BIG BOY, MAC ● Term of address used to any man, usu with a view to flattering him **2** *n phr* =DADDY **3** *n phr* =DADDY-O

big deal **1** *n phr* Anything very important; consequential event or circumstance ● Often used ironically to deflate someone or something, esp in the retort "Big deal" after someone has made an earnest reference: *Getting good grades is a big deal around here/ So you just bought an Audi. Big deal* **2** *n phr* An important person; =BIG SHOT: *George thinks he's a very big deal since he got the promotion* **3** *modifier: his big-deal pomposity/ a big-deal salary*
See MAKE A BIG PRODUCTION, NO BIG DEAL

Big Dick *n phr crapshooting* The point or roll of ten

the **Big Ditch** *n phr* Variously the Erie Canal, Atlantic Ocean, or Panama Canal

bigdome *n* An important person, esp a manager or business executive; =BIG SHOT: *if the NBA bigdomes are concerned about their image and popular appeal*—New York Daily News

big doolie *n phr* An important person, esp a winning athlete; = BIG SHOT: *I got a gold today, so I'm a big doolie*—New York Times [perhaps related to the earlier term *dooly* "dynamite"]

the **Big Drink** *n phr* Variously the Mississippi River, the Atlantic Ocean, or the Pacific Ocean

big drink of water *See* LONG DRINK OF WATER

big drive *n phr narcotics* A heavy or comparatively pure injection of a narcotic: *man, their eyes when that big drive hits*—Nelson Algren

big eights *n phr black* Long winter underwear

big enchilada *n phr* The chief; the head person; = BOSS: *The Big Enchilada is tied up with the Chief Honcho at the moment, but the Little Enchilada can see you now*—New Yorker cartoon

bigeye *n black* A greedy person

big fat *adj phr* Embarrassingly obvious; blatant and humiliating: *I couldn't keep my big fat mouth shut/ His big fat trademark heart greets you in this show*—Village Voice

big fish (or **frog**) *n phr* An important person; = BIG SHOT

big fish (or **frog**) **in a little** (or **small**) **pond** *n phr* An important person in a relatively unimportant place

big foot *n phr newspaper office* A senior editor, important editorialist or columnist, etc: *but many an editor or pundit, a "big foot" in the parlance of the bus*—Time [fr *bigfoot*, one of the designations of Sasquatch, a large hairy humanoid creature thought by some to inhabit the forests of the Pacific Northwest, and probably applied to senior newspaper persons because of metaphorical size and menace]

big George *n phr* A quarter of a dollar [fr the portrait of George Washington on the coin]

bigger (or **other**) **fish to fry** *n phr* Other and more pressing matters to attend to; more important things in prospect: *Anyway...we've got bigger fish to fry/ Tell him to relax, we've got bigger fish to fry*—Ed McBain

biggie **1** *n* A prominent or stellar person; = BIG SHOT: *Sullivan continues putting the bee on other Government biggies*—Variety **2** *n* Something important and successful; = BIG DEAL: *a tubular biggie, not only in LA and NY, but in Chicago, Detroit, and Atlanta*—Time **3** *n* Anything large and important: *if a real biggie, like Brazil, went to the wall*—Playboy
See NO BIGGIE

big gun *n phr* = BIG SHOT

big guns *See* HEAVY ARTILLERY

big H *n phr narcotics* Heroin

Big Harry *n phr narcotics* Heroin

bighead *n* A self-important, conceited person

a **big head** **1** *n phr* fr early 1800s Conceit: *The promotion gave him a big head* **2** *n phr* The discomfort consequent upon drinking too much liquor: *The rum gave me a big head next morning*

bigheaded *adj* Conceited

big hole *n phr truckers* The low gear of a truck

the **big house** or the **Big House** *n phr underworld fr middle 1800s* A state or federal penitentiary; = the BIG CAGE: *to go to the big house for the rest of his life*—Morris Bishop

bight *See* TAKE A REEF IN IT

the **big idea** *See* WHAT'S THE BIG IDEA

big if *n phr* A very important and unsure condition: *The big if is whether inflation will go up*

big John *n phr* A police officer or the police

the **big joint** *n phr* = the BIG HOUSE

big-league *adj* Serious; important; professional: *No more fooling around, now it's big-league stuff*

big-leaguer *n* = BIG-TIMER

the **big leagues** **1** *n phr* In baseball, the major leagues **2** *n phr* The higher, more serious and arduous reaches of a profession, business, government, sport, etc; = the BIG TIME, HARDBALL

the **big lie** *n phr* A major political untruth, usu of a demagogic sort, uttered frequently by leaders as a means of duping and controlling the constituency [fr a notion of Adolf Hitler in *Mein Kampf*]

big man **1** *n phr* An important or influential man; = BIG NUMBER **2** *n phr* fr students A male school or campus leader: *the prep school "big man"*—F Scott Fitzgerald

big man on campus *n phr college students* A male college student leader; = BMOC

big moment *n phr students fr 1930s* One's sweetheart or lover

big money *See* HEAVY MONEY

bigmouth **1** *n* A person who talks constantly and loudly **2** *n* A person who freely announces personal opinions and judgments; = KNOW-IT-ALL, SMART-ASS **3** *n* A person who can't keep a secret
See HAVE A BIG MOUTH

big name **1** *n phr* A celebrated person, personality or entity, esp a star entertainer: *Hollywood figures only the big names are bankable/ Harper & Row is a big name in publishing* **2** *n phr* A prominent reputation; fame: *The group has a big name in the Boston area* **3** *modifier*: *a big-name star/ They get a big-name fee*

big nickel *n phr gambling* A $5000 bet

big noise **1** *n phr* Important news: *Big Noise from Moscow*—New York Daily News **2** *n phr* An important person; most influential person: *Who's the big noise around here?*

big number *n phr* = BIG MAN

big O **1** *n phr railroad* A train conductor; = BIG OX **2** *n phr narcotics* Opium used for smoking

big one *n phr fr gambling* A thousand dollars, esp as a bet: *The highjackers are handed 50 cents a gallon, which is 15 big ones and OK for a couple hours' work*—Time/ *The next time you want me to do the Today show, it's going to cost you ten big ones*—Art Buchwald
See MAKE LITTLE ONES OUT OF BIG ONES

the **big one** *n phr* The most important or crucial item: *Having a winning season is fine, but now we've got to win the big one*

big ox **1** *n phr* Any large, strong man **2** *n phr railroad* A train conductor; = BIG O

the **big picture** *n phr* The large strategic situation as distinct from little details; inclusive of the surrounding circumstances

big pipe   *n phr cool musicians fr 1950s* A baritone saxophone

the **Big Pond**   *n phr fr middle 1800s* The Atlantic Ocean

the **Big Pretzel**   *n phr* Philadelphia

Big Pretzelite   *n phr* A Philadelphian: *several reasons for Big Pretzelites to swing into the Franklin Plaza*—Philadelphia

big production   *See* MAKE A BIG PRODUCTION

big rag   *n phr* = BIG TOP

the **bigs**   *n phr* The major leagues, in baseball or other areas; = the BIG TIME: *When Backman was in the bigs, he wasn't your regular Mr. Sunshine*—Village Voice

the **big school**   *n phr hoboes & underworld fr 1920s* = the BIG HOUSE

the **big score**   *n phr* Success; spectacular achievement: *Jobs' entrepreneurial flair and his instinct for the big score*—Time

big shot or **bigshot**   **1** *n phr* or *n fr early 1900s* A very important person; influential person; leader; = BIG CHEESE, BIGGIE: *eight big shots of various farmers', manufacturers', or veterans' organizations* —HL Mencken/ *"Hey, bigshot," his father would bellow on the telephone*—Joseph Heller   **2** *modifier* • Often used sarcastically: *a big-shot chest surgeon/ big-shot notions*

big stick   *n phr firefighters* An aerial ladder

the **big sticks**   *n phr lumberjacks* The forest, usu remote from civilized places

big stiff   *n phr* A large, rough man, esp one who is somewhat stupid as well • Sometimes used as a term of affection by a woman

big stink   **1** *n phr* A loud and prolonged complaint; an extensive fuss; = MAKE A FEDERAL CASE OUT OF something: *He made a big stink about my using his screwdriver*   **2** *n phr* A scandal: *There'll be a big stink about these tapes*

big talk   **1** *n phr* Boastful and extravagant talk; esp, promises or claims beyond one's capacity: *His promises were just big talk*   **2** *v: Don't big-talk a big-talker, man*

big (or **high**) **ticket**   *salespersons* **1** *adj phr* Expensive; high-priced: *very low for the promotion of a big-ticket item*—Fortune/ *More and more complete-text services are becoming available, especially in high-ticket fields like law*—Philadelphia   **2** *n phr* The sale of an expensive item: *He wrote up a couple of big tickets yesterday*

big time   *adv phr Army* Very much; extremely: *He's gonna complain big time*

the **big time**   **1** *n phr* The upper reaches of a profession, business, government, sport, etc; = the BIG LEAGUES   **2** *modifier: a big-time outfit/ big-time crime* [fr the outdated theater use designating certain important vaudeville circuits or houses]

big-time operator   *n phr* A person conspicuously active in affairs where trade-offs, special favors, private understandings, etc, are crucial; machinator; = BTO, MACHER, WHEELER-DEALER

big-timer   **1** *n* = BIG-LEAGUER   **2** *n* A professional gambler

big-time spender   *n phr* A person who is generous and extravagant, esp for lavish entertainment; = HIGH ROLLER

big top   **1** *n phr circus* The main tent of a circus; also, the circus and circus life in general: *hypnotized by life under the big top*—Hamilton Basso   **2** *n phr outdated underworld* A bank

the **big trouble**   *n phr hoboes fr 1930s* The Great Depression of the 1930s and 40s

big wheel   **1** *n phr* An important person; = BIG SHOT: *Up to that juncture I was boss man of the family and big wheel*—SJ Perelman   **2** *modifier: a big-wheel attitude/ Look at the big-wheel label on those jeans*

big white phone   *See* TALK TO THE BIG WHITE PHONE

big with someone   *prep phr* Popular with; preferred by; relished by: *That's big with her*—Armistead Maupin/ *Baggy sweaters are real big with the kids this year*

bike   **1** *n* A bicycle or motorcycle   **2** *n* A motorcycle police officer

    See DIRT BIKE, TOWN PUMP

biker   *n* A motorcycle rider and enthusiast: *Bikers in black leather roared through the town*

bikinis   *n* Very brief underpants

bilge   **1** *n* Nonsense; worthless and vain matter; = TRIPE, BLAH   **2** *v* (also **bilge out**) *Annapolis fr 1920s* To fail or expel a student   **3** *v* To use the toilet

    See PUMP BILGE

bilk joint   *n phr* A business place, esp a shop, that overcharges and cheats its customers; = GYP JOINT: *the Times Square tenderloin, the porno shops, the bilk joints, the freaks*—Pulpsmith [fr 16th century *bilk* "cheat, fraud" plus *joint*; see *joint*]

bill   **1** *n* The nose   **2** *n outdated black* A knife, esp a small one easily concealed   **3** *n* A hundred dollars: *I laid out four bills for that shearling*   **4** *n* A single dollar: *Can I borrow a couple of bills until tomorrow?*

    See HALF BILL, PHONY AS A THREE-DOLLAR BILL

Bill Daley   *n phr horse-racing* A long lead in a race: *She might go out on the Bill Daley and hang on*—J Lilienthal [after a jockey instructor who advised taking a long lead and holding it]

billies   *n high school students* Bills; currency; money

Bill Shears   *n phr hoboes* A farmer [fr *scissorbill*, by inversion and substitution of *shears*]

Billyball   *n* The style of baseball played under the management of Billy Martin

billycan or **billy**   *n hoboes fr Australian usage* A container for heating water or for cooking

billy club or **billy**   *n phr* or *n fr middle 1800s* A police officer's nightstick

billy-goat   *n armed forces* Mutton

bim   *n esp 1920s* A girl or woman, esp one's girlfriend [fr *bimbo*]

bimbette   *n* A frivolous or stupid young woman; a man's plaything • Regarded by some women as offensive: *itching to play something more demanding than bimbettes and stand-by wives*—Times

bimbo 1 *n fr early 1900s* A man, esp a mean and menacing one; =BABY, BOZO: *The bimbos once helped pluck a bank*—Dashiell Hammett/ *one of them bimbos which hurls a mean hammer*—H Witwer **2** *n fr early 1900s* An insignificant person; =NEBBISH: *Nobody listened to the poor bimbo* **3** *n 1920s* A baby ◁**4**▷ *n fr 1920s* A woman, esp a young woman: *What kind of a bimbo did he think I am?*—Hal Boyle **5** *n fr 1920s* A prostitute; =HOOKER: *Some escort services are just fronts for prostitution...men call up and the service just sends out some bimbo in blue jeans from Brooklyn*—New York [fr Italian, "baby, bambino"; the final sense is probably related to the common use of *Bimbo* as the name of a monkey or a monkey doll, in turn probably related to the monkey that accompanied street organ-grinders, typically Italians]

Bimmer *n* A BMW car: *Bum out a Bimmer driver. Unleash a Chevette*—Car and Driver

the **bin** *n phr* =LOONY BIN
See WEENIE BIN

bind *n* A very tight and awkward situation; cleft stick; =BOX, JAM: *This is a nasty sort of bind*
See IN A BIND

binder *See* HIGH-BINDER

binders *n police, hot rodders & students* The brakes of a car

bindle or **biddle 1** *n hoboes* A blanket-roll holding one's possessions; =BALLOON **2** *n* Any package or bundle **3** *n narcotics* A packet of narcotics, esp when folded as an envelope

bindlestiff *fr early 1900s* **1** *n* A migrant harvest worker, esp a hobo with his bindle: *I was a bindlestiff. That's the class that will do some work once in a while*—JR Kennedy **2** *n* Any hobo or derelict [fr *bindle* "blanket-roll, bundle" and *stiff* "worker, migratory worker"]

bing 1 *n outdated underworld* A packet of narcotics **2** *n prison* A prison cell used for solitary confinement; =the HOLE

binge *n* A spree, esp a drunken spree; =BAT, BENDER: *with the studios on an economy binge*—Variety/ *one last banana binge*—Philadelphia Bulletin

binged (BINGD) *adj armed forces fr WW1* Vaccinated

binger (BIN jər) *n* A person who goes on a spree or sprees: *situational sketches about stage mothers...and food bingers*—Village Voice

bingle 1 *n baseball* A base hit, esp a single **2** *n gambling* A poker chip, usu worth 25 cents **3** *n narcotics* A large supply or cache of narcotics

bingo *interj* An exclamation in reaction to something sudden and unexpected, or expressing sudden success: *Have your contracts and debts declared void and, bingo, you're back in business*—Newsweek
See BEACH BLANKET BINGO

bingo-boy *n street gang* A drunkard

bing spot *n phr outdated armed forces* A vaccination scar

binnacle list *n phr Navy* A list of sailors too sick for duty

binny *n underworld* A large or concealed pocket in a shoplifter's coat where stolen things may be hidden

bio *n* A biography, esp a brief one in a yearbook, theater program, etc: *By now Jenny had read my bio in the program*—Erich Segal

bioflick or **biopic** *n* A movie or television show based on some person's life story: *star in a bioflick on...Charlie Parker*—People Weekly/ *why so many biopics apocryphy their subjects*—Village Voice

bippy or **bibby** *n* The buttocks; =ASS
See BET YOUR BOOTS

bird 1 *n* A person of either sex, usu a man and often elderly: *I'm a literary bird myself*—F Scott Fitzgerald/ *She was a tall old bird with a chin like a rabbit*—Raymond Chandler **2** *n* A young woman; =CHICK ● Much commoner in British usage; regarded by some women as offensive **3** *n fr late 1800s* An odd or unusual person; an eccentric; =FLAKE, WEIRDO: *He was a funny bird in many ways*—Armistead Maupin ◁**4**▷ *n fr late 1800s* A male homosexual; =GAY **5** *modifier: a gaggle of the guys in a Third Avenue bird bar*—Judith Crist **6** *n armed forces fr WW1* The eagle as an insignia of rank **7** *modifier: a bird colonel* **8** *n* Any aircraft, esp a helicopter **9** *n astronautics* A rocket or guided missile **10** *n aerospace* A communications satellite: *A VTR operator in Vancouver is editing a local piece for The National. "Gotta make the bird," the guy says confidently*—Toronto Life/ *an agreement to put Satellite News Channel up on its bird*—Village Voice
See EARLY BIRD, FOR THE BIRDS, GOONEY BIRD, HAVE A BIRD, JAILBIRD, LOVEBIRDS, OFF one's NUT, RAILBIRD, TAKE OFF LIKE A BIGASS BIRD, WHIRLYBIRD, YARDBIRD

the **bird 1** *n phr* A rude flatulatory noise made with the tongue and lips to express disapproval, derision, or contempt; =BRONX CHEER, RASPBERRY: *Give him the boid, the raspberry*—Eugene O'Neill **2** *n phr* =the FINGER [first sense fr the mid-19th-century expression *give the big bird* "hiss someone like a goose"]

birdbrain *n* A person of meager intelligence; idiot: *whatever bird-brain is rendering one of the ditties of the day*—Robert Ruark

birdbrained *adj* Stupid: *Nancy Fox, an abducted bride, is unquestionably birdbrained*—Village Voice

birdcage 1 *n underworld* A prison cell **2** *n merchant marine* A small room rented by the day; sleeping space in a cheap lodging house **3** *n railroad* The lantern used by brake operators and switch handlers

bird colonel *n phr* =CHICKEN COLONEL

bird course *n phr Canadian students* An easy college course; =GUT COURSE

bird dog 1 *n phr* A person, like a detective, talent scout, etc, whose job is to find something or someone **2** *n phr students* A chaperon at a dance **3** *n phr service academy* A tactical office, enforcing order and discipline **4** *n phr WW2 Army Air Forces* A fighter or interceptor aircraft **5** *n phr airline* The automatic direction-finding instrument of an aircraft **6** *n phr gambling* A minor gambler who seeks the company and instruction of professionals

bird-dog **1** *v Army fr WW2* To become overly friendly with a superior's girlfriend or wife **2** *v students* To take or try to take another's girlfriend

birdfarm *n Vietnam War Navy* An aircraft carrier: *The days are gone when a carrier was called a flat-top. The craft is now a "birdfarm"*—New York Times

birdie or **birdy** *adj teenagers* Eccentric; weird; = FLAKY

birdies *n* = BIRD LEGS
See HEAR THE BIRDIES SING

bird legs *n phr* Thin bony legs

birds *See* FOR THE BIRDS, LOVEBIRDS

the **birds and the bees** *n phr* The basic facts about sex and reproduction, esp as explained to children

birdseed *n* Any dry breakfast cereal

birdseye *n narcotics* A small packet or portion of a narcotic

◁**birdseye maple**▷ *n phr black fr 1920s* A light-skinned black girl, esp if sexually attractive

◁**birdshit**▷ *n* = CHICKEN SHIT

◁**birdturd**▷ *n* A despicable person; = PRICK, SHIT: *Suppose those birdturds come back here today* —Bernard Malamud

birdwood *n narcotics* Marijuana cigarettes

birdyback *n* The transport of loaded containers or semitrailers by airplane

birthday suit *n phr fr middle 1800s* What one is wearing when completely nude; the state of naked-ness: *Naked as a jaybird, with nothing on over his birthday suit*

biscuit **1** *n prizefight* The face or head **2** *n railroad* A payroll timekeeper
See DOG BISCUIT, GROUND BISCUIT

biscuit hooks *n phr* The hands

biscuit-shooter *n outdated cowboy* A cook, esp on a ranch

bissel (BISS əl) *n* A bit; a little: *I'd hold onto your God's little acre a bissel longer*—Village Voice [fr Yiddish]

bistro (BEE stroh) *n* A restaurant or cafe [fr French]

bit **1** *n underworld* A prison sentence: *Ferrati, whose "bit" was three to seven years*—PL Quinlan **2** *n* (also **bit part**) *theater* A small part in a play or other show **3** *n fr theater* A display of pre-tended feeling, or an outright imitation; = ACT, SHTICK: *So he does his hurt-puppy-dog bit/ You should see my Jimmy Cagney bit* **4** *n fr 1950s beat & cool talk* A person's particular set of atti-tudes, reactions, behavior patterns, etc; style; life style; = THING: *Zen never was my real bit*
See FOUR-BIT, SIX-BIT, TWO-BIT

bit banger *n phr computer* A programmer who works out details of a computer program, rather than a subordinate or assistant programmer

bitch ◁**1**▷ *n* A woman one dislikes or disapproves of, esp a malicious, devious, or heartless woman ● The equivalent of the masculine **bastard** as a general term of opprobrium: *a cold-hearted bitch*
—Budd Schulberg ◁**2**▷ *n homosexuals* A wasp-ish or insolent male homosexual **3** *n* The queen of any suit in playing cards **4** *v* To complain; gripe; = BEEF, BELLYACHE: *College students always bitch about the food* **5** *n:* *What's your bitch today?* **6** *n* Anything arduous or very disagreea-ble: *That last mile was a bitch/ I had a bitch of a toothache* **7** *n* Anything pleasant or admirable; = BEAUT, HUMDINGER: *I just read his new book, and it's a bitch/ That's my new boat; ain't she a bitch?* **8** *v* To cheat; = CHISEL: *You never tried to bitch me out of anything*—Budd Schulberg
See BULL BITCH, DRUNK AS A FIDDLER'S BITCH, IT'S A BITCH, SON OF A BITCH

bitch box *n phr armed forces fr WW2* A public-address system; = SQUAWK BOX

bitchen or **bitchin'** or **bitching** **1** *adj teen-ager* Good; excellent; superior: *A bitchen new sin-gle from Southern California has been riding the airwaves to the max this summer*—Newsweek/ *Because of your bitchin' body, I'm going to put you on hold for a couple of days*—Easyriders/ *to borrow a term from the Valley Girls, one bitchen report* —Newsweek **2** *adv* Very; extremely: *That was a bitching good party*

◁**bitch in heat**▷ *n phr* A sexually predatory woman; promiscuous woman

bitch kitty ◁**1**▷ *n phr* An especially disliked or disagreeable woman **2** *n phr* An especially unpleasant or difficult task: *Taking the rusty muffler off the car was a bitch kitty* **3** *n phr* Anything especially pleasant or admirable; = HUMDINGER: *a real bitch kitty of a performance*
See IT'S A BITCH

bitch lamp *n phr hoboes* An improvised lamp; an oil lantern [see *slut lamp*]

a **bitch of a** or **one bitch of a** *adj phr* Very remarkable, awful, admirable, distressing, etc; = a HELL OF A, SOME KIND OF: *Getting the thing together was a bitch of a job/ She's wearing one sweet bitch of a dress!*

bitch session **1** *n phr* A meeting where com-plaints and grievances are voiced, esp by labor union representatives; = GRIPE SESSION **2** *n phr* = BULL SESSION

bitch up *v phr* To ruin; spoil; = LOUSE UP: *His goof bitched up the whole project*

bitchy ◁**1**▷ *adj* Having the traits of a bitch; mean; nasty; vindictive **2** *adj 1930s* Good-looking; chic; = CLASSY **3** *adj* Sexually provocative: *two bitchy strip queens*—Time

bite **1** *v* To accept a deception as truth: *She said she was rich, and he bit* **2** *v* To borrow money from; ask a loan from: *He bit me for six bills and left town* **3** *n* One's share of, or the amount of, a sum owed or demanded: *We owe ten thousand, so what's my bite?* **4** *v teenagers* = SUCK

the **bite** *n* Expense; charge; cost: *It's a good place, but the bite is fierce*
See PUT THE BITE ON someone

bite someone's **head off** *v phr* To react angrily; = JUMP DOWN someone's THROAT: *Don't mention the survey or she'll bite your head off*

◁**bite my ass**▷ *v phr* = KISS MY ASS

bite the bullet *v phr* To accept the cost of a course of action; do something painful but necessary: *Will he bite the bullet and become the...leader that Philadelphia's black community wants and needs?*—Philadelphia [fr the early surgical practice of having the patient bite hard on a bullet to divert the mind from pain and prevent screaming]

bite the dust **1** *v phr* *fr middle 1800s* To die or be killed **2** *v phr* To fail; be destroyed: *The ledgers showed too much red ink, and the company bit the dust*

bite your tongue *sentence* Retract or be ashamed of what you just said

bit-grinding *n* *computer* The processing of data into a computer

bit (or **piece**) **of fluff** *n phr* A girl or young woman; = CHIT

bit part *See* BIT

bits and pieces *n phr* A mixed collection; congeries: *My feelings about her are all bits and pieces since she left*

bitty *See* LITTLE BITTY

biz *n* *fr middle 1800s* Business
See SHOW BIZ, THAT'S SHOW BUSINESS

bizzer *n* An entertainer; veteran of show business: *It's kind of neat for a bizzer who's pushing 40...to come on as a dirty teen dream*—Village Voice

blab **1** *v* (also **blab off**) To talk on and on, without necessarily making sense **2** *n*: *That's stupid, just blab* **3** *v* (also **blab off**) To say more than one ought; esp, to incriminate oneself or others; = SING, SQUEAL: *We better leave town: the little rat blabbed*

blabbermouth *n* A person who talks too much, esp one who reveals personal or secret matters indiscreetly; = BIGMOUTH

black *narcotics* **1** *n* A grade or type of marijuana such as African Black **2** *n* A type of hashish
See IN THE BLACK

black and tan *adj phr* *esp 1920s* Occupied or patronized by both blacks and whites; interracial; = SALT AND PEPPER: *My place was black and tan, for colored and white alike*—A Lomax

black and white **1** *n phr* An ice-cream soda made with vanilla ice cream and chocolate syrup; = BLACK COW **2** *n phr* *narcotics* A capsule of an amphetamine and a sedative, or of two amphetamines

black bag job *n phr* A burglary or robbery done by government agents: *In the FBI...he'd never had anything to do with the famous black bag jobs*—New York Review of Books

blackball or **blacklist** *v* To punish someone by denial of work, boycotting of products, etc: *Some members of the* Twilight Zone *movie crew say they are being blackballed*—Washington Post

blackbirder *n* *fr late 1800s* A trader in black slaves ● Originally used of traders in Polynesian captives, esp Hawaiians sold into slavery: *The stinking ships of the blackbirders crossed the bars*—Stephen Longstreet

black book *See* LITTLE BLACK BOOK

black camp *n phr* *prison* A prison where most of the inmates are black

black-coat **1** *n* An undertaker **2** *n* A clergyman

black cow **1** *n phr* Root beer **2** *n phr* An ice-cream soda made with root beer and vanilla ice cream **3** *n phr* Chocolate milk **4** *n phr* = BLACK AND WHITE

black diamonds *See* DIAMONDS

black eye **1** *n phr* An eye surrounded with darkened areas of contusion; = MOUSE, SHINER **2** *n phr* A bad reputation; an adverse and damaging public image: *That story gave me a black eye*

black gang *n phr* The fireroom and boiler room crew of a ship

black hat **1** *n phr* A villain; = HEAVY: *The only way I can do that is to make you the black hat*—Philadelphia Journal/ *This time, perhaps, there are black hats on both sides*—New York Times **2** *v*: *They do not try to penetrate security systems or conduct clandestine tests..."There is no black-hatting"*—Associated Press **3** *modifier*: *the black-hat rustler in the horse opera* **4** *n phr* The badge or symbol of a villain: *Companies have this black hat on when they go to court*—New York Times [fr the Hollywood tradition that villains in Western movies always wore *black hats*]

blacklist *See* BLACKBALL

Black Maria (mə RĪ ə) **1** *n phr* *fr middle 1800s* A patrol wagon used to carry police prisoners **2** *n phr* A hearse

Black Mike *n phr* *hoboes* A meat and vegetable stew

black money (or **cash**) **1** *n phr* Money obtained illegally, esp by politicians and organized crime operations, that must be "laundered" before it can be used: *Money that derives from an illegal transaction...is considered "dirty" or "black" cash*—Philadelphia **2** *n phr* Income not reported for tax purposes; = SKIM

black operator *n phr* A secret agent: *At the Central Intelligence Agency, he was a "black operator" who never quite made it*—New York Times

black out **1** *v phr* To faint; lose consciousness **2** *v phr* To lose one's memory of something: *He totally blacked out that evening* **3** *v phr* To exclude an area from television coverage, esp of a sports event: *The whole region was blacked out for the final game*

blackshoe *n* *Navy* A nonflying member of an aircraft carrier's complement

blacksnake *n* *railroad* A train made up entirely of coal cars

blackstrap *n* *armed forces and lumberjack* Coffee

black stuff **1** *n phr* *narcotics* Opium ◀**2**▶ *n phr* A black woman or women as sex partner(s), esp for a white man

bladder[1] *n* *circus* A toy balloon [fr the fact that balloons were once made of animal bladders]

bladder[2] *n* A newspaper [fr German *Blatt* "leaf, page, newspaper"]

blade **1** *n* A knife considered as a weapon; = SWITCHBLADE **2** *n* *hospital* A surgeon

See SWITCHBLADE

blah (also **blah-blah** or **blah-blah-blah**) **1** *n* Idle and meaningless talk; falsehoods and vanities; =BALONEY, BUNK: *a lot of romantic blah*—Wolcott Gibbs **2** *adj* Unstimulating; bland; featureless; dull: *He seems stupefyingly blah* **3** *adj* Tired; mildly depressed; enervated: *fever, chills, sore throat...and an allover "blah" feeling*—A Fishbein

blahly *adj* In a tedious, colorless way; insipidly: *someone whose footsteps are blahly familiar*—New York

the **blahs** *n phr* A condition of dullness, fatigue, malaise, etc: *The radicals are suffering from a case of the blahs*—Life

blamed *adj fr early 1800s* =DARN

blank **1** *n* *narcotics* A weakened or diluted narcotic, or a non-narcotic substance sold as a narcotic; =FLEA POWDER **2** *v* *sports* To hold an opponent scoreless; =SCHNEIDER, SHUT OUT, SKUNK: *The hapless Tigers were blanked twice last week*
See DRAW A BLANK, SHOOT BLANKS

blank check *See* GIVE someone A BLANK CHECK

blanket **1** *n* A pancake; hotcake **2** *n* A cigarette paper **3** *n* An overcoat
See BEACH BLANKET BINGO, CALIFORNIA BLANKET, SECURITY BLANKET, WET BLANKET

blanket drill *n phr Army fr 1920s* Sleep; =SACK TIME

blanket stiff *n phr hoboes* A hobo or migratory worker, esp one who carries his belongings in a blanket roll; =BINDLESTIFF

blankety-blank *adj or n or v* A generalized euphemism substituted for a taboo or vulgar term; =BLEEP, BLEEPING: *You blankety-blank idiot!/ Stick it up your blankety-blank*

blap **1** *n* Stroke; bit: *little blaps of revelation and no affect*—Philadelphia **2** *v* To strike; =SOCK: *continually blapped about the head and shoulders with pig bladders wielded by clowns*—Philadelphia Bulletin

blast **1** *n* A blow; =SOCK: *a blast in the kisser* **2** *v*: *She blasted him in the gut* **3** *v* To shoot: *They blasted him with a sawed-off shotgun* **4** *n* In baseball, a long or strong hit, esp a home run **5** *v*: *So the Babe blasts it right out of there* **6** *v* To attack, esp with strong verbal condemnation: *He blasted the Secretary for saying that* **7** *n*: *He figures the opposition's blast won't hurt him* **8** *v* To defeat utterly; trounce; =CLOBBER **9** *v* To speed or speed up in a vehicle; =BARREL: *He got in the Porsche and blasted out of there* **10** *v* *narcotics* To take narcotics; use: *to start blasting opium from a water pipe*—H Braddy **11** *n* *narcotics* A single dose or portion of a narcotic or other stimulant; =BELT, FIX: *Maybe it's a little early in the day for that first blast*—D Harris **12** *n* A thrill; a transport of pleasure; =CHARGE, KICK: *Meeting her was a blast* **13** *n* A noisy and jolly party or other especially exciting occasion; =BALL **14** *n* Anything good or admirable; =GASSER **15** *n* A dismal failure; =BOMB, FLOP **16** *interj* An exclamation of dismay, irritation, frustration, etc ● Chiefly British use **17** *v* =DYNAMITE

See BEER BLAST, FULL BLAST

blasted **1** *adj and adv* =DARN **2** *adj* Entirely destitute; =FLAT BROKE **3** *adj* Drunk

blaster *underworld* **1** *n* A gunman; =HIT MAN **2** *n* A firearm
See GHETTO BOX

blastissimo *adj and adv musicians* Very, very loud; fortississimo: *You ought not to sing the berceuse blastissimo* [modeled on *fortissimo*]

blast off **1** *v phr* To ignite and rise from the launchpad: *The shuttle blasted off cleanly* **2** *v phr* To leave quickly; =SCRAM

blast (or **blasting**) **party** *n phr narcotics* A social gathering of narcotics users, esp of marijuana smokers; =POT PARTY

blat **1** *v* =BLAB **2** *n* A newspaper; =BLADDER

blaxploitation **1** *n* The commercial exploitation of putative black experience, esp in films with blacks in sensational heroic roles of police officers, criminals, gamblers, etc **2** *modifier*: *Most of the blaxploitation films...have been shoddy ripoffs*—Village Voice

blaze *See* LET'S BOOGIE

blazes *See* BLUE BLAZES

as **blazes** or **as hell** or ◁**as shit**▷ *adv phr* To a very great degree; =TO THE MAX: *the life now...hard as blazes*—Village Voice/ *cold as hell*/ *tough as shit*

blech (BLEKH or BLECH) *interj* An exclamation of disgust, revulsion, etc: *The House Democratic Caucus launched its response to Reaganomics: "BLECH!"*—National Review

bleed **1** *v* To take someone's money by overcharging or extortion: *His creditors bled him to death* **2** *n* *black* A black person; =BLOOD

bleeder **1** *n* *baseball* A lucky or weak base hit **2** *n* A person, esp a boxer, whose blood is easily drawn **3** *n* A hemophiliac

bleeding heart **1** *n phr* A person regarded as unduly softhearted, esp towards idlers who do not merit sympathy ● Very commonly used by the politically conservative to condemn the politically liberal **2** *modifier*: *a bleeding-heart wimpy liberal* [fr religious art showing the *bleeding heart* of Jesus]

bleed someone **white** *v phr* To take all of someone's money; exact everything: *The loan sharks bled him white*

bleep or **bleeping** or **blipping** *adj or n or v* A generalized euphemism substituted for a taboo or vulgar term; =BLANKETY-BLANK: *He bleeped right in my face so I told him to bleep off/ I was going to be a bleeping star*—Inside Sports/ *That 270 you recommended ain't no blipping good*—Sports Afield [fr the practice of erasing objectionable material on a tape or in a sound track with a high-pitched sound called echoically a *bleep*]

bletcherous *adj computer* Disgusting; nasty; ugly: *The whole design is bletcherous* [fr *bletch* or *blech*, a comic-book expression of disgust similar to *yuck*]

blimp *n* An obese person [fr the WW1 term for a nonrigid dirigible]

blind **1** *n* *post office* A letter with an incomplete or illegible address; =NIXIE **2** *adv* *esp students fr early 1900s* Completely; =COLD: *He had his story* *blind/ Goddam car was eating me blind*—George V Higgins **3** *adj* *homosexuals* Uncircumcised

See COLOR-BLIND, STEAL someone BLIND, STONE BLIND

blind baggage or **blind** *n phr* or *n hoboes* A railroad baggage car or mail car with no door or a locked door at one end; also, the relatively safe space thus provided, where hoboes may hide or ride: *to catch the blind baggage on the west-bound overland*—Jack London/ *must jump onto the blind again*—Jack London

blind Charley *n phr* *outdated underworld* A lamppost

blind date (or **drag**) *esp students fr 1920s* **1** *n phr* An arranged appointment for a show, dance, etc, where one's partner is a previously unknown person, usu the friend of a friend **2** *n phr* One's partner on such an occasion

blind drunk or **blinded** *adj phr* or *adj* Very drunk

blindfold a pair *v phr* *lunch counter* To fry two eggs on both sides

blind pig (or **tiger**) *n phr* *fr early 1900s* An unlicensed or illegal saloon; = SPEAKEASY

the **blinds** *See* RIDE THE BLINDS

blind-side 1 *v* (also **blind-pop**) *football* To tackle or block someone from an unseen quarter: *have to worry about gettin' blind-popped from a corner blitz*—Dan Jenkins **2** *v* To be burdened or attacked unexpectedly: *Business men began to be blind-sided by enormous legal bills*—Newsweek/ *The state...will be coming back sometime in the future to blind-side us*—Milwaukee Journal/ *Mitchell blindsided him on camera*—Washington Post

blind tiger *n phr* Cheap or inferior whiskey

See BLIND PIG

Blind Tom *n phr* *baseball* An umpire

blinger (BLING ər) *n* Something remarkable, wonderful, superior, etc; = HUMDINGER: *real blingers going through to the phase of secondary infection*—Paul de Kruif

blink *See* ON THE BLINK, TWO-BLINK

blinkers *n* The eyes

blinkie *n hoboes* A beggar who pretends to be blind

blip 1 *adj* *jive talk* Excellent; very good **2** *adj* = HIP **3** *n* A luminous signal on a radar screen: *Birds can cause blips on radar screens*—P Wagner **4** *n* A rapid increase and decrease; quick peaking: *It's not a form of communication, it's a temporary blip*—New York Magazine/ *despite temporary blips up and down*—Time **5** *v* To encroach upon, as one aircraft's image on a radar screen might enter the territory of another aircraft: *Cartridge-makers blip into Atari's airspace, attracted by the enormous profit potential*—New York Magazine **6** *v* To censor a taped word or passage by erasing it electronically from the tape and substituting a "bleep": *Occasionally Mr Carson's lines are "blipped"*—New York Times

blip (or **ping**) **jockey** *n phr* *armed forces* A person who monitors electronic detection devices

blip someone **off** *v phr* To kill, esp by shooting: *If he blipped Beno off, he knows me*—Dashiell Hammett

blipping *See* BLEEP

blissed out *adj phr* In a state of exaltation or blissful ecstasy: *blissed-out young pilgrims*—DS Greene/ *and lives a blissed-out life with Sue*—Washington Post

bliss ninny *n phr* A person ecstatic to the point of seeming idiocy

blissout *n* A state of exaltation or ecstasy; mystic daze

bliss out *v phr* To become ecstatic; go into a mystic daze, esp under the influence of a guru: *Don't get high, don't space out, don't get blissed out*—National Review

blister 1 *n* *fr middle 1800s* An annoying person without whom one could do nicely: *He's not quite a jerk, just a blister* **2** *n hoboes* A woman hobo **3** *n* A prostitute **4** *n* A bubble-shaped transparent covering on an aircraft cockpit, roof opening, etc

blisterfoot 1 *n* *WW1 Army* An infantry soldier; = PADDLEFOOT **2** *n* *police* A police officer who walks a beat

blitz¹ *v* *students around 1900* To absent oneself from a class or examination; = CUT, SHINE

blitz² *v* *armed forces* To polish one's brass buttons, etc; prepare for inspection [fr *Blitz Cloth*, trade name for a brand of metal-polishing cloth]

blitz³ 1 *v* To defeat decisively; = CLOBBER: *They blitzed the Mariners 12-zip* **2** *v* *football* To rush the quarterback in force, hoping to prevent him from completing a pass **3** *n* Any heavy onslaught or attack: *His best strategy was a blitz of TV spots just before the election* **4** *v*: *We blitzed her with questions* [fr German *Blitzkrieg* "lightning war," an overwhelmingly heavy and rapid attack]

blitzed *college students* **1** *adj* Drunk: *really blitzed. Six beers on an empty stomach*—Cameron Crowe **2** *adj* Completely exhausted; = WIPED OUT

blitzed out *adj phr* Intoxicated; = STONED: *We were pretty blitzed out by the time Lee walked in*—Richard Merkin [probably fr *blitz³*, perhaps influenced by *bliss out*]

blitzkrieg or **blitz** *n* = the RUSH ACT

blivit *n* Anything superfluous or annoying ● The word, when one is asked in puzzlement to define it, is said to mean "ten pounds of shit in a five-pound bag": *This is about as useful as a blivit*

blizzard-head *n* *television studio* A very blonde person for whom studio lighting must be subdued

bloated *adj* Drunk

blob 1 *n* *students early 1900s* A mistake **2** *v*: *He blobbed the second question* **3** *n* A mass of viscous matter; an amorphous portion; = GOB

block *n* The head

See GAPER'S BLOCK, KNOCK someone's BLOCK OFF, NEW KID ON THE BLOCK

blockbust *v* To persuade white property owners to sell their houses quickly by arousing a fear that blacks are moving into the neighborhood

blockbuster[1] *n* A great success; a lavish and popular film, show, etc: *A gangster movie can be a box-office blockbuster*—Saturday Review [fr the large high-explosive aerial bombs of World War 2 called *blockbusters*]

blockbuster[2] *n* A real estate dealer who blockbusts

blockhead *n* A stupid person; = KLUTZ

blocks *See* PUT THE BLOCKS TO someone

bloke[1] *n fr early 1800s* A man; fellow; = GUY ● More common in British use: *Look at the bloke ridin'*—Theodore Dreiser [perhaps fr Celtic *ploc* "large stubborn person"]

bloke[2] *n narcotics* Cocaine

blonde *See* BOTTLE BLONDE

blonde and sweet *n phr WW2 Navy* Coffee with sugar and cream

blood 1 *n college students fr early 1900s* A fashionable and popular man: *crew cut like the college blood*—John O'Hara **2** *n black* A fellow black; = BLOOD BROTHER: *and these cats...well, we was all bloods*—D Evans

See MAKE one's BLOOD BOIL, SMELL BLOOD, TIRED BLOOD, TOO RICH FOR someone's BLOOD

blood brother *n phr black fr about 1960* A fellow black; = BLEED, BLOOD

bloody (or blue) murder 1 *n phr* A shattering defeat; total destruction: *After the second quarter it was bloody murder* **2** *adv phr* As if announcing general slaughter and universal destruction: *yelling bloody murder/ screaming blue murder on the arms of their seats*—Village Voice

blooey *See* GO BLOOEY

bloom *n television studio* A glare from some white object in a television image; = WOMP

bloomer 1 *n outdated underworld* An empty or nearly empty safe **2** *n circus* A poorly attended show; a slow day or place of business **3** *n* A blunder; = BONER, GOOF: *a "bloomer" by Truman and Marshall about a grave that was not there*—United Press/ *This dictionary, I'm afraid, is scarcely free of bloomers*

bloomer boy *n phr WW2 armed forces* A paratrooper [fr the baggy style of their pants, reminiscent of the roomy trousers devised and worn by Amelia *Bloomer*, the 19th-century American feminist leader]

bloomers *n WW2 Navy* Gun covers

blooming *adj and adv* = DARN ● Chiefly British use

bloop 1 *n* An unwanted sound in a phonograph record, resulting from a poor splice between two pieces of magnetic tape **2** *n* = BLOOPER **3** *v* To hit a ball relatively weakly and slowly: *He blooped a lob over her head* **4** *v* To launch and land a long, curving blow: *Turner blooped a bolo to the heart*—New York Daily News

blooper 1 *n* A blow with the fist, esp a long, looping punch: *So I could hang a blooper on your kisser*—John O'Hara **2** *n baseball* A high, looping pitch, throw, or hit: *I poked an easy blooper over third* **3** *n* A blunder; = BONER, BOO-BOO: *He may have felt he pulled a blooper*—J Marlow

blort *n narcotics* Heroin [perhaps fr *blow* + *snort*]

blot out *v phr underworld* To kill; = RUB OUT

blotter 1 *n police* The daily record of arrests at a police station **2** *n* A drunkard **3** *n college students* LSD **4** *n* (also **blotter acid**) *college students* A sheet of absorbent paper to which liquid LSD has been applied and then allowed to dry

blotto *adj fr early 1900s* Drunk: *the drivers who are blotto*—Philadelphia

blow 1 *v jazz musicians fr early 1900s* To play a musical instrument, esp in jazz style and not necessarily a wind instrument: *There will be three kids blowing guitar, banjo, and washboard*—Ed McBain **2** *n esp 1950s beat & cool talk* To do or perform something, esp to do it well: *He blows great conversation*—E Horne ◁**3**▷ *v* To do fellatio or cunnilingus: SUCK OFF ◁**4**▷ *v* To be disgusting, nasty, worthless, etc; = SUCK: *This blows and you do too*—National Lampoon **5** *v* To treat someone to something; buy something expensive or unusual for someone: *I blew myself to a new pair of shoes* **6** *v* (also **blow** something **in**) *fr middle 1800s* To spend money, esp foolishly and all at once: *And blow it in on smokes*—Joseph Auslander **7** *v narcotics* To take a narcotic, esp but not necessarily by inhalation: *Jimi blew every kind of dope invented*—New York Times/ *You been blowing a little LSD?*—New York Times **8** *v narcotics* To smoke marijuana; = BLOW SMOKE: *He enjoys sex; he does not blow grass*—Commonweal **9** *v fr middle 1800s* To spend or lose money: *The state blew my money buying votes for Roosevelt*—Westbrook Pegler **10** *v fr middle 1800s* To leave; depart; = SPLIT: *I'm blowing, I got a job in Detroit*—Dorothy Parker **11** *v fr middle 1800s* To lose or ruin something by mistake, inattention, incompetence, etc; = BLOW IT: *I blew the best chance I ever had* **12** *v theater* To forget or botch one's part in a show **13** *v* To eliminate or cancel part of an agreement or business: *Let's just blow this next paragraph, OK?* **14** *v outdated underworld* To inform against someone; = SING **15** *v* To expose or publicize something secret, esp something scandalous: *Treat me right or I'll blow it about the love nest* **16** *v* To explode; blow up **17** *v* To lose one's temper; = BLOW one's TOP **18** *v* To brag; = TOOT one's OWN HORN **19** *v baseball* To pitch a ball so hard and fast that the batter cannot hit it: *He blew a fast ball right by the slugger*

See BLOW someone AWAY, BLOW one's COOL, BLOW someone's or something's COVER, BLOW someone's HAIR, BLOW something HIGH AS A KITE, BLOW someone's MIND, BLOW OFF one's MOUTH, BLOW ONE, BLOW ONE UP, BLOW OUT OF THE WATER, BLOW SMOKE, BLOW THE GAFF, BLOW THE LID OFF, BLOW THE WHISTLE, BLOW one's TOP, BLOW UP, BLOW UP A STORM, BLOW something WIDE OPEN, CIRCUIT BLOW, GIVE someone A BLOW, LET OFF STEAM, LOW BLOW, ONE-TWO, TOOT one's OWN HORN

Blow *See* JOE BLOW

blow a fix *v phr narcotics* To lose the effect of a narcotic injection by missing the vein

blow a gasket (or **a fuse**) *v phr* To lose one's temper; =BLOW one's TOP: *The higher-ups blew a gasket when they heard*—Bing Crosby

blow a hype *v phr* To become overexcited

blow away *v phr* To depart; =TAKE OFF

blow someone **away** **1** *v phr* To kill; assassinate; get rid of; =OFF: *and boom, Jack Blumenfeld gets blown away*—Philadelphia **2** *v phr* To defeat utterly; trounce; =CLOBBER: *He would be "blowing away" both Walter Mondale and John Glenn in the polls* **3** *v phr* To overcome, often with admiration: *I read the book and it blew me away*—Philadelphia Bulletin

blow-boy *n Army* A bugler

blow by blow **1** *adv phr* In a complete and detailed way: *I'll tell you what happened blow by blow* **2** *adj*: *a blow-by-blow account*

blow one's **cool** *v phr 1960s counterculture* To lose one's composure; become flustered, excited, or angry: *I always blow my cool when they honk at me*

blow one's **cork** *See* BLOW one's TOP

blow someone's or something's **cover** **1** *v phr espionage & police* To ruin or nullify one's disguise or assumed role; reveal one's true identity: *The undercover cop had to blow his cover by pulling his gun when he thought they might have spotted him/ She called out my name, which blew my cover* **2** *v phr* To reveal something, esp inadvertently or mischievously: *I'm not blowing the movie's cover story by giving you this information*—Philadelphia

blowed *See* SAUCERED AND BLOWED

blowed-in-the-glass *adj hoboes* Genuine; excellent [fr liquor bottles with the name wrought in the glass itself]

blower **1** *n hot rodders* A supercharger for a car engine; =HUFFER **2** *n* A handkerchief *See* MIND-BLOWER

blow fire *v phr black* To do something with particular skill and relish, esp to dance

blow grits *v phr college students* To vomit

blow someone's **hair** *v phr* To frighten someone; be scary: *When I think...things..could have happened, it blows my hair*—Playboy

blowhard *fr middle 1800s* **1** *n* A braggart; self-aggrandizer **2** *n* An insistent and aggressive talker

blow something **high as a kite** *v phr* To spoil or ruin something utterly by revealing it: *That discovery blew the scheme high as a kite*

blow hot and cold *v phr* To be indecisive; dither

blow in *v phr* To arrive and enter, esp from a distance: *Look who just blew in from Sri Lanka*

blow-in **1** *n lumberjacks* A spree **2** *n hoboes* A newly arrived person

blow something **in** *See* BLOW

blowing *n jazz musicians* The playing of jazz music: *This music is the culmination of all my writing and blowing*—Duke Ellington *See* HORNBLOWING, MIND-BLOWING

blowing cat *n phr outdated jazz musicians* A jazz musician

blow it *v phr* To fail; make a botch; ruin one's chances: *We are winning. If we don't blow it*—Village Voice/ *I think I blew it. I talked too much and said too little*—Erma Bombeck

blow it off *v phr college students* To fail to deal with or attend to something; neglect something deliberately: *He felt sort of blah so he decided to blow it off and skip his morning classes*

blow it out *interj* (Variations: **your asshole** or **your B-bag** or **your barracks bag** or **your ear** or **your tailpipe** may be added) *fr WW2 armed forces* A generalized exclamation of contempt, anger, incredulity, etc ● Most often uttered in challenge or rebuke

◁**blow job**▷ *n phr* An act of fellatio or of cunnilingus

blow someone's **mind** **1** *v phr fr narcotics & 1960s counterculture* To evoke deep feelings of awe, admiration, strangeness, etc; stir one profoundly: *The simplicity of the thing blew my mind* **2** *v phr* =BLOW one's COOL

blown *adj hot rodders* Having a supercharger: *a blown engine*

blown-out *adj narcotics* In a state of narcotic intoxication, trance, or exhilaration; =HIGH, STONED

blowoff **1** *n* A climax; a final provocation: *She said I was late, and that was the blowoff* **2** *n* A quarrel: *She and Hobart have had a big blow-off*—J Kelly **3** *n circus* A pitchman's first customer of the day, often given something free to attract others **4** *n teenagers* Something very easy; =PIECE OF CAKE

blow off *v phr* To avoid or shirk; not attend to: *He guessed he could blow off work that day and get away with it*

blow off one's **mouth** or **blow** one's **mouth off** *v phr* (Variations: **trap** or **yap** may replace **mouth**) =SHOOT OFF one's MOUTH

blow off steam *See* LET OFF STEAM

blow one *v phr* To draw a glass of draught beer and blow off the foam

blow one up *v phr prison* To light a cigarette

blowout **1** *n fr early 1800s* A noisy, festive occasion; =SHINDIG **2** *n underworld* An unsuccessful robbery

blow someone **out** *v phr fr cowboys* To kill or destroy; =BLOW someone AWAY: *The Redskins got blown out*—CBS Sports

blow out of the water *v phr* To defeat utterly; =SHOOT someone DOWN IN FLAMES: *Are you afraid of being blown out of the water?*—Playboy/ *Bradlee "blew him (Tavoulareas) out of the water"*—Washingtonian

blow one's **own horn** *See* TOOT one's OWN HORN

blow smoke **1** *v phr* To boast; brag; exaggerate: *four cops sitting around drinking, blowing smoke, and kidding*—Lawrence Sanders **2** *v phr* (also **blow smoke up** someone's **ass**) To mislead; confuse; deceive: *Anybody who tells you different's just blowing smoke up your ass*—George V Higgins **3** *v phr* To smoke marijuana or hashish: *Everybody blew smoke there. You could buy hash*—New Yorker [fr the presumed effects of smoking opium]

blow someone's **socks off** *See* KNOCK someone's SOCKS OFF

blow the gaff *v phr outdated underworld* To inform on someone; =SING: *didn't mind if I blew the gaff on this "common practice"* —Village Voice [to reveal the concealed cheating mechanism of a carnival game]

blow the lid off *v phr* To expose a scandal, esp political or governmental corruption

blow the whistle 1 *v phr underworld* To inform; =SING: *She hadn't been Dutch Schultz's wife for four years not to know the penalty for blowing the whistle*—NY Confidential **2** *v phr* To expose or begin to resist wrongdoing: *Somebody has to blow the whistle on this ruinous policy/ The detective who blew the whistle was also transferred* —Village Voice [fr the *whistle* signal of a sports official that an infraction, foul, etc, has been committed]

blowtop *n* A person who is easily angered; =HOT-HEAD

blow one's **top** (Variations: **cork** or **topper** or **stack** or **wig** may replace **top**) **1** *v* To go insane; become violently mad **2** *v* To become wildly excited or enthusiastic: *Here's an idea'll make you blow your cork* **3** *v* To become violently excited by narcotics; =FLIP, FREAK OUT **4** *v* To become violently and suddenly angry; have a tantrum [perhaps fr the violence of an oil well that *blows* as a gusher]

blowtorch *n 1950s Air Force* A jet aircraft or jet engine

blowup 1 *n* A fit of anger **2** *n* A quarrel; violent rift between persons **3** *n* A photographic or other enlargement: *He already has a blowup of your proverb...on a wall of his breakfast room* —Joseph Heller

blow up 1 *v phr* To enlarge a photograph **2** *v phr* To assign too much importance to; exaggerate; =MAKE A FEDERAL CASE OUT OF something, PUMP UP **3** *v phr* =BLOW one's TOP **4** *v phr* =BLOW one's COOL **5** *v phr theater* To forget or garble one's lines on stage; =BALLOON: *Barrymore "blew up" in his lines*—Gene Fowler

blow up a storm 1 *v phr jazz musicians* To play, esp jazz trumpet, cornet, clarinet, etc, with great skill and verve: *I first heard Buddy Bolden play....He was blowing up a storm*—Louis Armstrong **2** *v phr* =PISS UP A STORM

blow something **wide open** *v phr* To expose a scandal, esp political or governmental corruption; =BLOW THE LID OFF: *That'll be the perfect time to blow this thing wide open*—Washington Post

BLT (pronounced as separate letters) *n* A bacon, lettuce, and tomato sandwich

blubber 1 *v* To weep; snivel **2** *n* Fat; =AVOIR-DUPOIS

blubberhead *n* A stupid person; =FATHEAD

blue 1 *adj fr early 1800s* Drunk: *When you were blue you got the howling horrors*—Dorothy Parker **2** *adj fr middle 1800s* Lewd; rude; suggestive; =DIRTY ● The term covers the range from obscene to slightly risqué: *a blue movie/ blue gags* **3** *adj* Melancholy; depressed; woeful: *I feel a little blue and blah this morning* ◄**4**► *n* A very dark-skinned black person; =BLUE-SKIN **5** *n* A police officer: *By the time the first blues got there, there's like maybe ten people milling about*—Lawrence Sanders

See BAYOU BLUE, HEAVENLY BLUE

blue around the gills *See* GREEN AROUND THE GILLS

◄**blue-ball**► *n* A sexually frustrated male: *and a fellow blue-ball did things to each other that they wanted the girls to do to them*—Penthouse

◄**blue balls**► **1** *n phr* A turgid and painful condition of the testicles due to sexual excitement and frustration: *Sex will relieve testicular congestion, or blue balls*—Playboy **2** *n phr* Any of various venereal diseases, esp gonorrhea or lymphogranuloma inguinale

bluebird *n black* A police officer

blue blanket *n phr* A personal possession that gives a sense of safety; security blanket: *I like my stick closer to me...it's my blue blanket*—Joseph Wambaugh

blue blazes 1 *n phr fr early 1800s* An extreme situation, pace, pitch, etc **2** *n phr* Something extreme; the utmost: *It hurt like blue blazes* **3** *adv phr* To an extravagant degree: *lying blue blazes* —Ken Kesey [fr the *blue blazes* of Hell, an extreme environment]

bluebook *n college students* A college examination: *I'm cramming for a bluebook in Econ*

blue box *n phr* An electronic device enabling one to make long-distance telephone calls without paying: *the alleged use of an electronic "blue box" to avoid telephone tolls*—Arizona Wildcat

blue cheer *n phr narcotics* LSD

blue-chip *adj* Of the best sort; first rate: *a blue-chip stock* [fr the color of the highest denomination of gambling chip]

blue chipper *n phr* Persons or things of the highest quality, ability, etc: *But the crop does not contain many blue chippers*—Inside Sports

bluecoat *n fr middle 1800s* A police officer: *He told the damn bluecoat...he'd punch him all over the corner*—James T Farrell

blued *See* SCREWED, BLUED, AND TATTOOED

blue darter *n phr baseball* A low, hard-hit line drive: *A hard line drive is a blue darter, frozen rope, or an ungodly shot*—Jim Bouton

blue-devil *See* BLUE HEAVEN

blue-eyed 1 *adj* Innocent; unsophisticated **2** *adj black* White; Caucasian

blue-eyed boy *See* FAIRHAIRED BOY

blue-eyed devil *n phr black* A white person; a Caucasian

blue-eyed soul *n phr musicians* Black music with its style and mannerisms, as performed by white musicians: *Boz came on like an inspired amateur of blue-eyed soul*—Village Voice

blue flags *n phr narcotics* LSD

blue flick *See* BLUE MOVIE

blue flu *n phr* A mythical disease epidemic during a police job action when numbers of officers telephone to say that they are ill

blue funk *n phr* A profoundly melancholy state ● More common in British use: *Losing his girl put him into a blue funk for weeks*

bluegrass **1** *n* Music based on the songs and dances of the Southern Appalachians and played usu at a fast tempo by a string group **2** *modifier: the bluegrass sound/ bluegrass mandolin by Bob Applebaum* [fr the nickname of Kentucky, the *bluegrass state*]

◄**blue-gum**► *n* A black person

blue heaven or **blue-devil** *n phr* or *n* A capsule of Amytal (a trade name), a type of barbiturate

blue hell *n phr* An extremely nasty and trying situation: *It was more than tough, it was blue hell*

blue in the face *See* TILL one IS BLUE IN THE FACE

blue man *n phr* A uniformed male police officer

blue meany *n phr* A very, very cruel and nasty person; = BASTARD: *It's not that all landlords are blue meanies*—Washington Post [fr cartoon characters in the film *The Yellow Submarine* of the English rock group The Beatles]

blue movie (or **flick**) *n phr* A pornographic movie; erotic film; = SKIN FLICK

blue murder *See* BLOODY MURDER

bluenose *n fr early 1800s* A prude; prig: *The moral bluenoses were sniffing around*—Stephen Longstreet

Bluenose *n* A native of Nova Scotia, esp a Maritimes fisherman

blue note *n phr musicians* A flatted note of the sort common in blues music

the blues **1** *n phr* A state of melancholy; depression **2** *n phr* A usu slow style of singing, guitar-playing, and jazz originally reflecting in its melancholy and resignation the special plight of black people and the general vicissitudes of life and love; esp, songs having in each stanza a repeated opening statement and single closing statement **3** *n phr New York City narcotics* The police [first sense ultimately fr the *blue devils* "a fit of melancholy"]

◄**blue-skin**► *n fr early 1800s* A black person

blue sky *v phr* To hold a brainstorming session with no limit on the strangeness of the ideas proposed

blue-sky *adj fr early 1900s* Having no sound factual or value basis; recklessly imaginative: *a budget figure, as it turned out, and a blue-sky one at that* —Time

a **blue streak** *fr middle 1800s* **1** *adv phr* (also **like a blue streak**) In a very rapid or excessive manner; extravagantly: *She talked a blue streak/ She split out like a blue streak* **2** *n phr* An extreme amount, speed, etc: *He yelled a blue streak/ We ran a blue streak* [fr the *blue streak* of a lightning bolt]

blue ticket *n phr 1930s Army* A discharge without honor, a dismissal not as condemnatory as a dishonorable discharge

◄**blue veiner**► *n phr* A very stiff penile erection: *Even the Dragon Lady couldn't have given you a blue veiner*—Joseph Wambaugh

blue velvet *n phr narcotics* A mixture of paregoric with Pyrabenzamine (a trade name), an antihistamine, used as an injection

bluff **1** *v* To use confident pretense as a means of winning or succeeding **2** *n: His courage was all bluff*

See CALL someone's BLUFF

blurb *n* A statement in praise of something or somebody; esp an encomious passage from a book or theater review, used as advertising [coined by Gelett Burgess, early 20th century US humorist]

BMOC (pronounced as separate letters) *n phr* A college-student leader or idol [fr *big man on campus*]

B movie *n phr* A usu low-budget movie intended for the broad middle ground of taste and meant to be primarily entertaining and narrative rather than serious, artistic, etc

BMX *n bicyclists* Cross-country bicycle racing [fr *bicycle moto-cross*, fr *moto-cross* "cross-country motorcycle racing over a laid-out course," fr French *moto* "motorcycle" and English *cross* "cross-country"]

bo[1] or **'bo** *n hoboes* A hobo: *From some bo on the drag I managed to learn what time a certain freight pulled out*—Jack London

bo[2] **1** *n prison* A boy or young man, esp a prisoner's catamite; = PUNK **2** *n* A man; fellow ● Now outdated, but once used in direct address, like "mac" or "dad"

BO (pronounced as separate letters) **1** *n* Body odor, esp from underarm perspiration **2** *n show business* Box office, the gauge of how well a show is doing by its receipts **3** *adj show business* Theatrical appeal: *The show is really big BO*

board *n show business* A ticket to a show or game; = PASTEBOARD

See ACROSS THE BOARD, IDIOT CARD, JINKY-BOARD, JOGGLING BOARD, PASTEBOARD, PUNCHBOARD, SANDWICH BOARD, TOTE[3]

boards *n gambling* Playing cards; = PASTEBOARDS

boat **1** *n esp 1920s* A car: *The little boat (automobile, in the argot of '22)*—SJ Perelman **2** *n* A big car: *Barbara can't get rid of her boat. No one's buying them anymore*

See GRAVY TRAIN, LIFEBOAT, MAN IN THE BOAT, MISS THE BOAT, ON THE GRAVY TRAIN, RIDE THE GRAVY TRAIN, ROCK THE BOAT

boat people *n phr* Political refugees who escape by small boat

boat race *n phr horse-racing* A race with a prearranged winner

bob *See* BOOB JOB, DITTYBOP, FLY COP, NOSE JOB

bobber *See* DEELY BOPPER

bobble **1** *v* To blunder, esp in baseball, to mishandle or drop the ball: *The shortstop bobbled an easy out* **2** *n: The President's denial was a bad bobble*

bobby socks *n phr* White cotton socks worn below the knee, and esp worn folded over shoes [origin unknown; perhaps related to *bobbed* "short, cut short,'' influenced by the diminutive name *Bobby*]

bobby-soxer *n esp 1940s* An adolescent girl [fr the 1930s and 40s fashion of wearing *bobby socks* folded down over saddle shoes]

bobtail 1 *n armed forces fr WW1* A dishonorable discharge ● So called because the phrase ''service honorable and faithful'' was deleted from the discharge form **2** *n truckers* A truck tractor without a semitrailer **3** *v: He bobtailed back to the terminal/ Returning with just the tractor (bobtailing) represented a loss*—Smithsonian

◁**Boche**▷ (BAHSH) *WW1 armed forces* **1** *n* A German, esp a soldier **2** *modifier: the Boche infantry* [fr French, a shortening of *Alboche*, a contemptuous modification of *Allemand* ''German'']

bod 1 *n* A person ● Chiefly British use **2** *n* The body; physique
See WARM BODY

bodacious (boh DAY shəs) *adj chiefly Southern fr middle 1800s* Extreme; audacious; blatant: *as complicated as ''Gaucho'''s bodacious cowboy Custerdome business*—Village Voice [fr early 19th-century *bodyaciously* ''bodily, totally'']

bodega (boh DAY gə) **1** *n* A liquor store **2** *n* A grocery store, esp in Puerto Rican areas of New York City [fr Spanish, ''shop'']

bodgie *n 1930s jive talk* A male jitterbug: *A bodgie is a jitterbug-crazy boy*—Hal Boyle

bodice-ripper or **bodice-buster** *n publishing* A romantic-erotic novel, esp one with a historical plot; = HEAVY BREATHER: *the offensive term bodice-ripper* —Publishers Weekly/ *literary set that swoons over such bodice-busters as ''Rapture's Slave,'' ''Love's Sweet Agony''*—Philadelphia Journal

body *See* KNOW WHERE THE BODIES ARE BURIED, WARM BODY

body and soul *n phr* One's boyfriend or girlfriend [probably fr the title of a 1930s song, ''Body and Soul'']

body-shake *See* SKIN-SEARCH

boff 1 *n* A blow with the fist or open hand **2** *v: LaGuardia bade his cops to muss them up and boff them around on sight*—Westbrook Pegler **3** *v* To do the sex act: *professors boffing coeds in their offices*—New York Magazine/ *I was trying for the world boffing championship*—John D MacDonald **4** *n* A sex act; coupling: *a quick bathroom boff* —Playgirl **5** *v* To vomit; = BARF **6** *n show business* A laugh, esp one following a comedian's joke; = BOFFOLA **7** *n show business* A joke or witty remark **8** *n show business* A show that pleases the audience
See THROW A FUCK INTO someone

boffer *n* A man who does the sex act; = COCKSMAN: *The All-American boffer*—John D MacDonald

boffin *n* An expert, esp in a scientific or technical field: *Computer boffins...play a game called hunt the wumpus*—Time [fr WW2 British RAF slang, possibly fr a humorous comparison between the laboratories and shops of experts and the enormous trash heaps of Mr and Mrs Boffin in Dickens's *Our Mutual Friend*]

boffo 1 *n* A dollar: *That's worth a million boffos* —Joel Sayre **2** *n underworld* A year, esp a one-year prison sentence **3** *n show business* A laugh, esp a loud laugh in response to a comedian; = BOFFOLA **4** *n show business* A joke or a witty remark; = BOFF **5** *adj: Hey, that's a very boffo line* **6** *adj* Loud and appreciative: *The zany Brewsters...still get laughs, boffo laughs*—Philadelphia Evening Standard **7** *n show business* A successful entertainment; = BOFF, HIT: *her string of box-office boffos*—Bob Thomas **8** *adj: Red-blooded boffo entertainment for both sexes*—SJ Perelman **9** *adj* Highly favorable; laudatory [fr a 19th-century carnival term based on the idea of a good *box office*]

boffola or **buffola** *show business* **1** *n* A loud appreciative laugh; = BELLY LAUGH, BOFF: *This ability brought out the old boffola from coast to coast*—B Herndon **2** *n* A joke or remark that provokes such laughter: *All I need is a funny hat and a buffola* —Fred Allen

bogart or **Bogart** or **bogard** *fr black* **1** *v* To behave truculently; get something by intimidation: *some hotshot from Brooklyn trying to Bogart a game from the regulars*—Village Voice **2** *v* (also **bogart a joint**) To take more than one's share, esp of a marijuana cigarette; = HOG [fr the tough roles played in films by Humphrey *Bogart*]

bogey or **bogie** or **bogy 1** *n underworld* A police officer **2** *n WW2 Army Air Forces fr British RAF* An enemy aircraft, esp an attacking fighter plane **3** *n fr late 1800s British* A golf score of one stroke over par on a given hole [Golf sense fr the golf score of an imaginary expert called Colonel *Bogey*, against whom one competes]

◀**bog-trotter** or **bog-hopper**▶ *n* An Irishman or -woman or person of Irish extraction; = MICK

bogue¹ 1 *adj narcotics* In need of narcotics; suffering from deprivation: *I'm bogue....I'm trying to kick*—Clarence Cooper **2** *adj* False; fake; = BOGUS, PHONY [origin unknown]

**bogue² ** *adj teenagers* Disgusting; unattractive; = GROSS [fr *bogus*]

bogue³ *high school students* **1** *n* A cigarette **2** *v* To smoke a cigarette [fr Humphrey *Bogart*, who smoked so often in his films]

bogue out *v phr computer* To become bogus, that is, false, misleading, useless, etc

bogus 1 *adj fr early 1800s* False; fake; counterfeit; = PHONY **2** *adj teenagers* Ignorant; not up-to-date; unattractive; = LAME, SQUARE: *''Bogus'' is a different shading of ''lame''*—Time [origin unknown; perhaps from *bagasse*, perhaps fr *Borghese*, the name of a forger of the 1830s]

boho *n* An ineffectual person; = LOSER: *Leave it to bohos like the Clash to give the class war its first cavalry charge*—Village Voice/ *Jamie Lee as a goofball boho intellectual*—Washington Post [origin unknown; perhaps an alteration of *hobo*, like the attested *bo* and *bohobo*]

◀**bohunk**▶ *fr loggers* **1** *n* An immigrant from central or eastern Europe, usu a Czech, Slovak,

Hungarian, or Pole; =HUNKY **2** *n* A stupid, clumsy person

boiled *adj* Drunk
See HARD-BOILED, HARD-BOILED EGG

boiled leaves *n phr lunch counter* Tea

boiled shirt (or **rag**) **1** *n phr* A dress shirt, esp with a starched front; =FRIED SHIRT **2** *n phr* Stiff, chilly, and pompous behavior; stuffiness: *not arrayed in the "boiled shirt" of formality*—Robert Lynd

boiler 1 *n lumberjacks* An inferior cook **2** *n* A car, esp an old one; =HEAP, JALOPY **3** *n railroad* A steam locomotive: *sneak a boiler out of the roundhouse*—Merrill Blosser **4** *n* A liquor still
See POTBOILER

boilermaker 1 *n* (also **boilermaker and his helper**) A drink of whiskey with or in a glass of beer **2** *n* =BOILERMAKER'S DELIGHT

boilermaker's delight *n phr* Any very strong or rough drink; inferior whiskey; =ROTGUT [because it would clean the scales from the inside of a *boiler*]

boiler room See BUCKET SHOP

boil someone **in oil** *v phr* To punish or rebuke severely

boil up *v phr hoboes* To wash one's clothes

boing or **boing-boing** *interj WW2 armed forces* An exclamation of appreciative delight and intentness at the sight of an attractive woman: *dropped what they were doing and their eyes went "Boing, boing"*—Pete Martin [fr the sound a plucked spring makes, suggesting tenseness and quivering response, with a hint perhaps of penile erection]

boite (BWAHT) *n* A nightclub [fr French *bôite de nuit* "nightclub"]

bojie See BOOJIE

boke or **boko** *n underworld* The nose

bollixed (or **bolaxed** or **bolexed**) **up** *adj phr* In a thoroughly confused and futile condition; =BALLED UP, FUCKED UP: *You're getting your cues all bollixed up*—Jerome Weidman [ultimately fr old English *bealluc* "testicle"; see *balled up*]

boll weevil 1 *n phr labor union* A nonunion worker; =SCAB: *the boll weevils, the scabs*—A Lomax **2** *n phr labor union* Any unwelcome fellow worker, esp one who threatens the job of a senior employee **3** *n phr esp 1980s* A conservative Southern Democrat who votes with Republicans in Congress [fr the insidious reputation of the *boll weevil*, an insect that eats cotton bolls]

bolo 1 *n armed forces fr 1920s* A very inaccurate rifleman **2** *n prizefight* A long, looping punch: *Turner blooped a bolo to the heart of Jim Jennings*—New York Daily Mirror [probably fr *bolo*, the long, heavy knife of the Philippines, as suggesting a looping stroke]

boloney See BALONEY

bolter *v Vietnam War Navy* To fail to hook the arresting cables on the deck of an aircraft carrier

bolts See BUCKET OF BOLTS, NUTS AND BOLTS

bolus *n underworld fr middle 1800s* A physician [fr Latin *bolus* "pill"]

bomb 1 *n* =BOMBSHELL **2** *n football* A very long forward pass intended to score a quick touchdown **3** *n* A conspicuous and total failure; =BLAST, FLOP **4** *v: The show bombed everywhere on the road/ I took the test, and bombed* **5** *v* To do very well at or on: *I really bombed the math test, aced it* **6** *n hot rodders* A car, esp a hot rod [in the sense of failure, perhaps fr the outdated expression *make a baum of it* "fail"]
See DROP BOMBS, DUMB BOMB, STINK BOMB

bombed *adj* Drunk

bombed out *adj phr narcotics* Very much intoxicated by narcotics; very dozy or exhilarated; =SPACED-OUT, STONED

bomber *n narcotics* A marijuana cigarette; =JOINT

bombita (bahm BEE tə) *n narcotics* Any amphetamine pill or capsule used by addicts [fr Spanish, "little bomb"]

bomb out *v phr* To fail; =BOMB: *Stephanie Moody ..."bombed out" last year: failed to complete her opening lifts*—New York Magazine

bombshell 1 *n* A startling, striking event; something that makes one gape: *Her entrance astride the crocodile was a bombshell* **2** *n* A sexually stimulating woman

bond See JUNK BOND

bondage *n* Sexual practice in which a participant is tied up or otherwise restrained, usu for whipping or other "discipline"

bone¹ 1 *n teenagers* Money; cash **2** *n* A dollar, esp a silver dollar ◁**3**▷ *n* The erect penis
See FILE-BONE, HAVE A BONE ON, HAVE A BONE TO PICK WITH, JAWBONE, PRAYER BONES, TAIL BONE

bone² college students fr late 1800s 1 *n* A diligent student **2** *v* (also **bone up**) To study, esp to study intensely for an examination [fr the student's use of *bohns* "translations, ponies," named after *Bohn's* Classical Library]

bone-bender *n* A physician

bone-breaker 1 *n* A physician **2** *n* A very difficult task; =BALL-BUSTER **3** *n* A wrestler

bone-cracker 1 *n* A wrestler **2** *n* A chiropractor

bone-crusher *n* A wrestler

bone-eater *n* A dog

bone factory 1 *n phr* A hospital **2** *n phr* A cemetery

bonehead 1 *n* A stupid person: *four sons, all bone-heads*—F Scott Fitzgerald **2** *modifier: a bonehead idea/ bonehead play* **3** *n* A stubborn person; =PIGHEAD
See PULL A BONER

boneheaded *adj* Stupid

bonehead play *n phr sports* An error, esp one caused by bad judgment: *Merkel's throw was the most renowned bonehead play in history*

◁**bone-on**▷ *n* An erect penis: *Sometimes he could still get a pretty respectable bone-on*—Stephen King

bone-orchard *n* A cemetery

bone-polisher *n hoboes* A vicious dog

boner 1 *n fr early 1900s baseball* A blunder; error; =BLOOPER, HOWLER **2** *n college students* A diligent student; =BONE ◁**3**▷ *n* An erect penis; =HARD-ON: *the time you coveted your neighbor's*

wife. You had a big boner—Stanley Elkin/ *He walks around with a boner all the time*—Cameron Crowe
See PULL A BONER

bones 1 *n* Dice **2** *n* Any thin person **3** *n* Two sticks held between the fingers and used to make a clacking rhythm **4** *n* Dollars; money
See MAKE NO BONES ABOUT, PRAYER BONES, SAWBONES

Bones *n merchant marine* A ship's doctor

bone-shaker *n* Any badly sprung, springless, or violently jerking vehicle, esp a very early form of bicycle

bone-top *n* A stupid person; =BONEHEAD

bone up *See* BONE²

boneyard *n* A cemetery: *lie on a blanket out on the boneyard*—Tennessee Williams

bonfire *n* A cigarette, esp a lighted stub

bong 1 *n narcotics* A water pipe for smoking narcotics: *the array of glass and plastic water pipes or bongs*—New York Times **2** *v teenagers* To smoke marijuana using a water pipe **3** *v teenagers* To drink beer from a keg through a hose

bonged-out *adj* Intoxicated by a narcotic, esp one smoked through a bong: *You feel like a bonged-out Cubist painting*—Penthouse

bongoed *adj* Drunk

bonkers *adj fr British use* Crazy; insane; =NUTS: *Folks are going slightly bonkers these days over anything that glitters*—Newsweek [probably fr *bonk* "to hit on the head" + the British slang suffix *-ers*]

bonnet *See* BEE IN one's BONNET

bonzer 1 *adj WW2 armed forces fr Australian* Good; excellent **2** *n* Anything superior or useful

bonzo *adj* Crazy; =NUTS: *almost drove me bonzo*—Philadelphia Bulletin

boo 1 *adj esp early 1950s* Excellent; remarkable: *Something that used to be known as the cat's whiskers is now called..."deadly boo"*—Hal Boyle **2** *n narcotics* Marijuana or another narcotic: *I got over there and she lays this dynamite boo on me, I mean super shit*—Richard Price [second sense said to be fr black English *jabooby* "marijuana, so called because it induces a state of fear or anxiety," of unknown origin]
See TICKETY-BOO

boob 1 *n fr the late 1800s* A stupid person; =DIMWIT: *There are still boobs, alack, who'd like the old-time gin-mill back*—Sinclair Lewis **2** *n* A person who is too innocent and trusting; =SUCKER: *The poor boob fell for his line and gave him the money* ◁**3**▷ *n* A woman's breast; =BUB, KNOCKER **4** *n* A blunder; error; =BOO-BOO **5** *n underworld* A jail [sense 3 perhaps fr German dialect *bubbi* "a woman's breast"]

boobie¹ or **bubbie** (Bōō bee) *n* Friend; buddy; =SWEETIE ● A term of affection with general application [fr Yiddish *bubele*, an endearing epithet]

◁**boobie²** or **bubbie**▷ (Bōō bee) *n* A woman's breast [fr boob]

boo-bird *n* A spectator who boos; an adverse heckler: *A trade might satisfy the boo-birds*—New York Daily News

◁**boob job** (or **bob**)▷ *n phr* A mastectomy: *saying that Julie had had a boob job*—Playboy

boo-boo 1 *n fr early 1900s* A dollar **2** *n* Any error or misstep, esp one with embarrassing consequences; faux pas: *The original boo-boo that started all this public confusion*—HR King **3** *n* A minor flesh wound, or the accident causing such a wound [senses 2 and 3 perhaps from *boo-hoo*, a weeping over a costly error, or a child's crying over a minor hurt; perhaps fr Yiddish *bulba* "faux pas"]

boob trap *n phr* A nightclub

the **boob tube** *n phr* Television or a television set; =the TUBE

booby hatch 1 *n phr* An insane asylum; mental hospital: *King Bolden cut hair in the booby-hatch*—Stephen Longstreet **2** *n phr underworld* A jail or prison

booby trap 1 *n phr esp WW2 Army fr middle 1800s British* A hidden explosive charge designed to be set off by some ordinary act, such as starting a vehicle or driving down a street, used originally in wartime to harass invaders **2** *v:* *They booby-trapped his car and six people died* **3** *n phr* The seemingly harmless appearance that conceals vexations arranged for an unsuspecting opponent: *Don't debate him, it's a booby trap*

boodle 1 *n* An entire lot; a large number or amount; =CABOODLE **2** *n underworld fr middle 1800s* Counterfeit money **3** *n fr late 1800s* Bribe money or other money obtained by graft and corruption **4** *n* =BOODLER **5** *n fr late 1800s* Money in general **6** *n prison & students* Sweets; treats; delicacies **7** *v 1940s students* To hug, kiss, etc; =NECK [fr Dutch *boedel* "estate, lot"]

boodler 1 *n fr late 1800s* A corrupt politician **2** *n hoboes* A hobo who lives at public expense by spending winters in a warm jail

boodlers *n* Receivers of ill or easy gain, esp from political sinecures: *Weiss claims that the Fink boodlers were continued on the state payroll*—Village Voice

boog *v 1930s* To dance: *to go booging*—Life [fr *boogie-woogie*]

boogaloo or **bugaloo** (BōōG a lōō, BōōG-) **1** *n* A shuffling, shoulder-swinging dance: *feet doing a fast boogaloo in the grass*—Stephen King **2** *v:* *They boogalooed down the street* **3** *modifier:* *That's really voodoo music, man, boogaloo music*—Rolling Stone **4** *v* To carry on jocularly; play; tease; =FOOL AROUND **5** *modifier:* *go out and have a bugaloo good time*—Village Voice

booger *See* BUGGER

boogerboo (Bōō gər bōō, Bōō-) *black* **1** *v* To pretend; fake **2** *n* An insincere person; =PHONY

boogie or **boogey** (Bōō gee, Bōō-) **1** *n fr early 1900s black* Syphilis, esp advanced syphilis ◀**2**▶ *n* A black person ◁**3**▷ *modifier: a boogie hairstyle/ boogie music* **4** *n* =BOOGIE-WOOGIE **5** *v* To move, shake, and wriggle the body in time to rock-and-roll music; do a sort of boogaloo: *Amanda boogies and bangs a tambourine while her 39 sisters sit on steps and force shattered smiles*—G Mitchell **6** *v* =BREAK **7** *v* To carry on jocularly; play; tease; =FOOL AROUND: *back from a long weekend and ready to boogie*—Philadelphia Journal **8** *v* To do the sex act: *a lot of heavy boogieing going on at Iowa State*—Playboy ◁**9**▷ *n* The buttocks; behind; =ASS: *a little stomach, a high boogey...and thin legs* ◁**10**▷ *v* To do anal intercourse; =BUGGER: *Would Ronnie be averse to being boogied by Kiss during his acceptance speech* —National Lampoon **11** *n* WW2 Army Air Forces An enemy aircraft, esp a fighter plane; =BOGEY **12** *n* A piece of solid mucus from the nose

See FADED BOOGIE, LET'S BOOGIE

boogie board *n phr* A skateboard

boogie box *See* GHETTO BOX

boogie-woogie (Bŏŏ gee Wŏŏ gee, Bŏŏ-, Wŏŏ-) **1** *n fr early 1900s black* Syphilis, esp advanced syphilis **2** *n jazz musicians* A fast jazz piano style with a heavy rolling bass played eight beats to the measure, often used as a song accompaniment **3** *modifier: Jimmy Yancey...created the boogie woogie blues*—Stephen Longstreet **4** *n* Any jazz, swing, or jive music **5** *v black* To enjoy oneself thoroughly

boogily-woogily (Bŏŏ gə lee Wŏŏ gə lee, Bŏŏ- Wŏŏ-) *adv* In a confused and hasty manner; disorderly: *"Boogily-woogily"...means "pell-mell"*—Stephen Longstreet

boojie (Bŏŏ zhee, Bŏŏ-) (Variations: **bojie** or **boochie** or **booj** or **boojy** or **bourgie** or **buzhie**) *black* **1** *n* A middle-class black person; also, such persons collectively: *the black bourgeoisie...better known to most of us as the bourgie* —Washington Post **2** *n* Any middle-class person **3** *modifier: a bourgie couple mourning their 20-year-old daughter's comatose state*—Village Voice/ *exaggerating the slumminess of the tenements and playing down the boojy trappings of our apartment* —Richard Price/ *Kids my age don't wear fur....It's just white bourgie trash*—Philadelphia/ *upwardly mobile "bourgie" types*—Newsweek

book 1 *n underworld* A one-year prison sentence **2** *n gambling* =BOOKIE **3** *n gambling* A bookie's function and place of business: *Joey keeps a book* **4** *v* To be certain of something; bet on something: *It'll happen, you can book on it* **5** *n police* The daily logbook of a police station **6** *v police fr middle 1800s* To charge someone with a crime or misdemeanor at a police station: *They took the bum in and booked him for vagrancy* **7** *v* To engage in advance; reserve: *Please book me a table for 7 at 8* **8** *v* To arrange in advance, esp a performer, show, lecture, etc: *They booked eight readings in three days for the visiting poet* **9** *v students* To study hard; =HIT THE BOOKS **10** *v fr students* To run or depart, esp rapidly: *and the couple booked off into the sunset for their honeymoon* —Easyriders

See BY THE BOOK, CALIFORNIA PRAYER BOOK, CRACK A BOOK, DUKIE BOOK, HIT THE BOOKS, IN someone's BAD BOOKS, KEEP BOOK, LITTLE BLACK BOOK, ON BOOK, ONE FOR THE BOOK, POUND THE BOOKS, READ someone LIKE A BOOK, RUN A BOOK, STROKE BOOK, TAKE A PAGE FROM someone's BOOK, THROW THE BOOK AT someone, WISH BOOK, WRITE THE BOOK

the book 1 *n phr underworld* The maximum sentence allowed by law, esp a life sentence to prison **2** *n phr* Instructions or conventional wisdom about someone's performance; =FORM: *The "book" on this player...was to leave him alone, treat him politely, and pick him up if you happened to block him*—Lou Cannon

See THROW THE BOOK AT someone

bookie *n gambling* A person who accepts and handles bets on horse-races; bookmaker

book it 1 *v phr students* To depart quickly **2** *v phr* To be confident of something; count on something: *I'll be back. Book it*—Albuquerque Tribune

bookkeeper *n railroad* A flagman

boola-boola *n* Noisy partisan support for one's college teams: *too much panty-raiding, fraternities, and boola-boola and all of that*—Malcolm X [fr a Yale University song]

boom *See* FALL DOWN AND GO BOOM, LOWER THE BOOM

◁**boom-boom**▷ *n* Sexual activity; copulation; =ASS: *dragging girls into the woods "for a little boom-boom"*—Time

boomer 1 *n hoboes* A migratory worker **2** *n hoboes* A railroad or construction worker, logger, etc, who continually shifts from one place of work to another **3** *n esp 1930s* A womanizer; ladies' man

boom stick 1 *n phr hoboes* A railroad worker who continually shifts from one place of work to the next **2** *n phr* A firearm

boom sticks *n phr cool musicians & rock and roll* Drumsticks

◁**boon coon**▷ *See* ACE BOON COON

boondagger *n* A tough woman or aggressive lesbian; =BULLDYKE: *the boondaggers, you know, like bulls that come offa the street*—L Berry

boondock *modifier* Suitable for rough outdoor use: *Marines use boondock clothes and boondock shoes for hikes and maneuvers*—HL Miller

boondocker *n fr WW2 Navy and Marine Corps* A person who lives or works in a remote region, esp by preference

boondockers or **boon dockers** *n* or *n phr fr 1930s Marine Corps* Shoes suitable for rough outdoor use, esp heavy duty military shoes or boots

the boondocks or **the boonies** *n fr Marine Corps* Remote places; rural regions: *The people out there in the boonies may not know you're past it* —Washingtonian [fr Tagalog *bundok* "mountain"]

boondoggle *esp 1930s* **1** *v* To spend public funds on futile activity or outlandishly **2** *n: The public's got the idea that this is a boondoggle, a Rube Goldberg*—Time

booshwa or **booshwah** *See* BUSHWAH

boost 1 *v* To steal, esp by shoplifting: *Someone had boosted my tape recorder out of the room* —Harry Crews/ *slept on park benches and boosted from the A&P*—Herbert Gold **2** *v* To praise highly: *to boost one's home town* **3** *n: I'll give you a good boost*

booster 1 *n* A shoplifter; pilferer: *Got a booster for you. The chunky girl in blue at the lace counter* —Dashiell Hammett **2** *n* carnival A huckster's or auctioneer's assistant who pretends to buy in order to stimulate others; =SHILL **3** *n* A person who praises extravagantly; =FAN

boot 1 *v* To kick: *Let's boot a football around* **2** *n*: *Give him a boot in the ass* **3** *v* To discharge; =FIRE, SACK **4** *v* To dispraise; disrecommend **5** *n*: *I needed a boost but got a boot* **6** *v* To lose or waste by incompetence, inattention, etc; botch; bungle; =BLOW: *I booted three good chances* **7** *v* baseball To commit an error, esp in handling a ground ball **8** *n*: *Dark atoned for his boot by making a good play on Kiner's slow roller*—J McCulley **9** *n* A thrill; surge of pleasure; =BANG, KICK: *I get a boot from boats* **10** *v* (also **back-track**) narcotics To inject a narcotic gradually by pulling back and reinjecting blood again and again to increase the drug's effect: *The technique, known as "booting," is believed to prolong the drug's initial effect*—J Mills **11** *n* Navy & Marine Corps A recruit **12** *adj* *fr* Navy & Marine Corps Newly recruited; fresh on the job ◀**13**▶ *n* black A black person **14** *v* computers =BOOT UP **15** *n* (also **Denver boot**) A metal locking device put on the wheels of a scofflaw's car to prevent driving
See HARDBOOT, RUBBER BOOTS, TO BOOT

the boot *n phr* Dismissal, discharge
See GET THE BOOT, GIVE someone THE BOOT

boot and saddle *v phr* To leave; depart; =BOOK
• Often an injunction or command: *Boot and saddle, folks, it's time* [fr a cavalry command meaning "Mount your horse," said to be a folk etymology of French *boute-selle* "put the saddle on"]

boot camp *n phr* Navy & Marine Corps A basic training center

booter 1 *n* A football kicker **2** *n* A soccer player **3** *n* =BOOTLEGGER

boot it *v phr* To walk or go by foot

bootleg 1 *v* esp 1920s To make or sell illegal whiskey **2** *n* esp 1920s Whiskey illegally made or sold **3** *modifier*: *a bottle of bootleg hooch* **4** *v* football To carry the ball deceptively by holding it against the leg, esp after pretending to hand it off to another player [fr the idea of concealment in the upper part of one's boots; the phrase *on the bootleg plan* to describe illegal whiskey sales is attested from the mid-19th century]

bootlegger or **booter** or **bootie** *n* esp 1920s A person who bootlegs: *5,000 booters on Manhattan Island alone*—HL Mencken/ *That new bootie...carries a powerful line of hooch*—Saturday Evening Post

bootlick *v* students about 1900 To serve and flatter a superior; curry favor

boots *n* A shoeshine boy
See BET YOUR BOOTS, HAVE one's BOOTS LACED, JESUS BOOTS, RUBBER BOOTS

boot strapper *n phr* A person who succeeds by his own efforts; self-made person: *black "boot strappers," teachers, city workers, professionals who have to struggle to make it*—George Vecsey [fr the expression *lift oneself by one's own bootstraps*]

boot up or **boot** *v phr* or *v* computers To start up or input a computer's operating system: *The typical first step in working with a computer, then, is to load the DOS programs (this is called "booting up")*—Computers at Home/ *showed me how to log in and boot the operating system*—New York Times [perhaps fr *boot* "kick," with the sense of energizing or awakening with a kick; perhaps influenced by *boot up* "put on one's boots in preparation for action"]

◁**booty**▷ *esp black* **1** *n* The female body as a sex object **2** *n* The vulva **3** *n* The sex act; sex; =ASS: *The heroines are giving up some booty*—San Francisco

booze 1 *n* Any alcoholic drink, esp whiskey and other spirits **2** *v* To drink alcoholic beverages, esp to drink whiskey heavily [fr *bowse* "drink, carouse," reinforced by the name of a 19th-century Philadelphia distiller, EG Booze]
See HIT THE BOTTLE

boozed or **boozed up** *adj* or *adj phr* Drunk

boozehound or **booze-fighter** *n* A person who habitually drinks a great deal of whiskey; =LUSH: *Among American governors, the booze-fighters are plainly the best*—HL Mencken

boozery *n* A saloon, esp an illegal or after-hours saloon; =SPEAKEASY

booze up *v phr* To drink a great deal of liquor

booze-up *n* A drinking spree; =BINGE: *the morning booze-up which was still fouling his blood*—Robert Stone

boozy *adj* Drunk

bop 1 *v* To strike, esp with the fist: *Nina reached out and bopped her on the head*—Hal Boyle **2** *n*: *a bop on the beezer* **3** *v* To defeat: *The home team got bopped again* **4** *n* street gang A fight among gangs; =RUMBLE **5** *v*: *You gotta go on bopping and hanging around street corners all your life?*—Life **6** *n* (also **bebop**) A style of modern jazz characterized by complex harmonics, sudden changes in register, the use of fast and nearly unintelligible lyrics, etc: *Bop is "cool" jazz*—American Speech **7** *modifier*: *a bop musician* **8** *v* To walk or go, esp in a slow and relaxed mood: *They bopped over to the bar* [echoic]
See DIDDLYBOP, DITTYBOP, HARD BOP, TEENYBOPPER, THROW A FUCK INTO someone

bop cap *n phr* =APPLEJACK CAP

bop glasses *n phr* Horn rimmed spectacles: *The horn-rims of the intellectual came to be known as bop glasses*—Herbert Gold

bop off *v phr* To depart; =BOOK

bopper *See* DEELY BOPPER, TEENYBOPPER

bopping 1 *n* The act of a person who bops **2** *n* Philadelphia cabdrivers Tampering with taxicab meters to register illegally high charges: *The United Cab Association here has expelled about 40 cab drivers in the last two years for "bopping"*—Philadelphia Inquirer **3** *modifier*: *"bopping" cabbies expelled*—Philadelphia Inquirer

boppo *n underworld fr 1930s* A one-year prison sentence, or one year of a longer sentence

borax *fr 1920s furniture business* **1** *n* Cheap or inferior material; shoddy merchandise **2** *n* Exaggeration; misrepresentation; =HORSESHIT **3** *n* Any gaudy item; tasteless bric-a-brac **4** *modifier: strictly a piece of borax junk* [origin unknown; perhaps from the use of *borax* to conceal defects in furniture, or fr a tie-in between cheap furniture sellers and marketers of *borax* which was a cheap and plentiful product being touted as an ingredient of soap; perhaps related to British WW1 army use of *borax* "tell something false to a credulous person," apparently fr an Australian aborigine word *borak* "fun, banter," used in the late-19th-century British phrase *poke borak*, having the same meaning as the army use noted above]

border *See* SOUTH OF THE BORDER

bored stiff *adj phr* Very bored [fr the notion of being *bored to death*]

born loser *See* LOSER

borscht belt *n phr* The region in and near the Catskill Mountains north of New York City where many predominantly Jewish resort hotels are found [fr Russian *borshch* "beet soup," which was frequently on the menu of such hotels, in its Yiddish spelling]

borscht circuit *n phr* The resort hotels of the borscht belt, regarded as a circuit for entertainers, lecturers, etc

bosh *n* Nonsense; poppycock; =BULLSHIT

boss **1** *n* The chief; the person in charge **2** *n* A person or thing regarded as the best: *Of all the poets, Moss is the boss* **3** *modifier: Geoff's the boss drummer* **4** *adj teenagers fr black and jazz musicians* Excellent; wonderful; =COOL: *Aw, this is boss*—Rolling Stone/ *Japan has leaped into the implements-for-bosser-living gap*—San Francisco [fr Dutch *baas* "master"]

See CRUMB BOSS, STRAW BOSS

boss trick *See* CHAMPAGNE TRICK

bossy[1] *adj* Domineering; autocratic: *She's very bossy, a take-charge gal*

bossy[2] **1** *n* A cow **2** *n lunch counter* Beef [fr Latin *bos* "cow"]

Boston strawberries *n lunch counter* Beans

bot *n* A bottle

BOT (pronounced as separate letters) *n prison* The balance of time remaining to be served in prison

bothered *See* HOT AND BOTHERED

both hands **1** *n phr* Ten: *How many? Both hands* **2** *n phr underworld* A ten-year prison sentence

both sides of the street *See* WORK BOTH SIDES OF THE STREET

both ways *See* HAVE IT BOTH WAYS, SWING BOTH WAYS, WORK BOTH WAYS

bottle **1** *n* A bottle of liquor; =JUG: *He had a bottle on him* **2** *n line repairers* A glass insulator for electric or communications line **3** *n radio operators* A vacuum tube

See FIGHT A BOTTLE, POP BOTTLE

the **bottle** **1** *n phr* Liquor; =BOOZE **2** *n phr* Prostitution, esp male prostitution [sense 2 perhaps fr cockney rhyming slang *bottle and glass* "ass"]

See HIT THE BOTTLE

bottle baby *n phr police* A derelict alcoholic; =SKID ROW BUM

bottle blonde *n phr* A person whose hair is dyed blonde

bottle club *n phr* A social club where members may drink after legal hours

bottled *adj* Drunk

bottle-man *n* A habitual drinker; =LUSH: *a profound bottle-man*—Gene Fowler

bottom *n* The buttocks; =ASS

Bottom *See* FOGGY BOTTOM

bottom dollar *See* BET one's BOTTOM DOLLAR, BET YOUR BOOTS

bottom-end *n hot rodders* The crankshaft, main bearing, and connecting rod bearings of an automobile engine

bottomless *adj* Wearing nothing; nude: *a bottomless waitress*

the **bottom line** **1** *n phr* The bookkeeping figure showing profit or loss **2** *n phr* The result of any computation or estimate, esp one showing total costs: *I'll go half if the bottom line's OK* **3** *n phr* Any final decision or judgment: *Let me tell you the bottom line* **4** *n phr* A fundamental or crucial point of fact; the essence; =the NITTY GRITTY: *The bottom line is I am paid to win games, not for good will*—Inside Sports **5** *modifier: a bottom-line matter*

bottom man on the totem pole *See* LOW MAN ON THE TOTEM POLE

bottom of the barrel *See* SCRAPE THE BOTTOM OF THE BARREL

bottom out *v phr* To get as low or bad as possible; reach nadir: *If [Watergate] ever bottoms out, we might be all right*—Time

bottoms *n jazz musicians* Shoes; a pair of shoes

◁**bottoms up**▷ *adv phr* =DOG FASHION

bottom woman *n phr* The best patronized and most dependable woman in a pimp's covey of prostitutes

bounce **1** *v* To expel; throw out: *When he started swearing they bounced him* **2** *v* To discharge or dismiss; =FIRE **3** *n* Energy; vitality; =PISS AND VINEGAR, PIZZAZZ: *more bounce to the ounce* **4** *v* To be rejected for lack of funds in the bank: *His checks never bounce*

the **bounce** **1** *n phr* Forcible ejection, esp by a person hired to remove unwanted customers; =the BUM'S RUSH **2** *n phr* A dismissal, polite or otherwise; =KISS-OFF: *After a brief dialogue with my boss I got the bounce*

bounce something **around** *v phr* To think about and discuss an idea, project, etc: *Let's bounce it around a little before we decide*

bounce for *v phr* To pay for; treat; =PICK UP THE TAB: *somewhere that doesn't bounce for bluecoats*—Joseph Wambaugh/ *I'll bounce for the check this time*

bounce something **off** someone *v phr* To try out an idea or scheme by seeing how someone reacts; seek a quick evaluation: *Let's bounce the name off some typical housewives*

bounce off the walls 1 *v phr* *Army* Be in a nervous and confused condition; = BE HYPER **2** *v phr* *hospital* To be in a very agitated condition; be psychotically frantic and disturbed

bouncer 1 *n* *fr late 1800s* A person employed to eject unwanted customers from a saloon, restaurant, dance hall, etc **2** *n* A check that is returned for lack of funds; = RUBBER CHECK **3** *n* *underworld* A forged check **4** *n* *railroad* A caboose
See CHECK BOUNCER

◁**bouncy-bouncy**▷ *n* The sex act
See PLAY BOUNCY-BOUNCY

bouquets *See* THROW BOUQUETS AT someone or something

bourgie *See* BOOJIE

bovine extract *n phr* Milk

bow-and-arrow squad *n phr* A police assignment involving unarmed duty: *They pull an officer's weapon and send him off to a desk-bound bow-and-arrow squad*—Newsweek

bowels *See* GET one's BALLS IN AN UPROAR

Bowery bum *n phr* = SKID ROW BUM

bowl *n* Marijuana, esp when smoked in a pipe: *You wanna smoke a bowl?*
See CHILI-BOWL, FISH TANK, GOLDFISH BOWL, RUST BOWL

bowlegs *n* *outdated Army* A cavalry soldier

bowwow 1 *n* A dog ◁**2**▷ *n* An unattractive or obnoxious young woman; = DOG **3** *n* *fr around 1900* A frankfurter

bowwows 1 *n* The feet **2** *adj* Beautiful; attractive: *an athletically built blonde who was just bow-wows*—James T Farrell

bowzed *adj* = BOOZED

bowzered *adj* Drunk

box 1 *n* A coffin: *Keep that up and you'll go home in a box* **2** *v* *hospital* To die: *Oh, she boxed last night*—New York Times **3** *n* *underworld* A safe; vault; bank vault ◁**4**▷ *n* The vulva; vagina ◁**5**▷ *n* *homosexuals* The male genitals, esp as displayed by tight pants; = BASKET **6** *n* *jive & cool talk* Any stringed instrument, esp a guitar **7** *n* An accordion; = GROAN BOX **8** *n* A camera, esp one with a simple shutter and lens at the front of a small box **9** *n* An icebox or refrigerator **10** *n* A phonograph **11** *n* = GHETTO BOX: *Hey, man, don't mess with my box*—Wall Street Journal/ *were allowed to keep their boxes because their age exempted them from normal court procedures*—New York Times **12** *n* *police* A police telephone operator **13** *n* A very tight and awkward situation; cleft stick; = BIND: *Those guidelines put me in a hell of a box* **14** *adj* *hospital* Dead
See BITCH BOX, BLUE BOX, BRAIN-BOX, COLD-MEAT BOX, FIRST CRACK OUT OF THE BOX, GIT-BOX, GODBOX, GO HOME FEET FIRST, GOOLA BOX, GROAN BOX, IDIOT BOX, IN A BIND, IN THE BOX, JUICE-BOX, NUT HOUSE, OUT OF THE BOX, PETE, SHINE BOX, SOAPBOX, SQUAWK BOX, STUFF THE BALLOT BOX, THINK-BOX, WIND-BOX, WISDOM BOX

the **box** *n phr* Television or a television set

boxcar 1 *n* *WW2 Army Air Forces* A large cargo aircraft or bomber **2** *adj* *gambling* In high numbers: *boxcar odds* [second sense from the high numbers seen on the sides of railroad boxcars]

boxcar numbers (or **figures**) *n phr* Very high numbers: *bringing in the kind of boxcar numbers that advertisers like*—Village Voice

boxcars 1 *n* *crapshooting* A throw of two sixes **2** *n* Very large shoes
See GRAB AN ARMFUL OF BOXCARS

boxed *adj* Drunk

boxed in *adj phr* Incapacitated; trapped: *Without a car I'm boxed in*

boxed out *adj phr* *narcotics* Totally free and uninhibited, esp because of narcotic intoxication: *"Brush 'em easy, he boxed out," he says of a Pensacola dude, a dealer in contraband*—Village Voice

boxer *n* *hoboes* A box car

box someone **in** *v phr* To put someone in a tight and awkward situation; incapacitate someone

◁**box lunch**▷ *n phr* Cunnilingus

box man 1 *n phr* *underworld* A criminal specializing in opening safes; = PETE-MAN **2** *n phr* *gambling* A professional blackjack or twenty-one dealer **3** *n phr* *gambling* A cashier or croupier at a gambling table: *the box men, who are the cashiers of the tables*—J Cannon

box of dominoes *n phr* The mouth

box office *n phr* *fr show business* A popular and financial success, esp in the entertainment field: *just because you're no longer box office*—Roddy McDowall

boy ◂**1**▸ *n* A black man: *Don't call me "boy"...I'm as old as you are if not older*—Langston Hughes ◁**2**▷ *n* Any male, regardless of age, working as a porter, elevator operator, etc **3** *n* *homosexuals* A male who takes the subservient role in a homosexual relationship; = PEG BOY **4** *n* *narcotics fr 1920s* Heroin: *But now he had the boy; he could lie around*—C Cooper
See BIG BOY, BLOOMER BOY, BUG BOY, CLINKER BOY, FAIRHAIRED BOY, FLY-BOY, GOOD OLD BOY, JEWBOY, NOT BAD FOR A COUNTRY BOY, OLD BOY NETWORK, ONE OF THE BOYS, PADDY, PEG BOY, PERCY, POOR BOY, PRETTY-BOY, THAT'S MY BOY, TOMBOY, WALKBOY

boychik or **boychick** *n* A boy; youngster; = KID [fr Yiddish]

boyfriend *n* *fr early 1900s* A girl's or woman's sweetheart, lover, male friend, etc

boyo *n* A fellow; man; friend ● Often used in address [fr Anglo-Irish]

the **boys 1** *n phr* Any group of men, esp a group of drinking companions, poker players, etc: *an evening out with the boys* **2** *n phr* A group of criminals or other disreputable types
See ONE OF THE BOYS

the **boys in the backroom** *n phr* Any group of men, esp politicians and their aides, who are privy to and control the inner workings of an enterprise or place: *the salad boys in the back room, oiling up the cabbage*—WT Tyler

the **boys uptown** **1** *n phr* The political bosses of a city, and their staffs; =CITY HALL **2** *n phr* Any group of influential and unnamed criminals: *The tricksters...were "the boys uptown," not yet identified*—New York Daily News

bozette *n* A girl; a woman, esp a somewhat vulgar one; a female bozo: *A drunk babe is a happy babe, whether it's Babe Ruth or some bozette you've snagged at the five-and-dime*—National Lampoon

bozo *n fr early 1900s* A fellow; a man, esp a muscular type with a meager brain: *This bozo right here next to me [Rep. Thomas P. O'Neill incognito] could probably be a better Congressman than those guys in Congress*—Cheers (TV program) [fr Spanish *boso,* a version of *vosotros* "you" plural]

bra (BRAH) *n* A brassiere

bra-burner (BRAH bər nər) *n* A derogatory term for a very militant feminist: *The media decided henceforth to label feminists as "braburners"*—Esquire [fr the putative symbolic burning of brassieres as a protest against the restriction of women's freedom]

brace **1** *v* To stop or approach a person and beg for money: *This panhandler came up to me and braced me*—John O'Hara **2** *v* To confront someone with an accusation: *When I braced the guy he proved that Decker had paid him back*—Mickey Spillane **3** *n armed forces & service academies* A very stiff and exaggerated standing at military attention **4** *v: The sergeant ordered her to brace* See SPLICE THE MAIN BRACE, TAKE A BRACE

bracelets *n underworld fr late 1800s* A pair of handcuffs

bracer *n* A drink of liquor

brack-brain *n* A stupid, silly person: *this particular brack-brain*—Village Voice

brack-brained *adj* Stupid and silly: *April Fool's Day...makes some characters go completely brack-brained*—Village Voice

brackbrainer *n* Something that appalls, stupefies, or maddens: *The enormous new mural...is really some kind of brackbrainer*—Village Voice

bracket creep *n phr* The raising of wage-earners into higher income-tax brackets, esp because of wage-raises triggered by inflation: *Tax payments will mount next year from "bracket creep," the tendency of inflation to push people into higher tax brackets*—Wall Street Journal

brad *n outdated underworld* A small saw, such as might be used to cut off handcuffs

brag-rags *n* =FRUIT SALAD

braid See GOLD BRAID

brain **1** *n* An intelligent person; intellectual; good scholar: *The publicity of being a brain did not further her movie career as a glamor girl*—Bob Thomas **2** *v* To injure with a hard blow to the head: *The left hook really brained him* See BIRDBRAIN, BUBBLE BRAIN, HAVE something ON THE BRAIN, LAMEBRAIN, NOT HAVE BRAIN ONE, PICK someone's BRAIN, RATTLEBRAIN, SCATTERBRAIN

brain-box **1** *n* The head **2** *n railroad* A caboose **3** *n* The pilot house of a river towboat

brain bucket *n phr Army* A steel helmet

brain drain *n phr fr British* The loss of useful educated persons, esp professionals, from a place, esp a developing nation, or organization because they can find better conditions elsewhere: *Stalled Economy Speeds Puerto Rico's Brain Drain*—New York Times

brained See AIRHEADED, BIRDBRAINED, CRACK-BRAINED, DICK-BRAINED, LAMEBRAINED, NUMB-BRAINED

brainery *n fr late 1800s* A college or university

brain-fade *n* Stuporous boredom; tedium: *She and her colleagues fight brain-fade by sizing up customers*—Time

brain one *n phr* The most elementary intelligence; a minimum of sagacity: *Our leader doesn't have brain one* See NOT HAVE BRAIN ONE

brain-picker *n* A person who exploits the creative notions of others: *nothing but scorn for brain-pickers and imitators*—A Lomax

brains **1** *n* Intelligence; mind; =SAVVY, SMARTS **2** *n* The person who does the thinking and planning; guiding mind: *The brains of this outfit is the secretary* **3** *n railroad* A train conductor **4** *n merchant marine* A ship's officer; the official in authority See BEAT one's BRAINS OUT, FUCK someone's BRAINS OUT, HAVE SHIT FOR BRAINS, NOT HAVE BRAINS ENOUGH TO COME IN OUT OF THE RAIN, SHIT-FOR-BRAINS

one's **brains out** *adv phr* To one's utmost; extremely much; spectacularly; =one's HEAD OFF: *Everyone across this great nation shortly would be "partying" their brains out*—Village Voice

brainstorm **1** *n* A sudden idea, esp one that is apt and useful; a happy insight **2** *v* To examine and work on a problem by having a group sit around and utter whatever relevant thoughts they have, spontaneously: *We'll brainstorm the drop in enrollment*

brain tablet *n phr* A cigarette

brainwash **1** *v* To cause profound attitudinal changes, usu in a prisoner, by psychological conditioning, supplemented by drugs and physical abuse **2** *v* To change or influence someone's opinions or attitude by methods less stringent than those used on prisoners: *They were brainwashed into joining that crazy cult* **3** *n: Your line is persuasive, virtually a brainwash* [fr Chinese *hsi nao* "wash brain," which came into US use during and after the Korean War, apparently because of its use by North Koreans and their Chinese allies as custodians of US prisoners of war]

brain wave *n phr* A sudden useful idea; =BRAIN-STORM: *Lou had a brain wave. He offered the boy a C note to let him drive*—Raymond Chandler

brainy *adj* Intelligent; sagacious

brakes See STAND ON one's BRAKES

brakie or **brakey** *n railroad* The brake operator of a train

brand X **1** *n phr Army* The infantry insignia, crossed rifles **2** *n phr narcotics* Marijuana [fr the phrase used in television advertising for unnamed and inferior products]

brannigan or **branigan** *fr early 1900s* **1** *n* A spree: *a prolonged crossword puzzle brannigan* —Benjamin de Casseres **2** *n* A brawl or fracas; =DONNYBROOK: *Republicans and Democrats alike are guilty of this brannigan*—P Edson

brass 1 *n fr 1500s* Impudence; effrontery; =CHUTZPAH **2** *n outdated fr 1700s* Money • More common in British usage **3** *n* High officials or managers in general; =the BRASS: *There's lots of vice presidents here but they're not really brass* **4** *n hoboes & carnival* Cheap or fake jewelry
See BELLY BRASS, DOUBLE AS, FREEZE THE BALLS OFF A BRASS MONKEY

the **brass** *n phr armed forces fr WW2* The upper ranks of the military or other uniformed services: *Many a GI hated the brass and the enemy [equally]* —JB Douds
See the TOP BRASS

◁**brass balls**▷ *n phr* Courage; audacity; =GUTS: *But I had the brass balls to hold out for a piece of the action*—Rolling Stone

brass collar *n phr railroad* A railroad officer or high manager

brassed off *adj phr fr WW2 Air Forces* Ready to quit; sated; bored; =FED UP

brass hat 1 *n phr armed forces fr WW2* A high-ranking officer in the military or other uniformed services **2** *n phr* Any high-ranking official; manager; chief; =BOSS

brass monkey *See* FREEZE THE BALLS OFF A BRASS MONKEY

brass-pounder *n* A telegrapher; amateur radio operator [because sending keys are made of *brass*]

brass tacks *See* DOWN TO BRASS TACKS

brawl *n* A noisy, riotous party [fr *brawl* "a noisy fight," of obscure origin; perhaps related to Dutch *brallen* "brag," and Low German *brallen* "shout, roar"; perhaps fr French *branle* "an energetic circle dance"]

bread *n cool talk & 1960s counterculture* Money; =DOUGH [perhaps related to earlier *gingerbread* "money"]
See the BEST THING SINCE SLICED BREAD, SMALL POTATOES

breadbasket *n* The stomach; abdomen

bready *See* WHITE BREADY

break 1 *n* A prison escape **2** *n* A brief period of rest or relaxation: *Take a five-minute break* **3** *v*: *Let's break while I think about it all* **4** *v* To interrupt or abandon some regular practice: *to break training/ break an old routine* **5** *n* A stroke of luck, good or bad: *I got a break and made it on time/ Football's a game of breaks to some extent* **6** *n* A stroke of mercy or favor: *Give me one break and I'll never flunk again* **7** *v* To happen; occur; fall out: *If things break right I'll be OK* **8** *v* To tame a wild horse; subdue someone's spirit **9** *v* To bankrupt a company or person **10** *v* To ruin someone; destroy someone's chances and standing: *If you cross me on this I'll break you*

11 *v esp armed forces* To demote; reduce in rank: *They broke him back to buck private* **12** *v* To separate, esp from a clinch: *The boxers broke and came at each other again* **13** *n jazz musicians* An improvised passage; solo; =LICK **14** *v esp 1980s black teenagers* (also **breakdance** or **boogie**) To do a kind of dancing that evolved in the inner-city ghettos, and characterized esp by intricate writhings and shows of balance and strength close to the floor: *You can go running. You can swim. Or you can break*—New York Times **15** *n horse-racing* The start of a horse-race or other race
See COFFEE BREAK, EVEN BREAK, TAKE A BREAK

break a hamstring *v phr lumberjacks* To do one's best; =BUST one's ASS, BUST HUMP

break a leg *sentence fr theater* Best wishes; good luck; I hope you do very well [perhaps fr German *Hals und Bein brechen* "break your neck and leg," a similar good-luck formula]

◁**break one's ass**▷ (or ◁**balls**▷ or **buns** or **butt** or **cork** or **hump** or **nut** or ◁**sweet ass**▷)
See BUST one's ASS

breakaway 1 *modifier theater* Made to break or collapse easily: *bashed with a breakaway chair* **2** *adj* Unconventional; schismatic; rebellious: *a breakaway rock group/ breakaway mind set*

break (or **bust**) **chops** *v phr* To injure; punish; literally, to break someone's face or mouth: *Whoever did this hoax on NYPD was someone who wanted to break chops or who stood to gain from it* —New York Times

break (or **bust**) someone's **chops 1** *v phr* To verbally assault someone; harass: *His old man was starting to break his chops about the union*—Richard Price/ *I love it here. I can work hung over and nobody busts my chops*—National Lampoon **2** *v phr* =BUST one's ASS

breakdance *See* BREAK

break something **down** *v phr fr black* To explain something; present something in detail: *Break it down for me, Baby*—Eldridge Cleaver

breaker *n esp black teenagers* A person who dances with intricate writhings and shows of balance and strength close to the floor, esp and originally to rhythmic, staccato songs spoken rather than sung, in a style indigenous to the urban ghetto: *the night he and other breakers showed up...ready to boogie* —New York Times
See BACK-BREAKER, BONE-BREAKER, JAWBREAKER

breakfast *See* FROM HELL TO BREAKFAST, MEXICAN BREAKFAST, SHOOT one's COOKIES

break in *v phr* To surrender voluntarily for imprisonment

break-in *n* A burglary; forcible entry

break someone or something **in** *v phr* To put through an initial period of easy use or training before requiring full function

break it up 1 *v phr* To stop fighting, quarreling, chatting, etc • Usu a stern command **2** *v phr gambling* To win so much money that the other players are unable to continue

break luck *v phr prostitutes* To get the first client of the day

breakout *n* An escape

break out **1** *v phr* To escape from prison or some other confining situation **2** *v phr* To show symptoms of disease or discomfort: *He broke out in a purple rash* **3** *v phr* To bring out; produce for use: *When I came he broke out the Scotch*

◁**break out into assholes**▷ *v phr* To become very frightened [an allusion to the loose bowels associated with fear]

break out the jams *See* KICK OUT THE JAMS

the breaks **1** *n phr* Good luck; special favors: *If I get the breaks I'll prevail* **2** *n phr* Bad luck: *Them's the breaks*

break one's **shovel** *v phr* To lose favor: *You broke your shovel with me when you told that lie*

break the back *v phr* To achieve the hardest part of a job, journey, etc: *We got the back broken, the rest is a piece of cake*

break the ice *v phr* To dissipate the sense of strain among people who do not know each other: *I broke the ice by saying she looked like Charlemagne's mother*

break the news *v phr police* To beat someone up

break the points *v phr sports & gambling* To score enough points to cover the point-spread

breakthrough *n* An abrupt solution or surge of progress: *Understanding the reaction was a breakthrough*

break up **1** *v phr* To separate or to cause separation or dissolution of a close relationship: *to break up a marriage/ After ten years they broke up* **2** *v phr* To laugh or cause to laugh uncontrollably: *His doctor's shtick broke them up*

break-up *n* A separation or dissolution

break wind *v phr* To flatulate; = FART

◁**breastworks**▷ *n* The female breasts; = BAZOOM

breath *See* CHANGE BREATH

breathe easy *v phr* To be relieved of concern; relax

breather *n* A person who makes obscene telephone calls and merely breathes, rather than talking, into the mouthpiece

See HEAVY BREATHER, MOUTH-BREATHER

breathing *adj* Alive, at least: *They'll take any warm body that's breathing*

See MOUTH-BREATHING

breeder *n homosexuals* A heterosexual person; = STRAIGHT: *They are ridiculous things, and they are meant for breeders*—Armistead Maupin

breeze **1** *n* An easy task; anything easy; = CINCH, CAKEWALK **2** *v* To go or move rapidly and easily: *to breeze through work/ I breezed out* **3** *v prison* To escape from prison **4** *n:* *They had a breeze today at Ossining* **5** *n railroad* Compressed air for brakes

the breeze *See* BAT THE BREEZE, BURN THE BREEZE

breeze off *v phr* To leave; depart; = BOOK

breezy *adj* Very easy-going and jovial; cheery: *a breezy "Good morning"*

brekkie *n* Breakfast: *It was brekkie with Ed Meese* —Washington Post

a brew (or **brewskie**) *n phr esp college students* A glass, bottle, or can of beer; a beer: *She treated me to a brew*

brew out *n phr college students* A beer party; = BEER BUST

briar *n underworld* A file or hacksaw

brick **1** *n* A decent, generous, reliable person **2** *n narcotics* A kilogram (2.2 pounds) of tightly compacted marijuana

See DROP A BRICK, HIT someone LIKE A TON OF BRICKS, HIT THE BRICKS, PRESS THE BRICKS, THREE BRICKS SHY OF A LOAD

brick agent *n phr* An FBI agent of the lowest rank: *brick agent, the Federal infantry who...knock on doors, track down mysterious emigrés*—Philadelphia

the bricks **1** *n phr* The streets and sidewalks of a city: *I had to get out on the bricks and hustle* **2** *n phr prison* The world outside prison

See HIT THE BRICKS, PRESS THE BRICKS

bricks and mortar *n phr* Buildings and construction, esp as an item of expenditure and administrative emphasis for an institution

◁**brick shithouse**▷ *See* BUILT LIKE A BRICK SHITHOUSE

bricktop *n* A redheaded person

brickyard *See* HOGAN'S BRICKYARD

the Brickyard *n phr* The motor speedway at Indianapolis, Indiana, site of the annual 500-mile race [fr the *brick* construction of the track]

bridge *n lunch counter* Four of anything

brig *fr middle 1800s* **1** *n* The detention cell of a ship **2** *n* A naval prison **3** *n* Any jail or prison

bright *n black* A light-skinned black person

bright-eyed and bushy-tailed *adj phr* Eager and energetic; in splendid fettle

See STREET-SMART

brights *n* The bright or upper-beam headlights of a car: *into the brights of an oncoming car*—Village Voice

brig rat *n phr armed forces* A military prisoner

bringdown *esp 1950s beat & cool talk* **1** *n* A cutting rebuke or comment; a deflation: *Polite applause is a bit of a bringdown* **2** *n* A disappointing or depressing performance **3** *modifier: a bringdown scene* **4** *n* A morose person: *A "bringdown" is a depressing character*—Stephen Longstreet **5** *modifier: that bringdown face*

bring someone **down** *v phr students fr beat & cool talk* To depress; dispirit; sadden: *I'm afraid your jolly word brings me down*

bring down the house *v phr fr theater* To score a resounding theatrical success: *Old Man Dillinger strode onto the stage and brought down the house* —A Hynd/ *first heard on a Broadway stage in 1930, when she brought down the house singing "I Got Rhythm"*—New York Times

bring home the bacon (or **the groceries**) **1** *v phr* To achieve a tangible goal or task: *Their new tailback brought home the bacon* **2** *v phr* To earn enough to support oneself and one's family

bring it *v phr baseball* To throw a baseball fast

bring scunnion (or **smoke**) **1** *v phr* To inspire fear or anxiety in others **2** *v phr* To concentrate fire, esp artillery fire

bring up *v phr* To vomit; regurgitate

bring (or **keep**) someone **up to speed** *v phr* To give necessary information; brief; =FILL someone IN, PUT someone IN THE PICTURE: *Well, look, I appreciate your keeping me up to speed*—Washingtonian [fr the need to increase gradually the speed of a machine or phonograph turntable, video recorder, etc, to the proper rate]

the **briny** *n phr fr early 1900s* The ocean; the sea

Brit 1 *adj* British: *the Brit rock scene* **2** *n: two Brits and a Yank*

the **British** *See* BURN THE BRITISH

bro' or **bro 1** *n* Brother **2** *n black* A black person: *the slick-speaking bro who scores points off the ofay*—Time **3** *n motorcyclists* A motorcyclist; =BIKER: *the pack of twenty-seven bros jamming along the freeway*—Easyriders

◁**broad**▷ *fr early 1900s* **1** *n* A woman ● Used almost entirely by men, and considered offensive by many women: *Sorry lady, no broads allowed in here/ So here was this suburban broad*—Saul Bellow **2** *n* A promiscuous woman; prostitute [probably from the notion "*broad in the beam*"] *See* SQUARE BROAD

broad-gauge *adj* Very competent and versatile: *We're looking for a few broad-gauge people for an exciting project*

brodie or **Brodie 1** *n* A total failure; fiasco; =FLOP, TURKEY **2** *v* To commit suicide, esp by jumping from a high place [fr Steve Brodie, who claimed to have leaped off the Brooklyn Bridge in 1886, but failed to have the act witnessed]

broke *adj fr late 1800s* Entirely out of money; destitute *See* ALL HELL BROKE LOOSE, DEAD BROKE, FLAT BROKE, GO BROKE, GO FOR BROKE, STONY COLD BROKE

broken arms *n phr fr early 1900s* Table scraps

broken record *n phr* Something or someone repetitive, tedious, and importunate: *He kept asking for a raise, like a broken record*

broken-striper *n Navy* A naval warrant officer

bromide *esp early 1900s* **1** *n* An old, stale joke or scrap of wisdom: *Grandfather and his bromides* **2** *n* A boring, tedious person: *Clutterbuck, with his wilted wit, was a total bromide* [fr the use of bromide as a sedative]

bronc or **bronk 1** *n* =BRONCO **2** *n hoboes* A catamite; =PUNK

bronco 1 *n cowboys* A horse not tamed for riding **2** *n homosexuals* A young male not accustomed to nor complaisant in homosexual relations [fr Spanish *broncho* "rough, rude"]

bronco buster *n phr* (Variations: **peeler** or **snapper** or **twister** may replace **buster**) *cowboys* A cowboy who tames broncos to riding; also, a rodeo performer who rides unruly horses in competition

Bronx cheer 1 *n phr* A loud, rude, flatulating noise made with the tongue and lips; =BIRD, RASPBERRY: *The Duchess was startled but serene when the crowd greeted her with a fortissimo Bronx cheer* **2** *n phr* Any outright and precise expression of derision: *That book will get Bronx cheers from every critic*

brookie *n* A brook trout

broom *v black* To run or walk away, esp to escape by running *See* HAVE A BROOM UP one's ASS

broomstick *n* =BEANPOLE

broom tail *n phr cowboys* A mare

brother 1 *n* A man; fellow; =GUY ● Used in addressing strangers: *I don't know you, brother, but you said a mouthful* **2** *n black* A black person; =BLOOD: *All you brothers here, and you white people too, got to take care of business* *See* SOUL BROTHER

Brother *See* BIG BROTHER

brow *See* HIGHBROW, LOWBROW, MIDDLEBROW

◁**brown** or **brown-hole**▷ *v* or *v phr* To do anal intercourse; =BUGGER, BUNGHOLE *See* BUTTER BROWN

brown Abe *n phr fr 1930s jive talk* A penny

brown-bag or **brown-bag it** *v* or *v phr* To take one's lunch to the office, or one's liquor to a club or restaurant, in a paper bag: *for brown-bagging booze at places that allow this practice*—Esquire/ *to reduce the dangers of brown-bagging it for lunch*—Wall Street Journal

brown bagger 1 *n* A person who brown-bags **2** *n* A very ugly person; =DOUBLE-BAGGER [second sense fr the notion that such a person should wear a bag over the head to hide the face]

brown bucks *n phr lunch counter* Buckwheat cakes

browned off 1 *adj phr WW2 Army Air Forces fr British forces* Restless from waiting or wasting time; bored **2** *adj phr fr 1930s* Angry; =PISSED OFF: *He got browned off at the way they treated the kids*

brown eyes *See* BIG BROWN EYES

Brownie[1] *n railroad* A demerit [fr the name of a man who set up a disciplinary system]

Brownie[2] *n WW2 armed forces* =BROWN-NOSER

Brownie points *n phr* A fancied unit of credit and approval: *I'll get Brownie points for helping him/ a place where you get big shiny brownie points, cash, sex, and adulation*—Village Voice [fr merit points awarded to *Brownies* toward promotion to Junior Girl Scouts]

brown-nose 1 *v* To flatter and pamper in order to gain approval and advantage; curry favor; =APPLE-POLISH: *He's just like any other person who's in a position to screw you. You gotta brown nose*—John R Powers **2** *n: He got there by being a pious and effective brown-nose*

brown-noser *n* A person who brown-noses

brown off *v phr jazz musicians* To make a mistake; blunder; =GOOF

Brown Top *n phr show business* The main tent at a chautauqua

brud *n* Brother

bruh *n* Brother: *The man had me and I know what it's like, bruh*—Rolling Stone

bruised *adj* Drunk

bruiser *n fr middle 1800s* A big, strong man

brush 1 *n* A beard **2** *n* A fight; squabble; disagreement

the **brush 1** *n phr* The backwoods; jungle; = the BOONDOCKS **2** *n phr* A snub; quick dismissal; = BRUSH-OFF

See GIVE someone THE BRUSH

brush ape *n phr* A rustic or backwoods person

brushback 1 *modifier* *baseball* Pitched very close to the batter, as if to hit him: *knocked me over like a good brushback pitch*—New Yorker **2** *n: Throw another brushback and you're out of the game*

brush someone **back** *v phr* *baseball* To pitch close to a batter in order to force him or her away from home plate and upset the batting poise

brusher *See* SAGEBRUSHER

brush someone **off** *v phr* To pointedly snub or dismiss someone; = GIVE someone THE BRUSH

brush-off *n* = the BRUSH

brush up 1 *v phr* To clean; make neat and clean **2** *v phr* (also **brush up on**) To improve, review, or perfect one's mastery: *Brush up your Shakespeare. Start quoting him now*—Cole Porter

bruss *n* *Army* An extremely stiff and exaggerated military position of attention; = BRACE [fr *brace*]

brutal *adj* *students* Excellent; great

BS or **bs** (pronounced as separate letters) *n* = BULL-SHIT

B-side *n* The second or other side of a phonograph record; = FLIP SIDE

BT or **B and T** *n* *lunch counter* A bacon and tomato sandwich

BTO or **bto** (pronounced as separate letters) *n* = BIG-TIME OPERATOR

bub *n* A man; fellow; brother; = GUY ● Used in direct address, with a slightly insulting intent: *Okay, bub, get the hell outa my way* [fr *bubba* fr *brother*]

bubba *n* Brother ● Not uncommon as a nickname: *Here comes big Bubba Jones*

bubbie *See* BOOBIE

bubble brain *n phr* A stupid and vapid person; = AIRHEAD: *Did I want to establish that, bubble brain though I seemed to him, there were sound reasons?* —Saul Bellow

bubble-dancer *n* *lunch counter & WW2 Army* A dishwasher; = PEARL-DIVER [fr the ironic relation between the bubbly soapsuds of the dishwasher and the balloons used artistically by a cabaret *bubble-dancer*]

bubblegummer *n* A young teenager; = TEENYBOP-PER

bubble-gum music or **bubble gum 1** *n phr* Rock-and-roll music that appeals to young teenagers: *young adult audience dissatisfied with "bubble-gum music"*—New York Times/ *so fundamental that one might refer to it as "heavy bubble gum"* —Aquarian **2** *modifier: The rap itself is sheer bubble-gum monotony*—Variety

the **bubble-gum set** *n phr* Young teenagers; adolescents; = TEENYBOPPERS

bubblehead *n* A stupid person, esp one who is frivolous and flighty; = AIRHEAD: *Linda was, a polite word for dumb cunt, a bubblehead*—Richard Merkin

bubble queen *n phr* A woman who works in a laundry

bubbly *n* Champagne; sparkling wine

bubkes (BŌŌB kəs, BŌŌP-) **1** *n* Something trivial; nothing; = BEANS: *We've gone from bubkes to big deals in a year*—People Weekly/ *They've waved bye-bye to the likes of Julius Irving...and gotten bubkes in return*—Village Voice **2** *adv* Absurdly little: *That it sold bubkes...may say just as much for his laziness and his hubris*—Village Voice [fr Yiddish fr Russian, "beans"]

◁**bubs**▷ (BŌŌBZ, BŌŌBZ) *n* A woman's breasts; = BOOBS

buck 1 *n* *fr middle 1800s* A dollar **2** *n* *gambling* A hundred dollars, esp as a bet **3** *n* = BUCK PRIVATE **4** *n* *hoboes* A Roman Catholic priest **5** *n* A young male Indian; Native American brave **6** *n* A young black man **7** *n* Any young man, esp a strong and spirited one **8** *v* To resist; defy; go up against ● Usu in the negative: *You can't buck the system* **9** *v* *fr WW2 armed forces* To work for personal advancement; aspire eagerly; covet: *I'm bucking for that dealership* **10** *v* *fr WW2 armed forces* To pass along a letter, memorandum, problem, etc, usu without taking action; = PASS THE BUCK: *Let's buck this one to the Committee on Hot Potatoes*

See BANG FOR THE BUCK, BIG BUCKS, the BUCK STOPS HERE, FAST BUCK, HALF-BUCK, PASS THE BUCK, SAW-BUCK

bucked *adj* *WW1 armed forces* Pleased; proud; braced

bucker *n* (Variations: **buckayro, buckhara, buckeroo**) *cowboys* A cowboy [probably fr Spanish *vaquero* "cowboy"; perhaps fr *buckra*]

bucket 1 *n* A car, esp a big, old car **2** *n* *merchant marine & Navy* A ship, esp an old and slow ship; = RUST BUCKET **3** *n* *Navy* A destroyer; = CAN, TIN CAN **4** *n* The buttocks; rump: *Knocked him on his bucket* **5** *v* To speed; = BARREL: *They bucketed right through the light* **6** *n* *basketball* The basketball net **7** *n* *basketball* A basketball goal: *He'll make ten buckets a game* **8** *n* *baseball* The rearmost part of the batter's box: *had his foot way back in the bucket/ Emily steps into the bucket when going for a pitch*—New York Times

See BRAIN-BUCKET, someone CAN'T CARRY A TUNE IN A BUCKET, DROP one's BUCKETS, FOR CRYING OUT LOUD, GO TO HELL IN A HANDBASKET, GUTBUCKET, KICK THE BUCKET, LARD-BUCKET, RUST BUCKET, SLEAZE-BUCKET, SLIMEBAG, TAR BUCKET

the **bucket** *n phr* Jail; = the COOLER

buckethead *n* A stupid person; = BLOCKHEAD

bucket of bolts *n phr* An old car, airplane, etc

bucket of warm spit *See* WORTH A BUCKET OF WARM SPIT

bucket shop or **boiler room 1** *n phr* *from late 1800s* A place where very dubious stocks, real estate, etc, are sold, often by telephone solicitation **2** *modifier: what law enforcement officials call a "boiler room" operation*—Time [fr comparison with cheap saloons]

buck general *n phr Army* A brigadier general

buckle down *v phr* To set seriously to work; put slothful ease behind one

buck naked *n phr* Entirely nude; =BARE ASS: *My God, Sal, them women is buck naked in them magazines*

◀**buck nigger**▶ *n phr* A black man, esp a strong young one

bucko *fr 1800s merchant marine* **1** *n* Fellow; friend; comrade; buddy, guy **2** *n* A mean and dangerous man: *The mate aboard the Pride of Hoboken was a notorious bucko* **3** *modifier: The bucko skipper was a nasty sadist*

buck private *n phr Army fr late 1800s* An Army private; soldier of the lowest rank

buckra *n outdated black fr late 1700s British* A white man, esp a poor and mean one; =CRACKER, PADDY [probably fr *mbakara* "master," fr several West African languages]

bucks *See* BIG BUCKS, BROWN BUCKS, IN THE BUCKS, LIKE A MILLION BUCKS

buck sergeant *n phr Army fr WW1* An Army sergeant, wearing three stripes [fr *buck* "dollar" as the symbolic relative value of the most junior type of sergeant]

buck slip *n phr esp WW2 Army* A note, memorandum, printed form, etc, that passes an item of business along to someone else [fr *pass the buck*]

the **buck stops here** *sentence* This is the place where responsibility must be accepted; a decision must be made here ● Attributed usually to President Harry S Truman

buck up *v phr* To cheer up; brace: *Buck up, old chap, it may be good news*

buckwheater *n lumberjacks* A beginner; novice

bud[1] **1** *n* Friend; fellow; =GUY ● Used only in direct address, often with hostile intent: *Okay, bud, that'll do* **2** *n* A very close friend; =PAL: *Just be glad I'm your bud*—Cameron Crowe [fr *brother*]

bud[2] *n teenagers* Marijuana

◀**buddahead** or **buddhahead**▶ *n black & police* An Asian person

buddy *fr middle 1800s* **1** *n* =BUD[1] **2** *n* A man's closest male friend; =PAL ● During WW1 this term took on a particularly strong sentimental value **3** *n* A male's partner in work or sport **4** *v* =BUDDY UP [fr earlier *butty* "partner, chum," said to be fr Romany; probably influenced by *brother*]

See ACE BOON COON, ASSHOLE BUDDY, GOOD BUDDY, OLD BUDDY

buddy-buddy *fr WW2 armed forces* **1** *n* A close friend; =BUDDY **2** *n* A person who is too friendly; an importunate acquaintance **3** *v: Look at that guy buddy-buddying Joe* **4** *adj: It's just one of his buddy-buddy moves* **5** *adj* Very friendly; amenable to companionship: *He is not buddy-buddy...although he...insisted that the photographer take their pictures together*—Irwin Shaw

buddyroo *n* =BUDDY, PAL: *You should've seen the way they said hello....Old buddyroos*—JD Salinger

buddy seat *n phr* A passenger portion on a motorcycle seat

See IN THE DRIVER'S SEAT

buddy store *n phr Vietnam War Air Force & Navy* A military refueling facility for aircraft

buddy up *v phr* To share living quarters and conditions with; form a close association or two-person team: *These guys are alike; OK if they buddy up?/ Swimmers, buddy up*

buddy up to *v phr* To become close and comradely with; ingratiate oneself with: *He's hanging out with Watson now and buddying up to him*—Edmund Wilson/ *Lawrence smarmily buddies up to these women*—Washington Post

buff[1] *n* A devotee or enthusiast; hobbyist; =FAN, NUT: *I like to think I'm a people buff* [originally *fire buff*, because 19th-century New York City volunteer firefighters wore *buff*-colored coats; transferred to persons who like to watch fires, then to enthusiasts in general]

buff[2] *adj* Naked [probably fr the pale yellowish color of the leather called *buff*, likened to skin]

See IN THE BUFF

buff[3] or **buff up** *v or v phr hospital* To make a patient's chart look good, esp in preparing him or her for discharge [fr *buff* "to polish"]

Buff *n Air Force* An HH53 long-range rescue helicopter, called a "big ugly fat fellow"

buffalo **1** *v fr middle 1800s* To confuse someone purposely, esp in order to cheat or dupe **2** *v fr early 1900s* To intimidate; cow; =BULLDOZE **3** *n* A heavy or fat woman; =COW

buffalo butt *n phr students* A person with large buttocks; =FAT-ASS

buffaloed *adj* Baffled; puzzled

buffalo head *n phr* A nickel

buffer **1** *n outdated underworld* A dog or watchdog **2** *n Navy* A chief boatswain's mate

bug **1** *n* Any insect whatever **2** *n* Any bacterium, microbe, virus, etc: *Syph is caused by a bug* **3** *n* Any upper-respiratory or flulike complaint, esp one that is somewhat prevalent: *There's a bug going around* **4** *n* Any fault or defect in a machine, plan, system, etc: *You've got to get the bugs out of the program before trying to run it on the computer* **5** *n circus & carnival* Any small, cheap item sold by a vendor or huckster **6** *n poker* A joker or a wild card **7** *n outdated teenagers* A girl: *Boys prowl for "bugs"*—Time **8** *n radio operators* A semiautomatic or automatic radiotelegraph key used for fast sending **9** *n print shop* Any small symbol or label, such as a copyright or trademark symbol **10** *n print shop* An asterisk **11** *n horse-racing* An asterisk printed beside the weight a horse is to carry, showing that a five-pound decrease has been granted because the jockey is an apprentice **12** *n horse-racing* An apprentice jockey who has ridden his or her maiden race during the current year or has not yet won his or her fortieth race **13** *n horse-racing* A horse that has never won a race; =MAIDEN **14** *n hot rodders* A hot rod **15** *n* A Volkswagen beetle, or any small foreign car **16** *n astronautics* A small two-person lunar excursion vehicle **17** *n fr middle 1800s* An enthusiast; devotee; hobbyist;

=FAN, NUT: *Momma's a football bug* **18** *n* A compelling idea or interest: *His bug is surf-casting* **19** *n* A current fashion; epidemic preference or interest: *I never gave in to the hula-hoop bug* **20** *n* An insane person; =NUT: *Only a bug is strong enough for that*—Eugene O'Neill **21** *n prison fr 1930s* An irrational, touchy mood; bad mood **22** *n prison* A psychiatrist **23** *v prison* To do a psychiatric evaluation; pronounce one insane **24** *v 1960s counterculture fr black* To irritate or anger someone; pester or harry someone: *I suspected something was bugging her*—Louis Armstrong **25** *n underworld* A confidential message or signal; confidential information **26** *n underworld* A burglar alarm **27** *v: They've got that safe bugged eight ways* **28** *v police & espionage* To prepare a room or other place for electronic surveillance by installing hidden microphones; equip for electronic eavesdropping: *to bug a room/ Bug the Secretary's telephone* **29** *n: The team planted bugs in about six flowerpots* **30** *n* A large industrial crucible [the sense "irritate, pester" may be a shortening of black English *humbug*, attested in such uses as "Him wife de humbug him too much"; *humbug* itself, attested in English fr the mid-18th century, is apparently found in and may derive fr Pacific Pidgin English and West African Pidgin English]

See BIG BUG, FIREBUG, HAVE A BUG UP one's ASS, JITTERBUG, LITTERBUG, PUT A BUG IN someone's EAR, SHUTTERBUG

-bug *combining word* A devotee or energetic practitioner of what is indicated: *firebug/ money-bug*

bugaboo *n* Something that frightens or defeats one

bugaloo *See* BOOGALOO

bug boy (or **rider**) *n phr horse-racing* An apprentice jockey [fr the fact that an asterisk, or *bug*, appears beside their names in racing programs, showing that the horses are carrying reduced weight]

bug doctor *n phr prison* A psychologist or psychiatrist; =SHRINK

bugeyed **1** *adj* Having protruding eyeballs; exophthalmic; =POPEYED **2** *adj* Startled; astonished: *He looked all bugeyed* [fr humorous or dialectal pronunciation of *bulge*]

bugged *adj* Fitted with a concealed microphone or otherwise equipped for electronic surveillance: *do-it-yourself sex manuals, bugged phones*—WH Auden

bugged up *adj phr* Confused; flustered; upset

bugger[1] (BUH gər) *n* A person who bugs, esp one who installs electronic surveillance devices

bugger[2] (BUH gər, Bŏŏ-, Bŏŏ-) **1** *n* Fellow; man; child; thing ● Used affectionately: *What have been up to, you old bugger?/ Ain't he a cute little bugger?* **2** *n* An object, esp something admired, wondered at or scorned; =FUCKER, SUCKER: *Give that bugger a push, will you?* ◁**3**▷ *n* A male with a taste for anal intercourse; sodomite ◁**4**▷ *v* To do anal intercourse or sodomy; sodomize; =BUNGHOLE: *The proprietor...wins the right to bugger him* —Newsweek/ *who immediately announced that the Reverend Mr. Alger had been "buggering" him* —Village Voice **5** *v* (also **bugger up**) *fr cow-boys* To spoil; ruin; confuse; abuse; impair; =BOLLIX UP: *Between them they buggered up the mimeo machine/ The practice of how you bugger these numbers of US-Soviet armaments*—Village Voice

bugger[3] or **booger** or **boogie** (BUH gər, Bŏŏ-, Bŏŏ-) *n* A piece of solid mucus from the nose

bugger off *v phr chiefly British* To leave; depart; =FUCK OFF ● Often a contemptuous command: *pay no attention to my piteous Dont's, but bugger off quickly*—WH Auden

buggy[1] **1** *n railroad* A caboose **2** *n* A car, esp an old and rickety one; =HEAP, JALOPY: *I wouldn't exactly call my Maserati a buggy*

See BUZZ-BUGGY, HELL BUGGY, HORSE-AND-BUGGY, IRISH BUGGY, STRUGGLE-BUGGY, ZOOM BUGGY

buggy[2] *adj* Crazy; =BUGHOUSE, NUTS

buggy whip **1** *n phr* A long radio antenna on a car **2** *modifier:* *a buggy-whip antenna* **3** *adj* Old-fashioned; outmoded; antique; =OLD-TIMEY: *still manages to epitomize buggy-whip thinking in an increasingly sophisticated high-tech communications world*—Village Voice

bughouse *fr late 1800s* **1** *n* An insane asylum: *Who cares whether you're free or locked in a bughouse?*—Calder Willingham **2** *adj* Crazy; =NUTS: *He's a bughouse pimp*—William Kennedy/ *The local constabulary haul the bughouse blighter off to prison*—Washington Post

See GO BUGHOUSE

bug-hunter *n* An entomologist; naturalist; lepidopterist

bugjuice **1** *n fr late 1800s* Liquor, esp inferior whiskey; =ROTGUT **2** *n* A synthetic and highly colored soft drink [fr resemblance to the *juice* secreted by grasshoppers]

bugle *n fr middle 1800s* The nose; =BEAK, SCHNOZZ

bug man *n phr circus & carnival* A concessionaire who sells chameleons and turtles

bug off *v phr* To leave; depart ● Often an irritated command: *I'm done with you, so bug off* [perhaps fr late-19th-century British slang *bugger off*, of the same meaning; perhaps fr early-19th-century US *bulge* "to rush, dash"]

bugologist *n college students* An entomologist

bugology *college students* **1** *n* Entomology **2** *n* Biology

bugout *fr Korean War Army* **1** *n* A person who usually withdraws and evades; a slacker **2** *n* A military retreat **3** *modifier: a bugout plan*

bug out[1] *v phr fr middle 1800s* To bulge; protrude: *His eyes bugged out like a frog's*

bug out[2] **1** *v phr fr Korean War Army* To retreat; turn one's back and run **2** *v phr esp teenagers & hot rodders fr 1950s* To leave rapidly, esp to drive away in a hurry [Probably related to *bug off*]

bugs or **bugsy** *adj* Crazy; =NUTS: *The idea is so bugs it might work/ Don't act bugsy*

See STIR-CRAZY

bug test *prison* **1** *n phr* An intelligence test **2** *n phr* A psychological test or evaluation

bug torch *n phr railroad* A lantern

build **1** *n* One's physique, esp one's figure or shape: *a husky build/ sexy build* **2** *n theater* A show whose earnings continue to increase: *The revue was a build once word-of-mouth took hold* **3** *v* *underworld* To prepare someone for swindling, extortion, etc; = SET someone UP **4** *n:* *It's been a long build, but we can make our move now*

build a collar *v phr police* To gather evidence for an arrest

builder *See* STEW-BUILDER

builder-upper *n fr 1930s* Anything or anyone that strengthens someone or increases someone's confidence

buildup **1** *n* Publicity and other provisions for introducing a new product, entertainer, etc: *the buildup for a concert* **2** *n* The careful preparation of a potential customer or victim

build up *v phr* To increase, esp someone's self-esteem: *to build up earnings/ He's shy, needs building up*

built *adj* Physically well developed, esp in a sexually attractive way; = HUNKY, STACKED: *She wasn't especially smart, but she was built*

◁**built like a brick shithouse**▷ *adj phr* Very solidly and well constructed; = BUILT ● Said usually of a woman

bulb *n* = DIM BULB

bulge **1** *n* *fr middle 1800s* An advantage; a lead: *running up a 20-0 bulge*—New York Daily News **2** *n* A usu fatty surplus on the waist, buttocks, etc; = SPARE TIRE

See BATTLE OF THE BULGE

bull **1** *n* *fr 1700s* A peace officer of any kind, esp a uniformed police officer **2** *n* *lumberjacks* An ox **3** *n* *circus* An elephant, of either sex **4** *n* *poker* An ace **5** *n* Bull Durham, a very popular brand of tobacco for rolling cigarettes **6** *n* *railroad* A locomotive **7** *n* *lumberjacks & cowboys* The chief; head man; = BOSS **8** *n* *stock market* A dealer who favors higher prices and quicker selling **9** *modifier:* *a bull market* **10** *n* = BOONDAGGER, BULLDAGGER **11** *n* = BULLSHIT **12** *v:* *We were sitting around bulling/ He was bulling about his enormous talent*

See ALL THAT KIND OF CRAP, BULL OF THE WOODS, BULL SESSION, BULLWORK, CINDER BULL, COCK-AND-BULL STORY, FULL OF SHIT, HARNESS BULL, SHOOT THE BULL, SLING IT, THROW THE BULL, YARD BULL

◁**bull bitch**▷ *n phr* A woman with masculine traits; virago

bull cook *cowboys and lumberjacks* **1** *n phr* A male cook **2** *n phr* A cook's helper or menial

bulldagger *n black* A lesbian, esp a tough and aggressive one; = BOONDAGGER, BULLDYKE: *That's a bull-dagger, baby*—Claude Brown

bulldog **1** *n* *newspaper office* The earliest daily edition of a newspaper **2** *modifier:* *the bulldog edition* **3** *v* *gambling* To advertise horse-race winners falsely; = DYNAMITE **4** *v* *fr early 1800s & esp cowboys* To attack like a bulldog, esp to wrestle a steer to the ground by the horns **5** *n* *police & underworld* A snub-nosed revolver

bulldoze *v fr late 1800s* To intimidate; overcome by force: *to bulldoze employees* [fr *bulldose* "to

beat," perhaps fr the notion of the *dose* of force needed to cow a *bull*]

bulldozer *fr late 1800s* **1** *n* A person who bulldozes **2** *n* A revolver

bulldyke *n fr black* A lesbian, esp an aggressive one; = BOONDAGGER, BULLDAGGER, DYKE

bullet **1** *n* *poker* An ace **2** *n* *outdated underworld* Money; dollars **3** *n* *WW2 aircraft workers* A rivet **4** *n* Anything thrown very fast, esp a baseball: *He's throwing bullets out there* **5** *n* *recording industry* A record rising very fast on the popularity charts **6** *v:* *currently bulleting up the charts*—Rolling Stone

See BITE THE BULLET

bullet bait *n phr WW2 armed forces* Soldiers, esp young novice soldiers; = CANNON FODDER

bullets *fr early 1900s prison & Navy* **1** *n* Beans **2** *n* Peas, esp chickpeas and cowpeas

See SHIT BULLETS, SWEAT BULLETS

bullfest *n* = BULL SESSION

bull fiddle *n phr* The double bass; bass fiddle

bull-fighter *n railroad* A freight car

bullfrog *n truckers* A male hitchhiker

bullgine *n railroad* A locomotive

bullhead **1** *n* *railroad* A train conductor **2** *n* *fr middle 1800s* A stupid, obstinate person

bullheaded *adj* Obstinate

bullhorn *n fr Navy* An electronic megaphone; loud hailer

bullish **1** *adj* *stock market* Favoring and exhibiting high prices and relatively quick turnover: *a bullish market/ bullish advice* **2** *adj* Showing a positive and hopeful attitude; encouraging ● Often used with "on" or "about": *She tends to be bullish about our prospects/ He's quite bullish on the new restaurant* **3** *adj* Strong; stubborn; bull-like

bull of the woods **1** *n phr* *lumberjacks & truckers* The foreman or chief; = BOSS **2** *n phr* Any chief or supervisor: *Oakes is bull of the woods in the proofroom*

bullpen **1** *n* *prison* A cell or secure area where prisoners are kept temporarily: *We're in the bullpen waiting to go to court* **2** *n* *baseball fr late 1800s* A usu enclosed area where pitchers practice and warm up: *The bullpen's getting active now* **3** *n* *baseball* The relief pitching staff of a baseball team: *They've got starters but no bullpen* **4** *n* *lumberjacks* A bunkhouse **5** *n* *railroad* Dressing or sleeping rooms used between shifts **6** *n* *esp 1940s students* A living room, lounge, etc, where a girl's escorts and suitors are appraised by friends and family [baseball sense perhaps fr the fact that some baseball clubs would admit latecomers very cheaply and herd them like *bulls* into foul territory beyond first and third bases, where some bullpens are still located]

bullrag *n* Bovine excrement; = BULLSHIT, COWFLOP: *didn't mean bullrag in a pasture to him*—Stephen King

bull session *n phr* A discussion, esp one among good companions passing time idly but investigating important topics

bullseye *See* HIT THE NAIL ON THE HEAD

bullshine *n* Nonsense; pretentious talk; =BULL-SHIT: *the perpetual motion, nonstop, all-American bullshine machine*—Washington Post [a euphemism for *bullshit*]

◁**bullshit**▷ **1** *n* Nonsense; pretentious talk; bold and deceitful absurdities; =BALONEY: *I'm afraid your theory is chiefly bullshit* **2** *v*: *He tried to bullshit his way out of it* **3** *interj* An exclamation of disbelief, derision, and contempt in retort to some proposition

◁**bullshit artist**▷ *n phr* A person who habitually and effectively exaggerates, cajoles, seduces verbally, etc: *A good college president must be something of a bullshit artist*

bullshooter *n* A person given to exaggeration, boasting, or pompous inanity [fr *shoot the bull*, and a euphemism for *bullshitter*]

bullwork 1 *n lumberjacks, miners, cowboys & merchant marine* Hard work needing a bull's strength **2** *n* Tedious work requiring little thought or skill; =DONKEYWORK, SCUT: *sees computers taking over only the bullwork of secretaries*—Westworld

bully 1 *adj fr middle 1800s* Excellent; good **2** *interj*: *Bully for you!* **3** *n railroad* A track worker; =GANDY DANCER [the adjective sense may be related to *bullish*]

bullyrag *v* To harass; pester; =RAG [fr *ballyrag*, of unknown origin; influenced by *bully* "ruffian, blustering tyrant"]

bully up *v phr* To press one's way forward; =BELLY UP: *Sharkey...was bullying up to the bar*—George Warren

bum¹ 1 *n fr middle 1800s* A person who seldom works, seldom stays in one place, and survives by begging and petty theft; drifter; vagrant; hobo **2** *v* To live as a tramp, drifter, etc: *It wasn't easy bumming that winter/ He bummed for a couple of years, then got a job* **3** *v* To beg or borrow; cadge: *That's the third drink you've bummed in an hour* **4** *v* To hitchhike: *They bummed a ride to Nashville* **5** *n* A promiscuous woman, esp a cheap prostitute: *picking up bums in public dance halls*—James T Farrell **6** *n* Any male who is disliked by the speaker, esp for lack of energy, direction, or talent ● Often used of inept or despised athletes: *The bum strikes out three times in a row* **7** *n* A person who lives or tries to live by his or her sports talent and charm, without being genuinely professional: *ski bum/ tennis bum* **8** *n* An inferior animal, breed, racehorse, etc **9** *n* Anything inferior or ineffectual: *Money is a bum, a no-good bum*—Hal Boyle **10** *adj*: *a bum record/ bum heart* **11** *adj* False; invalid: *I told a bum story first*—James M Cain/ *bum rap* **12** *v* To deceive; victimize: *anyone who's seen this half-baked ode to mixed marital relations realizes that (the star) has been bummed into a bit role*—Us **13** *v computer* To improve something, esp by exploiting its full potential or rearranging its parts: *I bummed the whole program to show up all possible mistakes* [probably fr German *Bummler* "loafer"]

See BEACH BUM, CRUMB-BUN, ON THE BUM, SKID ROW BUM, SPECK BUM, STEWBUM, STUMBLEBUM

bum² *n* The buttocks or anus; =ASS ● More common in British usage: *after getting a shot of something in her bum*—Philadelphia [fr Middle English *bom* "anus"]

bum around *v phr* To go about idly; loaf: *I just bummed around last summer*

bumble-bee *See* KNEE-HIGH TO A GRASSHOPPER

bumblepuppy *cardplayers* **1** *n* A bridge game played haphazardly **2** *n* An indifferent or erratic player [fr a late-19th-century British term for inexpert whist]

◀**bumfuck**▶ *v* =ASSFUCK

◀**Bumfuck, Egypt**▶ *Army* **1** *n phr* A very distant and remote place; dead-end **2** *n phr* The destination of or a point along a long and circuitous march

bummed or **bummed out** *adj* or *adj phr* In a bad mood; dejected; depressed: *I'm heavily bummed...if I've realigned anybody's karma*—Playboy/ *belonging to the most bummed-out generation*—Chicago [fr narcotics and teenager senses of *bummer*]

bummer 1 *n fr middle 1800s* A bum: *an old bummer named Rumson*—AJ Lerner **2** *n narcotics* An unpleasant or depressing experience with a narcotic, esp with LSD; =BAD TRIP **3** *n teenagers fr 1960s counterculture* Any bad experience or occasion; bad situation or place: *May 17: Trip was a bummer. Instead of being off by ourselves, we met another couple*—Erma Bombeck/ *Her little soiree was a bummer/ This school's a bummer*

bum out *v phr* To depress; discourage; irritate: *At a fraternity...the things you observe totally bum you out*—Esquire/ *It bums the fuck out of me sometimes*—Rolling Stone

bum-out *n 1940s prison & Army* An assignment to easy work

bump 1 *v* To discharge; dismiss; =FIRE: *They bumped him for insubordination* **2** *v fr middle 1800s* To take away one person's status in order to accommodate someone of greater importance or seniority: *A person is bumped by someone with a larger number of retention points*—Jane Eads/ *The colonel bumped the corporal off the plane* **3** *v* To cancel a reserved seat on an airline, bus, etc because the vehicle has been oversold: *To be bumped...means to be put off a flight because too many seats have been sold*—Wall Street Journal **4** *v* To displace a sports opponent by defeat: *The Indians bumped the Tigers out of third place* **5** *v* To kill; =BUMP OFF **6** *n*: *They blew him away, gave him the bump* **7** *v* To make pregnant; =KNOCK someone UP: *She had to blame someone for bumping her*—Len Yinberg **8** *v* To promote: *He got bumped to assistant manager* **9** *n*: *I see old Pipkin has got the bump to full professor*—Morris Bishop **10** *v poker* To raise a bet **11** *v show business* In dancing, esp in striptease, to thrust the pelvis forward and up ● Nearly always in combination with **grind 12** *n*: *She unreeled about fifty bumps in dazzling staccato* **13** *n* A drink; =SLUG: *They go out...and have a bump of whiskey*—Garrison Keillor

See HUMP AND BUMP, LIKE A BUMP ON A LOG

bump along *v phr* To progress haltingly: *The interest rate has been bumping along*—New York Times

bump and grind *v phr* To thrust out and rotate the pelvis in dancing, esp the striptease, imitation of the sex act: *She bumped and ground faster as the bass drum upped its tempo*

bumper 1 *n outdated cardplayers* A two-game rubber of bridge **2** *n show business* A striptease dancer or other erotic dancer **3** *n railroad* The coupling mechanism of a railroad car

bump one's **gums** *See* BAT one's GUMS

bumpman 1 *n esp 1920s underworld* A professional killer; =HIT MAN **2** *n* A pickpocket

bumpoff *n fr early 1900s underworld* A killing; murder; assassination

bump off *v phr fr early 1900s underworld* To kill, esp to murder

bump on a log *See* LIKE A BUMP ON A LOG

bumps *See* DUCK BUMPS, GOOSE BUMPS

bumpy *See* GOOSE-BUMPY

bum rap 1 *n phr underworld* An erroneous conviction or sentence **2** *v: he had been bum-rapped*—Stephen King **3** *n phr* Any unjustified condemnation: *Reagan said, "Nancy's taken a bit of a bum rap on that buying White House china"* —Newsweek **4** *v: the Philadelphia Navy Yard has been bum-rapped*—Philadelphia

bum-rush *v* To eject someone, esp from a restaurant or other public place

the **bum's rush** *fr early 1900s* **1** *n phr* The ejection of a person by force, esp from a public place: *Dey gimme de bum's rush*—Eugene O'Neill **2** *n phr* Any discourteous or summary dismissal: *Those not in sympathy with the strike got the bum's rush*—Westbrook Pegler/ *with Stanfill telling the press that she had given her husband "the bum's rush"*—Washington Post

bum steer *n phr fr early 1900s underworld* Erroneous guidance or advice

bum trip *See* BAD TRIP

bun 1 *n fr early 1900s* A state of drunkenness; alcoholic exhilaration: *A bun is a light jag*—R Connell **2** *n* The buttocks; =BUM **3** *n* A single buttock; =CHEEK: *a boil on my left bun*

See CHEESE BUN, CRUMB-BUN, HAVE A BUN IN THE OVEN, HAVE A BUN ON

bun-buster *n* A very hard task or job; =BALL-BUSTER: *This job is a bun-buster*—People Weekly

bunch 1 *v 1920s hoboes* To quit a job **2** *n* A group, family, set: *I like my bunch, but yours is elitist* **3** *n* =MOB **4** *n* Money, esp a large sum; =BUNDLE: *He must have paid a bunch for that mink*

bunch of fives *n phr* A fist

bunco or **bunko 1** *v esp late 1800s* To swindle; defraud; =FLIMFLAM: *He was buncoed out of his seat in the House*—Greenough and Kittredge **2** *n* A swindle; =CON GAME, SCAM **3** *modifier: a bunco scheme/ instead of bunko artists*—Herbert Kastle [perhaps fr *bunkum* fr *Buncombe.* See bunk]

bunco (or **bunko**) **artist** *n phr* A professional swindler; =CON MAN: *The other fellow is, in most instances, a bunko artist*—Time

buncombe *See* BUNK

bunco-steerer *n phr outdated police* An accomplice in a confidence game, esp one who makes the first contact with the victim; =SHILL: *became entangled with a bunco-steerer*—Theodore Dreiser

bundle 1 *n fr early 1900s* A large amount of money: *I hear you made a bundle in real estate/ Can the Pentagon Save a Bundle?*—New York Times/ *He's dropped a bundle that way*—WT Tyler **2** *n* A large, quick profit; =KILLING: *I made a bundle yesterday on the market* **3** *n* An attractive woman: *I saw Charley yesterday with this cute bundle* **4** *n narcotics* Twenty-five $5 packets of a narcotic, esp marijuana or cocaine

See DROP A BUNDLE

bung or **bung up** *v* or *v phr* To dent; hurt by hitting; =BANG: *He bunged up the left fender pretty good*

◁**bung fodder**▷ *n phr* Toilet paper

◁**bunghole**▷ **1** *n* The anus **2** *v* To do anal intercourse; =BUGGER

bunhead *n* A stupid person

bunk[1] *fr late 1900s* **1** *n* Nonsense; pretentious talk; =BALONEY, BULLSHIT **2** *v* To cheat; defraud; =BUNCO: *couldn't possibly have done a better job of bunking the American people*—Chicago Tribune [fr the explanation by a 19th-century politician that his extraordinary statements were meant only for his constituents in *Buncombe County, North Carolina*]

bunk[2] *v* To leave; depart

Bunker *See* ARCHIE BUNKER

bunk fatigue (or **habit**) *n phr WW2 armed forces* A period of sleep or rest in bed; =BLANKET DRILL, SACK TIME

bunk flying *n phr WW2 Army Air Forces* Talk, esp dramatic and exaggerated talk, about one's flying

bunkie *n students fr WW2 armed forces* A roommate or bunkmate

bunk lizard *n phr WW2 armed forces fr Navy* A habitual shirker; =GOLDBRICK, GOOF-OFF

bunko *See* BUNCO

bunkum or **buncombe** *n* =BUNK

bunned *adj* Drunk

bunny 1 *n early 1900s students* Welsh rabbit **2** *n* A habitually puzzled or victimized person: *She is always criticizing some poor bunny*—Sinclair Lewis ◁**3**▷ *n* Any young woman, esp a pert and attractive one **4** *n* A young woman who associates with the men in some exciting, daring, or otherwise glamorous activity, sometimes as a participant; =GROUPIE: *snow bunny/ surf bunny/ to eliminate any chance that newsroom chauvinists could tag her as an electronic bunny*—Time **5** *n homosexuals* A prostitute who serves his or her own sex **6** *n basketball* A layup shot

See BEACH BUNNY, CUDDLE-BUNNY, DUMB BUNNY, DUST KITTY, FUCK LIKE A BUNNY, GUNBUNNY, JUNGLE-BUNNY, PLAY SNUGGLE-BUNNIES, QUICK LIKE A BUNNY, SEX KITTEN, SKI BUNNY

bunny (or **rabbit**) **food** *n phr* Lettuce, salad, green vegetables, etc

◄**bunny fuck►** **1** *n phr* A very quick sex act; =QUICKIE **2** *v: They pulled beside the road and bunny-fucked* **3** *v* To stall; waste time; =FUCK THE DOG: *Quit bunny-fucking and let's move*

buns *n* The buttocks, esp male buttocks: *I'll grab Ron's or Alan's buns sometimes and they're firm and hard*—Playboy
See one's ASS OFF, BUST one's ASS, WORK one's ASS OFF

one's **buns off** *adv phr* Very energetically; with maximum effort; =TO THE MAX: *You'll be playing your buns off with your left hand*—Toronto Life

bun-struggle *n esp around 1920* A formal tea

Bunyan camp *n phr lumberjacks* A logging or construction camp that does not furnish bedding for workers [fr the legendary lumberjack Paul *Bunyan*, who lived primitively]

'burb *n* A suburb: *the 'burbs (my pet name for LA-Boston-Frisco)*—Village Voice

burbed out *adj phr teenagers* Middle-class; bourgeois; pretentious: *non-stop wisecracks about burbed-out or boojy students*—Richard Price

burg *n fr middle 1800s* A city; town; village ● Usu expresses contempt: *stuck two days in this ghastly burg*

-burger *combining word* A sandwich made with cooked portions of what is indicated: *beefburger/ cheeseburger/ snakeburger* ● The definition does not apply to **hamburger**, the source of the term

burglar *n* A person who cheats or victimizes others: *Don't shop there, he's a burglar*
See GUT-BURGLAR

burgle *v fr middle 1800s* To break into a place for robbery; burglarize

buried **1** *adj underworld & prison* Serving a life sentence or other long prison sentence **2** *adj underworld* Languishing in solitary confinement; incommunicado

burleycue or **burlecue** or **burlicue** **1** *n* A burlesque show; the burlesque stage or circuit **2** *modifier: burleycue top banana/ burlicue stripper*

burly *n* Burlesque: *even when Buttons was in burly*—Gilbert Milstein

burn **1** *v* To cook or heat food **2** *v* To put or be put to death in the electric chair; =FRY **3** *v* To kill; assassinate **4** *v* To become angry; =BURN UP: *He began making cracks....I burned but went on singing*—John O'Hara **5** *n: He didn't blow up, just did a slow burn* **6** *v* To anger; infuriate; =PISS-OFF: *You must have done something to burn him*—Elizabeth Morgan **7** *v fr middle 1800s* To cheat; swindle; victimize; rob; =RIP OFF: *If you go along with that guy you'll get burned* **8** *n: It was a burn, but it didn't start out to be*—Rolling Stone Interviews **9** *v street gang* To assault or fight a rival gang or gang member **10** *v* To harass a person relentlessly; hound: *I'll burn you right off the force*—Ira Wolfert **11** *v teenagers & students* To insult; =PUT DOWN: *I burned this chick...."Whereja get those jeans, like Sears or something?"*—The Valley Girls' Guide to Life **12**

n: I didn't mean it as a burn **13** *v* To infect or become infected with a venereal disease **14** *v* To pass; spend; waste: *I'll start a conversation just to burn time*—Washington Post/ *if it burns tomorrow afternoon*—George V Higgins **15** *v* To move very rapidly; speed; =BARREL: *He wasn't just running, he was burning* **16** *v black fr jazz musicians* To perform, esp to improvise, superbly; excel; =be HOT: *The cat was getting down and burning* **17** *v* To borrow; beg **18** *v* To throw something, esp a baseball, very fast: *He burned the fastball right down the middle* **19** *v* To outdo; outshine in competition: *in the direction of the Spanish kids, who are already looking humiliated. Tony has burned the guy*—Village Voice
See BURNOUT

a **burn** *n phr* A cigarette; =a SMOKE: *They stepped outside for a burn*
See DO A SLOW BURN

burn a mark *v phr police* To frighten a shoplifting suspect into dropping a pilfered object

burn artist *n phr* A professional swindler or confidence man; a person who makes fraudulent sales, esp of spurious narcotics

burn someone's **ass** *v phr* To anger someone; irritate someone extremely: *It burns a girl's ass...when she's not supposed to go around with anybody else*—Noel Gerson/ *Still, it burns my ass to be so close and miss it*—Lawrence Sanders

burn someone **down** **1** *v phr* To shoot someone **2** *v phr* To deflate; humiliate: *He's so cocky someone has to burn him down*

burned *adj* Very angry: *Everyone is sitting there really pissed, really burned*—WT Tyler

burned out **1** *adj phr* Tired; exhausted; =POOPED **2** *adj phr* At the end of one's vigor and productivity: *The coach said he quit because he was burned out/ an old burned-out teacher* **3** *adj phr narcotics* Depressed and exhausted after the effects of a narcotic have worn off **4** *adj phr* Bored

burner **1** *n* The electric chair **2** *n black* A superlative performer; =the TOPS **3** *n football* A pass receiver whose speed is excellent for the first few yards run, but then is not notable
See COOK WITH GAS, FAST BURNER, GREASE-BURNER, HAY BURNER, IRON-BURNER, OAT-BURNER, ON THE BACK BURNER

burnese *See* BERNICE

burnie *narcotics* **1** *n* A partially smoked marijuana cigarette **2** *n* A marijuana cigarette shared among smokers

burning out *n phr narcotics* An older addict's voluntary withdrawal from narcotics after years of use; =AGE OUT

burn one *v phr fr 1930s* To draw a glass of beer

burn one in (or **over**) *v phr* In baseball, to throw a fastball

burnout **1** *n* Total and incapacitating exhaustion; inability to go on: *Many report lawyer burnout after two or three years in practice/ high rate of teacher burnout* **2** *n* Boredom; satiation; end of tolerance ● The currency of this and the previous sense are due to the various narcotics-users' meanings of **burn out:** *I feared polka burnout, but it never happened...I became a polkaholic*—Village Voice **3** *n* (also **burn**) *teenagers* A user or abuser of drugs, liquor, etc: *There are two groups in my school, the jocks and burn-outs. The burn-outs smoke and take pills and drink*—New York Times/ *except for the long hairs (or "burns," shorty for "burnouts") who hang out on the steps and smoke*—Washington Post **4** *n* *hot rodders* A very high-speed hot rod race **5** *n* An informal match where players try to throw a baseball so hard that it cannot be caught without undue pain **6** *n* *astronautics* The point where a rocket or missile has exhausted its fuel

burn rubber *v phr* To leave; depart, esp very precipitately: *When I got back to the flat, you had burned rubber out the back*—Village Voice [fr the scorching of tires in the fast acceleration of a car]

burn the breeze *v phr* To run or drive at very high speed

burn the British *v phr* *lunch counter* To toast an English muffin

burn the road *v phr* To drive a car very fast

burn up 1 *v phr* To perform very well; do superbly well: *His club is burning up the league this season* **2** *v phr* To go very fast on: *to burn up the base paths/ burn up the road* **3** *v phr* To become angry

burn someone **up 1** *v phr* (also **burn** someone **off**) To anger someone: *His egocentricity burns me up* **2** *v phr* To put someone to death in the electric chair **3** *v* *circus* To cheat; swindle; victimize

burp *fr early 1900s* **1** *n* A belch, esp a gentle one **2** *v:* *She burped thrice and smiled* **3** *v* To cause a baby to belch, esp by holding it over the shoulder and patting its back

burp gun 1 *n phr* *WW2 Army* A German Schmeisser machine pistol, with a very high rate of fire **2** *n phr* Any submachine gun; = TOMMY GUN

◀**burrhead**▶ *n* A black person

bury *v* *underworld* To sentence someone to a very long prison term or to solitary confinement

bus 1 *n* A car: *Whose old bus is in the drive?* **2** *n* An aircraft **3** *v* To clear dirty dishes and tableware from the tables in a restaurant or cafeteria [the restaurant sense probably fr the four-wheeled cart often used to carry dishes]
See JITNEY, RUBBERNECK WAGON

busboy *n* A person who clears dirty dishes and tableware from restaurant tables

buscar *fr early 1900s armed forces* **1** *n* Borrowed money **2** *n* Unexpected or forbidden pleasure; = BOODLE **3** *n* A close friend [perhaps fr Italian *buscare* "to give"]

bush 1 *n* A beard; whiskers ◀**2**▶ *n* The pubic hair, esp of a female; = BEAVER ◀**3**▶ *modifier:* *Bush shot. You could see the pubic hair, but not the sex parts*—John Irving **4** *adj* Rural; provincial; = BUSH LEAGUE: *a bush town* **5** *adj* Mediocre; second-rate; amateur: *seemed pretty bush for...pros* —John D MacDonald **6** *v* To fatigue; exhaust; sap; = POOP: *The climb bushed him/ Our dialogues always bush me*

See BEAT AROUND THE BUSH, BEAT THE BUSHES, TAKE THE RAG OFF THE BUSH

the **bush** *n phr* The back country; = the BOONIES

bushed *adj fr loggers* Tired out; exhausted; = POOPED [perhaps fr middle-19th-century meaning "lost in the woods"]

busher or **bush leaguer 1** *n* or *n phr* A baseball player in a minor league **2** *n* or *n phr* Any mediocre or second-rate performer; amateur: *He's a busher at the piano*

the **bushes** *n phr* Rural regions; small towns and villages: *When I was...working 12-hour tricks as a newspaper cub in the bushes*—Westbrook Pegler

bush league 1 *n phr* A baseball minor league of professional or semiprofessional players **2** *n phr* Any subordinate, apprentice, or amateur enterprise: *The road companies are sometimes bush leagues for aspirants to Broadway* **3** *adj phr* Mediocre; second- or third-rate; = BUSH, SMALL-TIME: *a bush-league hoodlum/ Your ideas are invariably bush league*

the **bush leagues** *n phr* The mediocre and inferior reaches of business, entertainment, sports, etc; = the SMALL TIME: *For years he made a perilous living as a singer in the bush leagues*

bush parole *n phr* *prison* An escape

bush patrol[1] *n phr* Hugging and kissing; = NECKING [fr the notion that a couple might hide in the bushes]

◀**bush patrol**[2]▶ *n phr* The sex act; copulation [fr *bush* "pubic hair"]

bushwah (BŏŏSH wah, BŏŏSH-) (Variations: **booshwah** or **bushwa** or **booshwa**) *n fr around 1920* Nonsense; pretentious talk; bold and deceitful absurdities; = BALONEY, BULLSHIT: *But the President's own managers concede this is so much bushwah*—Washingtonian [a euphemism for *bullshit* fr a cowboy corruption of French *bois-de-vache* "dried cow dung"]

bushwhack 1 *v fr middle 1800s* To assault, esp from ambush: *Two guys jumped out and bushwhacked him* **2** *v* To attack violently: *After that speech the President felt bushwhacked*

bushy-tailed *See* BRIGHT-EYED AND BUSHY-TAILED

business *n* Excrement, esp that of a house pet
See IN BUSINESS, KNOW one's ONIONS, MONKEY BUSINESS, TAKE CARE OF BUSINESS, THAT'S SHOW BUSINESS

the **business** *n phr narcotics* The equipment used for giving oneself a narcotic injection
See GET THE BUSINESS, GIVE someone THE BUSINESS

the **business end** *n phr fr middle 1800s* The dangerous or crucial part of something, esp the muzzle of a gun

businessman's bounce *n phr jazz musicians* Dance music or a popular song played in a fast tempo

bussy *n* A bus driver: *Where the blazes was that bussy?*—Sports Illustrated

bust 1 *v fr late 1800s* To break: *I busted my nose* **2** *v* *Army fr late 1800s* To reduce in rank; demote: *He got busted from buck sergeant to buck private* **3** *v* *cowboys fr late 1800s* To tame a wild horse for riding: *Two rides will usually bust a bronco*

so that the average cow-puncher can use him
—Harper's Magazine **4** *v underworld* To break
open a safe, vault, etc; also, burglarize a place **5**
n street gang To disperse or chase a rival street
gang **6** *n* A police raid: *One whiff (of marijuana)
and we get a bust*—Meyer Berger **7** *n* An arrest;
= COLLAR: *Beating a Bust: Two Views*—Rolling
Stone **8** *v: I've been busted, bring bail* **9** *v
teenagers fr 1950s* To catch someone in an illegal
or immoral act **10** *v* To hit someone: *She
busted me in the kishkes* **11** *n: That one bust
decked me* **12** *n fr middle 1800s* A failure;
fiasco: *My try for her sweet favors was a total bust*
13 *n* A person who fails; = NONSTARTER, LOSER:
At baseball I was a risible bust **14** *v college students* To fail an examination or course; = FLUNK: *I
miserably busted the econ final* **15** *n fr middle
1800s* A spree; drinking bout: *took his paycheck
and went on a bust* **16** *adj* Out of funds; destitute; = BROKE
See BEER BUST, GO BROKE

bust a cap *v phr narcotics* To take a narcotic, esp
heroin: *Why don't you bust a cap with me? It's
choice*—C Cooper [fr the breaking off of the *cap* of
a narcotics vial]

bust a gut *v phr* = BUST one's ASS

bust along *v phr* To travel fast; speed: *Ab Jenkins...busting along at 120 or so*—Sports Illustrated

◁**bust** one's **ass**▷ *v phr* (Variations: **break** may
replace **bust**; ◁**balls**▷ or **buns** or **butt** or **chops**
or **conk** or **hump** or **nuts** or ◁**sweet ass**▷ may
replace **ass**) To work or perform to one's utmost;
exert oneself mightily: *If They Break Their Asses
They Might Get into College Program*—John R
Powers/ *I'm finished busting my hump on that kind
of work*—Rolling Stone

◁**bust balls**▷ *v phr* To discipline harshly; punish:
They gonna be bustin' balls, man—David Rabe

bust caps *v phr Army* To fire the main gun of a
tank [see *bust a cap*; reference perhaps also to taking cannon shells out of sealed containers]

bust chops *See* BREAK CHOPS

bust someone's **chops** *See* BREAK someone's
CHOPS

buster 1 *n fr middle 1800s* A big person, esp a
boy: *He was a buster...nigh as big as his Mammy*
—Robert Penn Warren **2** *n* (also **Buster**) Man;
fellow; = GUY, BROTHER ● Used in direct address
with a somewhat hostile tone: *That'll just about do,
buster* **3** *combining word* Someone or something that destroys, thwarts, or otherwise defeats
what or who is indicated ● Popularized by an early
1980s film comedy called *Ghostbusters: troll
buster/ gridlock buster/ fuzz buster/ virus buster*
See BALL-BUSTER, BELLY-WHOPPER, BRONCO BUSTER,
BUN-BUSTER, CLOUD-BUSTER, CONK-BUSTER, KIDNEY-
BUSTER, SKULL-BUSTER

busthead 1 *n fr middle 1800s* Cheap or inferior
whiskey; = PANTHER PISS **2** *n* A drunkard, one
who is a hobo or drifter; = SKID ROW BUM

bust hump *v phr* To work extremely hard; = BUST
one's ASS: *Nobody's ever accused you of being
unwilling to bust hump*—Hannibal Boris

bust out 1 *v phr* To be dismissed from a school
for academic failure **2** *v phr* To lose all one's
money gambling, esp at craps; = TAP OUT **3** *v phr*
= BREAK OUT

bust someone **out** *v phr gambling* To win all of
someone's money in a crap game, esp by cheating

bust-out *n police* The climax of a swindle, when the
victim hands over the money

bust-out joint *n phr gambling* A dishonest gambling house

bust-outs *n gambling* Loaded or otherwise tam-
pered-with dishonest dice

busy bee *n phr narcotics* The powdered form of
Phencyclidine, a tranquilizer used in veterinary medicine, which as a narcotic is either sniffed or smoked
in a tightly rolled cigarette; = ANGEL DUST: *angel
dust, also known as busy bee*—New York Times

but *adv* Really; definitely: *He noticed it and began
making cracks but loud*—John O'Hara

butch 1 *n* A rough, strong man; = TOUGH
● Often used as a nickname **2** *n homosexuals*
An aggressive lesbian; = BULLDYKE, DYKE **3** *adj:
short round blonde of butch self-sufficiency*—Saul
Bellow [fr *butcher*]

butcher 1 *n outdated railroad & circus* A vendor
of small items like newspapers and candy **2** *n*
An incompetent surgeon **3** *n* A brutal and san-
guinary ruler: *They called Bokassa a worse butcher
than Amin* **4** *n* A person who is crude and
clumsy at work that needs finesse: *As a carpenter
I'm a butcher* **5** *v: I butcher their language/ I try
to paint but butcher the canvas*
See WOOD BUTCHER

butcher shop *n phr* A hospital

butcher wagon *n phr* An ambulance

bute *n* Butazolidin (a trade name), a drug sometimes used to stimulate race horses

but good *adv phr* Very well; extremely; really:
*They hate us but good/ Your brother fucked you
but good*—Saul Bellow

butt 1 *n* The buttocks; rump; = ASS: *So drunk he
couldn't find his butt with both hands*—H Allen
Smith **2** *n* The remainder of a smoked cigarette
or cigar **3** *n* A cigarette: *a pack of butts* **4** *n
armed forces & prison* The final year of a prison
sentence or a term of military enlistment
See BUST one's ASS, DUCK-BUTT, DUSTY BUTT, GET OFF
one's ASS, GOOD BUTT, GOOFY-BUTT, GRIPE one's ASS,
NO SKIN OFF MY ASS, SCUTTLEBUTT, SPRINGBUTT

butt can *n phr esp WW2 armed forces* A large tin
hung in a barracks or elsewhere to receive cigarette
butts

butter *n* Flattery; cajolery; = SOFT SOAP
See LIKE SHIT THROUGH A TIN HORN

butter-and-egg man *esp 1920s* **1** *n phr* A
wealthy business executive or farmer from the provinces: *The visiting Butter and Egg Men [making]
Whoopee in New York*—C Bragdon **2** *n phr* A
person who finances a theatrical production;
= ANGEL

butterball *n* Any plump person

butter bar *n phr Army* A second lieutenant

butter brown *n phr lunch counter* Buttered toast

buttercup *n* A girl, esp an innocent and attractive one

butterfingers *n fr cricket fr middle 1800s* A clumsy, unhandy person, esp one who regularly drops things: *Brunhilde is a regular butterfingers*

butterflies *n* Dull spasms in one's stomach, caused by anxiety and nervousness; flutters: *I sure got butterflies thinking about it*

butterfly *See* PUSSY BUTTERFLY

butterfly ball (or **pitch**) *n phr baseball* A slow and erratic pitch; =KNUCKLEBALL: *All this exertion took the butter off his butterfly ball*—New York Daily News

butterfly case *n phr* An insane person; =NUT: *At first Rupert Pupkin...doesn't seem like a butterfly case*—Philadelphia [fr the conceit that insane persons go about chasing *butterflies*]

butterfly kiss *n phr* A caress made by winking an eye so that the lashes brush one's partner: *She worked her eyelashes and made butterfly kisses on my cheeks*—Raymond Chandler

◁**butterhead**▷ *n black* A black person regarded by other blacks as a discredit to the black community

Butternut *n* A Confederate soldier [fr the fact that many such soldiers, esp fr rural areas, were dressed in homespun colored with dye made fr *butternuts*]

butter up *v phr* To flatter someone, esp in view of some special advantage; cajole: *You butter up the boss, you get the raise*

◀**buttfuck**▶ *v and n* =ASSFUCK, BUMFUCK

◀**buttfuck buddy**▶ *See* ASSHOLE BUDDY

◁**butthole**▷ *n* The anus; =ASSHOLE: *Did those buttholes score again?*—Dan Jenkins
See ASSHOLE

butt in *v phr* To intrude oneself; proffer unwanted counsel; =BARGE IN: *The Wagner Act forbade any employer to butt in on such matters*—Westbrook Pegler/ *"Greenspan, don't butt in," said Gold*—Joseph Heller

buttinsky *n* (Variations: **butterinsky** or **buttinski** or **butt-in**) *fr early 1900s* A person who rudely intrudes himself, esp one who does so habitually [fr *butt in* + the Slavic or Yiddish suffix *-sky*, added for humorous effect]

button **1** *n* The chin; point of the chin: *I got clipped square on the button* **2** *n* The clitoris; =CLIT **3** *n narcotics* A small quantity of a narcotic: *There exists some traffic, however, in "buttons," or small amounts*—H Braddy **4** *n narcotics* The rounded top of the peyote plant **5** *n* A police officer's badge
See BELLY BUTTON, CHICKEN SWITCH, HIT THE PANIC BUTTON, ON THE BUTTON, PUSH one's BUTTON

button chopper *n phr WW2 Army* A laundry; also, a laundry owner or worker

buttondown or **buttoned-down** *adj* Conventional; of unmistakable respectability; conservative; =SQUARE: *The button-down, dispassionate, country club racism of the nouveau riche*—Paul Good/ *One of the most squeaky-clean and buttoned-down of US corporations is a partner*—Wall Street Journal [fr the wearing of *buttondown* collars by business executives and other conservatives]

button down **1** *v phr* To classify; =PEG, PIGEONHOLE: *I buttoned him down from the start as a probable bore* **2** *v phr* To make precise; discard all but one alternative: *First we decide to buy, then we button down the price* **3** *v phr* To prepare for action; get ready: *He was all buttoned down and ready to go* [third sense fr a military term for closing all ports and hatches for action]

buttoned-up *adj* Neat; trim; prim: *Betty Crocker's very serious, buttoned-up, orderly*—Wall Street Journal

buttonhook *n football* A maneuver in which a pass receiver runs downfield and then suddenly spins and runs back toward the line of scrimmage [so called fr the resemblance of the path to a *hook* used for pulling *buttons* through the buttonholes of a pair of shoes]

button one's **lip** *v phr* To stop talking; not tell what one knows: *Tell that gasbag to button his lip*

button man (or **player** or **soldier**) *n phr underworld* A low-ranking member of the Mafia; =SOLDIER [probably fr the fact that such humble associates would be paid in *buttons* rather than valid coin]

buttons *See* HAVE ALL one's BUTTONS, HAVE SOME BUTTONS MISSING

button up **1** *v phr* To keep quiet; =BUTTON one's LIP, CLAM UP: *If you don't button up they'll shut you up* **2** *v phr* To finish something, esp tidily and handsomely: *We buttoned it up in a couple days* **3** *v phr* To lock up, close up, or make secure: *I told John Sanderson to button up the generator*—JC Clark

butt out **1** *v phr* To stop intruding; reverse one's butting in ● Usu an exasperated command: *Look, I'm busy, so butt out* **2** *v phr* To depart, esp abruptly; =BUG OUT: *I butted right out of there when it went off*

butt-room *n* A smoking room

butts or **butts on** *interj* The declaration that one has or wants first rights to something; =DIBS: *The kids hollered "Butts on the drumstick!"* [fr the claiming of a cigarette *butt* seen in the street]

buy **1** *v* To believe; accept as true: *These guys bought the myth and now it's costing them dearly*—Toronto Life **2** *v* To agree to; acquiesce in: *If that's the plan I'll buy it* **3** *v* To do; effectuate: *She pointed her gun at me. I said, "What are you trying to buy with that?"*—J Evans **4** *v* To hire; engage: *He bought him a lawyer and filed suit* **5** *v* To bribe: *He tried to buy a couple of jury members*

buy a pig in a poke *v phr* To accept or agree to something without careful examination; risk the unknown: *It is unfair for anyone running for president "to ask people to buy a pig in the poke"*—Associated Press [fr dialect *poke* "bag, sack"]
See CAN'T BUY

buy into *v phr* To accept; acquiesce in ● Thought of and perhaps coined as the opposite of **sell out**, which has a more contemptuous suggestion of betrayal: *lots of guilt and I bought into that*—San Francisco/ *I bought into the whole materialistic trip*—San Francisco

buy it *See* COP IT

buy jawbone *v phr* To buy on credit [perhaps fr the notion that one has to *jawbone* the merchant into taking a credit risk]

buy off on *v phr Army* To agree to; =BUY: *Will you buy off on letting us go back to garrison?*

buy the farm (or **the ranch**) *v phr fr armed forces* To be killed; die: *the cat that bought the farm when Harvey hit him on his bike*—Cyra McFadden/ *Luna crash confirmed. They bought the ranch* —Playboy [fr earlier Air Force term *buy a farm* "to crash"; probably from the expressed desire of wartime pilots to stop flying, buy a farm, and live peacefully]

buy time *v phr* To be dilatory or evasive in order to gain time; temporize; =STALL

buzhie *See* BOOJIE

buzz 1 *v* To call someone on the telephone; =RING: *Why not buzz Eddy for the brawl?*—HT Webster **2** *n*: *I think I'll give the Guided Child a buzz*—K Brush **3** *v* To talk; converse: *The crowd was buzzing about some pretty raunchy divorces* **4** *n* Subject of talk; gossip; rumor: *What's the dirtiest buzz?* **5** *n* A feeling or surge of pleasure, esp a pleasant sense of intoxication; =HIGH: *After two Scotches he got a nice buzz* **6** *v*: *I was pleasantly buzzed by a belt of Bourbon* **7** *n teenagers fr 1950s* A police squad car **8** *n* A kiss, esp a quick kiss on the cheek **9** *v* To flatter; court **10** *v* To inform someone in confidence, esp by whispering: *You'll buzz me later*—Mickey Spillane **11** *v* To announce one's arrival or summon someone by or as if by sounding a buzzer: *Buzz when you want me* **12** *v hoboes* To beg **13** *v underworld* To pilfer; rob; =HOLD UP **14** *v outdated police & underworld* To question or investigate someone **15** *v* To fly an aircraft alarmingly close to something, esp to the ground **16** *v WW2 armed forces* To roister drunkenly at: *They were all buzzing the bar*

buzz along *See* BUZZ OFF

buzzard 1 *n* A dislikable person, esp an old man: *a stingy and predatory old buzzard* **2** *n prison, Army & students* Chicken or turkey **3** *n armed forces* The eagle worn as insignia by a colonel or a naval captain
See JUNGLE BUZZARD

buzzard colonel *n phr armed forces* =CHICKEN COLONEL

buzz around the barrel *v phr 1950s rock and roll talk* To get something to eat; snack

buzz bomb *n phr* A German WW2 V-1 winged robot bomb powered by a ramjet engine

buzz book *n phr* A best-selling book; a book everyone is talking about: *The nation's latest buzz book is not a fast summer read*—Time

buzz-buggy or **buzz-wagon** *n* A car

buzz-buzz *n esp early 1900s* Unintelligible or tedious noise, esp continuous vociferation: *All the buzz-buzz from without may be said to go in one ear and out the other*—Atlantic Monthly

buzzed *adj* Intoxicated, esp mildly so: *Getting a little buzzed on a second Bloody Mary*—Peter de Vries

buzzer *n* A police or other law-enforcement badge: *I brought out the 1928 deputy sheriff's star I carried to show people who wanted to see a buzzer*—J Evans
See MOLL-BUZZER

buzzin' *See* WHAT'S BUZZIN', COUSIN

buzz in *v phr* To arrive: *Old JK buzzed in from Syracuse*

buzz someone in *v phr* To unlock an outer door for someone by actuating an electric unlatching device

buzz off (or **along**) *v phr* To depart; =TODDLE OFF

buzz-saw *See* MONKEY WITH THE BUZZ-SAW

buzzword or **buzzphrase** *n* A modish technical or arcane term used to make one appear sophisticated: *The rhetoric has sputtered with buzzwords like "anticolonialist" and "progressive"*—Time/ *I avoid buzzphrases like "this point in time"*

buzzy *adj* Drunk

BVDs (bee vee deez) *n* A suit of men's underwear, esp one-piece long underwear; =BEEVEEDEES [fr a trade name]

by 1 *prep* With; as far as concerns: *Five skins is jake by me*—American Mercury **2** *prep* At; to; at the place of: *I'll buy you a drink by Antek*—Nelson Algren [fr direct transcription of Yiddish prepositional use into English]
See GET AWAY WITH something, GET BY

not by a long shot (or **a jugful**) *See* NOT BY A LONG SHOT

by a nose *adv phr* By a narrow margin; barely: *win by a nose*

by cracky *interj fr early 1800s* By Christ ● A euphemistic form: *By cracky, he hit the jackpot!*

bye *See* TAKE A BYE

by ear *adv phr* By instincts and feelings, without the benefit of formal training or procedures: *He sort of made his judgments by ear*
See PLAY IT BY EAR

by George *interj* A mild exclamation of surprise, approval, determination, emphasis, etc: *By George, I'll do it/ I think she's got it, by George* [A euphemism for *by God*]

-by God- *infix* Used for emphasis: *I was born in West-by God-Virginia*

by guess and by God *adv phr* By approximation and instinct; not by precise or infallible means: *She didn't know exactly how to make a quiche, so had to do it by guess and by God*

bylow *n outdated black* A kind of folding knife: *Mary Jack whipped out a bylow, a big knife with a large blade*—Louis Armstrong [fr *Barlow*, a trade name]

BYOB (pronounced as separate letters) **1** *v phr* Bring your own bottle, or your own booze **2** *modifier*: *a BYOB party*

◁**by the balls**▷ *See* HAVE someone BY THE BALLS

by the bell *See* SAVED BY THE BELL

by the book *adv phr* According to correct procedures; as one should under regulations, law, contract, etc: *He said there would be no more corner cutting, we'd do everything strictly by the book*

by the numbers *adv phr fr WW1 armed forces* In a prescribed way; mechanically: *He even makes love by the numbers* [fr the military training device of analyzing a complex action by breaking it into a numbered series of simpler actions, performed as the *numbers* are called out]

by the seat of one's **pants** *See* FLY BY THE SEAT OF one's PANTS

C

C *n* Cocaine

See BIG C, C-NOTE, GENTLEMAN'S C, H AND C

caballo *n narcotics* Heroin [fr Spanish, "horse," translating *horse* "heroin"]

cabbage *n* Money; =LETTUCE: *the salad boys in the back room, oiling up the cabbage. And it's big cabbage, too*—WT Tyler

See FOLDING MONEY, HAPPY-CABBAGE, POCKET CABBAGE

cabe *See* ABE'S CABE

cabinet *See* KITCHEN CABINET

cabin fever *n phr* Restlessness, impatience, and other signs of having been restrained too long

caboodle *n fr middle 1800s* A totality; discrete unit; =BOODLE: *Keep the whole caboodle* [perhaps fr *boodle*; see *boodle*]

See KIT AND CABOODLE

caboose *n* A jail [prob fr *calaboose* "jail"]

ca-ca or **caca** or **kaka** **1** *n* Excrement; =SHIT: *not worth ca-ca* **2** *n narcotics* Heroin; =HORSE, SHIT [fr late-19th-century *cack* "to defecate," perhaps fr Latin *cacavi* "to defecate," used as a euphemism in the presence of children; ultimately fr the Indo-European root *kakka* or *kaka*, designating defecation]

cackle-broad or **cack-broad** *n outdated black* A wealthy woman or society woman: *I knocks de pad with them cack-broads up on Sugar Hill*—Zora Neale Hurston

cackle factory *n phr* An insane asylum; =LAUGHING ACADEMY

cackler *n hoboes* An office worker; white-collar worker

Cad or **Caddy** or **Caddie** *n* A Cadillac car

cadet *See* SPACE CADET

cadge (CAJ, CAYJ) *v fr early 1800s* To borrow; beg; =BUM, MOOCH

Cadillac *n narcotics* An ounce of heroin

cage **1** *n fr 1600s* A prison **2** *v*: *The punk concealed a genuine terror of being caged*—Nelson Algren **3** *n motorcyclists* A car or van: *The cage behind me bleated its horn*—Easyriders **4** *v* =CADGE **5** *n sports fr early 1900s* A basketball basket or net **6** *n sports fr early 1900s* Basketball **7** *modifier*: *a big cage star/ the cage standing*

See LOUSE-CAGE, MONKEY CAGE, RATTLE someone's CAGE, RATTLE CAGES

caged *adj* Drunk

cager **1** *n sports* A basketball player: *The eight-foot cager sped down the court like a maddened giraffe* **2** *n* A drunkard

cage rattler *n phr* A person not content with the humdrum or conventional: *The governor wants "cage rattlers"...thinkers, dreamers, and gadflies*—Newsweek

cagey or **cagy** *adj fr late 1800s* Shrewd; wary; pawky: *a quiet, cagy observer*

cahoots *See* IN CAHOOTS

Cain *See* RAISE CAIN

cake ◁**1**▷ *n black* The female genitals **2** *n black* A sexually attractive woman; =FOX **3** *n esp 1920s* A ladies' man; =DUDE: *his brown hat, fixed square-shaped the way the cakes were wearing them*—James T Farrell **4** *n college students* =PIECE OF CAKE

See BABYCAKES, COFFEE AND CAKES, CUT CAKE, FLY CAKE, FRUITCAKE, HEAVY-CAKE, ICE THE CAKE, NUTBALL, PIECE OF CAKE, TAKE THE CAKE

cake-cutter *n circus* A cashier or other person who gives short change

cake-eater *n esp 1920s* A ladies' man; =DUDE

cakewalk *n* Something very easy; =BREEZE, CINCH, PIECE OF CAKE: *Casey on his way to a cakewalk with the Senate Intelligence Committee*—Time/ *Our players thought this season was going to be a cakewalk*—Sports Illustrated [fr the name of a 19th-century dance contest, influenced by *piece of cake*]

calaboose *n fr 1700s* A jail or prison; cell [fr Spanish *calabozo*]

calf *See* SHAKE A WICKED CALF

calf love *n phr* =PUPPY LOVE

calico *See* PIECE OF CALICO

California blanket *n phr hoboes* Newspapers used as bedding: *spent his nights on park benches under California blankets*—World's Work

California kiss-off *See* KISS-OFF

California prayer book (or **bible**) *n phr fr middle 1800s* A deck of playing cards

calk off *See* CAULK OFF

call **1** *n hoboes* A stew **2** *n* =NATURE'S CALL

See CATTLE CALL, CLOSE SHAVE

call someone's **bluff** *v phr* To force someone to justify or validate a pretense; require the truth: *When she called his bluff, he had to admit he was lying*

call-down *n* A reprimand; rebuke

call someone **down** *v phr* To reprimand; rebuke

call girl *n phr* A prostitute, esp one who may be engaged by telephone

call house (or **joint**) *n phr* A brothel, esp one where a prostitute may be engaged by telephone: *that call joint*—Jerome Weidman

call in one's **chips** *v phr* To finish something; declare an end: *The Administration is calling in its chips, and people are lining up*

calliope *n railroad* A steam locomotive with a multitoned whistle

call it quits *v phr* To stop or terminate something; declare one has had enough: *After four years they called it quits*

call someone **on the carpet** *v phr* To reprimand or summon for a reprimand; =CHEW someone OUT [probably fr early-19th-century British *walk the carpet*, having the same sense and based upon a servant's being called into the parlor to be reprimanded]

call one's **shots** *v phr* To explain or predict what one will do: *She'll never try to trick you, she always calls her shots* [fr the announcement of a targetshooter where the next *shot* will hit]

call the shots *v phr* To be in charge: *Who's calling the shots around here?*

cally *n outdated hoboes* A jail or police station [fr *calaboose*]

calm as a Christian with aces wired *See* COOL AS A CHRISTIAN WITH ACES WIRED

◄**Cambo**► *n Vietnam War armed forces* A Cambodian

camelback or **camel** *n railroad* A locomotive having the cab in the center rather than at the rear

◄**camel-jammer**► *n* An Arab or Iranian

camp 1 *n homosexuals fr 1940s* A male homosexual **2** *adj: a camp bar/ the camp scene* **3** *n homosexuals fr 1930s* Effeminate behavior, such as mincing gait, fluttering gestures, or pronounced lisp **4** *v* (also **camp it up**): *Malcolm was camping perilously in the blue-collar bar* **5** *n fr 1960s* Something, esp in art, decoration, theater, etc, so naively stylized, artificial, affected, old-fashioned, and inadequate to good modern taste as to be highly amusing and inviting to parody: *television's inexhaustible supply of crash courses in camp* —Washington Post **6** *adj: a camp advertisement/ camp clothing* **7** *v* (also **camp it up**) To behave in a humorously affected, exaggerated way, esp imitating the acting and oratorical styles of the 1800s: *She started camping, vamping me like Theda Bara*

See BLACK CAMP, BOOT CAMP, BUNYAN CAMP, HIGH CAMP, LOW CAMP, MITT-CAMP

campaign *See* WHISPERING CAMPAIGN

campus *v college students* To confine a student to the college premises as a disciplinary measure

campy 1 *adj homosexuals* Effeminate; overtly homosexual **2** *adj* Displaying naive, affected, and old-fashioned style: *a campy evocation of WW1 patriotism*

can 1 *n* A toilet; =JOHN **2** *n* The buttocks; rump; =ASS **3** *v fr early 1900s* To discharge an employee; =FIRE: *He is not the first commentator*

to be canned by an editor—Heywood Broun **4** *v fr early 1900s* To stop; cease, esp some objectionable behavior ● Usu a stern command: *Let's can the noise* **5** *n* A jail or prison; cell **6** *v: They caught him and canned him for two weeks* **7** *n Navy* A destroyer **8** *n hot rodders* A hot rod **9** *n narcotics* An ounce of marijuana

See ASH CAN, BUTT CAN, GET A CAN ON, IN THE CAN, KICKING CAN, OIL CAN, SHITCAN, TIE A CAN ON someone, TIN CAN, TOMATO CAN

canal water *See* SUCK CANAL WATER

canary¹ 1 *n fr late 1800s* A girl or woman; =CHICK **2** *n* A woman singer, esp of popular music **3** *v: She used to canary with Stan Kenton* **4** *n underworld* An informer; =STOOL PIGEON

See MOUNTAIN CANARY

canary² *n* A compliment; critical approval [fr Yiddish *kayn aynhoreh* "(may you have) no bad luck or no evil eye," a formula used to ward off bad luck]

can be *See* EASY AS PIE

can do 1 *sentence fr late 1800s armed forces* I can do it; I'm the one you want: *We asked them to design a whole new bridge in a week, and they said "Can do"* **2** *adj: The CIA was a can-do outfit* —The New Republic

See NO CAN DO

candy *narcotics* **1** *n* Cocaine or hashish **2** *n* A sugar cube soaked with LSD; LSD **3** *n* Any barbiturate drug

See NEEDLE CANDY, NOSE CANDY, ROCK CANDY

candy ass *n phr* A timid person; weakling; =WIMP

candy-assed or **candyass** *adj* Timid; feeble; cowardly; =WIMPY: *not that candy-assed dreck played by legions of Spandexed clones*—Worcester Magazine/ *Some candyass Barry Manilow type might be at ease in this setting*—New York Times

candy man *n phr narcotics* A narcotics supplier; =CONNECTION, PUSHER

candy stripe *n phr Army* A secondary road on a map

candy striper *n phr* A young woman who is a volunteer nurse's aide in a hospital [fr the *stripe* on her uniform, resembling those on peppermint *candy*]

cane corn *n phr* Corn whiskey made from corn and cane sugar; =MOONSHINE

can house *n phr* A brothel: *him playing the races and going to can houses*—James T Farrell

canned 1 *adj* Drunk: *They was already pretty canned*—James M Cain **2** *adj* Recorded; played from a phonograph record or magnetic tape: *canned music* **3** *adj* Not fresh for the occasion; kept for easy and general use: *The candidate uttered one or two canned one-liners, to small effect* **4** *adj movie studio* Filmed; completed: *That scene is already canned*

canned cow *n phr fr cowboys* Canned milk; condensed milk

canned goods *n phr* A virgin, either male or female

canned up *adj phr esp 1920s* Drunk: *They got canned up a little more*—James M Cain

cannery *n* A jail

cannibal *n* =SIXTY-NINE

cannon[1] *n* A pistol; firearm; = PIECE: *He holstered his own cannon*—Raymond Chandler

See LOOSE CANNON

cannon[2] **1** *n* *underworld fr early 1900s* A professional thief, esp a pickpocket: *grand larceny, when a cannon lifts a wallet from a pocket*—New York Times **2** *v*: *You're too small to cannon the street-cars*—Nelson Algren [an extension of *gun* "thief," fr Yiddish *gonif*]

cannonball 1 *n* *hoboes* A fast express or freight train **2** *n* *prison* A message sent from one prisoner to another, or from a prisoner to friends outside

cannon fodder *n phr fr 1930s* Common soldiers, esp young and relatively untrained infantry soldiers; = BULLET BAIT

canoe *v* To kiss and caress, etc; = MAKE OUT, NECK: *Her old man had been hearing about me and Daisy canoeing*—Louis Armstrong [probably fr *canoodle*]

can (or **tall can**) **of corn** *n phr baseball* A high, easy fly ball

can (or **bag**) **of worms** *n phr* A complex and troublesome matter; a Pandora's box: *The Social Security problem is a can of worms/ the current bag of worms*—Armistead Maupin

See OPEN UP A CAN OF WORMS

canoodle *fr middle 1800s* **1** *v* To hug, caress, etc; make love **2** *v* To coax, esp by lavishing affection

can-opener *n underworld* Any tool used to open a safe

one **can really** (or one **sure knows how to**) **pick 'em** *sentence* One is very selective, accurate, and successful in choices ● Nearly always used ironically: *Is this turkey your idea of a good show? You can really pick 'em*

cans ◁**1**▷ *n* A woman's breasts; = TITS: *that chanteuse with the huge cans* **2** *n* Earphones worn over the ears

See KNOCK someone FOR A LOOP

can't buy *v phr* To have no possibility of; be totally denied: *From then on, I couldn't buy a good review*—Saturday Review/ *You couldn't find a job. You couldn't buy a job*—Newsweek

someone **can't carry a tune in a bucket** *sentence* Someone is tone-deaf; someone sings very badly: *Ashley can't carry a tune in a bucket*—New York Times

you **can't fight city hall** *See* YOU CAN'T FIGHT CITY HALL

can't fight (or **punch**) one's **way out of a paper bag** *v phr fr prizefight* To be a very weak or ineffective puncher; put up a poor showing

you **can't get there from here** *See* YOU CAN'T GET THERE FROM HERE

someone **can't hit the side of a barn** (or **a barn door**) *sentence* Someone is unable to throw accurately enough to hit anything at all

you **can't make an omelet without breaking eggs** *See* YOU CAN'T MAKE AN OMELET WITHOUT BREAKING EGGS

canto *n sports* A round, inning, period, or other division of a contest: *Lefty got decked in the third canto*

[fr Italian, "song," with reference to the 100 poetic divisions of Dante's *Commedia*]

someone **can't win for losing** *sentence* Someone seems unable to make any sort of success; someone is persistently and distressingly bested: *We busted our humps, but we just couldn't win for losing*

Canuck 1 *n* A Canadian, esp a French-Canadian **2** *modifier*: *Canuck booze/ my Canuck pal* ● Regarded as offensive by some, but apparently becoming more acceptable

can you read lips *See* READ MY LIPS

cap[1] **1** *n* Captain **2** *n* Mister; sir ● Used in direct address to a man one wishes to flatter

cap[2] *narcotics* **1** *n* A capsule of narcotics: *I didn't have the money to buy a cap with*—D Hulburd **2** *v* To buy narcotics; = COP: *I capped me some more pot*—H Braddy **3** *v* To open or use a capsule of narcotics; = BUST A CAP

See BUST CAPS

cap[3] *v* To best or outdo, esp with a funnier joke, stranger story, etc; = TOP: *She told a lie that capped mine*

See APPLEJACK CAP, GIMME CAP, GO-TO-HELL CAP, OVERSEAS CAP, TIT CAP

◁**cap**[4]▷ *n* Fellatio; = HEAD: *Give Jerry some cap*—Donald Goines

Cape Cod (or **Cape Ann**) **turkey** *n phr fr middle 1800s* Codfish

capeesh *See* COPPISH

caper 1 *n* A drunken spree **2** *n* Any spree; = BINGE **3** *n* *fr middle 1800s* A prank; stunt **4** *n* *fr underworld fr 1920s* A crime, esp a robbery

caper-juice *n late 1800s* Whiskey

capo (KA poh, KAH-) *n* The head of a local unit of the Mafia; Mafia captain [fr Italian, "head, chief"]

capon *n* An effeminate man; male homosexual

capper 1 *n* *carnival & gambling fr middle 1800s* A huckster's or professional gambler's helper, who attracts clients; = SHILL **2** *n* The climax or end of something **3** *n* A story, joke, etc, that outdoes another one

captain 1 *n* *hoboes* A generous man; free spender **2** *n* *railroad* A train conductor

captain of the head (or **heads**) *n phr fr late 1800s British Navy* A person in charge of the ship's toilets, hence someone rather stupid and minimally competent

car *See* FUNNY CAR, POP CAR, PROWL CAR, WAY CAR

carbo *n* A carbohydrate food: *She knew she shouldn't be munching out on carbos like this*—Cyra McFadden

carborundum *See* ILLEGITIMATI NON CARBORUNDUM

car catcher *n phr railroad* A train's brake operator

card 1 *n* *fr middle 1800s* A remarkable person, esp an eccentric or amusing one **2** *n* *narcotics* A portion of a narcotic; = DECK **3** *n* *sports* A schedule; program of events: *six fights on the card* **4** *v* To require someone to show identification, esp at a bar

See FACE CARD, GET one's CARD PUNCHED, IN THE CARDS, MEAT CARD, PAINT CARDS, PIE CARD, STACK THE DECK, WILD CARD

card-carrying *adj* Authentic; genuine and long-standing: *These women tend not to be card-carrying feminists*—New York Daily News/ *a service for all us card-carrying optimists*—James Michener [fr the *carrying* of a membership *card* in an organization]

carder *n fr middle 1800s* A professional gambler; = CARD SHARP

card sharp (or **shark**) *n phr fr late 1800s* A very clever cardplayer, esp an unscrupulous poker or bridge player

care *See* TAKE CARE, TAKE CARE OF BUSINESS

career girl *n phr* A woman, esp a young woman, who pursues a business or professional career, and often remains unmarried

carhop *fr 1920s* **1** *n* A waitress or waiter who serves food to patrons in parked cars at a drive-in restaurant; = CURBIE **2** *v*: *She carhopped at Beef Babylon* [formed on the model of *bellhop*]

carny or **carney** or **carnie** *carnival* **1** *n* A carnival **2** *n* A carnival worker or member of such a worker's family: *outdoor show people, the "carnies," who travel from town to town with carnivals*—AJ Liebling **3** *modifier*: *carny talk/ a carney family* **4** *n* The occupational idiom or jargon of carnival people: *I thought you talked carney by now*—F Brown

carpet *See* CALL someone ON THE CARPET, DANCE THE CARPET, ON THE CARPET, RED CARPET, ROLL OUT THE RED CARPET

carpetbag *v 1930s students* To try to make a good impression

carpet-rat *See* RUG APE

carps *n theater* A stage carpenter • Used as a nickname, as **Chips** is for a ship's carpenter

carrier *See* BAT CARRIER, JEEP CARRIER

carrot-top *n* A redhead

carry **1** *n police* A person who needs to be carried on a stretcher **2** *v underworld* To be armed

carry a load *v phr fr 1930s* To be drunk

carry a lot of weight *v phr* To be important; be influential: *My opinions don't carry a lot of weight*

carry a tune in a bucket *See* someone CAN'T CARRY A TUNE IN A BUCKET

carrying *See* CARD-CARRYING

carry the banner *v phr hoboes* To walk the street all night for lack of a bed: *I have "carried the banner" in infernal metropolises*—Jack London

carry the difference *v phr* To be armed: *If you're going to fool around with that guy, don't you think you ought to carry the difference?*—Johnny Eager (movie)

carry the load (or the **ball**) *v phr* To do or be responsible for the major part of a job: *His wife carried the load in that family*

carry (or **haul**) **the mail** **1** *v phr* = CARRY THE LOAD **2** *v phr* To go very fast; = BARREL

carry the stick *v phr, hoboes* To be a hobo; = BUM AROUND [fr the *stick* on which the hobo carried his or her bindle]

carry the torch *v phr fr 1930s* To love in a suffering way, esp because the desired one does not reciprocate: *She was carrying the torch for WC Fields*—E Johnson [origin unknown; said to have been coined by a Broadway nightclub singer named Tommy Lyman, but the semantic links are not apparent; Venus, of course, carried a torch regularly]

cart *v* To transport; take: *I carted him over to the drug store/ Why did you cart all that crap in here?* *See* COLD-MEAT CART, GO-CART

car toad *n phr railroad* A terminal worker who inspects or services railroad cars

cartwheel *n fr late 1800s* A dollar, esp a silver dollar

carve *v esp 1930s jive talk* To give one a thrill; = SEND: *He carves me. Does he carve you?*—Max Shulman

not **carved in stone** *See* NOT CARVED IN STONE

cas (CAZH) *adj teenagers* Casual; informal; = LAID-BACK

Casanova or **casanova** *n* A ladies' man and seducer; = LOVER-BOY: *Do ravish me, you bold casanova you* [fr the name of Giacomo Girolamo Casanova, legendary debaucher]

case **1** *n fr middle 1800s* An odd, eccentric person; = CARD, CHARACTER **2** *v underworld* To inspect, scrutinize, esp a place with a view to robbery or burglary **3** *n*: *Lefty gave the bank a case* *See* BUTTERFLY CASE, COUCH CASE, DROP CASE, FIVE-CASE NOTE, GET DOWN TO CASES, GET OFF someone's CASE, GET ON someone's CASE, HAVE A CASE OF THE DUMB-ASS, HAVE A CASE ON someone, HEADCASE, MAKE A FEDERAL CASE OUT OF something, NUTBALL, OFF someone's CASE, ON someone's CASE, SHOWCASE, WORST-CASE SCENARIO

case ace *n phr cardplayers* The fourth ace after three have been dealt, esp in stud poker [fr the dealing box or *case* used in the game of faro]

case dough *n phr* A small amount of money set aside for emergencies; = MAD MONEY

case note *n phr* A dollar; dollar bill

case out *v phr* To accompany someone, esp in order to share winnings, luck, etc: *Can't I case out wit' you, Frankie?*—Nelson Algren

case someone or something **out** *v phr* To examine or inspect; find out the facts: *I'll case the situation out and let you know*

cash *See* COLD CASH

cash cow *n phr* A source of money, esp a generous one: *But all this leaves The New Republic Inc without a cash cow*—New Republic

cash in one's **chips** **1** *v phr* (also **cash it in**) *fr middle 1800s* To die; = KICK THE BUCKET **2** *v phr* To withdraw from some arrangements, esp a business deal

cash in on something *v phr* To get profit or advantage from something, esp from something unexpected

cast a kitten *See* HAVE KITTENS

casting couch *n phr* The fancied lounge in a theatrical or film decision-maker's office upon which he appraises the talent of young women seeking roles:

only slightly detoured by a refusal to join Darryl F Zanuck on the casting couch—New York Times

cast-iron balls *See* HAVE BRASS BALLS

cast-iron overshoes *See* WIN THE PORCELAIN HAIRNET

cat¹ **1** *n* *outdated hoboes* A hobo or a migrant worker **2** *n* *fr 1500s* A prostitute ◁**3**▷ *n* (also **catty-cat**) *black* The vulva **4** *v* (also **cat around**) To spend time with women for amatory purposes; chase and stalk women; = TOMCAT **5** *n* A woman who, often subtly, attacks and denigrates other women; spiteful and malicious woman: *Dorothy Parker was a super cat* **6** *n* *black* A man who dresses flashily, and ostentatiously pursues worldly pleasure; = DUDE, SPORT: *I was a sharp cat*—Louis Armstrong/ *The cool chick down on Calumet has got herself a brand new cat*—Gwendolyn Brooks **7** *v* *black* To move stealthily: *began to cat toward the door*—Donald Goines **8** *v* *street gang* To loaf and idle; spend one's time on street corners admiring young women **9** *n* *jazz musicians* A jazz musician: *It was all right to the early cats*—Stephen Longstreet **10** *n* = HEPCAT **11** *n* = HIPSTER **12** *n* *fr jive and cool talk* Any man; fellow; = GUY: *Who's that cat sitting next to the Pope?* **13** *n* A sailboat with one fore-and-aft sail; a catboat: *He sails a little cat* [black sense, "dude," may be influenced by a Wolof term; see *hepcat*]

See ALLEY CAT, ASH CAT, BLOWING CAT, FAT CAT, FRAIDY CAT, HELLCAT, HEPCAT, HIP CAT, HOLY CATS, KICK AT THE CAT, LET THE CAT OUT OF THE BAG, LOOK LIKE SOMETHING THE CAT DRAGGED IN, STRAW-CAT, TOUGH CAT

cat² or **Cat** *n* A bulldozer or Caterpillar tractor [fr *Caterpillar*, trade name for a kind of continuous-track tractor]

cat³ *n* A catamaran boat

Cat *n* *black* A Cadillac: *Tia Juana pulled up in his long green Cat*—CB Himes

catbird seat *n phr* An enviable position; a controlling position: *The owners are in the catbird seat*—Sports Illustrated

See SIT IN THE CATBIRD SEAT

catch **1** *v* To see or attend a particular entertainment: *I caught Mickey Rooney on TV* **2** *n* A highly desirable acquisition or engagement: *Getting Von Karajan for our benefit would be a catch* **3** *n* *fr middle 1800s* A hidden cost, qualification, defect, etc; something to make one think twice: *It looks like all gravy, but there's a catch to it* **4** *v* *police* To do desk duty, answering the telephone and receiving complaints: *Thompson was catching in the squad room at Manhattan South*—Richard Lockridge **5** *v* *homosexual* To be penetrated in an anal sex act

See SHOESTRING CATCH

catch someone somewhere, doing something, etc *sentence* You will never discover this person in the situation or activity named ● A vigorous denial with nearly interjectional force: *Catch Eddie allowing himself to be dated like that!*—Saul Bellow/ *Catch me in a tux!*

catch a rail *See* TAKE GAS

catcher *See* CAR CATCHER, COOTIE-CATCHER

catch flies **1** *v phr* *theater* To distract the audience's attention from another performer by making unnecessary gestures and motions **2** *v phr* To gape and yawn, esp from boredom

catch hell (Variations: **holy hell** or **it** or **merry hell** may replace **hell**) **1** *v phr* To be severely rebuked or punished **2** *v phr* To be severely damaged or injured: *The dock caught holy hell in that last approach*

catch it (or **get it**) **in the neck** *v phr* To be very severely rebuked or punished: *One more time and you catch it right in the neck*

catch on **1** *v phr* To see and understand, esp with insightful suddenness; grasp: *As long as they don't catch on, we can cheat them forever* **2** *v phr* To be accepted and approved; succeed with the public: *Lots of artists catch on only after they're dead*

catch someone **redhanded** *v phr* To find or seize someone in the act of doing something criminal or reprehensible; catch in flagrante delicto

catch-22 or **Catch-22** **1** *n* A condition or requirement very hard to fulfill, esp one which flatly contradicts others: *It's a catch-22; I need experience to get a job, and I need a job to get experience* **2** *modifier*: *puts me in a Catch-22 fix*—William Appel [fr the title of a satirical novel by Joseph Heller]

catch-up *See* PLAY CATCH-UP

catch someone **with** someone's **hand in the till** *See* WITH one's HAND IN THE TILL

catch someone **with** someone's **pants down** *v phr* To find someone in the wrong with no possibility of evasion; catch someone in flagrante delicto: *Every time someone catches us with our pants down, catches us in an outright lie, up pops Ron to admit it*—Earl Thompson

catch Zs *See* COP ZS

cat fight *n phr* A particularly noisy and vicious struggle or squabble: *to judge from the cat fight that erupted among members of the advisory council*—Washington Post

catfit *n* A violent fit of rage or other strong feeling; = DUCK-FIT: *If he doesn't get that job he'll have a catfit*

cathaul *v* To subject someone to prolonged and rough questioning [fr the mid-19th-century literal term *cathaul* "drag a clawing cat down the bare back of a prone victim"]

Catholic *See* IS THE POPE POLISH

cathouse **1** *n* *early 1900s hoboes* A cheap lodging house; = FLOPHOUSE **2** *n* *fr early 1900s* A brothel: *New Orleans was proud and ashamed of its cathouses*—Stephen Longstreet **3** *n* *outdated jazz musicians* An insinuating style of jazz music; = BARRELHOUSE [second sense fr earlier *cat* "prostitute, vulva"]

cat plant *n phr* An oil refinery [fr *catalysis*, a refining process]

cats and dogs **1** *n phr* *stock market* Low-priced stocks, such as those returning no dividends at all **2** *n phr* = ODDS AND ENDS

See RAIN CATS AND DOGS

cats' eyes *n phr* Tapioca pudding

the **cat's meow** *n phr* (Variations: **balls** or **eyebrows** or **nuts** or **pajamas** or **whiskers** may replace **meow**; the phrase may be shortened to **the cat's**) *fr 1920s* Something or someone that is superlative: *He thinks he's the cat's pajamas*

cattle call 1 *n phr show business* An audition announcement, esp for a number of extras; also the crowd resulting from such an announcement: *Mr Allen is having what is known in show business as a cattle call*—Wall Street Journal/ *I can't speak for the other agencies,...but we've just about done away with the cattle call*—Toronto Life **2** *modifier: Nonprofessionals may vie for spaces...in "cattle-call" auditions*—Washington Post

cattle show *n phr* A convention or other occasion where political candidates display their notions, charisma, etc: *raise money for themselves by holding "cattle shows"*—Washingtonian

cattle train *n phr black* A Cadillac

catty *adj* Inclined to discredit others; malicious; spitefully gossipy

catty-cat *See* CAT ¹

be **caught dead** *See* NOT BE CAUGHT DEAD

cauliflower ear *n phr fr early 1900s* A boxer's or wrestler's ear deformed by injuries and accumulated scar tissue

caulk (or **calk** or **cork**) **off** *Navy fr middle 1800s British* **1** *v phr* To sleep; go to sleep **2** *v* To rest from work; = TAKE A BREAK

cavalier *n prizefight fr 1920s* A skillful boxer as distinct from a slugger or caveman

cave *n black & cool talk* A room; = PAD

caveman 1 *n* A strong, crude man, esp one who is sexually rough and masterful; = MACHO **2** *n prizefight* A strong hitter or slugger [fr the conventional image of the brutal, fur-draped troglodyte dragging a woman by the hair]

cayuse (KĪ yōōs) *n cowboys fr middle 1800s* A horse, esp a small and hardy beast descended from the wild horse of the Pacific Northwest: *From Oregon came the horse's name, "cayuse." That state was the home of the Cayuse tribe of Indians, an equestrian people*—PA Rollins

Cecil or **Cee** *n narcotics* Cocaine

ceiling *n* An upper limit: *The Gov put a two-billion-dollar ceiling on office expenses*
See HIT THE CEILING

celeb (sə LEB) *n fr early 1900s* A celebrity: *each a certified celeb from the realms of cafe, style, or theatrical society*—New York Daily News/ *surrounded by giggling celebs*—New York

the **cellar** *n phr* The lowest standing in a sports league, esp in a baseball league: *struggling not to finish in the cellar*

cellar-dwellers *n* The team in last place in a sports league

cement *See* IN CEMENT

cement mixer 1 *n phr* A dance or other act that includes a swiveling of the pelvis; = GRIND **2** *n phr truckers* A noisy car or truck

cement overcoat (or **kimono**) *n phr* A casing of cement containing a corpse for disposal in deep water

cent *See* a RED CENT

center *See* DEAD CENTER, FRONT AND CENTER

centerfold *n* A sexually desirable person: *a woman with a centerfold's chest going for her*—Dan Jenkins [fr the photographs of such persons decorating the *centerfolds* of erotic magazines]

cents *See* PUT one's TWO CENTS IN, TEN CENTS

century *n fr middle 1800s* A hundred dollars: *For two centuries a week I had me a bodyguard*—Jerome Robbins

certain *See* FOR CERTAIN

Cessna repellent *n phr airline* The landing lights of an airliner when switched on in a busy area to warn other aircraft of its presence [fr *Cessna*, trade name for a line of relatively small airplanes, and *repellent* fr the model *insect repellent*]

chain *See* BALL-AND-CHAIN, DAISY CHAIN, PULL someone's CHAIN

chain-drink *v* To have drink after drink without pause: *a man who chain-drinks Pepsis*—C See

chain lightning *n phr fr middle 1800s* Inferior whiskey

chain locker *n phr merchant marine* A wretched dockside bar [fr the filthy and dangerous compartment where anchor *chain* is stowed aboard ship]

chain man *n phr outdated underworld* A watch thief

chain-smoke *v fr early 1900s* To smoke cigarette after cigarette, lighting the next one from the previous one

chair *See* BARBER CHAIR

the **chair 1** *n* The electric chair; = the HOT SEAT **2** *n* Death by legal electrocution: *They convicted him, and he got the chair*

chair-warmer *n* An idle and dispensable person; = WARM BODY

chalk 1 *n horse-racing* A horse favored to win **2** *n prison* Milk

chalk-eater or **chalk-player** *n horse-racing* A person who bets only on the horse favored to win

chambermaid *n railroad* A machinist in a roundhouse

Chamber of Commerce *n phr* A toilet [fr *chamber pot*]

chamber pot *See* WIN THE PORCELAIN HAIRNET

champ *n fr middle 1800s* A champion, esp a boxing titleholder

champagne (or **boss**) **trick** *n phr prostitutes* A rich or high-paying client: *I take only champagne tricks, $100 an hour*—Gail Sheehy

chance *See* CHINAMAN'S CHANCE, the GENTLEMAN WILL TAKE A CHANCE, OUTSIDE CHANCE, a SNOWBALL'S CHANCE IN HELL

change *n* Money: *a sizable chunk of change*—Bob Thomas
See LOOSE CHANGE, PIECE OF CHANGE, SMALL POTATOES

change breath *v phr* To have a drink of liquor

change the channel *v phr esp 1950s teenagers* To shift the topic of conversation

change-up 1 *n* *baseball* A slow pitch delivered after a motion that might precede a fast pitch; a change of pace **2** *v:* *Holy cow! He changed him up for a strike!* **3** *n* Any change, esp a pronounced one: *McDowell exhibits a first-rate change-up*—Richard Schickel/ *Four costume changes served as a change-up in the manic pace*—Rolling Stone

chank or **shank** (SHANK) **1** *n* A syphilis chancre **2** *n* Syphilis or a case of syphilis

channel 1 *n* *narcotics* A vein, usu in the crook of the elbow or the instep, favored for the injection of narcotics; = MAIN LINE **2** *v* *esp 1950s hot rodders* To lower the body of a car by opening channels around parts of the frame: *Johnny Slash, the punk in wraparound shades, lusts for a chopped and channeled '49 Merc*—Village Voice

chaplain *See* SEE THE CHAPLAIN

chapped *adj* Angry; = PISSED OFF

chappie or **chappy** *n* A man; fellow ● More common in British use: *which may amuse the chappies around Labuses*—John O'Hara

chaps *See* CHOPS

chapter 1 *n* A division of a sports contest, esp an inning of baseball; = CANTO **2** *n* An episode, period, or passage: *Please don't remind me of that revoltingly squalid chapter in my life*

chapter and verse 1 *n phr* An exact detailed account: *I can give you chapter and verse about that night* **2** *adv phr:* *He knew it chapter and verse* **3** *n phr* The guiding documents or principles; rules: *I know the chapter and verse of the university's policy*

character 1 *n* *fr 1700s* A person who behaves oddly and often amusingly; an eccentric: *My uncle's quite a character* **2** *n* A person; = JOKER: *You know a character name of Robert Ready?*

charge 1 *n* *narcotics* An injection of a narcotic **2** *n* *fr 1930s jazz musicians* An acute thrill of pleasure; = BLAST, RUSH: *What kind of ol' creep'd get a charge out of this stuff?*—SJ Perelman **3** *n* *narcotics* Marijuana ◁**4**▷ *n* The semen produced by an orgasm; = LOAD ◁**5**▷ *n* A penile erection **6** *v* *underworld* To rob
See GET A BANG OUT OF someone or something, LARGE CHARGE

charge account *underworld* **1** *n phr* Access to bail money **2** *n phr* A person or group likely to provide bail money

charged up 1 *adj phr* *narcotics* Intoxicated by a narcotic; = HIGH **2** *adj phr* Agitated and upset: *He got all charged up about my silly mistake* **3** *adj phr* In a state of excited preparedness and heightened keenness; = PUMPED UP: *They lost, the coach declared, because they were not charged up*

charger *n* *hot rodders* A driver, esp of a hot rod

chariot *n* A car

charity *See* COLD AS HELL, VERMONT CHARITY

charity girl *n phr* *esp 1940s* A sexually promiscuous young woman

Charley *n* = CHARLEY HORSE
See BLIND CHARLEY, GOOD-TIME CHARLEY

Charley coke or **Charlie** *narcotics* **1** *n phr* or *n* Cocaine **2** *n phr* or *n* A cocaine addict

charley (or **Charley**) **horse** *n phr* A stiff and painful inflammation of a muscle, esp of the large thigh muscle

Charley Noble *n phr* The galley chimney, funnel, or exhaust pipe of a ship or boat

Charlie *n* *Vietnam War armed forces* The Vietcong or a Vietcong soldier [fr Victor *Charlie*, military voice alphabet designation for VC]

Charlie Nebs 1 *n phr* *outdated underworld* The police **2** *n phr* *black* A police officer

Charlies *n* *Army* Army C-rations, packages of tinned and dried food

charm the pants off someone *v phr* To ingratiate oneself decisively

chart 1 *n* *fr horse-racing* Figures and other material showing past performance, esp of a race horse; = FORM, TRACK RECORD **2** *n* *cool musicians* A musical arrangement or score

the charts *n phr* The listings which show the popularity of a song, a record, etc: *Stevie's latest single is way, way up on the charts*
See OFF THE CHARTS

chase *See* GO CHASE oneself, PAPER CHASE

chaser 1 *n* A drink, usu of water, taken immediately after a measure of whiskey **2** *n* A man in amatory pursuit of women; = SKIRT-CHASER: *Mark always was a lady-killer, a chaser*—AR Hilliard **3** *n* *truckers* An employee assigned to hurry others in their work **4** *n* *show business* An exit march; music played as the audience is leaving **5** *n* *prison* A guard
See AMBULANCE CHASER, DOG-CHASER, FLY-CHASER, MONKEY-CHASER, SKIRT-CHASER, WOMAN-CHASER

chase the dragon *v phr* *narcotics* To use a narcotic, esp heroin: *I was chasing the dragon, strung out on junk*—Philadelphia Journal

chassis *n* The human physique, esp the body of a well-built woman; = BUILD
See CLASSY CHASSIS

chat up *v phr* To charm and seduce with talk ● More common in British use, fr 1930s: *You hear Elvis laughing, chatting up the crowd*—Rolling Stone/ *while Dartmouth seniors, a little tight, chatted up Smithies*—Time

chauvinist pig *See* MALE CHAUVINIST PIG

chazeray or **chazerei** *See* KHAZERAY

cheap 1 *adj* Stingy; overly frugal; = CHINTZY: *Cheap old bastard won't give you the time of day* **2** *adj* Reputedly easy of sexual conquest; = ROUNDHEELED: *a cheap tramp with a heart of gold* **3** *adj* Squalid; repulsive; = CRUMMY: *Sheesh, what a cheap joint you've got here*
See DIRT CHEAP, ON THE CHEAP

cheap date (or **drunk**) *n phr* A person who needs very few drinks to become intoxicated: *All it took was one small sherry, she's such a cheap date*

cheapie or **cheapo 1** *n* Any cheaply made or cheaply sold item: *No ticket in town is a cheapie these days/ the problem with retreads, ethnic shoes, and Woolworth cheapos is*—Village Voice **2**

modifier: *cheapie ripoffs of The Godfather*—T Meehan/ *Our Tenth Annual Cheapo Guide* —Toronto Life *See* EL CHEAPO

cheapjack or **Cheap John** *adj* or *adj phr* Inferior and cheap; obscure and third-rate; shoddy

◁**cheapshit**▷ *adj* Inexpensive and inferior: *ten million pair of cheapshit jeans without any labels on them*—National Lampoon

cheap shot 1 *n phr* A malicious insult or action; something crude, underhanded, and damaging: *Well, the race for governor isn't a festival of cheap shots*—New York Magazine/ *Keenan shouted, "Didn't you just take what is known as a cheap shot?"*—New York Times **2** *v phr:* *see his players take illegal runs at his son. He'd say "Hey, don't cheap shot my son"*—Philadelphia Journal/ *If a person's going to cheapshot me, it just shows how low he is*—Playboy **3** *modifier:* *some dirtymouth comedian who made cheap-shot race jokes*—Village Voice

cheat *v* To be sexually unfaithful; = GET A LITTLE ON THE SIDE

cheaters *fr early 1900s underworld* **1** *n* Spectacles **2** *n* Marked playing cards

cheat stick 1 *n phr* A slide rule; = SLIPSTICK **2** *n phr* *lumberjacks* A scaler's rule used to find the board-feet of lumber a log will yield, by which pay is determined **3** *n phr* A wage scale by which any employee's pay is calculated

check 1 *interj* An expression of understanding, approval, etc: *I'll say check to that!/ It's time to leave? Check!* **2** *v* (also **check that**) *esp broadcasting* To cancel; introduce a correction: *He made eight yards; check that, six yards* **3** *v* To look at; pay attention to; = CHECK OUT: *Check the guy at the end of the counter* **4** *n narcotics* A small quantity of a drug *See* GIVE someone A BLANK CHECK, PICK UP THE TAB, RAIN CHECK, RUBBER CHECK, TAKE A RAIN CHECK

check bouncer *n phr* A person who writes checks on bank accounts with insufficient funds or none whatever

check crew *n phr* A work crew having black and white members [fr the black and white squares of a *checkerboard*]

checkerboard *n* A neighborhood, town, or other place with both black and white people; an integrated place

checkers *See* PLAY CHECKERS

check into the net *v phr Army* To announce one's arrival or departure; keep others informed

check out 1 *v phr* To look closely at, esp for evaluation; scrutinize; = GIVE someone or something THE ONCE-OVER: *Check out the guy at the counter. Do you know him?/ Before you buy anything, check out our low, low prices/ If you're in doubt, check it out* **2** *v phr* To prove valid; be accurate: *Your story checks out* **3** *v phr* To examine and approve one's competence: *I'm checked out on that machine* **4** *v phr* To add up purchases and collect money at a supermarket or similar store: *I'll check you out over here* **5** *modifier:* *a check-out counter/ check-out man* **6** *n:* *express check-out/ slow sloppy check-out* **7** *v phr* To pay for one's purchases at a supermarket or similar store: *It took me an hour to check out of that place* **8** *v phr* To pay one's bill and leave a hotel or motel: *When did Almendorfer check out of this fleabag?* **9** *v phr* To leave; depart; = BOOK: *Let's check out of this joint and find a livelier one* **10** *v phr* To die: *She checked out before they reached the hospital*

check six *v phr* To be on guard against treachery [fr a fighter pilot's request that the rear of the aircraft, designated as *six o'clock*, be guarded by a comrade]

check the plumbing *v phr* To go to the toilet

cheeba *n narcotics* Marijuana

cheechako *n fr late 1800s* A newcomer; = GREENHORN [fr Chinook jargon *chee chahco* "newcomer"]

cheek 1 *n fr late 1800s* Impudence; audacity; = BRASS, CHUTZPA: *She had the infernal cheek to stick out her tongue at me* **2** *n* A buttock; = BUN: *I took the injection in the left cheek*

cheek it *v phr late 1800s college students fr middle 1800s British* To deceive by pretending more knowledge than one has; = BLUFF, FAKE IT, WING IT

cheeky *adj* Impudent; impertinent; rude ● More common in British use, fr middle 1800s

cheer *See* BRONX CHEER

cheerio or **cheery-bye** *interj* Good-bye ● Used as a conscious Briticism: *Cheerio, pip-pip, and all that!*

cheers *interj* A salute or toast on taking a drink ● Originally British, from the late 1940s: *Cheers and bottoms up, one and all!*

cheese 1 *n* Nonsense; lies; exaggerations; = BALONEY: *What a line of cheese*—Richard Bissell **2** *n baseball* A fastball **3** *v* = CHEESE IT **4** *v* (also **cut the cheese**) To flatulate; = FART **5** *v* To vomit; = BARF **6** *n:* *There was cheese all over the floor in the subway station* *See* BIG CHEESE, EAT CHEESE, GET one's CHEESE, HARD CHEESE, MAKE THE CHEESE MORE BINDING, RAT CHEESE

the cheese *n phr esp 1920s fr early 1800s British* An important person; something or someone genuine: *She's the real cheese*—A Lewis [perhaps fr Anglo-Indian slang *chiz* fr Hindi fr Persian, "the thing"]

cheese bun (or **eater**) *n phr dock workers* An informer or other despicable person; = RAT

cheesecake 1 *n fr early 1900s* Photographs and photography of women in clothing and poses that emphasize their sexuality: *a magazine full of cheesecake* **2** *modifier:* *unless one perceives in cheesecake photographs illicit and limitless pleasures*—Toronto Life **3** *n* A woman's legs, breasts, hips, etc: *standing on the corner scoping out the cheesecake* [apparently fr the appreciative comments of one or another early-20th-century New York City newspaper photographer at the ocean-liner docks who posed women so that their legs were featured, and pronounced the pictures to be "better than *cheesecake*"]

cheesed off *adj phr* WW2 Air Forces fr British armed forces Bored; disgusted

cheesehead *n* A stupid person: *You let this cheesehead...insult me?*—Raymond Chandler

cheese it *fr early 1800s underworld* **1** *interj* An exclamation of alarm and warning uttered when properly constituted authorities are approaching: *Cheese it, Muggsy, the cops!* **2** *v phr* To leave; depart; = SCRAM

cheesy **1** *adj* Lacking in taste; vulgarly unesthetic: *an altogether hideous room, expensive but cheesy* —JD Salinger **2** *adj* Of inferior workmanship; shoddy: *Where'd you get this cheesy pair of pliers?* **3** *adj* Shabby; ugly: *Why stay in this cheesy neighborhood?*

chef *n narcotics* A person who prepares opium for smoking

See DEEPSEA CHEF

chemistry *n* Feelings between persons; attractions and repulsions: *Miss McElderry feels the unusual chemistry between her and Mr Pfeiffer has been beneficial*—New York Times/ *He also struck up what one aide calls "instant chemistry" with US Secretary of State George Shultz*—New York Times

cher (SHEHR) *adj teenagers* Personable; attractive: *He's a real cher cat* [fr French "dear"]

cherry ◁**1**▷ *n* A virgin, of either sex ◁**2**▷ *n* Virginity: *Does he still have his cherry?* ◁**3**▷ *adj* Virgin; sexually uninitiated: *She confessed she was cherry* ◁**4**▷ *n* The hymen **5** *adj* In an unproved or maiden state of any sort: *He hasn't published anything yet; still cherry* **6** *n* Army An inexperienced soldier sent to the front lines as a replacement: *A Cherry who survived long enough earned the right to harass the next rookie*—New York Times Magazine **7** *n* The red light atop a police car [sexual senses fr the fancied resemblance between the hymen and a *cherry*]

See COP A CHERRY, HAVE one's CHERRY, POP someone's CHERRY

cherry-picker ◁**1**▷ *n* A man who especially prizes the sex act with young girls **2** *n railroad* A switch operator **3** *n* An articulated crane with a bucket-like platform: *a guy in a cherry-picker fixing the phone lines*

cherry pie **1** *n phr* Something easily done or gotten; = PIECE OF CAKE **2** *n phr circus* Money easily obtained

cherry-top *n teenagers* A police car; = PROWL CAR

chest *See* PLAY CLOSE TO THE CHEST

chestnut *n fr late 1800s* A trite old story, joke, song, etc; = OLD TURKEY

chesty **1** *adj* Having large breasts; bosomy: *a chesty blonde* **2** *adj* Prone to boast about one's virility, boldness, etc: *He's a chesty little guy, particularly when he's been drinking*

chev *See* SHIV

chevy *See* CHIVVY

Chevy (SHEH vee) *n* A Chevrolet car

chew **1** *v* To chew tobacco **2** *n:* *He had big chew in his cheek* **3** *v* hoboes To eat **4** *v* To talk; converse; = JAW

chewallop or **chewalloper** (chee WAH ləp) *n* A fall or dive that makes a loud splat

chew a lone something *v phr esp teenagers* To do alone what is ordinarily done in company: *Old Rick's chewing a lone drink*

◁**chew** someone's **ass** (or **ass out**)▷ *v phr* = CHEW someone OUT

chew someone's **ear off** *v phr* To talk overlong and tediously to someone: *I just wanted the time, not to get my ear chewed off*

chewed *adj 1940s black* Tired; defeated; = BEAT: *I know you feel chewed*—Zora Neale Hurston

chewed fine *n phr lunch counter* A hamburger

chewed up **1** *adj phr* Badly damaged or worn: *The transmission's all chewed up* **2** *adj phr* = CHEWED

chew gum at the same time *See* NOT HAVE BRAINS ENOUGH TO WALK AND CHEW GUM AT THE SAME TIME

chewing *See* RAG-CHEWING

chewings *n hoboes* Food

chew someone **out** (or **up**) *v phr fr WW2 armed forces* To reprimand severely; rebuke harshly; = EAT someone OUT, REAM: *In the boss's office he got chewed out good*

chew something **over** *v phr* To discuss thoroughly: *Let's chew over the budget*

chew the fat (or **the rag**) *v phr fr late 1800s* To converse, esp in a relaxed and reminiscent way

chew up the scenery *v phr show business* To overact; = HAM: *Beery...and Lionel Barrymore chew up all the scenery that isn't nailed down*—Village Voice [originally fr a 1930 theater review by Dorothy Parker: *"more glutton than artist...he commences to chew up the scenery"*]

chewy *adj* Substantial and desirable; rich: *Hepburn...may have a less chewy part than has Fonda*—Richard Schickel

chib *See* SHIV

chiba (CHEE bə) *n narcotics* Marijuana; = POT

chiba shop *See* SMOKE SHOP

Chicago *n lunch counter* A pineapple sundae or soda [fr gangsters' use of *pineapple* "hand grenade"; *Chicago* was the most famous gangster milieu during the 1920s and 30s]

Chicago flats *See* ST LOUIS FLATS

Chicago overcoat *n phr* A coffin: *A Chicago overcoat is what blasting would get you*—Raymond Chandler

Chicago piano *n phr* A submachine gun ● Used in WW2 in British Navy for a rapid-fire automatic antiaircraft gun

Chicago pineapple *n phr esp 1930s* A small grenade or bomb

chichi (SHEE SHEE, CHEE CHEE) **1** *n* Something frilly, fancy, precious, and overdecorated: *Another bit of chichi that has come to our notice lately is Eleanor Roosevelt's letterhead*—New Yorker/ *So much chichi. The pretty glass people* —New York Magazine **2** *adj:* *a chichi concern for his poses/ chichi little chapeau* [fr French]

◁**chi-chi**▷ (CHEE chee) *late 1940s & Korean War armed forces* **1** *n* A woman's breasts; = TITS **2** *n* Anything sexually attractive [fr a corruption of Japanese *chisai chichi* "little breasts"]

chick 1 *n underworld* Prison food **2** *n esp beat, cool & 1960s counterculture* A woman, esp a young woman

See HIP CHICK, SLICK CHICK

chickabiddy *n fr British fr middle 1800s* =CHICK

chicken 1 *n fr early 1900s* A young woman, esp an attractive one; =CHICK **2** *n homosexuals* An adolescent boy regarded as a sexual object for an adult homosexual **3** *modifier:* had I written extensively about the mechanics of chicken sex—Village Voice **4** *n* A coward; an overly timid person; =SISSY: *Don't be a chicken; dive right in* **5** *adj: He seems like a chicken guy* **6** *n esp hot rodders* A trial of valor in which two persons drive cars at each other down the middle of a road, the first to swerve aside being designated "chicken" **7** *n Army fr 1920s* The eagle worn as insignia of rank by an Army colonel **8** *n* =CHICKEN SHIT **9** *adj* =CHICKEN-SHIT **10** *n underworld* The victim of a robbery or swindle; =MARK, SUCKER **11** *n* A person, esp a durable one: *John's a tough old chicken* [homosexual senses perhaps fr late 19th-century sailor term for a boy who takes a sailor's fancy and whom he calls his *chicken*]

See RUBBER CHICKEN

chicken colonel *n phr Army* A full colonel; =BIRD COLONEL

chicken coop *n phr truckers* A weighing station for trucks

See RAIN CATS AND DOGS

chicken feed (or **money**) *n phr* A small amount of money; =PEANUTS, SMALL POTATOES: *Two million? That's chicken feed in this milieu*

chickenhawk *n homosexuals* An adult homosexual who relishes young boys as sex partners

chickenhead *n* A stupid person

chickenheart *n* A coward

chickenhearted 1 *adj* Cowardly; =SISSIFIED: *Here's a potbellied, chickenhearted slob*—J & W Hawkins **2** *adj* Squeamish; overly fastidious

chicken-livered *adj* Cowardly; =CHICKEN-HEARTED

chicken out *v phr* To cancel or withdraw from an action because of fear; =HAVE COLD FEET: *You'll think of something to chicken out*—Erma Bombeck/ *The Senator chickened out and changed his vote*

◁**chicken shit**▷ *fr WW2 armed forces* **1** *n phr* The rules, restrictions, rigors, and meanness of a minor and pretentious tyrant, or of a bureaucracy: *The new regulations are so many parcels of chicken shit* **2** *n phr* An excessive display of authority; a hectoring insistence **3** *adj: a chicken-shit requirement/ chicken-shit new task force*

chicken (or **egads**) **switch** (or **button**) **1** *n phr* A control used to destroy a malfunctioning rocket in flight; a destruct switch **2** *n phr* A control used to eject an astronaut or pilot from a damaged vehicle [*chicken* fr the sense "coward"; *egads* an acronym for *electronic ground automatic destruct sequencer* and coincides with an archaic interjection of dismay]

chicken tracks *See* HEN TRACKS

chickie 1 *n* A young girl; =CHICK: *But I do not really envy the guys my age who...are making out with the young chickies*—San Francisco **2** *interj esp New York City teenagers* An exclamation of alarm and warning, uttered when properly constituted authorities are approaching; =CHEESE IT, JIGGERS

See LAY CHICKIE

chicklet or **chiclet** *n* A young girl; =CHICK: *Teenies and chicklets came into fashion*—Gail Sheehy [normal diminutive form, reinforced by *Chiclet*, trade name of a brand of chewing gum sold in small sugared bits]

Chic Sale *n phr esp 1920s* An outhouse; privy [fr the name of a humorist who wrote of such amenities]

chief 1 *n* A man; fellow; =GUY ● Usu used in direct address to a stranger, with a sense of ironic deference **2** *n narcotics* LSD

See TOO MANY CHIEFS AND NOT ENOUGH INDIANS

chief itch and rub *n phr* The most important person about; =BIG ENCHILADA, BOSS

chief of staff *n phr Army* An army officer's wife

child *See* FLOWER CHILD

children *See* FLOWER CHILDREN

◀**chili**▶ *adj* Mexican

chili-bowl 1 *n* A haircut that looks as if someone had put a bowl over one's head and cut off what hair showed below **2** *n* A dirty, slovenly person; =DIRT-BALL

chill 1 *v* To resolve or relax a perilous situation: *They agreed to talk, and that chilled the riot* **2** *v* To frighten: *a sight that chilled him* **3** *v underworld* To render someone unconscious; =KNOCK someone OUT: *She chilled him with a kick on the chin* **4** *v fr 1940s black* To kill; murder: *Remember the night Stein got chilled out front?*—Raymond Chandler **5** *v* To quench enthusiasm and amiability abruptly: *He chilled me with a glance* **6** *v* =CHILL OUT **7** *v esp black teenagers* To do a move in dancing intended to show one's ease and nonchalance **8** *n students* A glass or can of beer **9** *adj teenagers* Wonderful; excellent; =COOL, NEAT: *A "chill" outfit for a girl is tight Sergio Valente or Tale Lord jeans*—New York Times

See PUT ON THE CHILL, PUT THE CHILL ON someone

chiller *n fr 1950s* A film, play, etc, intended to evoke delicious shudders of fear; horror show or story

chiller-diller *n fr 1950s* A chiller, esp a very effective one

chill out *v phr teenagers fr black* To relax; calm oneself; =COOL OUT: *offers her a lit joint. "Chill out," he says*—New York Magazine

chilly mo *n phr* An aloof and unengaged person; =COLD FISH [fr *mo* "motherfucker"]

chime in 1 *v phr* To interrupt and intrude one's counsel; =BUTT IN, KIBITZ **2** *v phr* To offer comment: *Chime in whenever you want*

chimney *n black* The head

chin 1 *v fr late 1800s* To talk; converse: *happily chinning in the corner* **2** *n fr early 1900s* A talk;

a chat **3** *v* To talk to: *The cop was chinning...a nurse*—James M Cain

See TAKE IT ON THE CHIN, WAG one's CHIN

china 1 *n* The teeth **2** *n* *esp jazz musicians* Money **3** *n* *lunch counter* A cup of tea

china chin *See* GLASS JAW

china-clipper *n WW2 armed forces* A dishwasher; =PEARL-DIVER [fr the *China Clipper*, a Pan American Airways seaplane that flew a regular service to the Far East beginning in the 1930s, because the dishwasher was apparently thought to be *clipping* "hitting, bashing" the dishes]

China (or **china**) **doll** *n phr* A woman of very delicate beauty; a pretty and fragile woman

◀**Chinaman**▶ **1** *n* *merchant marine* A sailor who works in a ship's laundry **2** *n* *police* A police officer's patron and influential political friend; =RABBI: *police officer...needed a Chinaman, or sponsor*—Chicago Magazine

◀a **Chinaman's chance**▶ *n phr fr middle 1800s* No chance at all ● Nearly always in the negative: *He hasn't got a Chinaman's chance of landing that job* [fr the unfortunate situation of Chinese prospectors in the California gold rush, who were forced to work exhausted or unpromising claims]

China White *n phr narcotics* A very high grade of heroin: *"It's China White," he said....Jesus, I thought, I'm out here with junkies*—Hunter S Thompson

chinch *n fr early 1800s* A bedbug

chinch pad *n phr hoboes* A cheap hotel or lodging house; =FLOPHOUSE

chinchy *adj esp black fr 1930s* Parsimonious; stingy; mean; =CHINTZY [perhaps related to *chinch* "bedbug" and associated notions of squalor]

chine (SHEEN) *n teenagers* A machine, esp a car

◀**Chinee**▶ **1** *n* A Chinese person **2** *n* (also **chinee** (or **Chinese**) **ducket**) *show business* A complimentary ticket; =ANNIE OAKLEY: *a chinee being a ducket with holes punched in it like old-fashioned Chink money*—Damon Runyon

◀**Chinese ace**▶ *n phr aviators fr WW1 armed forces* A pilot who lands an airplane with one wing low [fr the possible Chinese name Wun Wing Low or the purportedly humorous invention Wun Hung Low referring to the low wing]

Chinese arithmetic *See* HARDER THAN CHINESE ARITHMETIC

◀**Chinese fire drill**▶ *n phr* Something incredibly confused and confusing: *an eight-page letter with a Chinese fire drill of your life*—Chicago Tribune/ *did their Chinese fire drill of calling the fix-it man*—Richard Merkin [perhaps fr the WW2 Marine Corps expression "fucked up like *Chinese fire call*"]

◀**Chinese landing**▶ *n phr aviators* A landing made with one wing low [see *Chinese ace*]

◀**Chinese opera**▶ *n phr Army* An extremely elaborate event, parade, briefing, etc

Chinese pagodas *See* KNOCK someone FOR A LOOP

◀**Chinese three-point landing**▶ *n phr aviators* An airplane crash, esp one due to pilot error

chinfest *n* A session of talk and gossip; =BULL SESSION, GABFEST

chinjaw *n lumberjacks* Talk, esp inconsequential chatting

◀**Chink** or **chink**▶ **1** *n* A Chinese person **2** *adj*: *Chink food/ a chink chick*

chin music *n phr fr middle 1800s* Talk, esp inconsequential chatter; =CHITCHAT: *chin music calculated to allay her trepidation*—SJ Perelman

◀**Chino** or **chino**[1]▶ (CHĬ noh) *narcotics* **1** *n* A Chinese person **2** *adj*: *chino dope*

chino[2] (CHEE noh) **1** *n* A kind of cotton twill cloth, esp as used for summer military uniforms **2** *modifier*: *chino pants* [fr American Spanish]

chinos (CHEE nohz) *n* Trousers made from chino cloth

chintzy[1] *fr 1950s adj* Parsimonious; stingy; =CHEAP [perhaps fr *chinch* "bedbug," hence the semantic equivalent of "lousy"; the sense is either derived fr or is a partial source of *chintzy*[2]]

chintzy[2] **1** *adj* Cheap and ill-made, but showy: *the window filled with chintzy plastic couches* **2** *adj* Lacking chic and style; unfashionable: *White shoes with a dark dress is considered very definitely..."chintzy"*—Syracuse Post-Standard [fr the printed cotton fabric *chintz*, regarded as cheap, gaudy, and unstylish]

chin-wag *n* A conversation, esp a long and intimate chat: *You haven't had a good chin-wag with your sister-in-law since she got the joystick for her Apple*—Washington Post

chip 1 *n* A flat piece of dung **2** *v golf* To hit a short, usu high shot onto the green **3** *v narcotics* To use a drug or drugs clandestinely while abstaining from using the drug for which one is being treated or is undergoing psychotherapy: *The men and women of the group...also look at the man who is chipping. There is some palpable dismay*—Washington Post

See BARGAINING CHIP, BLUE-CHIP, HAVE A CHIP ON one's SHOULDER

chiphead *n* A computer enthusiast: *I'm not a chiphead, but if you don't keep up with the new developments...you're not going to have the competitive edge*—Time [fr silicon *chip* + *head* "addict"]

chip in 1 *v phr fr middle 1800s* To contribute, esp a share of some expense: *We each chipped in twenty bucks and got him a new suit* **2** *v phr* To interject a comment; contribute to a colloquy: *She chipped in some honeyed reminiscences* [fr the adding of poker *chips* to the pot]

a **chip off the old block** *n phr* A child that resembles one or both parents, esp a boy that resembles his father

chipper[1] *n narcotics* An occasional user of narcotics; =JOY-POPPER: *Amy, who is only a "chipper,"...wanted to meet somebody*—Rolling Stone [fr *chip* "small quantity, bit"]

chipper[2] *adj fr early 1800s* Energetic and jaunty; lively; =PERKY [fr British dialect *kipper*]

chippy or **chippie 1** *n fr late 1800s* A woman presumed to be of easy virtue; woman who frequents bars, public dance halls, etc: *the same as in Storyville except that the chippies were cheaper* —Louis Armstrong **2** *v* To be sexually unfaithful to one's wife; = CHEAT, GET A LITTLE ON THE SIDE **3** *n fr early 1900s* A simple buttoned dress: *A chippie is a dress that women wore, knee length and very easy to disrobe*—A Lomax **4** *v narcotics* To take narcotics only occasionally [origin unknown; senses relating to women possibly from the chirping sound of a sparrow, squirrel, or other small creature, suggesting the gay frivolity of such women]

chippy (or **chippie**) **joint** *n phr* A brothel

chips *See* CASH IN one's CHIPS, IN THE CHIPS

Chips *n merchant marine* A ship's carpenter ● Used as a nickname, as Sparks is for a radio officer and Bones for a ship's doctor

the **chips are down** *sentence* The time of final decision and hard confrontation has come; resolution is at hand: *When the chips are down he goes to pieces* [fr the final bets of a poker hand]

chip shot 1 *n phr golf* A shot, usu a high shot made onto the green **2** *n phr football* An easy field goal or field goal opportunity [perhaps fr hitting under the ball as if to chop a *chip* from it]

chirp 1 *v* To sing: *She chirps with the orchestra* —Bob Thomas **2** *v underworld* To inform; = SING

chirpy *adj* Bright and energetic; vivacious: *a nice, wholesome, chirpy, reasonably intelligent woman* —Philadelphia Magazine

chisel 1 *v fr early 1800s* To cheat or defraud, esp in a petty way; deal unfairly: *Every time I buy a part he chisels a buck or two* **2** *v* To get without intending to repay or return: *Can I chisel a cigarette from you, pal?*

chisel in *v phr underworld fr 1920s* To intrude oneself; = MUSCLE IN

chit 1 *n* An impudent and spirited young woman: *a saucy chit* **2** *n* A bill for food or drink, which one signs or initials instead of paying immediately

chitchat *n* Talk, esp relaxed and idle conversation; = CHIN MUSIC: *The members were enjoying a bit of chitchat when the gavel sounded*

chitlin circuit *n phr* Theaters and clubs featuring black entertainers

chiv or **chive** *See* SHIV

chivvy or **chivey** or **chevy** (CHIH vee, CHEH vee) *v* To harry and annoy; badger; = BUG

◁**chocha**▷ (CHOH chah) *n* The vulva [fr Spanish]

chockablock *adj fr early 1800s nautical* Crammed; crowded full: *The plays and stories...are chockablock with figures*—Washington Post [fr a nautical rhyming phrase used to mean that the two *blocks* of a block and tackle are touching after the device has been tightened to its limit]

◀**chocolate drop**▶ *n phr* A black person

chogie (CHOH gee) *v Army* To go fast

choi oy *interj Vietnam War armed forces* An exclamation of disgust, dismay, etc [fr Vietnamese]

choke a horse *v phr* To be very large: *That bankroll would choke a horse*
See ENOUGH TO CHOKE A HORSE

choke-dog *n fr early 1800s* Strong raw whiskey, usu homemade

choker *n* Anything worn about the neck, such as a collar, necktie, or a short necklace
See HERRING CHOKER

◁**choke the gopher**▷ *v phr* To masturbate

choke up 1 *v phr esp sports* To become tense and ineffective under pressure; = SWALLOW THE APPLE, TAKE THE PIPE: *He choked up, lost his concentration, and got clobbered in the third* **2** *v phr* To cause one to be speechless with pleasure: *Your new book doesn't exactly choke me up* **3** *v phr* To become speechless with grief

chompers *n* Teeth, whether genuine or false

◁**chooch**▷ *n fr 1920s* The vulva; = CHOCHA: *Ah, yuh mudduh's chooch*—Sidney Kingsley [fr chocha]

choo-choo *See* PULL A TRAIN

chop *n* Grade or quality [fr Hindi, "seal"]

the **chop** *See* GIVE something THE CHOP

chop-chop *adv* Quickly; at once ● Used as a command or exhortation as well as a modifier: *They cut out chop-chop* [fr Pidgin English, "fast," fr Chinese]

chopped 1 *adj hot rodders* Of a car, having the chassis lowered or the fenders removed or both **2** *adj motorcyclists* Of a motorcycle, having the front brake and fender removed, the wheel fork extended forward, and the handlebars raised

chopped liver 1 *n phr* A beaten and scarred person; one who has undergone a humiliating defeat: *That mugger made chopped liver of him* **2** *n phr* An insignificant person or thing ● Often in the negative: *Even if he didn't win, being the first black nominee wasn't chopped liver/ She may be great, but her sister's not exactly chopped liver*
See THAT AIN'T HAY

chopped top *n phr hot rodders* A car with the windshield, windows, upper body, etc, removed

chopper 1 *n esp 1920s* A submachine gun, esp a Thompson; = TOMMY GUN **2** *n* A gangster who uses a submachine gun: *Johnny Head had met the "chopper"*—John Gunther **3** *n* A helicopter: *the traffic reporter from the chopper* **4** *n hot rodders & motorcyclists* A chopped car or motorcycle
See BUTTON CHOPPER, PORK-CHOPPER

choppers *n* Teeth, esp false teeth

chops 1 *n* (also **chaps**) The jaws; the mouth; the cheeks beside the mouth; jowls: *old turkey with pendulous chops/ Open your chops and sing* **2** *n jazz musicians fr 1920s* Musical technique or ability: *With electronically amplified music you lose your chops, your right hand, you lose your dexterity* —Philadelphia Journal **3** *n* Talent or skill in general: *We'll see what kind of chops they got*—Jimmy Breslin [senses related to skill fr notion of a jazz musician's lips, *chops*, the essential for technique in "blowing" the instrument; see ax]
See BAT one's GUMS, BREAK CHOPS, BREAK someone's CHOPS, BUST one's ASS, KLOP IN THE CHOPS, LICK one's CHOPS

chop shop 1 *n phr* A place where stolen cars are dismantled to be sold as parts: *I started off takin' 'em to a chop shop for $100*—Philadelphia

Magazine **2** *modifier: mixed up with chop shop operators in the Midwest*—Saul Bellow

chop one's **teeth** *v phr* = BAT one's GUMS

chord *See* PINK CHORD

chow **1** *n* *fr middle 1800s* Food; meals; fare: *How's the chow at Maxim's these days?* **2** *v: OK gang, let's chow* [fr Pidgin English *chow-chow* "a mixture (of foods)"]

chowderhead *n* *fr early 1800s* A stupid person

chow down *v phr* *fr Navy* To eat; have a meal: *They should bundle up, chow down, and stay home* —Fran Lebowitz

chow hall *n phr* *Army* A room where meals are served, esp a military mess hall

chow hound *n phr* *WW2 armed forces* A person keenly and actively interested in eating; glutton

chow line *n phr* *fr armed forces* A line of persons waiting to get food

Christer *n* *college students* A straitlaced person, esp a religious one: *Nondrinkers are called all sorts of names, one in popular use is "Christer"*—Cornell Daily Sun

Christian with aces wired *See* COOL AS A CHRISTIAN WITH ACES WIRED

Christmas goose *See* as FULL OF SHIT AS A CHRISTMAS GOOSE

Christmas tree **1** *n phr* *oilfield* The assembly of valves, pipes, and gauges used to control the output of an oil well **2** *n phr* *car-racing* A display of colored lights which flash in sequence, used to start drag races **3** *n phr* *Navy* The control panel of a submarine
See LIT UP

chub *n* *fr middle 1800s* A Texan [origin unknown]

chubbette *n* A chubby woman, esp a small one: *The poor thing was petrified that Graig would find out what a chubbette she'd become*—Armistead Maupin/ *a chubbette with "railroad tracks" across her teeth*—New York

chuck **1** *n* *fr middle 1800s fr British* Food; a meal; = CHOW, EATS: *She invited us in for some chuck* **2** *v* To throw, esp to throw or pitch a ball: *chuck a mean slider* **3** *v* To discard; throw away: *Is it possible she has chucked her aloofness*—Sinclair Lewis **4** *v* To vomit; = UPCHUCK [relation of the food sense to the others is obscure and uncertain]

chuck a dummy *v phr* *hoboes* To pretend to faint in order to get sympathy and food

chuck-a-lug *See* CHUG-A-LUG

chucker-out *n* ● More common in British use = BOUNCER

chuck habit or **chuck horrors** or **chucks** **1** *n phr* or *n* *narcotics* The intense hunger felt by a drug addict whose narcotics intake is cut off: *He'd gotten the chuck horrors: for two full days he'd eaten candy bars, sweet rolls and strawberry malteds*—Nelson Algren **2** *n phr* or *n* *hoboes* The voracious eating that comes from extreme hunger: *the "chuck horrors," that awful animal craving for food that comes after missing half a dozen meals*—J Black **3** *n phr* or *n* *prison* Insanity

resulting from imprisonment or fear of imprisonment

chucklehead *n* *fr early 1900s* A stupid person

chuck wagon **1** *n phr* Any small diner or lunch counter **2** *n phr* *esp Western US* A buffet meal something like a smorgasbord: *You can eat chuck wagon at the Sham Chaparral for twelve bucks* [fr the *food wagon* that accompanied cowboys on roundups and drives]

chuck you, Farley *interj* (Variation: **and your whole famn damily** may be added) May you and yours be reviled, abused, humiliated, rejected, etc; = FUCK YOU, UP YOURS ● This amusing variant of the damning formula goes beyond the brevity of an interjection but retains the force [based on earlier *fuck you, Charley* and the euphemism *whole famn damily*]

chug *v* To move along, esp slowly and laboriously and in the water: *The USS Saratoga came chugging up the Delaware*—Philadelphia [echoic of a steam engine operating]

chug-a-lug or **chug** or **chuck-a-lug** *v* To drink the whole of what is in a glass or bottle without pausing: *He chugged a liter of vodka and dropped dead*

chukker *n* *sports* A division of a sports contest; = CANTO, STANZA [fr a division of a polo game, fr Hindi *cakkar* "circular running course"]

chum **1** *n* *fr 1700s* A very close friend; = BUDDY, PAL **2** *v* (also **chum around**): *He chums with Georgie Ogle* **3** *n* Man; fellow; = GUY ● Used in direct address esp to strangers, usu with mildly hostile overtones: *Knock it off now, chum* **4** *v* To throw ground-up bait into the water to attract fish: *to chum for blues* **5** *n: Augie, start dumping the chum over*

chum-buddy *n* A particularly close friend: *Yesterday's villains are tomorrow's chum-buddies*—Robert Ruark

chummy **1** *adj* Very friendly; = BUDDY-BUDDY, PALSY-WALSY **2** *n: Hey, chummy, how about a drink?*

chump **1** *n* *fr late 1800s fr British* A stupid person, esp a dupe; = SUCKER: *If he wasn't such a chump he wouldn't be tempted/ I look like a chump these days*—William Kennedy **2** *n* *carnival & circus* A customer [origin unknown; perhaps a blend of *chunk* and *lump*, both referring to blockheadedness]

◄**chungo bunny**► *n phr* A black person: *looked like he hadda be the biggest chungo bunny inna world*—George V Higgins [fr *jungle bunny*]

church key *n phr* A bottle or can opener that punches a triangular hole in the lid of a can

churn *v* To increase the level of activity in a law firm or other enterprise in order to seem busy and productive

chute *See* POOP CHUTE

chutzpa (HŏŏTS pə, KHŏŏTS-) *n* (Variations: **chuzpa** or **hutzpa** or **hutzpah**) Extreme and offensive brashness; arrogant presumption; hubris: *Chutzpa is that quality enshrined in a man who, having killed his mother and father, throws himself on* the mercy of the court because he is an orphan —Leo Rosten/ *The hutzpah of using Studio 54...was much commented on*—Pulpsmith

ciao (CHOW) *interj* A salutation either on meeting or parting [fr Italian]

cider barrel *n phr merchant marine* An ocean-going tugboat

cig *n* A cigarette

cigaroot *n* A cigarette [influenced by *cheroot*]

cinch *fr late 1800s fr cowboys* **1** *n* A certainty; something sure to happen; =SURE THING: *It's a cinch they'll win* **2** *n* Something easily done; =BREEZE, PIECE OF CAKE: *Going up is a bother, coming down's a cinch* **3** *v* To make something certain; =CLINCH, NAIL something DOWN: *We cinched it with a last-second field goal* [fr Spanish *cincha* "saddle girth," which, when tight, fosters certainty]
See HAVE something CINCHED, LEAD-PIPE CINCH

cinched *See* HAVE something CINCHED

cinchers *n esp 1930s truckers & bus drivers* The brakes of a truck, car, or bus

cinder bull *n phr hoboes* A railroad police officer or detective

cinder crusher *n phr railroad* A switch tender

cinder dick *n phr hoboes* A railroad detective

◁**circle jerk**▷ **1** *n phr esp teenagers* A sex party of mutual masturbation **2** *n phr* Any futile occasion, meeting, session, etc

circuit *See* BORSCHT CIRCUIT, CHITLIN CIRCUIT, CLOUT FOR THE CIRCUIT, STRAW-HAT CIRCUIT

circuit blow (or **clout** or **wallop**) *n phr baseball* A home run

circuit slugger *n phr baseball* A talented home-run hitter: *Gil Hodges...became the greatest circuit slugger ever to wear Dodger flannels*—New York Daily News

circular file *n phr* A wastebasket

circus **1** *n* Any bright and uproarious occasion: *You should have been there, it was a circus* **2** *n hoboes* A pretended fainting spell

citizen *n esp black & counterculture* A person of a more conservative, established, and prosaic caste than oneself; =SQUARE

Citizen *See* JOHN Q CITIZEN

city **1** *combining word* The place or milieu of what is indicated: *hamburger city* **2** *combining word* A prevalence or instance of the thing indicated: *trouble city/ dumb city* [coined on the model of the -sville suffix]
See FAT CITY, FUN CITY, SOUL CITY, TAP CITY, WRINKLE CITY, YUCKO CITY

city cow *n phr WW2 armed forces* Canned milk; =ARMORED COW

city hall *n phr* The political powers and their haunts; those who control purse strings and patronage: *See how city hall reacts*
See YOU CAN'T FIGHT CITY HALL

city slicker *n phr fr early 1900s* A shrewd and modish urban person, esp as distinct from the honest and gullible provincial

civvies *n fr WW1 armed forces* Civilian dress; mufti

claim agent *n phr horse-racing* A bettor who claims to have won but has lost the ticket that would

prove it [fr ironic reference to the government official with whom mining *claims* or land *claims* were filed]

clam **1** *n fr early 1900s* A silent, secretive person, esp one who can be trusted with a confidence **2** *v* =CLAM UP **3** *n* A dollar: *That'll be eight clams for the oil* **4** *n broadcasting* A verbal mistake; =HOWLER **5** *n jazz musicians* A wrong or sour note; =CLINKER
See BEARDED CLAM, HAPPY AS A CLAM

clambake **1** *n* Any gathering, meeting, convention, party, etc, esp a happy and noisy one **2** *n jazz musicians* =JAM SESSION **3** *n broadcasting* A blatant failure, esp one resulting from insufficient rehearsal

clamp down *v phr fr 1940s* To increase the severity of measures against persons who break rules and laws; punish rather than tolerate: *The whole country's clamping down now on drunk drivers*

the **clamps** *See* PUT THE CLAMPS ON

clam shells (or **trap**) *n phr fr early 1800s* The mouth and jaws

clam up *v phr fr early 1900s* To stay or become silent; stand mute; =BUTTON UP: *When I ask for details he just clams up*—HL Wilson

clank or **clank up** *v or v phr students fr Air Force* To panic; be paralyzed by fear; =FREEZE UP

clanked *adj esp 1960s students* Exhausted; =BEAT, POOPED

clanker *n outdated hoboes & circus* A dollar

the **clanks** *n phr* Delirium tremens; =the SHAKES: *He had the clanks from Purple Passions*—Hal Boyle/ *The old rum-bum was sick with the clanks*

◁the **clap**▷ *n fr late 1500s* Gonorrhea [fr early French *clapoir* "bubo, swelling"]
See NO-CLAP MEDAL

clapped-out *adj fr British fr 1940s Air Force* Worn-out; ready for the junk heap; =BEAT-UP: *The civilian jumped into his clapped-out Mercury*—Car and Driver

◁**clapped-up**▷ *adj* Infected with gonorrhea: *In reality she's a gotch-eyed...clapped-up...hooker*—Dan Jenkins

claptrap *n* Nonsense; mendacious cant; =BULLSHIT

claret *n prizefight fr middle 1800s* Blood [fr the red color of *claret* wine]

class **1** *n fr late 1800s* High quality; admirable style; cachet: *quiet dignity under fire, real class* **2** *modifier: a real class joint*
See HIGH-CLASS, WORLD-CLASS

a **class act** *n phr fr show business* A person or thing of admirable style, quality, competence, etc: *48 HRS. clicks anyway. It's a class act*—Playboy/ *Monaco was, as Arthur Lewis said, a class act*—Philadelphia

classy **1** *adj* Of high quality; first-rate; superior: *That's a very classy speech you just made* **2** *adj* Having or showing prestige; aristocratic; =POSH: *a classy school/ classy manners*

classy chassis *n phr* A good figure; trim body: *sassy lassie with a classy chassis*

Claus *See* SANTA CLAUS

claw 1 *n* A police officer **2** *v* To arrest
See HAVE one's CLAWS OUT, PUT THE CLAW ON someone

clawhammer *n fr middle 1800s* A men's dress
coat

◄**clay eater**► *n phr* A native of southern US low
country

clay pigeon 1 *n phr* A person who is easily
duped; = EASY MARK **2** *n phr Navy* An aircraft
catapulted from a ship **3** *n phr* Something easily
done; = CINCH

clean 1 *adj* Not carrying anything forbidden, esp
a firearm: *Cops gave him a body-shake and he
came out clean* **2** *adj* Innocent; unincriminated
3 *adj* Not producing radioactive contamination: *a
clean bomb* **4** *adj* Lacking money; = BROKE,
CLEANED OUT **5** *adj* Not lewd or obscene; morally unexceptionable: *a couple of clean jokes/ a
clean old man* **6** *adj* Trim; neat; elegant: *Mies's
clean lines and crisp angles* **7** *adv: I was crazy
about Lester. He played so clean and beautiful*
—Charlie Parker **8** *adj narcotics* Free of drug
addiction **9** *adj black* Well-dressed; clad in the
latest style: *Danny, he was really clean. He had new
clothes*—Claude Brown
See COME CLEAN, KEEP one's NOSE CLEAN, SCRUB THE
SLATE CLEAN, SQUEAKY-CLEAN

Clean *See* MISTER CLEAN

clean as a hound's tooth *adj phr* Perfectly
clean: *His record is clean as a hound's tooth now*

clean someone's **clock 1** *v phr* To attack and
punish someone: *Carlson suddenly really wanted to
clean Ron Connelly's clock*—Earl Thompson **2** *v
phr* To defeat; trounce; = CLOBBER: *The DA...had
his clock cleaned for him*—George V Higgins/ *"She
just cleaned my clock,"* Mrs King said—New York
Times

clean dozens *n phr black* An elaborate word
game in which personal insults are bandied, but
without reference to the opponent's mother

cleaned out *adj phr* Lacking money, esp having
lost it gambling or speculating; = BROKE, TAPPED
OUT: *Georgie was cleaned out after the third race*

the **cleaners** *See* GO TO THE CLEANERS, TAKE someone TO THE CLEANERS

cleaning *See* HOUSE-CLEANING

clean someone **out 1** *v phr* To win all of someone's money at gambling, esp in a crap game **2** *v
phr* To require or use up all of someone's money:
Buying the condo just about cleaned them out

cleanup 1 *n* An intensive effort or campaign
against crime, filth, etc, of the sort periodically
undertaken by the authorities: *The Mayor vowed a
definitive cleanup of the Times Square area* **2**
modifier: another cleanup campaign **3** *modifier baseball* Batting fourth in the lineup: *He did
better as the cleanup hitter* [baseball sense fr the
notion and hope that the first three hitters will reach
base and the bases will be emptied, *cleaned up,* by
the fourth hitter]
See BAT CLEANUP

clean up *v phr fr early 1800s* To make a large
profit; get an impressive return on one's money;

= MAKE A KILLING: *The West today knows many a
ghost town where men of too much enterprise
cleaned up and cleared out*—Sierra Club Bulletin

clean up one's **act** (or ◄one's **shit**►) *v phr* To
correct one's behavior; act properly and decently;
= STRAIGHTEN UP AND FLY RIGHT: *I told the kid to
clean up his act or leave*

clean up on someone *v phr fr late 1900s* To
defeat someone decisively; trounce; thrash;
= CLEAN someone's CLOCK: *We really cleaned up on
them in the second half*

the **cleanup spot** (or **slot**) *n phr baseball* The
fourth position in the batting order: *The manager
didn't have a very reliable hitter for the cleanup spot*
[fr the fact that the batter in this position may, or
ought to, get a hit and *clean* the runners off the
bases by driving them in to score]

clean up the floor with someone *v phr* To
defeat someone decisively; = CLEAN UP ON someone:
*If he said that to me I'd clean up the floor with the
bastard*

clear *n outdated labor union* A member of the
Industrial Workers of the World; = WOBBLY
See READ someone LOUD AND CLEAR

clear out *v phr fr late 1800s* To depart; = HIT THE
ROAD

clear sailing *n phr* Easy and unimpeded progress;
easy going: *After a rough couple of months it was
clear sailing*

clear up 1 *v phr* To make understandable: *Can
you clear this matter up for me?* **2** *v phr* To
become more orderly and comprehensible: *when
the Persian Gulf situation clears up* **3** *v phr* To
become cloudless and fair: *The weather cleared up
in the afternoon* **4** *v phr* To heal: *The rash
cleared up by itself* **5** *v phr narcotics* To stop
using narcotics; get help in withdrawing from drug
addiction

clem *circus & carnival* **1** *n* A fight between show
people and the local citizenry: *It'd start a clem, with
me in the middle*—F Brown **2** *v* To disperse riot-
ing customers at a circus or carnival

Clem *circus* **1** *n* A small-town resident; rural person, esp one who is easily duped **2** *n* An inhabi-
tant of the place where the circus is playing **3**
interj A cry used by circus people to rally forces in
a fight with townspeople

clemo *prison* **1** *n* Executive clemency **2** *n* A
prison escape

clerks and jerks *n phr Army* Soldiers in other
than front-line units; rear-echelon troops

click 1 *v early 1900s* To succeed; please an audience or constituency: *If I can click with a wholesal-
ers I should be ready to open up in about 3 weeks*
—George Orwell **2** *v* To evoke or precede a
flash of insight: *Something clicked and I knew what I
had to do next* **3** *n* An insight, esp a sudden
one; flash of comprehension: *She gifts us with this
click: most men want their wives to have a jobette*
—Gloria Steinem/ *a turbulent period of feminist
clicks*—Ms **4** *v fr early 1900s* To fit together precisely; go well together: *Those two really click, like a
well-oiled machine* **5** *n fr 1920s* A clique **6** *n*

(also **klick**, **klik**) *armed forces* A kilometer: *a hundred and sixty clicks north of Saigon*—George Warren

cliffdweller *n* A resident of a tall apartment house; high-rise dweller

cliffhanger *n fr early 1900s* A very suspenseful story, film, book, situation, etc: *The election was a cliffhanger, right through the recount* [fr the fact that the actress Pearl White actually ended some episodes of her early serial movies *hanging* from the Palisades above the Hudson River]

climb someone *v phr WW2 Army* To reprimand severely; = CHEW OUT, REAM: *The old man really climbed me for that stupid trick*

climb on the bandwagon *See* GET ON THE BANDWAGON

climb (or **go up**) **the wall** *v phr* To become frantic, esp from frustration or anxiety; = GO OUT OF one's SKULL: *By the time the cops came I was about to climb the wall*

clinch **1** *n fr early 1800s* A close contact of two boxers, where they hold each others' arms to stifle blows **2** *v*: *Two palookas clinched through six rounds* **3** *n fr 1930s* An embrace; passionate hug **4** *v* To determine conclusively; finish definitively and positively; = NAIL something DOWN: *They claim new evidence that'll clinch their case* [fr the bending over, *clinching*, of the point of a nail to ensure it does not pull out; ultimately fr *clench*]

clincher *n fr early 1800s* The deciding or conclusive element; = BOTTOM LINE: *One smudged fingerprint was the clincher*

clink *n black* A black person; = BROTHER

the **clink** *n phr* A jail or prison; = the SLAMMER [fr the old prison on *Clink* Street in the Southwark district of London]

clinker **1** *n fr late 1800s* A biscuit **2** *n* = the CLINK **3** *n telephone workers* An unwanted noise on a long-distance telephone line **4** *n musicians* A squeak or unintended reed sound made on the clarinet, saxophone, or oboe **5** *n musicians* An obvious wrong or sour note: *One of the louder sopranos hit an excruciating clinker* **6** *n* An error; = BONER **7** *n* Anything inferior in workmanship, esp a play, movie, or other show; = LEMON, TURKEY **8** *n* Something damaging, esp when unseen or unforeseen; a hidden flaw: *There was a clinker in the works apart from his writing, a sort of catch*—Earl Thompson **9** *n* An incompetent person; a failure; = LOSER: *There have been some ultraconservative judges, but there has been an absence of real clinkers*—Time [fr *clinker* "unburnable cinder"]

clinker boy *n phr railroad* A fire stoker

clip **1** *v* To hit; strike sharply and neatly: *He clipped and decked the local goon* **2** *n*: *You hit him a good clip*—P Starnes **3** *v* To steal; = SWIPE: *Where'd you clip the new car?* **4** *n underworld* A thief **5** *v* To cheat someone, esp by overcharging: *That joint'll clip you every time* **6** *v* To arrest **7** *v* To kill, esp by shooting ◀**8**▶ *n* = CLIPPED DICK **9** *n* Pace; rate: *She took off at a real good clip* **10** *n* Each one; each occasion;

= POP: *two treatments at $100 a clip/ Every clip cost him half a day's pay* **11** *n* A clipping from a newspaper, magazine, etc: *Thanks for sending the clips about the kid's wedding* **12** *n* A portion of a movie or television tape: *television clips from the period of the accident*—New York Times **13** *n* A brief news item on televison: *Now for a couple of clips to end the show* [senses denoting fraud and theft are probably fr the practice of *clipping* bits of metal off coins and passing them at face value]
See PUT THE CLIP ON someone, ROACH CLIP

clip-artist *n underworld* A professional swindler or thief

clip joint *n phr* A business establishment that regularly overcharges, or where one is likely to be robbed or swindled: *One man's gourmet noshery is another man's clip joint*

◀**clipped dick**▶ *n phr* A Jewish male

clipper *n police* A pickpocket: *accused her of being a clipper, or pickpocket*—New York Times

clipping **1** *n sports* Illegal blocking or checking from behind **2** *n* The repairing of a car by joining together two undamaged halves after either the front or the rear end has been damaged: *Front and rear clips are attached to the remains of vehicles that have been seriously damaged...but clipping...is dangerous*—Washingtonian

◁**clit**▷ *n* The clitoris; = BUTTON

◁**clit-licker**▷ *n* A person who does cunnilingus; = MUFF-DIVER

clobber **1** *v fr British fr early 1900s* To hit or attack very hard; = BASH **2** *v* To defeat decisively; trounce; = MURDER, WIPE OUT: *Rommel got clobbered at El Alamein*

clobbered *adj esp 1950s* Drunk: *those who are, to use a word presently popular with the younger drinking set, clobbered*—James Thurber

clock **1** *v fr Australian fr 1920s* To hit; = SOCK: *who clocked me when I wasn't looking*—R Starnes **2** *v from early 1900s* To time, esp with a stopwatch: *They clocked her at 6:05:03.65* **3** *v* To achieve a specified time: *I clocked a two-minute lap yesterday* [first sense perhaps fr the notion of a *clock's* striking, sound of the bell when struck]
See CLEAN someone's CLOCK

clock in (or **out**) *v phr* To come or go at a certain recorded time, esp to or from a job where a time clock is used; = PUNCH IN (or OUT)

clock-watcher *n phr* A person who vouchsafes more attention to the time of quitting than to work: *a hard worker, no clockwatcher*—Ira Wolfert

clod *n* A stupid person [fr *clodpate* or *clodpole*, fr 17th century]

clodhopper **1** *n fr late 1600s* A farmer; rustic **2** *n* A strong, heavy shoe, esp a workshoe; = BOONDOCKER **3** *n* An old vehicle, suitable for only short passages

clone *n* An imitation, esp a person who imitates or emulates another; a mindless copy: *Not a clone in sight. No one has the same color hair*—Village Voice [fr *clone* "the asexually produced offspring of an organism," ultimately fr Greek *klon* "twig, branch"]

clonesome *adj* Tending to copy; unoriginal; robot-like: *a tall, dark, clonesome actor*—Village Voice

clong *n politics* The impact of a powerfully inept speech, line, phrase, etc: *Clong is speechwriter talk for "the rush of s--- to the heart when a line drops dead in the hall"*—Globe and Mail/ *His call is a grand clong*—Washington Post [probably echoic of something falling with a loud, dull clang, like *clonk* and *clunk*]

clonish *adj* Inclined to copy; unoriginal and duplicative: *The crowd was decidedly clonish*—Armistead Maupin

clonk *v* = CLUNK

close 1 *adj* Warm and humid: *a very close day* **2** *adj fr 1700s* Parsimonious; stingy

close but no cigar *adv phr* Very nearly correct; not quite the thing: *one package that was acceptable, too many amounted to her idea of close-but-no-cigar*—Washington Post/ *If you answered George Lucas's Star Wars you're close, but no cigar*—Washingtonian [fr carnival feats where one gets a *cigar* as a prize]

close shave (or **call**) *n phr fr late 1800s* A very narrow avoidance or evasion of some danger; = SQUEAKER

closet *modifier* Secret; unsuspected: *Puddin' calls me his closet red neck*—Dan Jenkins/ *fellow who was known around the White House as a "closet liberal"*—New York Times

the **closet** *n phr* The condition of concealment in which a homosexual or other nonconforming person lives: *If you're out of the closet, you're out of the armed service*—Ms
See COME OUT OF THE CLOSET

close to the chest *See* PLAY CLOSE TO THE CHEST

closet queen (or **queer**) *n phr* A secret homosexual

close-up 1 *n* A photograph or movie or television sequence shot close to the subject **2** *modifier* Made or done from very near: *a close-up view/ close-up study* **3** *n fr 1930s* A biography: *It is becoming commonplace for a literary critic to describe a biography as a "close-up"*—Ernest Weekley

clothes *See* SOFT-CLOTHES, SUNDAY CLOTHES

clotheshorse *n fr 1930s* A fashionably dressed person; a person who wears clothes becomingly and perhaps does nothing else

clothesline 1 *n baseball* A very flat, fast line drive **2** *v football* To block or tackle by holding out one's arm in the path of a running player: *He clotheslined him*—Esquire

cloud *See* ON CLOUD NINE, UNDER A CLOUD, UP IN THE CLOUDS

cloud-buster 1 *n baseball* A very, very high fly ball **2** *n* A skyscraper

cloud nine (or **seven**) *See* ON CLOUD NINE

clout 1 *v* To hit; strike; = BASH: *My old man would have clouted the hell out of me*—Calder Willingham **2** *n:* *She gave him a clout on the snoot* **3** *v* To steal, esp to shoplift or steal a car **4** *n* Force; power; impact; = PUNCH: *This wimpish paragraph lacks clout* **5** *n* Influence or power, esp of a political sort: *He has lots of friends in high places, but no clout*
See CIRCUIT BLOW

clouter *n underworld* A person who examines a place to find how it may best be robbed

clout (or **hit**) **for the circuit** *v phr* To hit a home run in baseball

clover *See* IN CLOVER, LIKE PIGS IN CLOVER

clover-kicker *n* = SHITKICKER

clown 1 *n* A person for whom the speaker feels mild contempt, esp one whose behavior merits derision: *So these clowns start in about karma or something* **2** *v* (also **clown around**) To behave frivolously; persist in inappropriate levity

clown wagon *n phr railroad* The caboose of a freight train

club *See* BOTTLE CLUB, DEUCE OF CLUBS, FIVE OF CLUBS, KEY CLUB, MILE-HIGH CLUB, RAP CLUB, SCRUB CLUB, WAR CLUB, WELCOME TO THE CLUB

clubhouse lawyer *n phr baseball* A baseball player who is a prominent self-appointed authority on the game and its regulations, and who generously instructs his associates

club-winder *n railroad* A train's brake operator

cluck or **cluckhead** or **kluck 1** *n* A stupid person; idiot **2** *n black* A very dark black person
See DUMB CLUCK

cluck and grunt *n phr lunch counter* Ham and eggs

cluckish *adj* Stupid

clue *v* or *v phr* (also **clue in**) To inform someone of pertinent facts; = PUT someone IN THE PICTURE: *Neil Sheehan and I were terribly clued-in. We had a lock on that story*—David Halberstam
See GET A CLUE, HAVE A CLUE, NOT HAVE A CLUE

clueless *adj college students* Ignorant • Possibly connected with WW2 British Army and Air Force use
See TOTALLY CLUELESS

clunk 1 *v* (also **clonk**) To hit; strike; = CLOCK: *She clunked him in the teeth* **2** *n:* *He hit me a good clunk* **3** *n* A stupid person; = CLUCK: *scheming maids who have been working on the poor clunks all spring*—Robert Ruark **4** *n* An old and worn-out machine, esp a car; = CLUNKER: *Look at that fuckin' broad in the clunk next to us*—Rolling Stone/ *hauled a junk car on the ice and took bets....This contest was called "Dunk the Clunk"*—Village Voice

clunk down *See* PLANK DOWN

clunker 1 *n* Anything inferior; = LEMON, TURKEY: *His last clunker was Lolly Madonna*—New York Magazine **2** *n* An old, worn-out machine, esp a car; = CLUNK, JALOPY: *let in someone in an old clunker with a broken muffler and a fuming exhaust*—New York Times **3** *n* A clumsy person, esp an unskillful athlete; = DUFFER, HACKER: *Tell one of those clunkers what a great stroke he has*—G Edson

clunkhead *n* A stupid person: *Some clunkhead sent me three live quail*—Arthur Godfrey

clunkily *adv* Ungracefully; stolidly: *Her clunkily earnest lyrics are very big on concepts like the Necessity of Being Your Own Person*—Ms

clunky or **clunkish** *adj* Blockish and ungraceful; stolidly unsophisticated: *I don't like clunky shoes or heavy soles—Village Voice/ a clunkish magazine called Pick-Up Times—Village Voice/ The ads are so clunky and quaint that they transport one back to a seemingly more innocent consumer past—*Washington Post

clutch **1** *n* An embrace; =CLINCH **2** *n* A group; bunch: *a clutch of drunken sailors* **3** *n* restaurant A customer who does not tip, or tips too little **4** *v* (also **clutch up**) To panic; be seized with anxiety

the **clutch** **1** *n phr* A moment when heroic performance under pressure is needed: *You could always depend on Gladys when the clutch came* **2** *modifier:* *a clutch hitter/ clutch play*

clutched *adj* Nervous; tense; =UPTIGHT

clutcher *See* DOUBLE-CLUTCHER

clutching *See* DOUBLE-CLUTCHING

clutchy **1** *adj* Likely to become nervous or anxious **2** *adj* Difficult; dangerous; =HAIRY **3** *adj* Clinging; needy

clutz *See* KLUTZ

clyde *n fr rock and roll & cool talk* A person who does not appreciate rock-and-roll music, culture, etc; =SQUARE

C-note *n* A hundred-dollar bill

coach *See* SLOW COACH

coal *See* DEAL IN COAL, HAUL someone OVER THE COALS, POUR ON THE COAL

coalhole *n* A prison, guardhouse, cell, etc

coast **1** *v* To go along without effort: *I coasted through the two exams* **2** *v narcotics & jazz musicians* To be exhilarated by a narcotic, by music, etc; be euphoric: *That first fix...had sent him coasting one whole week—*Nelson Algren **3** *n:* *The flip side gave us a coast*

the **coast** (or **Coast**) *n phr* The Pacific coast, esp California, or the Atlantic coast
See LEFT COAST

coaster *n teenagers* A person living on or near the beach

coat *See* PINE OVERCOAT

coattail **1** *v musicians* To keep the same musical tempo: *You're still keeping the same time. We called it coattailing—*Downbeat **2** *modifier* Based on another person's achievement or quality; derivative: *but the Sephardim are not likely to remain contented with coattail power for long—*Newsweek
See ON someone's COATTAILS

cob *See* OFF THE COB, ON THE COB, ROUGH AS A COB

cobber *n* =PAL, BUDDY ● Chiefly Australian [fr Yiddish fr Hebrew *chaber* "comrade"]

cobbler *n underworld* A forger

cock ◁**1**▷ *n* The penis; =PRICK **2** *n* A friend; =PAL ● Chiefly British: *How goes it, old cock?*
See DROP YOUR COCKS AND GRAB YOUR SOCKS, HORSE COCK, POPPYCOCK

cockalorum *See* HIGH COCKALORUM

cockamamie or **cockamamey** or **cockamamy** (kahk ə MAY mee) *adj* Crazy; confused: *The picture ends with a cockamamie implication that love will conquer all—*Time [fr New York City dialect, perhaps fr British; somehow connected with *decalcomania*; perhaps because decalcomanias as given in candy boxes and chewing-gum packets were used by children for antic self-decoration]

cock-and-bull story *n phr* An improbable account, usu an alibi; a mendacious farrago: *He gives me this cock-and-bull story about six flat tires* [said to be fr the stories that would be told in the barrooms at the *Cock* Hotel and the *Bull* Hotel, nearby establishments on the high street of Stony Stratford in England]

cocked *adj* Drunk
See HALF COCKED

cocked hat *See* KNOCK something INTO A COCKED HAT

cocker *See* ALTER KOCKER, OLD COCKER

cockeye *n baseball* A lefthanded pitcher; =SOUTHPAW

cockeyed **1** *adj* Crosseyed; walleyed; strabismic **2** *adj* Crazy; weird; all wrong; =SCREWY: *Anybody who thinks I'm kidding is cockeyed—*Heywood Broun/ *This plan appears to be completely "cockeyed"—*AH Marckwardt & FG Cassidy **3** *adj* Drunk **4** *adj* Unconscious: *Izzy knocks him cockeyed* **5** *adv* Askew; crooked; =SLONCHWAYS: *He put his hat on cockeyed and got a polite chuckle* **6** *adv* Very; extremely: *That is cockeyed silly*
See I'LL TELL THE WORLD

◁**cocksman**▷ **1** *n* A man regarded and evaluated as sex partner **2** *n* An ardent womanizer and copulator; =STUD

◀**cocksucker**▶ **1** *n* A person who does fellatio, esp a male homosexual **2** *n* A man held by the speaker in extreme contempt; =BASTARD, PRICK: *Oh, Sid, you fucking cocksucker....You nailed me again—*Joseph Heller

◀**cocksucking**▶ **1** *adj* Despicable; contemptible: *So I told the cocksucking little pimp to get lost* **2** *adj* Wretched; =DAMNED ● A very general intensive use, often for euphony: *Don't give me no cocksucking grief/ Here, take your cocksucking money* **3** *adv:* *Don't talk so cocksucking silly*

cocktail *narcotics* **1** *n* A cigarette of marijuana and tobacco, with marijuana put into the end of an ordinary cigarette **2** *n* A cigarette of more than a single narcotic
See MOLOTOV COCKTAIL

◁**cock-teaser** or **prick-teaser**▷ *n* A woman or a male homosexual who arouses a man sexually by granting certain favors, then denies him the sex act

coco *n* The head

coconut **1** *n fr early 1800s* The head **2** *n* One dollar: *the whole hundred thousand coconuts—*Joel Sayre

coffee *See* COWBOY COFFEE, CUP OF COFFEE

coffee and *n phr lunch counter* Coffee and doughnut, cake, roll, etc

coffee-and-cake job *n phr* A job paying very little

coffee-and-cake joint *n phr* (Variations: **layout** or **place** or **spot** may replace **joint**) A business or place of business that is not very remunerative

coffee and cakes *n phr* Small wages; a pittance; =PEANUTS: *playing for coffee and cakes in an obscure Washington nightspot*—A Lomax

coffee break *n phr* A respite of ten or twenty minutes during the workday

coffee cooler *n phr* A person devoted to easy work; shirker; =GOLDBRICK

coffee grinder **1** *n phr* A strip teaser or other performer who features slow pelvic gyration; =CEMENT MIXER **2** *n phr* A prostitute **3** *n phr* *movie studio* A cinematographer **4** *n phr* WW2 *Army Air Forces* An aircraft engine

coffee pot **1** *n phr* A lunch counter or diner: *The Marx brothers ate in coffee pots and greasy spoons*—Joel Sayre **2** *n phr* *railroad* A small steam locomotive

coffin **1** *n* Any vehicle regarded as unsafe **2** *n* WW2 *Army* A tank or armored car

coffin corner *n phr* *sports* Any corner of the football field

coffin nail (or **tack**) *n phr* *fr late 1800s* A cigarette; =BUTT

coffin varnish *n phr* *early 1900s* Inferior whiskey, esp bootleg or homemade whiskey

coin *n fr early 1900s* Money; =BREAD, LOOT

coin money *v phr* =MAKE MONEY HAND OVER FIST

cojones (coh HOH neez) *n* Courage; audacity; =BALLS: *requiring cojones the size of the award-winning cabbages at the state fair*—Car and Driver/ *since even he doesn't have the cojones to sell Beame or Biaggi to the Liberal Party*—Village Voice [fr Spanish "testicles"]

coke *fr early 1900s* **1** *n* Cocaine **2** *modifier*: *coke peddlers/ coke sniffer* **3** *n* =COKE

Coke *n* Coca-Cola, a trade name

See CHARLEY COKE

coke-bottle glasses *n phr* Very thick eyeglass lenses: *He had thinning hair, Coke-bottle glasses, a big nose*—New York Review [fr their resemblance to the thickness of the bottom of a soft-drink bottle]

coked or **coked-up** or **coked-out** *adj* Intoxicated with cocaine; =HIGH: *the new generation of "coked"...gunmen*—E Lavine/ *the pair of strippers, a coked-out Pakistani princess and a coked-up Fire Island queen*—Village Voice

cokehead **1** *n* *narcotics* A cocaine addict **2** *n* Any dull, stupid person

cokie or **cokey** *narcotics* **1** *n* A narcotics addict, esp a cocaine addict: *the horde of Hollywood cokies* **2** *modifier*: *a cokey friend/ cokie chat* **3** *adj* Relaxed and sleepy-looking; inattentive

cola *n* *narcotics* Cocaine: *paying upwards of $75 for a gram of cola*—Head

colaholic *n* A person who drinks a great deal of cola: *Many colaholics revealed that they would find it difficult to give up the habit*—P Horn

cold **1** *adj* Unconscious; =OUT: *The snowball knocked him cold* **2** *adj* Having or displaying no emotional warmth: *He's a cold sort of fish* **3** *adj* Undergoing a spell of bad luck: *I got out of that game because I was cold and Pop was hot* **4** *adj* Without rehearsal, practice, or warmup: *When the*

star got sick, this woman had to take over the part cold **5** *adj* Perfectly; in every detail; =BLIND: *She knew the subject cold* **6** *adv* With no possibility of evasion; definitively; =DEAD TO RIGHTS: *After that slip they had him cold*

See BLOW HOT AND COLD, HOT AND COLD, STONY COLD BROKE

cold as (or **colder than**) **hell** (Variations: **charity** or **Kelsey's ass** or **a welldigger's ass** or **a witch's tit** may replace **hell**) *adj phr* Very cold: *In Chicago, that December 1955, it was cold as a well-digger's ass in the Klondike*—Earl Thompson

cold cash *n phr* Unmistakably valid money, as distinct from checks, promises, etc; =HARD CASH: *The place wants payment in cold cash, nothing less* [fr the notion that definite and inalterable things are cold and hard]

coldcock **1** *v* To knock someone unconscious; =KNOCK someone OUT: *He told me to step aside and I wouldn't, so he cold cocked me*—Village Voice **2** *n* The act of knocking someone unconscious quickly before the victim can resist [perhaps fr the hammering of *caulking* into a boat's or ship's seams; perhaps related to Canadian lumberjacks' *put the caulks to* someone "stamp in someone's face with spiked boots"]

cold day in hell *n phr* An impossible time; never: *It'll be a cold day in hell when you catch me taking dope*

cold deck **1** *n phr* *fr middle 1800s* A dishonest deck of playing cards, usu stacked or marked **2** *v phr* To take advantage of someone; dishonestly assure one's own winning; =RIG, STACK THE DECK

cold-decker *n fr early 1900s* A swindler; cheat

cold feet *See* HAVE COLD FEET

cold fish *n phr* A person who lacks emotional warmth, compassion, sociability, etc; =ICEBERG

cold haul **1** *v phr* To take advantage of; dupe **2** *v phr* To do something in a slipshod way, and esp to miss a good opportunity **3** *v phr* (also **cold haul it**) *black* To leave; depart; =HAUL ASS: *He cold hauled it!*—Zora Neale Hurston

cold in hand *adj phr* *black* Lacking money; =BROKE

cold meat *n phr fr early 1800s* A cadaver; corpse

cold-meat box *n phr fr early 1800s* A coffin

cold-meat cart *n phr fr early 1800s* A hearse

cold-meat party *n phr fr early 1800s* A wake or funeral: *You were at that cold-meat party, I spotted you coming out of the cemetery*—J Evans

cold pack **1** *n phr* *prizefight* A knockout or knockout punch **2** *n phr* *esp 1920s* A certainty; =SURE THING, CINCH

cold pricklies *n phr* Unpleasant and unwelcome comments; adverse criticism: *The cast needed strokes, but they got cold pricklies*

cold shoulder **1** *n phr fr early 1800s fr British* A deliberate snub; display of chilly contempt **2** *v*: *I cold-shouldered him and he looked puzzled*

cold sober *adj phr* Completely sober

See STONE COLD SOBER

cold storage *See* IN COLD STORAGE

cold turkey **1** *adv phr* Without warning, rehearsal, overture, etc: *simply walk in cold turkey and talk things over*—DH Beetle **2** *n phr* narcotics Total and abrupt deprivation of narcotics, as distinct from gradual withdrawal **3** *adv phr:* *He kicked his habit cold turkey* **4** *adj* narcotics Requiring abrupt and complete deprivation: *They tried the cold-turkey cure* **5** *v phr* auctioneers To stop auction bidding and sell at a previously set price **6** *adj* *fr early 1900s* Basic; unadorned; =HARD-CORE: *Stalin didn't like certain cold-turkey facts Kennan reported*—New York Daily News [perhaps fr the contrast between the unadorned *cold turkey* and the warm, prepared, tasty bird served at the feast]

coll *n* hoboes A stew or hash

collar **1** *n* A police officer **2** *n* police An arrest: *The bull makes a collar on me*—American Mercury **3** *v:* *He collared the muggers in the next block* **4** *v* To comprehend; grasp: *I don't collar your meaning, Sam*
See ACCOMMODATION COLLAR, BRASS COLLAR, DOG COLLAR, HOT UNDER THE COLLAR, WHITE-COLLAR

collar a nod *v phr* black To sleep: *You can't collar nods all day*—Zora Neale Hurston

collar the jive *v phr* 1930s jive talk To understand and approve; =DIG

college *n* outdated underworld A jail, prison, or reformatory
See COW COLLEGE, NUT HOUSE

College *See* JOE COLLEGE

college try *See* the OLD COLLEGE TRY

collision mat *n phr* Navy fr WW2 A waffle or pancake

colly *v* black To understand; =DIG

colonel *See* CHICKEN COLONEL, LIGHT COLONEL

color *See* OFF COLOR

color-blind **1** *adj* Unable to distinguish one's own money from someone else's, hence likely to cheat or steal **2** *adj* Making no prejudicial distinctions among races: *The law is, in design, perfectly color-blind*

colors *See* WITH FLYING COLORS

color-struck *adj* black Harboring prejudice against darker-skinned black persons

Columbia *See* HAIL COLUMBIA

combo **1** *n* fr 1940s musicians A musical group or band: *a combo like Led Zeppelin* **2** *n* The combination of a safe, lock, vault, etc **3** *n* Any combination: *gin and tomato juice combo/ boy-girl combo*

◁**come**▷ **1** *v* To have an orgasm; ejaculate semen **2** *n* (also **cum**) Semen, or any fluid secreted at orgasm **3** *n* An orgasm **4** *n* (also **cum**) Any viscid food or other substance resembling semen
See HOW COME, WHAT GOES AROUND COMES AROUND

come a cropper **1** *v phr* To take a sudden violent fall **2** *v phr* To fail; suffer a setback • Some US use, chiefly as a conscious Briticism [probably fr a British dialect word *crop* "neck"]

come across **1** *v phr* To give something, esp to do so somewhat reluctantly: *When will you come across with the rent, you bum?* **2** *v phr* To accede to the sex act; bestow oneself sexually: *She came across without more fuss* **3** *v phr* To impress one; appear to be: *Walter doesn't come across as a crusader, or muckraker*—Esquire

come again *v phr* To repeat something; =RUN something BY AGAIN • Nearly always a request, or an expression of disbelief at what one has heard: *Come again? Did I hear what I hope I didn't?*

come apart at the seams *v phr* To lose one's normal poise and competence: *It was rather a long kiss. Silas felt himself coming apart at the seams*—S McNeil

comeback **1** *n* A regaining of success, fame, health, etc: *He's trying another comeback at 38* **2** *n* A quick and witty retort; a withering riposte: *Dorothy Parker was famous for devastating comebacks* **3** *n* salespersons A customer who returns merchandise; also, the returning itself **4** *n* citizens band A response to a call: *Thanks for your comeback, Dead Duck*

come back *v phr* To regain success, renown, health, etc: *It's hard to come back after a fiasco like that*

come clean *v phr* To tell the truth, esp the whole truth; make a plenary confession

comedian *See* STAND-UP COMIC

comedown **1** *n* A reduction of one's status; loss of prestige: *Riding the bus was a comedown for her* **2** *n* =LETDOWN **3** *n* narcotics The ending of a drug experience: *I cooled it with Quaalude...the comedown wasn't too bad*—Saturday Review

come down **1** *v phr* narcotics To experience the ending of a drug intoxication: *as if he had just come down off methedrine*—J Bradshaw **2** *v phr* narcotics To become firmly established: *when a chick's habit came down on her*—Claude Brown **3** *v phr* fr black To happen: *Sir Morgan's cove, where the Great Event was coming down*—Worcester/ *Something weird had to be coming down*—Cyra McFadden

come down hard *v phr* To punish or suppress severely; =CLAMP DOWN: *He always comes down real hard on two-time losers*

come down the pike *v phr* To appear; come on the scene: *every dumbass little news story that comes down the pike*—Armistead Maupin

come hell or high water *adv phr* No matter what happens; in any event: *I'll find out come hell or high water*

come-hither *adj* Inviting; seductive: *Courage and come-hither eyes Have a genius for taking pains*—WH Auden

come-in circus **1** *n* The line of people waiting to buy tickets **2** *n* The time between the opening of the main tent and the beginning of the entry procession

come in out of the rain *See* NOT HAVE BRAINS ENOUGH TO COME IN OUT OF THE RAIN

come-lately *See* JOHNNY-COME-LATELY

come off ◁**1**▷ *v phr* To have an orgasm; ejaculate semen **2** *v phr* To succeed: *To everybody's astonishment, the scheme came off*

come off something *v phr* To stop doing or saying something immediately ● Usu a stern command: *Come off that crap. Keep your jaw shut* —Calder Willingham

come off one's **perch** *v phr* To stop behaving in a superior or haughty manner; = GET OFF one's HIGH HORSE

come on 1 *v phr* To show as; present oneself as; act: *Your friend comes on real dumb* **2** *interj* An exclamation of disbelief, disapproval, request, etc: *Come on, Arnold, don't give me that shit* **3** *v phr* horse-racing To gain: *Aching Axel is coming on real strong in the home stretch*

come-on 1 *n* Anything designed to attract or seduce; an enticement: *I gave her a big grin, but she knew it was a come-on* **2** *modifier: football bowls baited with $100,000 or so of come-on money*—Arthur Daley

come on like gangbusters *v phr* To begin or proceed in a vigorous fashion: *The campaign's coming on like gangbusters* [fr the radio program *Gangbusters* of the 1930s and 40s, which was introduced by a noisy miscellany of sirens, shots, screeches, music, etc]

come on strong 1 *v phr* horse-racing To gain steadily and rapidly in a race **2** *v phr* To be vehement and positive: *He always comes on a little too strong about taxes*

come out 1 *v phr* fr homosexuals To become an acknowledged homosexual; = COME OUT OF THE CLOSET: *Their eldest son had "come out"*—Shana Alexander **2** *v phr* To end; eventuate: *How'd that whole deal come out?* **3** *v phr* To declare oneself; take a position: *Did she come out for the Equal Rights Amendment?*

come out ahead (or **on top**) *v phr* To win: *Who came out ahead in the poll?*

come out of the closet 1 *v phr* fr homosexuals To become an acknowledged homosexual; = COME OUT: *He came out of the closet last year and his parents damn near died* **2** *v phr* To reveal or acknowledge some personal conviction, political position, etc: *In 1978 Timmy came out of the closet and showed a genuine interest in the club*—Sports Illustrated/ *James Robinson, a fiery, red-faced orator with a Bible clenched in his upraised hand, thundered that it was "time for God's people to come out of the closet and the churches and change America"*—Washington Post

come out of the woodwork *See* CRAWL OUT OF THE WOODWORK

◁ **come-queen** ▷ *v* A person who prefers and practices fellatio: *a nutty come-queen named Linda Lovelace*—Deep Throat Papers

comer *n* A person doing very well and promising to do better in a certain field: *She's a comer, a potential champ*

comes around *See* WHAT GOES AROUND COMES AROUND

come through 1 *v phr* To succeed as expected and desired: *Jim Thorpe always came through to win*—Bill Stern **2** *v phr* To cope successfully with perils and troubles; weather adversity: *All seems bleak, but we'll come through unscathed* **3** *v phr* = COME ACROSS

come to a screeching halt *v phr* To finish abruptly and immediately: *All this damn foolishness must come to a screeching halt*

come unglued (or **unstuck** or **unwrapped**) *v phr* To go out of control; deteriorate to chaos: *Mr Foster...succeeded in keeping the proceedings from coming unglued*—New York Times/ *Everybody knew she was bound to come unwrapped*—John Farris

comeuppance or **come-uppings** *n fr middle 1800s* A deserved chastening, esp some event that checks a wrongdoer; just deserts

come up smelling like a rose (or **with the five-dollar gold piece**) *v phr* To have extraordinarily good luck; emerge from peril with profit [fr the traditional image of the happy person who "falls in the shitpile and *comes up smelling like a rose*"]

come up to the wire *v phr* To approach the finish; come near the end: *The crucial project is coming up to the wire and we're a bit nervous* [fr the *wire* that marks the finish line of a race]

come within an ace *v phr fr late 1600s* To come very near to doing something, winning something, etc: *She came within an ace of getting the world title* [probably a version of the 13th-century term *within ambs ace* "very close to," *ambs ace* being the lowest point in dice, two ones or snake-eyes, fr Old French fr Latin *ambas as* "both ace"]

come with the territory *See* GO WITH THE TERRITORY

comfy *adj* Comfortable and comforting; pleasant and easy: *Just reeling off their names is ever so comfy*—WH Auden

comic 1 *n* A comedian, esp one who does a solo act in clubs, etc **2** *n* A comic book or comic strip *See* HEAD COMIC, STAND-UP COMIC

the comics *See* the FUNNIES

coming from *See* WHERE someone IS COMING FROM

coming out of someone's **ears** *See* STEAM WAS COMING OUT OF someone's EARS

comma-counter *n* A person who overstresses minor details; a pedantic and picayune perfectionist

commando *n students fr WW2 Army* A person who behaves roughly and overeagerly, esp in love-making [fr the *Commandos*, elite British shock troops of WW2] *See* BEDPAN COMMANDO, PICCADILLY COMMANDO

Commerce *See* CHAMBER OF COMMERCE

commercial 1 *n* Any endorsement or recommendation: *I like the idea, so spare me the commercial* **2** *n* jazz musicians A musical piece played at audience request **3** *adj fr jazz musicians* Obviously designed for wide audience approval: *How can it be commercial? It's Jelly Roll*

Commie or **Commy 1** *n* A communist **2** *adj: Commy plot/ Commie rhetoric*

commo[1] *n prison* Treats, cigarettes, etc, from the prison commissary

commo[2] *n* Commotion: *What's the commo about?*

commo³ 1 *n Army* Communications: *Commo okay?* **2** *modifier fr Army: a commo platoon/ went over the commo signals for the fiftieth time* —Richard Merkin/ *Murphy's selling commo systems out of a place out in Rockville*—WT Tyler

communist *n Army* Any despised person; =BAS-TARD: *Some communist swiped my typewriter*

commy *n* A cheap glass playing marble: *Commies was our word for those cheap ten-for-a-cent marbles* —James Thurber

comp 1 *n* A complimentary ticket; =ANNIE OAKLEY **2** *n* A nonpaying guest at a restaurant, casino, club, etc **3** *n* Something given free to a privileged guest or customer: *The first was the comps he got in the casino for dropping his $2000* —Philadelphia Journal **4** *v:* Now, *because I'm a high roller, everything is comped. I don't pay for anything*—Philadelphia

the **Company** *n phr espionage* The US Central Intelligence Agency

company man *n phr labor union* One who is, esp from the point of view of union members, devoted to the interests of the employer

compleat *See* REET

compo *n* A cheap dress shoe that is pasted or nailed together rather than sewn [fr *composition*]

comps *n students* The comprehensive examinations in their field that must be passed by candidates for advanced degrees

con¹ *n* A convict or former convict; prison inmate

con² 1 *n* A swindle; confidence game; =SCAM: *It's a clever con and you're a greedy rat* **2** *v:* We *conned the old fart out of three big ones* **3** *n* A dishonest sort of persuasion; =PUT-ON: *a slick young man with a line of deferential con*—Pete Hamill/ *His pretense of concern was all con* **4** *v: He conned her into thinking he'd marry her*

con artist *See* CON MAN

concern *See* a GOING CONCERN

conchy or **conchie** *n fr WW2 British* A conscientious objector to military service

condo *n* A condominium apartment, house, etc

cone *See* GIVE CONE

conehead *teenagers* **1** *n* An intellectual; =POINTY HEAD: *These coneheads are retards*—Village Voice **2** *n* A stupid person

Coney Island 1 *n phr* A lunch wagon **2** *n phr* A large hot dog **3** *n phr* A glass of beer with much foam and little substance **4** *n phr outdated underworld* A room where the police interrogate a suspect harshly and at length

confab (KAHN fab) **1** *n fr early 1900s* A talk; discussion **2** *v: Let's confab a bit about that idea* [fr *confabulation*]

confetti *See* IRISH CONFETTI

confisticate *v* To confiscate

con game (or **job**) **1** *n phr* A confidence game; swindle; =SCAM **2** *n phr* An easy job; sinecure

conk¹ 1 *n* The head **2** *v* To hit on the head: *I got conked by the bat* **3** *v* To defeat utterly; =CLOBBER [probably fr *conch*] *See* BUST ONE'S ASS

conk² or **gonk** *black* **1** *v* To apply a mixture sometimes containing lye to the head in order to straighten kinky hair **2** *n: I couldn't get over marveling at how their hair was straight and shiny like white men's hair; Ella told me this was called "conk"*—Malcolm X [probably fr *Congolene*, trade name of a preparation used to straighten hair, influenced by *conk¹*]

conk-buster *black* **1** *n* Cheap and inferior liquor **2** *n* Any difficult problem **3** *n* An intellectual

conked *adj* Of hair, straightened by application of lye or other chemicals: *pegged pants, conked heads, tight skirts*—Village Voice

conk off 1 *v phr* To stop work; rest when one should work; =GOOF OFF **2** *v phr* To go to sleep; sleep: *You been conking off for eight hours* —Mickey Spillane

conkout *n* An act or instance of conking out: *I did a swift conkout when I got to bed*

conk out *fr WW1 British RAF* **1** *v phr* To stop running or operating: *The engine conked right out* **2** *v phr* To lose energy and spirits suddenly; become abruptly exhausted **3** *v phr* To go to sleep; =CONK OFF **4** *v phr* To die: *So she's conked out, eh?*—Agatha Christie/ *John Le Mesurier wishes it to be known that he conked out on Nov. 15. He sadly misses family and friends*—Time [probably echoic]

con man (or **artist**) **1** *n phr* A confidence man **2** *n phr* One adept at persuasion, esp at dishonest or self-serving persuasion **3** *n phr* One who manages to lead an easy and indolent life

connect 1 *v* To hit very hard: *He connected with a rude one to the jaw* **2** *v narcotics* To buy narcotics or other contraband **3** *v* To get along with; establish rapport with: *She's never been able to connect with her tenant*

connection *n narcotics* A seller of narcotics; a person who can get drugs; =PUSHER *See* KILO CONNECTION

cons *See* MOD CONS

constant *See* FINAGLE FACTOR

constructed *adj* Having an attractive body; generously built; =STACKED

contact high *n phr narcotics* A seeming intoxication induced by being with persons who are intoxicated with narcotics: *that sympathetic vibration known as the "contact high"*—Tom Wolfe

contract 1 *n* An arrangement to have someone murdered by a professional killer: *The word is there's a contract out for Taffy Taylor* **2** *n police* Any illegal or unethical arrangement: *contract, any favor one policeman says he'll do for another*—GY Wells *See* SWEETHEART CONTRACT, YELLOW DOG CONTRACT

conversation piece *n phr* Something unusual or bizarre, esp in the decoration of a room, which can at least be justified as a topic of discussion

conversation pit *n phr* A sunken area in the floor of a living room where people may gather to chat

convict *n circus* A zebra

cooch **1** *n* Any sexually suggestive or imitative dance; =HOOTCHIE-COOTCHIE **2** *modifier: a slow hot cooch dance* ◁**3**▷ *n* The female crotch; vulva

coo-coo *See* CUCKOO

cook **1** *v* To be put to death in the electric chair; =FRY **2** *v* To suffer and quake while awaiting some outcome **3** *v fr jive talk* To happen; occur: *Is anything cooking on the new tax rule?* **4** *v fr jive talk* To do very well; excel: *if the performers begin cooking together and most of the director's intuitions and skills pay off*—Washington Post **5** *v* To falsify; tamper with ● Chiefly British use: *The British government cooked press stories shamelessly in order to deceive the Argentine enemy*—Newsweek/ *She cooked the statistics*—New York Times
See BULL COOK

cookbook *students* **1** *n* A chemistry laboratory manual **2** *adj* Routine; mechanical; unimaginative: *All he did was adopt the cookbook solution*

cooked *fr middle 1800s* **1** *adj* Ruined; hopelessly beaten; =FINISHED: *After the fourth fumble they were cooked* **2** *adj* Drunk

cooked-up *adj* Specially contrived; expedient and dishonest: *It's insane why we give ourselves cooked up reasons for not moving the issue*—Westworld

cooker *See* FIRELESS COOKER, PRESSURE COOKER

cook someone's **goose** *v phr fr middle 1800s* To ruin or destroy someone; =FINISH ● Very often in the passive form, "our goose is cooked": *If he doesn't like it our goose is cooked*

cookie or **cookey** **1** *n* (also **cookee**) *merchant marine, lumberjacks & cowboys fr middle 1800s* A cook or cook's helper **2** *n narcotics* A person who prepares opium for smoking; opium addict **3** *n* An attractive young woman **4** *n* A person; =GAL, GUY: *real tough cookie/ shrewd cookie* ◁**5**▷ *n* (also **cookies**) *black* The female genitals; vulva **6** *n baseball* A base hit: *knowing I was going to get at least one cookie every game*—Sports Illustrated
See GRIPE one's ASS, THAT'S THE WAY THE BALL BOUNCES, TOUGH COOKIE

cookie-cutter or **cooky-cutter** **1** *n circus* A police officer's badge **2** *n* A weak and unenterprising person; =COOKIE-PUSHER, WIMP **3** *n* An inadequate weapon, esp a knife **4** *modifier* (also **cookie-cut**) Identical and unoriginal; standardized; stereotyped: *Friedman has created a cookie-cutter version of one of the most complex personalities*—New York/ *Each store is a cookie-cutter copy, laid out according to plans devised at the corporate headquarters*—New York Times/ *I'd never want to read that kind of cookie-cut magazine*—Philadelphia

cookie jar *See* WITH one's HAND IN THE TILL

cookie-pusher or **cooky-pusher** **1** *n* A weak and unenterprising person; =WIMP **2** *n* A person who pampers and flatters superiors; =APPLE-POLISHER, BROWN-NOSE **3** *n* A government career person, esp in the Department of State

cookies *See* COOKIE, SHOOT one's COOKIES

cooks *See* WHAT'S COOKING

Cook's tour *n phr* A complete and detailed viewing, esp when regarded as excessive: *I just wanted a look, not a damn Cook's tour* [fr the British travel agency Thos. *Cook* and Sons]

cook the books *v phr* To tamper with and falsify records, esp financial accounts: *The managers had cooked the books to the tune of $34 million*—Newsweek/ *He's been cooking the books for so many of those companies*—WT Tyler

cook up *v phr* To devise; fabricate; =HOKE UP: *We'll cook up a story to explain your swollen lip*

cook up a pill *v phr narcotics* To prepare opium for smoking

cook with gas (or **on the front burner**) *v phr fr 1930s jive talk* To perform very commendably; =GROOVE

cool **1** *v* To postpone; await developments in: *Let's cool this whole business for a week or so* **2** *v fr 1930s* To kill **3** *adj* In control of one's feelings; stoic: *Learn to be cool under fire* **4** *n: He lost his cool and bolted like a rabbit* **5** *adj beat & cool talk* Aloof and uninvolved; disengaged, as an expression of alienation; =BEAT, HIP: *He's cool, don't give a shit for nothing* **6** *n: My guru drifted me to a total spiritual cool* **7** *n 1940s cool musicians* Jazz marked by soft tones, improvisation based on advanced chord extensions, and revision of certain classical jazz idioms **8** *adj: cool jazz/ a real cool passage* **9** *adj beat & cool talk & counterculture* Excellent; good: *a cool shirt/ cool sermon* **10** *adj* Pleasant; desirable; =COPACETIC
See BLOW one's COOL, EYES TO COOL IT, LOSE one's COOL, PLAY IT COOL, ZERO COOL

cool (or **calm**) **as a Christian with aces wired** *adj phr* Serenely assured; tranquilly confident: *"We will take care of that," he says, cool as a Christian with aces wired*—Edward Abbey

cooled-out *adj* Relaxed; passionless: *a cooled-out sign linked to the mass media*—Time

the **cooler** *fr middle 1800s* **1** *n* A jail; =the SLAMMER **2** *n prison* A cell or cellblock for solitary confinement
See COFFEE COOLER

cool hand **1** *n phr* A person not easily disconcerted **2** *modifier: these four cool-hand lunatics*—Newsweek

cool one's **heels** *v phr* To wait, esp to be kept waiting: *I cooled my heels for two hours before the great one would see me*

cool it *beat & cool talk* **1** *v phr* To relax; stop being excited or angry **2** *v phr* To slow one's pace; stop being strenuous **3** *v phr* To stop what one is doing, esp what is annoying the speaker ● In all three senses often an exhortation or irritated command

cool off **1** *v phr* To become calmer and less explosive; moderate: *When he cooled off I spoke sweet reason* **2** *v phr* To kill: *The mob cooled off the late whoremaster*

cool out **1** *v phr horse-racing* To walk a horse after a race to calm and moderate it gradually **2** *v* *phr* beat & black To do the sex act **3** *v phr* To relax; become calm; =COOL IT: *I told him to cool out and stop complaining*

cool-out *n* A device or strategy intended to relax someone, esp to calm justified apprehensions: *cooperating in an Uncle Tom cool-out this late in the game*—Eldridge Cleaver/ *begins what he calls the "cool out." This prepares the man to accept defeat philosophically*—Wall Street Journal

cool someone **out** *fr beat & cool talk* **1** *v phr* To mollify and appease someone; calm someone's apprehensions or anger: *White Americans found a new level in which to cool the blacks out*—Eldridge Cleaver/ *He is the one who has to cool people out and pay off State officials*—New York **2** *v phr* To relax; become calm: *We've got to cool Bobby out before the teacher gets pissed off* **3** *v phr* To kill someone

coolville or **Coolville** *n* (also **coolsville** or **Coolsville**) Excellent; splendid: *Your little scheme's coolville*

◀**coon**▶ *n fr middle 1800s* A black person
   See ACE BOON COON

◀**coon box**▶ *See* GHETTO BOX

coop **1** *n* Any small and wretched building; hovel **2** *v* *police* To sleep while on duty; nap on the job, esp in a police car: *A couple of cops were cooping in the park/ There were the cats, the milkmen, and the cops cooping in a police car at the corner*—Earl Thompson **3** *n* A coupe car: *It's a Plymouth convertible coop*—John O'Hara
   See CHICKEN COOP, FLY THE COOP, HENCOOP, IN THE COOP, RAIN CATS AND DOGS

co-op or **coop** (KOH ahp) **1** *n* A cooperative apartment house, store, etc **2** *modifier*: *co-op prices/ coop apartment complex* **3** *v* To convert an apartment or building from a rental to a cooperative unit: *The old Sussex Arms got co-oped last year*
   See GO CO-OP

coop-happy *adj prison* =STIR-CRAZY

coot *n fr late 1700s* A stupid or silly person, usu an aged one: *a harmless old coot*
   See CRAZY AS A LOON

cootchie *See* HOOTCHIE-COOTCHIE

cootie *n esp WW1 Army fr British* A body louse [fr Malay, "dog tick"]

cootie-catcher *n* A folded-paper toy made by children and used to pretend to catch lice on other children

◁**cooz**▷ (Variations: **cooze** or **cou** or **couz** or **couzie** or **couzy** or **cuzzy**) **1** *n* A woman: *killed two quarts of tequila last night in Olvera Street, this Mexican cooz and I*—SJ Perelman/ *He runs. He screams like a cooze*—Robert Stone **2** *n* The female genitals; vulva **3** *n* A person, esp a woman, viewed solely as a sex object: *a piece of beautiful, dumb eighteen-year-old cooze*—Jackie Collins

cop **1** *n fr middle 1800s* A police officer **2** *v* To steal: *He copped six PCs from the shop* **3** *v* To win; be awarded: *to cop second place* **4** *v* To comprehend; grasp: *I don't quite cop your sense, pal* **5** *v narcotics* To buy or get narcotics: *The*

pusher has appeared,...they will make their roundabout way to him to "cop"*—J Mills [origin uncertain; perhaps ultimately fr Latin *capere* "seize," by way of French]
   See GOOD COP BAD COP

copacetic (KOH pə SET ik) *adj* (Variations: **copesetic** or **kopasetic** or **kopesetic** or **kopasetee** or **kopesetee**) *fr 1920s* As it should be; quite satisfactory; =COOL, OK [origin unknown]

◁**cop a** (or someone's) **cherry**▷ *v phr* To deprive someone of virginity; deflower someone

cop a feel *v phr* To feel or caress someone's body, esp the sex organs, usu in a sly or seemingly inadvertent way: *I thought he wanted to help me into the car, but I think he just wanted to cop a feel*

cop a heel (or **a mope**) *v phr outdated underworld* To escape from prison or the law

cop an attitude *See* HAVE AN ATTITUDE

cop and heel *outdated underworld* **1** *n phr* An escape from prison or the law; =GETAWAY **2** *n phr* =CLOSE CALL

cop a plea *v phr police & underworld* To plead guilty to a lesser charge than one might otherwise be tried for; escape a worse punishment by accepting a lesser one

copeck *n early 1900s* A silver dollar [fr the name of a Russian coin]

cop-heat *n* Police activity: *When there's cop-heat here, the prostitutes go there*—Los Angeles Times

copilot *n truckers* An amphetamine taken in order to stay awake

cop (or **buy**) **it** *v phr fr WW1* To die, esp to be killed in battle or otherwise: *He had a feeling he wouldn't cop it that day/ The guy who buys it...does it off camera*—Washington Post

cop-killer *n* A bullet capable of penetrating bulletproof vests: *the apple-green bullets they call cop-killers*—Chicago Tribune

cop out **1** *v phr underworld* To be arrested **2** *v phr* =COP A PLEA **3** *v phr esp 1960s counterculture* To avoid trouble and responsibility; evade an issue or problem; disengage oneself: *When his friends really needed help he copped out*

cop-out *n* An evasion; an excuse for inaction: *Arguing about standards is a "cop-out"*—P Sourain

copper[1] **1** *n fr middle 1800s* A police officer **2** *v*: *My old man coppered for thirty years* **3** *n underworld* An informer; =STOOL PIGEON **4** *n underworld* Time taken off a prison sentence for good behavior or because one has informed on colleagues

copper[2] *v gambling fr middle 1800s* To bet against a card, roll of the dice, person, etc [fr the use of a special metal chip by a gambler to indicate a "lose" bet in faro]

copper a tip *v phr gambling* To bet against a hunch or strong advice

copper-bottomed *adj* Genuine; authentic: *a copper-bottomed scoundrel* [fr the covering of a ship's bottom with copper plates to frustrate the shipworm]

copper-hearted *adj underworld* Likely to be an informer; untrustworthy

copper-on copper-off *n phr* gambling A system where one alternatively bets for and against, or bets and doesn't bet, etc

coppish or **capeesh** (kə PEESH) **1** *question* Do you understand?: *All right, class, that's all there is to it. Coppish?* **2** *affirmation* I understand: *Ten tonight? Capeesh* [fr Italian informal or dialect fr *capito* "I understand"]

cops *See* ON THE COPS

cop shop *n phr* A police station

copycat **1** *n* fr late 1800s An imitator; mimic **2** *modifier*: *a copycat inventor/ copycat crime*

copycat crime *n phr* A crime committed in imitation of another crime, esp one which is sensational and highly publicized: *Copy-Cat Crimes of the Heart* —Time

copy the mail *v phr* citizens band To listen to radio traffic; monitor

cop Zs (or **some Zs**) *v phr* (Variations: **bag** or **catch** or **cut** or **get** or **pile up** or **stack** may replace **cop**) fr black To take a nap; sleep; = SNOOZE: *got to peck a little, and cop me some Z's* —Malcolm X/ *sits around all day cutting Zs*—Motorcross Action Magazine [see some Zs]

core *See* HARD-CORE, SOFT-CORE

core dump **1** *v phr* computers To empty out the central memory of a computer **2** *v phr* fr computers To explain oneself fully; say one's piece, esp in the mode of complaint: *One of the semiconductor makers here went to see her manager the other day. Later she told a friend that she had "core dumped" on the boss*—New York Times

Corine *n* narcotics Cocaine

cork *See* BEHIND THE CORK, BLOW one's TOP, POP one's CORK

corked *adj* fr early 1900s Drunk

corker *n* fr early 1800s A person or thing that is remarkable, wonderful, superior, etc; = HUMDINGER, PISS-CUTTER [perhaps fr nautical slang *caulk* "do the sex act," whence notion of something special or prodigious]

corking fr late 1800s **1** *adv* Extremely; very: *to have a corking good time* **2** *adj* Excellent; wonderful: *a corking party*

corking mat *n phr* WW2 Navy A sleeping pad or a mattress

cork off *See* CAULK OFF

cork opera *n phr* A minstrel show [fr the burnt *cork* used to blacken skin]

corksacking *adj* Disgusting; depraved; = COCKSUCKING ● Euphemistic form of **cocksucking**: *you effing corksacking limey effer*—Anthony Burgess

corn **1** *n* Corn whiskey; moonshine **2** *n* fr jive talk Music, poetry, sentiment, etc, that is maudlin and naively affirmative of old-fashioned values; banal and emotionally overwrought material; = SCHMALTZ: *His ethical sincerity verges on corn* [second sense probably from the notion of *cornfed* as indicating rural simplicity and naivete]
See CANE CORN, CAN OF CORN

cornball fr jive talk **1** *n* A person who admires or produces markedly sentimental material and utters relatively simpleminded moral convictions:

Eisenhower on no account can be called a cornball —Robert Ruark **2** *adj*: *Where did you get those cornball notions?*

corn bill *See* CORN WILLIE

corned *adj* fr late 1700s Drunk
See HALF-CORNED

corner **1** *v* To turn corners on a street or road ● Used most often to characterize the behavior of a car in turning: *This car does not corner well* **2** *n* A person's special place or niche
See COFFIN CORNER, HOT CORNER

corn-fed **1** *adj* Plump and sturdy; rural or as if rural: *a corn-fed beauty* **2** *adj* Naive and sentimental; = CORNY

cornfield meet *n phr* railroad A head-on collision of trains

◀**cornhole**▶ *v* fr early 1900s To do anal intercourse; = BUGGER, BUNGHOLE: *so the Germans would get castrated when they cornholed him*—Trevanian/ *if Bartley had corn-holed the Irish maid in full view of wife and child*—Gore Vidal

corn juice (or **mule**) *n phr* fr middle 1800s Corn whiskey; moonshine

corn shucks *n phr* Tobacco

corn willie (or **bill**) *n phr* fr WW1 Army Corned beef [origin unknown]

corny *adj* fr jive talk Overly sentimental; banal; devoted to or expressing old-fashioned moral convictions; = CORNBALL: *He uses a corny ethos to get himself elected*

corporal *See* HOLLYWOOD CORPORAL

corporal's guard *n phr* A very small group: *a corporal's guard of adherents*

corpse *v* theater To embarrass a fellow performer by forgetting one's lines and failing to deliver a cue

corral (kə RAL) *v* To find; gather: *to corral votes*

cosh **1** *n* chiefly British fr late 1800s A bludgeon; blackjack **2** *v* To hit with a blackjack: *as these samurai cosh, ignite, bludgeon and blow away a host of contemptible nincompoops*—Washington Post

cosmo *n* The admired quality of cities; urbanness; cosmopolitanism: *the fashion runway of highstyle and cosmo*—Nashville

cotics *n* narcotics Narcotics

cotton *See* IN TALL COTTON, SHIT IN HIGH COTTON

cotton mouth *n phr* Dryness of the mouth caused by a hangover, use of marijuana or drugs, fear, etc

cotton-picking or **cotton-pickin'** *adj* Despicable; wretched; = DAMNED: *Take your cotton-pickin' hands off me/ none of your cotton-picking business/ They're out of their cotton-picking minds* —Washington Post [fr the inferior status of the field hand or poor farmer in southern US society]

cotton to *v phr* fr late 1700s British Approve of; like; appreciate; fancy: *We just didn't cotton to one another/ I don't cotton to your ogling my little sister* [perhaps fr Welsh *cytuno* "agree, consent"]

◁**cou**▷ *See* COOZ

couch *See* CASTING COUCH

couch case *n phr* An emotionally disturbed person

couch doctor *n phr* A psychoanalyst; = SHRINK

couch potato *n phr* A habitual lounger, esp a person who spends much time watching television: *They're not couch potatoes. They're mobile, they go out*—Washington Post/ *the period that Anglophile couch potatoes find most fascinating*—Book World

cough syrup *n phr 1920s underworld* Bribe or blackmail money paid to silence someone

cough up **1** *v phr fr late 1800s* To pay money or produce goods, esp with some reluctance: *When'll you cough up the rent?/ I saw you taking those pens. Cough them up* **2** *v phr fr 1300s* To tell or relate, esp under interrogation

could be *sentence* It is possible • Often a reply to a speculative question: *Is he still alive? Could be/ Could be they don't like us out there*
See EASY AS PIE

could not (or **could**) **care less** *v phr* One simply does not care; one is sublimely indifferent • In a curious development, the original British negative form has been changed to affirmative by many US speakers, without change of meaning: *I couldn't care less if you like me or not/ I could care less about his comfort, the old bastard*

count **See** DOWN FOR THE COUNT, NO-COUNT, TAKE THE LONG COUNT

countdown *n* The backward calling off of time units, esp of seconds, to the triggering of some event

be counted **See** STAND UP AND BE COUNTED

counter **See** COMMA-COUNTER

not count for spit **See** NOT COUNT FOR SPIT

country *adj* Very competent; reliable: *He's a country ball player; gets his pitches over the plate*
See ANOTHER COUNTRY HEARD FROM, GO OUT IN THE COUNTRY

country boy **See** NOT BAD FOR A COUNTRY BOY

a country mile *n phr* A very long distance: *She chased him a country mile*

count ties *v phr hoboes* To walk along a railroad track

county mounty *n phr citizens band* A county sheriff or deputy sheriff [second element fr *Mounty* or *Mountie* "member of the Royal Canadian Mounted Police"]

coupe **See** DEUCE

courage **See** DUTCH COURAGE

course **See** BIRD COURSE, CRIB COURSE, GUT COURSE, PAR FOR THE COURSE, PIPE COURSE, SNAP COURSE

court **See** the BALL IS IN someone's COURT, FULL COURT PRESS, HOME-COURT ADVANTAGE, KANGAROO COURT

cousin **1** *n* Friend; person • An amiable form of address: *How you doin', cousin?* **2** *n* A dupe; = MARK, PIGEON
See KISSING COUSIN, WHAT'S BUZZIN', COUSIN

◁**couz** or **couzie** or **couzy**▷ **See** COOZ

cove *n fr British fr 1500s* A man; fellow; = GUY • much more common in British use [fr Romany *kova* "thing"]

cover **1** *v* (also **cover up**) To protect someone with one's testimony: *I'll cover for you if you're* caught **2** *v* To substitute for someone; replace someone temporarily and protectively: *I'll cover if you want to take a day off* **3** *v* To attend to, esp temporarily: *Will you cover the switchboard while I'm at the dentist?* **4** *v* To travel: *I covered two miles in one minute* **5** *v* To complete an account; provide pertinent information: *That about covers what happened* **6** *v* To aim at with a firearm: *Freeze, I got you covered* **7** *n* A popular song recorded by artists other than those who made it famous: *third album, like the first two, contains many covers of recent chart-busters*—Rolling Stone **8** *v*: *They did best covering Springsteen and Stones hits* **9** *n espionage* An identity, usu an elaborate falsification, assumed by a secret agent for concealment: *To improve his cover he "resigned" from the agency*—C McCrystal
See BLOW someone's COVER

◁**cover** one's **ass**▷ (or **tail**) (also **CYA**) **1** *v phr* To provide or arrange for exculpation; devise excuses and alibis: *Some call it "risk management," others "covering your ass"*—Toronto Life/ *The FBI may have to let you be destroyed to cover its own ass*—Nat Hentoff/ *The one aspect I don't like up here is the covering-your-tail cautiousness*—Washington Post/ *CYA, you know, that old French expression that means making sure that when historians write about it all it won't be seen as happening on your shift*—Washington Post **2** *modifier: writing long cover-your-ass memos*—Village Voice

covered wagon *n phr WW2 Navy* An aircraft carrier

cover girl *n phr* A photographer's model or celebrity whose likeness appears on the cover of a magazine; a beautiful and glamorous young woman

cover story **1** *n phr espionage* The biography and plausible account devised for a secret agent for concealment **2** *n phr* An alibi; a false narrative explanation: *We agree on the cover story, that you haven't seen me for three weeks*

cover the waterfront *v phr* To be a complete account of something; be the whole story: *Lake covers premarital agreements, no-fault divorce...even a...will. That covers the waterfront*—Playboy [fr the title of a 1932 book by Max Miller, a journalist, exposing crime and corruption on the *waterfront*]

cover-up *n* Anything designed to conceal or obfuscate the truth by replacement: *Sending the Navy south instead of north was an obvious cover-up*

cow **1** *n fr early 1900s* Milk **2** *n* Cream or butter **3** *n* Beef: *a hunk of cow* ◁**4**▷ *n* A heavy, ungraceful person, esp a woman: *Easy, you big cow* ◁**5**▷ *n 1930s underworld* A young woman ◁**6**▷ *n* A woman, esp a dim and placid woman who appears to have been victimized by her female role: *The poor cow had eight kids before she figured out what was happening*
See ARMORED COW, BLACK COW, CANNED COW, CASH COW, CITY COW, HOLY CATS, SEA COW, TIN COW, WHITE COW

cowabunga **1** *interj surfers fr 1960s Australian* A surfer's exclamation of delight and commitment at the beginning of a ride, often used as a generalized cry of delight: *It was the real Andy Griffith, too: cowabunga*—Village Voice **2** *n* Energetic popular success in music: *make their most open bid yet for commercial cowabunga*—Village Voice

cowboy 1 *n* A reckless person, esp a driver or pilot: *Here comes that cowboy in his Porsche/ City Subway Mishaps Attributed To Speeding "Cowboy" Motormen*—New York Times **2** *n* The king of a suit of playing cards **3** *v underworld* To murder recklessly and openly: *even if we had to cowboy them (which) means that we were to kill them any place we found them even if it was in the middle of Broadway*—CA Wyer
See DRUGSTORE COWBOY

cowboy coffee *n phr* Black coffee: *air, self-esteem, cigarette butts, cowboy coffee*—Joseph Mitchell

cowboy job *n phr underworld* A robbery done recklessly and clumsily

cow-cage *n railroad* A cattle car

cow college (or **tech**) *n phr college students* A college rurally located and of humble distinction, esp an agricultural college: *Every instructor in every cow college is trying to get to be an assistant professor*—Philadelphia

cowflop or **cowflap** or **cowplop 1** *n* Cattle dung: *He is dumb as cowflop and hopeless at foot shufflin' and finger snappin', but he tries hard*—John Skow **2** *n* Nonsense; pretentious talk; = BULLSHIT: *I don't believe that cowflap*—Paul Theroux/ *Urban Cowplop*—Rolling Stone

cowhide *n* A baseball

◁**cow pilot**▷ *n phr airline* An airline stewardess; woman cabin attendant

cowpuncher or **cowpoke** *n* A cowboy [fr the use of metal-tipped prods to drive cattle into railroad cars]

cow-simple *adj 1930s underworld* In love with a woman or with women in general

cozy up *v phr* To become very friendly; court: *He started cozying up to the boss*

crab 1 *v fr early 1800s* To complain, esp to do so regularly; nag; = BITCH: *Crab, crab, crab, that was all she ever did*—Dorothy Parker **2** *n*: *He's an awful crab, never gives her a moment's peace* **3** *n* A resident of Annapolis, Maryland **4** *v* To spoil; ruin: *He's trying to crab the deal* **5** *v* To pilfer: *I crabbed six TVs* **6** *n hoboes* A type of flea

crabs *n* An infestation of crab lice in the pubic area: *Her friends slobbered, ripped off girls' dresses at parties, had crabs*—Philip Wylie

crack 1 *v* To enter or leave a place by force, esp to enter a place for robbery **2** *v* To open a safe or vault by force **3** *n* A try; attempt; = SHOT: *It looks impossible, but I'll take a crack at it* **4** *v* To go uninvited to a party; = CRASH **5** *v* To gain admittance to some desired category or milieu: *He finally cracked the best-seller list* **6** *v* To solve; reveal the secret of: *if they ever crack the problem of nuclear fusion* **7** *v circus & carnival* To reveal; disclose **8** *v* To change a banknote; = BREAK: *Can you crack a fifty?* **9** *v* (also **crack up**) To suffer an emotional or mental collapse; go into hys-

teria, depression, etc: *After six months of that it's a wonder she didn't crack* **10** *v* To give information, or to confess, after intense interrogation: *Buggsy cracked and spilled everything* **11** *v* To speak; talk; make remarks: *Listen, Ben, quit cracking dumb*—James M Cain **12** *n* A brief, funny, pungent, and often malicious remark; = WISECRACK: *What kind of a crack is that?/ One more crack like that and I'm going to sock you*—K Brush **13** *n* A great pleasure; a notable treat or regalement; kick: *That really gives me a crack!* **14** *v card players* In bridge, to double ◁**15**▷ *n* The vulva; = CUNT ◁**16**▷ *n* The deep crease between the buttocks **17** *n narcotics* Very pure cocaine intended for smoking rather than inhalation; = COKE: *Crack's low price and quick payoff make it especially alluring to teenagers*—Time
See FALL BETWEEN THE CRACKS, GIVE something A SHOT, HAVE A CRACK AT something, WISECRACK

crack a book (or **the books**) *v phr students* To study ● Nearly always in the negative: *He tried to pass the course without cracking a book/ The exam's coming up and I better crack the books*

crack a deal *See* CUT A DEAL

crack a smile *v phr* To start to smile: *I wiggled my ears but she wouldn't crack a smile*

crackbrained *adj fr 1600s* Crazy; eccentric; wild; = CRACKPOT

crackdown *n* A particular instance or severity of punishment, law enforcement, etc: *The Mayor again vowed a crackdown on the porn shops*

crack down *fr 1920s* **1** *v phr* To enforce the law more vigorously; = CLAMP DOWN: *Cops will crack down on drunk drivers* **2** *v phr* To exercise a prerogative of severity not ordinarily used: *If there's any more tardiness I'll crack down*

cracked 1 *adj* Crazy; eccentric: *You're cracked if you think I'll stay now* **2** *adj* Stupid; foolish
See GET one's NUTS

cracked up *part phr* Said; praised ● most often in the negative: *The beer ain't what it's cracked up to be* [fr earlier sense of *crack*, "boast, brag"]

cracker *n late 1700s* A Southern rustic or poor white; = REDNECK [probably from their use of whips with a piece of buckskin at the end for *cracking*]
See BONE-CRACKER, DIAMOND-CRACKER, JAWBREAKER, SAFECRACKER

cracker-barrel 1 *adj* Unsophisticated; basic: *a cracker-barrel philosophy* **2** *adj* Intimate; gossipy: *a cracker-barrel discussion of family* [fr the archetypical image of rural discussants sitting on or around the *cracker barrel* in the general store]

cracker box *n phr Army* An Army ambulance

cracker factory *n phr* A mental hospital; = LOONEY BIN, NUT HOUSE

crackerjack or **crackajack 1** *n fr late 1800s* A person or thing that is remarkable, wonderful, superior, etc: *Signorelli is a crackerjack* **2** *modifier: Orne...estimates that a crackerjack examiner working under optimum conditions would find 10 to 15 percent of his cases to be inconclusive*—Washingtonian/ *I'm a crackerjack story teller*—Pulpsmith [apparently a reduplication of *cracker* in the mid-

19th-century British sense "something approaching perfection," which is also reflected in terms like *crack shot*, *crack troops*, etc, and based on an echoic expression of speed; hence also *cracking*; the term is reinforced in the US by late-19th-century trade name *Cracker Jack* for a popcorn and peanut confection]

crackers *adj* Crazy; =CRACKED ● Chiefly British use: *You must wed me, for I'm crackers over you/ Also he was plain crackers*—Saul Bellow [formed with the British suffix *-ers*, like *bonkers*, *preggers*, etc]

cracking *fr late 1800s British* **1** *adj* Excellent; first-rate: *a cracking meal* **2** *adv* Very: *a cracking good meal*
See GET CRACKING

crack one's **jaw** *v phr* To brag

crack off *v phr* To make nasty or boastful remarks

crackpot **1** *n* A crazy idiot; an addled fool; eccentric: *He's a crackpot about flying saucers* **2** *adj*: *my colleague's crackpot notions*

cracks *See* FALL BETWEEN THE CRACKS

crackup **1** *n* A collision, crash, etc: *a bad car crackup/ airline crackup* **2** *n* A mental or emotional breakdown: *Have you read Fitzgerald's The Crackup?* **3** *n* A very funny person or thing: *His Cagney sketch is a crackup*

crack up **1** *v phr* To collide; crash: *The trucks cracked up head-on* **2** *v phr* (also **crack**) To suffer an emotional or mental breakdown; go into hysteria, depression, etc: *Jimmy felt that he was cracking up*—Calder Willingham **3** *v phr* To have a fit of uncontrollable laughter: *He cracked up when he heard Richard Pryor*

crack wise *v phr* To make quick, pungent, witty, and often malicious remarks: *All you do is crack wise*—Raymond Chandler

cradle *n railroad* A gondola car
See ROB THE CRADLE

cradle-robber or **cradle-snatcher** **1** *n* A person who prefers relatively younger sex or courtship partners **2** *n* A recruiter or sports scout who solicits very young persons
See ROB THE CRADLE

cram *fr early 1800s* **1** *v* To study intensively for an upcoming examination **2** *modifier: a cram session/ cram book* **3** *n* A very diligent student; =GRIND

cram it *See* STICK IT

cramp someone's **style** *v phr fr 1920s* To be a hindrance or distraction: *Your blank stare cramps my style*

crank **1** *n fr late 1800s* An eccentric person, esp one who is irritable or maliciously mischievous: *That crank wants a yogurt shampoo/ All kinds of cranks took credit for the murder* **2** *modifier: crank letters/ crank phone calls* **3** *n* narcotics Methamphetamine, a stimulant; =SPEED [fr earlier English, "twisted, bent"; hence the bent lever for turning or starting machines with associated senses of producing, commencing, speeding, etc]

crank back *v phr* To return to an earlier stage: *We've got to crank right back to where we started*

cranked up *adj phr* Excited and eager; keen for action; =CHARGED UP, PUMPED UP: *Those guys are really cranked up for the finals*

crank something **out** *v phr* To produce or make something, esp with mechanical precision and regularity: *with the kind of junk the studios are cranking out*—J Bell

crank someone or something **up** **1** *v phr* To get someone started; instigate someone's action: *The people around Reagan...talk about "We'll crank him up on this"*—Washington Post **2** *v phr* To make excited, eager, keenly ready for action, etc: *You better crank the quarterback up if you want this team to score* **3** *v phr* To get something started; put something in operation: *Let's crank up the dog project tomorrow*

cranky *adj* Very irritable; touchy: *The baby was cranky all day*

◁**crap**▷ **1** *n fr middle 1800s British* Feces; excrement; =SHIT **2** *v*: *Where's the bathroom, I have to crap* **3** *interj* An exclamation of disbelief, disgust, disappointment, rejection, etc: *Oh, crap, I broke it again* **4** *n fr early 1900s* Nonsense; pretentious talk; bold and deceitful absurdities; =BULLSHIT: *I'm not interested in stories about the past or any crap of that kind*—Arthur Miller **5** *v* To lie, exaggerate; try to deceive: *You can't crap an old crapper* **6** *n* Offensive and contemptuous treatment; overt disrespect: *but I don't take crap from anybody*—Us **7** *n* Anything of shoddy quality; pretentious and meretricious trash: *Her new show is pious crap* [by extension fr Middle English *crap* "chaff, siftings of grain, residue"]
See ALL THAT KIND OF CRAP, FULL OF SHIT, SHOOT THE BULL

crape-hanger **1** *n* A habitually morose person; pessimist; =KILLJOY **2** *n* An undertaker

crap game *See* FLOATING CRAP GAME

◁**crap list**▷ *See* SHIT LIST

◁**crapoid**▷ *adj* Disgusting; nasty; wretched; =CRAPPY: *Clover said they were crapoid for thinking that*—Paul Theroux

◁**crapola**▷ **1** *n* Lies and exaggeration; =BULLSHIT: *odious even by the usual standards of feminist crapola*—Village Voice/ *grinding out the old heartfelt crapola*—Peter De Vries **2** *modifier: the latest trends in crapola entertainment*

◁**crapper**▷ **1** *n* A toilet: *We'd just like to know if the governor of the state is aware of that damned thing in the crapper*—Earl Thompson **2** *n* A person who regularly lies and exaggerates; a boaster and self-advertiser: *I call your great guru a mean little crapper* **3** *n* Something disgusting, nasty, or shoddy: *Oh, Mondays are a crapper*—Westworld [fr *crap*]

◁**crappy**▷ **1** *adj* Of inferior quality; shoddy: *the crappiest shoes I ever had* **2** *adj* Very unpleasant; nasty: *my crappy hometown/ a crappy thing to say*

crash **1** *v* To break into a building; enter by force: *Hoover's men crashed Doc's apartment*—A Hynd **2** *v* To rob a place, esp by breaking in; =CRACK **3** *v* To gain admittance to some desired category or milieu: *In LA she tried to crash TV* **4** *v* (also **crash the gate**) To go to a party or other event uninvited or without tickets **5** *v* *beat talk & counterculture* To sleep or live at a place for a day or so, usu without invitation: *I heard about this place and hoped I could crash here for a day or two* —P Curtis **6** *v* To go to sleep **7** *v* *narcotics* To lose consciousness from narcotics or alcohol **8** *n* *narcotics* The empty feeling, depression, etc, felt when a euphoric intoxication ends; =LETDOWN: *The "crash" from coke...is grim*—Time **9** *v* *computer* To fail suddenly: *The spacecraft's No 1 computer..."crashed" or shut down*—Time/ *computers that can alert a mainframe owner to an impending computer "crash"*—New York Times

crash and burn *Army* **1** *v phr* To fail entirely; =BLOW IT **2** *v* To collapse from exhaustion; =POOP OUT: *I was just about to crash and burn* —Armistead Maupin **3** *v* To concentrate entirely on one task

crashed *adj* Drunk

crashout *n underworld & prison* A prison escape; jailbreak

crash out *v phr underworld & prison* To escape from prison

crash pad *n phr beat talk & counterculture* A place to sleep or live for a day or so, esp for young people traveling about more or less aimlessly and with little money

crash program (or **project**) *n phr* An intense and extraordinary effort to a specific end: *Getting the refugees housed needed a crash program*

crate **1** *n* A car, bus, airplane, etc, esp an old rickety one **2** *n hoboes* A jail

crate of sand *n phr truckers* A truckload of sugar

crawfish *v fr middle 1800s* To renege; retreat; =BACK OUT: *He started to crawfish when he realized who the competition was*

crawl **1** *v* To go or move very slowly: *Traffic was crawling that day* ◁**2**▷ *v* To do the sex act with; mount: *He crawled her once or twice* **3** *v WW1 Army* To reprimand severely; =CHEW OUT **4** *n 1930s college students* A dance; =HOP
See PUB CRAWL

crawl someone's **hump** *v phr cowboys* To assault someone; =CLOBBER

crawling with *adj phr* Well provided with; =LOUSY WITH: *He's crawling with guilt*

crawl (or **come**) **out of the woodwork** *v phr* To appear, materialize, interfere, etc, as or like something very loathsome: *A lot of them are weirdos who just crawled out of the woodwork*—WT Tyler/ *Any time there's a juicy scandal a lot of creeps come out of the woodwork* [fr the notion that worms, spiders, maggoty creatures, rats, etc, dwell in hidden places]

crazy **1** *adj esp 1940s bop talk* Excellent; splendid; =COOL **2** *n* An inmate of a mental hospital; psychiatric patient **3** *n* A destructive and irrational person; =LOONY: *Some crazies took over the US Embassy/ We're going to prevent the right-wing crazies from bombing and destroying* —Playgirl

See LIKE CRAZY, STIR CRAZY

-crazy *combining word* Inordinately devoted to or manic over what is indicated: *boy-crazy/ kill-crazy/ speed-crazy*

crazy about (or **over** or **for**) *adj phr* Very enthusiastic about; infatuated with; =NUTS ABOUT: *I'm crazy about Ronnie*

crazy as a loon (or **a coot** or **a bedbug**) *adj phr fr middle 1800s* Insane; =NUTTY: *If you think that, you're crazy as a loon* [fr the loon's or coot's cry, like an insane laugh, and the bedbug's frantic rushing about when exposed]

crazy-house *n* A mental hospital; insane asylum

creak *v* To be worn out; be near collapse: *indications that their marriages are creaking*—Philadelphia Journal

creaker *n* An old person or old thing: *That plot is something of a creaker*

cream **1** *v esp 1920s* To cheat or deprive someone of something, esp by silky glibness: *I got creamed out of the hotel spot in Ohio*—John O'Hara/ *a smoothie who wolfed on a friend and creamed his lady*—World's Work **2** *v esp students* To do very well against; overcome; =CLOBBER: *I creamed the philosophy exam/ The basketball team got creamed* ◁**3**▷ *v* To be sexually aroused, esp so as to secrete sexual fluids, either semen or lubricants: *He thinks we're gettin' all agitated...over here creamin' in our drawers*—John Sayles/ *It made me cream in my panties, isn't that fun?*—Interview
See HEAVY CREAM, ICE CREAM, ICE CREAM HABIT

creamie *n* A white or clear playing marble

◁**cream** one's **jeans** (or **silkies**)▷ *v phr* To become sexually excited; exude sexual fluids: *any idea how them ladies cream their silkies watching a muscular and handsome guy*—Tom Aldibrandi

cream puff **1** *n phr* A weakling; =SISSY, WIMP: *Opponents might get the idea...Lemonick is a cream puff*—D Cresan **2** *n phr salespersons* Something for sale, esp a used car in splendid condition and a tremendous bargain: *before you believe, much less see, any of the "creampuffs" in the...classifieds*—Philadelphia

cream-puff hitter *n phr baseball* A weak hitter

cream up *v phr* To execute perfectly: *You guys know what you're supposed to do and when, so let's cream this up*—New Yorker

creative accounting *n phr* Fraudulent or dubious bookkeeping; falsification of financial records: *secret takeover deals, creative accounting just this side of Internal Revenue Service rules*—New York Times

creek *See* UP SHIT CREEK

creep *n fr 1930s students* A disgusting and obnoxious person; =CRUD, JERK, NERD: *The man is nothing but a creep*—Quentin Reynolds/ *poets loyal to Blake and Whitman, the "holy creeps"*—Saul Bellow [fr the notion of making one's flesh *creep*]

creeper **1** *n truckers* The lowest gear on a truck **2** *n radio studio* A performer who moves closer and closer to the microphone **3** *n underworld fr 1930s* A sneak thief

creepers *n* =SNEAKERS

Creepers *n* & *interj* Christ ● A euphemistic form: *Creepers, but that was a nasty moment*
See JEEPERS CREEPERS

creeping *adj* Slow and gradual: *creeping idiocy/ creeping socialism*

creeping crud *n phr fr WW2 armed forces* Any disease, esp an unnamed and prevalent flulike disorder or an unexplained and nasty rash [a reduplicating expansion of *crud*]

creep-joint *n underworld fr 1920s* A gambling meet that moves about to avoid arrest; =FLOATING CRAP GAME

the **creeps** **1** *n phr fr middle 1800s* Sensations of fear and loathing, such that one's flesh seems to formicate; revulsion: *His smarm gives me the creeps* **2** *n phr* Delirium tremens: *He was not in with the creeps but with a broken leg*—John McNulty

creepy **1** *adj* Frightening; scary; =HAIRY: *a creepy show about necrophiles* **2** *adj* Loathsome; disgusting: *a creepy little chap with an enormous bow tie*

creepy-crawly **1** *adj* Loathsome; repellent; =CREEPY: *The trio plunges into the creepy-crawly high life of Acapulco*—Richard Grenier **2** *n* A nasty creature, esp the caterpillar, snake, or centipede sort: *the lair, maybe, Of creepy-crawlies or a ghost*—WH Auden

cretinoid *college students* **1** *n* A cretin; idiot; =SPASTIC **2** *modifier: El Presidente, and others too cretinoid to mention*—Drew Acorn

cretinous *adj computer* Wrong; inoperative; wretchedly designed; =BLETCHEROUS

crew *See* CHECK CREW

crib **1** *n students fr early 1800s* A set of answers used to cheat on an examination **2** *v: He cribbed on the econ exam and got caught* **3** *n hoboes & underworld fr 1920s* A place where thieves and hoodlums congregate; cheap saloon: *a sleazy crib on Second Ave* **4** *v fr 1700s* To steal **5** *n fr Australian fr early 1900s* A brothel **6** *n* A nightclub; =DIVE: *I am singing for coffee and cakes at a crib on Cottage Grove Avenue*—John O'Hara **7** *n railroad* A caboose **8** *n teenagers* Home

crib course *n phr college students* An easy college course; =GUT COURSE: *Even at Stanford or Johns Hopkins the student in desperate need of a crib course can be sure to find one*—Washington Post [fr student senses of *crib*]

crib crime (or **job**) *n phr* The robbing or mugging of an old person

not **cricket** *See* NOT CRICKET

Crikey *n* & *interj* Christ ● Chiefly British euphemism: *Crikey but it was a rum go*

crime *See* COPYCAT CRIME

Criminy or **Crimus** (KRI mə nee, KRĪ məs) *n* & *interj* Christ ● A euphemistic form: *Criminy, I've been hoodwinked/ Crimus but it's cold*

crimp **1** *n* A restriction; obstacle: *He kept putting crimps into my plan* **2** *v: I'll crimp him good with this nasty rule*

crip **1** *n esp hoboes & underworld* A cripple; =GIMP: *"Phony crips" as the fraudulent cripples call each other*—New Yorker **2** *n* A pool ball so positioned as to be easy to win **3** *n* (also **crip course**) *outdated college students* An easy course; =CRIB COURSE, GUT COURSE, SNAP

Cripes or **Cripus** *n* & *interj fr 1840s* Christ ● A euphemistic form: *Cripes, what a rotten deal*

crip-faker *n hoboes* A professional beggar who feigns being badly crippled

Crisco *n* An obese person; =FATTY [fr *Crisco*, trade name for a kind of shortening sold in cans, hence, "fat in the can"]

Crisco disco *n phr* A nightclub or discotheque frequented by male homosexuals [fr the presumed use of *Crisco* as a lubricant for anal intercourse]

croak **1** *v fr early 1800s* To die: *I had the horse trained, then he up and croaked on me* **2** *v* To murder: *He croaked a screw at Dannemora*—Joel Sayre

croaker *n underworld, hoboes & circus* A physician: *Don't say "croaker," say "doctor"*—Nelson Algren

crock **1** *n* A disliked person, esp an old person: *a lot of old crocks with baggy eyes*—R Starnes **2** *n* A drunkard: *a rummy crock* **3** *n merchant marine* A bargelike cargo ship made of cement **4** *v* To hit; =CLOBBER, CLOCK: *I crocked the orderly with a bedspring*—Raymond Chandler **5** *v* To ruin; wreck; =QUEER: *Calling the pitch...lies, as you might imagine, crocked the job*—Philadelphia **6** *n* =CROCK OF SHIT **7** *n computer* Something, esp a program, that functions erratically **8** *n computer* An overly complicated and inalterable program

crocked *adj* Drunk

crockery **1** *n* The teeth **2** *n baseball* A pitcher's arm that becomes lame and ineffective; =GLASS ARM

crockie *n* A playing marble with a blue or brown glazed surface

◁**crock of shit**▷ *n phr* Nonsense; lies and exaggerations; mendacious cant; =BULLSHIT: *characterized reports of TJ Club activity in Weinstein's campaign as a "crock of shit"*—Village Voice/ *Asked about Burns's contention...he replied, "That's a crock of shit"*—Toronto Life

cronk *adj fr middle 1800s* Drunk [fr German *krank* "ill"]

crook **1** *n fr late 1800s* A habitual or professional criminal; a consistently dishonest person: *The chief said, "I'm not a crook"* **2** *v: He crooked my socks*—E Kasser

crooked (KRŏŏ kəd) *adj* Dishonest; fraudulent; criminal

crooked arm *n phr baseball* A lefthanded pitcher

crooker *See* PINKY-CROOKER

crook the elbow *See* BEND THE ELBOW

croon **1** *v* To sing in a relaxed and mellow style: *Rudy Vallee crooned his way to immortality* **2** *v* To sing

cropper *See* COME A CROPPER

croppy *n railroad* A corpse: *If you don't want a croppy on your hands, start firing the locomotive* —G Jones

cross *v* To act contrary to someone's wishes; attempt to thwart someone; contradict: *You must not cross me on this*
See DOUBLE CROSS, NAIL someone TO THE CROSS

cross-dresser *n* A transvestite: *I'm constantly getting calls from cross-dressers who think I could use their talents*—Village Voice

crossed idiotsticks *n phr Army* The crossed rifles of the infantry insignia

cross-eyed *See* LOOK AT someone CROSS-EYED

cross my heart or **cross my heart and hope to die** *sentence* I am telling the truth; I swear this is the truth: *I love you, baby. Cross my heart*

cross someone's **palm** *See* GREASE someone's PALM

crossroader *n police* A person who cheats slot machines: *one of the world's greatest crossroaders, or slot-machine cheats*—Wall Street Journal

cross-up **1** *n* An error, esp one caused by misunderstanding: *nobody's fault, just a cross-up* **2** *n* = DOUBLE CROSS

cross someone **up** *v phr* To confuse or deceive someone: *He had to cross up the blocking backs*

crotch worker *n phr police* A shoplifter who conceals loot under her dress

Crow **1** *n fr WW1 Navy* The eagle on naval insignia **2** *n Navy* A naval petty officer or captain who wears the eagle insignia **3** *n WW2 armed forces* Chicken **4** *v* To boast in exultation; flatter oneself: *That poem's nothing to crow about*
See JANE CROW, JIM CROW

crowbait *n cowboys* An old, mean, or ugly horse

crowd **1** *n* A group, faction, clique, etc: *I got no crowd, I'm a very private person* **2** *n* An audience: *The crowd loved you tonight, darling* **3** *n lunch counter* Three of anything
See GO ALONG WITH THE CROWD

crowd someone *v* To press or importune someone; encroach on someone's territory or safety: *Don't crowd me now, just let me handle it*

Crow Jim *n phr* Strong antiwhite prejudice among blacks: *the form of reverse prejudice known as Crow Jim*—Esquire

crown *v* To hit someone, esp on the head; = BEAN, CONK: *If she finds out she'll crown me*

crown fire *n phr lumberjacks* A severe hangover

crow tracks *n phr Army* Chevrons showing noncommissioned officers' rank; = STRIPES

crud or **crut** ◁1▷ *n* Dried semen **2** *n Army fr 1920s* Any venereal disease **3** *n* (also **the crud**) Any disease, esp one featuring a rash or obvious skin eruption; any unnamed disease: *I probably picked up the crud that's going around* **4** *n* A dirty and slovenly person; = DIRTBALL: *I used to be a smelly crud* **5** *n* Anything loathsome or markedly inferior: *His new show's a piece of crud* **6** *modifier:* *It's in your ballpark, since you love the crud detail*—Erma Bombeck [fr Middle English, "coagulated milk or other substance, curd," of unknown origin]

See CREEPING CRUD

cruddy **1** *adj* Nasty; loathsome; repellent **2** *adj* Somewhat ill and indisposed; under par; = BLAH: *I'm not exactly sick, I just feel cruddy*

cruft **1** *n computer* A repellent substance; = CRAP, CRUD: *Clean that cruft up off the floor* **2** *n* The consequences of inferior construction: *He tried for elegance in that design, but ended up with cruft*

cruise **1** *v* To drive slowly and watchfully in the streets, walk about vigilantly in bars and parties, etc, looking for a sex partner: *He started cruising the singles bars* **2** *v* To make a subtle or casual sexual approach: *I dated girls but at the same time was still cruising guys*—Deviant Reality **3** *v Philadelphia black* To sleep **4** *v counterculture* To be smoothly going about one's business: *He was still "cruising nice and mellow" from an acid trip two nights before*—New York Magazine/ *Times were tough, but now I'm cruising along*
See LET'S BOOGIE, SHAKEDOWN CRUISE

cruiser *n* A person who cruises: *"Looking for Mr Goodbar," which was told from a female cruiser's point of view*—New York Magazine

cruising for a bruising *v phr teenagers & college students* Looking for trouble; courting violence, esp while riding about in a car

cruit (KRo͞oT) *n Army fr WW1* A recruit

crumb or **crum** **1** *n hoboes, cowboys & armed forces fr late 1800s* A louse or bedbug **2** *n hoboes* A blanket roll or pack; = BINDLE **3** *n* A dirty, slovenly person; = CRUD, DIRTBALL **4** *n* A loathsome, contemptible person; = CREEP

crumb boss **1** *n phr lumberjacks* A bunkhouse janitor **2** *n phr railroad* A person in charge of a work-crew's car

crumb-bun or **crum-bun** *n* A contemptible person; = BUM, CRUMB: *Boxing also attracts some of the nicest, but they still can't outnumber the crum-buns* —Arthur Daley/ *Unlike the other critic crumb-buns, he has a soul*—Saul Bellow

crumbcrusher *n* (Variations: **crumbcruncher** or **crumbgrinder** or **crumbsnatcher**) *esp students fr 1930s black* A baby; small child: *when your own li'l crumbcrushers suffered through fatherless periods*—Douglas Turner/ *Here comes one crumbsnatcher, then two*—Joseph A Walker

crumb joint (or **house**) *n phr hoboes* A cheap lodging house; = FLEABAG, FLOPHOUSE

crumb-roll *n hoboes* A bedroll or blanket roll; bed

crumbs *n* A little money; a pittance; = COFFEE AND CAKES, PEANUTS: *Hell no. I won't work for crumbs, I want bread*

crumb (or **crum**) **the deal** *v phr* To spoil a plan; = LOUSE UP

crumb (or **crum**) **up** **1** *v phr* To spoil; confuse; = MESS UP: *He tried too hard and crumbed the whole thing up* **2** *v phr hoboes & WW1 Army* To clean clothing thoroughly, esp to delouse

crummy or **crumby** **1** *adj esp hoboes, cowboys & armed forces fr middle 1800s British* Infested with body lice; lousy **2** *adj* Loathsome; disgusting; = LOUSY: *I'd be dead of the dirty monotony around this crummy neighborhood*—Nelson

Algren **3** *adj* Of inferior quality; shoddy; =CHEAP: *This crumby razor doesn't work/ Where'd you get that crummy camera?* **4** *adj* Insignificant; trifling; paltry; =PISSY: *Just two days, two crummy days, an' I woulda been here myself*—WT Tyler **5** *n* hoboes A caboose: *expecting that thousands of the so-called "crummies" will soon be rolling off into the sunset*—Newsweek **6** *n* railroad A work-crew bunk car [origin unknown; perhaps fr the resemblance of a louse to a *crumb*]

crumped out *adj phr* Drunk

crunch *fr outdated black* **1** *n* A crisis; a desperate climax: *Then came the political conventions that summer, and more crunches*—Clay Felker **2** *n* A critical situation, esp one where two seemingly contrary forces are in play; =SQUEEZE: *A "crunch" is characterized by a skyrocketing of interest rates and a choking off of the availability of credit*—L Silk **3** *n* Tension and strife between opposing interests: *The "crunch" between press and Government is inevitable in American affairs*—J Raymond **4** *v* computer To process, usu in a wearisome way

cruncher *See* NUMBER CRUNCHER

crunchie *n* Army An infantry soldier

crunching *See* NUMBER-CRUNCHING, NUT-CRUNCHING

crupper *n* line repairers A body belt; safety harness

crush **1** *n* *fr early 1900s* A passing infatuation: *It's only a schoolgirl crush* **2** *n* A thick crowd; heavily crowded place **3** *v* To humiliate someone; reduce someone to helpless dismay: *Her snub crushed me*

See HAVE A CRUSH ON someone, ORANGE CRUSH

crusher *See* BONE-CRUSHER, CINDER CRUSHER, ROCK CRUSHER

crush out *v phr* underworld To escape from prison: *who had crushed out of Leavenworth*—Dashiell Hammett

crush-out *n* underworld An escape from prison; =JAILBREAK

crust *n* *fr early 1900s* Bold audacity; gall; =CHUTZPA: *You've got a hell of a crust assuming I'll go down there*—Raymond Chandler

See the UPPER CRUST

crusty *adj* Gruff; surly; =FEISTY: *Crusty George Meany....The downturned lips, the jowls, the half-closed lids, all were dour*—Time

crut *See* CRUD

crutch **1** *n* *outdated black* A car **2** *n* narcotics A container for a hypodermic needle **3** *n* narcotics =ROACH CLIP

crybaby **1** *n* A person given to weeping or lamenting at the least adversity, esp from self-pity **2** *modifier*: *None of your crybaby pleas, please/ The Georgetown basketball team...has continued its crybaby act*—Milwaukee Journal

cry in one's **beer** *v phr* To indulge in a session of lamentation or weeping; feel keenly sorry for oneself

crying *See* FOR CRYING OUT LOUD

crying jag *n phr* A fit of uncontrollable weeping, often accompanying drunkenness: *Florence got reg-*

ular crying jags and the men sought to cheer and comfort her*—Dorothy Parker

crying room *n phr* A fancied place where one can go to bewail a defeat, disappointment, etc

crying towel *n phr* A fancied towel offered in ironic sympathy to one who laments undeserved ill fortune, unbearable reverses, etc: *Get out the crying towel, old Frank got another parking ticket*

crystal *n* narcotics Narcotics in powdered form, esp amphetamines

◁ **ct** or **CT** ▷ *n* =COCK-TEASER

CTD *adj* hospital Nearly dead [fr *circling the drain,* that is, about to go down]

cub **1** *n* *newspaper office* A novice reporter **2** *n* Any novice or apprentice **3** *modifier*: *a cub reporter/ cub professor*

cubby *n* black A room or dwelling; =PAD [fr *cubbyhole* fr middle 19th century]

cube **1** *n* A very conformistic and conventional person; =SQUARE **2** *n* narcotics A portion of a narcotic: *He wanted a couple cubes, two cubes I had*—Prison

cubehead *n* narcotics A frequent user of LSD [fr sugar *cube,* into which LSD can be soaked before taking]

the cubes *n phr* Dice; a pair of dice: *He chose to stake his hopes...on one throw of the cubes*—G Talbot

cuckoo or **coo-coo** **1** *adj* *fr early 1900s* Crazy; very eccentric; =NUTTY **2** *n*: *Stop acting like a cuckoo*

cuckooed *adj* Drunk

cuddle-bunny *n esp 1940s teenagers* An attractive young woman, esp one who is generous with sexual favors

cue *v baseball* To hit a baseball hard and straight, as if with a pool cue

cueball **1** *n* *WW2 armed forces & students* A man or boy with a bald, shaven, or close-clipped head **2** *n* An eccentric person; =ODDBALL

cue in *v phr* To add to, or interpolate into, a script, film, etc: *Change the setting to Arizona and cue in some songs for Doris Day*—Richard Bissell

cue someone **in** *v phr* To explain: *I didn't understand until she cued me in to the procedure*

cuff *fr early 1900s* **1** *v* To borrow money from someone, usu in an urgent way **2** *v* To charge something, esp on an expense account: *No man...feels he is getting ahead until he can cuff a few tabs on the firm*—Hal Boyle [fr the notion of keeping track of debts by notations on the *cuff* of one's shirt]

See FOR THE CUFF, OFF THE CUFF, ON THE CUFF, PUT THE CUFF ON someone, STUFF CUFF

cuffers *n* Short socks; anklets

◁ **cuff** one's **meat** ▷ *v phr* To masturbate: *He'd still be cuffing his meat in Spain*—Tom Aldibrandi

cuffo or **cufferoo** *adj* Free of charge; nonpaying; on credit: *not a spending party, strictly cufferoo*—John O'Hara/ *before you caught your cuffo flight*—Paul Sann

cuffs *n* Handcuffs

culture vulture *n phr* An enthusiastic devotee of the arts and of intellectual pursuits, esp a pretentious one: *Culture vultures to the contrary, there is more integrity to the guy*—San Francisco

◁**cum¹**▷ *See* COME

cum² (KYo͞oM) *college students* **1** *n* The cumulative academic average of a student **2** *v* To study hard; strive for a high grade-point average

cumshaw *n Navy fr British fr early 1800s* Irregular acquisitions; = MIDNIGHT REQUISITIONS

◀**cunt**▶ **1** *n* The vulva **2** *n* A woman: *Why didn't he spin off this stupid cunt*—Saul Bellow **3** *n homosexuals* A fellow male homosexual one dislikes: *and this one is from Max, the cunt*—Arthur Maling **4** *n* Sexual favors and indulgence; = ASS, FUCKING: *But some of their daughters were giving away more cunt than Dixie was selling*—Claude Brown

◀**cuntface** or **cunthead**▶ *n* A despicable person; = BASTARD: *cunthead...you wretched fart*—John Irving

◀**cunt-hair**▶ *n* A very small amount or distance; minute amount; = SMIDGEN, TAD: *knows when it's off center, even when it's only a cunt hair off*—William Kennedy

◀**cunt-lapper**▶ *n* A person who does cunnilingus; = MUFF-DIVER

◀**cunt-lapping**▶ *n* Cunnilingus: *nor induced Maurice White to advocate cunt-lapping*—Village Voice

◀**cunt meat**▶ *n phr* Women; women's quality: *He was drowning in cunt meat. Tina's and his mother's, waves of it*—Patrick Mann

◀**cuntmobile**▶ *n* = RAPE WAGON

◀**cunt-struck**▶ *n* Dominated by a woman; henpecked; = PUSSY-WHIPPED

a **cup** *n phr lunch counter* A cup of coffee

cupcake **1** *n* An eccentric person; = NUTBALL: *regarding puppeteers as kind of weird cupcakes who play with dolls*—Washington Post/ *the publishing cupcake...who nailed you on the couch and then fired you*—R Grossbach **2** *n* An attractive young woman; = CHICK: *Flossie was a saucy blonde cupcake then*—William Kennedy/ *In her...don't-think-I'm-just-another-cupcake suit, Geraldine A. Ferraro...gave a pep talk*—Philadelphia

cup of coffee *n phr* A very short visit or tenure: *After his years with the Tigers, the outfielder had a cup of coffee with the Yankees in 1950 and the Giants in 1952*—New York Daily News

one's **cup** (or **dish**) **of tea** *n phr fr British fr 1920s* One's special taste, predilection, etc; = THING: *Ugaritic paleography is not my cup of tea/ Harlem is...his forte and his dish of tea*—Carl Van Vechten

cups *See* IN one's CUPS

curbie *n* = CARHOP

curbstone *n* A cigarette made from the tobacco of found stubs

curdle *v* To offend; disgust: *"It curdles me"* [means] *"I loathe it"*—Life

cure *See* TAKE THE CURE

curl someone's **hair** *v phr* To shock or appall: *The prices here will curl your hair*

curlies *See* HAVE someone BY THE SHORT HAIRS

currency *See* HARD CURRENCY, SOFT MONEY

the **curse** *n phr* A woman's menstrual period; menstruation: *Is it any wonder that menstruation is commonly called "the curse"*—Saturday Review

curtain *See* BAMBOO CURTAIN, IRON CURTAIN, LACE-CURTAIN IRISH

curtain climber *n phr esp students* A baby or small child, esp one who is just learning to walk; = CRUMBCRUSHER, RUG APE

curtains *n* Death; disaster; the bitter end: *It looked like curtains for Ezra then and there*—J Lilienthal [fr the final *curtain* of a show; or perhaps fr the crape *curtains* formerly hung by undertakers at the dead person's door]

cush (Ko͝oSH) **1** *n fr early 1900s* Money; cash: *They've put up their good cush to send me on tour*—H McHugh **2** *n* A wallet [probably fr *cash*]

cushion **1** *n* One of the bases in baseball; = BAG **2** *n* Anything, esp money, kept as a safeguard against hard times: *He kept one bank account just as a cushion*

See the KEYSTONE, WHOOPEE CUSHION

the **cushions** *n phr railroad* A passenger coach or train; first-class train travel

cushy (Ko͝oSH ee) *fr British fr early 1900s* **1** *adj* Easy; easeful; supplying comfort and pleasure: *I landed a cushy post, a soft sinecure at the foundation* **2** *adj* Fancy; luxurious; = HIGHFALUTIN, POSH: *I may not know a lot of cushy words*—Budd Schulberg [perhaps fr Hindi *khush* "pleasure" or Romany *kushto* "good," or perhaps fr a shortening of *cushiony*]

cuspy *adj computer* Neat and clean; elegant; efficiently designed [fr *commonly used system program*, a program designed for wide use and typically with a useful simplicity]

cuss *n fr 1700s* A man; fellow; = GUY

customer *n* A person; = COOKIE: *a tough customer/ She's a shrewd customer* [probably fr an expansion of *cuss*]

cut **1** *v* To absent oneself from without permission or legitimate excuse: *She cut choir practice twice/ to cut class* **2** *n*: *Anybody with more than four cuts flunks* **3** *n* A share or portion, esp of criminal or gambling profits **4** *v*: *They cut the million eight ways* **5** *v* To dilute something, esp whiskey or narcotics: *They cut the pure stuff before they sell it on the street* **6** *adj*: *cut whiskey/ heavily cut cocaine* **7** *v* To shorten a movie, book, manuscript, etc **8** *n*: *How much of a cut did you make?* **9** *adj*: *a brutally cut film/ a cut version* **10** *v* To injure someone with an insult or sarcasm: *That crack really cut me* **11** *n*: *What a nasty cut she gave me* **12** *v* To ignore someone pointedly, esp an acquaintance: *Next time I saw him I cut him* **13** *n*: *That wasn't a snub, it was a cut* **14** *v* To remove someone from a team, cast, group, etc: *I'll be happy if Coach doesn't cut me* **15** *n*: *I survived the cut!* **16** *v* To stop doing something; desist ● Usu an irritated command: *Cut the foolishness now, and listen* **17** *v* To leave; depart: *Let's cut....We ain't no more than* just time, providing we step lively—W Henry **18** *n* A turn; time; = CRACK: *Have a cut at it yourself* **19** *v* baseball To swing at the ball **20** *n*: *What a thunderous cut that was!* **21** *v* musicians To outdo someone; best; surpass: *Lydia Lunch, who I feel cuts Yoko on every possible level*—Village Voice **22** *v* To make a phonograph record or tape recording; record: *He cut a couple of demos yesterday* **23** *n* A recording date or session **24** *n* A phonograph record or side, or a separate band on a record

See WHITTLE someone or something DOWN TO SIZE

cut a (kut AY) *See* CUT ASS

cut a beef *v phr* early 1900s underworld To complain; = BEEF, BITCH

cut someone **a break** *v phr* To give someone special favor: *He petitioned...Judge Michael Wallace to cut me a break*—Philadelphia Journal

cut (or **crack**) **a deal** *v phr* To make or conclude an arrangement; transact an agreement: *Doesn't it make more sense to cut a deal with the Soviets?* —Philadelphia Journal/ *The city has done its entrepreneurial turn by cutting a deal with the Republicans in which it must approve all souvenirs*—New Republic

◁ **cut a fart** ▷ *See* LAY A FART

cut a figure *v phr* fr middle 1700s To be important; be imposing; make an impression: *I cut quite a figure in this town, but nowhere else*

cut and dried (or **dry**) *adj phr* Regular, predictable, and uninteresting; pro forma

cut and run *v phr* fr middle 1800s To leave; depart, esp hastily: *If you hear a whistle, cut and run at once* [fr the *cutting* of the anchor cable in the swift departure of a ship]

◁ **cut** someone **a new asshole** ▷ *v phr* To rebuke someone harshly; reprimand severely; = REAM

◁ **cut ass** (or **a**) ▷ *v phr* To leave; depart; = HAUL ASS

cut a take 1 *v phr* recording industry To record a performance, song, number, etc **2** *v phr* cool talk To explain something carefully

cutback *n* A reduction or decrease: *no cutback in prices*

cut back *v phr* To reduce; decrease: *They'll cut back the interest rate*

cut bait *v phr* To cease some activity; stop; discontinue: *Westway Trial: Lawyers Cut Bait*—Village Voice

See FISH OR CUT BAIT

cut cake *v phr* circus To give short change

cut didoes (DĪ dohz) *v phr* fr British Navy fr middle 1800s To frivol and frolic; = HORSE AROUND [originally fr the very smart appearance of the British corvette *Dido*]

cut someone **down to size** *See* WHITTLE someone or something DOWN TO SIZE

cute 1 *adj* Shrewd; sly; tricky **2** *adj* Disrespectfully frivolous; = SMART-ASS: *Don't be cute with me, you slimy pimp*

cuter or **kyuet** or **quetor** (KYōō tər) *n* fr circus, carnival & hoboes A quarter; 25-cent piece

the **cutes 1** *n phr* Arch and simpering behavior; kittenish ways: *Lina began flapping her dress to give*

herself air. Then she got the cutes and asked if that was allowed*—James M Cain/ *Some of the musical background, like the narration, also suffers from the cutes*—New York Times **2** *n phr* The tendency or habit of constant joking; tasteless frivolity: *born with an incurable case of the cutes*—Time

cutesey or **cutesie 1** *adj* Archly coy and kittenish; overtly charming: *and the children cutesy freaks* —Judith Crist/ *a cutesey fun book* **2** *n*: *The author oversimplifies everything and gets carried away with his own cutesies*—Playboy

cutesy-poo or **cutesy-pie** *adj* Designedly arch and simpering to a nauseating degree: *saying anything narsty about so cutesy-poo an endeavor* —Judith Crist/ *felt that those cutesy-poo tops with puffed sleeves were more suitable for Bo Peep than for the boardroom*—Philadelphia/ *McWilliams writes in a cloying cutesy-pie style*—New Republic

cutie or **cutey** or **cuty 1** *n* A person or thing that is charming, attractive, clever, etc: *I'm no beauty, but am counted a cutie* **2** *n* A person who is shrewd, deceptive, wily, and not to be trusted: *Watch out for that dumb-looking one, he's a cutey*

cutie-pie *n* A very attractive person, esp a woman, esp a doll-like one: *my new cutie pies*—Dan Jenkins

cut in 1 *v phr* To intrude into a conversation or discussion; = BARGE IN **2** *v phr* To take someone's partner away while dancing

cut-in *n* The right to share something: *We've each got a cut-in on the profits*—Jerome Weidman

cut someone **in** *v phr* To award someone a share, esp of winnings, loot, etc: *They cut me in for 25 percent of the take*

cut it 1 *v phr* (also **cut it out**) To stop doing something; desist ● Usu a stern command: *I said cut it right now, that hollering* **2** *v phr* fr loggers To achieve or finish something; succeed; = HACK IT: *They've been warned that a string group won't cut it with jazz fans*—Peter Occhiogrosso/ *But I think that you probably could cut it*—National Review

cut it up *v phr* To analyze and discuss something; take a close look: *Let's cut it up and see how serious the problem is*

cut something **loose** *v phr* fr black To give something up; free oneself from something: *I want to save some bread so I can cut the hustling thing loose altogether*—New York Magazine

cut one's **losses** *v phr* To make the best compromise in a losing situation; salvage or extricate at least something

cut no ice (or **smoke**) *v phr* To have no influence or effect; make no difference: *His Nobel Prize don't cut no ice with me/ but that doesn't cut any smoke with the Gov*—New York Daily News

cut oneself **off at the knees** *v phr* To disable oneself; = SHOOT oneself IN THE FOOT: *I don't want to cut myself off at the knees by giving figures* —Washingtonian

cut someone **off at the knees** *v phr* To deflate or reduce someone, esp surprisingly; = TAKE someone DOWN A PEG: *the nebbish with a disarming wit that could cut you off at the knees*—Philadelphia

cut-offs *n* Pants, usu blue jeans, cut off above the knees and left to unravel

cut (or **turn**) **off** someone's **water** *v phr* To subdue someone; deal decisively and damagingly with someone: *I just smiled sweetly and turned off his water*

'**cutor** or **cutor** (KYoῡ tər) *n* A prosecuting attorney

cut out 1 *v phr* To leave; depart, esp hastily: *So you think you're cutting out? You're not leaving until I leave with you*—Tennessee Williams **2** *v phr fr late 1800s* To stop doing something; desist: *If you cut out the booze maybe it'll work*

cut-out *n espionage & police* A person, business, etc, used to conceal the identity or purpose of a secret operation; =COVER: *The firm operated as a cut-out, or front, for the FBI's purchase*—Time

cut out dolls (or **paper dolls**) *v phr* To be insane; behave dementedly: *She has her cutting out paper dolls*—Raymond Chandler

cut one's **own throat** *v phr* To ruin oneself; hoist oneself with one's own petard; =SHOOT oneself IN THE FOOT: *If you try to get him that way you'll cut your own throat*

cut someone's **papers** (or **orders**) *v phr police & Army* To prepare and distribute official papers such as warrants, writs, assignment orders, etc: *They're still cutting her papers*—The Gauntlet (movie) [probably fr the *cutting*, perforation by typing, of a duplicating-machine stencil]

cut-plug *n fr middle 1800s* An inferior horse

cut-rate *adj* Cheap; offered at discount

cutter *See* CAKE-CUTTER, COOKIE-CUTTER, DAISY-CUTTER, FOG-CUTTER, PISS-CUTTER, RUG-CUTTER

cut the cheese *See* CHEESE

cut (or **cut up**) **the melon** (or **the pie**) *v phr* To divide and share out receipts, profits, loot, etc

cut the mouth *v phr reformatory* To become silent; =CLAM UP

not **cut the mustard** *See* NOT CUT THE MUSTARD

cut the (or **a**) **rug** *v phr esp 1930s jive talk* To dance, esp in jitterbug style

cutthroat *adj* Very harsh and barbarous: *a cut-throat game/ cutthroat competition*

cut two ways *See* WORK BOTH WAYS

cut up 1 *v phr fr middle 1800s* To behave frivolously; frolic; =HORSE AROUND **2** *v phr underworld* To divide profits, loot, etc **3** *v phr underworld* To discuss; go over carefully **4** *v phr* To speak ill of; analyze maliciously: *Or they can collectively "cut up" the girls they see around*—Sexual Behavior

cut-up 1 *n* A prankster; practical joker; antic rogue: *Uncle is a cut-up, owner of all kinds of gimmicks* **2** *n esp late 1800s* An energetic and entertaining person: *a great cut-up. He could dance a bit, sing better than average, and had a sense of comedy*—HR Hoyt **3** *adj* Upset; hurt; distressed: *She was pretty cut up about not getting a paper*—Richard Peck

cut up the touches (or **jackpots** or **pipes**) *v phr underworld* To divide loot, spoils, etc, esp at a special meeting

cuty *See* CUTIE

cut Zs *See* COP ZS

◁**cuzzy**▷ *See* COOZ

CV (pronounced as separate letters) *n* A curriculum vitae or brief biography, esp of education and work; resumé; =VITA [fr Latin *curriculum vitae*, literally "course of life"]

CYA *See* COVER one's ASS

the **cycle** *See* HIT FOR THE CYCLE

D

D *n* A dollar

See BIG D, TAKE A D, THREE D

DA (pronounced as separate letters) *n* District Attorney

daaa *See* TAH-DAH

dab *See* SMACK

dab hand *n phr esp British fr late 1600s* An expert; a skilled person; an adept: *He is reportedly a dab hand at setting lofty prices*—New York Magazine [fr British slang *dab* "an expert," of unknown origin]

dad 1 *n* An old man ● Used as a disrespectful address towards older men. The similar term **pop** is not similarly disrespectful: *Okay, dad, outa the way and you won't get hurt* **2** *n* God ● Used euphemistically as an element in various old-fashioned mild oaths like **dad-blamed**

See HO-DAD

dad-blamed or **dad-blasted** *adj* (also **dag-blamed** or **dag-blasted**) Wretched; accursed; =DARN: *Git outa my dad-blamed way*

dad (or **dag**) **burn** *interj* An exclamation of surprise, irritation, frustration, etc ● A euphemism for **goddamn**: *Well, dad burn it, come on*

daddy 1 *n fr black* A male lover, esp one who keeps a younger mistress; =SUGAR DADDY **2** *n* The most respected man in a field; cynosure; dean: *Gary Cooper, the daddy of all cowboys*

See DISNEYLAND DADDY, HO-DAD, ZOO DADDY

Daddy-o or **daddy-o** *n fr bop talk* Man; old guy; =GUY ● Used in addressing men, sometimes older men, respectfully and amiably

daffy *adj fr British fr late 1800s* Crazy; =NUTS: *He tries to convince her that she is not daffy*—SJ Perelman/ *Most of his cherished tenets are quite daffy* [fr British dialect *daff* "fool, simpleton"; *daffish* is attested fr the 15th century]

See STIR-CRAZY

daffydill *n* An insane person; =NUT

dag-blamed or **dag-blasted** *See* DAD-BLAMED

dag burn *See* DAD BURN

dagged *adj* Drunk

dagger *See* BULLDYKE

daggone *See* DOGGONE

dagnab *See* DOGGONE

◀**dago** or **Dago**▶ *fr early 1700s* **1** *n* An Italian or person of Italian descent: *Hey, Fiorello, you're a dago*—Fiorello H LaGuardia **2** *adj* Italian **3** *n* The Italian language **4** *n fr middle 1800s* A person of Hispanic birth or descent [fr *Diego* "James,"

used in the 17th century to mean "Spaniard"; the narrowing to "Italian" occurred in the 20th century]

◀**dago** (or **Dago**) **bomb**▶ *n phr* A white spherical firecracker

◀**dago** (or **Dago**) **red**▶ *n phr* Cheap red table wine, esp of Italian origin or type

dagwood *n* A large thick sandwich of many ingredients [from *Dagwood* Bumstead, a comic-strip character who made tall and complex sandwiches]

dah *See* TAH-DAH

daisies *See* PUSH UP DAISIES

the **daisies** *n phr baseball* The outfield

daisy 1 *n fr middle 1700s* A person or thing that is remarkable, wonderful, superior, etc; =DILLY, HONEY: *My new car's a daisy* ◁**2**▷ *n* A male homosexual; =PANSY ◁**3**▷ *n* A weak, effeminate, or cowardly man; =SISSY, WIMP

daisy chain *n phr* Sexual acts shared or partly shared by more than two people at the same time in the same place; group sex

daisy-cutter 1 *n baseball* A grounder or very low line drive **2** *n* A very low tennis shot **3** *n* A horse that trots with its hooves near the ground **4** *n WW2 Army* An antipersonnel bomb or mine that ejects shrapnel close to the ground

dally *See* DILLY-DALLY

damaged *adj* Drunk

dame *n* A woman; =BROAD, DOLL

damn 1 *interj* (also **damn it**) An exclamation of disappointment, irritation, frustration, etc: *Damn, it's gone!* **2** *adj* (also **damned**) Cursed; accursed; wretched: *What do I do with this damned thing?* **3** *adv*: *You seem damn stupid all of a sudden*

See HOT DAMN

a **damn** *See* NOT GIVE A DAMN, WORTH A DAMN

damned *See* I'LL BE DAMNED

damn-fool *adj* =DAMN, DAMNED

damn tootin' *See* YOU'RE DAMN TOOTIN'

damper 1 *n* A person or thing that depresses, takes the edge off joy, chills one's enthusiasm, etc: *The news was a damper on our hopes* **2** *n circus, hoboes & underworld fr 1920s* A cash register or till; cash drawer **3** *n* A bank or money depository: *dropping bonds into the damper which are then sold to the public*—Westbrook Pegler [fr the *damper* control on a stove or furnace]

See PUT A DAMPER ON, TURN someone's DAMPER DOWN

damper pad *n phr underworld* A bankbook

damp rag *n phr* A disappointment; a blighted hope: *That...was a little bit of a damp rag*—Washington Post

Dan *See* DAPPER DAN

dance 1 *v* =DANCE TO someone's TUNE **2** *n street gang* A fight between rival gangs; =RUMBLE *See* GET THE LAST DANCE, GO INTO ONE'S DANCE, RAIN DANCE, SONG AND DANCE, TAP DANCE

dancehall *prison* **1** *n* A death-house or execution chamber **2** *n* The cells or cell block adjoining an execution chamber; =DEATH ROW [fr outdated underworld *dance* "die by hanging"]

dance off *v phr* To die, esp by legal execution

dance on air (or **on nothing**) *v phr* To die by hanging

dancer *n prizefight* A boxer who spends most of his time and energy nimbly evading the opponent *See* BUBBLE-DANCER, DOLLY DANCER, GANDY DANCER, GO-GO GIRL

dance the carpet *v phr fr 1920s railroad* To appear before one's superior for reprimand

dance to someone's **tune** *v phr* To be in the power and at the will of someone else

dancing *See* TOUCH DANCING

D and D¹ or **dee-dee** *adj phr* or *adj police* Drunk and disorderly

D and D² or **dee-dee** *dock workers & underworld fr 1950s* **1** *adj phr* or *adj* Deaf and dumb **2** *adj phr* or *adj* Timorous of fighting for one's rights; deaf and dumb to injustice

dander *See* GET one's DANDER UP

dandy 1 *n* A person or thing that is remarkable, wonderful, superior, etc: *You should get one, it's a dandy* **2** *adj*: *a dandy idea* **3** *adv*: *He does it dandy/ We get on just dandy See* HOTSIE-TOTSIE, JIM-DANDY

◁**dang¹**▷ **1** *n* The penis; =DONG **2** *adj* Sexually stimulating; =FOXY

dang² **1** *interj* (also **dang it**) An exclamation of disappointment, irritation, frustration, etc: *Dang, we missed the Welk show* **2** *adj* (also **danged**) Wretched; nasty; silly **3** *adv* Extremely: *You looked dang silly* [a euphemism for *damn*, which is regarded by some as taboo]

a **dang** *See* NOT GIVE A DAMN

danged *See* I'LL BE DAMNED

dangler *n circus* A trapeze artist; =FLYER

Dan O'Leary *See* DO A DAN O'LEARY

dap *black* **1** *adj* Stylish; well-dressed; dapper **2** *n* A white person

dapper (or **fancy**) **Dan** *n phr* An ostentatiously well-groomed man, usu one not inured to hard work: *the fancy Dans, dressed fit to kill*—A Lomax

darb *n esp 1920s* A person or thing that is remarkable, wonderful, superior, etc; =LULU [perhaps fr Ruby *Darby*, the name of an Oklahoma showgirl much admired by oil-drillers, who would praise a new gusher as a "Ruby Darby" or "a Darb"; perhaps fr *dab* "an expert"]

darbies or **derbies** *n* Handcuffs [fr a form of British usurer's bond called *Father Derby's* (or *Darby's*) bands]

dark 1 *adj theater* Closed; not in operation: *Monday is a "dark" day at Heinz Hall*—New Yorker **2** *adj lunch counter* With less than the usual amount of cream *See* IN THE DARK

dark horse 1 *n phr fr horse-racing* A person or team, esp in sports or politics, that seems very unlikely to win but might nevertheless do so **2** *modifier*: *a dark-horse candidate/ dark-horse odds*

dark meat ◀**1**▶ *n phr* A black person, esp a woman, regarded solely as a sex partner ◀**2**▶ *n phr* A black person's body and genitals

dark-thirty *See* OH-DARK-THIRTY

◀**darky**▶ *n* A black person

darn or **dern** or **durn** *fr middle 1700s* **1** *interj* (also **darn it** or **dern it** or **durn it**) An exclamation of disappointment, irritation, frustration, etc: *Darn, I've dropped my glockenspiel!* **2** *adj* (also **darned** or **darnfool** or **derned** or **durned**) Wretched; nasty; silly: *Where does this darn lamp go?/ sentimental songs, darnfool ditties, revival hymns*—Virgil Thompson **3** *adv*: *She was darn excited* [euphemism for *damn*, which is regarded by some as taboo]

a **darn** or **a dern** or **a durn** *See* NOT GIVE A DAMN

darned *See* I'LL BE DAMNED

darning needles *See* RAIN CATS AND DOGS

darn tootin' *See* YOU'RE DAMN TOOTIN'

darter *See* BLUE DARTER, JOE-DARTER

dash *n* The dashboard of a car: *I keep a gun under the dash See* SLAPDASH

dash it or **dash it all** *v phr* =DAMN, DARN ● Chiefly British use

dat (DAT) *n Army* A tank-crew member [fr *dumbass tanker*]

date 1 *n* An engagement or rendezvous, esp with a member of the other sex **2** *n* A man or woman with whom one has an engagement or rendezvous: *He's her date for tonight* **3** *v*: *How many girls have you dated this week?* **4** *n* A booking or engagement of a speaker, musical group, etc: *Tonight she's got a date speaking at Syracuse See* BLIND DATE, CHEAP DATE, HEAVY DATE

date bait *n phr 1940s teenagers* A popular and attractive young woman

date mate *n phr 1940s teenagers* One's partner on a social rendezvous, esp a regular partner: *finds himself a date mate who'll wait to be dated*—SJ Daly

date someone **up** *v phr* To schedule a social engagement or rendezvous with someone

Dave or **David** *n shoeshop* The shoe width D

day *See* EAGLE DAY, HAVE A FIELD DAY, MAKE MY DAY, MOTHER'S DAY, NINETY-DAY WONDER, NOT GIVE someone THE TIME OF DAY, PUNK DAY, RED-LETTER DAY

day-glo *adj* Blatantly gaudy; cheaply flashy: *smoldering pageant turns totally day-glo*—Village Voice/ *plenty of sequins and day-glo fur*—Rolling Stone/ *day-glo glamor*—Us [fr the trade name of a brand of paint that makes things glow under a black light and produces lurid, psychedelic color effects]

daylight *v* To work at a second job during the day: *who is daylighting in an ad agency as a producer of commercials*—Playboy
See LET DAYLIGHT INTO, PUT DAYLIGHT BETWEEN

the **daylights** or **the living daylights** See BEAT THE SHIT OUT OF someone or something

days See DOG DAYS, ORAL DAYS

◁the **day the eagle shits**▷ (or **screams**) *n phr esp armed forces* Payday [fr the *eagle* as symbol of the US government]

dazzle See RAZZLE-DAZZLE

deacon seat *n phr hoboes & lumberjacks* The long seat along the edge of bunks in a bunkhouse

dead 1 *adj* Very tired; = BEAT, POOPED **2** *adj* Not operating; not startable: *Damn battery's dead* **3** *adj* Ruined; destroyed: *As far as another chance goes, I'm dead* **4** *adj* No longer under consideration: *The ERA's dead again* **5** *adj* Dull; tedious and uninteresting: *another dead sermon* **6** *adj* Lacking brilliance and overtones; flat; dull: *The trumpets sounded dead* **7** *adj* Absolute; assured: *It's a dead certainty he'll run again* **8** *adv*: *I'm dead broke/ dead set against it* **9** *n post office* A letter or package that can neither be delivered nor returned [the sense "absolute, assured, certain" probably developed fr expressions like Middle English *ded oppressed* "completely overcome," 16th-century *dead drunk*, and others suggesting the inertness of death; when inertness suggested fixedness, unchangingness, certainty, etc, the term took on these present senses]
See DROP DEAD, KNOCK someone DEAD, NOT BE CAUGHT DEAD, STONE DEAD, STOP someone or something DEAD IN someone's or something's TRACKS

dead as a dodo (or **doornail**) *adj phr* Absolutely lifeless; entirely hopeless: *The Philadelphia Bulletin is dead, dead as a doornail*—Philadelphia

◁**deadass**▷ **1** *n* A stupid, boring person; an absolute dullard: *Get some action going among these deadasses in the loony bin*—Tom Wolfe **2** *adj*: *There are so many deadass people out there, boring each other to death*—San Francisco **3** *adv* Completely; totally: *You're deadass wrong when you say I got nothing to go on*—William Brashler
See GET OFF one's ASS

deadbeat *fr middle 1800s* **1** *n* A person who habitually begs or gets money from others, does not pay his or her debts, etc; = MOOCHER, SCHNORRER: *a chance to demand immediate payment if the clerk looks like a deadbeat*—Time **2** *n* A tramp or hobo, esp one riding on a freight train **3** *v* To sponge, loaf, etc: *Living off interest is not exactly deadbeating* [fr *dead* "complete, completely" and *beat* "sponger"]

dead beat *adj phr* Completely exhausted: *My poor ass is draggin' and I'm dead beat*

dead broke *adj phr* Totally without money; destitute

dead cat *n phr circus* A lion, tiger, etc, that does not perform but is only exhibited

dead center *n phr* A point at which nothing is happening: *Let's try to get this negotiation off dead center*

dead duck (or **pigeon**) *n phr fr middle 1800s* A person or thing that is ruined; = a GONER: *Just one more little push and she was a dead duck*—Changes/ *Unless somebody would start this mob to the sugar bowl, I was a dead pigeon*—Max Shulman

deadfanny *adj* Dull; stupid: *the hilariously deadpan, deadfanny fall guy*—Newsweek

dead from the neck up *adj phr* Stupid; dull; = KLUTZY

dead giveaway *n phr* An unmistakable and definitive clue: *His blushing was a dead giveaway*

deadhead 1 *n fr middle 1800s* A nonpaying spectator at a game, show, etc; = FREELOADER **2** *n railroad fr middle 1800s* A nonpaying passenger **3** *n fr railroad fr late 1800s* A train, bus, etc, carrying no passengers or freight, usu returning from a paying trip **4** *modifier: a deadhead cab/ deadhead freight train* **5** *v: I'll deadhead your hack back to the garage* **6** *n* A stupid person; an incompetent; = KLUTZ **7** *n* An extremely boring person

Deadhead *n* A devotee of the rock-and-roll group the Grateful Dead

dead heat *n phr fr horse-racing fr middle 1800s* A tied race, contest, etc: *The election ended in a dead heat* [fr *dead* "absolute, total, thorough," related to the finality of death, and *heat* "a single course of a race," related either to a single firing or heating of a mass of metal, or to the heating of the body in running, or to both]

dead horse (or **letter**) *n phr* A matter no longer of concern or currency; a bygone issue: *I'm afraid free love is a dead letter these days*
See BEAT A DEAD HORSE

dead hour *n phr college students fr 1920s* A college period during which one has no class: *By dead hour I didn't mean Professor Chapman's class, only that I had no class at all at 9*

dead in the water *adj phr* Unable to move; stalled; defunct: *Right now, the economy is dead in the water, with 10.8 percent unemployment*—New York Times/ *Once I saw you, you were dead in the water*—The Lost Honor of Kathryn Beck (TV movie) [fr the image of a disabled ship, unable to proceed]

deadlights *n merchant marine* The eyes [fr the heavy glass set in a ship's hull to admit light]

deadly 1 *adj* Boring; extremely tedious; dull: *I came prepared for a long and deadly meeting* **2** *adj 1940s jive talk* Excellent; admirable; = COOL

dead man's hand *n phr poker fr late 1800s* A hand containing a pair of aces and a pair of eights [fr the tradition that Wild Bill Hickock held such a hand when Jack McCall shot him in 1876]

dead man switch *n phr railroad* A throttle control on a train or other vehicle that automatically goes to the "stop" position if not gripped and held

deadneck *n* A stupid person; dullard: *They were awake and lively; they weren't deadnecks*—James T

Farrell [probably fr the expression *dead from the neck up*]

dead one 1 *n phr* hoboes A retired hobo **2** *n phr* hoboes A stingy, ungenerous person **3** *n phr* A dull, ineffective person; = DULL TOOL

deadpan 1 *n* An expressionless face; = POKER FACE **2** *n* A person with an expressionless face: *Buster Keaton and Fred Allen were classic deadpans* **3** *v*: *With kids packing his audiences, he deadpanned "I promise to lower the voting age to 6"*—Newsweek **4** *adj*: *a deadpan delivery/ This is known as the deadpan system of prevarication*—AJ Liebling

dead pigeon *See* DEAD DUCK

dead president *n phr* Any US banknote

dead ringer *n phr* fr early 1900s An exact duplicate, esp a person who is the double of another: *He was such a dead ringer for my ex-boss*—Jerome Weidman [fr *dead* "precise, exact" and *ring in* "substitute, esp fraudulently," an early-19th-century slang term for gambling]

dead soldier (or **marine**) *fr British Navy fr early 1800s* **1** *n phr* An empty or emptied bottle, esp a liquor bottle **2** *n phr* Food or plates of food only partially eaten: *on the way to the kitchen with the dead soldiers, or leftovers*—Louis Armstrong

deadsville *adj* Dull; boring: *the young people who always felt that cruises were deadsville*—Newsweek

dead (or **bang**) **to rights** *adv phr fr middle 1800s* With no possibility of escape or evasion; in flagrante delicto; redhanded: *was caught "dead to rights" and now languishes in the city Bastille*—San Francisco City Argus

dead to the world 1 *adj phr* Drunk, esp stuporous from drink **2** *adj phr* Fast asleep

dead wagon *n phr fr late 1800s* A hearse; vehicle for carrying dead bodies: *calling the dead wagon for a nice ride downtown to the morgue*—H Johnson

deadwood 1 *n fr late 1800s* Unproductive persons; lazy and useless staff **2** *n* Anything useless, esp something useless which must be kept **3** *n theater* An unsold ticket or block of tickets [fr the fact that *dead* or rotten *wood* does not produce much heat when burned]

deal 1 *v* To negotiate, esp over a purchase or sale; chaffer: *"Okay," said Mack, "let's deal"* **2** *v* To be active and aggressive in making arrangements, tradeoffs, sales, etc; = WHEEL AND DEAL: *Sophie did all the dealing there*—Nelson Algren **3** *v* narcotics To sell narcotics; be a peddler **4** *v* To pitch a baseball: *The big lefthander deals a smoker* **5** *n fr late 1800s* A usu secret arrangement between politicians, rulers, business executives, etc: *He made a deal with the Republicans...to suppress the charges*—RG Spivack **6** *n* Situation; thing in hand or at issue: *Hey, what's the deal here? My car's gone/ The deal is that I'm tired of this whole farce*

See BIG DEAL, CRUMB THE DEAL, GOOD DEAL, MAKE A BIG PRODUCTION, NO BIG DEAL, NOT MAKE DEALS, PLAY WITH A FULL DECK, RAW DEAL, SWEETHEART DEAL, TIE-IN DEAL

deal someone **a poor deck** *v phr* To treat someone cruelly and unjustly *Take a thirty-year-old nurse...who's bitter and thinks she's been dealt a poor deck*—AT Fleming

dealer 1 *n gambling* A person who makes a living from gambling, whether or not an actual dealer-out of cards: *A bookmaker, who is known as a dealer in refined usage*—T Betts **2** *n* A person involved actively and aggressively in a range of negotiations, trades, purchases, etc; = WHEELER-DEALER **3** *n narcotics* A person who sells narcotics; peddler; = PUSHER: *The "dealer" (not "pusher") is the man who sells all this*—New York Times

See JUICE DEALER, WHEELER-DEALER

deal someone **in** *v phr* To make someone a participant; let someone share: *He heard we were going and said deal him in*

deal in coal *black* **1** *v phr* To mix and consort with black persons when one is not black oneself **2** *v phr* To associate with very dark-skinned black persons

dealing *See* DOUBLE-DEALING

deal with a full deck *See* PLAY WITH A FULL DECK

deaner *See* DEEMER

deano *n underworld* A month [perhaps fr *deaner deemer*, etc, because a month is about as much of a year as a dime is of a dollar]

dearie *n* Dear person; cherished one ● A somewhat vulgar term of address used chiefly by women: *If you wore it you can't return it, dearie*

Dear John 1 *n phr fr WW2 armed forces* A letter or other means of informing a fiance, spouse, boyfriend, etc, that one is breaking off the relationship **2** *modifier: Dear-John letter*

death *See* the KISS OF DEATH, LOOK LIKE DEATH WARMED OVER, SUDDEN DEATH

death row *n phr* The part of a prison housing convicts condemned to death; = DANCEHALL

death snow *n phr narcotics* Poisoned or contaminated cocaine

death warmed over *See* LOOK LIKE DEATH WARMED OVER

the **death warrant** *n phr* The cause of termination; the doom: *Looks like that's the death warrant for our plan*

deb 1 *n* A debutante **2** *n street gang* A member of a girl's street gang: *The Assassins...were organized with sub-gangs of..."debs"*—New York Times

◁**de-ball**▷ *See* DE-NUT

debunk *n fr 1920s* To clear away lies, exaggerations, vanities, etc: *The author neither glorifies nor debunks*—Saturday Review [coined by WE Woodward in a book published in 1923]

Decatur *See* EIGHTER FROM DECATUR

deceivers *See* FALSIES

decibel level *See* RAISE THE DECIBEL LEVEL

deck 1 *n* hoboes The roof of a railroad car **2** *n narcotics* A package of narcotics; portion of a drug, esp three grains of heroin; = BAG: *a deck of nose candy for sale*—J Evans **3** *n* A package of cigarettes **4** *v* To knock someone down, esp with the fist; = FLOOR: *Remember that guy I decked in*

the restaurant?—Lawrence Sanders/ *The quarterback got decked eight times in blitzes*
See COLD DECK, DEAL someone A POOR DECK, the GREEN DECK, HIT THE DECK, ON DECK, PLAY WITH A FULL DECK, WET DECK

decker *See* DOUBLE-DECKER, JOKER

deck hand *n phr theater* A stagehand

decks awash *adj phr* Drunk

decode *v* Explain: *Hans, will you please decode that?*

decrease the volume *v phr teenagers* To speak lower ● Usu a command or request

deduck (DEE duck) *n* A deduction, esp from one's taxable income: *more deducks or we're dead ducks*

dee-dee *See* D AND D

deejay *See* DISC JOCKEY

deek *n* A detective; = DICK

deely bopper or **deely bobber** or **beely bopper** *n phr* A small hat equipped with bobbing wire antennas like those of an insect or some extraterrestrial creature: *a decor of remaindered Deely Bobbers and airsick bags*—Newsweek

deemer or **deaner** or **deener** *hoboes, circus & carnival fr early 1800s British* **1** *n* A dime **2** *n* A niggardly tip **3** *n* A person who gives an insufficient tip; = CHEAPSKATE **4** *n* Ten [fr British tramps' term for "shilling"]

deep *See* KNEE DEEP

deep end *See* GO OFF THE DEEP END, JUMP OFF THE DEEP END

deep freeze *See* IN COLD STORAGE

deepie or **depthie** *n esp 1950s* A three-dimensional movie: *The deepies released so far have been gimmick pictures*—Associated Press

deep pocket *n phr* Wealth; available riches and financial security: *He felt more comfortable with the deepest pocket available*—Wall Street Journal/ *a deep pocket, that of an insurance company*—New York Times

deep pockets *n phr* Sources of much money; rich persons: *He didn't hit the really deep pockets, as divorce lawyers say, until 1964*—Washington Post/ *greater news-gathering assets than CNN and deeper pockets to offset losses*—Time

deepsea chef *n phr hoboes* A dishwasher

deepsea turkey *n phr WW2 armed forces* Salmon

deep six *fr Navy & merchant marine* **1** *n phr* A grave **2** *v phr* To discard; jettison; throw overboard: *One White House disposal crew even unblushingly planned to deep six a file in the Potomac*—Jack Anderson/ *If any publication is deep-sixed, it will almost certainly be "The Car Book"*—Mother Jones [probably fr the combined notions of a grave as *six feet deep* and a fathom as *six feet in depth*]
See GIVE something THE DEEP SIX

deep-think **1** *n* Profound intellectuality ● Used ironically: *a good example of university deep-think* **2** *modifier:* *do some deep-think social criticism* [probably based on *goodthink, crimethink*, and other terms coined by George Orwell in *Nineteen Eighty-Four*]

deep trouble (or ◁**shit**▷) *n phr* Very serious trouble: *One slip and you're in deep trouble/ He was in deep shit with Big Lou*—Rolling Stone

deep water *See* IN DEEP WATER

defense *See* NICKEL DEFENSE

defi or **defy** (DEE fī) *n esp 1920s* Defiance; notice of act of defiance: *on a signboard, a defi to the On Leongs*—E Lavine [apparently fr French *défi*]

defuse *v* To ease or eliminate the danger of something menacing: *We might not stop it, but we might defuse it*

degree *See* THIRD DEGREE

dehorn **1** *n hoboes* Bootleg whiskey or denatured alcohol **2** *n* A drunkard; = BUM: *patronized largely by vagrants, winos, dehorns, grifters*—Max Shulman **3** *n 1920s* Anything inimical to the Industrial Workers of the World, esp alcohol and gambling **4** *v* To do the sex act after long abstinence

deke *v fr Canadian hockey* To trick, esp by decoying; = FAKE someone OUT: *My friend, you deked me. You're not supposed to do that*—George V Higgins [fr *decoy*]

delay *See* GAPER'S BLOCK

Delhi belly *n phr* Diarrhea

deli or **delly** or **dellie** (DELL ee) **1** *n* A delicatessen: *a nice smelly deli* **2** *modifier:* *deli food/ treat from the deli counter*

delight *See* BOILERMAKER'S DELIGHT

delish (dee LISH) *adj* Delicious

deliver or **deliver the goods** *v* or *v phr* To perform successfully, esp after promising; = COME THROUGH: *It's a very tough assignment, but he thinks he can deliver/ He talks big, but can he deliver the goods?*

Dem or **Demo** **1** *n* A Democrat **2** *adj:* *the Dem boss/ Demo congressmen*

demi-rep *n fr 1700s* A woman of somewhat shady reputation

demo[1] (DEH moh) *n* A demolition worker

demo[2] (DEH moh) **1** *n* A record or tape made to demonstrate the abilities of musicians, the quality of a song, etc: *Mark's got a good demo to pitch the new song with* **2** *n* A computer disk or tape cassette made to demonstrate the abilities of a particular program: *I tried out their software demo before I bought their package* **3** *modifier:* *Let's try the demo disk* **4** *n* A demonstration of protest or other conviction, esp by a large crowd with banners, etc: *a no-nukes demo*

demon *n 1930s jive talk* A dime

Denmark *See* GO TO DENMARK

den mother *n phr homosexuals* The head and sometimes provider or supporter of a group of male homosexuals, often an older man: *They had a sort of den mother. A middle-aged writer type who had given up the straight life*—Patrick Mann

◁**de-nut** or **de-ball**▷ *v* To castrate

Denver boot *See* BOOT

depth *See* OUT OF one's DEPTH

depthie *See* DEEPIE

derail *v* To throw off the proper course; wreck: *He managed to derail the proposal just before Christmas*—Time

derbies *See* DARBIES

Derbyville *n* Louisville, Kentucky

dern *See* DARN

a **dern** *See* a DARN, NOT GIVE A DARN

derned *See* DARN

derrick **1** *n* *underworld* A successful thief of expensive things **2** *n* *underworld* A shoplifter **3** *v* *sports* To remove a player from a game: *Shotton derricked him in favor of Cookie Lavagetto*—Arthur Daley

derriere or **derrière** (deh ree EHR) *n* The buttocks; rump: *what Mr Irvine would no doubt delicately call our derrieres*—AE Gower/ *So gangway everybody, mother's off her derriere again*—American Home [fr French]

desert rat *n phr* A person who lives in or frequents the desert

designer **1** *n* *underworld* A counterfeiter **2** *modifier* Of high quality; bearing a famous label: *Ah, designer ennui*—Village Voice/ *You got a designer body, honey*

designer drug *n phr* A synthesized narcotic, often of much higher potency than those produced from plants: *These new "designer drugs" or "super narcotics" are triply dangerous*—Good Housekeeping

desk jockey *n phr* An office worker: *Let some desk jockey in the home office envy you*—Hal Boyle

desperado *n* *gambling* A person who gambles or borrows more than he can pay, and is certain to default [fr earlier *desperado* "outlaw, fugitive," literally "desperate man," fr Spanish]

detainer *n railroad* A train dispatcher

detox *v narcotics* To free someone of a narcotics addiction; detoxify: *I jumped in and out of opium habits but eventually de-toxed for good*—Saturday Review/ *We can detox a heroin addict...in three weeks*—G Hoenig

deuce **1** *n* A two of playing cards **2** *n poker* A pair of cards of the same value **3** *n* Two dollars **4** *n prison* A two-year prison sentence: *did a deuce together at Joliet*—Kansas City Confidential **5** *n street gang* A quitter; coward; petty thief **6** *n* (also **deuce coupe**) *hot rodders* A powerful or handsome specially prepared car, esp a 1932 Ford *See* ACE-DEUCE, FORTY-DEUCE

the **deuce** **1** *n phr fr British fr 1700s* = the HELL **2** *n phr esp teenagers* Forty-second Street in New York City, mecca for many teenage runaways; = FORTY-DEUCE: *in the peep shows and urinals and bars of the Deuce*—Village Voice

deuce and a half *n phr Army* A two-and-a-half ton truck

deuce it **1** *v phr theater* To come second in order, esp on the bill of a show **2** *v phr* To do something as one of a couple

deuce of clubs *n phr reformatory* Both fists

deucer *n* Two dollars; a two-dollar bill

deuce spot **1** *n phr theater* The second act in a vaudeville show **2** *n phr* Second place in a contest

Devil *See* RED

the **devil** *See* the HELL

devil-may-care *adj fr middle 1800s* Reckless; cavalier: *a devil-may-care insouciance*

the **devil's bedposts** *n phr 1930s cardplayers* The four of clubs

devil's dozen *n phr fr British fr 1600s* Thirteen; baker's dozen

devoon (də VōoN) *adj 1940s teenagers* Divine; great: *"Devoon," said Jeanie languidly*—Billy Rose

dew *n narcotics* Marijuana *See* MOUNTAIN DEW

dexie or **dexy** *n students* A tablet of Dexedrine, trade name of a brand of amphetamine: *You can take dexies, but you can get hooked on them*—Stephen Longstreet

DI (pronounced as separate letters) *n Marine Corps* A drill instructor; noncommissioned officer in charge of recruits

dial something **out** *v phr* To put firmly out of one's mind; ignore designedly: *All I had to do was concentrate on driving. I had a real excuse to dial it all out*—Sports Illustrated

diamond-cracker *n* (Variations: **pusher** or **thrower** may replace **cracker**) *railroad* A fire stoker

diamonds **1** *n* (also **black diamonds**) Coal: *throwing diamonds in the firebox*—Casey Jones **2** *n* The testicles; = FAMILY JEWELS

diarrhea of the mouth *See* VERBAL DIARRHEA

dib **1** *n* Money, esp a share of money: *I ought to collect the kid's dib, too*—Dashiell Hammett **2** *n* A dollar: *fifty sweet dibs*—Samuel Hopkins Adams [fr *divvy*]

dibs **1** *n fr British fr early 1800s* Money: *How did you make your dibs?*—Raymond Chandler **2** *n* (also **dibs on**) A claim; a preemptive declaration: *It's mine, I said dibs first/ Dibs on the front seat* [perhaps fr *dibstones*, a children's game played with small bones or other counters]

dice *v fr British 1950s car-racing* To jockey for position in a race: *I had no really sharp feeling about dicing with Parnelli*—Sports Afield [fr the amusing melodramatic phrase "to dice with death"] *See* LOAD THE DICE, NO DICE, SLICE AND DICE FILM

dice house *n phr 1920s cowboys* A bunkhouse

dicer *fr early 1800s British n* A stiff hat, or a military helmet

dicey *adj fr British* Risky; perilous: *African investment is dicey*—Newsweek/ *Updike indulged in many dicey curlicues*—Commonweal/ *the dicey art of writing a farce*—New York Times

dick[1] or **deek** *fr early 1900s underworld* **1** *n* A detective **2** *n* Any police officer; = BULL [fr a shortening and altering of *detective*] *See* HARNESS BULL

◁**dick**[2]▷ **1** *n fr middle 1800s British armed forces* The penis **2** *v* To do the sex act with; = SCREW: *If he went and dicked your twelve-year-old sister...he wouldn't tell you all about it*—Richard Merkin **3** *v* (also **dick around**) To potter or meddle; play; = MESS, SCREW AROUND: *That's federal merchandise you're dicking with, right, marshal?*—WT Tyler/ *still*

in the kitchen, dicking around with the sushi—Armistead Maupin **4** *n* A despised person; = PRICK: *You dick!*—Cameron Crowe [perhaps fr the nickname *Dick*, an instance of the widespread use of affectionate names for the genitals; perhaps fr earlier British *derrick* "penis"; perhaps fr a dialect survival of Middle English *dighten* "do the sex act with," in a locution like "he dight her," which would be pronounced "he dicked her"]
   See CLIPPED DICK, DOES A WOODEN HORSE HAVE A HICKORY DICK, DONKEY DICK, LIMP-DICK, STEP ON IT

Dick *See* BIG DICK, EVERY TOM, DICK, AND HARRY

◁**dick-brained**▷ *adj* Stupid; crazy; = NUTTY: *coke-snorting super freaks, dick-brained Bob Marley tribute, and jive ooh-la-la*—Village Voice

◁**dickey**▷ *n* = DICK²

◁**dickhead**▷ *n* A despised person; = BASTARD, PRICK: *Why would I possibly want to check out a dickhead like you?*—Richard Merkin

◁**dick-licker** or **dickey-licker**▷ *n* A person who does fellatio, most often a male homosexual; = COCKSUCKER

dicty or **dickty** or **dictee** *black* **1** *adj* Stylish; wealthy; = CLASSY: *"Dicty" is high-class*—Stephen Longstreet **2** *adj* Haughty; snobbish; imperious: *these dickty jigs*—Zora Neale Hurston **3** *n* A snob; aristocrat: *I don't want to be a dicty*—Mezz Mezzrow [origin unknown]

diddle **1** *v* (also **diddle around**) *fr early 1800s British* To waste time; idle; loaf **2** *v* *fr early 1800s British* To cheat; swindle ◁**3**▷ *v* *fr late 1800s* To do the sex act; = SCREW ◁**4**▷ *v* *fr early 1900s* To insert a finger into a woman's vulva; = FINGERFUCK

diddle with **1** *v phr* To handle casually, idly, or nervously; play with: *Stop diddling with the silverware* **2** *v phr* (also **diddle around with**) To interfere with; have to do with; = FOOL AROUND WITH: *Don't diddle with that button, it controls the power for the whole building*

diddly or **diddley** (Variations: **damn** or **poo** or **poop** or **shit** or **squat** or **squirt** or **whoop** may be added) **1** *adj* Trivial; insignificant: *Tennis was a diddly sport back then*—Sports Illustrated/ *If you had a choice between...IBM or a diddly-squirt upstart*—Newsweek **2** *n* Nothing at all; very little; = ZILCH: *Rock critics don't mean diddley*—Rolling Stone/ *I don't know a diddly damn about theater*—Washingtonian/ *And Hannibal, he didn't do diddly-squat*—Pulpsmith
   See NOT GIVE A DAMN, NOT KNOW BEANS

diddlybop *students fr bop talk* **1** *v* To waste time; idle **2** *v* To do something pleasant and exciting **3** *n:* *They had a nice diddlybop at Gino's after work*

diddy bag *See* DITTY BAG

diddybop *See* DITTYBOP

diddybopper *See* DITTYBOPPER

didie *n* A baby's diaper

DIDO (DĪ doh) **1** *sentence fr computer* A product can be no better than its constituents; esp, the validity of a computer's output cannot surpass the validity of the input; = GIGO **2** *modifier:* *The DIDO principle still applies to its contents*—Village Voice [fr the abbreviation of *dreck in, dreck out* "shit in, shit out"]

didoes *See* CUT DIDOES

die **1** *v* To laugh uncontrollably: *When he puts a lampshade on his head you could die*—Max Shulman **2** *v* To desire very strongly: *She was dying to become Miss Pancake* **3** *v* *baseball* To be left on base at the end of an inning **4** *v* Of a ball, to stop moving, rolling, bouncing, etc
   See CROSS MY HEART, ROOT-HOG-OR-DIE

die for something *v phr* To have a very strong desire for something: *I'm dying for a drink/ Kids die for Sugar Glops*

die on someone *v phr* To die or cease to function, to the disadvantage of the speaker: *Damn motor died on me halfway up*

die on one's **feet** *v phr* To become absolutely exhausted; carry on although one can hardly move

◁**diesel dyke**▷ *n phr* An aggressive, masculine lesbian; = BULLDYKE: *a man fighting with a diesel-dyke over a girl they both wanted*—Maledicta

die standing up *v phr show business* To fail in a show or performance; = BOMB

die with one's **boots on** *v phr* To die while still active and vital

diff or **dif** *n fr middle 1800s* Difference: *don't make no diff*

difference *See* the SAME DIFFERENCE

the **difference** *n phr* A clear advantage; something that gives an advantage, esp a gun
   See CARRY THE DIFFERENCE

different strokes for different folks *interj fr black* A comment on the inevitable and tolerable variety of people and their ways: *Different strokes for different folks, I remarked*—Arthur Maling/ *Different strokes for different folks, he chirped mentally*—Earl Thompson

diffugalty (dih FYōō gəl tee) *n fr 1920s* Difficulty; trouble; problems [a humorous mispronunciation]

diffy *n Navy* A sickbay attendant

dig **1** *v* *fr middle 1800s* To study very diligently; exert oneself: *I had to dig to master even the rudiments* **2** *v* To interrogate or inquire vigorously: *She won't tell you, no matter how hard you dig* **3** *n* A derogatory, irritating, or contemptuous comment: *It wasn't quite an insult, more a dig* **4** *n* An archeological excavation **5** *v* *cool talk & counterculture fr jive talk* To understand; comprehend: *I dig your sense, but not its pertinence* **6** *v* *cool talk & counterculture fr jive talk* To like; admire; prefer: *Do you dig gazpacho and macho?* **7** *v* = DIG UP **8** *v* To hear or see in performance; = CATCH: *dug a heavy sermon at Smoky Mary's last week* [the cool senses, originally black, are probably related to the early-19th-century sense, "study hard, strive to understand"]
   See TAKE A DIG AT someone

dig at *v phr* To derogate; harass verbally; = PUT DOWN: *Why are you always digging at me about my mustache?*

dig dirt *v phr esp 1920s* To gossip

digger 1 *n fr WW1* An Australian **2** *n* =GOLD-DIGGER **3** *n* A pickpocket **4** *n* A person who buys tickets to be sold at prices higher than is legally permitted; =SCALPER: *They use diggers, dozens of guys who stand in lines and buy the maximum* —New York Times

diggety or **diggity** *See* HOT DIGGETY

digging *See* EASY DIGGING

dig out *v phr fr middle 1800s* To leave; depart; =CUT OUT, SPLIT: *supposing we dig out*—Owen Johnson

digs or **diggings** *n fr early 1800s* Lodgings; quarters: *Your digs, or mine?*

dig someone or something **the most** *v phr cool talk & counterculture* To like or prefer; have the closest affinity: *Adam and I dig each other the most* —Hazel Scott

dig up *v phr* To find or discover: *She dug up a shirt and we went out*

dike *See* DYKE

dikey *See* DYKEY

dildo or **dildoe 1** *n* An artificial substitute for an erect penis **2** *n* (also **dill**) A stupid and despicable person; =JERK, PRICK

diller *See* CHILLER-DILLER, KILLER, THRILLER-DILLER

dillion 1 *n* A very large sum; =JILLION **2** *modifier: I'd walk a dillion miles*

dilly or **dill** *n* A person or thing that is remarkable, wonderful, superior, etc; =BEAUT, LULU: *The last one is a dilly if you don't have an appointment*—RS Prather

dilly-dally *v* To idle; dither in an aimless or pointless fashion: *Stop dilly-dallying and get to the point*

dim *adj* Stupid; uncomprehending: *a nice man, but a trifle dim*

dim bulb *n phr* A stupid person; =DIMWIT: *a peculiar combination of dim bulb and bump-on-a-log* —Washington Post/ *Heroes meant to be swankily sexy tend to come off as tight-lipped dim bulbs*—Village Voice

dime 1 *n underworld* A ten-year prison sentence **2** *n gambling* A thousand dollars, esp as a bet **3** *v* (also **drop a dime**) *underworld & prison* To inform on someone; =SING, SQUEAL: *Frankie would have been okay if somebody hadn't dimed on him* [final sense from the *dime* dropped into the pay telephone for the call to the police] *See* FIVE-AND-TEN, GET OFF THE DIME, NICKEL AND DIME, ON someone's DIME, ON one's OWN TIME AND OWN DIME, STOP ON A DIME, a THIN DIME, TURN ON A DIME

a dime a dozen *adj* Very common; very cheap; in surplus: *PhDs are a dime a dozen now/ Copycats are a dime a dozen*—Sports Illustrated

dime bag or **dime** *n phr* or *n narcotics* Ten dollars' worth of a narcotic

dime dropper *n phr* An informer; =FINK: *Somebody that talks, turns state's evidence on you, a dime dropper*—Village Voice

dime-note *n* A ten-dollar bill; =TEN-SPOT

dime store *n phr* =FIVE-AND-TEN

dime up *v phr hoboes* To offer a dime for a meal, then try to get the dime back as well as the meal

dimmer 1 *n* (also **dimmo**) A dime; =DEEMER **2** *n prison* An electric light

dim view *See* TAKE A DIM VIEW OF someone or something

dimwit *n* A stupid person; =BOOB

dinah or **dine** *n lumberjacks & miners* Dynamite or nitroglycerine

dinch *fr underworld* **1** *v* To crush out a cigar or cigarette **2** *n* A cigarette or cigar butt

din-din *n fr late 1800s British* Dinner: *kisses, candlelight, din-din, liqueurs*—Philadelphia

diner *n railroad* A caboose

dinero (dee NAIR oh) *n* Money [fr Spanish]

ding 1 *v hoboes* To go on the road as a hobo; =BUM: *When you go bumming, you go dinging* —New Yorker **2** *modifier: in the ding camp at San Jose*—New Yorker **3** *v hoboes* To beg; =BUM, PANHANDLE **4** *v college students* To vote against a candidate for membership; blackball **5** *n: She got six yeahs and five dings* **6** *n college students* A letter rejecting one's application for a job or interview: *most disappointed in the dings that come on postcards*—Wall Street Journal **7** *n* A blow; a buffet: *We get a ding a day from the Chinese*—Time/ *the dings and dodges of daily life* **8** *v fr Army* To administer a reprimand or an adverse appraisal: *If we dinged people, very seldom did they get jobs*—Washingtonian *See* RING-A-DING-DING, RING-DANG-DO, RING-DING

ding-a-ling 1 *n* An eccentric person; =NUT, SCREWBALL: *The impression left by all this is that Wolman and Kuharich must be a couple of ding-a-lings*—True/ *great for teeny-boppers and cute little ding-a-lings*—Jackie Collins **2** *adj: to maintain the dingaling Holly Goheavily manner of life*—Life/ *It's the ding-a-ling capital of the universe*—Dan Jenkins [fr the notion that such a person hears bells ringing in the head]

dingbat 1 *n fr middle 1800s* An unspecified or unspecifiable object; something one does not know the name of or does not wish to name; =DINGUS, GADGET: *I don't think any wire and glass dingbat is going to "oontz" out cheek-to-cheek dancing*—Billy Rose/ *You can take your pulse now with a little dingbat stuck on your finger* **2** *n fr early 1900s Australian* A stupid person, esp a vague and inane simpleton; =DIMWIT: *"All in the Family" was re-exported to the BBC complete with "Polack pinko meatheads,"..."dingbats," and "spades"*—D Taylor **3** *n print shop* Any of various typographic symbols used as decorations, separators, emphasizers, trademark and union-done indicators, etc [first sense fr German or Dutch *dinges* "thing"]

ding-dang *interj* =DANG

ding-ding *n* A stupid person; idiot; =DINGBAT: *or have that ding-ding of a driver inform the cops* —Glendon Swarthout

ding-dong 1 *n* A bell **2** *n railroad* A gas-powered or gas-electric coach **3** *adj* Vigorous and spirited; =KNOCK-DOWN-DRAG-OUT: *A ding-dong battle is in prospect*—Fortune **4** *n* An eccentric person; =DING-A-LING, NUT ◁**5**▷ *n* The penis; =DONG: *couldn't find his own ding-dong if you told* *him to look between his legs*—Calvin Trillin/ *Forget his ding-dong. Think of it as a technically superior game*—Village Voice

ding-donger *n hoboes* An energetic and aggressive hobo

◄**dinge**► (DINJ) **1** *n fr 1920s* A black person **2** *modifier: You say this here is a dinge joint?*—Raymond Chandler [fr *dingy* "dark," used as a term for black persons fr early 1900s]

dinger 1 *n* = HUMDINGER **2** *n railroad* A yardmaster or assistant yardmaster **3** *n baseball* A base hit **4** *modifier: He was in an 11-game dinger drought*—Sports Illustrated

dingey 1 *n hoboes, railroad & truckers* A small vehicle, such as a locomotive, train, or truck **2** *n cowboys* Substandard, unregistered, or unbranded cattle

ding how (or **hao**) *adj phr fr WW2 armed forces* Very good; splendid: *It was a ding how operation all the way* [fr Chinese]

dingo 1 *n hoboes* A hobo; tramp **2** *n* A petty confidence man: *One dingo got a dollar*—Meyer Berger [related to the hobo sense of *ding* and probably ultimately to the 17th-century British slang *ding-boy* "rogue, sharper"]

ding-swizzled *adj* or *adv* = DARNED, DAMNED *See* I'LL BE DAMNED

dingus *n fr middle 1800s* Any unspecified or unspecifiable object; something one does not know the name of or does not wish to name; = GADGET, GIZMO: *What's that dingus in the corner?/ Hey, don't touch my dingus* [fr Dutch *dinges*, of the same meaning, essentially "thing"]

ding ward *n phr* The psychiatric ward of a hospital

dink¹ 1 *n college students* A tiny cap worn by freshmen ◄**2**► *n* The penis **3** *n* A despised person; = JERK, PRICK: *Nor, he insists, does he believe that any witless dink could learn to play like Ringo Starr within a week*—Rolling Stone **4** *n* Very little; nothing; = ZILCH: *He knows dink about weapons* **5** *v* To move slowly and jerkily: *after finding that the campaign was dinking along like a Toonerville trolley*—Time [fr *dinky*]

◄**dink²**► *n Vietnam War armed forces* A Vietnamese; = GOOK, SLOPE [related to Australian *Dink* "a Chinese," perhaps fr *dinge* or fr *Chink*]

dink³ *n* A yacht's tender; dinghy

dink⁴ *See* INKY-DINK, RINKY-DINK

dinkey 1 *n railroad fr late 1800s* A small locomotive for switching, etc **2** *n* = DINK³ [the railroad sense may be the source of the meaning "small"]

dinkum *adj* = FAIR DINKUM

dinky 1 *adj* Small; undersized: *a dinky foreign car/ dinky little town* **2** *adj* Inadequate; substandard: *What a dinky joint!*

dinner *See* SHOOT one's COOKIES

◄**dino¹**► (DEE noh) *n* An Italian or other southern European, or a person of such extraction; = DAGO: *Someday he'll shake down the wrong dino*—Nelson Algren [probably fr *Dino*, a common Italian given name; the term became confused with *dyno* "railroad section hand," probably because southern European immigrants became construction laborers

in great numbers; similarly, *wop* and *spick* are outdated terms for railroad section hands]

dino² *See* DYNO

dip¹ 1 *n fr middle 1800s underworld* A pickpocket **2** *v: Frankie dipped two men on the 37 bus* [fr *dipping* one's hand into a pocket]

dip² 1 *n fr 1920s* A stupid person; simpleton; = DIPSHIT: *That goddamned dip's worse than the Cowboys*—WT Tyler **2** *n* An eccentric person; = NUT: *My grandmother was a woefully crazy lady...a bit of a dip*—Carol Burnett **3** *n teenagers* A slovenly, untidy person; = DIRTBAG **4** *adj* = DIPPY

dip³ *n* Diphtheria

dip⁴ *n* = DIPSO

dip⁵ *v* To chew tobacco or take snuff orally

dip⁶ *See* DOUBLE-DIP, I'LL BE DAMNED, SHEEP-DIP, SKINNY-DIP

dipped or ◄**dipped in shit**► *See* I'LL BE DAMNED

dipper *n* = DIPPERMOUTH *See* FANNY-DIPPER, HIPPER-DIPPER

dippermouth *n* A person with a large mouth: *Dipper, that was my nickname, short for Dippermouth*—Louis Armstrong

dippiness *n* Craziness; silliness: *the sweet season of general dippiness*

dippy *adj fr early 1900s British* Crazy; foolish; whimsically silly; = KOOKY: *so strange and dippy as to have come from the brain of Tolkien*—Toronto Life/ *Depardieu at his dippiest*—Village Voice [origin unknown; perhaps fr *dipsomaniac*; perhaps fr Romany *divio* "mad, madman"]

dipsey *n hoboes* A short jail sentence

◄**dipshit**► or **dipstick 1** *n* A stupid, obnoxious person; = JERK: *You dipshit dog*—Stephen King/ *The other guy is the dipshit*—Village Voice/ *We're broke, dipstick*—Toronto Sun **2** *modifier: The dipshit broads took their lives in their own hands*—Easyriders [*dipshit* is an emphatic form of *dip²*, and *dipstick* is a euphemism for *dipshit*]

dipso *n fr early 1900s* A drunkard; dipsomaniac; = LUSH: *Madeline Kahn is his dipso wife, Gilda Radner his ditsy daughter*—Time

dipsy 1 *adj* Drunken; bibulous; alcoholic; = DIPSO: *Beryl Reid's appearance as a dipsy researcher*—Time **2** *adj* Foolish; silly; = DITSY: *Kelly, her dipsy counterpart at NBC*—Pulpsmith

dipsy-do or **dipsy-doo** *n baseball* A deceptive curveball that dips sharply

dipsy-doodle 1 *n* Fraud; deception; chicanery: *I opened the front door, leaving the key in the lock. I wasn't going to work any dipsy-doodle in this place*—Raymond Chandler/ *This dipsy-doodle allowed the Democratic candidate to preach a different sermon in every church*—Rolling Stone/ *Jennifer is as much a dipsy-doodle as everybody else on Square Pegs*—New York **2** *n* A deceiver; swindler; = CON MAN: *He's a marriage counselor, this dipsy-doodle*—New York Magazine **3** *v: That smooth chap might just have dipsy-doodled us* **4** *n* = DIPSY-DO **5** *n prizefight* A fight with predetermined outcome; a fixed fight **6** *n* A dance featuring dipping motions

◁**dip** one's **wick**▷ *v phr fr middle 1800s* To insert one's penis; do the sex act; =SCREW: *The Army forbade dipping one's wick in a WAC*

dirt 1 *n* Obscenity; pornography: *All you see in the movies these days is dirt* **2** *n* Gossip; intimate or scandalous intelligence; =SCOOP: *What's the dirt about your neighbors?* **3** *n* A despicable person; scum; filth: *He's dirt, no better*
    See DIG DIRT, DISH THE DIRT, DO SOMEONE DIRT, EAT DIRT, HIT THE DIRT, MOVE DIRT, PAY DIRT, TAKE SHIT

◁**dirtbag** or **dirtball**▷ **1** *n WW2 armed forces* A garbage collector **2** *n phr* A despicable person; filthy lout; =CRUD, SCUMBAG: *Those people in the store must have thought I was some kind of dirt bag* —New York Times/ *Why don't you throw this dirtbag in jail, deputy?*—Playboy/ *He ended up being chased down the hall by a dirtball with a knife*—Your Week in Ocean City

dirt bike *n motorcyclists* =SCRAMBLER

dirt cheap 1 *adj phr* Very cheap: *dirt-cheap prices* **2** *adv phr:* *buy it dirt cheap*

dirt under one's **feet** *n phr* A person or persons held in absolute contempt: *He treats me like dirt under his feet*

dirty 1 *adj* Aimed at getting an unfair advantage; dishonest; shady: *a few dirty tricks/ real dirty deal* **2** *adv:* *They fight dirty/ play dirty* **3** *adj* Lewd; obscene; =BLUE, RAUNCHY: *This dictionary dotes on dirty words/ Eschew dirty thoughts* **4** *adv:* *He talks dirty* **5** *adj 1920s jazz musicians* Sexually insinuating in sound and intonation; =CATHOUSE, BARRELHOUSE: *dirty blues* **6** *adj* Personally malicious or snide; nasty: *a dirty crack* **7** *adj narcotics* Addicted to narcotics **8** *adj narcotics* Having narcotics in one's possession: *Cops did a bodyshake and he was real dirty* **9** *adj* Well supplied with money; =FILTHY RICH: *Paddy was dirty with fifteen thousand or so*—Dashiell Hammett **10** *adj* Leaving much radioactive contamination or waste: *dirty bombs*
    See DO THE DIRTY ON someone, DOWN AND DIRTY, QUICK-AND-DIRTY

the **dirty dozens** *See* PLAY THE DOZENS

dirty heavy *n phr 1920s movie studio* A villain, esp in the movies; =HEAVY

dirtyleg *n* A promiscuous woman or prostitute; =FLOOZY: *flirting with a dirtyleg while in the company of a lady*—Dan Jenkins

dirty linen (or **wash**) *n phr* Personal or family matters; intimate details: *I won't hang out our dirty linen in front of this bunch*
    See WASH one's DIRTY LINEN

dirty little secret 1 *n phr* Something shameful that must be concealed; an embarrassing fact: *Power...has been a dirty little secret among modern economists*—New York Times **2** *n phr* Anything held secret personally or communally because it is patently shameful; a skeleton in the closet: *Everybody will know the dirty little secret of American journalism*—Time/ *Class Act: America's Last Dirty Little Secret*—New York Times [phrase propagated

by DH Lawrence, esp in his long essay "Pornography and Obscenity"]

dirty mind *n phr* A head full of sexual, malicious, and other reprehensible thoughts and fantasies

dirty-minded *adj* Inclined toward sexual, odious, or dubious notions

◁**dirty-neck**▷ **1** *n* A laborer or farmer **2** *n* An immigrant

dirty old man 1 *n phr* A lecherous man, esp an elderly one; =OLD GOAT **2** *n phr homosexuals* A male homosexual whose partner is much younger than himself: *Christopher is 20 years younger than Leo....He asks Leo to be his dirty old man*—New York Times

dirty pool *n phr* Unethical and dubious practice; =DIRTY TRICKS: *triggered ugly accusations of dirty pool*—TV Guide

dirty (or **low-down dirty**) **shame** *n phr* A person or thing that is much to be lamented; a pity; a disgrace: *He did? Ain't that a dirty shame?/ Man, you're a low-down dirty shame, you're nasty*

dirty tricks 1 *n phr* Dishonest or underhanded practices, esp in politics; malicious tactics: *make into federal crimes many "dirty tricks" in presidential and congressional elections*—Time/ *Mr Clarke called the indictment "one of the greatest political dirty tricks of all times"*—New York Times **2** *modifier:* *the Senate Watergate Committee's chief "dirty tricks" investigator*—Newsweek

dirty work *n phr* Dishonest, unethical, underhanded, or criminal acts: =SKULLDUGGERY

disappear *v underworld* To be murdered, esp in such a way that no trace is left

a **disaster** *n* A person or thing that fails utterly; =a TOTAL LOSS: *My debut was a disaster/ The dean's a disaster*

disc or **disk** *n* A phonograph record; =PLATTER

disc jockey *n phr* (Variations: **deejay** or **Dee-Jay** or **DJ** or **dj**) A radio performer who plays and comments on phonograph records; also, the person who plays records at a discotheque: *the thunder-voiced DJ*—Saturday Review

disco 1 *n* A discotheque, a kind of nightclub where patrons dance to recorded music, sometimes with synchronized psychedelic and strobe lighting: *There's not much jazzing around at the disco* —Vogue **2** *modifier:* *show up...for a disco party and fashion show*—Look **3** *v:* *We discoed the night away*
    See CRISCO DISCO

discombobulate or **discomboberate** *fr early 1800s* **1** *v* To disturb; upset; =BUG **2** *v* To perplex; puzzle: *The fancy words discombobulated me*

discombobulated *adj* Disturbed; upset; weird: *In this discombobulated society, it is far easier to get a piano shipped out to sea and lowered into the water beside the drowning man*—Washington Post

discombobulation *n* The condition of being discombobulated: *the Skinner course responsible for their emotional discombobulation*—Time

discouraged *adj* Drunk

disease *See* BLOOD DISEASE, FOOT-IN-MOUTH DISEASE, SOCIAL DISEASE

dise-drag *n* hoboes A freight car

disguised *adj* Drunk

disgusto *adj* Disgusting: *disgusto special effects aside*—Village Voice

dish **1** *n* A particularly attractive woman • Regarded by some women as offensive: *This was going to be my favorite dish*—John O'Hara/ *I love this book and I think its 80-year-old author is a dish* —Washington Post **2** *n* A person or thing that one especially likes; what exactly meets one's taste; = CUP OF TEA: *Now, there is a book that is just my dish*—George S Kaufman **3** *n* baseball The home plate of the baseball diamond **4** *v* To say something; tell something: *What the hell is he dishing us now?* **5** *v* To gossip; have an intimate chat; = DISH THE DIRT: *She sat and dished with the girls*—H Selby **6** *v* To give; purvey: *He took everything we gave and dished it right back*—D Cresap **7** *v* fr late 1700s British To cheat; thwart: *I'm afraid that blackguard has dished us again* **8** *n* lunch counter An order of ice cream
See one's CUP OF TEA

dish it out *v phr* To administer punishment, injury, or abuse: *Jenny, you can dish it out, but you can't take it*—Erich Segal

one's **dish of tea** *See* one's CUP OF TEA

dish out (or **up**) **1** *v phr* To distribute; issue: *The brand of drool they dished out*—Joseph Auslander/ *What line are they dishing up today?* **2** *v phr* To inflict; give: *They dished her out a horrid trouncing*

dishrag *See* LIMP DISHRAG

dish the dirt *v phr* To gossip; enjoy a cozy chat about personalities: *We sat around dishing the dirt until the gavel sounded*

dishwasher *n* railroad An engine wiper

dishwater *n* Weak and scarcely drinkable soup, coffee, etc
See DULL AS DISHWATER

dishy *adj* Very attractive; sexually desirable • Chiefly British use; regarded by some women as offensive: *exactly what it is to be a dishy girl bored stiff*—Penelope Gilliatt

disk *See* DISC

Disneyland daddy *n phr* A divorced or separated father who sees his children rarely; = ZOO DADDY

dispatcher *n* gambling A dishonest pair of dice

dissolve **1** *n* movie & television studio The gradual blending of one scene into the next; also, a device that causes this effect **2** *v*: *Dissolve to a closeup of the house*

ditch **1** *v* fr early 1900s To dispose of; get rid of; = CHUCK: *We'll ditch this Greek and blow*—James M Cain **2** *v* To land an aircraft on the water in an emergency **3** *v* To play truant; fail to go to school or to a class

Ditch *See* the BIG DITCH

dit-da artist *n phr* A radio-telegraph operator

ditsy *adj* Vapid and frivolous; silly; = AIRHEADED: *Charles Ruggles's ditsy bimbo*—Village Voice/ *Is there something in the air that makes Washington*

wives ditsy?—Philadelphia Journal [perhaps a blending of *dizzy* and *dotty*]

ditty (or **diddy**) **bag** *n phr* fr merchant marine fr middle 1800s A small bag for one's personal belongings, usu exclusive of clothing [origin uncertain; perhaps short for *commodity*, fr the earlier British naval term *commodity box*, which became *ditty box*]

dittybop or **dittybob** or **diddybop** black ◁1▷ *n* A stupid person, esp a crude and unsophisticated black person: *the diddybop image of JJ*—Amsterdam News **2** *v* To move, sway, etc, to music; = BOP: *A young man with earphones on his head...was ditty bopping in front of Saks*—New York Magazine

dittybopper or **diddybopper** black **1** *n* A person who dittybops ◁2▷ *n* A pretentious or pompous black person, esp one who aspires to enter the mainstream white culture **3** *n* = DITTYBOP

ditz *n* A silly and inane person; a frivolous ninny: *a brainy ditz involved with a vulnerable hunk*—Village Voice/ *little more than a likable, spoiled ditz who allows herself to ruled by...chemicals*—New York Review

dive **1** *n* fr late 1800s A vulgar and disreputable haunt, such as a cheap bar, nightclub, lodging house, or dancehall; = CRIB: *the girl who danced in a dive in New Orleans*—K Brush **2** *n* = SPEAK-EASY **3** *n* prizefight A knockdown or knockout, esp a false prearranged knockout: *A dive is a phantom knockout*—Arthur Daley **4** *v*: *They fixed it so he'd dive in the fourth* [origin uncertain; perhaps fr the notion that one could *dive* into a disreputable cellar haunt and lose oneself among lowlifes and criminals; perhaps a shortening of *divan* "a smoking and gaming room," a usage popular in London in the middle and late 19th century; the places were so called because furnished with *divans* "lounges," the name ultimately fr Turkish]
See NOSE DIVE, TAKE A DIVE

diver *See* MUFF-DIVER, PEARL-DIVER

divot (DIV ət) *n* A toupee [fr the Scottish word, "a piece of turf or sod, esp one cut out by a golf club," of unknown origin]

divvy **1** *v* (also **divvy out** or **divvy up**) To divide; apportion; = PIECE UP: *The governor and the Paris crook divvy the swag*—Alva Johnson/ *We would pass our hats and divvy up*—Louis Armstrong **2** *n* A share of profits or spoils **3** *n* A dividend

Dix or **dix** *n* A ten-dollar bill [fr French *dix* "ten," printed on ten-dollar bills once issued in New Orleans]

dixie *n* outdated Army A mess tin or small pot

Dixie¹ *n* New Orleans

Dixie² **1** *n* The southern United States **2** modifier: *a Dixie drawl* [probably because the region is south of the Mason-*Dixon* line]
See NOT JUST WHISTLING DIXIE, WHISTLING DIXIE

Dixieland **1** *n* The southern United States; = DIXIE **2** *n* The style of jazz played by the street bands in New Orleans, marked by a simple two-beat rhythm, ragged syncopation, improvised ensemble passages, etc **3** *adj*: *Dixieland trumpet*

Dixie mafia *n phr* A confederation or category of criminals operating in the southern United States, esp in urban centers and esp in the narcotics traffic: *a new criminal class, which some Southern law officials, for lack of a better term, term the Dixie mafia* —New York Times

dizzy *adj* Silly; foolish; inane; = DITSY: *some dizzy broad*—Jerome Weidman

dizzy-wizzy *n esp early 1900s narcotics* Any narcotic in pill form

DJ or **dj** *See* DISC JOCKEY

DMT *n narcotics* Dimethyltryptamine, a hallucinogen like LSD but with shorter effects

do 1 *v fr early 1800s British* To cheat; swindle: *He is hated by all the beggars above him, and they do him every chance they get*—J Flynt **2** *v narcotics* To use or take narcotics: *The straights do dope, ball a lot*—Saturday Review/ *I'd wonder why and do another line. But I never looked at it as if I were some big drug addict*—Playboy **3** *v* To serve a prison sentence: *He did six years up at San Quentin* **4** *n fr early 1900s British* A party or other gathering; affair; = SHINDIG: *a few of the other main do's* —Budd Schulberg/ *The Tweed do was held early last December*—Village Voice **5** *n esp black* A hairdo **6** *n* Excrement; feces: *I stepped in doggy-do* **7** *n* Something one should do or must do: *Being friendly is a do, but being possessive is a don't*

See DO someone DIRT, DO-GOODER, DO IT ALL, DO one's NUMBER, DOODAD, DO someone OUT OF, DO-RAG, DO one's STUFF, DO one's THING, DO TIME, DO UP, DO something UP BROWN, WHOOP-DE-DO

DOA (pronounced as separate letters) **1** *adj* Dead on arrival **2** *n*: *Don't risk being a DOA by driving drunk*

do a Dan O'Leary *v phr police* To work diligently, esp as a uniformed police officer

do a job on 1 *v phr* To injure; treat roughly: *Those motherf..in' scorpions really do a job on you* —New York Times **2** *v phr* = DO A NUMBER ON **3** *v phr* To destroy: *The pup did a job on the rug*

Doakes *See* JOE BLOW

do (or **run**) **a number on 1** *v phr* To take advantage of, esp by deception; mistreat; = SCREW: *You people ran a number on us. Whenever we brought it up, you walked away*—New York Times/ *get even with Leonard for doing that...number on her*—Cyra McFadden **2** *v phr* To affect adversely, esp as to morale and self-esteem: *He really did a number on her when he told her the boss didn't like her report* **3** *v phr* To defeat decisively; trounce; = CLOBBER: *They really did a number on the poor old Sox*

do a slow burn *v phr* To become very angry gradually: *And I do a real slow burn*—Leo Rosten

doby (DOH bee) *v merchant marine fr British* To wash clothing by hand: *He dobied a couple of blue shirts* [fr Hindi *dhobi* "washerman"]

doc 1 *n* A physician; doctor **2** *n* Man; fellow; = GUY ● Used in address to strangers: *Hey, doc, where's the exit?/ What's up, doc?*

dock *v* To reduce one's pay for some infraction: *I'm docking you six bucks for being sassy* [fr *dock* "to cut off part of the tail," fr a Middle English word meaning "docked tail"]

dock rat *n phr* A vagrant; drifter; = BUM

dock-walloper *n* A dockworker: *strolled among the dock-wallopers swinging a cane*—O McIntyre/ *As a dock-walloper he was the king of Greenpernt's waterfront*—Time

doctor 1 *n horse-racing* A person who drugs racehorses to improve their performance **2** *v* To alter or tamper with something dishonestly; = COOK: *We doctored the receipts/ He doctored the booze* **3** *v* To repair; mend: *Somebody's got to doctor this furnace*

See BUG DOCTOR, COUCH DOCTOR, PLAY-DOCTOR, SPIN DOCTOR, ZIT DOCTOR

Dr Feelgood 1 *n phr* A physician who prescribes amphetamines, vitamins, hormones, etc, to induce euphoria: *No Dr Feelgood was in the White House administering amphetamines*—William Safire **2** *n phr* Any person who soothes and pleases by hedonic ministrations: *the Dr Feelgood of American politics*—New York Times [fr the title of a 1960s song popularized by Aretha Franklin]

docu or **docudrama** (DAHK yoo) *n* A documentary film, TV program, play, etc: *Each of the...programs is half docu, half drama*—People Weekly/ *one vidfilm, plus a docu on Theodore Roosevelt*—Variety

do-dad *See* DOODAD

dodge *n fr early 1800s* A person's way of making a living, esp if illegal or dubious: *We used to run gin, but when prohibition ended we had to give up that dodge*

dodger *See* ROGER

do someone **dirt** *v phr* To cause someone trouble or embarrassment, esp by malice and slander; serve someone ill: *Don't repeat that unless you want to do him dirt*

dodo 1 *n fr late 1800s British* A stupid, inept person; = TURKEY **2** *n* A boring person; = FOGY: *I'm a respectable old dodo*—Philip Wylie **3** *n 1940s Army Air Corps* A student pilot who has not yet made a solo flight [fr the extinct *dodo* bird, rather sluggish and flightless]

See DEAD AS A DODO

◁**does a bear shit in the woods**▷ *sentence* That was a stupid question; isn't the answer very obvious?

◁**does a wooden horse have a hickory dick**▷ *sentence* That was a stupid question; isn't the answer very obvious?; = DOES A BEAR SHIT IN THE WOODS

◁**does Howdy Doody have wooden balls**▷ *sentence* That was a stupid question; isn't the answer very obvious?; = DOES A BEAR SHIT IN THE WOODS

do-funny *See* DOODAD

dog **1** *n* An unappealing or inferior person or thing; =DUD, LOSER: *The new show's a total dog* ◁**2**▷ *n* An unattractive woman: *Why'd you tell him his girl's a dog?* **3** *n* *esp jazz musicians* An attractive woman; =FOX **4** *n* A man; fellow; =GUY: *dirty dog/ handsome dog* **5** *n* *esp black* An untrustworthy man; seducer **6** *n* *black* A sexually aggressive man: *before the dogs on the ward showed their hand*—Donald Goines **7** *n* A foot: *His left dog pained* **8** *n* =HOT DOG **9** *v* *Army* To pester; =BUG, HASSLE

See BARKING DOGS, BIRD DOG, CATS AND DOGS, DOG IT, DOG-ROBBER, DOG SHOW, DOG'S-NOSE, DOG TAGS, DOG UP, DOG-WAGON, FUCK THE DOG, the HAIR OF THE DOG, HONG KONG DOG, HOT DIGGETY, HOT DOG, HOUND DOG, IT SHOULDN'T HAPPEN TO A DOG, LINE DOG, NERVOUS AS A DOG SHITTING RAZORBLADES, PUPPY-DOG FEET, PUP TENT, PUT ON THE RITZ, RAIN CATS AND DOGS, RED DOG, ROAD DOG, SEE A MAN ABOUT A DOG, SHORT DOG, TOP DOG, YELLOW DOG CONTRACT

the **Dog** *See* the HOUND

dog and pony act (or **show**) *n phr* An elaborately prepared or staged presentation, event, etc: *Bring them in here and do a dog and pony act*—Ed McBain/ *The company rep gave us a dog and pony show*

See GO INTO one's DANCE

◁**dog-ass**▷ *adj* Wretched; inferior; pitiable: *boning up on the dog-ass Jets*—Dan Jenkins

dog biscuit **1** *n phr* *1920s Army & students* Hardtack, a hard biscuit or bread made of flour and water **2** *n phr* A soda cracker ◁**3**▷ *n phr* *1940s students* An unattractive woman

dog-chaser *n* *railroad* A relief crew sent to bring in a train that cannot, under legal or union regulations, be moved by its own crew

dog collar *n phr* A collar fastening at the back, like a Roman collar; also, a very high collar like the one on a Marine Corps uniform

dog days *n phr* The hot and humid days of late summer [fr the rising of Sirius, the *dog* star]

dog-eared **1** *adj* Worn, creased, and rumpled; shabby; unkempt **2** *adj* Old; outworn; hackneyed: *even a clean reading of a dog-eared tune is deepened*—Village Voice [fr the look of a book whose pages have been repeatedly folded at the corners]

dog eye *n phr* A reproachful or pleading look

dogface **1** *n* *esp WW2 Army* A soldier, esp an infantry private: *Few wanted to be dogfaces*—Time **2** *modifier*: *a dogface, paddlefoot private*

◁**dog fashion** (or **style**)▷ *adv phr* With one partner in a sex act entering the other from the rear; =BOTTOMS UP

dogfight **1** *n* *fr WW1 air forces* An aerial combat among fighter planes **2** *n* Any confused and riotous brawl; =DONNYBROOK

dog food *n phr* *WW2 Navy* Corned-beef hash

◀**dogfuck**▶ *v* To do a sex act with one partner entering the other from the rear: *including how to 69 and dogfuck*—Playboy

dogger *See* HOT DOGGER

doggie **1** *n* A sailor or merchant seaman **2** *n* =DOG **3** *n* =HOT DOG **4** *n* =DOGFACE

See LINE DOG

doggo **1** *adj* Inferior; unpromising; wretched; =DOG-ASS: *Even doggo prospects like anthropologists and landscape architects, we learn, are still in demand*—Washington Post **2** *adj* *fr late 1800s British* In hiding; quiet and unobtrusive; low-profile: *The three that got away are doggo somewhere*

See LIE DOGGO

doggone or **daggone** or **dagnab** *fr middle 1800s* **1** *interj* (also **doggone it** or **daggone it** or **dagnab it**) An exclamation of disappointment, irritation, frustration, etc; =DANG, DARN: *Doggone it, leave me be!* **2** *adj* (also **doggoned** or **daggoned** or **dagnabbed**) Wretched; nasty; silly: *This doggone thing's busted* **3** *adv*: *They left here doggone fast* [a euphemism for *God damn*]

doggy **1** *adj* *late 1800s college students* Stylish; well dressed and groomed **2** *adj* Inferior; wretched; =DOGGO: *selling off the doggy companies Geneen had bought*—Newsweek

doggy bag *n phr* A paper or plastic bag given a restaurant customer to take home leftovers

doghouse **1** *n* Any small structure resembling in some way a dog's individual kennel: *The boat has a doghouse over the main cabin* **2** *n* *jazz talk* The bass viol: *Cole on doghouse was a miracle*

See IN THE DOGHOUSE

dogie *n* *cowboys* A motherless calf in a herd; =BUM

dog it **1** *v phr* =PUT ON THE RITZ **2** *v phr* To avoid or evade work; refuse to exert oneself; =COAST: *The whole shop's been dogging it today* **3** *v phr* To leave hastily; flee **4** *v phr* To live as a parasite; =SPONGE: *He was dogging it, mooching his room and board*

dognaper or **dognapper** *n* A stealer of dogs, esp for profitable selling

do-good *adj* Overtly benign and altruistic: *This "do-good" laundry list draws sneers*—Saturday Review

do-gooder *n* A person whose selfless work may be more pretentiously than actually altruistic; an ostentatiously rightminded citizen: *a professional do-gooder*—Billy Rose

dog out (or **up**) *v phr* To dress fancily; =DOLL UP: *He would have been feeling much better if he were dogged out in a new outfit*—James T Farrell

◁**dog-robber**▷ **1** *n* *outdated Army fr middle 1800s* An officer's orderly **2** *n* *baseball* An umpire [military sense fr the notion that these soldiers, who ate at the second table in the officers' mess, were *robbing the dogs* of the table scraps; the baseball sense seems merely contemptuous, and derived fr the military]

dogs *n* The feet

See BARKING DOGS, CATS AND DOGS, GO TO THE DOGS, RAIN CATS AND DOGS

the **dogs** *n phr* The greatest thing; a marvel: *Wouldn't it be the dogs to be paged like that?* —James T Farrell

dogsbody *n* A menial; lowly pawn • Chiefly British usage

dog's breakfast *n phr* A wretched mixture; an unpalatable combination: *that dog's breakfast of fact and fancy...docudrama*—Meg Greenfield/ *The plot is a dog's breakfast of half-baked ideas*—San Francisco

◁**dogshit**▷ *n* Despicable matter; pretentious trash; =CRAP: *none of this fancy-pants bullshit, poodle-top haircuts and flashy clothes. None of that dogshit*—Rolling Stone

dog show *n phr WW2 Army* Foot inspection

dog's-nose *n* A drink of beer or ale mixed with gin or rum

dog style *See* DOG FASHION

dog tags *n phr armed forces fr WW1* Identification tags, esp metal tags worn around the neck by members of the armed forces: *vets, if you still have your dog tags*—New York Sunday News

dog tent *See* PUP TENT

dog up *See* DOG OUT

dog-wagon **1** *n* A modest or cheap diner, such as might occupy an old railroad car or street car, that serves hot dogs **2** *n truckers* An antiquated truck

do-hickey or **do-hinky** *See* DOODAD, DOOHICKEY

do one's **homework** *v phr* To be ready and informed, esp for a meeting, interview, report, etc: *It was sketchy and we knew the chairman hadn't done his homework/ Shana Alexander has done her homework well*—National Public Radio

do someone **in** **1** *v phr fr late 1800s British* To kill someone: *She did in the old woman too*—Agatha Christie **2** *v phr* To ruin someone; destroy: *Another flop will do us in/ why you let your brother do you in the way he did*—Saul Bellow

doing *See* NOTHING DOING, TAKE SOME DOING

do it *v phr* To do the sex act; =FUCK ● An arch euphemism very popular for a time in a series of bumper-stickers: *Divers do it deeper/Professors do it fifty minutes at a time*

do it all **1** *v phr underworld* To serve a life term in prison **2** *v phr* To be versatile; be variously skilled: *Take that shortstop. He'll do it all for you*

do it up *v phr* To do something decisively and well: *Some of us really did it up in grand style*—Saturday Review

do-jigger *See* DOODAD

doke or **dokey** or **dokie** *See* OKEY-DOKE

doker *n carnival & circus* =SHILL

dokle *See* OKEY-DOKE

doll **1** *n* (also **dolly**) A conventionally pretty and shapely young woman, esp a curly, blue-eyed blonde, whose function is to elevate the status of a male and to inspire general lust; =BABY DOLL, BIMBO: *If a blonde girl doesn't talk we call her a doll*—F Scott Fitzgerald **2** *n* Any woman, esp an attractive one; =BABE, CHICK ● Considered offensive by many women **3** *n* Any notably decent, pleasant, generous person; =LIVING DOLL: *Isn't he a doll?* **4** *n* An attractive boy or young man **5** *n* (also **dolly**) *narcotics* An amphetamine or barbiturate drug in pill or capsule form

See BABY DOLL, CHINA DOLL, LIVING DOLL

Doll *See* BARBIE DOLL

dollar *See* ADOBE DOLLAR, BET one's BOTTOM DOLLAR, HOT AS A THREE-DOLLAR PISTOL, PHONY AS A THREE-DOLLAR BILL, TOP DOLLAR

dollar-spinner *n* Commercial success; seller: *All spectator sports combined to become the No 1 dollar-spinner...in entertainment*—People Weekly

dollar to rub against another *See* NOT HAVE ONE DOLLAR TO RUB AGAINST ANOTHER

dollface *n* A person with regularly pretty features of a feminine sort

dollop **1** *n* A lump or glob **2** *n* A portion, esp a small portion of food [origin unknown]

dolls *See* CUT OUT DOLLS

doll up (or **out**) *v phr fr early 1920s* To dress fancily and in one's best clothes; =GUSSY UP: *This year the girls are dolling up in calico patchworks*—New York Magazine

dolly *See* DOLL

dolly dancer *n phr WW2 Army* A soldier who gets easy duty, esp by pleasing officers

-dom *suffix used to form nouns* The range, establishment, scope, or realm of what is indicated: *fandom/ moviedom/ klutzdom*

dome *n fr late 1800s* The head: *What's going on in that dome of hers?*

See IVORY-DOME, MARBLE-DOME

dominoes **1** *n* The teeth **2** *n* Sugar cubes having the thinnish rectangular shape of dominoes **3** *n crapshooting* Dice

See AFRICAN DOMINOES, BOX OF DOMINOES, GALLOPING DOMINOES

donagher *See* DONNICKER

donar or **donah** (DAH nər, -nə) *n street gang fr 1950s* A girl, esp one's steady girl or fiancee, or a street-gang girl ● Used in London slang fr middle 1800s, and Australian fr late 1800s [prob fr Italian *donna* "woman, lady"]

done in **1** *adj phr* (also **done up**) Very tired; =POOPED: *I was done up*—SJ Perelman **2** *adj phr* Killed **3** *adj phr* Ruined; wrecked: *My plans are done in but good*

◁**dong**▷ *n* The penis [origin unknown; possibly fr *ding-dong* fr *dingus*, a euphemism for the unnamable thing; perhaps echoic to suggest striking; compare *wang*]

See FLONG one's DONG, PULL one's PUD

donk *n* Whiskey, esp raw or corn whiskey [because it has a kick like a *donkey*]

donkey *n railroad* A section hand

◁**donkey dick**▷ **1** *n phr WW2 armed forces* Salami and other cold-cut sausages; =HORSE COCK **2** *n phr narcotics* A very durable penile erection, due to an effect of heroin use: *a reward known in smack circles as "donkey dick"*—High Times

donkey-puncher *n lumberjacks* The operator of a donkey engine, an auxiliary engine for traction or lifting

donkey roast *n phr* A large, fancy, or noisy party: *at $100 a ticket...promises to be a real fine donkey roast*—New York Post

donkey's breakfast *n phr merchant marine* A straw mattress

donkey's years *n phr* A very long time ● Chiefly British use: *I got interested in his apprenticeship donkey's years ago*—Robert Ruark [a punning allusion to the long *ears* of a *donkey*]

donkeywork *n* Tedious work needing little skill or wit; = SCUT: *He uses computers to do what the "whiz kids" call their "donkey work"*—US News and World Report

donna *See* PRIMA DONNA

donnicker or **doniker** or **donagher** **1** *n* *underworld, carnival & circus fr late 1800s* A toilet **2** *n* *railroad* A freight-train's brake operator [fr diminutive of 18th-century British *danna* "feces," applied to a privy]

donnybrook *n* A riotous scene, esp a general and energetic brawl; = BRANNIGAN: *A donnybrook began when police arrested the operators*—R McCarthy [fr the reputation of a fair held annually at *Donnybrook* in Ireland]

do someone **nothing** *v phr* To leave one unaffected, unmoved, unpleased, etc: *This book does me nothing*

don't *n* Something one should not or must not do = a NO-NO: *The do's and don'ts of sailing a leaky barge*

don't give it a second thought *interj* An exclamation of pardon; a token of forgiveness for some presumed insult, offense, etc; = FORGET IT: *You didn't mean to, I know. Don't give it a second thought*

don't knock it *sentence* Don't be critical of it; appreciate its value: *Don't knock it. Nobody who lived in the past would want to live in the past*—A Brien/ *Don't knock it. You haven't even tried it yet*

don't take any wooden nickels *sentence fr 1920s* Take care of yourself; goodbye, and watch yourself ● Used as an amiable parting salutation

do one's **number** *v phr* To behave in an expected way; play a role; = GO INTO one's ACT: *He was doing his number about how you have to alienate no one* [fr *number* "theatrical act or routine, shtick"]

doo *See* HOOPER DOOPER

doobie or **dubee** or **duby** **1** *n* *narcotics* A marijuana cigarette; = JOINT: *I smoke a doobie at lunch*—Armistead Maupin/ *and rolled myself an ample doobie*—Richard Merkin **2** *n* *computer* A data base

doodad **1** *n* (Variations: **do-dad** or **do-funny** or **doofunny** or **do-hickey** or **doohickey** or **do-hinky** or **doohinky** or **do-jigger** or **doojigger** or **doowhangam** or **do-whistle** or **doowhistle** or **do-willie** or **doowillie**) Any unspecified or unspecifiable thing; something one does not know the name of or does not wish to name; = GADGET, THINGAMAJIG: *We may have turned into what looks like a nation of doohickeys*—Time/ *Imagination and art aren't worth those little doowhangams you put under a sofa leg*—National Review **2** *n* Something useless or merely ornamental: *Just a flourish, a little doodad*

doodah *See* ALL OF A DOODAH

doodle **1** *v* To cheat; swindle; = DIDDLE **2** *v* To make drawings and patterns while sitting at a meeting, talking on the telephone, etc: *From your doodle the shrink sees what's in your noodle* **3** *n* Wretched material; = SHIT: *How can he write such doodle?*—Washington Post

See DIPSY-DOODLE, WHANGDOODLE, WHOOP-DE-DO

doodle-brained *adj* Stupid; silly: *singing a doodle-brained folk song about "travelin'"*—Village Voice

doodlebug **1** *n* *railroad* A self-propelled railroad car; a one-car train **2** *n* *WW2 armed forces* A small reconnaissance car **3** *n* *WW2 armed forces* A military tank, esp a light tank **4** *n* A divining rod or other device used for locating underground water, gas, etc

◁**doodle-shit**▷ *n* (Variations: **doodily-shit** or **doodley-shit** or **doodly-squat** or **doodly**) Nothing; very little; = SQUAT, ZILCH: *I don't care doodily-shit about Jews and Nazis*—Ira Levin/ *A whole lot of doodley-shit*—Richard Fariña

doodling *n* Idle playing; = FOOLING AROUND, NOODLING: *When Sinatra entered the wings,...the doodling ceased*—Village Voice

doodly-squat **1** *n* *carnival* Money **2** *n* = DOODLE-SHIT

doo-doo *n* Excrement; = DO, SHIT: *I think doo-doo is coming out of your ears*—R Grossbach

doo-doo head *n phr* A stupid person; an idiot: *Let's face it, we're doo-doo heads for playing*—Washington Post

doofunny *See* DOODAD

doohickey *n* (Variations: **do-hickey** or **do-hinky** or **doohinky**) A pimple, blackhead, or other minor skin lesion; = ZIT

See DOODAD

doohinky *See* DOODAD, DOOHICKEY

doojee or **doojie** or **dujie** (DOO jee) **1** *n* *narcotics* Heroin **2** *n* A baby born addicted to heroin [perhaps fr *do* "feces," since heroin is also called "shit"]

doojigger *See* DOODAD

dookie *See* DUKIE

doolie *n* *Air Force Academy* A first-year cadet

See BIG DOOLIE

do something **on top of** (or **standing on**) one's **head** *v phr* To accomplish something easily: *You can do that shit on top of your head*—Donald Goines/ *That climb? I can do that standing on my head*

doop *See* WHOOP-DE-DO

dooper *See* HOOPER DOOPER, SUPER-DUPER, WHOOPER-DOOPER

door *See* someone CAN'T HIT THE SIDE OF A BARN, KATIE BAR THE DOOR, REVOLVING-DOOR, SHOW someone THE DOOR, SIDE-DOOR PULLMAN

doorknob *See* WIN THE PORCELAIN HAIRNET

doormat **1** *n* A person who is regularly and predictably exploited by others; constant victim: *the soulful Earth Mother doormat of the kind played by Shirley MacLaine in the fifties*—New York Magazine **2** *modifier*: *Cornell University's doormat status on the gridiron*—People Weekly

See TREAT someone LIKE A DOORMAT, WIN THE PORCELAIN HAIRNET

do someone **out of** *v phr* To deprive by cheating, fraud, stealing, etc: *They did the poor jerk out of his pay*

doowhangam or **doowhistle** or **doowillie** *See* DOODAD

doo-wop or **do-whop** **1** *n fr 1950s black musicians* A style of street jazz-singing, esp by black ensembles **2** *modifier: from the do-whop music and lovingly customized cars*—Time/ *lead singer of her Sixties doo-wop outfit, Patti Labelle and the Bluebelles*—Rolling Stone [echoic fr a common rhythm phrase of the songs]

doozie or **doozy** or **doosie** *n fr 1930s* A person or thing that is remarkable, wonderful, superior, etc; = BEAUT, HUMDINGER: *a little 30-page doozey called "Making Chicken Soup"*—Village Voice/ *Want a swell Naval Air Station? I got two doozies up for grabs*—Esquire [fr *Deusenberg*, the name of a very expensive and desirable car of the 1920s and 30s]

dope **1** *n fr late 1800s* Any narcotic drug: *They searched him for dope* **2** *modifier: a dope fiend/ dope stash* **3** *n* A sedative or painkilling drug, esp when prescribed or given by a physician **4** *v: The nurse doped him so he could sleep* **5** *v* To give drugs, vitamins, etc, to horses or athletes to improve their competitive prowess: *He couldn't run that fast if he wasn't doped* **6** *n* Coca-Cola (a trade name): *Jim Bob sat down and ordered a large dope* **7** *n fr middle 1800s* Any liquid, esp a viscous one, used for a special purpose: *airplane dope/ pipe dope* **8** *n fr late 1800s* = DOPER **9** *n fr early 1900s* A stupid person; idiot; = TURKEY: *Only a dope would refuse that chance* **10** *n* A cigarette; = DOPE STICK **11** *n fr early 1900s* Information; data: *Get me all the dope you can on her colleagues* **12** *n* Gossip; news; = the LOWDOWN: *What's the latest dope about Ruth?* **13** *n* A prediction, esp about a race or a game, based on analysis of past performance; = FORM: *The dope says Dream Diddle in a romp* **14** *v: I dope it like this, Ali all the way* [fr Dutch *doop* "sauce for dipping"; with elaborate semantic shifts] *See* HIT THE DOPE

dopenik *n narcotics* A narcotics addict

dope off **1** *v phr fr WW1 Navy & Marine Corps* To sleep; fall asleep: *I fill my stomach before I go in there and I'll start to dope off and yawn or something*—Earl Thompson **2** *v phr WW2 armed forces* To neglect one's duty and concerns; = GOOF OFF

dope out **1** *v phr fr early 1900s* To explain or clarify; figure out: *I can't dope out how they got in* **2** *v phr* To predict a sports result from the available information

doper *narcotics* **1** *n* A narcotics addict or user: *alerting dopers of every stripe that where the penalties had been stiff, they would now be feudal*—T Ferris **2** *modifier: with all these doper cops loose*—Rolling Stone/ *seemed merely a statement of doper hipness*—Rolling Stone

dope sheet *n phr* Printed information or instructions, esp about the past performance of race horses; = FORM

dopester *n fr early 1900s* A person who makes predictions based on available information, esp about races and games

dope stick *n phr esp early 1900s* A cigarette

dopey or **dopy** *fr late 1800s* **1** *adj* Stuporous, esp from narcotic intoxication: *I was dopy after they gave me the shot* **2** *adj* Stupid; idiotic: *What a dopey thing to say*

Dora *See* DUMB DORA

do-rag **1** *n black* A cloth or scarf worn over a processed hairdo or "conk": *wears a "do-rag" on his new hairdo as he pours out hatred of whites*—Life **2** *modifier: that famous do-rag militant, Sammy Davis*—Village Voice

do-re-mi *n* Money: *Get the rubber band off the do-re-mi*—John Kieran [fr the first three sol-fa notes, with a pun on *dough* "money"]

◁**dork**▷ **1** *n esp teenagers* The penis: *the glorious acrobatics she can perform while dangling from the end of my dork*—Philip Roth **2** *n* A despicable person; = JERK, PRICK: *a frightened, virtuous dork* —New Yorker

dorky *adj* Stupid; awkward; = KLUTZY: *a dorky kid with Dumbo ears*—Armistead Maupin

dorm **1** *n* A dormitory, esp at a college **2** *modifier: a dorm picnic/ dorm rule*

dory *See* HUNKY-DORY

dose **1** *v* To give a horse, dog, athlete, etc, a drug or other stimulant before a competition; = DOPE ◁**2**▷ *v* To infect with a venereal disease, esp gonorrhea: *What's going to happen is that you'll get dosed*—Richard Fariña

a dose ◁**1**▷ *n phr* A case of venereal disease, esp of gonorrhea: *Don't Give a Dose to the One You Love Most*—New York Daily News **2** *n phr* An excess; surfeit: *I got a real dose of that in freshman year and don't want any more* *See* LIKE SHIT THROUGH A TIN HORN

do-se-do (DOH see DOH) *n prizefight* A dull fight, with more dancing than punching [fr the square-dance figure, fr French *dos-à-dos* "back to back"]

dose of salts *See* LIKE SHIT THROUGH A TIN HORN

doss *hoboes fr late 1800s* **1** *n* Sleep: *find good barns for a doss at night* **2** *n* (also **doss house**) A cheap lodging house; = FLOPHOUSE **3** *n* A brothel **4** *n* A bed; = KIP [ultimately fr Latin *dorsum* "back"]

do (or **strut**) one's **stuff** *v phr* To display one's virtuosity; show one's skill: *Get in there and do your stuff* [ultimately fr a black expression for showing off one's sexual attraction]

the **dot** *n phr* The exact moment: *midnight to the dot* *See* ON THE DOT

do the dirty on someone *v phr* = DO someone DIRT

do the Dutch (or the **Dutch act**) *v phr* To commit suicide: *Why did the old man do the Dutch?* —Lawrence Sanders/ *She only came aboard to do the Dutch act*—John O'Hara [narrowed meaning of an earlier phrase meaning "to depart, abscond"]

do one's (or one's **own**) **thing** *v phr esp 1960s counterculture fr black* To follow one's special inclinations, esp despite disapproval; fulfill one's peculiar destiny: *Doing your own thing may be all right in prescribed doses*—AJH Brown

do time *v phr* To serve a prison sentence

do tricks *See* GO DOWN AND DO TRICKS

dotty *adj fr middle 1800s British* Crazy; insane; very eccentric: *a dotty old fellow*

double 1 *n* A person or thing that strongly or exactly resembles another; duplicate; =DEAD RINGER, LOOK-ALIKE: *She's Grace Kelly's double* **2** *n* An actor or stunt person who does the dangerous things required in a part: *He never uses a double. He does his own stunts* **3** *v*: *We got a guy'll double for you jumping off the cliff* *See* ON THE DOUBLE

a **double** *n phr* A double portion or pair of anything: *scored a double, riding the winners of the fourth and seventh races*—New York World-Telegram/ *Gimme a Scotch, a double*

double (or **double in brass**) **as** *v phr* To perform or work as, in addition to one's primary job: *He doubled in brass as a waiter when the cooking was done* [fr the skill of a circus performer who does an act and plays in the band]

double-bagger *n esp teenagers* A very ugly person; =TWO-BAGGER [fr the fact that one needs two *bags* to obscure the ugliness, one to go over the subject's head and one over one's own head]

double-clutcher[1] *n fr black* A despicable person; =BASTARD, PRICK [a rhyming euphemism for *motherfucker*]

double-clutcher[2] *n black* A person who takes more than his or her share of puffs from a marijuana cigarette, esp one who takes two puffs in quick succession [perhaps because the arm motion of a quickly repeated puff resembles the leg motion of a person who *double-clutches* a truck or other vehicle]

double-clutching *adj fr black* =MOTHERFUCKING

double cross 1 *n phr fr middle 1800s British* A betrayal or cheating of one's own colleagues; an act of treachery: *The two suspected dealers were planning a double-cross*—New York Magazine **2** *v*: *I would never double-cross a pal* [fr the reneging on an agreement to lose, a *cross*, by actually winning] *See* GIVE someone THE DOUBLE CROSS

double-dealing 1 *n* Deceitful or treacherous behavior **2** *modifier*: *a double-dealing little crum*

double-decker 1 *n* Anything, like a sandwich or a bus, having two levels or layers rather than the normal one **2** *modifier*: *a double-decker ham sandwich/ double-decker red bus*

double dip *n phr* An ice-cream cone with two scoops of the confection

double-dip *v* To collect more than one income at a time, esp by drawing a military pension and holding a job

double-dipper *n* A person who double-dips: *Federal pensioners are "double-dippers" who also collect Social Security checks*—Time

double-dome 1 *n* An intellectual; scholar; =EGGHEAD: *Princeton, NJ, where the double domes congregate*—New York Post **2** *modifier*: *None of your double-dome pomp, please* **3** *v*: *legitimate double-doming I suppose, but totally without fact*—Philadelphia

double Dutch *n phr* Language that cannot be understood, esp overly technical jargon: *Plain English will do; cut the double Dutch*

double-gaited 1 *adj* Bisexual; =AC-DC: *Duilio is not double gaited as far as I know*—John O'Hara/ *Was Danny simply double-gaited?*—Charles Beardsley **2** *adj* Strange; eccentric; =WEIRD: *These double-gaited gonzos are perpetrating a plague of best-selling takeoffs*—Newsweek [fr the various *gaits* of a horse]

doubleheader 1 *n railroad* A train pulled by two locomotives **2** *n sports* Two contests, esp baseball games, played at one meeting **3** *n salespersons* A customer who buys more than one of the same item at a time

double in brass as *See* DOUBLE AS

double-minus *See* X-DOUBLE-MINUS

double nickel *n phr fr citizens band* The 55-mile-per-hour speed limit

double-o *v* To examine carefully; scrutinize: *I stop a second to double-o the frame*—Lionel Stander [fr the abbreviation of *once-over*]

the **double-o** *n phr* A close examination; =the ONCE-OVER: *You mean give him the double-O*—John O'Hara

double sawbuck (or **saw**) *n phr* Twenty dollars; a $20 bill: *so many sheets of dollars, ten-spots and double saws*—Westbrook Pegler

double scrud *See* SCRUD

double (or **fast**) **shuffle 1** *n phr* =DOUBLE CROSS **2** *n phr* Deception; duplicity; =RUN-AROUND: *The dean gives me a quick double shuffle/ I don't want you to think I'm giving you a fast shuffle*—Lawrence Anderson **3** *v*: *He was fast shuffling me, but I caught him* [fr the deceptive *shuffle* of a card sharp]

double-take 1 *n* A sudden second look or a laugh or gesture over something one has at first ignored or accepted; a belated reaction: *She suddenly caught the reference and did a double-take* **2** *v*: *I double-took a little bit when she ordered a cigar*—Robert Ruark

double-team *v sports fr middle 1800s politics* To attack or defend against a formidable athlete with twice the usual forces: *He was gaining every play till they double-teamed him* [originally fr *doubling* the *team* of horses used for a purpose]

double-time *v* =DOUBLE-CROSS, TWO-TIME

double-trouble 1 *n* Serious difficulty; =DEEP TROUBLE **2** *modifier*: *a double-trouble day* **3** *n* A source or cause of great difficulty or menace; =BAD NEWS: *Watch that clown, he's double trouble*

double whammy *n phr* A two-part or two-pronged difficulty; a dual disadvantage: *the double-whammy of steep home prices and steeper interest rates*—Washingtonian

double X *n phr* =DOUBLE CROSS

douche *See* TAKE A DOUCHE

◁**douche bag**▷ *n phr* A despicable and loathsome woman; =SCUMBAG: *dirty, filthy douchebag*—Herbert Kastle

douchie *n prison* A dupe; a victim; =PATSY

dough **1** *n fr late 1800s* Money; =BREAD: *And to get the dough we'll put our watch and chain in hock*—HS Canby **2** *n* =DOUGHBOY
See CASE DOUGH, HEAVY MONEY

doughboy *n fr middle 1800s & esp WW1* An infantry soldier; =GRUNT, PADDLEFOOT [origin unknown; perhaps fr a resemblance between the buttons of the infantry uniform and *doughboys* "suet dumplings boiled in seawater," a term fr the British merchant marine]

doughfoot *n WW1* =DOUGHBOY

dough-head **1** *n* A stupid person; idiot; =KLUTZ **2** *n hoboes* A baker

doughnut *n truckers* A truck tire
See TAKE A FLYING FUCK

doughnut factory (Variations: **foundry** or **house** or **joint** may replace **factory**) **1** *n phr* A cheap eating place; luncheonette **2** *n phr hoboes* A place where free food is distributed

dough-pop *v* To defeat; hit, =CLOBBER: *dough-popped Arkansas 37 to 21*—Dan Jenkins

dough-puncher *n armed forces* An Army or Navy baker

dough-roller *n lumberjacks* A logging-camp cook

do up **1** *v phr* To pummel and trounce; =CLOBBER **2** *v phr narcotics* To take narcotics: *We'll do up some hash* **3** *v phr* To enhance; prepare, esp to wrap or package: *I'll do it up real nice. It's a present*

do something **up brown** *v phr fr middle 1800s* To do something very thoroughly: *He didn't just finish it, he did it up brown* [fr the *brown* color of something well baked]

douse or **dowse** *v fr middle 1800s* To extinguish a light, lamp, candle, etc [specialized fr an earlier sense, "hit"]

dove (DUHV) **1** *n* Dear one; honey; love: *There at once, my dove* **2** *n* A person who advocates peace and nonviolence; an irenic soul
See TURTLE DOVES

dovetail *v Army* To say something linked and sequential: *Let me dovetail on what you just said*

dovey *n* =LOVEY-DOVEY

dovish *adj* Tending to advocate peace over war; irenic: *more and more room for dovish interpretations*—Stewart Alsop

dow *See* ROW-DOW, ROWDY-DOW

dowdy *See* ROWDY-DOW

do-whistle or **do-histle** *See* DOODAD

do whop *See* DOO-WOP

down **1** *v* To defeat; trounce: *She downed the bruiser* **2** *v* To knock or bring to the ground; =DECK: *They finally downed him at the three-yard line* **3** *v* To eat or drink: *I downed an enormous pizza* **4** *v* To criticize; complain of; =PUT someone or something DOWN: *My friends downed me for listening to country music*—HE Roberts **5** *v* To sell **6** *adj* Depressed; melancholy; =BLUE: *He's real down about losing that chance* **7** *adj* Lacking vitality; exhausted; =BEAT: *You look down today, old buddy* **8** *adj* Not functioning; =ON THE BLINK: *The power plant has been down for two months/ The computer's down again today* **9** *adv* Behind one's opponent in score: *They were down by six at the end of the first half* **10** *adj* Finished; dealt with • Referring always to a series of tasks, requirements, etc: *They're well into the triathlon, with two events down and only one to go* **11** *adj lunch counter* Toasted **12** *n lunch counter* Toast **13** *adj cool talk & counterculture* Coolly cognizant; at ease in one's own skin; =COOL: *a down cat* **14** *adj cool talk & counterculture fr black* Excellent; good; profoundly satisfying: *The way she sang it was real down* **15** *adj black & teenagers* Ready; able to respond without inhibition: *They were down for it, so I got down too* **16** *adj* Depressing; pessimistic; dampening; =DOWNBEAT: *I don't see the point of making such a "down" picture*—Xaviera Hollander **17** *n narcotics* =DOWNER [sense "nonfunctional" probably fr a shortening of *broken down*; cool and teenager senses perhaps fr jazz musicians' terms like *low down* and *down and dirty* used to praise gutbucket and other jazz when especially well played; see *get down*]
See DOWN ON someone, GET DOWN, GO DOWN ON someone, HAVE something DOWN, LOOK DOWN ON someone, the LOWDOWN, LOW-DOWN, MELTDOWN, PUT-DOWN, PUT someone DOWN FOR something, TURN THUMBS DOWN, UP-AND-DOWN

down (or **up**) one's **alley** *adv phr* Of the sort one prefers or is best at; =TAILOR-MADE: *That job's right down his alley*

down and dirty **1** *adj phr* Nasty; low; vicious and deceptive: *Mississippi: A Down And Dirty Campaign*—Newsweek/ *This is down-and-dirty time. Just witness Rizzo's angry characterization of Goode*—Philadelphia **2** *adj phr poker* With the face down, and probably nasty for someone • Uttered in stud poker as the last cards are dealt face down

down and out *adj phr fr early 1900s* Penniless and hopeless; destitute: *When you're down and out, remember what did it*—Arthur Miller [fr the condition of a fighter who is knocked out]

down-and-outer *n fr early 1900s* A complete failure; derelict; =BUM

down a peg *See* TAKE someone DOWN A PEG

downbeat *adj* Depressing; pessimistic: *a triumph of upbeat pictures over the downbeat*—Bob Thomas

down-dressed *adj* Avoiding the obvious appearance of luxury; understated

downer **1** *n narcotics* A depressant drug, esp a barbiturate; sedative; =DOWN **2** *n fr narcotics* A depressing experience; =BUMMER, DRAG: *The opening scene's a downer* **3** *n* =BAD TRIP

down for the count *adj phr* Utterly defeated; ruined; =DOWN AND OUT [fr the *count* of ten made over a *downed* boxer]

downhill **1** *n prison & armed forces* The final half of a prison sentence or a military enlistment **2** *adj* Simple and easy: *nearly done and all downhill from here* **3** *adv* To a worse condition; to the

bad: *all trends ineluctably downhill* **4** *adj:* a
downhill prospect
See GO DOWNHILL

down home *esp black* **1** *adv phr* In the southern US; in Dixie **2** *n phr:* old buddy *from down
home* **3** *modifier: He was getting away from all
that old down-home stuff*—Claude Brown **4** *adv
phr* In a Southern regional or ethnic manner:
*funkier than blues and playing about as down home
as you can get*—Rolling Stone **5** *adj phr* Simple;
homey: *a down-home meal of roast chicken, potatoes, and peas*

down in flames *See* GO DOWN IN FLAMES

down in the kitchen *adv phr truckers* Driving in
lowest gear

down one's **nose** *See* LOOK DOWN one's NOSE

down on someone or something *adj phr* Angry
with or critical: *Everybody's down on Mary since she
reported Sue to the boss*

down on all fours *adv phr* In a depressed position or state: *Du Pont found itself down on all fours
with the rest of the industry*—M Ways

downputter *n* A person who regularly criticizes
and disparages; = KNOCKER

down the drain *adv phr* To a futile end; to waste:
All his best efforts seemed to go down the drain
See POUR MONEY DOWN THE DRAIN

down the Goodyears (or **the rollers**) *v phr
airline* To lower the landing gear ● Esp the command to do so

down the hatch *interj* A toast, followed by the
swallowing of a whole drink

down the line **1** *adv phr* From the higher to the
lower in a hierarchy: *down the line to the doorman*
2 *adv phr* In a certain direction along a road:
*Ain't no gas station here, but there's one down the
line about two miles* **3** *adv phr* In the brothel
district: *Saw her down the line last week, looking
bad*

down the pike *See* COME DOWN THE PIKE

down the river *See* SELL someone DOWN THE
RIVER

down the tube (or **tubes** or **chute**) *See* GO
DOWN THE TUBE

down someone's **throat** *See* JUMP DOWN someone's THROAT

down-thumb *v* To disapprove; veto; = TURN
THUMBS DOWN: *We down-thumbed the shaky marriage last December*—McCall's

downtime **1** *n* Time during which a machine,
factory, etc, is not operating **2** *n* Time away
from work; leisure time: *He spends most of his
downtime with Toby, his wife*—People Weekly/ *He
has more downtime than he did four years ago*
—Time

down to brass tacks *adv phr fr early 1900s*
Dealing with the essentials; concerned with the
practical realities: *highbrow sermons that don't
come down to brass tacks*—Sinclair Lewis

down to size *See* WHITTLE someone or something
DOWN TO SIZE

down to the ankles *See* BEATEN DOWN TO THE
ANKLES

down to the ground *adv phr* Totally; utterly:
That'll suit me down to the ground

down to the wire *adv phr fr 1940s* Near the finish; at or to the last possible moment: *The project is
getting down to the wire and things are getting frantic* [fr the imaginary line marking the end of a horse-
race; horses were said to pass "under the *wire*"]
See GO TO THE WIRE

down trip *See* BAD TRIP

Down Under **1** *adv phr* In Australia and/or
New Zealand; in the Antipodes **2** *n phr: They're
from Down Under*

down with it *adj phr jive talk* Coolly cognizant;
absolutely in touch; = WITH IT

down yonder *adv phr* = DOWN HOME

do you want an engraved invitation *question*
Must you be especially asked and pleaded with?;
you are being too standoffish and scrupulous

dozen *See* CLEAN DOZENS, DEVIL'S DOZEN, a DIME A
DOZEN, PLAY THE DOZENS

dozer **1** *n* A powerful blow, esp with the fist;
= BELT, BIFF **2** *n* = DOOZIE **3** *n* A bulldozer

DPT *n* Dipropylphyptamine, a hallucinogen like LSD
but having an effect lasting only an hour or two

draft *See* FEEL A DRAFT

draft bait *n phr esp 1940s* A person subject to
immediate conscription

drag **1** *n fr late 1900s* Influence; weight; = CLOUT,
PULL: *We had a big drag with the waiter*—Ernest
Hemingway **2** *n fr early 1900s* A street: *from
some bo on the drag I managed to learn*—Jack
London **3** *n* An inhalation of smoke; puff;
= TOKE: *The ponies took last drags at their cigarettes and slumped into place*—F Scott Fitzgerald **4**
v: dragging on cigars and feeling grown up **5** *n*
A cigarette; = BUTT: *a drag smoking on your lip*
—Stephen Longstreet **6** *n homosexuals fr late
1800s* A party or gathering, usu of homosexuals,
where everyone wears clothing of the other sex; a
clustering of transvestites **7** *n homosexuals*
Clothing worn by someone of the sex for which the
clothing was not intended; transvestite costume, esp
women's clothing worn by a man **8** *modifier: a
drag queen/ drag party* **9** *n esp students* A
dance or dancing party; prom **10** *v esp students*
To escort a partner to a dance **11** *n: I asked
Jeannie to be my drag tomorrow night* **12** *adv*
With a partner; escorted: *Can't come stag, have to
be drag* **13** *v teenagers & hot rodders* To race
down a straightaway **14** *n* = DRAG RACE **15** *n
police* A roll of money, purse, etc, used to lure the
victim in a confidence game **16** *n fr middle
1800s* A situation, occupation, event, etc, that is
tedious and trying; = DOWNER: *Life can be such a
drag one minute and a solid sender the next*—Louis
Armstrong **17** *n* A dull, boring person: *Don't
ask John to the party, he's such a drag*
See MAIN DRAG

◁**drag ass**▷ **1** *v phr* To depart, esp in a hurry;
= HAUL ASS **2** *v phr* To be morose, sluggish,
and whiny: *Quit drag-assing and get to work*

drag one's **feet** *v phr fr loggers* To shirk; make
less than a good effort, perhaps in the spirit of sabo-

tage: *The project failed because even the managers were dragging their feet* [fr the action of an unenergetic member of a two-person sawing team, who would *drag his feet* or "ride the saw" rather than contribute the proper effort]

drag one's **freight** *See* PULL one's FREIGHT

dragged in *See* LOOK LIKE SOMETHING THE CAT DRAGGED IN

dragged out *adj phr fr middle 1800s* Exhausted; = BEAT: *I feel awful dragged out today*

dragger *n restaurant* A customer who asks for change when giving a tip *See* KNUCKLE-DRAGGER

dragging *See* one's ASS IS DRAGGING

draggy *adj* Slow; monotonous; sluggish: *a draggy movie*

drag in *v phr* To arrive: *Where'd you drag in from?*

drag it *v phr* To quit; break off; = DRAG ASS

drag someone **kicking and screaming into the twentieth century** *v phr* To force someone to recognize or adapt to change; educate a rigid reactionary: *the group that drags the ABA kicking and screaming into the 20th century*—New York Times

Dragon Lady *n phr* A powerful, intimidating woman [fr a character in the popular comic strip "Terry and the Pirates" which originated in the 1930s]

dragon wagon *n phr teenagers* An automobile tow truck

drag out 1 *v phr* To extend something tediously; make something last too long: *He dragged out the story excruciatingly* **2** *v phr* To extract; elicit: *She couldn't drag the truth out of him*

drag-out *See* KNOCK-DOWN DRAG-OUT

drag party *n phr homosexuals* A party where merrymakers wear the dress of the other sex; also, any party for homosexuals

drag queen *homosexuals* **1** *n phr* A male homosexual who enjoys dressing like a woman **2** *n phr* A male homosexual who affects pronounced feminine behavior; = QUEEN

drag race *n phr hot rodders & teenagers* A speed competition between or among cars, esp vehicles with very powerful engines and very elongated, skeletal bodies

dragster *n hot rodders & teenagers* A car used in drag races, esp one purposely built for such competition

drag strip *n phr hot rodders & teenagers* The straight track or portion of highway on which a drag race is held

dragsville *adj* Very dull; tedious; = DRAGGY, DULLSVILLE: *My much touted party proved dragsville*

drag-tail *v* To move or work sluggishly; = DRAG ASS: *Jimmy is drag-tailing it up Main Street*—Billy Rose

drag one's **tail** (or ◁**ass**▷) *v phr* To work sluggishly; loaf; = DRAG ASS, DRAG-TAIL: *Two hours off with pay, why the hell are they draggin' their tails?* —Pietro di Donato

drain *See* BRAIN DRAIN, DOWN THE TUBE, POUR MONEY DOWN THE DRAIN

drama *See* DOCU, DROOPY DRAMA, MACHODRAMA

drape 1 *n jive talk* A suit; ensemble of suit, shirt, necktie, and hat **2** *n jive talk* A young man wearing black, narrow-cuffed slacks, a garish shirt, a loose jacket without lapels, and no necktie: *Drapes resent any comparison with zoot-suiters*—Time **3** *n* A dress; gown *See* SET OF THREADS

drape ape *n phr college students* A baby or small child; = CRUMBCATCHER

drapes *n black* Clothes; dress

drape shape 1 *n phr jive talk* A severely draped garment, as worn by zoot-suiters **2** *modifier: designing the first drape-shape coat*—New Yorker

draw *See* BEAT someone TO THE DRAW, GET A BEAD ON someone or something, the LUCK OF THE DRAW, be QUICK-DRAW, QUICK ON THE DRAW, SLOW ON THE DRAW

draw a blank 1 *v phr* To fail completely in recall: *I'm trying to remember, but keep drawing a blank* **2** *v phr* To get nothing; have a negative result: *I drew a blank when I solicited him*

draw a picture *v phr* To explain something in very simple terms; make things transparently clear: *I just don't like him. Do I have to draw a picture?*

drawer *See* TOP-DRAWER

drawers *See* INTO HER DRAWERS, MAGGIE'S DRAWERS

draw one *v phr* To fill a glass with draft beer

draw play *n phr football* A play in which the quarterback feints a pass but gives the ball to a running back

dreadlock or **dredlock 1** *n* A mat or clump of long ungroomed hair as worn by Rastafarians, reggae musicians, etc: *grown his hair in long dredlocks, Rasta style*—Village Voice **2** *modifier: a British skinhead playing the dreadlock music of Jamaica*—Playboy [fr the *dread* presumably aroused by the wearers]

dream *See* PIPE DREAM, WET DREAM

dream and cream *v phr* To have sexual fantasies: *the kind of man you dream and cream about*—Tom Aldibrandi

dream bait (or **puss**) *n phr esp students fr 1940s* An attractive, desirable person

dream beads *n phr outdated narcotics* Pellets of opium; opium

dreamboat 1 *n* Any very desirable vehicle: *A dreamboat for hot-rodders is a chromed roadster* —Life **2** *n fr 1940s* A very attractive person: *will star opposite James Mason, who she says is a "dreamboat"*—Associated Press

dreambox *n jive talk* The head

dream-stick *n outdated narcotics* An opium pill

dream up *v phr* To invent; confect in the mind: *Julian has to start dreaming up a story*—Budd Schulberg/ *conceptions of living dreamed up by such groups as the Mormons*—JB Roulier

dreck or **drek 1** *n* Wretched trash; = GARBAGE, JUNK, SHIT: *the ugliness, dreck and horror of New York City*—People Weekly/ *They may bring with them a pile of overfinished drek*—Toronto Life/ *the sad glitter of desert drek*—WH Auden **2** *modifier: no point in my keeping every drek album* —Rolling Stone/ *an opponent of the ticky-tacky* *world of dreck-tech architecture* —Toronto Life [fr Yiddish, "feces"]

dress *v theater* To increase attendance by reducing admission prices and/or giving away free tickets: *The show was slumping and they had to dress it* **See** GRANNY DRESS

dress down **1** *v phr* To reprimand; rebuke; = CHEW OUT **2** *v phr* To dress less formally or arrestingly than one might

dressed to the teeth (or **to kill** or **to the nines**) **1** *adj phr* Extremely well and fancily dressed; = DOLLED UP: *She's dressed to the teeth in magenta silks*—Village Voice **2** *modifier: our dressed-to-the-teeth test car*—Car and Driver **3** *v phr: when she wrote articles about textured stockings and dressed to the nines*—Gloria Steinem [*to the teeth* implies "completely, from the bottom up"; *to the nines* is probably based on *nine* as a nearly perfect number just under ten, or on *nine* as a mystical or sacred number in numerology, the product of three times three; see the *whole nine yards*]

dress-off *n black* A competition among flashily-garbed persons

dried **See** CUT AND DRIED

drift **1** *n car-racing* A controlled sidewards skid: *Maserati or Ferrari into a corner with a four-wheel drift*—Life **2** *n* Meaning; intent: *Get my drift, chum?* **3** *v* (also **drift out**) To leave; depart: *Drift out, pal* **See** GET THE DRIFT

drifter *n* A derelict; = BUM

drift off track *v phr* To deviate from proper conduct: *I sometimes drift off track a bit, but I really try to do what is right*—Westworld

drifty *adj* Stupidly inattentive; silly; = SPACED-OUT: *It makes Dede and me both look a little drifty*—Armistead Maupin

drill **1** *v hoboes fr middle 1800s* To walk; hike; slog: *I had to drill 20 miles*—J Flynt **2** *v* To speed with force, esp through obstacles: *skimmed by his head and drilled through the closed window* —New York Daily News **3** *v* To shoot; kill by shooting: *whirled and drilled him between the eyes* **4** *v baseball* To hit a hard, straight grounder or line drive: *Lockman drilled a single past Hodges* —Associated Press **5** *n* The way of doing something; the plan of action ● Still chiefly British use: *Now I'll show you the drill for closing the place up* **See** BLANKET DRILL, MONKEY DRILL, SACK DUTY

drink **See** CHAIN-DRINK, I'LL DRINK TO THAT, RUBBER DRINK, TAKE A DRINK

Drink **See** the BIG DRINK

the drink *n phr fr early 1800s* Any body of water, from a rill to the ocean

drink one's **beer** *v phr* To stop talking; = SHUT UP ● Usu an exasperated command: *Finally I had to tell him to drink his beer*—Hal Boyle

drink of water **See** LONG DRINK OF WATER

drink up *v phr* To finish one's drink: *Drink up and we'll get started*

drip **1** *n esp 1940s students* A tedious, unimaginative, conventional person; = SQUARE, WIMP: *the biggest drip at Miss Basehoar's, a school*

ostensibly abounding with fair-sized drips—JD Salinger/ *such drips...they're just sort of dull*—Calder Willingham **2** *n hoboes* Useless and idle talk; gossip

drippy **1** *adj* Tedious; unimaginative; conventional; = WIMPY **2** *adj* Sentimental; lachrymose; = CORNY

drive **1** *n* Dynamism; insistent power: *a song with drive* **2** *v jazz & jive talk* To play music, esp jazz, with strong forward impetus and rhythms **3** *n narcotics* A thrill or transport of pleasure and energy; = KICK, RUSH **4** *n basketball* To dribble strongly and rapidly downcourt **See** BIG DRIVE

drive in *v phr baseball* To cause a run or runs to score by hitting: *Willie Randolph drove in three runs on two hits*

drive-in **1** *n* A place where one eats, watches movies, worships, etc, while sitting in one's parked car **2** *modifier: drive-in bank/ drive-in church/ drive-in movie*

driven *adj* Pressed along by some despotic or urgent force; hag-ridden: *She works as if driven*

drive someone **over the hill** *v phr* To drive to distraction; drive mad: *That kid is going to drive me over the hill. I'm at my wits' end*—Psychology Today

driver **1** *n railroad* A leg **2** *n Vietnam War Air Force & Navy* An airplane pilot **See** BACKSEAT DRIVER, HACK-DRIVER, PENCIL-PUSHER, SUNDAY DRIVER, TRUCK DRIVER

driver's seat **See** IN THE DRIVER'S SEAT

drive the big bus *v phr* Vomit into the toilet, esp from drunkenness [fr the resemblance of a toilet seat to a steering wheel]

drive the train *v phr Army* To be the determinative factor; be crucial: *The time element here will drive the train*

drive someone **up the wall** *v phr* To cause someone to become irrational or hysterical; madden: *Leave him alone and let him work. Quit driving him up the wall*—JJ Roget

driving at **See** WHAT one IS DRIVING AT

drizzle or **drizzle-puss** *n* = DRIP

droid **1** *n esp teenagers* An inferior, mechanical sort of person; robot; a semi-human drone; = CLONE: *for all its ecumenical menagerie of creatures and droids*—People Weekly **2** *modifier: tends to get people in the droid positions...and pay little*—San Francisco [fr *android* "humanlike," esp as used by science-fiction writers]

drone **1** *n 1940s students* A boring person; = DRIP, WIMP **2** *n* A small unmanned aircraft used as a target for gunnery practice

drool **1** *v* To talk foolishly or stupidly; utter inanities **2** *n: It gives me sharp and shooting pains, to listen to such drool*—Morris Bishop **3** *n* = DRIP

drool over *v phr* To show keen appreciation; show desire: *He's still drooling over Marilyn Monroe*

drooly *1940s teenagers* **1** *adj* Very attractive; = YUMMY: *Rain can turn the sharpest dressed drooly dreamboat into a drizzly drip from the knees down* —New York Daily News **2** *n* A popular and attractive boy: *Who's the chief drooly at Cooley?*

droop or **droopy-drawers** *n esp 1940s* A somewhat dull and stupid person: *He's such a droop, he can't even discuss the weather intelligently*

droopy drama *n phr esp 1940s* A radio or television daytime serial

drop 1 *v underworld* To be arrested; be caught with loot: *Just as I was climbing back out the window, I got dropped* **2** *v* To knock someone down; =DECK: *He was getting away with it until he mentioned my mother. Then I just spun around and dropped him with a quick left* **3** *v* To kill someone; =BUMP **4** *v underworld* To supply stolen or contraband goods to someone **5** *n*: *We made the drop and then waited to see if they'd keep their part of the bargain* **6** *v* To lose, esp money: *He dropped a bundle in the market yesterday* **7** *v* To collapse, esp with fatigue: *I'll drop if I don't sit down* **8** *v* To stop seeing or associating with someone: *She dropped her boyfriend* **9** *v narcotics* To take any narcotic, esp in pill or capsule form: *We want a society where you can smoke grass and drop acid*—New York Times **10** *n* (also **drop joint**) *underworld* A seemingly honest place used as a cover for illegal matters, esp as a depot for stolen goods **11** *n* =MAIL DROP **12** *n* A drink or drinks: *I could see by his careful walking he'd taken a drop* **13** *n black* A homeless slum boy: *accepting anywhere from 25 cents to $1 a week for taking in drops, rustles, fetches*—W Davenport **14** *n cabdrivers* A paying passenger **15** *n cabdrivers* The base fee on a taxi meter registered when the cabdriver activates the meter

See CHOCOLATE DROP, GET THE DROP ON someone, KNOCKOUT DROPS

drop a brick *v phr* To blunder; commit a gaffe: *He rather dropped a brick when he mispronounced Lady Fuchs's name*

drop a bundle *v phr* To lose a large amount of money, esp by gambling: *She went to play the slot machines and dropped a bundle/ He's dropped a bundle that way*—WT Tyler

drop a (or **the**) **dime 1** *v phr* To inform; give information, esp to the police; =DIME, RAT: *Chaney questioned the man who had dropped the dime on Madison*—Washingtonian/ *and then he dropped the dime (made the phone call) and turned Vinnie in*—Village Voice **2** *v phr Army* To point out the faults and failures of another; criticize [fr the *dime* put into a pay telephone] • New York City teenagers have equated **dime** with an amount of information, and also speak of **dropping a quarter**, more information, and **dropping a dollar**, the maximum of information

drop beads *homosexuals* **1** *v phr* To use homosexual code words to elicit whether someone is homosexual **2** *v phr* To reveal oneself as homosexual inadvertently, esp during conversation

drop bombs *v phr jazz musicians* To place accents in music, esp during improvised passages, using the foot pedal of a bass drum: *Joe Jones? He was the first drummer to drop bombs*—A Basie Dozen (radio program)

drop one's **buckets** *v phr* To make an embarrassing mistake; =GOOF: *You really dropped your buckets when you replied*—Washington Post

drop case (or **shot**) *n phr* A stupid person; idiot; =TURKEY: *Nobody...was a big enough drop case to bet*—Dan Jenkins/ *Mr Williams called Mr Mallard a drop shot, which had been established as a derogatory term*—New York Times [perhaps fr the notion that a stupid person had been *dropped* on his head when a baby, with some added connection with the ignominious *drop shot* in tennis]

drop one's **cookies** *See* SHOOT one's COOKIES

drop dead 1 *interj* Go to hell; screw you; =GET LOST • Nearly always an exclamation of curt refusal or sharp disapproval: *At that rude suggestion she told him to drop dead* **2** *adj phr* Unusually striking; sensational: *A drop-dead mansion in Beverly Hills, complete with his-and-hers whirlpools*—People Weekly/ *the soulful voice and the drop-dead campiness*—Time • So called because it is an affront to some canons of taste

drop-dead list *n phr* A usu fancied list of persons one does not wish to associate with or favor; =SHIT LIST

drop-in 1 *n* A place of temporary and often dubious resort: *drop-ins for youths wishing marijuana revels*—NY Confidential! **2** *n students* A person who attends classes and other college events without being registered: *NBC did some research on college drop-ins*—D Kallman [the opposite of a *dropout*]

drop someone **in** someone's **tracks** *v phr* To knock down or kill someone suddenly and sharply: *One kick dropped him in his tracks*

drop joint *See* DROP

drop someone or something **like a hot potato** *v phr* To divest or get rid of very quickly: *When she frowned I dropped the topic like a hot potato*

◁**drop** one's **load**▷ **1** *v phr* To ejaculate semen; have an orgasm **2** *v phr* =DUMP A LOAD

dropout *n* A person who withdraws; voluntary self-excluder, esp from school or college

drop out *v phr* To remove oneself from the conventional competitive world of politics, business, education, etc: *rush back from every excursion into Big Power and drop out with town meetings and backyard picnics*—Hugh Sidey/ *Kids dropped out and went to ashrams*

dropper *n underworld* A criminal who injures or kills his victims; =COWBOY, MUGGER

drops *See* KNOCKOUT DROPS

drop some iron *v phr* To spend some money

drop one's **teeth** *v phr* To be very astonished; be gapingly shocked: *I do drop my teeth at the notion that Shakespeare is busted and needs to be fixed*—Washington Post

drop (or **put**) **the lug on** someone *v phr* To beg money; =PUT THE BITE ON someone: *How's about dropping the lug on you for thirty-five thousand?*—C Carson

drop the other shoe *v phr* To conclude or round out something in suspense: *The city...dropped the* *other shoe*—Village Voice/ *The President dropped the other budget shoe yesterday*

◁ **drop your cocks and grab your socks** ▷ *sentence WW2 armed forces* Get out of bed immediately ● A jovial instruction issued by a noncommissioned officer or barracks orderly to troops quite early in the morning

drownder *See* GOOSE-DROWNDER

drowned rat *See* LOOK LIKE A DROWNED RAT

drown one's **sorrows** (or **troubles**) *v phr* To alleviate or obscure the chagrins of one's life by getting drunk

drug[1] *v* To annoy and nag at; = BUG: *His constant bitching really drugs me*

See DESIGNER DRUG, HARD DRUG, LOVE DRUG, ORPHAN DRUG, SOFT DRUG, YOU'RE ON DRUGS

drug[2] *adj* Displeased; angry; = PISSED OFF: *If other players are drug about it or feel that I'm trying to horn in...then it's not much fun*—Downbeat [past participle of *drag*, in one of its pejorative connotations]

druggie or **druggy** *n narcotics* A narcotics user or addict; = DOPER

drughead *n* A heavy user of narcotics or other drugs; = HOPHEAD: *every front-page report of violence by some freaked-out drughead*—P Horn

drugola *n narcotics* Money paid by narcotics dealers for protection, esp to the police

a **drug on the market** *n phr* Anything so plentiful as to have little value; surplus or surfeit

drugstore cowboy *n phr fr 1920s* A young man who frequents public places trying to impress and entice women; a Romeo of the street corners: *bell-bottom trousers so much in vogue with the drugstore cowboys*—A Hynd

drugstore race *n phr horse-racing* A race in which one or more of the creatures has been given drugs or alcohol: *what racketeers call "a drug store race"*—A Hynd

drum *See* BEAT THE DRUM, POP A DRUM

drum-beater *n* A person, esp a press agent, who insistently lauds someone or something: *Phil's a drum-beater for jogging now*

drummer **1** *n fr middle 1800s* A traveling salesperson **2** *n railroad* A yard conductor

drum up *v phr fr early 1800s* To stimulate; promote: *Go drum up a little enthusiasm for this turkey*

drunk *fr early 1800s* **1** *n* A drinking bout; spree; = BENDER **2** *n* A case of intoxication: *He'd quite a drunk on him at the time* **3** *n* A drunken person **4** *n* A habitual alcoholic; = LUSH: *The old drunk weaves along the curb*

See CHEAP DATE, PUNCH-DRUNK

drunkard *n railroad* A late Saturday night train

drunk as a fiddler's bitch *adj phr fr middle 1800s British* Very drunk: *It's all over, and nobody knows it but me, drunk as a fiddler's bitch, lasted too long*—Washington Post [the phrase is essentially a bit of rhyming fun, with *fiddler* probably not meaning "violinist" but "trifler, trivial person"]

drunk as a skunk *adj phr* Very drunk; = SNOCKERED: *They bring beer and cigarettes, are drunk as skunks*—Village Voice

drunk tank *See* TANK

druthers *n fr Southern dialect* Wishes; desires; preferred alternatives: *We know your druthers, The Marketplace*—Philadelphia [fr a dialect pronunciation of *rather* or *had rather*]

See HAVE one's DRUTHERS

dry **1** *n* A person who favors the prohibition of alcoholic drink **2** *adj* Not permitting the sale of alcoholic drink: *a dry state/ dry county* **3** *adj* Thirsty

See ON THE DRY

not **dry behind the ears** *See* NOT DRY BEHIND THE EARS

◀ **dry fuck** (or **hump**) ▶ **1** *n phr* To approximate the sex act, without penetration or divestiture, and typically without orgasm: *what he would call...the dry humps*—Stephen King **2** *v*: *Did attack-crazy kamikazes crash into dry-humping kids on the Hell's Kitchen shore?*—Village Voice

dry-gulch **1** *v* To murder, esp by pushing off a cliff **2** *v* To knock senseless; = BUSHWHACK, CLOBBER: *Then one of them got into the car and dry-gulched me*—Raymond Chandler [fr the practice of killing the animals of another rancher by stampeding them over a cliff into a *gulch*]

dry out *v phr fr late 1800s* To refrain from alcohol, esp in a hospital as a part of treatment for alcohol abuse: *He dried out a couple of weeks up in the Valley*

dry run **1** *n phr* A tryout, practice version, or rehearsal of something planned: *One more dry run, then tomorrow we do it* **2** *v*: *so the hospital staff could "dry run" their equipment*—Associated Press **3** *n phr* = DRY FUCK

dry up *v phr fr middle 1800s* To stop talking; = SHUT UP ● Usu an irritated command: *Finally I just told him to dry up*—Hal Boyle

DT's *n* Delirium tremens; = the CLANKS: *When Bix got the DT's Whiteman treated Bix to a drunk cure*—Stephen Longstreet

duals *n truckers* A pair of wheels and tires mounted as a unit on a truck or semitrailer axle

dub[1] **1** *n* A form of reggae music marked by weird, unexpected, and discontinuous sounds: *The hypnotic weirdness of such music has helped make dub the most popular form of reggae*—Newsweek **2** *modifier*: *A flood of dub versions followed*—Newsweek [probably fr the electronic technique of *dubbing* sound tracks]

dub[2] **1** *v* To replace or augment an original sound track with another, esp to substitute a movie sound track in a language other than the original **2** *v* To add a singer, instrumental part, etc, to the tape for a recording: *They dubbed the final vocals last week* [fr *double*]

dub[3] *n fr late 1800s* An awkward performer; novice; = DUFFER

See FLUBDUB, FLUB THE DUB

dubee or **duby** *See* DOOBIE

dubok (Doo bahk) *n underworld fr espionage* A seemingly innocent place where clandestine activity may be shielded; = DROP [fr Russian, "oak tree"]

ducat or **ducket** or **duket** (DUH kət) **1** *n* *fr late 1800s British* A ticket or pass to a show, game, race, etc **2** *n* *hoboes* A union card **3** *n* *hoboes* A printed card begging alms for a deaf or blind person **4** *n* A dollar; money: *keep him in ducats for the rest of his life*—Ellery Queen [fr the name of an originally Italian gold coin]
See CHINEE

ducat-snatcher *n* A ticket-taker

duchess *n* *street gang* A female member of a street gang

duck **1** *n* *fr middle 1800s* A man; fellow; =GUY: *That duck isn't a critic*—H McHugh **2** *n* (also **ducks**) Dear one; precious; pet; =DUCKY: *How does that grab you, duck?/ and his wife, a darling duck of a homebody*—Village Voice **3** *n* =DUCK EGG **4** *n* A hospital bedpan **5** *n* An amphibious vehicle, esp a WW2 troop carrier designated DUKW 1942, whence the nickname **6** *v* To move, weave, squat, etc, so as to avoid a blow **7** *v* (also **duck out**) *fr late 1800s* To evade or escape: *He ducked over the wall/ They always felt she was trying to duck work*
See DEAD DUCK, FUCK A DUCK, HAVE one's DUCKS IN A ROW, KNEE-HIGH TO A GRASSHOPPER, LAME DUCK, RUPTURED DUCK, SITTING DUCK

duck bumps *n phr* =GOOSE BUMPS

duck-butt *n* A person of short stature

duck-egg *n* A score or grade of zero; =GOOSE-EGG, ZIP

duck-fit *n* A noisy fit of anger: *Clarice...would throw a duck-fit, if she knew*—Elmer Rice

ducks **1** *n* White flannel trousers **2** *n* Dear one; precious ● Chiefly British use: *Try this one, ducks*
See HAVE one's DUCKS IN A ROW

duck soup *n phr* Anything easily done; =CINCH, PIECE OF CAKE: *She made it look like duck soup*

duck squeezer *n phr* *college students* A conservationist and environmentalist; =ECOFREAK

ducky or **duckie** **1** *adj* Excellent; splendid ● Often used ironically: *What a perfectly ducky notion!/ Cutting off my phone is just ducky* **2** *adj* Cute; too cute; =CORNY: *Pastel phials tied with ducky satin bows*—Raymond Chandler **3** *n* Dear one; precious; =DEARIE: *Are you quite ready, duckie?*

ducrot (DŌŌ kraht) *n West Point* Anything or anyone whose name is not known and not worth knowing; =DUMBJOHN [fr French *du crotte* "a portion of excrement"]

dud **1** *n* *fr middle 1800s* A failure: *The show's a dud/ He was a bit of a dud* **2** *n* *fr WW1* A shell or bomb that fails to explode **3** *modifier*: *a dud bomb*

duddy *See* FUDDY-DUDDY

dude **1** *n* *fr late 1800s* A dapper man, esp one who is ostentatiously dressed; dandy **2** *n* *fr late 1800s* A guest at a Western or Western-style ranch **3** *n* *esp black* A man; fellow; =CAT, GUY: *I'm sittin' in the bus stop...just me an' these other three dudes*—D Evans

dude heaver *n phr* =BOUNCER

dude up *v phr* To don fancy clothes, or one's best clothes; =DOLL UP

Dudley *See* YOUR UNCLE DUDLEY

duds *n* Clothing; =THREADS [perhaps fr *dude up*]

dues *See* PAY one's DUES

duff *n* The buttocks; rump; =ASS: *A bunch of lazy guys sitting around on our duffs*—Time

duffer *fr middle 1800s British* **1** *n* An elderly man; =GEEZER, JASPER ● Used rather affectionately: *He's a sweet old duffer, isn't he?* **2** *n* A mediocre or downright poor performer, esp at golf; =HACKER [perhaps fr Scots *duffar* "dolt"]

dufus **1** *adj* (also ◁**dufus-assed**▷) Stupid; blundering: *many another dufus play among friends*—Richard Merkin **2** *n*: (also ◁**dufus-ass**▷) *He's a real dufus*

dujie *See* DOOJEE

duke **1** *n* A hand, esp when regarded as a weapon **2** *n* *prizefight* The winning decision in a boxing match, signaled by the referee's holding up the victor's hand: *Even if I lose the duke I get forty per cent*—Jim Tully **3** *v* To hand something to someone: *Duke the kid a five or ten*—George V Higgins **4** *v* To fight with the fists **5** *v* *circus* To try to collect money from a parent for something given to a child **6** *v* *circus* To short-change someone by palming a coin owed him **7** *v* To shake hands; =PRESS THE FLESH [fr Romany *dook* "the hand as read in palmistry, one's fate"]

the duke *n phr* On a farm, the bull

duke someone **out** **1** *v phr* To beat someone unconscious; =KNOCK someone OUT: *What should I do, duke him or her out?*—National Review **2** *v phr* To damage or injure someone: *Dirk Hamilton dukes himself out, adopts a...style in which he's inferior*—Village Voice

dukes *n* *fr middle 1800s British* The fists or hands: *He put up his dukes to defend himself* [said to be Cockney rhyming slang fr *Duke of Yorks* "forks"]

dukes-up *adj* Combative; =FEISTY: *Her salty language and dukes-up style endeared her*—Time

duket *See* DUCAT

dukie or **dookie** **1** *n* *outdated carnival* A meal ticket **2** *n* *circus* A box lunch

dukie book *n phr* *circus* A book of meal tickets

dull as dishwater *adj phr* Very tedious and unexciting; boring: *The sermon today was dull as dishwater, Your Eminence*

dullsville *adj* Very dull; tedious; =DRAGSVILLE: *a dullsville wimp* [see -sville]

dull tool *n phr* An ineffective person; =DEAD ONE, LOSER

dumb **1** *adj* *fr early 1800s* Stupid; mentally sluggish; =DIM: *You think I'm pretty dumb, don't you?*—F Scott Fitzgerald/ *a dumb trick* **2** *adv*: *He acts dumb sometimes* **3** *adj* & *adv* =DAMN, DARN [fr Pennsylvania German *dumm*]

dumb act *n phr* *outdated theater* Any act without words

◁**dumb-ass**▷ **1** *adj* Stupid; inane; tedious: *a dumb-ass trick/ Our private life has to take a back seat to every dumbass little news story*—Armistead

Maupin **2** *n:* *to understand how a dumb-ass like Newton can have a following*—Playboy
See HAVE A CASE OF THE DUMB-ASS

dumbbell *n fr 1920s* A stupid person; idiot: *He's slow, but no dumbbell*

dumb bomb (or **missile**) *n phr* A bomb or missile lacking a sophisticated and accurate guidance system [fr contrast with *smart bomb*]

dumb bunny *n phr* A naive and unwary person; silly little fool: *Only a dumb bunny would fall for that crap*

dumb cluck *n phr* A stupid person; clumsy bungler; =KLUTZ: *all those dumb clucks snickering at you*—Sinclair Lewis

Dumb Dora *n phr esp 1920s* A stupid or vapid young woman: *What's the percentage of Dumb Doras at Radcliffe?/ You're just an average Dumb Dora from north-suburban Chicagoland*—Saul Bellow [probably jocular reduplication, like *nervous Nellie* or *Handy Andy*; David Copperfield's wife was a sort of *dumb Dora*, probably not implicated in this coinage]

dumb down *v phr* To make simpler, esp to alter a textbook to make it more elementary: *There has been a real "dumbing down" of the texts*—Village Voice/ *what some educators have called the "dumbing down" of textbooks*—New York Times [attributed to Los Angeles Times reporter William Trombley]

dumbhead *n* A stupid person: *This dumbhead has just gone nuts*—Ellery Queen [perhaps fr German *Dummkopf*]

dumbjohn **1** *n* A person easily duped; =EASY MARK, PATSY **2** *n* =DUCROT **3** *n* Army A recruit; =CRUIT, POGGIE

dumbo (DUM boh) **1** *n* A stupid person: *an ace dumbo friend named Cleo*—Time **2** *n* A blunder; stupid mistake; =BLOOPER: *if you think you've seen dumbos pulled on the highways*—Saturday Evening Post

dumb ox *n phr* A stupid, sluggish person, esp a hulking one

dum-dum or **dumdum** or **dumb-dumb** **1** *n* A stupid or foolish person **2** *adj:* *his dumdum ideas/ a dum-dum crack/ The only man safe enough to see is this dumdum cop*—Saul Bellow

dummy **1** *n* A stupid person; idiot; =CLUCK ◁**2**▷ *n* A deaf-mute or a mute **3** *n* hoboes Bread **4** *n* railroad A train carrying railroad employees ◁**5**▷ *n* The penis **6** *n* A weakened or diluted narcotic; also, a non-narcotic substance sold as a narcotic; =BLANK **7** *n* newspaper office & publishing A pasted-up page, a blank book, or other preliminary representation of material to be published **8** *v:* *The designer dummied the new book* **9** *n* A model or representation; =MOCK-UP **10** *modifier:* *a dummy machine gun/ dummy windows*
See BEAT one's MEAT, CHUCK A DUMMY

dummy up **1** *v phr* To keep silent; =CLAM UP: *You can't dummy up on a murder case*—Raymond Chandler/ *When questioned, they invariably dummy up*—SJ Perelman **2** *v phr* To make a

representation or model: *The carpenter dummied up a Victorian facade/ Have layout dummy up those pages*

dump **1** *n* fr late 1800s Any place so shabby or ugly as to be comparable to a depository for trash and garbage; a repulsive venue: *What a dump my hometown is now!* **2** *n* Any building or place: *Nice little dump you got here/ fanciest dump in town* **3** *n* underworld A prison **4** *v fr middle 1800s* To sell goods, stock, etc, in order to manipulate or depress a market **5** *n* gambling A race, game, etc, that is intentionally lost, usu for gambling advantage; =FIX: *When he took a dive in the first I knew we had a dump on our hands* **6** *v:* *Players accepting bribes to "dump" games*—Associated Press/ *Some people would think that Goliath dumped, for that matter* **7** *v* To bunt a baseball: *Dehoney dumped one toward third* **8** *v* To kill **9** *v* To rid oneself of someone or something; =DEEP-SIX: *He dumped the whole cabinet* **10** *n* A defecation; =a SHIT: *To start the morning with a satisfactory dump is a good omen*—WH Auden
See CORE DUMP, TAKE A DUMP

◁**dump a load**▷ *v phr* To defecate; =CRAP

dumper **1** *n* gambling An erratic and extravagant gambler: *Professional gamblers describe the Colonel as a dumper*—Albert Goldman **2** *n* A container for trash; dumpster: *It was determined...that disco would be in the dumper*—Playboy
See IN THE DUMPER

dumping *n* Harsh criticism; severe derogation: *A coupon is provided on page 47 for your dumping*—Diner's Choice

dump on (or **all over**) *v phr* To criticize harshly, often unfairly; complain and carp at; =PUT DOWN: *If he does something right, I'm not going to dump on him*—Time/ *Don't dump on the teachers we have*—New York Times/ *an acknowledgement of the fact that he had dumped on us all year*—Judith Martin

dune buggy *n phr* A small and squat open car, usu with a Volkswagen engine, equipped with very fat tires for traveling on sand

duner *n* A dune-buggy driver or rider: *Duners go out on runs, trips by a half-dozen dune buggies*—Calvin Trillin

dunk **1** *v fr 1920s* To dip something into a liquid, esp to dip food into a drink: *I dunk doughnuts in Scotch/ Scientific temperature readings cannot be taken just by dunking a thermometer on a string*—G Hill **2** *v* To go into the water: *Be right back, just want to dunk* **3** *n:* *Leroy had a quick dunk in the creek* **4** *n* sports A basketball field goal scored by putting the ball into the hoop from just beside or above it: *Almost all of the baskets were dunks*—Sports Illustrated/ *basketball courts...where the dunks have been so fierce lately*—Philadelphia **5** *v:* *He jumped up and dunked another one* [fr Pennsylvania German *dunken* "dip"]
See SLAM DUNK

dunnigan *n* A repulsive thief who plies his trade in public toilets: *Sam is not like the sleazy dunnigans,* who work toilets—Los Angeles Times [fr earlier *dunnakin* "toilet"]

dupe *n* A duplicate copy, esp of a letter or other text

duper *See* SUPER-DUPER

durn or **durned** *See* DARN

a **durn** *See* NOT GIVE A DAMN

dust 1 *v* *fr middle 1800s fr 1600s British* To leave quickly; flee; fly: *Dillinger...used a Ford...when dusting from a job*—A Hynd **2** *v* To hit; swat: *dusted one of the lieutenants with an old shoe for trying to talk them back to work*—Time **3** *v* To spray insecticide from a low-flying aircraft **4** *n narcotics* Narcotics in powder form
See ANGEL DUST, EAT someone's DUST, HAPPY-DUST, HEAVEN DUST, SAWDUST

the **dust** *n phr* The ground; the dirt: *One must not trail his glory in the dust*
See BITE THE DUST

duster 1 *n baseball* A pitch purposely thrown at or close to the batter, to intimidate him or force him back from the plate; = BRUSHBACK **2** *n* A woman's smock or housecoat
See EAR-DUSTER, FEATHER DUSTER, KNUCKLE-DUSTERS

dusters *n underworld & street gang* Brass knuckles; = KNUCKLE-DUSTERS

dust someone's **jacket** *v phr* To beat and pummel someone

dust kitty (or **bunny**) *n phr* One of the tufts of dust that accumulate under beds, tables, etc

dust someone **off 1** *v phr* To give someone a beating; thrash someone **2** *v phr baseball* To pitch a ball at or close to the batter; = BRUSHBACK

dust someone's **pants** (or **trousers**) *v phr* To hit or kick in the rump; esp, to spank a child

dust-raiser *n railroad* A fire stoker

dustup *n* A quarrel or fight; altercation; = SCRAP: *a big dustup in the office of a vice-president*—New Yorker

dusty *See* RUSTY-DUSTY

Dusty 1 *n* A common nickname for a person named Rhodes, Rhoades, Rodes, etc **2** *n* A nickname for a short person, a "dusty butt"

dusty butt *n phr* A person of short stature; = SHORTY

dutch 1 *v outdated horse-racing* To bet on each horse in a race proportionately, so that any winner will return more than the total amount **2** *v* To ruin or spoil

Dutch 1 *adj* German: *Ann Arbor's a Dutch town* **2** *n* A nickname for anyone with a German surname: *Big Dutch Klangenfuss* **3** *v gambling* To place a careful series of bets such that the gambling house or owner of the game is ruined **4** *v* To ruin someone's business, health, reputation, etc, maliciously **5** *adv* With each person paying his or her own share: *This meal is Dutch, okay?*
See DOUBLE DUTCH, GO DUTCH, IN DUTCH, TO BEAT THE BAND

the **Dutch act** *See* DO THE DUTCH

Dutch book *n phr gambling* A minor horse-betting establishment, esp one that will take bets of less than one dollar

Dutch courage *n phr* False or fleeting bravery resulting from liquor: *A man in liquor...is full of Dutch courage*—FK Secrist [like many other pejorative uses of *Dutch*, this comes from the 17th century, when the English and the Hollanders were chronically at war. In some uses, though, *Dutch* means "German" rather than "Netherlandish," and the cases are not easily sorted]

Dutch rub *n phr* The trick or torment of holding someone's head and rubbing very hard and painfully at a small area of scalp with the fist; = NOOGIE, BARBERSHOP QUARTET

Dutch treat 1 *n phr* A meal, show, etc, where each person pays his or her own way **2** *adv*: *We'll eat Dutch treat tonight*
See GO DUTCH

Dutch uncle *n phr* A severely censorious person, usu a man: *A "Dutch uncle" whose every word is reproof*—FK Secrist

duty *See* PAD DUTY, RACK DUTY, SACK DUTY

dweeb *n teenagers* A despised person; = CREEP, NERD

◁**dyke** or **dike**▷ **1** *n* A lesbian, esp one who takes an aggressive role; = BULLDYKE **2** *modifier*: *That woman lives with her dyke daughter and her dyke daughter-in-law*—Armistead Maupin [origin uncertain and much debated; perhaps fr a shortening of *morphodyke*, dialectal and substandard pronunciation of "hermaphrodite," perhaps influenced by *dick* "penis"]

◁**dykey** or **dikey**▷ *adj* Resembling or having the nature of an aggressive lesbian: *a dykey sort of woman/ doing calisthenics with the dikey-looking brunette*—Earl Thompson

dynamite 1 *n narcotics* Heroin or cocaine of high quality: *a connection who deals in good-quality stuff, "dynamite"*—J Mills **2** *n narcotics* Marijuana, esp a marijuana cigarette **3** *adj* (also **dyno-mite**) Excellent; superior; = SUPER: *a dynamite scheme* **4** *n* Something very disturbing or dangerous; a sensation: *Don't talk about it, it's dynamite* **5** *n gambling* A portion of bets that a bookmaker has covered elsewhere in order to minimize his risk **6** *n outdated horse-racing* The luring of customers with false information: *Touts were allowed to advertise winners they did not have. This was called..."dynamite"*—T Betts
See SCANDINAVIAN DYNAMITE

dynamiter *n truckers* A driver who abuses a truck by rough handling or speeding

dyno or **dino** (DĪ noh) *n esp railroad* A railroad section hand or any other construction or excavation worker, esp one who uses dynamite [fr *dynamite*; but see *dino*[1]]

E

each *See* PER EACH

eager beaver 1 *n phr esp WW2 armed forces* An energetic and willing worker; ambitious striver **2** *modifier: her eager-beaver sincerity/ eager-beaver gung-ho spirit*

the **eagers** *n phr* Eagerness; exaggerated willingness

eagle *See* the DAY THE EAGLE SHITS, LEGAL EAGLE, WHEN THE EAGLE FLIES

◀**eagle-beak**▶ *n* A Jew: *Catch me workin' for one of them eagle-beaks*—James T Farrell

eagle day *n phr WW2 armed forces* Payday [fr the *eagle* depicted on US currency]

eagle-eye 1 *n* A person noted for keen vision or one who keeps a close watch: *It took a real eagle-eye to catch that* **2** *n railroad* A locomotive engineer **3** *n* A detective, esp one assigned to watch for shoplifters or pickpockets

eagle-eyed 1 *adj* Having very keen vision **2** *adj* Keeping a close watch

eagle freak *n phr* A conservationist and environmentalist; = ECOFREAK, DUCK SQUEEZER

ear 1 *n* The handle of a cup: *around the ear of my coffee cup*—Peter De Vries **2** *v* To listen; hear: *Rosen Tapes To Be Eared By The Judge*—New York Daily News
See ALL EARS, BEND someone's EAR, BLOW IT OUT, CAULIFLOWER EAR, CHEW someone's EAR OFF, ELEPHANT EARS, HAVE something COMING OUT OF one's EARS, IN A PIG'S ASS, NOT DRY BEHIND THE EARS, PIN someone's EARS BACK, PLAY IT BY EAR, POUND one's EAR, PRETTY EAR, PULL IN one's EARS, PUT A BUG IN someone's EAR, PUT IT IN YOUR EAR, RABBIT EARS, STAND AROUND WITH one's FINGER UP one's ASS, STEAM WAS COMING OUT OF someone's EARS, STICK IT, TALK someone's EAR OFF, WARM someone's EAR

ear-banger 1 *n WW2 armed forces* A person who tries to advance himself by flattery; = BROWN-NOSE **2** *n* A braggart

ear-bender *n* An overly loquacious person; = GABBER, WINDBAG: *James Joyce was something of an ear-bender, no?*

ear-duster 1 *n baseball* = DUSTER **2** *n* A gossip **3** *n* An item of gossip: *Any juicy ear-dusters today?*

eared *See* DOG-EARED

an **earful** *n phr* A large or impressive quantity of talk, esp of a rambling or gossipy sort

early bird 1 *n phr* A person who habitually gets up early in the morning; one who greets the dawn **2** *modifier: an early-bird session/ early-bird radio program* **3** *n phr* A person who arrives early at a gathering, the office, etc **4** *n phr* The first train, bus, airplane, etc, of the day

earn one's **wings** *v phr* To prove oneself competent and reliable in one's work [fr the *wing*-shaped badge awarded to graduating air cadets]

ease *v* To move or walk slowly; = OOZE: *Ease over to the store and get a six-pack/ He eased himself into my chair*

ease on (or **out** or **on out**) *v phr fr black* To depart; = MOSEY ALONG: *easing on down the road to the Land of Oz*—Philadelphia

ease someone **out** *v phr* To dismiss or remove someone from a post or place gradually and gently

Eastern Western *n phr* A Japanese or Chinese movie featuring the sort of violence and machismo typical of cowboy movies

East Jesus *n phr* An archetypical small rural town; = PODUNK

East Jesus State *n phr* Any small college regarded as inferior and backward; the mythical, archetypical small provincial college; = SIWASH

easy *See* BREATHE EASY, FREE-AND-EASY, GO EASY, OVER EASY, SPEAKEASY, TAKE IT EASY, TAKE THINGS EASY

easy as pie *adj phr* & *adv phr* (Variations: **can be** or **could be** or **falling off a log** or **hell** or **rolling off a log** may replace **pie**) Very easy or easily: *He did it easy as pie/ The thing's easy as can be*

easy digging *n phr* Anything easily done; = PIECE OF CAKE

easy make 1 *n phr* (also **easy lay**) A woman easily persuaded to engage in the sex act **2** *n phr* = EASY MARK

easy mark *n phr* A person easily victimized or cheated; = PATSY, SUCKER: *He was...an "easy mark"*—Jack London

easy meat *fr 1920s British* **1** *n phr* Something done or acquired very easily **2** *modifier: their easy-meat score in the aerial spraying issue*—Los Angeles Times [fr the earlier sense that something or someone is vulnerable, easily hunted and caught, etc, esp in the sexual sense where *meat* means "sexual victim, conquest, object, etc"]

easy street *See* ON EASY STREET

eat 1 *v* To preoccupy or upset; engross; fret: *She asked what was eating me when I frowned so* **2** *v* To be forced to accept something; swallow something: *He couldn't get any redress, and just had to eat the damage* **3** *v sports* To be unable to pass the ball along: *They blitzed and the quarterback had to eat the ball* **4** *v* To accept and enjoy; =SWALLOW: *You really eat this shit, don't you?*—CDB Bryan ◁**5**▷ *v* To do fellatio or cunnilingus; =GO DOWN ON someone: *So Little Red Riding Hood said to the wolf, "Eat me"*

eat cheese *v phr Army* To inform on someone; tattle; =RAT [fr the *cheese-eating* of the rodent]

eat dirt *v phr* To accept rebuke or harassment meekly; swallow one's pride; =EAT SHIT: *I ate dirt and apologized to that bastard*—Calder Willingham

eat someone's **dust** *v phr* To be behind someone in a race or chase: *After two laps they ate Coghlan's dust*

eater *See* BONE-EATER, CAKE-EATER, CHALK-EATER, CHEESE BUN, CLAY EATER, FIRE-EATER, FROG, GRASS-EATER, HAY-EATER, MEATEATER, MOTHERFUCKER, PETER-EATER, SAWDUST EATER, SNAKE EATER

eat one's **hat** *See* EAT one's WORDS

eat (or **live**) **high on the hog** (or **off the hog** or **on the joint**) *v phr* To live very well; thrive, prosper; =SHIT IN HIGH COTTON: *You will...eat high on the hog, as a member of the ruling mob*—Westbrook Pegler/ *The institute will eat high off the hog*—Harvey Breit

eating *See* FROG, MOTHERFUCKING

◁**eatin' stuff** or **eating pussy** or **table grade**▷ *n phr* A woman of great sexual appeal ● Although the reference is ambiguous, these terms need not connote cunnilingus

eat it ◁**1**▷ *v phr* To do fellatio or cunnilingus; =GO DOWN ON someone ◁**2**▷ *interj* (also **eat this**) An exclamation of contempt and defiance ● A hostile invitation to fellatio: *"Gee, Les, you're such a charming guy," Frank says. "Eat it"*—Atlantic Monthly/ *When the cop questioned him he said, "Eat this, buster"* **3** *v phr* To dispose of something in an embarrassing way; swallow something: *The quarterback just had to eat the football when he found no receivers/ Nobody wants that complaint, so you'll just have to eat it*

eat (or **have**) someone's **lunch** *v phr* To defeat decisively; =CLOBBER, FINISH: *Dole would eat our lunch if pitted regularly against Byrd on the nightly news*—New York Times/ *The hitters have been having his lunch*—New Yorker

eat nails *v phr football* To be very tough and durable

eat out *v phr* To have a meal away from home, esp at a restaurant

eat someone **out 1** *v phr* To reprimand someone severely; rebuke harshly; =CHEW someone OUT: *Out came Joe McCarthy from the Boston dugout all set to eat me out*—Gilbert Millstein ◁**2**▷ *v phr* To do cunnilingus or analingus

eats *n* Food; provender: *A soft bed and good eats were paradise enow*

◁**eat shit**▷ **1** *v phr* =EAT DIRT **2** *v phr* To be repulsive and contemptible ● Usu a loud oral insult: *You eat shit, you son of a bitch!* *See* TAKE SHIT

eat the Bible *See* SWALLOW THE BIBLE

eat up 1 *v phr* To use entirely; deprive of completely; =GOBBLE UP: *The rent ate up half my pay* **2** *v phr* To accept and enjoy; have delectation for: *He really ate that show up*

eat one **up** *v phr* To be strongly bothered or affected by: *His pontificating really eats me up*

eat someone **up** (or **up with a spoon**) *v phr* To be especially devoted to someone: *She's so sweet I could just eat her up*

eat one's **words** (or **hat**) *v phr* To be forced either to retract or to suffer for what one has said: *They showed him proof and he had to eat his words/ I'll eat my hat if I'm wrong*

ech (EK) *See* YUCK

ecofreak or **econut** *n* An environmentalist and conservationist; =DUCK SQUEEZER, EAGLE FREAK: *Eco-freaks will love the clean-burning engine*—National Review

ecstasy *n narcotics* A variety of amphetamine narcotic: *Ecstasy...by emergency order of the Drug Enforcement Administration, illegal*—Washington Post

Ed *See* OP-ED PAGE

Eddy or **Edgar** *n shoeshop* The shoe width E

edge 1 *n fr late 1800s* An advantage: *The insurgents seem to have the edge* **2** *n* An irritated or sarcastic tone; sharp timbre: *She answered with a slight edge to her voice* *See* HAVE AN EDGE ON, HAVE AN EDGE ON someone

edged 1 *adj* Drunk: *When he was nicely edged he was a pretty good sort of guy*—Raymond Chandler **2** *adj teenagers* Very angry; =PISSED OFF

edge someone **out** *v phr* To defeat by a close margin; barely surpass: *We edged them out by just three votes*

edgy or **on edge** *adj* or *adj phr fr early 1900s* Tense and irritable; nervous; =UP TIGHT: *I saw he was getting a bit edgy, so I agreed to include him*

Edsel *n* Something useless; a fiasco: *We have to win out. We're not selling Edsels, you know*—Time [fr the *Edsel* car, which fell short of commercial success]

-ee *suffix used to form nouns* The object of what is indicated: *baby-sittee/ kickee/ muggee*

eel 1 *n prison* A clever prisoner **2** *n* A slippery person, esp a criminal who regularly evades arrest or a politician who equivocates over an issue or fact *See* MANHATTAN EEL

◁**eff**▷ *v & n* =FUCK ● This curt euphemism is also the base for equivalents of **fucked**, **fucking**, and **fucker:** *eff off back to effing Russia*—Anthony Burgess/ *otherwise effed around until...Bill Veeck was forced to*—Playboy

egads switch (or **button**) *See* CHICKEN SWITCH

egg 1 *n fr late 1800s* A person: *Evelyn's a good egg* **2** *n* Anything roughly egg-shaped, such as the head, a baseball, an aerial bomb, etc: *bopped him on the egg/ reared back and chucked the old*

egg 3 *n* =EGGHEAD [first sense altered fr the mid-19th-century term *bad egg* "bad or rotten person"]
See BAD EGG, DUCK-EGG, FISH-EGGS, FRIED EGG, FULL AS AN EGG, GOOSE EGG, HARD-BOILED EGG, HAVE EGG ON one's FACE, LAY AN EGG, NEST EGG, SUCK EGGS, WALK ON EGGS, YOU CAN'T MAKE AN OMELET WITHOUT BREAKING EGGS

eggbeater 1 *n* WW2 *Army Air Forces* An aircraft propeller **2** *n* A helicopter: *The "egg-beater" took off for Inchon with its burden*—Associated Press **3** *n* An outboard motor; =KICKER: *wouldn't be caught dead with an eggbeater on their boat*—RW Carrick

egger *See* HAM-AND-EGGER

eggery *See* HAM-AND-EGGERY

egghead 1 *n* A bald man **2** *n* An intellectual; thinker; =DOUBLE DOME: *An egghead is "one who calls Marilyn Monroe Mrs Arthur Miller"*—P Sann [presumably fr the putative high, domed, *egg*-shaped *heads* of such persons; the term was used in a letter of Carl Sandburg about 1918]

egg in someone's **beer** *n phr* The height of luxury or pleasure; everything one could desire • Often part of an impatient question addressed to someone who asks for more than is merited or available: *So it's got no air-conditioning. You want egg in your beer?/ I don't call two weeks' vacation exactly egg in my beer*

egg orchard *n phr outdated hoboes* A chicken farm

egg-sucker *n* A person who seeks advancement through flattery; =BROWN-NOSE

ego trip (or **jag**) **1** *n phr* Something done primarily to build one's self-esteem or display one's splendid qualities: *The pie-thrower...said the guru was on an ego trip*—Time/ *This isn't any ego trip, taking a job in this administration*—WT Tyler **2** *v*: *I was showing off, ego-tripping*

eight *See* FORKED-EIGHT, FORTY-EIGHT, NINETY-EIGHT

eightball ◀**1**▶ *n* A black person **2** *n* A chronically unfortunate and ineffective person; =LOSER, SAD SACK **3** *n* =SQUARE
See BEHIND THE EIGHT BALL

eighteen wheeler *n phr truckers & citizens band* A semitrailer truck; cab and trailer: *The driver of the eighteen-wheeler to my left was wearing the uniform of the West Virginia Highway Patrol*—Penthouse

eighter (or **Ada**) **from Decatur** *n phr crap-shooting & poker* The card, roll, or point of eight

eight-hundred-pound gorilla *See* SIX-HUN-DRED-POUND GORILLA

◀**eight-rock**▶ *n black* A very dark-skinned black person

eights *See* BIG EIGHTS

eighty-eight or **eighty-eights** *n* A piano

eighty-four *n* WW2 *Navy* A naval prison

eighty-one or **eighty-two** *n lunch counter* A glass of water

eighty-seven *n lunch counter* A signal meaning "a good-looking woman has come in; take note"

eighty-six 1 *n lunch counter* A cook's term for "none" or "nix" when asked for something not available **2** *v*: *We had to eighty-six the French dip*—John Sayles **3** *n bartenders* A person who is not to be served more liquor • This use may come from the relatively weaker 86-proof whiskey as compared with 100-proof: *known as an "eighty-six," which...means: "Don't serve him"*—Gene Fowler **4** *v* (also **eight-six**) To eject or interdict someone: *I'll have you eighty-sixed out of this bar*—John Rechy/ *I been eighty-sixed out of better situations*—George V Higgins **5** *v* To kill; destroy; annihilate: *There'd been serious pragmatic reasons for not eighty-sixing the man then and there*—Richard Merkin [probably fr the rhyme with "nix"]

eighty-two *See* EIGHTY-ONE

elbow 1 *n* A police officer or detective **2** *v* To associate with someone as a friend; =RUB ELBOWS
See BEND THE ELBOW, NOT KNOW one's ASS FROM one's ELBOW, RUB ELBOWS

elbow-bender *n* A convivial person; drinker

elbow-bending *n* Drinking liquor: *the gentlemanly art of refined elbow-bending*—Esquire

elbow grease *n phr fr late 1700s British* Muscular exertion; physical effort

elbow someone **out** *v phr* To eliminate or replace someone by aggressive pressure: *She looked pretty secure, but he elbowed her out of the vice presidency*

elbow room *n phr fr 1700s* Barely enough space for the occupant; a minimum of space: *This office is so crowded I couldn't find elbow room for anyone else/ Don't crowd so, give me elbow room* [propagated in the US because it was a nickname for General John Burgoyne, who boasted in the 1770s that he would find *elbow room* in this country]

El Cheapo *n phr* A cheap product; a piece of shoddy merchandise: *They bought the El Cheapos and found they didn't work*—New York Times [see *el -o*, mock-Spanish combining form]

electric 1 *adj outdated jazz talk* Played smoothly and sensuously **2** *n* Electricity: *Who's gonna pay for the electric?*

elephant *See* SEE PINK ELEPHANTS, WHITE ELEPHANT

elephant ears *n phr astronautics* Large, thick metal discs on the outer shell of a rocket or missile

elephant hunt *v phr outdated fr late 1800s* =SLUM

elephant tranquilizer *n phr* =ANGEL DUST

elevate *v esp 1920s* To rob: *go out and "elevate" a bank*—J Black [probably a play on *heist*]

elevated *adj* Drunk

elevator music *n phr* Bland, pretty music, of the sort played over speakers in elevators; =MUZAK: *Please don't call us "elevator music." We play instrumental versions of popular hits*

el foldo *See* PULL AN EL FOLDO

Elk *n beat talk* A conventional person; =SQUARE: *kill themselves later with laughter over the amount of money the Elks spent*—S Boal [fr a scornful judgment of the Benevolent and Protective Order of Elks]

el -o *combining form* An amusing variation of whatever is infixed: *travel el cheapo*—Time/ *flatchested el birdos in long dresses*—Stephen King/ *You still* seeing El Sleazo these days?—Cyra McFadden/ *universal emptiness...el zilcho*—Stephen King/ *Our President...did his famous el foldo*—Sports Illustrated/ *If it is calm, it is el snoro*—Time [fr a common pattern in Spanish]

El Ropo *n phr* A name for any inferior cigar, or for any cigar at all that one does not like [imitation of a typical cigar name, of a cigar made of *rope*]

else *See* OR ELSE

Elsewhere *See* MOUNT SAINT ELSEWHERE

embalmed *adj* Drunk

embalming fluid *n phr* Strong coffee, whiskey, or other potent drink

embrangle *v* To involve; entangle: *The investigation threatened to embrangle...the Duke of Argyll* —Time [a blend of *embroil* with *entangle*]

emcee *See* MC

emery ball *n phr* baseball A pitch thrown with the ball partially roughened

emote 1 *v* To play a theatrical role, esp one calling for a strong display of emotion; = HAM: *all been panting to see her emote in the gangster film* —Louella Parsons 2 *v* To indulge in a display of feeling, esp a pretense: *Now she's emoting about the electric bill*

empty nester *n phr* Parent whose children have grown up and moved from home: *We are getting a lot of empty-nesters moving into a Leisure World development*—Washingtonian/ *elderly "empty nesters" who sell their suburban homes and come to the city*—New York Times

enchilada *See* BIG ENCHILADA, the WHOLE ENCHILADA

end 1 *n* A share; = CUT: *Eddie would be entitled to half an end*—E DeBaun 2 *n* Particular concern or portion; sector: *Selling's his end of it* *See* FRONT-END, GO OFF THE DEEP END, HAVE one's END OFF, HIND END, JUMP OFF THE DEEP END, the LIVING END, REAR END, SEE THE LIGHT AT THE END OF THE TUNNEL, SHORT END OF THE STICK

the **end** *n phr* beat & cool talk The best; the greatest; = the LIVING END: *Mr Secretary General, you're the end!*

ends *n* beat & cool talk Shoes: *When a hipster buys clothes, he begins with "ends"*—E Horne

endville or **endsville** *adj esp 1950s cool talk* Superb; unsurpassed: *His last gig was endsville* [see -*sville*]

enforcer *n* A person, esp a gangster or an athlete, assigned to intimidate and punish opponents

English[1] *n lunch counter* An English muffin

English[2] *n* A spin imparted to a billiard ball, tennis ball, etc, to make it curve [fr French *anglé* "angled," similar to *Anglais* "English"]

English spliff *n phr narcotics* A cigarette combining tobacco with some narcotic: *rolls an English spliff, tobacco mixed with hashish*—Rolling Stone

an engraved invitation *See* DO YOU WANT AN ENGRAVED INVITATION

enough to choke a horse 1 *adv phr* To a very great degree; in a very large quantity: *His ego is big enough to choke a horse* 2 *n phr* A very

large quantity; a plethora: *Does he have money? Enough to choke a horse*

enough to gag a maggot *adv phr* Very disgusting; repulsive: *His excuse was enough to gag a maggot*

equalizer *n* A pistol or other firearm

erase *v* To kill; = RUB OUT

eraser *n prizefight* A knockout or a knockout punch

Erie *See* ON THE ERIE

-erino *suffix used to form nouns* (also -**arino** or -**orino**) A humorous version or a remarkable specimen of what is indicated: *peacherino/ bitcherino* [probably fr the Italian diminutive suffix -*ino* combined with the agentive suffix -*er*]

-eroo *suffix used to form nouns* (also -**aroo** or -**roo** or -**oo**) Emphatic, humorous, or affectionate form of what is indicated: *babyroo/ jivaroo/ screameroo/ sockeroo*

-erooney *See* -AROONEY

-ers *suffix used to form adjectives* In the condition humorously indicated ● These are all British imports, coming ultimately from public school slang: *bonkers/ preggers/ starkers*

-ery 1 *suffix used to form nouns* Place or establishment where the indicated thing is used, done, sold, etc: *boozery/ eatery/ minkery* 2 *suffix used to form nouns* The collectivity or an instance of what is indicated: *claptrappery/ jerkery*

-ess *suffix used to form nouns* A woman member of the indicated group or calling ● A standard suffix now used most often in slang partly because the standard use is regarded as, and sometimes meant to be, offensive: *loaferess/ muggess/ veepess*

estate *See* REAL ESTATE

etaoin shrdlu (ə TAY oh ən SHƏRD lōō) *n phr* Confusion; mistakes: *98 percent accurate and 2 percent etaoin shrdlu*—New York Post [fr the phrase typeset by sweeping one's finger down the two lefthand columns of Linotype keys, in a gesture made by compositors when they have erred and must begin again]

-eteria *See* -ATERIA

Ethel *esp 1920s* 1 *n* A coward, esp a cautious prizefighter 2 *n* An effeminate man; = PERCY, SISSY

◄**Ethiopian paradise**► *n phr* The topmost gallery or balcony of a theater [a tasteless euphemism for the equally offensive "nigger heaven"]

Euro *adj & combining word* European: *The majority of the Euro children hit the black box first*—Psychology/ *Eurobrat/ Eurobucks/ Eurofunk/ dancing Europop strings*—Village Voice

even *adj* On the same footing: *When you hit me we'll be even* *See* GET EVEN

even break *n phr* A fair and equal chance; honest treatment; = a FAIR SHAKE: *The Bible, I think it is, says never to give a sucker an even break*

evened out *adj phr* Restored to balance and health; rational: *"I was really emotionally fucked up." "Are you evened out now?"*—Diana Clapton

evening *See* LARGE EVENING

even-stephen or **even-steven** **1** *adj* *fr middle 1800s* Fair; even; equable: *Give me the hundred and fifty and we'll call it even-steven*—Dashiell Hammett **2** *adv*: *And we'll do likewise for San Francisco and Odessa, or any places we want, always even-stephen*—D Fairbairn

even the score *v phr* = GET EVEN

evergreen *n* A perennial favorite, esp a song; = GOLDEN OLDIE

every Tom, Dick, and Harry *n phr* Every and any man, esp a very ordinary one; = ORDINARY JOE: *letting every Tom, Dick, and Harry in on the election*—Max Shulman

Eve with the lid on *n phr* *lunch counter* A piece of apple pie [fr biblical *Eve*'s traffic with the fateful apple]

evil **1** *adj* Excellent; splendid; = MEAN, WICKED: *Geoffrey beats an evil set of skins* **2** *adj* homosexuals Biting and sarcastic; catty; = BITCHY

ex[1] or **x** *n* A former wife or husband, girlfriend or boyfriend, etc: *He introduced his ex rather casually, considering they were together 27 years*

ex[2] *n* *circus* An exclusive concession

exam **1** *n* An examination **2** *modifier*: *exam results/ exam book*

excess baggage *n phr* A person or thing regarded as unnecessary and likely to impede: *He thought his wife and kids were excess baggage*

excuse[1] (ek SKYo͞oZ) *v* *railroad* To disconnect and separate

excuse[2] (ek SKYo͞oS) *n* A version or example of: *He's a rotten excuse for a lawyer*

excuse (or **pardon**) **me all to hell** *sentence* I apologize; I am sorry ● Most often said ironically, when one thinks an accusation has been undeserved or too strong

exec **1** *n* *Navy fr 1920s* An executive officer **2** *n* A business executive: *They'd never heard of female execs*—New York Magazine/ *I find parking space for senior execs*—New Yorker **3** *modifier*: *exec perks/ exec burnout*

expedition *See* GO FISHING

extra **1** *n* A special edition of a newspaper or special broadcast of news made immediately on learning of an important event; news-break **2** *n* *movie studio* A person appearing in a crowd scene or otherwise in a minor capacity in a play or movie: *I was an extra in the Budapest showcase of "Godot"*

extract *See* BOVINE EXTRACT

extracurricular *adj* Irregular; irresponsible: *not an affair, but an extracurricular fling*

the **extra mile** *See* GO THE EXTRA MILE

-ey *See* -IE

eye **1** *n* A private detective; = PRIVATE EYE: *an eye named Johnny O'John*—Anthony Boucher **2** *n*

railroad A signal light **3** *n* A television set or screen

See BIG BROWN EYES, BLACK EYE, CATS' EYES, DOG EYE, EAGLE-EYE, FISH-EGGS, FOUR-EYES, GET THE EYE, GIVE someone THE EYE, GIVE someone THE FISH-EYE, GIVE someone THE GLAD EYE, GIVE WITH THE EYES, the GLAD EYE, a GLEAM IN someone's EYE, GOGGLE-EYE, GOO-GOO EYES, HAVE EYES FOR, IN A PIG'S ASS, KEEP AN EYE ON, MAKE GOO-GOO EYES, MUD IN YOUR EYE, NOT BAT AN EYE, PRIVATE EYE, PULL THE WOOL OVER someone's EYES, PUT THE EYE ON someone, REDEYE, the RED-EYE, ROUND-EYE, SHORT EYES, SHUT-EYE, SNAKE EYES, STONED TO THE EYES, a THUMB IN one's EYE

the **Eye** or **the eye** *n* The Pinkerton National Detective Agency, or one of its detectives

eyeball *v* *teenagers fr black* To look at; look over; = SCOPE ON: *He would eyeball the idol-breaker*—Zora Neale Hurston/ *You locate trophies before they eyeball you*—Sports Afield

See GIVE someone THE FISH-EYE, UP TO one's EYEBALLS

eyeball to eyeball **1** *adv phr* Face to face; in confrontation: *We're eyeball to eyeball and I think the other fellow just blinked*—Dean Rusk **2** *adj phr*: *our eyeball-to-eyeball chat*

eyed *See* COCKEYED, GLASSY-EYED, GOTCH-EYED, HOARY-EYED, ONE-EYED MONSTER, OWL-EYED, PIE-EYED, WALL-EYED

eye-opener **1** *n* A drink of liquor taken upon awaking: *He fumbled for the jug and slurped an eye-opener* **2** *n* *narcotics* An addict's first injection of the day **3** *n* Anything that informs or enlightens one: *Listening to that story was a real eye-opener*

eyepopper *n* Something that makes one's eyes bulge in astonishment: *The president added a further eyepopper*—Washington Post

eye-shut *n* = SHUT-EYE

◁**eyes like pissholes in the snow**▷ *n phr* Very bleary eyes; tired and dim eyes, esp those of a severe hangover: *Your eyes look like two piss holes in the snow*—Rex Burns

eyes only *adj phr* Very personal and confidential [fr the phrase "for your *eyes only*"]

eyes open *See* WITH EYES OPEN

eyes to cool it *n phr* *cool talk* A wish to relax or withdraw: *eyes to cool it, the desire to relax*—E Horne

eyewash **1** *n* = HOGWASH **2** *n* Flattery; cajolery: *eyewash to soften him up for the touch*

◁**Eytie** or **Eyetie**▷ (Ī tee, Brit Ī tī) **1** *n* An Italian **2** *adj*: *an Eytie village/ Eyetie chick*

F

fab *adj* & *interj* *esp teenagers* Excellent; wonderful; fabulous: *a man who would think it a fab idea to rent a silver limo*—Village Voice

face 1 *n* *show business* A celebrity, esp a show-business notable **2** *n* *student* & *cool talk* A person: *bad face...a surly, mean, no-good cat*—E Horne **3** *n* *black* A white person; = FAY

See BALD FACE, BAG YOUR FACE, DOLLFACE, FEED one's FACE, FLANGE-FACE, GET OUT OF one's FACE, GET OUT OF someone's FACE, GO UPSIDE one's FACE, HAVE A RED FACE, HAVE EGG ON one's FACE, JUST ANOTHER PRETTY FACE, LAUGH ON THE OTHER SIDE OF one's FACE, LET'S FACE IT, MINISTER'S FACE, OPEN one's FACE, PALEFACE, PIEFACE, POKER FACE, PRUNEFACE, RAT-FACE, RED FACE, SHE CAN SIT ON MY FACE ANY TIME, SHIT-FACED, SHOOT OFF one's MOUTH, a SLAP IN THE FACE, STRAIGHT FACE, SUCK FACE, TILL one IS BLUE IN THE FACE, WHAT'S-HIS-NAME, WHITE-FACE

face card *n phr* An important person; star; = BIG SHOT: *Oh, don't be so modest...you're a face card yourself now*—Philadelphia Journal

faced *See* POKER-FACED, RED-FACED, SHIT-FACED

face hanging out *See* STAND THERE WITH one's BARE FACE HANGING OUT

face-off *n* Confrontation, esp one before action: *continuing face-off and stalemate*—Philadelphia [fr the poised situation in a hockey game, where two players prepare to drive the puck when it is dropped between them by an official]

face the music *v phr* fr middle 1800s To endure whatever punishment or rigors one has incurred; take what one has coming [perhaps fr the necessity of forcing a cavalry horse to face steadily the regimental band; perhaps fr the plight of a performer on stage]

fack *v* *black* To tell the truth; utter facts: *Negroes know...that facking means speaking facts*—Time [fr the normal pronunciation of *fact* in Black English]

factor *See* FINAGLE FACTOR

factory 1 *n* *narcotics* The apparatus used for injecting narcotics; = WORKS **2** *combining word* Place where what is indicated is done, pursued, used, etc ● A jocular appropriation of the term: *brain factory/ freak factory/ nut factory*

See BONE FACTORY, CRACKER FACTORY, GARGLE-FACTORY, JOINT FACTORY, NUT HOUSE

facts *See* HARD FACTS

faddle *See* FIDDLE-FADDLE

fade 1 *v* To leave; depart: *He faded to Chicago*—A Hynd **2** *v* *crapshooting* To take one's bet; cover one's offered bet: *When I saw I was faded, I rolled the dice* **3** *v* To lose power and effectiveness: *They faded in the second half/ Damned engine's fading fast* **4** *n* *black* A white person **5** *n* *black* A black person who prefers white friends, sex partners, attitudes, etc; = OREO

fadeaway *n* *baseball* A pitch that moves away from the batter so that he would have to reach out for it

fade away (or **out**) *v phr* fr late 1800s To depart, esp gradually

◁**faded boogie**▷ *n phr* *black* A black police informer [fr the suggestion that the subject is no better than a white person]

fag 1 *n* fr late 1800s A cigarette; = BUTT, COFFIN NAIL: *He passed them swell fags around*—Langston Hughes ◁**2**▷ *n* fr 1920s A male homosexual; = FAGGOT, QUEER: *and fags are certain to arouse the loathing of all decent fiction addicts*—Gore Vidal/ *sicker by a long shot than any fag, drag, thang, or simple gay man or woman*—Ebony ◁**3**▷ *modifier: frenetic hot-rhythm dancing, the cheap fag jokes*—Playboy/ *like a fag party*—Raymond Chandler **4** *v* (also **fag out**) To fatigue; exhaust: *This sort of work fags me quickly* [origin unknown; the "homosexual" sense may be connected with the British term *fag* "the boy servant, and inferentially the catamite, of a public-school upperclassman"; perhaps influenced by Yiddish *faygele* "homosexual," literally "bird, little bird"]

fag along *v phr* *cowboys* To ride fast

◁**fag bag**▷ *n phr* *homosexuals* A woman married to a homosexual

fag end *n phr* The useless, dreary, or extreme end of something: *The fag ends of my days are irretrievably grungy*

◁**faggot**▷ *n* A male homosexual: *Hot faggot queens bump up against chilly Jewish matrons*—Albert Goldman/ *an amazing job of controlling the faggots*—Tennessee Williams [origin unknown; perhaps fr *fag*]

◁**faggotry**▷ *n* Male homosexuality: *Faggotry was at the very least a terrible embarrassment*—RA Arthur

◁**faggoty**▷ *adj* Homosexual, esp in an overt way ● Used only of males: *who lives with his faggoty American friend*—Playboy

◁**fag hag** or **faggot's moll**▷ *n phr* A heterosexual woman who seeks or prefers the company of homosexual men: *Zeffirelli seems to have created a sort of limp-wrist commune, with Clare as the fag hag* —Judith Crist/ *Michael once referred to her...as "the fag hag of the bourgeoisie"*—Armistead Maupin

fagin *n* A teacher of crime; a nasty old crook [fr the character in Dickens's *Oliver Twist*]

fail *n* stock market A failure of a broker to deliver stocks within a customary period: *the amount of what Wall Street calls "fails"*—New Yorker

faint *adj* Drunk

fair dinkum *adj phr* WW1 fr Australian Honest; fair and just ● Still chiefly Australian use

fairhaired (or **blue-eyed** or **white-haired**) **boy** **1** *n phr* A favored or favorite man or boy: *the latest "fairhaired boy" of the musical world*—D Bittan/ *the white-haired boy of the happy family* —Budd Schulberg/ *If I could possibly pull it off, I'd be the fair-haired boy*—Lawrence Sanders **2** *n phr* A man destined for and being groomed for principal leadership or other reward; =COMER

fair hell *n phr* A person who is energetic and successful

a **fair shake** *n phr* fr early 1800s Equal treatment; the same chance as others; =EVEN BREAK: *He complains he didn't get a fair shake* [fr an honest *shake* of the dice]

◁**fairy**▷ *n* fr early 1900s fr hoboes A male homosexual, esp an effeminate one; =FAG, QUEER: *Too bad you weren't a fairy*—Philip Wylie

fairy godfather *n phr* show business A potential sponsor, advertiser, or financial backer, esp in show business

◁**fairy godmother**▷ *n phr* homosexuals A male homosexual's homosexual initiator and tutor

◁**fairy lady**▷ *n phr* A lesbian who plays a passive role in sex

fake fr early 1800s British **1** *n* A sham or deception; something spurious **2** *v* To make something spurious; imitate deceptively: *He was good at faking Old Masters* [fr earlier *feak, feague*, or *fig* "to spruce up, esp by deceptive artificial means"; perhaps ultimately fr German *fegen* "clean, furbish"]

fake it 1 *v phr* To make a pretense of knowledge, skill, etc; bluff; =CHEEK IT **2** *v phr* (also **fake**) jazz musicians fr early 1900s To improvise more or less compatible chords or notes as one plays or sings something one really has not learned

fake off *v phr* To loaf; idle; =GOOF OFF

fake someone **out** *v phr* To bluff or deceive someone; mislead: *Bailey...had faked out Keuper into using a preempt*—John D MacDonald/ *He faked the cops out by dressing like a priest*

faker *See* MUSH-FAKER, POODLE-FAKER

fall 1 *v* underworld fr late 1800s To be arrested; be imprisoned; =DROP: *When you have bad luck and you fall, New York is the best place*—New York Times/ *the best thief in the city till he fell*—WR Burnett **2** *n: This your first fall, ain't it?*—The American Scholar/ *Another fall meant a life sentence*—D Purroy **3** *v* underworld To fail in a robbery attempt: *The whole mob may fall*—E DeBaun **4** *v*

To become enamored; become a lover: *Once Abelard saw her he fell*

See PRATFALL, the ROOF FALLS IN, TAKE A FALL, TAKE THE RAP

fall apart *v phr* To lose one's usual poise and confidence; lose control; =LOSE one's COOL: *Even the seasoned troupers fall apart*—A Hirschfeld

fall (or **slip**) **between** (or **through**) **the cracks** *v phr* To be ignored, overlooked, mismanaged, or forgotten, esp because of ambiguity in definition or understanding: *The entire problem...simply fell between the cracks*—New Yorker/ *a conviction that otherwise might have fallen through the cracks* —Washingtonian

fall down and go boom esp 1920s & 30s **1** *v phr* To take a tumble; fall heavily **2** *v phr* To fail, esp utterly and obviously

fall down on the job *v phr* To fail at one's responsibilities; shirk an obligation

fall for 1 *v phr* fr early 1900s To become enamored; become a lover of: *He's constantly falling for long-legged brunettes* **2** *v phr* To be deceived or duped by; acquiesce to: *Americans would continue to "fall for" this*—Robert Lynd/ *Don't fall for his limp excuses*

fall guy 1 *n phr* fr early 1900s An easy victim; =EASY MARK, SUCKER **2** *n phr* fr underworld A person who willingly or not takes the blame and punishment for another's misdoings; =PATSY: *He said he would not be the president's fall guy*

falling off a log *See* EASY AS PIE

fall money *n phr* underworld Money set aside to deal with the expenses of being arrested: *Mike set aside a percentage of his takings for "fall money"* —TJ Courtney

fall off the roof *v phr* To menstruate, esp to begin a menstrual period [probably a fanciful way to explain bleeding]

fall off the wagon *v phr* To begin drinking liquor again after a period of abstinence; also, to breach abstinence or moderation in anything: *But like most of us, she falls off the wagon from time to time, and heads for a stadium hot dog*—Toronto Life

◁**fall on** one's **ass**▷ **1** *v phr* (also **fall flat on** one's **ass**) To fail, esp ignominiously and spectacularly: *He'll fall on his ass if he tries to take on that kind of competition*/ *They want to see you fall on your ass*—Interview **2** *v phr* airline To deteriorate beneath operational limits ● Said of the weather conditions at an airport

fallout 1 *n* An accompanying or resultant effect of something; an aftermath: *Talking to oneself is a fallout of watching too many primaries on TV* —Goodman Ace **2** *n* Incidental products, esp when copious and of little value: *reports, memoranda, and other printed fallout from the executive suite*—Saturday Review [fr the radioactive dust and other debris of a nuclear explosion]

fall out 1 *v phr* narcotics To go to sleep or into a stuporous condition from narcotic intoxication: *Only those who are uptight fall out*—Saturday Review/ *If you resist falling out and pass the barrier, the curve is up to a mellow stupor*—New York **2** *v phr* To become helpless with laughter or emotion; = CRACK UP: *I tried double tempo and everybody fell out laughing*—Charlie Parker

fall up *v phr* (Variations: **by** or **down** or **out** may replace **up**) *cool talk fr 1930s black* To come for a visit; arrive: *The bash is in the basement, Dad. Fall up anytime*—E Horne

faloosie *See* FLOOZY

falsie or **falsy** **1** *n* Anything false or artificial; a prosthesis: *Its tail, a falsy, fell off*—Newsweek **2** *n* A brassiere padded to give the appearance of large breasts; also, padding worn in other places to increase the generosity of a woman's body

falsies or **gay deceivers** *n* A pair of breast pads worn to give the appearance of large breasts

family *See* PLAY THE DOZENS

family jewels *n phr* The testicles; = NUTS: *A kick in the family jewels will often dampen a man's ardor*

fan¹ *n fr late 1800s* A devotee or enthusiast, esp of a sport; aficionado; = BUFF, BUG: *a tennis fan / cathedral fan* [fr *fanatic*, or perhaps fr *the fancy* "sports followers or fanciers"]

fan² **1** *n* *WW2 Army Air Forces* An aircraft propeller or engine **2** *v* *baseball* To strike out; = WHIFF **3** *v* To fire a revolver by working the hammer with the hand that is not holding the firearm: *Gary Cooper fanned off six shots* **4** *v* *underworld* To search someone; = FRISK: *The gendarmes fan them to see if they have any rods on them*—Damon Runyon **5** *n* *underworld* A quick brush or pat used by pickpockets to find the place of the victim's wallet **6** *v*: *You will be fanned by hands feeling for an impression of your wallet*—New York **7** *v* To chat; gossip; = BAT THE BREEZE: *all the other chauffeurs I'd stand around fanning with*—H Larkin **8** *v* To manipulate the coin-return lever of a pay telephone in the hope of dislodging coins: *Mary was embarrassed at being observed at her fanning activities*—New York Post *See* BAT THE BREEZE, FAN someone's TAIL, IRISH BANJO, the SHIT HITS THE FAN

fancy Dan *n phr* *prizefight* A skillful boxer with a weak punch *See* DAPPER DAN

fancy-Dan *adj* Pretentious; = HIGHFALUTIN: *It's fancy-Dan nomenclature*—National Review

fancy (or **fast**) **footwork** *n phr fr prizefighting* Very adroit evasion; clever dodging and maneuver: *It will take fancy footwork to explain this one/ The American Medical Association tried a little fast footwork before Congress last week*—New York Times

fancy man *n phr* A lover, esp the adulterous sex partner of a married woman

fancy pants **1** *n phr* A dressed-up or overdressed person **2** *n phr* An effete man; = SISSY **3** *modifier:* *one of your fancy-pants diplomats*

fancy-schmancy *adj* Very elegant or ornate, esp pretentiously so; = HIGHFALUTIN: *mostly fancy-schmancy Roman numbers like IIs and IIIs*—Philadelphia [fr the humorous and derisive Yiddish rhyming of a first word with a second one beginning *shm-*, as in "Oedipus-shmoedipus, just so he loves his mother"]

fandangle¹ *n* An ornamental object; gew-gaw

fandangle² *n* A confused profusion; generous lively miscellany: *cranes, firebirds, foxes, flamingos, a fauna fandangle hard to believe*—New York [fr middle 1800s eastern US dialect *fandango* "a boisterous assembly," fr the Spanish dance]

fandom *n* Devotees and aficionados collectively: *All fandom welcomes the new summer football*

faniggle *See* FINAGLE

fanner **1** *n* A fan dancer **2** *n* *underworld* A person who locates wallets for a pickpocket to steal **3** *n* A person who manipulates coin-return levers on pay telephones, hoping to dislodge coins: *little old lady of about 80 who was dubbed Mary the Fanner*—New York Post

fanny *n fr 1920s* The buttocks; rump; = ASS: *I can hardly sit down, my fanny is so sore*—Associated Press [fr earlier British *fanny* "vulva," perhaps fr John Cleland's 18th-century heroine *Fanny Hill*]

fannybumper **1** *n* A crowded occasion; = MOB SCENE: *The reception was a fannybumper* **2** *modifier:* *organized a fannybumper vernissage*—Interview

fanny-dipper *n surfers* A conventional swimmer, as distinct from a surfer

fan someone's **tail** *v phr* To spank someone; = TAN: *Don't let him out of your sight, or I'll fan your tail*—Ellery Queen

fan the breeze *v phr* = BAT THE BREEZE

the **fantods** *n phr fr late 1800s* Fidgety nervousness; uneasy restlessness; = the WILLIES: *You just got the fantods, that's all*—W Henry [fr British dialect, "indisposition, restlessness," perhaps fr *fanteague* "commotion, excitement" or fr *fantasy*]

fanzine **1** *n* A fan magazine: *wants to start his own fanzine*—Village Voice **2** *modifier:* *The fanzine set is not scared off by raunchy lyrics*—Rolling Stone

fare-thee-well or **fare-you-well** *See* TO A FARE-THEE-WELL

Farley *See* CHUCK YOU, FARLEY

farm *v Army* To be killed in action; die in the armed services; = BUY THE FARM: *Just about my whole company farmed that day* [fr *buy the farm*] *See* BET THE FARM, FAT FARM, FUNNY FARM, NUT HOUSE

farmer *n* A stupid person; ignorant rustic; clown

Farmer *See* JOHN FARMER

farmisht (far MISHT) *adj* Confused; mixed up; ambivalent and/or ambiguous: *I'm afraid she's a little farmisht* [fr Yiddish]

far out **1** *adj* Very unconventional; unorthodox and strange; = WEIRD: *Drake liked "Suzie Q." Which to us was really far out*—Rolling Stone/ *a curious combination of far-out medicine, pampering, and very shrewd doctoring*—Fortune **2** *adj* Excellent; splendid; = COOL: *The next thing I heard from her was "Far out!"*—American Scholar/ *His latest film is very far out*

◁**fart**▷ **1** *v fr 1300s* To expel gas through the anus; relieve flatulence by the most immediate expedient **2** *n* A man; fellow; person; = GUY: *What's that stupid fart up to?* **3** *n* The least thing; nothing;

= DIDDLY, ZILCH: *I don't give a fart for that notion/ It isn't worth a fart*

See FIDDLE AROUND, LAY A FART, OLD FART

◁**fart around**▷ **1** *v phr* = HORSE AROUND **2** *v phr* = GOOF AROUND

◁**fart sack**▷ *n phr Army* A sleeping bag

fashion plate *n phr* A well-dressed person, esp a stylish one: *The present-day...racketeer is a veritable fashion plate*—E Lavine

fast *adj* Morally lax; libertine: *on Long Island with the fast younger married set*—F Scott Fitzgerald

fast (or **quick**) **buck 1** *n phr* Money gotten quickly, esp without too fine a concern for ethics or the future: *tryin' to hustle me for a fast buck*—Arthur Kober **2** *modifier: Fast-buck speculators were getting rich on inflated FHA appraisals*—Reader's Digest

fast burner *n phr Army* A person whose success is rapid; = BALL OF FIRE

fast food 1 *n phr* Food like hamburgers, fried chicken, etc, cooked and served very rapidly and uniformly, usu by large catering corporations **2** *modifier: a fast-food chain*

fast footwork *See* FANCY FOOTWORK

fast lane (or **track**) **1** *n phr* A pace and quality of life emphasizing quick success against strong competition, along with the trappings of wealth and style: *amazing woman, lives on a fast lane*—Village Voice/ *Jean Piaget...started academic life on a fast track*—Time **2** *modifier: its glittery fast-lane image*—Time/ *fast-track people/ fast-track male*—William Safire [fr the left-hand or *fast lane* of a superhighway, which slower drivers enter at their risk]

fast one *n phr* A trick or deception; clever subterfuge; = DIPSY DOODLE: *That was sure a fast one, you wearing the false mustache* [probably fr *fast shuffle*] *See* PULL A FAST ONE

fast shuffle *See* DOUBLE SHUFFLE

fast talk *n phr* Talk meant to deceive or confuse; glib and plausible nonsense: *Ignore the fast talk and don't sign a thing*

fat 1 *n* The best and most rewarding part; = CREAM: *He just took the fat; screw the long term* **2** *adj: fat profits/ fat prospects* **3** *adj fr 1920s* Wealthy; in funds, esp temporarily so; = FLUSH: *Hit him up now, he's pretty fat* **4** *n* A fat person; = FATTY: *I met the other 18 women or fellow fats*—AD Botorff

See BIG FAT, CHEW THE FAT, LIVE OFF THE FAT OF THE LAND, SIT FAT

fat Albert 1 *n phr* A kind of guided bomb **2** *n phr* airlines A Boeing 747 jet aircraft, or other jumbo jet [fr a character used in stories by the comedian Bill Cosby]

fat-ass 1 *n* A fat person **2** *adj: Get your fat-ass self out of here* **3** *n* A person with large buttocks; = BUFFALOBUTT

fatback *adj* Redolent of southern black ethnic tastes; = FUNKY: *The song became progressively funkier with Guerin laying down a dirty fatback beat*—San Francisco [fr the particularly *fat* sort of pork that characterizes some sorts of black ethnic food]

fat cat 1 *n phr fr 1920s* Any privileged and well-treated person, esp a wealthy benefactor; tycoon: *a millionaire fat-cat who, when the revolution comes, will probably be allowed to keep at least one of his chauffeurs*—New York/ *the late arrival even of such famous "fat cats"*—New York Times/ *had jousted with Nelson Rockefeller at a formal dinner for fat cats*—Joseph Heller **2** *modifier: the fat-cat cases, where big money is involved*—New York Times/ *whether fat-cat contributors or New Hampshire coffee-klatschers*—Meg Greenfield **3** *v: "fat-catting"...a term applied...to higher leaders who try to pad themselves with special privileges and comforts*—Hal Boyle

fat city 1 *n phr* esp students fr jazz musicians An ideal situation; splendid state of affairs: *You're in fat city while other poor slobs sweat on assembly lines*—Sports Illustrated/ *Johnny came marching home from college...and announced he was in "fat city"*—New York Times **2** *n phr* Poor physical condition, esp because of being overweight: *Its principal characters wind up in "fat city" (argot for "out of condition")*—American Scholar

fat, dumb, and happy *adj phr* Blissfully and rather bovinely contented

fat farm *n phr* A resort or treatment center where people go to lose weight: *It'll be adventures of me, and takes place at a fat farm*—Blair Sabol/ *I went to a California fat farm a couple years ago*—New York Times

fathead *n* A stupid person; = BLUBBERHEAD

fatheaded *adj* Stupid: *some fatheaded motorist*—J Evans

◀**fatherfucker**▶ *n* = MOTHERFUCKER

fatigue *See* BUNK FATIGUE

fat lady sings *See* the OPERA'S NEVER OVER TILL THE FAT LADY SINGS

fat-mouth 1 *v* To blab and chatter; = CHEW THE FAT **2** *v* To cajole verbally; = BULLSHIT, SWEET-TALK: *I ain't asking you to fatmouth me, just as I am not interested in getting into any argument*—Bernard Malamud

Fats *n* (Variations: **Fat** or **Fatty** or **Fatso** or **Fat stuff**) A nickname for a fat person

fatso *adj* Fat, in any sense: *a fatso deal in six figures*—New York Daily News

fatter *See* HAM-FATTER

fatty *n* A fat person: *designed to keep all us fatties from committing hara-kiri*—Esquire

faunet or **faunlet** (FAW nət, FAWN lət) *n homosexuals* An adolescent or preadolescent boy as a homosexual sex object [on analogy with *nymphet*, probably influenced by *fawn*]

faust (FOUST) *adj cool talk* Ugly; disgusting: *"Faust"...means ugly*—Stephen Longstreet

fave or **fave rave 1** *n* or *n phr* A favorite song or musical number, film, person, etc: *group scats Mozart, Vivaldi, Bach and other fave raves*—Saturday Review/ *includes many of the quintet's faves*—Variety **2** *modifier: My absolute fave-rave model was printed boldly*—Village Voice

◀**fay[1]**▶ *n black* A white person; = HONKY, PECKERWOOD [fr *ofay*]

fay² *adj homosexuals* Homosexual; = GAY [fr earlier *fay* "fairy"]

featherbed 1 *v* To work languidly and sluggishly; seek easy tasks **2** *v labor union* To create or retain unnecessary jobs; do essentially fictitious jobs: *featherbedding clauses in labor agreements* —Labor's Special Language

feather duster *n phr military school* The high plume worn on a full-dress military hat

feather-legs *n 1940s students* An unfair or deceitful person

feather merchant 1 *n phr WW2 armed forces* A civilian, esp one who evades military service **2** *n phr WW2 Navy* A reserve officer, or a person commissioned directly into the Navy **3** *n phr Navy* A sailor who has a desk job [perhaps fr a group of small rather parasitic persons called *feather merchants* in the comic strip "Barney Google"]

feather (or **line**) one's **nest** *v phr fr 1600s* To be primarily concerned with one's own gain; take care of oneself

feathers *See* HORSEFEATHERS, PITTSBURGH FEATHERS

feature *v fr 1920s* To understand; take note of: *He shoved the picture in my face and said "Feature that!"*

Fed *n* Any federal government worker or agent, esp in law enforcement or taxation: *right up to the day the Feds dragged him into court*—Esquire

the Fed *n phr* The Federal Reserve System, Board, or Bank: *Now the Fed has apparently decided to let the market carry interest rates upward*—New York Times/ *The Fed was reluctant to raise its discount rate*—Wall Street Journal

Federal case *See* MAKE A FEDERAL CASE OUT OF something

fed up *adj phr fr WW1 fr British* Disgusted; tired; surfeited; = BRASSED OFF: *A number of people suddenly became fed up with a slang phrase like "fed up"*—J Greig/ *I'm fed up and I won't take it any more*

feeb 1 *n* A feeble-minded person; idiot: *Then why are you treating me like a feeb?*—Life **2** *n* = FEEB

Feeb or **Feebie** *n* An agent of the Federal Bureau of Investigation; = G-MAN: *the agents of the Federal Bureau of Investigation, whom they call "Feebs"* —FC Shapiro/ *our heroes, the feebs, however*--Village Voice/ *make sure the Feebies didn't get any credit for it*—Patrick Mann

feebles *n* A hangover: *his several disquisitions on the jeebies, or feebles*—H Allen Smith

feed 1 *n fr early 1800s* A meal: *Stop by for a feed, anytime* **2** *n fr late 1800s* Money **3** *v* To board; take one's meals: *He feeds over at Mrs Ackerman's*
See CHICKEN FEED, OFF one's FEED

feedback *n* Response, esp information and opinion: *We'll wait for feedback before we try anything else* [fr the portion of output *fed back* to the input in an automatic control circuit or system]

the feedbag *n phr* A meal: *I'm ready for the feedbag*—WR Burnett [fr the *bag* of feed hung on the head of a horse]
See PUT ON THE FEEDBAG

feedbox (or **feedbag**) **information** *n phr horse-racing* Supposedly dependable advance information on a horse race: *Neither of us had ever heard of Clam giving out feed-box information to anybody*—J Lilienthal [because such information was virtually from the horse's mouth]

feed one's **face** *v phr* To eat

feed the kitty *v phr fr poker* To contribute to a fund, esp to put what one owes into the pot of a card game

◁**feel** or **feel up**▷ *v or v phr* To touch, caress, or handle the buttocks, breasts, legs, crotch, etc; = COP A FEEL

◁a **feel**▷ *n phr* A caress or touch, esp of the buttocks, breasts, or crotch: *The eager amorist entreated a quick feel*
See COP A FEEL

feel a draft 1 *v phr black* To sense racial prejudice against oneself **2** *v phr* To feel unwelcome, snubbed, etc; sense coolness: *I felt a draft as soon as I walked into his office*

feeler *n* A finger, esp the middle finger

Feelgood or **feelgood 1** *n* = DR FEELGOOD **2** *n* A condition of contentment or euphoria: *a purveyor of religious feelgood* **3** *modifier*: *a general "relax, feelgood" vibe*—Village Voice/ *The President is running a feel-good campaign*—Charles MacDowell

feel good *v phr* To be slightly and pleasantly drunk: *Old Charley was feeling good that night*—Mickey Spillane

feelie *See* TOUCHIE-FEELIE

feel no pain *v phr fr 1940s* To be drunk: *three men who were feeling no pain*—Christopher Morley/ *The anticipated audience...should be feeling no pain*—GQ

feel one's **oats** *v phr fr early 1800s* To be active and high-spirited; act brashly and confidently: *The manufacturer was just feeling his oats, having accomplished his happy intention*—Village Voice [fr the vigor of a just-fed horse]

feel out *v phr* To inquire or investigate tentatively: *Let's feel out the market first*

feel someone **out** *v phr* To examine someone's opinions, knowledge, etc, esp indirectly: *Touch bases with Riemer and feel him out on this*

feep 1 *n computer* The electronic bell- or whistle-like sound made by computer terminals **2** *v*: *The machine feeped inexplicably but insistently*

feet *See* DRAG one's FEET, GET one's FEET WET, GO HOME FEET FIRST, HAVE COLD FEET, HOLD someone's FEET TO THE FIRE, PUPPY-DOG FEET, VOTE WITH one's FEET

fegelah or **feygelah** (FAY gə lə) *n* A male homosexual; = FAG: *The guy must be a real whacko. A fegelah, you figure?*—Lawrence Sanders [fr Yiddish, "little bird"]

feh or **fehh** *interj* An exclamation of disgust: *Thus, soccer. Feh*—Village Voice/ *Well, fehh, Petro thinks* *that Dr Scholl's spray seems to work*—Village Voice [fr Yiddish]

feisty *adj* Truculent; irascible: *They said the president was a feisty little chap/ He was having trouble with a feisty old lady who didn't want to move* [fr Southern dialect *fice*, a small, worthless cur, esp a lapdog on which the owner's flatulence could be blamed]

fellow *See* BEST FELLOW, HAIL-FELLOW, REGULAR FELLOW

fellow traveler *n phr esp 1930s to early 1950s* A person who sympathizes with a cause or doctrine, without openly identifying himself with it: *These people are not hipsters, they are fellow travelers* —Eugene Burdick [said to have been coined by Leon Trotsky in Russian as *sputnik*, and translated into English as "fellow traveler"]

◁**femme** or **fem**▷ **1** *n* A woman: *He has aired the fem that got him the job*—John O'Hara **2** *modifier: looks more like a post deb than a femme comic*—H Gardner/ *whereas women with big heads of fat hair always look femme*—San Francisco **3** *n homosexuals* A lesbian who takes a passive, feminine role in sex **4** *modifier: butch-femme role players are sad relics of the uptight past* —Village Voice **5** *n homosexuals* An effeminate homosexual male: *active or passive, manly ("stud") or womanly ("fem")*—Saturday Review [fr French, "woman"]

fenagle *See* FINAGLE

fence 1 *n fr 1600s* A person or place that deals in stolen goods: *But even big fences like Alphonso can get stuck*—New York/ *The loot had disappeared and been handled by a fence*—Associated Press **2** *v: The clown that stole the Mona Lisa found it hard to fence* **3** *v* To maneuver for advantage; spar: *Their lawyers fenced for a couple hours* [all senses are shortenings of *defence*; in the case of criminal act, the notion is probably that of a secure place and trusty person, well defended; the other sense is from *fence* "fight or defend oneself with a sword"] *See* GO FOR THE FENCES, ON THE FENCE, OVER THE FENCE

fence-straddle *v* To maintain a neutral attitude; not take a position; = STRADDLE THE FENCE: *The candidate resolutely fence-straddled on that point*

fence-straddler or **fence-hanger** *n* = MUGWUMP

fender-bender *n* A minor car accident; trivial collision: *I've only had one fender-bender since I got it* —Don Pendleton

fer instance *See* FOR INSTANCE

fer sure (or **shure** or **shurr**) *See* FOR SURE

fess (or **'fess**) **up** *v phr* To confess; admit the truth: *Then why doesn't the judge come clean and fess up?*—Village Voice

-fest *combining form fr late 1800s* A celebration or extensive exercise and indulgence of what is indicated: *slugfest/ gabfest/ fuckfest/ jazzfest* [fr German, "festival"] *See* BULL SESSION

fetching *adj fr late 1800s* Attractive: *a fetching appearance*

fetch-me-down *See* HAND-ME-DOWN

fever 1 *n poker* The five of a playing-card suit **2** *n crapshooting* Five or the point of five; = PHOEBE *See* CABIN FEVER, SHACK FEVER

a few *See* HANG A FEW ON, WIN A FEW LOSE A FEW

feygelah *See* FEGELAH

fi *See* HI-FI, LOW-FI

the fickle finger of fate *n phr* The dire and unpredictable aspect of destiny: *It wasn't anything she specially deserved, just the fickle finger of fate at work* [regarding *finger* as both a pointer and a violator of the body] *See* FUCKED BY THE FICKLE FINGER OF FATE

fiddle 1 *v* To cheat; defraud ● Chiefly British **2** *n: His new boat is a tax fiddle* *See* BELLY FIDDLE, BULL FIDDLE, GIT-BOX, PLAY SECOND FIDDLE, SECOND FIDDLE, STEAM FIDDLE, SWEDISH FIDDLE

fiddle around *v phr* (also ◁**fiddle fart around** or **fiddle-fart**▷) To loaf or idle about; also, tinker or tamper; = MONKEY AROUND: *He fiddled around all week/ She was fiddling around with the gearshift/ The dentist fiddle-farted for two hours while I suffered*

fiddle-faddle 1 *interj* An exclamation of irritation, disapproval, dismissal, etc **2** *n* Nonsense; foolishness; = BULLSHIT: *such homemade fiddle-faddle*—Alexander Woolcott

◀**fiddlefucking**▶ *adj* Particular and accursed; = DAMN ● Used for vehement and vulgar emphasis: *Not one swingin' dick will be leavin' this fiddlefuckin' area*—Philip Roth

fiddler's bitch *See* DRUNK AS A FIDDLER'S BITCH

fiddlesticks *n* Nonsense; foolishness; = BULLSHIT ● Often a dismissive response to a contemptible comment: *When I explained, she only said, "Fiddlesticks!"*

fiddle with *v phr* To play or tamper with; = FIDDLE AROUND: *Don't fiddle with that grenade*

field *v* To handle; receive and answer; cope with: *The secretary fielded the questions rather lamely* *See* OUT IN LEFT FIELD, PLAY THE FIELD

field day *See* HAVE A FIELD DAY

fiend *combining word* A devotee or user of what is indicated: *camera fiend/ dope-fiend/ sex fiend*

fierce *adj esp 1920s* Nasty; unpleasant; awful: *Gee, it was fierce of me*—Sinclair Lewis *See* SOMETHING FIERCE

the fifth *See* PLEAD THE FIFTH

fifth wheel *n phr* A superfluous person or thing: *I feel as though I'm a fifth wheel*—Wall Street Journal

fifty-five *n lunch counter* Root beer

fifty-one *n lunch counter* Hot chocolate

fifty-six *n police* The time off that substitutes for the weekends of those who work Saturdays and Sundays [because the time adds up to *fifty-six* hours]

fifty-two *n lunch counter* An order for two cups of hot chocolate

fig *See* MOLDY FIG

fight *n* A party; = STRUGGLE: *the cocktail fights attended by the old man*—R Starnes *See* CAT FIGHT, DOGFIGHT, TANK FIGHT, YOU CAN'T FIGHT CITY HALL

fight a bottle *v phr* To drink liquor, esp to excess: *after fighting a bottle all evening*—R Starnes

fighter *See* BOOZEHOUND, HOP FIEND, NIGHT PEOPLE

fightin' tools *n phr armed forces* Eating utensils; silverware

fightin' words *n phr* Provocative speech; words inviting combat ● Often said in a broad cowboy style: *I can go along with a little ribbing, but them is fightin' words, son*

can't **fight** one's **way out of a paper bag** *See* CAN'T FIGHT one's WAY OUT OF A PAPER BAG

figure 1 *v* To make sense; be plausible and reasonable: *It figures he'd be next in line* **2** *v* To be expected; be very likely: *The pup figured to be in the room when Einstein discussed the bomb with the president*—Billy Rose

See BALLPARK FIGURE

file 1 *n underworld fr 1600s British* A pickpocket **2** *n* A wastebasket ● Often humorously called **file 17, the circular file** etc [first sense perhaps fr the tool; perhaps related to French *filou* "pickpocket"]

See CIRCULAR FILE

file and forget *v phr* To consign to oblivion; to refuse to take as serious and consequent

file-bone *n esp service academies* Anything that may improve one's standing in a class

fileboner *n esp service academies* A diligent and serious student: *Everyone was surprised that a fileboner as hivey as Cunningham was D in math*—C Macon

file 17 (or **13**) *n phr esp WW2 armed forces* A wastebasket; = CIRCULAR FILE

fill in *v phr* To substitute; replace temporarily: *I'll fill in for you*

fill-in 1 *n* A summary account; information meant to supply what one does not know: *A friend gives me a fill-in on how Costello is running the country*—Saturday Evening Post **2** *n* A substitute worker: *Get a fill-in, I gotta split*

fill someone **in** *v phr* To complete someone's knowledge; brief someone; = PUT someone IN THE PICTURE: *Fill me in so I know what's up here*

filling station *n phr* A very small town; = JERKWATER TOWN

fillmill *n* A bar; saloon; = GIN MILL

fill the squares *v phr armed forces* To finish a set of compulsory routine tasks

filly *n fr Brit fr 1600s* A girl; young woman [fr French *fille* "girl"]

film *See* SLICE AND DICE FILM, SNUFF FILM, SPLAT MOVIE

filthbag *n* A despicable person; = DIRTBAG, SCUMBAG: *Tony called Strumpet a filthbag*—San Francisco

filthy 1 *adj* Wealthy; rich; = LOADED: *He's filthy with dough*—Eugene O'Neill **2** *adj* Obscene; salacious; = BLUE, DIRTY: *filthy movies/ filthy minds*

the **filthy** *n phr* Money; = FILTHY LUCRE: *just trying to make a bit of the filthy*—PG Wodehouse

filthy lucre *n phr* Money [fr the Pauline epistle to Titus]

filthy rich *adj phr* Very rich; = LOADED

fin[1] **1** *n fr 1700s fr sailors* The hand: *Reach out your fin and grab it* **2** *n* The arm and hand

fin[2] *n fr 1920s underworld* A five-dollar bill; five dollars: *I gave my pal a fin*—John O'Hara/ *It was the fin seen round the world. Where Reagan got the five bucks is a mystery*—Time [fr Yiddish *finif* "five"]

finagle (fə NAY gəl) (Variations: **faniggle** or **fenagle** or **finigal** or **finagel** or **phenagle**) **1** *v* To manage or arrange, esp by dubious means; contrive: *He finagled it so she got the job/ He finagled the driver into doing it for him*—Hannibal and Boris **2** *v* To acquire, esp by trickery: *She finagled a couple of choice seats* [origin unknown; perhaps related to British dialect *finegue* "to evade" or *fainague* "to renege"]

finagle factor or **Fink's constant** *n phr* The putative mathematical constant by which a wrong answer is multiplied to get a right answer

find 1 *n* A remarkable discovery, esp of something unexpected **2** *v West Point* To discharge a cadet for deficiency of one sort or another ● Because in official terminology the cadet is "found deficient"

See IF YOU CAN'T FIND 'EM, GRIND 'EM

fine *See* CHEWED FINE

a **fine how-de-do** (or **how-do-you-do**) *n phr fr early 1800s British* A situation; set of circumstances: *which is a fine how-de-do in a country that prides itself on progress*—David Dempsey

fine kettle of fish *n phr* A nasty predicament; lamentable situation

the **fine print** *See* the SMALL PRINT

the **finest** *n phr* The police force ● Often in city name plus **finest** phrases like **San Francisco's finest**, **Madison's finest**

fine-tune *v* To make delicate and careful adjustments: *knowledge and techniques to fine-tune the economy*—New York Times

finger 1 *v underworld* To locate and point out someone, esp for a professional killer: *You're the guy that fingered Manny Tinnen*—Raymond Chandler/ *He got so mad he fingered her to the cops* **2** *v underworld* To tell thieves about the location, value, etc, of potential loot **3** *n underworld* A police informer; = STOOL PIGEON **4** *n underworld* A person who tells thieves about potential loot **5** *n underworld* A police officer ◁**6**▷ *v* To insert a finger into the vulva; = FINGERFUCK: *With one hand Larry was fingering me*—Xaviera Hollander **7** *n* About a half-inch of liquor in a glass: *Maybe I'd better have another finger of the hooch*—Raymond Chandler

See BUTTERFINGERS, FIVE FINGERS, FUCKED BY THE FICKLE FINGER OF FATE, GIVE FIVE FINGERS TO, GIVE someone THE FINGER, NOT LAY A GLOVE ON someone, ON THE FINGER, PLAY STINKY-PINKY, PUT one's FINGER ON something, PUT THE FINGER ON someone, STAND AROUND WITH one's FINGER UP one's ASS

the **finger 1** *n phr underworld* The act of identifying or pointing out potential loot, a hired killer's victim, a wanted criminal, etc **2** *n phr* A lewd insulting gesture made by holding up the middle finger with the others folded down, and meaning "fuck you" or "up yours"; = the BIRD

See GIVE someone THE FINGER, PUT THE FINGER ON someone

fingered *See* LIGHT-FINGERED, STICKY-FINGERED

◀**fingerfuck**▶ *v* To insert a finger into the vulva; = FRIG, PLAY STINKY-PINKY: *She wants you to finger-fuck her shikse cunt till she faints*—Philip Roth

finger man *n phr underworld* A person who points out potential loot, potential victims, wanted criminals, etc

finger mob *n phr underworld* A criminal group working under police protection, usu in return for informing on other wrongdoers

finger of fate *See* FUCKED BY THE FICKLE FINGER OF FATE

finger-popper *cool talk n* A listener who is sent into finger-snapping transports by music; an enthusiastic devotee

fingerprint *v truckers* To load or unload a truck oneself, without using paid dockside labor ● Said of independent truckers: *An independent driver...may "fingerprint" the boxes on or off the trailer himself*—Smithsonian

fingers 1 *n underworld* A ten percent share of loot **2** *n musicians* A jazz piano player ● Often a nickname

See BUTTERFINGERS, FIVE FINGERS, GIVE FIVE FINGERS TO

finger up one's **ass** *See* STAND AROUND WITH one's FINGER UP one's ASS

finger-wringer *n movie studio* A performer prone to overly emotional performance

finif or **finiff** or **finnif** *n fr British fr middle 1800s* A five-dollar bill; five dollars; = FIN [fr Yiddish *finif* "five"]

finigal *See* FINAGLE

finish *v* To put a disastrous end to something or to someone's prospects; = COOK someone's GOOSE

finished *adj* Occupationally ruined; no longer able to function or compete; = DEAD: *After two tries he was finished/ She couldn't act any longer and was finished at thirty*

finisher *n prizefight* A blow that knocks one unconscious; quietus

See TABLE FINISHER

finish last *See* NICE GUYS FINISH LAST

fink 1 *n fr late 1800s* A strikebreaker; = SCAB **2** *n fr late 1800s* A labor spy; worker who is primarily loyal to the employer: *unpopular with the other waiters, who thought him a fink*—New Yorker **3** *n fr late 1800s* A police officer, detective, guard, or other law enforcement agent: *This Sherlock Holmes...this fink's on the old yocky-dock*—J Cannon **4** *n underworld* An informer; = STOOL PIGEON: *Now he's looking for the fink who turned him in*—Raymond Chandler/ *The glossary runs to such pejorative nouns as fink, stoolie, rat, canary, squealer*—Time **5** *v*: *Dutch knew I worked for his friend...and I wouldn't fink*—George Raft **6** *n* Any contemptible person; vile wretch; = RAT FINK, SHITHEEL: *All men are brothers, and if you don't*

give, you're a kind of fink—Bennett Berger **7** *n hoboes* A tramp who begs food at kitchen doors **8** *n circus & carnival* A piece of shabby small merchandise; = LARRY [origin unknown; perhaps fr *Pink* "a Pinkerton agent engaged in strikebreaking," or fr German *Fink* "finch," a university students' term for a student who did not join in duelling and drinking societies]

See RAT FINK

fink out 1 *v phr esp 1960s counterculture* To withdraw from or refuse support to a project, movement, etc, esp in a seemingly cowardly and self-serving way; = BACK OUT: *or if he will "fink out," as Kauffman believed he had done so far*—Society **2** *v phr underworld* To become untrustworthy and a potential informer **3** *v phr* To fail utterly

Fink's constant *See* FINAGLE FACTOR

Finn *See* MICKEY FINN

finnagel *See* FINAGLE

finiff or **finnif** *See* FINIF

fire 1 *v fr late 1800s* To discharge someone from a job; dismiss, usu with prejudice; = CAN, SACK **2** *v* To throw something with great force: *The big lefthander fired a fastball down the middle* **3** *v* To ask or utter with bluntness and vehemence: *The panel fired questions at me and I soon wilted*

See BALL OF FIRE, CROWN FIRE, HANG FIRE, HOLD someone's FEET TO THE FIRE, HOLD FIRE, ON THE FIRE, PULL something OUT OF THE FIRE, SURE-FIRE, TAKE FIRE

fire away 1 *v phr fr late 1700s* To begin; go ahead ● Usu an invitation: *"Fire away!" said I when she threatened to denounce me* **2** *v phr* To attack verbally: *As soon as I walked into the room he began to fire away at me*

fireball *n* = BALL OF FIRE

fire blanks *See* SHOOT BLANKS

firebug *n fr late 1800s* An arsonist; pyromaniac

firecracker *n WW2 armed forces* A bomb; torpedo

fired up 1 *adj phr fr middle 1800s* Drunk **2** *adj phr* Angry **3** *adj phr* (also **all fired up**) Full of enthusiasm, energy, and resolve: *If he gets fired up he's unbeatable*

fire-eater 1 *n* A fire fighter; = SMOKE-EATER **2** *n fr early 1900s* A notably pugnacious and courageous person; a quarrelsome dynamo

fireless cooker *n phr* An outdoor toilet; = BACK-HOUSE

fireman *n baseball* A relief pitcher, esp an effective one: *a four-run blast against fireman Joe in the eighth inning*—Associated Press

See VISITING FIREMAN

fire on *v phr black* To strike; hit: *looking at this one dude Huey had fired on*—Bobby Seale

fire stick *n phr street gang fr 1950s* A firearm; gun; = PIECE

firestorm *n* An intense and often destructive spate of action or reaction: *report...has already generated a firestorm of criticism*—New York Times [fr the catastrophic and unquenchable *fires* caused by aerial bombing of cities in World War 2]

fire up *v phr WW2 Army Air Forces & hot rodders* To start an engine: *Fire up and split, dudes*

fire someone **up** *v phr* To fill someone with energy and enthusiasm; excite someone: *She fired them up with promises of huge winnings*

firewater *n fr early 1800s* Liquor; = BOOZE

fireworks 1 *n* Excitement; furor; noisy fuss; = HOOPLA: *speeches that...would produce the "fireworks" supporters have demanded*—J Devlin/ *low profile, please, no fireworks* **2** *n* Anger; quarrels; rancorous rhetoric **3** *n* Shooting; gunfire or cannon fire: *The riot ended when the National Guard showed up and the fireworks began*

first base *See* GET TO FIRST BASE

first crack out of the box *adv phr* Immediately; before anything else: *Get him back home and first crack out of the box he's run away again*

firstest (or **fustest**) **with the mostest** *adv phr* First with the most; soonest and best equipped [fr explanation by General Nathan B Forrest of how he won a skirmish]

first john *n phr* Army A first lieutenant

first lady *n phr* lunch counter An order of spare ribs [because Eve was made from a rib]

first luff *n phr* Navy A naval first lieutenant

first man (or **shirt** or **soldier**) *n phr* Army A first sergeant; = TOP-KICK

first off *adv phr* First in order; to begin with: *I said that first off I wanted an apology*

first-of-May *circus & carnival* **1** *n* A novice; neophyte, esp one who stays on the job only a short time: *A beginner at barking is known as a "first of May"*—M Bracker/ *a short-timer, a "First-of-May"*—Society **2** *adj:* *These first-of-May guys are a little off time*—RL Taylor [related to the early May beginning of the season]

first-rate 1 *adj* Excellent; of best quality **2** *adv:* *That'll do first-rate*

first sacker *n phr* baseball A first baseman

fish 1 *n* prison A new inmate: *As a "fish"...at Charlestown, I was physically miserable*—Malcolm X **2** *n* street gang A nonmember of a street gang; a person regarded as inimical and distasteful by a street gang **3** *n* A stupid person, esp one easily victimized; = PATSY, SUCKER: *Why should he be the fish for the big guys?*—Ira Wolfert **4** *n* A person, esp a criminal, thought of as being caught like a fish: *The cops catch a lot of very interesting fish*—Life **5** *n* homosexuals A heterosexual woman **6** *n* students A promiscuous woman **7** *n* sports A weak opponent: *The superteams get stronger. They can pad their schedules with the occasional fish*—Sports Illustrated **8** *n* A dollar: *The job paid only fifty fish*—Lionel Stander **9** *n* = TIN FISH **10** *v* To seek information, esp by a legal or quasi-legal process having a very general aim; = GO FISHING **11** *v* To ask for something, usu a compliment, esp in an indirect and apparently modest way

See BIG FISH, BIGGER FISH TO FRY, COLD FISH, FINE KETTLE OF FISH, GO FISHING, GONE FISHING, KETTLE OF FISH, LIKE SHOOTING FISH IN A BARREL, POOR FISH, QUEER FISH, TIN FISH, YELLOWFISH

fishball *n* A contemptible person; = CREEP

fish bowl *See* FISH TANK

◀**fisheater**▶ *n* A Roman Catholic [fr the fact that Roman Catholics were formerly forbidden to eat meat on Fridays]

fish-eggs or **fish-eyes** *n* prison, armed forces & students Tapioca pudding

fishery *n* hoboes A religious mission in a working-class neighborhood [ultimately fr the concept of St Peter as a *fisher* of men]

the **fish-eye** *See* GIVE someone THE FISH-EYE

fish-eyed *adj* Cold, staring, and inhuman: *have to persuade a fish-eyed insurance claims adjustor*—New York

fishhooks *n* The fingers

fishing *See* GO FISHING, GONE FISHING

fishing expedition *See* GO FISHING

fish music *n phr* An early form of rock and roll, not as fast and loud as the developed version

fish or cut bait *sentence* Do one thing or another, but stop dithering; take action; = SHIT OR GET OFF THE POT ● Usu a firm or irritated demand: *The union leader warned that the city had until Feb 1 to "fish or cut bait"*—New York Times

fish scale *n phr* A very small denomination of coin; a penny or nickel

fishskin 1 *n* A dollar bill **2** *n* A condom

fish story (or **tale**) *n phr fr early 1800s* A series of lies or exaggerations; a false or improbable explanation: *His whole alibi is a fish story* [fr the tendency of an angler to exaggerate the size of the catch]

fishtail 1 *n* railroad A semaphore flag **2** *n* esp 1950s A women's dress or skirt style featuring a flare at the bottom **3** *n* hot rodders Flaring rear fenders on a car **4** *v* To swing a car, motorcycle, etc, from side to side at the rear: *causing his rear wheels to spin or the rear end to fishtail, that is swing back and forth*—Life

fish tank (or **bowl**) *n phr* underworld The part of a jail or prison where new inmates are kept for classification, testing, etc: *I'm in the fish tank....There are forty of us in the diagnostic center*—Ann Rule/ *They keep 'em in the fish tank for five weeks or so*

fish to fry *See* BIGGER FISH TO FRY

fish trap *n phr* The mouth

fishwife *n* homosexuals The wife of a homosexual man

fishy *adj fr middle 1800s British* Very probably false or dishonest; very dubious: *The whole proposition is decidedly fishy* [probably fr the unpleasant odor of spoiled *fish*]

fishyback *n* The transport of loaded containers or semitrailers by ship or barge [modeled on *piggyback*]

fist 1 *n* telegraphers & radio operators The hand used for operating a telegraphic key **2** *n* railroad A signature

See MAKE MONEY HAND OVER FIST

fisted *See* HAM-HANDED

◀**fist-fucking** or **fisting**▶ *n* Anal intercourse, usu homosexual, in which the hand is inserted into the partner's anus

fistful 1 *n* A large amount: *I've got a fistful of overdue bills* **2** *n* A large amount of money: *The* digital stereo set me back a fistful **3** *n* underworld A five-year prison sentence

fistiana *n* The sport or business of prizefighting; the boxing game: *that hotbed of fistiana known as Las Cruces*—New York Daily News

fit *n* narcotics The devices used for injecting narcotics; drug paraphernalia; =WORKS [probably a shortening of *outfit*]
See CATFIT, DUCK-FIT, HAVE A SHIT FIT, MEAT-FIT, THROW A FIT

five 1 *n* lunch counter A large glass of milk **2** *n* jive talk The hand; the five fingers
See FIFTY-FIVE, FORTY-FIVE, GIVE someone FIVE, HANG FIVE, NINE-TO-FIVE, NINETY-FIVE, PLEAD THE FIFTH, SLIP (or GIVE) ME FIVE, TAKE FIVE

five-and-ten or **five-and-dime 1** *n* A variety store selling relatively cheap items; =DIME STORE **2** *adj* Cheap; paltry; second-rate: *Dr Ruth is strictly a five-and-dime affair*—New York

five-by-five 1 *adj* jive talk Fat: *In this emaciated culture nobody wants to be five-by-five* **2** *adj* radio operators =FIVE SQUARE

five-case note *n phr* A five-dollar bill

five-dollar gold piece See COME UP SMELLING LIKE A ROSE

five-finger *n* A thief; a shoplifter or pickpocket

five-finger discount *n phr esp teenagers* Shoplifting

five fingers underworld **1** *n phr* A five-year prison sentence **2** *n phr* A thief
See GIVE FIVE FINGERS TO

five it *v phr* To refuse to answer on grounds of the Fifth Amendment: *How many questions would they be able to get in before DeMeo began to "five it"*—New York

Five-O *n teenagers* A police officer [fr the TV police-adventure series *Hawaii Five-O*]

five of clubs *n phr* A fist

five-ouncers *n prizefight* The fists [fr the minimum weight of boxing gloves]

five-percenter *n esp 1940s & 50s* A person, close to an important government official, who uses dubious influence, esp for a five-percent share of illegal payments

five-pound bag See BLIVIT, LOOK LIKE TEN POUNDS OF SHIT IN A FIVE-POUND BAG

fiver 1 *n* A five-dollar bill; five dollars: *For a fiver, cash, you could ride*—Nelson Algren **2** *n prison* A five-year prison sentence
See NINE-TO-FIVER

fives See BUNCH OF FIVES

five-sided puzzle palace *n phr Army* The Pentagon

five-spot 1 *n* A five-dollar bill **2** *n underworld* A five-year prison sentence **3** *n* A five of playing cards

five square (or **five**) **1** *adj phr radio operators* Of a radio signal, strong and easy to understand; loud and clear **2** *adj phr* Perfectly clear; well understood; loud and clear: *The president's message is five square* **3** *adv phr*: *Yes my dear, I hear you five five* [fr the military radio operator's double scale, of one to *five*, for reporting both strength and clarity of a signal]

fix 1 *v fr late 1800s* To prearrange the outcome of a prizefight, race, game, etc **2** *n* A fight, game, etc, of which the winner has been fraudulently predetermined: *The World Series that year was a blatant fix* **3** *v fr 1920s* To arrange exoneration from a charge, esp by bribery; have a charge quashed: *He had a pal could fix tickets for five bucks* **4** *n narcotics* A dose of a narcotic, esp an injection of heroin; =BLAST: *a fix to calm her jittery nerves*—San Francisco Examiner **5** *n* Anything needed to appease a habitual need or craving: *He had to have his daily fix of flattery* **6** *v* To castrate an animal, esp a cat **7** *v* To punish; injure; =FIX someone's WAGON: *Make him wash the dishes, that'll fix him* **8** *n* A difficult situation; a nasty position or dilemma: *I'm afraid her lying has gotten her in a bad fix* **9** *n* A clear idea; an accurate notion: *I can't get a fix on this guy's intentions* **10** *n police* A police officer's assignment that does not require patrolling
See QUICK FIX

the fix 1 *n phr* Arrangements, esp illicit payments, assuring the prearranged outcome of a prizefight, game, race, etc; =ALYO: *It's in the bag. The fix is on*—WR and FK Simpson **2** *n phr* Arrangements assuring exoneration from a police charge: *The super hisself couldn't put the fix in any faster*—Nelson Algren

fixer 1 *n circus* A lawyer; =SHYSTER **2** *n* A person who arranges shady and illegal affairs: *He's a fixer you have to see if you want to open a gambling hall*—Raymond Chandler **3** *n narcotics* A person who sells narcotics to users; =CONNECTION: *My fixer's got the best dope on the Lower East Side*

fix someone's **hash** See SETTLE someone's HASH

fixings *n fr early 1800s* Things, esp food, normally accompanying some central or focal object: *turkey and all the fixings*

fixing to (or **like**) *v phr* Readying; preparing; on the verge of: *Looks like he's fixing to get drunk/ She's fixing like she's going to leave here very suddenly*

Fixit See MISTER FIXIT

fix-up *n narcotics* A dose of narcotics; =FIX

fix someone **up 1** *v phr* To provide an escort or date for **2** *v phr* To provide a sex partner for **3** *v phr* To provide anything needed: *Gas? Yeah, we can fix you up*

fix someone's **wagon** *v phr* To punish; injure; ruin; =CLEAN someone's CLOCK

fizz *n* A failure; =FIZZLE: *"It was a big fizz," the ambassador said*—Time

fizzle 1 *v fr middle 1800s* To fail; lose effect; =FLOP, PETER OUT: *The covert operation fizzled unspectacularly* **2** *n*: *Our monster bash was a fizzle* [fr the lackluster sibilance of a damp firecracker]

fizz-water or **sizz-water** *n* Carbonated water; club soda; seltzer: *crowded the sizz-water into the wood alcohol*—H McHugh

flack or **flak 1** *n* Publicity; public relations material; =BALLYHOO, HYPE: *Mr Mogul's latest epic was* preceded by wheeling galaxies of affecting flack **2** *modifier:* *The flack description is also worth quoting*—Variety **3** *n* (also **flacker**) A publicity person or press agent: *something that would cause your basic, self-respecting flack to want to slit his throat*—Calvin Trillin/ *I'm a flak...a publicity man*—Irwin Shaw/ *"He's shown steady improvement," said a hospital flak*—New York Daily News **4** *v:* *his publishers, who flack it...into a best seller*—Atlantic Monthly/ *He's not flakking for ulterior motives*—Toronto Life [said to be fr the name of Gene Flack, a moving picture publicity agent, and first used in the show-business paper *Variety*; perhaps fr or influenced by *flak*]

flack or **flack out 1** *v* or *v phr* *fr cool & beat talk* To fall asleep; lose consciousness **2** *v phr* To be tired or depressed **3** *v phr* To die

flackery *n* Publicity; = FLACK, HYPE: *A White House insider's name, with enough flackery, can be sold like mouthwash*—Hugh Sidey

flag 1 *v* (also **flag down**) To hail a vehicle, person, etc; signal a stop: *He was barreling along till she flagged him down* **2** *v underworld* To arrest; = BUST: *They flagged my reefer man yesterday*—New York **3** *n baseball* The pennant awarded annually to a league championship team **4** *n underworld* An assumed name; alias

See JEWISH FLAG

flagged *adj* Forbidden further drinks, because already drunk

flagger *n cabdrivers* A person hailing a cab

flag it *v phr college students* To fail an examination or a course; = FLUNK

flagpole *See* RUN something UP THE FLAGPOLE

flagship 1 *n* The most imposing constituent; premier specimen: *The Ritz is the flagship of my caravansery chain* **2** *modifier:* *and not one damn word in the nation's flagship papers*—Village Voice

flag-up *adj cabdrivers* With the taxi meter not started: *a flag-up ride*

flag-waver 1 *n* A conspicuously patriotic person; superpatriot **2** *n* A book, play, etc, that is strongly patriotic

flak 1 *n* An antiaircraft gun or guns; antiaircraft fire; = AA, ACK-ACK **2** *n* (also **flack**) Severe criticism; angry blame: *This order provoked little political flack*—Harper's/ *Little recreation clubs like ours draw a lot of flack*—John D MacDonald **3** *n* Trouble; fuss; dissension; = STATIC: *Let's not have a lot of flak about this* [fr German *Fliegerabwehrkanonen* "antiaircraft gun"]

flake 1 *n fr baseball* An eccentric person, esp a colorful individualist; = BIRD: *what is known in the trade as a flake, a kook, or a clubhouse lawyer*—Christopher Lehmann-Haupt **2** *n fr baseball* The quality of flamboyant individualism: *The Yankees have acquired...an amount of "flake"*—Leonard Koppett **3** *adj:* *Don't act so flake* **4** *n teenagers* A stupid, erratic person; = RETARD **5** *n narcotics* Cocaine **6** *v police* To arrest someone on false or invented charges; = FRAME **7** *v police* To plant evidence on a suspect **8** *n police* An arrest made in order to meet a quota; = ACCOM-

MODATION COLLAR [origin unknown; perhaps fr various associations with the narcotics sense]

flaked-out *adj fr beat & cool talk* Asleep; unconscious

flake off *v phr teenagers* To leave; depart ● Often an irritated command: *Want to brush off such friends? Suggest that they...flake off*—J Gray [probably a euphemism for *fuck off*]

flake out 1 *v phr* = FLACK OUT **2** *v phr jazz musicians* = FLAKE OFF **3** *v phr* To fail

flake-out *n* A total failure; = FLOP

flak jacket *n phr* A bulletproof vest or other protective garment for the chest: *the flak jacket Oiler QB Dan Pastorini wore last year*—New York Daily News [fr the protective *jacket* worn by air-crew members in WW2]

flaky or **flakey 1** *adj fr baseball* Colorfully eccentric; buoyantly individualistic **2** *adj* Insane; = SCREWY, WACKY: *a flaky old professor, a snake expert*—New York **3** *adj* Disoriented; barely conscious; dizzy: *played the last 23 minutes of the game in a condition that was described as "flaky" and "fuzzy"*—New York Times

flam *See* FLIMFLAM

flamdoodle *See* FLAPDOODLE

flame 1 *n fr 1600s* A sweetheart; beloved **2** *v* (also **flame it up**) *homosexuals* To flaunt or exaggerate effeminate traits; = CAMP IT UP **3** *v esp computer* To talk long and noisily; rant; carry on, esp in a computer bulletin board or other communication network

See SHOOT someone DOWN

◁**flamer** or **flaming asshole** or **flaming fruitbar**▷ *n* or *n phr* A male homosexual; = QUEEN: *It doesn't have anything to do with me being a flamer*—Richard Merkin

flames *See* GO DOWN IN FLAMES

flamethrower *n baseball* A pitcher with a very fast fastball

flaming 1 *adj* Blatantly homosexual, esp in an effeminate way; = SWISH: *in hiding the fact that Babe Ruth and Lou Gehrig were flaming homosexuals*—National Lampoon **2** *adv* Very ● Used as an intensifier, usu preceded by "so": *I can't believe he'd be so flaming stupid* **3** *n computer* The use of rude, strong, obscene, etc, language on a computer bulletin board, in computer mail, etc ● This sort of verbal license is said to be common and apparently to be an effect of the medium itself

◁**flaming pisspot**▷ *n phr Army* The insignia of the Ordnance Corps, a flaming grenade bomb

flammer *See* FLIMFLAMMER

◁**flange-face**▷ *n esp WW2 Navy* An ugly sailor

◀**flange-head**▶ *n WW2 Army Air Forces* A Chinese person

flanker *n West Point* A tall person

flap 1 *n fr late 1800s British Navy* Disturbance; tumult; fuss: *Law was one direction open to me with the least amount of flap*—Good Housekeeping **2** *n street gang* A fight between street gangs; = RUMBLE **3** *v* To become flustered; lose one's composure: *I've seen him under hostile pressure before.*

He doesn't flap and he doesn't become a doormat —DE Kneeland

flapdoodle or **flamdoodle** *n fr early 1900s British perhaps fr earlier US* Nonsense; foolishness; =BALONEY: *He then goes on to utter other flapdoodle for the nourishment of the mind*—New York Times

flap one's **gums** *See* BAT one's GUMS

flapjaw **1** *n* Talk; discourse; chat: *We caught Mannone and Moore for a moment's flapjaw before we left*—New Yorker **2** *n* A loquacious person; =MOTOR-MOUTH

flapjawed *adj* Talkative; notably loquacious: *to describe the flap-jawed Turner as outspoken*—People Weekly

flap one's **lip** *See* FLIP one's LIP

flapper **1** *n fr early 1800s* The hand; =FLIPPER **2** *n esp 1920s* A young woman of the type fashionable in the 1920s, with pronounced worldly interests, relatively few inhibitions, a distinctive style of grooming, etc **3** *modifier: the flapper era/ flat flapper chest* [origin uncertain; perhaps from the idea of an unfledged bird *flapping* its wings, as one did while dancing the Charleston]

flaps *n* The ears

flares *n* Flared trousers or slacks

flareup *n outdated fr jazz musicians* The climax of intensity in a jazz performance

flarp *adj musicians* Quavering, tentative, and off-pitch: *Please sing an E-natural, not an E-flarp* [fr combining *flat* and *sharp*]

flash **1** *n fr early 1800s* Thieves' argot **2** *n* A look; quick glance: *We slid into the cross street to take a flash at the alley*—James M Cain **3** *n* A person who excels at something; =WHIZ: *He's a flash at math* **4** *n circus* A display of gaudy merchandise or prizes: *expensive flash that the mark couldn't win*—E Brown **5** *v circus* To set up a display of presumed prizes: *Flash the joint*—American Mercury **6** *v* To vomit **7** *v narcotics* To have a hallucinatory experience from a narcotic: *He flashed he was as big as a mountain* **8** *v narcotics* To feel the sudden pleasurable effect of a narcotics injection: *As soon as the needle went in, she flashed* **9** *n: Harry shot up a couple of the goof balls and tried to think a bigger and better flash than he got*—Hubert Selby, Jr **10** *adj teenagers* Excellent; wonderful; =DYNAMITE **11** *n fr narcotics* Distinctive personal style and charm; charisma: *Flash is in the clothes, the cars, the walk, the talk*—R Woodley **12** *v esp narcotics* To have a sudden idea, insight, or impulse **13** *n: if he should get a sudden flash to commit Cat...and wants to call her*—S Werbin **14** *n fr narcotics* Something one is currently doing; =BAG, THING: *His current "flash," as he calls it, tends toward gaucho suits*—New York Post **15** *v fr middle 1800s British* To expose one's genitals, breasts, etc ● The earlier British forms were **flash it** and **flash** one's **meat**: *Judy thought she was gonna flash me. She started unbuttoning her blouse*—Dolly Parton **16** *n: He gave her a flash and she squawked* **17** *v* To display suddenly and briefly: *The cop flashed his badge/ She flashed me a big smile* **18** *n* Urination; =PISS: *and said he'd pay double in case of a "flash," which is a delicate way of describing one of nature's indelicate imperatives*—Washington Post

flashback **1** *n* A scene or passage in a novel, movie, etc, that depicts events earlier than those in the main time frame **2** *n narcotics* A hallucination or sensation originally induced by LSD or other drugs but recurring after the drug experience has ended

flasher *n* A person who exposes the genitals in public; exhibitionist

flashforward *n* A scene or passage in a novel, movie, etc, that depicts events later than those of the main time frame

flash in the pan *n phr* A person or thing that does not fulfill an apparent potential: *If he's not a flash in the pan he'll be the best poet we ever had* [fr the igniting charge in an old gun that goes off *in the pan* or holder without igniting the main charge]

flash on *v phr* To recall; realize vividly: *I flashed on all that stuff in basic about it being better dead than captured*—Rolling Stone/ *She just flashed on it for once in her life, she ought to put her own needs right up front*—Cyra McFadden

flash rider *n phr fr late 1800s cowboys* A professional horse-breaker or bronco-rider

flash roll or **flash money** or **front money** *n phr* A bundle of cash suddenly shown as proof that the holder is in funds: *money advanced as a "flash roll" to be shown*—FC Shapiro/ *showed suspects six million in cash as front or flash money to prove that they indeed had funds*—Portland Journal

flash-sport *n black* A gaudily groomed man; =DUDE, SPORT: *The gals would begin to say, "My, my, who's this new flash-sport"*—A Lomax

flashy *adj* Gaudy; meretriciously showy: *flashy rings/ a flashy new car*

flat **1** *adj* =FLAT BROKE **2** *adj carnival* Having to do with any gambling game, esp one in which money rather than prizes may be won [carnival sense fr earlier meaning of *flats* "playing cards" or fr earlier meaning "dishonest dice"]
See GRANNY FLAT, IN NOTHING FLAT

◁**flat-ass**▷ *adj* Totally: *Some farmers are absolutely flat-ass broke*—Time

flatbacker *n* A prostitute: *His prostitutes are well known for being unhooked flatbackers*—I Ianni

flat broke *adj phr fr middle 1800s* Entirely without funds; penniless

flatfoot *n fr early 1900s* A police officer or detective: *The flat-feet scratched their heads*—NY Confidential

flatfooted *adj fr early 1900s* Unprepared; surprised

flathead **1** *n fr late 1800s* A stupid person; =FATHEAD **2** *n* A police officer; =FLATFOOT **3** *n restaurant* A nontipping patron at a restaurant or club **4** *n hot rodders* An L-head or side-valve car engine

flatheaded *adj* Stupid: *The speaker was a flatheaded idiot*—P Curtiss

flat-joint or **flatstore** *carnival* **1** *n* A game one plays for money rather than a prize **2** *n* Any gambling concession, esp a dishonest one

◁**flat on** one's **ass**▷ **1** *adj phr* Penniless and exhausted; =DOWN AND OUT: *He blew his pay pack and he's flat on his ass* **2** *adj phr* Army Incompetent; feckless: *That platoon's a loser, flat on its ass*

See FALL ON one's ASS

flat out *fr early 1900s* *adv phr* At full speed; =ALL OUT, WIDE OPEN: *The economy is running flat out and revenues are pouring in*—Wall Street Journal/ *Flat out, working on it myself, it will take a week* —John McPhee [perhaps fr the elongated shape of a horse going at top speed]

flat-out **1** *adj* Open and direct; unambiguous; plain: *Bunuel resorts to flat-out assertions in the last scene*—American Scholar/ *Richard Allen's plea of being flat-out dumb* **2** *adj* Total; unrestricted: *a husband who was a flat-out failure*—Time

flats **1** *n* *lumberjacks* Pancakes **2** *n* *horse-racing* Horse-racing in which the jockey is mounted and the horse runs, rather than trotting **3** *n* The feet **4** *n* Women's shoes with no heel or a low heel **5** *n* *gamblers fr early 1700s* A pair of dishonest dice

See ST LOUIS FLATS

flattener *n* *prizefight* A blow that knocks one down and unconscious; knockout punch

flat tire (or **hoop**) *n phr* A tedious person; an insipid companion

flattop *n fr WW2* An aircraft carrier

flatty or **flattie** **1** *n* *street gang* A police officer; =FLATFOOT **2** *n* *carnival* A gambling concession; =FLAT-JOINT: **3** *n* *carnival* A concession agent who operates a flat-joint: *Performers suggest that "flatties" are no more than common thieves* —Society

◁**flavor**▷ *n* *black* A sexually attractive woman

FLB (pronounced as separate letters) *n* *hospital* Strange or arhythmic heartbeats [fr *funny-looking beats*]

flea *n* An annoying person, esp a small nagging one

fleabag or **fleahouse** or **fleatrap** **1** *n* *armed forces fr WW1* A bed; mattress; bunk or hammock **2** *n* *horse-racing* An inferior racehorse **3** *n* A cheap and wretched hotel or rooming house; =FLOPHOUSE: *my last French hotel of the war: a fleabag two rooms wide*—Albert Guerard/ *He has transformed the motel from the old wayside fleabag into the most popular home away from home* —Time **4** *modifier*: *will no longer take her dates to fleabag hotels*—New York Times **5** *n* Any cheap, dirty, or ramshackle public place: *unveiled at an owl show in a Forty-second Street flea bag*—SJ Perelman

flea powder *n phr* *narcotics* A weakened or diluted narcotic, or a nonnarcotic substance sold as a narcotic; =BLANK

fleece *v fr 1600s* To cheat or swindle: *get back the money he'd fleeced me out of*—J Scarne/ *For these traders the function of the outside public speculator is to be fleeced*—Washington Post

flesh *See* IN THE FLESH, PRESS THE FLESH

flesh flick *See* SKIN FLICK

flesh-peddler **1** *n* A pimp or prostitute **2** *n* A person in charge of a show featuring unclad women **3** *n fr 1930s* An actor's or athlete's agent: *The old Hollywood flesh peddlers never stop talking money*—Raymond Chandler **4** *n* A person working at an employment agency

flesh-pressing *modifier* Handshaking, meeting and flattering voters, etc, in politics: *The flesh-pressing process remains invariable, as you will glean from the weekly schedule of City Alderman Joe Pantalone*—Toronto Life

flex one's **muscles** *v phr* To give a sample of one's power, esp in a threatening way: *I'm not sure they mean harm, probably just flexing their muscles*

flextime or **flexitime** *n* Flexible working time that varies as to hours and days worked: *flextime for working mothers and fathers in business*—Time

flic *n* A police officer: *if the flic had the slightest suspicion*—R Fish [fr French slang]

flick *fr 1920s* **1** *n* A movie: *a cheapie hard-core porno flick*—Saturday Review/ *He will play a role in the flick*—Associated Press **2** *n* A movie theater [fr the *flickering* of early movie images]

See SKIN FLICK

flicker **1** *n fr early 1900s* *hoboes* A beggar who pretends to faint or have a fit **2** *n fr 1920s* =FLICK

the **flicks** or **flickers** or **flix** *n phr fr 1920s* The movies; the cinema: *When I went to the flicks, I was forced to sit far back*—Goodman Ace/ *the getting-away-from-it-all surcease we seek at the flicks* —Judith Crist

flier *See* FLYER

flies *See* CATCH FLIES, NO FLIES ON, SWAT FLIES, WHEN THE EAGLE FLIES

flight *n* *narcotics* A hallucinogenic drug experience; =TRIP

See WHITE FLIGHT

flimflam **1** *v fr 1600s* To cheat or swindle; defraud; =BAMBOOZLE, CON: *We've been flim-flammed*—James M Cain **2** *n*: *Don't fall for that flimflam* **3** *modifier*: *a flimflam game/ flimflam man*

flimflammer *n* A confidence man; cheater; swindler: *an expert flimflammer who worked up crime's ladder*—New York Daily News

flimsy *n* A copy of a bill, art work, etc, on thin paper

fling **1** *n* A period of pleasure and indulgence, often as relaxation after or before stern responsibilities: *He had a last fling before going to the monastery* **2** *n* A try; =CRACK, GO: *Ms Ready, will you have a fling at climbing that wall?* **3** *n* *students* A dance; party; =SHINDIG

fling woo *See* PITCH WOO

flip **1** *adj fr early 1900s* Flippant; impudent; =CHEEKY: *Mr Lawrence...is flip and easy*—Clive Barnes/ *Someone else thought he was too flip at press conferences*—New York Times **2** *v* To change or switch diametrically; =FLIP-FLOP: *So I flipped over to the opposite opinion* **3** *v* To respond enthusiastically; feel great excitement and pleasure: *"They flipped over it," Riveroll recalls* —Forbes/ *I flip over this record*—T Brown **4** *v* To cause one to respond with enthusiasm; give one great pleasure: *My imitation of Mr Kissinger flipped the assemblage* **5** *n* Something that causes hilarity or pleasure: *The big flip of the year is Peter Arno's book of cartoons*—Gilbert Milstein **6** *v* To become angry: *When he told me what he had done, I flipped* **7** *v fr cool talk* To go insane; behave irrationally; =FLIP OUT: *I was flipping at first...but then the marvelous vibes got to me* —Whitney Balliett **8** *v hoboes* To board a train, esp when it is moving **9** *n 1930s teenagers* A small favor ◀**10**▶ *n* A Filipino

flip-flop 1 *n* A complete reversal of direction; about-face: *Commodities have been doing flip-flops on the price ladder*—K Scheibel **2** *v:* *So Kennedy's flip-flopped again*—Time **3** *modifier:* *whose flip-flop views and reluctance to confront the issues*—New Yorker

flip-flops *n* Bathing sandals, esp the kind where a strap fits between one's toes: *in a flowered housedress and Dr Scholl flip-flops*—New York Times

flip one's **lid** (or **wig** or **raspberry**) *fr bop & cool talk* **1** *v phr* To become violently angry; =BLOW one's TOP: *When she told him he flipped his lid* **2** *v phr* To go insane; behave irrationally: *When he started mumbling I was sure he'd flipped his wig/ flipped his lid and blew a whole list of nuclear warhead targets*—WT Tyler **3** *v phr* To show great enthusiasm and approval: *When she finished reading, the crowd flipped its raspberry*

flip (or **flap**) one's **lip** *v phr* To talk, esp idly or foolishly

flip-lipped *adj* Flippantly loquacious; =FLIP, SMART-ASS: *Pine was a flip-lipped bastard who should have had his ears pinned back long ago*—J Evans

flip out *fr bop & cool talk* **1** *v phr* To evoke an enthusiastic response: *I flipped out these guys with my crazy stories*—Xaviera Hollander **2** *v phr* To display enthusiasm; crow: *My junkie brother continues to flip out about what a cool dude I am*—Saturday Review **3** *v phr* To go insane; =FLIP, FREAK OUT: *and I flipped out and went crazy*—Rolling Stone

flip-out 1 *n fr bop & cool talk* A spell of anger, disturbance, craziness, etc: *Harriet has a minor flip-out and flees*—New Yorker **2** *n* An exciting or wondrous experience: *Her performance was a real flip-out*

flipper 1 *n fr early 1900s* A hand; =FLAPPER: *I manfully gripped his flipper* **2** *n* An arm and hand **3** *n* A slingshot

flipping *adj* Accursed; wretched; =DAMN, FREAKING: *Give me the flipping thing and I'll get it fixed* [a euphemism for *fucking*]

flip side 1 *n phr* The reverse surface of a phonograph record; =B-SIDE: *a golden oldie on the flip side* **2** *n phr* The other side of a question, issue, etc: *it is true that...the flip side is that*—People Weekly/ *That's the good news. The flip side is the bad news*

flip the bird *v phr students* To make a contemptuous sign with the hand, middle finger extended; =GIVE someone THE FINGER: *The six ladies flipped the bird to all their earthling viewers, lifting their minis*—National Lampoon

flip-top *See* POP-TOP

◁**flit**▷ *n* A male homosexual; effeminate man

◁**flitty**▷ *adj* Homosexual; effeminate; =GAY: *This isn't some weird kind of flitty pass, is it?*—Toronto Life/ *Do you know the ballet? All those flitty people up on their toes*—John Irving

fliv 1 *n* =FLIVVER **2** *v show business* To fail; =FLOP

flivver 1 *v fr early 1900s show business* To fail; =FLOP: *If the production flivvers, I'll need that thirty cents*—LJ Vance **2** *n* A failure **3** *n fr early 1900s* A Model-T Ford car **4** *n* Any car, airplane, or other vehicle, esp a small or cheap one [origin unknown]

the **flix** *See* the FLICKS

FLK (pronounced as separate letters) *n hospital* An abnormal, sick, or ugly child [fr *funny-looking kid*]

float 1 *v* To be so happy and contented that one feels light as air; be ecstatic **2** *v* To loaf on the job; =GOOF OFF **3** *n salespersons* A customer who leaves while one is looking for merchandise **4** *n students* A period in which a student has no class; a free period **5** *v* To disseminate; send out: *Reporters have been told to float their resumes* —Washingtonian

floater 1 *n fr middle 1800s* A person who habitually moves about; vagabond; =DRIFTER **2** *n hoboes* A police order to leave town within one or two days, with suspension of a jail sentence **3** *n fr early 1900s British universities* A blunder: *made an error, slip...or floater*—Sterling North **4** *n baseball fr early 1900s* A slow pitch that appears to float in the air **5** *n* A loan; money loaned or borrowed **6** *n* An insurance policy valid no matter where one may take the insured items **7** *n fr middle 1800s* A corpse taken from the water

floating 1 *adj* Drunk **2** *adj narcotics & black* Intoxicated with narcotics; =HIGH **3** *adj* Ecstatic; euphoric

floating crap game *n phr* A professional crap game that moves about to thwart police interference: *The floating crap game run by an underworld gambling syndicate*—WR and FK Simpson

floating on air *adj phr* Ecstatic; euphoric; =ON CLOUD NINE

floating on the clouds 1 *adj phr* Putting credence in mere hopes and dreams; deluded **2** *adj phr* =FLOATING ON AIR

a **flock** *n phr* A large number; =HEAPS: *buys him a flock of drinks afterwards, and hopes for the best* —John Crosby

flog *v fr 1930s British fr late 1800s armed forces* To sell; peddle, esp in the sense of public hawking: *I went to the...convention to flog a new book*—Art Buchwald/ *Motel and bus companies flog special charter rates*—Newsweek [fr British slang *flog the clock* "move the clockhands forward in order to deceive," applied later to the illicit selling of military stores]

flogger *n outdated underworld* An overcoat

◁**flog** one's **meat**▷ *See* BEAT one's MEAT

◁**flong** one's **dong**▷ *v phr* To masturbate: *If it weren't for flonging my dong, I don't know what I'd do*—Playgirl

flood pants *See* HIGH WATERS

flooey *adj* Drunk
See GO BLOOEY

flookum or **flookem** *See* FLUKUM

floor **1** *v fr 1700s* To knock down; = DECK **2** *v* To shock, surprise, or hurt to the point of helplessness: *His divorce floored him* **3** *v* (also **floorboard**) To drive at full speed; push the throttle pedal to the floorboard: *She floored the Porsche on the freeway and got caught*
See CLEAN UP ON someone, IN ON THE GROUND FLOOR, MOP THE FLOOR WITH someone, PUT someone ON THE FLOOR

floozy (Variations: **faloosie** or **floogy** or **floosie** or **floozie** or **flugie**) **1** *n fr late 1800s* A self-indulgent, predatory woman, esp one of easy morals; cheap and tawdry woman: *He'd learn more about their psychology by taking a floozie to Atlantic City*—WB Johnson/ *the central figure of an adult whodunit, an obviously no-good floosie*—S Helfrich **2** *n* A prostitute

flop **1** *v fr early 1900s hoboes* To lie down for rest or sleep; sleep; = CRASH: *"Kip," "doss," "flop," "pound your ear," all mean...to sleep*—Jack London **2** *n*: *need a good flop tonight, and I'll be OK/ I went through $30 in 20 minutes one day buying drinks and flops for everyone*—Wall Street Journal **3** *n* A place to sleep, esp a cheap and sordid hotel or shelter: *I went into the flops and the shelters and was shocked*—New York/ *living...in a three-dollar-a-week flop*—J Roebert **4** *v fr late 1800s* To fail completely; = BOMB: *The show flopped, ran one night only* **5** *n*: *My great idea was a total flop*
See BELLY FLOP, MAKE THE FLOP

flophouse *n* A cheap and sordid rooming house or hotel, esp one with dormitories for men; = CHINCH PAD, FLEABAG: *I'm spending my nights at the flophouse*

flopper *See* BELLY-FLOPPER

flopperoo *n* A particularly spectacular failure; = FLOP: *three subdivisions: flop, flopperoo, and kerplunk*—W Holbrook

floppola *n* A failure, esp a severe one; = FLOP-PEROO: *And Fortune's worst floppola seems apocalyptic: Who will care for the poor?*—Washington Post

flop sweat *n phr* An actor's anxiety; fear of failure: *Flop sweat is what an actor gets when he's nervous on stage*—Henny Youngman

floss **1** *n circus & carnival* Cotton candy; spun sugar **2** *n* Stylish adornment; frills; fretwork: *just a simple dress, no floss/ The building was stark, without floss*

flossy or **flossie** *adj* Fancy; frilly; = HIGHFALUTIN: *It may be highly important to know a flossy name*

for the boss—F Tripp/ *Delete the flossy enhancements*

flour *n* Face powder

the **flow** *See* GO WITH THE FLOW

◁**flower**[1]▷ **1** *n* An effeminate man or boy; = SISSY **2** *n* A male homosexual

flower[2] *See* HEARTS AND FLOWERS, WALLFLOWER

flower child *n phr esp 1960s and 70s* A member of the hippie movement or counterculture, who typically advocated love, peace, and nonviolence: *a caricature of a London flower child who is about as interesting as a boiled potato*—New Yorker

flower children (or **people**) *n phr esp 1960s and 70s* Members of the 1960s hippie movement collectively: *Woodstock is long over, and the bloom has gone off these flower children*—Penelope Gilliatt/ *the flower people of the late 1960s, mostly middle-class kids trying to create a gaudy secular religion*—Time

flower power *n phr* The influence and merits of the pacifistic, altruistic values of the 1960s hippie movement

the **flu** *n fr middle 1800s* Influenza

flub **1** *n fr early 1900s* A stupid blunderer; = LUMMOX, KLUTZ: *Pick up your feet and don't be such a flub* **2** *v* To blunder; err; commit a gaffe; = GOOF: *I flubbed as soon as I opened my big mouth* **3** *v* To ruin by blundering; spoil with mistakes: *She flubbed the introduction, but did okay afterwards* **4** *n*: *How many flubs do they allow us?/ The flub, as generally defined, is a mistake*—Pulpsmith **5** *v* To avoid work or duty; shirk; = GOOF OFF

flubdub **1** *n* Incompetence; ineptitude: *They would remove much of the amateur flub-dub*—New York Daily News **2** *n* An awkward person; blunderer; = GOOF-UP, KLUTZ

flubdubbed *adj* Awkward; blundering; inept = KLUTZY: *I made flubdubbed and increasingly abashed efforts to make myself feel good again*—St Clair McKelway

flub the dub *esp WW2 armed forces* **1** *v phr* To avoid one's work or duty; shirk; = GOLDBRICK: *He learned to flub the dub, but still stay pals with his associates* **2** *v phr* To think, work, move, etc, sluggishly and haplessly **3** *v phr* To fail by blundering; ruin one's best chances: *I think I flubbed the dub again, bidding so late*

flub-up **1** *n* A blunder: *The attempt was one big flub-up* **2** *n* A blunderer; = GOOF-UP, KLUTZ: *a kooky police cadet flub-up*—People Weekly

FLUF (FLUHF) *n airline* The Boeing 737 airliner [fr *fat little ugly fucker*]

fluff ◁**1**▷ *n* A girl or young woman: *A wan little fluff steals a dress so as to look sweet in the eyes of her boyfriend*—RL Woods **2** *n* An oral error, esp one made by an actor, announcer, etc; lapsus linguae: *a hell of a fluff, talking about Montezuma's revenge to the president of Mexico* **3** *v*: *Show me an actor that never fluffed a line* **4** *adj* Vague, lacking in intellectual content, insubstantial: *Frankly, I found the book to be nothing but fluff*
See BIT OF FLUFF

the **fluff** *n* An easy job or task
See GIVE someone THE FLUFF

◁**fluffhead**▷ *n* A frivolous or stupid young woman; =DITZ: *To judge masculinity you need a woman, and not some little fluffhead either*—Village Voice

fluff off *v phr fr WW2 armed forces* To avoid work or duty; shirk; =GOOF OFF [probably a euphemism for *fuck off*]

fluff-off *n fr WW2 armed forces* A sluggard; shirker; =GOLDBRICK, GOOF-OFF

fluff someone **off** *v phr* To snub or cut someone; reject someone haughtily: *He thought he was pretty good, so he fluffed us all off*

flugie *See* FLOOZY

fluid *See* EMBALMING FLUID

fluke *n fr middle 1800s British* A good or bad stroke of luck; an extraordinary and unpredictable event: *My winning was just a fluke/ We got onto that flight by a fluke* [origin unknown, but perhaps fr *fluke* "flatfish" by way of an early 1800s British slang sense of *flat* "easy dupe, victim," altered in billiards jargon to *fluke* to characterize the seeming chicanery of a good stroke of luck]

flukum or **flookum** or **flookem** (FLŌō kəm) **1** *n fr early 1920s pitchmen* Cheap and gaudy merchandise **2** *n* Powder to which sugar and water are added to make a soft drink **3** *n* A failure

fluky or **flukey** *adj* Uncertain, unpredictable, and often unexpected: *It would have been a very fluky shot, even if he happened to have the camera in his hand*—Raymond Chandler

flummadiddle *n fr middle 1800s* Nonsense; foolishness; =BOSH

flummox *fr early 1800s* **1** *v* To spoil; upset; confound: *Fu-Manchu tries to abduct a missionary who has flummoxed his plans in China*—SJ Perelman **2** *n* A failure; disaster; =FUCK-UP: *The solemn commemoration was a total flummox* [fr British dialect, "maul, bewilder"]

flummoxed *adj* Confused and turbulent; baffling or baffled

flunk **1** *v fr early 1800s* To fail; make a botch of: *I tried selling, but flunked at that* **2** *v college students fr early 1800s* To fail an examination, a course, etc; =BUST: *He flunked the final but passed the course* **3** *v college students fr middle 1800s* To give a student a failing grade **4** *n*: *I've got three passes and two flunks* [origin unknown; perhaps a blend of *fail* with *funk*, perhaps echoic of a dull collapse]

flunk out *fr early 1800s* **1** *v phr* To fail; make a botch **2** *v phr college students* To be dismissed from school for failing work: *The great man had flunked out of Wittenberg*

flunky *n* A failed or failing student

flush **1** *adj fr late 1600s* Having plenty of money; affluent, esp temporarily; rich: *It took money, and the jazzman wasn't ever too flush*—Stephen Longstreet **2** *n* A wealthy person: *Morny took [the house] over from a busted flush*—Raymond Chandler **3** *v college students* To stay away from class; =CUT **4** *v college students* =FLUNK **5** *v* To reject or ignore someone socially [first two

senses fr the notion of a full or overfull container; other senses fr the notion of *flushing* a toilet to be rid of unwanted or useless material]
See FOUR-FLUSH, IN A FLUSH

flusher *n* A toilet: *right in the old flusher*—Dan Jenkins
See FOUR-FLUSHER

flush it **1** *v phr students* To fail a course, examination, etc; =FLUNK **2** *interj* An exclamation of contempt and disbelief: *I started to explain, but the cop told me to flush it*

◁**flute** or **fluter**▷ *n fr musicians* A male homosexual [fr metaphor of *flute* as "penis," and a homosexual as one who *plays the skin flute*]
See PLAY THE SKIN FLUTE, SKIN FLUTE

fly **1** *adj fr early 1800s British* Clever; alert; shrewd **2** *adj esp black fr early 1900s* Stylish; very attractive; =SHARP, SUPERFLY: *driving a Cadillac that's fly*—R Woodley/ *They tell each other they're fly when they look sharp*—Philadelphia Inquirer **3** *v narcotics* To act in a strange or bizarre way: *The broad must be flying on something*—Philadelphia Journal **4** *v narcotics* To feel the effects of narcotic intoxication: *About a minute after the fix he was flying* **5** *v* To succeed; persuade; =GO OVER ● Often in the negative: *They're experts on what will fly and what won't*—Art Buchwald/ *It's a great idea, but it won't fly/ He glanced at Keenan to see if that statement was going to fly*—Playboy **6** *n* (also **green fly**) *baseball* An annoying, importuning fan; pest **7** *v* To run or travel very fast [the sense "clever, alert, etc" is of unknown origin, though it is conjectured that it may refer to the difficulty of catching a *fly* in midair, that it may be cognate with *fledge* and hence mean "accomplished, proven, seasoned," and that it is a corruption of *fla*, a shortening of *flash*, the sense "succeed, persuade, etc" is fr a cluster of jokes and phrases having to do with the Wright Brothers' and others' efforts to get something off the ground and make it *fly*; the two adjective senses involve either a survival or a revival of an early-19th-century British underworld term of unknown origin]
See BAR-FLY, CATCH FLIES, FRUIT FLY, LET FLY, NO FLIES ON, ON THE FLY, SHOO-FLY, STRAIGHTEN UP AND FLY RIGHT, SUPERFLY

fly a kite *v phr underworld* To smuggle a letter into or out of prison
See GO FLY A KITE

fly-bait **1** *n* A member of Phi Beta Kappa **2** *n* A corpse [first sense fr a pun on the name]

fly-boy *n fr WW2 armed forces* An aircraft pilot, esp an intrepid one in the US Air Force: *The generals are no full-throttle "fly-boys"*—Time

flyby *n* A ceremonial or demonstrational passage overhead by an airplane or a group of airplanes: *They saluted the President with a flyby of the newest jets*

fly by the seat of one's **pants** **1** *v phr fr British fr 1930s Army Air Corps* To pilot an airplane by feel and instinct rather than by instruments: *The old-time barnstormers had to fly by the seat of their pants* **2** *v phr* To proceed or work by instinct

and improvisation, without formal guides or instructive experience: *The teachers are not trained to recognize it....They're flying by the seat of their pants*—Washington Post
See SEAT-OF-THE-PANTS

fly cake *n phr* Raisin cake

fly-chaser *n* baseball An outfielder

flychick *n fr 1940s black* = HIP CHICK

fly cop *n phr* (Variations: **ball** or **bob** or **bull** or **dick** or **mug** may replace **cop**) *fr middle 1800s British* A detective; plainclothes police officer: *an offer to make him a "fly-cop" or detective*—E Lavine [probably fr *fly* "clever, shrewd," because of the presumed intelligence of detectives]

flyer or **flier** *n circus* A trapeze performer
See TAKE A FLYER

flying 1 *n* Free and exhilarating experience, such as drug or liquor intoxication, sexual or spiritual ecstasy, etc: *I told him he'd better stop that flying and get practical* **2** *n police* Duty in places remote from one's usual post
See HAVE THE RAG ON

flying colors See WITH FLYING COLORS

◁**flying frig**▷ **See** TAKE A FLYING FUCK

◀a **flying fuck**▶ **See** NOT GIVE A DAMN, TAKE A FLYING FUCK

flying-jinny *n* A merry-go-round; carousel: *The wooden horses of the flying-jinny revolved in the circle to the mechanical music*—Carson McCullers

flying time *n phr WW2 armed forces* Sleep

fly light *v phr* To go hungry; miss a meal

fly mug See FLY COP

fly off the handle *v phr fr early 1800s* To lose one's temper; = LOSE one's COOL

fly out *v phr baseball* To hit a fly ball that is caught for an out

fly pie *n phr lunch counter* Huckleberry pie

fly right *v phr* To be honest, dependable, etc: *He's my son...I want him to fly right*—J and W Hawkins
See STRAIGHTEN UP AND FLY RIGHT

fly the coop *v phr fr early 1900s* To leave, esp to escape from confinement: *He had flown the coop...via a fire-escape*—A Hynd

fly trap *n phr* The mouth

fodder See BUNG FODDER, CANNON FODDER

fofarraw See FOOFOORAW

fog 1 *v* (also **fog it**) *early 1900s Western* To run; speed; hurry **2** *v* To throw with great force: *Ole Diz was in his prime then, fogging a fastball*—Hal Boyle **3** *v early 1900s Western* To attack; assault, esp with gunfire: *I takes me heat an' fogs 'em*—American Mercury [origin unknown; possibly a substitution for *smoke* in all senses]
See IN A FOG

fog away *v phr early 1900s Western* To commence shooting; shoot: *I fogged away with my gun*—CG Givens

fog-cutter *n outdated fr middle 1800s* A drink of liquor taken in the morning [supposed to protect one against the danger of the morning *fog*]

the foggiest See NOT HAVE THE FOGGIEST

Foggy Bottom *n phr* The US Department of State: *little affinity for the "career boys" of Foggy*

Bottom—HS Villard [fr the name of a marshy region in Washington, DC, where the State Department and other federal buildings are located; also an allusion to the murkiness of some policies and pronouncements]

fog it in *v phr baseball* To pitch a fastball

fogle (FOH gəl) *n* A silk handkerchief [possibly fr Italian *foglia* "pocket"]

fog up *v phr* To light a cigarette, cigar, etc [fr 18th-century *fog* "smoke, light a pipe"]

fogy or **fogey 1** *n fr late 1700s* An old person; any very conservative, outdated person; = DODO: *College students today are young fogies* **2** *n armed forces fr late 1800s* A military longevity allowance, awarded for units of service: *He got his pension and eight fogies* [origin unknown]

foil *n narcotics* A small packet of narcotics; = BAG

fold 1 *v* To fail or close, esp in business or show business: *The show folded after two nights* **2** *v* To lose effect and energy; wilt; fade: *She said she was about to fold*

folding *n* Money; = FOLDING MONEY: *The socialites lose a handsome wallet stuffed with a liberal supply of folding*—John O'Hara
See GREEN FOLDING

folding money *n phr* (Variations: **cabbage** or **green** or **lettuce** may replace **money**) Paper money; banknotes, esp in large quantities: *They leave their folding money at home*—John O'Hara/ *lacks the folding green to pick up a nightclub tab*—Hal Boyle

folkie *n* A folk singer or folk-music devotee: *The precious youth audience was lost to the folkies and the rockers*—New York

folknik *n* A folk-music devotee or enthusiast

the **folks 1** *n phr outdated underworld* A band of hoodlums **2** *n phr* (also one's **folks**) Parents
● Usu used affectionately

follow through (or **up**) **1** *v phr* To carry on with the next useful action; finish an action completely; pursue: *Follow up these hints, and you'll find the answer* **2** *n*: *What's the logical follow-through to what he said?*

follow-up *n* A result; a consequence: *The follow-up could be horrible*

follow something **up 1** *v phr* To carry one's investigation further; pursue a lead **2** *v phr* (also **follow**) To do something appropriate subsequent to something else, or better than something already done: *How will she follow up her bestseller?*/ *I can't follow that line*

fonk See FUNK

fonky See FUNKY

food See ANGEL FOOD, BUNNY FOOD, DOG FOOD, FAST FOOD, JUNK FOOD, SEAFOOD, SOUL FOOD, SQUIRREL-FOOD

foodaholic *n* A compulsive eater; glutton

food for the squirrels *n phr* = SQUIRREL-FOOD

fooey See PHOOEY

foofooraw or **fofarraw** or **foo-foo-rah** (FŌŌ fə raw) *fr middle 1800s Western* **1** *n* A loud disturbance; uproar **2** *n* Gaudy clothing and accessories, esp the latter **3** *n* Ostentation; proud show: *The refreshing thing about it is the lack of drumbeating and foo-foo-rah*—Saturday Evening Post [probably fr Spanish *fanfarrón* "braggart"]

fool *See* DAMN-FOOL, TOMFOOL

fool around **1** *v phr* To pass one's time idly; putter about; loaf **2** *v phr* To joke and tease; = KID AROUND: *Mark, stop fooling around and get to work* **3** *v phr* To adventure sexually, esp adulterously: *He had never fooled around or seen a prostitute until he came to us*—Xaviera Hollander **4** *v phr* To flirt or coquette with; make a faint or casual try at seduction: *She wasn't serious, just fooling around*

fool around with *v phr* To play or tamper with; = FIDDLE WITH: *I told you not to fool around with that gun; now you've shot Aunt Bessie*

foolish powder *n phr* 1930s underworld Heroin

◁**foop**▷ *v* college students To do homosexual sex acts [probably a backward version of British *poof* "male homosexual, effeminate male," fr early-20th-century Australian, perhaps fr the exclamation *poof* or *pooh,* regarded as effeminate]

◁**fooper**▷ *n* college students A homosexual

foot *See* BIG FOOT, BLISTERFOOT, DOUGHFOOT, FLAT-FOOT, GIVE someone THE FOOT, HAVE ONE FOOT IN THE GRAVE, HEAVY-FOOT, HOTFOOT, PADDLEFOOT, PUT one's FOOT IN IT, PUT one's FOOT IN one's MOUTH, RABBIT-FOOT, SHOOT oneself IN THE FOOT, SLEWFOOT, TANGLE-FOOT, TENDERFOOT, WEB-FOOT

football *See* GUINEA FOOTBALL, ITALIAN FOOTBALL

football around *v phr* To tout or hawk loudly and often: *The product will fall flat if it's footballed around too much* [perhaps fr the notion of *kicking something around* rather than dealing with it sensibly and seriously]

footed *See* LEAD-FOOTED, LIGHT-FOOTED

foot-in-mouth disease *n phr* The uttering of embarrassing, stupid, or indiscreet speech: *The president had another of his attacks of foot-in-mouth disease when he talked about "freedom fighters"* [blend of the veterinary term *hoof-and-mouth disease* and the idiom *put one's foot in one's mouth*]

foot it **1** *v phr* To walk: *A bus is OK during non-rush-hours if you've been footing it too long*—New York Times **2** *v phr* To escape by running; = BEAT IT: *He stopped all of a sudden and said, "Foot it, Sonny! Foot it!"*—Claude Brown

footshot *n* Army An act, choice, utterance, etc, that damages one's reputation or standing: *Saying "stuff it" out loud was a real footshot* [fr *shoot oneself in the foot*]

footsie (Variations: **footsy-footsy** or **footsy-wootsy** or **footy-footy,** or all these spelled with **ie** replacing the final **y**) ● Nearly always in the expression **play footsie, footsy-footsy,** etc **1** *n* Amorous and clandestine touching and rubbing of feet between a couple; pedal dalliance: *I played footsie with her during Carmen*—Gene Fowler/ *We had a quiet bout of footsie under the table* **2** *n* Any especially close relationship between persons or parties: *Truman is plenty burned up over the way*

Chiang Kai-shek...played footy-footy with the Republicans—Drew Pearson

footwork *See* FANCY FOOTWORK

fooy *See* PHOOEY

foozle *fr early 1800s* **1** *v* To blunder; spoil by bungling; botch: *I rather foozled my first attempt at acting* **2** *n* An error; = BONER **3** *n* A conservative, out-of-date person; = DODO, FOGY

for a loop *See* THROW someone FOR A LOOP

for certain *adv phr* Certainly; surely; = FOR SURE: *I don't know for certain if she does or not*

for crying out loud (or **in a bucket**) *interj* An exclamation of emphasis, surprise, disbelief, impatience, etc; = FOR THE LOVE OF PETE: *For crying out loud, what half-assed thing has he done now?* [a euphemism for *for Christ's sake*]

forecastle (or **sea**) **lawyer** *n phr* fr merchant marine fr early 1800s A sailor or other person who habitually complains and criticizes, pretends to an intricate knowledge of rules and regulations, demands rights, etc; = LATRINE LAWYER

for free *adv phr* Without charge; gratis; = FREE GRATIS: *They gave him a sandwich absolutely for free*—Arthur Daley

forget it **1** *interj* An injunction to put something out of one's hopes, concern, etc, esp because it is impossible: *If you thought you were next in line around here, forget it/ Forget it, she never did intend to go/ I can get up there most of the time, but in winter, forget it* **2** *interj* An exclamation of pardon; a token of forgiveness; = DON'T GIVE IT A SECOND THOUGHT: *Hell no, I didn't mind. Forget it*

forget you teenagers **1** *interj* An invitation or command to leave; = BUG OFF **2** *interj* An exclamation of rejection or refusal; = NO WAY

for one's **health** *adv phr* fr early 1900s Lightly or frivolously; for one's delightful good ● Always used ironically and in the negative: *I didn't make this damn stupid trip for my health, you know*

for (or **fer**) **instance** *n phr* An example; an instance: *I'd understand the point better if you gave me a couple of concrete for instances*

for it *adj phr* chiefly British fr early 1900s = IN FOR IT

fork[1] *outdated underworld* **1** *v* To pick a pocket **2** *n* A pickpocket

◁**fork**[2]▷ *v* To cheat; maltreat; take advantage of; = FUCK, SHAFT: *I hoped he'd take care of us, but we got forked* [a euphemism for *fuck*]

forkball *n* baseball A pitch thrown from a forklike finger grip

forked-eight or **bent-eight** *n* hot rodders A V-8 engine or a car having such an engine

for keeps *adv phr* Forever; permanently: *They put him away for keeps/ She wanted to be married for keeps*
See PLAY FOR KEEPS

forkhander *n* baseball A lefthanded pitcher; = SOUTHPAW

◁**forking**▷ **1** *adj* Wretched; disgusting: *I won't eat this forking stuff* **2** *adv* Very; extremely: *He sounded forking mad* [a euphemism for *fucking*]

fork over (or **up** or **out**) *v phr fr early 1800s* To pay; give; contribute: *Fork up the cash*—E Conradi/ *I imagine he used a picture...to make you fork over the dough*—RS Prather

forks *n fr 1940s black* Fingers: *Get your forks off that*

See RAIN CATS AND DOGS

◁**fork you**▷ *interj* =FUCK YOU

form *n fr horse-racing* The record of past performances by a horse, team, competitor, etc; =TRACK RECORD: *What's the form on General Electric this quarter?/ The form on the little gelding is super*

form sheet *n phr fr horse-racing* A printed record of past performance; =CHART, DOPE SHEET

for openers (or **starters**) *adv phr* As a beginning; as a first move or suggestion: *For openers, there's the approach via the Staten Island ferry*—New York Times/ *So, try this for openers*—Pulpsmith/ *expensive...for starters*—Armistead Maupin

for real 1 *adj phr* Believably existent; as good or bad as seems; authentic: *I often wondered if the bastard was for real* **2 *adv phr*** Really; truly: *I'm gonna for real do it, right now*

for serious 1 *adv phr* Seriously; with a sober intent: *The Yanks took the field for serious*—Robert Ruark **2 *adj phr:*** *He was for serious but she wasn't*

for (or **fer**) **sure** (or **shure** or **shurr**) *teenagers* **1 *adv*** Definitely; certainly: *He is for sure a nerd* **2 *affirmation*** Yes: *When he asked if I'd do it I said fer sure I would*

fort *n truckers* An armored truck or car

for the birds *adj phr fr WW2 armed forces* Inferior; undesirable; of small worth; =LOUSY: *I won't buy it....It's for the birds*—John Crosby/ *A single bed is for single men, it's for the birds*—Sidney Skolsky [a euphemistic shortening of *shit for the birds*, a version of *birdshit* or *chickenshit*]

for the cuff *adj phr* Confidential; not to be mentioned

for (or **just for**) **the hell of it** *adv phr* For no definite or useful reason; for fun; casually: *And just for the hell of it she told him he could come again*

for the long ball *See* GO FOR THE LONG BALL

for (or **over**) **the long haul** *adv phr* For a long and arduous effort; for a period of difficulty and strain: *He's the kind of guy you can count on for the long haul*

for the love of Pete *interj* An exclamation of emphasis, surprise, impatience, disbelief, dismay, etc; =FOR CRYING OUT LOUD: *I already did it, for the love of Pete!*

for (or **on**) **the record** *adv phr* Not confidential; meant for publication and attribution: *Is that for the record, or not for the record?/ No matter how hard the media questioned her, she wouldn't put anything on the record* [probably fr the specification by a US representative that a certain statement was or was not to be published in the *Congressional Record*]

forthwith *n police* An order to report immediately

forty *n lunch counter* Milk

forty-deuce *n* Forty-second Street in New York City: *Forty-deuce is what its seamy inhabitants call 42d Street*—Newark Star Ledger

forty-eight *n WW2 Navy* A weekend pass

forty-five or **45** **1** *n* (also **.45**) A .45-caliber pistol, esp a Colt automatic **2** *n* A phonograph record made to be played at 45 revolutions a minute

forty-four[1] **1** *n* *lunch counter* A cup of coffee **2** *n* (also **44** or **.44**) A .44-caliber pistol: *Frankie went down to the hotel, pulled out her big forty-four*

forty-four[2] *n* A prostitute [fr the rhyme with *whore*]

forty-'leven 1 *n* An indefinite large number **2** *modifier:* *about forty-'leven times*

forty-one *lunch counter* **1** *n* Lemonade or orangeade **2** *n* A glass of milk

forty-two *n lunch counter* Milk for two

forty (or **six**) **ways to Sunday** *adv phr fr middle 1800s* In every possible manner, direction, etc; comprehensively: *She had him beat forty ways to Sunday* [origin unknown]

forty winks *n phr fr early 1800s British* A short sleep; nap: *He caught forty winks and perked right up*

forward in the saddle *See* LEAN FORWARD IN THE SADDLE

forwards *n narcotics* Pills of amphetamine or its derivatives [probably an allusion to *speed* in the same sense, with perhaps a by-reference to the *fast forward* control of a tape player]

fossil *n* An old person; =ALTER KOCKER, FOGY: *If I got to kiss old fossils to hold this job I'm underpaid*—Hal Boyle

fotog *See* PHOTOG

foul ball 1 *n phr* *prizefight fr 1920s* An inferior fighter; =PALOOKA **2 *n phr*** A useless and inadequate person; =DULL TOOL, LOSER: *It is Scotty's boast that he hasn't sent a sponsor a foul ball yet*—J McCallum **3 *n phr*** A person having deviant convictions and attitudes; outsider; =ODDBALL

fouled up 1 *adj phr* Spoiled by bungling; confused; hopelessly tangled; =FUCKED UP: *never seen anything more fouled up than what happened yesterday at the White House*—J Marlow **2 *adj phr*** Damaged; impaired: *The kids were fouled up...came from bad homes, went to bad schools*—New York Times [a euphemism for *fucked up*]

foulmouth *n* A person inclined to utter obscenities, profanity, etc

foulmouthed *adj* Obscene and profane in speech; filthy: *a foulmouthed retort*

foul up *v phr* To ruin and confuse a project, assignment, etc; display one's ineptitude and futility; =FUCK UP, SNAFU: *I fouled up my very first chance to be a reporter* [a euphemism for *fuck up*]

foul-up 1 *n* A confused, tangled, hopeless situation; botch: *It's supposed to be a concert series, but it's a total foul-up* **2 *n*** A person who consistently blunders; bungler; =FUCK-UP: *Why put that notorious foul-up in charge?*

foundling *n West Point* A dismissed cadet

foundry *See* HASH FOUNDRY, NUT HOUSE

four *See* TEN FOUR

four-and-one *black* **1** *n* Friday, the fifth day of the week **2** *n* Payday

four-bagger *n baseball* A home run: *It was Bobby's 31st four-bagger and his fourth at Ebbets Field*—J Reichler

four-banger *n* A four-cylinder motor or car

four-bit *adj* Costing 50 cents; half-dollar: *to smoke four-bit cigars*—James T Farrell

four bits *n phr fr early 1800s* Half a dollar; 50 cents [originally a *bit* was a Mexican or Spanish *real*, worth 12½ cents, or a part of a more valuable coin, such that eight would make a dollar; ultimately fr 18th-century British slang *bit* "a small piece of money"]

four-by-four *n Army & truckers* A four-wheel-drive vehicle having four forward gears

four-eyes *n* A person who wears eyeglasses

four-flush *fr early 1900s* **1** *v* To live by sponging off others, or by pretense and fraud **2** *v* To cheat; swindle; victimize **3** *modifier: Four-flushing hustlers who really knew how to gamble*—Louis Armstrong [fr a poker player's attempt to bluff when he has *four* cards of one suit showing and one of another suit not showing]

four-flusher *n fr early 1900s* A bluffer or fraud; cheat; swindler

the four hundred *n phr* The set of socially prominent people, esp in a given place; the social elite [fr the list, attributed to Ward McAllister, of *four hundred* socially desirable people]

four-letter man 1 *n phr* A stupid man ● From the four letters of **dumb 2** *n phr* A detestable man; a contemptible wretch; = PRICK, SHIT ● From the four letters of **shit**

four nines *n phr* Something pure or very nearly pure: *That is four nines, or 99.99 pure gold*—Time

four-O *adj WW2 Navy* Perfect; splendid; = A-OK [fr the point system used in Navy efficiency ratings, where 4.0 is the top rating]

four on the floor *n phr* A gearshift lever emerging from the floor of a car, and controlling four speeds; hence, standard as distinct from automatic shift: *This little baby's got four on the floor and leather bucket seats*

four-pointer *college students* **1** *n* A grade of A for an examination or course **2** *n* A superior student [fr the grade-point system where an A rates at four points]

fours *See* DOWN ON ALL FOURS

four sheets to the wind *See* THREE SHEETS TO THE WIND

four-square *adj* Conventional; unimaginative; stolid; = SQUARE: *Undeniably the conducting is a bit four-square and heavy*—Village Voice

four-striper *n Navy* A naval captain, wearing four stripes as insignia

fourteen *lunch counter* A special order

four-time loser *See* THREE-TIME LOSER

four-wheeler *n truckers* An automobile; = CAGE

four wide ones *n phr baseball* A base on balls; a walk, esp an intentional pass

fox 1 *v* To deceive; mislead; outwit; = OUTFOX: *He tried to fox me with that phoney accent, and did* **2**

n teenagers & black fr 1940s black A beautiful, sexually attractive woman, or in teenage use, man

foxhole *n esp WW2 armed forces* A hole in which one conceals oneself, esp one dug for that purpose by a soldier

fox paw *n phr* A faux pas

foxy *adj fr 1940s black* Attractive; sexually desirable; = DANG[1]: *She was 22 years old, a real foxy little chick with auburn hair*—J Eszterhas

fracture 1 *v* To elicit loud laughter from; = LAY THEM IN THE AISLES: *We're a riot, hey. We play all kinds of funny stuff. We fracture the people*—Max Shulman **2** *v bop & cool talk* To evoke a strong reaction: *That flips me out and fractures me, man*

fractured *adj* Drunk

frag 1 *v Vietnam War armed forces* To kill or wound someone, esp a detested officer of one's own unit, typically by throwing a fragmentation grenade at him **2** *v* To kill; = ICE, WASTE: *If I hadn't've done it, he would've fragged me*—George V Higgins

fragged *adj car-racing* Ruined; blown-out: *countless fragged Ferrari engines, including two that disintegrated under a CD tester's heavy foot*—Car and Driver

fraidy (or **'fraidy**) **cat** *n phr* A timorous person, esp a boy; coward

frail *n fr 1920s college students* A woman, esp a young woman: *in persuading frails to divulge what they know*—E Lavine

◁**frail eel**▷ *n phr black* An attractive woman; = FOX: *I can get any frail eel I wants*—Zora Neale Hurston

◁**frail job**▷ **1** *n phr* A woman, esp a sexually attractive one **2** *n phr* The sex act with a woman

frame 1 *n* The human body; physique; build, esp that of a woman **2** *n homosexuals* A heterosexual man attractive to homosexuals **3** *n* A unit of a game or other contest; = STANZA: *Mel Queen lined a single to right field to open that frame*—R McGowen **4** *n fr early 1900s* The incrimination of an innocent person with false evidence; = FRAME-UP: *just the victim of a frame*—J Evans **5** *v: I was framed*—Joseph Auslander **6** *v carnival* To put in running order

frame-up 1 *n fr early 1900s* The incrimination of an innocent person with false evidence: *I'll prove to you it's a frame-up*—W Weeks **2** *n pitchmen* A display of goods for sale

frame someone **up** *v phr fr early 1900s* To incriminate an innocent person with false evidence: *They couldn't get him legally, so they framed him up with a phony burglary charge*

frank *n* A frankfurter; = WEENIE

frantic *bop & cool talk* **1** *adj* Excellent; wonderful; = COOL **2** *adj* Conventional; bourgeois; = UNCOOL: *The man who cares is now derided for being "frantic"*—Herbert Gold

frapping *adj* Wretched; accursed; = DAMN, FUCKING: *I need a frapping medic like a hole in the head*—People Weekly [a euphemism for *fucking*]

frat *college students* **1** *n* A college fraternity **2** *n* (also **frat rat**) A fraternity member **3** *n teenagers* A male student who conforms to middle-class norms of conduct and dress: *A "frat"...is a youth who dresses neatly and conforms to the accepted patterns*—New York Times

fraternize *v esp WW2 armed forces* To associate closely with inhabitants of an enemy country, esp to consort sexually with the women

frau (FROU) **1** *n* A woman **2** *n* One's wife: *and escort your incomparable frau to a tea dance* —K Brush/ *his reward from the frau*—Hal Boyle [fr German]

to a **frazzle** *adv phr fr middle 1800s* Completely; totally; to a ruined condition: *After the marathon I was beat to a frazzle* [fr dialect *frazzle* "frayed end of a rope"]

frazzled 1 *adj* Exhausted; tired in nerve and flesh; = PLAYED OUT: *He was frazzled after three weeks without a break* **2** *adj* Drunk

freak 1 *n* A drink made of Coca-Cola (a trade name) and orange flavoring ◁**2**▷ *n jazz musicians* A male homosexual: *"Freak" is a homosexual* —Stephen Longstreet **3** *n* = HIPPIE **4** *v* To behave strangely and disorientedly as if intoxicated by a psychedelic drug; = FREAK OUT: *His publisher for the last two books "sort of freaked" when they got a look at this one*—New York

-freak *combining word* A devotee or enthusiast; addict; = BUG, BUFF, NUT: *plant freak/ radio freak/ porn-freak*
See ACID FREAK, ECOFREAK, HARD-ROAD FREAK, JESUS FREAK, METH HEAD, PEEK FREAK, SOAP FREAK, SPEED-FREAK

freaking *adj* Wretched; accursed; = DAMN, FUCKING: *who's got so much freaking talent it just turns your stomach*—Car and Driver/ *all the freaking way to the bank*—Playboy [a euphemism for *fucking*]

freak out (or **up**) *fr narcotics* **1** *v phr* To have intense and disturbing hallucinations and other reactions from psychedelic drugs **2** *v phr* To go out of touch with reality with or without narcotics; become irrational, esp frantically so; be intoxicated; = FLIP OUT: *plus the chance to freak out, speak in tongues or talk nonsense*—Herbert Gold/ *I saw those golden arches and I freaked out, because I'd just seen the buttes and all that great stuff*—New Yorker **3** *v phr* To become very excited and exhilarated, as if intoxicated with narcotics **4** *v phr* To abandon conventional values and attitudes; = DROP OUT

freak-out *fr narcotics* **1** *n* An instance of freaking out: *a period which one feminist writer has called one of "mass freak-outs all over the place"* —Esquire/ *the same freakouts, the same strange clothes*—New Yorker **2** *n* A person who is freaked out **3** *n* A frightening or nightmarish drug experience; = BAD TRIP, BUMMER **4** *n* A congregation of hippies

freak someone **out** *v phr fr narcotics* To cause someone to show the irrationality, lethargy, excitement, withdrawal, etc, of a psychedelic experience: *The heavy metal sound freaked him out*

freak trick *n phr prostitutes* A man who demands very exotic or brutal sexual activity: *the victim of a*

"freak trick," a customer who gets his kicks from brutally beating girls—Xaviera Hollander

freaky *adj fr narcotics* Having the qualities of a freak or a freak-out; = FAR OUT: *I think it would be freaky to have an affair with my barber*—Playboy/ *There is nothing bohemian, or beat, or hippie, or freaky about them. They are straights, uptight*—Saturday Review

freckles *n WW2 Navy & Marines* Tobacco for rolling cigarettes

free *See* FOR FREE, HOME FREE

free-and-easy *n fr late 1700s* A saloon or other bibulous social center

freebase or **free base it** *v* or *v phr narcotics* To use cocaine by heating it and inhaling the smoke, its most powerful essence: *The addiction problem seems to be compounded by the fact that so many cokeheads are freebasing it*

freebie or **freebee** or **freeby** *n fr early 1900s black* Anything given or enjoyed free of charge: *That meal was a freebie and it didn't cost me anything*—Louis Armstrong/ *Holiday Inn bartenders are enjoined from giving freebies to customers, no matter how much they spend*—Time

free gratis (GRA təs) **1** *adv phr fr late 1800s* Without charge; = FOR FREE: *The Congressmen traveled free gratis* **2** *adj phr*: *a free-gratis perk/ free-gratis tickets* [fr combination of *free* with Latin *gratis* "free"]

freeload 1 *v* To be fed, entertained, supported, etc, without charge; live parasitically; = SPONGE: *They will successfully free load the rest of their lives* —Hal Boyle **2** *n*: *During the depression women free loads were rare*—J Cannon

freeloader 1 *n* A person who freeloads; = MOOCHER, SPONGER: *Congressmen are great free-loaders*—L Mortimer **2** *n* A gathering or party with free refreshments: *Somebody was tossing a free-loader over on Park Avenue*—J Bainbridge

freeloading 1 *v* Eating, drinking, etc, without paying: *Free loading has diminished*—J Cannon **2** *modifier*: *my freeloading cousins/ your freeloading pals*

free lunch *n phr* Something had without paying for it; an uncompensated pleasure; a perk or gratuity: *pushing the free lunch*—Wall Street Journal [fr the former custom of giving customers free food called *free lunch* in saloons]
See THERE'S NO FREE LUNCH

free-o *n* Something received without charge; = FREEBIE: *So he picks up a few free-o's here and there*—California

free (or **freeworld**) **people** *n phr prison* People who are not prison inmates, esp guards, wardens, etc

free ride *See* GET A FREE RIDE

free-rider *n labor union* A nonunion worker who benefits from the pay and advantages gained by a union

freeside *adv prison* Outside the walls of a prison: *He yearns to live freeside again*

free ticket 1 *n phr* General freedom of action, esp of forbidden action; license; carte blanche: *He* *thinks the uniform gives him a free ticket to be a shitheel* **2** *n phr* (also **free transportation**) *baseball* A base on balls; walk

free-vee *n* Nonpay television: *Well, pay-TV proved free-vee wrong*—Toronto Star

free-wheeling **1** *n* Independence of action and initiative; blithe and unconstrained indulgence: *No free-wheeling here, you do things strictly our way* **2** *modifier:* *Jonathan himself tries opium, hash, freewheeling sex, gliders*—Playboy **3** *n* Liberal spending; easy munificence: *the free-wheeling of the new rich* **4** *modifier:* *the free-wheeling out-of-towner*—Hal Boyle [fr the feature of certain 1930s cars permitting them to coast *freely* without being slowed by the engine]

freeworld **1** *n* *prison* Life outside prison; uncarcerated living **2** *modifier:* *what they called free-world punks, guys who'd been queer even before they got sent up*—Ezra Hannon

freeze **1** *n* A stopping of change, esp in various monetary matters: *a freeze on profits/ nuclear freeze* **2** *v:* *The government denies it wants to freeze interest rates* **3** *v* To stay or become motionless: *The cop hollered to him to freeze right there* **4** *v* To stay where one is: *Your best bet is to freeze and wait. You can't get away*—Nelson Algren **5** *v* To treat someone with deliberate hauteur; snub; cut; = PUT THE FREEZE ON someone: *Next time she froze me mercilessly* **6** *v* To inspire terror: *His scream froze me*
See IN COLD STORAGE

freeze-out *n* The absence of cooperation, information, etc; a blank: *this total freeze-out on details for big Ray*—Erich Segal

freeze someone **out** *v phr fr late 1800s* To exclude someone; discriminate against someone: *When I wanted to get into the game they froze me out*

◁**freeze the balls off a brass monkey**▷ *v phr* To be very cold: *It was the kind of clear winter day that would freeze the balls off a brass monkey*

freeze up *v phr* To become paralyzed by fear; be immobilized by panic; = CLANK

freight *See* PAY THE FREIGHT, PULL one's FREIGHT

◁**French**▷ **1** *n* Cunnilingus; = the FRENCH WAY **2** *v:* *Then the perverse chap actually Frenched her!*
See PARDON MY FRENCH

French-inhale **1** *n* The trick of exhaling smoke by mouth and immediately reinhaling it by nose **2** *modifier:* *He continued to smoke in this "French inhale" style*—JD Salinger

French kiss **1** *n phr fr 1920s* A kiss in which the tongue of one person explores the oral cavity of another, and vice versa; = MOUTH-TO-MOUTH RESUSCITATION, SOUL KISS **2** *v:* *They French-kissed and perhaps more*

French leave *n phr fr late 1700s* Departure without notice or permission, esp going AWOL from a military post

French letter *n phr fr middle 1800s* A condom

French postcard *n phr* A pornographic photograph, such as was fancied to be sold by furtive characters pulling at one's sleeve in the streets of Paris ● In the form **French print**, used fr the middle 1800s

◁**French tickler**▷ *n phr* A condom with added variegated surfaces, spirals, fins, etc, to increase vaginal stimulation

French (or **Spanish**) **walk** **1** *n phr* A pained and humiliating gait used by one whose seat and neck are strongly grasped and raised to urge him along; = the BUM'S RUSH **2** *v* (also **walk Spanish**): *Mike Spanish-walked him swiftly across the little space*—WR Burnett/ *Smith...was an expert at walking 'em Spanish*—New Yorker ● **walk Spanish** is attested from the early 1800s [said to be fr the custom of pirates, in the *Spanish* Main, of forcing prisoners to *walk* while holding them by the neck so that their toes barely touched the deck]

◁the **French way**▷ *n phr* Cunnilingus [fr the conviction expressed in the classic couplet: The French they are a funny race/ They fight with their feet and fuck with their face]

fresh **1** *adj* Impudent; disrespectful; saucy; = CHEEKY: *Don't be fresh to your Momma or I'll belt you one* **2** *adj* Flirtatious; sexually bold; = FAST: *I'm not that kind of girl, so don't be fresh* **3** *adj* Aloof and uninvolved; = COOL: *"We hang out with him because he's fresh," said Jesse MMC*—New York Daily News [first two senses perhaps related to German *frech* "impudent"]

fresh and sweet *adj phr prostitutes* Just released from jail ● Used by prostitutes of other prostitutes

freshie *n college students* A first-year college student [fr *freshman*]

fresh one *n phr prison* A new prisoner

fresh out *adv phr* Without; = OUT: *We're fresh out of bananas, Missus*

fribble *n* A trifle; a piece of inanity: *For every zap-pow fribble, there were equal servings of socially redeeming food for thought*—Newsweek

Friday *See* GAL FRIDAY, TGIF

fried **1** *adj* Drunk **2** *adj esp underworld* Electrocuted **3** *adj teenagers* Confused; muddled; exhausted; = BURNED OUT

fried egg *esp WW2 armed forces* **1** *n phr* A showy brass military cap decoration **2** *n phr* The Japanese flag: *sunk about everything the Japs owned with a fried egg on its masthead*—Robert Ruark

fried shirt *n phr* = BOILED SHIRT

friendly *n armed forces fr WW2* In wartime, a plane, ship, soldier, civilian, etc, of one's own side: *Friendlies...sometimes used to designate townspeople who cooperate with the Americans*—New York Times

◁**frig**▷ **1** *v* To stimulate the female genitals manually or digitally **2** *v fr middle 1800s* To masturbate **3** *v fr early 1900s* To do the sex act **4** *v* To cheat or trick someone; take advantage of someone; = DIDDLE, SHAFT **5** *interj* = FUCK [ultimately fr Latin *fricare* "rub"]
See TAKE A FLYING FUCK

◁**frigging**▷ **1** *adj* Wretched; accursed; = DAMN, FUCKING: *if we could find the frigging truck*—Arthur Hailey/ *You're a walkin', friggin' combat zone*

—Time **2** *adv*: *Ain't it frigging stupid?/ They friggin' loved it*—Washington Post

◁**frill**▷ *n* A woman, esp a young woman

fringe *n* A fringe benefit added to one's pay

Frisco *n* San Francisco, California: *Ever been to Frisco?*—James M Cain ● This nickname is said to be disapproved by the residents of the place

frisk *fr late 1700s British* **1** *v* (also **frisk down**) To search, esp for firearms or contraband, by patting or rubbing the person in places where these might be concealed: *raise your hands high, frisk him*—R Wallace/ *without getting taken-off, frisked-down or punched-out*—New York Times **2** *n:* *They did a quick frisk and let him go* **3** *v* To inspect a building, apartment, etc, for evidence or loot: *Let's go up and frisk the apartment*—Raymond Chandler

frit *n* A male homosexual; = FLIT

fritz *v* To make something inoperative; put out of working order: *Lightning hit some wires and fritzed the generator*—F Brown

See ON THE BLINK

◁**Fritz**▷ *n fr WW1* A German, esp a German soldier; = KRAUT

fritzer *n underworld* Something false; = PHONY

frivol *v* To behave frivolously; jape and frolic: *I wish I could frivol away my summer*

'fro or **fro** *n* A frizzy style of coiffure; = AFRO: *humongous earrings, and, of course, a gigantic fro/ the curly 'fro which has found particular favor among the men*—Ebony

frobnitz *n computer* An unspecified or unspecifiable object; something one does not know the name of or does not wish to name; = GADGET, GIZMO

frog **1** *n* = FROGSKIN ◁**2**▷ *n* (also **Frog** or **froggy** or **Froggy** or **frog-eater**) *esp WW1 fr middle 1800s British* A Frenchman or -woman: *My dad was in France during the last war. He knows those Frogs*—Calder Willingham **3** *modifier:* *frog wine/ a Frog chick* ◁**4**▷ *n* The French language: *He asked me in Frog* **5** *n teenagers* A dull and conventional person: *Anybody who still wears saddle shoes is...a "frog"*—New York Times [senses referring to the French fr their eating of *frog-legs*]

See BIG FISH, BIG FISH IN A LITTLE POND, IS A FROG'S ASS WATERPROOF, KNEE-HIGH TO A GRASSHOPPER

frogging *adj* Wretched; accursed; = DAMN, FUCKING: *Baseball is a froggin' silly little game*—Milwaukee Journal [a euphemism for *fucking*]

frogman *n fr WW2 Navy* A scuba diver, esp a professional or military diver

frogskin *fr early 1900s* **1** *n* A one-dollar bill; one dollar: *I'll give you five hundred frogskins for the good will and fixtures*—SJ Perelman **2** *n* Any piece of paper money; = FOLDING MONEY: *He not only got his quail, but a handful of frogskins as well*—Associated Press [fr the green color]

frog-sticker **1** *n fr early 1800s* A long-bladed knife, esp a pocket knife: *Out comes your liver on the end o' this frogsticker*—Chicago Tribune **2** *n WW2 Army* A bayonet

frog up *v phr 1930s black* To become confused; be deceived [probably fr humorous mispronunciation of *fog up*]

from Adam *See* NOT KNOW someone FROM ADAM

from A to Z *adv phr* Completely; thoroughly; all the way

from hell to breakfast *adv phr* Thoroughly and vehemently; violently: *Police...clubbed the Gophers from hell to breakfast*—H Asbury

from hunger **1** *adj phr fr 1930s musicians* Inferior; unpleasant; contemptible: *I started giving the three witches at the next table the eye again. That is, the blonde one. The other two were strictly from hunger*—JD Salinger **2** *adv phr:* *playing from hunger...in a style to please the uneducated masses*—Peabody Bulletin

from nothing *See* KNOW FROM NOTHING

from scratch **1** *adv phr* From the earliest stages; from the very beginning: *We had to do it all again, from scratch* **2** *adv phr* Using the separate basic ingredients or parts: *I never tired of watching my grandmother make the bread "from scratch" to feed the whole family*—San Francisco **3** *adj phr:* *his first from-scratch musical venture*—Philadelphia

from the git-go (or **get-go**) *adv phr* From the very beginning: *It was his bust from the git-go*—R Woodley/ *Right from the get-go he came out smoking....It all went down in milliseconds*—New York Times

from the hip *See* SHOOT FROM THE HIP

from (or **out of** or **straight from**) **the horse's mouth** *adv phr* From the most authentic source: *I got the tip straight from the horse's mouth*—WR Burnett [fr the fact that a *horse's* age can be determined most precisely and directly by examining its teeth]

from the shoulder *See* STRAIGHT FROM THE SHOULDER

from the top *adv phr esp musicians* From the beginning: *Let's hear it again from the top* [perhaps fr the musical instruction *da capo* "from the beginning," literally, "from the head"]

from the word go *adv phr fr middle 1800s* From the very beginning; ab ovo: *He was lying from the word go*

front **1** *n hoboes* A suit of clothes **2** *n fr 1920s* The appearance and impression one presents publicly; facade: *This and his stickpin, his two diamond rings, and his shirts and the gabardine suit composed his "front"*—Ira Wolfert/ *a real coon type. But that's just front*—Lawrence Anderson **3** *n* (also **front man**) A respectable and impressive person who represents or publicly supports persons lacking social approval: *Inability to hire a professional bondsman and "good front" results in a quick trial*—E Lavine **4** *v:* *If you ask them to front for you, they know you're going to do something*—Playboy **5** *n fr 1920s* An ordinary and unexceptional business used as a cover for gambling, extortion, etc, esp as a way of decontaminating ill-gotten money: *The candy store was a front for his bookie business* **6** *v fr narcotics* To give something, esp narcotics, on promise of payment: *I'll front you some of this shit if you pay me by Thursday*

See OUT-FRONT, UP FRONT

frontal *adj* Candid; direct; open: *He's a very direct and forceful guy, a very frontal person*—Washington Post [fr *up front*]

See FULL FRONTAL

front and center *n phr* The place where one is most conspicuously alone, esp before one's superiors ● Usu a command to present oneself at once [fr the position in *front* of a military formation where a singled-out soldier presents himself or herself]

front-door *adj* Legitimate; respectable: *a front-door operation*

the **front door 1** *n phr* *circus* The management of a circus, as distinct from the performers **2** *n phr* *truckers* The first truck in a convoy

front-end *adj* *circus* On or concerning the part of the midway that is near the main entrance

front gee (JEE) *n phr* *underworld* A pickpocket's confederate [fr *gee* "guy"]

front money *n phr* An initial and impressive amount of money; cash as an earnest: *He had agreed...to help the manufacturer get the $1.2 million loan in return for 7 percent of the total, plus "green" or "front money"*—New York Times/ *in the drive for $4.5 million in "front money" by Labor Day*—New York Times

See FLASH ROLL

front name *n phr* The first name; given name: *What is your front name?*—Groucho Marx

front office 1 *n phr* The chief administrative offices of a company **2** *n phr* Managers; executives: *What's the front office think?* **3** *adj phr*: *front-office memos* **4** *n phr* *underworld* A police station

front runner *n phr* The leader in a contest, election, etc: *That left as front runners Runcie and England's second-ranking churchman*—Time

front-running *adj* Leading; first in a competition: *universally considered to be the GOP's front-running candidate*—Time

frosh *n* *students fr early 1900s* A first-year student, or such students collectively

frost 1 *n* *fr late 1800s British* A total failure; something not well received: *My idea was a dismal frost* **2** *n* Social hauteur; chill; = COLD SHOULDER: *He smiled at her and got frost* **3** *v* To anger; irritate: *That tone of voice really frosts me* [first sense fr the notion of "a killing frost"]

frosted over *adj phr* Irritated; annoyed

frosty 1 *adj* Unperturbed: *Stay frosty. Relax* —Joseph Wambaugh **2** *adj* In a reserved manner; haughty; cool: *her frosty glance*

frou-frou *n* Frilly dress and adornment; frivolous bedizenment: *Is that what you want in a girl, chi-chi, frou-frou, fancy clothes, permanent waves?*—Max Shulman [fr French, imitative of the rustling of silk]

frowsy *n* A slovenly, unkempt woman: *a few frowsies in skirts*—New Yorker

frozen rope *n phr* *baseball* A hard line drive: *A hard line drive is a blue darter, frozen rope, or an ungodly shot*—Jim Bouton

the **frug** *n phr* *esp 1960s* A discotheque dance derived from the twist: *The dignified dances include...the Frug (the movement is in the hips, the derivation of the name is shady)*—New York Times [origin unknown; perhaps a blend of *frig* and *fuck*]

fruit 1 *n* An eccentric person; = FRUITCAKE, ODDBALL: *I'll bet we get a lot of fruits*—O Johnson ◁**2**▷ *n fr 1930s* A male homosexual; = FAIRY [first sense short for *fruitcake*, as in "nutty as a fruitcake"]

See HEN-FRUIT

fruitbar *See* FLAMER

fruitcake 1 *n* An insane person; = NUT: *The shrink himself is a certified fruitcake* **2** *n* An eccentric person; = FRUIT, ODDBALL **3** *modifier*: *those fruitcake sandal makers in the tractor-gear factory*—Calvin Trillin ◁**4**▷ *n* A male homosexual; = FRUIT **5** *modifier*: *his fruitcake mannerisms*

See NUTTY AS A FRUITCAKE

◁**fruit fly**▷ *n phr* *homosexuals* = FAG HAG

fruit-picker *n* *homosexuals* A basically heterosexual man who occasionally seeks out homosexual partners

fruit salad 1 *n phr* *fr WW2 armed forces* Ribbons and other badges worn on the breast of a military jacket **2** *n phr* *narcotics* A mixture of tranquilizers, painkillers, and other drugs from the family medicine cabinet used secretly by adolescents ◁**3**▷ *n phr* (Variations: **potato patch** or **rose garden** or **vegetable garden**) *hospital* A group of stroke victims or otherwise totally disabled patients

fruit-salad party *n phr* *narcotics* A party at which adolescents experiment with drugs garnered from the family medicine cabinet

fruit wagon *n phr* *dockworkers* An ambulance: *If you squawk you leave the docks, most likely in the fruit wagon*—MH Vorse

fruity 1 *adj* Eccentric; odd; = NUTTY, WEIRD ◁**2**▷ *adj* Homosexual; = GAY **3** *adj* *esp British fr early 1900s* Very rich; unctuous: *a fruity upperclass accent*

frump *n* A dowdy woman: *that floppy-looking frump he left you for*—James M Cain

frumpy *adj* Dowdy; run-down; unattractive: *The message is that soft frumpy fellows are not only lovable but sexually attractive*—Village Voice

fry 1 *v* To be executed in the electric chair, or to execute someone in the electric chair: *I built up a case against Sandmark. You probably could have fried him with it, too*—J Evans/ *Apparently everybody in Texas thinks everybody should be fried* —Washington Post **2** *v* *esp teenagers* To punish or injure, esp in revenge **3** *v* *computer* To fail; = GO DOWN **4** *v* *black* To remove the kinks from hair with a hot comb or curling iron

See BIGGER FISH TO FRY, SMALL FRY

FTA (pronounced as separate letters) *sentence* *Army fr 1950s* Fuck the Army; also, fuck them all

fu (Fōō) *n narcotics* Marijuana [perhaps a shortening of Portuguese *fumo d'Angola* "Angola smoke," referring to marijuana and the smoking habit brought by slaves fr Angola to Brazil]

fubar (Fōō bar) *adj fr WW2 armed forces* Totally botched and confused; =SNAFU [fr *fucked up beyond all recognition*]

fubb *adj fr WW2 armed forces* =FUBAR, SNAFU [fr *fucked up beyond belief*]

fubis (Fōō bis) *sentence Army fr 1950s* An irritated or defiant comment [fr *fuck you, buddy, I'm shipping*]

◀**fuck**▶ **1** *v fr 1200s* To do the sex act with or to someone **2** *n* An instance of the sex act: *a quick fuck* **3** *n* A sex partner: *She said he's not a bad fuck* **4** *n* A despicable person; =BASTARD, PRICK: *Why don't you fucks find a cure for that already?* —Joseph Heller/ *Get out, you stupid fuck!* **5** *v* To cheat; swindle; maltreat; take advantage of; =FUCK OVER, SCREW: *I was with them twenty years, but they fucked me anyhow* **6** *v* To curse and vilify; revile extremely; =DAMN ● Strongest of the cursing terms that include wishing the person or thing to eternal damnation; "damn," "to hell with," and mentally subjecting the person or thing to an act of sodomy: "fuck, screw," and British "bugger": *Fuck the money, I'm gone go on this ride*—Claude Brown/ *Ah, fuck that noise*—Philip Roth **7** *interj* An exclamation of disgust, disappointment, dismay, etc: *Oh fuck, the thing's busted!* **8** *v* To botch and confuse; ruin; =FUCK UP: *My God, if the doctor sent out a bill...it might fuck the whole thing*—Lawrence Sanders [origin unknown; perhaps fr or related to German *ficken* "strike, copulate with"]
See DRY FUCK, FINGERFUCK, a FLYING FUCK, GOAT FUCK, GO FUCK oneself, HONEY-FUCK, MIND-FUCK, NOT GIVE A DAMN, NOT GIVE A FUCK FOR NOTHING, RAT FUCK, TAKE A FLYING FUCK, THROW A FUCK INTO someone

◀a **fuck**▶ *See* NOT GIVE A DAMN, NOT GIVE A FUCK FOR NOTHING

◀the **fuck**▶ *See* the HELL

◀**fuck a duck**▶ *interj* An exclamation of surprise and incredulity: *He did? Well fuck a duck!*

◀**fuck-all**▶ *n esp British* Nothing; =ZILCH: *A good extra...can pull in good money to not do fuck-all* —Playboy/ *He knows fuck-all about the case*

◀**fuck around**▶ **1** *v phr* To idle and loaf about; =MESS AROUND: *Although I do fuck around in home studios and things like that, I think that it's of no importance*—Rolling Stone **2** *v phr* To tease; fool around annoyingly; =HORSE AROUND
See FUCK WITH

◀**fuck book**▶ *n phr* A pornographic book or magazine

◀**fuck** someone's **brains out**▶ *v phr* To do the sex act busily and for a long time: *We can spend the whole night together, fuck our brains out*—Earl Thompson/ *two people who'd just fucked each other's brains out*—Richard Grossbach

◀**fucked by the fickle finger of fate**▶ *adj phr* Victimized by bad luck; very unfortunate

◀**fucked out**▶ *adj phr* Exhausted; =PLAYED OUT, POOPED

◀**fucked up**▶ **1** *adj phr* Confused; botched; ruined; =BALLED UP: *A good idea, but now it's totally fucked up* **2** *adj phr* Mentally and emotionally disturbed; neurotic: *I was so fucked up I couldn't talk sense* **3** *adj phr* Intoxicated, esp by narcotics: *I was so drunk and fucked up and shaken with tenderness*—Rolling Stone

◀**fucker**▶ **1** *n* A detestable person; =BASTARD, PRICK: *And the fuckers are really, really twisting us up*—Rolling Stone **2** *n* Any person or thing ● Often used affectionately: *The cop's really a nice old fucker/ Look at that little fucker go!*
See FATHER-FUCKER, MIND-FUCKER, MOTHERFUCKER, PIG-FUCKER

◀**fuck film**▶ *n phr* A pornographic movie; =SKIN FLICK: *Calling it an erotic film festival made it possible for people...to dig a good fuck film*—Changes

◀**fuckhead**▶ *n* A despicable person; =JERK: *some back-country fuckhead with a stethoscope*—Stephen King

◀**fucking**▶ **1** *adj* Wretched; rotten; accursed; =DAMN: *hectic fuckin' business*—Changes/ *I hate this fucking place* **2** *adv* Extremely; very: *It's fucking difficult to get a raise these days*
See MOTHERFUCKING, a ROYAL FUCKING

◀**-fucking-**▶ *infix* Used for emphasis: *Chinese fuckin' fire drill/ trans-fucking-continental/ in-fucking-credible*—Dan Jenkins/ *"Un-fucking-believable," they say in the booth*—Toronto Life

◀**fucking a** (or **ay**)▶ *fr 1940s fr British* **1** *affirmation* Absolutely; definitely: *Fucking a, no one's gonna shoot Keith*—Playboy **2** *adv phr: Fucking ay right I did*—Patrick Mann **3** *interj* An exclamation of pleasure, triumph, joy, etc; =GREAT: *We won? Fucking a!* [fr an affirmatory phrase *your fucking arse*]

◀**fucking well**▶ *adv phr* Nearly; precisely; just about: *not afraid of fucking well anything*—George Warren

◀**fucking well told**▶ *adv phr* Absolutely right; definitely; =FUCKING A: *Is he stupid? You're fucking well told he is*

◀**fuck like a bunny**▶ *v phr* To copulate readily and vigorously ● Said of both sexes [fr the amatory eagerness of rabbits, also referred to in the catch-phrase "Shoot the habit to me, rabbit" as a response to "Sex is just a habit"]

◀**fuck like a mink**▶ *v phr fr early 1900s* To copulate readily and vigorously ● Said only of women

◀**fuck off**▶ **1** *v phr* =FUCK AROUND **2** *v phr* =FUCK UP **3** *v phr fr late 1800s* To leave; depart: *Tell 'em to fuck off, I don't want anything to do with them*—Xaviera Hollander **4** *interj: Scat, Sophie! Fuck off, Jack!*

◀**fuck-off**▶ *n fr WW2 armed forces* A habitual shirker; sluggard; =GOOF-OFF: *I mean, everybody's a fuck-off*—Rolling Stone

◀**fuck over**▶ *v phr* To victimize and maltreat, sexually or otherwise; =FUCK: *so accustomed to being used and fucked over that they probably would do* nothing—Howard S Becker/ *let people know who might be fucking them over*—Village Voice

◀**fuck the dog**▶ *v phr* To waste time; idle about; temporize: *We better quit fucking the dog and get cracking*

◀**fuck up**▶ *fr late 1800s* **1** *v phr* To fail by blundering; ruin one's prospects: *They are the prime reasons that people fuck up in bands*—Rolling Stone **2** *v phr* To confuse; botch; =BALL UP: *I had it right, but he fucked it up*

◀**fuck-up**▶ **1** *n* A bungler, esp a chronic one: *The sergeant was a confirmed fuck-up* **2** *n* A confused situation; botch; =MESS: *The operation was a royal fuck-up* **3** *n* A blunder; =GOOF: *These things are my ideas...they've all got the same fuck-ups*—Rolling Stone

◀**fuck** someone **up**▶ *v phr* To injure or maltreat someone; =FUCK OVER: *If anybody was to mess with your sister, you had to really fuck him up*—Claude Brown/ *They didn't do it, so they fucked me up*—Rolling Stone

◀**fuck up, move up**▶ *sentence* Army If you blunder badly, you'll be promoted

◀**fuck** (or **fuck around**) **with**▶ **1** *v phr* To play or toy with; meddle with: *Stop fucking around with that switch!/ Floyd was a little crazy and just liked to fuck with people by talking a lot of nonsense*—Claude Brown **2** *v phr* To defy or challenge; provoke; =MESS AROUND WITH: *Don't fuck with me, buster, unless you're tired of living*

◀**fuck you**▶ *interj* An exclamation of very strong defiance and contempt: *Fuck you, friend, if that's your attitude*

Fudd *See* WILLIE FUDD

fuddy-duddy or **fuddy-dud** **1** *n* An old-fashioned, esp a meticulous, person; an outdated conservative: *To this little squab, I evidently rated as a fuddy-duddy*—Billy Rose **2** *adj:* *There were a few fuddy-duddy requests for documentation*—Village Voice

fudge **1** *v* *fr middle 1800s* To cheat or misrepresent slightly; deviate somewhat: *so I could fudge three or four inches on my height*—James M Cain/ *if you're fudging on your income tax return*—Associated Press **2** *interj* *fr late 1700s British* A mild exclamation of surprise, disappointment, etc; =DARN **3** *v* To rub someone to orgasm; =FRIG [first sense recorded as used by boys playing marbles; other senses perhaps euphemisms for *fuck*] *See* OH FUDGE

fudge one's **pants** (or **undies**) *v phr* To become frightened; =SHIT one's PANTS

fuggle *See* HONEY-FUCK

fuie *See* PHOOEY

full *adj* Drunk

full as an egg (or **a tick**) *adj phr* Drunk

full blast **1** *adv phr* To the limit of capacity; with no restraint; =ALL-OUT **2** *adj:* *a full-blast campaign for mayor*

full court press *n phr* Very great or maximum pressure: *an inclination not to resume a full court press for the peace plan*—Wall Street Journal/ *Only two of the candidates mounted a full-court press*

looking to the Iowa caucuses [fr an aggressive pressing defense in basketball, using both halves of the *court*]

full deck *See* PLAY WITH A FULL DECK

full frontal *adj phr* Total; complete; unrestricted: *a variety of forms including iambic pentameter, full frontal rhyme and ballads*—New York Times [fr the phrase "*full frontal nudity*" used to describe the ultimate grade of nakedness, as seen in art, moving pictures, television, etc]

full-mooner *n* An insane or very eccentric person; =LOONY, NUT: *in San Francisco, where there are full-mooners on every street corner*—Washingtonian/ *This issue goes beyond the full-mooners*—Robert Nowak [fr the belief that some people go crazy at the time of the *full moon*]

full of beans **1** *adj phr* *fr middle 1800s British* Vibrant with energy; peppy: *The old man's full of beans and bitching up a storm* **2** *adj phr* (also **full of hops** or **full of prunes**) Wrong; mistaken, esp chronically so; =FULL OF SHIT [first sense fr the belief that a *bean*-fed horse is particularly frisky and strong; second sense fr a connection with *beans*, *hops*, etc., as promoting excretion]

full of hot air *adj phr* Wrong; mistaken; pompously in error: *If she says that, she's full of hot air*

◁**full of piss and vinegar**▷ *adj phr* Brimming with energy; very peppy and assertive: *full of the piss and vinegar her mother lacks*—Village Voice/ *full of piss and vinegar and occasionally now, a little weed*—Inside Sports

◁**full of shit**▷ *adj phr* (Variations: **crap** or **bull** or **it** may replace **shit**) Wrong; mistaken; not to be credited: *Oh, he's so full of shit, that self-seeking schmuck*—Joseph Heller/ *Anyone who says it doesn't matter is full of it*—Erich Segal/ *They're all fulla shit anyway, all them goddam politicians*—WT Tyler

◁as **full of shit as a Christmas goose**▷ *adj phr* =FULL OF SHIT ● An intensive use

full-ride *adj* Total; full: *accused of receiving a full ride scholarship from Michigan*—B Fay

full up **1** *adj phr* Completely full: *The plane was full up by then* **2** *adj phr* =FED UP **3** *adj phr* Sentimental; nearly weeping

full yard *See* GO THE FULL YARD

fumble-fingered *adj* Clumsy; =BUTTERFINGERED: *directions for the fumble-fingered*—Time

fume or **fumigate** *v esp around 1900* To smoke a cigarette, cigar, etc

fumtu (FUHM tōō) *adj phr* WW2 armed forces Totally confused; botched; =SNAFU [fr *fucked up more than usual*]

fun *adj* With which, with whom, in which, etc., one can have fun: *a fun place/ Mickey and his chums introduce each other as "a real fun guy"*—Saturday Review *See* LIKE HELL, POKE FUN

fun and games *n phr* *fr early 1900s* Pleasure; delightful diversion ● More commonly British than US, and most often ironic: *His job looks like constant fun and games/ We had some fun and games a few months ago*—Rex Burns [based on the talk and attitude used toward children by hearty people, and analogous with *show and tell*]

Fun City or **fun city** *n phr fr late 1960s* Any city, esp New York City, fancied to be a venue for pleasure, often ironically [first used as a public-relations motto for the administration of New York City Mayor John Lindsay, and felt to be in ironic contrast with increasing urban shabbiness, poverty, crime, etc]

fund *See* SLUSH FUND

fun fur *n phr* Cheap synthetic fur for casual use

fungo 1 *n baseball fr middle 1800s* A ball hit to give practice to fielders, usu by tossing it up and swinging **2** *v*: *They used to fungo that ball over your head*—Philadelphia Journal **3** *n* A long, light bat used to hit practice balls to fielders [origin unknown; perhaps fr dialect *fonge* "catch," fr Old English *fon* "seize, catch," or fr the German cognate *fangen* in the same sense; the *-o* ending might indicate a shouted warning, the whole meaning "Now catch!"]

fungo stick *n phr baseball* A bat used to hit balls for fielding practice

fungus-faced *adj teenagers* Repulsive; = GROSS: *The kids call Baker a fungus-faced toadsucker*—Washington Post

funk[1] **1** *v chiefly British fr middle 1700s* To fail through panic; be frightened to immobility: *She would have won, but suddenly funked* **2** *n* Depression; moroseness; = the BLUES: *He paled and fell into a funk/ This levelheaded man of logic, however, is also a creature of moods and funks*—Playboy [perhaps fr Flemish *fonck* "perturbation"]

See BLUE FUNK, IN A FUNK

funk[2] or **fonk 1** *n esp musicians fr 1950s* A style of urban black music that relies heavily on bass guitar and exhibits black elements like African rhythms, the blues, early rock and roll, jazz, etc: *There is no denying...the influence of Instant Funk*—Aquarian/ *the Minister of Super Heavy Funk, the legendary James Brown*—Afrika Bambaataa/ *The Night Tripper has been making good records longer than most of us have been listening. He is New Orleans "fonk"*—record jacket **2** *v* To play or move to an urban black music that features a dominant bass guitar: *I think it's all right to funk all night*—Aquarian [fr *funky*]

Funk *See* PETER FUNK

funkadelic *adj* Musically hard-edged and urban while also reminiscent of the effects of hallucinogenic drugs; = FUNKY: *breaks into his best funkadelic solo as the mood changes*—Village Voice [fr a blend of *funky* and *psychedelic*]

funk hole *n phr fr early 1900s* A hiding place when one is frightened

funkified *adj* Tending toward a hard-edged, urban, black 1970s style in music: *Ornette Coleman, whose current funkified direction*—Downbeat

funkiness *n* The excited, hard-edged, soulful, or rhythmically compelling mood associated with funk: *Cannonball's alto sax has lost its old zesty funkiness*—Time

funky (also **fonky** or **funky-butt** or **funkyass**) **1** *adj* Repulsive; malodorous; stinking: *What a stinking, dirty, funky bitch she was*—Claude Brown/ *The Baths, though, are funky enough without booze*—Saturday Review **2** *adj fr 1950s black musicians* In the style of the blues; earthy; simple yet compelling, with a strong beat and powerful bass guitar: *He has combined a basically funky sound with experimentation*—Ebony/ *the funky-butt tune high wide an' lonesome*—George Warren **3** *adj* Excellent; effective; = GROOVY: *He wanted to get down and get funky*—Sports Illustrated/ *There's a funkyass biker after my own heart*—George Warren **4** *adj* Musically hard-edged and urban: *the gently funky, Latin-flavored rhythms*—Variety/ *but soulful to a degree, and a little bit funky so you could kinda sway your head to it*—Rolling Stone **5** *adj* Old-fashioned; quaintly out-of-date; having a nostalgic appeal: *for those of you who are not familiar with its funky splendor*—Village Voice/ *my love for funky Forties clothes*—Playboy/ *the great old funky restaurant called Harrigan's in Southwest DC*—Washingtonian **6** *adj* Pleasantly eccentric or unconventional; = OFFBEAT **7** *adj* Deviant; = KINKY: *That guy's a little too funky for my taste* **8** *adj* Highly emotional; lacking affective restraint: *He hints that it may have its funky moments*—New Republic [fr US dialect, "musty, mouldy, old and malodorous," fr early-17th-century British *funk* "stifling tobacco smoke, strong stench," of unknown origin though perhaps fr French dialect and Old French *funkier* "smoke," perhaps fr Latin *fumicare* "smoke"]

the funnies (or **comics**) *n phr* Comic strips; section or page of a newspaper with comic strips

funny 1 *adj* Eccentric; odd; = WEIRD **2** *adj* Insane; = NUTS **3** *adv* In a strange way: *He looked at her real funny*

a funny *n* A joke; wisecrack; witty remark

See DOODAD

funny business *See* MONKEY BUSINESS

funny car 1 *n phr* A car resembling a production model but having a very powerful engine, esp a drag racer so modified: *the "funny" car, built for speed*—Dick Tracy (comic strip) **2** *n phr* A dramatically modified car, usu having a powerful engine, oversized wheels, a raised rear suspension, etc

funny farm (or **house**) *n phr* A mental hospital, rest home for alcoholics, etc; = LAUGHING ACADEMY: *Who put me in your private funny house?*—Raymond Chandler/ *They must all have died in flophouses or on state funny-farms*—Saul Bellow

funny money *n phr* Worthless, counterfeit, or play money

funnypaper 1 *n* A newspaper with comic strips **2** *n Air Force* A map

◁**fur**▷ *n* The vulva; pubic hair

◁**furburger**▷ *college students* **1** *n* The vulva **2** *n* A very attractive woman; = EATIN' STUFF

fur-lined bathtub *See* WIN THE PORCELAIN HAIRNET

furnace *n gambling* An event that heavy betting

◁**fur pie**▷ **1** *n phr* The vulva **2** *n phr* Cunnilingus

furry *adj* Frightening; terrifying; =HAIRY

fuse *See* BLOW A GASKET, HAVE A SHORT FUSE

fuss *See* KICK UP A FUSS

fusspot *n fr late 1800s British* A very meticulous and finicky person; fussbudget

fustest with the mostest *See* FIRSTEST WITH THE MOSTEST

◁**futy**▷ (Fōō dee) **1** *n* The vulva **2** *v* To do the sex act; =FUCK **3** *v* =FUTZ AROUND **4** *v* To fuss; grumble; =BITCH

◁**futz**▷ (FUTS) **1** *n* The vulva **2** *v* =FUCK **3** *v* (also ◁**futz with**▷) To meddle or alter wrongfully; damage; =FUCK UP: *What is clear is that this movie has been futzed with*—Newsweek **4** *n* A repulsive man, esp an old one; =ALTER KOCKER: *Inside of every American...is a scrawny, twanging old futz like me*—Kurt Vonnegut, Jr

futz around **1** *v phr* To loaf and idle; =FUCK OFF: *Stop futzing around and get to work* **2** *v phr* To experiment; try tricks; play; =MESS AROUND: *The foundation folk may get to futzing around with their computers*—Book World/ *You never really had time to sort of futz around in the sets*—Playbill **3** *v phr* To defy or challenge; provoke; =FUCK WITH: *I am nobody to futz around with*—Philip Roth

futzed up *adj phr* Confused; botched; ruined; =FUCKED UP: *I've got her all futzed up. She does everything I tell her*—Calder Willingham

fuzz *n fr 1930s black* A police officer; the police: *Cops must be annihilated. Kill the Fascist fuzz*—Newsweek [fr black slang *man with the fuzzy balls* "white man"]

See LIP FUZZ

fuzzbuster *n* A device that detects police radar signals: *Rauch discovered that I had a Fuzzbuster, designed to warn me of radar traps*—Penthouse

fuzzled *adj* Drunk

◁**fuzznuts**▷ *n* A contemptible person; =JERK [fr the notion that a boy or young man is incompetent and contemptible fr the standpoint of a mature man, and also has no proper hair on his genitals; see *fuzz*]

◁**fuzz nutted**▷ *adj phr* Inexperienced; callow; green: *a fuzz nutted rookie*—Joseph Wambaugh [fr *fuzznuts*]

fuzzy **1** *n* (also **fuzzie**) A police officer; =FUZZ **2** *n gambling* A certainty, esp a horse sure to win; =SURE THING **3** *adj* Vague; unsure: *I'm a little fuzzy on the details* **4** *adj* Drunk

G

gabber *n* A talkative person; = GASBAG, MOTOR-MOUTH

gabby *adj* Talkative; noisily garrulous; gossipy: *They have spoken of any gabby party*—Westbrook Pegler/ *Shaw is a gabby playwright*

gabfest *n fr late 1800s* A session of conversation; a loquacious occasion; = CHINFEST

gaboon *See* GOBOON

Gabriel *n jive talk* A trumpet player

gabs *See* GOB¹

gadget **1** *n fr middle 1800s British merchant marine* Any unspecified or unspecifiable usu small object; something one does not know the name of or does not wish to name; = THINGAMAJIG **2** *n* An unnecessary but presumably impressive item added as decoration or inducement: *The car's full of silly gadgets* [perhaps fr French *gachette* "a small mechanical part of a rifle, lock, etc"]

gadgetry *n* Ingenious or impressive devices, esp electronic or mechanical: *an age in love with gadgetry*

gaff **1** *n carnival & hawkers* A concealed device or operation that makes it impossible for the customer to win; = GIMMICK: *People started looking for a gaff* —New Yorker **2** *v* To cheat; swindle; trick, esp by short-changing **3** *v* To use a concealed device, esp for an illusion: *The volcano was "gaffed" with steampipes*—AJ Liebling **4** *v Navy* To reprimand; rebuke severely [fr *gaff* "a hook"]

See BLOW THE GAFF, STAND THE GAFF

gaffer **1** *n* One's father; = OLD MAN: *Studs felt that Mr O'Brien was different from his own gaffer* —James T Farrell **2** *n* An old man: *Look at that gaffer trying to stand on his head* **3** *n* A foreman or boss, such as the manager of a circus, head glassblower, chief electrician on a movie set, etc [fr British dialect, "grandfather, godfather"]

See OLD COCKER

gag **1** *n fr late 1800s fr early 1800s British* A joke; wisecrack; trick: *I'll tell you gags, I'll sing you songs* —Mel Brooks **2** *n hoboes* An old, trite alibi [First sense perhaps fr obsolete *geck* "dupe," related to German *geck* "fool"; in the late 19th century a *gag* was "a line interpolated into a play"]

gaga *adj fr 1920s British* Crazy; silly; irrational: *When prohibition comes up, the wets go gaga*—A Briggs/ *not to mention a ga-ga French gamine in Mickey Mouse ears*—Village Voice/ *I'm not exactly gaga over the idea* [fr French, "fool"]

gag a maggot *See* ENOUGH TO GAG A MAGGOT

gage or **gauge** (GAYJ) **1** *n* Cheap whiskey **2** *n* Tobacco **3** *n narcotics fr black* Marijuana: *I could not see how they were more justified in drinking than I was in blowing the gage*—Eldridge Cleaver **4** *adj* (also **gaged**) *narcotics* Intoxicated with marijuana [fr 17th-century British senses "quart pot, pipeful of tobacco," based either on the notion of *gauge* "measure" or that of "enough to pledge or toast with"]

See GET one's GAGE UP, STICK OF GAGE

gage (or **gauge**) **butt** *n phr narcotics* A marijuana cigarette; = JOINT

gaged (GAYJD) *adj* Drunk

See GAGE

gagers (GAY jərz) *n* The eyes

gag me with a spoon *sentence teenagers* I am disgusted; I am about to retch

gago *n gypsy* A non-Gypsy

gaited *See* DOUBLE-GAITED

gal *n* A woman ● The equivalent of **guy** for a man: *She's a good gal, don't you think?/ a tough old gal*

gal (or **girl**) **Friday** *n phr* A woman assistant or secretary, esp in an office; female factotum; = GOFER [fr Daniel Defoe's novel *Robinson Crusoe* where the servant and companion was named *Friday*]

gall *n* Arrogant self-assurance; effrontery; = CHUTZPAH: *How do you like the gall of those Aussies*—S Smith

gallery *See* PEANUT GALLERY, PICTURE GALLERY, ROGUE'S GALLERY, SHOOTING GALLERY

galley-west *adj* Confused; turbulent; = FUCKED UP: *The whole place was galley-west when we got there* [probably by folk etymology fr British dialect *collywest* or *collyweston*, of unknown origin and defined as "a term used when anything goes wrong"]

See KNOCK someone GALLEY-WEST

galloping dominoes *n phr* Dice

galoot (gə LŌŌT) *n fr middle 1800s* A person, esp an awkward or boorish man ● Very often in the phrase **big galoot**: *large enough for the galoots to fit through and take over*—New York Times/ *So she told the big galoot to get lost* [fr early 1800s British, "inexperienced seaman," of unknown origin; perhaps fr the Sierra Leone Creole language Krio *galut* fr Spanish *galeoto* "galley slave"]

galumph *v* To move or cavort ungracefully; crash heavily about: *Linda Evans galumphing around the edges...like a wounded rhino*—Village Voice [coined by Lewis Carroll in *Through the Looking Glass*]

galumphing *adj* Ungraceful; heavy and cumbersome: *his dead eyes, croaky voice, and large galumphing body*—Village Voice

gam[1] **1** *v* *black* To boast; show off **2** *v* *black* To flirt **3** *v* To gossip; visit **4** *n* A social visit; party [origin unknown]

gam[2] *n* *fr late 1800s fr British* A leg, esp a woman's leg ● Most often in the plural: *regarding her superb gams with affection*—V Faulkner/ *Gavilan has spindly gams, a thin neck and a wasp waist*—New York Daily News [perhaps fr Italian *gamba* or Northern French *gambe* "leg"]

gambler *See* TINHORN

game *n* One's occupation; business; = RACKET: *He's in the computer game these days*
See AHEAD OF THE GAME, BADGER GAME, BALL GAME, CON GAME, FLOATING CRAP GAME, the NAME OF THE GAME, ON one's GAME, the ONLY GAME IN TOWN, PLAY GAMES, SKIN GAME, a WHOLE NEW BALL GAME, a WHOLE 'NOTHER THING

game plan *n phr* A strategy for winning; plan for conducting some project or affair: *That type of a game plan gave us the option to point out how badly we need a responsible press*—Tom Wicker [fr football]

gamer *n* *baseball & football* A brave and enterprising player, esp one who works with pain or against the odds: *what is known in the business as a gamer, a guy who pitches with pain...who wants the ball*—New York Daily News/ *When Jean Fuggett played for the Dallas Cowboys...his teammates called him a gamer*—Arthur Pincus

gander 1 *n* *fr early 1900s* A look; close scrutiny; glance: *I'll have a gander at the prices* **2** *v*: *Want to gander at TV for a while?* **3** *n* *underworld* A criminal lookout [fr the stretched, goose-like neck of someone gazing intently]
See TAKE A GANDER

gandy dancer 1 *n phr* *hoboes, railroad & lumberjacks fr early 1900s* A railroad track worker **2** *n phr* *lumberjacks* Any manual laborer **3** *n phr* *carnival* A seller of novelties [origin unknown]

ganef or **ganof** *See* GONIFF

gang *See* BLACK GANG, JERRY GANG

◁ **gang bang** ▷ (Variations: **shag** or **shay** may replace **bang**) **1** *n phr* An occasion when several males do the sex act serially with one woman; = TRAIN **2** *v phr*: *tear the place apart, leave the owner for dead, gangbang the waitress*—Joan Didion **3** *n phr* A group-sex orgy: *We all ended up in a big profitable gang-bang*—Xaviera Hollander

gangbusters *n* A great and conspicuous success; = HIT: *and "Breakfast Time" does that well. I think it's going to be gangbusters*—Newsweek
See LIKE GANGBUSTERS

gangland 1 *n* The world of organized crime; the gangster milieu **2** *modifier*: *a gangland-style slaying/ gangland gorillas*

gang plank *n phr* *truckers* A toll bridge

gangster 1 *n* *fr 1920s* A member of a criminal gang; an organized-crime figure; = MOBSTER **2** *modifier*: *gangster movie/ the gangster menace* **3** *n* *narcotics* A marijuana cigarette: *Just go on and smoke that gangster and be real cool*—C Cooper

gang up on someone or something *v phr* To combine against an opponent: *The nonaligned nations ganged up on Sri Lanka*

ganja (GAHN jə) *n* *narcotics* A strong type of marijuana obtained from a cultivated strain of Indian hemp [fr Hindi]

ganze macher (GAHN sə MAH kər) **1** *n phr* A person busy with many affairs, esp officiously and conspiratorially; = BIG-TIME OPERATOR **2** *n phr* An important person; = BIG SHOT, VIP [fr Yiddish, "total busybody"]

gaper *n* *jive talk* A mirror

gaper's block or **gaper delay** *n phr* Traffic congestion caused by drivers slowing down to inspect an accident or other matter of interest; = RUBBERNECKING

garage *See* COOTIE GARAGE

garbage (GAR bəj, gar BAHZH) **1** *n* *hoboes* Food or meals **2** *n* Nonsense; pretentious talk; = BULLSHIT: *The speech was nine-tenths garbage* **3** *n* Anything inferior and worthless; = CRAP, JUNK: *You call that piece of garbage a sonnet?* **4** *modifier*: *She uses a lot of tricky garbage shots to win games and sets/ I call it a garbage movie*

garbage down *v phr* *Navy & students fr WW2 Navy* To eat; have a meal; = CHOW DOWN

garbage furniture *See* STREET FURNITURE

garbage habit *n phr* *narcotics* The taking of narcotics in medleys and mixes: *an increase in the garbage habit, where people mix a variety of drugs to achieve a high*—New York Times

garbage head *n phr* *narcotics* A person who mixes various narcotics: *I'm an old garbage head from way back, taking booze and Quaaludes*

garden 1 *n* = OUTER GARDEN **2** *n* *railroad* A freight yard

gardener 1 *n* *baseball* An outfielder **2** *n* *narcotics* A person who plants narcotics on an airplane for smuggling

garden-variety *adj* Of the usual kind; ordinary; = RUN-OF-THE-MILL

gargle 1 *n* A drink, esp of liquor **2** *v* *truckers* To drain and flush the radiator of a truck

gargle-factory *n* A saloon; bar

garlic-burner *n* *motorcyclists* A motorcycle made in Italy

garter *See* WIN THE PORCELAIN HAIRNET

gas 1 *n* *fr late 1700s* Empty and idle talk; mendacious and exaggerated claims; = BULLSHIT: *Most of what I say is pure gas, my friend* **2** *n* *fr middle 1800s* Talk of any sort, esp conversation: *Let's get together for a good gas* **3** *v*: *I haven't gassed this long for a year*—Sinclair Lewis **4** *n* *fr early 1900s* Gasoline **5** *n* *hoboes* Denatured alcohol or some other substitute for liquor **6** *v* *cool talk* To impress one's hearers very favorably; overcome with admiration: *Bird gassed them*—Metronome

Yearbook/ *She gassed me, she was that good*—P Martin **7** *v* To impress an audience very unfavorably; fail with; =BOMB: *Our show appears to have gassed the critics and the public*
See COOK WITH GAS, RUN OUT OF GAS, STEP ON IT

a **gas** *n phr cool talk fr black* Something very impressive, pleasurable, effective, etc: *Therefore it's a gas for me to be the scribe of this weekly space*—Amsterdam News/ *Cool salt-air breezes came through the open windows...."It's a gas!" she cried*—New Yorker

gasbag **1** *n* An energetic and persevering talker; =WINDBAG **2** *v* To talk energetically and perseveringly: *although we have of course plenty of gasbagging about morality*—Newsweek

gas-guzzler *n* A car, esp a large American model, that uses a great deal of gasoline

◀**gash**¹▶ **1** *n fr 1700s* The vulva: *Plus ball the gash off a real foxy chick?*—Easyriders **2** *n* Women regarded as sex partners: *that St Paul gash*—Richard Bissell/ *all that fine gash, just wasted*—Esquire **3** *n* The sex act; =ASS: *Don't you ever think of anything but gash?*—James T Farrell

gash² *n WW2 Army fr early 1900s British Navy* Extra or unexpected portions, bits of luck, etc; dividends; bonuses [origin unknown; perhaps fr French *gaché* "spoiled," since it occurs in *gash bucket* "garbage bin"]

gas hound *n phr hoboes* A person who drinks denatured alcohol or other substitutes for liquor

gas house *n phr WW2 armed forces* A saloon; bar; beer tavern

gasket *See* BLOW A GASKET

gas man *n phr* A publicist; press agent; =FLACK

gasper *n* A cigarette: *handed Lt Edward Psota a nice, fresh marijuana gasper*—A Smith

gassed **1** *adj* Drunk: *I begged them not to get gassed or start any fights*—Bing Crosby **2** *adj* Overcome with admiration: *After her speech the crowd was gassed*

gasser **1** *n* =GASBAG **2** *n cool talk fr 1930s black* Anything or anyone exceptionally amusing, effective, memorable, etc; =a GAS: *or examine this gasser*—Leo Rosten **3** *n* Anything or anyone exceptionally dull, mediocre, inept, etc; =CORNBALL, BOMB: *We planned a blast, and got a gasser*

gassy *adj fr middle 1800s* Garrulous; loudly self-important and pretentious

gas something up *v phr* To make more interesting, exciting, etc; =JAZZ something UP: *Warner Brothers has been around to gas things up a little*—John McCarten

gat *n fr early 1900s underworld* A pistol: *poking his gat your way*—Saturday Evening Post [probably fr *Gatling gun*]

gate **1** *n fr early 1800s* The money collected from selling tickets to a sporting or other entertainment event **2** *n jazz musicians & jive musicians* A performing engagement; =GIG **3** *n jazz talk & jive talk fr early 1920s* A musician, a musical devotee, or any man; =CAT **4** *n railroad* A switch **5** *v* =GIVE someone THE GATE [musicians' senses fr the

simile *swing like a gate* "play or respond to swing music well and readily," with some influence of '*gator* and *alligator*; or perhaps fr *gatemouth*, a nickname for Louis Armstrong; first musical sense said to have been coined by Louis Armstrong]
See CRASH, GET one's TAIL IN A GATE, GIVE someone THE GATE, SWING LIKE A RUSTY GATE

-gate *combining word* An exposed affair of corruption, venality, etc, of the sort indicated: *Allengate/ Billygate/ Koreagate/ Lancegate* [fr the *Watergate* scandals of the early 1970s]

gate-crasher *n* A person who attends a party, entertainment, etc, without invitation or ticket; uninvited guest

gatemouth *n black* A person who knows and tells everyone else's business; a chronic and active gossip

gator or '**gator** *n black fr 1920s* =ALLIGATOR

gatoring *n* A sort of ballroom divertissement in which the participants writhe about among one another on the floor: *Gatoring is over*—Parade

gat up *v phr outdated underworld* To arm oneself with a pistol

gat-up *n outdated underworld* An armed robbery; holdup

gauge butt *See* GAGE BUTT

gawk *v fr late 1700s* To stare; gape stupidly [fr dialect *gawk, gouk* "fool, idiot," literally "cuckoo"]

gay *homosexuals fr 1930s or earlier* **1** *adj* Homosexual; homoerotic: *gay men and women/ gay attitudes* **2** *adj* Intended for or used by homosexuals: *a gay bar/ gay movies* **3** *n* A male homosexual or a lesbian: *a hideaway for live-together couples and middle-aged gays*—Albert Goldman ● Widely used by heterosexuals in preference to pejorative terms [perhaps by extension fr earlier British *gay* "leading a whore's life"]

gay-bashing **1** *n* The harassment of homosexuals **2** *modifier*: *after his arrest in a gay-bashing case*—Village Voice

gay-cat **1** *n hoboes fr early 1900s* A hobo, esp a novice: *Were not these other tramps mere dubs and "gay-cats"?*—Jack London **2** *n* (also **gey-cat**) A homosexual boy; catamite **3** *n outdated underworld* A novice criminal who acts as lookout, decoy, etc **4** *n jazz talk & cool talk* A jovial, relaxed, and hedonistic man; =DUDE

gay deceivers *See* FALSIES

gay (or **Gay**) **lib** **1** *n* The movement that advocates the rights and protection of homosexual persons: *the presence of Gay Lib and advocates for legalization of abortion*—Commentary/ *Your reporter needs to open his closet a little wider to find out how great gay lib is*—Rolling Stone **2** *modifier*: *gay-lib banners/ a gay lib alliance* [modeled on *women's lib*]

gayola **1** *n* Bribery, blackmail, and extortion paid by homosexuals and homosexual businesses, esp to police: *for blackmail and for shakedowns by real or phony cops, a practice known as "gayola"*—Time/ *Homosexual bars...pay "gayola" to crime syndicates and to law enforcement agencies*—Saturday Review **2** *adj* Homosexual; =GAY: *There have* *to be some fulfilling alternatives to the gayola fun fair*—Village Voice [first sense modeled on *payola*]

gazabo (gə ZAY boh) *n fr early 1800s Southwestern* A man; fellow; =GUY: *The gazabos they put on the jury'll know all about me*—WE Weeks [fr Mexican Spanish *gazapo* "smart fellow"]

gazer *n narcotics* A federal narcotics agent; =NARC *See* SHADOW GAZER

gazonga *n* The buttocks; =ASS: *I don't get these women to sweat their gazongas off*—Village Voice

gazoo or **gazool** *See* KAZOO

gazooney or **gazoonie** **1** *n early 1900s* A catamite; =PUNK **2** *n hoboes* A young and callow tramp **3** *n merchant marine* An ignorant man **4** *n circus* An animal-trainer's assistant [said to be a variant of *gunsel*; see *gunsel*[1]]

GB or **gb** (pronounced as separate letters) *n* =GOOFBALL

gd or **g-d** (pronounced as separate letters) *adj* Goddamned: *The biggest gd engine in the West*—Stephen Longstreet

gear *adj esp 1960s teenagers fr 1950s British* Excellent; wonderful; superb: *The opposite of "gear" is "grotty"*—Village Voice [fr the equipment and costume, the *gear*, used and preferred as a sort of uniform of the cognoscenti; see the WW1 British Army phrase *that's the gear* "that's right"] *See* IN HIGH GEAR, SHIFT INTO HIGH GEAR

gear oneself or **gear** oneself **up** *v phr* To ready oneself psychologically; =PSYCH oneself: *I'm gearing myself for the big chance*

gearbox or **gearhead** *n* A stupid person; idiot; =DIMWIT: *only gearboxes greet strangers*—Toronto Life/ *translating that into monosyllables for you gearheads*—Car and Driver

geared or **geared up** **1** *adj* or *adj phr* Drunk **2** *adj* or *adj phr* Excited; ecstatic; =HIGH: *a sexy rock star, and he got the audience so geared*—Rolling Stone [probably fr the notion of the higher, faster *gears* of a car; but *gear* "any narcotics, esp marijuana" occurs in 1940s British slang]

gear-jammer *n truckers* A truck or bus driver

gear up *v phr* To prepare; equip oneself: *seem ready to gear up realistically for the very tough political fight ahead*—New York Daily News/ *Geriatric Gearing Up*—New York Daily News

gedunk (gee DUNK) *n WW2 Navy* Ice cream, pudding, and the like

gee[1] (JEE) **1** *n esp 1930s* A fellow; man; =GUY: *He was the mayor, and he was one smart gee*—James T Farrell **2** *n underworld* The leader of a gang in prison; an influential inmate; =the MAN [abbreviation of *guy*] *See* FRONT GEE, HIP GEE, WRONG GEE

gee[2] (JEE) *n hoboes* A gallon of liquor [abbreviation of *gallon*]

gee[3] (JEE) **1** *n* A thousand dollars; =GRAND **2** *n* Money [abbreviation of *grand*]

gee[4] (JEE) *interj* An exclamation of surprise, pleasure, sheepishness, etc; =GEE WHIZ [a euphemism for *Jesus*] *See* HOLY CATS

gee[5] *adj teenagers* Disgusting; rebarbative; =GROSS [abbreviation of *gross*]

gee[6] *n underworld* A pistol; =GAT [abbreviation of *gun* or *gat*]

◀**geechee** or **geechie**▶ (GEE chee) **1** *n esp black* A black person, esp a Southern rural black: *obsessed with hatred for the "geechees," those he feels are holding back the race*—Washington Post **2** *n* The dialect, culture, etc, of Southern rural or seacoast blacks **3** *n* A low-country South Carolinian, esp one from the Charleston area [origin uncertain or mixed; perhaps fr the *Ogeechee River* in northern Georgia or another place name and ultimately fr a Native American language; perhaps fr *geejee* "the Gullah dialect or a speaker of that dialect," and ultimately fr the name of a language and tribe in the Kissy region of Liberia]

◀**geechie**▶ (GEE chee) *n WW2 armed forces* A woman of the South Pacific region, esp of the islands occupied by US forces in World War 2 [fr *geisha girl*, perhaps influenced by *geechee*]

geed (or **g'd**) **up**[1] (JEED) **1** *adj phr* Crippled **2** *adj phr hoboes* Battered and bent [perhaps from *gimp* "limp"]

geed (or **g'd**) **up**[2] (JEED) *adj phr narcotics* Intoxicated with narcotics, esp stimulants [perhaps fr *geared up*]

geedus or **geetis** or **geetus** (GEE təs) *n fr 1930s fr underworld & hawkers* Money: *Pitchman must give the store a 40% cut on the "geedus"*—M Zolotow

gee-gee (JEE jee) *n horse-racing fr middle 1800s British* A horse, esp a mediocre race horse: *I like to follow the gee-gees*—J Evans/ *You can go to bet the gee-gees at Hialeah or Gulfstream*—Washingtonian [fr the turning command *gee* given to a horse]

geek **1** *n carnival & circus* A sideshow freak, esp one who does revolting things like biting the heads off of live chickens **2** *n 1920s carnival & circus* A snake charmer **3** *n* A pervert or degenerate, esp one who will do disgusting things to slake deviant appetites; =CREEP, WEIRDO: *When the campus paper called the Prez a geek, he went to this dictionary, then went bananas* **4** *n* A drunkard; =LUSH [origin unknown; perhaps related to British dialect *geck, geke* "fool"]

geep *n dock workers* A sailor who leaves his ship to work as a dock worker

geepo *n underworld* An informer; =STOOL PIGEON: *In the underworld most of them are geepos*—M Lipsius

gee string or **G-string** *n phr* or *n fr middle 1800s* A breech-cloth, or brief covering for the genitals, worn esp by striptease dancers: *Thus the G-string became an integral part of a stripper's apparatus*—Toronto Life [origin unknown]

geets (GEETS) *n beat & cool talk* Money; =GEEDUS [said to be a comic mispronunciation: "Money *geets* you things"]

gee whiz[1] or **gee willikers** **1** *interj* (also **Gee whiz**) An exclamation of approval, surprise, mild disapproval, emphasis, etc; =GOSH: *But gee willikers, he does arithmetic like lightning*—Washington

Post **2** *adj* Enthusiastic; very much impressed; youthfully optimistic: *With a very gee-whiz kid, you're not talking about a very long period*—Philadelphia Journal/ *Finch's willed naiveté frequently leads to gee-whiz insights*—Village Voice [a euphemism for *Jesus*]

gee whiz[2] *n phr underworld* An armed pickpocket [fr *gee* "gun" and *whiz* "pickpocket"]

geez or **geeze** (GEEZ) *v narcotics* To have or give a dose of narcotics, esp an injection: *They drop acid, go up on DMT and "geeze" (mainline) meth*—Newsweek/ *I need to geez now, Bumper. Real bad*—Joseph Wambaugh/ *I geezed that scum*—Newark Star Ledger

geezed or **geezed up** **1** *adj* or *adj phr* Drunk **2** *adj* or *adj phr narcotics* Intoxicated with narcotics; = GEED UP, HIGH

geezer[1] *n fr late 1800s* A man; fellow; = DUFFER, GUY: *It gave him all kinds of confidence just to hear the big geezer spout*—J Lilienthal/ *He is a tall geezer with chin whiskers*—H Allen Smith [fr earlier and dialect *giser* "mummer, one who puts on a guise or mask," hence, a quaint figure]

geezer[2] **1** *n* A drink of liquor; = SNORT **2** *n narcotics* A dose or injection of a narcotic

geezo *n prison* An inmate, esp an experienced one [probably fr *geezer*[1]]

gel *v* To come to a firm and useful form; = WORK: *In this highly partisan county, it just didn't gel*—Chicago Tribune/ *If this doesn't gel, the local people...will be stuck*—Philadelphia Journal

gelt (GELT) *n fr late 1600s* Money: *To let you guys get away with the gelt?*—WE Weeks [fr German and Yiddish]

general **1** *n* Anyone in chief authority: *Better ask the general if I can go* **2** *n railroad* A yardmaster *See* ARMCHAIR GENERAL, BUCK GENERAL

gent (JENT) *n* A man; fellow; = GUY: *A hefty, tough-talking gent of not quite 50*—P Edson

gentleman's C *n phr* A satisfactory rating, but not a high one: *The Sierra Club gives Ruckelshaus only a "gentleman's C"*—Time [fr the passing but mediocre grade traditionally given in college to well-bred but not serious students]

the **gentleman will take a chance** *sentence lunch counter* The man has ordered hash

the **gents** *n phr* The men's toilet

geometry *See* HARDER THAN CHINESE ARITHMETIC

george *v black* To invite to sexual activity; = PROPOSITION: *One of the girls georged him, just for kicks*—C Cooper

George **1** *interj* = BY GEORGE **2** *adj* (also **george**) *outdated bop talk & teenagers* Excellent; great; superb: *Dinner tonight was just George* **3** *n aviators* The automatic pilot of an aircraft **4** *n 1950s rock and roll* A theater usher [aviation sense fr *let George do it*]
See BIG GEORGE, LET GEORGE DO IT, the REAL GEORGE, SHORTY GEORGE

◁**German goiter**▷ *n phr* A protuberant paunch; = BEER BELLY

get **1** *v fr early 1900s* To seize mentally; grasp; understand: *Do you get me?*—Zora Neale Hurston

2 *v* To take note of; pay attention to: *Get him, acting like such a big shot* **3** *v* To have vengeance on someone; retaliate destructively against: *He can't say that. I'll get him* **4** *n* Offspring; progeny **5** *n show business* = GATE, TAKE **6** *n outdated underworld* The route taken by criminals in fleeing the scene of their efforts: *The get, or getaway route*—E DeBaun

get one's **1** *v phr* To get the punishment one deserves: *Don't worry, he'll get his before this is all over* **2** *v phr* To become rich; get one's large share of worldly goods: *She went into this business determined to get hers by the time she was thirty*

get a bag on *See* TIE A BAG ON

get a bang (or **charge**) **out of** someone or something *v phr* To enjoy especially; get a thrill out of: *The younger set is not "getting a bang" out of things anymore*—New York Times

get (or **draw**) **a bead on** something or someone *v phr* To take very careful aim at something or someone; concentrate successfully; = ZERO IN: *She has, however, got a bead on her five original characters*—Washington Post

get a broom up one's **ass** *See* HAVE A BROOM UP one's ASS

get (or **have**) **a can on** *v phr esp 1920s* To get drunk: *A gal used to throw herself out the window every time she got a can on*—Dorothy Parker

get a clue *v phr teenagers* To understand; grasp

get something **across** (or **over**) *v phr* To explain successfully; = PUT something ACROSS: *He decided to devote all his energy to getting his own platform across*—Howard Fats

get a crush on someone *See* HAVE A CRUSH ON someone

get (or **have**) **a free ride** *v phr* To enjoy something without paying; get something gratis

get a handle on something *v phr* To find a way of coping; discover how to proceed: *Sometimes I think I haven't got a handle on things anymore*—Armistead Maupin/ *"I haven't got a handle on it," Mr Barry said*—New York Times

get (or **take**) **a hinge at** *v phr esp 1930s* To look at; glance at: *I only write you letters instead of getting a hinge at yr...kisser*—John O'Hara/ *a fast hinge at the sodden courtyard*—R Starnes [perhaps fr the action of turning the head, as if on a *hinge*]

get a hump on *v phr fr late 1800s* To speed up; hurry; = GET A MOVE ON: *Get a hump on with that assignment, OK?*

get a hustle on *See* GET A MOVE ON

get a kick out of someone or something *v phr* To enjoy immensely; take great pleasure in: *I sure get a kick...out of the way you guys kid each other along*—Joseph Heller/ *I get a kick out of you*—Cole Porter (from a song lyric)

get (or **have**) **a little on the side** *v phr* To be sexually unfaithful; = CHEAT

get a load of *v phr* To examine; attend to; = GET: *Let him get a load of the new suit of clothes*—James M Cain

get along (or **on**) **1** *v phr* To live without any great joy nor grief; pass through life more or less adequately; cope; =GET BY **2** *v phr* To be compatible; associate easily: *He didn't get along with the boss* **3** *v phr* To grow old; age

get a move on *v phr* (Variations: **hump** or **hustle** or **wiggle** may replace **move**) *fr early 1900s* To hurry; speed up; =GET GOING: *Tell him to damn well get a wiggle on*—Laurence Stallings & Maxwell Anderson

get an offer one **can't refuse** *See* MAKE AN OFFER one CAN'T REFUSE

get a rise out of someone *v phr fr early 1800s British* To get a response from someone, esp a warm or angry one: *His limp joke got a rise and some projectiles out of the crowd* [fr the *rising* of a fish to the bait in fly-fishing]

◁**get** (or **have**) one's **ashes hauled**▷ *v phr* To do the sex act: *that spider climbin' up that wall, goin' up there to get her ashes hauled*—Jelly Roll Morton [*ashes* may be a euphemism for *ass*]

◁**get** one's **ass in a sling**▷ *See* HAVE one's ASS IN A SLING

◁**get** one's **ass in gear**▷ *v phr* To get into action; stop loafing and wasting time: *If we get our ass in gear we'll win this thing*

get (or **have**) **a toehold** *v phr* To get or have a precarious grip on something; get or have an uncertain command: *You've got a good toehold on the job, now let's see you take over* [fr the sort of unsure footing one has when only the *toes* are planted and the precarious seizure one has made when only the *toe* of the quarry is in one's grip]

getaway **1** *n fr early 1900s* The act of fleeing, esp from the scene of a crime; =COP AND HEEL: *How about a quiet getaway from this mad scene?* **2** *modifier:* *our getaway car/ getaway route/ getaway vacation package*

See MAKE one's GETAWAY

getaway day *n phr horse-racing* The last day of a race meeting

get away with something **1** *v phr* (also **get by with** something) To go uncaught and unpunished after doing something illegal or indiscreet: *I didn't get away with hassling the committee* **2** *v phr* To steal or run off with something: *He came for a friendly visit and got away with my stereo*

get away with murder *v phr* To go unpunished or unharmed after some risk or impudence: *He lets her get away with murder/ bitter complaints that Reagan was getting away with murder in the press*—Washingtonian

get one's or someone's **back up** *v phr* To become angry or make someone angry, esp in a way to cause one to resist: *When they said he was lying, that got his back up*

◁not **get** one's **balls in an uproar**▷ *See* NOT GET one's BALLS IN AN UPROAR

get one's **banana peeled** *See* HAVE one's BANANA PEELED

get behind **1** *v phr narcotics* To have a pleasurable narcotic intoxication **2** *v phr* To enjoy something: *I can't get behind this, I keep trying to tell you*—Cyra McFadden

get behind something or someone *v phr* To support or advocate a person, cause, etc; =PUSH: *If we all get behind the amendment it'll pass*

get by **1** *v phr* To do just acceptably well; neither succeed nor fail, but survive; =MAKE OUT: *We were barely getting by on two salaries* **2** *v phr* To barely escape failure; scrape by **3** *v phr* To pass inspection; stand up to scrutiny: *His work didn't get by the manager* **4** *v phr* To pass something very closely: *I barely got by that truck*

get someone **by the short hairs** (or **curlies** or **knickers**) *See* HAVE someone BY THE SHORT HAIRS

get by with something *See* GET AWAY WITH something

get (or **have**) one's **card punched** *v phr* To have one's credentials, merit, etc, verified: *I'm not here to get my civil-rights card punched*—Walter Mondale [fr the periodic punching of one's *union card* to show that one has paid one's dues]

get one's **cheese** *v phr* To attain one's goal; be rewarded

get cold feet *See* HAVE COLD FEET

get one's **cookies** (or **jollies** or **kicks**) *v phr* To enjoy one's keenest pleasure; indulge oneself; =GET OFF ● Usually with a hint of perversion: *The owner...gets his jollies by walking around...in a Sioux war bonnet*—D Welch/ *This how you get your cookies?*—George V Higgins

get cracking (or **cutting**) *fr 1920s British RAF* **1** *v phr* To commence: *Let's get cracking with this unloading* **2** *v phr* To go or work faster: *and if we don't get cracking, get serious, and get leadership*—Washingtonian

get one's **dander** (or **Irish**) **up** **1** *v phr* To cause anger; infuriate; =PISS-OFF: *That law gets my dander up* **2** *v phr* To become angry; =BLOW one's TOP: *The lewd gesture got Luciano's Irish up/ They got their dander up and decided to fight the case in court*—Washington Post

get down **1** *v phr gambling* To stake one's money or chips; bet: *All right, get down on this card*—A Lomax **2** *v phr fr black musicians* To make an effort; get serious; attend to the task: *so I get down now and then to try to block a couple of shots*—Village Voice/ *She's gonna get down. She just plans for it*—Cameron Crowe **3** *v phr fr black* To let oneself be natural and unrestrained: *to really get down and relate*—Cyra McFadden/ *It's really egalitarian that you can come here and just get down with regular people*—CoEvolution Quarterly **4** *modifier:* *a get down player for those who enjoy that thumping sound*—Downbeat **5** *v phr teenagers* To enjoy oneself; have fun **6** *v narcotics* To use a narcotic, esp heroin [perhaps fr *get down to it* "begin to work seriously"; perhaps from an unattested *get down and dirty; see down*]

get someone **down** *v phr* To depress or annoy; =MIFF: *That constant whine gets me down*

get down on someone **1** *v phr* To show strong disapproval or lack of trust; rebuke; upbraid: *Mama used to get down on me about hanging out with Reno*—Claude Brown **2** *v phr* To nag

See GO DOWN ON someone

get down to brass tacks *See* DOWN TO BRASS TACKS

get down to cases *v phr fr 1930s* To talk seriously; = TALK TURKEY

get (or **have**) one's **ducks in a row** *See* HAVE one's DUCKS IN A ROW

get even *v phr* To take revenge; = EVEN THE SCORE: *His motto was "Don't get mad, get even"*

get one's **feet wet** *v phr* To initiate oneself or be initiated into something; have a first and testing experience of something: *Try one or two, just to get your feet wet* [fr the image of a person who goes into the water very carefully rather than plunging in]

get one's **gage up 1** *v phr* = GET one's DANDER UP **2** *v phr* To become drunk [probably from the condition shown by a rising pressure *gauge* on a steam boiler, influenced by *gaged* "drunk"]

get someone's **goat** (or **nanny**) *v phr fr early 1900s* To annoy: *His bitching gets my goat sometimes* [perhaps fr depriving a racehorse of its goat mascot; perhaps fr French *prendre sa chèvre* "take one's source of milk or nourishment"]

get going 1 *v phr* To leave; depart **2** *v phr* To begin a job or assignment **3** *v phr* To stop loafing, idling, etc; = GET CRACKING: *When the going gets tough, the tough get going*

◁**get** one's **head out of** one's **ass**▷ *v phr* To start paying attention; become aware and active; = GET ON THE BALL: *Make the system work. Get your head out of your Hollywood ass*—Pulpsmith

get one's **hooks into** *v phr* To get possession of, esp in a predatory way; get hold of: *If they get their hooks into you, you're a goner*

◁**get in** or **get it in**▷ *v phr* To succeed in penetrating someone sexually

get in someone's **face** *v phr* To be in someone's presence, esp in a provocative way: *Don't you get in my face no more...I'll kill you*—Donald Goines

get in someone's **hair** *v phr* To annoy someone; nag at someone: *That squeaky voice gets in my hair*

get one's **Irish up** *See* GET one's DANDER UP

get it in the neck *v phr fr late 1800s* To be severely punished or injured: *The poor wimp got it in the neck again* [probably an allusion to hanging]

◁**get it off**▷ **1** *v phr* To have an orgasm; ejaculate semen; = COME OFF **2** *v phr* To do the sex act **3** *v phr* To masturbate

get it on ◁**1**▷ *v phr* To become sexually excited; get an erection ◁**2**▷ *v phr* To do the sex act; = GET IT OFF: *I couldn't believe that the whole time he was getting it on with Joe's wife* **3** *v phr* (also **get it off**) To enjoy something greatly; have a good time; = JAM: *three, five, fifteen guys in a studio just get it off*—Ringo Starr/ *And they overlay their daring with pure joy. They're getting it on*—Sports Illustrated

get it together (or **all together**) *v phr* (Variations: **one's act** or **one's head** or **one's shit** or **one's stuff** may replace **it**) *fr 1960s counterculture fr black* To arrange one's life or affairs properly; integrate and focus oneself: *Get your shit together, said Junior Jones*—John Irving/ *why the executive*

departments of government don't get their act together—Lewis Powell/ *Congress has to get its shit together*—WT Tyler

◁**get it up**▷ *v phr* To achieve and retain an erection: *I couldn't get it up in the State of Israel*—Philip Roth/ *He was so bashful he could not get it up*—Xaviera Hollander

get one's **jollies** or **kicks** *See* GET one's COOKIES

get lost 1 *v phr* To leave; depart; = SCRAM
● Usually an exasperated command: *I offered him five bucks and he told me loudly to get lost* **2** *interj* An exclamation of severe and abrupt rejection; = DROP DEAD

get one's **lumps** *v phr* To be severely beaten, punished, rebuked, etc: *Their greatest fun is to see a cop getting his lumps*—H Lee

get mileage out of something *v phr* To gain advantage or profit; exploit: *All of us down here can start getting mileage out of that one right away*—Joseph Heller

get naked *v phr* To have a good time; really enjoy oneself; = JAM

get next to oneself or **get next** *v phr* To realize that one has been stupid, duped, tedious, etc; = WISE UP: *She took me for a hundred before I got next*—Jim Tully

get next to someone *v phr* To become familiar with someone, esp in view of sexual favors: *I'm telling you you were liable to get next to that broad*—A Lomax

get nowhere fast *v phr* To make no progress whatever; be stuck: *He was getting nowhere fast and was more depressed*—Charles Beardsley

◁**get** one's **nuts**▷ *v phr* (Variations: **cracked** or **off** may be added) To have an orgasm; ejaculate semen: *He'd get his nuts just looking at her/ When I'd gotten my nuts off about six times, we got hungry*—Claude Brown

get off 1 *v phr narcotics* To get relief and pleasure from a dose of narcotics: *How we s'posed to get off with no water to mix the stuff with?*—Philadelphia Bulletin ◁**2**▷ *v phr* To do the sex act; have an orgasm; = GET IT OFF: *It is led by trendy bisexual types, who love to get off amidst the chic accouterments of a big smack-and-coke party*—Albert Goldman **3** *v phr musicians* To play an improvised solo **4** *v phr* To avoid the consequences of; = GET AWAY WITH something: *He thinks he can get off with charging $150 for this junk*
See TELL someone WHERE TO GET OFF

get someone **off** ◁**1**▷ *v phr* To bring someone to sexual climax: *She was really eager and it didn't take long to get her off* **2** *v phr* To please greatly; move and excite: *Ron sings so fast because it gets us off*—Village Voice/ *I've got to write stuff...that will get people off*—Aquarian

get off one's **ass** *v phr* (Variations: **butt** or **dead ass** or **duff** may replace **ass**) To stop being lazy and inert; = GET CRACKING: *He wasn't able to get his class off their dead ass*

get off someone's **back** (or **neck**) *v phr* To leave alone; stop nagging or annoying: *All they need is for Government to get off their backs*—Time

get off someone's **case** *v phr fr black* To leave alone; =GET OFF someone's BACK: *I hope you will...tell your mother to get off your case*—Ann Landers/ *Get off my case, O.K., Dad?*—New Yorker

get off one's **high horse** *v phr* To stop being haughty and superior; deal informally; =COME OFF one's PERCH

get off on *v phr* To enjoy greatly; like very much: *They're getting off on wordsmithing*—Saturday Review/ *She really got off on Eddings*—Cyra McFadden
　　See TELL someone WHERE TO GET OFF

get off the block *v phr* To start, esp to start quickly: *My game plan was to get off the block first and stay out there*—Toronto Life [fr the *starting blocks* used by runners for initial impetus]

get off the dime *v phr* To start; stop wasting time: *How do we get off the dime we're on?*—New York Times/ *with word from the Mayor to get off the dime*—Philadelphia Journal [alteration of the expression *stop on a dime*, used to praise the brakes of a car]

get off the ground *v phr* To succeed, esp to do so initially: *projects misfired or didn't get off the ground at all*—Saturday Review/ *CBS Early Morning News, which didn't get off the ground until late*

get something **off the ground** *v phr* To make a successful start: *As Wilbur said to Orville, "You'll never get it off the ground"*

get someone **off the hook** *v phr* To aid someone in evading or preventing punishment, responsibility, etc: *He falls for Ilona...and winds up trying to get her off the hook*—J Kelly

get on *See* GET ALONG

get on one's **bicycle** *v phr prizefight fr 1920s* To keep retreating from one's opponent in the boxing ring; fight defensively

get on someone's **case** *v phr fr black* To meddle in someone's affairs; pay unwanted, annoying attention to someone; criticize; =BUG, HASSLE: *There are times when I get on his case pretty hard*—Sports Illustrated [fr early 1900s black expression *sit on [someone's] case* "make a quasi-judicial study and judgment"]

get on one's **high horse** *v phr fr early 1700s British* To become dignified and formal; assume a haughty and arrogant mien: *As soon as I said a little slang to her she got on her high horse*

get on one's **horse** *v phr* To hurry; start at once: *You better get on your horse if you're going to make that plane*

get on someone's **nerves** *v phr fr late 1800s British* To be an irritant; annoy: *This word processor's humming gets on my nerves*

get on the ball *v phr* To pay closer attention to doing something right; improve one's performance ● Often an exasperated command [fr baseball or other ball sports]

get on the bandwagon *v phr* (Variations: **climb** or **hop** or **leap** or **jump** may replace **get**) To join a person, party, cause, etc, esp one that is currently popular

get on the stick *v phr* To get actively to work; stop loafing; =GET one's ASS IN GEAR

get out *interj* An exclamation of disbelief; =GO ON: *Oh, get out, you can't mean that!*
　　See ALL GET OUT

get out from under *v phr* To extricate oneself from troubles, esp financial troubles

get out of one's **face** *v phr* To stop annoying or importuning; leave alone: *Why don't you get out of my face?*—TJ Hooker (TV program)

get out of someone's **face** *v phr* To leave alone; stop annoying; = GET OFF someone's CASE: *He turned to the cop and told her to get out of his face*

get outside of *v phr fr late 1800s* To eat or drink heartily: *as he got outside of a bowl of chili*—AJ Liebling

get out with one's **eyeteeth** *v phr* To escape relatively unharmed; extricate oneself: *I was lucky to get out with my eyeteeth, seeing those prices!*

get over 1 *v phr* To recover or rebound from something; be restored to the previous norm: *She was in love with him for a few months, but finally got over him/ We couldn't get over how well he managed all that/ It took me weeks to get over that head cold* **2** *v phr* To succeed; make a favorable impression: *He did everything he could think of, but still couldn't get over her* **3** *v phr Army* To evade duty; =FUCK OFF, GOLDBRICK [Army sense perhaps fr *get over someone*]

◁**get over** someone▷ *v phr* To do the sex act with someone

get something **over with** *v phr* To finish or end something; come to the stopping point: *It was a very tough job, but we had to get it over with*

get physical *v phr* To use the body and body contact, esp roughly or amorously: *The type who might want to get physical early in a relationship, like during the first five minutes*—New York Times

get psyched *v phr teenagers* To get excited; become enthusiastic

get religion *v phr* To be chastened; learn proper behavior, at last; become a convert: *It appears that Mr. Reagan has got religion on the subject of environmentalism*—National Public Radio

◁**get** one's **rocks** (or one's **rocks off**)▷ **1** *v phr* To have an orgasm; =GET one's NUTS: *Go out, have a few drinks, and if you're lucky, maybe even get your rocks off*—Advocate/ *people who'd never be caught dead at a 42d Street skinflick to get their rocks off and feel intellectual about it*—E McCormack **2** *v phr* To enjoy very much; =GET one's COOKIES: *while everyone else was getting...their rocks off at the Muse concerts*—Village Voice/ *I think she gets her rocks off turning squid inside out*—John Irving

◁**get** one's **shit together**▷ *v phr* To organize and manage one's affairs and life properly; =HAVE one's DUCKS IN A ROW

get sidetracked *v phr* To be diverted from one's goal or proper aim; lose concentration

get smart *v phr* To become wisely aware of one's situation, the possibilities, etc: =WISE UP: *Tell him if he doesn't get smart he'll get clobbered*

get stuffed *interj* = FUCK YOU ● Chiefly British

get one's **tail in a gate** ◁(or **tit in a wringer**)▷
v phr To get into a perilous plight; be in a painful
situation: *With the whole bunch against it you got
your tail in a gate/ Katie Graham's gonna get her tit
caught in a big fat wringer if that's published*—John
Mitchell

get taken off at the knees *v phr* To be severely
injured; be destroyed: *That guy is just waiting to get
taken off at the knees*—Peter Gent

getter *See* GO-GETTER

get the air *v phr* To be dismissed, esp to be jilted:
When she found out, he got the air

get the ax *v phr* To be dismissed, discharged,
expelled, etc: *Three more VPs got the ax this morning*

get the boot *v phr* To be discharged or dismissed:
He got the boot from his job and his girl both

get the business *v phr* To be treated roughly; be
punished or rebuked: *When they found out his record he got the business*

get the (or one's) **drift** *v phr* To understand, esp
what one is hinting at ● Often a question asked
with or as if with a wink: *And it won't show up. Get
my drift?*

get the drop on someone *v phr* To get someone
in an inferior or threatened position; seize the
advantage: *I got the drop on him with that question
about oil*

get the eye *v phr* To be looked at in an insinuating, seductive way

get the goods on someone *v phr* To find or collect decisive evidence against: *The cops got the
goods on him and he had to go to jail*

get the hang of something *v phr fr middle 1800s*
To master the particular skill needed: *He couldn't
get the hang of the new machines*

get the hook *v phr fr show business* To be dismissed, silenced, or rejected, esp suddenly: *Just
when he thought he was doing so well, he got the
hook* [fr the notion that a wretched performer, esp
at an amateur night, was pulled forcibly off the stage
with a *hook*]

get the hungries *v phr* To become hungry: *I get
the hungries for some breakfast*—TV ad

get the jump on someone or something *v phr*
To get the lead, or an advantage, esp by alert early
moves: *She got the jump on the other runners by
perfect maneuvering at the start/ Never let the
other guy get the jump on you*—Village Voice

get the last dance *v phr* To be the winner in the
end; triumph finally: *But Dorsey got the last dance,
telling jurors Mary had "died a noble death"*
—Washington Post [fr the awarding by the belle of
the *last dance* at the ball to the favored suitor]

get the lead out *v phr* (Variations: **of** one's **ass**
or **of** one's **pants** or **of** one's **feet** may be added)
To stop loafing; = GET one's ASS IN GEAR, HUSTLE
● Often an irritated command: *Get the lead out and
start writing*

get the monkey off (or **off** one's **back**) *v phr*
narcotics To break a narcotics habit: *so hooked on*

morphine that there would be no getting the monkey off without another's help*—Nelson Algren

get the munchies *See* HAVE THE MUNCHIES

get the nod *v phr* To be approved; be chosen:
*There were a dozen other bids...but McCulloch got
the nod*—Saturday Review

get the picture 1 *v phr* To understand; = COP-
PISH, DIG ● Often a question: *After I told him about
six times he got the picture/ Well, you won't ever be
promoted here. Get the picture?* **2** *v phr* To
mentally grasp something injurious or repellent to
oneself; = GET WISE: *After she caught him with that
whore she got the picture*

get the pink slip *v phr* To be dismissed or discharged: *When they discovered the shortage of
funds he got the pink slip*

◁**get** (or **have**) **the red ass**▷ *v phr* To become
irritated and angry; be irritable: *If any of us gets the
red ass about something, then we ought to talk it
over*—Dan Jenkins/ *An angry man has the red ass
or the RA*—Jim Bouton

get there from here *See* YOU CAN'T GET THERE
FROM HERE

get the shaft *v phr* To be ill-treated; be abused,
esp by cruel deception: *He thought he'd get promoted, but he got the shaft instead* [a euphemism
for sodomization]

get to someone **1** *v phr* To disturb or anger
someone; = BUG, HASSLE: *It's impossible to "get to"
Oliver Barrett III*—Erich Segal/ *I think it is starting to
get to me*—Eliot Fremont-Smith **2** *v phr* To
affect; make an impression: *The puppy really got to
me; I couldn't send him to the shelter*

get to first base 1 *v phr* To begin well; take a
successful first step ● Usually in the negative: *I
couldn't get to first base with the committee* **2** *v
phr* To initiate sexual activity successfully, esp by
hugging, caressing, kissing, etc ● In the same baseball analogy, **get to third base** means touching
and toying with the genitals, and **get to home
plate** means to do the sex act, that is, "score"

get-together *n* A meeting or session, often social;
party

get under someone's **skin** *v phr* To trouble or
irritate; annoy; = BUG: *That cackle of his soon got
under my skin*

get up 1 *v phr outdated underworld* To finish a
prison term **2** *v phr street gang* To establish
one's individual signature, esp with graffiti

get-up 1 *n outdated underworld* The end of a
prison term **2** *n* Dress; costume and grooming:
Why the fancy get-up today?

get someone **up** *v phr* To inspire and energize
someone, esp for a game, examination, or other
ordeal; = PSYCH someone UP: *Steinbrenner thinks he
can get the players up for games*—Inside Sports

get-up-and-go *n* Energy and initiative; pep; = PISS
AND VINEGAR, PIZZAZZ: *My get-up-and-go has got up
and went*

get up someone's **nose** *v phr* To irritate someone; provoke hostility: *Put us together and we'd get
up each other's noses in a minute*—George Warren

get up off something *v phr* Army To relinquish something; make something available: *He was able to convince the supply sergeant to get up off some fuel*

get wise 1 *v phr fr late 1800s* To become aware, esp in matters of survival and advancement; look to one's own interest; = WISE UP ● In the form **get wise with yourself** often an exhortation: *I hope you'll get wise and learn to keep your mouth shut/ If you don't get wise with yourself they'll fire you* ● Often a command or bit of strong advice: *Get wise! Haven't you noticed what he's been up to* **2** *v phr* To become impudent or defiant; be saucy: *Get wise with me, punk, and you're dead*

get with it *v phr* To pay active attention to what is happening or what needs doing; = GET ON THE BALL: *We'll all have to get with it if we want this to turn out right*

get Zs *See* COP ZS

gevalt (gə VAHLT) *interj* An exclamation of woe, distress, shock, etc: *He breaks open a mezuzah, nothing inside, gevalt! but a piece of paper that says "Made in Japan"*—R Alter [fr Yiddish, "powers," hence an invocation of a higher force]

gey-cat *See* GAY-CAT

◁**ghetto box**▶ *n phr* (Variations: **boogie box** or **box** or **coon box** or **ghetto blaster**) A large portable stereo radio and cassette player often carried and played loudly in public places: *Hey, man, don't mess with my box*—Wall Street Journal/ *that guy in the streets with his ghetto blaster*—Village Voice

ghost 1 *n fr late 1800s British* A writer paid for a book or article published under someone else's name; professional anonymous author **2** *v: I "ghosted" my wife's cookbook*—P Darrow **3** *n theater fr middle 1800s British* The treasurer of a theatrical company [Theater sense said to be fr a line in *Hamlet*: "The *ghost* walks" implying that pay is at hand; analogous with "the eagle shits" referring to the source of pay]

◁**ghost turds**▶ *n phr Army* = HOUSE MOSS

GI (pronounced as separate letters) **1** *adj fr WW1 armed forces* Of, in, or from the US armed forces, esp the Army; government issue: *GI shoes/ His officious ways are very GI* **2** *n* A member of the US armed forces, esp an enlisted Army soldier serving since or during World War 2: *The GIs fought furiously to hold Taejon*—Associated Press **3** *v WW2 Army* To scrub and make trim: *They Gled the barracks every Friday night*
See GI PARTY, the GIS

GIB (pronounced as separate letters) *adj* Sexually proficient [fr *good in bed*]

GI can *n phr Army fr early 1900s* A large refuse or garbage can [abbreviation of *galvanized iron*]

gidget 1 *n* = GADGET **2** *n* A lithe and pert young woman

gift *See* GOD'S GIFT

gift of gab (or **the gab**) *n phr fr 1700s British* The ability to talk interestingly, colorfully, and/or persuasively

gig¹ 1 *n jazz musicians* A party for jazz musicians and devotees; = JAM SESSION: *Kid Ory had some of the finest gigs, especially for the rich white folks* —Louis Armstrong **2** *n musicians fr 1930s* A playing date or engagement, esp a one-night job: *on a gig, or one night stand*—Louis Armstrong/ *We found some musicians and I was able to finish the gig*—Whitney Balliett **3** *v: Gave him a clarinet to gig on*—Metronome Year Book/ *I forget whether we're gigging in Basin Street or Buenos Aires* —Dizzy Gillespie **4** *n* Any job or occupation: *it's better to take some kind of main gig for their sake* —New York **5** *n* A criminal act; swindle; = SCAM: *It ain't no gig, lady, and I don't really care what you think*—Sports Illustrated/ *On my first solo gig I was bagged...beaten shitless, and dumped in jail*—Bernard Malamud **6** *n armed forces* A demerit; report of deficiency or breach of rules [origin unknown; musicians' senses are extensions of earlier meanings, "spree, dance, party"]
See LIVING-ROOM GIG

◁**gig²**▶ *n fr late 1600s British* = GIGGY [origin unknown; perhaps fr Irish or Anglo-Irish, as attested by the name *sheila-na-gig* given to carved figures of women with grotesquely enlarged vulvae found in English churches]
See UP YOURS

gig³ *n* An old car [fr *gig* "one-horse carriage"]

◁**giggy**▶ **1** *n* The vulva **2** *n* The anus
See UP YOURS

GIGO or **gigo** (GĪ goh) *sentence computer* The output is no better than the input [fr *garbage in, garbage out*]
See MEGOGIGO

GI Joe *n phr fr WW2* A US soldier, esp an enlisted soldier of and since World War 2; = DOGFACE

gilguy (GILL gī) *n late 1800s merchant marine* = THINGAMAJIG [origin uncertain; used in the mid-19th century to designate a *guy* rope or wire supporting a boom, and often applied to an inefficient *guy*]

gilhickey *n* = THINGAMAJIG

gilhooley 1 *n* = THINGAMAJIG **2** *n car-racing* A skid in which a car ends up facing in the reverse direction

gillion *See* JILLION

gills *See* GREEN AROUND THE GILLS, LIT TO THE GILLS, SOUSED, STEWED

gilly *circus* **1** *n* A small circus traveling in cars **2** *n* A vehicle hired to carry circus or show equipment

Gilroy's kite *See* HIGHER THAN A KITE

gimme or **gimmie 1** *n* An acquisitive tendency: *They got da gimmies...always take, never give* —James M Cain/ *With her it's always gimme, gimme, gimme* **2** *modifier: The extent to which the "gimme" spirit has banished rationality*—New York Times

gimmick 1 *n circus, carnival & hawkers fr early 1900s* A secret device or hidden trick that causes something to work and assures that the customer will not win; = GAFF: *A new gimmick, infra-red contact lenses which...enabled a card player to read markings on the backs of cards*—Billy Rose **2** *n fr 1920s* Any device; = GADGET **3** *n narcotics*

Apparatus used for preparing and injecting narcotics; = WORKS: *A small red cloth bag with his spike needle and "gimmicks" fell out*—New York **4** *n* A feature in a product, plan, presentation, etc, believed to increase appeal although it is not necessarily useful or important: *This promo isn't bad, but we sorely need a gimmick* **5** *v*: *Get a fairly good item, then gimmick the hell out of it* **6** *n* One's selfish and concealed motive; = ANGLE, PERCENTAGE: *This looks fine, Mr Mayor. What's your gimmick, anyhow?* [perhaps fr *gimcrack*]

gimmickery or **gimmickry** *n* The use of gimmicks: *To juxtapose this...is sheer gimmickry*—Time

gimmie hat (or **cap**) *n phr* A peaked cap like a baseball cap, bearing the trademark or name of a manufacturer and distributed as an advertising device: *She made him stop wearing his John Deere gimmie hat in public places*—New Yorker/ *a "macho" gimmie cap emblazoned with "Cat"* (for Caterpillar Tractors)—New York Times [probably fr the request "*gimme one of those!*" often heard when these were available free from dealers]

gimp *fr early 1900s hoboes & underworld* **1** *n* A limp **2** *v*: *The old guy was gimping across the street* ◁**3**▷ *n* A lame person; = CRIP: *He'd just kick a gimp in the good leg and leave him lay*—JK Winkler

gimper *n Air Force* A competent and efficient airman [see early 1900s British Army phrase *gimp up* "dress oneself up smartly," fr British dialect *gimp* "neat"]

gimp stick *n phr* A crutch or cane

gimpy *adj* Having a limp or being lame

gin **1** *n* *black & street gang* A street fight; = RUMBLE **2** *v* To fight; scuffle [perhaps related to earlier *gin up* "make things rough and dangerous; stir around like trapped animals," fr British dialect *gin* "trap," fr *engine*]

See BATHTUB GIN

◁**ginch**▷ *esp motorcyclists* **1** *n* A woman, esp solely as a sexual object; = CHICK: *the fifth ginch I'd had on those eerie sand barrier islands*—Easy Riders/ *cop can't afford that kind of ginch*—George V Higgins **2** *n* The vulva, and sexual activity; = ASS, CUNT: *all the free groupie ginch south of Bakersfield*—George Warren/ *Hagen...prowls the Stampede for ginch ahoof*—Tom Wolfe [origin uncertain; perhaps related to 1950s Australian and British sense, of surfer origin, "elegance, smartness, skill"]

ginchy *adj* Excellent; admirable; elegant; = SEXY: *Annie and I were the cat's pajamas and ginchy beyond belief*—Richard Merkin

ginder *See* CRUMBCRUSHER

◀**ginee**▶ *See* GUINEA

ginger *n fr middle 1800s* Energy; pep; = PIZZAZZ: *the effervescent quality that used to be called "ginger"*—LF McHugh [fr the practice of putting ginger under a horse's tail to increase its mettle and showiness]

gingerbread **1** *n fr 1600s* Money **2** *n* Fussy decoration, esp on a house; frillwork **3** *modifier*: *the gingerbread stacks of the old river steamers*

ginger-peachy *adj outdated teenagers* Excellent; splendid; = NEAT

ginhead *n* A drunkard; = LUSH: *a busted romance that makes her become a ginhead*—Damon Runyon

gink (GINK) *fr early 1900s* **1** *n* A man; fellow; = GUY: *Does a gink in Minsk suffer less from an appendectomy?*—Hal Boyle **2** *n* A tedious, mediocre person; = JERK [origin unknown; perhaps somehow fr Turkish, "catamite, punk," found in early 1800s sources both British and US]

gin mill *n phr* A saloon, barroom; tavern: *There still are some boobs, alas, who'd like the old-time gin-mill back*—Sinclair Lewis/ *In some gin mill where they know the bartender*—New York Times

ginned or **ginned up** *adj* or *adj phr fr late 1800s* Drunk: *Hold me up, kid; I'm ginned*—P Marks

◀**ginnee** or **ginney**▶ *See* GUINEA

◀**ginzo** or **guinzo**▶ **1** *n* An Italian or person of Italian descent: *Gonna have at least eight hot ginzos looking for me*—George V Higgins **2** *adj*: *What ginzo broad didn't?*—Patrick Mann **3** *n* Any apparently foreign person; = HUNKY: *a Roumanian or some kinda guinzo*—Joel Sayre

gip *See* GYP

GI party *n phr fr WW2 Army* A bout of scrubbing and cleaning

girene *See* GYRENE

girl **1** *n homosexuals* A male homosexual **2** *n narcotics* Cocaine: *They call cocaine girl because it gives 'em a sexual jolt when they take a shot*—C Cooper **3** *n* A queen of playing cards

See BACHELOR GIRL, BAR-GIRL, BEST GIRL, B-GIRL, CALL GIRL, CHARITY GIRL, GAL FRIDAY, GLAMOR GIRL, GO-GO GIRL, IDIOT GIRL, OOMPH GIRL, PLAYGIRL, SWEATER GIRL, TOMBOY, V-GIRL, WORKING GIRL

girl Friday *See* GAL FRIDAY

◁**girlie**▷ **1** *n* A girl: *this girlie and her mother*—Sinclair Lewis **2** *adj* Featuring nude or otherwise sexually provocative women: *To some extent, "girlie" magazines are information-getting*—US News & World Report

the GIs or **the GI shits** *n phr WW2 Army* Diarrhea: *An all-night bout with the GIs left him weak and weary*—Time [so called because soldiers often got diarrhea after eating with unclean mess-gear]

gism *See* JISM

gismo *See* GIZMO

git-box or **git-fiddle** *n fr 1920s jazz musicians* A guitar

git-go *See* FROM THE GIT-GO

give *See* SOMETHING'S GOT TO GIVE

give (or **write**) someone **a blank check** *v phr* To give someone leave to do whatever he or she wishes; give carte blanche: *The man gave me a blank check to order whatever I needed*

give someone **a blow** *v phr* To call someone; greet or salute someone

not **give a damn** *See* NOT GIVE A DAMN

◀not **give a fuck**▶ *See* NOT GIVE A DAMN

◀not **give a fuck for nothing**▶ *See* NOT GIVE A FUCK FOR NOTHING

give someone **a grease job** *v phr* To flatter; = BUTTER UP

give someone **a hand 1** *v phr* To help: *Gimme a hand with this huge crate* **2** *v phr* To applaud someone by clapping the hands

give someone **a hard time 1** *v phr* To scold or rebuke; quarrel with: *He was giving her a hard time about drinking too much* **2** *v phr* To make difficulties for someone, esp needless ones; =HASSLE: *I hope you won't give me a hard time this trip*

give someone **a hotfoot 1** *v phr* To do the practical joke of clandestinely sticking a match into the crevice between the heel or sole and upper of the victim's shoe, then lighting the match and watching the pained and startled reaction: *Kids give them hotfoots with kitchen matches*—Joseph Mitchell **2** *v phr* To arouse someone from lethargy; stimulate someone sharply to activity: *The project's stalled and we'd better give Joe a hotfoot*

give someone or something **a miss** (or **the go-by**) *v phr* To avoid; not opt for ● **the go-by** variant is attested from the mid-1600s: *Give these girls a miss*—Pan American Travel Guide/ *become fed up with a slang phrase...and resolve to give it the go-by in future*—J Greig

give someone **a pain** *v phr* (Variations: **in the neck** or **in the ass** may be added) To be distasteful, repellent, tedious, etc: *That guy gives me a swift pain in the ass/ one of those bragging polymath types who gave everybody a pain in the ass*—Saul Bellow

give someone **a ring** *v phr* To call on the telephone

give something **a shot** *v phr* (Variations: **crack** or **go** or **rip** or **ripple** may replace **shot**) To have a try at; make an attempt: *He gave the exam a good shot, but flunked it/ Let's give it a rip. We've nothing to lose*

give someone **a slap on the wrist** *v phr* To give a light and insufficient punishment; =RAP someone's KNUCKLES: *They caught a couple more Mafiosi and I'm sure they'll give them a real good slap on the wrist*

give someone **a tumble** *v phr fr early 1900s* To show a sign of recognition or approval; acknowledge: *The newspaper guys had the Bone Crusher pegged as a plant and wouldn't give him a tumble*—H Witwer/ *Both knew me, but neither gave me a tumble*—Dashiell Hammett [probably fr the earlier *take a tumble to oneself* "examine oneself closely, esp with respect to one's faults," after which *tumble* was taken to mean "scrutiny, acknowledgement"]

giveaway 1 *n* Anything that reveals something concealed; clue: *She talked harsh, but the smile was a giveaway* **2** *n* A gift, prize, etc, esp one given to attract business; =FREEBIE **3** *modifier*: *a giveaway show/ giveaway offer* *See* DEAD GIVEAWAY

give something one's **best shot 1** *v phr* To try one's hardest; do the best one can: *For three months, they had given it their best shot*—Toronto Star **2** *v phr* To do one's very best; make one's finest and utmost effort: *Anyway, I gave it my best shot*—Village Voice/ *A lot of people will be watching you. Give it your best shot*—Pat Conroy **3** *v*

phr To make a maximum effort; =BUST one's ASS: *The whole thing is not easy....But you must give it your best shot*—New York Times

◁**give cone**▷ *v phr teenagers* =GIVE HEAD

give someone **five 1** *v phr* =GIVE someone A HAND **2** *v phr* (Variation: **slap** can replace **give**) *fr black* To shake hands with someone or slap someone's hand in greeting, congratulation, etc; =GIVE someone SOME SKIN: *Reno put out his hand for me to give him five*—Claude Brown

give five fingers to *v phr* To thumb one's nose at: *Then you could give five fingers to every cop*—A Hynd

give someone **grief** *v phr* To make difficulties for someone; harrass; =HASSLE: *Don't let the prof give you any grief about this*

◁**give head** (or **good head**)▷ *v phr* To do fellatio; =SUCK: *Not that Linda has anything against balling customers...but she just loves to give head*—Xaviera Hollander/ *She must give extra good head or something*—Joseph Wambaugh

give someone **heat** *v phr* To criticize; complain; =BITCH: *though she gave me heat about it not being "man's work"*—Erich Segal

give someone **hell** (or **merry hell** or **holy hell**) *v phr* To rebuke or punish severely; =CHEW OUT: *The skipper gave him merry hell for crud and drunkenness*

give (or **read**) someone **his** (or **her**) **rights** *v phr* To inform an arrested person formally of his or her legal rights, esp by reading him or her a "Miranda card" detailing them: *The judge threw it out because they hadn't given the crook his rights* [fr the requirement based on the Supreme Court decision in the Miranda case of 1966]

give someone **his** (or **her**) **walking papers** *v phr* (Variation: **running shoes** or **walking ticket** may replace **walking papers**) To dismiss or discharge; reject: *If he doesn't stop seeing other women she'll give him his walking papers/ When he objected to the new policy they gave him his running shoes*

give it a rest *v phr* To stop; ease up on ● Often a firm command: *OK, give it a rest, huh Joe?*

don't give it a second thought *See* DON'T GIVE IT A SECOND THOUGHT

give it the gun *v phr* To speed up an engine abruptly; accelerate to highest speed; =FLOOR

give it to someone **1** *v phr* To beat, punish, or rebuke: *He really gave it to me yesterday after I totaled his car* ◁**2**▷ *v phr* To do the sex act with or to someone: *one minute he'd be giving it to her in his cousin's Buick*—JD Salinger

give someone **leg** *v phr* To deceive someone; fool someone; =PULL someone's LEG: *Last time I saw you, you're giving me a little leg about there's nothing going on*—George V Higgins

give someone **lip** *v phr* To speak to someone in an impertinent and offensive way: *People get on here all day long and all they do is give me lip*—Washington Post/ *Don't be giving me lip*—James T Farrell

give me five *See* SLIP ME FIVE

give out *v phr* Collapse; cease to function; die: *His old ticker gave out/ The bus gave out halfway up the hill*
See PUT OUT

gives *See* WHAT GIVES

give some skin *v phr* To shake hands; greet; =GIVE someone FIVE: *Everybody gave some skin all around*—Richard Fariña

give someone **some skin** *v phr esp black* To shake or slap hands in salutation

not **give spit** *See* NOT GIVE SPIT

give someone **the air** *v phr* To jilt or reject: *His last girl gave him the air*

give someone **the ax** *v phr* To dismiss or discharge; =CAN, CUT, FIRE: *The school gave six profs the ax yesterday*

give someone **the boot** *v phr* To dismiss or discharge; =GIVE someone THE AX: *The Oval Office should give him what he really deserves: the boot*—Newsweek

give someone **the brush** *v phr* To snub; treat icily and curtly; =KISS OFF: *I got the brush in about two seconds in that fancy dump*

give someone **the business** *v phr* To give someone rough treatment; punish; rebuke: *I really gave him the business when I caught him cheating on my exam*

give something **the chop** *v phr* To eliminate; =CUT: *A vast trade and business complex...was given the chop*—Westworld

give something **the deep six** *v phr fr Navy & merchant marine* To dispose definitively of; jettison; throw overboard: *They gave those files the deep six*

give someone **the double cross** *v phr* To betray or cheat one's own colleagues; act treacherously: *if you feel tempted to give the old gentleman the double cross*—H McHugh

give someone **the eye** **1** *v phr* To look at in an insinuating and seductive way: *I could see he was giving you the eye* **2** *v phr* To signal with a look: *Get up when I give you the eye*

◁**give** someone **the finger**▷ **1** *v phr* To treat unfairly, dishonestly, etc; =SCREW, SHAFT: *Let me show you how to give that guy the finger*—Budd Schulberg **2** *v phr* To show contempt and defiance by holding up the extended middle finger toward someone; =FLIP THE BIRD: *When they honk at me I give them the finger/ It's a sort of collective giving of the finger to liberalism in all its forms*—Toronto Life [fr the figurative insertion of a finger punitively into the anus]

give someone **the fish-eye** (or **beady eye** or **hairy eyeball**) *v phr* To look or stare at someone in a cold, contemptuous, or menacing way: *A well-fed man in tails opened the door, gave them the fish eye*—G Homes/ *who gave me such hairy eyeballs that I want to slink back*—Village Voice

give someone **the fluff** *v phr* To snub; dismiss; = BRUSH OFF: *I gave him the fluff*—Hal Boyle

give someone **the foot** *v phr* To kick someone

give someone **the gate** *v phr* To discharge, jilt, or eject someone: *After the last goof they gave him the gate*

give someone **the glad eye** *v phr* To look or glance at invitingly; gaze enticingly at: *A tipsy actress gives her man, Donald, the glad eye*—New York Times

give someone **the glad hand** *v phr* To greet and welcome effusively: *I gave 'em all the glad hand, but they voted for the bum anyway*

give someone or something **the go-by** *See* GIVE someone or something A MISS

give someone **the heat** *v phr prison* To kill by shooting

give someone **the hook** *v phr fr show business* To dismiss, silence, or otherwise reject someone, esp suddenly: *I was pretty bad, and not surprised when they gave me the hook* [see get the hook]

give someone **the needle** *v phr* To nag at someone; criticize regularly and smartingly; =HASSLE, NEEDLE: *The only needle she knows is the one she gives grandpa for stopping off at the bar on his way home*—Hal Boyle

give the nod *v phr* To give approval; confer permission: *Detroit has tightened the reins...on the boys in the sheet metal design department...while giving the nod to the engineers*—Ebony

give someone or something **the once-over** *v phr* To examine closely; scrutinize, esp with a view to evaluation or identification; =CHECK OUT: *That guy in the corner is giving us the once-over/ I gave her papers the once-over and figured she qualified*

give someone **the pink slip** *v phr* To discharge or dismiss; = CAN, FIRE

give someone **the shaft** *v phr* To swindle, maltreat, or otherwise deal punishingly with someone; =FUCK, SHAFT: *He wasn't expecting much praise, but he sure didn't think they'd give him the shaft like that*

give someone **the shake** *v phr* To rid oneself of someone; get away from someone: *He gave the cops the shake a block or so away*

give someone **the shirt off** one's **back** *v phr* To be extremely generous ● Usu in a conditional statement: *Open-handed? Why he'd give you the shirt off his back if you needed it*

not **give** someone **the time of day** *See* NOT GIVE someone THE TIME OF DAY

give someone **the works** *v phr fr 1920s* To mistreat or beat severely; =CLOBBER; WORK someone OVER: *They took him into the adjoining room and gave him the works* [probably fr the thoroughness suggested by the works; see the works]

give someone **what for** *v phr fr middle 1800s British* To beat or punish severely; drub either physically or verbally; =CLOBBER, LET someone HAVE IT: *two or three of us would pitch on him and give him "what-for"*—Jack London

give with *v phr esp 1940s fr jive talk* To give; impart: *He wouldn't give with the information*—I, Mobster [perhaps modeled on *make with* fr Yiddish *machen mit*]

give with the eyes *v phr* To look; glance at: *gives with the big blue eyes as if to say: "Her didn't mean to"*—E DeBaun

gizmo or **gismo** or **giz** **1** *n* *fr Navy & Marine Corps* An unspecified or unspecifiable object; something one does not know the name of or does not wish to name; = DINGUS, GADGET: *"Why weren't you using the gizmo?" "I was. It didn't work"*—New York Times/ *"What's this gizmo?" I asked. "The hand brake"*—Billy Rose/ *Guy tried to shove a Pepsi bottle in his wife's giz*—Joseph Wambaugh **2** *n* *gambling* = GIMMICK **3** *n* A man; fellow; = GUY: *What's this gizmo have in mind?* [origin unknown]

the **glad eye** *n phr* A welcoming and enticing look; seductive glance: *She gave me the glad eye and I wondered what she had been up to now*

glad-hand **1** *modifier:* Effusive and warm; cordial: *He gave me that glad-hand business* **2** *v:* *After...glad-handing the local dignitaries, he heads for the fence*—Associated Press
  See GIVE someone THE GLAD HAND

glad-hander *n* A person who evinces a warmth and heartiness that is probably insincere; one who is designedly cordial: *He is what is known as a glad-hander, meaning that he merely shakes hands and talks*—TV Guide

glad rags *fr late 1800s* **1** *n phr* One's best and fanciest clothing; party clothes **2** *n phr* Formal evening wear

glahm *See* GLOM

glamor (or **glamour**) **girl** *n phr* A woman whose looks and life are glamorous, esp a movie star or other professional beauty: *She was a beautiful thing when she started her career as a glamor girl*—New York Daily News

glamor-puss or **glamour-puss** **1** *n* A person whose looks and life are regarded as glamorous: *Joe's a glamor-puss and a hunk/ She's a certified glamour-puss, with brains* **2** *modifier:* *They are augmented by Daryl Hannah as Rourke's glamorpuss girlfriend*—Washington Post

glass arm **1** *n phr* *baseball* A pitcher's arm that is prone to injury and inflammation; = CROCKERY **2** *n phr* *dock workers* An inferior worker; weakling

glasses *See* BOP GLASSES, GRANNY GLASSES, HAVE one's GLASSES ON

glassie *n* A glass playing marble

glass jaw or **china chin** *n phr* *prizefight* A boxer's chin that cannot tolerate a hard punch: *His glass jaw gives him excruciating pain when struck/ He protects his china chin by clinching*

glass-jawed *adj* *prizefight* Having a very tender or vulnerable chin: *the glass-jawed bimbo which can't take it and dives into a clinch when shook up*—H Witwer

glassy-eyed *adj* Drunk

glaum *See* GLOM

glazed *adj* Intoxicated by alcohol or narcotics; stuporous

glaze someone **over** *v phr* To make someone ecstatic; intoxicate: *Said one enthusiastic participant: "Doesn't this just glaze you over?"*—Washington Post

a **gleam in** someone's **eye** *n phr* An exciting idea or prospect; passionate impulse: *At that time he wasn't even born, wasn't even a gleam in his father's eye*

glim **1** *n* *fr 1600s* A light, lamp, etc: *"Douse the glim, Mugsy," said a voice from my youth* **2** *n* (also **glimmer**) *truckers* A headlight **3** *n* (also **glimmer**) *fr middle 1800s* An eye **4** *v: I glimmed her from across the room*

glims *n fr 1920s underworld & hoboes* Eyeglasses: *Dark glasses, of course, are rimmed dimmed glims*—Philadelphia Bulletin

glim worker *n phr* *carnival* A person who sells eyeglasses of plain glass

glitch **1** *n* *fr 1960s aerospace* An operating defect; malfunction; a disabling minor problem: *despite such "glitches" (a spaceman's word for irritating disturbances)*—Time/ *Most had assured themselves that the trouble signal was only a "glitch"*—Newsweek **2** *n* *computer* A sudden interruption of electrical supply, program function, etc: *the term "bug" to refer to a computer glitch*—Newsweek [fr German *glitschen* (or Yiddish *glitshen*) "slip"]

glitter *n* A gaudy style of dress and grooming affected by some musicians, comprising dyed hair, jewels on face and body, and refulgent jump- and cowboy suits

the **glitterati** *n* Famous and glamorous people; outstanding celebrities: *among the glitterati*—People Weekly/ *to film the glitterati at a Derby bash*—Newsweek [based on *literati*]

glitter rock *n phr* Music played by rock groups that affect a spectacular style of dress

glitz **1** *n* High gaudy finish; flashy surface: *some optional Hollywood glitz*—Car and Driver/ *applied Vegas and hot tub glitz to the old Jack La Lanne*—Village Voice **2** *v* (also **glitz up**): *the Pirates of Penzance newly glitzed*—California/ *He said if we glitz the place up a little we can charge more*

glitzy *adj* Blatantly scintillant; flashy; gaudy: *and a glitzy sister...who has backed into degeneracy*—New York Times [fr German or Yiddish *glitzern* "glitter, glisten"]

◁**globes**▷ *n* A woman's breasts: *I'd even seen Elena's soft globes*—HK Fink

glom or **glaum** or **glahm** *fr early 1900s underworld & hoboes* **1** *n* A hand, regarded as a grabbing tool **2** *v* To grasp; seize: *She glommed the kid and held on tight* **3** *v* = GLOM ON TO **4** *v* To steal: *"Where'd you glahm 'em?" I asked*—Jack London/ *under the pretext of glomming a diamond from the strongbox*—SJ Perelman **5** *v* To be arrested **6** *v* To look at; seize with the eyes; = GANDER, GLIM: *or walk around the corner to glom old smack heads, woozy winos and degenerates*—New York Times/ *two new collections for the fashionable to glom*—Village Voice **7** *n: Have a glom at that leg, won't you?* [fr British dialect *glaum*, *glam* "hand," ultimately fr Old English *clamm* "bond, grasp," related to *clamp*]

glommer or **glaumer** or **glahmer** *fr underworld & hoboes* **1** *n* A hand, as used for grabbing or stealing **2** *n* A person who works at grasping or picking, like a fruit picker

See MITT-GLOMMER

glom (or **glaum** or **glahm**) **on to** *v phr fr underworld & hoboes* To acquire; =LATCH ON TO: *Glom on to a couple jugs and we'll have a party*

gloomy Gus *n phr* A morose, melancholic person; pessimist; =CRAPE-HANGER

glop 1 *n* Any viscous fluid or mixture; =GOO, GOOK, GUNK: *dimes that rolled into the glop*—William Kennedy/ *What's that glop on your face?* **2** *n* Sentimentality; maudlin trash; =SCHMALTZ: *That is very dull. I hate glop*—Hal Boyle/ *My poetry tends to be glop compounded with kitsch*

glory *n railroad* A train of empty cars

glory hole 1 *n phr homosexuals* A hole between stalls in a toilet, through which the penis may be put for oral sex **2** *modifier:* *A private glory-hole club makes a lot more sense*—Playboy

glory wagon *n phr railroad* A caboose

glossy 1 *n* A magazine printed on shiny coated paper; a high-quality magazine; =SLICK: *female editors of the powerful "glossies"*—K Fraser **2** *n* A photograph printed on shiny paper

glove See NOT LAY A GLOVE ON someone

glow *n* Mild intoxication; =TIDDLINESS: *After a couple of bourbons I had a nice glow*

glued *adj* Drunk

gluepot *n* A racehorse: *pay the cost the old gluepot rates when he toes the line*—Robert Ruark [fr the conventional belief or suspicion that horses go to the *glue* factory as raw material when no longer of use]

gluey or **glutinous** *adj* Sentimental; maudlin; =CORNY, SCHMALTZY: *He tells a gluey little tale of home*

glug 1 *n* A drink of liquor; =PULL, SNORT **2** *n* The quantity of liquor poured as the bottle makes one dull gurgle

G-man *n esp 1930s* A Federal Bureau of Investigations agent; =FEEB

gnarly *adj teenagers* Excellent; wonderful; =GREAT

gnome *n* An anonymous expert, esp a statistician or an industrious observer of trends; =BEAN COUNTER ● The term is being extended from the first use, **gnomes of Zurich**, designating the faceless little men who take account of and in part determine the curiosities of the international money market: *The Gnomes of Baseball*—Time/ *the inhibitions of sports announcers whose minds have been studied by small-town station managers and network gnomes*—New York Times

go 1 *n* A fight: *a ripsnorting go*—WR Burnett **2** *n* A try; =CRACK, WHACK: *She gave it a good go, and made it* **3** *v* To die **4** *v* To relieve oneself; go to the bathroom: *The dog had to go. We set him in the sink*—Nelson Algren **5** *v* To happen; transpire; =GO DOWN: *What goes here?*—WR Burnett **6** *v teenagers esp fr late 1960s* To say; utter: *So he goes "Let me breathe!"/ You wake up one morning and you go, "Wait a minute"*—Playgirl **7** *v* To weigh: *She'll go maybe 300, 400 pounds* **8** *v* To pay: *I went five bills for that*—Hy Sobol **9** *adj fr astronauts* Functioning properly; going as planned; =A-OK: *As the astronauts say...all signs are*

go in the National League—Sporting News **10** *adj* Appropriate; fitting: *beatniks, whose heavy black turtle-neck sweaters had never looked particularly go with white tennis socks*—Time

See FROM THE GIT-GO, FROM THE WORD GO, GIVE something A SHOT, GO MAN GO, HAVE A CRACK AT SOMETHING, HAVE something GOING FOR someone or something, LET FLY, LET oneself GO, NO GO, NO-GO, ON THE GO, TELL someone WHERE TO GET OFF, THERE YOU GO, TO GO, WAY TO GO, WHAT GOES AROUND COMES AROUND

the **go-ahead 1** *n* Permission or a signal to proceed; consent: *She pleaded her case before state officials and got the go-ahead*—Associated Press/ *His wife Joan had given him the go-ahead to make the race*—Time **2** *modifier* Putting a competitor in the lead: *The Tigers got the go-ahead run in the eighth and held the lead to win 9 to 8*

goal See KNOCK someone FOR A LOOP

go all the way 1 *v phr* To do the utmost; make a special effort; =GO THE EXTRA MILE: *If you decide to do it, I'll go all the way for you* **2** *v phr* =GO THE LIMIT

go along for the ride *v phr* To do something or join in something in a passive way: *I don't expect much, but I'll go along for the ride*

go along with 1 *v phr* To agree with some suggestion or statement **2** *v phr* To accept or comply with some proposal; acquiesce

go along with the crowd *v phr* To lack or eschew individual judgment; do what everyone else does: *What the hell, I figured I'd go along with the crowd and vote yes*

go ape (or ◁**ape-shit**▷) **1** *v phr* To behave stupidly, irrationally, and violently; go wild: *When they told him, he went ape and wrecked his room* **2** *v phr* To be very enthusiastic; admire enormously: *People are going quietly ape over the girl*—HG Brown/ *Everyone we met, experienced native and green tourist alike, went ape for it*—Popular Science

go around Robin Hood's barn *v phr* To act or speak in a roundabout way; make complexity out of something simple; =MAKE A FEDERAL CASE OUT OF something [fr the fact that *Robin Hood's barn* would be a large and pathless forest]

go around the bend *v phr fr British* To become insane; go crazy; =FREAK OUT: *Jessica Lange, who goes around the bend with more style, insight, and intensity*—Washingtonian

◁**go around the world**▷ *v phr* To kiss or lick the whole body of one's partner, esp as a prelude to fellatio or cunnilingus

go around together *v phr* To be partners frequently on dates, at parties, etc; keep company

go around with someone *v phr* To be someone's frequent escort or date; be linked romantically or sexually

goat 1 *n hot rodders & teenagers* A car, esp an old one or one with an especially powerful engine **2** *n* A person who takes the blame for failure or wrongdoing; scapegoat; =PATSY: *After the latest flop they elected me goat* **3** *n Army* The most junior officer in an Army unit **4** *n railroad* A switch engine or yard engine **5** *n* *horse-racing* A racehorse, esp an aged or inferior beast

See GET someone's GOAT, OLD GOAT, YARD GOAT

◄**goat fuck** (or **screw** or **rope**)► *n phr* *Army* A very confused situation, operation, etc; =CHINESE FIRE DRILL

goat-smelling *adj* *Army* Malodorous; stinking: *Get your goat-smelling ass out of here*

gob[1] *fr British dialect fr 1500s* **1** *n* A mass of viscous matter; =BLOB: *She chucked a big gob of plaster at me* **2** *n* (also **gabs**) A quantity, esp a large quantity: *I think he's got gobs of money*

gob[2] *n* The mouth ● Chiefly British use [fr Irish]

gob[3] *n fr early 1900s* A US Navy sailor; =SWABBY [perhaps fr earlier British *gabby* "coast guard; quarterdeckman," of unknown origin]

go back to (or **be at**) **square one** *v phr* To be forced to return to one's starting point, usu after a waste of effort; make a new beginning; =SCRUB THE SLATE CLEAN

go bananas **1** *v phr* To become wildly irrational; =FREAK OUT, GO APE: *speculation that maybe old Strom had gone bananas at last*—John Corry **2** *v phr* To be extremely enthusiastic; admire enormously: *She went bananas over the dress and bought one in every color* [fr the spectacle of an ape greedily gobbling *bananas*]

gobble **1** *v* *baseball* To make a catch ◄**2**► *v* To do fellatio or cunnilingus; =EAT IT

gobbledegook *n* Pretentious and scarcely intelligible language, esp of the sort attributed to bureaucrats, sociologists, etc [coined in 1944 by Representative Maury Maverick of Texas]

◄**gobbler**► *n* A person who does fellatio or cunnilingus

gobble up *v* =EAT UP

go belly up *v phr* To die; collapse; cease to operate; =BELLY UP: *two major credit-card firms had gone belly up*—Wall Street Journal

go blooey *v phr* (Variations: **flooey** or **kablooey** or **kerflooey** or **kerflooie** or **kerfooey** may replace **blooey**) To end abruptly in failure or disaster; break down; collapse: *The peace talks went blooey today/ Damn telephone went kerflooey/ Will I make it...without the air conditioner in the car going kablooey*—Washington Post/ *Then, of course, the whole thing all goes flooey*—Village Voice [echoic imitation of an explosion]

go boom *See* FALL DOWN AND GO BOOM

goboon or **gobboon** or **gaboon** (gah BŌŌN) *n* A spittoon

go broke (or **bust**) *v phr* To become penniless; become insolvent; =GO BELLY UP, TAKE A BATH: *His newest escapade into the fashionable world of trade and manufacturing had again gone bust*—Joseph Heller

gobs *See* GOB

gob-stick *n* A clarinet [a *stick* to put in the *gob* "mouth"]

go bughouse *v phr* To become insane; go crazy: *Four years earlier, Travis...had gone bughouse*—Washington Post

go bust *See* GO BROKE

the **go-by** *See* GIVE someone or something A MISS

go-cart *n* *railroad* A caboose

go chase oneself *v phr* To depart; =GET LOST ● Almost always a command: *He told the guy to go chase himself*

go co-op (or **coop**) *v phr* To be converted from a place, esp an apartment house, where tenants pay rent to one where they own accommodations on the cooperative principle: *My place down at the beach is going co-op and I haven't decided whether or not to buy*

God *See* BY GUESS AND BY GOD, OLDER THAN GOD

god-awful *fr early 1900s* **1** *adv* Extremely: *Ain't it god-awful cold in here?* **2** *adj* Wretched; miserable; inferior: *"It was god-awful," Newman recalls*—New York Times/ *cases that would never have come up but for this god-awful legislation*—Toronto Life

god box **1** *n* A pipe organ or other organ **2** *n* A church

God-damn or **God-damned** *adj* Accursed; wretched; nasty; =FUCKING ● Often used for euphony and rhythm of emphasis: *Take your God-damn foot off my God-damn toes*

goddess *See* SEX GODDESS

godfather *n* The chief; highest authority; =BOSS: *He was Life's first publisher, the godfather of the radio and film March of Time series*—Time

See FAIRY GODFATHER

godfer *n fr outdated British* A child; one's offspring: *I took the trouble and the godfers for a whisper in the fields before Rosie*—John Lardner [fr rhyming slang *God forbid* for kid]

godmother *See* FAIRY GODMOTHER

go down[1] *v phr* *esp computer* To become inoperative; stop functioning *See* WHAT'S GOING DOWN

go down[2] *v phr fr black* To happen; =GO: *He wanted this scam to go down as rigged*—Lawrence Sanders/ *You can't define it in terms of what kind of rap is going down*—Bobby Seal

go-down *n* *black* A basement apartment or room

◄**go down and do tricks**► *v phr* =GO DOWN ON someone

go downhill *v phr* To deteriorate; worsen: *It looks like his health is going downhill fast*

go down in flames *v phr* To be utterly ruined; be wrecked: *He became Washington bureau chief of ABC News and promptly went down in flames*—Washingtonian [fr the fate of WW1 combat pilots, who wore no parachutes]

◄**go down on** someone► *v phr* To do fellatio or cunnilingus; =EAT IT, SUCK: *Only she won't go down on me. Isn't that odd?*—Philip Roth/ *By the time the stewardess removed our trays, I already wanted to go down on him*—Xaviera Hollander

go down the tube (or **tubes** or **chute**) *adv phr* To wrack and ruin; to perdition; =KAPUT: *Bache was in danger of going down the chute with the price of silver*—Nicholas von Hoffman/ *speaks of a whole generation going down the tube*—New York Times

God's gift *n phr* A very special blessing; premier offering ● Nearly always ironical: *He thought he was God's gift to pedagogy*

God's medicine *n phr narcotics* Narcotics of any sort: *The joy-poppers had the will-power, they felt, to use God's medicine once or twice a month and forget it the rest of the time*—Nelson Algren

go Dutch (or **Dutch treat**) *v phr* To pay one's own way at a dinner, show, etc: *Nobody had much money, so we all went Dutch*

go easy 1 *v phr* To restrain oneself; control one's anger: *Go easy, fellow, he was just jiving* **2** *v phr* To be lenient with; spare: *Why do the judges go so easy with these perverts?*

goes around *See* WHAT GOES AROUND COMES AROUND

gofer or **go-for** or **gopher** *n* An employee who is expected to serve and cater to others; a low-ranking subordinate: *running the robo machine and acting as a receptionist, secretary, and general go-for*—Nicholas von Hoffman/ *attractive go-fers for executive editor Frank Waldrop*—Washingtonian

go fishing (or **on a fishing expedition**) *v phr fr late 1800s* To undertake a search for facts, esp by a legal or quasi-legal process like a grand-jury investigation

go fly a kite *sentence* Go away at once; = GO TO HELL, GET LOST: *I asked for more, and he told me to go fly a kite*

go for *v phr fr early 1800s* To be in favor of; admire; be attracted to: *I really go for her*—John O'Hara
See HAVE something GOING FOR someone or something

go for broke (or **all the marbles**) *v phr* To make a maximum effort; stake everything on a big try: *We went for broke on that deal, and won/ He goes for all the marbles*—CBS News [fr a gambler's last desperate or hopeful wager]

go for it *v phr* To make a try for something, esp a valiant and risky one ● Often an encouraging imperative: *Will we play it safe, or go for it?/ Go for it! You've almost got it knocked!*

go for the fences *v phr baseball* To try to make long base hits; = SLUG

go for the long ball *v phr* To take a large risk for a large gain; = GO FOR BROKE: *entering the fall campaign might decide to go for the long ball*—Washingtonian [fr a *long* desperation pass thrown in a football game]

◄**go fuck** (or **impale**) oneself► *sentence* May you be accursed, confounded, humiliated, rejected, etc; = GO TO HELL: *Ah, go impale yourselves, the bunch of you*—John Le Carré/ *If people were only interested in it 'cause she balled Paul McCartney "then they could go fuck themselves"*—Village Voice

go-getter *n fr 1920s* A vigorous and effective person; = WINNER: *sometimes enviously referred to as a go-getter, a hot shot, a ball of fire*—Fact Detective Mysteries

goggle-eye *n* Raw and inferior whiskey; = REDEYE

goggle-eyed *adj* Impressed; incredulous; agog

go-go *esp 1960s* **1** *adj* Having to do with discotheques, their music, style of dancing, etc **2** *adj* Stylish; modish; = TRENDY: *She may be getting on in years but she certainly is a go-go dresser* **3** *adj* Showing vitality and drive, esp in business and commerce; urgent and energetic: *Religion is a really go-go growth industry these days*—LR Hills/ *Japan's go-go entrepreneurs can turn their operations into the new Goliaths*—Newsweek
See A GO-GO

go-go girl (or **dancer**) *n phr* A scantily clad or partly naked young woman employed to do solo gyrational dancing in a discotheque or club on a small stage or platform, in a cage, etc

go great guns *v phr* To do extremely well; succeed remarkably: *He's going great guns as a wine-taster* [fr the early 1800s expression *blow great guns*]

go gunning for someone *See* GUN FOR someone

go halfies (or **halvies** or **halvsies**) *v phr* To award an equal share; divide in two equal parts: *I may go halvsies*—Atlantic Monthly

go haywire *fr early 1900s* **1** *v phr* To become inoperative; break down unexpectedly; = GO BLOOEY: *This radio's gone haywire*—JC Hixson **2** *v phr* To go crazy; become confused and disoriented: *Remember that I tried to talk you out of it, and don't go haywire*—S McNeil [fr the ramshackle condition of something that must be hastily repaired with *haywire*]

go (or **run**) **hog-wild** *v phr fr late 1800s* To act audaciously and unrestrainedly: *I went hog-wild and spent the whole week's pay/ I'm going to take a roundhouse wallop at the first thing I see and run hog-wild on the bases*—Everybody's Magazine

go home feet first (or **in a box**) *v phr* To die: *Make one wrong move and you go home feet first*

goifa *See* GREEFA

going *See* GET GOING, HAVE something GOING FOR someone or something

a **going concern** *n phr* A project, business, operation, etc, that is successfully launched and functioning smoothly: *Just an idea last year, now it's a going concern*

going down *See* WHAT'S GOING DOWN

going out of style *See* LIKE IT'S GOING OUT OF STYLE

a **going-over 1** *n phr* A beating; trouncing: *The goons gave him a brutal going over* **2** *n phr* An examination; scrutiny: *Give these records a going-over, please*

go in the tank *v phr fr prizefight* To lose a fight, game, etc, deliberately; = THROW: [fr the resemblance between a fighter hitting the canvas and a person *taking a dive into a tank*]

go into one's **act** *v phr* = DO one's NUMBER

go into one's **dance** *v phr* (Variations: **dog and pony show** or **song and dance** may replace **dance**) To begin a prepared line of pleading, explanation, selling, seduction, etc: *He went into his dance, but she wasn't convinced*

go into orbit *v phr* To reach very extreme and apparently uncontrolled heights: *those whose stocks* can absorb, say, $50 million or more without going into orbit—Fortune

go it alone *v phr fr middle 1800s gambling* To do something arduous or tricky by oneself: *She tried going it alone but found it scary* [fr the game of euchre, where one may play against combined opponents]

goiter *See* GERMAN GOITER, MILWAUKEE GOITER

go kerplunk *v phr* To fail; =FLOP: *If they go kerplunk, someone will have to scrape up the pieces* —Arthur Daley

gold 1 *n* Money **2** *n narcotics* A high grade of marijuana *See* ACAPULCO GOLD

◀**Goldberg**▶ *n black* A Jew, esp one who employs blacks or has a shop in a black neighborhood: *sweeping the floors for Goldberg*—Claude Brown *See* RUBE GOLDBERG

gold braid *n phr* Naval officers, esp high-ranking ones: *It is evident that the gold braid doesn't think enough of the order*—GW Hibbitt

goldbrick 1 *n* (also **goldbricker**) *fr WW1 armed forces* A shirker; a person who avoids work or duty; =GOOF-OFF **2** *v:* *She made him promise to quit goldbricking* **3** *v esp early 1900s* To swindle; cheat; =CON [fr the convention of the confidence trickster who sells spurious *gold bricks*]

gold chamberpot *See* WIN THE PORCELAIN HAIRNET

gold-digger *n fr 1920s* A woman who uses her charms and favors to get money, presents, etc, from wealthy men: *Lorelei Lee...the crazy-like-a-fox gold-digger*—Billy Rose

golden-ager *n* An elderly person, usu retired

golden handcuffs *n phr* Arrangements, options, perquisites, etc, that induce one to stay in one's job: *These ties that bind have become known in industry as golden handcuffs*—Time

golden oldie or **oldie but goodie** *n phr fr 1960s* An old record, song, etc, still regarded as good, esp one that has revived or sustained popularity: *a golden oldie like "Honeysuckle Rose"*—FP Tullius/ *All the golden oldies are replayed and the untied threads neatly resolved*—Newsweek/ *oldies but goodies such as "Down by the Riverside"* —Pulpsmith [probably influenced by association with the *gold* phonograph record struck for a recording that has sold a million copies and more]

golden parachute (or **handshake**) *n phr* Very high sums, benefits, etc, offered for taking early retirement: *"Golden parachutes" or severance packages...are all becoming more common*—New York Times/ *parting golden handshake with GM included a valuable Cadillac franchise*—Time

◁**golden shower**▷ *n phr homosexuals & prostitutes* Urination on someone who sexually enjoys such a wetting: *what girls do through the bladder, which is otherwise known as the "golden shower"* —Xaviera Hollander/ *Golden showers...Not me* —Philadelphia

goldfinger *n narcotics* A type of synthetic heroin

goldfish *n fr WW1 Army* Canned salmon

goldfish bowl *n phr* A place or situation where one is exposed; a venue without privacy: *Celebrities must live in a goldfish bowl*

goldilocks *n* Any pretty blond woman ● Often used ironically: *Well, thought Jimmy, it won't be because of you, goldilocks*—Calder Willingham

gold piece *See* COME UP SMELLING LIKE A ROSE

go levers *n phr airline* The throttles of an aircraft

golf *See* AFRICAN GOLF, BARNYARD GOLF

golf ball *n phr* A globular firecracker that explodes on impact

golf widow *n phr* A woman often left alone while her mate plays golf

go light *v phr poker* To bet on credit using money out of the pot

golly *interj fr middle 1800s British fr middle 1700s black* A mild exclamation of surprise, dismay, pleasure, etc; =GOSH: *Golly, Mom, did you really win it?* [a euphemism for *God*] *See* HOLLY-GOLLY

go-long *n black* A police patrol wagon; =PADDY WAGON: *Joe Brown had you all in the go-long last night*—Zora Neale Hurston

goma (GOH mah) *n narcotics* Crude opium

go man go *interj fr jazz musicians* An exclamation of praise, encouragement, rapport, etc; =WAY TO GO

gomer *n hospital* A patient needing extensive care, and usu sent to a nursing home [origin unknown; perhaps related to British *gomers* "going-home clothes"]

goms *n underworld fr 1920s* A police officer

gon or **gond** *n railroad* A gondola car: *a string of gonds went past*—James M Cain *See* GUN²

go native *v phr* To take on the behavior and standards of the place one has moved to or is visiting, esp when this means a loss of rigor, respectability, etc: *On Bleecker Street he went native and donned a black sweatshirt and sneakers*

gone 1 *adj jazz musicians* Intoxicated, esp with narcotics **2** *adj cool talk* In a trancelike condition; meditative: *gurgling forth a flow of words, a "gone" expression on his face*—Calder Willingham **3** *adj cool talk* Excellent; wonderful; =COOL: *a real gone chick*

gone fishing *adj phr* Not working; unaccountably absent from duty; very relaxed

gone goose *n phr* =DEAD DUCK [an alliterative phrase modeled on *dead duck*]

gone on (or **over**) *adj phr* In love with; enamored of: *I was so gone over her*—Louis Armstrong

a **goner** *n fr middle 1800s* Someone or something that is doomed; someone dead or about to die; =DEAD DUCK: *pray...or you're a goner*—San Diego Herald/ *for Rome will be a goner*—WH Auden

gong 1 *n* (also **gonger**) *narcotics* An opium pipe **2** *n chiefly British WW2 use* A military decoration; medal or ribbon [both senses probably fr *gong* "saucer-shaped metal bell," of Malayan origin; the sense "opium pipe" may be related to the general association of *gongs* with Chinese matters, and the

military sense to the notion that a decoration is something like the ceremonial sounding of a *gong*]
See BEAT THE GONG, KICK THE GONG AROUND

gonged *adj narcotics* Intoxicated with narcotics; =HIGH, STONED: *She's sitting in the front row gonged to the gills with acid*—Albert Goldman

goniff (GAH nəf) **1** *n* (Variations: **gonef** or **gonif** or **gonof** or **gonoph** or **ganef** or **ganof** or **guniff**) *fr middle 1800s* A thief; a person who is in effect a thief, like an unethical salesperson: *And who is this arch-goniff?*—Dashiell Hammett/ *a gonof like Glick*—Budd Schulberg/ *all the other gonophs, consultants who peddle bullshit, builders who build badly*—Village Voice **2** *v:* *Are you trying to goniff me, pal?* ◁**3**▷ *n* A male homosexual [fr Yiddish, "thief," fr Hebrew *gannabh* "thief"]

gonk *See* CONK

go no-go *adj phr fr astronauts* Pertaining to the last critical moment at which a project, plans, etc, can still be cancelled; relating to the point of no return: *It's go no-go. Either we do it or we kill it*

gonsil or **gonzel** *See* GUNSEL

Gonzalez *See* SPEEDY GONZALEZ

gonzo (GAHN zoh) **1** *adj fr early 1970s* Insane; wild; bizarre; confused: *established Hunter Thompson as the father of gonzo journalism, a flamboyant if controversial style*—New York Daily News/ *the gonzo idea of a cross-country street race*—Car and Driver/ *incorrigibly gonzo, cuckoo, bananas*—Rolling Stone **2** *n:* *The Gonzo and the Geeks*—Vivian Gornick/ *These double-gaited gonzos are perpetrating a plague of best-selling takeoffs*—Newsweek [fr Italian, "credulous, simple, too good"]

goo 1 *n fr early 1900s* Any sticky and viscous substance; =GLOP, GUNK: *fell in the goo rounding third*—New York Daily News/ *a layer of goo on the skin*—R Adler **2** *n* Sentimentality; maudlin rubbish; =GLOP, SCHMALTZ **3** *n* Fulsome flattery; overly affectionate greetings: *They ladle out the old goo*—Bing Crosby [perhaps sound symbolism, influenced by *glue*; perhaps fr *burgoo* "oatmeal porridge"]

goober *teenagers* **1** *n* A minor skin lesion; =ZIT: *whiteheads, blackheads, goopheads, goobers, pips*—New York Times **2** *n* A stupid and bizarre person; =WEIRDO [fr *goober* "peanut" fr Kongo *nguba* "kidney, peanut," apparently because of the resemblance of the lesion to a peanut]

◁**goober-grabber**▷ *n phr* A Georgian [fr the general association of Georgia with its important product the peanut]

goober-grease 1 *n* Butter **2** *n* Peanut butter

gooby *n prison* Food

good *See* BE GOOD, DO-GOOD, DO-GOODER, FEEL GOOD, HAVE IT GOOD, MAKE GOOD, NO-GOOD

good buddy *n phr esp citizens band* The person one is cordially addressing

good butt *n phr narcotics* A marijuana cigarette; =JOINT

goodbye *See* KISS something GOODBYE

good cop bad cop or **nice cop tough cop** *modifier* Marked by alternations between friendliness and hostility, easiness and rigor, etc: *Successful management requires a variation of the "good cop, bad cop" routine*—New York Times/ *In short, a "nice cop" Rousseau and a "tough cop" Rousseau*—New York Review/ *I think that she's the good cop and he's the bad one, and I think it's quite deliberate*—New York [fr the interrogation technique by which one police officer pretends to sympathize with the suspect and to protect him from a pitiless and menacing fellow-officer]

good deal *fr WW2 armed forces* **1** *n phr* A pleasant and favorable situation, life, job, etc: *He had a good deal there at the bank, but blew it* **2** *interj* An exclamation of agreement, pleasure, congratulation, etc: *You made it? Good deal!*

good egg *n phr* A decent and kindly person; a reliable and admirable citizen: *Henry Fonda frequently was cast as the good egg*

gooder *See* DO-GOODER

good hair *n phr black* Straight or nearly straight and shiny hair

good head *n phr esp 1950s teenagers* A pleasant and agreeable person

goodie or **goody 1** *n* =GOODY-GOODY **2** *n* A special treat; something nice to eat: *a huge basket of goodies*—New Yorker **3** *n* Something nice; a pleasant feature; something very desirable: *headlight with a middle beam, the goodie you've been waiting for*—Popular Science/ *the goody he had saved for them*—New York/ *The local population took to the goodies of Western culture with avidity*—J Williams **4** *modifier:* *Then I got out my goodie bag*—Xaviera Hollander **5** *n* Someone on the side of virtue and decency, in contrast with a villain: *It's much easier to make a girl a baddie than a goodie*—Time

See GOLDEN OLDIE

good Joe *n phr* A pleasant, decent, reliable man; =GOOD EGG

good-looker *n fr late 1800s* Someone or something that is handsome and attractive, esp a woman; =LOOKER: *Is she a good looker?*—S Smith

good night *interj* An exclamation of surprise, irritation, emphasis, etc: *Good night! Must you chew that gum so loud?* [a euphemism for *good God*]

good old (or **ole**) **boy** *n phr* A white Southerner who exemplifies the masculine ideals of the region: *The helpful truck driver was a good old boy from around Nashville*

good pay *n phr* A person who pays readily and faithfully what is owed

goods *n narcotics* Narcotics of any sort
See CANNED GOODS, GREEN GOODS, PIECE OF CALICO, STRAIGHT GOODS

the goods 1 *n phr fr late 1800s* Something or someone of excellent quality; just what is wanted: *She's the real goods*—A Lewis **2** *n phr* The evidence needed to arrest and convict a criminal: *We've got the goods on him*—Erle Stanley Gardner **3** *n phr* Stolen property; contraband: *They caught him with the goods in his pocket*
See DELIVER THE GOODS, GET THE GOODS ON someone

good shit 1 *interj* =GOOD DEAL **2** *n phr* Anything favorable or pleasant; something one approves of: *This place is real good shit, ain't it?*

good sport *n phr* A person who plays fair, accepts both victory and defeat, and stays amiable: *I just want to be a good sport and get along with people*—Hal Boyle

good time *n phr* *prison fr late 1800s* Time deducted from a prison term for good behavior: *a period of solitary confinement and a loss of "good time"*—American Scholar

good-time Charlie *n phr* A man devoted to partying and pleasure; bon vivant

good word *See* WHAT'S THE GOOD WORD

Goodyears *See* DOWN THE GOODYEARS

goody-goody *n fr late 1800s* A prim and ostentatiously virtuous person: *I'm not a mammy boy nor a goody-goody*—O Johnson/ *what might have been a goody-goody role*—Time

goody two-shoes 1 *n phr* An obviously innocent and virtuous young woman; =GOODY-GOODY ● Most often used mockingly or contemptuously **2** *modifier:* *in spite of its Goody Two-Shoes ecological image*—Toronto Life [fr the name of the heroine of a middle-1700s child's story, probably by Oliver Goldsmith, about a little girl who exulted publicly at the acquisition of a second shoe]

gooey *adj* Consisting of, covered with, or resembling goo: *gooey pie/ These passages seem affected and a bit gooey*—New Yorker/ *the story of Teresa Stratas, without gooey heaviness*—Toronto Life

goof 1 *n fr early 1900s* A stupid person; =BOOB, KLUTZ: *He's a goof, but harmless* **2** *n* An insane person; mental case **3** *n 1930s prison* One's cellmate **4** *n narcotics* A narcotics addict **5** *v: He was goofing then, and had a $100 habit* **6** *n fr jive talk* A blunder; bad mistake; =BOO-BOO: *they covered their goof quite well*—Esquire **7** *v: You goofed again, it's a one-way street* **8** *v* To pass one's time idly and pleasantly; =GOOF OFF: *In Sarajevo, members of a student volunteer brigade goofed and joked as they worked*—Time **9** *v* =GOOF AROUND **10** *v* To fool; =KID: *Don't goof your grandpa*—James T Farrell [fr British dialect *goof, goff* "fool"]

goof around 1 *v phr* To pass one's time idly and pleasantly; potter about; =BEAT AROUND, FART AROUND **2** *v phr* To joke and play when one should be serious; =FUCK AROUND, HORSE AROUND: *The monarch ordered the field marshal to quit goofing around and win the goddamn war*

goof at *v phr* To examine; look at; =GAWK

goofball 1 *n* A stupid and clumsy person; =GOOF: *roles that earned him the affectionate labeling as a "goof ball"*—Washington Post **2** *n* An eccentric person; =ODDBALL, WEIRDO **3** *n narcotics* A pill or capsule of Nembutal (a trade name) **4** *n narcotics* A barbiturate, tranquilizer, etc, used as a narcotic: *took over three hundred goof balls*—A Stump **5** *n narcotics* A portion or dose of a narcotic; =BALL, GB: *A goof ball is a nar-*

cotics preparation which is burned on a spoon and inhaled—New York Daily News

goof-butt *See* GOOFY-BUTT

goofed *adj narcotics* Intoxicated with a narcotic, esp marijuana; =HIGH, STONED

goofer or **goopher 1** *n* A fool; =GOOF: *Don't be a critical goopher or you can't go*—F Scott Fitzgerald **2** *n WW2 Army Air Forces* An intrepid fighter pilot

go off ◁1▷ *v phr* To have an orgasm; =COME OFF **2** *v phr* To occur; succeed: *Did everything go off as planned?*

go off half-cocked *v phr* To make a premature response, esp an angry one: *She went off half-cocked before she even knew what happened* [fr the accidental firing of a gun at *half cock*]

go off the deep end 1 *v phr fr early 1900s* To go into a violent rage; =BLOW one's TOP **2** *v phr* To have a mental breakdown: *The old lady just went off the deep end after her family died in that car crash* [perhaps fr the notion of jumping into a pool at the *deep end*, hence being in *deep* water, in trouble] *See* JUMP OFF THE DEEP END

goofiness *n* The acts, ways, ideas, etc, of those who are goofy: *an unparalleled tolerance for goofiness*—AJ Liebling

goof off *v phr fr WW2 armed forces* To pass one's time idly and pleasantly; potter about; shirk duty; =GOOF AROUND: *My goofing off in the final period had knocked down a possible A average*—Life/ *Are you trying to tell me my son is goofing off?*—Erma Bombeck

goof-off *fr WW2 armed forces* **1** *n* A person who regularly or chronically avoids work; =BUNK LIZARD, FUCK-OFF: *getting kicked out of seminary as a goof-off*—Inside Sports **2** *n* A period of relaxation; respite: *A little goof-off will do you good*

goof on someone *v phr teenagers* To play a joke on someone; fool someone

goof-proof *v* To insure against mistakes; forestall errors: *her own formulas for goof-proofing a party*—Philadelphia

goof up 1 *v phr* To spoil; disable; =BITCH UP, QUEER: *He goofed up the whole deal by talking too soon* **2** *v phr* To blunder; =GOOF: *that can look at a child when he goofs up and reflect, "I understand and I love you"*—Erma Bombeck

goof-up 1 *n* =FUCK-UP **2** *n* A blunder, esp a serious one; =FUCK-UP, SNAFU

goofus 1 *n* =THINGAMAJIG **2** *n early 1900s circus* A small calliope **3** *n circus & carnival* A rural person; naive spectator; =EASY MARK **4** *n show business* Tasteless and meretricious material or entertainment designed for the unsophisticated

goofy *adj* Silly; foolish; crazy; =DOTTY ● Nearly always has an affectionate and amused connotation: *a goofy grin*—HC Witwer/ *a goofy awkward kid*—Chances/ *And he looked, well, goofy*—JD Salinger

goofy about *adj phr* =CRAZY ABOUT

goofy-butt or **goof-butt** *n narcotics* A marijuana cigarette; =JOINT

googlum *See* GOOZLUM

googly *adj fr late 1800s* Protruding; exophthalmic: *her great big googly eyes* [origin uncertain; perhaps fr *goggle*, which meant "stare at admiringly or amorously"; perhaps fr mid-19th-century *google* "the Adam's apple," where the eyes are thought of as similarly protruding; perhaps influenced by *goo* in the sense of "sentimental, amorous"; popularized by the hero of a comic strip]

goo-goo or **gu-gu** ◁1▷ *n 1920s Navy* = GOOK[2] **2** *adj* Silly; crazy; = GAGA **3** *adj fr middle 1800s* Infantile; cooing: *talking goo-goo talk to her, like you would to a baby*—Saturday Evening Post

goo-goo eyes *n phr fr late 1800s* Eyes expressing enticement, desire, seduction, etc [probably fr *googly*, with which it is synonymous in early uses] *See* MAKE GOO-GOO EYES

googs *n hawkers* Eyeglasses [probably fr *goggles*]

gook[1] (GUCK, GŌŌK) **1** *n* Dirt; grime; sediment; = GLOP: *Glim gets the gook off*—New York Daily News/ *got gook all over my shoes* **2** *n* Cheap and inferior merchandise; = SCHLOCK **3** *modifier: wearing gook jewelry*

◀**gook**[2]▶ (GŌK, GŌŌK) *fr late 1800s* **1** *n* An Asian or Polynesian; = SLOPE ● Originally a Filipino insurrectionary, then a Nicaraguan, then any Pacific Islander during WW2, embraced Koreans after 1950, Vietnamese and any Asian fr 1960s: *take it on the chin better than an American or a Zulu or a gook*—Hal Boyle/ *the way he felt about Vietnam. The gooks*—New York Times/ *It was there that I first heard of dinks, slopes, and gooks* —New Yorker **2** *modifier: Give it to the gook hospitals*—New York Times [fr *gugu*, a term of Filipino origin, perhaps fr Vicol *gugurang* "familiar spirit, personal demon," adopted by US armed forces during the Filipino Insurrection of 1899 as a contemptuous term for Filipinos, and spread among US troops to other places of occupation, invasion, etc; probably revived after 1950 by the Korean term *kuk* which is a suffix of nationality, as in *Chungkuk* "China," etc]

gooky (GŌŌK ee) *adj* Sticky; viscid; greasy: *Greaseless. Nongooky*—Cosmetics advertisement

goola *n jive musicians* A piano

goola box *n phr black* A juke box

goombah or **goombar** or **gumbah** (GŌŌM bah) **1** *n* A friend; companion; trusted associate; patron; = PAL: *They called him Joey Gallo's rabbi or his goombah*—Saturday Evening Post/ *trying to make these old goombars understand*—Patrick Mann/ *We want all our gumbahs to come over and get rich*—George V Higgins **2** *n* An organized-crime figure; Mafioso: *I'm gonna kill any greasy Guinea goombah that tries to stop me*—George Warren [fr dialect pronunciation of Italian *compare* "companion, godfather"]

goomer *n hospital* A hypochondriac [fr *get out of my emergency room*]

goon 1 *n fr early 1920s* A strong, rough, intimidating man, esp a paid ruffian **2** *modifier: goon squad/ his goon tactics* **3** *n* Any unattractive or unliked person; = JERK, PILL: *He had the face of a pure goon*—H Allen Smith [fr the name of Alice the Goon, a large, hairy creature in EC Segar's comic strip "Thimble Theatre"; perhaps fr *gooney*]

go on *interj* A mild exclamation of disbelief, esp when one is praised: *Oh, go on, I'm not that good*

go something or someone **one better** *v phr fr middle 1800s* To surpass or outbid; raise the standard: *That wasn't a bad offer, but I'll go you one better* [fr the raising of bets in poker]

gooney *n fr late 1800s* A stupid person; simpleton; fool [fr earlier *goney, gonus* "simpleton," as old as the late 1500s]

gooney bird *n phr aviators* The DC-3 airplane: *Pilots everywhere refer to it with great affection as the "Gooney Bird" after the albatross*—New York Post [fr the slow but sure flight of the *gooney bird* "black-footed albatross," the bird so called because of its foolish look and awkward behavior when on the ground]

goonk *See* GUNK

goonlet *n* A young hoodlum or ruffian: *Cops handle young goonlets gently*—W Davenport

goon squad *n phr* A group of ruffians: *A few weeks later, another "goon squad," as they have been rightly labeled*—New York Times/ *What some doctors deride as investigative "goon squads"* —Time

go on the hook for someone or something **1** *v phr* To go into debt: *So you'll go on the hook for one of those eighty-dollar sports-car coats*—S McNeil **2** *v phr* To endanger oneself for another; go out on a limb

go on track *v phr prostitutes* To patrol an area seeking prostitution customers; = HOOK: *Then I'd go on track till 4 AM, sleep two more hours, and start over*—Milwaukee Journal

goony *adj* Like a goon or a goon's behavior

goop[1] or **goup** *n* A nasty viscid substance; = GLOP, GOO: *suck up the goop and then spill it over*—John D MacDonald

goop[2] **1** *n* A stupid and boorish person; = CLOD, KLUTZ **2** *n* Stupidly sentimental material; sugary rubbish: *who can't transcend the Positive Mental Attitude goop she is forced to utter*—Village Voice [first sense fr the name of an unmannerly creature invented by the humorist Gelett Burgess in the late 1800s]

goophead *n* A minor skin lesion; = ZIT: *whiteheads, blackheads, goopheads, goobers, pips*—New York Times

goopher *See* GOOFER

goopy 1 *adj* Viscid; nastily sticky: *You certainly tend to get goopy fancy food these days*—Arizona Republic **2** *adj* Stupidly sentimental; maudlin; = GOOEY: *There's no way to talk about that without sounding goopy*—Tom Wolfe/ *please, not another goopy eulogy to the past*—Village Voice

goose ◁1▷ *v* To prod someone roughly and rudely in the anal region, usu as a coarse and amiable joke: *As she was bending over her lab table, a playful lab assistant goosed her*—Max Shulman ◁2▷ *n: He threatened a goose, and I cringed* **3** *v* To exhort strongly and irritably; goad harshly:

and goosed the media into hyping them—Washington Post/ *every once in a while goose it with defense spending*—Village Voice **4** *n: The whole bunch needed a good goose* **5** *v* To run an engine at full speed or with spurts of high speed; = GUN: *Vroom-vroom-vroom, he goosed the engine to full-throated life*—Earl Thompson **6** *v* railroad To stop a locomotive suddenly, esp by putting it into reverse

See COOK someone's GOOSE, as FULL OF SHIT AS A CHRISTMAS GOOSE, GONE GOOSE, YARD GOOSE

gooseberry 1 *n* A clothesline with clothing hanging out to dry: *Hoboes would rob a "gooseberry" if they needed a new shirt*—C Ashleigh **2** *v: The bum got caught gooseberrying a pair of pants*

gooseberry lay 1 *n phr* An expedition for stealing clothing off clotheslines **2** *v phr: But no gooseberry laying, since most of the characters are trying desperately not to hang their dirty linen in public*—Saturday Review ● A metaphoric extension of the hobo term **3** *n phr* outdated underworld An easily committed crime [fr an earlier expression *as easy as picking gooseberries*, because gooseberries are large and the plants have no thorns]

goose bumps *n phr* A roughness of the skin or the production of small pimples on the skin as the result of fear, cold, or excitement; gooseflesh

goose-bumpy *adj* Frightened; panicky: *goes goose-bumpy at the thought of hooking a 50-pound sailfish*—Time

goose-drownder *n* fr early 1900s A very heavy rainstorm; cloudburst

goose egg *n phr* fr middle 1800s Zero; nothing; a score of zero; = ZILCH: *My contribution appears to have been a great big goose egg*

goose something **up** *v phr* To make something more exciting, intense, impressive, etc; = JAZZ something UP: *If we tried to goose it up too much...it wouldn't help anybody*—Newsweek

goosy or **goosey** *adj* Touchy; jumpy; sensitive: *I feel a little goosy about the whole thing*—Time/ *Hennessey was goosey anyway, and he jumped*—James T Farrell

See LOOSE AS A GOOSE

go out *v phr* To lose consciousness; = PASS OUT: *Last thing I heard before I went out was the siren*

go out in the country *v phr* To murder someone in the classical gangster way of kidnapping the victim and disposing of the corpse in a remote place; also, to be murdered in this way; = TAKE someone FOR A RIDE

go out like a light *v phr* To lose consciousness very suddenly and totally: *Something swished and I went out like a light*—Raymond Chandler

go out of one's **skull** fr 1960s **1** *v phr* To become very tense; get nervous: *You can go out of your skull while they're doing that*—R Musel **2** *v phr* To become very excited; be overcome with emotion; = GO APE: *They went out of their skulls when she grabbed the mike to sing* **3** *v phr* To be overcome with tedium; fret with boredom: *The silence made him go right out of his skull*

go out of one's **way** *v phr* To make a special effort; try very hard; = BEND OVER BACKWARDS: *I went out of my way to be nice to the guy*

go out on a limb *v phr* To put oneself in a vulnerable position; take a risk: *OK, I'll go out on a limb and vouch for you*

go over *v phr* To succeed; be accepted: *This demonstration will never go over with the hard hats*

go over big *v phr* To succeed very well; be received with great approval: *Her proposal went over big with the biggies*

go overboard 1 *v phr* To be smitten with love or helpless admiration: *He went overboard for her right away* **2** *v phr* To commit oneself excessively or perilously; overdo: *Take a couple, but don't go overboard* **3** *v phr* = JUMP OFF THE DEEP END

go over like a lead balloon *v phr* To fail miserably; = FLOP: *My appeal to his better nature went over like a lead balloon*

go over the hill *v phr* fr armed forces fr 1920s To go absent without leave from a military unit

go over the wall *v phr* To escape from prison

go over with a bang *v phr* To succeed splendidly; be enthusiastically approved: *My idea for a new bulletin board went over with a bang*

goozle *n* The throat

See WET one's GOOZLE

goozlum or **googlum** *n* lumberjacks Syrup; molasses; gravy

go pfft *v phr* esp 1930s To end; dissolve; break up; = FIZZLE: *Their romance went pfft after that* [used by gossip columnists; fr late 1900s British echoic phrase *go phut* "come to grief, fizzle out"]

gopher[1] **1** *n* fr late 1800s A young thief or hoodlum: *tough West Side gophers who wouldn't hesitate to use a gun*—E Lavine **2** *n* underworld A safecracker **3** *n* underworld A safe or vault **4** *n* lumberjacks A helper who digs under logs so that a rope may be tied around them **5** *n* = GOFER

gopher[2] *v* baseball To pitch a gopher ball: *only about the fifth or sixth that Orosco had gophered home the eventual gamer*—Village Voice

gopher ball *n phr* baseball A pitch that is hit for a home run; a batter's favorite pitch or an easy pitch to hit [because the batter will *go for* the pitch]

go piss up a rope *sentence* Go away and do something characteristically stupid; = GET LOST, GO FLY A KITE: *He asked for a contribution and I told him to go piss up a rope*

go pittypat (or **pitterpat**) *v phr* To beat strongly and excitedly; pump with joy and anticipation: *My veteran heart went pittypat*—San Francisco

go places *v phr* To do very well in one's work; have a successful career; make good

go pound salt (or **sand**) *sentence* (Variation: **up** one's **ass** may be added) May one be accursed, confounded, humiliated, etc: *told Glazer and the feds to go pound sand in legal terms, of course*—Philadelphia

go public *v phr* To reveal onself; acknowledge openly; = COME OUT OF THE CLOSET: *how she* adjusted to going public as a single-breasted woman —Ms [fr the financial idiom *go public* "offer stock for sale in the stock market after it had previously been held in a family or otherwise privately"]

gorilla 1 *n* *fr middle 1800s* An extremely strong person, esp one who is not very clever **2** *n* (also **gorill**) *fr 1930s* A ruffian; =GOON: *Strong-arm men, gorillas, and tough gangsters*—E Lavine/ *Those gorills do not care anything about law*—John O'Hara **3** *n* *fr 1930s* A hired killer; =HIT MAN **4** *v* To steal or rob with threat and violence: *if you let somebody gorilla you out of some money*—Claude Brown **5** *v* To beat someone up; savage someone; =CLOBBER: *If that doesn't work, we'll gorilla a little bit*—New York Times **6** *n* Anything very powerful and unstoppable; anything very forceful and intimidating: *It is very simple to create the appearance of a "gorilla," a product with a lot of momentum*—Wall Street Journal

See SIX-HUNDRED-POUND GORILLA

gork *hospital* **1** *n* A stuporous or imbecilic patient; patient who has lost brain function: *The gork in that room has the "O" sign, did you notice?* —Elizabeth Morgan **2** *v* To sedate a patient heavily [originally fr *God only really knows,* referring to a patient with a mysterious ailment]

gorked or **gorked out** *adj* or *adj phr* *hospital* Stuporous; semi-conscious; heavily sedated; =SPACED-OUT

gorm *v* *fr middle 1800s* To eat voraciously [fr *gormandize*]

gormless *adj* *fr 1930s* Stupid; slow-witted; =DUMB [fr British dialect *gaumless* "half-silly," lacking *gaum* "understanding"]

go-round *n* A turn; a repetition: *That was nice, let's have another go-round*

See MERRY-GO-ROUND

go round and round *v phr* To quarrel; squabble; fight: *They went round and round the same issues for hours*

gorp[1] *v* To eat greedily; =GORM [perhaps related to *gulp*]

gorp[2] *n* A food mixture of dried fruit, nuts, and seeds, consumed esp by hikers, alpinists, etc [thought to be fr *good old raisins* and *peanuts* and probably related to *gorp*[1]]

gorp gobbler *n phr* A hiker; backpacker: *A Nature-Loving Backpacker is a Gorp Gobbler* —Nevada

gosh *interj* *fr middle 1700s* A mild exclamation of pleasure, disbelief, surprise, etc: *Gosh but I'm tickled, Reverend* [a euphemism for *God*]

go shank's mare *See* RIDE SHANK'S MARE

gosh-awful 1 *adv* Extremely: *Wasn't it gosh-awful dark in there?* **2** *adj* Wretched; miserable; =DARNED: *Isn't that picture gosh-awful?*

◁**go shit in your hat**▷ *See* SHIT IN YOUR HAT

go slumming *See* SLUM

go snooks (or **snucks**) *v phr* *fr middle 1800s* To share equally; go half-and-half: *We are going to go snooks on an electric golf cart*—Milwaukee Tribune [fr British dialect *go snacks,* where *snacks* is related

to earlier US *snook* "a bite to eat"; hence the idiom has to do originally with sharing something to eat]

go soak yourself (or **your head**) *sentence* Cease annoying me; =GO TO HELL: *When I asked for a date she told me to go soak my head*

go sour *v phr* To become unsatisfying; fail; disappoint: *After a couple of years of fame it all went sour*

go south *v phr* To disappear; fail by or as if by vanishing: *He played unbelievably...then all of a sudden he just went south*—Sports Illustrated/ *publicly accused him of going south on me*—Philadelphia Journal/ *concern about injury went south*—Sports Illustrated [probably fr the notion of disappearing *south of the border,* in particular the Mexican border, to escape legal pursuit and responsibility; probably reinforced by the widespread Native American belief that the soul after death journeys to the south, attested in American Colonial writing fr the mid-18th century]

go south with something *v phr* To abscond with something; steal something and disappear: *She went south with a couple of silk pieces*—Dashiell Hammett

gospel *See* BIBLE

gospel-pusher *n* A preacher; minister

go steady *v phr* To have a constant and only boyfriend or girlfriend: *Going steady means taking out one girl until a better one comes along*—Woman's Day

go straight *v phr* *fr underworld* To renounce a life of crime; reform; =SLIPPER

got *See* NO GOT

gotcha 1 *n* A wound or injury, usu minor like a slight razor slice incurred while shaving: *Remember the gotchas you got from that worn old wrench?* **2** *n* A capture; arrest: *"This is a gotcha," Johnson allegedly told Jaffee*—Time [fr *got you*]

gotch-eyed *adj* Having protuberant eyes; exophthalmic: *she is a gotch-eyed...clapped up...hooker* —Dan Jenkins [fr British dialect *gotch* "pitcher, round jug"]

go the extra mile 1 *v phr* To make an extra effort; do more than usual: *It is time to communicate that. It is time to go that extra mile*—Garrison Keillor/ *but for women, you have to go the extra mile to prove your credibility*—Nancy Landon Kassebaum **2** *v phr* To make an extraordinary effort; persevere: *When elected, my friends, I promise to go the extra mile for you all and your beloved families*

go the full yard *v phr* To do the utmost; pursue something to the limit; =GO THE WHOLE HOG [compare with *the whole nine yards*]

go the hang-out road *v phr* *fr 1960s* To make a complete disclosure; abandon all concealment; =LET IT ALL HANG OUT

go the limit (or **all the way**) *v phr* To do the sex act, as distinct from heavy petting, foreplay, etc: *all-American girl must not..."go the limit"*—Frederic Morton

go the whole hog or **go whole hog** *v phr* *fr early 1800s* To do the utmost; not slacken; pursue to the limit; =GO THE FULL YARD: *He decided to go the whole hog and buy a real big boat* [origin uncertain; *whole hog* may be primarily an amusing alliteration with suggestions of something impressively huge]

go the whole nine yards *v phr fr armed forces* To do the utmost; =GO THE LIMIT, GO THE WHOLE HOG: *I went the whole nine yards*—St Elsewhere's (TV program) [see the *whole nine yards*]

go through changes 1 *v phr* To work very hard; strive; =HUSTLE **2** *v phr* To pass through various emotional difficulties; be unstable and unsure: *Since last July 31, he has "gone through every change, from suicidal to who gives a shit"*—Toronto Life

go (or **be**) **through the mill** *v phr fr early 1800s* To have practical experience of something; be thoroughly seasoned: *I think you can rely on her, she's been through the mill*

go to bat *v phr underworld* To be sentenced to prison

go to bat against *v phr* Oppose; contend against: *None of her victims would go to bat against her*—Dashiell Hammett

go to bat for *v phr* To support or defend; help: *He knew his boss would go to bat for him*

go to bed *v phr newspaper office* To be in final form ready for the press: *I can predict before the paper goes to bed*—Westbrook Pegler [probably a reference to the *bed*, the flat surface under the sheet to be printed, of a printing press]

go to bed with someone *v phr* To do the sex act with someone; =SLEEP WITH someone

go to Denmark *v phr* To have a sex-change operation; become a transsexual [fr the fact that such operations were originally done primarily in Denmark]

go toe to toe *v phr* To fight, esp to fight hard; =SLUG IT OUT: *They are going toe-to-toe with Cosmo, Glamour*—Philadelphia/ *Men in the courtroom can go toe to toe and then go off patting each other on the back*—Philadelphia

go together *v phr* To have dates, court, etc

◁**go to hell**▷ **1** *v phr* To deteriorate; be ruined: *The whole town's gone to hell, with that new mayor/ Old Joe's gone to hell a bit lately* **2** *sentence* May you be accursed, confounded, humiliated, etc; =DROP DEAD, GO FUCK oneself: *He wanted me to lie, but I told him to go to hell*

go-to-hell cap *n phr fr WW1 armed forces* A military garrison cap; overseas cap

go to hell in a handbasket (or **a bucket**) *v phr* To deteriorate badly and rapidly; =GO DOWNHILL: *The country's going to hell in a handbasket with this damned inflation/ You'll go to hell in a bucket if you don't get those debts settled/ White people can go to hell in a handbasket, they can go to Burger King and not have their way*—Washington Post

go to pot *v phr* To deteriorate; worsen; =GO DOWNHILL: *A group of men who had literally and figuratively let themselves go to pot get back into good physical condition*—Psychology Today/ *A middle-aged man going to pot gets more than muscle tone from heavy exercise*—Psychology Today [fr the condition of an animal no longer useful for breeding, egg-laying, etc, that will now be cooked in the *pot*]

go (or **be taken**) **to the cleaners** *v phr* To lose all one's money, esp gambling at craps; =TAKE A BATH

go to the dogs *v phr fr 1500s* =GO TO HELL, GO TO POT [fr the notion that something unfit for human food would be given to the lowly *dogs*]

go to the mat *v phr* To fight; contend mightily: *They soon stopped sparring and went to the mat* [fr the *mat* used as a wrestling site]

go to the wall 1 *v phr* To be ruined and destitute; collapse: *if a real biggie, like Brazil, say, went to the wall*—Playboy **2** *v phr* To do the utmost; =GO ALL THE WAY: *We've gone to the wall for you*—Cagney and Lacey (TV program) [first sense fr the plight of someone being executed by being shot, against a *wall*]

go to (or **down to**) **the wire** *v phr* To be in very close competition until the very end; =be NIP AND TUCK: *The 1928 pennant race between the A's and the Yanks went to the wire*—Philadelphia/ *They were absolutely evenly matched and went right down to the wire*

go to town 1 *v phr* To do very well; succeed; perform impressively **2** *v phr* To throw off restraint; let go

got to give *See* SOMETHING'S GOT TO GIVE

got up on (or **out of**) **the wrong side of the bed** *v phr fr late 1800s* To be peevish, perverse, etc; be in a nasty mood: *He just about bit my head off, must have got on the wrong side of the bed*

goulash 1 *n fr 1920s underworld* False information; unreliable data **2** *n police* A place where criminals, gamblers, etc, congregate, esp an eating place **3** *n gambling* A way of dealing a hand of cards so that everyone gets an unusual hand [fr the name of the Hungarian dish, with the general sense of "mess, strange mixture"]

goulashes or **goolashes** (G⌢OO lash əz) *n* Galoshes, as amusingly mispronounced

go under *v phr fr late 1800s* To fail; sink; esp, to lose consciousness

go underground *v phr* To take up a concealed life; go into hiding, typically with a false identity, esp in order to avoid arrest: *His partners were caught, but he was able to go underground until the amnesty went into effect*

goup *See* GOOP

go up 1 *v phr narcotics* To become intoxicated from narcotics **2** *v phr musicians* To make a mistake in playing; =FLUFF **3** *v phr theater* =GO UP IN one's LINES

go up against *v phr* To confront; face; challenge: *So that's the kind of piffle actors have to go up against*—H McHugh/ *He wants to go up against the champ*

go up in one's **lines** *v phr theater fr early 1900s* To forget or badly misspeak one's lines during a performance; =GO UP IN THE AIR

go up in smoke *v phr* To be ruined; be destroyed: *He just saw his careful scam go up in smoke*

go up in the air 1 *v phr theater* To miss a cue, forget one's lines, etc; = FLUFF **2** *v phr fr early 1900s* To lose one's composure; become angry; = LOSE one's COOL: *You will rouse his anger, and he may "go up in the air"*—DS Martin

go (or **hit**) **upside** one's **face** (or **head**) **1** *v phr black* To beat and pummel, esp around the head **2** *v phr* To defeat utterly; trounce; = CLOBBER

go up the wall *See* CLIMB THE WALL

gourd *n fr middle 1800s* The head; skull
See LOSE one's GOURD, OUT OF one's HEAD

governor 1 *n fr early 1920s* One's father **2** *n fr 1920s circus & carnival* Any superior or supervisor; = BOSS

gow (GOU) **1** *n outdated narcotics fr early 1900s underworld* Opium **2** *n outdated narcotics* Any narcotic **3** *n outdated narcotics* A marijuana cigarette; = JOINT **4** *n* Pictures of unclad or scarcely clad women; = LEG ART: *this type of artwork, which in the newspaper field is called "cheesecake" and in the paperbooks field is "gow"*—Publishers Weekly [fr Canton Chinese, *yao-kao*, "sap, opium"]

gowed up *adj phr outdated narcotics* Intoxicated with a narcotic; = HIGH, HOPPED UP: *some gowed-up runt*—Raymond Chandler

go whole hog *See* GO THE WHOLE HOG

go with the flow *v phr fr 1960s counterculture* To consign oneself to the order and pace of things; be passive: *They pondered a while and decided to go with the flow and they all went back to sleep*—Tom Wolfe

go (or **come**) **with the territory** *v phr* To be an integral part of some occupation or status, esp a part which is not especially delightful: *At EPA It Goes With the Territory*—New York Times/ *Tierney's answer was that such speculation "goes with the territory"*—New York/ *Being blamed for everything comes with the territory* [fr the conditions implicit in a sales representative's covering of a certain *territory*, popularized by use in the Requiem section of Arthur Miller's play, *Death of a Salesman*]

gow job *n phr hot rodders* = HOT ROD

go wrong 1 *v phr* To become a criminal, deviant, etc: *a good preacher till he went wrong* **2** *v phr* To make a mistake; err: *Where did we go wrong, oh where?*

gowster *n outdated narcotics* A marijuana user; = POTHEAD

◁**goy**▷ **1** *n* A non-Jew; Gentile: *My dad reads the Talmud all the time and hates goys*—Sinclair Lewis/ *He knows no more about the Torah than a goy*—Budd Schulberg **2** *adj: The mob's strictly goy*—American Mercury [fr Hebrew]

◁**goyische**▷ (GOI ish ə) *adj* Non-Jewish; Gentile: *hotsy-totsy free weekend in Atlantic City, to a fancy goyische hotel*—Philip Roth

◁**goyische kop**▷ *n phr* Gentile attributes as perceived by Jews in a somewhat hostile vein, esp when found in a Jewish person: *The first Jewish mayor will be one with a "goyische kop"*—Dick Schaap [fr Yiddish, "Gentile head"]

grab 1 *v police* An arrest; = BUST, PINCH: *We will get credit for the grab, and we will also profit*—Lawrence Sanders/ *The only thing worse than no grab is a bad grab*—Cosmopolitan **2** *v* To seize the admiration or attention of; impress: *How does that grab you?*—New Yorker/ *to reflect on a whole lot of things that had been grabbing me*—New York Times

grab a handful of air *v phr truckers* To apply the brakes of a truck or bus quickly [fr the fact that such vehicles have *hand*-operated *air* brakes]

grab a handful of rods *v phr hoboes* To ride on the rods of a freight car; = RIDE THE RODS: *I grabbed myself a handful of rods*—Jack Dempsey

grab an armful of boxcars *v phr hoboes* To jump on a moving freight train

◁**grab-ass** or **grabarse**▷ *n* Sexual touching and clutching: *Nothing serious, just a little grab-ass between them/ less anxious, less suspicious about my merry games of grabarse*—John Cheever
See PLAY GRAB-ASS

grab-bag *n* A miscellaneous mixture; random collection: *the grab-bag of memories in my muddled head*

grabber 1 *n railroad* A passenger-train conductor **2** *n* Anything that seizes and rivets the attention; something that commands immediate admiration; = HOOK: *Dance within the regular format is a solid grabber*—Variety/ *He's found a real grabber*—Westworld
See GOOBER-GRABBER, MOTHERFUCKER

grabby 1 *adj* Greedy; acquisitive; selfish: *Share that, don't be grabby* **2** *adj* Seizing; arresting; riveting: *spent hours working on a goddamn grabby lead*—Armistead Maupin

grab-joint *n circus & carnival fr 1930s* A booth that sells souvenirs, cotton candy, food, etc

grabs *See* UP FOR GRABS

grab shot *n phr* A photograph taken in great haste, without time for proper focusing, exposure-setting, etc; a photograph of opportunity

grab your socks *See* DROP YOUR COCKS AND GRAB YOUR SOCKS

grad 1 *n fr late 1800s* A graduate: *college grad* **2** *modifier: a grad student/ grad reunion*

grade *See* EATIN' STUFF

the **grade** *See* MAKE THE GRADE

graft 1 *n fr late 1800s British* One's occupation; = GAME, RACKET **2** *n fr early 1900s* The acquisition of money by dishonest means, esp by bribery for political favors: *the usual charges of graft at City Hall* [origin unknown]

gramps *n* Grandfather; any old man: *Need any help, gramps?*

grand *n fr early 1900s underworld & sports* A thousand dollars; = GEE: *A banker would scarcely call one thousand dollars "one grand"*—JC Hixson [said to have originated with Peaches Van Camp, a criminal who flashed such *grand* notes for ostentation]

the **grand bounce** *n phr* = the BOUNCE

Grand Central Station *n phr* Any place that is overcrowded and busy: *My office was like Grand Central Station this morning*

grandfather or **granddaddy** **1** *n* The prime example of something; the oldest, biggest, chief; dean; doyen: *That must be the grandfather of all excuses* **2** *v* To give someone a special status or privilege because of service prior to the time a new or definitive arrangement was made: *They gave all the newly qualified a license on examination, and grandfathered the experienced ones* [the second sense is fr the *grandfather clause* often written into new arrangements in order to be fair to older incumbents or practitioners]

grandma **1** *n* truckers The lowest and slowest gear of a truck **2** *n* Any old woman: *Can I carry your groceries, grandma?*

grand slam **1** *n phr* The winning of all the goals, games, prizes, etc, available; total comprehensive victory: *Nobody won the tennis grand slam last year* **2** *n phr* baseball =GRAND SLAMMER **3** *modifier: grand-slam home run* [fr a bridge term for the winning of all the tricks in one hand]

grand slammer *n phr* baseball A home run hit when all the bases are occupied, and scoring four runs

grandstand **1** *v* fr late 1800s To play or perform in a brilliant and spectacular way, esp in order to get the approval of an audience; =HOT DOG, SHOW OFF: *Coach told him to stop grandstanding and take care of business* **2** *modifier: a grandstand catch*

grandstander *n* A person who habitually grandstands; =HOT DOG, SHOW-OFF

grandstand play **1** *n phr* A play made with special brilliance and brio, esp in order to impress the spectators **2** *n phr* Any action, speech, tactic, etc, designed to appeal to spectators; a tour de force: *The President's pronouncement's just a grandstand play*

granny dress *n phr* fr 1960s A floor-length dress, usu with long sleeves and a high neckline

granny flat *n phr* A small cottage or apartment where elderly people may live near but not actually with their childrens' family; =MOTHER-IN-LAW APARTMENT

granny glasses *n phr* fr 1960s Eyeglasses with small, circular steel or gold frames

grape *n* Wine or champagne
See IRISH GRAPE

grapefruit league *n phr* baseball The association of major league teams as they play each other in preseason training [fr the fact that most spring training camps are held in citrus-growing regions]

the **grapes** *n phr* Champagne

grapevine *adj* Coming from an unofficial source of rumor or news: *a grapevine item/ grapevine gossip*

the **grapevine** *n phr* fr Civil War The source and route of rumors and unofficial news: *The grapevine says we're moving soon/ I heard it through the grapevine*—Norma Whitfield and Barrett Strong

grappo *n* hoboes Wine [perhaps fr Italian *grappa* "brandy"]

grass **1** *n* Lettuce or other salad material; =BUNNY FOOD **2** *n* black The straight hair typical of Caucasians **3** *n* narcotics Marijuana; =POT: *smoking a little grass and passing on venereal disease*—New York Times/ *Scoring grass here is easier than buying a loaf of bread*—New Yorker
See one's ASS IS GRASS

grass-cutter or **grass-clipper** *n* baseball A very low and hard line drive

grasseater *n* A corrupt police officer who accepts graft money but does not demand it: *repeated the distinction between the "grass eater" and the "meat eater"*—New York Times/ *The grasseaters are turning themselves in*—New York Post

grasshopper *n* narcotics A person who smokes marijuana; =POTHEAD: *My wife was a little grasshopper herself. But she didn't go on to become an addict*—RV Winslow

grass weed *n phr* outdated narcotics Marijuana; =GRASS

grass widow *n phr* fr late 1800s A woman who is alone because of divorce, separation, rejection, etc [because her husband is still above the *grass* rather than under it]

gratis *See* FREE GRATIS

graum *v* To worry; fret: *All a bookmaker graums about is they don't drop a atom bomb*—J Cannon [perhaps fr Middle English *gramen* "be afflicted or tormented," fr Old English]

grave *See* HAVE ONE FOOT IN THE GRAVE

gravel *See* HIT THE DIRT

graveyard shift *n phr* A working shift that begins at midnight or 2 AM

graveyard watch *n phr* railroad & Army A period of guard or watch duty from midnight to 4 AM or 8 AM

gravy *n* fr early 1900s Money or other valuables beyond what one actually earns or needs; a bonus or excess: *Once we make back our expenses, everything is gravy*

gravy ride *n phr* A life or period lived on unearned or abundant funds

gravy train (or **boat**) *n phr* fr early 1900s sports A chance, job, business, etc, that gives a very ample return for little or no work; an obvious sinecure: *His job's a permanent gravy train*
See ON THE GRAVY TRAIN, RIDE THE GRAVY TRAIN

◄**gray**► **1** *n* black A white person; Caucasian; =OFAY **2** *adj: What about that gray girl in San Jose who had your nose wide open?*—Eldridge Cleaver

graybeard *n* airline A very senior pilot

gray market *n phr* The sale of reputable products, esp cameras and electronic equipment, by persons who have not bought them from the manufacturers' authorized distributors, and hence offer lower prices because the products do not qualify for the makers' guarantees

gray matter *n phr* Intelligence; =BRAINS, SMARTS

gray mule *See* WHITE MULE

graze *v* Army, prison & students To eat a meal

greafa or **greapha** *See* GREEFA

grease 1 *n esp 1800s* Money **2** *n underworld fr 1930s* Bribe or protection money; money given for corrupt purposes **3** *n WW2 Army* Butter **4** *n* Influence; =PULL: *You can't get a job here without plenty of grease* **5** *v police* To shoot, esp to kill by shooting: *He has a gun and might try to grease you*—Rolling Stone **6** *n: You handled the grease real good, but not good enough, you didn't kill them*—Robert Daley [police senses fr the notion of *greasegun*, whether for lubricant or for bullets] *See* AXLE GREASE, ELBOW GREASE, GOOBER-GREASE, GREASE someone's PALM, HOT GREASE, SKID GREASE

greaseball ◀1▶ *n* A dark-skinned, dark-haired person of Mediterranean or Latin American origin; =DAGO, GREASER: *taking knives away from greaseballs in zoot suits*—Raymond Chandler **2** *n hoboes* A dirty tramp **3** *n WW2 Navy* A cook or kitchen worker **4** *n circus* A hamburger stand or concession **5** *n theater fr 1920s* An actor who uses too much makeup or greasepaint

grease-burner *n* A cook, esp one who fries food at a lunch counter

greased *adj* Drunk

greased lightning *n phr* Something or someone extraordinarily fast; =A BLUE STREAK: *He got out of there like greased lightning*

greasegun *n phr fr WW2 armed forces* A submachine gun, esp one with a cylindrical body resembling a lubricating grease gun: *The Army's present standard model, the M-3 "greasegun"*—Associated Press

grease it in *v phr aviators* To land an aircraft smoothly

grease job *n phr Air Force* A very smooth landing *See* GIVE someone A GREASE JOB

grease joint 1 *n phr circus & carnival fr early 1900s* The cookhouse and eating tent **2** *n phr* Any inexpensive diner or food stand; =GREASY SPOON

grease monkey 1 *n phr* A worker who lubricates machines, esp automobiles: *Good grease monkeys all, they could think better with a grease rack to lean against*—J Ellison **2** *n phr merchant marine* A stoker, oiler, or wiper on a ship **3** *n phr* Any mechanic, esp an automotive mechanic

grease (or **cross** or **oil**) someone's **palm** *v phr* To pay someone for a corrupt purpose; bribe; buy favors: *If you grease the commissioner's palm, you can get anything fixed*—Jim Tully/ *Officials whose palms have been crossed*—A Hynd

grease-pusher *n theater* A theatrical makeup person

◀greaser▶ 1 *n fr early 1800s* =GREASEBALL ● Used esp in referring to a Mexican or an Italian **2** *n esp 1950s teenagers* A hoodlum, petty thief, etc; =PUNK [second sense fr the *grease* used for their typical combed-back hairstyle]

grease the skids *v phr* To cause or cooperate in the rapid decline or failure of someone or something: *When your time comes, you bastard, I hope I can grease the skids*

grease trough (or **pit**) *n phr* A lunch counter or lunch room: *Imagine yourself in the grease trough again*—Saturday Evening Post/ *a shadowy grease pit midway between*—Time

greasy 1 *adj* Repellent in an unctuous and cunning way; =OILY **2** *adj horse-racing* Muddy and slippery: *to negotiate a "greasy" mile before an approving audience*—Morning Telegraph

greasy grind *n phr fr early 1900s* A very diligent student

greasy spoon *n phr* A small, cheap restaurant, lunchroom, or diner: *The Marx brothers ate in coffee pots and greasy spoons*—Joel Sayre/ *your above-average greasy spoon in Boston's Back Bay*—Time

great 1 *adj* Excellent; wonderful: *Hey, that's really great* **2** *n* A famous person, esp an athlete or entertainer: *Weiss, a former football "great"*—Philadelphia Inquirer

the **greatest** *n phr fr bop & cool talk* A person or thing of superlative quality; =the MOST

the **greatest thing since sliced bread** *See* the BEST THING SINCE SLICED BREAD

great guns *See* GO GREAT GUNS

great shakes *See* NO GREAT SHAKES

greedball *n* Professional baseball as administered and played by very high-paid and wealthy persons

greefa *n* (Variations: **goifa** or **greafa** or **greapha** or **greefo** or **greeta** or **grefa** or **griefo** or **griffa** or **grifo**) *narcotics* Marijuana or a marijuana cigarette [fr Mexican Spanish *griffa* "weed"]

Greek 1 *n college students* A college fraternity member ◁**2▷** *v* To do anal intercourse, esp heterosexually

◁**Greek fashion** (or **style**)▷ *adv phr* Anally: *They did it Greek fashion*

◁the **Greek way** (or **style**)▷ **1** *n phr* Anal intercourse, esp heterosexual: *Another request is for Greek style. That is, anal sex*—Xaviera Hollander **2** *adv phr* =GREEK FASHION

green *n fr 1920s underworld & sports* Money, esp ready cash; =FOLDING MONEY: *plus "green" or "front money" to pay off others*—New York Times *See* FOLDING MONEY, JERSEY GREEN, LONG GREEN, MEAN GREEN, SHIT GREEN

green apples *See* SURE AS GOD MADE LITTLE GREEN APPLES

green (or **blue**) **around the gills** *adj phr* Sick-looking; pale and miserable; nauseated: *He was looking green around the gills so I told him to lie down*

◁**green-ass**▷ *adj* New and inexperienced; callow; green: *I spent thirty-four months havin' green-ass corporals chew me up*—Nelson Algren

the **green deck** *n phr* Grass

green fly *See* FLY

green folding *n phr* =FOLDING MONEY

green goods *n phr fr late 1800s* Counterfeit paper money

greenhorn *n fr middle 1800s* An inexperienced person; newcomer; neophyte; =ROOKIE

greenhouse *n aviators* The transparent cockpit cover of an airplane

green ice *n phr underworld* Emeralds

greenie 1 *n* =GREENHORN **2** *n* narcotics A heart-shaped green stimulant pill of dextroamphetamine: *Do you take something, like greenies?* —Sports Illustrated/ *Greenies are pep pills...and a lot of baseball players couldn't function without them*—Jim Bouton

the **green light** *n phr* Permission, esp a superior's approval to proceed; =the GO-AHEAD: *Once she gives us the green light, we crank it up/ He got the green light on a three-and-oh pitch and whacked one out of here*

greenmail *n* The buying, at a premium price, of the stock holdings of someone who is threatening to take over a company, in order to induce the person to cease the attempt: *The most cited recent case of greenmail...occurred this spring and summer as Walt Disney Productions fought to escape a take-over*—New York Times/ *But Wall Street analysts agreed that CBS was unlikely to consider such action, since it amounts to "greenmail"*—New York Daily News [modeled on *blackmail*]

green money *n phr* Paper money; ready cash; =FOLDING MONEY: *shooting for green money*—A Hynd

the **green stuff** *n phr* Money; ready cash; paper money; =FOLDING MONEY, LONG GREEN: *He really poured the green stuff to the bookies*—S Frank

a **green thumb 1** *n phr* A special talent for gardening **2** *n phr* The ability to make projects succeed, like flourishing plants: *possessor of a green thumb when it comes to making musicals blossom* —H Ormsbee

greeta or **grefa** *See* GREEFA

gremlin 1 *n* WW2 Army Air Forces fr British perhaps fr WWI An imaginary imp who caused malfunction in machines, problems in projects, confusion in arrangements, etc **2** *n* surfers A person, esp a girl, who frequents surfing beaches without surfing; =BEACH BUNNY: *gremlins, usually girls, those hangers-on who may never get wet*—Time [origin unknown; probably modeled on *goblin*, with the first syllable perhaps fr Irish *gruaimin* "irascible little creature"]

gremmy or **gremmie** *n* =GREMLIN

grette *See* GRIT

greyhound 1 *n* circus A fast-working salesperson **2** *v* To run, esp in escape or pursuit: *The cop went greyhounding after the purse-snatcher* [fr the speed of the *greyhound*, a racing dog]

greyhound therapy *n phr* The practice by some municipalities or other governmental groups of ridding themselves of the homeless and other potentially burdensome persons by giving them a bus ticket to another place: *Greyhound therapy...giving the homeless a one-way bus ticket to Los Angeles* —New York Times [fr the name of the *Greyhound* bus company]

grid or **gridiron 1** *n* A football field **2** *modifier: the grid squad/ gridiron victories*

gridlock *n* A blockage; paralysis: *Until the emotional and psychological gridlock over the Federal deficit is broken*—Newsweek [fr the traffic term designating a total blockage of traffic caused by cars stopping in intersections behind other stopped cars, and blocking traffic on the intersecting street]

grief *See* GIVE someone GRIEF

griefo or **grifo** or **griffa** *See* GREEFA

grift fr carnival & circus **1** *n* Money gotten dishonestly and by one's wits, esp by swindling **2** *n* Any dishonest way of getting money by cunning, esp the deceptions of confidence tricksters, hawkers, etc **3** *v: He grifted a couple years then got a regular job*

See ON THE GRIFT

grifter 1 *n* circus A gambler **2** *n* A confidence trickster, hawker, minor criminal, etc **3** *n* A hobo; vagabond; =DRIFTER

grind 1 *v* fr middle 1800s To rotate one's pelvis in the sex act or in imitation of the sex act ● Nearly always in combination with **bump**: *the strippers bumping and grinding away* **2** *n: to wow the audience with her bumps and grinds*—Trans-Action **3** *v* fr middle 1800s To study diligently: *Five days to grind and two days to be social...the way it was at Yale*—Sexual Behavior **4** *n: No one except a few notorious grinds studied that night*—P Marks **5** *v* circus To attract and address a crowd at a show or concession; =SPIEL **6** *n: They heard the hawker go into his grind* **7** *n* circus A hawker or barker **8** *n* Any obnoxious or annoying person; =JERK, a PAIN IN THE NECK, PILL: *The prof's a tedious old grind* **9** *n* Any very difficult and trying task, esp one that lasts a long time and is slowly and painfully done: *Writing dictionaries is indeed a grind*

See BUMP AND GRIND, GREASY GRIND, IF YOU CAN'T FIND 'EM, GRIND 'EM

grinder 1 *n* circus & carnival fr 1920s A barker or hawker **2** *n* A stripteaser; =STRIPPER **3** *n* A car, esp an old and ramshackle one: *bought a brand new Chev to take the place of her old grinder*—J Lilienthal **4** *n* =HERO SANDWICH **5** *n* Marine Corps A parade ground; drill field

See COFFEE GRINDER

grind-house or **grind movie** *n* or *n phr* theater A theater that runs continuously without intermissions, holidays, etc: *Four years ago, it would have been restricted to a few downtown grind-houses* —Time/ *He dragged me to the Times Square grind-house to which it had been relegated*—San Francisco [probably fr *grind show*, perhaps influenced by the burlesque and sexual connotations of *grind*]

grinding *See* BIT-GRINDING

grind something **out** *v phr* To produce or make something, esp with uninspired precision or long and painful effort: *They sat down and ground the script out in two days/ They just grind them out...ten a day*

grind show *n phr* outdated carnival A show that runs continuously [probably because the show *grinds* along like a machine]

grip 1 *n* theater & movie studio A stagehand or stage carpenter: *crowded with assistant directors, character actors, movie stars, grips and electricians* —H Niemeyer **2** *n* fr middle 1800s A travelling bag; valise [second sense a shortening of *gripsack*]

gripe **1** *v fr late 1800s* To complain, esp habitually and trivially; groan; =BITCH, KVETCH, PISS: *He got good and sore and griped*—Morris Bishop **2** *n*: *I want to clear my desk of various matters, mostly gripes*—Bernard DeVoto **3** *v* To annoy or disgust; exasperate: *What's griping him is that he can't do anything for the kids*—James T Farrell **4** *n* =GRIPER [ultimately fr *griping of the gut* "colic, bellyache, stomach cramp"]

◁**gripe** one's **ass**▷ *v phr* (Variations: **balls** or **butt** or **cookies** or **left nut** or **middle kidney** or **soul**, or some other organ or possession at the whim of the speaker, may replace **ass**) To disgust or annoy someone extremely: *His sycophancy gripes my ass*

griper *n* A chronic complainer; malcontent; =KVETCH

the **gripes** **1** *n phr* A spell of complaining; =BITCHING **2** *n phr* The habit of frequent or trivial complaining

gripe session *n phr* A conversation or discussion consisting primarily of complaints

gripper *See* GROUND-GRIPPER

grit **1** *n fr late 1700s* Courage; fortitude and stamina **2** *n railroad* The roadpath beside a railroad track **3** *v black* To eat **4** *n* (also **grits**) *black fr 1930s* Food **5** *n* A Southerner: *He's a hotshot down here among the grits. A good Yankee guard would eat him alive*—Pat Conroy **6** *n* (also **Grit**) *Southern* A Northerner: *It's a God's wonder some Grit didn't kill us*—Harry Crews **7** *n* (also **grette**) A cigarette [food senses at least partially fr *hominy grits*, although *grit* was British military slang for "food" in the 1930s; Southern dialect sense probably ironically fr Civil War use of the expression *true Yankee grit* by Northern soldiers and writers]

See HIT THE DIRT

gritty *See* the NITTY GRITTY

groady or **groaty** or **groddy** *See* GROTTY

groan box *n phr* An accordion

groaner *n* A singer, esp a crooner of the 1930s

See GRUNT-AND-GROANER

groceries *n* A meal or meals: *I got hooked for the groceries*—Sherman Billingsley

See BRING HOME THE BACON

grogged **1** *adj* Drunk **2** *adj* Sleepy; =GROGGY [fr British naval *grog* "rum and water," so called because it was introduced in the mid-18th century as a sailor's ration by "Old *Grog*," Admiral Sir Edward Vernon, who habitually wore a *grogram* coat]

groggy *adj fr late 1700s British* Sleepy; dazed; semiconscious

groghound *n students* A drinker of alcohol, esp of beer

grog-mill **1** *n* A saloon; tavern **2** *modifier*: *no grog-mill cuties*—J Evans

◀**groid**▶ *n esp Southern & college students* A black person: *The groids sure love to fish*—John McPhee [fr *Negroid*]

grok (GRAHK) **1** *v esp 1960s counterculture & students* To communicate sympathetically: *all rapping and grokking over the sound it made*—Tom Wolfe/ *All the Romans grokked like Greeks*—Pulp-

smith **2** *v esp 1960s counterculture & students* To get into exquisite sympathy with: *She met him at an acid-rock ball and she grokked him*—Playboy **3** *v esp computer* To understand: *You've come to grok that Cronenberg's narrative is merely the pretense for his imagery*—Village Voice [coined by Robert A Heinlein as a Martian word in the science-fiction novel *Stranger in a Strange Land*]

grollo *n* =GROWLER

gronk out *v phr computer* To cease functioning; =GO DOWN: *The terminal gronked out about ten minutes ago*

grooby *adj fr jive talk* Excellent; =GROOVY: *You, too, can get on the grooby side*—Time

groove **1** *n* Any habitually preferred activity; what excites and gratifies one; =BAG, KICK **2** *v* To enjoy intensely; take gratification, esp rather passively and subjectively; =GO WITH THE FLOW: *To groove means to yield yourself to the flow of activity around you*—New York Times/ *If you want to groove, go get yourself some groovy clothes*—New York **3** *v* To like and approve; =DIG: *They see the spade cat going with ofay chicks and they don't groove it*—R DeWolf **4** *v* To perform very well; be effective: *really grooving on that funny trumpet* [fr the sense that a musician is in a definite and exciting track, has hit a perfect stride, when playing well, esp a solo; perhaps influenced by the *grooves* of a phonograph record]

See IN THE GROOVE

a **groove** *n phr* Something excellent, desirable, exciting, etc: *Working at ABC is "a groove"*—New York/ *Your hat is a groove*—Harper's Bazaar

groove on something or someone *v phr* To enjoy intensely; =GROOVE: *I can really groove on the Beatles*—New York Times/ *She walks for blocks grooving on Reality*—Gail Sheehy

groovy **1** *adj jive talk fr 1930s* Playing and enjoying music well and with concentration; =HEP, IN THE GROOVE **2** *adj* Excellent; wonderful; =FAR OUT: *"Hey, groovy," said Sally*—Max Shulman **3** *adj teenagers* Obsolete; out-of-date: *She was wearing groovy saddle-shoes*

grope *v* To touch, feel, caress, fondle, etc, with seeming or actual sexual intent

See GROUP-GROPE

grope-in *n* =GROUP-GROPE

gross *adj esp teenagers fr 1960s* Disgusting; rebarbative; =GROTTY: *at this moment (how gross!) blowing kisses into the phone*—Erich Segal

grossed out *adj phr esp teenagers & students fr 1960s* Disgusted; revulsed

gross-out *esp teenagers fr 1960s* **1** *n* Something particularly disgusting; repellent trash: *He attempts...the ultimate gross-out: "self-expression" of the kind found in Greenwich Village*—Newsweek **2** *modifier*: *The Animal House gross-out movies are all about groups*—New York/ *gross-out scenes of the Dalmatian mounting the smaller dog*—Toronto Life

gross someone **out** *v phr esp teenagers fr 1970s* To disgust or offend, esp with crude and obscene language and behavior: *They're grossing me out* *too, you know*—Cyra McFadden/ *Being a mother really grosses me out*—Erma Bombeck

grotty (GROH dee, -tee) **1** *adj* (Variations: **groady** or **groaty** or **groddy**; **to the max** may be added) *esp teenagers fr 1960s* Disgusting; nasty; repellent; bizarre; = GRUNGY, SCUZZY: *The magazines had covers with those grotty weirdos on them*—Philadelphia **2** *noun:* *the introspective hedonism and political individualism of the second group...called groddies*—Trans-Action [fr *grotesque*; popularized by the Beatles in the 1960s; perhaps fr Merseyside dialect]

grouch-bag *circus* **1** *n* A small bag in which money for an emergency is carried: *Circus roustabouts took their money out of grouch-bags, pouches...like tobacco pouches*—Nelson Algren **2** *n* The money in a grouch-bag; = MAD MONEY

ground *See* BEAT TO THE GROUND, DOWN TO THE GROUND, NOT KNOW one's ASS FROM one's ELBOW, NOT KNOW someone or something FROM A HOLE IN THE GROUND, RUN something INTO THE GROUND, STAMPING GROUND

ground someone *v phr* To deny privileges to someone, esp to keep someone confined at home as a punishment: *If my father got a pair of bell-bottoms, I think I'd ground him*—McCall's/ *I got grounded in my room for three days because I whispered to somebody* [fr the practice of not permitting a pilot to fly, as a punishment]

ground apple *n phr lumberjacks* A rock

ground biscuit *n phr* = ALLEY APPLE

grounder **1** *n hoboes* A cigarette butt **2** *n* A batted baseball that rolls along the ground

ground floor *See* IN ON THE GROUND FLOOR

ground-gripper *WW2 Navy* **1** *n* A landlubber **2** *n* A sailor who neither flies in an airplane nor sails in a ship

groundhog *n railroad* A train's brake operator

ground out *v phr baseball* To hit a ball along the ground and make an out, usu by a fielder's throwing to first base

ground rations *n phr black* The sex act [probably fr the sexual sense of *grind* plus the frequent association of the sex act with eating]

groundskeeping *n sports* Meticulous smoothing and adjusting of turf and dirt where one is to hit, throw, bat, etc, esp when done to fluster an opponent

group *See* IN GROUP, RAP GROUP

group-grope **1** *n* Mutual touching and caressing by a group of people, either plainly orgiastic or with some sort of psychotherapeutic intent; = GROPE-IN **2** *n* Intimate intertwining of entities: *Harvard will reestablish an independent department of sociology, ending 24 years of interdisciplinary group-grope*—John Leonard

groupie *fr 1960s rock and roll* **1** *n* A young woman who seeks to share the glamor of famous persons, esp rock musicians, by offering help and sexual favors; = BUNNY: *a story about "groupies"...youthful females committing sexual aggression against juvenile rock musicians/ No fool, no groupie, no teeny-bopper, she takes rock music, rightly, seriously*—Vogue **2** *n* An ardent devotee and votary; = FAN: *like many of Hollywood's young trendies, a political groupie*—Newsweek/ *the American literary groupies*—Saturday Review **3** *modifier: the "groupie" syndrome, personified by adulatory novices of science flocking around the luminaries*—Dan Greenberg

grouse *v fr late 1800s British armed forces* To complain; = BITCH: *No grousing, no foot-dragging, both signs of a solid pro*—Harper's

growl *v* To complain; mutter angrily

growler **1** *n* (also **grollo**) *esp late 1800s* A container used to carry beer home from a bar: *A can brought in filled with beer at a barroom is called a growler*—B Matthews **2** *n WW2 Navy* A public-address loudspeaker or system; = BITCH BOX, SQUAWK BOX **3** *n* A small iceberg

See RUSH THE GROWLER

growler-rushing **1** *n esp late 1800s* A drinking spree **2** *modifier: Heslin was the contemptible, growler-rushing type of petty thief*—E Lavine

growth *modifier* Becoming or likely to become more vigorous, valuable, profitable, etc: *Cancer research is a growth industry/ Buy some growth stocks*

grub **1** *n fr late 1800s cowboys* Food: *goods one can exchange at the kitchen door for grub*—Jack London/ *nonchalantly gobble up mounds of this grub*—CoEvolution Quarterly **2** *v black: Come over and grub with us*—O Johnson [fr *grub stake*, the food provided for miners or prospectors who would go out to dig (*grub*) for useful ore]

grub-pile *n cowboys* A meal

grub-slinger *n cowboys* A cook

grubstake *n fr middle 1800s* The money needed for a new venture, new start, etc: *Nobody knows how much he gave away in grubstakes*—T Betts

grunge or **grunch** (GRUHNJ, GRUHNCH) *teenagers* **1** *n* A dull, tedious person; = NERD, PILL **2** *adj* Boring **3** *adj* = GRUNGY **4** *n* Slovenliness; sloppiness **5** *n* Something nasty: *Look at the grunge at the bottom of that bottle/ Those globs of guitar grunge get me off every time*—Village Voice

grungy (GRUHN jee) *adj teenagers fr 1960s* Shabby; squalid; dirty; = GROTTY, SCUZZY: *I put down in my grungy little notebook that Max Frisch was a wise man*—C Vetter/ *the peerless, fearless, slightly grungy Grodin to investigate*—Richard Grenier [origin unknown; perhaps sound symbolism resembling *gross, mangy, mung, stingy*, etc]

grunt **1** *n line repairers* A line repairer's helper who works on the ground and does not climb poles **2** *n railroad* A locomotive engineer; = HOGGER **3** *n fr Vietnam War armed forces* An infantry soldier; = PADDLEFOOT: *I was drafted...and served twelve months as a grunt in Vietnam*—Newsweek/ *Now there's a willingness to tell the story of the poor grunt who got his tail shot off*—New York Times **4** *n* Any low-ranking person, neophyte, etc: *The attitude among the reporter grunts was pretty much "them against us"*—Washingtonian **5** *n* Pork or ham; pig meat **6** *n* A bill for food or drink: *I just hope Toots didn't bring along any of the grunts I must have left in that oasis*—Paul Sann **7** *n* A diligent student; =GRIND: *A grunt is a student who gives a shit about nothing except his sheepskin*—Stephen King **8** *n* A wrestler, esp an inferior one; =GRUNT-AND-GROANER **9** *n* Wrestling, as sport and entertainment **10** *modifier: the grunt scene/ grunt show on TV* **11** *v* To defecate *See* CLUCK AND GRUNT

grunt-and-groaner *n* A wrestler

grunter *n* A wrestler

grunt-horn or **grunt-iron** *n musicians* A tuba

grunts *n* Bacon

grunt work (or **labor**) *n phr* Hard and/or tedious toil; =SCUT WORK: *The machine will do the grunt work, filing, typing lists, comparing, sorting*—San Francisco

G-string *See* GEE STRING

guard *See* CORPORAL'S GUARD, HOME GUARD

guardhouse lawyer *n phr fr middle 1800s Army* =LATRINE LAWYER

guck (GUHK) *n* Any sticky, viscous substance; =GOO, GLOP: *Joan has white guck all over her face*—Philadelphia

guess *See* BY GUESS AND BY GOD

guess-stick *n college students* A slide rule; =SLIP-STICK

guff **1** *n fr late 1800s* Nonsense; pretentious talk; bold and deceitful absurdities; =BULLSHIT: *his ability to listen to all the guff, through all the tedium*—Time **2** *n* Complaints, abuse: *Don't take any guff from him*—New Yorker **3** *v* To lie; exaggerate; =BULLSHIT: *Quit your guffing and tell it right* [perhaps fr British dialect *guff* "fool," or Scots "a puff of wind"]

guide *See* TOUR GUIDE

the guilties *n phr* Feelings or pangs of guilt: *Sometimes...we get the guilties on this account*—Newsweek

◀**Guinea**▶ (GIHN ee) (also **ghinney** or **ginee** or **ginnee** or **ginney** or **guin** or **guinea** or **guinie**; any of the variants may begin with a capital letter) *fr late 1800s* **1** *n* An Italian or person of Italian descent **2** *adj: a tough Ginney bootlegger*—Damon Runyon **3** *n WW2 armed forces* A native of a Pacific island, including Japan [perhaps fr contemptuous association with the outdated term *Guinea Negro* "black slave from the Guinea coast"]

◀**guinea football**▶ *n phr* A small bomb, esp a homemade one; =ITALIAN FOOTBALL

guinney *n horse-racing* A racetrack stable hand

◀**guinzo**▶ *See* GINZO

gulch *See* DRY-GULCH

gull **1** *n merchant marine* Chicken or other fowl **2** *n WW2 Navy* A prostitute

gully *See* HOLLY-GOLLY

gully-jumper *n* A farmer

gully-low *adj jazz musicians* Sensuous; insinuating; =DIRTY, SEXY

gum **1** *v* To talk; chatter: *The he-gossips at the Press Club have been gumming about another romance*—R Starnes **2** *v* =GUM UP

See BAT one's GUMS, BUBBLE-GUM MUSIC, the BUBBLE-GUM SET

gumbah *See* GOOMBAH

gumball **1** *n* The lights carried atop a police car; =PARTY HAT: *Don't believe in gumballs. I kinda like to sneak around, you know*—Car and Driver **2** *v: a dozen police cars blocking the streets, their red-and-blue lights gumballing in all directions*—Playboy

gum-beater *n* A persistent talker, esp a pompous braggart; =BLOWHARD

gum-beating **1** *n jive talk* A conversation; chat; =RAP **2** *n* Vain and exaggerated talk; =BALONEY, BULLSHIT

gumby *n Canadian teenagers* A dull, tedious person, esp one out of touch with current fashions; =NERD, PILL: *You can become a gumby...by wearing the wrong plaid stretch pants*—The Globe and Mail [perhaps fr a repulsive character, Mr *Gumby*, in the television series "Monty Python's Flying Circus," and somehow related to a person-shaped toy rubber figure named *Gumby*]

gummixed (or **gummoxed**) **up** *adj phr* Confused; chaotic; ruined; =BOLLIXED UP, FUCKED UP [perhaps from a blend of *gummed up* with *bollixed up*]

gummy **1** *adj esp 1930s* Inferior; tedious; unpleasant: *He found himself in a very gummy situation, with both of them berating him* **2** *adj esp 1940s* Sentimental; maudlin; =CORNY: *a gummy, gooey tearjerker of a film* **3** *n* Glue of any sort **4** *n carnival* A hawker who sells glue [first two senses, like *icky* and *sticky*, fr the unpleasant feel of glue or slime]

gump **1** *n* A fool; dolt; =KNUCKLEHEAD **2** *n hoboes* A chicken, esp a stolen one **3** *n prison* A male homosexual **4** *adj* Good; fine: *I'm feeling gump today* [fr British dialect, "fool"]

gump light *n phr miners* A lantern or lamp

gums *See* BAT one's GUMS

gumshoe **1** *n* (Variations: **gum boot** or **gumfoot** or **gumheel** or **gumshoe man**) *fr early 1900s* A police officer, esp a detective or plain-clothes officer **2** *v* (also **gumheel**) To work as a police officer or detective: *Still gumheeling?*—R Starnes **3** *v* To walk a police beat: *Police now ride prowl cars instead of gumshoeing around the block*—EB White **4** *v* To walk quietly and stealthily [fr *gumshoe* "rubber-soled shoe"]

gum up or **gum up the works** *v phr* To ruin; spoil; throw into confusion; =BOLLIX UP, FUCK UP

gun[1] **1** *n fr middle 1800s* An armed criminal: *They hired a gun to blast the competition* **2** *v fr late 1800s* To shoot someone: *Canales had no motive to gun Lou*—Raymond Chandler **3** *n* An important person; =BIG GUN: *He's quite a gun around there now* **4** *n fr 1920s* The throttle of a car, airplane, etc: *Get your stupid foot off the gun* **5** *v* To speed up an engine or vehicle, esp abruptly; =GOOSE: *He gunned the Rolls into the parking spot* **6** *n railroad* An explosive warning device placed on the tracks; torpedo **7** *n narcotics fr 1930s* A hypodermic needle **8** *n surfers* A long, heavy surfboard

See BIG GUN, BURP GUN, GIVE IT THE GUN, GREASEGUN, JUMP THE GUN, SCATTERGUN, SIX-SHOOTER, SMOKING GUN, SON OF A BITCH, TOMMY GUN, ZIP GUN

gun² *n* (also **gon**) *fr early 1800s* A professional thief, esp a pickpocket [fr Yiddish *gonif*]

gunboat *n railroad* A coal car or gondola; = GON

gunboats *fr late 1800s* **1** *n* A pair of shoes or galoshes, esp of large size: *He brought some of the 14EE gunboats with him from the States*—Associated Press **2** *n* A pair of large feet

gunbunny *n Army* An artillery operator

gunch **1** *n* An attempt to influence the roll of a pinball **2** *v*: *the body English, the nudging, gunching, and infinite alternations of the ways to flip the flipper*—Time

gun someone **down** *v phr* To shoot so as to fell or kill: *They gunned him down in a barber chair*

gun (or **go gunning**) **for** someone *v phr* To seek out or pursue with harmful intent; aim to punish: *He gunned for her after she slapped him with a lawsuit*

gung ho *adj phr fr WW2 Marine Corps* Very zealous; totally committed; enthusiastic: *They were gung ho about the opportunity, their talk charged with an eagerness*—New Yorker [fr the name of a Chinese industrial cooperative organization, adopted as *Gung ho!* to be the battle cry of a Marine Corps raiders group in World War 2]

guniff *See* GONIFF

gunk or **goonk** **1** *n* Any sticky, viscous liquid, esp hair tonic, cosmetics, lubricants, or cleaning fluids; = GLOP, GUCK **2** *n* Dirt; slime; oily grime; muck: *The anchor was clotted in noisome gunk* [fr a trade name, *Gunk*, and part of a cluster of nearly synonymous terms beginning with g-; perhaps a blend of *goo* and *junk*]

gunkhole **1** *v yachting* To cruise rivers, creeks, tidal estuaries, etc, in a small yacht, anchoring in remote spots **2** *n*: *We found a nice gunkhole near the Kennebec*

gun moll *n phr fr late 1800s* A female criminal or a criminal's consort [fr *gonif* rather than fr the firearm]

gunner *n* A flashy performer; = GRANDSTANDER, HOT DOG: *the reputation of a gunner and a hot dog, playground terms for players who showboat*—New York Times

gunny **1** *n Marine Corps* A gunnery sergeant: *Whenever you try to explain something...the gunny accuses you of trying to skate*—New York Times **2** *n* An armed criminal: *Tell us the rest about the two gunnies*—Raymond Chandler

gunpoke *n* An armed criminal: *sends a gunpoke around to take the money*—Raymond Chandler

guns *See* HEAVY ARTILLERY

gunsel¹ *n* (also **gonsil** or **gonzel** or **guncel** or **guntzel** or **gunzl**) *underworld fr early 1900s hoboes & prison* A sexually vulnerable boy or young man; catamite; = PUNK [fr Yiddish *gantzel* "gosling"]

gunsel² *n* (Variations: see **gunsel¹**) An armed criminal; hoodlum: *The reformed gunzl took a quick gander*—Paul Sann/ *scores of hoodlums, gunsels,*

informers, shyster lawyers, and crooked shamuses—SJ Perelman/ *The gunsels killed each other off*—Don Pendleton [fr a blend of *gonif*, *gunsel¹*, *gunman*, etc]

gun-slinger *n fr cowboys* An armed criminal: *The gun-slinger will spend...his life behind bars*—Associated Press

guru **1** *n fr 1960s* A leader, expert, or authority in some field, esp a charismatic or spiritual figure who attracts a devoted following: *turning for guidance to such gurus as Paul Goodman and Herbert Marcuse*—John Fischer/ *That genial guru of the right, Barry Goldwater*—Tom Wicker **2** *n* A psychiatrist; = SHRINK **3** *n narcotics & counterculture* A person who aids and supports someone having a psychedelic drug experience [fr Sanskrit, "venerable"]

Gus *See* GLOOMY GUS

gussy up **1** *v phr* To dress in one's best clothes; adorn oneself; = DOLL UP **2** *v phr* To clean or make neat: *We gussied up the room before they came* **3** *v phr* To decorate or elaborate on a plain design **4** *v phr* To refurbish, renovate; polish: *They're gussying up the same old tiredness*—Village Voice **5** *v phr* To decorate; make fancy: *It resembled a gussied-up Studebaker*—Philadelphia [origin unknown; perhaps fr *gusset*, a triangular insert that might be used to prettify a dress; perhaps fr someone or some place named Augusta]

gut **1** *n* The stomach; abdomen; paunch; = BAY WINDOW, POTBELLY **2** *adj* Basic; essential; most immediate: *the gut issues in the forthcoming election*—Newsweek **3** *adj* Deep and not essentially rational; visceral; intuitive: *this deep, gut feeling that they want to be part of things*—WH Honan/ *He has to convince me on a gut level that I can do things my mind resists*—Playboy **4** *n hoboes* Sausage **5** *n* = GUT COURSE **6** *adj*: *a "gut" humanities course where the professor is said to put on a good show*—David Riesman **7** *v beat & cool talk fr hot rodders* To remove all unessentials; = STRIPPED DOWN

See BUST A GUT, PINCH-GUT, POTBELLY, PUS-GUT, ROTGUT, SPILL one's GUTS, SPLIT A GUT, TUB OF GUTS

gutbucket **1** *n jazz musicians fr early 1900s* A strongly rhythmic, emotionally evocative, uninhibited style of jazz: *puts toe-tapping tunes atop the complicated counterpoint....I've started calling this music avant-gutbucket for its brains, historical sweep, and down-home emotion*—New York Times **2** *n* A fat, pompous person [first sense fr a New Orleans name for a low resort, where a *gutbucket*, that is, a beer bucket or a chamber pot, would be used to collect contributions for the musicians; second sense fr the notion of *a bucket of guts*]

gut-burglar *n lumberjacks* A cook

gut course *n phr* (also **gut**) *college students* An easy course in college: *In his senior year, he needed all the gut courses he could find/ Basic religion course was considered a "gut"*—WE Chilton III

gut-hammer *n lumberjacks* A gong or iron triangle used as a dinner bell

gut it out *v phr* To be strong and resistant; be sturdily stoic; persist; = TOUGH IT OUT: *Cook claimed that he was innocent of any wrongdoing and until last week insisted that he would "gut it out"*—Time

gut reaction *n phr* An immediate and instinctive response; an intuition; = HUNCH: *if the public-opinion polls and gut reaction count for anything*—Philadelphia

guts 1 *n* The insides of a person, machine, etc; viscera; = INNARDS: *He removed the cover and exposed the guts* **2** *n* The most essential material or part; essence: *The guts of the matter is that they are not here* **3** *n fr late 1800s* British Courage; nerve; = BALLS: *the guy who had guts enough to croak "Tough Tony"*—E Lavine
See HATE someone's GUTS, SPILL one's GUTS, TUB OF GUTS

gutsy 1 *adj* Brave: *a gutsy lady* **2** *adj* Energetic and tough; = ZINGY: *a gutsy car*

gutter *n* A dive in which one lands flat on the water; = BELLY-WHOPPER
See HAVE one's MIND IN THE GUTTER

guttersnipe or **gutterpup** *n fr middle 1800s* A vulgar person; a vile wretch

gutty 1 *adj* Forceful and assertive: *a good gutty rock number*—John Clellon Holmes **2** *adj* = GUTSY **3** *adj* = GUT **4** *adj* hot rodders Capable of high speed; having a powerful engine

guy 1 *v esp late 1800s* To mock; ridicule **2** *n fr late 1800s* A person of either sex, esp a man; fellow ● Used of and to women in address, and then almost invariably in the plural, but seldom in reference or in the singular **3** *n* A woman's fiance, husband, lover, etc: *Just remember he's my guy* [ultimately fr the name and reputation of *Guy Fawkes,* and esp of his ugly effigies burnt in England on November 5 to commemorate the foiling of the Gunpowder Plot, his plot to blow up the houses of Parliament]
See BIFF-GUY, FALL GUY, JIGGER-MAN, ONE OF THE BOYS, ONE-WAY GUY, PAPPY GUY, REGULAR FELLOW, RIGHT GUY, SMART GUY, TOUGH GUY, WISE GUY

guyed out *adj circus* Drunk [fr *guy out* "tighten"]

guzzle 1 *v fr 1500s* To drink, esp rapidly: *He guzzled a Coke* **2** *v* To drink liquor, esp to excess: *He guzzled a lot when he got worried* **3** *n* = GOOZLE [fr French *gosier* "throat," or, perhaps like the French word, echoically based on the sound of swallowing]

guzzled *adj* Drunk

guzzlery or **guzzery** *n* A saloon or bar; = GIN MILL

guzzle shop *n phr early 1900s* A saloon or bar: *No lower guzzle shop was ever operated*—H Asbury

gweebo *n college students* A tedious and contemptible person; = DORK, NERD

gyp or **gip** or **jip 1** *n* A gypsy **2** *n* (also **gyp artist** or **gypster**) *fr late 1800s* A swindler; cheater; = CROOK: *denunciations of punks, tinhorns, and gyps*—Westbrook Pegler **3** *modifier: a gyp joint/ gyp terms* **4** *v fr 1920s* To cheat; swindle; = CON: *We got gypped out of it all in two days*—F Scott Fitzgerald **5** *n: the victim of any such gyp*—James M Cain **6** *n cabdrivers* A cabdriver who does not start the meter, hence can pocket the fare [fr *gypsy; grip* "thief" is attested fr the mid-19th century]

gyp joint *n phr* Any business place that overcharges, cheats, etc; = CLIP JOINT: *Cops tried to shut down the midtown gyp joint*

gyppo or **jippo 1** *n 1920s hoboes & lumberjacks* Part-time work **2** *n* An itinerant worker or pieceworker **3** *modifier: They discussed gyppo logging*—Time **4** *v* To cheat; swindle; = GYP: *The contract worker is...being unmercifully gyppoed by the boss*—American Mercury

gyppy tummy *n phr* Diarrhea, esp as it afflicts travelers ● Chiefly British, reflecting former Empire territory: *In the Middle East, it's gyppy tummy and Basra belly*—New York Times [fr British *gyppy* "Egyptian"]

gypsy 1 *n* = GYPSY CAB **2** *n truckers* A truck driven by its owner rather than a union driver **3** *n truckers* An owner-driver; an independent trucker **4** *v gambling* To make a risky bet or call: *You will find players consistently gypsying, flat-calling with kings up or less*—Gambling Times

gypsy cab *n phr* A taxicab operating without a taxi license or medallion, or with only a livery license that does not entitle them to pick up passengers on the street: *the advent of the latest taxi competitor: the gypsy cab*—Society

gypsy moth *n phr esp 1980s* A Republican from the Northern states who votes against an incumbent conservative President and with the more liberal Democrats, esp on budgetary matters [based on *boll weevil,* as a sort of Northern equivalent]

gyrene or **girene** (jī REEN) *n fr 1920s Annapolis* A US Marine; = LEATHERNECK [perhaps fr alteration of *GI Marine*]

gyve *See* JIVE

H

H *n narcotics* Heroin

    See BIG H

haba-haba (HAH bə HAH bə) *interj WW2 armed forces* An exhortation or request for speed or immediate action [*see hubba-hubba*]

habit *n narcotics* Drug addiction: *I had a great big habit*—Nelson Algren

    See BUNK FATIGUE, CHUCK HABIT, GARBAGE HABIT, ICE CREAM HABIT, OFF THE HABIT

ha-cha-cha *See* HOTCHA

hack¹ 1 *n fr early 1900s* A taxicab **2** *v: I worked in an office for years....Then I took to "hacking"*—Hal Boyle **3** *n* A taxicab driver **4** *adj: a hack license* **5** *n bus drivers* A bus **6** *n railroad* A caboose [ultimately fr *hackney* "horse", fr *Hackney*, a village incorporated into London, fr Old English "Haca's island" or "hook island"; presumably the horses were associated with the place]

    See YARD BULL

hack² 1 *n* A persistent, often nervous, cough: *oughta see someone about that hack* **2** *v: If you quit smoking maybe you won't hack like that* **3** *n fr early 1800s* A try; attempt; = WHACK: *Let Mark take a hack at it* **4** *v* To cope with, esp successfully; manage; = HANDLE ● Most often in the negative: *"I can't hack this," Sandy remarked*—New Yorker/ *I couldn't hack the lines, so I used mother nature's privy*—Andy Gordon **5** *v* (also **hack at**) To attempt; do persistently but mediocrely: *Do I play tennis? Well, I hack at it* **6** *n* A mediocre performer or worker; tiresome drudge: *they are not the hacks that Eric's scholarship would make them*—Changes **7** *v: They hacked for some of our most respected...leaders*—Washington Post **8** *n* (also **hack writer**) *fr early 1800s* A professional, usu free-lance, writer who works to order ● This sense belongs to **hack¹**, reflecting the notion that such a writer was for hire like a horse, but is placed here because its own derivatives blend with those of **hack²**, esp "try, stroke, etc" **9** *n computer* A computer program, esp a good one: *A well-crafted program, a good hack, is elegant*—Rolling Stone **10** *v computer* To work with a computer or computer program, esp to do so cleverly, persistently, and enthusiastically ● The term has many specialized senses in computer slang, which alter too rapidly for practical account **11** *v fr late 1800s Southern* To annoy; anger; = BURN: *That attitude really hacks me* **12** *n prison* A guard: *The*

guards, the hacks, as they called them—Claude Brown/ *The hacks didn't worry about the old convicts too much*—Donald Goines **13** *n black & prison* A white person; = HONKY, OFAY [nearly all senses ultimately fr *hack* "cut, chop"; black and prison senses fr identification of prison guards with white persons in the pattern identical with that of *the man*; prison guards perhaps so called because they sometimes beat prisoners]

hack around *v phr* To do nothing in particular; idle; loaf; = BEAT AROUND: *He says he's been hacking around in some bar*—George V Higgins/ *So I quit Butter, hacked around for a while*—Rolling Stone

hack-driver *n Navy* A chief petty officer

hacked *adj* (also **hacked off**) *fr 1940s black* Annoyed; angered; chagrinned: *I don't know what made him so hacked about it/ How come you're so hacked off about Combs?*—WT Tyler

hacker¹ *n* (also **hackey** or **hackie**) A taxicab driver: *He enriched another hacker by an even $5,000*—Associated Press/ *He actually found a hackie named Louis Schweitzer*—World

hacker² *n* A persistent but generally unskillful performer or athlete; = DUFFER

hacker³ 1 *n computer* An energetic and skillful computer programmer, often perfectionistic: *When a hacker programs, he creates worlds*—Rolling Stone/ *As a hacker, McLachlan is a member of an intense, reclusive subculture of the computer age*—Time **2** *n computer* Anyone who works with computers or computer programs, esp one who does so enthusiastically ● The term has many senses in computer slang, which change too rapidly for practical account [said to be fr *hack²*, computer jargon for a clever and subtle correction of a flow in a computer program]

hackery *n* Routine mediocrity; esp the dull performance and tone of an average political professional: *the grey, self-serving hackery of previous City Councils*—Toronto Life

hack hand *n phr truckers* A trucker

hack it *v phr fr loggers* To cope successfully; = CUT IT, HANDLE ● Often in the negative: *John Fist can't hack it any more*—Webster Schott/ *It was a good job, but she couldn't hack it/ It's a tough assignment. Do you think you can hack it?*

hack-skinner *n bus drivers* A bus driver [fr *mule-skinner*] be **had** (or **taken** or **took**) **1** *v phr* To become a partner in the sex act **2** *v phr* To be duped or cheated; be victimized: *You practically need a finance degree to know that you are being had* —Newsweek

had it *See* one HAS HAD IT

ha-ha 1 *n* A joke; something funny; stroke of wit: *That's a ha-ha all right*—Ira Wolfert **2** *adj: even made a ha-ha pass at him*—Psychology Today/ *ha-ha candles made to look like penises*—Saturday Review

See the MERRY HA-HA

the **Haight** *n phr* =HASHBURY

hail Columbia 1 *interj* A mild exclamation of emphasis, annoyance, etc: *Hail Columbia, can't I ever go?* **2** *n phr* Punitive measures; a rebuke; =HELL: *They'll give me hail Columbia when they know* [a euphemism for *hell*]

hail-fellow or **hail-fellow-well-met 1** *n* A very jovial man; good companion **2** *adj: his hail-fellow-well-met pretense*

haimish or **heimish** (HAY mish) *adj* Friendly and informal; unpretentious; cozy: *No one in his right mind would ever call Generals de Gaulle or MacArthur haimish*—Leo Rosten [fr Yiddish, with root of *haim* "home"]

hair *n computer* Complexity: *a system with a lot of hair*

See CURL someone's HAIR, FAIRHAIRED BOY, GET IN one's HAIR, GOOD HAIR, HAVE A BUG UP one's ASS, HAVE someone BY THE SHORT HAIRS, IN someone's HAIR, LET one's HAIR DOWN, LONGHAIR, NOT HAVE A HAIR ON one's ASS

hair bag *n phr police* A veteran police officer [fr the image of a person who would save all his or her *hair* after combing, in a triumph of self-centered triviality]

haired *See* LONGHAIR

hairnet *See* WIN THE PORCELAIN HAIRNET

the **hair of the dog** (or **of the dog that bit one**) *n phr* A drink of liquor taken as a remedy for a hangover [fr the belief that the bite of a *dog* could be healed by applying its *hair* to the wound]

◁**hair on** one's **ass**▷ *See* NOT HAVE A HAIR ON one's ASS

◁**hair pie**▷ **1** *n phr* Cunnilingus; =BOX LUNCH **2** *n phr* The female genitalia; the vulva; =PUSSY

hairpin 1 *n hoboes* A housewife **2** *v cowboys* To mount a horse

See DROP BEADS

hair-pounder *n lumberjacks* The driver of a team of horses; teamster

hairy 1 *adj* Old; hoary: *a hairy tale* **2** *adj* Difficult; rough; =TOUGH: *We had a hairy time getting it all organized* **3** *adj esp teenagers fr 1960s* Frighteningly dangerous; hair-raising; scary: *campus guards would comb the dorm...."It was hairy"* —New Yorker/ *the hairy strip of 42d Street*—New York Times [last sense probably fr the *hairy* monsters of horror films, but the sense of "difficult" was used in 19th-century Oxford, and that of "dangerous" in the British armed forces of the 1930s]

hairy eyeball *See* GIVE someone THE FISH-EYE

half *See* BETTER HALF, DEUCE AND A HALF, a LAUGH, ONE-AND-A-HALF-STRIPER, OTHER HALF, TWO-AND-A-HALF-STRIPER

◁**half-and-half**▷ *n prostitutes* Fellatio plus the sex act

half a shake *n phr* A moment; a trice: *I'll be there in half a shake* [fr the expression *two shakes of a lamb's tail* "a very short time"]

◁**half-assed**▷ *adj fr late 1800s* Foolish; ineffectual; stupid: *You first ran into censorship problems with the words "half-assed games"*—Rolling Stone [perhaps fr a humorous mispronunciation of *haphazard*]

half a yard *n phr fr early 1900s hawkers* Fifty dollars: *a "yard" and "half a yard" meaning one hundred dollars and fifty dollars respectively*—Society

half-bagged *adj* Drunk: *They keep half-bagged all day and bore their new friends silly with stories* —Lawrence Sanders

half-baked *adj fr early 1600s* Foolish; ill-conceived; not completely thought out; =HALF-ASSED

half bill or **half a bill** *n phr* Fifty dollars: *Half an hour after I'd lent Reno the half bill, he was back uptown*—Claude Brown

half-buck or **half a buck** *n or n phr* A half-dollar; fifty cents

half cocked 1 *adv* Prematurely; unprepared: *not going into this half cocked*—Max Shulman **2** *adj: a half-cocked start* [see go off half cocked]

half-corned *adj* Drunk

half crocked *adj phr* Drunk; half-drunk: *laying around on a settee, sort of half crocked*—SJ Perelman/ *I came out at twelve, one o'clock, half-crocked, really snockered*—WT Tyler

halfies or **halvies** or **halvsies** *n fr late 1800s* One half of what is indicated, esp as an equal share: *She found it, but I claimed halvsies because I did most of the work*

See GO HALFIES

half in the bag *adj phr* Drunk; half-drunk: *He was half in the bag. He always is at Christmas*—Playboy

half load *n phr narcotics* Fifteen packets of a narcotic, esp of cocaine or heroin

half-pint 1 *n* A short person: *the little half-pint that she was*—John O'Hara **2** *modifier: half-pint showman*—United Press **3** *n* A boy

half seas over *adj phr fr 1600s British naval* Drunk [fr the notion that one is like a ship low in the water and burdened so that relatively low waves, *half seas,* sweep over its deck]

half-shaved *adj* Drunk; half-drunk

half-shot 1 *adj* Drunk; half-drunk: *when they were half shot with beer*—James M Cain **2** *adj* Nearly ravaged; deteriorating: *Her nerves are half shot*

half-stewed *adj* (Variations: **screwed** or **slewed** or **snaped** or **sprung** may replace **stewed**) Drunk; half-drunk

half under 1 *adj phr* Drunk; half-drunk **2** *adj phr* Semiconscious; stuporous: *He was half under when they pulled him out*

hall *n* Alcohol

See CHOW HALL, JOHN HALL

ham[1] **1** *n* An amateur, esp an amateur radio operator **2** *modifier:* *a ham radio operator/ ham network* [fr *amateur*]

ham[2] **1** *n* *fr late 1800s* An actor who overacts, dramatizes himself, emotes too broadly, etc: *had been roasted by the critics as a ham*—Russell Baker/ *Variety never referred to actors as "hams"* —Abel Green **2** *modifier:* *ham actor/ ham performance* **3** *v* (also **ham it up**): *The famous star was hamming all the way* **4** *n* A person who uses overtheatrical and overly expressive airs and actions: *Miss Moment was no doubt the biggest ham of a teacher*—A Lomax **5** *v* (also **ham it up**): *The prof strode into the lecture hall hamming and mugging*

ham and or **ham an** *n phr* *lunch counter* Ham and eggs

ham-and-egger **1** *n* *fr 1920s* An average person; =ORDINARY JOE **2** *n* *prizefight fr 1920s* An average or mediocre prizefighter

ham-and-eggery *n* A small restaurant or lunch counter

hambone *n* A person who fancies himself an actor; histrionic self-advertiser; =HAM: *Every hambone from the deep sticks was constrained to make a speech for the benefit of the cameras*—Robert Ruark

hamburger **1** *n* *prizefight* A scarred and unvictorious prizefighter **2** *n* A hobo or mendicant **3** *n* An inferior racing dog **4** *n* A mixture of mud and skin nutrients, used for facial treatment in beauty parlors

See MAKE HAMBURGER OUT OF someone or something

ham-fatter *n* *fr late 1800s* =HAM, HAMBONE [fr a minstrel song of 1887, *The Hamfat Man*, having to do with a second-rate actor; see *ham joint*]

hamfist *n* A large fist, big as a ham: *His huge hamfist had landed me a vicious blow*—Xaviera Hollander

ham-handed or **ham-fisted** *adj* Crude and clumsy; lacking in finesse: *his hamfisted approach to a delicate matter*

ham-handedness *n* Crudeness; clumsiness; lack of polish: *In selecting the rottenest apples...one seeks the pretension and the exploitation rather than mere ham-handedness*—Judith Crist

ham joint *n phr* *1920s* A cheap restaurant or pool hall, used as a loitering and gathering spot by criminals: *rendezvous is a "ham joint"*—H McLellan [origin uncertain; perhaps related to late-19th-century *ham* or *ham-fatter* "vagrant, loafer," which may reflect a notion that fat is both slippery and unnourishing compared with lean meat]

hammer **1** *n* *black* A sexually desirable woman; =FOX ● Regarded by some women as offensive **2** *n* *truckers* The accelerator of a truck **3** *n* The penis: *How's your hammer hangin', Tiger?* —George Warren

See GUT-HAMMER

hammer down *adv phr* *fr truckers* Going full speed; with throttles to the floor; =WIDE OPEN: *a*

herd of LA rednecks, all of 'em pie-eyed and hammer down—Esquire

hammered *adj* Drunk

hammerhead *n* A very hard-headed person: *The best way out is for one of the three to be a hammerhead*—Jerome Weidman

hammer lane *n phr* *truckers* The fast lane of a superhighway [fr the trucker sense *hammer* "accelerator"]

hammer-man *n* *black* An authoritative person; strong man

hammertails *n* A formal dress coat; swallowtail coat: *Several men in cutaway coats, called "hammertails"*—Stephen Longstreet

ham up *v phr* To make histrionic; overexpress; =HAM: *The baseball umpire was hamming up his signals for the benefit of the television audience* —New Yorker

hand *v* To give, esp something not desired; bestow forcefully, fraudulently, etc: *The Red Sox handed the Yankees a 12 to 3 shellacking/ What kind of con job was he trying to hand you?*

See BOTH HANDS, COLD IN HAND, COOL HAND, DEAD MAN'S HAND, DECK HAND, GIVE someone THE GLAD HAND, GLAD-HAND, HACK HAND, HAVE one's HANDS FULL, NOT LAY A GLOVE ON someone, SOFT HANDS, TIP one's MITT, WITH one's HAND IN THE TILL, WITH ONE HAND TIED BEHIND one's BACK

a **hand** **1** *n* A round of applause: *Well she got a big hand*—John O'Hara **2** *n* Help; aid

See GIVE someone A HAND

hand someone **a lemon** *v phr* To take advantage of; cheat; =GYP: *if they hand me a lemon*—Erle Stanley Gardner

handbasket *See* GO TO HELL IN A HANDBASKET

handbook **1** *n* *horse-racing & gambling fr late 1800s* A place, other than a legal betting office, where bets are made away from the racetrack; =HORSE ROOM: *I was in the handbook near Loomis and Madison*—Fact Detective Mysteries **2** *n* =BOOKIE [probably fr the fact that betting records were kept in small, concealable notebooks for secrecy and portability]

H and C *n phr* *narcotics* A mixture of heroin and cocaine; =SPEEDBALL

handcuffs *See* GOLDEN HANDCUFFS

handed *See* HAM-HANDED, LEFT-HANDED, RED-HANDED, RIGHT-HANDED

hander *See* FORKHANDER, GLAD-HANDER

handful **1** *n* *underworld* A five-year prison sentence or term **2** *n* *lunch counter* Five of anything **3** *n* A very difficult job or heavy responsibility: *That kid of yours is a handful*

See GRAB A HANDFUL OF AIR

hand someone someone's **head** *v phr* To destroy; figuratively to decapitate someone and hand him his own head; =CLOBBER: *Do what they want, or they'll hand you your head*—Village Voice/ *when the press is handing Francis Coppola his head* —Village Voice

handies *See* PLAY HANDIES

hand it to someone *v phr* To compliment; praise someone for a success ● Often said with overtones of reluctance: *I got to hand it to you*—James M Cain/ *You have to hand it to me, I can at least lie well*

◁**hand job**▷ *n phr* An act of masturbation, usu done for one person by another: *rolled over on top of me and started giving me a real good hand job*—Lon Albert/ *if you were unlucky, all you got was a hand job*—Philadelphia

◁**handkerchief-head**▷ *black* **1** *n* A black person who is obsequious towards white people; =UNCLE TOM: *A "handkerchief-head" is an old-fashioned Negro who doesn't know his rights*—Stephen Longstreet **2** *n* A black man who wears a cloth or scarf on his head to protect his processed hairdo

handle 1 *n fr early 1900s* A person's name, nickname, or alias: *He is known by that handle ever since to all his pals*—Associated Press/ *The CB freaks took handles, like Sweet Slats and Kimono Katey* **2** *n fr 1920s* The gross receipts or the profit of a sporting event, a gambling game, an illegal operation, etc: *A total handle of...between 4 and 10 billion a year in the handbooks, the numbers, and the slots*—Westbrook Pegler **3** *n gambling* The amount of money bet on a specific race or game, or in a particular day or week, etc: *The handle at Belmont dropped today on account of the blizzard* **4** *n* A way of approaching or grasping something; an initial and relevant insight: *I just can't find the handle to this problem* **5** *v* To cope with; manage; =HACK: *He can handle Tom's temper tantrums very well*/ *My wife left me and I don't know how to handle it*

See FLY OFF THE HANDLE, GET A HANDLE ON something, LONG-HANDLE UNDERWEAR, PANHANDLE

handler *See* PANHANDLER

handles *See* LOVE HANDLES

hand-me-down or **fetch-me-down** **1** *n* Something, esp clothing, used by one person and then passed to another, usu a younger sibling: *I wore mostly my brother's hand-me-downs* **2** *modifier*: *a pair of hand-me-down pants*/ *fetch-me-down ski boots*

handout 1 *n hoboes fr late 1800s* Food, money, or other donations received or given ● Nearly always with the implication that the giver is over-generous or self-interested, and the recipient undeserving: *Damn hippies lived on food stamps and other bleeding heart handouts* **2** *n* A leaflet or flyer passed out on the streets **3** *n* An official press release or communiqué: *The newspaperman's slightly derogatory slang term for the news release is "handout"*—Daniel J Boorstin

hand over fist *adv phr fr late 1800s* Very energetically, persistently, and rapidly: *It was a treat to see them go at it hand over fist*

See MAKE MONEY HAND OVER FIST

hand-painted doormat *See* WIN THE PORCELAIN HAIRNET

hands *See* BOTH HANDS, HAVE one's HANDS FULL, SIT ON one's HANDS

hands down *adv phr* Very easily; without effort ● Most often in the phrase **win hands down**: *She entered the race unheralded, and won it hands down*/ *We just loafed along, but beat them hands down* [probably fr the notion of winning a fight, besting someone in a confrontation, etc, without raising a *hand*]

handshaker *n fr early 1900s armed forces* A person who characteristically gets on by being amiable, making friends, pleasing superiors, etc; =GLAD-HANDER

hands-off *adj* Noninterfering; passive: *the president's hands-off policy*

handsome *See* HIGH, WIDE, AND HANDSOME

hands on 1 *adv phr* Manually, by direct control rather than automatic control: *The ship was then flown hands on* **2** *modifier*: *hands-on landing of the aircraft* **3** *adj* Practical and active rather than theoretical: *what we labeled a hands-on mayor*—San Francisco/ *No Hands-On Achiever Need Apply*—Newsweek

hand trouble *n phr* A pronounced tendency to touch and caress; generalized tactile amorousness: *Bonnie had encountered men with hand trouble*—A Hynd

hang 1 *v* To spend time; frequent; =HANG OUT: *Who runs the coffepot where they hang?*—Scene of the Crime **2** *v horse-racing* To lack reserve speed during the last stretch **3** *v cool talk* To wait; await: *Let's hang here until Mary Beth gets off work*

See HAVE IT ALL HANGING OUT, LET IT ALL HANG OUT

hang a few on *v phr* To have several drinks of liquor: *He had only hung a few on and was, for him, slightly sober*—Stephen Longstreet

hang a left (or **a right**) *v phr esp teenagers* To turn left or right, to round a corner [perhaps fr surfers' phrases *hang five, hang ten*]

hang around 1 *v phr fr late 1800s* To idle about; loiter; =HACK AROUND **2** *v phr* To stay where one is; remain: *I decided to hang around and see what went down*

hang around with or **hang with** *v phr* To seek and prefer the company of; consort with: *Who you hanging around with these days?*/ *Sondra didn't hang with nobody but doctors*—Ms

◁**hang-down**▷ *n* The penis; =PRICK: *like the horse's hang-down that I am, get myself shit-faced*—George V Higgins

hanged *See* I'LL BE DAMNED

hanger *See* CLIFFHANGER, CRAPE-HANGER, FENCE-STRADDLER, PAPERHANGER

hangers *See* APE HANGERS

hang fire *v phr* To be delayed or stalled; fail to materialize: *The whole deal's hanging fire till the jerk decides what to do next*

hang five *v phr surfers* To ride forward on the surfboard so that the toes of one foot are over the edge

hang in (or **in there**) *v phr* To endure in some difficult action or position; persist tenaciously; =HANG TOUGH: *He didn't pack it up, of course, he hung in there and saw the story through*—Playboy/ *Rosemary Woods is hanging in*—Nora Ephron

hang it *v phr hospital* To administer intravenous medicine: *As soon as the nurse is free, he'll be in to hang it*

hang it easy *v phr teenagers* =TAKE IT EASY

hang it up *v phr* To retire; cease working, competing, etc: *since Joe Namath and Sonny Jurgenson hung it up*—Dan Jenkins/ *After a serious injury they wanted me to hang it up*—Washington Post [probably a shortened and generalized form of *hang up one's shoes* or *spikes* "retire from baseball"]

hang (or **stay**) **loose** *v phr fr 1960s counterculture* To be relaxed and nonchalant; be uninvolved; =COOL IT ● Often heard as a genial exhortation: *I needed to hang loose, breathe free, get lost, take a trip*—Xaviera Hollander/ *You're healthier and happier when you hang loose*—Harper's/ *Stay loose, man*—Richard Fariña

the **hang** of something *See* GET THE HANG OF something

hang on 1 *v phr* To endure; persist; =HANG IN **2** *v phr* To make an accusation; inculpate; =PASTE ON: *Let's see what felonies we can hang on this creep now that we've got him*

hang (or **tie** or **pin**) **one on 1** *v phr* To get very drunk; go on a drinking spree **2** *v phr* To hit someone hard; =CLOBBER: *Will you hang one on my jaw?*—James M Cain

hang onto your hats *sentence* Get ready to hear something shocking or amazing

hangout[1] **1** *n fr late 1800s hoboes & underworld* A place for loitering, loafing, and passing time, esp with congenial companions: *a grad student hangout on Mirandola Lane/ a gay hangout* **2** *n fr 1920s* One's home; =DIGS

hangout[2] *n* Complete disclosure; total openness: *a "modified limited hang-out," meaning a response that would satisfy Watergate investigators while disclosing as little as possible*—Newsweek

See GO THE HANG-OUT ROAD

hang out *v phr* To pass time; loaf pleasantly about; loiter: *just us five hangin' out*—Rolling Stone/ *The best hours of my youth were spent loitering in front of Simon's Candy Store...doing nothing, just hanging out*—Saturday Review

See HAVE IT ALL HANGING OUT, LET IT ALL HANG OUT

hang out the laundry *v phr fr WW2 Air Forces* To drop paratroops from an aircraft

hang out the wash *v phr baseball* To hit a hard line drive [because the ball's path resembles a taut clothesline]

hangover 1 *n fr early 1900s* The headache, morbid sensitivity, nausea, etc, felt upon awakening some hours after drinking too much liquor **2** *n* A remnant or survival, often an undesirable one: *The problem is a hangover from the high birthrate of the 50s*

hang ten *v phr surfers* To ride forward on a surfboard so that the toes of both feet are over the edge

hang tough *v phr* To endure in a difficult plight; show plucky and stoic persistence; =HANG ON, TOUGH IT OUT: *You've got a friend at Chase Manhattan, if you've still got a Traveler's Check to cash. Otherwise, hang tough*—J Horn/ *Mr Shannon glorifies Kennedy for his ability to "hang tough"*—Book World

hang up 1 *v phr esp 1960s* To become fixated: *Why did you hang up on Proust, anyhow?* **2** *v phr* To cease annoying or chattering; =SHUT UP ● Often an irritated command [second sense fr the cessation of a telephone call]

hang-up 1 *n esp 1960s counterculture* A mental block; a psychological disturbance, fixation, or problem: *ribald anecdotes concerning his hang-up on strong women*—Changes **2** *n* Anything encumbering, frustrating, distressing, etc: *You couldn't carry around an amplifier and electric guitar and expect to survive, it was just too much of a hang-up*—Bob Dylan/ *The only hang-up we can see right now is that business of paying the doctors*—Lawrence Sanders

hang someone or something **up** *v phr fr middle 1800s* To stall or immobilize; frustrate; paralyze: *The four would not be able to hang the entire jury up*—Ebony/ *or some other means of transcending the realities that hang one up*—Trans-Action

hang up (or **out**) one's **shingle** *v phr* To commence professional practice; open up a law office, doctor's office, etc: *He's passed his bar exam now, so he can hang up his shingle*

hank 1 *n* Illicit activity, esp sexual; =HANKY-PANKY: **2** *modifier: a hank book/ hank flicks*

hankie or **hanky** *n* A handkerchief

hankty *See* HINCTY

hanky-pank 1 *n carnival* Any game that is cheap to play, esp one where the customer gets a prize each time he or she plays: *Typical hanky-panks are the fish-pond, the ring-toss and dart-throwing games*—Society **2** *n carnival* A barker's exhortations; =SPIEL **3** *adj fr carnival* Cheap and gaudy; trashy; =SCHLOCKY: *hanky-pank costume jewelry*

hanky-panky *n fr middle 1800s British* Anything dishonest, deceptive, or unethical, esp sexual infidelity; =HANK, MONKEY BUSINESS: *She seems just to be along for some hanky-panky with her pal, General Von Griem*—Ms/ *can be an assurance against clandestine wrongdoing and political hanky-panky*—Nation [fr the conjurer's use of a *handkerchief* in prestidigitation]

happenings *n narcotics* Narcotics; =JUNK

happies 1 *n shoeshop* Arch supporters **2** *n* =JOLLIES

happy *adj* Drunk, esp slightly so; =TIDDLY *See* SAP-HAPPY

-happy *combining word* Somewhat insane over or excessively wrought upon by what is indicated: *bomb-happy/ car-happy/ power-happy/ trigger-happy* [probably modeled on *slap-happy*]

happy as a clam *adj phr* Very happy; euphoric: *On the boat she's happy as a clam* [fr earlier locution *happy as a clam at high tide*, that is, when it cannot be dug]

happy-cabbage *n* Money; =CABBAGE

happy-dust *narcotics* **1** *n* Cocaine **2** *n* Morphine

happy hour 1 *n phr* The hour or so of relaxation with drinks after work; cocktail hour **2** *n phr* A specified period of time, usu in early evening, in some restaurants and bars when drinks are sold at lower prices or when free food is provided

happy-juice *n* Liquor: *The increased taxes on happy-juice has cut the revenues from liquor sales* —Robert Ruark

happy-money *n* Money saved or reserved for personal pleasures

happy talk *television studio* **1** *n phr* Informal chat and chaffing among news broadcasters during the program, as an element of entertainment: *Later, happy talk evolved, to break the tension created by the action, that is the violence, shown on TV news* —Washingtonian **2** *modifier:* *as for the happy-talk format that sandwiches cheerful repartee between the fire and robbery reports*—Philadelphia

hard 1 *adj* Demonstrable; verifiable; not dependent on subjective judgment, emotion, etc: *hard facts/ hard sciences* **2** *adj* =TOUGH **3** *adj* *jive talk* Excellent; good; =COOL ◁**4**▷ *n* =HARD-ON
See COME DOWN HARD, TAKE IT HARD

hard as nails *adj phr* Extremely durable and grim; =TOUGH

◁**hard-ass**▷ **1** *n* A severe and often pugnacious person; =HARDNOSE: *I've gotten the reputation as being a hard-ass*—Aquarian **2** *adj:* *He had a hard-ass way of getting what he wanted*

hardball 1 *n* Serious and consequential activity, work, etc; perilous and responsible doings: *It's hard-ball now, it's not games anymore*—Philadelphia Journal/ *It's going to be hard ball....We're talking about physicians losing income*—New York Times **2** *adj:* *fields hardball questions in a practice TV interview*—Time/ *despite his hardball attitude toward sponsors of offensive TV shows*—Time **3** *v* =PLAY HARDBALL

hard-boiled *adj* Severe and uncompromising; strict and pugnacious; =TOUGH: *The rather hard-boiled painting that hangs in Father's office*—F Scott Fitzgerald/ *Hemingway is usually thought of as a hard-boiled guy* [fr hard-boiled egg]

hard-boiled egg *n phr* A severe and pugnacious person; =TOUGH GUY: *Our basic idea of a hero is really a "hard-boiled egg"*—P Curtiss

hardboot *horse-racing* **1** *n* A Southern horseman or jockey **2** *n* A devotee of horses and of horse-racing: *Granted hardboots can be sentimental about a horse on the lead*—Time

hard bop *n phr jazz musicians* A type of music resembling the blues that is related to, but more earthy and modal in approach than, straight bop: *swing, bop, cool jazz, hard bop, funky jazz*—BW Bell

hard (or **heavy**) **breathing** *n phr* Passionate love-making

hard cash *n phr* =COLD CASH

hard cheese *n phr* An unfortunate outcome or situation ● Still chiefly British; often an interjection: *This is hard cheese indeed*—Village Voice

hard coin *n phr* Large amounts of money; =MEGABUCKS: *There's some hard coin being made by the music magnates*—Motive

hard-core 1 *adj* Essential and uncompromising; without evasion or admixture: *a hard-core Republi-*

can/ *hard-core pornography* **2** *n* Pornography that openly depicts complete sex acts: *He sort of likes dirty stuff, but not real hard core*

hard currency (or **money**) *n phr* A national currency that is strong in the market and backed by considerable metal and economic power: *Sterling isn't the leading hard currency any more* [along with *hard cash* and *hard coin*, fr 17th-century terms distinguishing gold and silver from paper *currency*]

hard drug *n phr* A narcotic like heroin or morphine, that is powerfully addictive and injurious: *The American problem is heroin, as "hard" a drug as there is*—New York Times

harder than Chinese arithmetic (or **Japanese geometry**) *adj phr* Very hard; rocklike ● Used esp to describe a penile erection

hard facts *n phr* Information that is dependable and verifiable

hard hat 1 *n phr* A derby hat: *The boys with the hard hats always ask a lot of questions about murders*—J Evans **2** *n phr* The steel or plastic helmet worn by various sorts of workers, esp construction workers **3** *modifier:* *Caution, this is a hard-hat zone* **4** *n phr* A worker who wears a hard hat: *The hard hats sat around whistling at the passing girls* **5** *n fr early 1970s* A very conservative right-winger; a reactionary: *He knows he can count on the hard hats to support him* **6** *n phr Vietnam War armed forces* A regular Viet Cong soldier, who wears a military helmet, as distinct from a guerilla or reservist: *some 50,000 are "hard-hats" (full-time fighters)*—Time [the political sense fr the vocal and sometimes violent opposition of many construction workers to the US peace movement during the Vietnam War, reinforced by terms like *hard line* and *hard core*]

hardhead 1 *n* An obstinate or stupid person ◀**2**▶ *n* A black person ◀**3**▶ *n black* A white person

hard-headed 1 *adj* Obstinate; stubborn; =PIG-HEADED **2** *adj* Realistic; practical; unevasive; =HARD-NOSED

hard John *n phr underworld* An FBI agent; =FEEB, G-MAN

hard legs *n phr black* A man; =CAT, DUDE

hard line 1 *n phr* A policy or attitude based on severity and lack of compromise: *Take a hard line with them or they'll murder you* **2** *adj:* *the President's hard-line views on abortion*

hard liquor *n phr* Whiskey, rum, gin, brandy, as distinct from wine and beer; spirits; strong waters

hard look 1 *n phr* An intense and unblinking scrutiny; strict examination ● Most often with **a**: *Take a hard look at what's going on upstairs/ We'll have a hard look at the income and expenses* **2** *n phr* A menacing or hostile stare: *She gave me a real hard look when I blurted her name*
See LONG HARD LOOK

hardnose *n* A severe, durable, and often pugnacious person; =TOUGH GUY: *The pussycat turned into a hardnose overnight*

hard-nosed 1 *adj* Stubborn; obstinate **2** *adj* Severe and pugnacious; harshly realistic; =HARD-

HEADED, TOUGH: *They'll take a hard-nosed look, then report*

◁ **hard-on** ▷   *n* An erection of the penis: *It was another one of those subway things. Like having a hard-on at random*—Saul Bellow

See HAVE A HARD-ON FOR someone or something

hard-road freak   *n phr* A drifting young person who has rejected conventional society and has typically been arrested for vagrancy, drug use, etc; = HIPPIE

hard rock   *n phr rock and roll* A form of rock and roll music with a simple, driving beat, usu played on heavily amplified guitars

hard-rock   *adj* Severe; dour and pugnacious; = TOUGH: *the old hard-rock guy who would line up all the cocaine users and shoot them*—Time [probably fr the difficulty of *hard-rock* mining as distinct fr other kinds; influenced by *rock-hard*]

a **hard** (or **tough**) **row to hoe**   *n phr* A difficult task; a period of trouble and travail; = HARD TIMES: *With inflation and all they had a mighty hard row to hoe*

hard science   *n phr* A science like chemistry or physics where the data and conclusions are supportable by objective criteria

hard sell   *n phr* An act or policy of selling aggressively, forcibly, loudly, etc: *Joe is a master at hard sell*

hard-shell   *adj* Strict; conservative; = HARD-CORE

hard stuff   **1**   *n* Whiskey and other strong liquors; spirits; = HARD LIQUOR: *The troubles the hard stuff inflicts on men with no defense against it*—John McCarten   **2**   *n phr* = HARD DRUG   **3**   *n phr underworld* Money, esp loot or other illicit gain

hardtack   *n late 1800s* Money, esp silver money

hard time   See GIVE someone A HARD TIME

hard times   *n phr* A period of economic depression, poverty, etc

hardtop   *n esp 1950s & 60s* A car resembling a convertible, but having a metal roof

hard up   **1**   *adj phr fr early 1800s British* Poor; penniless: *It was no disgrace to be hard up in those times*   **2**   *adj phr* Sexually frustrated; needing sexual gratification; = HORNY: *He declared he was so hard up he'd fuck mud* [apparently fr a nautical expression meaning the helm is *hard up*, that is, held all the way to windward while beating and so pinched as tight as possible]

hard up for something   *adj phr* Lacking; deficient in: *We're hard up for booze around here*

hardware   **1**   *n fr middle 1800s* Weapons and other war matériel: *military "hardware," tanks, planes, guns, rockets, weapons*—WF Arbogast   **2**   *n WW2 armed forces* Military insignia or medals worn on a uniform   **3**   *n fr 1930s* Badges and other identification jewelry   **4**   *n computers* Computers and computer equipment, as distinct from programs and other material used for computer operation

the **hard way**   **1**   *n phr crapshooting* The repetition of an even number that came up on the first roll, made by rolling two even dice that add up to it

2   *n phr* The most difficult and strenuous way of doing anything: *My motto is "Anything worth doing is worth doing the hard way"*

hardy-har or **hardy-har-har** or **har-har-har**   **1**   *adj* Funny; hilarious: *a mildly hardy-har gag*   **2**   *adv:* *how hardy-har funny a little quick witted humor can be*—Village Voice   **3**   *n* Joviality; laughter; jolly spirits: *Underneath the har-har-har... there was anything but fun and games*—Washingtonian

Hare Krishnas or **Hare Krishna kids** (or **people**)   *n phr* Persons who belong to a cult called the International Society for Krishna Consciousness [fr the Sanskrit prayer *Hare Krishna* "hail krishna"]

harness   *n* The dress and equipment of special categories of persons, such as telephone line repairers, police officers, train conductors, motorcyclists, etc: *Wise detectives, who dread going back into "harness" or uniform*—E Lavine

See IN HARNESS

harness bull (or **cop** or **dick**)   **1**   *n phr underworld & hoboes fr early 1900s* A uniformed police officer   **2**   *modifier: the harness-bull secretary*—WR Burnett

harp ◀**1**▶   *n* An Irishperson or one of Irish descent   **2**   *n* A harmonica

Harry   See BIG HARRY, EVERY TOM, DICK, AND HARRY

Hart, Schaffner and Marx   *n phr poker* Three jacks [fr the name of a men's clothing manufacturer]

has-been   **1**   *n* A person who was once famous, successful, courted, etc, but is no longer so: *Some has-beens make spectacular comebacks*   **2**   *n* A person whose preferences, style, etc, are passé; = BACK NUMBER

hash   **1**   *v* To discuss, esp at length; = HASH OVER: *they had hashed and rehashed for many a frugal conversational meal*—F Scott Fitzgerald   **2**   *v* = HASH UP   **3**   *n narcotics* Hashish   **4**   *adj cool talk* Excellent; wonderful; = COOL

See MAKE HAMBURGER OUT OF someone or something, SETTLE someone's HASH, SLING HASH

one **has had it**   **1**   *sentence* (Variations: **up to here** or **up to** one's **ass** or **up to** one's **eyebrows** or some other anatomical feature may be added) One is exhausted, disgusted, unwilling to put up with any more: *All at once I've had it up to here with psychiatry*—New Yorker   **2**   *sentence* One has been given a last chance and has failed: *That's the ball game, buddy, you've had it* [fr shortening of World War 2 British Royal Air Force slang *He's had his time* "He's been killed"]

Hashbury   *n esp 1960s counterculture* The Haight-Ashbury section of San Francisco, a haunt of hippies during the 1960s; = the HAIGHT

hasher   **1**   *n* A waiter or waitress: *going to give them jobs as hashers*—G Weisberg   **2**   *n* A cook or kitchen worker

hashery   *n* A restaurant or lunch counter, esp a small or cheap place: *We'll inhale a few hamburgers at some fashionable hashery*—"Our Boarding House" (comic strip)

hash foundry 1 *n phr* =HASHERY **2** *n phr* hoboes A charitable establishment where free meals may be had

hash head *n phr* narcotics A frequent user of hashish or marijuana

hash-house *n fr middle 1800s* Western A restaurant or lunch counter, esp a cheap one; =HASHERY: *the sort of language that one would expect to hear from a hobo in a Bowery hash-house*—Bookman

hash mark (or **stripe**) **1** *n phr* armed forces A service stripe, worn on the sleeve of a military uniform to mark each four-year period of service: *the voice of a subaltern of God, hashmarks running down his arm for a thousand miles*—Pat Conroy **2** *n phr* football An inbounds line marker used to help fix the point where the ball is put in play, and spaced one yard from the next mark [military sense fr the humorous inference that the soldier has not cleaned the uniform of accumulating food stains]

hash over *fr early 1900s* **1** *v phr* To discuss, esp repeatedly and lengthily: *We kept hashing over the same tired old topics* **2** *v phr* To rehash, review: *Asked him in to hash over a point or two* —New Yorker

hash session *n phr* =GABFEST

hash-slinger 1 *n fr middle 1800s* Western A waiter or waitress, usu in a cheap restaurant or lunch counter: *Hash-slingers are plentiful but well-trained waitresses are scarce*—Associated Press **2** *n fr late 1800s* A cook or kitchen worker

hash up *v phr* To ruin; spoil; =FUCK UP, MESS UP

hassle or **hassel** *fr middle 1800s* **1** *n* A disagreement; quarrel; fight: *A hassel between two actors touched off...the riot*—Billy Rose/ *The hassle over putting fluoride in drinking water*—N Boynton **2** *v*: *They were hassling about who would pay the bill* **3** *v* To harass; treat rudely and roughly: *I went to an assistant DA and told him I wanted to discuss being hassled by the police* **4** *n* A difficult or tedious task or concern: *Getting those tickets was a real hassle* **5** *v* narcotics To get narcotics with difficulty: *He finally hassled one bag* [origin unknown; perhaps fr French *harceler* "importune, attack constantly"; perhaps a blend: *haggle* and *tussle, haggle* and *wrestle* have been proposed; perhaps fr a Southern dialect word meaning "pant, breathe noisily"]

hat *See* BRASS HAT, GIMMIE HAT, HANG ONTO YOUR HATS, HARD HAT, HERE'S YOUR HAT WHAT'S YOUR HURRY, HIGH-HAT, IRON HAT, KNOCK something INTO A COCKED HAT, OLD HAT, PARTY HAT, PASS THE HAT, PLUG HAT, PUT A HAT ON IT, SHIT IN YOUR HAT, STRAW HAT, TALK THROUGH one's HAT, THROW one's HAT IN THE RING, TIN HAT, UNDER one's HAT, WEAR TWO HATS, WHITE HAT, WOOL HAT

hatch *n* The mouth and throat: *DeCasseres would hurl the first legal drink down his hatch*—HA Smith *See* BOOBY HATCH, DOWN THE HATCH, NUT HOUSE

hatchet job 1 *n phr* A malicious attack; a diatribe or indictment meant to destroy: *By hatchet job is meant here...a calculated attempt to demolish the author*—Wilfred Sheed **2** *n phr* A discharge or dismissal; =the AX

hatchet man 1 *n phr fr 1920s* A professional killer; =HIT MAN **2** *n phr* A person whose task and predilection is to destroy an opponent, often by illegitimate means

◀**hatchet-thrower**▶ *n black* A Puerto Rican or other Hispanic

hate someone's **guts** *v phr* To have an extreme hatred for someone; absolutely execrate someone: *I dislike him, but I don't hate his damn guts*

hat in hand *adv phr* Obsequiously; tamely; pleadingly: *He expects me to come asking hat in hand/ The President stands there, hat in hand, begging the Congress for their votes*—National Public Radio

hatrack *n* A thin or frail person; =BEANPOLE

hat trick *n phr sports fr late 1800s* British The scoring of three goals in a single game by the same player ● Commonly used of hockey or soccer [fr cricket, "the bowling down of three wickets with successive balls," a feat which entitled the player to the proceeds of a collection, i.e., a passing of the *hat*, or to a new *hat*]

hatty *See* HIGH-HAT

haul *n* Profits or return, esp illicit ones; loot: *The show yielded a huge haul* *See* COLD HAUL, FOR THE LONG HAUL, GET one's ASHES HAULED, LONG HAUL, OVER THE LONG HAUL

haul one's **ashes** *v phr* To leave; depart; =HAUL ASS

haul someone's **ashes 1** *v phr* To harm or injure someone, esp by beating ◀**2**▶ *v phr* To do the sex act with someone *See* GET one's ASHES HAULED

◀**haul ass**▶ **1** *v phr fr WW1* Navy To leave; depart; =CLEAR OUT, DRAG ASS **2** *v phr* To act quickly, esp in response to a command: *I want it now, so haul ass!* **3** *v phr* To drive or travel very fast: *They were really hauling ass when they hit that curve*

hauler *n hot rodders* A very fast car; =HOT ROD

haul someone **in** *v phr* To arrest someone; =RUN someone IN: *The police decided to haul them all in* —Life

haul it *v phr black* To run away; flee; escape [fr *haul ass*]

haul off *v phr fr middle 1800s* To launch an attack, diatribe, etc: *The parson hauled off and told that bunch of jerks they were a bunch of jerks/ She hauled off and decked him* [probably fr the action of stepping back to make more room for launching the fist, and *haul* suggests a nautical origin]

haul off on someone *v phr* To hit or beat someone; launch a blow at someone: *counting fifty before they hauled off on a Red*—James T Farrell

haul (or **rake**) someone **over the coals 1** *v phr fr late 1700s* British To rebuke someone harshly; castigate; =CHEW OUT **2** *v phr* To put someone through an ordeal [fr the old ordeal by fire]

haul the mail *See* CARRY THE MAIL

hausfrau (HOUS frou) *n* A woman whose primary interests are keeping house, raising children, etc ● Often used in mild contempt, and to suggest a lack of chic [fr German, "housewife"]

have ◁**1**▷ *v* To do the sex act with; possess sexually: *I had Mary Jane in her own bathtub ten times* —Calder Willingham/ *I must have you, you sultry vamp!* **2** *v* To cheat; deceive; =DIDDLE: *I'm afraid it's a scam, they had us*
See be HAD

have a bag (or **half a bag**) **on** *v phr* To be drunk: *He had half a bag on and looked it*—Mickey Spillane

have a ball *v phr* To enjoy oneself particularly well and uninhibitedly: *After the dean left we had us a ball*

have a big mouth *v phr* To be inclined to say embarrassingly too much, esp about others' personal affairs: *Marcel Proust sure had a big mouth/ When he heard, my pal told me I had a big mouth*

have a bird *v phr* To exhibit shock or anger; =HAVE KITTENS: *Charlie will have a bird when he learns she died*—William Goldman

◁**have a bone on**▷ *v phr* To have an erect penis [fr a hubristic anatomical misstatement]

have a bone to pick with someone *v phr* To have a matter to complain about or go into with someone

◁**have a broom up** one's **ass**▷ *v phr* (Variations: **get** may replace **have**; **stick** may replace **broom**; **in** one's **tail** may replace **up** one's **ass**; **butt** may replace **ass**) To work diligently and eagerly; be an overachiever [fr the willing or harried worker in a joke, whose hands are full, but who would sweep the floor if one placed a *broom* in the worker's nether cavity]

◁**have a bug** (or **hair**) **up** one's **ass** (or **up** one's **nose**)▷ *v phr* To be very irascible and touchy: *He must have had a bug up his ass, he nearly took my head off when I just asked politely/ Cheatham had a hair up his ass, was the consensus*—Earl Thompson

have a bun in the oven *v phr* To be pregnant: *The outspoken Miss Bow, who...had a bun in the oven, replied*—Ms

have a bun on **1** *v phr* *fr early 1900s* To be drunk **2** *v phr* To be intoxicated with narcotics

have a can on *See* GET A CAN ON

◁**have a case of the dumb-ass**▷ *v phr Army* To do something stupid; err idiotically

have a case on someone *v phr* To be infatuated with or in love [*case* was specialized to mean "a case of being in love" by the mid-19th century]

have a chip on one's **shoulder** *v phr* To be very touchy and belligerent; be easily provoked

have a clue *v phr chiefly British fr 1940s armed forces* To know; be aware or apprised of: *Do you have any clue about what's going on here?*
See NOT HAVE A CLUE

have a cow *See* HAVE KITTENS

have (or **take**) **a crack at** something *v phr* (Variations: **go** or **rip** or **ripple** or **shot** or **whack** may replace **crack**) To make an attempt at something; have a try: *He said he wasn't sure he could, but he'd have a crack at it*

have a crush on someone *v phr fr late 1800s* To be infatuated or enchanted with someone, esp to be secretly in love with someone older and more worldly than oneself

have a few buttons missing *See* HAVE SOME BUTTONS MISSING

have a field day *v phr* To indulge oneself freely and successfully; have it entirely one's way; go all out: *When the news gets out, the press will have a field day/ I'm afraid the bunnies have had a field day with the hyacinths* [fr late-19th-century *field day*, when a school or college, a fire company, etc, would indulge in hearty outdoor sports and drills, inferentially not against the strongest competition or genuine dangers]

have a free ride *See* GET A FREE RIDE

◁not **have a hair on** one's **ass**▷ *See* NOT HAVE A HAIR ON one's ASS

have a hair up one's **ass** *See* HAVE A BUG UP one's ASS

◁**have a hard-on for** someone or something▷ **1** *v phr* To be very much enamored of or attracted to: *I'm afraid the chief executive officer has a hard-on for this idea* **2** *v phr* To be very eager for; lust after: *He knows I'm a federal cop, so he's got to figure I got a hard on for Panthers*—George V Higgins **3** *v phr* *Army* To dislike; make problems for someone

have a head *v phr* To suffer from a hangover

have a heart *interj* A pleading exclamation: *Have a heart, baby, I only did it once!*

have a hole in one's **head** (or **wig**) *v phr* To be very stupid; be insane; =HAVE ROCKS IN one's HEAD

have a lech for someone or something *v phr* To be especially desirous of; lust after [*lech* is a shortening of *lechery* or *lecherous*]

have a leg up on someone or something *v phr* To have a good start on some project, process, in some competition, etc; be well on the way to a goal: *She just started, and they already have a leg up on it*

have a little on the side *See* GET A LITTLE ON THE SIDE

have all one's **buttons** (or **marbles**) *v phr* To be normal or mentally sound; be sane; be shrewd and aware ● Most often in the negative: *When I'm sure I no longer have all my buttons I'll quit this line of work/ The old guy doesn't seem to have all his marbles, the way he mumbles to himself* [*buttons* probably refers to the neatness and completeness of a normal mind compared with the uncertainty and slovenliness of clothes lacking buttons; the lack of *marbles* is probably a reference to the lack of testicles as evincing abnormality]

have all one's **ducks in a row** *See* HAVE one's DUCKS IN A ROW

not **have all** one's **switches on** *See* NOT HAVE ALL one's SWITCHES ON

have all the answers *See* KNOW ALL THE ANSWERS

have all the moves *v phr* To be very skillful; be expert, esp and originally in a sport or game

have a load on *v phr* To be drunk; =FEEL NO PAIN

have a lock on something *v phr* To be assured of some result; be certain of success: *Looks like the Pirates have a lock on the pennant*

have a mind like a sieve *v phr* To be very forgetful

have a monkey on one's **back** *v phr narcotics* To be addicted to narcotics

have (or **cop**) **an attitude** **1** *v phr Army fr black* To dislike and complain about one's plight; = BITCH, KVETCH: *If you'd put up as many bonds for nothing...as I have, you'd have a fucking attitude too*—Donald Goines/ *"Go ahead, cop an attitude," she says and pulls away from him*—Village Voice **2** *v phr* to be arrogant or haughty

have an edge on *v phr* To be slightly drunk

have an (or **the**) **edge on** someone *v phr* To have an advantage; enjoy a superior or winning position

have a (or one's) **nerve** *v phr fr early 1900s* To be impudently aggressive: *You sure have your nerve, telling him off that way*

not **have any** *See* NOT HAVE ANY

have a party *v phr* To do the sex act

◁not **have a pot** (or **without a pot**) **to piss in**▷ *See* NOT HAVE A POT TO PISS IN

have a prayer *v phr* To have a chance; be able
• Very often in the negative: *If everything goes right, we may just have a prayer/ The Eagles don't have a prayer, and neither will Murray*—Philadelphia

have a red face *v phr* To be embarrassed; have a guilty and sheepish mien; = HAVE EGG ON one's FACE: *The Chief had a red face when...he was found in possession of stolen property*—A Hynd

◁**have a rod on**▷ *v phr* To have an erect penis; = HAVE A BONE ON

have a screw loose *v phr* To be crazy; be eccentric: *that his brains, in her opinion, were twisted, or that he had a screw loose*—Joseph Heller

have one's **ashes hauled** *See* GET one's ASHES HAULED

◁**have a shit fit**▷ *v phr* To become very upset or furious; = SHIT A BRICK, SHIT GREEN: *Some people are going to have a shit fit when they read it*—Anne Bernays

have a short fuse *v phr* To have a quick temper; be irascible

◁**have** someone's **ass**▷ *v phr* To punish someone; retaliate severely: *If you utter one word, I'll have your ass*

◁**have** one's **ass in a sling**▷ *v phr* (Variations: **get** or **put** may replace **have**; the locution may be **one's ass is**, **was**, etc, **in a sling**) *fr 1930s* To be in serious trouble: *If she catches you changing that report you'll have your ass in a sling/ Allen has taken an introspective, but not innocent, bystander, and put his ass in a sling*—Playboy

have a thing about *v phr* To be especially concerned with, in love, hate, or fascination; be strongly emotional about: *She really has a thing about pyramids*

have a tiger by the tail *v phr* To be in a nasty situation, esp innocently or unexpectedly, that will get much worse before it gets better

have oneself **a time** *v phr* To enjoy oneself hugely: *Everybody had himself a time*—Billy Rose

have a toehold *See* GET A TOEHOLD

◁**have** (or **get**) one's **banana peeled**▷ *v phr* To do the sex act; copulate

have bats in one's **belfry** *v phr* To be crazy; be eccentric

have one's **boots laced** *v phr* To be alert and aware

not **have brain one** *See* NOT HAVE BRAIN ONE

◁**have brass** (or **cast-iron**) **balls**▷ *v phr* To have audacity; be foolhardy: *Which one of you worthless nits had the brass balls enough to cough when I was talking*—Pat Conroy

◁**have** someone **by the balls**▷ *v phr* To have someone in a very perilous and painful position; have a firm grip on someone; = HAVE someone BY THE SHORT HAIRS: *I didn't want to do it, but they had me by the balls*

◁**have** (or **get**) someone **by the short hairs** (or **curlies** or **knickers**)▷ *v phr first form fr late 1800s* To have someone in a painful and helpless situation; have absolute control over; = HAVE someone BY THE BALLS: *When life gets you by the short hairs, it doesn't let go*—Playboy/ *Someone nasty and ruthless has him by the short hairs*—Village Voice/ *You're in no position to make deals. We got you by the curlies*—Joseph Wambaugh/ *We've got him by the knickers and he's hurting*—Wall Street Journal [fr the *short hairs* growing on the scrotum]

have someone or something **by the tail** **1** *v phr* = HAVE someone BY THE BALLS **2** *v phr* To have control of: *I know all young people are sure they can have it by the tail*—Stephen Longstreet

have one's **card punched** *See* GET one's CARD PUNCHED

◁**have** one's **cherry**▷ **1** *v phr* To be a virgin **2** *v phr* To be unproved or untried in the sense indicated: *He's never been bankrupt, still got his cherry*

have something **cinched** *v phr* (Variations: **iced** or **knocked** or **made** or **taped** or **wired** may replace **cinched**) To be entirely sure of a favorable outcome; be sure of success, well-being, etc: *Then you see the helicopter...and you know you've got it knocked*—The Bridges at Toko-ri (movie)/ *a veteran bank shot artist who has the back boards at West 4th Street wired, does anything he pleases*—Village Voice/ *One more mile and we've got it made/ I thought I had it iced*—Washington Post [*have* something *cinched* is fr cowboy usage, referring to a tightly and securely *cinched* saddle; the variants *have* something *made*, *taped*, and *wired* fr poker terms, also fr cowboy use]

have one's **claws out** *v phr* To be intent on committing injury; be in a damaging or fighting mood: *Maggie Siggins certainly had her claws out when she wrote about Bill*

have (or **get**) **cold feet** *v phr* To be timorous or afraid; have second thoughts: *Ella was coming too, but she had cold feet*

have something **coming out of** one's **ears** *v phr* To have a surplus of something: *He's got talent coming out of his ears*

have something **down** (or **down pat**) *v phr* To know something or be able to do something perfectly; be perfect master of something: *I had my story down pat so I almost believed it myself*

have one's **druthers** *v phr* To have one's preference; have it one's way: *if George Bush had his druthers*—National Review/ *But personally, if I had my druthers, I would like nothing better than to run off to the country with some guy*—Washington Post [fr dialect pronunciation of *I'd rather* as *I'd druther*]

have (or **get**) one's **ducks in a row** *v phr* (Variations: **have** (or **get**) one's **ducks all in a row** or **have** (or **get**) **all** one's **ducks in a row**) *Army* To be fully prepared; to be organized; = DO one's HOMEWORK: *Be sure you have your ducks all in a row when the General comes around/ You have five years to get all your ducks in a row*—Time/ *Getting all your ducks in a row has never been easier*—television commercial [perhaps fr a mother duck's marshaling of her *ducklings* in a neat flotilla behind her; perhaps fr some game]

have one's **ears on** *v phr citizens band* To have one's receiver turned on

have egg on one's **face** *v phr* To be caught in an embarrassing or guilty plight; be rueful and embarrassed: *Steve Brill, the editor...should have egg on his face this week*—Village Voice/ *He left President Reagan with egg on his face*—Washington Post

◁**have** one's **end off**▷ *v phr* To do the sex act; = FUCK

have eyes for *v phr* To desire; wish for; = HAVE A LECH FOR: *But the chick who has eyes for some cat would be uncool if she told him so directly*—S Boal

have one's **glasses on** *v phr black* To behave in a stiff and formal way

have something **going** (or **working**) **for** someone or something *v phr* To enjoy a certain advantage; have particular assets: *You've got more going for you with NTS home training*—Popular Science/ *The best thing this mall has going for it is it's just a test*—New Yorker

have one's **hands** (or **plate**) **full** *v phr* To be occupied up to one's limit, esp in an emergency: *When the water main burst, the utility workers had their hands full/ They wanted me to take on another case but I had my plate full*

have one's **head pulled** *v phr* (Variation: **out of** one's **ass** may be added) *Army* To be intelligent and sensible; be aware

◁**have** one's **head up** one's **ass**▷ *v phr* To behave stupidly and blindly; be chronically wrong: *We lost because the whole team had its head up its ass/ Why you gommy, stupid shit...Your head is up your ass*—William Kennedy

have hot pants *v phr* To be very lustful; crave carnally: *He has hot pants for her and she for someone else, alas*

have it *v phr* To be talented; be competent and effectual: *He tries hard, but he just doesn't have it See* HAD IT, LET someone HAVE IT

have it all hanging out *v phr* To be concealing nothing; be entirely candid and undefensive; = LET IT ALL HANG OUT: *As the current saying goes, NCR has it all hanging out*—Forbes

have it all over someone or something *v phr* To be superior; surpass or outstrip: *In advanced technology, the North has it all over the South*

have (or **get**) **it all together** *v phr* To have one's life, feelings, energies, etc, satisfactorily arranged; be free of emotional and behavioral dysfunctions: *Dr Jung says we'll all be OK when we have it all together*

have it bad *v phr* To be very much in love; be powerfully infatuated: *He had it bad for her, though she was indifferent/ He warbled the old song, "I got it bad and that ain't good"*

have it both ways *v phr* To hold or esp to profit from two contrary positions; = WORK BOTH SIDES OF THE STREET: *Make up your mind which one you'll support, because you can't have it both ways*

have it for someone *v phr* To be in love with: *They would say that mouse has got it for Joey but bad*—John O'Hara

have it good *v phr* To enjoy prosperity, health, regular meals and pleasures, etc: *I had it real good up there, till they canned me/ We never had it so good!*

have it in for someone *v phr* To be angry with; feel vindictive towards; bear a grudge: *Hatfield had it in for McCoy*

◁**have it off**▷ *v phr fr 1930s British* To do the sex act; copulate ● Still chiefly British: *who has had it off with both of them*—Us [fr earlier use, "to achieve a crime or shady transaction, pull something off," probably transferred to sexual activity on analogy with *cheating* and *hanky panky*, and by psychological suggestions related to *pull off* and *come off*]

have kittens (or **a cow**) or **cast a kitten** *v phr* To manifest strong and sudden feeling; have a fit of laughter, fear, anger, etc: *He got so mad I thought he was going to have kittens*

have lead in one's **pants** (or ◁**in** one's **ass**▷) *v phr* To be very sluggish and lazy; move or work slowly; be unresponsive: *Frank's got lead in his ass, go jazz him up*

◁**have lead in** one's **pencil**▷ **1** *v phr* To be sexually potent; have an erect penis **2** *v phr* To be keenly needful of sexual gratification

have someone's **lunch** *See* EAT someone's LUNCH

have something **made** *See* HAVE something CINCHED

have one's **mind in the gutter** *v phr* To be preoccupied with or devoted to crudeness and smut

have no bones about *See* MAKE NO BONES ABOUT

have someone's **nose open** *v phr black* To excite someone's sexual appetite: *What about that gray girl in San Jose who had your nose wide open?*—Eldridge Cleaver [perhaps fr the involuntary flaring of the nostrils as a symptom of strong desire, anger, etc]

have-not 1 *n* A poor person, region, etc **2** *modifier: the have-not nations of the Third World*

have someone's **number** *v phr* To know the exact truth about someone, though it be disguised;

know someone completely: *She knew what I meant, and she knew I had her number*—James M Cain [perhaps fr one's telephone *number*; perhaps fr one's serial or other *number* used for identification]

have one foot in the grave *v phr* To be nearly dead; be doomed

have something **on the brain** *v phr fr middle 1800s* To be obsessed with: *She's got folk-dancing on the brain*

have papers (or **papers on**) *v phr black* To be married, or married to: *I will not be number two, I got papers on you*—Washington Post

have one's **plate full** *See* HAVE one's HANDS FULL

have problems with something *v phr* To find hard to accept; be unable to agree immediately: *Even after talking it over, she still had problems with the board's decision*

have pups *v phr* = HAVE KITTENS

have rocks in one's (or the) **head** *v phr* To be wrong, stupid, crazy, etc: *Kid, you got rocks in your head*—Max Shulman
See ROCKS IN one's HEAD

◁**have shit for brains**▷ *v phr* To be very stupid: *You suffer from chronic cranial rectalitis, you have shit for brains*

have some (or **a few**) **buttons** (or **marbles**) **missing** *v phr* To be insane; be eccentric

have the edge on someone *See* HAVE AN EDGE ON someone

◁**have the hots for** someone▷ *v phr* To desire someone sexually: *the stocky instructress was glaring at them. "Think she's got the hots for you"*—Earl Thompson/ *I know Grodin has the hots for you*—Village Voice

have the inside track *n phr* To have a strong advantage, esp one based on some fortuitous circumstance: *All the candidates look OK, but Hester has the inside track because she's single* [fr the advantage that a racer has by being nearest the *inside* of the *track* and having therefore the shortest distance to run]

have the jump (or **jump on**) *v phr* To enjoy a lead or advantage; be ahead of: *Who has the jump in this election?/ I got the jump on him right away, and never looked back*

have them in the aisles *See* LAY THEM IN THE AISLES

have (or **get**) **the munchies** *v phr narcotics & counterculture* To be hungry, esp for sweets and starches after using marijuana: *I just smoked the smoke and got the munchies and I got real fat*—New York Times

◁**have the rag on** (or **Baker flying**)▷ *v phr* To menstruate; = FALL OFF THE ROOF [*Baker flying* is fr the red-colored B flag, called *Baker* flag in the military phonetic alphabet]

◁**have the red ass**▷ *See* GET THE RED ASS

◁**have the world by the balls**▷ *v phr* To be in a very profitable and dominant situation; = HAVE something CINCHED, SHIT IN HIGH COTTON: *Dunning had the world by the balls*—Don Pendleton/ *With a good agent, you've got the world by the balls*—John Irving

have one's **ticket punched** *v phr* To be a legitimate member of something; be fully warranted in experience, qualification, etc; = PAY one's DUES: *These women have had their "tickets punched" in the corporate world*—Washington Post

hawk[1] *v* To clear one's throat; cough up and spit: *let out of their cells to wash...hawk...stretch*—Nelson Algren

hawk[2] **1** *n* A person who advocates a strong and bellicose policy or action: *Some were doves on Vietnam and hawks on Iran* **2** *n* A person who attracts and procures young men and boys for homosexuals, esp older men: *The police believe he was acting the role of a "hawk," finding "chickens" (young boys) for older men*—New York Times

the hawk *n phr black* The cold winter wind: *Well, looks like the hawk is getting ready to hit the scene and send temperatures down*—Ruby Dee [origin unknown; perhaps fr the strong biting quality of such a wind]

Hawkins *See* MISTER HAWKINS

hawkish *adj* Having the attitudes of one who advocates strong action on national policy: *These people...are as hawkish as Lyndon Johnson*—Stewart Alsop

hawkishness *n* The quality of being an advocate of a bellicose policy; belligerence: *A few of the Republicans objected to Nixon's hawkishness*—Saturday Evening Post

hay 1 *n narcotics* Marijuana; = HERB **2** *n lunch counter* Strawberry or strawberries **3** *n* A small amount of money; = NICKELS AND DIMES, PEANUTS: *What they offered was just hay*
See HIT THE HAY, INDIAN HAY, LOAD OF HAY, MAKE HAY, a ROLL IN THE HAY, THAT AIN'T HAY

the hay 1 *n* Bed: *He is in his hotel room in the hay*—Damon Runyon **2** *n* Sleep; semiconsciousness
See HIT THE HAY

haybag *n hoboes* A woman hobo

hay burner 1 *n phr* (also **oat-burner**) *fr early 1900s* A horse, esp a race horse: *preferred the company of hay-burners to that of humans*—Billy Rose **2** *n phr* A person who smokes marijuana: *About half the guys in the troupe were hay burners*—New Yorker

◀**hay-eater**▶ *n black* A white person; = OFAY

haymaker *fr early 1900s prizefight* **1** *n* A very strong blow with the fist: *Smashes the...kid with a wild haymaker*—H Witwer **2** *n* Any powerful stroke or felling blow: *Having her arrested...would be a haymaker to your father*—J Evans **3** *n* Any supreme or definitive effort, performance, etc; = WINNER: *Her blues number was a haymaker*

hayseed 1 *n* (also **hayseeder**) *fr late 1800s* A farmer; country person: *There's still a lot of hayseed in Senator Chance*—R Starnes **2** *adj*: *a hayseed routine/ hayseed simplicity* **3** *adj* Rural; provincial: *The bad actors perform worse plays in hayseed theaters*—Robert Ruark

haywire 1 *adj fr early 1900s* Functioning erratically; out of order; = ON THE BLINK: *This meter's haywire* **2** *adj* Makeshift; precariously operative: *What sort of haywire gadget are you using for a*

pump? **3** *adj* Crazy; confused; =COCKEYED: *He never looked inside an almanac, and was sure that anyone who did was haywire*—Stewart Holbrook
See GO HAYWIRE

haze *See* IN A FOG

head 1 *n* A headache, esp as a component of a hangover; = a BIG HEAD: *You won't believe the head I had next morning* **2** *n* The mouth: *Keep your head shut* **3** *n* The foam on a glass of beer **4** *n* One person as a unit in an audience, group, etc: *at twenty-five cents a head, no reserved seats*—J Lilienthal **5** *n* A person: *One head that used to claim to sell stockings called*—AJ Liebling ◁**6**▷ *n* The erect penis, esp the glans ◁**7**▷ *n* Fellatio or cunnilingus; = BLOW JOB, HAIR PIE: *Some quiff is going to give you head*—Lawrence Sanders **8** *n* narcotics A narcotics user, esp an addict: *My trip is to reach as many heads in this country as I can, and turn them around*—New York Times **9** *n* narcotics The feeling of euphoria produced by a narcotic; = HIGH, RUSH: *I take two Tuinals and get a nice head*—New York/ *much of the head, or psychic lift, that users experience*—Wall Street Journal
See ACID FREAK, ACIDHEAD, AIRHEAD, APPLEHEAD, BAKEHEAD, BALLOONHEAD, BANANAHEAD, BEANHEAD, BIGHEAD, a BIG HEAD, BITE someone's HEAD OFF, BLIZZARD-HEAD, BLOCKHEAD, BLUBBERHEAD, BONEHEAD, BUBBLEHEAD, BUCKETHEAD, BULLHEAD, BUNHEAD, BURRHEAD, BUSTHEAD, CAPTAIN OF THE HEAD, CHEESEHEAD, CHICKENHEAD, CHIPHEAD, CHOWDERHEAD, CHUCKLEHEAD, CLUNKHEAD, COKEHEAD, DEADHEAD, DOO-DOO HEAD, DUMBHEAD, FATHEAD, FLANGEHEAD, FLATHEAD, GARBAGE HEAD, GET one's HEAD OUT OF one's ASS, GINHEAD, GIVE HEAD, GOOD HEAD, GO SOAK YOURSELF, HANDKERCHIEF-HEAD, HARDHEAD, HASH HEAD, HAVE A HEAD, HAVE A HOLE IN one's HEAD, HAVE one's HEAD PULLED, HAVE ROCKS IN one's HEAD, one's HEAD IS UP one's ASS, HEAD SHOP, HEADSHRINKER, HIT THE NAIL ON THE HEAD, HOPHEAD, HOTHEAD, IN OVER one's HEAD, JARHEAD, JUICEHEAD, KINKY-HEAD, KNOTHEAD, KNUCKLEHEAD, LARDHEAD, LUNKHEAD, MEATHEAD, METAL HEAD, METH HEAD, MINISTER'S FACE, MUSCLEHEAD, MUSH-HEAD, MUTTONHEAD, NEED someone or something LIKE A HOLE IN THE HEAD, NOODLEHEAD, NUMBHEAD, OFF one's NUT, OFF THE TOP OF one's HEAD, OPEN one's FACE, OUT OF one's HEAD, OVER one's HEAD, PIGHEAD, PILLHEAD, PINHEAD, POINTHEAD, POINTY-HEAD, POTATO-HEAD, POTHEAD, PUDDINGHEAD, PUMPKINHEAD, PUTTY-HEAD, RAGHEAD, ROCKHEAD, ROCKS IN one's HEAD, ROTORHEAD, SAPHEAD, SHITHEAD, SHOVELHEAD, SOFT IN THE HEAD, SOREHEAD, STAND ON one's HEAD, TALKING HEAD, TREADHEAD, USE one's HEAD, WEEDHEAD, WHERE someone's HEAD IS AT, WOODENHEAD, WOODHEAD, YELL one's HEAD OFF

-head *combining word* Addicted to or using the narcotic specified: *acidhead/ pothead*

the head *n phr fr merchant marine & Navy* The toilet; = CAN [fr the location of the crew's toilet in the bow or *head* of a ship]

headache *fr 1930s* **1** *n* Any trouble, annoyance, vexation, etc: *another headache for pro coaches*—Associated Press **2** *n* A tedious, obnoxious person; = PILL: *My learned associate is something of a headache*

headbone *n* The skull

headcase *n* An insane or very eccentric person; = NUT: *dedication to a cause that marked them as fanatics of a sort...the wealthy headcases and professional haters*—Don Pendleton

head (or **underground**) **comic** *n phr narcotics & 1960s counterculture* An underground comic book designed to be read while smoking marijuana, and featuring bizarre drawings, black humor, sex, etc

-headed *combining word* Having a head, esp a mind, of the specified defective sort
See AIRHEADED, BALLOONHEADED, BIGHEADED, BONEHEADED, BULLHEADED, FATHEADED, FLATHEADED, MEATHEADED, MUSH-HEADED, MUTTONHEADED, NUMBHEADED, PIGHEADED, PINHEADED, POINTY-HEADED, WOOLLY-HEADED

header 1 *n fr middle 1800s* A head-first dive, fall, or plunge **2** *n* A more or less desperate try; a gamble: *They took a header on the stock market* **3** *n soccer* A pass, shot at the goal, etc, made by batting the ball with one's head
See DOUBLEHEADER

head for *v phr* To start out for or toward; = HIT FOR: *I headed for the door/ He's headed for a disappointment*

headhunter 1 *n* A person or agency that seeks out and recruits employees, esp business executives and highly paid professionals, as candidates for usu high-paying or prestigious jobs: *Headhunters head for Washington as a capital place to find executives*—Wall Street Journal **2** *n football* A very rough player, usu a defensive player

◁one's **head is up** one's **ass**▷ *sentence* One is behaving stupidly and blindly: *were even saying that, skill-wise, the FBI's head was up its ass*—Village Voice

◁**head job**▷ *n phr* Fellatio or cunnilingus; oral sex: *receiving a listless headjob from an aging black prostitute*—Joseph Wambaugh

head kit *n phr narcotics* The set of implements used for taking narcotics; = WORKS: *Head kits are constantly being found*—LJ Berry

headlight 1 *n black* A light-skinned black person **2** *n* A large diamond, esp in a ring or clasp: *A lurid "headlight" in his tie*—Abel Green

headlights 1 *n fr 1920s prizefight* The eyes ◁**2**▷ *n* A woman's breasts **3** *n* Large diamonds

headliner *n* The main or chief performer; main attraction: *She was headliner last week at the Seven Seas*

one's **head off** *adv phr* To one's utmost; extremely much; spectacularly; = one's ASS OFF, one's BRAINS OUT: *one time when Joey was vomiting his head off*—San Francisco

head someone or something **off at the pass** *v phr* To forestall or prevent by anticipation: *A single mother has to establish control fast...Before the coercive cycle...builds...you have to head it off at the pass*—New York Times [fr the stock situation in

Western movies, where typically the leader of a force pursuing thieves or rustlers through rough ground declares "We'll *head them off at the pass*"]

head shop *n phr esp 1960s teenagers & counterculture* A shop selling various accessories of the drug culture and hippie culture, such as water pipes, holders for marijuana cigarettes, psychedelic posters, incense, etc

headshrinker or **headpeeper** *n* Any psychotherapist, psychiatrist, psychoanalyst, etc; = SHRINK: *with a good deal more understanding than any clergyman or headshrinker*—Sports Afield/ *you lousy smug headpeeper*—Stephen King

heads up *interj* A warning of some impending danger or need to be alert: *Heads up, folks, I'm firing this thing*

heads-up *adj* Clever; alert; shrewd: *They're playing real heads-up football*

heads will roll *sentence* People will be dismissed, punished, ruined, etc: *If eventually the authorities catch up with you, no heads will roll*—Punch/ *If this package is not delivered on time, heads will roll*

head trip 1 *n phr* A mental exploration; an adventure of thought, esp of a new sort; a delectable fantasy: *Private head trips seemed to be adjuncts or companions of social movements*—Andrew Kopkind **2** *modifier*: *The Head-Trip Dodge, verbalizing without involvement, the educated filibuster*—New York **3** *v phr*: *man seeks companion for headtripping, studying together, Scrabble, etc*—Psychology Today

head up *v phr* To be the chief of; supervise; direct: *Stan Baker will head up our new Verbal Economy Division*

heap 1 *n* A car, esp an old ramshackle one; = JALOPY **2** *n* Any old vehicle
See JUNK HEAP

a **heap** *adv phr* Very much: *Thanks a heap, old buddy*

heaps 1 *n* Very many; = a FLOCK, OODLES: *I've got heaps of scratch* **2** *adv* Very much: *She loved him heaps, but kept mum*

hearse *n railroad* A caboose

heart 1 *n* Courage; stamina; pluck **2** *n* Generosity; charity; kindness: *The old dame's full of heart* ◁**3**▷ *n* The erect penis, esp the glans; = HEAD **4** *n narcotics* A tablet of an amphetamine, esp Dexedrine (a trade name)
See BLEEDING HEART, CROSS MY HEART, HAVE A HEART, PURPLE HEART

hearted *See* CHICKENHEARTED, COPPER-HEARTED

hear the birdies sing *v phr* To be knocked unconscious; be unconscious

hearts and flowers 1 *n phr fr early 1900s* Sentimentality; maudlin appeals, etc: *I believed all the hearts and flowers you gave me about being in love with your husband*—J Evans **2** *n phr prizefight* A knockout [first sense fr the name of a popular sentimental song of about 1910]

heart-throb *n* One's deeply beloved: *Who's your heart-throb this week?*

heat 1 *n underworld fr 1920s* Pursuit, prosecution, and other sorts of involvement with the law:

types of cash mark which do not involve federal heat—E DeBaun **2** *n carnival* Mob violence, esp in resentment for being cheated **3** *n* Any sort of trouble and recrimination, esp the angry complaining of irritated persons; = FLAK, STATIC: *We better expect heat when this report gets out* **4** *n underworld fr 1920s* A firearm, usu a pistol: *I was packing about as much heat as you find in an icicle...without a gun*—J Evans **5** *n sports* A round in boxing, inning in baseball, etc
See BITCH IN HEAT, DEAD HEAT, GIVE someone HEAT, PACK HEAT

the **heat** *n phr fr black* The police; a police officer: *Try operating an American city without the heat, the fuzz, the man*—Eldridge Cleaver/ *until the heat pulls up in one of those super paddy wagons*—Esquire
See GIVE someone THE HEAT, IF YOU CAN'T STAND THE HEAT STAY OUT OF THE KITCHEN, PUT THE HEAT ON someone, TAKE HEAT, TAKE THE HEAT OFF

heat artist *n phr hoboes* A drinker of jellied alcohol [jellied alcohol is called *canned heat*]

heater 1 *n* A firearm, esp a pistol; = HEAT **2** *n* A cigar: *those long Havana heaters*—Mike Todd
See ARMSTRONG HEATER

the **heat is on** *sentence* Extreme pressure and pursuit are afoot, esp by the police against criminals: *We better stop purse-snatching while the heat is on/ The heat is on dope. That's a big bust if they get hold of you*—New York

heat merchant *n phr* A chronic complainer and critic; = KVETCH

heat-packer *n* An armed criminal

heave 1 *v* To vomit; = BARF **2** *n police* A shelter: *Heave. Any shelter used by a policeman to avoid the elements*—GY Wells

the (or the **old**) **heave-ho** *n phr* Forcible ejection; summary and emphatic dismissal; = the BOUNCE: *If you make any noise...you get the heave-ho*—WJ Slocum [*heave and ho*, the sailors' cry when hauling, is attested from the 16th century]

heaven *See* BLUE HEAVEN, HOG HEAVEN, NIGGER HEAVEN, STINK TO HIGH HEAVEN, TO HELL

heaven dust *n phr narcotics* Cocaine

heavenly blue *n phr narcotics* Morning glory seeds, used as a narcotic

heavy 1 *n* A thug; hoodlum; = GOON **2** *n fr theater fr 1920s* The villain in a play, movie, situation, action, etc; = BADDIE, DIRTY HEAVY: *It mattered not at all that his employers were the heavies of the piece*—Don Pendleton **3** *adj* Serious; intense: *heavy petting/ heavy correcting* **4** *adj cool talk & counterculture fr black* Excellent; wonderful; = COOL: *These guys were not simply cool...they were heavy, totally hip, and totally trustworthy*—San Francisco **5** *adj cool talk & counterculture fr black* Important; consequential; prominent: *The heaviest art form on the planet is certainly films*—D Crosby/ *You said we were meeting this heavy actress*—Paul Theroux/ *He must have been blowing some heavy politics*—Bobby Seale **6** *n* An important person; = BIG SHOT, HEAVYWEIGHT: *will continue to stitch up the local heavies*—Village Voice **7** *n surfers* A big wave: *good set of heavies*—Life

See ON THE HEAVY, WALK HEAVY

heavy artillery or **big guns** *n phr* The most impressive and persuasive arguments, evidence, persons, etc, available: *They're wheeling out the heavy artillery for the debate on withholding/ Against these big critics' big guns I offer Serban & Co some shelter*—Village Voice

heavy breather *n phr* =BODICE-RIPPER

heavy breathing *See* HARD BREATHING

heavy-cake *n 1920s* A ladies' man; =LOVER-BOY

◁**heavy cream**▷ *n phr* A fat woman

heavy date 1 *n phr* A very important rendezvous, esp with someone of the other sex for sex: *A heavy date with a light lady*—K Brush **2** *n phr* One's partner on a heavy date **3** *n phr* Any important, urgent engagement: *a heavy poker date for this afternoon*—WC Burnett

heavy-foot *n police* A habitually fast driver; speeder

heavy (or **heavily**) **into** *adj phr* Much engaged in; prominent in: *his family very heavy into potato chips*—A Arthur

heavy leather 1 *n phr* Leather clothing and various metal accoutrements as or in imitation of motorcycle gangs, esp by extravagantly masculine homosexuals: *He's gone beyond butch, won't wear anything but heavy leather these days* **2** *modifier:* *A psychopathic killer cruises heavy-leather homosexual bars*—New York Times

heavy metal 1 *n phr rock and roll* A style of simple music characterized by extreme loudness, distortion, pounding drums, and played through great banks of amplifiers and speakers: *With all the sudden interest in heavy metal...Deep Purple has decided to give it a go once again*—Aquarian/ *a degree of internal intricacy that belies popular conceptions of heavy metal*—Rolling Stone **2** *modifier:* *As the prototypical heavy metal band, Led Zeppelin has created its fair share*—Rolling Stone

heavy money *n phr* (Variations: **big** or **important** or **real** may replace **heavy**; **dough** or **jack** or **sugar** may replace **money**) A large amount of money; impressive sums; =MEGABUCKS: *Why did she walk out on a movie career which was paying her heavy money?*—P Martin/ *I've been busy cleaning up some heavy dough*—Jerome Weidman

heavy petting (or **necking**) *n phr* Very passionate kissing, fondling, etc, stopping short of the sex act proper

heavy sugar *n phr* A possession or condition indicating wealth: *Six Mercedeses is heavy sugar*

See HEAVY MONEY

heavyweight *n* An important person; =BIGGIE: *He's some sort of heavyweight in the rag trade*

◀**Hebe** or **Heeb**▶ *n* A Jew

heck *interj* =HELL

the **heck** *See* the HELL

hedge 1 *v* (also **hedge off**) *gambling* To transfer part of one's bets to another bookmaker as a means of reducing possible losses if too many of one's clients were to win **2** *n* Something that offsets expected losses: *People were buying gold as a hedge against inflation*

hedgehop *v* To fly an airplane very low

the **heebie-jeebies** (Variations: the **heebies** or the **jeebies** or the **leaping heebies**) *fr early 1900s* **1** *n phr* A very uneasy and jumpy feeling; nagging frets; =the WILLIES: *His several disquisitions on the jeebies*—H Allen Smith/ *I always get the heebies there*—Harold Robbins/ *First night I had a fit of the heebie-jeebies* **2** *n phr* Delirium tremens [said to have been coined by a cartoonist named Billy De Beck]

heel 1 *n underworld fr early 1900s* A sneak-thief; petty criminal; =PUNK **2** *n carnival* A petty hawker; =SHILL **3** *n fr early 1900s* A contemptible man; blackguard; =BASTARD, PRICK, SHITHEEL: *His friend turned out to be a heel, and ran off with his wife and money* **4** *v underworld* To escape from prison **5** *n:* *They made a clean heel from Leavenworth* **6** *v fr late 1800s* To get a gun for oneself or another person **7** *v* To get money for another person: *I heeled him, got a sawbuck from Jim*

See COOL one's HEELS, COP A HEEL, COP AND HEEL, ROUNDHEEL, RUBBER HEEL, SHITHEEL, TARHEEL

heeled 1 *adj fr middle 1800s* Armed; carrying a weapon: *I can talk better when I know this guy isn't heeled*—J Evans **2** *adj fr late 1800s* Wealthy; in funds; =FLUSH: *Having two bills in the kick I counted myself heeled* **3** *adj narcotics* Possessing narcotics; =DIRTY, HOLDING [said to be fr the spur attached to the "heel" of a fighting cock, hence a weapon]

See WELL-HEELED

heeler *n newspaper office* An apprentice; novice reporter; =CUB [perhaps fr the obedience of a trained dog who stays at the heel of the master]

See WARD HEELER

heeltap *n* A few drops of liquor left in a glass: *drink three martinis...absolutely no heeltaps*—American Mercury [origin uncertain; a heeltap glass was one without a flat base, so that it could not be set down until entirely empty (such was presumably also a tumbler), and probably so called because the narrow bottom resembled the narrow tap of a shoeheel]

heesh *n narcotics* Hashish

hefty 1 *n* A stout or obese person: *While other hefties count their calories, he counts the dollars*—Hal Boyle **2** *adj* Obese: *a hefty matron over at the corner table* **3** *adj* Large; considerable: *not only romance, but a hefty dose of fantasy these days*—New York

◁**heifer**▷ *n fr early 1800s* A young woman, esp an attractive one; =FILLY

See ARMORED COW

heimish *See* HAIMISH

a **Heinz 57 variety** *n phr* A mutt; a dog of no discernible lineage; a mongrel: *Chloe's her dog..."a Heinz 57 variety," says Ivey*—New York Daily News [fr a promotional phrase for the many kinds of food packaged and sold by the Heinz company]

heist (HĪST) **1** *v fr early 1900s underworld* To steal; stick up; rob **2** *v* To highjack **3** *n* A robbery or hold-up: *Led Zeppelin...was the victim of* *the heist*—New York Post [fr an early and dialectal pronunciation of *hoist*, with the sense that a thief lifts and takes his booty]

See SHORT HEIST

heist man *n phr underworld* A professional thief or hold-up man

hell **1** *interj* An exclamation of disgust, regret, emphasis, etc: *Oh hell, they're back/ Hell, darling, I didn't mean it* **2** *n* Strong rebuke or punishment; =MERRY HELL: *Your old man'll give you hell/ I caught hell from the tax people* **3** *n* A bad experience: *Dinner with my in-laws is usually pure hell* **4** *v* =HELL AROUND **5** *v* To speed; =BARREL: *An ambulance, helling out the state road* —R Starnes

See ALL HELL BROKE LOOSE, BEAT THE SHIT OUT OF, as BLAZES, BLUE HELL, CATCH HELL, COME HELL OR HIGH WATER, EASY AS PIE, EXCUSE ME ALL TO HELL, FAIR HELL, FOR THE HELL OF IT, FROM HELL TO BREAKFAST, GIVE someone HELL, GO-TO-HELL CAP, GO TO HELL IN A HANDBASKET, HOT AS HELL, LIKE A BAT OUT OF HELL, LIKE HELL, MERRY HELL, PLAY HELL WITH something, RAISE HELL, a SNOWBALL'S CHANCE IN HELL, TAKE OFF LIKE A BIGASS BIRD, TO HELL

the hell **1** *adv phr* (also ◀**the fuck**▶) Completely and immediately • A hostile intensifier: *Get the hell out of here/ Get the fuck off my back, you jerk* **2** *adv phr* (Variations: **deuce** or **devil** or ◀**fuck**▶ or **heck** may replace **hell**; **in God's name** or **in hell** may replace **the hell**) In fact; really • Mainly used for rhythmic fullness in a hostile question: *What the hell do you mean by that?/ What the deuce are you about, you blackguard/ Tell me what the devil you have in mind/ How the fuck would he meet the taxes and pay so many salaries?*—Joseph Heller/ *He never told me where in God's name he was going/ Where in hell is that paper clip?* [probably derived from expressions of incredulity like "in the world," which altered to "in hell"]

hellacious *adj college students* Excellent; wonderful; =GREAT: *It was a hellacious picnic*

hell around *v phr fr late 1800s* To lead a life of low pleasures; frequent bars, chase sex partners, etc: *I'd like to hell around a couple years, then settle down*

hell-bender *n* A wild spree

hell-bent-for-leather *See* HELL-FOR-LEATHER

hell-buggy *n WW2 Army* A military tank

hellcat *n* A volatile and dangerous woman

heller **1** *n* An energetic and aggressive person, esp one who is mischievous and menacing: *He was quite a heller when young* **2** *n college students* An exciting and action-packed party

hell-for-leather or **hell-bent-for-leather** *adv fr late 1800s British* Rapidly and energetically; =ALL-OUT, FLAT OUT: *You're heading hell-for-leather to a crack-up* [origin unknown; perhaps related to British dialect phrases *go hell for ladder, hell fallader ly, hell faleero*, and remaining mysterious even if so, although the *leather* would then be a very probable case of folk etymology with a vague sense of the *leather* involved in horse trappings]

hellhole *n* Any unpleasant or morally degenerate place; =DUMP: *I was so glad to get out of this hell-hole*—Calder Willingham/ *Emerson is a hellhole* —New York Times

a **hell of a** or **helluva** or **one hell of a** *adj phr* Very remarkable, awful, admirable, distressing, etc; =a BITCH OF A, SOME KIND OF: *We had one hell of a good time/ They could have done a helluva lot better than cold cereal*—Armistead Maupin

a **hell of a note** *n phr* Something amazing, disgusting, surprising, etc: *She drank it, ain't that a hell of a note?/ What a hell of a note this is, a lousy flat tire*

a **hell of a** (or **no**) **way to run a railroad** *n phr* An incompetent, overcomplex, or disastrous way of doing something; a flawed and botched methodology: *When she saw how our department was organized she told us it was a hell of a way to run a railroad, and she suggested some improvements*

the **hell of it** *n phr* The worst part of something; what makes something very nasty: *The hell of it is that I tried all week to renew my license before they caught me*

hell on wheels *n phr* A very impressive, nasty, violent, etc, situation or event: *That party was hell on wheels/ This house is going to be hell on wheels in six months*—Lawrence Sanders [said to be fr mid-19th-century characterization of the gambling places and houses of prostitution loaded on flat-cars for railroad workers in the West]

hell or high water *See* COME HELL OR HIGH WATER

hell-raiser **1** *n* A person likely to cause trouble and disturbance, esp by an active and defiant spirit: *This town needs a few hell-raisers to liven it up* **2** *n* A person who leads a life of low pleasures; profligate; libertine; =HELLER: *He was barred from the Muskie train after lending his press pass to a drunken hell-raiser*—Saturday Review

hell's bells *interj fr early 1900s* An exclamation of impatience, anger, emphasis, etc: *Hell's bells, Maude, I did that two whole years ago*

hell to pay *n phr* A very large fuss with dangerous implications; violent repercussions: *When you come late there'll be hell to pay*

hell to split *adv phr* Very rapidly; =HELL-FOR-LEATHER, LICKETY-SPLIT: *She looked back, and I piled after her hell to split*—James M Cain

helper *See* BOILERMAKER

he-man **1** *n* A very masculine man; =HUNK, MACHO **2** *adj*: *a he-man pose/ a regular he-man cop*—E Lavine

hemp **1** *n* A cigar **2** *n narcotics* Marijuana [*hemp* plants produce both rope and marijuana]

See INDIAN HAY

the **hemp** **1** *n phr* Death by hanging; the noose **2** *n phr narcotics* Marijuana or a marijuana cigarette

hen **1** *n* A woman, esp a fussy or gossipy woman • This and other senses regarded as offensive to some women: *That old hen made him sick*—P Marks **2** *n* A young woman; =CHICK **3** *v* To chat and gossip **4** *modifier* By, of, and for women: *hen party/ hen talk*

hen-apple *n* An egg

hencoop or **hen ranch** *n* or *n phr* college students *fr late 1800s* A woman's dormitory

hen-fruit *n* Eggs

hen party *n phr* A party for women only: *Men have stag parties; girls have hen parties*—JG Rothenberg

hen-pen *n 1940s students* A girl's school, esp a private boarding school

hen tracks *n phr* (Variations: **chicken** may replace **hen**; **scratches** or **scratchings** may replace **tracks**) Illegible handwriting; scrawl

hep *adj jive talk fr early 1900s jazz musicians* Aware; up-to-date; = HIP, WITH IT: *By running with the older boys I soon began to get hep*—Louis Armstrong/ *but I'm hep, man; for example, I had my vasectomy already*—Herbert Gold [origin uncertain; perhaps fr the drillmaster's *hep, hep*, with the sense "in step"; early jazz musicians often marched in parades, esp funeral parades]
See UNHEP

hepcat *n jive talk* A man who appreciates the right sort of music, leads a life of fashionable pleasure, etc; = CAT, DUDE: *a big-timer, a young sport, a hep cat, in other words, a man-about-town*—Langston Hughes [fr *hep cat*; a possible supplementary origin fr Wolof *hipicat* "man who is aware" has been suggested]

hepster *n jive talk* A hep person; = HEPCAT

hep to *adj phr* Aware of; cognizant of: *How little we've been personally hep to what's actually going on*—New Yorker

hep to the jive *adj jive talk* Aware; informed; initiated; = WITH IT: *I commenced getting hep to the jive*—Louis Armstrong

herb or **herbs** *n narcotics* Marijuana; = POT: *So you get fines to pay and you've lost your herbs*—Wall Street Journal

herd *See* RIDE HERD ON someone

herder *n prison* A prison guard

here *See* UP TO HERE

here's mud in your eye *See* MUD IN YOUR EYE

here's your hat what's your hurry *sentence* Why are you leaving so soon? but leave at once • Ironic and jocular combination of a polite question and rude request

Herkimer Jerkimer *n phr* Any rustic, fool, or eccentric [based on a *jerk* from *Herkimer*, that is, from a distant provincial place]

herky-jerky *adj* Jerky; spasmodic; not smooth: *bellow and quiver with those herky-jerky spasms*—Village Voice/ *herky-jerky instability of Shepard's plays*—New Yorker

hero sandwich or **hero** or **Hero** *n phr* or *n* A sandwich made with a loaf of bread cut lengthwise and filled with a variety of cheeses, sausages, vegetables, etc; = GRINDER, HOAGIE, POOR BOY, SUBMARINE, TORPEDO [perhaps because one needs to be a bit of a *hero* to eat a whole *sandwich*]

herpie *n* A person infected with herpes virus

◁**Herring Choker** or **herring chocker**▷ **1** *n* A Scandinavian **2** *n* A New Brunswick native or ship **3** *n phr* A Nova Scotian person or ship;

= BLUENOSE: *No price for lobster, cause of the Herring-Chokers*—Philip Wheelwright

the **herring pond** *n phr fr early 1700s British* The Atlantic Ocean

Hershey bar 1 *n phr* WW2 armed forces A stripe, worn on a military uniform to indicate units of time spent on overseas service ◀**2**▶ *n phr* A black person [fr a *bar* of *Hershey* (a trade name) chocolate, the brown of the chocolate in the second sense and the yellow of the wrapper of some such bars in the first; first sense probably influenced by the name of General Lewis B *Hershey*, director of the selective service system from 1941 to 1970]

hess *See* MELL OF A HESS

hex *n* A jinx or curse; = the INDIAN SIGN, WHAMMY: *I lose every time, must be a hex on me* [ultimately fr German *Hexe* "witch"]

hey *interj* An exclamation used to get attention, to show surprise, delight, greeting, disapproval, etc • Increasingly used as a placative or apologetic analogue of "Listen" or "Believe me": *Hey, you can't go in there!/ Hey, how you doing?/ Hey, it's okay, I didn't mean it/ Hey, you were never better*

hey Rube *n phr fr late 1800s* The traditional warning and rallying cry of circus and carnival people, used esp when they are attacked by righteously indignant citizens [fr *Rube* "Reuben," used to designate the archetypal noncircus citizen, esp in the provinces]

hi or **hiya** *interj fr early 1900s* A salutation upon meeting: *The staccato cry of "Hi!," which we...judged to be the almost universal greeting*—New Yorker

hick 1 *n fr late 1600s British* A rural person; a simple, countrified man or woman; = APPLEKNOCKER, RUBE: *The automobile...largely nullified the outward distinctions between hick and city slicker*—DL Cohn **2** *modifier*: *wasn't bad looking in a hick way*—H Witwer/ *that hick chief of police*—Erle Stanley Gardner [fr a nickname of Richard, thought of as a country name, as Reuben is the base of "rube"]
See WOODHICK

hickey or **hickie 1** *n fr early 1900s* Any unspecified or unspecifiable object; something one does not know the name of or does not wish to name; = DOODAD, DOOHICKEY, GADGET: *We have little hickeys beside our seats*—Atlantic Monthly **2** *n* A blackhead, pimple, or other minor skin lesion; = ZIT **3** *n* A mark on the skin made by biting or sucking during a sex act: *line of hickeys, or love bites*—John Irving

hickeymadoodle *n* = DOODAD, HICKEY

◁**hickory dick**▷ *See* DOES A WOODEN HORSE HAVE A HICKORY DICK

hicksville or **Hicksville 1** *adj* = DULLSVILLE **2** *adj* = CORNY

hick town *n phr fr early 1900s* A small or rural town: *any hick town in Kansas*—American Mercury

hicky *adj* Rural; mean and meager: *This man is from some hicky farm in Shit Creek, Georgia*—Eldridge Cleaver

hide *n* = HORSEHIDE

See TAKE IT OUT OF someone's HIDE, TAN

hideaway 1 *n* A private retreat; personal refuge; =HIDEOUT **2** *n* A small, remote place, esp a small nightclub, restaurant, etc: *The vaudeville performer on the two-a-day has played to punks in the hideaways*—World's Work

hideout 1 *n prison fr early 1900s* An inmate who hides with the intention of escaping at night **2** *n fr 1920s* A place of relative obscurity and safety; =HIDEAWAY: *The gang had a hideout in a ruined warehouse near Hoboken*

hide out *v phr* To hide, esp from the police or other pursuers

hides *n jazz musicians* Drums, esp a complete drum set as used by a jazz musician

hide the weenie *See* PLAY HIDE THE WEENIE

hidey hole 1 *n phr fr middle 1800s British* A place to hide; =HIDEAWAY **2** *modifier: conceal themselves in one of the hidey hole apartments of their proliferating step-parents*—Village Voice

hi-fi or **hi fi** or **high-fi 1** *n* or *n phr fr late 1940s* A record player that reproduces sound without much distortion or alteration from the original **2** *modifier: a hi-fi amplifier/ hi fi recording* [fr *high fidelity*]

higgledy-piggledy *adj fr late 1500s British* Confused; chaotic; =MESSY: *I was walking in dark corridors that were all higgledy-piggledy*—San Francisco [origin uncertain; perhaps fr humorous echoic reduplication based on the squalor of the traditional *pig*]

high 1 *adj* Drunk, esp slightly so: *high, slightly alcoholic, above the earth!*—Arthur Miller **2** *adj narcotics fr 1920s* Intoxicated by narcotics, esp in an easy and lighthearted condition induced by drugs; =GEEZED: *An actor has less license to get high during working hours than does a musician*—Saturday Review/ *the smoker uses them in big puffs getting high*—Stephen Longstreet **3** *n: He took a few tokes and got a pretty good high* **4** *n* A nonintoxicated feeling of exhilaration or euphoria; =LIFT: *Weddings are a high*—Saturday Review **5** *adj: The congregation was all high on gospel enthusiasm*
See MILE-HIGH CLUB, SHIT IN HIGH COTTON, YOU'RE ON DRUGS

high as a kite *adj phr* Intoxicated or exhilarated to an important degree
See BLOW something HIGH AS A KITE

highball 1 *n railroad fr late 1800s* A signal denoting a clear track or clearance to start or accelerate **2** *n railroad* A train running on schedule, or an express train **3** *v fr 1920s fr railroad* To speed; rush: *A train was thirty yards away, highballing down the track*—Calder Willingham/ *One New York distributor highballed 30 trucks through the Holland Tunnel*—Associated Press **4** *n fr late 1800s* An iced, mixed alcoholic drink taken in a high glass: *He quaffed a couple of rye highballs and left* **5** *n fr WW1 Army* A military salute [fr the former use of a railroad track-side signal using a two-foot globe, raised or lowered, to instruct the engineer; the military sense fr the use of a railroad conductor's raised hand or fist as a signal to the engineer to start, the

term transferred from the mechanical signal; the origin of the beverage sense is uncertain, though the reference may be to the drink in a *high* glass raised *high* in a toast, and resembling the train conductor's *highball* signal]

high-binder *n fr early 1800s* A corrupt politician or functionary: *covered the winter meeting of the grand inner circle of high-binders at Miami Beach*—Westbrook Pegler [of obscure origin, at first referring to ruffians and gang members]

highbrow 1 *n fr early 1900s* An intellectual; person of notable education and culture; =DOUBLE DOME, EGGHEAD: *One does not need to be a "highbrow" to read this book*—AG Kennedy **2** *adj* (also **highbrowed**): *all them high-brow sermons*—Sinclair Lewis **3** *adj* Impractical; idealistic; unrealistic: *another silly highbrow scheme* [coined by the humorist Will Irwin around 1905]

high camp *n phr* Art work, theater performance, items of decoration, etc, that are so outrageously old-fashioned, so blatantly injurious to good contemporary taste, as to assume a sort of special value by their very egregiousness: *His way of lisping Shirley Temple lyrics is high camp*

high-class *adj* Of first quality; esp of refined and elevated culture; =CLASSY: *a high-class show/ a very high-class guy*

high cockalorum *n phr fr late 1800s* A pompous, self-important person [ultimately fr a mid-19th-century British schoolboys' game in which boys leapfrogged on top of one another, and the highest was called *high cockalorum*, suggesting a triumphant, crowing rooster]

high cotton *See* SHIT IN HIGH COTTON

higher than a kite (or **than Gilroy's kite**) *adj phr* Very drunk or very much intoxicated by narcotics

higher-up *n* One of the persons in charge; a member of the upper echelon; =BIG SHOT ● Most often in the plural: *A conference with the Higher-ups and Tammany Hall*—E Lavine/ *She always fought with the movie higher-ups*—Associated Press

highfalutin or **highfalutin'** or **hi-foluting** *adj fr middle 1800s* Overblown and pretentious; bombastic; stilted: *take one with ideas less "highfalutin'"*—Scribner's/ *stilted, overstrained, and as the Americans would say, hi-foluting*—Anthony Trollope [origin unknown; originally a gerund, seemingly based on a verb *high falute*, suggesting a humorous alteration of *flute*; perhaps fr a blend of *highflown* with some other element]

high five 1 *n phr* A way of greeting by slapping raised palms together ● Chiefly used by and adopted from athletes, who themselves adopted the style from black colleagues: *handshaking, even a few high-fives from the younger alums*—Rutland Herald **2** *n phr: Hey, Jim, high five me*

highflag *v cabdrivers* To convey a customer and collect the fare without using the meter; =ARM IT, RIDE THE ARM

high gear *See* IN HIGH GEAR, SHIFT INTO HIGH GEAR

highgrade *v lumberjacks* To remove the best trees of a forest

high-hat 1 *n* (also **high-hatter**) A person who behaves arrogantly and snobbishly; a putatively important person: *a lot of lowbrows pretending to be intellectual high-hats*—P Marks **2** *v fr 1920s*: *How come you're high-hatting me, old buddy?* **3** *adj* (also **high-hatty**) *fr 1920s*: *his high-hat posturings/ high-hatty pretentions* **4** *n fr jazz musicians* A set of two cymbals, the upper of which is crashed on the lower by operating a foot-pedal; = SOCK

high-hatter *n* = HIGH-HAT

high heaven *See* STINK TO HIGH HEAVEN, TO HELL

high horse *See* GET ON one's HIGH HORSE

highjack *See* HIJACK

high-jinks *See* HI-JINKS

high muckety-muck *n phr* (Variations: **muck-a-muck** or **muckie-muck** or **mucky-muck** or **monkey-monk** may replace **muckety-muck**) *fr middle 1800s Western* A very important person, esp a pompous one; = BIG SHOT, HIGHER-UP: *I'm gonna meet a couple of the high muckety-mucks at the university tomorrow* [fr Chinook jargon *hiu muckamuck* "plenty to eat," transferred to the important individual who has plenty to eat; the *monkey-monk* variant is a case of folk etymology]

high on someone or something **1** *adj phr* Very favorable towards; enthusiastic about: *I'm not as high on Wallace Stevens as I once was* **2** *adj phr* Intoxicated by; exhilarated with: *He says he's high on Jesus/ She gets high on wine and pot*

high on the hog *See* EAT HIGH ON THE HOG

high pitch *n phr hawkers* A hawker's street display set up on a box, wagon, or car: *40,000 men standing on the sidewalks...with high pitch*—JT Flynn

highpockets *n* A tall person, esp a man or boy

high-rent *adj phr* Chic and expensive; = CLASSY, HIGH-CLASS: *with some kind of high-rent bitch from a women's magazine*—Dan Jenkins

high roller 1 *n phr fr late 1800s* A person who gambles for high stakes: *for the high rollers in the mysterious world of wheat and corn futures*—Time/ *The casinos give generous freebies to the high rollers* **2** *n phr* = BIG-TIME SPENDER

the **high sign** *n phr fr early 1900s fr southern Appalachian* A signal to an associate, esp one given inconspicuously by gesture: *waiting by prearrangement in the dark blue Lincoln Town Car, and George gave him the high sign*—San Francisco

hightail or **hightail it** *fr early 1900s fr cowboys* **1** *v* or *v phr* To leave quickly; = LIGHT OUT: *She took one look and hightailed for home* **2** *v* or *v phr* To speed; rush; = HIGHBALL: *We better hightail it if we want to make the first show* **3** *v* or *v phr* = TAILGATE

high tech or **hitech 1** *n phr* or *n* Advanced technology: *From OPEC to High Tech*—Washington Post **2** *adj*: *takes us through three high tech happenings, a computer room, a radiology unit, an intensive care unit*—Village Voice/ *a chic, high-tech version of The Creature from the Black Lagoon*—New York/ *a downsized, hitech, ultraswoopy model next year*—Car and Driver **3** *n phr* or *n* An object or design, usu of synthetic or fabricated material, designed to look like an example of high technology: *This chair is high tech*

high ticket *See* BIG TICKET

high-toned or **high-tony** *adj* Very refined and genteel; aloof and superior; = TONY: *Look at the high-tony bum*—Toots Shor

high-up *n* An important person; = BIG SHOT, HIGHER-UP ● Most often plural: *Rico got in touch with some of the high-ups*

high water *See* COME HELL OR HIGH WATER

high waters *n phr* (also **high water pants** or **high waders** or **flood pants**) Trousers that are shorter than current fashion dictates [fr the notion that the trousers have been chosen or rolled up for walking through *high water*]

high, wide, and handsome 1 *adv phr* Easily, triumphally, and masterfully; = WITH FLYING COLORS **2** *adj phr*: *a high-wide-and-handsome win*

high-wine *n hoboes* Coca-Cola (a trade name)

◁**high yellow** (or **yaller**)▷ *black n phr* A light-skinned black person, esp an attractive young woman: *I mean high-yellow girls*—Langston Hughes/ *took some little high-yaller girl in the closet one day*—Claude Brown

hijack or **highjack 1** *v fr 1920s* To rob, esp to rob a vehicle of its load: *Hijack the truck*—E Lavine **2** *v* To commandeer a public vehicle, esp an airliner, for some extortionary or political purpose: *Two more planes were hijacked to Cuba last week* [said to be fr the command *High, Jack*, telling a robbery victim to raise his hands; an early-20th-century hobo sense, "traveling hold-up man," is attested, which suggests that the source may be railroad and hobo slang; see *ball the jack*]

hi-jinks or **high-jinks** *n fr middle 1800s* Boisterous fun; uninhibited jollification; pranks and capers: *the dashing hi-jinks of the Katzenjammer Kids*—Ebony/ *the out-of-towner...cuts the hi-jinks here*—Hal Boyle [fr the name of a dice game played for drinks]

hike 1 *v line repairers fr 1920s* To work as a line repairer, esp to climb poles and towers in such work **2** *v* To raise: *They won't hike our wages this year* **3** *n*: *The government got a big tax hike* **4** *v* = HIKE A CHECK [fr mid-19th-century term *hike up* "go or raise up," related to *hoick* of the same meaning, both probably fr the basic dialectal sense "go, go about"]

hike a check *v phr underworld* To illegally raise the amount shown on a check: *Did you hike those checks?*—Associated Press

hiker 1 *n line repairers* A telephone or electric line repairer **2** *n hoboes* A town marshal

hill *n baseball* The pitcher's mound
See DRIVE someone OVER THE HILL, GO OVER THE HILL, OVER THE HILL

Hill *See* SAM HILL, SUGAR HILL

the **Hill 1** *n phr* Capitol Hill in Washington, DC: *They're all over the Hill, and can frighten members*—Fortune **2** *n phr* The US Congress: *Republicans or Democrats on the Hill*—Playboy

hillbilly 1 *n fr late 1800s* A southern Appalachian hill dweller **2** *adj*: *hillbilly music/ hillbilly* *crafts* **3** *n* A country bumpkin **4** *adj* Countrified; unsophisticated; =HICK: *This ain't no hillbilly joint. We got some class here*—J Cannon

a **hill of beans** *See* NOT GIVE A DAMN

hi-lo *n* A forklift vehicle

himself *See* HIS NIBS

hincty (Variations: **hinkty** or **hinktyass** or **hankty**) *black* **1** *adj* Snobbish; aloof; =STUCK-UP: *hinkty motherfucker*—George Warren/ *like you do a hankty heifer in the bed and make her like it*—Village Voice **2** *adj* Pompous; overbearing **3** *adj* =HINKY **4** *n* A white person; =OFAY [origin unknown]

hind end *n phr* The buttocks; =ASS

hinders or **hind legs** *n* or *n phr* The legs
• Often in phrases connoting resistance or defiance: *He stood up on his short little hinders and got himself a lawyer/ The Packer defense rose on its hind legs again*—Milwaukee Journal

hind hook *n phr* railroad A train's brake operator

hindsight *See* TWENTY-TWENTY HINDSIGHT

◁ **hind tit** ▷ *See* SUCK HIND TIT

hinge *n* A look or glance; =GANDER
See GET A HINGE AT

hinky *adj* Suspicious; curious: *Something hinky is going down*—The Renegades (TV program)/ *driver of the pimpmobile looks hinky*—Joseph Wambaugh [origin unknown]
See DOODAD

hip *beat & cool talk fr black* **1** *adj* =HEP **2** *adj* Being and/or emulating a hipster, hippy, beatnik, etc; =COOL, FAR OUT: *"I'm hip"...means....Cool. In* —Herbert Gold/ *to be hip is to be "disaffiliated"* —Eugene Burdick **3** *v* To make aware; inform: *educating the masses of America, hipping black people to the need to work together*—Bobby Seale [fr *hep*]
See SHOOT FROM THE HIP

hip cat or **hipcat** *beat & cool talk* **1** *n phr* or *n* =HEPCAT **2** *n phr* or *n* =HIPSTER

hip chick *n phr* *beat & cool talk* An alert and up-to-date young woman, esp in matters of popular culture, music, etc; =FLYCHICK

hipe *See* HYPE

hip gee[1] *n phr* A man who can be trusted; a well-informed man [fr *hip* plus *gee* "guy"]

hip gee[2] *n phr* Money well used or bet; =the SMART MONEY [*gee* meaning "grand," hence a large amount of money]

hip-hop or **Hip Hop** **1** *n* or *n phr* =RAP SONG **2** *n* or *n phr* =BREAK DANCING **3** *adj* or *adj phr* Of or pertaining to contemporary black urban youth culture in the 1980s: *Hip-hop clubs feature rappin' DJs and bad-dressin' dudes* **4** *n* or *n phr* The activities that are emblematic of contemporary black urban youth culture: *What is "hip-hop"? That phrase includes such activities as break dancing, rap music, and graffiti art*—New York Daily News/ *Most of them...are young Hispanics, more connected to Hip Hop than High culture*—New York Daily News

hip-huggers *n* Pants having a low waistline, usu below the navel

hipped *See* UNHEP

hipped on *adj phr* *fr early 1900s* Enthusiastic about; obsessed with: *I ain't hipped on her, sort of hypnotized by her, any more*—Sinclair Lewis/ *I'm hipped on Freud and all that*—F Scott Fitzgerald [ultimately fr *hip* or *the hip* "hypochondria," hence obsession]

hipper-dipper *esp 1940s* **1** *adj* Excellent; superb; =SUPER-DUPER: *a hipper-dipper display* —John Kieran **2** *n* *prizefight* A prizefight where the result is prearranged; =TANK FIGHT: *the last fight being a "hipper-dipper"*—Philadelphia Record [the boxing sense perhaps related to *dipper* "small swimming pool," in which one goes up to the *hips*; modeled on *take a dive* and *tank*]

hippie or **hippy** **1** *n* *esp 1960s counterculture* One of a group of usu young persons who reject the values of conventional society and withdraw into drifting, communes, etc, espouse peace and universal love, typically wear long hair and beards, and use marijuana or psychedelic drugs; =BEAT, BEATNIK **2** *modifier: Saigon has acquired an elaborate hippie culture*—New Yorker/ *freaky hippie posters*

hippiedom or **hipdom** **1** *n* Hippies collectively **2** *n* The hippie movement, world, culture, etc

hippings *n* *hoboes* Anything used as bedding under the hips

hippo *n* A hippopotamus

hip-pocket bookie *n phr* *gambling* A betting agent who has only a few large bettors as clients

hippooed *adj* Cheated; deceived; =BUFFALOED

hippy *adj* Having wide and prominent hips
See HIPPIE

hips *n* *esp 1920s* The woeful end; =CURTAINS: *Well, that's hips for Sam*—WR Burnett

hip shooter *n phr* A person inclined to act and respond impulsively and aggressively; =HOTHEAD

hipster **1** *n* =HEPCAT, HEPSTER, HIP CAT **2** *n* =BEATNIK, HIPPIE

hip to *adj phr* *beat & cool talk* Aware of; knowledgeable and informed of: *Why don't you get hip to yourself?*—P Dunning & G Abbott/ *They were hip to me too and just waiting for the right moment* —Macleans

hired gun **1** *n phr* A professional killer; =HIT MAN **2** *modifier: elaborated on his "hired gun" reference in an interview*—Washingtonian **3** *n phr* An employee, esp one who does persuasional and promotional sort of work: *We're not just "hired guns" out to raise a few bucks for the place*—Washingtonian

his nibs or **himself** *n phr* A very important person; supervisor or chief, esp one who insists on deferential treatment; =the MAN: *Take it in to his nibs yourself/ Has himself seen this?* [origin uncertain; perhaps *nibs* is related to *nob* "important person, esp a rich one"]

hit **1** *n* Anything very successful and popular, esp a show, book, etc: *He wrote two Broadway hits* **2** *v: I think this show will hit* **3** *modifier: a hit musical/ hit song* **4** *n* A win at gambling, on the stock market, etc: *a big hit on the commodities exchange* **5** *v: She hit real big at the track last* week **6** *n* *narcotics & underworld* A meeting between criminals, esp for the purpose of transferring loot or contraband **7** *n* *underworld* A premeditated murder or organized-crime execution, esp one contracted for with a professional killer: *"He can order a hit," a police officer says*—New York Times/ *There is no set price for a hit*—Playboy **8** *v*: *The mob figure got hit last night in his car* **9** *n* *narcotics* A dose of narcotics; = FIX: *The current price of cocaine was about $10 a "hit"*—HM Schmeck **10** *n* *narcotics* A puff of a marijuana cigarette; = TOKE: *He held a long hit in his mouth, then expelled it slowly*—Cameron Crowe **11** *n* *fr narcotics* A pleasurable sensation; = RUSH: *People jockeyed for position around the foyer to get a little hit of darshan*—Ramparts **12** *n* *narcotics* A cigarette into which heroin has been introduced: *GIs sit smoking the mixed tobacco-and-heroin cigarettes called "hits"*—I Peterson **13** *v* To reach; visit; attain: *He hit Frisco on the third day/ His new book...hit the best-seller list*—Philadelphia Bulletin/ *The market hit a new high today* **14** *n* Each separate occasion; each time; = SHOT: *You should be on a tour, where you can get 2000 people a hit* **15** *v* *students* To pass an examination, esp with a good grade; = ACE: *I really hit the eco final* **16** *v* To cause a strong reaction: *The injection hit the heart like a runaway locomotive*—Nelson Algren *See* BANJO HIT, CLOUT FOR THE CIRCUIT, MAKE A HIT, PINCH HIT, SMASH

hit someone **1** *v phr* (also **hit** someone **up**) To solicit money, a favor, etc: *I'll hit Joe for ten bucks/ She hit him up for a big raise* **2** *v phr* To have a strong impact on; distress; overwhelm: *Kennedy's death hit me pretty hard* **3** *v phr* To present; reveal: *I wanna hit you with a very profitable idea* **4** *v phr* *poker* To deal another card **5** *v phr* To serve another drink: *He signaled the bartender. "Hit us again"*—JE Grove **6** *v phr* *narcotics* To administer a narcotic, esp by injection

hitch 1 *n* A problem or difficulty; delaying defect; = CATCH, GLITCH: *Everything went off without a hitch* **2** *n* *armed forces* A period of enlistment: *42 percent have "reupped" for another hitch*—New York Times **3** *n* A ride, esp one gotten by hitchhiking; = LIFT **4** *v* = HITCHHIKE **5** *v* *fr middle 1800s* To marry; be married

hitch a ride (or **a lift**) *v phr* To get a free ride, esp by hitchhiking

hitched *adj fr middle 1800s* Married

hitchhike *v* To get free rides by standing beside a road and signaling drivers; = HITCH, THUMB

hitch-up *n* A connection; alliance; marriage

hitchy *adj* Nervous; jumpy [probably fr *itchy*]

hitfest *n* A baseball game with many hits and runs; = SLUGFEST: *pathetic parodies of the old hitfests*—Robert Ruark

hit for (or **out for**) *v phr* To start for or toward; = HEAD FOR: *One time we hit for KC*—James M Cain

hit for the circuit *See* CLOUT FOR THE CIRCUIT

hit for the cycle *v phr* *baseball* To hit personally a single, a double, a triple, and a home run all in one game

hi there *interj* An emphatic salutation in greeting

hit it *v phr* To begin playing music; attack

hit it a lick *v phr* To hit something very hard: *I hit it a hell of a lick, right out of the place*

hit it off 1 *v phr* To like one another: *The pair hit it off right from the start*—Billy Rose **2** *v phr* To work well together **3** *v phr* To succeed with others: *He hit it off with the whole class*

hit someone **like a ton of bricks** *v phr* To have a great sudden impact on, esp by surprise: *Then the answer hit me like a ton of bricks* [based on the mid-19th-century term *fall upon* someone *like a thousand of bricks*]

hit list *n phr* A putative or actual list of persons who are to be removed from office, punished, murdered, etc: *EPA officials maintained a "hit list" of employees*—New York Times

hit man *n phr* An assassin, esp a professional killer; = HIRED GUN: *Like every professional hit man I've ever known, I've always used a gun*—Playboy/ *a State Police detective, posing as a hired killer "flown in as a hit man"*—New York Times

hit on someone **1** *v phr* To ask for a favor; = HIT someone: *I hit on her to take my classes that day* **2** *v phr* To make advances to; = PROPOSITION: *What if muscle-bound jocks hit on her all day long?*—Cameron Crowe/ *I fired my last studio manager for hitting on one of the girls*—Susan Peters/ *It's amazing that a man of my own age would be hitting on me*—San Francisco **3** *v phr* To steal from someone

hit on all six (or **on six**) *v phr fr early 1900s* To do very well; operate smoothly and effectively: *He's sure hittin' on all six*—Literary Digest [fr the smooth operation of a *six*-cylinder engine]

hit (or **head**) **out** *v phr* To start; depart; get on the way

hit pay dirt *v phr* To find what one is looking for or needs; = STRIKE OIL: *I didn't hit pay dirt until near the bottom of the second box*—J Evans

hitter *n* = HIT MAN *See* CREAM-PUFF HITTER, NO-HITTER, SWITCH-HITTER

hit the books *v phr* *students* To study, esp in an intensive way

hit the bottle (or **the booze** or **the sauce**) *v phr* To drink liquor, esp rapidly and to excess; = BOOZE: *If he keeps hitting the bottle they'll have to dry him out*

hit the bricks 1 *v phr* To go out and start walking on a street or sidewalk **2** *v phr* *prison* To be released from prison: *He'll hit the bricks tomorrow, having been paroled* **3** *v phr* To go out on strike: *teachers...won't be as quick to hit the bricks*—New York Times **4** *v phr* *hoboes* To live in the streets because one is homeless

hit the bullseye *v phr* = HIT THE NAIL ON THE HEAD

hit the ceiling *v phr* To become violently angry; = BLOW UP: *and, according to one source, hit the ceiling with rage*—New York Times

hit the deck 1 *v phr* To be knocked down **2** *v phr* To get down on the ground quickly; duck down flat: *When I heard that airplane shoot I hit the* deck **3** *v phr* *fr Navy* To get out of bed; rouse oneself

hit the dirt (or **gravel**) **1** *v phr* *baseball* To slide into a base **2** *v phr* *hoboes* (also **hit the grit**) To jump off a train, esp a moving one **3** *v phr* To get down and take cover, esp from gunfire

hit the dope *v phr* To use narcotics

hit the fan *v phr* To cause or experience extensive trouble and chaos: *A month later it all hit the fan* —Esquire/ *Meanwhile the mailings had hit the fan* —New York
See the SHIT HITS THE FAN

hit the hay (or **the sack**) *v phr* To go to bed

hit the hump *v phr* To escape from prison, desert from military service, etc; = GO OVER THE HILL

hit the jackpot *v phr* To win or succeed spectacularly; get the most available: *I hit the jackpot with this new job*

hit the mat *v phr* = HIT THE DECK

hit the nail on the head *v phr* To be exactly right; say precisely the most accurate thing: *His few quiet remarks hit the nail on the head*

hit the pad *v phr* = HIT THE HAY

hit (or **push**) **the panic button** *v phr* To give way to alarm and terror; declare a general emergency: *He hit the panic button when he saw the month's figures*/ *a move characterized by many as pushing the panic button*—Inside Sports

hit the pipe *v phr* To smoke a narcotic, esp opium

hit the road 1 *v phr* To leave; get on one's way: *We better hit the road, it's a long way home* **2** *interj* An irritated request that one leave: *They found me and told me to hit the road*/ *Hit the road, Jack, and don't you come back no more*—Percy Mayfield

hit the rods *See* RIDE THE RODS

hit the sauce *See* HIT THE BOTTLE

hit the sidewalks *v phr* To start walking about, esp looking for a job; = HIT THE BRICKS, POUND THE PAVEMENT

hit the silk *v phr* *esp WW2 paratroops & Army Air Forces* To make a parachute jump

hit the skids 1 *v phr* To fail; = GO BELLY UP: *But if HBJ hit the skids, could the building ensure the integrity of retirees' pensions?*—Newsweek **2** *v phr* To show a precipitous decline; fall disastrously: *Home sales are down and sales of large cars have hit the skids*—Time/ *Eventually they had hit the skids*—AJ Liebling

hit the spot *v phr* To be very satisfying, esp to some appetitive need: *That cup of coffee really hit the spot*

hit the ties *v phr fr late 1800s* To travel by walking along railroad tracks: *It was up to me to hit the ties to Wadsworth*—Jack London

hit up *v phr narcotics* To inject a narcotic; = SHOOT UP

hit upside one's **face** (or **head**) *See* GO UPSIDE one's FACE

hit someone **where he lives** *v phr fr middle 1800s* To deliver a very painful blow, insult, insinuation, etc

hit someone **with** something *v phr* To present something; reveal something, esp a suggestion: *I want to hit you with a very intriguing proposition*

hive *v West Point* To understand

hivey *adj West Point* Sharp-witted; perceptive

hiya *See* HI

hizzoner *n* The mayor: *Hizzoner threw them out of the meeting*

◁ **hn** ▷ (pronounced as separate letters) *n black* A black person who adopts or reflects white society's values; = OREO, UNCLE TOM [fr *house nigger*, a reference to the slavery-era distinction between slaves who worked in the plantation house and those who worked in the fields]

ho[1] or **hoe** *n* A prostitute or other disreputable woman: *like many of her sisters of the streets (she calls them "ho's")*—New York Times/ *The bar was a hangout for players and hos*—Time [fr Southern or black pronunciation of *whore*]

ho[2] *See* the HEAVE-HO, RIGHT-O

hoagie *n* = HERO SANDWICH

hoary-eyed or **orie-eyed** or **orry-eyed** *adj* Drunk: *He would be orry-eyed before nightfall*—H Allen Smith [origin uncertain; perhaps fr *hoary* "frosty, hence icy, glazed," with later dropping of the *h* to avoid *whore*]

hobo *n fr late 1800s* A person who wanders from place to place, typically by riding on freight trains, and who may occasionally work but more often cadges sustenance ● The hobo is sometimes distinguished from bums and tramps by the fact that he works [origin unknown; perhaps fr the call "Ho, boy," used on late-19th-century Western railroads by mail carriers, then altered and transferred to vagrants; perhaps putative *hoe-boy*, a migrant farm worker in the West, who became a *hobo* after the harvest season]

hock[1] **1** *v fr middle 1800s* To pawn: *I hocked my diamond ring*—John O'Hara **2** *n* The state of pawn: *I've got to get my typewriter out of hock* [apparently fr Dutch *hok* "prison"; the earliest US use was in *in hock*, "in prison"; perhaps also fr the underworld phrase *in hock* "caught," fr the notion that one is taken "by the heels," or *hocks*]
See IN HOCK

hock[2] or **hok** *v* To pester; nag: *whom my mother kept hocking my father to promote to director* —Budd Schulberg/ *Stop already hocking us to be good*—Philip Roth/ *with her hokking and her kvetching*—National Lampoon [fr Yiddish *hok* in the idiom *hok a chynik* "knock a teapot," meaning "chatter constantly, talk foolishness," perhaps because such talking resembled the loud whacking of a pot]

hockable *adj* Pawnable: *The "ice" was always hockable*—Abel Green

◁ **hockey** or **hocky** ▷ **1** *n* Feces; excrement; = SHIT: *Great big blooping hunks of dog hockey* —William Styron **2** *n* Empty and pretentious nonsense; = BULLSHIT: *any of that hocky about being a white man*—Calder Willingham **3** *n* Semen; = CUM [origin unknown; perhaps fr a variant pronunciation of the *hokum, hokey, hocus-*

pocus cluster, suggested by some spellings, and hence originally "falsehood, pretentious exaggeration, etc," whence "bullshit," whence "shit"]

hockshop *n fr late 1800s* A pawnshop

hocus-pocus *n fr middle 1600s British* Sleight-of-hand; trickery; = MONKEY BUSINESS [originally a term for a juggler, and probably derived fr a juggler's spoken formula imitating the Church Latin phrase *hoc est corpus* "this is the body"]

◄**hod**► *n cabdrivers fr 1920s* A black passenger; = SCUTTLE [probably because a *hod* is a container for coal]

ho-dad (also **hodad** or **ho dad** or **ho-daddy**) *fr surfers* **1** *n* A person who claims knowledge and authority he or she does not possess; = BLOWHARD, WISE GUY: *"ho-daddy" (intruding wise guy)*—Life **2** *n* A nonparticipant who seeks the company of athletes and performers; hanger-on: *The true surfer is scornful of the "ho-daddies"*—Time **3** *n esp teenagers* An obnoxious and contemptible person; = JERK, PHONY, WIMP [perhaps fr a surfer's cry *Ho, dad*!]

hoe *See* A HARD ROW TO HOE

hoedown **1** *n* (also **hoe-dig**) A country square dance; = HOODANG **2** *n* A lively and noisy argument **3** *n* A riotous fight; brawl **4** *n street gangs* A fight between gangs; = RUMBLE: *Anything can start a hoedown*—H Lee

hog **1** *n railroad & hoboes fr late 1800s* A locomotive, originally a heavy freight engine **2** *n railroad & hoboes fr late 1800s* = HOGGER **3** *n motorcyclists* A Harley Davidson (a trade name) motorcycle: *Harley, perhaps best known for its big-engine "hogs"*—Time/ *a hundred Hell's Angels on their Hogs*—Esquire **4** *n black* A large car, esp a Cadillac (a trade name): *"I got a Hog...a Cadillac"*—Clarence Cooper **5** *v* To take or eat everything available, for oneself; claim and seize all: *appeared simultaneously with ET and suffered as the little fungiform geek hogged the box office*—Washington Post/ *That creep's hogging the booze* **6** *n* (also **the hog**) *narcotics* PCP or a similar addictive drug: *climbed on stage and threw thousands of caps of "the hog"...into the crowd*—Esquire [railroad and hobo sense fr the fact that large locomotives consumed a great deal of coal]
See EAT HIGH ON THE HOG, ON THE HOG, ROOT-HOG-OR-DIE, SEWER HOG, SWITCH HOG, WHOLE HOG

hogan *See* MOLLY-HOGAN

Hogan's brickyard *n phr* A rough baseball diamond; = SANDLOT

hogger *n* (also **hog** or **hog-head** or **hogshead** or **hog-jockey**) *railroad & hoboes* A railroad engineer; = GRUNT

hog (or **pig**) **heaven** *n phr* A place of total bliss; paradise; = FAT CITY: *For the sports junkie, this is Mecca. For the gambler, it is hog heaven*—Philadelphia Journal/ *One American woman talks gleefully of finding some Victorian pressed glass for almost nothing. "We are in pig heaven"*—Time

hog (or **hog's**) **leg** *n phr fr cowboys* A pistol, esp a large one: *his hog's leg looking like a fire plug against his ribs*—Raymond Chandler/ *He got his hog leg out and came over*—RV Winslow/ *a .45-caliber hogleg out of his coat pocket*—Stephen King

hogs *n bop talk* Dollars, esp only a few dollars

hogwash *n* Empty and pretentious talk; nonsense; = BALONEY, BULLSHIT: *He said most of my theory is pure hogwash*

hog-wild *See* GO HOG-WILD

ho-hum **1** *adj* Unexciting; mediocre; dull: *ho-hum sex and the dregs of countless six-packs*—RJ Battaglia/ *After a ho-hum second quarter, stocks have perked up*—Time **2** *v* To be bored with; be indifferent to: *On the other hand, we shouldn't ho-hum the situation*—Paul Engeler **3** *n* Boring matter; dull tripe

hoist **1** *v fr underworld fr 1700s* To rob; steal; = HEIST: *The stall...distracts the sales force while the hoister hoists*—RL Woods **2** *n: Crooks...speak of a job of hold-up as a "hoist"*—J Wilstach **3** *v* To drink some beer or liquor: *Let's stop at Harry's and hoist a few*

hoisted *adj fr underworld fr 1700s* Stolen: *among the hoisted articles recently*—C Adams

hoity-toity *adj fr late 1800s British* Snobbishly exclusive; haughty; uppish; = SNOOTY: *in the hoity-toitiest of Fifth Avenue shops*—S Dawson/ *Will he go all hoity-toity on us?*—Washington Post [fr earlier *highty-tighty* "peremptory, quarrelsome," perhaps related to the notion of being *high* in the sense of "superior"]

hoke *n* = HOKUM

hoked-up *adj* False; dishonestly confected; = PHONY: *hoked-up or fictionalized biographies*—Jay Jacobs/ *a zest for hoked-up violence*—Playboy

hoke up *v phr* To make something artificial or meretricious; confect; falsify: *Halaby hoked up a special ceremony*—RG Sherrill/ *I'll hoke up a good alibi* [fr *hoke* fr *hokum*]

hokey *adj* False and meretricious; very dubious; = PHONY: *hokey confections that public taste ought to repudiate*—Albert Maltz/ *The radio is jammed with hokey copies of US and European rock and roll songs*—New Republic

hokey-dokey *See* OKEY-DOKE

hokey-pokey or **hoky-poky** **1** *n fr late 1800s British* Cheap ice cream and sweets made primarily to attract children **2** *modifier: candy bars on the hokey-pokey counter*—Westbrook Pegler **3** *n* A seller of such provender **4** *n* Any cheap, gaudy items **5** *n* False and meretricious material; = HOKUM: *too much of... "Hollywood hokey-pokey"*—Philadelphia Bulletin [fr an earlier sense of *hokey-pokey* "cheat, swindle," ultimately fr *hocus-pocus*]

the hokey-pokey *n phr* A simple, informal sort of circle dance: *people across the globe will join hands, form huge human circles....The hokey-pokey*—Philadelphia

hokum *fr theater fr early 1900s* **1** *n* Pretentious nonsense; insane trash; = BUNK: *more hokum from the Department of State* **2** *n theater* A trick, gag, routine, etc, sure to please a gullible public: *There is some hokum in "King Penguin"*—New

York Times **3** *n* =HOKEY-POKEY [perhaps fr a blend of *hocus* and *bunkum*]

hokus *n narcotics* Any narcotic

hold *narcotics* **1** *v* To have narcotics for sale **2** *v* To have narcotics in one's possession *See* ON HOLD

holder *See* ROACH CLIP

hold someone's **feet to the fire** *v phr* To subject someone to strong and painful persuasion; use maximum pressure: *helping hold the President's feet to the fire*—New York Times

hold fire *v phr* To delay or be delayed; postpone: *Let's hold fire a couple more days*

hold one's **horses** *v phr* To be patient; stop importuning; =HOLD one's WATER ● Often an irritated command: *He kept on asking though she told him to hold his horses*

holding 1 *adj* Wealthy: *Respect...for people who are "holding"*—AJ Liebling **2** *adj narcotics* Possessing narcotics

holding pattern *See* IN A HOLDING PATTERN

holdout 1 *n* A person, esp a professional athlete, who refuses to sign a contract until the salary is raised **2** *n* A person who refuses to agree to something: *coerce reluctant hold-outs into "kicking in"*—E Lavine **3** *n gambling* A playing card sneakily kept from the deck by the dealer

hold out 1 *v phr* To refuse to do something until one certain conditions: *The union held out for a 10 percent raise* **2** *v phr* To endure; persist: *This tire won't hold out another mile*

holds *See* NO HOLDS BARRED

hold the bag (or **the sack**) **1** *v phr fr late 1800s* To be deceived so that one takes all the losses; be duped to one's disadvantage: *Don't you let them leave you holding the bag*—Erle Stanley Gardner **2** *v phr* To be so maneuvered that one takes individual blame for a failure or a crime [fr 17th-century *give the bag to hold* "victimize in a game of snipe-hunt"]

hold the lumber *v phr lunch counter* Include no toothpicks

hold the phone *v phr* To wait a minute; delay ● Often a request for respite and thinking space: *My body jerked back in a kind of WC Fields double take. "Hold the phone," I said*—Newsweek

holdup 1 *n fr late 1800s* A robbery, esp the armed robbery of a person, bank, store, etc; =STICKUP: *Give us no nonsense. This is a holdup*—Philadelphia Bulletin **2** *modifier: the full-fledged hold-up business*—E Lavine **3** *n* The demanding of exorbitant prices, wages, etc: *That was no sale, it was a holdup* **4** *n* A delay; stoppage; cause of delay: *a brief holdup in our magnificent progress/ What's the holdup?*

hold up 1 *v phr fr late 1800s* To rob, esp at gunpoint: *They were holding an old man up at the corner* **2** *v phr* To extort or demand higher prices, wages, etc: *That shop held me up!* **3** *v phr* To delay; cause a delay or stoppage: *The strike held up our flight for six days* **4** *v phr* To point to; single out: *Is this the one you held up as such a great example?*

hold one's **water** *v phr* To be patient; stop importuning; =HOLD one's HORSES ● Often an irritated command: *I know that, fuckface. Just hold your water*—Paul Sann

hole 1 *n* Any nasty or unpleasant place; =DUMP, JOINT: *The restaurant turned out to be a loathsome little hole* ◁**2**▷ *n* The vulva ◁**3**▷ *n* The anus ◁**4**▷ *n* A person regarded merely as a sex object or organ; =ASS ◁**5**▷ *n* Sexual activity; genital gratification; =ASS **6** *v* To shoot someone: *Those two cops are bound to get holed*—John Farris

See ACE IN THE HOLE, BIG HOLE, BROWN, BUNGHOLE, CORNHOLE, IN A HOLE, IN THE HOLE, the NINETEENTH HOLE, NOT KNOW ONE'S ASS FROM ONE'S ELBOW, NOT KNOW someone or something FROM A HOLE IN THE GROUND, RATHOLE

the hole 1 *n prison* Solitary confinement or a cell used for it; =BING: *I was slapped with the organizing label and put in the "hole"*—Huey P Newton/ *I was thrown in the hole for it*—Eldridge Cleaver **2** *n phr railroad* A spur or sidetrack; siding **3** *n phr fr underworld* A subway

See ACE IN THE HOLE, IN THE HOLE

hole card *n phr poker* A card dealt face down in stud poker

hole in the ground *See* NOT KNOW one's ASS FROM one's ELBOW, NOT KNOW someone or something FROM A HOLE IN THE GROUND

a hole in the (or **one's**) **head** *See* HAVE A HOLE IN one's HEAD, NEED someone or something LIKE A HOLE IN THE HEAD

hole in the wall *n phr* A small and usu unpretentious dwelling, shop, etc: *Nothing fancy, just a hole in the wall on Park Lane*

hole out *v phr golf* To finish a hole by putting the ball in the cup

hole up (or **in**) **1** *v phr* To hide; take refuge; =HIDE OUT: *Long Island, where...he might hole up for a day or two*—NY Confidential **2** *v phr* To stay for a time; lodge; =CRASH: *thinking about holing up for the night*—Sinclair Lewis/ *Kesey holes up at his old friend's house in Palo Alto*—Tom Wolfe

holiday 1 *n* A small area missed while painting **2** *n Navy* A forgotten or neglected task

holler 1 *v* To shout **2** *v* To inform; =SING, SQUEAL: *You think he wouldn't holler if they turned the heat on him?*—WR Burnett **3** *v* To complain; =BITCH: *What's he hollering about now?* **4** *n* (also **holler-song**) A Southern black folk song with spoken or shouted words, a precursor of the blues song: *You find hollers in many of Leadbelly's recordings and songs*—Stephen Longstreet

hollow *See* BEAT ALL HOLLOW

holly-golly or **hully-gully 1** *n* Nonsense; =BALONEY, BUNK **2** *n* Disturbance; upset; racket; =FLAP: *What's this ghastly holly-golly all about?* [probably echoic symbolism for a fuss, influenced by *hullabaloo, hurly burly*, etc]

Hollywood corporal *n phr WW2 Army* An acting corporal

Hollywood kiss (or **kiss-off**) *n phr* =KISS-OFF

holy cats *interj* (Variations: **cow** or **gee** or **mackerel** or **Moses** or **shit** or **smoke** may replace **cats**) An exclamation of surprise, wonder, dismay, admiration, etc: *All he could manage to say upon seeing the nude blonde was "holy cow!"*—B Price/ *holy shit, the police*—Richard Fariña [euphemisms for *holy Christ*]

holy hell *n phr* Vehement rebuke; severe punishment; = HELL, MERRY HELL: *I caught holy hell when the thing broke*
See CATCH HELL, GIVE someone HELL

Holy Joe **1** *n phr* *fr middle 1800s British nautical* A clergyman; chaplain: *needs twelve Holy Joes to get him past them Pearly Gates*—J Evans **2** *n phr* A sanctimonious, pietistic person: *In the east they're all holy Joes and teach in Sunday schools*—Stephen Longstreet **3** *modifier:* *these Holy Joe voices* —JD Salinger

◁**holy shit**▷ *interj* An exclamation of surprise, dismay, discovery, etc: *And I think holy shit, this could be a Hitler*—Village Voice

holy terror *n phr* A troublesome, energetic, and aggressive person: *He's a holy terror around home*

hombre (HAHM bray, AHM bray) **1** *n* A Hispanic person **2** *n* A man; fellow; = GUY: *a real cool hombre*
See WISE GUY

home *adj* Familiar; domestic; unpretentious; cozy: *home cooking/ home folks*
See BRING HOME THE BACON, HOME BOY, MONEY FROM HOME, NOBODY HOME, NOTHING TO WRITE HOME ABOUT

home boy or **homeboy** *fr Southern, esp black* **1** *n phr* or *n* A person from one's home town **2** *n phr* or *n* (also **home**) A close friend, or someone accepted like a friend: *Home boy, them brothers is taking care of business!*—Eldridge Cleaver **3** *n phr* or *n* *chiefly college students* An easygoing, unpretentious person **4** *n phr* *police* A male homosexual, esp the friend or lover of another male homosexual [homosexual sense *fr homo*]

home-court advantage *n phr* *fr sports* The psychological and other favorable elements that come from being in familiar surroundings, with a sympathetic audience, etc: *Yojimbo is less than sympathetic here* (*it's clear who has the home-court advantage*)—Village Voice

home free *adv phr* Successfully arrived or concluded; at or assured of one's goal; out of trouble: *A couple more good days' work and I'm home free*

home guard **1** *n* *circus & hoboes fr early 1900s* A resident of a place; native; = LOCAL **2** *n phr* *fr early 1900s* A person who works for the same employer for a long period; = OLD HAND

home plate *n phr* *Air Force fr 1950s* The landing field, aircraft carrier, etc, where an aircraft is based [*fr* the baseball sense, regarded as a goal and safe haven]
See GET TO FIRST BASE

homer **1** *n* *baseball* A home run; = CIRCUIT BLOW **2** *v:* *Kaline homered in the sixth*

homework *n* *students* Kissing, embracing, etc; = NECKING, PETTING
See DO one's HOMEWORK

homey or **homie** **1** *n* An innocent, unsophisticated person; home body **2** *n* *black* A close friend or a fellow townsperson; = HOME BOY: *is expecting more than her homies to support her* —Amsterdam News **3** *n* *black* A new arrival from the South

◁**homo**▷ **1** *n* A homosexual man or woman: *I knew nothing about "homos" at that time*—HK Fink **2** *adj:* *homo slang/ a homo bar*

hon (HUHN) *n* Sweetheart; honey ● Used in direct address

the Hon (HAHN) *n phr* The Honorable: *I want you to meet the Hon P Jensen, our mayor*

honcho (HAHN choh) **1** *n* *fr Korean War armed forces* The person in charge; chief; = BIG ENCHILADA, BOSS: *better known as the honcho of Scientific Anglers, Inc*—Sports Afield **2** *v:* *He honchoed the whole deal* [fr Japanese *hancho* "squad leader"]

honey **1** *n* One's sweetheart, beloved, spouse, etc **2** *n* Any pleasant, decent person; = PUSSYCAT, SWEETIE **3** *n* A person or thing that is remarkable, wonderful, superior, etc; = DILLY, HUMDINGER: *Ain't this a honey of a Scotch?*

honey barge *n phr* *Navy* A garbage scow

honey bucket *n phr* A chamber pot or other container for excrement

honeycakes *See* BABY CAKES

◂**honey-fuck**▸ **1** *v* To do the sex act in a romantic, idyllic way **2** *v* (also **honey-fuggle**) To do the sex act with a very young girl: *mysterious pains and penalties attached to "honeyfuggling"*—Philip Wylie [fr the early-19th-century *honeyfuggle*, of obscure origin, which meant "cheat, swindle"; the present sense must come fr assimilation with *fuck*]

honey man *n phr* A kept man; pimp

◁**honeypot**▷ *n fr later 1700s* The vulva or vagina

honey wagon **1** *n phr* A manure wagon or manure spreader **2** *n phr* A garbage truck

Hong Kong dog *n phr* Diarrhea, esp of the kind travelers get

honk **1** *v* To sound the horn of a car **2** *v* To make a sexual, esp a homosexual, advance by handling or pressing a man's genitals: *He's making a move to honk you, just grab his hand*—Joseph Wambaugh

◂**honky** or **honkie**▸ **1** *n* *black* A white person; = GRAY, OFAY **2** *adj:* *No talkin' or we'll bust your honky heads*—Time [fr *hunky*[1], as often normally pronounced in black English]

honky-tonk *fr black fr late 1800s* **1** *n* A cheap, usu disreputable saloon and gambling place; = JOINT: *rode to my honky-tonk on a bus*—Philip Wylie **2** *v:* *his honky-tonking ended, naturally, at Filly's, the urban cowboy saloon*—Philadelphia Journal **3** *n* A cheap, small-town theater: *playin' the sticks...the honky-tonks*—Gypsy Rose Lee **4** *n* A brothel **5** *modifier:* *the honky-tonk district* [origin unknown]

hon-yock or **hon-yocker** **1** *n* *fr late 1800s* A rustic person; farmer; = HICK: *speaking as a purebred hon-yock out of the Middle West*—H Allen

Smith **2** *adj:* *a kind of dumb hon-yock accent* [origin unknown]

hoo-boy *interj esp 1950s* An exclamation of surprise, consternation, amazement, etc [perhaps a blend of *hoo ha* with *oh boy*]

hooch[1] *n fr late 1800s* Liquor; strong drink; = BOOZE: *and the bottles of hooch, and the free food on the job*—New York Times/ *or guzzles hooch that he hides inside a big toy duck*—Time [fr the liquor made by the *Hoochinoo* Indians of Alaska]

hooch[2] or **hootch** *fr Korean & Vietnam War armed forces* **1** *n* A Korean house, room, shack, etc: *giggle timidly and plead: "Come on to my hooch"*—Time **2** *n* A Vietnamese village hut **3** *n* An American barracks, esp a Quonset-style barracks in Vietnam [fr Japanese *uchi* "house"]

hooch[3] *See* HOOTCHIE-COOTCHIE, the HOOTCHIE-COOTCHIE

hood (HŏŏD, HŏŏD) **1** *n fr early 1900s* A hoodlum: *those St Louis hoods*—American Mercury/ *the procession of hoods...on the witness stand*—Bruce Bliven **2** *modifier:* *has been in the hood hierarchy for decades*—New York Post [fr *hoodlum*, origin unknown; perhaps fr Bavarian German *hodalum* "scamp"]

hoodang or **houdang** (Hŏŏ dang) *n* Any jolly gathering; a party; barn dance; = HOEDOWN

hoody *adj* Hoodlumish; like a hood: *imitating a hoody Tony Curtis*—Time

hooey *n esp 1920s & 30s* Nonsense; foolishness; = BALONEY: *lip-smacking imps of mawk and hooey write with us what they will*—WH Auden/ *a dangerous mix of electioneering hooey and religious claptrap*—Time [perhaps based on *phooey*]

hoof **1** *n fr late 1800s* A foot: *Take your goddam hoof the hell off my fender*—J Evans **2** *v* To walk; = HOOF IT: *I better hoof over to the garage* **3** *v fr 1920s* To dance: *She's hoofing in that show about cats*

See SHAKE A WICKED CALF

hoofer *n* A dancer, esp a professional dancer in nightclubs, musical plays, etc: *The hoofers and the chorines of a cabaret*—John Mason Brown

hoof it *fr early 1900s* **1** *v phr* To walk: *She hoofed it over to the next house/ get off the bus...and hoof it home*—Philadelphia **2** *v phr* To dance: *then hoofed it a bit herself with old friend Gene Kelly*—Newsweek

hoo-ha[1] *interj* An exclamation of astonishment, admiration, envy, scorn, deflation, etc: *So your boy's on TV, hoo ha/ Does she gossip? Hoo-ha* —Leo Rosten [fr Yiddish]

hoo-ha[2] **1** *n fr early 1900s* British armed forces Disturbance; brouhaha; uproar: *What was I supposed to do in the middle of such a hoo-ha?*—Leo Rosten/ *in case you're wondering what all the hoo-ha is about*—A Sainer **2** *n* A noisy celebration; a raucous fete: *But Northampton, Mass, held a week-long hoo-ha for its favorite son*—Newsweek [perhaps influenced by *hoo-ha*[1]; first attested in early-20th-century British armed forces as "an argument; an artillery demonstration," and probably echoic-

symbolic of a loud fuss, like *hoopla, to-do, brouhaha, foofaraw,* and *hooley*]

hoohaw *n* An important person; = POOH-BAH: *and the rest of the town's hoohaws*—William Brashler

hook **1** *n merchant marine & Navy* An anchor **2** *n baseball* A curveball **3** *n narcotics* A hypodermic needle or bent pin used for injecting a narcotic **4** *n narcotics* A narcotic, esp heroin **5** *v fr 1600s* To steal, esp to shoplift: *Hooking merchandise from department stores requires no training* —Forum **6** *v* To get; find: *Since Swede had no car, he either hooked rides from the waiters who did, or walked*—New Yorker **7** *v* To arrest; stop and ticket: *My cab driver got hooked for speeding* —WR Burnett **8** *v* To entice successfully; procure more or less against one's will: *They hooked me for the main speech* **9** *v* To cheat; deceive ● Most often in the passive voice: *He got hooked into paying the whole bill* **10** *n* A prostitute; = HOOKER: *Janie Ruth looked at the hook*—Dan Jenkins **11** *v* To work as a prostitute; whore: *They stress the fact that they strip and don't hook* —Trans-Action/ *Carl supplemented their income by...hooking from the notorious bus bench*—San Francisco **12** *n esp musicians* Something that strongly attracts, esp something catchy in the lyrics or music of a song: *the musicians push a good hook, a high, ragged guitar line*—Rolling Stone/ *You just won't tell me much at a time about life. It's your hook*—Larry McMurtry/ *There are no hooks, either, like the mechanical bull or dancing*—Milwaukee Journal **13** *n college students* A grade of C **14** *v* To drink, esp quickly at a gulp: *You pour a half-glass of Dewar's, hook it down and fan out the flames with a bottle of beer*—Albert Goldman

See BUTTONHOOK, HIND HOOK, MUD-HOOK, ON one's OWN HOOK, SHITHOOK, SKYHOOK

the **hook** *n phr* A violent football tackle in which the head of the ball-carrier is caught and held in the crook of the tackler's arm

See GET someone OFF THE HOOK, GET THE HOOK, GIVE someone THE HOOK, GO ON THE HOOK FOR someone or something, LET someone OFF THE HOOK, OFF THE HOOK, ON THE HOOK, RING OFF THE HOOK

hook arm *n phr baseball* A pitcher's throwing arm

hooked **1** *adj narcotics* Addicted to a narcotic: *Once a week wasn't being hooked*—Nelson Algren/ *I was the pusher who got you hooked*—WH Auden **2** *adj* Captivated as if drug-addicted: *a shock to discover my wife was hooked on needlepoint* —Good Housekeeping/ *Once you buy his preposterous premise and get to know his pleasantly insane characters, you're hooked*—Playboy **3** *adj* Married; = HITCHED

hooker **1** *n fr middle 1800s* A prostitute: *drunken sportswriters, hard-eyed hookers, wandering geeks and hustlers*—Hunter S Thompson/ *the thirtyish ex-hooker was answering questions*—New York Post **2** *modifier:* *hooker district* **3** *n* A person who recruits, enlists, snares, etc: *Hooker, a person who induces union members to act as spies*—Labor's Special Language **4** *n* A drink of liquor; = SNORT: *It took a stiff hooker of whiskey...to thaw* her—Dashiell Hammett [first sense apparently fr a resident of Corlear's *Hook* in New York City, in the 19th century the site of many brothels, esp frequented by seamen]

hook someone **for** *v phr* To cheat someone out of; take away, esp by shady means: *At Atlantic City they hooked him for everything he had*

hook (or **rook**) someone **into** something *v phr* To obligate or involve someone by force or trickery: *They hooked me into paying for everybody's lunch/ She got rooked into a very boring cocktail party*

hook it *v phr fr middle 1800s* To depart hastily; run away: *Better hook it, Joan, the heat's arrived*

◄**hooknose**► *n* A Jew

hooks *n* The hands
  See BISCUIT HOOKS, FISHHOOKS, GET one's HOOKS INTO, LUNCH-HOOKS, MEATHOOKS, POTHOOKS, THROW THE HOOKS INTO someone

hookshop *n* A brothel, esp a cheap one: *one of the cheap hookshops*—American Mercury

hooky 1 *adj* Captivating; very attractive; catchy: *It's also more insinuatingly hooky than Led Zep ever was*—Village Voice/ *But it's hooky, the formidable Graham Parker*—Village Voice **2** *v* =PLAY HOOKY

hooligan 1 *n fr late 1800s British* A hoodlum; ruffian: *Beat me up with your hooligans*—Ira Wolfert **2** *n* =GUN **3** *n circus* The Wild West tent of a circus or show [perhaps fr a rowdy Irish family named *Hooligan* of Southwark, London, England; circus sense perhaps related to Western *hoolian* or *hooley-ann* or *hoolihan* "throw a steer by leaping on its horns, bulldog"; all senses perhaps related to Irish *hooley* "noisy party, carousal"]

hooligan Navy *n phr Navy* The US Coast Guard

hoop 1 *n fr underworld* A finger ring: *the old hoop on that finger*—Joseph Auslander **2** *n* The basketball net or basket; =BUCKET **3** *n* A basketball goal; =BUCKET: *He made six hoops last night* **4** *modifier* Having to do with basketball: *a hoop team/ hoop scores*
  See FLAT TIRE

hoop-a-doop or **hoop-de-doop** or **hoopty-do** *See* WHOOP-DE-DO

hooperdooper or **hooperdoo 1** *n* A person or thing that is remarkable, wonderful, superior, etc; =HONEY, HUMDINGER: *Next Saturday's Barn Dance is going to be another hooper-doo*—National Barn Dance (radio program) **2** *modifier:* *we got a hooperdoo quarter hour left*—Uncle Walter's Doghouse (radio program) **3** *n* A very important person; =BIG SHOT: *The hooperdooper in front is the celebrated poet*

hoopla or **whoopla 1** *n* A joyous and boisterous clamor; =HOO-HA: *Is this hoopla for my birthday?* **2** *n* A noisy fuss; a commotion: *His arrival started a big hoopla* **3** *n* Advertising or promotion; =BALLYHOO, FLACK: *I say this is a lot of unnecessary hoopla*—Sports Afield

hoop-man or **hoopster** *n* A basketball player

hoops *See* JUMP THROUGH HOOPS

hoopty-doo *See* WHOOP-DE-DO

hoosegow (HōōS gou) *n fr early 1900s cowboys* A jail [fr Mexican Spanish *juzgao* "tribunal, court"]

hoosier 1 *n outdated fr lumberjacks, carnival, circus & hoboes* A rustic; =HICK **2** *n 1930s prison* A prison guard [origin uncertain; perhaps fr southern Appalachian term *hoozer* "anything unusually large, humdinger"]

Hoosier *n* A native or resident of Indiana

hoot *n* A person; =COOT: *Milo O'Shea makes a canny old hoot of the judge*—People Weekly
  See SKYHOOT

a **hoot** *n fr 1960s British* Something very funny and pleasant; plain fun: *Life is a hoot*—Village Voice/ *Wouldn't it be a hoot to wake up one morning and find yourself in Gracie Mansion?*—Denison Hatch
  See NOT GIVE A DAMN

hootch *See* HOOCH

◄**hootchee** or **hotchee**► *n esp Korean War armed forces* The penis

hootchie-cootchie or **hooch** *n* Sexual activity; =ASS: *He propositioned her for a little hootchie-cootchie*

the **hootchie-cootchie** (or **hootchy-kootchy** or **hooch**) *fr late 1800s* **1** *n* An erotic dance in which the woman rotates her hips, etc **2** *n* A woman who dances the hootchie-cootchie [origin unknown; *The Hootchy-Kootchy* was the name of a song associated with the dancer Little Egypt at the Chicago World's Fair of 1893, but the term is attested several years earlier in the context of the minstrel show]

hootenanny (HōōT ən annee) *n* Any unspecified or unspecifiable object; something one does not know the name of or does not wish to name; =GADGET, GIZMO: *He took a little hootenanny off the shelf and blew into it* [one of many fanciful coinages for something unspecified; probably related to *hooter* "anything trifling," attested fr the mid-19th century, and to *hewgag* "an indeterminate, unknown mythical creature," similarly attested; the syllable *hoo-*, which is prominent in such coinages, probably represents the interrogative pronoun *who*]

hooter *n students* A marijuana cigarette

◄**hooters**► *n* A woman's breasts: *Hooters (a synonym, I learn, for knockers...) is a nice little play*—New York

hooty *adj* Excellent; delightful; amusing: *Wasn't that a hooty rendition?*

hoover 1 *v chiefly British* To eat or drink up, esp greedily: *instead of the moussaka and lamb that everyone else was hoovering*—Car and Driver ◄**2**► *v* To do fellatio or cunnilingus with or to; =EAT: *Will you hoover me immediately, before I pay any attention to you*—National Lampoon [fr the *Hoover* (a trade name) vacuum cleaner]

Hooverville *n esp 1930s* A slum of makeshift shacks where unemployed workers live [fr President Herbert *Hoover* who was president during the early years of the Depression]

hop¹ 1 *n fr middle 1700s* A dance or dancing party: *We went to a hop*—James T Farrell **2** *n* A hotel desk porter; =BELLHOP: *The hop was tall and thin*—Raymond Chandler **3** *n* A trip; stage of a

journey; airplane flight: *a long hop to Singapore* **4**
v: *They hopped over to Brussels* **5** *v* To board:
to hop a plane **6** *n* A short flight, as distinct from
a long one

See BELLHOP, CARHOP, MUD HOP, SEAGOING BELLHOP,
SOCK HOP, TABLE-HOP

hop² **1** *n* *fr late 1800s* Opium: *So long as any
smoker can obtain his hop*—The Lantern **2** *n*
narcotics Any narcotic; =DOPE: *A little hop or dope
was slipped to an anxious prisoner*—E Lavine **3**
modifier: *a hop fiend/ hop dream* **4** *n* narcotics A drug addict; =HEAD, HOPHEAD **5** *n* Nonsense; lies; =BALONEY, BULLSHIT: *Go peddle your
hop somewhere else*—J Roeburt [fr a shortening of
Cantonese Chinese *nga pin,* pronounced HAH
peen, "opium," literally "crow peelings," a Chinese
folk etymology for English *opium;* in a subsequent
US folk etymology this was changed to *hop* by
assimilation with the plant used to make beer, with
its suggestions of intoxication]

hope to die *See* CROSS MY HEART

hop fiend (or **fighter**) *n phr* A drug addict;
=HOPHEAD

hophead *n* narcotics A drug addict; =HEAD:
deprive a "hophead" of narcotics—E Lavine/ *the
bench with its bittersweet words: winos, hopheads,
the omnipresent graffiti*—New York

hop it *v phr* chiefly British fr early 1900s cockney
To leave; depart hastily; =BEAT IT

hopjoint **1** *n* A cheap saloon **2** *n* An opium
den

hop on the bandwagon *See* GET ON THE BAND-
WAGON

hopped up **1** *adj* narcotics Intoxicated by narcotics; =GEEZED, GOWED UP: *The newer generation of
"coked" or "hopped up" gunmen*—E Lavine **2**
adj Excited; highly stimulated: *What are you so
hopped up about?* **3** *adj* Made very exciting;
deliberately intensified; =JAZZED UP: *those hopped-
up novels in which passion is named but not felt*
—WG Rogers **4** *adj* hot rodders =SOUPED UP

hopper **1** *n* hoboes A partly smoked cigarette **2**
n baseball A ground ball that hops along

See WHORE-HOPPER

the hopper *n phr* The imagined place where proposed ideas, actions, etc, are placed; =PIPELINE:
Can't look at it now, put it in the hopper [fr the *hopper* device that feeds mills, etc, so called fr its shak-
ing]

hops **1** *n* fr early 1900s Opium; =DOPE **2** *n*
Beer

See FULL OF BEANS

hopscotch *v* To leap about; make long and diverse
transits: *The show...hopscotches from Toronto and
Boston to Lake Tahoe and Las Vegas*—RK Doan

hop-stick *n* narcotics An opium pipe

hop toad **1** *n phr* railroad A bar used for derail-
ing cars **2** *n phr* A big drink of liquor

hopup (HAHP up) *modifier* hot rodders Used to
increase the power and speed of a car engine: *a
pretty good selection of hopup and speed equipment*—Village Voice

hop up **1** *v phr* narcotics To administer narcotics:
He hopped himself up on heroin **2** *v phr* horse-
racing To drug a horse for speed; =DOPE: *to hop
up or slow down their horses*—A Hynd **3** *v phr*
hot rodders To increase the speed and power of a
car; =SOUP UP: *How to Hop Up Chevrolet and
GMC Engines*—Floyd Clymer Motorbook

horn **1** *n* musicians Any wind instrument **2** *n*
jazz musicians The trumpet ◁**3**▷ *n* A penile erection; =HARD-ON: *I could have beat up five guys with
the horn I had on*—George V Higgins

See GRUNT-HORN, LIKE SHIT THROUGH A TIN HORN, TIN-
HORN, TOOT ONE'S OWN HORN

the horn *n phr* The telephone: *Regional representatives got on the horn with the Louisville headquarters*—Philadelphia

hornblowing *n* Aggressive advertising; high-pressure selling

horndog *n* armed forces A dedicated fornicator;
sexual athlete; =COCKSMAN

horner *n* narcotics A person who has a tender,
runny nose from inhaling cocaine

horn in *v phr* fr early 1900s cowboys To intrude;
thrust oneself in; =BUTT IN: *Some wallie tried to
horn in on our gang*—Philadelphia Bulletin

horniness *n* Sexual craving; lust and lustfulness;
=HOT ROCKS: *the lure of High Art to mask the visceral odors of simple human horniness*—New York

hornswoggle *v* fr early 1800s To cheat; swindle;
dupe; =CON

◁**horny**▷ *adj* Sexually excited and desirous; keenly
amorous; lustful; =HOT ● Of recent years applied
to women as well as men, despite being derived fr
horn "erect penis": *his horny teen-age daughter*
—Time/ *At first it eased my head and made me less
horny*—Mike Aron/ *a few scenes between a horny
housewife and a guy in a Lone Ranger mask*—Playboy

horrors *See* CHUCK HABIT

horse **1** *n* circus A thousand dollars; =GRAND **2**
n narcotics Heroin; =SHIT: *They shoot horse in
the john at the local high school*—Judith Crist/ *After
about 1952, nobody called it horse any more*
—Claude Brown **3** *n* narcotics A hard-drug
addict **4** *n* prison A prison guard paid by
inmates to smuggle letters and other contraband in
and out **5** *n* truckers A truck or a tractor **6** *n*
police An honest, hard-working police officer: *We
know who the horses are around here, every cop in
the department knows*—Providence Journal-Bulletin
7 *v* To play and idle; =FOOL AROUND, HORSE
AROUND: *He wasn't just horsing now*—W Henry
◁**8**▷ *v* To do the sex act with or to; =SCREW:
They caught him horsing his secretary **9** *v* To
hoax; fool **10** *v* =IN A FOG [the sense "heroin"
may have derived fr *shit* "heroin" by way of *horseshit,* although the derivation might well have gone in
the other direction; or perhaps the sense is based
on the sobriquet of a Damon Runyon character
Harry the Horse by way of the partial rhyme of
Harry with *heroin*]

See DARK HORSE, DEAD HORSE, DOES A WOODEN
HORSE HAVE A HICKORY DICK, ENOUGH TO CHOKE A

HORSE, FROM THE HORSE'S MOUTH, GET ON one's HIGH HORSE, GET ON one's HORSE, IRON HORSE, ONE-HORSE, ONE-HORSE TOWN, PINTO, RED HORSE, SALT HORSE, WARHORSE

horse-and-buggy *adj* Old-fashioned: *a horse-and-buggy leisureliness*

horse apple 1 *n phr* A ball of horse feces **2** *n phr* Pretentious trash; = HORSESHIT: *all that particular pile of horseapples boiled down to*—Stephen King

horse apples *interj* = HORSESHIT

horse around *v phr* To joke and caper pleasurably; indulge in horseplay; = FOOL AROUND: *He wouldn't stop horsing around, so they let him go*

horse cock *n phr fr WW2 Navy* Salami and other cold-cut sausages; = DONKEY DICK

horsefeathers *esp 1920s* **1** *interj* An exclamation of disbelief, rejection, contempt, etc: *Mail comes urging that something be done to "rescue children from guns, daggers, and soldier worship." Horsefeathers!*—F Tripp **2** *n* Nonsense; = BALONEY, BUNK, HORSESHIT: *Don't give me that horsefeathers about your saintly momma*

horsehide *n* A baseball

the **horselaugh** *n phr* A loud, nasty, and dismissive laugh at someone; = the MERRY HA-HA: *When I asked for more time I just got the horselaugh*

horseman *n Canadian* A member of the Royal Canadian Mounted Police

horse opera (or **opry**) **1** *n phr fr early 1900s* A cowboy movie; Western; = BANG-BANG, OATER **2** *n phr circus* A circus

horse piano *n phr circus* A steam calliope

horseplayer *n* A person who bets on horse races

horserace *n* A serious contest; a hard-fought competition: *Suddenly what looked like a shoo-in for Mondale turned into a real horserace*

horse room (or **parlor**) *n phr horse-racing* A bookmaker's establishment; = HANDBOOK

horses *n gambling* A pair of dishonest dice, esp of mismatched dice that can produce only specific combinations: *Karnov explained the use of "horses"*—Associated Press

See HOLD one's HORSES, WILD HORSES COULDN'T DRAG IT OUT OF someone

◁**horse's ass**▷ *n phr* A contemptible person; a persistent and obnoxious fool; = JERK: *The philosopher has inquired why the world has so many more horses' asses than horses/ I just regard the critic privately as being the biggest horse's ass in the western world*—Interview/ *If, however, he wanted to present himself in Texas as a real horse's ass, none of us would dispute him*—Joseph Heller

◁**horseshit**▷ **1** *n* Nonsense; pretentious talk; bold and deceitful absurdities; = BALONEY, BULLSHIT: *You give me all that horseshit about the conditions here*—Calder Willingham **2** *modifier:* *Superstar! What a horseshit idiot!*—Saul Bellow **3** *v:* *He was horseshitting about what a great sailor he is* **4** *interj* An exclamation of disbelief, disapproval, and contempt: *Horseshit! I'll never believe that* **5** *n* Trivialities; nonessentials; = CHICKEN SHIT: *Don't bother me with that niminy-piminy horseshit*

◁**horseshit and gunsmoke**▷ *n phr Army* Excitement and confusion; chaos [fr an evocation of a cavalry skirmish or a cowboys-and-Indians battle]

horse's mouth *See* FROM THE HORSE'S MOUTH

hose 1 *v* To cheat; deceive; dupe; = SCREW, SHAFT: *The IRS tried to hose me* **2** *v college students* To turn down; reject; snub: *They're afraid of getting hosed*—New York Times [origin uncertain; perhaps fr a rare but attested *hose* "penis," whereupon the term would be analogous to *diddle, fuck, screw, shaft,* etc]

hoser 1 *n* A person who cheats and deceives; = CON MAN: *Reagan is a hoser*—Drew University graffito **2** *n Canadian* A Canadian, esp a simple and durable northern type: *unavailable to us hosers, but can be bought down south*—Westworld/ *unlike their hoser cousins*—Toronto Star

a **hosing** *See* TAKE A HOSING

hostess *See* BALL-BEARING HOSTESS, BANG THE HOSTESS

the **hostess with the mostest** *n phr* The most successful, lavish, and well-connected party-giving woman [fr a popular song fr the 1950s show *Call Me Madam*, "The Hostess with the Mostest on the Ball"]

hot 1 *adj fr middle 1800s* Capable of high speed; moving very fast: *Hot crate, a fast plane*—A Ostrow/ *the hottest car on the track* **2** *adj* Selling very rapidly and readily, hence very much in demand: *paralleled the rise of the "hot" ticket*—New York Times/ *Xaviera Hollander...is the hottest thing in the business promoting her own work*—New York **3** *adj fr late 1800s* Performing extremely well; certain to win: *When you're hot you're hot/ The fork-baller is real hot today, folks* **4** *adj fr late 1800s* Angry; furious; = PISSED OFF: *Don't get so hot about it, it was just a goof* **5** *adj* Lively; vital; vibrant: *This is a hot town*—Ernest Hemingway/ *A "hot" magazine is one that's sizzling and bubbling with activity*—New York Herald Tribune **6** *adj* Sexually excited; afire with passion; lustful; = HORNY: *Hot faggot queens bump up against chilly Jewish matrons*—Albert Goldman/ *the hottest little devil I ever met*—P Marks **7** *adj* Pornographic; salacious; = DIRTY: *a real hot movie* **8** *adj* Eager; = ANTSY: *Why so hot to get started?* **9** *adj jazz musicians* Exciting, rapid, strongly rhythmical, eliciting a visceral response: *The old jazz was mostly hot, then it was cool, and now even cool cats blow hot licks now and then* **10** *adj underworld* Stolen, esp recently stolen; contraband: *Stolen bonds are "hot paper"*—H McLellan **11** *adj underworld* Wanted by the police: *Where would a hot can of corn like Dillinger hide out*—A Hynd **12** *adj* Dangerous; menacing; potentially disastrous: *Things were getting too hot*—Erle Stanley Gardner/ *It's so hot out there, man, I'm thinking about getting into another game*—New York **13** *adj* New, esp both brand-new and interesting: *a hot tip/ the hot news from upstairs* **14** *adj* Having electrical potential; live; switched on: *Is this mike hot?/ Can I touch this wire, or is it hot?* **15** *adj* Radioactive

See BLOW HOT AND COLD, NOT SO HOT, RED HOT, SQUAT HOT

a hot   *n phr hoboes & jive talk* A meal: *He might have staked him to a hot*—Zora Neale Hurston

hot air   *fr middle 1800s* **1**   *n phr* Nonsense; pretentious talk; bold and deceitful absurdities; = BALONEY, BULLSHIT: *The Jefferson family tree will never be blown down by any hot air from me*—H McHugh   **2**   *n phr* Pomposity and vanity; bombast: *The old fraud talks a lot of hot air*
See FULL OF HOT AIR

hot and bothered   *adj phr* Angry; fiercely indignant; = PISSED OFF, STEAMED UP: *Now don't get all hot and bothered just because he didn't call*

hot and cold   *n phr narcotics* A mixture of heroin and cocaine; = SPEEDBALL
See BLOW HOT AND COLD

hot as a three-dollar pistol   *adj phr* Very hot; red-hot: *The rumor is hot as a three-dollar pistol*

hot as hell   *adj phr* Very hot indeed

hot baby   *n phr students fr late 1800s* A wild and sexy young woman

hotbed   **1**   *n   black & hoboes* A bed used both day and night, by shifts of sleepers   **2**   *n* A place that produces or is prominently rich in specified things: *College these days is a hotbed of sobriety*

hotcha   *esp 1920s & 30s* **1**   *interj* (also **hotcha-cha** or **ha-cha-cha**) An expression of pleasure, approval, relish, etc   **2**   *adj* Sexually attractive and energetic: *He run Sternwood's hotcha daughter, the young one, off to Yuma*—Raymond Chandler [a derivation fr Yiddish *hotsa* "hop!" has been suggested, based on the joyous repetition of the word as one bounces an infant on one's knees; perhaps fr *hot*]

hot corner   **1**   *n phr baseball* Third base, esp as a fielding position   **2**   *n phr* Any very dangerous and crucial place: *The North African front...is a "hot corner"*—Word Study

hot damn   *interj* An exclamation of pleasure, gratification, etc; = HOT DOG, HOT SHIT

hot diggety (or **diggity**)   *interj* (Variations: **dog** or **doggety** or **damn** may be added; **ziggety** or **ziggity** may replace **diggety**) = HOT DOG

hot dog   **1**   *interj* An exclamation of delight, gratification, relish, etc; = HOT DAMN, HOT SHIT: *Did you have a good time? "Hot dog!"*—Philadelphia Bulletin   **2**   *n phr* A frankfurter or a frankfurter sandwich   **3**   *modifier: a hot-dog stand/ embattled hot-dog vendor*   **4**   *n phr* = HOT SHOT   **5**   *v phr* To perform in a brilliant, spectacular way, esp in order to seize the admiration of an audience; = GRANDSTAND, SHOW OFF: *a little careless against Bob Cousy's Royals, hot-dogging their passes and loosening their defenses*—New York Times   **6**   *n: Walter is one of the good guys, not a hot dog*—John Chancellor   **7**   *modifier: I don't appreciate that hot-dog garbage in my ball park*—Newsweek   **8**   *v surfers* To surf spectacularly: *Surfers may..."hot dog," do acrobatics*—National Geographic   **9**   *v phr* To do hot-dog skiing

hot dogger   *n phr* = GRANDSTANDER, HOT SHOT

hot-dog skiing   *n phr* Free-style skiing that features somersaults, midair turns, ballet-like figures, and other feats rather than speed: *A whole new style of baroque skiing has developed. Known as "free-style," "exhibition," or "hot-dog" skiing*—Time

hotfoot   **1**   *v* (also **hotfoot it**) *fr early 1900s* To go fast; hurry: *The boys would hotfoot back...when they heard the mess call*—Louis Armstrong/ *Tell him to hotfoot it to the sheriff's office*—G Homes   **2**   *adv* At once; immediately: *I'll walk hotfoot to the doctor's office*   **3**   *n* A bail-jumper   **4**   *v* = GIVE someone A HOTFOOT

hot for   **1**   *adj phr* Very desirous of; lusting for; wishing to possess: *She seemed hot for you*—Calder Willingham   **2**   *adj phr* Very eager over; enthusiastic about: *He's real hot for the new promotion policy*

hot grease   *n phr* Trouble, esp impending trouble

hothead   **1**   *n* An irascible person; one quick to anger; = BLOWTOP   **2**   *n* A fanatical, emotional person; fiery militant

hot iron   *n phr* = HOT ROD

hot knife through butter   *See* LIKE SHIT THROUGH A TIN HORN

hot line   *n phr* An emergency telephone line or number, esp the one between the White House and the Kremlin or one modeled on it: *Clearly, hot lines are no cure for the complex, overall problem of drug abuse*—Parent/ *a community "hot line" to head off gang wars*—New York Times

hot number (or **item**)   **1**   *n phr* A very sexy man or woman; = HOT PANTS   **2**   *n phr salespersons* Something that is selling rapidly and well

hot one   *n phr* A very funny story, piece of news, etc

hot pants   **1**   *n phr* Strong sexual desire; lust; carnal craving: *His hot pants will get him in trouble*   **2**   *n phr* A very passionate, lustful, and potentially promiscuous person: *Catherine the Great was apparently an imperial hot pants*   **3**   *n phr esp 1960s & 70s* Very brief women's shorts
See HAVE HOT PANTS

hot patootie   *n phr esp 1920s* A sexually attractive and sexy woman: *He calls the object of his affection a "hot patootie"*—Nation [fr *hot potato*, with a play on potato as used, like *tomato*, to mean "a person"]

hot (or **hot-rock**) **pilot**   *n phr fr WW2 Air Forces* A very skillful and daring aviator: *Gabreskie was a very hot pilot/ a vanishing breed of hot-rock pilot in an age of increasingly automated flight*—Time

hot poo   **1**   *n phr & interj* = HOT SHIT   **2**   *n phr* Recent and authoritative information; the latest word

hot potato   *n phr* Something embarrassing and troublesome; a tricky and sticky matter: *Everyone can see how the boss looks when he handles a hot potato*—Associated Press
See DROP someone or something LIKE A HOT POTATO

hot property   *n phr* Someone or something very valuable and marketable, esp an athlete, desirable executive, entertainer, etc: *Timmons and Co, know-*

ing a hot property when it signs one up—Washington Post

hot rock *n phr* =HOT SHOT

◁**hot rocks** (or **nuts**)▷ *n phr* Male sexual craving; powerful lust; =HORNINESS: *At that time I had real hot rocks*

hot rod *hot rodders* **1** *n phr* A car specially modified and fitted with a powerful or rebuilt engine so as to be much faster than one of the same stock design; =A-BOMB, CAN, ROD: *Special Racing Cars and Hot Rods, a technical book...explains the principles of supercharging, carburetion, suspension, shock absorbers. A complete speed manual*—advertisement for Floyd Clymer books **2** *modifier: hot-rod manual/ hot-rod club* **3** *n phr* (also **hot rodder**) A driver or devotee of hot rods: *Right away he thinks he's a hot rod*—JA Maxwell [fr the notion of a *hot* connecting *rod* as symbolic and typical of such special engines]

the **hots 1** *n phr* Strong liking; predilection: *I'd never got the deep undying hots for that rah rah collitch boy*—Hal Boyle **2** *n phr* Lust; =HOT PANTS: *A bare-chested photograph of this guy can give 2,300 women the hots*—Philadelphia Journal
See HAVE THE HOTS FOR someone

the **hot seat 1** *n phr* The electric chair; =the HOT SQUAT **2** *n phr* A place where one is under uncomfortable scrutiny and pressure, esp the witness stand: *Deane was succeeded in the hot seat by a very small pot from the State Department*—R Starnes/ *always on the cutting edge, always in the hot seat*—Washington Post
See ON THE HOT SEAT

hot shit 1 *n phr* & *interj* =HOT DOG **2** *n phr* Someone or something very remarkable and attractive, irresistible, etc; =HOT STUFF: *He thinks he's real hot shit/ Ain't my new boat hot shit?* **3** *n phr* An aggressive, self-assured person; =BIG SHOT: *something sensitive and probing like all the rest of these hot shits*—Rolling Stone

hot short *n phr* esp 1920s & 30s underworld A stolen car

hot shot 1 *n phr* An especially gifted and effective person; a notably successful person; =BALL OF FIRE, WINNER ● Often used ironically: *What has been written about executives has usually dealt with the hot shots*—CW Morton/ *You're not pushing around some crummy client to show him what a hot-shot you are*—J Evans/ *You're dead, hotshot*—Don Pendleton **2** *modifier: In just a year I'm claiming to be a hot-shot Columbia man myself*—Dwight David Eisenhower/ *a young, hot-shot second lieutenant*—American Legion Magazine **3** *n phr* railroad A fast train or express train **4** *modifier: a hot-shot freight* **5** *n phr* A news bulletin; a news flash: *When that hot-shot came in about Monahan's death*—Scene of the Crime (movie) **6** *n phr* narcotics A narcotics injection that is fatal because of an impurity or poison: *You got a hot shot! You're dead*—C Cooper

hot-shot Charlie *n phr* WW2 Air Forces A flashy braggart; egotist

hotsie-totsie or **hotsie-dandy** *adj* esp 1920s Satisfactory; fine; =COPACETIC: *All's hotsie-totsie here, thank you so much*

hot sketch *fr early 1900s* **1** *n phr* A remarkable, colorful person; =CARD **2** *n phr* An attractive young woman; =HOT NUMBER

hot spit *n phr* & *interj* =HOT SHIT

hot spot 1 *n phr* =TIGHT SPOT **2** *n phr* A popular night club, esp one with sexy entertainment: *became 52d Street's hot spot*—Louis Sobol

the **hot squat** *n phr* The electric chair: *You couldn't ever rise from the hot squat*—A Hynd

hot stove league *n phr* The off-season entity of devotees, arguments, etc, that keeps baseball serious and topical from October to April

hot stuff 1 *n phr* fr late 1800s A person of exceptional merit, talents, attractions, etc; =HOT SHOT ● Almost always used ironically: *I guess they think they are hot stuff*—John O'Hara/ *Don't you think I'm hot stuff*—RS Prather **2** *n phr* Material, entertainment, etc, that is very exciting, esp salacious: *Those magazines are real hot stuff* **3** *n phr* fr underworld Stolen goods; contraband **4** *n phr* News or information that is very important, fresh, sensational, forbidden, etc: *I peeked in your brief case, and that's hot stuff!* **5** *n phr* Food, drinks, etc, that are very hot: *Hot stuff coming through*

hot to trot *adj phr* Afire with craving, esp for sexual activity; lustful: *to ask her bluntly if she was hot to trot*—Cyra McFadden/ *Somebody...was hot to trot for a Japanese sedan*—Car and Driver/ *who claims her hot-to-trot boss gave her a chase around the office*—New York Post

hot under the collar *adj phr* Very angry: *The Puerto Ricans who get hot under the collar and curse aloud if anyone should question their being Puerto Rican*—Village Voice

hot up 1 *v phr* To become more exciting: *Then things really hot up and January falls in love with an aging macho novelist*—Saturday Review **2** *v phr* To make something hot or hotter: *I'll just hot up some soup for lunch*

hot walker *n phr* horse-racing A person who walks a horse after a race or strong exercise in order to cool it off gradually: *She has worked at the King Ranch and at Churchill Downs as a "hotwalker" grazing thoroughbreds*—Washingtonian

hot war *n phr* A war with combat and killing; =SHOOTING WAR

hot water *n phr* Difficulty; trouble; embarrassment: *got herself into hot water by marrying a Siamese prince*—Time
See IN HOT WATER

hot-wire 1 *v* To start a car, truck, etc, by electrically by-passing the ignition lock: *He could hot-wire any car in about 20 seconds* **2** *v* To activate illegally; tamper with: *let the affected corporations hot-wire the regulatory process*—New York Times [fr the notion of attaching an electrically *hot* wire to the starter-motor relay; notice the earlier term *hot short*]

houdang *See* HOODANG

hound *v* To harass, pester, or annoy someone; = BURN

See BOOZEHOUND, CHOW HOUND, GAS HOUND

-hound *combining word* A person devoted to or addicted to what is indicated: *autograph hound/ boozehound/ nicotine hound/ thrill-hound*

the **Hound** or the **Dog** *n phr black & students fr truckers* A Greyhound bus (a trade name)

hound dog *n phr* A man who thinks of little but sex; a woman-chaser ● A Southernism popularized by an Elvis Presley song "Ain't nothin' but a hound dog"

hounds *adj teenagers fr 1950s* Very satisfying; wonderful; great; = NEAT

hounds on an island *n phr lunch counter* Frankfurters on a heap of baked beans

hound's tooth *See* CLEAN AS A HOUND'S TOOTH

hour *See* DEAD HOUR, ZERO HOUR

house 1 *n* A brothel; = CATHOUSE, WHOREHOUSE **2** *n* The audience at a theater

See BARRELHOUSE, BED HOUSE, the BIG HOUSE, BRING DOWN THE HOUSE, BUGHOUSE, CALL HOUSE, CAN HOUSE, CATHOUSE, CRAZY-HOUSE, CRUMB JOINT, DICE HOUSE, DOSS, FLEABAG, FLOPHOUSE, FUNNY FARM, GAS HOUSE, GRIND-HOUSE, HASH-HOUSE, IRON HOUSE, JAG HOUSE, JOY HOUSE, JUKE HOUSE, LIGHTHOUSE, MONKEY-HOUSE, NOTCH-HOUSE, NUT HOUSE, ONE ON THE HOUSE, ON THE HOUSE, PAPER HOUSE, POWERHOUSE, ROUGHHOUSE, ROUNDHOUSE, SCRATCH HOUSE, SKIN HOUSE, SPORTING HOUSE, STROKE HOUSE, WHEELHOUSE, WHOREHOUSE

house ape *n phr* A small child; an infant; = CURTAIN CLIMBER, RUG APE

house-cleaning *n* A reorganization of a business or government department, esp with dismissal of incompetent or dishonest employees; = SHAKE-UP: *Honest cops, instead of welcoming a house-cleaning...resent it*—E Lavine

housefrau *n* = HAUSFRAU

house larry *n phr salespersons* A man who frequents a store without buying: *The "house larry"...drops in two or three times a week not to buy*—G Milstein

house moss *n phr* The tufts and whorls of dust that accumulate under beds, tables, etc; = BEGGAR'S VELVET, GHOST TURDS

house-sit *v* To live in and care for a house free of charge while the owner is away

how *See* AND HOW, DING HOW, KNOW-HOW

how about that or **how do you like that** *interj* An exclamation of surprise, pleasure, admiration, etc: *We've only got a year to go. How about that!/ It's a first! How do you like that!*

how something **can you get** *sentence* It is impossible to be or behave to a more extreme degree; this is the utmost: *"How tacky can you get?" Maddie said disgustedly*—Lawrence Sanders/ *He did? How stupid can you get?*

how come *sentence fr middle 1800s* What is that?; what is the reason?

how do you like them apples *interj* An exclamation of pleasure and triumph, usu inviting admiration for something one has done or acquired: *He* spread the full house on the table and crowed *"How do you like them apples!"*

Howdy Doody *See* DOES HOWDY DOODY HAVE WOODEN BALLS

a **howl** *n teenagers* Something amusing; a funny event; = a HOOT

howler *n* A very funny mistake, esp in something written or spoken rather solemnly: *His misuse of "Rappaport" for "rapport" was the season's howler*

how's about *prep phr* What do you feel or think about: *How's about a new needle?/ How's about a drink?*—Budd Schulberg

how's tricks *sentence* How are you?; how are things going for you?

◁**how they hanging**▷ *sentence* How are you? ● A genial greeting, usu from one man to another; an inquiry as to the condition of the testicles: *Madeline Kurnitz said, "How they hanging, kiddo"*—Lawrence Sanders

HUA (pronounced as separate letters) *adv phr* Stupidly; blindly; inattentively: *You're driving pretty HUA today* [fr *head up ass*]

hubba-hubba *WW2 armed forces* **1** *interj* An exclamation of delight, relish, etc, esp at the sight of a woman **2** *adv* Quickly; immediately; = HABA-HABA, ON THE DOUBLE [origin unknown; perhaps a version of a Chinese greeting *how-pu-how*, apparently adopted by US airmen from Chinese pilot trainees; perhaps originally a bit of gibberish used to imitate the clamor of conversation, esp when soldiers get the command "Parade rest," after which one can talk, as distinct from the command "At ease," after which one must remain silent and contribute to no *hubbub*]

Hubbard *See* MOTHER HUBBARD

hubby *n* Husband

huckleberry *fr early 1800s* **1** *n* A man; fellow; = GUY: *Well, I'm your huckleberry, Mr Haney*—Jim Tully **2** *n* A fool; a dunce; = JERK ● A very mild and affectionate insult

huckster *n fr 1950s* An advertising person or publicity agent: *so the television hucksters can peddle their shaving cream*—New York Times

huddle 1 *n* A conference; closed and intense discussion: *He went into a huddle with his aides* **2** *v*: *We'll have to huddle on that one* [fr the *huddle*, esp of the offensive team, before most plays in football]

Huey *n esp Vietnam War armed forces* A US military helicopter of a certain model: *The Huey...combination of shuttle bus, supply truck, ambulance, and weapon of war*—New York Times

huff *See* IN A HUFF

huff-duff *n WW2 Army Air Forces* A high-frequency radio direction finder [fr the initials making up the name]

huffer *n hot rodders* An automobile supercharger; = BLOWER

huffy *adj fr middle 1800s* Angry; petulant; irritable; = IN A HUFF: *I didn't mean to get huffy*—Sinclair Lewis

huggy-huggy *adj* Very affectionate; = BUDDY-BUDDY, PALSY-WALSY: *We are all very huggy-huggy with each other*—People Weekly

the **hully-gully** *n phr esp 1960s* A discotheque dance derived from the twist: *The dignified dances include...the Hully-Gully (like Wyatt Earp drawing his guns, Dean Martin downing drinks, and Esther Williams knocking water out of her ear)*—New York Times [origin unknown; perhaps related by some of its gestures to a southern children's game, *hull-gull*, in which the players guessed at the number of chinkapin nuts held in a closed hand]
See HOLLY-GOLLY

humdinger *n fr early 1900s* A person or thing that is remarkable, wonderful, superior, etc; = BEAUT, LOLLAPALOOZA: *Arnold Moss gave us a humdinger of a talk*

humdinging *adj* First-rate; superior: *a real, humdinging corner*—Ira Wolfert

hummer *n* A person or thing that is remarkable, wonderful, etc; = HUMDINGER: *This is Mason's first book, and it's a hummer*—Village Voice

hummy **1** *adj black* Content; happy; ignorant of danger **2** *adv*: *She lives real hummy*

humongous (hŏŏ MAWN gəs) *adj esp teenagers* Very large; gigantic: *a humongous chain*—Industrial Research [perhaps a sort of echoic-symbolic blend of *huge* with *monstrous*]

hump **1** *v* (also **hump it** or **hump along**) To move or go, esp with difficulty; slog: *lack the nerve to hump it through to the end*—Partisan Review/ *put on that pack and hump for miles through the boonies*—Life ◁**2**▷ *v* To do the sex act with or to; = FUCK: *from the brave pilots who hump the nubile hostesses to the dialect-spouting steerage passenger*—Judith Crist **3** *n circus* A camel **4** *n* A Camel (a trade name) cigarette
See BUST one's ASS, BUST HUMP, CRAWL someone's HUMP, DRY FUCK, GET A HUMP ON, GET A MOVE ON, HIT THE HUMP, OVER THE HILL

hump and bump *v phr* To work hard and progress or propel haltingly: *He says it costs him $10,000 a month to hump and bump his business along*—Village Voice

◁**humpery**▷ *n* The sex act; coupling; = FUCKING: *refused to change the X rating on "Fritz the Cat" on the ground that it depicted "anthropomorphic humpery"*—Judith Crist

◁**humpy**▷ *adj* Sexually arousing; lubricious; sexy: *flashy, precise, and humpy as...in a Czardas*—Village Voice

hunch **1** *n fr late 1800s* An intuitive premonition; a shrewd idea or notion: *I gotta hunch she won't come back* **2** *modifier*: *This was too good a hunch play to let drop*—E Selby **3** *v*: *As I hunch it, the answer is triple*—Billy Rose [said to be fr a gamblers' belief that touching a *hunchback's* hump would bring good luck]

hung **1** *adj jazz talk* Annoyed; peeved **2** *adj* Exhausted; tired out **3** *adj* = HUNG OVER **4** *adj rock and roll* In love ◁**5**▷ *adj fr early 1800s* Having impressive male genitals; = HUNG LIKE A BULL, WELL-HUNG

hunger *See* FROM HUNGER

◁**hung like a bull** (or **a horse**)▷ *adj phr* Possessing large genitals; = WELL-HUNG

hung over *adj phr* Suffering the ill effects of a hangover: *looking as hung over as you can get*—R Starnes

the **hungries** *See* GET THE HUNGRIES

hungry **1** *adj* Very ambitious; extremely eager to succeed: *If you don't like this job, I know a couple of hungry guys that do* **2** *adj* Impoverished; = BROKE

hung up **1** *adj phr fr beat & cool talk* Limited by conventional beliefs and attitudes; = SQUARE, UNCOOL: *Either you're way out, pops, or you're hung up*—E Klein **2** *adj phr fr beat & cool talk* Agitated or immobilized by emotional disturbance; stalled: *She suddenly got all hung up around Xmas* **3** *adj phr* Delayed; detained: *He got hung up with a phone call as he was leaving*

hung up on *adj phr fr beat & cool talk* Obsessed with; stalled or frustrated by; suffering a hangup over: *I'm hung up on fried rice*—Harper's Bazaar

hunk **1** *n* A man or woman considered primarily as a sex partner; = PIECE, PIECE OF ASS: *He came back to the hot little hunk he used to run around with*—J Evans **2** *n* A very attractive man, esp a muscular and sexually appealing one: *Wherever she goes she always manages to pick up a hunk*—Aquarian

hunker down **1** *v phr* To squat on one's haunches: *He heads for the inevitable mariachi square, hunkers down in the dark, wet and shivering*—Tom Wolfe **2** *v phr* To get into the mood and posture for hard work: *Now that summer's gone we must hunker down and get that report finished* **3** *v phr* To take a sturdy defensive attitude; become hard to move: *As the public responds...the defense lawyers hunker down*—Philadelphia/ *"We'll just have to hunker down," said Jody Powell*—Newsweek [fr southern US fr northern British dialect *hunker* "haunch"]

hunk of change *See* PIECE OF CHANGE

hunk of cheese *n phr* A stupid, obnoxious person

◁**hunky¹**▷ (also **hunkie** or **Hunky** or **Hunkie** or **Hunk** or **hunks**) **1** *n* A foreigner, esp a Hungarian, Slavic, or Baltic laborer; = BOHUNK, GINZO **2** *modifier*: *hunky talk/ dumb hunkie brain* **3** *n black* A white person; = HONKY: *99 white workers got killed in a coal-mine disaster, man! Do you know what I mean? So I can't call everybody no Hunkie*—Ishmael Reed [fr *bohunk*]

hunky² *adj* = HORNY

hunky³ *adj* Attractive, esp sexually desirable; = MACHO ● Used most often of men: *hunky, bearded actor-troubadour*—Time/ *the hunky blond who cranks the ferry*—Advocate

hunky-dory *adj fr middle 1800s* Satisfactory; fine; = COPACETIC: *That may be hunky-dory...with the jumping and jiving youngsters*—Bosley Crowther

hunt *See* ELEPHANT HUNT

hunter *See* HEADHUNTER, IVORY-HUNTER, MANGO HUNTER, POTHUNTER

hurl *v baseball* To pitch: *after hurling five frames in three games*—F Eck

hurler *n baseball* A pitcher

a **hurrah's nest** *n phr outdated fr early 1800s* Confusion; chaos; =SNAFU

hurry *See* HERE'S YOUR HAT WHAT'S YOUR HURRY

hurtin' for certain *adj phr college students* =HURTING

hurting *adj esp armed forces & college students fr black* In great need; in distress: *If they find out about this you'll be hurting/ We were all hurting for a little praise*

husband 1 *n prostitutes* A pimp: *She has a pimp she calls her "husband"*—New York Times **2** *n homosexuals* The dominant, masculine member of a homosexual couple, male or female

hush-hush 1 *adj* Very secret; classified: *a hush-hush border meeting*—Associated Press **2** *n: Why all the hush-hush about Walden?*—Raymond Chandler

husk *v* To undress; =PEEL

hustle 1 *v* To hurry: *We better hustle, the thing leaves in five minutes* **2** *n: Put a little hustle in it now* **3** *v fr late 1800s* To behave, play, perform, etc, very energetically and aggressively: *The reason they're losing is they don't hustle* **4** *v* To beg: *You'll hustle for an overcoat*—J Flynt **5** *v* To work as a prostitute; =HOOK: *whores that hustle all night long*—Louis Armstrong **6** *v* To sell; hawk **7** *v* To cheat; swindle; victimize; =CON: *It took a hell of a caddy to hustle a pro and a greenkeeper*—Saturday Evening Post/ *Larabee, he decided, was trying to hustle him*—WT Tyler **8** *n: I guess one man's "hustle" is another man's "promotion"*—Village Voice **9** *v fr early 1900s* To steal: *We must hustle us a car* **10** *n: You know I can't pay out five bills for a wash if I wasn't planning a hustle*—Lawrence Sanders [criminal senses may be related to early-19th-century *hustle* "do the sex act, fuck"]

See GET A HUSTLE ON, GET A MOVE ON, ON THE HUSTLE

hustler 1 *n fr early 1900s* A thief or a dealer in stolen goods: *and sells to hustlers like Tommy at about one-third its retail value*—New York **2** *n fr 1920s* A confidence trickster or swindler, esp one who pretends ignorance of a game where he or she is in fact an expert and sure to win; =CON MAN, SHARK **3** *n* A prostitute; =HOOKER: *I ain't nothing but a hustler*—Langston Hughes **4** *n* An energetic, aggressive performer or worker: *We need more hustlers in this department*

hut 1 *n railroad* A caboose **2** *n prison* A prison cell

hutzpa or **hutzpah** *See* CHUTZPA

hype[1] 1 *n fr early 1900s* A hypodermic needle; =HYPE-STICK **2** *n fr 1920s* An injection of narcotics **3** *n* An addict who injects narcotics: *and heroin substitutes don't work with a stone hype*—Joseph Wambaugh **4** *n* A seller of narcotics; =CONNECTION: *any hype that wants to get you hooked*—D Hulburd [fr *hypodermic* referring to a needle or an injection]

hype[2] 1 *n* Advertising or promotion, esp of a blatant sort; =BALLYHOO, FLACK: *without any advance*

p r hype—H Smith **2** *v: exercises no stock options, hypes no quick secondary stock offering*—New York/ *unless Margaret's hyping the gate for a rematch*—Sports Illustrated **3** *v fr early 1900s* To trick; deceive; originally, to short-change **4** *v* =HYPE UP [origin unknown; perhaps related to *hyper* "hustle," of obscure origin, attested from the mid-19th century; recent advertising and public relations senses probably influenced by *hype[1]* as suggesting supernormal energy, excitement, etc, and by *hyper[2]*]

See MEDIA HYPE

a **hype 1** *n phr* A high-pressure advocacy or urging; a publicity or public relations invention: *The nostalgia for the fifties is not entirely a media hype*—New York Times/ *This is gonna sound like a hype*—Rolling Stone **2** *n phr* A person or thing promoted by hype **3** *n phr* A swindle; =CON, SCAM **4** *n phr* A lie

hyped-up 1 *adj* False; fake; =HOKED-UP, PHONY: *no hyped-up glamour*—Billy Rose/ *the woman's archly hyped-up language*—Village Voice **2** *adj* Excited; overstimulated; =HYPER: *I leave early...hyped-up, impressed, nauseated*—Commentary/ *The game gets him "hyped up," and "releases energy" in the same way that football does*—Games

hyper[1] or **hype artist** *n* or *n phr* A publicist; promoter; advertiser; =FLACK [fr *hype[2]*]

hyper[2] 1 *adj fr 1920s* Overexcited; manic; overwrought; =HYPED-UP: *She tells how the grownups gave her Nembutal when she was eight years old, because "I was hyper"*—New York/ *It's this flaky hyper hour*—New York/ *She's a hyper-person, accustomed to constant activity*—Good Housekeeping **2** *adj* Exceeding most; very superior; =SUPER: *with harem cushions, a hyper-hi-fi set, ha-ha candles*—Saturday Review [fr Greek *hyper* "super," and in the first sense probably fr medical terms like *hyperkinetic, hyperthyroid*, etc; in some sources this term is associated with *hipped* and *hippish*, fr *hypochondriac* "melancholic," first attested in the early 18th century]

See THROW A FIT

hype-stick *n narcotics* A hypodermic needle

hype up 1 *v phr* To fake; manufacture; invent; =HOKE UP: *They had to hype up a convincing story* **2** *v phr* To promote or advertise by blatant, obnoxious means **3** *v phr* To give something a false impact, appeal, energy, etc: *other chemicals to hype up the produce and fool the buyer*—Saturday Review

hypo *fr early 1900s* **1** *n* A hypodermic needle **2** *n* A hypodermic injection **3** *n narcotics* A drug addict; =HYPE **4** *v* To stimulate or strengthen; =BEEF UP: *a wilted record player hypoed by a pooped-out public address system*—John R Powers [fr *hypodermic*, referring to a needle or an injection]

I

IC (pronounced as separate letters) *n lunch counter* An irate customer: *There were usually about two ICs a night*—Cameron Crowe

I Can Catch *n phr truckers* The Interstate Commerce Commission

ice 1 *n* Diamonds; a diamond: *a two-carat hunk of ice* **2** *n* Gems and jewelry in general: *Gonna wear your ice?* **3** *n* Extra payment given for a desirable theater ticket: *a slight fee, say $100 worth of tickets for $120. The $20 is the "ice"*—M Zolotow **4** *v* To make something certain; =CINCH, SEW something UP: *They iced the game in the ninth with two more runs* **5** *v* (also **ice** someone **out**) To ignore someone; snub; cut; =COLD SHOULDER: *how women were "iced" by peers during corridor conversations*—Newsweek **6** *v* To defeat utterly; trounce; =CLOBBER: *Nebraska iced Kentucky 55 to 16* **7** *v underworld* To kill; =OFF: *Ice a pig. Off a pig. That means kill a cop*—Robert Daley **8** *adj cool talk* Excellent; fine; =COOL

See BREAK THE ICE, CUT NO ICE, GREEN ICE, ON ICE

iceberg *n* An unemotional, chilly person; =COLD FISH

icebox 1 *n prison* A solitary confinement cell; =the HOLE: *When a prisoner is sent to the "icebox"*—E Lavine **2** *n prison* A prison **3** *n* The imagined place where persons and things are held in reserve: *I got a lefthander in the icebox* **4** *n* A very cold place: *This building's an icebox*

ice cream *n phr early 1900s narcotics* The crystalline form of a narcotic: *the ice cream eaters, who chewed the crystal*—H Asbury

ice cream habit *n phr narcotics* The occasional, nonaddicted, use of narcotics

iced *See* HAVE something CINCHED

ice maiden (or **queen**) *n phr* A very cool and composed woman; a chilly woman: *Margaret Thatcher, the Ice Maiden/ branded the conservative Gorsuch "the Ice Queen"*—Newsweek

iceman 1 *n* A jewel thief **2** *n* A very calm person, performer, etc: *An iceman...is a gambler who never loses his head*—J Lilienthal **3** *n* A professional killer= HIT MAN: *Maybe I hadn't seen the iceman with Bobb*—Richard Merkin/ *Go play iceman*—TJ Hooker (TV program)

ice (or **put the icing on**) **the cake** *v phr* To put a victory beyond question; insure a favorable result: *He iced the cake with a knockdown in the seventh*

icky (Variations: **ickie** or **icky-poo** or **icky-sticky** or **ickey-wickey**) **1** *adj jive talk fr 1930s* Oversentimental; maudlin; =SCHMALTZY: *That music pleased my icky, lachrymose sensibility/ The prose gets a mite too icky-poo for comfort*—New York **2** *n* A conventional, tedious person; =SQUARE: *She turned out to be an icky* **3** *adj* Unpleasant; revolting; nasty; =GROSS, GRUNGY: *Those cool comedies and quizzes became dumb, boring, icky, weird*—Good Housekeeping/ *refuse to get involved in anything outside their own little ickey-wickey bailiwicks*—Village Voice/ *The acting is icky*—San Francisco [fr baby-talk, "sticky, nasty"; although perhaps fr Yiddish *elken* or *iklen* "nauseate, revolt"]

ID (pronounced as separate letters) **1** *n* An identity card **2** *n* Identification; evidence for one's identity: *You can't cash it here without ID* **3** *v:* *Who'll ID this clown?*

idea *See* WHAT'S THE BIG IDEA

idiot box *n phr* A television set; television; =the BOOB TUBE

idiot card (or **board**) *n phr television studio* A large sheet of heavy paper held up out of range of the television camera, to prompt actors or speakers; cue card: *"Idiot boards" are held out of camera range*—Saturday Evening Post/ *The scripts are gone, but now there are idiot cards*—Saturday Review

idiot girl *n phr television studio* A young woman who holds up idiot cards for television performers

idiot light *n phr* A usu red light on a car's dashboard that glows to announce some sort of fact, such as the discharge of a battery, overheating, etc: *replaced by too-late-to-react idiot lights*—Car and Driver

idiot mittens *n phr* Children's mittens connected by a cord that runs through the sleeves of a coat or jacket, to prevent loss of the mittens

-ie (also **-ey** or **-y** or **-sie** or **-sey** or **-sy**) **1** *suffix used to form nouns* Diminutive, affectionate, or familiar versions of what is indicated: *auntie/ cubby/ tootsie/ folksy* **2** *suffix used to form adjectives* Having the quality indicated: *comfy/ creepy/ swanky* **3** *suffix used to form nouns* Coming from the place or background indicated: *Arky/ Okie/ Yalie* **4** *suffix used to form nouns* A person of the sort indicated: *weirdie/ hippy/ sharpy*

if *See* BIG IF

223

if bet *n phr gambling* A bet on two or more horses, stipulating that part of the winnings be wagered on one or more later races

iffy 1 *adj* Uncertain; doubtful; improbable: *His chances...were a bit iffy*—Time **2** *adj* = DICEY

-ific or **-iffic** *suffix used to form adjectives* Extremely marked by what is indicated: *horrific/beautific* [fr *terrific*]

if you can't find 'em, grind 'em *sentence* If something cannot be done smoothly or readily, do it roughly; let push come to shove if necessary [fr the action of a truck driver who, if the gears do not shift smoothly, forces them and lets them *grind*]

if you can't stand the heat stay out of the kitchen *sentence* Do not undertake a hard job if you lack the stamina and thick skin to endure sharp criticism [a favorite saying of President Harry S Truman, referring to the Presidency]

ig or **igg** *v jive talk fr black* To ignore; refuse to notice

iggle *v teenagers fr 1950s* To persuade: *See if you can iggle him into it*

Ike *See* ALIBI IKE

◀**Ikey**▶ *n fr middle 1800s British* A Jew [fr a nickname for *Isaac*]

I kid you not *sentence fr 1950s* I am perfectly serious; I am not misleading nor joking with you: *It's the best thing that ever happened to me. I kid you not*

ill *adj underworld* Arrested or detained on suspicion; jailed

I'll be damned *sentence* (Variations: **danged** or **darned** or **ding swizzled** or **dipped** or **dipped in shit** or **fucked** or **jiggered** or **jig-swiggered** or **hanged** or **hornswoggled** or **a monkey's uncle** or **switched** may replace **damned**; **damned** may be omitted) May I be maltreated, confounded, accursed, etc; an exclamation of surprise or determination: *I'll be damned, we made it!/ I will be dipped in shit*—Larry Niven and Jerry Bournelle/ *I'll be a monkey's uncle if you put that over on me!/ Well I'll be, he made it!* [*dipped* forms fr 17th-century British *be dipped* "get into trouble"]

I'll drink to that *sentence* I agree; you are quite right; I approve

illegitimati non carborundum *sentence* Don't let the bastards grind you down ● Offered as a proposed motto or a pearl of wisdom [fr mock-Latin *illegitimatus* "bastard" and *Carborundum*, trade name of a brand of abrasives]

I'll tell the world (or **the cockeyed world**) *sentence fr early 1900s esp WW1 armed forces* You are absolutely right; it is entirely correct: *I'll tell the cockeyed world he's a crook*

immatesticle *adj* Of no concern; not relevant; immaterial: *Whether I get called or not is immatesticle* [a play on *immaterial*]

immie 1 *n* A kind of playing marble: *The correct answer is marble aggies and immies*—Jack Paar **2** *n* An eye: *a guy who could be junked up to where his immies turn into little beads*—Rocky Graziano

impact on *v phr* To affect or influence; = HIT: *The cut will not impact on our department*

import *n college students* An out-of-town date brought to a dance, party, etc

important money *See* HEAVY MONEY

in 1 *n* An advantage, esp through an acquaintance; entree: *He has an in at that place, since his mother owns it* **2** *adj* In fashion at the moment; now preferred: *Violence is in, sentiment is out* **3** *adj* Belonging to a select circle of the most fashionable: *one of the in people* **4** *adj* (also **in like Flynn**) Accepted; acceptable: *Suck up the right people and you're in/ "Are you in or out right now?" "I'm in like Flynn. Didn't you notice the picture on my desk?"*—Art Buchwald **5** *adj police* Arrested: *Come along now, you're in* [police sense from *run someone in*]

See GET IN, HAVE IT IN FOR someone

-in *combining word* A communal occasion where one does what is indicated: *be-in/ lie-in/ pray-in*

in a big way *adv phr* Very much; extremely: *The soldiers went for pin-ups in a big way*—United Press International

in a bind (or **box**) *adj phr fr loggers* In a very tight and awkward situation; stalled by a dilemma: *I'm in a bind, damned if I do and damned if I don't* [fr the situation of a logger whose saw is caught and held tight by the weight of a tree or branch]

in a box *See* GO HOME FEET FIRST

in a bucket *See* FOR CRYING OUT LOUD

in a flush *adj phr* Confused; troubled; bewildered

in a fog (or **haze**) *adj phr* In a dazed, disoriented, confused state; inattentive: *He was so tired he was walking around in a haze*

in a funk 1 *adv phr fr British fr middle 1700s* In a depressed, nervous, or frightened state: *Jackson left San Francisco in a funk, he...looked tired and sounded like a morose, defeated candidate*—Washington Post **2** *adj phr* Depressed; melancholy: *Steve's been in a funk since he lost his dog*

in a holding pattern *adv phr fr aviators* In abeyance; not in an active status; = ON THE BACK BURNER [fr the aviation term for airplanes that are flying a prescribed c.rcling route while awaiting clearance to land]

in a hole *adj phr* In grave and probably insurmountable difficulties; = UP SHIT CREEK: *Without their help I was sort of in a hole/ The death of my brother leaves me in a deep legal-financial hole*—Saul Bellow

in a huff *adj phr* Angry; petulant; grumpy

in a jam *adj phr* In trouble, esp serious trouble: *If you're in a jam, he'll fight for you*—P Jones

in a jiffy *See* JIFFY

in a lather (or **lava**) *adj phr fr 1600s* Angry; upset; = IN A SWEAT: *this business of you being in a lather about it*—J Evans/ *The editors say they are not in a lava over the coincidence*—Time [fr the resemblance between an agitated sweat, esp the frothy sweat of horses, and frothy washing *lather* thought of as the result of vigorous agitation; the earliest attested use is in the form in a *lavour*]

◁**in-and-out**▷ *n* The sex act; copulation; = FUCKING: *The pages of romances offered less in-and-out than a downtown parking garage*—San Francisco/ *Her* *refreshing answers about the old in-and-out bluntly demystified any last glitches*—Village Voice [fr the 17th-century British idiom *play at in-and-out* "do the sex act, copulate"]

in-and-outer *n* An erratic performer: *30 knockouts among his 52 victories, but he has been an in-and-outer*—Associated Press

in an uproar *See* NOT GET one's BALLS IN AN UPROAR

◁**in a pig's ass**▷ (or **ear** or **eye**) *adv phr* Not at all; never; =LIKE HELL ● Used for vehement denial: *In a pig's ass, I did*—Village Voice/ *Yeah, we'll get it back. In a pig's eye*—Jerome Weidman

in a pinch 1 *adv phr* If necessary; if need be: *In a pinch we could make that do* **2** *adv phr* =IN A JAM

in a poke *See* BUY A PIG IN A POKE

in a row *See* HAVE one's DUCKS IN A ROW

in a state 1 *adj phr* fr early 1800s British Agitated; upset; tense: *She got home and found her husband in a state* **2** *adj phr* fr late 1800s British Untidy; disheveled; chaotic: *I'm afraid my room's in a state*

in a stew 1 *adj phr* Chaotic and muddled; in disarray; =IN A FLUSH: *The whole place is in a stew about the new appointment* **2** *adj phr* Angry and irritable; upset; =IN A SWEAT: *Well don't get in such a stew about it*

in a sweat *adj phr* Upset; irritated; tense; scared: *Don't get in a sweat, I'll return it at once*

in a tizzy *adj phr* fr early 1900s Very much upset; distractingly disturbed; in a state: *I have been in a tizzy since reading his accusations*—Saul Bellow [origin unknown]

in at the kill *adv phr* Participating in the finish of something, esp when it is very satisfying and vindictive: *Tell me when the thing'll be signed, I want to be in at the kill* [fr a fox-hunting term]

in a walk *See* WIN IN A WALK

in a whoosh *adv phr* Very rapidly; in an easy rush: *He went through in a whoosh and obviously with attention to all the arcane mumbo jumbo he had to memorize*—William Kennedy [echoic]

in a zone *adj phr* Daydreaming, esp from narcotics; =SPACED-OUT [said to be fr *ozone*, implying very high up in the sky or towards outer space]

in someone's bad books *adv phr* esp Canadian & British Regarded as hostile by someone; hated and menaced by someone: *nervous about getting in the bad books of the mob guys*—Toronto Life

in bed *See* one SHOULD HAVE STOOD IN BED

in business *adj phr* In operation; under way: *One more day or so of prep and we're in business/ The space shuttle is finally in business*

in cahoots *adj phr* fr cowboys In partnership; acting in a common purpose: *I told you those two were in cahoots*

in cement *adj phr* Fixed and immovable; intractable; uncompromising: *The President seems to be in cement*—Congressman Thomas P O'Neill

in clover *adv phr* In a position of ease and affluence; =HAPPY AS A CLAM

in cold storage (or **the deep freeze**) *adv phr* Held in abeyance; reserved to be dealt with later; =ON HOLD: *The plan's in cold storage for now/ Well, let's just keep that one in the deep freeze for a few months*

in one's **cups** *adj phr* Drunk

indeedy *adv* fr early 1800s Indeed; certainly: *No, indeedy*—Sinclair Lewis

in deep water *adv phr* In a difficult situation, esp where one is not fitted to cope; =OUT OF one's DEPTH

Indian *See* LIKE A WOODEN INDIAN

Indian hay (or **hemp**) *n phr* narcotics Marijuana: *a couple of Indian hay cigarettes*—American Journal of Psychiatry

Indians *See* TOO MANY CHIEFS AND NOT ENOUGH INDIANS

the **Indian sign** *n phr* A baleful spell or curse; =HEX, JINX, WHAMMY: *You'd think the Indian sign was on the whole operation*

indie 1 *n* movie studio An independent, esp an independent movie producer **2** *modifier:* *one indie pic company*—Variety

in (or **into**) someone's **drawers** (or **pants**) *adv phr* Into the venue of venereal delight; enjoying sex with someone: *You wouldn't believe how easy it is to get into her drawers*

in Dutch *adj phr* fr early 1900s In disfavor; in trouble: *You have to promise, Pop, not to get me in Dutch with Mrs Skoglund*—Saul Bellow [origin unknown]

the **Indy** or **Indy 500** *n phr* The annual Indianapolis 500 car race

in one's **ear** *See* STAND AROUND WITH one's FINGER UP one's ASS, STICK IT

in one's **eye** *See* a THUMB IN one's EYE

in flames *See* GO DOWN IN FLAMES

info *n* Information; =POOP: *I can slip you the info*—Saturday Evening Post

in for it *adj phr* fr late 1600s About to be caught and punished; about to suffer trouble, attack, etc: *When they saw the black clouds they knew they were in for it/ If they nab us with the pope's ring, we'll really be in for it*

information *See* FEEDBOX INFORMATION

in front *See* UP FRONT

in God's name *See* the HELL

in group *n phr* An exclusive group or clique of influential persons

in someone's hair *adj phr* fr late 1800s Constantly annoying; nagging at: *You'll have one of these...professors in your hair*—Mark Twain

inhale *v* To eat or drink, esp rapidly: *He inhaled a couple of Martinis*
See FRENCH-INHALE

in harness *adj phr* Working; actively employed rather than resting, retired, on holiday, etc: *He didn't know how to relax after all those years in harness*

in heat *See* BITCH IN HEAT

in heck *See* the HECK

in hell *See* the HELL

in high gear *adj phr* In the most active, rapid, impressive phase; at full tempo: *The advertising campaign is in high gear*
See SHIFT INTO HIGH GEAR

in hock 1 *adj phr* Accepted for pawn; in a pawnshop **2** *adj phr* In debt; mortgaged: *We're deeply in hock to the bank*

in hot water 1 *adv phr* In trouble, esp with the law, one's superiors, etc: *He had the knack of always being in hot water with his wife* **2** *adv phr* In difficulties, esp in serious trouble; = IN THE SOUP: *He's got in hot water with the manager again*

ink 1 *n* hoboes Coffee **2** *n* black Cheap wine: *a cheap local "ink"*—Meyer Berger ◄**3**► *n* A black person **4** *v* To write; sign, esp a contract: *He also inked the plays*—New York Daily News/ *has inked to helm two more pictures*—Variety
See PINK INK, RED INK

ink-slinger 1 *n* fr middle 1800s A writer; author; newspaper reporter or writer **2** *n* lumberjacks, cowboys & hoboes fr early 1900s A clerk; office worker

inkstick *n* hawkers A fountain pen: *At 15, Nellie was "making a pitch" with inksticks*—SS Jacobs

◄**inky-dink**► *n* A dark-skinned black person

in like Flynn See IN

in line 1 *adj phr* Within appropriate bounds; acceptable; = IN THE BALLPARK: *Yes, those prices are about in line* **2** *adj phr* Behaving properly; out of trouble: *How did you keep your kids in line?*

in line for *adv phr* In position to get; about to get: *Hey, you're in line for a big bonus*

in luck *adj phr* Lucky

in mothballs *adj phr* In reserve; = ON ICE

innards *n* The viscera; = GUTS, KISHKES: *got a feeling in my innards it won't work*

inning *n* prizefight fr early 1900s A round of a prizefight

in nothing (or **no time**) **flat** *adv phr* Very quickly: *I got over there in nothing flat*

-ino See -ERINO

in one piece See ALL IN ONE PIECE

in on the ground floor *adv phr* fr middle 1800s Engaged early and profitably in a project, investment, etc: *You better act now if you want to be in on the ground floor*

in orbit *adj phr* teenagers Having a free and exhilarating experience; = HIGH, WAY OUT: *One slurp of gin and he's in orbit*

◄**in-out**► *n* The sex act; copulation; = IN-AND-OUT: *the endlessly hypnotic spectacle of the old in-out*—Changes

in over (or **above**) one's **head** *adv phr* In a situation one cannot cope with; helplessly committed and likely to lose: *He tried to stop, but he was in over his head*

in one's **pants** See ANTS

in pictures *adv phr* In the movies: *After years in pictures he went back to the theater and bombed*

in place *adj phr* Available; ready for use; effectuated or installed; = ON LINE: *We've got a couple of new procedures in place*

in someone's **pocket** *adv phr* Under someone's absolute control: *Don't worry, I have him in my pocket/ He's in the hip pocket of the networks* —Washington Post

inside See ON THE INSIDE

inside job *n phr* A robbery, stroke of espionage, etc, done by someone or with the aid of someone within the target organization: *The cops think the hotel murder is an inside job*

insider *n* A person who has special knowledge, authority, etc, because he is within or part of some privileged group: *The insiders are saying that the President will veto it*

insides *n* = INNARDS

the inside track See HAVE THE INSIDE TRACK

in spades *adv phr* To the utmost; in the highest degree: *What Aleksandr Solzhenitsyn did for the Gulag he has now done in spades for the Soviet Union as a whole*—National Review/ *I detest them right back, in spades*—Saul Bellow

inspection See SHORT-ARM INSPECTION

instant replay *n phr* Immediate repetition: *If anyone mistakes the new regimen for freedom, the full trappings of martial law remain available for instant replay*—New York Times

insurance 1 *n* Something that makes an outcome sure and safe: *I bought a few extra for insurance* **2** *modifier*: *They got a pair of insurance runs in the eighth*

in sync (or **synch**) *adv phr* In order; in harmony; synchronized; without jar or clash: *to bring the author back into sync with his existentialist colleagues*—National Review/ *perfectly in sync with Thicke's outrageous style*—Newsweek

inta See INTO

in tall cotton *adj phr* Very successful; enjoying excellent fortune; = FAT, DUMB, AND HAPPY: *would greet them from this office, this desk, this chair, high and dry in tall cotton*—Washington Post

intercom *n* An intercommunication system: *Marc yelled into the intercom*—Billy Rose

in the air See a BEAR IN THE AIR

in the altogether *adj phr* Naked

in the bag 1 *adj phr* Certain; sure; = ON ICE: *My election is in the bag/ It's in the bag. The fix is in* —WR and FK Simpson **2** *adj phr* Ruined; destroyed; = FINISHED, KAPUT, OUT OF THE BOX: *If an actor is hurt or killed doing a stunt the whole film is in the bag*—Entertainment Tonight (TV program) [fr game shot and stuffed *into the game bag*; second sense fr the use of the heavy plastic body bag for the handling of military and other fatal casualties]
See HALF IN THE BAG

in the ballpark *adj phr* Within general appropriate limits; not exorbitant, outrageous, etc: *react to an analyst's estimate by telling him whether it is too high, too low, or "in the ballpark"*—Fortune

in the barrel *adj phr* black Without money; = BROKE: *A red hot pimp like you ain't got no business being in the barrel*—Zora Neale Hurston

in the black *adj phr* Profitable; solvent; not in debt: *We toyed with bankruptcy for a while, but now* we're in the black [fr the color of ink traditionally used by bookkeepers to record assets, profits, etc]

in the boat *See* MAN IN THE BOAT

◁**in the box**▷ *adj phr* Doing the sex act with a woman; =SCREWING

in the bucks *adj phr* Having money, esp a lot of it; in funds; =FLUSH, LOADED: *right after Christmas and we're not in the bucks*

in the buff *adj phr* Naked; =BARE-ASS, BUCK NAKED: *There we stood, in the buff and abysmally embarrassed*

in the can *adj phr fr movie studio* Successfully finished; ready for release, consumption, etc [fr the large, flat, circular tin *can* into which finished movie film is put]

in the cards *adj phr* Very probably; likely to or about to happen: *Another tax hike is in the cards*

in the catbird seat *See* SIT IN THE CATBIRD SEAT

in the chips *adj phr* Having money; affluent; =FLUSH, LOADED

in the chops *See* KLOP IN THE CHOPS

in the coop *adj phr police & underworld* Sleeping on the job; off duty for unauthorized rest: *The cruise car for that street was supposed to be in the coop*—Lawrence Sanders

in the dark **1** *adj phr* Uninformed; ignorant; uncognizant: *We'll keep 'em in the dark about this until the time is right* **2** *adj phr* Mystified; puzzled: *You maybe told me, but I'm still sort of in the dark*

in the doghouse *adj phr* In a position or status of obloquy; out of favor, esp temporarily: *The press secretary is in the doghouse for cussing out a reporter*

in the driver's (or **buddy**) **seat** *adj phr* In the position of authority; in control: *With that kind of vote we're in the driver's seat/ You don't make it very easy, do you? Always in the driver's seat*—WT Tyler

in the dumper *adj phr* Bankrupt; ruined; insolvent; =IN THE TUB

in the face *See* A SLAP ON THE FACE, TILL one IS BLUE IN THE FACE

in the flesh **1** *adv phr* In person; in propria persona: *The great movie star appeared there in the flesh* **2** *adj phr*: *an in-the-flesh presentation*

in the foot *See* SHOOT oneself IN THE FOOT

in the groove *fr 1930s jive talk* **1** *adj phr* Making good sense; saying what needs saying: *Right! You're in the groove now* **2** *adj phr* In good form; working smoothly and well: *The professor of Classics was, as she would have put it, "in canaliculo," in the groove* **3** *adj phr jive musicians* Playing well and excitingly; =HEP

in the gutter *See* HAVE one's MIND IN THE GUTTER

in the hay *adv phr* In bed, either sleeping or cavorting: *Joe's in the hay, zonked out/ a toss in the hay with her boss*—Neal Travis
See A ROLL IN THE HAY

in the hole **1** *adv phr poker* Dealt face down, in stud poker: *What's he got in the hole?* **2** *adv phr* In debt: *We're in the hole to the tune of $9000*
See ACE IN THE HOLE

in the hopper *See* IN THE WORKS

in the hot seat *See* ON THE HOT SEAT

in the know *adj phr* Well informed, esp having current, advance, or confidential information: *My source has an inside track and is truly in the know*

in the life *adj phr* Occupied or engaged in some specialized and usu socially despised way of living, such as the homosexual subculture or prostitution: *By the time strippers are "in the life" they have developed an exploitative attitude to men and people in general*—Trans-Action

in the long run *adv phr* After a long period of time, trial, endurance, etc: *It looks grim now, but in the long run you'll see it'll get better*

in the loop *adv phr* In the select company, esp in the circle of the powerful: *no force in the administration, observes simply, "He's not in the loop"*—Chicago Tribune/ *Sometimes they are not even "in the loop" to get important information*—New York Times [probably an alteration of the military idiom *in the net*, of the same meaning, fr the use of radio *nets* or communications nexuses that include or exclude certain headquarters]

in the money **1** *adj phr* Having money, esp in large amounts; =IN THE BUCKS, FLUSH: *I'm in the money at last*—H Allen Smith **2** *adv phr gambling & horse-racing* Providing winnings to bettors: *None of his horses finished in the money today at the track*

in the mud *See* STICK IN THE MUD

in the picture **1** *adv phr* In a position to understand what is happening; in an informed position ● Chiefly British: *OK, now that you're one of us, I want you in the picture* **2** *adj phr* Probable; distinctly conceivable: *It just isn't in the picture that they'll get married/ I'd like to travel, but it doesn't seem like it's in the picture for a year or so*
See PUT someone IN THE PICTURE

in the pink *adj phr* In good health; ruddy and in fine fettle

in the pipeline **1** *adj phr* (also **in the hopper** or **in the works**) Being prepared, processed, or worked on; =ON THE FIRE: *There could be a good raise in the pipeline for you/ We got a little gizmo in the works that'll give them a duck-fit* **2** *adv phr surfers* Riding inside the curled-over front of a wave

in the pocket *adj phr narcotics* Enjoying the best part of a psychedelic intoxication: *It was a golden time, and I was right in the pocket*—Rolling Stone [probably fr the sense of safety and pleasure associated with catching and holding a baseball *in the pocket*, or concave niche, of a mitt or glove]

in the raw **1** *adj phr* Naked; =IN THE BUFF: *prancing around the common in the raw* **2** *adj phr* Without amenity or polish; relatively crude and primitive: *Up there they lived life in the raw/ His work is sculpture in the raw*

in there **1** *adv phr* =IN THERE PITCHING **2** *adv phr baseball* Pitched across home plate for a strike
See HANG IN

in the red *adj phr* In debt; losing money; insolvent: *The huge corporation has been in the red for eight* *years* [fr the color of ink traditionally used by book-keepers to record debts, losses, etc]

in there pitching *adv phr* (also **in there** or **right there** or **right in there**) Making a great effort; coping energetically and successfully; = ON TOP OF: *I'm on the go night and day, and I'm in there pitching*—Calder Willingham/ *When they needed a strong guide, he was in there*

in the ring *See* THROW one's HAT IN THE RING

in the road *See* WIDE PLACE IN THE ROAD

in the soup 1 *adv phr* fr late 1800s In trouble; under reproach: *You had better report right now, or you'll be in the soup* **2** *adj phr* In difficulties, esp in serious trouble; = IN HOT WATER: *Jeeves cocks an eyebrow, and Bertie knows he's in the soup*—Village Voice

in the straight lane *adv phr* Of a normal and respectable sort, esp not criminal nor homosexual nor drug-addicted: *referred her to Booth Street for another chance at life in the straight lane*—Milwaukee Journal

in the tank *See* GO IN THE TANK

in the tooth *See* LONG IN THE TOOTH

in the trenches *adv phr* In the workplace; in contact with the people or problems in a situation; unprotected by distance or illusion: *I needed to be back in the trenches where I could really relate to a community*—Philadelphia Journal/ *More retrospective accounts are elegant and noble. Watson told it like it was in the trenches*—Edward Yoxen

in the tub *adj phr* Bankrupt; ruined; = IN THE DUMPER

in the water *See* DEAD IN THE WATER

in the wind *See* TWIST SLOWLY IN THE WIND

in the woods *See* DOES A BEAR SHIT IN THE WOODS

in the works *See* IN THE PIPELINE

in the wrong 1 *adj phr* Mistaken; wrong; erring: *He's usually in the wrong when he discusses music* **2** *adv phr* In an unfavorable light or position: *This guy is always putting me in the wrong*

into or **inta** (IN tōō, IN tə) *prep* Currently interested or involved in; now practicing or absorbed in: *a former Ivy Leaguer named Crimpcut who is into Buddha*—Russell Baker/ *Cool it, woman, I'm inta my thing*—D Evans/ *if you're into Chinese cuisine* —Esquire

into someone **for** *adj phr* Indebted to; owing, esp money: *He's into Citibank for ten grand*

into the ground *See* RUN something INTO THE GROUND

into the twentieth century *See* DRAG someone KICKING AND SCREAMING INTO THE TWENTIETH CENTURY

intro 1 *n* An introduction or prelude of any sort: *"Listen to that intro," she says. "How awful"* —Whitney Balliett/ *the kind of intro which is important*—Rolling Stone **2** *v:* *Who'll intro the archbishop?*

invent *v* To falsify; = HOKE UP: *They invented a sweet little alibi*

invent the wheel *v phr* To labor unnecessarily through the obvious and elementary stages of something: *If you guys will stop inventing the wheel we can get on with this operation*

invitation *See* DO YOU WANT AN ENGRAVED INVITATION

invite (IN vīt) *n* An invitation: *You can't go in there without an invite*

in wrong *adv phr* In trouble; in disfavor: *I don't get in wrong with no fuzz*/ *He must have done something horrible to get that much in wrong*

in your ear *See* PUT IT IN YOUR EAR

IOU (pronounced as separate letters) *n* A promise to pay; written acknowledgment of a debt: *had won $800,000, in cash, not IOUs*—John Scarne

Irish *See* GET one's DANDER UP, LACE-CURTAIN IRISH, SHANTY IRISH

Irish banjo *See* BANJO

◁**Irish buggy** (or **local**)▷ *n phr* A wheelbarrow

◁**Irish confetti**▷ *n phr* Bricks; brickbats, esp when thrown in a fight

Irisher *n* fr early 1800s An Irish person or one of Irish descent: *the most exemplary Irisher in Hollywood*—J Bacon

◁**Irish grape**▷ *n phr* A potato

◁**Irish pennant**▷ *n phr* yachting The end of a rope, sheet, etc, carelessly left loose or trailing off a boat

◁**Irish turkey**▷ *n phr* hoboes Corned beef and cabbage

◀the **Irish way**▶ *n phr* Heterosexual anal copulation [fr the notion that such a mode of intercourse was used to prevent pregnancy]

iron 1 *n* motorcyclists fr 1920s A motorcycle; motorcycles collectively: *on old British and American iron*—Cycle World **2** *n* A car **3** *n* A pistol; = SHOOTING IRON **4** *n* The weights used in weight-lifting
See HAVE BRASS BALLS, HOT IRON, PIG-IRON, PUMP IRON, SHOOTING IRON, WAFFLE-IRON

iron betsy *n phr* Army An Army rifle

iron-burner *n* lumberjacks A blacksmith

iron hat *n phr* A derby hat; = HARD HAT

iron horse 1 *n phr* fr middle 1800s A railroad engine **2** *n phr* WW2 Army A military tank

iron house *n phr* A jail; prison

iron maiden (or **lady**) *n phr* A strict, severe, and unremittingly sober woman [in part probably fr the rigid expression and the menace of the *iron maiden*, an instrument of torture]

iron man 1 *n phr* A dollar: *two hundred iron men snatched...out of his mitt*—Charles MacArthur **2** *n phr* A very durable and tough man; tireless worker and player, esp in sports **3** *n phr* musicians A West Indian musician who plays an instrument made out of an oil drum

iron off *v phr* To pay; pay off

iron out 1 *v phr* To kill, esp with a gun: *You weren't at home when he was ironed out*—J Evans **2** *v phr* To arrange satisfactorily; straighten out; = WORK OUT: *They will meet and iron out all the problems*

iron out the kinks *v phr* To solve and settle the problems; straighten things out: *Ironing out the kinks this way made them aware of just how weak their endgame was*—Games

iron pony *n phr* A motorcycle

iron-pumper *n* A weight lifter

iron up *v phr truckers* To put on tire chains

Irvine or **Irv** *n black* A police officer

ish kabibble (ISH kə BIB əl) *interj fr early 1900s* An exclamation of indifference, nonchalance, etc: *"Ishkabibble," or "I should worry"*—CT Ryan/ *It was a pretty abrupt transition from la belle époque into the Space Age, but ish kabibble*—SJ Perelman [origin unknown; perhaps an alteration of Yiddish *nit* or *nisht gefidlt*; apparently introduced and perhaps coined by the comedienne Fanny Brice]

island *See* HOUNDS ON AN ISLAND

Island *See* CONEY ISLAND

iso *n prison* Solitary confinement or isolation cells

Isro (IZ roh) *n* A hairstyle similar to the Afro, worn by Jewish males

Is the Pope Polish (or **Italian** or **Catholic**) *sentence* That was a stupid question; isn't the answer very obvious?; = DOES A BEAR SHIT IN THE WOODS ● First variant used since the accession of John Paul II

it **1** *n fr early 1900s* A stupid person; = BOOB **2** *n fr early 1900s, esp 1920s & 30s* Sex appeal, esp female: *a girl with lots of it* **3** *modifier:* Clara *Bow, the original it girl* **4** *n fr 1400s* The sex act; copulation; = SCREWING ● Used in numberless unmistakable but quasi-euphemistic contexts like **do it**, **go at it**, **want it**, **have it off**, **make it**, etc [first sense fr the distinction in pronoun between a person and a mere thing; sexual senses fr euphemistic and often arch uses where the indefinite pronoun takes on intense explicit meaning from the sexual referent and finally supplants the referent entirely, a process attested as early as the mid-15th century]

◀**Italian football**▶ *n phr* A bomb; grenade, as used by criminals; = GUINEA FOOTBALL

itch *See* SCRATCH

itch and rub *See* CHIEF ITCH AND RUB

itchy *adj* Eager; restless; = ANTSY

it couldn't happen to a nicer guy *sentence* What punishment or damage was received was richly deserved ● The sentiment is quite ironical: *Joe got canned? It couldn't happen to a nicer guy!*

item *See* HOT NUMBER

an item *n phr* A matter of interest and comment, esp a sexual relationship; = a NUMBER: *Book Says Ava and Adlai Were An Item*—New York/ *She and I used to be an item*

it girl *n phr esp 1920s & 30s* A young woman with sex appeal

-itis *suffix used to form nouns* An excessive and probably unhealthy involvement with or prevalence of what is indicated: *committeeitis/ symbolitis*

it's a bitch (or **bitch kitty**) *sentence* The thing referred to is very impressive, very difficult, very complicated, very sad, or in some other way extraordinary: *She shook his knee playfully. "It's a bitch, isn't it?"*—Armistead Maupin/ *The last couple of laps are a real bitch kitty*

it's at *See* KNOW WHERE IT'S AT

it's been real or **it's been** *sentence* It has been nice to meet you, it has been a nice time or party, etc ● Often used ironically

it shouldn't happen to a dog *sentence* What has happened, often to the speaker, ought not to happen even to the lowliest of creatures; it is atrocious: *The trouble I had getting this ticket, it shouldn't happen to a dog* [fr Yiddish speech patterns]

it's you *sentence* The thing is precisely appropriate or integral to you: *Oh my sweet, that mauve cummerbund, it's you!*

it takes two to tango *sentence* This cannot happen or have happened without more than one person; cooperation or connivance is indicated: *It takes two to tango, said the mediator*—Philadelphia Journal/ *Now, it takes two to tango, but I still think it was more her fault*—San Francisco [the name of a song popular in the 1930s]

it up *suffix used to intensify verbs* Doing energetically, vehemently, loudly, etc, what is indicated: *camping it up/ laughing it up*

◁**it will be** (or **it's**) someone's **ass** *sentence* That will be the end or ruination of someone; someone will be severely punished: *You write anything about me in an article again and it'll be your ass*—Joseph Heller/ *We have to find this outlaw an hour after daybreak or it's our asses!*—Don Pendleton [fr an elliptical way of saying *that will be the end of you* based on the notion that the *ass* equals the person]

ivories **1** *n fr late 1700s* The teeth: *as fine a display of ivories as we've seen in our time*—New Yorker **2** *n fr early 1800s* Dice; a pair of dice

the ivories *n fr early 1900s* Piano keys; the piano *See* TICKLE THE IVORIES

ivory **1** *n fr late 1800s* A billiard ball **2** *n* The skull **3** *n* A tooth

ivory-dome **1** *n early 1900s* A stupid person; = BONEHEAD **2** *n esp 1940s* An intellectual; = EGGHEAD

ivory-hunter *n* A recruiter or scout, esp a baseball scout

ivory-thumper *n* A piano player: *some cheap little ivory thumper*—James M Cain

ixnay *negation* No; no more; none: *Ixnay on the kabitz*—American Mercury [pig Latin for *nix*]

izzatso *interj* An exclamation of defiance or disbelief: *I'm a crud? Izzatso!*

J

J *n* (Variations: **jay** or **jay smoke** or **J smoke**) A marijuana cigarette; =JOINT [fr the *J* of *Mary Jane* "marijuana" or the *j* of *joint*]

jab a vein *v phr narcotics* To inject narcotics, esp heroin; =SHOOT UP: *smoke marijuana or opium...or jab a vein*—Stephen Longstreet

jabber 1 *n narcotics fr early 1900s* A hypodermic needle **2** *v* To talk incessantly; chatter on *See* JIBBER-JABBER

jabberjack *n* Foolish talk; nonsense; =BULLSHIT: *When I hear all the false jabberjack, all the phony cries and squawks*—Newsweek

jab-off *n narcotics* An injection of a narcotic

◁**jaboney** or **jiboney** or **jibone**▷ **1** *n* A newly arrived immigrant; a naive person; =GREENHORN: *Vinny, you're a real jibone, you know that?*—Richard Price **2** *n* A hoodlum; thug; =GORILLA: *He had a couple of his jiboneys with him*—Lionel Stander [origin unknown; perhaps fr Italian dialect]

jack 1 *n* Money: *the fans which paid their jack*—H Witwer/ *I figured it would be an easy way to make some jack*—Village Voice **2** *v Air Force fr Vietnam War* To take twisting evasive action in an airplane; =JANK, JINK [first sense probably fr an 18th-century idiom *make one's jack* "succeed, get rich," perhaps fr the game of bowls; but see mid-19th-century British *jack* "a gambling counter resembling a sovereign"; second sense perhaps related to mid-19th-century British criminal slang *jack* "run away, escape," or perhaps by folk etymology fr *jank*, an echoic companion of *jink*; compare *jink-jank* with *yin-yang* and *zig-zag*] *See* ACTING JACK, BALL THE JACK, HEAVY MONEY, HIGHJACK, PIECE OF CHANGE, SINGLE-JACK

Jack¹ *n* Man; friend; fellow; =MAC ● Used in addressing any man, whatever his name: *Man, he's murder, Jack*—Max Shulman/ *Looking for trouble, Jack?*

Jack² *n lunch counter* A grilled cheese sandwich [fr *grilled American cheese*]

jack around *fr students* **1** *v phr* To idle about; =FART AROUND, SCREW AROUND: *He and LD had been jacking around in practice and LD fell on his leg*—Peter Gent **2** *v phr* To meddle with; =FOOL AROUND: *and jack around with somebody else's wife*—Dan Jenkins/ *until the lawyers started jacking around with the structure*—Toronto Life

jack someone **around** *fr students* **1** *v phr* To tease; =KID: *These guys are only trying to jack you around*—Dan Jenkins **2** *v phr* To harass; pester; victimize; =JERK someone AROUND: *Don't you think I know when people are jacking me around?*—Armistead Maupin

jackass *n fr early 1800s* A stupid person; idiot; dolt; fool

Jack Benny (or **Back**) *n phr lunch counter* A grilled cheese sandwich with bacon [lunch counter *Jack* fr *grilled American cheese* plus *Benny* or *Back* for *bacon*, the first fr the name of the popular radio and television comedian *Jack Benny*]

jacked up 1 *adj phr* Stimulated; exhilarated; =HIGH: *all the parents jacked up on coffee*—Cameron Crowe **2** *adj phr* Elevated, esp by artifice; =JUMPED-UP: *That he is a jacked-up cowboy and minor film star is a libel*—National Review

jackeroo *n cowboys* A cowboy [perhaps fr Spanish *vaquero*; see buckeroo]

jacket *See* DUST someone's JACKET, MONKEY JACKET, YELLOW JACKET

◁**jack off**▷ *v* To masturbate; =JERK OFF ● Said chiefly of males [ultimately fr *jack* "penis"]

◁**jack-off** or **jagoff**▷ *n* A stupid, incompetent person; =JERK: *What's that jack-off up to now?*/ *those two slick-haired jagoffs*—William Brashler

jack out *v phr* To pull out; seize and expose: *could jack his gun out kind of fast*—Raymond Chandler

jackpot *n fr late 1800s* A very large payoff in a gambling game, esp the largest win available in a slot machine [fr the *progressive jack pot* in poker, which stipulates that if no player has a pair of jacks or better to open, then on the next hand, after anteing again, someone must have queens or better, and so on; thus the *pot* could become quite large] *See* CUT UP THE TOUCHES, HIT THE JACKPOT

jackroll *v fr middle 1800s Canadian* To rob, esp a drunken man; =ROLL: *Father had recently been "jackrolled" while drunk*—WJ Slocum

◁**jack shit**▷ *n phr fr esp southern college students* Nothing at all; =DIDDLY, ZILCH: *They had it, but jack shit was what they had*—Robert Stone/ *I didn't know jackshit about it*—Richard Merkin/ *"Ex-model" means jackshit*—Jessica Lange

jack up 1 *v phr narcotics* To inject a narcotic; =SHOOT UP **2** *v phr* To stimulate; exhilarate: *Aren't you getting jacked up?...Ain't it great?*—Washington Post **3** *v phr* To raise; increase:

Did they jack up the price of booze again? **4** *v phr* police = TAKE ON

jack someone **up 1** *v phr* fr late 1800s To rebuke, esp to revive a sense of duty: *The sergeant had to jack the whole platoon up* **2** *v phr* To rob, esp at gunpoint **3** *v phr* To thrash; trounce; = CLOBBER **4** *v phr* black To search and question a suspect: *On the way home a couple of cops jacked me up*

jag *fr late 1800s fr 1600s British dialect* **1** *n* A drinking spree; = BENDER **2** *n* A spell or spree of a specified sort: *One had a "crying jag"*—P Marks/ *the annual Christmas gift-buying jag*—Hal Boyle
See CRYING JAG

jagged (JAGD) *adj fr early 1700s* Drunk

jag house *n phr* homosexuals A house of male prostitution [probably fr *jack* "penis"]

jagoff *See* JACK-OFF

jail bait ◁**1**▷ *n phr* A girl below the legal age of sexual consent, copulation with whom would constitute statutory rape **2** *n phr* Any person or thing likely to tempt one to crime and imprisonment

jailbird *n fr 1600s British* A convict or ex-convict

jailhouse lawyer *n phr* A prisoner who, authoritative or not, is disposed to lengthy discussion of his legal rights and those of other inmates; = GUARD-HOUSE LAWYER: *an avid reader of good literature and a "jailhouse lawyer"*—E Ranzal

jake 1 *adj* outdated fr early 1900s Excellent; very satisfactory; = HUNKY-DORY: *She said the whole college seemed jake to her*—P Marks **2** *adv:* *You never can tell on a day like this, things could be goin' jake one minute, then presto, before you know it you're history*—Village Voice [origin unknown]

jalopy or **jaloppy** or **jalop 1** *n fr 1920s* An old and battered car or airplane; = HEAP: *A jalopy is a model one step above a "junker"*—New York Times **2** *n* Any car; any vehicle; = BUGGY: *Let them search every jalop on the road*—Gangbusters (radio program) [origin unknown]

jam¹ 1 *n fr late 1800s British* A predicament; = BIND, TIGHT SPOT **2** *n* A tight crush of cars, people, etc; = JAM-UP **3** *n* underworld Small objects like rings and watches that are easy to steal **4** *v* jazz musicians fr 1930s To play jazz with great spontaneity, esp to improvise freely with other musicians and usu without an audience **5** *modifier:* *Jam bands do have styles*—C Smith **6** *n* jazz musicians fr 1930s A party or gathering where jazz musicians play for or with one another; = JAM SESSION: *Bix and the boys would blow it free and the jam was on*—Stephen Longstreet **7** *v* esp students fr 1930s black To have a good time; party joyously; = GET IT ON **8** *n:* *The kids were having a jam upstairs* **9** *v* esp New York teenagers To make up a rap song, esp in a competitive situation **10** *v* To make trouble for; coerce or harass, esp with physical force: *than when they're jammin' me for a penny every time I walk down the street*—Newsweek/ *He knows what to say that will jam you and not jam you*—New York ◁**11**▷ *n fr black possibly fr late 1800s British* The vulva; a woman's

genitals ◁**12**▷ *v* esp college students: To do the sex act; copulate; = SCREW: *Did what? Jammed* —Paul Theroux **13** *n* narcotics Cocaine **14** *v* hawkers To auction; act as an auctioneer **15** *v* To send an interfering signal on a broadcast channel one wishes to make unintelligible: *An attempt was made to jam The Voice of America* [all senses have some relation to the basic notion of squeezing or crushing so as to make *jam*]
See IN A JAM, JIM-JAM, LOGJAM, TOE JAM

jam² *n* homosexuals A heterosexual man [said to be fr *just a man*]

jam auction (or **pitch**) *n phr* hawkers A hawker's business carried on in a store, esp one where cheap knickknacks, souvenirs, jewelry, etc, are sold

jamble *See* JIMBLE-JAMBLE

James *See* JESSE JAMES

jammed *adj* Drunk: *He got jammed*—Philadelphia Bulletin

jammed up 1 *adj phr* In a glutted condition; immobilized or burdened by some sort of excess: *Traffic's jammed up for six miles on the thruway/ I can't have lunch today, I'm too jammed up at the office* **2** *adj phr* = IN A JAM

jammer *n* jazz talk A musician who takes part in jam sessions: *the likely jammers being the four ex-Beatles, Leon Russell, Mick Jagger, and a few other "friends"*—Rolling Stone
See CAMEL-JAMMER, GEAR-JAMMER

jammy *adj fr middle 1800s British* Very lucky

jamoke or **Jamoke** (jə MOHK) **1** *n fr armed forces & hoboes* Coffee **2** *n* A man; fellow; = GUY: *If I was going to find out what kind of jamoke Marlin was*—J Evans/ *I don't rate your chances none too good if that jamoke's going to defend you*—George V Higgins [first sense perhaps a blend of *java* and *mocha*; second sense perhaps echoic-symbolic fr *jerk, joker,* and the like]

jam-packed *adj* Very tightly packed; very crowded: *those jam-packed suburban classes*—New York

the **jams** *See* the JIM-JAMS, KICK OUT THE JAMS

jam session *n phr* jazz musicians fr 1930s A gathering of musicians, esp jazz musicians, playing freely and for one another, but sometimes in a public performance; = JAM: *Here's Dodo on the piano and Tiny on the bass. Looks like we'll have a fine jam session*—Slim Gaillard

jam-up *n* A tight crush of people, cars, etc, preventing normal movement; = JAM: *to forestall the possibility of another jam-up*—James M Cain

jane 1 *n* A young woman; = CHICK, DOLL: *some jane that was kind of simple*—A Lomax/ *Ladies from Long Island, janes from New Jersey*—New York Times **2** *n* A man's sweetheart, fiancée, etc: *make earrings for our janes out of them studs* —Langston Hughes **3** *n* A women's toilet; = JOHN

Jane *n* An average woman
See MARY JANE

Jane Crow *n phr* Discrimination against women: *segregation by sex, describing it as "Jane Crow"* —Life [fr *Jim Crow*]

Jane Doe *n phr* Any woman; the average woman; =JANE

Jane Q Citizen (or **Public**) *n phr* Any woman, esp the average or typical woman: *The president seems very popular with Jane Q Citizen*

janfu *n WW2 armed forces* Confusion; chaos; =SNAFU [fr *joint Army Navy fuck-up*]

◁**jang**▷ *n* The penis
See YING-YANG

jangle **See** JINGLE-JANGLE

jank *v Air Force fr Vietnam War* To maneuver an airplane about evasively; =JACK, JINK: *I was janking...when I got hit*—Time

janney *v railroad* To couple cars, an engine, etc

◀**Jap**▶ (JAP) *n* A Japanese or person of Japanese descent; =NIP
See JEWISH AMERICAN PRINCESS

Japanese geometry **See** HARDER THAN CHINESE ARITHMETIC

jarhead **1** *n* A mule ◀**2**▶ *n* A black man **3** *n WW2 armed forces* A US Marine; =GYRENE

jasper **1** *n* A fellow; man; =GUY: *two jaspers with a grudge*—H Birney **2** *n* A rustic; =HICK

java or **Java** *n fr middle 1800s* Coffee [fr *Java*, an Indonesian island whence some coffee was exported]

jaw **1** *v fr late 1800s* To talk; chat; converse: *Can't stand here jawing with you all day*—SJ Perelman **2** *n: ain't had a good jaw together*—WR Burnett **3** *v* To exhort; lecture; strive to persuade orally; =JAWBONE: *had kept sober for several months by jawing drunks, unsuccessfully*—J Alexander
See BAT one's GUMS, CRACK one's JAW, FLAPJAW, GLASS JAW, RATCHET-MOUTH, REST one's JAW

jawbone **1** *v fr late 1800s cowboys* To borrow; obtain on credit: *He jawboned enough...to set up an office*—Robert Ruark **2** *n fr late 1800s* Credit or trust, esp financial: *Try as he might he got no jawbone from the bankers* **3** *n fr late 1800s* A loan **4** *adv fr late 1800s* On credit or trust: *He bought the machine jawbone* **5** *v* To discuss; talk over, esp extensively and profoundly: *a distinguished group of presidential biographers to jawbone about the situation*—Washington Post **6** *v* To exhort and earnestly urge in order to persuade ● Used predominantly to describe high-level pressure applied on economic issues: *the Presidential promise not to "jawbone" business into not raising prices*—Commonweal/ *chiefly direct controls on all pay and prices or "jawboning" against individual wage and price rises*—Wall Street Journal **7** *n: The President launched a sustained and hot jawbone on the budget cuts* **8** *v WW2 Army* To fire a weapon in practice, esp for formal qualification to use it [the senses having to do with credit and trust are related to *jawbone* "talk without action," attested in the 19th century]

jawboning *n* Strong exhortation; potent oral pressure: *The technique was called "jawboning." Lyndon Johnson and Mr Nixon used it*—Newsweek

jawbreaker or **jawcracker** **1** *n* A long word or a word difficult to pronounce: *Diphenylpentoactomaggetoneplangianoliosis is something of*

a jawbreaker **2** *n fr middle 1800s* A piece of hard candy, esp a spherical piece with bubble gum in the center

jawed **See** GLASS-JAWED

jay[1] **1** *n fr late 1800s* A rustic; simpleton; =HICK, RUBE **2** *n underworld* An easy victim; =MARK, PATSY, SUCKER [probably fr the stupid, raucous bird]

jay[2] *n* Marijuana or a marijuana cigarette; =J: *Let's do up a jay and truck on down to the libo*—Esquire

Jayhawker *n fr middle 1800s* A native or resident of Kansas [fr a term for "freebooter, guerilla," applied during the Civil War to pro-slavery raiders]

jay smoke **See** J

jaywalk *v fr early 1900s* To walk into or across a street at a forbidden place or without the right of way [fr the naive behavior of a *jay* "rustic"]

jazz ◁**1**▷ *v* To do the sex act with or to; =FUCK: *I jazzed her, too*—James T Farrell **2** *v* To increase the tempo, animation, or excitement of something; =JAZZ something UP: *Come on, jazz yourself, we're late* **3** *n: This place needs more jazz and pizzazz* **4** *n jazz musicians fr early 1900s* A kind of popular, often improvised, and emotive instrumental music originating among southern black people in the late 19th century, and still evolving as an American and a world style **5** *v* To arrange or play in a jazz style: *They jazzed the National Anthem* **6** *modifier: a jazz trumpet/ jazz riffs* **7** *n* Empty talk; nonsense; lies; =BALONEY, BULLSHIT, JIVE: *You mean her most eloquent pledges were jazz?* **8** *v: Stop your jazzing and merely adduce the data* **9** *n* Ornamentation; embellishment, esp when merely superficial: *a clean design, without a lot of jazz* [origin unknown; *jass* was an earlier spelling]
See ALL THAT JAZZ

jazz-bo **1** *n* A flashily groomed man or woman; =CAT, DUDE: *her stage image as a witchy little jazzbo with a boxer's shuffle and a baseball player's kick*—Time ◀**2**▶ *n* A black man, esp a black soldier

jazzed *adj teenagers* Alert and energetic; =PSYCHED UP

jazzed up *adj phr* Made faster, more exciting, interesting, active, etc; =HOPPED UP, HYPED: *A jazzed up version of Little Women might just work*

jazz it *v phr* To play or sing a piece of music in a jazz style

jazz something **up** **1** *v phr* To make faster, more exciting or stimulating, etc: *He tried to jazz the meeting up* **2** *v phr* To play in the musical style indicated

jazzy **1** *adj* Resembling or partaking of the musical style indicated: *He could turn a Beethoven sonata into a jazzy little number* **2** *adj* Exciting; stimulating: *He wore bow ties and...jazzy suits*—Truman Capote

jeans **1** *n fr middle 1800s* Trousers; pants: *I had the price in my jeans*—Jack London **2** *n* Blue denim work pants or trousers that are modifications of these [fr *jean fustian*, a cloth originating in *Gene* (Genoa), Italy]
See STRETCH SOME JEANS

jeasly or **jeasely** *adj* Of little worth; trivial: *here is his jeasely ol' pie and biscuit irons*—Stewart Holbrook [probably echoic-symbolic]

Jebby *n* A Jesuit

jeebies *See* the HEEBIE-JEEBIES

jeep 1 *n* *fr WW2 Army* A useful and durable small open US military vehicle of World War 2, later adapted to civilian use and still evolving **2** *v*: *jeeping...through Maquis-held territory*—Time **3** *n* = JEEP CARRIER [fr the name and cry of a small versatile creature in the comic strip "Thimble Theatre" by EC Segar, and the military designation *GP* "general purpose" in the designation of the little vehicle]

jeep carrier *n phr* *WW2 Navy* A US Navy escort aircraft carrier

Jeepers Creepers or **Jeepers** *interj* An exclamation of surprise, dismay, emphasis, etc: *Jeepers Creepers, another busted leg!* [a euphemism for *Jesus Christ*]

jeep-jockey *n* *WW2 Army* A jeep driver

Jeez *interj* (Variations: **jeez** or **Jeeze** or **jeeze** or **Jees** or **jees** or **jeezy-peezy** or **Jeezy-peezy**) An exclamation of surprise, dismay, emphasis, etc; = JEEPERS CREEPERS [fr *Jesus*]

jeff or **Jeff** *black fr 1930s* **1** *n* A white person **2** *v* To take on the values of the dominant white society; = TOM: *same people Profilin' and Jeffin' for their survival*—Amsterdam News **3** *n* A tedious person; = SQUARE [fr *Jefferson* Davis, president of the Confederacy during the Civil War]

See SILVER JEFF

jelly 1 *n* An easy, pleasant task; sinecure; = CINCH **2** *n* Anything gotten free or without effort; = GRAVY **3** *n* = JELLY-ROLL

jellybean 1 *n* *early 1900s* A gaudily dressed man; faddish dresser **2** *n* *fr early 1900s* A stupid person; fool; = SAP: *The jelly beans I went to school with*—Richard Bissell **3** *n* *baseball* A novice; = ROOKIE

jelly-belly *n* A fat person

jelly-roll *black fr late 1800s* ◁**1**▷ *n* The vulva; vagina ◁**2**▷ *n* The sex act; copulation; = FUCKING **3** *n* A man obsessed with women; woman-chaser; = COCKSMAN, LOVER-BOY **4** *n* A lover or mistress; = SWEET PAPA, SWEET MAMA

jeppo 1 *n* *lumberjacks* A cook **2** *v*: *He jeppoed awhile in Oregon*

jerk 1 *n* *early 1900s* A short branch railroad line: *a small "jerk" with only two locals a day*—Jack London **2** *n* *cabdrivers fr 1920s* A short ride **3** *n* *fr 1930s* A tedious and ineffectual person, esp a man; fool; ninny; = BOOB, TURKEY: *Jeez, what a jerk!* —American Scholar/ *The poor jerk just made a wrong turn* **4** *n* *fr 1930s* A contemptible and obnoxious person, esp a man; = ASSHOLE, BASTARD: *I'm not talking to that jerk since he ran out on his family* **5** *modifier*: *my jerk cousin/ a couple of jerk wops*—I, Mobster **6** *n* = SODA JERK ◁**7**▷ *v* = JERK OFF **8** *v* To draw or pull out: *He jerked a gun and that's all she wrote* [the derogatory term comes fr *jerk off* "masturbate"]

See CIRCLE JERK, KNEE-JERK, PULL someone's CHAIN, SODA JERK

jerk around *v phr* To idle about; play casually; = FOOL AROUND: *if kids are jerking around and enter a system as a lark with no intent to deprive*—Newsweek

jerk someone **around** (or **off**) *v phr* To victimize or harass: *Salespeople feel that men who want hand holding are often jerking them around*—Philadelphia/ *bumming cigarettes...and generally jerking him around throughout the broadcast*—Rolling Stone/ *I think Coyle was jerking you off*—George V Higgins

jerk (or **yank**) someone's **chain** *v phr* To victimize or harass; = JERK someone AROUND: *You came out to jerk my chain tonight*—George V Higgins/ *Are you guys yanking my chain?*—Hill Street Blues (TV program) [fr the notion of a chained man, monkey, etc, being harassed]

Jerkimer *See* HERKIMER JERKIMER

Jerk McGee *n phr* A stupid person; = JERK: *Some Jerk McGee like you just got off the boat*—J Cannon

◁**jerk off**▷ **1** *v phr* To masturbate; = JACK OFF: *I went ahead as usual and jerked off into my sock* —Philip Roth/ *KB was always trying to jerk off* —Claude Brown **2** *v phr* To idle about; = FUCK OFF, GOOF OFF

◁**jerk-off**▷ **1** *modifier* Useful for masturbation: *an electric suction jerk-off device*—Village Voice **2** *adj* Stupid; = JERKY: *It's too much of a jerk-off idea* —Rolling Stone/ *preparing an answer to the jerkoff question*—Easyriders **3** *n* A person who jerks off, either literally or figuratively: *I'd be tickled to death to lose the jerk-offs*—Rolling Stone

jerk soda *v phr* *fr late 1800s* To work at a soda fountain: *They had spent their tender years jerking sodas*—American Mercury

jerk (or **jerkwater**) **town** *n phr* *fr late 1800s* A small town; an insignificant village: *to fool around a jerk town*—J Flynt

jerkwater *adj* Insignificant; trivial: *These seem like jerkwater sentiments*

jerk water (or **soup**) *v phr* *railroad* To take on boiler water, esp by scooping from a trough between the rails

jerky *adj* Having the traits of a jerk: *any jerky Joe* —Billy Rose

See HERKY-JERKY

jerry 1 *n* *railroad* A track laborer; = GANDY DANCER **2** *n* *hoboes* Any laborer **3** *n* *underworld* A small pistol that can be easily concealed

jerry gang *n phr* *railroad* A track-laying crew

Jersey green *n phr* *narcotics* A type of marijuana

Jersey lightning *n phr* *fr middle 1800s* Applejack brandy [fr the fact that applejack brandy was (and still is) distilled in New Jersey]

Jerusalem Slim *n phr* *hoboes* Jesus Christ

Jesse James *n phr* *miners* Anyone who cheats, esp one who cheats workers

Jesus *n* = the BEJESUS

See EAST JESUS, EAST JESUS STATE

Jesus boots *n phr* *esp 1960s counterculture* Men's sandals

Jesus freaks (or **people**) *n phr esp 1960s counterculture* Members of an evangelical Christian religious movement among young people, esp exhippies and drug addicts: *in this light the herds of Jesus freaks*—M Rossman/ *Jesus freaks, gypsies, lunatic right-wingers, leering conventioneers*—Psychology Today

the **jet set** *n phr* The group of wealthy, chic people who move about from one costly venue to another: *a charter member of the international jet set*—Time

the **jetties** *n phr* Jet fatigue; jet lag: *She was disoriented a couple days by a bad case of the jetties*

◀**Jewboy**▶ *n* A Jewish boy or man

◀**Jew** (or **jew**) **down**▶ *v phr fr late 1800s* To bargain and haggle in an attempt to get a lower price: *but then the guy started jewin' me down*—Philadelphia

jewels *See* FAMILY JEWELS

Jewfro *n police* A hairstyle similar to the Afro; = ISRO: *wild curly hair that stood out from their heads like pyramids of Brillo, what police slang called a Jewfro*—Beth Gutcheon

Jewish Alps *n phr* The Catskill Mountains in southern New York State; = BORSCHT BELT: *I could never go back to the Jewish Alps with any woman whose name was Birdye*—Paul Sann

◀**Jewish American Prince**▶ *n phr* A pampered and usu wealthy young man who feels he deserves special treatment

◀**Jewish American Princess** or **JAP** or **Jap**▶ *n phr* A pampered and usu wealthy young woman who feels she deserves special treatment: *plenty of Jewish American Princesses in their wigs and false eyelashes*—Xaviera Hollander/ *the unofficial, secret JAP within me*—Village Voice

◀**Jewish flag**▶ *n phr hoboes* A dollar bill

◀**Jewish lightning**▶ *n phr* What causes buildings, usu old ones, to burn so that insurance can be collected; arson

Jewish penicillin *n phr* Chicken soup

◀**jibagoo**▶ *See* JIGABOO

jibber-jabber **1** *v* To talk nonsense; = JABBER: *Time for Congress to quit jibber-jabbering*—Philadelphia Bulletin **2** *n:* *Cut out the jibber-jabber*

jiboney *See* JABONEY

jice *See* NEW JICE

a **jiffy** **1** *n phr* (Variations: **jif** or **jiff** or **jiffin** or **jiffing**) *fr 1700s* A short space of time; an instant: *drop off to sleep for a jiffy*—SJ Perelman/ *I'll be ready in a jif/ I'll have coffee ready in a jiff*—Lawrence Sanders **2** *modifier:* *a jiffy dessert/ jiffy pronouncements* [said to be fr thieves' slang *jeffey* or *jiffey* "lightning"]

jiffy bag **1** *n phr* A small canvas or leather bag for carrying toilet articles, etc, while traveling **2** *n phr* (also **Jiffy**, a trade name) A heavy-walled paper bag used for mailing items, esp books

jig **1** *n* A dancing party or public dance ◀**2**▶ = JIGABOO

◀**jigaboo**▶ (Variations: **jibagoo** or **jigabo** or **jig** or **zig** or **zigaboo** or **zigabo**) *fr early 1900s* **1** *n* A black person **2** *modifier:* *a jig band*

jigger **1** *n late 1800s hoboes* An artificially made sore, usu on the arm or leg, useful in begging; *whether it will pay to use his "jigger"*—J Flynt **2** *n students* An ice-cream sundae **3** *n* A liquor glass of one-and-a-half ounce capacity; = SHOT GLASS **4** *v hoboes* To interfere with; = QUEER: *jigger our riding on the railroad*—J Flynt **5** *v* To tamper with or falsify: *There is pressure from Casey...to jigger estimates*—New York Times

See DOODAD, I'LL BE DAMNED

jiggered *See* I'LL BE DAMNED

jigger-man or **jiggers guy** *n* or *n phr underworld* A lookout: *acted only as "the two-block jiggers guy"*—LF McHugh

jiggers or **jigs** *interj* An exclamation of alarm and warning: *Jiggers, the heat's here*

jiggery-pokery *n fr late 1800s British* Deception; trickery; = SKULLDUGGERY: *or what some term jiggery-pokery*—Time/ *could have prevented most of the jiggery-pokery*—New Yorker [fr Scottish *joukery-paukery* fr *jouk* "trick"]

jiggins *See* JUGGINS

jiggle or **jiggly** **1** *n* The bouncing and shaking of a woman's parts, esp of the breasts ● Hence the whole tone and style of blatant female sexual exploitation: *help put the jiggle back in the series "Charlie's Angels"*—People Weekly **2** *modifier:* *the ads for comedies in the jiggle genre*—TV Guide **3** *v:* *She swims, jumps rope, and practices jiggling in front of the mirror*—Philadelphia **4** *n* A TV program featuring the bouncing and shaking of a woman's parts: *when advertisers see wall-to-wall jigglies in prime time*—New York Times

◀**Jiggs**▶ *n outdated carnival* A black carnival worker

◁**jig-jig** or **zig-zig**▷ *n* The sex act; copulation; = FUCKING

jigmaree *n fr early 1800s* A new gadget

jig-swiggered *See* I'LL BE DAMNED

jillion *n* (also **gillion** or **skillion** or **zillion**) A great many; an indefinitely large number; = SCADS: *a jillion jackpots*—Time/ *The beautiful people who would be at her cocktail party ("A zillion horny studs!")*—Lawrence Sanders

jim *v underworld* To ruin; spoil; = JIMMY UP

jimble-jamble *adj* Mixed; motley: *a jimble-jamble sort of crowd*—Village Voice

Jim Crow ◀**1**▶ *n phr fr early 1800s* A black person **2** *n phr* Segregation and discrimination against black people, and the laws and practices that accompany them: *My first experience with Jim Crow*—Louis Armstrong/ *Jim Crow killed Bessie Smith*—Tennessee Williams **3** *modifier:* *Jim Crow statutes/ Jim Crow toilets* **4** *v:* *I would like to...say that the people who Jim Crow me have a white heart*—Langston Hughes **5** *n phr railroad* A wooden railroad tie unfit for sale or use [fr a character in a minstrel-show song]

See CROW JIM

jim-dandy **1** *n fr late 1800s* A person or thing that is remarkable, wonderful, superior, etc; = BEAUT, HUMDINGER **2** *adj:* *a jim-dandy speech/ Anacin is a jim-dandy remedy*—Philip Hamburger

jim-jam *v* = JAZZ, JAZZ something UP

the **jim-jams** *n phr fr middle 1800s* =the HEEBIE-JEEBIES

jimjick *n* Something one does not know the name of or does not wish to name; =GIZMO, THINGAMAJIG: *this jimjick here, the trigger*—SJ Perelman

jimmies *n* Bits of candy put onto ice cream as a topping

the **jimmies** *n phr* Nervous frets; =the HEEBIE-JEEBIES: *Frankly it gives me the jimmies*—Wolcott Gibbs

jimmy *n shoeshop* A cork inner sole

jimmy up *v phr* To spoil something; damage; =BUGGER: *This scale's all jimmied up*

jingle *n* A telephone call; a ring; =TINKLE: *We never hear from you, not even a jingle*—Any Number Can Play (movie)

jingle-jangle 1 *n* Money; coins **2** *adj* In poor condition; ramshackle: *driving down to Big Sur in their funky bus or some jingle-jangle car*—Rolling Stone

jink *v fr Vietnam War Air Force fr earlier British* To take evasive action; dodge; zig-zag: *went jinking down the field, shot and missed*—Paul Theroux [fr northern English dialect *jink* "make a quick evasive turn," adopted into the idiom of rugby football]

jinks *See* HIGH-JINKS

jinky-board *n* A seesaw

jinny *n 1920s* A speakeasy
See FLYING-JINNY

jinx 1 *n fr early 1900s* A cause of bad luck: *Somebody around here is a jinx* **2** *n* A curse; assured ill fortune: *Looks like the place has a jinx on it* **3** *v*: *Somebody jinxed him* [apparently fr *jynx* or *iynx* "wryneck woodpecker," fr the use of the bird in divination]

jip *See* GYP

jippo *n esp WWI armed forces fr British* Fat or grease; drippings: *He dipped his bread in the jippo and sighed with pleasure* [fr the mid-19th-century nautical sense "gravy," of obscure origin]
See GYPPO

jism ◀1▶ *n* Semen; =CUM **2** *n* (also **gism**) *fr middle 1800s* Liveliness; excitement; spunk; =ZING [origin unknown]

jit 1 *n* A nickel; five cents ◀2▶ *n* A black person

jitney 1 *n fr late 1800s* A nickel; =JIT **2** *n* (also **jitney bus**) *fr early 1900s* A small bus used as public transportation ● Formerly, jitneys were cars operating for low fare in more or less unregulated competition with taxis, buses, and street cars **3** *modifier*: *cracked down today on illegal jitney service*—Philadelphia Bulletin **4** *n* Any car, esp a small or cheap one **5** *n* A cheap cigar; nickel cigar **6** *adj* Cheap: *a jitney dance hall*—G Millburn [origin unknown; perhaps fr French *jeton* "token"]

jitter 1 *v* To tremble; quiver: *A line of...half-washed clothes jittered on a rusty wire*—Raymond Chandler **2** *v* To be nervous; be agitated; fret: *I jittered around the house...unable to concentrate on anything*—H Allen Smith [echoic-symbolic]

jitterbug *1930s jive talk* **1** *n* A devotee of swing music, esp one who dances to swing: *Jitterbugs are the extreme swing addicts*—Life **2** *v* To dance to swing music: *Do you feel like jitterbugging a little bit?*—JD Salinger

the **jitterbug** *n phr 1930s jive talk* A fast, freely improvisational, and vigorous dance done to swing music, with passages where the couple separates to do more or less spectacular solo figures

the **jitters** *n phr* A state of nervous agitation; acute restless apprehension: *I had the jitters*—Philip Wylie

jittery *adj* Nervous: *He felt all jittery and uptight*

jive[1] *fr black fr early 1900s* **1** *v* To banter; jest; tease; =KID: *She told him to quit jiving* **2** *v* To deceive, but not seriously; mislead, esp playfully **3** *n* Empty and pretentious talk; foolishness; =BALONEY, BULLSHIT: *Sugar Mouth Sammy with the same ol' tired jive*—D Evans/ *male chauvinist, damsel in distress, and all that jive*—Village Voice **4** *n* Trifles; trash: *I bought a lot of cheap jive at the five and ten cent store*—Louis Armstrong **5** *n* Swing music of the 1930s and 40s, esp as played by the big bands and played fast and excitingly: *Man, what solid jive!*—Max Shulman **6** *modifier*: *jive records/ jive dancers* **7** *v* To play or dance to fast, exciting swing music **8** *n* (also **gyve**) Marijuana or a marijuana cigarette: *So Diane smoked jive, pot, and tea*—Orville Prescott [origin unknown; perhaps fr Wolof *jev* "talk disparagingly"]
See JUKING AND JIVING, SHUCK

jive[2] *v* To jibe: *The two answers do not jive*

jive and juke *v phr college students* To have a very good time
See JUKING AND JIVING

◁**jive-ass**▷ *fr black* **1** *n* Pretentious and deceitful talk; =BULLSHIT, JIVE: *That's like jive-ass*—Rolling Stone **2** *adj* Deceitful; undependable: *Damn his lazy, jiveass soul*—Armistead Maupin/ *You better find out some place else, you jiveass punk*—Society

jive stick *n phr narcotics* A marijuana cigarette

jive talk *n phr* A fast, pattering way of talking, accompanied with finger-snapping and bodily jerks, and using the swing and jive vocabulary, affected by teenagers during the swing and jive era of the 1930s and 40s

◀**jizz** or **jizzum**▶ *n* Semen; =CUM, JISM: *puts a little body in his jizz, pumps a baby a year into the wife*—John Sayles

joanie *adj teenagers* Out-of-date; passé

job 1 *n* (also **jobbie**) A specimen or example, either of a thing or a person: *I lost two $110 imported jobs before a locksmith told me what I was doing wrong*—Saturday Review/ *She's a tough little job*—Dashiell Hammett/ *one of those big 18-wheel jobbies* **2** *n underworld fr middle 1800s* A crime; a criminal project; =CAPER: *a big payroll job* **3** *v fr underworld* To deceive; cheat; =DOUBLE-CROSS, FRAME: *Crying...that he had been jobbed*—H Asbury/ *You got jobbed, pal*—Paul Sann/ *got absolutely jobbed out of the Heisman*—Sports Illustrated **4** *n* A bowel movement
See BAG JOB, BLOW JOB, BOOB JOB, COFFEE-AND-CAKE JOB, CON GAME, COWBOY JOB, DO A JOB ON, FRAIL JOB,

GIVE someone A GREASE JOB, GOW JOB, GREASE JOB, HAND JOB, HATCHET JOB, INSIDE JOB, LAY DOWN ON THE JOB, LUBE, MENTAL JOB, NOSE JOB, PUT-UP JOB, SEX JOB, SHACK JOB, SNOW JOB, STRAIGHT JOB, TORCH JOB, TURNKEY JOB

jobbie *v* To befoul: *any ladies out there who will jobbie their pants for the camera*—Village Voice
See JOB

job pop *v phr narcotics* To inject narcotics intravenously, usu into the arm

jock **1** *n* A jockey **2** *n* = DISC JOCKEY **3** *n fr late 1700s British* The penis; the crotch: *I'll be beating the bushes with snow to my jock*—George V Higgins **4** *n* An athletic supporter; = JOCKSTRAP: *I asked him if he wanted some sweat clothes, or a jock*—Esquire **5** *n* An athlete ● Now used of both men and women, despite the phallic derivation: *The players themselves are a curious blend of woman and jock*—New York Times/ *the lucrative job proper to an all-Ivy jock*—Clara Park [the basic etymon is jock "penis," fr *jack*, probably the diminutive of *John*, which fr the 14th century has been applied to males, male-like things, and male organs; the sense "athlete" is fr *jockstrap*]
See VIDEO JOCK

jocker *hoboes* **1** *n* A homosexual hobo who lives off the begging of his boy companion **2** *n* An aggressive male homosexual

jockey *n* The driver or pilot of any vehicle: *airplane jockey/ tank jockey*
See BLIP JOCKEY, DESK JOCKEY, DISC JOCKEY, HOGGER, JEEP-JOCKEY, PSYCH-JOCKEY, SOUP JOCKEY

jockocracy *n* The athletes and former athletes who play a large role in television broadcasting: *bored with the games, utterly bored with the jockocracy*—Washington Post

jockstrap **1** *n* An athletic supporter **2** *n* An athlete; = JOCK **3** *v* To make one's living in the less glamorous and lucrative reaches of professional sports: *He spent a couple of years jockstrapping in the minor leagues*

jody *Army fr WW2 fr black* **1** *n* A civilian who is thought to be prospering back home with a soldier's sweetheart, wife, job, etc: *Jody was the guy going in the back door while you were walking down the front walk*—Soldiers **2** *n* = JODY CALL [fr the full name *Jody Grinder*, that is, fornicator, probably fr an earlier black and prison character of similar import *Oolong the Chinese Grind-boy* or *Chinese Joe the Grinder*]

jody call *n phr Army* An antiphonal song or chant done while marching or running [fr the character *Jody* used in the chant]

Joe or **joe** **1** *n* Coffee **2** *n* Man; fellow; = GUY: *Seems like a good Joe/ never seemed to share much of the problems of the ordinary joe*—Robert Ruark **3** *n fr WW2* = GI JOE **4** *n fr WW2* Any American, esp any US military man **5** *adj underworld* Informed; aware; = HEP **6** *v:* *Let me Joe you to that racket*—DW Maurier
See GI JOE, GOOD JOE, HOLY JOE, LITTLE JOE, OLD JOE, ORDINARY JOE, SLOPPY JOE

Joe Blow¹ *n phr* (Variations: **Doakes** or **Storch** or **Zilch** may replace **Blow**) *fr 1920s black jazz musicians* Any man; the average man; = JOHN DOE: *the average black "Mr Joe Blow"*—Ebony [fr the blowing of the musician, later probably thought of as referring to big talk]

Joe Blow² *n phr circus* Mealtime

Joe College *n phr esp 1920s & 30s* A young man whose dress and manner betoken the nonacademic aspects of college life: *a real Joe College type*—Leonard Feather

joe-darter *n fr middle 1800s* = HUMDINGER

joepot *n* A coffee pot

Joe Sad *n phr black* An unpopular person

Joe Schmo (or **Schmoe**) *n phr* An undistinguished and unfortunate person

◁**Joe Shit the Ragman**▷ *n phr* (Variations: **Snuffy** or **Tentpeg** may replace **Shit the Ragman**) *Army* An ordinary soldier; = BUCK PRIVATE, GI

Joe Six-pack *n phr* An ordinary American male; = JOE, JOE BLOW: *Do you think that Joe Six-pack in Illinois cares?*—National Public Radio/ *a sleazy bar where go-go girls perform for goggle-eyed Joe Six-packs*—New York Times [fr the six-bottle or -can packets of beer these men typically consume]

joey or **Joey** *n circus fr late 1800s* A clown [fr the name of *Joseph* Grimaldi, famous early-19th-century British clown and pantomimist]

Joe Yale *n phr* A young man whose dress and manner betoken the nonacademic aspects of life in the Ivy League: *this very Joe Yale-looking guy*—JD Salinger

jog *v teenagers* To annoy; bother

joggling board **1** *n phr* A seesaw; = JINKYBOARD **2** *n phr* A swing

john¹ *n fr 1930s* A toilet; = CAN: *I made a brief visit to the john*—J Evans [probably an amusing euphemism for *jack* or *jakes*, 16th-century terms for toilet]

john² *n fr WW2 Army* An Army lieutenant
See FIRST JOHN, SECOND JOHN

John **1** *n* (also **john**) *fr black* Any man; an average man; = JOE: *We don't want no poor johns on here*—A Lomax **2** *n* A man regarded as an easy victim, a potential easy sale, etc: *He's pretty smart at figurin' out what a John'll pay*—Langston Hughes **3** *n Army* Any man who keeps a girl; = DADDY, SUGAR DADDY **5** *n prostitutes fr early 1900s* (also **john**) A prostitute's customer: *even for girls turning their first tricks, pulling their first real John*—Claude Brown/ *shot an 18-year-old hooker...then plugged a john who was present*—New York Times **6** *n homosexuals* An older homosexual male who keeps a younger one **7** *n* = JOHN LAW
See BIG JOHN, DEAR JOHN, HARD JOHN, PLAY WHO SHOT JOHN, POOR JOHN, SQUARE JOHN

John B *n phr* A hat [fr *John B* Stetson, the hat maker]

John Doe or **Richard Roe** *n phr* Any man; the average man; = JOE

John dogface *n phr WW2 Army* A recruit

John Farmer *n phr* A farmer

John Hall *n phr* Alcohol

John Hancock (or **Henry**) *n phr* One's signature [fr the fact that *John Hancock* of Massachusetts was the first to sign the Declaration of Independence in 1776; *John Henry*, possibly by confusion with Patrick *Henry*, because of the prominence of *John Henry* as a folklore hero, and by near-rhyming resemblance]

John Hollowlegs *n phr* hoboes A hungry man

John Law *n phr fr* hoboes & circus A police officer; the police: *had been gathered in by John Law*—Jack London

John L's *n phr* = LONG JOHNS

Johnny or **johnny** *n* Any man; = JOE, JOHN: *The big johnny came over to talk*

Johnny-come-lately 1 *n* A person or thing only recently arrived, esp as compared with the more seasoned: *Postwar planning...was no Johnny-come-lately*—Max Shulman **2** *modifier:* a *Johnny-come-lately quasi-solution* **3** *n* An upstart

Johnny O'Brian *n phr* hoboes A boxcar

Johnny-on-the-spot *n fr late 1800s* A person who is ready and effective when needed: *Ed was Johnny-on-the-spot and we got it cleaned up quick*

Johnny Trots *n phr* = the TROTS

John Q Citizen (or **Public**) *n phr* Any man, esp the average or typical man: *John Q Citizen seems to yearn for the big cars*

John Roscoe *n phr* underworld = ROSCOE

johns *See* LONG JOHNS

◁**johnson** or **Johnson** or **jones**▷ *n esp black* The penis: *beat out time with their titties and their johnsons*—Village Voice/ *I've only got one Johnson, and he winks*—Village Voice/ *Enough is enough, turn my jones loose*—Donald Goines [origin unknown; such a use is recorded fr Canada in the mid-19th century, perhaps as a euphemism for the British euphemism *John Thomas* "penis"; the US black use may be related to the name of the boxer *Jack Johnson*, and hence to such penile terms as *jack* and *jock*]

Johnson *n* underworld A hobo; drifter; = BUM

Johnson rod *n phr* A mythical and fragile part of a machine ● Used jocularly, esp to confuse novices: *Could it be that the Johnson rod is bent?*

John Wayne Army **1** *adj phr* Very tough and durable; militarily exemplary **2** *v phr* To handle a weapon, esp a machine gun, in an ostentatiously unconventional way

John Wayne it *v phr* To be very tough, taciturn, and virile: *I'm supposed to go around John Wayneing it all the time*—San Francisco

John Wayne's brother *n phr* Army A good soldier; ideal fighting man

John Wayne's sister (or **mother**) *n phr* Army A weak, lazy, self-indulgent person

joie *See* MAISON JOIE

joinout *v phr* circus To join; join up

joint 1 *n fr late 1800s* Any disgusting or disreputable place; = DIVE, DUMP: *That evening the joint buzzed with sedition*—American Scholar/ *I took one look at the joint and nearly retched* **2** *n fr late* 1800s Any place or venue, esp of a commercial sort: *It's a swell joint, all right*—H McHugh **3** *n* One's home; residence: *Come by my joint later and I'll give you a drink* **4** *n* narcotics A marijuana cigarette; = REEFER: *inhale a joint or two of cannabis*—Time/ *I've had to hold joints in my hand...but I never smoked even one*—New York Times **5** *n* narcotics The apparatus for injecting narcotics; = HEAD KIT, WORKS ◁**6**▷ *n* The penis [place senses fr early-19th-century Anglo-Irish *joint* "low resort," perhaps from its being a nearby, joined room rather than a main room]

See BEER JOINT, the BIG JOINT, BUST-OUT JOINT, CALL HOUSE, CLIP JOINT, CREEP-JOINT, CRUMB JOINT, EAT HIGH ON THE HOG, FLAT-JOINT, GRAB-JOINT, GREASE JOINT, GYP JOINT, HAM JOINT, HOPJOINT, JUICE-JOINT, JUKE JOINT, LEAD JOINT, MITT-CAMP, MUG JOINT, ONE-ARM JOINT, PULL one's PUD, PUT someone's NOSE OUT OF JOINT, RIB JOINT, RIGHT JOINT, RUB JOINT, RUG JOINT, SCATTER-JOINT, SCHLOCK SHOP, SQUARE

-joint *combining word* Place where the indicated activity goes on, the indicated thing may be had, having the indicated quality, etc: *clip-joint/ hamburger joint/ gyp joint*

the **joint** *n phr* Prison: *in the joint*—Joseph Wambaugh

joint factory *n phr* narcotics = SMOKE SHOP

joint hop *v phr* outdated students To go from one bar or club to another, then another, etc; = BARHOP

joke *See* SICK JOKE

joker 1 *n* (also **joker in the deck**) A hidden cost, qualification, defect, nasty result, etc; = CATCH: *It all looks very sweet, but there's a joker* **2** *n fr* early 1800s A man; fellow; = GUY, CHARACTER, CLOWN ● Often derogatory: *Ask that joker who the hell he thinks he is*

jollies *n* Pleasure and gratification; thrills, esp when somewhat disreputable; = BANGS, KICKS: *People that drive Buicks are getting some kind of jollies*—A Sherman

See GET one's COOKIES

jollop *n* A large portion of food

jolt 1 *n* narcotics The initial impact of a narcotic injection; = RUSH **2** *n* narcotics A narcotic injection **3** *v: We didn't want to jolt*—D Hulburd **4** *n* narcotics A marijuana cigarette; = JOINT **5** *n* A drink of liquor; = SNORT: *a wee jolt of Bourbon*—F Scott Fitzgerald **6** *n* underworld A prison sentence: *to get a jolt in the stir*—E Booth

Jonah *n* rock and roll = HIPSTER, CAT

Jones or **jones** narcotics **1** *n* A drug habit: *works at two jobs to keep up with the "Jones"*—J Lelyveld **2** *n* Any intense interest or absorption

See JOHNSON

Joneses *See* KEEP UP WITH THE JONESES

jook *See* JUKE

josan *n* Korean War armed forces A girlfriend [fr Korean]

Jose *See* NO WAY

Josephine *See* NOT TONIGHT, JOSEPHINE

josh 1 *v* To joke; banter; = KID **2** *n: It was just a tasteless little josh*

joskin *n fr early 1800s British* A rustic; =HICK [fr British dialect *joss* "bump," with wordplay on *bumpkin*]

jostle *v* To pick pockets: *a junkie vocation known as "jostling"*—J Markham/ *always looking for cats who were down there jostling*—Claude Brown

jowls *See* BAT one's GUMS

joy house *n phr* A brothel: *I ain't been in a joy house in 20 years*—Raymond Chandler

joy-juice *n* Liquor

◁**joy knob**▷ *n phr* The penis

joy pop *v phr narcotics* To take narcotic injections occasionally, esp intramuscularly

joy-popper *narcotics* **1** *n* A newcomer among narcotics users, esp among marijuana smokers **2** *n* A person who takes, or claims to take, only an occasional dose of narcotics: *For the "joy-poppers" had no intention of becoming addicts in the true sense*—Nelson Algren

joy-powder *n narcotics* Morphine

joy ride *n phr fr early 1900s* A ride or trip taken solely for pleasure, esp a fast and merry junket that is in some way forbidden: *They stole the police car and had themselves a joy ride*

joy-rider *n narcotics* An occasional and nonaddicted user of narcotics

joy smoke *n phr narcotics* Marijuana

joy-stick **1** *n fr early 1900s* The control lever of an airplane **2** *n hot rodders* The steering wheel of a car, esp a hot rod **3** *n* The control lever of a computer game **4** *n narcotics* An opium pipe ◁**5**▷ *n fr late 1800s* The penis [the origin of the control-lever senses is uncertain; perhaps fr the tremulous shaking of the stick, perhaps fr the joyful sensation experienced while flying]

J smoke *See* J

juane *n narcotics* Marijuana or a marijuana cigarette: *a half-smoked juane on the side*—Philip Wylie

Judy *sentence fr WW2 Air Forces* I have you in sight or on the radar screen [origin unknown]

jug **1** *v fr early 1800s* To put in jail; imprison: *I get jugged for parking in the wrong places?*—Lawrence Sanders **2** *n* A bottle of liquor: *Fetch me my jug* **3** *n* A relatively cheap wine, usu bought in large bottles; =JUG WINE: *Far more people drink jugs these days*—San Francisco **4** *n underworld* A vault or safe; =CRIB **5** *n police* A bank **6** *n hot rodders* A carburetor

the jug *n phr fr early 1800s* Jail; prison: *Refusal will result in a quick trip to the jug*—Rolling Stone

jugful *See* NOT BY A LONG SHOT

juggins or **jiggins** **1** *n fr late 1800s British* A stupid person; dolt; =JUGHEAD **2** *n* A dupe; =EASY MARK, PATSY

juggler *n narcotics* =PUSHER

jughandle *n* A circular portion of road shaped like the handle of a jug, used for making turns from and into a busy highway

jughead *n* A stupid person; fool; =KLUTZ

◁**jugs**▷ *n fr early 1900s Australian* A woman's breasts; =HOOTERS

jug wine *n phr* A relatively cheap domestic wine, usu bought in large bottles

juice¹ or **juicer** *n theater & movie studio* A stage or studio electrician: *He treated the grips and juicers the way he had always treated them*—A Morgan

juice² **1** *n* Liquor; =BOOZE, the SAUCE: *liquor much stronger than the present-day juice*—Louis Armstrong **2** *n underworld* Money, esp illegally obtained and used by gamblers, loan sharks, etc **3** *modifier*: *a juice dealer/ juice man* **4** *n underworld* The interest paid on a usurious loan; =VIGORISH: *interest, known in the trade as vigorish, vig, or juice*—Wall Street Journal **5** *n fr late 1800s* Electricity; current and voltage: *Turn on the juice so we can see something* **6** *n* Gasoline; motor fuel: *If you have a light supply of juice you climb at about 200 mph*—New York Times **7** *n hot rodders & car-racing* A fuel additive for cars, esp hot rods; =POP **8** *n miners* Nitroglycerin **9** *n* Influence; =CLOUT, PULL: *"What's juice?" "I guess you'd call it pull. Or clout"*—John Gregory Dunne **10** *n narcotics* Methadone, often administered in fruit juice

See BUG JUICE, CAPER-JUICE, CORNJUICE, HAPPY-JUICE, JOY-JUICE, JUNGLE-JUICE, JUNIPER-JUICE, LIMEY, MOO-JUICE, TORPEDO JUICE

juice-box *n electricians* An electrical junction box

juiced or **juiced up** *adj* or *adj phr* Drunk: *Crabs was already pretty juiced up*—Easyriders

juice dealer *n phr underworld* A racketeer who loans money at very high interest; usurer; =LOAN SHARK, SHYLOCK

juicehead *n* A heavy drinker; =LUSH: *He had a raving juice-head for a wife*—Rolling Stone/ *All wayfarers, outlaws, broken-down poets and juiceheads looking for a free drink were welcomed*—Changes

juice-joint **1** *n circus* A soft-drink concession or stand **2** *n esp 1920s* =SPEAKEASY

juice loan *n phr underworld* A loan made by a racketeer; a usurious loan

juice man *n phr underworld* A hoodlum who collects money owed to a racketeer: *a "juice man" (loan collector) for syndicate hoodlum bosses*—Chicago Tribune

juice up **1** *v phr* To energize; invigorate: *A thing like that can really juice you up*—Time/ *He seems, if anything, to be juicing up the pace these days*—Philadelphia Journal **2** *v phr* To fuel: *They juiced the car up and set out*

juju **1** *n outdated narcotics* A marijuana cigarette: *I knew a guy once who smoked jujus*—Raymond Chandler **2** *n* Any object which a person nervously plays with or manipulates; fetish; amulet [both senses probably fr Hausa, "fetish"]

juke or **jook** *fr early 1900s* **1** *n* =JUKE HOUSE **2** *n* =JUKE JOINT **3** *n* =JUKEBOX **4** *v* To tour roadside bars, drinking and dancing: *I want you to go juking with me*—Tennessee Williams **5** *v college students* To have a good time; disport oneself, esp at a party **6** *v college students* To dance **7** *v sports* To swerve and reverse evasively; trick a defender or tackler; =JINK: *rather than to juke a defensive back, then duck inside*—Sports Illustrated/ *Zaffuto juked past...Peters on the right side*—Sports Illustrated [fr Gullah fr Wolof and/or

Bambara, "unsavory"; the sports sense is probably fr the dancing sense and the echoic-symbolic force shown also in *jack, jank,* and *jink*]

See JIVE AND JUKE, JUKING AND JIVING

jukebox *n fr early 1900s Southern* A coin-operated record player in a restaurant, bar, etc

juke house *n phr esp early 1900s Southern* A brothel

juke joint *n phr fr early 1900s Southern* A usu cheap bar, roadside tavern, etc, with a jukebox

juking and jiving 1 *n phr* Frivolity and evasiveness; triviality and inanity **2** *modifier:* Hart despises "the jukin' and jivin' phoniness of politics" —Time

See JIVE AND JUKE

jumbo *adj* Very large; gigantic; = HUMONGOUS: *I had a jumbo portion* [fr PT Barnum's great elephant *Jumbo,* fr the word for "elephant" in various West African languages, for example Kongo *nzamba*]

jump 1 *v fr late 1800s* To attack; assault: *We jumped him as he left the place* **2** *v* To rob, esp at gunpoint; = HOLD UP **3** *v jive talk* To be furiously active; be vibrant with noise and energy: *Before long the joint was jumpin'*—H Allen Smith **4** *n jive talk* = SWING **5** *modifier: a jump tune/ jump music* **6** *n jive talk* A dance where the music is swing or jive; = HOP **7** *n street gang* A street fight between teenage gangs; = RUMBLE ◁**8**▷ *v* To do the sex act with or to; = SCREW: *She admitted she always wanted him to jump her*

See GET THE JUMP ON someone or something, HAVE THE JUMP

jump all over someone *v phr* To rebuke and berate someone very severely; savage someone: *He jumped all over her for not telling him*

jump bail *v phr underworld fr middle 1800s* To default on one's bail

jump band *n phr jive talk* A band playing fast and heavily accented swing music: *A "jump band" is a big and powerful jazz band*—Stephen Longstreet

jump (or **jump on**) someone's **bones 1** *v phr* To make strong sexual advances; sexually assault: *All these spades is gonna jump on your bones and pull your pants off*—Playboy/ *Have I tried to...jump your bones?*—The Gauntlet (movie) **2** *v phr* To do the sex act with someone

jump down someone's **throat** *v phr fr early 1800s* To make a violent and wrathful response: *When I hinted he might be mistaken he jumped down my throat*

jumped-up 1 *adj* = JACKED UP **2** *adj* Hastily organized; impromptu

jumper *See* GULLY-JUMPER, PUDDLE-JUMPER, STUMP-JUMPER, TREE JUMPER

jump (or **go**) **off the deep end** *v phr* To act precipitately; take drastic action: *He jumped off the deep end and got married again* [see *go off the deep end*]

jump on someone *v phr* = JUMP ALL OVER someone

jump on someone's **meat** *v phr* To rebuke severely; savage; = CHEW OUT: *Chickenshit lieuten-*

ant...used to jump on our meat every night at roll-call—Joseph Wambaugh

jump on the bandwagon *See* GET ON THE BANDWAGON

the **jumps** *n phr* = the JITTERS

jump salty *v phr black* To lose one's temper: *if you're trying to jump salty*—Zora Neale Hurston

jump smooth *v phr street gang* To give up crime and violence; adhere to the law: *tells why he decided to "jump smooth"*—Life

jump-start *v* To start a car by attaching cables to the battery from a car that runs; start anything that resists going: *Santa's in the driveway jump-starting one of the reindeer/ Mubarak Tries to Jump Start Stalled Mideast Peace Talks*—New York Times

jump suit *n phr* A one-piece coverall modeled on those worn by paratroopers and parachute jumpers

jump the gun *v phr fr early 1900s* To act prematurely: *We planned it well, but jumped the gun and ruined it*

◁**jump through** one's **ass**▷ *v phr Army* To make a very quick response to a sudden difficult demand: *Old Man says we'll have to jump through our ass to get that done by tomorrow*

jump through hoops 1 *v phr* To serve, obey, or accommodate someone without question, esp in a harried, frantic way: *You had to jump through hoops to please that guy* **2** *v phr* To exert oneself mightily; strain: *I had to jump through hoops to get you that job* [fr the image of a trained animal jumping through hoops in a show, circus, etc]

jump up *v phr* To increase the force of; = JAZZ something UP: *He decides to jump up the tune just as he jumped up "That's All Right, Mama"*—Albert Goldman

jump-up *n Army* A job that must be done at once, with little time to think and prepare

jumpy *adj* Nervous; apprehensive; = JITTERY: *One of our pals...is jumpy and he needs a bodyguard tonight*—George Raft

jungle 1 *n hoboes* A camp or regular stopping place near the railroad on the outskirts of a town: *always leaves the jungle like he found it*—James M Cain **2** *n* Any place of notable violence, lawlessness, etc: *The neighborhood's becoming a jungle*

◀**jungle-bunny**▶ *n* A black person

jungle buzzard *n phr hoboes* A hobo who lives permanently in a camp or regular stopping place and begs from transient hoboes

jungle-juice *n WW2 Army fr earlier nautical* Liquor made by prisoners, soldiers, etc, from any available alcohol and flavorings [originally African rum]

jungle stiff *n phr hoboes* A hobo living or staying in a camp or regular stopping place

juniper-juice *n* Gin

junk 1 *n fr middle 1800s* Worthless and shoddy things; useless and inept productions; trash; = DRECK, SHIT: *Why do you always buy such junk?* **2** *modifier: junk jewelry/ junk mail* **3** *n tennis* Tricky serves and lobs; soft, hard-to-reach shots: *He is a master of control and of dealing "junk"*—New York Times/ *looping junk, the players' term for soft, short shots*—Esquire **4** *n baseball* = JUNK-

BALL **5** *n* *narcotics* Narcotics; =DOPE: *Canales has a noseful of junk a lot of the time*—Raymond Chandler/ *Sherlock Holmes...All he does is play a fiddle and take junk*—J Cannon **6** *modifier:* one *of the most dangerous junk neighborhoods in the city*—Esquire **7** *n* Unspecified heaps and objects; stuff; crap: *What's all that junk in the corner?*

junk-ball 1 *n* *baseball* A deceptive and unorthodox pitch; =JUNK **2** *modifier: a junk-ball artist*

junk bond *n phr* A bond having high yield but relatively little security, used as payment for one company by another in a corporate merger: *Fed adopts "Junk Bond" curbs*—New York Times

junked up *adj phr* *narcotics* =HOPPED UP

junker 1 *n* *narcotics fr 1920s* =JUNKIE **2** *n narcotics* A narcotics dealer; =JUGGLER **3** *n* A car or other machine that is worn out and ready to be discarded, or that has been discarded: *You can't litter the countryside with the kind of crap that the junkers are*—Fortune/ *driving a junker around and around one of the chicken coops*—Newsweek

junk food *n phr* Foods like potato chips, popcorn, sugar-coated cereals, and the like, esp popular with children and having little nutritional value

junk heap 1 *n phr* A worn and ramshackle old car; =HEAP, JALOPY **2** *n phr* Any unsightly or chaotic place: *His room was always a fetid junk heap*

junkie or **junky 1** *n* *narcotics* A narcotics addict: *I didn't want to be a junkie*—Saturday Review/ *The man I was to find was both a junkie and pusher*—A Halsey **2** *n* A devotee or addict of any sort: *Zuckerman describes himself as a "newspaper and magazine junkie"*—Time/ *Growth junkies, snipes one former insider, go-go boys*—Wall Street Journal

junk mail *n phr* Mail, usu third class, consisting of advertising circulars, appeals for money, etc, and sometimes addressed to "resident"

junk shop *n phr* A shop where old discarded things and miscellaneous bits of potential trash are sold; second-hand store

junque *n* Old and discarded odds and ends; rummage; =JUNK: *a wonderful collection of white elephants, trash, treasures and, as the antique dealers spell it, "junque"*—Washington Post [the pseudo-French spelling lends a certain chic and dignity to the material]

just another pretty face *n phr* Someone or something of no particular distinction; a mediocre person or thing: *He had a time convincing them he was a genuine expert, not just another pretty face* [fr the plight of a young woman, esp in popular fiction or film, who has intelligence, talent, etc, but fears she is being treated by males as only an ordinary sex object]

just for the hell of it *See* FOR THE HELL OF IT

just one of those things *n phr fr 1930s* Something that can hardly be predicted, justified, explained, or avoided, but is an intrinsic and sometimes a distressful part of living ● The gestural equivalent is a shrug: *Their divorce was just one of those things*

just whistling Dixie *See* NOT JUST WHISTLING DIXIE, WHISTLING DIXIE

juve or **juvie** or **juvey 1** *adj* Juvenile; youthful: *the next monster juve act would be*—Village Voice/ *Andrews became the archetypal juve lead on British television*—People Weekly **2** *n* A young person; child; juvenile, esp a juvenile offender: *I'm a juve*—Hill Street Blues (TV program) **3** *n* A juvenile court or a reformatory **4** *modifier: juvey hall/ juvey books*

K

K 1 *n* A thousand dollars: *Four bastards no smarter'n you and me got ninety-seven K out of some little bank*—George V Higgins **2** *n* narcotics A kilogram, esp such a quantity of narcotics: *even occasional Ks (kilograms) of cocaine*—New York Times [fr the Greek prefix *kilo-* "one thousand"]

kabibble *See* ISH KABIBBLE

kablooey *See* GO BLOOEY

kack 1 *n outdated black* A refined or pleasant person **2** *n cowboys* A saddle

kafooster *n* Useless talk; babble; =BULLSHIT: *There has been a great deal of kafooster about emasculating the price-control act*—Robert Taft

kaka *adj* Bad: *Overweight is kaka*—Village Voice [fr Greek]

See CA-CA

kale or **kale-seed** *n* Money; =the GREEN STUFF: *trite slangisms, among'em kale, dough, mazuma, etc*—Abel Green

kangaroo *v prison* To convict someone with false evidence; =FRAME

kangaroo court or **club** *fr middle 1800s* **1** *n phr prison fr hobo* A mock court: *The toughest prisoner announced that he was president of the Kangaroo Club and would hold court*—E Lavine **2** *n phr* A small-town police court where traffic fines to transients are high, and usu divided among the police **3** *n phr* Any local court that is severe with hoboes and transients **4** *n phr* Any court where procedures are arbitrary and defective [origin unknown; perhaps connected with the fact that Australia was for some time a prison colony]

kaput (kah PŏŏT) *adj fr WW2 armed forces* Inoperative; ineffective; =FINISHED: *I would be "kaput" without a folding machete*—SJ Perelman [fr echoic-symbolic German slang]

karma *n* =VIBES [fr Sanskrit "work"]

Katie bar the door *sentence* Get ready for trouble; a desperate situation is at hand: *If you fall too far behind, it'll be Katie-bar-the-door real quick*—New York Times/ *If they were on to him, well that's all she wrote. Katie bar the door*—William Kennedy

kayducer *n underworld* A train conductor, esp one who colludes with gamblers and confidence tricksters aboard his train

kayo or **kay** *n prizefight* A knockout; =KO

kazoo or **gazoo** or **gazool 1** *n* The buttocks; anus; =ASS: *an impossible, unreliable, self-destructive pain in the kazoo*—Washington Post/ *We have subcommittee staff running out the kazoo*—New York Times **2** *n* Toilet; =CAN: *I tore it up and flushed it down the kazoo*—Lawrence Sanders [origin unknown; perhaps *kazoo*, known in its standard sense fr the 1880s, suggested the anus in being tubular and emitting sounds, and *gazool* in a sort of blend with *asshole*]

See UP THE KAZOO

k-balling *n Air Force* The cannibalizing of one aircraft to repair another

kee *See* KEY

keed *n* =KID

keel over *fr late 1800s v phr* To fall down; collapse: *He was so tired he was about to keel over* [fr nautical careening of a ship so that the *keel* is raised]

keen *adj outdated teenagers & students* Excellent; wonderful; =NEAT: *I think she's a keen kid*—Max Shulman/ *"Keen?" Blanche said. "I haven't heard that word in 20 years"*—Lawrence Sanders

See PEACHY

keep someone *v phr* To support and maintain someone for sexual purposes: *She has "an old man"...who "keeps" her*—New York Times/ *Maybe some day some guy'll even keep me*—Xaviera Hollander

keep (or **maintain**) **a low profile** *v phr* To stay inconspicuous; try not to attract much attention: *Better keep a low profile until this blows over*

keep an eye on someone or something *v phr* To watch; guard over: *Will you keep an eye on my cat while I'm away?*

keep (or **make**) **book** *v phr fr gambling* To bet or be willing to cover bets; have confidence: *I wouldn't make book that he'll get the nod*

keep one's **eye on the ball** *v phr* To pay strict attention to what one is doing; be alert and undistracted

keep someone **honest 1** *v phr* To pose a requirement or test so that someone does not go unchallenged: *We'll ask her a few questions just to keep her honest* **2** *v phr baseball* To pitch close to a batter; throw at a batter: *Keep him honest, which means, make the batter afraid of you*—Jim Bouton

keep one's **nose clean** *v phr* To avoid doing wrong or seeming to do wrong; stay above reproach: *Good boy, Billy. Keep your nose clean* —Lawrence Sanders [fr the traditional injunction of a mother to a child to wipe its *nose*, wash behind its ears, etc]

keep on trucking *v phr* To carry on; continue what one is doing, esp working, plugging away, etc

keeps *See* FOR KEEPS, PLAY FOR KEEPS

keep one's **shirt** (or **pants**) **on** *fr middle 1800s* **1** *v phr* To stay unruffled; be calm; =COOL IT: *He was beginning to holler, so I told him to keep his shirt on* **2** *v phr* To be patient; wait a bit; =HOLD one's HORSES: *Keep your pants on and the guy will be back*

keep tabs on *v phr fr late 1800s* To keep informed about; keep watch on or over: *Who's gonna keep tabs on the receipts?*

keep up with the Joneses *v phr* To strive, esp beyond one's means, to keep up socially and financially with others in the same neighborhood or in the same social circle: *Never keep up with the Joneses; drag them down to your level...it's cheaper* —Quentin Crisp [fr the title of a comic strip of the early 20th century]

kee-rect (KEE rekt) *adj* Correct

kef (KEEF, KAYF) *n* (also **keef** or **kief** or **kif**) *narcotics* Marijuana, hashish, or opium [fr Arabic, "pleasure"]

kegger *n teenagers & students* A beer party; =BEER BUST

keister (KEE stər) (also **keester** or **keyster** or **kiester** or **kister**) **1** *n* The buttocks; rump; =ASS: *I've had it up to my keister with these leaks* —Ronald Reagan **2** *n pickpockets* A rear trousers pocket **3** *n hawkers and hoboes* A suitcase that opens into a display of goods: *the typical "keister" of the street hawker*—Collier and Westrate **4** *n underworld* A safe; strongbox; =CRIB [fr British dialect *kist* or German *Kiste* "chest, box," transferred to the buttocks perhaps by the pickpocket sense or by the notion that something may be concealed in the rectum]

◁**Kelsey's ass**▷ *See* COLD AS HELL

◁**Kelsey's nuts**▷ *See* TIGHT AS KELSEY'S NUTS

◁**kelt** or **keltch**▷ *black fr early 1900s* **1** *n* A white person **2** *n* A light-skinned black person who might or does pass as white [origin unknown]

Ken *n* A conformist, conventional man; a man lacking any but bland typical characteristics [fr the male counterpart of the Barbie doll]

kennel *n hoboes* A house or room

ken-ten lamp *n phr narcotics* A lamp used to prepare opium for smoking: *over the little ken-ten lamp made of a sardine tin*—Stephen Longstreet [origin unknown; the form suggests a Chinese source]

Kentucky windage *n phr* A slight adjustment made on instinct rather than strict measurement: *Let's apply some Kentucky windage and raise that figure a little* [fr the skillful adjustments of aim made by good sharpshooters]

keptie *n* A woman kept as a mistress: *the place to hole up your "keptie"*—NY Confidential

kerflooie or **kerflooey** *See* GO BLOOEY

kerflummoxed *adj* =FLUMMOXED

kerplunk *See* GO KERPLUNK

kettle **1** *n underworld* A pocket watch **2** *n railroad* A small locomotive; switch engine

kettle of fish *See* FINE KETTLE OF FISH

key[1] *n college students fr 1950s* A typical Ivy League student; =WHITE SHOE
See CHURCH KEY

key[2] or **kee** or **ki** *n narcotics* A kilogram (about 2.2 pounds) of a narcotic: *enough opium to produce a key (kilo) of heroin*—Time/ *Anybody who can handle a key of pure coke is dealing big*—New York [fr kilo]

key club **1** *n phr* A loose association of married couples in which keys to dwellings are exchanged more or less at random, for sexual purposes **2** *n phr* A private social organization to which one can purchase a membership

keyster *See* KEISTER

the keystone (or **keystone sack** or **keystone cushion**) *n phr baseball* Second base

key-swinger *college students* **1** *n* A person who ostentatiously wears the keys of honor societies **2** *n* A boaster; braggart

khazeray or **khazerei** (KHAH zə rī) *n* Odious and worthless material; =CRAP, SHIT: *All that airtime talk, all that khazeray, wasn't worth doing* [fr Yiddish, ultimately fr Hebrew *khazer* "pig"]

ki *See* KEY

kibitz **1** *v* To give intrusive and unrequested advice while watching a game, performance, etc **2** *v* To banter, comment [fr Yiddish fr German *Kiebitz* "peewit, lapwing," a noisy little bird]

kibitzer *n* A person who gives intrusive advice: *I don't mind admitting that a good kibitzer has 20-20 hindsight*—New York Post

kibosh (KĪ bahsh) *v* To eliminate; =KILL: *that was kiboshed promptly by White House spokesman* —Philadelphia Journal

the kibosh *n phr* The termination; sad end; sudden doom: *This latest goof is probably the kibosh* [origin unknown, and very extensively speculated upon; perhaps, eg, fr Irish *cie bais* "cap of death," referring to the black cap a judge would don when pronouncing a death sentence]
See PUT THE KIBOSH ON someone or something

kick **1** *v fr late 1700s* To complain; protest; =BITCH: *She can just kick all she wants to*—Sinclair Lewis **2** *n:* *If you got any kicks, you can always quit* **3** *n fr middle 1800s* A pocket, esp a pants pocket: *I have a hundred thousand boo-boos in the kick*—H McHugh **4** *n fr jive talk* A surge or fit of pleasure; a feeling of joy and delight; =BELT, CHARGE: *He was having a real kick*—RS Prather/ *I get a kick out of you*—Cole Porter **5** *n* Anything that gives one a feeling of pleasure, joy, etc: *That's a kick....Ridin' a guy down Wilshire in daylight*—Raymond Chandler **6** *n fr jive talk* A strong personal predilection; =THING: *Arthur...is on the Paris kick* —John Crosby/ *several opportunities to let her wail on a comic kick*—Bob Salmaggi **7** *n* Power; impact; potency: *One of those...stories with a kick*

—P Marks **8** *n* A shoe: *Hey, nice kicks* [pocket sense fr late-17th-century *kicks* "breeches"]
See GET A KICK OUT OF someone or something, ON A ROLL, PRAT KICK, SIDEKICK, TOP-KICK

kick around 1 *v phr* To idle about; drift around rootlessly; = BAT AROUND: *He put in a couple years just kicking around California* **2** *v phr* To acquire experience; become seasoned: *sound like a band that's kicked around for a long time*—Changes **3** *v phr* To abuse; repeatedly maltreat: *Mr Nixon said the press wouldn't have him to kick around any more*

kick something **around** *v phr* To discuss or think about something; consider from all angles: *Let's kick Merrill's idea around for awhile*

kick ass 1 *v phr* To assert power; be rough; punish: *He once again kicked ass with the Wagner 6 to 1 triumph*—Village Voice/ *Geometry and algebra were kicking my ass*—Claude Brown/ *We kicked a little ass last night*—George Bush **2** *v phr* To have power; have unpolished vigor: *just country that kicks ass and entertains*—Aquarian

kick-ass 1 *adj* (also **kick-yer-ass**) Rough; powerful; = ROUGH-ASS, TOUGH: *that kick-ass attitude*—Sports Illustrated/ *gave up its last drop of kick-ass Gewurztraminer*—Car and Driver/ *I wanted it to be kick-ass country, high energy country*—Rolling Stone **2** *n* Power; energy; virility: *He's the guy who coaxed the kick-ass back into the torque*—Car and Driver/ *with the gall to label such Muzak kick-ass*—Worcester

◁**kick ass and take names**▷ *v phr* To behave very roughly and angrily; = KICK ASS: *screaming, berating, threatening, kicking ass and taking names*—Sports Illustrated/ *Paschal ain't gonna do nothing but kick ass and take names*—Dan Jenkins [fr the image of a rough and punitive police officer, drill sergeant, prison guard, etc]

kick at the cat *n phr* A turn; a chance: *When the pages are pasted up, the Engraving Department gets its second kick at the cat*—Milwaukee Journal

kickback *n* Money given to someone illegally or unethically: *Buying another poor devil's job for $50 or a kick-back from his pay*—Westbrook Pegler/ *All the cops were on the pad, getting kickbacks from the hookers*

kick back 1 *v phr* underworld To return or restore, esp to give back stolen property: *Stolen goods returned to the rightful owner are "kicked back"*—H McLellan **2** *v phr* To give part of wages, fees, etc, illicitly to another in return for one's job or other advantage: *The cabbies had to kick back a lot to the dispatchers* **3** *v phr* college students fr black To relax: *Use the pool, kick back....Who knows?*—Armistead Maupin

kick booty *v phr* = KICK ASS

kick down *v phr* truckers To shift into a lower gear in a truck or car

kicker 1 *n* A small motor, esp an outboard, used for a boat; = EGGBEATER **2** *n* Anything that gives great pleasure; = KICK: *The kicker...was the station wagon*—R Starnes **3** *n* A hidden cost, qualifica-

tion, defect, etc; = CATCH: *The kicker is that if you are subject to this requirement...your homeowner's policy will not cover the injuries*—Washingtonian/ *The kicker to this one is simple*—Gilbert Milstein/ *It may look like a good deal, but there's a kicker* **4** *n* = PUNCH LINE **5** *n* A pocket; = KICK: *Keep it in yer kickers*—Car and Driver

kickers *n* college students Shoes, esp tennis shoes

kick in 1 *v phr* fr early 1900s To pay up money; make one's proper contribution; = FORK OVER: *to ask you guys to kick in your share of the expenses*—Jerome Weidman **2** *v phr* To contribute orally; = CHIME IN **3** *v phr* To die

kicking ass *n phr* college students A good time; = a BALL: *We went downtown and had a kicking ass*

kicking can *n phr* An object of attack, esp a habitual object; whipping boy: *The young alderman's chief kicking can has been four oil companies*—Toronto Life [fr the child's game *kick the can*]

◁a **kick in the ass**▷ **1** *n phr* A surprising and dampening rebuff, misfortune, etc; a slap in the face **2** *n phr* A strong stimulus or impetus; = a SHOT IN THE ARM: *If this campaign doesn't get a kick in the ass we're dead*

kick it 1 *v phr* narcotics To rid oneself of narcotic addiction: *I don't think anybody knew anyone who had kicked it*—Claude Brown **2** *v phr* jazz talk & jive talk To play swing or jazz very vigorously

kickoff 1 *n* The beginning; inauguration: *He planned the kickoff of his campaign for Texas* **2** *modifier*: *kickoff dinner/ kickoff speech*

kick off 1 *v phr* To die: *after his wife kicked off*—New Yorker **2** *v phr* To leave; depart **3** *v phr* To begin something; inaugurate: *the chain of thought kicked off by it*—Eldridge Cleaver

kick-out *n* WW2 armed forces A dishonorable discharge

kick someone **out** *v phr* To eject, expel, or dismiss someone; = BOUNCE

kick (or **break**) **out the jams** *v phr* esp musicians To behave in an unrestrained way; be uninhibited; = LET oneself GO: *Kick out the jams, motherfookers*—Village Voice/ *On Side Two they kick out the jams, or at least shake the Jello*—Rolling Stone

kick over *See* KNOCK OVER

kick pad *n phr* narcotics A place where one is detoxified from narcotics: *I was clean three more days, left the kick pad*—Joseph Wambaugh

kick party *n phr* narcotics A party where LSD is used

kicks 1 *n* fr bop talk fr narcotics Pleasure and gratification; = BANGS, JOLLIES: *Sock cymbal's enough to give me my kicks*—Douglass Wallop **2** *n* Shoes ● Attested as an early 1900s hobo term *See* GET one's COOKIES

kick stick *n phr* outdated narcotics A marijuana cigarette

kick the bucket *v phr* fr late 1700s British To die: *Old man Mose done kicked the bucket* [origin uncertain; perhaps fr the *bucket* a suicide might kick from under in hanging himself]

kick the gong around *v phr outdated narcotics* To smoke opium or marijuana: *He helped the world kick the gong around, Jack did*—William Kennedy

◁**kick the shit out of** someone or something▷ *See* BEAT THE SHIT OUT OF someone or something

kick the tires *v phr* To make a quick and superficial inspection; do cursory checking: *simplistic agrarian vision bought by the war-weary nation without kicking the tires*—Michael M Thomas [fr such an examination made while appraising a car]

kick-up 1 *n* A dance or dancing party **2** *n* A commotion; disturbance; = RUCKUS

kick up a fuss *v phr* To make a disturbance; complain loudly and bitterly; = RAISE CAIN: *I don't want his lawyer to kick up a fuss about this*—E Lavine

kick up a storm *See* PISS UP A STORM

kick someone **upstairs** *v phr* To remove someone from office by promotion to a nominally superior position: *It is conceivable but not likely that Mr Gromyko has been kicked upstairs where...he'll no longer influence Soviet foreign policy*—New York Times

kicky 1 *adj* Very chic and modish: *a lot of kicky clothes, many of them imports*—New York Times/ *so easy and smooth in their short, kicky skirts, pantyhose*—Village Voice **2** *adj* Exciting; ravishing; = FAR OUT: *It's very kicky to be able to drive right over sand dunes*—Playboy/ *a kicky way to spend a couple of years*—Mpls St Paul

kid 1 *n fr late 1500s* A child: *She's a cute little kid* **2** *n fr late 1800s* Any young or relatively young person: *the kids in college* **3** *modifier:* *his kid sister/ my kid cousin* **4** *v fr middle 1800s British* To joke; jest; banter; = JOSH: *a funny guy, always kidding* **5** *v* To attempt to deceive; try to fool: *Are you kidding me?* **6** *n:* *That's no kid, neither* —Dunning and Abbott [bantering and fooling senses perhaps fr an alteration of dialect *cod* "hoax, fool"]
See I KID YOU NOT, NEW KID ON THE BLOCK, WHIZ KID

the **Kid** *n phr WW2 Army Air Forces* A copilot; = METER-READER

kid around *v phr* To jest and banter; avoid seriousness; = FOOL AROUND

kiddie or **kiddy** *n* A child

kidding *See* NO KIDDING

kiddo or **Kiddo** *n fr early 1900s* A person, esp one younger than oneself ● Used nearly always in direct address: *OK, kiddo, you can leave now*

kidney *See* GRIPE one's ASS

kidney-buster *truckers* **1** *n* A rough road **2** *n* A hard-riding truck

kid show *n phr circus* A sideshow

kid stuff 1 *n phr* Something too easy to challenge an adult; = CINCH, PIECE OF CAKE: *That swim to Catalina's kid stuff* **2** *n phr* Activity not appropriate for an adult; childish concerns: *Give up the kid stuff and find a real job*

kid top *n phr circus* The sideshow tent

kidvid 1 *n* Children's television: *a year when kidvid is being publicly scolded*—TV Guide/ *The three networks are offering the public more kidvid* —New York Times **2** *modifier:* *The trade jour-nals call the children's program segment on television the "kidvid ghetto"*—American Scholar

kief or **kif** *See* KEF

kiester *See* KEISTER

kife 1 *v circus* To swindle **2** *v* To steal

◀**kike**▶ **1** *n fr early 1900s* A Jew ● Sometimes used by Jews of other Jews they regard with contempt **2** *adj:* *kike neighborhood* [origin unknown and much speculated upon; perhaps fr Yiddish *kikel* "circle" because Jews who could not sign their names would make a circle; perhaps an alteration of *Ike* "Isaac"; perhaps because so many Jewish immigrant names ended in *-ky* or *-ki*; perhaps fr British dialect *keek* "peep," used for a spy on a rival's designs in the clothing business]

kill 1 *v* To drink or eat up: *He killed a couple beers* **2** *v* To spoil or ruin: *One bad grade killed his chances for med school* **3** *v* To demoralize totally; make hopeless: *The third defeat killed him* **4** *v* To be extremely successful with: *That curtain speech always kills them/ The Evergreen Review kills him*—Eldridge Cleaver **5** *v* To make an audience helpless with laughter; = FRACTURE: *My McEnroe act kills 'em* **6** *v* To eliminate: *Kill half these lights/ Kill that whole paragraph* **7** *n* A murder: *for the Shannon kill*—Raymond Chandler **8** *n fr WW2 armed forces* An enemy airplane, ship, tank, etc, destroyed
See IN AT THE KILL, KILLER, THAT KILLS IT

to **kill** *See* DRESSED TO KILL, DRESSED TO THE TEETH

killer 1 *n* A very attractive person: *Ain't she a killer?* **2** *n* (also **killer-diller**) A person or thing that is remarkable, wonderful, superior, etc; = BEAUT, DOOZIE: *The song's a killer!* **3** *adj* (also **killer-diller**) *not only was it a killer version*—Village Voice/ *The killer idea of the century is about to be laid on you*—William Goldman/ *What a killer dude, fer shurr* **4** *n narcotics* A marijuana cigarette
See LADY-KILLER

killing *n* A very large and quick profit; = BUNDLE: *It wasn't just a fair return he made, it was a killing*
See MAKE A KILLING

killjoy *n* A morose pessimist; = CRAPE-HANGER, GLOOMY GUS

killout *n black* A remarkable person or thing; = KICK

kilo connection *n phr narcotics* A wholesale narcotics dealer, who dilutes the pure drug by about 50 percent

kilter *See* OUT OF KILTER

kimono *See* PINE OVERCOAT

kin *See* KISSING COUSIN, SHIRTTAIL KIN

the **kind** *adj phr teenagers* Excellent; superior; = SOME KIND OF: *He's got the kind car*

kind (or **sort**) **of** *adj phr* Somewhat: *I think he's kind of stupid/ We're sort of stuck with it*
See SOME KIND OF

king 1 *n* (also **king pin**) The leader; chief: *king of the motorcycle jumpers* **2** *n underworld* A prison warden **3** *n railroad* A yardmaster or freight conductor

King Kong *n phr black* Cheap and strong liquor: *No six-year-old child got no business drinking that King Kong*—Claude Brown

kings *n* A pack of king-size cigarettes

◁**King Shit**▷ *See* THINK one IS KING SHIT

king-size or **king-sized** *adj* Very large; extra large: *Your nagging gives me a king-size headache*

king snipe *n phr railroad* The leader of a railroad section gang or track-laying crew

kink 1 *n* (also **kinko**) A person with deviant or bizarre tastes, esp sexual: *I'm not some kind of kink* —John D MacDonald **2** *modifier: a kinko diner who tries to attract Chong's attention*—Washington Post **3** *n* A deviant practice or predilection, esp sexual: *a Nazi with a kink for prepubescent girls*—A Bailey/ *the female staffer whose kink is making love down in the morgue*—New York **4** *n* A defect or flaw, esp a minor one; =BUG: *We'll work the kinks out of the plan before we announce it*

kinker *n circus* Any circus performer

the **kinks** *See* IRON OUT THE KINKS

kinky 1 *adj* Dishonest; illegal; =CROOKED: *"kinky" gambling paraphernalia*—WR Simpson **2** *adj underworld* Stolen: *a kinky car* **3** *adj fr middle 1800s* Eccentric **4** *adj* Bizarre; weird: *no offense so kinky that the Maximum Enchilada and his consigliores wouldn't commit it*—G Wolff **5** *adj* Deviant and abnormal, esp sexually: *a very kinky guy, likes being beat up* **6** *adj* Showing or pertaining to sexual deviation: *kinky photos/ kinky porn*

◀**kinky-head**▶ *n* A black person

kip *esp underworld & hoboes fr middle 1800s* **1** *n* A bed: *in the kip*—John O'Hara **2** *n* Sleep; a sleep or nap **3** *v: find a place to "kip"*—Jack London **4** *n* A night guard [origin uncertain; perhaps fr Danish *kippe* "hut, mean alehouse," whence the early-19th-century sense "brothel"]

kipe *v* To steal, esp something of little value; =NICK, SWIPE

kishkes or **kishkas** *n* The entrails; innards; =GUTS: *His kishkas were gripped by the iron hand of outrage and frustration*—Philip Roth [fr Yiddish]

kiss *n* =KISS-OFF

See BUTTERFLY KISS, FRENCH KISS, SOUL KISS

KISS (KIS) *sentence* Keep it simple, stupid or keep it simple and stupid

◁**kiss ass**▷ *v phr* To flatter one's superiors; =BROWN-NOSE: *He likes to be perfect and kiss ass* —Pat Conroy

◁**kiss-ass**▷ or **kiss-butt 1** *n* A toady; sycophant; =BROWN-NOSE, ASS-KISSER: *and not have people think, "Oh, what a kiss-butt"*—Washington Post **2** *modifier: another kiss-ass review of an extremely bad album*—Rolling Stone **3** *n* Sycophantic flattery: *using the old kiss-ass with the colonel*

◁**kiss** someone's **ass**▷ *v phr* To flatter someone; curry favor with superiors: *I didn't kiss anybody's ass and I didn't expect anybody to kiss mine*—People Weekly

kisser *n fr middle 1800s* The mouth; the face: *It would be a pleasure to drop one on your kisser, I admit*—Leo Rosten/ *show the good side of my kisser*—John O'Hara/ *Reagan had that quizzical "do I talk now?" look on his kisser*—Washington Post

See ASS-KISSER, BABY-KISSER, MOTHERFUCKER

kiss something **goodbye 1** *v phr* To abandon or renounce: *When he finally found out it was bad for him he kissed it goodbye* **2** *v phr* To accept or infer the fact that something is irrevocably gone: *You can kiss that promotion goodbye, after the way you talked to her*

kissing *See* MOTHERFUCKING

kissing cousin (or **kin**) **1** *n* A relative close enough to be kissed in salutation, hence anyone with whom a person is fairly intimate: *The two species will often prove to be kissing cousins for they'll crossbreed*—Sports Afield **2** *n* A close copy: *He had a kissing cousin of Montgomery's mustache* —JA Kugelmass

kissing trap *n phr* The mouth; =TRAP

◁**kiss my ass**▷ *sentence* I invite you to perform an obsequious and humiliating act; =GO FUCK oneself ● Always an insulting challenge and rejection: *"What should I say?" asked Belle. "Tell him to kiss my ass"*—Joseph Heller

the **kiss of death** *n phr* Something that looks helpful but is in fact fatal; a lethal benefaction: *His endorsement will be the kiss of death* [fr the *kiss* given Jesus by Judas]

kiss off 1 *v phr* To dodge; evade: *had kissed off all raps*—J Evans **2** *v phr* To kill: *who kissed off Martin*—J Evans

kiss-off 1 *n* (also **California kiss-off** or **New York kiss-off**) A dismissal, esp a rude one; =the BOUNCE, BRUSH-OFF: *She's given hundreds of suitors the royal kiss-off* **2** *v black fr 1940s* To die **3** *n: How is cholesterol related to kiss-off, Doc?*

kiss someone or something **off 1** *v phr* To dismiss rudely; =BRUSH someone OFF: *The receptionist kissed me off quite cheekily* **2** *v phr* To let go of, to attempt to forget; =KISS something GOODBYE: *You can kiss that money off*

kiss someone **out** *v phr underworld* To deny someone their share: *When a member of a mob is deprived of his share he is "kissed out"*—H McLellan

kiss the canvas (or **the resin**) *v phr* To be knocked unconscious, esp in a boxing match

kiss the dust *v phr* =BITE THE DUST

kissy-face or **kissy-facey** or **kissy-poo 1** *n teenagers & students* Kissing and cuddling; =MAKING OUT, NECKING: *Let's have a little kissy-face* **2** *n* A kiss: *The symbol of welcome...is a handshake, not a kissy-poo*—Washington Post **3** *v: I've trained poodles so that they won't kissy-face everybody* —Time

See PLAY KISSIE

kister *See* KEISTER

kit *See* HEAD KIT

kit and caboodle (or **boodle**) *n phr fr middle 1800s* The totality; everything: *the whole kit and caboodle, go hang*—George Jean Nathan/ *the whole kit and boodle of 'em*—Ellery Queen [fr 18th-century British *kit* "outfit of equipment" plus early-19th-century *boodle* "lot, collection," perhaps fr Dutch *boedel* "property, effects"]

kitchen 1 *n railroad* The cab of a locomotive **2** *n hoboes* The stomach **3** *n baseball* The space over home plate where a batter finds it easiest to hit a fair ball; a batter's preferred point of delivery; = WHEELHOUSE: *He'd throw it in my kitchen, so I moved up a step toward the plate*—Associated Press *See* DOWN IN THE KITCHEN, IF YOU CAN'T STAND THE HEAT STAY OUT OF THE KITCHEN

kitchen cabinet *n phr fr late 1800s* An unofficial set of advisers to a president or chief, made up of close friends and cronies

kitchen sweat *n phr lumberjacks* A dance or dancing party

kite 1 *n underworld* A letter or note, esp one smuggled into prison **2** *n* An airplane **3** *v* To write a check when one does not have the funds to cover it, hoping to find them before the check is cashed: *The bill was due before payday, so I had to kite the check* **4** *v* To raise the value of a check illegally before cashing it *See* BLOW something HIGH AS A KITE, FLY A KITE, GO FLY A KITE, HIGH AS A KITE, HIGHER THAN A KITE

kited *adj* Drunk

kitsch or **Kitsch** (KITCH) *n* Literature or art having little esthetic merit but appealing powerfully to popular taste: *It stands unchallenged as a masterpiece of kitsch*—Playboy/ *The closest I can come to America is through its Kitsch*—Harper's

kitschy *adj* Being or resembling kitsch: *Visconti's kitschy film*—Harvey Gross/ *Its kitschy Lupe Velez ambiance*—Armistead Maupin

kitten *See* HAVE KITTENS, SEX KITTEN

kitty *n fr gambling* The pot or pool of money in a gambling game, made up of contributions from the players; a contributed fund: *We made up a kitty of a few hundred bucks for her/ Each put $25,000 in the kitty*—Philadelphia *See* BITCH KITTY, DUST KITTY, FEED THE KITTY, IT'S A BITCH

Kitty *n* A Cadillac car: *If I had my way I'd take a Kitty*—CB Himes

kiwi *n Air Force fr WW1 British* An Air Force member, esp an officer, who shuns airplanes [fr the name of a flightless bird of New Zealand, fr Maori]

klepto *n* A kleptomaniac: *"Bloody klepto," says Siddhartha*—New Yorker

klick or **klik** *See* CLICK

◁ **klooch** ▷ (KLo͞oCH) *n lumberjacks* A woman: *I've sent my klooch to town*—RW Service [fr Chinook jargon]

klop in the chops *n phr* A blow to the face; a severe attack: *starting with a klop in the chops from San Francisco*—Ann Landers [fr Yiddish *klop* "a blow," plus the *chop* phrase for rhyme]

kluck *See* CLUCK, DUMB CLUCK

kludge or **kloodge** or **kluge** (KLo͞oJ, KLUJ) *computer* **1** *n* A term of endearment for a favorite computer, esp a somewhat defective one **2** *n* A computer program that has been revised and tinkered with so much that it will never work **3** *n*

A ludicrous assortment of incompatible and unworkable components: *You see this mechanical kluge (contraption), stop, think, and decide to do something*—Newsweek

klutz or **clutz** (KLUTS) **1** *n* A stupid person; idiot; = BLOCKHEAD: *Now, klutz that I am, I thought of Neal*—Esquire/ *A small crowd of first-class clutzes*—John D MacDonald **2** *n* A clumsy person; a lubberly lout: *I am the world's biggest klutz...I trip over my own feet, drop things*—New York Post [fr Yiddish, "blockhead," literally "block"]

klutz around *v phr* To behave stupidly; tamper with clumsily

klutzy 1 *adj* Stupid; idiotic: *any clever kid playing a klutzy kid*—New York Times **2** *adj* Clumsy; unhandy

knee-bender *n hoboes* A church-goer; = CHRISTER

kneecap *v* To shoot someone in the kneecap or legs ● Typically done by terrorists or gangsters as a disabling measure short of assassination

knee deep *adj phr* Overwhelmed; oversupplied; very much involved: *I never even tried to make money, and now I'm knee deep in the stuff*—Saul Bellow

knee-high to a grasshopper *adj phr* (Variations: **bumble-bee** or **duck** or **frog** or **mosquito** or **spit** or **splinter** or **toad** may replace **grasshopper**) *fr early 1800s* Very short or small, esp because young: *He's been smoking since he was knee-high to a grasshopper*

knee-jerk 1 *n* A reflexlike action or response: *Being nasty to women is a knee-jerk with him* **2** *modifier:* one more gesture to the knee-jerk hawks in the Congress—W Jackson/ *Yet McDonald is no mere knee-jerk critic of the evangelicals*—Washington Post **3** *n* A person who reacts with a reflexlike response: *a seventy-year old knee-jerk best remembered for castigating the Reverend Bill Moyers for dancing the frug in the White House*—LL King [fr the patellar reflex]

knees *See* CUT oneself OFF AT THE KNEES, CUT someone OFF AT THE KNEES

kneesies *n* Clandestine amorous friction of the knees: *We got back to the table and played kneesies while we talked*—Mickey Spillane

knee-slapper *n* Something very funny, esp a joke; = BOFFOLA: *That's a knee-slapper*—Matt Crowley/ *If she ever told a knee-slapper, I wasn't there*—Washingtonian

knickers *See* HAVE someone BY THE SHORT HAIRS

one's **knitting** *See* STICK TO one's KNITTING

knob *n* The head: *Can you get that through your ugly knob? See* JOY KNOB

knobber *n* A male homosexual transvestite prostitute: *It is where the knobbers, or transvestites, hang out*—New York Times [perhaps fr their wearing of false *knobs* "female nipples or breasts"; perhaps because they give *knob jobs*]

knobby *See* NOBBY

◁ **knob job** ▷ *n phr fr homosexuals* An act of fellatio; = BLOW JOB

◁**knobs**▷ *n* A woman's breasts or nipples; =KNOCKERS
See WITH BELLS ON

knock 1 *v fr late 1800s* To deprecate; criticize severely; dispraise; =PUT someone or something DOWN: *Their film critic knocks every flick in sight* **2** *n: It wasn't a disinterested comment, it was a knock/ The knock on Fernandez is he can't field* **3** *v black* To borrow or lend; ask or beg **4** *v* To give: *C'mon, baby, knock me a kiss*
See BEAT THE SHIT OUT OF, DON'T KNOCK IT, HAVE something CINCHED

the **knock** *n phr* The bill for food, drinks, etc; =TAB: *By the way, I'm picking up the knock*—Lawrence Sanders

knock around *v phr* To idle about; loaf; =KICK AROUND

knock someone **around** *v phr* To abuse someone; =KICK someone AROUND

knock back *v phr* To drink in one gulp: *The Colonel got his drink, and after he had knocked it back with one swift motion, he began to feel better*—AJ Liebling/ *there to mull their downside risks and knock back free champagne*—Toronto Life

knock someone's **block off** *v phr* To hit very hard; give a severe trouncing; =CLOBBER: *One more word and I'll knock your block off*

knock someone **cuckoo** *v phr* To knock unconscious or semiconscious

knock someone (or **knock 'em**) **dead** *v phr* To delight or impress someone extremely; =KILL, KNOCK someone's SOCKS OFF, WOW: *a fantastic scenery number for my life's movie. Something that'll knock 'em dead*—Washington Post/ *This new video will knock them dead, believe me*

knockdown 1 *n outdated fr late 1800s* An introduction: *You want a knockdown to something*—Jerome Weidman **2** *n* An invitation **3** *n fr late 1800s* Money stolen from one's employer: *considered the "knock-down" a perfectly legitimate source of profit*—EA Powell **4** *modifier* Designed to be sold unassembled, and be easy to assemble and disassemble: *a knockdown kitchen set*

knock down 1 *v phr fr middle 1800s* To pocket money taken from one's employer: *clerk who was knocking down on the till*—J Evans **2** *v phr* To earn: *Hommuch he knock down a week?*—Arthur Kober **3** *v phr* To reduce a price, salary, figure, etc: *Let's knock down the estimate a bit* **4** *v phr* To criticize; =KNOCK **5** *v phr* To drink: *I have knocked down one quart of Scotch whiskey every day for the last week*

knock something **down** *v phr* To sell something, esp at a price favorable to the buyer: *I'll knock it down to you for three bucks* [probably fr the gavelblow given by an auctioneer to signal and conclude a sale]

knock-down-drag-out 1 *adj phr* Very violent; unrestrained; =ALL-OUT: *They were having a knock-down-drag-out argument when I got there* **2** *n: Seems the neighbors were having a knockdown-drag-out*—Washington Post

knocked *See* HAVE something CINCHED

knocked out 1 *adj phr* Drunk **2** *adj phr* Intoxicated with a narcotic; =HIGH, STONED **3** *adj phr* Overcome with delight; extremely pleased: *and were really knocked out with it*—Rolling Stone/ *Everybody was knocked out to be asked*—Rolling Stone **4** *adj phr* Very tired; exhausted; =POOPED

◁**knocked up**▷ *adj phr* Pregnant

knocker[1] *n* A consistently negative critic; detracter: *that pack of knockers that have been howling*—The Billboard
See APPLE-KNOCKER

knocker[2] (KNAH kər) *n* A very important person; =BIG SHOT, MACHER: *Knocker means a big shot, either real or imagined, and you pronounce that first "k"*—C McHarr [fr Yiddish, literally "one who cracks or snaps a whip"]

◁**knockers**▷ *n* A woman's breasts; =HOOTERS: *Dumb broads with big knockers, that's what guys go for*—A Leslie

knock someone or something **for a loop** (Variations: **throw** may replace **knock** and **goal** or **row** or **row of ashcans** or **row of milk cans** or **row of Chinese pagodas** or **row of tall red totem poles** may replace **loop**) **1** *v phr fr early 1900s* To hit someone or something very hard; =CLOBBER: *We knocked the villain for a row of ash cans*—H Witwer/ *You certainly knocked him for a row of tall red totem poles*—K Brush **2** *v phr fr early 1900s* To unsettle severely; disrupt calm and confidence; =DISCOMBOBULATE: *It must have thrown him for a loop, but he asked*—Earl Thompson **3** *v phr* To delight extremely; thrill and amaze; =KILL, KNOCK someone's SOCKS OFF: *if this climactic sequence doesn't knock you for a loop*—Playboy/ *Wouldn't that knock the boys for a row or two*—James T Farrell/ *guaranteed to knock the keenest mind for a loop*—Raymond Chandler **4** *v phr* To cope with very well; =ACE, CREAM: *Would he hit Math 1 in the eye? He'd knock it for a loop*—P Marks

knock someone or something **galley west** (or **skywest**) *v phr fr middle 1800s* To hit someone or something very hard, esp to knock unconscious; trounce; =CLOBBER: *Jimmy likewise knocked him galley-west*—Foy and Harlow/ *something that will knock somebody around here skywest*—L Ford

knock something **into a cocked hat** *v phr fr early 1800s* To disprove, invalidate, or show the falsity of a statement, plea, etc: *This knocks our whole case into a cocked hat* [literally "flatten," since a naval officer's cocked hat could be flattened]

knock someone or something **into the middle of next week** *v phr* To hit extremely hard; =CLOBBER

knock it off or **knock it** *v phr fr middle 1800s Navy* To stop doing or saying something; desist; =CUT IT OUT ● Often a stern command: *I told you creeps to knock it off, now I'm gonna waste you*

knock someone's **lights out 1** *v phr* To beat severely; =BEAT THE SHIT OUT OF someone, CLOBBER **2** *v phr* To impress enormously; =KNOCK someone's SOCKS OFF: *I have a story that would knock your lights out*—Sam Shepard

knock off 1 *v phr* To stop, esp to stop working; desist **2** *v phr* To produce, esp with seeming ease and rapidity: *He knocked off a couple of portraits at $40,000 each* **3** *v phr* To consume, esp to drink; =KNOCK DOWN: *after knocking off a glass of...wine*—John McCarten/ *while I knock off two or three or four drinks*—Esquire **4** *v phr* To delete; shorten by: *Let's knock off this last paragraph* **5** *v phr* To kill; murder; assassinate; =RUB OUT: *Before long the spiders knock off Michael*—Judith Crist/ *sent to a lonely spot and knocked off*—E Lavine **6** *v phr* To die; pass away **7** *v phr* To arrest, esp after a raid: *Local cops...had free authority to knock them off*—Westbrook Pegler **8** *v phr* To rob; =HOLD UP, KNOCK OVER: *The pair knocked off several shops, a bank, and jewelry stores*—Associated Press ◁**9**▷ *v phr* To do the sex act with, esp as a prostitute; satisfy a sex client: *if you're a street hooker and knock off twenty or thirty guys a day*—Xaviera Hollander/ *She couldn't see anybody just knocking her off one time*—Claude Brown **10** *v phr* To defeat; overcome: *The Tigers knocked off the Yankees today* **11** *v phr* To attain; operate at: *The old tub was knocking off 12 knots and groaning like a cow in labor*

◁**knock off a piece**▷ *v phr* To do the sex act; copulate; =SCREW

knockout 1 *n* An especially attractive person or thing; =DISH: *Saaay, you know, you're a knockout*—Jerome Weidman **2** *modifier*: *That was a knockout plot*—K Brush/ *a knockout wife and two daughters*—Ira Levin

knock oneself **out 1** *v phr* To work very hard; do one's utmost: *They like "knocking themselves out" for Variety*—Abel Green **2** *v phr* To have a splendid and exhausting time: *They knocked themselves out drinking and dancing*

knock someone **out 1** *v phr* (also **knock** someone **stiff**) To make someone unconscious, esp with a blow **2** *v phr* To delight or impress someone extremely; =KILL, KNOCK someone's SOCKS OFF: *I read a lot of war books and mysteries and all, but they don't knock me out too much*—JD Salinger/ *He knocked me out. He just killed me!*—Rolling Stone

knock something **out** *v phr* To make or produce, esp rather quickly and crudely: *I haven't got time to knock the script out myself*—Budd Schulberg

knockout drops *n phr* Chloral hydrate or another stupefacient drug, esp when put into a drink of liquor; =MICKEY FINN

knockover *n underworld* A robbery; =HEIST

knock over 1 *v phr* (also **kick over**) *fr underworld* To rob; =HOLD UP, KNOCK OFF: *made regular sweeps by jet, knocking over airport motels*—Time/ *We kick over the spot*—American Mercury/ *to prevent people from coming in to case the joint so they can knock it over later*—Washington Post **2** *v phr* To raid: *knocked over a reputed...bookmaking parlor*—J Martin

knocks *n* Extreme pleasure; gratification; =COOKIES, JOLLIES, KICKS: *They get their knocks that way*—Pete Martin

knock (or **blow**) someone's **socks off** *v phr* To delight extremely; thrill and amaze; =KILL, SEND: *It's undressing that really knocks your socks off*—Playboy/ *We got a sound that's gonna knock your socks off*—Rolling Stone/ *a "surprise special" that we think will blow your socks off*—Playboy [these senses fr mid-19th-century sense "defeat utterly," fr the notion of hitting someone so hard that he is lifted right out of his shoes and socks]

knock them in the aisles *See* LAY THEM IN THE AISLES

knock the props from under (or **out from under**) *v phr* To make a position, argument, opinion, etc, invalid; call into serious question: *What he found out knocks the props from under her story*

◁**knock the shit out of** someone or something▷ *See* BEAT THE SHIT OUT OF someone or something

knock (or **throw**) **together** *v phr* To make or produce something quickly: *what you said about knocking something together that we could eat*—James M Cain/ *In the few minutes available they threw together a cover story*

knock someone **up** ◁**1**▷ *v phr* To make pregnant **2** *v phr* To awaken someone; arouse by knocking ● Used with arch jocularity by Americans who know that it is a British term, meaning to awaken someone with a knock at the door, with a vulgar US meaning

knothead *n* A stupid person: *Look at Petey, a knothead*—Max Shulman/ *The movie states the knothead's case in its early passages*—Time

know *See* IN THE KNOW

know (or **have**) **all the answers 1** *v phr* To claim or affect special intimate knowledge: *That little creep over there always thinks he knows all the answers* **2** *v phr* To have a jaded, cynical, spiritless sort of wisdom: *She don't bother any more, knows all the answers* **3** *v phr* To know a case or subject thoroughly ● Most often in the negative: *Even your doctor doesn't have all the answers*

◁not **know** one's **ass from** one's **elbow** (or **from a hole in the ground**)▷ *See* NOT KNOW one's ASS FROM one's ELBOW

not **know beans** *See* NOT KNOW BEANS

not **know** someone **from Adam** *See* NOT KNOW someone FROM ADAM

not **know** someone or something **from a hole in the ground** *See* NOT KNOW someone FROM A HOLE IN THE GROUND

know (or **not know**) **from nothing** *v phr* To be ignorant; be deeply uninformed or ill-informed: *That pompous bastard knows from nothing* [fr Yiddish *fun gornisht*]

know-how *n fr middle 1800s* Skill, esp technical skill; practical competence: *Takes know-how to run that thing*

know-it-all *n* A person who pretends to virtual omniscience; =BIGMOUTH, SMART-ASS

know one's **onions** *v phr* (Variations: **beans** or **business** or **stuff** may replace **onions**) *fr early*

1900s To be very competent and authoritative in one's work: *I'm glad the tax accountant knows his onions*

◁not **know shit from Shinola**▷ *See* NOT KNOW SHIT FROM SHINOLA

know the ropes *v phr fr middle 1800s nautical* To be seasoned and informed; know the intricacies of a job, situation, etc; = KNOW one's WAY AROUND [fr the myriad *ropes* of a sailing vessel]

know the score *v phr* To have essential and current information; understand what is important: *You look like a smart lad who knows the score*—J Evans

know one's **way around** *v phr* To be informed and experienced; be seasoned and reliable: *He's been at the job for two years but still doesn't know his way around*

know what one **can do with** something *v phr* (Variations: **where** one **can put** (or **shove** or **stick** or **stuff**) may replace **what** one **can do with**) To know that one's offer, request, possession, etc, is held in extreme contempt ● A euphemized way of saying that one can take something and **stick it up** his or her **ass**: *I saw the contract, and he knows what he can do with it/ I told him where he can shove that great idea of his*

know where it's at *v phr esp 1960s counterculture* To be up-to-date and cognizant; = be HIP: *the NOW generation, who, like, know what's happening and where it's at*—Trans-Action

know where the bodies are buried *v phr* To have intimate and secret knowledge, esp of something criminal, scandalous, etc: *The president reckoned he had to keep that lawyer quiet, because he knew where the bodies were buried*

knucker or **knucksman** *n underworld fr middle 1800s* A pickpocket [fr late-18th-century English criminal slang *knuckler* or *knuckle* "pickpocket," perhaps referring to the suppleness and sleight of the fingers of an expert]

knuckle 1 *n* The head: *one clonk on the knuckle*—Saturday Evening Post **2** *n* Bone: *nothin' upstairs but solid knuckle*—The Asphalt Jungle (movie)
See WHITE KNUCKLE

knuckleball or **knuckler 1** *n baseball fr early 1900s* A pitch thrown from the knuckles that moves slowly and erratically; = BUTTERFLY BALL: *Leonard's tantalizing knucklers*—L Effrat **2** *modifier*: *a knuckleball artist*

knuckle-buster *n* An end wrench

knuckled *See* WHITE-KNUCKLED

knuckle down *v phr fr middle 1800s* To work hard and seriously; stop loafing; = BUCKLE DOWN [fr the act of putting one's *knuckles* down to the taw or marble preparing for a careful shot in the game of marbles, a use dating fr the mid-18th century]

knuckle-dragger *n fr college students* A rough, somewhat stupid and crude man; = GORILLA, STRONG ARM MAN: *the tendency of some covert agents, "the knuckledraggers" of the Special Oper-*ations Group, *to revel in deception*—Washingtonian [from the image of a gorilla whose *knuckles drag* on the ground when it walks]

knuckle-duster *n baseball* A pitch thrown inside near the batter's knuckles

knuckle-dusters *n fr middle 1800s* Brass knuckles

knucklehead *n* A stupid person; = BONEHEAD: *Movies are made by unappreciative knuckleheads*—Pete Martin

knuckler *See* KNUCKLEBALL, WHITE KNUCKLER

knuckles *See* RAP someone's KNUCKLES

knuckle sandwich *n phr* A hard blow to the mouth or face: *I feed him a knuckle sandwich*—Lawrence Sanders/ *You keep that up and you're going to get a knuckle sandwich*—Newsweek

knucks *n* Brass knuckles; = KNUCKLE-DUSTERS: *The "knucks" were hidden in the heel*—Associated Press

KO (pronounced as separate letters) **1** *n prizefight* A knockout; = KAYO **2** *v*: *He KOed six in a row* **3** *modifier*: *a KO punch*
See TKO

kocker *See* ALTER KOCKER

Kong or **kong** *n black* = KING KONG

kook (Kō̄K) **1** *n fr 1950s teenagers* An eccentric person; = NUT, SCREWBALL: *The bomb cannot be exploded by a single "kook"*—Nation/ *The early Streisand played kook*—Look **2** *modifier*: *did a kook piece with dancers*—Village Voice **3** *n surfers* A novice surfer [fr *cuckoo*]

kookie or **kooky** *adj fr 1950s teenagers* Crazy; eccentric; = DIPPY, GOOFY: *make you seem a little kookie*—David Halberstam/ *the kooky stunt so pleased him*—Time

kootchy *See* the HOOTCHIE-COOTCHIE

kopasetic *See* COPACETIC

kosh *n* = COSH

kosher *adj* Proper; as it should be; legitimate: *Something about this arrangement ain't kosher/ It all looked kosher until Buzzy stepped on a mine* [fr Yiddish fr Hebrew *kasher* "fit, proper"]

◀**kraut** or **Kraut** or **krauthead**▶ **1** *n esp WW2 armed forces* A German, esp a German soldier: *Oh, that kraut-head*—Tennessee Williams **2** *adj*: *kraut wine* [fr *sauerkraut*, regarded as a favorite and characteristic German food]

Krishna *See* HARE KRISHNA KIDS

kvell (KVEL) *v* To display pride and satisfaction; beam: *The elderly couple...kvell also...upon making contact with a Jewish airstrip*—Philip Roth/ *Hollywood agents, kissing and kvelling*—New York [fr Yiddish, literally "gush, flow forth"]

kvetch (kə VECH) **1** *v* To whine; complain; be consistently pessimistic: *Dealing with a controversial idea of public importance, Mobil kvetched*—Village Voice **2** *n*: *Your sister's a nagging kvetch/ right in tune with the city hospital spirit, which is basically one of kvetch*—New York [fr Yiddish, literally "squeeze, press"]

kyuter (KYō̄ tər) *See* CUTER

L

lab 1 *n* A laboratory **2** *modifier:* *lab work/ a lab coat*

labonza *n* The belly; =GUT, KISHKES: *She let him have it right in the labonza* [probably fr Italian *pancia* "paunch," with attached article and dialectal pronunciation]

labor *See* GRUNT WORK

◁**lace-curtain Irish**▷ *n phr* Prosperous and respectable persons of Irish extraction: *become lace-curtain Irish...across the tracks*—AE Hutson [fr the fact that *lace curtains* in the windows would be a sign of prosperity and of social superiority relative to the laboring class]

lacy *adj* Effeminate; homosexual

la-de-da (Variations: **lah-de-dah** or **la-di-da** or **lah-di-dah**) *fr middle 1800s British* **1** *n* A dandyish or sissified man; super-refined and delicate person: *Some lah-de-da with a cane*—Hecht and MacArthur **2** *adj:* *lunch place of the la-de-dah literary set*—New York Confidential **3** *adj* Very refined and respectable: *Nobody weren't going to make her live in a lah-di-dah place like that*—RGG Price **4** *adj* Carefree and nonchalant: *Her emotions at the dissolution of her 25-year marriage are anything but la-de-da*—Us **5** *v* To treat in a nonchalant, off-hand manner: *The outfielder la-di-da'd the catch* **6** *interj* A phrase used to mean the equivalent of "It doesn't matter": *You're cancelling our date? Oh well, lah-di-da*

ladies' (or **lady's**) **man 1** *n phr* A man who pursues and otherwise devotes himself to women to an unusual degree; =LOVER-BOY **2** *n phr* A man who is attractive to many women: *He's so conceited...thinks he's a real ladies' man*

lady *n* Any woman; any grown-up female ● Often used in quasi-polite direct address: *Lady, will you please move your car?*
See BAG LADY, FAIRY LADY, OLD LADY, the OPERA'S NEVER OVER TILL THE FAT LADY SINGS

the lady *n phr narcotics* Cocaine

Lady H *n phr narcotics* Heroin: *urging teens to stay away from Lady H*—Los Angeles Times

lady-killer *n* =LADIES' MAN

laff riot 1 *n phr* A very funny show, event, etc: *the "Tristan und Isolde" of laff riots*—New Yorker **2** *n phr* Something very amusing; an occasion for hilarity ● Often used ironically: *Otherwise I might have turned into a "laff riot,"...a zany*—Saul Bellow/ *Oh yeah, the meeting was a regular laff riot* [fr a cliché based on an advertising misspelling of *laugh* for humorous effect]

lag *underworld* **1** *n* A convict **2** *n* Any criminal

lagger *n underworld* A convict, esp one on parole

lagniappe (LAN yap) *n fr middle 1800s* A dividend; something extra: *I hit her with a few real hard ones for lagniappe (or good measure)*—Louis Armstrong [fr New Orleans Creole, origin unknown and much speculated; originally a little present or gratuity given to a customer by a New Orleans merchant]

laid-back *adj* Relaxed; easy-going: *a sort of laid-back, not insane Janis Joplin*—V Aletti/ *relatively upbeat moods, laid-back-in-the-South-Seas*—New Times [perhaps fr the reclining posture of highway motorcyclists]

laid out *adj* Drunk

◁**laid, relaid, and parlayed**▷ **1** *adj phr* Very copiously and satisfactorily treated sexually **2** *adj phr* Thoroughly deceived and cheated

lallygag *See* LOLLYGAG

lam *underworld fr late 1800s* **1** *v* To depart; go, esp hastily in escaping: *lammed for Cleveland*—H Witwer **2** *v* To escape from prison [ultimately fr 16th-century British sense "beat," hence the same semantically as *beat it*]
See ON THE LAM, TAKE IT ON THE LAM

lamb 1 *n* A person who is easily victimized; =PATSY, SUCKER **2** *n* =LAMBIE **3** *n* A dear, sweet person: *Mary is such a lamb*

lambaste or **lambast** (lam BAYST, lam BAST) **1** *v fr middle 1800s* To hit very hard; =CLOBBER: *They lambasted the suspect mercilessly* **2** *v* To disparage strongly; castigate: *A woman psychologist today lambasted the idea that "mom is to blame"*—AL Blakeslee [ultimately fr British *lam* and *baste*, both "beat"]

lambie or **lambie-pie** *n* One's sweetheart; beloved: *a dithering meditation on a lackluster Don Juan. Are Reynolds and Edwards such unmanly lambie-pies?*—Washington Post

lame 1 *n esp teenagers fr black* An old-fashioned, conventional person; =SQUARE: *and not worry about anybody naming me a lame*—Claude Brown/ *not have been as quick to judge him as a lame*—Rolling Stone **2** *adj:* *He's so lame I can't believe he was born in this century* **3** *adj* Inept: *Their performances were sloppy, sometimes even lame*—Saturday Review

lamebrain *n* A stupid person; =DOPE, KNUCKLEHEAD: *Not all the lamebrains on Capitol Hill frequent the House or Senate*—Washington Post

lamebrained *adj* Stupid; =KLUTZY

lamed *adj* Stupid; dim

lame duck 1 *n phr fr middle 1800s* A public official who has lost an election or one who is not permitted by law to seek reelection for an additional term but is serving out a term **2** *modifier: lame-duck president/ lame-duck session* **3** *n phr stock market* A speculator who has taken options on stocks he or she cannot pay for

lamp *fr middle 1800s* **1** *n* An eye: *a beefsteak...for this lamp of mine*—P Marks **2** *n* A look; glance; =GANDER **3** *v: Lamp the lad in blue*—FK Secrist

See BITCH LAMP, KEN-TEN LAMP, SLUT LAMP

lamster *n underworld* An escaped convict [fr *lam*]

landing *See* CHINESE LANDING

landsman (LAHNTS mən) *n* A fellow countryman, townsman, etc; compatriot; =HOMEBOY, PAESAN: *You from Kalamazoo? Landsman!* [fr Yiddish]

land up *v phr* To conclude by being; end up: *shows Nina landing up pregnant by Blume*—New Yorker

lane *See* FAST LANE, HAMMER LANE, IN THE STRAIGHT LANE

lap 1 *n fr 1920s* A round of a prizefight **2** *n* A swallow of liquor; =SLURP

lap organ *n phr* An accordion

lapper *See* CUNT-LAPPER

lapping *See* CUNT-LAPPING

lard *See* TUB OF GUTS

lard-bucket *n* A fat person; =TUB OF GUTS

lardhead *n* A stupid person; =FATHEAD

large *adj fr theater & jazz talk* Very popular and successful; highly favored; =BIG: *His act was quite large in Boston*

large charge 1 *n phr esp 1940s students fr jive talk* Great pleasure; =CHARGE, KICK: *I can hardly do justice to the large charge I get out of you* **2** *n phr* =BIG SHOT

large evening *n phr* A festive, pleasant, exciting, etc, evening: *The good doctor had himself a large evening*—LF McHugh

large for *adj phr fr theater & jazz talk* Enthusiastic over; very much pleased with: *This week they're large for Renato Zero; next week, who knows*

large one *n phr underworld* A year in prison: *The Tiger got fifteen large ones*—George V Higgins

larky *adj chiefly British* Playful; frolicsome; bantering: *began making larky plunges into show business*—Time

larry 1 *n circus* Any shoddy or broken small article of merchandise **2** *adj salespersons* Worthless; shoddy: *pushing larry merchandise*—M Zolotow [origin unknown; formerly quite common in underworld and circus slang as a synonym for "bad, lousy"]

See HOUSE LARRY

lash-up *n WW2 Army fr British* Living quarters; barracks; =DIGS

last *See* NICE GUYS FINISH LAST, TRADE-LAST

the last dance *See* GET THE LAST DANCE

latch on to or **latch on** *fr 1930s black* **1** *v phr* To get; obtain; =GLOM ON TO: *Latch on to the first seat that's empty/ When you find the page, latch on* **2** *v phr* To comprehend; grasp; =DIG: *He finally latched onto the truth* **3** *v phr* To attach oneself to; be dependent on: *He latched on to me as soon as I arrived*

lately *See* JOHNNY-COME-LATELY

later *interj esp teenagers fr black* A parting salutation: *I dug right away what the kick was, so I said, "Later," and he split*—Eldridge Cleaver

lather *v fr late 1700s* To hit; strike: *He lathered the ball out of the park/ They caught him and lathered him* [fr the notion that frothy washing *lather* is produced by vigorous agitation or beating; see *in a lather*]

lathered *adj* Drunk

latrine (or **barracks**) **lawyer** *n phr Army* A soldier who is argumentative, esp on fine points, and tends to be a meddler, complainer, and self-server

latrine rumor *n phr WW2 Army* An idle rumor that probably has no basis in fact

lats *n* The latissimus dorsi muscles: *checking the cut of their lats in shiny windows*—San Francisco

laugh *See* BELLY LAUGH, the HORSELAUGH

a laugh or **a laugh and a half** *n phr* Something funny; a cause of amusement, esp of contemptuous derision: *You're gonna cook? That's a laugh*

laugher *n esp sports* A laughing matter, esp a game in which one team scores an annihilating victory: *The two games he mentioned were laughers, Oklahoma 41-7 over North Carolina*—Sports Illustrated/ *I like to see it about 16-0. I like laughers*—Inside Sports

laughing academy *n phr* A mental hospital; =FUNNY FARM, NUT HOUSE

laughing soup *n phr* Liquor; =BOOZE

laugh on (or **out of**) **the other side of** one's **face** *v phr* To lament and moan; suffer a change of mood from joy to distress; undergo a defeat: *When they get through with him he'll be laughing out of the other side of his face*

launching pad *n phr narcotics* =SHOOTING GALLERY

launder *v* To transfer or convert funds so that illegal or dubious receipts are made to appear legitimate: *the account money that had been "laundered" by being siphoned from this country into Mexico and returned under an alias*—W Barthelmes

laundry 1 *n* A bank or other place used for laundering illegal or dubious money **2** *n WW2 Air Forces* A board of faculty members that passes on flying cadets [second sense from the fact that some cadets were *washed out* "failed" by such a board]

See HANG OUT THE LAUNDRY

laundry (or **shopping**) **list** *n phr* A long bill of items to be obtained, discussed, done, or not done: *This "do-good" laundry list draws sneers*—Maurice Moskowitz/ *The cadets didn't need a laundry list of prohibitions*—New York Times/ *A shopping list is not a strategy*—New York Review

lava *See* IN A LATHER

lavender *See* LAY someone OUT

law *See* SQUEAL RULE, SUNSET LAW, SUNSHINE LAW

Law *See* JOHN LAW

the **law** *n phr fr underworld* Any police officer, prison guard, etc

the **lawn** *n phr horse-racing* The infield of a racetrack: *Bookies took places on "the lawn"*—T Betts

lawnmower **1** *n baseball* A grounder **2** *n* A sheep

lawyer *n salespersons* A friend who accompanies a customer to a store and gives much free advice *See* CLUBHOUSE LAWYER, FORECASTLE LAWYER, JAILHOUSE LAWYER, LATRINE LAWYER, SEA LAWYER

lay **1** *n outdated hoboes & underworld* A thieving expedition ◁**2**▷ *n* A person regarded merely as a sex partner or object: *The two girls looked like swell lays*—James T Farrell/ *She's a great lay*—Saturday Review ◁**3**▷ *n* A sex act; = PIECE OF ASS: *anyone who is looking for an easy lay*—New York ◁**4**▷ *v: five cadets who swore they'd all laid the girl one night*—Calder Willingham **5** *v* To bet: *I laid her six to one he wouldn't show up* *See* EASY MAKE, GOOSEBERRY LAY

lay a batch *v phr hot rodders* To leave black rubber marks on the road by accelerating a car rapidly

◁**lay (cut** or **let) a fart**▷ *v phr* To flatulate; = FART: *This guy...laid this terrific fart*—JD Salinger

not **lay a glove** (or **finger** or **hand**) on someone *See* NOT LAY A GLOVE ON someone

lay an egg *v phr fr late 1800s* To fail; = BOMB, FLOP: *The plan's going to lay an egg unless we give it a shot in the arm* [fr earlier British *lay a duck's egg* "make a score of zero"]

lay a trip (or **scene**) **on** someone *v phr fr 1960s counterculture fr black* To attribute something to someone; burden someone with something; accuse someone of something: *But if you try and lay a trip on somebody through psychoanalysis, it's nonsense*—Changes/ *Don't lay this scene on me. I did the best I could*—Paul Sann/ *Vote for...Walker....But don't lay any undue trips on him*—Amsterdam News

lay back *v phr fr black* To relax; take one's ease: *not a Southern-rock band. They don't lay back*—Rolling Stone

lay chickie *v phr street gang* To act as a lookout for criminals: *not having anyone to lay chickie for me*—Claude Brown [origin unknown]

lay down on the job *v phr* To loaf; dawdle and shirk

lay for someone *v phr* To watch for one's chance to take revenge; vigilantly stalk: *I'd lay for him in town some night*—Calder Willingham

lay it on *v phr fr middle 1800s* To exaggerate; = BULLSHIT

lay (or **put**) **it on the line** (or **on the table**) *v phr* To speak candidly and straightforwardly; = TELL IT LIKE IT IS: *OK, no more fancy footwork, I'll lay it on the line/ They are more likely to give it to you if you lay it on the table*—CoEvolution Quarterly

lay low *v phr* To stay out of sight; remain inconspicuous: *We're layin' low a couple days*—Nelson Algren

layoff **1** *n* A dismissal or furlough from a a job **2** *n gambling* The part of a bookmaker's bets placed

with another agent to forestall catastrophic loss **3** *n theater* An unemployed actor: *A couple of layoffs...were walking out of the hotel*—Lionel Stander

lay off **1** *v phr* To stop troubling or harrying someone; leave someone in peace ● Often an irritated command or entreaty: *So lay off or I'll split your head, baby*—Changes **2** *v phr gambling* To place a portion of the bets one has accepted with other agents, so as to reduce one's possible losses

lay someone **off** *v phr* To terminate someone's job

lay something **on** someone *esp 1960s counterculture fr black* **1** *v phr* To present an idea, point of view, etc: *And the sisters laid the revolutionary ideology right on them*—Bobby Seale **2** *v phr* To tell or inform: *I have something heavy to lay on you, I'm afraid*

◁**lay one**▷ *v phr* = LAY A FART

lay one on *v phr* To hit hard; punch; = HANG ONE ON: *She laid one on him, when he least expected it*

lay (or **put**) something **on the line** *v phr* To put deliberately at risk; put in peril as a wager or hostage: *If you try this, remember you are laying your ass on the line*

layout **1** *n* A place; house; living arrangements: *Nice little layout you got here* **2** *n* Place, equipment, apparatus, etc, for a particular purpose: *This layout is for writing dictionaries* *See* COFFEE-AND-CAKE JOINT

lay someone **out** (or **out in lavender**) **1** *v phr fr late 1800s* To knock down; = DECK: *If that woman gets the Republican nomination...I will lay her out in lavender*—Vivian Kellems **2** *v phr* To reprimand; castigate [fr the *laying out* of a dead person]

lay paper *v phr underworld* To pass counterfeit money, worthless checks, etc

lay pipe (or **tube**) ◁**1**▷ *v phr fr black* To do the sex act; copulate; = SCREW: *If you're up all night, laying pipe, you won't be worth a shit to me on the court*—Tom Aldibrandi/ *About eighty a them's gonna lay more tube than the motherfuckin' Alaska Pipeline*—Playboy **2** *v phr* To specify; spell out: *You can't just infer that; you gotta lay pipe*—Don't Touch That Dial (TV program)

lay rubber *v phr hot rodders* To accelerate rapidly and speed in a car, so as to leave black tire marks on the road

lay them in the aisles *v phr* (Variations: **have** or **knock** or **put** may replace **lay**) To entertain, amuse, or impress an audience extravagantly; = WOW

lead *n* Bullets; gunfire *See* GET THE LEAD OUT, HAVE LEAD IN one's PANTS, HAVE LEAD IN one's PENCIL, RED LEAD, THROW LEAD

lead balloon *n phr* A dismal failure; = FLOP: *His run for office was a lead balloon* *See* GO OVER LIKE A LEAD BALLOON

lead someone **down the garden path** *v phr* To deceive someone; hoodwink someone: *Will anyone know who led whom down the garden path?*—New Yorker

lead foot (LED fŏŏt) *n* A fast driver: *Make sure to wear your seatbelt. He's a real lead foot*

lead-footed (LED foŏt əd) **1** *adj* Sluggish and awkward; clumsy: *The bungling, lead-footed fellow* —R Wallace **2** *adj* Tending to drive very fast

lead joint *n phr* carnival A shooting gallery

lead-pipe cinch 1 *n phr* fr 1930s A certainty; inescapable fact: *not early enough to move no tables, that's a lead-pipe cinch*—Nelson Algren/ *calls ColecoVision a "lead-pipe cinch" for making a strong showing at Christmas*—Toronto Life **2** *n phr* Something very easy; =CINCH, PIECE OF CAKE: *It's a lead-pipe cinch for somebody that strong* [fr the fact that a *lead pipe* can be easily bent, in case one has bet on such a feat]

lead-poisoning *n* fr cowboys Gunshot wounds

the **leaf** *n phr* narcotics Cocaine

league *See* BIG-LEAGUE, BUSH LEAGUE, GRAPEFRUIT LEAGUE, HOT STOVE LEAGUE, OUT OF one's LEAGUE

leaguer *See* TEXAS LEAGUER

leagues *See* the BIG LEAGUES, the BUSH LEAGUES

leak 1 *v* To give information to the press or other recipient secretly: *Then the FCC report was "leaked" to the press*—RG Spivack **2** *n* A person, channel, etc, from which secret information is reaching places it should not: *A famous leak was called Deep Throat* **3** *n* A point of weakness in a system of information security: *a leak in the department* ◁**4**▷ *n* An act of urination; =a PISS ◁**5**▷ *v* To urinate; =PISS: *He said he had to leak, his back teeth were floating* *See* TAKE A LEAK

lean and mean *adj phr* Desperately and somewhat menacingly ambitious; =HUNGRY: *"Lean and mean" is the byword in publishing these days*—New York

lean forward in the saddle *v phr* Army To be eager and anxious; =be RARING TO GO

lean on someone **1** *v phr* To put pressure on someone, esp with violence or the threat of it: *and he thinks he can lean on me!*—Hannibal & Boris/ *Several restaurants and clubs...were being leaned on*—Jackie Collins **2** *v phr* To depend on for understanding, assistance, etc: *Well, we all need someone we can lean on*—Mick Jagger

the **leaping heebies** *See* the HEEBIE-JEEBIES

leap on the bandwagon *See* GET ON THE BANDWAGON

leap-tick circus **1** *n* A mattress on which clowns, acrobats, etc, fall **2** *n* The false paunch of a comedian or clown [fr *leap* plus *tick* "bed, mattress"]

leary *See* LEERY

the **least** *n phr* beat & cool talk The worst; the dullest, most conventional, etc

leather 1 *n* underworld A purse or wallet **2** *n* A football **3** *n* Boxing gloves **4** *n* The clothing and trappings of overt sado-masochism; =S AND M **5** *adj*: *a leather outfit/ leather porn* **6** *n* homosexuals A kind of male homosexual behavior, costume, etc, based on exaggerated masculinity as symbolized esp by black-leather-clad motorcycle gangs **7** *modifier*: *jokes about the heroine's harmless male roommate, leather men, etc*—New Republic/ *becomes part of the leather-bar homo-*

sexual underworld—New York Times/ *the sex clubs and leather bars of the gay ghetto*—New York *See* HEAVY LEATHER, HELL-FOR-LEATHER, THROW LEATHER

the **leather 1** *n phr* A kick: *what we called "the leather," meaning a few boots*—Damon Runyon **2** *n phr* A blow with the fist

leatherneck *n* fr late 1800s Navy A US Marine; =GYRENE [fr the *leather* collars of their early uniforms]

leave *See* FRENCH LEAVE

leave a strip *v phr* hot rodders To brake or decelerate a car very rapidly, so as to leave black rubber marks on the pavement

leaves[1] *See* BOILED LEAVES

leaves[2] *n* esp 1950s teenagers Denim dungarees; =LEVIS [fr *Levis*]

Leblang theater fr 1920s **1** *v* To sell theater tickets at reduced prices **2** *v* To reduce the price of admission to a theater [fr Joe *Leblang*, a New York ticket agent]

lech or **letch** fr early 1900s **1** *n* Strong desire, esp sexual; lust; =the HOTS: *his lech for cam shafts and turbines*—James M Cain **2** *v*: *when Henry goes letching after Anne*—Vincent Canby/ *keep Junior from leching*—Time **3** *n* A lecher: *under the illusion that the lech is as enamored as she is* —Inquiry/ *who also appears as a good-natured lech* —Newsweek [fr *lecher, lechery*, ultimately fr the notion of licking] *See* HAVE A LECH FOR someone or something

leech 1 *n* A human parasite **2** *v*: *insisted that MCI was not leeching off the successful campaign of its competition*—Philadelphia Journal

leery or **leary** *adj* fr late 1700s British Untrusting; suspicious; wary: *He was leery of toting so much money*—Dashiell Hammett/ *Cheyfitz and Farrell exchanged leery glances*—Hannibal and Boris [probably fr British dialect *lere* "learning, knowledge"]

left *See* HANG A LEFT

Left Coast *n phr* The Pacific Coast: *That's not what they're saying out on the Left Coast*—Playboy

left field *See* OUT IN LEFT FIELD

left-handed 1 *adj* merchant marine Undesirable; unlucky **2** *adj* Irregular; illicit: *left-handed honeymoons with someone else's husband*—J Evans **3** *adj* Homosexual

left-handed compliment *n phr* Praise that is subtle dispraise; reluctant and dubious praise: *Telling her she has the constitution of a horse is maybe a left-handed compliment*

left nut *See* GRIPE one's ASS

lefty or **leftie 1** *n* A left-handed person, esp a left-handed pitcher or other athlete **2** *modifier*: *a lefty hurler/ leftie tennis ace* **3** *n* A person of liberal or socialist political beliefs; radical; liberal: *such urban lefties as Bella Abzug*—National Review **4** *n* A shoe, glove, etc, for a left-side member

leg 1 *v* (also **leg it**) To go; travel: *I was legging down the line* **2** *n* Vietnam War Army An infantry soldier; =GRUNT **3** *n* college students fr black A woman, esp a sexually promiscuous one

See an ARM AND A LEG, BOOTLEG, DIRTYLEG, GIVE someone LEG, HAVE A LEG UP ON someone or something, HOG LEG, MIDDLE LEG, PANTS-LEG, PEG LEG, PULL someone's LEG, SHAKE A LEG, SHAKE A WICKED CALF, SHOW A LEG, TANGLE-FOOTED

legal eagle (or **beagle**) *n phr* A lawyer, esp a clever and aggressive one: *In 1979 Davis's legal eagles got him acquitted again*—Newsweek

leg-biter *n college students* A small child or infant; = CRUMB-CRUSHER

legger 1 *n* = BOOTLEGGER **2** *n* = LEG MAN

leggy *adj fr middle 1800s* Having prominent legs, esp long and shapely ones ● Nearly always used of women: *Not very chesty, but nicely leggy*

legit (lə JIHT) *fr early 1900s* **1** *adj* Legitimate; = KOSHER: *She's a legit farmer*—H Allen Smith/ *by legit, or honest, people*—E DeBaun **2** *adj* Having to do with or being of the legitimate theater: *a legit play/ specialists in legit reviewing*—Abel Green **3** *n* A legitimate theater

See ON THE LEGIT

leg man 1 *n phr newspaper office* A newspaper reporter who goes out to gather facts, and may or may not write the story **2** *n phr* Any person who works actively and outside, rather than in, an office **3** *n phr* A man whose favorite part of the female body is the legs

leg-off case *n phr lawyers* A major injury claim

leg-pull *n* The act of deceiving or fooling someone; = PUT-ON: *the wisecrack and the gag, the leg pull and the hotfoot*—James Thurber

Legree *See* SIMON LEGREE

legs *n show business* The ability of a show, song, public figure, etc, to be an enduring success; staying power: *whether a movie will have legs, the power to entice audiences week after week*—New York Times/ *runaway success, bigger than disco, with stronger legs*—Newsweek/ *Rep Jack Kemp...he's got legs*—Washington Post

See BIRD LEGS, FEATHER-LEGS, HARD LEGS, HINDERS

leg show *n phr* A performance featuring the bare legs, etc, of dancers or models

a leg up 1 *n phr* An advantage: *You can go in with a leg up on other people*—Washington Post **2** *n* Aid; a boost: *He'll do OK, but he needs a financial leg up to get started*

See HAVE A LEG UP ON something

lemo 1 *n* Lemonade **2** *n prison & Army* Lemon extract, drunk for its alcohol

lemon[1] **1** *n fr early 1900s* Anything unsatisfactory or defective, esp a car; = CLINKER: *His tale brought back memories of my first lemon*—Mother Jones/ *That show's a lemon* **2** *n black* A light-skinned and attractive black woman; = HIGH YELLOW **3** *n* A sour, disagreeable person **4** *n* (also **lemonade**) *narcotics* Weakened or diluted narcotics, or a nonnarcotic substance sold as a narcotic; = BLANK

See HAND someone A LEMON

lemon[2] *n narcotics* A Quaalude (a trade name) [*Lemmon* is the name of a pharmaceutical company that once manufactured the drug]

lens louse *n phr fr 1940s* A person who obtrusively puts himself into a photograph, television shot, etc, esp by clowning behind the speaker

◁**les** or **lez**▷ (LEZ) *n* A lesbian: *Mary is a les and John is a fairy*—Joe E Lewis/ *I'd have figured you for a lez*—Lawrence Sanders

◁**lesbo**▷ (LEZ boh) *n* A lesbian: *where the Lesbos even come and watch the dress rehearsals*—John O'Hara

let a fart *See* LAY A FART

letch *See* LECH

let daylight (or **sunlight**) **into** *v phr* To bring clarity and illumination to a subject: *They called a meeting to let daylight into the sewer mess/ Maybe if we brought in someone from outside the committee, she could let a little sunlight into the fundraising scheme*

letdown 1 *n* A disappointment; = COMEDOWN **2** *n* A period or sensation of dullness and emptiness after activity or excitement **3** *n* The gradual descent of an airplane toward a landing

let fly (or **go**) **1** *v phr* To launch vigorously into something; begin with projective energy: *She took a deep breath and let fly* **2** *v phr* To hurl; shoot; fire: *The gunman let go with both automatics*—E Lavine

let George do it *sentence fr early 1900s British* Let someone else besides me take care of it [perhaps fr a learned journalist's recall of the French *laissez faire à Georges* "let George do it," referring to Cardinal Georges d'Amboise, a church and government official under Louis XII in the late 15th and early 16th centuries]

let oneself **go** *v phr* To behave in an unrestrained way; be uninhibited: *Come on, Herbert, let yourself go, have another martini*

let someone **go** (or **out**) *v phr* To dismiss from a job; terminate someone

let one's **hair down** *v phr* To be very open and candid, esp about personal matters: *A lot of men that I have been with do not let their hair down*—Sexual Behavior/ *You can let your hair down in front of me*—Jerome Weidman

let someone **have it 1** *v phr* To hit someone, esp powerfully; = CLOBBER: *Then let him have it, right on the chin*—James M Cain **2** *v phr* To attack verbally, esp punitively; = GIVE IT TO someone: *He allows me to count on his affection. Then he lets me have it*—Saul Bellow

let her (or **'er**) **rip** *v phr fr middle 1800s* To let something go at full speed; take off all restraints: *He decided to buckle his seat belt and let her rip*

let it all hang out *v phr esp 1960s counterculture fr black* To be entirely candid; be free and unrestrained; = LET one's HAIR DOWN: *You'll feel better if you let it all hang out*

let it walk *v phr lunch counter* To prepare an order to take out

let moonlight into *v phr fr early 1900s* To shoot: *I'll let moonlight into a captain*—Lawrence Stallings

let (or **blow**) **off steam** *v phr fr early 1800s* To talk loudly and angrily, as a method of relieving the pressure of one's feelings; express one's anger or frustration: *I've blown off steam*—Woman's Home Companion/ *They're bored, just blowing off steam* —WT Tyler

let someone **off the hook** *v phr* To relieve someone of responsibility or menace: *They had already given me a lot. I wanted to let them off the hook*—Philadelphia

let on *v phr fr middle 1800s* To reveal; hint

letout 1 *n* Dismissal from a job: *other Metro executive letouts*—Variety **2** *n* =OUT

let something **ride** *v phr* To let something go on as it is; decline to change or intervene: *Let the same order ride for now*

let's boogie *sentence* (Variations: **cruise** or **blaze** may replace **boogie**) *teenagers* Let us leave

let's face it *sentence* Let us freely admit it; let us accept the unhappy truth: *Let's face it, kids, we're all to blame some*

let's get the (or **this**) **show on the road** *sentence* We should get started; we should become active

let sunlight into *See* LET DAYLIGHT INTO

letter *See* DEAD HORSE, FRENCH LETTER, POISON-PEN LETTER, RED-LETTER DAY

letter man *See* FOUR-LETTER MAN

let the cat out of the bag *v phr* To reveal a secret, usu without intending to: *Her guilty smile pretty much let the cat out of the bag*

lettuce *n* Money, esp paper money; =CABBAGE: *That's a lot of lettuce*—Kenyon Review/ *the man who nipped all this lettuce from the Playboy patch* —Newsweek
See FOLDING MONEY, POCKET CABBAGE

level 1 *v fr early 1900s* To tell the truth; be honest and candid: *Don't laugh. I'm leveling*—Joel Sayre/ *It's on this level that they tell you that they are "leveling" with you*—Saul Bellow **2** *adj* True: *There's never a place for guys like me....That's level*—H Lee
See ON THE LEVEL, RAISE THE DECIBEL LEVEL

someone's **level best** *n phr* The utmost one can do; one's honest greatest effort: *I'll do my level best to keep you*

'leven *See* FORTY-'LEVEN, SEVENTY-'LEVEN

levers *See* GO LEVERS

Levis (LEE vīz) *n* Blue denim dungaree pants; denim work pants [fr *Levi* Strauss, a mid-19th-century Western company that made and makes such garments]

lez *See* LES

◁**lezzie**▷ **1** *n* A lesbian **2** *adj*: *It was a fantastic turn-on, watching a lezzie scene*—Herbert Kastle

lib[1] *n* Liberation, esp as the aim of various movements: *animal lib*
See GAY LIB, MEN'S LIB

lib[2] *See* RADIC-LIB

◁**libber**▷ *n* A member of one of the liberation movements, esp of the women's lib movement: *Thus...did Golda Meir vent her view of women's libbers*—Newsweek/ *"The libber and the lobber." All those lines are mine*—Nora Ephron

libe *students* **1** *n* A library, esp a college library **2** *v* To study in a library

liberate *v fr WW2 Army* To steal or appropriate, originally something in conquered enemy territory

liberty *See* AT LIBERTY

a **license to print money** *n phr* A very lucrative business: *Having a liquor store on that corner is a license to print money*

lick 1 *n fr middle 1800s* A blow; stroke: *I got in a couple good licks before he decked me* **2** *n* A try; attempt; =CRACK, SHOT: *I probably won't make it, but I'll give it a good lick* **3** *n fr 1920s jazz musicians* A short figure or solo, esp when improvised; =BREAK, RIFF: *a few solid licks on the sliphorn* —C Smith/ *that I know are exactly the licks that I play*—Rolling Stone
See HIT IT A LICK

a **lick and a promise** *n phr fr middle 1800s* A hasty job; a cursory performance [fr the notion that one does one *lick* or stroke of what is appropriate, and *promises* to do the rest]

lick one's **chops** *v phr* To display hunger and anticipation, for food or for something else desired: *We all sat licking our chops as the turkey was carved/ I licked my chops when I thought of that huge bonus*

licker *See* ASS-KISSER, CLIT-LICKER, DICK-LICKER, TOKUS LICKER

lickety-split *adv fr middle 1800s* Very fast: *They ran lickety-split to the store*

licorice stick *n phr jive talk* The clarinet

lid 1 *n* A hat **2** *n narcotics* One ounce of marijuana: *a shutdown on grass, lids were going for thirty dollars*—Saturday Review/ *lifted out the back seat and found a lid of marijuana*—Rolling Stone
See BLOW THE LID OFF, EVE WITH THE LID ON, FLIP one's LID, PUT A LID ON something or someone, SKID LID

lie *See* the BIG LIE, a PACK OF LIES

lie doggo *v phr fr late 1800s British* To stay in hiding; secrete oneself; =LAY LOW: *You better lie doggo a while till it blows over* [probably fr the silent and unobtrusive behavior of a hunting or herding *dog* when stalking]

lieut (Lō͞oT) *n fr 1700s* Lieutenant; =LOOT

lieutenant *See* THIRD LIEUTENANT

life *See* BET YOUR BOOTS, LOW-LIFE, NOT ON YOUR LIFE

the **life** or **the Life 1** *n phr* Prostitution, esp as a business: *generally understood by those in the Life*—FAJ Ianni/ *this latter often purchased "hot" from others in the life*—Xaviera Hollander **2** *n phr* The homosexual life, esp that of an effeminate transvestite male prostitute: *She had lived the life so long now*—Patrick Mann
See IN THE LIFE

lifeboat *n underworld* A pardon from a prison or other sentence; a retrial

lifer 1 *n fr late 1700s* A convict serving a life sentence **2** *n Army* A career Army officer: *"lifers" (the contemptuous GI term for career officers)* —New York Times

lift 1 *n* A surge or feeling of exhilaration; a transport of exuberance; =HIGH, KICK, RUSH: *I get a lift from watching that kid* **2** *v* To steal: *He got*

caught lifting a chicken from the convenience store **3** *v* To plagiarize: *whole pages lifted from my book* **4** *n* A ride: *I need a lift to the bus terminal downtown*
See HITCH A RIDE

lifties or **lifts** *n* Men's shoes built up so as to increase the wearer's height: *Male movie stars are said to wear "lifties"*—Associated Press

light 1 *adj* hoboes Hungry; needing a meal **2** *adj* Lacking; having an insufficient amount: *I'm light about 20 bucks* **3** *adj* beat & cool talk =HEP **4** *n* The igniting of a cigarette, cigar or pipe: *Could you give me a light?* **5** *v* =LIGHT OUT **6** *adj* lunch counter With extra cream added: *light coffee*
See GO LIGHT, GO OUT LIKE A LIGHT, the GREEN LIGHT, IDIOT LIGHT, MAKE LIGHT OF, OUT LIKE A LIGHT, RED-LIGHT, SEE THE LIGHT, SEE THE LIGHT AT THE END OF THE TUNNEL

light colonel *n phr* Army A lieutenant colonel

light-fingered *adj fr 1500s* Inclined to steal; thievish; =STICKY-FINGERED

light-footed *adj* Homosexual

lighthouse *n outdated* hoboes A criminal accomplice who can recognize plainclothes police on sight

lightly *See* a ONCE-OVER

lightning *n* Cheap, raw whiskey; =WHITE LIGHTNING
See CHAIN LIGHTNING, GREASED LIGHTNING, JERSEY LIGHTNING, RIDE THE LIGHTNING, WHITE LIGHTNING

lightning-slinger *n* railroad A telegrapher

light out *v phr fr middle 1800s* To leave, esp hastily; =TAKE OFF, HIGHTAIL: *He lit out for the border* [fr earlier nautical *light out* "move out, or move something out," of obscure origin; perhaps "move or move something lightly, quickly, handily"]

lights out 1 *n phr* Bedtime: *Lights out is at 10:30* **2** *n phr* The end; death; =CURTAINS: *otherwise lights out for me*—Dashiell Hammett
See PUNCH someone's LIGHTS OUT, SHOOT THE LIGHTS OUT

lightweight 1 *adj* Inconsequential; unserious **2** *n*: *He seems like a lightweight to me, don't pay him any attention*

like 1 *modifier esp 1960s counterculture & bop talk* As if; really; you know; sort of ● A generalized modifier used to lend a somewhat tentative and detached tone to the speaker, to give the speaker time to rally words and ideas: *Like I was like groovin' like, you know?* **2** *v* To predict as winner; bet on: *You like the Mets?/ Who do you like in the title fight?*
See MAKE LIKE

like a bandit *adv phr* Very successfully; thrivingly: *coming out of the battle with Bendix like a bandit*—New York Times [see *make out like a bandit*]

like a bat out of hell *adv phr* Very rapidly; =LICKETY-SPLIT: *They were moving along like a bat out of hell*
See TAKE OFF LIKE A BIGASS BIRD

like a blue streak *See* a BLUE STREAK

like a bump on a log *adv phr* Idly; uselessly; inertly: *Don't sit there like a bump on a log, move*

like a bunny *See* FUCK LIKE A BUNNY, QUICK LIKE A BUNNY

like a hole in the head *See* NEED someone or something LIKE A HOLE IN THE HEAD

like a million bucks *adv phr* Very good; superb: *In that blouse she looks like a million bucks/ This new chair feels like a million bucks*

like a wooden Indian *adv phr fr late 1800s* Very stolidly and stiffly; silently and without expression: *When I addressed her she stood there like a wooden Indian* [fr the *wooden* statues of Native Americans holding out a bunch of cigars, put in front of tobacco stores as signs, and also called *cigar-store Indians*]

like crazy (or **mad**) *adv phr* Extravagantly; wildly; violently: *tearing around like crazy*—P Marks/ *Then everybody laughs like mad*—AJ Liebling

like gangbusters *adv phr* Very energetically and successfully: *Everyone knows I'm getting into your pants like gangbusters*—Earl Thompson/ *The rest of the year the economy will be going like gangbusters*—Newsweek
See COME ON LIKE GANGBUSTERS

like hell 1 *adv phr* In an extravagant way; very forcefully: *walleyes feed like crazy and "bite like hell"*—Sports Afield/ *Started screaming like hell*—Joyce Carol Oates **2** *adv phr* (Variations: **fun** or **shit** may replace **hell**) Never; it is impermissible that; =IN A PIG'S ASS: *Like hell you will!/ Like shit it's a good job/* when the prostitute says *"Like fun you are"*—D Costello

like it is *See* TELL IT LIKE IT IS

like it or lump it *adv phr* Whether or not one wishes: *We have to go now, like it or lump it*

like it's going out of style or **like there's no tomorrow** *adv phr* Extravagantly; wildly; recklessly; with abandon: *spending money like it was going out of style/ boozing like there was no tomorrow*

like pigs in clover (or ◁**in shit**▷) *adv phr fr early 1800s* In complete happiness; blissfully: *We'll go down there and we'll live like pigs in clover/ They were giggling and euphoric like pigs in shit*

◁**like shit through a tin horn**▷ *adv phr* (Variations: **a dose of salts** or **a hot knife through butter** may replace **shit through a tin horn**) Very rapidly and easily; effortlessly: *He went through the defense like shit through a tin horn/ The pension bill went through like a dose of salts*

like shooting fish in a barrel *adj phr* Very easy; much too easy: *Beating them was like shooting fish in a barrel*

like sixty *adv phr fr middle 1800s* Very rapidly; =LIKE A BAT OUT OF HELL: *They went after him like sixty* [*sixty* is probably used as an indefinite large number, as *forty* was in similar 19th-century contexts, to express extreme briskness]

like that *See* ALL LIKE THAT THERE

lily 1 *n* =SISSY **2** *n* Something remarkable, superior, etc; =LULU: *I told my best joke...it's never missed, it's a lily*—Lionel Stander

lily white 1 *adj phr* Innocent; immaculate **2** *adj phr* Having only Caucasian residents, workers, etc: *The town is lily white*

lily whites *n phr* Bed sheets
See SLIP IN BETWEEN THE LILY WHITES

limb See GO OUT ON A LIMB, OUT ON A LIMB

limey or **lime-juicer** ◀**1**▶ *n fr early 1900s* An English person: *The limeys are unhappy over the weakness of the pound sterling/ The "Doctor" was a lime-juicer—Scribner's* ◀**2**▶ *adj: a limey accent* ◀**3**▶ *n* An English ship **4** *n lunch counter* An English muffin [fr the ration of *lime-juice* given to British sailors as an antiscorbutic]

the limit *n phr* A person, thing, etc, that exceeds or outrages what is acceptable: *Ain't he awful, ain't he just the limit?*
See GO THE LIMIT

limmy *n outdated underworld* A burglar's jimmy

limo (LIHM oh) *n* A limousine: *disapproves of this vast fleet (789 limos) of luxury transportation—Saturday Review*
See STRETCH LIMO

limp *adj* Drunk

◁**limp-dick**▷ **1** *n* An ineffectual man; an impotent man; =WIMP **2** *adj: I called myself every limp-dick name I could think of—Richard Price*

limp dishrag *n phr* An ineffectual person; =NEBBISH, WIMP: *Sandy is discarded...as if she were, well, a limp dishrag—Village Voice*

limp-noodle 1 *n phr* Something feeble, tasteless, and without distinction **2** *adj: outdated postures, overused jokes, and limp-noodle romantic ballads—Village Voice*

limp wrist 1 *n phr* A male homosexual: *I reminded her that Boke Kellum was a limp wrist—Dan Jenkins/ Barbara Hutton could only marry herself seven or eight limp wrists—Paul Sann* **2** *modifier: a limp-wrist hangout*

limp-wristed *adj* Effeminate; slack and sinuous; homosexual: *His art always has this subtle, limp-wristed style to it—Village Voice/ the most limp-wristed "stud" in the Philadelphia metropolitan area—Philadelphia*

line 1 *n fr early 1900s* One's usual way of talking, esp when being persuasive or self-aggrandizing; =SPIEL: *of what in a later generation would have been termed her "line"—F Scott Fitzgerald/ You've got some line—Ira Wolfert* **2** *n* The public position of a party, faction, etc: *the Republican line* **3** *n* One's occupation, business, etc; =RACKET: *What's my line? Herring in brine* **4** *n jazz musicians & swing musicians* A musical solo or figure, esp personal and innovative: *Coasters talk of "lines," not licks, breaks, or riffs—Artie Shaw* **5** *v baseball* To hit the ball in a line drive **6** *n gambling* A bookmaker's odds on a sports event: *Baseball, basketball, and hockey lines are available on the day or night of the games—Harper's* **7** *n* A dose of cocaine, usu formed into a thin line on a mirror to be nasally ingested **8** *v: They lined twice last night, no wonder they're tired*
See someone's ASS IS ON THE LINE, the BOTTOM LINE, CHOW LINE, DOWN THE LINE, HARD LINE, HOT LINE, IN LINE, IN LINE FOR, LAY IT ON THE LINE, MAIN LINE, ON LINE, ON THE LINE, OUT OF LINE, PULL A LINE, PUNCH LINE, PUT one's ASS ON THE LINE, REDLINE, SHOOT someone A LINE, STAG LINE, TOE THE MARK

the line 1 *n phr* The chorus girls of a show **2** *n phr* An assembly line
See TOE THE MARK

line dog (or **doggie**) *n phr Army* A soldier, esp a sergeant, in a combat unit [combat units are trained to operate in the front *line*]

line-load *n cabdrivers* A passenger for the brothel district

linen See DIRTY LINEN, WASH one's DIRTY LINEN

line one's **nest** See FEATHER one's NEST

line out 1 *v phr* To sing, esp in a loud strong voice; =BELT OUT **2** *v phr baseball* To hit a line drive that is caught

liner See HEADLINER, ONE-LINER

lines See GO UP IN one's LINES

lineup 1 *n police* A number of persons displayed in line across a platform to find whether witnesses can pick a suspect from among them; =SHOWUP **2** *n sports* The roster of a team, esp for a particular game: *Just before the game started, the managers showed their lineups to the umpires*

line up with *v phr* To support; take sides with: *Who will you line up with on this thorny issue?*

lingo (LIN goh) *n* Language; jargon; idiom

lip 1 *n fr early 1800s* Insolent, impertinent, or presumptuous talk: *I don't want none of your lip—W Moore* **2** *n underworld* A lawyer; =MOUTHPIECE **3** *v jazz musicians* To play a musical instrument, esp in jazz; =BLOW: *He couldn't lip anything proper any more—Stephen Longstreet*
See BAT one's GUMS, BUTTON one's LIP, FLIP one's LIP, ZIP one's LIP

lip fuzz *n phr* A mustache

lip mover *n phr* A dull and stupid person; =BLOCKHEAD: *between those countless millions of lip-movers and the minuscule audience for better novels—New York Times* [fr the habit of uneducated or dull people of *moving their lips* while reading to themselves]

lippy 1 *adj* Insolent; brash and arrogant **2** *adj* Talkative

lip-splitter *n jazz musicians* A musician who plays a wind instrument

lip-sync or **lip-synch** (LIP sink) *v* To move the lips silently in synchronism with recorded singing or speaking, to give the illusion of performance: *Having taped his lines before the show, he lip-synched his pronouncements—Time/ staying home with her sister lip synching to Leon Russell records—Village Voice*

liquidate *v* To kill

liquor See HARD LIQUOR, POT LIQUOR

liquored up *adj* Drunk

list See HIT LIST, SUCKER LIST, WISH LIST

listen *v* To seem right; make sense; =FIGURE: *It don't listen—Raymond Chandler/ That listens, doesn't it?—Lawrence Sanders*

listen-in *n* An instance of eavesdropping or wire-tapping: *an occasional listen-in on the...line*—Philadelphia Bulletin

listen up *v phr fr armed forces fr black* To listen closely; pay strict attention: *He can make you listen up with that violin of his*—Village Voice

lit[1] *n students fr late 1800s* Literature: *comp lit/ black lit*

lit[2] *adj* Drunk

litter *See* POCKET LITTER

litterbug *n* A person who throws trash in the streets, parks, etc [modeled on *jitterbug*]

little bitty *adj phr* Very small: *I got four little bitty kids*—American Scholar

little black book *n phr* The private notebook in which one is supposed to keep telephone numbers and details of potential and actual sex partners

little green apples *See* SURE AS GOD MADE LITTLE GREEN APPLES

Little Joe *n phr crapshooting* The point four, or four on the dice [a shortening of *Little Joe from Kokomo*; the relation to four is not patent]

little Michael (or **Mickey**) *n phr* = MICKEY FINN

little ones *See* MAKE LITTLE ONES OUT OF BIG ONES

little Phoebe (or **fever**) *See* PHOEBE

little school *n phr underworld & hoboes* A reformatory; reform school

little secret *See* DIRTY LITTLE SECRET

little shaver *n phr* A young boy

the **little woman** *n phr fr late 1800s* One's wife: *tooling along with the kiddies and the little woman in his costly can*—Westbrook Pegler

lit to the gills *adj phr* Drunk

lit up or **lit up like a Christmas tree** **1** *adj phr* Drunk: *I found Uncle Peter and he was also lit up*—H McHugh **2** *adj phr narcotics* Intoxicated with narcotics; = HIGH

litvak (LIT vahk) **1** *n* A Lithuanian or person of Lithuanian background ◁**2**▷ *n* A clever fellow; a sharp, tricky trader [fr Yiddish fr Polish; the second sense, derogatory in force, is used by the Galitzianer Jews of Polish or Russian background, and Lithuanians would not agree with the definition]

live (LĪV) **1** *adj* Not yet fired or exploded: *a live shell* **2** *adj* Containing bullets or shot, as distinct from blank: *live ammunition* **3** *adj* Not recorded or taped: *live music/ a live telecast* **4** *adj* Having electrical potential; = HOT: *a live circuit/ live wire* **5** *adj esp teenagers* Lively; exciting: *a very live party/ a live dude*
See ALL THE WAY LIVE

live high on the hog *See* EAT HIGH ON THE HOG

live-in **1** *adj* Sharing one's domicile: *Coe's former live-in girlfriend*—Newsweek/ *J Edgar's "long-time live-in lover"*—Village Voice **2** *n* A housekeeper who lives in one's home: *After they had their second child, they hired a live-in*

live off the fat of the land (or **off the tit**) *v phr* To live very well, esp without working: *You been living off the tit too long, I think*—George V Higgins

live one **1** *n phr* A lively person; up-to-date person **2** *n phr* A likely target for a confidence scheme or fast sell: *Hey, Eddie, looks like we got us a live one here*

liver *See* CHOPPED LIVER, THAT AIN'T HAY

lives *See* HIT someone WHERE HE LIVES

live wire *n phr* An energetic, vibrant person: *Jimmy's a live wire, all right*—P Marks

the **living daylights** *See* BEAT THE SHIT OUT OF someone or something

living doll *n phr* A notably decent, pleasant person: *Isn't the emcee a living doll?*

the **living end** *n phr fr beat & cool talk* A person, thing, etc, that is about as much as one can stand; = the END, the LIMIT ● Usu highly complimentary

living-room gig *n phr jazz musicians* A television appearance: *living room gig, a guest shot on television*—E Horne

◁the **living shit**▷ *See* BEAT THE SHIT OUT OF someone or something, SCARE THE SHIT OUT OF someone

lizard *n horse-racing* A racehorse, esp an inferior one; = BEETLE
See ARKANSAS LIZARD, BUNK LIZARD, LOUNGE LIZARD

lizzie[1] or **Lizzie** *n fr early 1900s* A car, esp a cheap or ramshackle one: *the luxurious lizzie I've always dreamed about*—Billy Rose
See TIN LIZZIE

lizzie[2] *n esp 1920s* An indolent man; an effeminate man; = WIMP: *I hear the reporters in New York are all lizzies*—Hecht & MacArthur [probably fr *lounge lizard*]

load **1** *n* Enough liquor to make one drunk: *He's taking on a load again* **2** *n esp teenagers* A dose of narcotic smoked in a water pipe ◁**3**▷ *n* The semen of a single orgasm
See CARRY A LOAD, CARRY THE LOAD, DROP one's LOAD, FREELOAD, GET A LOAD OF, HALF LOAD, HAVE A LOAD ON, LINE-LOAD, a SHITLOAD, SHOOT one's LOAD, TAKE A LOAD OFF one's FEET, THREE BRICKS SHY OF A LOAD

loaded **1** *adj fr late 1800s* Drunk: *Men act different when they get loaded*—Lantern **2** *adj* Containing whiskey: *We sipped our loaded coffee*—Raymond Chandler **3** *adj narcotics* Intoxicated with narcotics, esp heroin; = HIGH: *And then you get loaded and like it*—D Hulburd **4** *adj fr early 1900s* Wealthy; = FILTHY RICH: *They're all loaded in that neighborhood* **5** *adj fr early 1900s* Having a great deal of money, if only temporarily; = FLUSH: *After the thing sold I was loaded for a few months* **6** *adj* Explosive; perilous: *The situation this fall is really loaded* **7** *adj* Carrying significance beyond the obvious or surface meaning ● Often meant to embarrass or baffle: *No loaded questions if you really want information/ That was a loaded remark* **8** *adj* Prearranged; biased: *The interview was loaded in my favor*

loaded dice *n phr* Dice of which the weight distribution has been altered so that the roll is predictable

loaded for bear *adj phr* Ready and anxious for a fight; heavily prepared for conflict, debate, etc: *I went to the board meeting loaded for bear* [fr the notion that a hunter must use particularly powerful ammunition, or *load*, to kill a *bear*]

loaded with *adj phr* Well provided with; having much of; =LOUSY WITH: *She's loaded with talent*

loader *See* FREELOADER, MUZZLE-LOADER

loadie or **loady** **1** *n* *esp teenagers* A person who uses narcotics, drinks beer and liquor, etc: *for every high school loadie you will find a National Merit Scholar*—Time **2** *n* *college students* A drunkard; an alcoholic; =LUSH

loading *See* FREELOADING

a **load off** someone's **mind** *n phr* A great mental and emotional relief; an end to fretting: *When I heard she was OK it was a great load off my mind*

load of hay **1** *n phr* A head of long hair **2** *n phr* Nonpaying and nontipping customers, guests of the management

a **load of VW radiators** (or **post holes** or **wind**) *n phr* *truckers* An empty truck; no cargo whatever [fr the fact that VW engines are air-cooled and have no *radiators*]

a **load of wind** *n phr* =WINDBAG

load the dice *v phr* To prearrange or bias some result: *a man who helped load the dice against the dissidents within the government*—David Halberstam

loan *See* JUICE LOAN

loan shark *n phr* An underworld usurer; =JUICE DEALER, SHYLOCK

lob **1** *n* A softly thrown ball or a tennis ball hit very high **2** *v*: *He lobbed the ball back near the baseline*

lobo *n* A hoodlum; thug: *A lobo's a gun, thug, hoodlum, downstate*—Scene of the Crime (movie) [fr Spanish, "wolf"]

lobster shift (or **trick**) *n phr* *esp newspaper office fr 1920s* A very late-night or early-morning working shift

local *n* A local resident; native; =HOME GUARD: *The locals are suspicious of the summer types* *See* IRISH BUGGY

local yokel **1** *n phr* *citizens band* A town or city police officer **2** *n phr* A resident of a small town or rural area

lock *v* *prison* To occupy a prison cell

a **lock** *n phr* A certainty; =SURE THING, SHOO-IN: *This guy looks like a lock now*—New York Post/ *no longer a lock to win the NFC East*—New York Daily News [fr the phrase *have it all locked up*] *See* HAVE A LOCK ON something, MORTAL LOCK

locker *See* CHAIN LOCKER

lock horns *v phr* To contend with; fight: *They had locked horns with a better man*—Albert Goldman/ *She has also locked horns with the network*—New York Daily News

lock-in *n* *prison* A form of protest in which prisoners refuse to leave their cells

lockup *n* A cell, esp a detention cell or holding cell; =the COOLER, TANK

loco[1] **1** *adj* *fr late 1800s cowboys* Crazy; =NUTS: *He took one look and just went loco* **2** *n*: *She's acting like a loco* [fr the name of a weed that made cattle behave strangely, fr Spanish, "insane"]

loco[2] *n* *railroad* A locomotive

locomotive **1** *n* *students* A cheer that resembles a steam locomotive starting: *We all had to stand up...and give him a locomotive*—JD Salinger **2** *n* A strong motive force; prime mover: *free trade, which has been a locomotive of prosperity since World War II*—Time

log *See* BEAT one's MEAT, EASY AS PIE

logjam *n* An immovable static situation; =GRIDLOCK: *He broke the logjam of negotiations with the cable companies*—Toronto Life

log roll *n phr* *hospital* A way of carefully turning a patient out of a cart onto a bed: *She said she needed my help with a log roll in Room 643*

loid **1** *v* To open a locked door by moving the catch with a strip of celluloid: *The cards...could be used to loid any door with a spring latch*—Ezra Hannon **2** *v* To burglarize an apartment, building, etc [fr *celluloid*]

lollapalooza (lah lə pə Lōō zə) *n* A person or thing that is remarkable, wonderful, superior, etc; =BEAUT, HUMDINGER: *He's got a lollapalooza of a cold*

lollop *n* =DOLLOP, JOLLOP

lollygag or **lallygag** (LAH lee gag) **1** *v* *fr middle 1800s* To idle about; =GOOF OFF: *the summer free for play, swimming, berry picking, and general lallygagging*—Frank Sullivan/ *when my nephew and his companion lollygagged back to my house*—Washington Post **2** *v* To kiss and caress; dally

lone *See* CHEW A LONE something

loner **1** *n* (also **lone wolf**) A person who prefers to be alone, do things alone, etc; a solitary: *He became more of a "loner," almost a man apart from the rest of the team*—Arthur Daley/ *that breed of loners who wandered through the Rockies in the first half of the nineteenth century*—Esquire **2** *n* One person or thing by itself: *"Make it two and I'll be true." "Here's a loner to get you started"*—Lawrence Sanders

lonesome *See* ALL BY one's LONESOME

as **long as your arm** *See* AS LONG AS YOUR ARM

the **long arm** *n phr* A police officer; =the LAW

long ball *See* GO FOR THE LONG BALL

long count *See* TAKE THE LONG COUNT

long drink of water *n phr* A very tall, thin person

long green *n phr* *fr late 1800s* Money; =FOLDING MONEY: *that dear old affectionately regarded long green*—Amsterdam News [perhaps influenced by earlier sense of a kind of large-leafed tobacco]

longhair **1** *n* *fr early 1900s* An intellectual; =EGGHEAD **2** *adj* (also **long-haired**): *longhair tastes in poetry* **3** *n* *fr 1920s jazz musicians* Classical music ● Originally the term was used for musicians who play from written music, and for the music they play: *sometimes called Western music, sometimes European music, and sometimes just longhair*—Stephen Longstreet **4** *adj* (also **long-haired**): *sonatas and other longhair stuff* **5** *n* *fr 1960s* A young man with long hair, esp a hippie: *another longhair, a member of our commune*—J Jerome [earlier senses fr the stereotype of an intellectual or esthete as being strange and wearing *long hair*]

long-handle (or **long-handled**) **underwear** *n phr fr 1940s* Long winter underwear: *coats and long-handle underwear to fill Norway's needs* —Time

long hard look *n phr* A very close and careful critical scrutiny: *I advise you take a long hard look at yourself, son*

long haul *n phr* A long and arduous period: *It looks like it'll be a long haul*
See FOR THE LONG HAUL, OVER THE LONG HAUL

longhorn *n* A Texan

longies 1 *n* Long pants **2** *n* Long underwear; = LONG JOHNS: *that day's version of today's longies* —C Lawry

long in the tooth *adj phr fr early 1900s British* Aged; advanced in age: *The actor is a bit long in the tooth to be playing Tom Sawyer* [fr the practice of judging age, esp of horses, by the *length* of *teeth*]

long johns or **long ones** *n phr* Long winter underwear: *A generation or so ago, men, women, boys and girls put on long ones in October and wore long ones until spring*—Wall Street Journal/ Pop, will you dig that dish out of your long johns —Saul Bellow

long pig *n phr* A person regarded as meat for cannibals: *he offered mammoth marrow, and, perhaps, Long Pig*—WH Auden

the **long run** *See* IN THE LONG RUN

long shot 1 *n phr fr middle 1800s British* A person, horse, project, etc, that seems not likely to win; = DARK HORSE: *The idea's a long shot, but it's worth a try* **2** *modifier:* *long-shot odds/ a long-shot victory* **3** *n phr* A scene photographed from a distance; a long-range photograph
See NOT BY A LONG SHOT

long time no see *sentence* I haven't seen you for a long time ● A quasi-Pidgin salutation

long underwear *jive talk* **1** *n phr* Jazz music played in a sweet or commercial way: *"long underwear" for concert stuff*—Stephen Longstreet **2** *n phr* An incompetent jazz musician **3** *n phr* Classical music; = LONGHAIR **4** *adj:* *She found out he was a long-underwear platterbug*—C Mason

loo *n* A toilet ● Chiefly British: *everything you'd find in a powder room except the loo*—Toronto Life [origin uncertain; probably fr *Waterloo* in proportionate analogy with *water closet*]

-loo *suffix used to form nouns and adjectives* A remarkable or emphatic instance of what is indicated: *fakeloo*

looey or **looie** or **louie** *n WW1 Army* A lieutenant; = LOOT: *They demoted me to second looey* —Stephen Lewis

loogan 1 *n* A stupid person; = BOOB **2** *n* A thug; = GOON, HOOD: *What's a loogan? A guy with a gun*—Raymond Chandler

look *See* HARD LOOK, LONG HARD LOOK

look-alike *n* A person who closely resembles another; = DEAD RINGER, DOUBLE: *Barratt had an interview with his noted look-alike*—B Thomas

look at someone **cross-eyed** *v phr* To commit even a tiny fault; offend in the least way: *who would yell copper if you looked at them cross-eyed*—Raymond Chandler

look down one's **nose** *v phr* To behave with hauteur; act condescendingly: *He looked down his nose at me as if I were some loathsome thing in his path*

look down on someone or something *v phr* To hold in contempt; scorn: *He looks down on us as newcomers*

looker 1 *n fr middle 1800s* A good-looking person of either sex, but esp a woman: *That waitress is a looker, a real dish* **2** *n salespersons* A person who inspects merchandise but does not buy: *A "looker" is to the used car lot what a browser is to a bookstore*—New York Times
See GOOD-LOOKER

looking good *interj* An exclamation of encouragement, praise, reassurance, etc: *They hollered "Looking good!" as the leader passed*

look like a drowned rat *v phr* To have a singularly disheveled, subdued, and unsightly appearance: *When they got off the boat after a weekend they looked like drowned rats*

look like death warmed over *v phr* To look miserable; look ill and exhausted; have a wretched mien: *I don't know what the news is, but Frank looks like death warmed over*

look like something the cat dragged in *v phr* To have a dirty and bedraggled appearance; present an unkempt mien

◁**look like ten pounds of shit in a five-pound bag**▷ **1** *v phr* To be sloppily dressed, esp dressed in clothing too small, bulging, and gapped **2** *v phr* To be overstuffed, overweight, bulging, etc

look see *v phr* To look; have a look: *I'm dropping down to look see*—Raymond Chandler

a **look-see** *n* A look; an inspection: *Let's have a look-see at our friend*—Ellery Queen/ *I stopped in at Jerry's for a lager and a look-see*—Billy Rose

loon *See* CRAZY AS A LOON

loony or **looney 1** *adj fr middle 1800s* Crazy; = NUTTY: *you looney punk*—Ira Wolfert **2** *n* (also **loon** or **loonball**) *fr late 1800s: the inspired looney who hated killing*—Billy Rose/ *would have shown up in a Mel Brooks epic had that loonball thought of it first*—Toronto Life [probably fr both *lunatic* and *crazy as a loon*]

loony bin *n phr fr late 1800s* A mental hospital; = NUT-HOUSE: *that fugitive from a loony-bin*—Arthur Kober/ *So how come I felt like a loony in a loony-bin?*—Esquire

loony-tune or **loony-tunes 1** *n* (Variations: **looney** may replace **loony**; **toon** may replace **tune**) A crazy person; = NUT: *Jesus, what a loony tune*—Richard Merkin/ *Some loony-toon's been showing off for his girl friend*—Kudzu (comic strip) **2** *modifier:* *the loony-toon acting debut of writer Stephen King*—Flare/ *It's been kind of a looney-tunes week*—William Goldman [fr *Looney Tunes*, trade name of a series of short cartoon-film comedies, a paraphrasing fr *Silly Symphonies*, also short cartoon-film comedies]

loop *n sports* An athletic league or conference: *the Big Ten loop*
See IN THE LOOP, KNOCK someone FOR A LOOP, OUT OF THE LOOP, THROW someone FOR A LOOP

looped or **looping** *adj* Drunk: *The end result is a looped group*—Hal Boyle/ *Was she drunk? Looping* —Irwin Shaw

looper *n baseball* A flyball hit between the infield and outfield

loopy *adj* Crazy; silly; =NUTTY: *that loopy guy whose handkerchief you cry into*—Raymond Chandler/ *visually complemented the singer's loopy Balkan bop*—Rolling Stone/ *even loopier bids for the few works in Wood's small mature oeuvre*—Time

loose 1 *adj cool talk* Relaxed; easy; =COOL: *No wonder you guys were really loose*—Rolling Stone/ *You are loose in the rush, misty and safe*—New York **2** *adj* Sexually promiscuous
See ALL HELL BROKE LOOSE, HANG LOOSE, a SCREW LOOSE

loose as a goose or **loosey-goosey** *adj phr* or *adj cool talk* Very relaxed; perfectly easy; =COOL: *The pitcher's got a nice loosey-goosey motion/ He was feeling fine, loose as a goose* [probably both fr the rhyme and the perception that a *goose* has *loose* bowels]

loose cannon *n phr* A person who is quite likely to cause damage; a wildly irresponsible person: *Haig is a loose cannon on a pitching deck*—Time/ *His detractors call him a loose cannon...who makes recommendations in public before consulting*—Washington Post

loose change *n phr* Money at hand and to spare; available money: *I wanted to help, but didn't have any loose change*

loose in the bean (or **upper story**) *adj phr* Crazy; =NUTTY

loose wig *n phr cool talk* A very much moved and madly inspired musician: *loose wig, completely uninhibited really way out musician*—E Horne [fr the notion that the musician has *flipped* his or her *wig*]

loot[1] *n fr 1920s jazz musicians* Money, esp a large amount of money: *Rich planters would come and spend some awful large amounts of loot*—Louis Armstrong

loot[2] *n fr 1700s* A lieutenant; =LIEUT

lord **See** TIGHT

lose one's **cookies** **See** SHOOT one's COOKIES

lose one's **cool** *v phr fr cool talk* To become angry or flustered; lose composure: *He was unflappable, never lost his cool*

lose one's **gourd** *v phr* To become insane; go crazy; =GO APE, FREAK OUT: *Have you lost your gourd?*—Pat Conroy

lose one's **marbles** *v phr* To become foolish, irrational, forgetful, etc, as if senile [fr an earlier phrase *let his marbles go with the monkey*, fr a story about a boy whose marbles were carried off by a monkey]

loser 1 *n* (also **born loser**) A person or thing that fails, esp habitually; =BUST, DUD, LEMON **2** *v: I don't want them to think I'm losered out*—New York Times

lose the ballgame *v phr* To end disastrously: *One puff, one gust, one very small disturbance, and I'd have lost the whole ballgame right there*—John McPhee

lose one's **wig** *v phr cool talk* =BLOW one's TOP

losing **See** someone CAN'T WIN FOR LOSING

losses **See** CUT one's LOSSES

lost **See** GET LOST

lot **See** ALL OVER THE LOT, PORTABLE PARKING LOT

lot louse *n phr circus* A person who wanders and watches but does not spend money

lot of weight **See** CARRY A LOT OF WEIGHT

loud *adj fr middle 1800s* Vulgar and gaudy in taste; garish: *blatant checked suits and loud ties*
See FOR CRYING OUT LOUD, READ someone LOUD AND CLEAR

loudmouth 1 *n* A loud and constant talker, esp a braggart and self-appointed authority; =WINDBAG: *Maybe poking Loud Mouth in the kisseroo would solve everything*—D Decker **2** *v: Don't you loudmouth me!*

loud-talk *v prison* To provoke trouble by talking loudly about real or supposed violations of rules

louie or **Louie** *n esp 1930s* A migrant worker: *Now the fruit tramps are called Okies and Arkies and Louies*—James M Cain [fr *Louisiana*]
See LOOEY

lounge lizard *n phr esp 1920s* =LADIES' MAN [fr the notion that such a man *lounges*, frequents ladies' *lounges*, and is as colorful, indolent, and reptilian as a *lizard* in the sun]

louse *n* An obnoxious and despicable person, esp one who is devious and undependable; =BASTARD, CRUMB
See LENS LOUSE, LOT LOUSE

louse-cage *n railroad* A caboose or bunkhouse

louse up 1 *v phr* To ruin or spill; botch; =BOLLIX UP: *Boy, you certainly loused that up*—John O'Hara **2** *v phr* To fail; =SCREW UP: *He'll get promoted next month if he doesn't louse up*

lousy 1 *adj fr middle 1800s* Bad; nasty; =CRUMMY: *Crab was all she ever did. What a lousy sport*—Dorothy Parker/ *yuh lousy boob*—Eugene O'Neill **2** *adv: I did pretty lousy on that test*—F Brown

lousy with *adj phr fr middle 1800s* Well provided with; swarming with: *Everybody will come home lousy with cash*—Dashiell Hammett/ *That hotel was lousy with perverts*—JD Salinger

love **See** CALF LOVE, FOR THE LOVE OF PETE, PUPPY LOVE

lovebirds *n* Lovers: *the two lovebirds*—Raymond Chandler

love drug *n phr esp students* A drug thought to be an aphrodisiac, such as methaqualone

love handle 1 *n phr* A bulge of fat at the side of the abdomen: *when I have strapped the metal thing to my love handles*—George V Higgins **2** *modifier: who come in rarely, and mostly for love-handle removal*—Village Voice

love-in *n esp 1960s counterculture* A gathering, esp of hippies, devoted to mutual love and understanding: *Tulsa...recently had its first love-in*—Jack Newfield

lovely *n* An attractive woman: *where flabby lovelies in polka-dot bikinis lobbed beachballs around*—New York

◁**love-muscle**▷ *n* The penis

love nest *n phr* A place where two can make love, esp adulterous love

lover *See* MOTHERFUCKER

lover-boy 1 *n* A handsome man; matinee idol **2** *n* A womanizer; woman-chaser; =LADIES' MAN, CASANOVA, STUD

lovey-dovey 1 *adj* Affectionate; amorous: *My, aren't they lovey-dovey?* **2** *n* Affection; friendship: *a reign of peace, prosperity, and lovey-dovey*—HL Mencken **3** *n* A wife, mistress, sweetheart, etc: *their foreign lovey-doveys*—D Fairbairn

loving *See* MOTHERFUCKING

low 1 *adj* *fr late 1800s* Sad; melancholy: *I was so...low and depressed*—Bill Nye **2** *n* *narcotics* A bad reaction to a narcotic; =BUMMER

See GULLY-LOW, KEEP A LOW PROFILE, LAY LOW

low-ball *v* To lower; reduce; aim for low standards: *Had Feldstein deliberately low-balled the original numbers?*—Newsweek/ *They may be guilty of "low balling," the term used to describe the modest management goals*—Wall Street Journal

low-belly strippers *n phr gambling* Marked playing cards; a marked deck

low blow *n phr* An unfair and malicious stroke; =CHEAP SHOT: *It wasn't exactly unethical, but it was a pretty low blow*

lowbrow *fr early 1900s* **1** *n* A person lacking education and refinement; an ignorant lout **2** *adj: lowbrow tastes/ What are you always pulling that lowbrow stuff for?*—P Marks

low camp *n phr* Entertainment or art characterized by very broad and vulgar features: *Low camp...would mean doing it with winks and leers at the audience, in jeering collusion*—John Simon

low-down 1 *adj* *fr middle 1800s* Dishonest; despicable; vile: *a dirty low-down trick* **2** *adj jazz musicians* Intense and insinuating, in the blues style: *a real low-down horn/ a babe with a low-down voice*—Mickey Spillane

See DIRTY SHAME

the lowdown *n phr* The truth; the authentic facts: *eager to get the low-down on new aircraft*—Philadelphia Bulletin

low-down dirty shame *See* DIRTY SHAME

lower the boom 1 *v phr prizefight* To deliver a knockout punch **2** *v phr* To punish; exact obedience and docility: *if we lower the boom on every nonconformist in society*—Arthur Schlesinger/ *My patience evaporated and I lowered the boom on them*—SJ Perelman

low-fi or **low fi 1** *n* or *n phr* Record- or tape-playing or other equipment that reproduces sound rather badly **2** *modifier: a room full of low-fi components* [based on *hi-fi*]

low five *n phr* A greeting or gesture of approval made by slapping hands at about waist level: *San Diego hand-slapping, high fives, low fives*—Newsweek

low-level Munchkin *n phr* A low-ranking employee, staff-member, etc; a menial: *Justice Department spokesman Thomas De Cair sniffed that Honegger was "a low-level Munchkin"*—Newsweek/ *When his calls were returned, it was by low-level Munchkins*—New Yorker [fr the name of the dwarfish helpers in L Frank Baum's *The Wizard of Oz*]

low-life 1 *n* A person of reprehensible habits; =BUM **2** *adj: fancies himself in love with the raucous, lowlife Doreen*—New Yorker

low (or **bottom**) **man on the totem pole** *n phr* The person having least seniority, importance, etc

low pitch *n phr hawkers* A street display set on the sidewalk or pavement

low profile 1 *n phr* Inconspicuousness; recessiveness; modesty: *He thought he'd do better with a low profile the first year or so* **2** *adj: a low-profile discreetness*

See KEEP A LOW PROFILE

low-rent *adj* Cheap; second-rate; inferior: *and from that low-rent lunch at the Century Plaza*—Dan Jenkins/ *Low-Rent Himalayas*—CoEvolution Quarterly

low ride *adj phr esp southern California* Socially inferior; vulgar; =TRASHY: *For teenagers any mixing with the Indians or low ride Mexicans down in the valley is slumming*—Time

low rider 1 *n phr esp southern California* A person who drives a car with a radically lowered suspension **2** *n phr* A car with a lowered suspension **3** *n phr* A motorcyclist, esp one who rides a customized motorcycle with the handlebars very high **4** *n phr* A rough young man from a black ghetto: *A group of low riders from Watts assembled on the basketball court*—Eldridge Cleaver/ *There are what the blacks call low riders, these people who run around pushing their weight around*—Prison [extended fr the ghetto style, among blacks and Chicanos, of the cool young man who wished, according to Calvin Trillin, "to *lower* his car to within a few inches of the ground, make it as beautiful as he knows how...and drive it very slowly"]

lox *n astronautics* Liquid oxygen, as a rocket fuel

LP or **lp** *n* A phonograph record that plays at 33⅓ revolutions per minute [fr *long playing*]

the Ls *n phr gambling* The losers, esp professional gamblers who get a 5 percent kickback from bookmakers on losing bets

LSD *n* Lysergic acid diethylamide, a hallucinogenic drug; =ACID: *There is no rite of passage, such as smoking pot or tripping with LSD*—Trans-Action

L7 1 *n black* An unpopular misfit; =SQUARE **2** *adj: an uncool L7 wimp* [fr the square visual pattern made by the joining of the capital *L* and the number 7]

LT *n college students* Living together: *the subject of living together ("LT" in college lingo)*—Washington Post

lube 1 *n* (also **lube job**) A lubrication; grease job **2** *modifier: lube rack* **3** *n* *students* Butter [last sense from the likening of *butter* and *grease*]

lubricant *n* *students* Butter

lubricated *adj* Drunk

luck *See* BREAK LUCK, IN LUCK, OUT OF LUCK, POT LUCK, SHIT OUT OF LUCK

luck into *v phr* To get something by luck: *Alain lucked into a goldmine with an idea for a magazine* —New York Times

the **luck of the draw** *n phr* The way fortune would have it; = THAT'S THE WAY THE BALL BOUNCES

luck out ● One of the slang expressions that can mean two opposite things **1** *v phr* To be lucky; get something by good luck: *that he will...luck out after his search and create operation*—Commonweal **2** *v phr* *WW2 Army* To be very unlucky; be doomed

luck up *v phr* To become lucky: *before I lucked up* —Louis Armstrong

lucre *See* FILTHY LUCRE

lude *n* Quaalude (a trade name), a depressant drug; any methaqualone capsule or pill: *Only this year "ludes" (Quaaludes or "downs") were the hot sellers*—Judy Klemesrud/ *Dropping the Last 'Lude* —Time

luded out *adj phr* Intoxicated with depressants, esp Quaalude (a trade name): *The folks who use it are usually too luded out or preoccupied*—Playboy

luff *See* FIRST LUFF

lug 1 *n* *fr 1920s* A stupid man; dull fellow; = BOZO: *Those lugs in the band would begin to kid me about it*—John O'Hara/ *a simple-minded lug like Moose Malloy*—Raymond Chandler **2** *n* *prizefight* The face, chin, or jaw **3** *n* *underworld* A demand for money, esp bribe or protection money: *a captain of detectives who was collecting the lug from the gambling houses*—Westbrook Pegler **4** *v* To solicit money; borrow [origins and derivations uncertain; the first sense is probably fr *lug* "something heavy and clumsy," attested in the 16th century and retained in several English dialects where it is used derogatorily of persons]

See DROP THE LUG ON someone

◀**lugan**▶ *n* A Lithuanian or person of Lithuanian descent [origin unknown; perhaps related to *lug* "stupid man"]

lugger *n* *horse-racing* A racehorse that bears into or away from the inner rail: *a rapid lugger*—AJ Liebling

lug in *v phr* *horse-racing* To bear into the inner rail of a racetrack

lug out *v phr* *horse-racing* To bear away from the inner rail of a racetrack

lulu¹ *n* *fr middle 1800s* A person or thing that is remarkable, wonderful, superior, etc; = DARB, HUMDINGER: *He said the aquarium was a lulu*—AJ Liebling/ *Burrows was permitted his own bower, and it was a lulu*—SJ Perelman [origin unknown; earlier *looly* "beautiful girl" is attested; perhaps fr the cowboy term *loo loo* "a winning hand," explained as a hand invented by local people in order to win a game from a stranger "for the good of the *loo*," where *loo* means "party, set, community"; this sense of *loo* is related to the popular 18th-century card game of the same name, fr *lanterloo* fr French *lanterlu*, a nonsense phrase in the refrain of a song]

lulu² *n* *New York State* A legislator's perquisite of goods, services, or a stipend "in lieu" of basic legitimate compensation: *decision to abandon the "lulus" of legislators*—New York Times/ *He may also get a "lulu" (a stipend in lieu of expenses)*—Village Voice [fr *lieu*, influenced by *lulu¹*]

lumber 1 *n* *baseball* A bat **2** *n* *lunch counter* Toothpicks **3** *v* *chiefly British* To take advantage of someone; make someone a scapegoat: *He was totally lumbered. It was a terrible travesty* —Washingtonian

See HOLD THE LUMBER

lumberman *n* *hoboes* A beggar with a crutch: *The "lumbermen" can beg $30 a day with ease*—WJ Slocum

lummox or **lummux** *n* A stupid, clumsy person; = KLUTZ [fr British dialect fr *lummock* "lump"]

lump 1 *n* *hoboes* A packet of food: *"Lumps"...are possible at any time during the day* —HF Kane **2** *n* A dull, stupid person; = CLOD, KLUTZ: *What an unspeakable lump I was*—Max Shulman

lumper *n* *truckers* A person who loads and unloads trucks: *"Lumpers" unload the trailer for him* —Smithsonian

lump it *v phr* *fr late 1700s* To accept or swallow something one does not like: *It was a lousy deal, but I just had to lump it* [fr earlier sense of *lump* "dislike, reject," probably related to the sense "strike, thrash"; see *lumps*]

See LIKE IT OR LUMP IT

lumps *n* Severe treatment; punishment; a beating: *Somebody was out to give him his lumps*—J Roeburt [fr late-18th-century *lump* "beat, thrash"]

See GET one's LUMPS, TAKE one's LUMPS

lumpy *adj* *cool talk* Badly played

lunch or **lunchy** *students* **1** *adj* Stupid; ineffectual: *A lunch guy might as well be out to lunch for all the good he's doing*—R Scott **2** *adj* Old-fashioned; passé; out of style: *That bow tie is stone lunchy*

See EAT someone's LUNCH, OUT TO LUNCH, SHOOT one's COOKIES

lunch-hooks *n* The hands; = MEATHOOKS: *get a set of predatory lunch-hooks into him*—Gilbert Milstein

lung *n* *railroad* A draw-bar connecting railroad cars

lunger (LUNG ər) *n* A person with tuberculosis: *at once a lunger and lifer*—J Black

See ONE-LUNGER

◁**lung-hammock**▷ *n* A brassiere

◁**lungs**▷ *n* A woman's breasts; = KNOCKERS: *pushed a whole blouse full of lungs against my arm*—Dan Jenkins/ *She has a great pair of lungs*—Lawrence Sanders

lunk 1 *n* A stupid person; = LUNKHEAD: *Lunks, Hunks and Arkifacts*—Time/ *a character whom Tristan describes as "a big lunk"*—Village Voice **2** *modifier: four books about a lunk hero Carlo Reinhart*—Time

lunker **1** *n* A very big fish, often the apocryphal one that got away: *In the ocean there's nothing but lunkers*—New York Times **2** *n* An old car; =CLUNKER, HEAP: *in old cars known as clunkers, lunkers, winter rats*—New York Times

lunkhead *n fr middle 1800s* A stupid person; =BOOB, DOPE: *a bulky, duckfooted lunkhead*—John Cheever/ *Tenors have been traditionally stereotyped as vain lunkheads*—Newsweek

lunky *adj* Stupid: *conflict between paternal authority and lunky adolescent waywardness*—Time

lurker *n computer* A person who enters a computer system illegally; an uninvited computer eavesdropper: *Ian had found a lurker in the system*—Toronto Life

luscious *adj* Very attractive; =DISHY, SEXY

lush **1** *n fr late 1800s* A drunkard; an alcoholic; =DIPSO: *She is still plastered, the little lush*—John O'Hara/ *The father was by no means a lush, but the son carried temperance to an extreme*—Joseph Mitchell **2** *v: lushing, stowing wine into our faces*—Henry Seidel Canby [origin unknown; fr early-19th-century British, "tipple, drink," perhaps fr the name of *Lushington*, a London brewer, or fr British dialect, "intoxicating drink," which is perhaps fr Romany or Shelta (tinkers' jargon)]

lushed or **lushed up** *adj* or *adj phr* Drunk

lusher *n* A drunkard: *City editors are roughnecks and urbane gentlemen, lushers and Puritans*—Stanley Walker

lush roller (or **worker**) *n phr underworld* A thief who specializes in robbing helpless drunks: *A lush roller rolls lushes*—AJ Liebling/ *when a...lush worker picks the pocket of a sleeping drunk*—New York Times

lushwell *n* =LUSH

luxo *adj* Luxurious; =POSH: *Sapporo/Challenger luxo-coupe*—Westworld

M

M 1 *n* narcotics Morphine: *You've got to get M to get that tingle-tingle*—Nelson Algren **2** *n* Money

ma'am *See* WHAM-BAM THANK YOU MA'AM

ma-and-pa *See* MOM-AND-POP

Ma Bell *n phr* A wry nickname for the Bell Telephone system: *Ma Bell, for instance, is fair game to many*—American Scholar/ *The quality of some phone lines is often below what Ma Bell promised*—Fortune

mac *n* A mackintosh: *His simple dream of naked girls in wet macs*
See MACK

Mac or **Mack** *n* Man; fellow; = BUSTER, JACK ● Used in direct address, often with a mildly hostile intent: *Take it easy, Mac*

macaroni 1 *n* lumberjacks Sawdust **2** *n* Any flexible and usu hollow item, such as electrical insulation, flexible tubing, etc

macher (MAH kər, -khər) *n* An active, usu self-important person; = BIG SHOT, OPERATOR: *the Muse to numerous folk-rock machers*—New Yorker/ *Put a schlep in a monkey suit and he thinks he's a macher/ I have become a big macher in the senior citizen's group*—New York Times [fr Yiddish, literally "maker, doer"]

machisma (mah CHIZ mə) *n* The female counterpart of machismo: *Machisma, Women, and Daring*—Grace Lichtenstein

machismo (mah CHIZ moh) *n* Aggressive masculinity; blatant virility: *machismo, a he-man complex*—Time/ *with Chicago machismo, also universal adolescent horniness*—Harper's [fr Spanish]

macho (MAH choh) **1** *n* An aggressively masculine man; = HE-MAN **2** *n* Aggressive maleness; = MACHISMO: *It was not just a question of executive macho*—New York **3** *adj*: *a typical macho Mailerism*—Pauline Kael/ *list of macho jobs as long as a master sergeant's sleeve of hash marks*—Nation [fr Spanish]

machodrama *n* A movie or play glorifying aggressive maleness

macho it out *v phr* To behave with masculine courage and stamina; = TOUGH IT OUT: *I machoed it out all the way into the men's room before I threw up*—Time

Machree *See* MOTHER MACHREE

mack *n* esp black fr late 1800s A pimp; = MACKMAN: *copped you a mack*—Donald Goines [fr 15th-century *mackerel* "pimp," fr Old French *macquerel*,

perhaps related to Dutch *makelaar* "trade, traffic," hence ultimately to *make, macher*, etc]
See MAC

mackerel *See* HOLY CATS

◀**mackerel-snapper**▶ *n* A Roman Catholic [fr the fact that Roman Catholics ate fish on Fridays]

mackman 1 *n* esp black A pimp; = MACK: *went back to...that young mackman?*—C Cooper/ *a mere player masquerading as a mack-man*—Village Voice **2** *modifier*: *for all his jackass mackman shit*—Village Voice

Mack truck *n phr* football A very tough and solid player, usu a defensive one [fr the trade name of a line of heavy trucks]

mad 1 *adj* Angry **2** *adj* bop & cool talk Excellent; exciting; = CRAZY
See LIKE CRAZY, SO MAD one COULD SPIT NAILS

-mad *combining word* Devoted to, manic over, obsessed with what is indicated: *money-mad/ computer-mad/ horse-mad*

mad about something or someone *adj phr* = CRAZY ABOUT: *Aren't you just mad about her new book?*

madam *n* fr late 1600s The female manager or owner of a brothel

mad as a wet hen *adj phr* Very angry; infuriated; = PISSED OFF

madball *n* carnival A crystal-gazer's glass globe: *made with the madball*—F Brown

made *n* black Straightened hair; a head of straightened hair
See HAVE something CINCHED, TAILOR-MADE

be **made** *v phr* = be TAKEN

made for one *adj phr* Exactly fitted to one's desires, looks, etc: *I love this town, it's made for me*

Madison Avenue or **Mad Ave 1** *n phr* The values, behavior, business, milieu, etc, of advertising and public relations **2** *modifier*: *Madison Avenue hype*

mad money 1 *n phr* Money carried by a woman with which to pay her way home if her escort becomes offensive **2** *n phr* Money saved by a woman against the time when she wants to make an impulsive or therapeutic purchase

Mae West *n phr* fr 1930s British aviators A bulky life preserver

mafia *n* A group prominent in and suspected of controlling some organization, institution, etc: *Chernenko was a member of the Brezhnev mafia in the*

Politburo—National Public Radio [fr Italian *mafia* or *maffia*, designating the Sicilian secret society supposed to be deeply involved in organized crime both in Italy and the US; the Italian word derives fr Old French *mafler* "to gluttonize, devour," perhaps cognate with German *maffelen* "chew"] *See* DIXIE MAFIA

mag 1 *n* A magazine **2** *n* A magneto **3** *n* A car wheel made of a magnesium alloy

magazine *See* SKIN MAGAZINE

Magellan *n airline* An aircraft navigator

Maggie or **maggie** *n underworld* An automatic pistol [perhaps fr the fact that bullets are put into a *magazine*, which fits into the pistol]

Maggie's drawers *n phr Army* A blatant red flag waved on a military firing range when the target is missed completely

maggot *n* A cigarette butt: *snapped the maggot over the rail*—Sterling Hayden *See* ENOUGH TO GAG A MAGGOT

magic *See* TRAGIC MAGIC

magnum-force *adj* Very powerful: *one of Thomas Hearns's magnum-force punches* [fr the powerful *Magnum* revolver]

magoo (mə GŌō) **1** *n* Custard pie, esp as used in comic stage and movie scenes **2** *n* An important person; = BIG SHOT: *Darryl Zanuck, chief magoo of the studio*—TM Pryor

maiden *n horse-racing* A racehorse, regardless of sex, that has never won a race; = BUG *See* IRON MAIDEN

maiden's delight *n phr* A cherry-flavored Coca-Cola (a trade name)

mail *See* AIRMAIL, CARRY THE MAIL, GREENMAIL, JUNK MAIL, PACK THE MAIL

mail drop *n phr* A place or address where one can receive mail clandestinely

main *adj black* Favorite; most admired; beloved: *This is my main nigger, my number one nigger*—Claude Brown *See* MAINLINE

main brace *See* SPLICE THE MAIN BRACE

main drag (or **stem**) *n phr hoboes* The major street of a town or city: *We begged together on the "main drag"*—Jack London/ *We sifted along the main stem*—Raymond Chandler

mainline or **main 1** *v narcotics* To inject narcotics into a blood vessel; = SHOOT UP: *after mainlining heroin the night before*—New York Post **2** *v* To take or administer stimulants or depressants of various sorts: *because the economy was mainlining bigger and bigger fixes of inflation*—Philadelphia

main line 1 *n phr* (also **Main Line**) The wealthy and fashionable elements of a place; high society and its area of residence, esp that of Philadelphia: *so young and handsome and so popular with the Main Line*—Stephen Longstreet **2** *n phr narcotics* A blood vessel, usu in the arm or leg, into which narcotics may be injected **3** *n phr prison* The mess hall [first sense fr the railroad between Philadelphia and the wealthy suburbs to the west]

main man 1 *n phr black* One's best friend: *Lou Reed, he my main man*—Aquarian **2** *n phr* A

woman's lover: *He's been her main man for two years. Do you think they'll get married?*

main queen 1 *n phr* One's steady girlfriend **2** *n phr homosexuals* A male homosexual who takes the passive role, esp one much sought after by other homosexuals

main squeeze 1 *n phr* The most important person; = BIG ENCHILADA, BOSS: *Vance seems to be the main squeeze*—Dashiell Hammett **2** *n phr* One's sweetheart, lover, etc: *which center on his main squeeze, a girl in his Shakespeare class*—Publishers Weekly

maintain a low profile *See* KEEP A LOW PROFILE

maisie *See* S AND M

maison joie (meh ZAWN JəWAH) *n phr* A brothel: *Countess Piazza's "maison joie"*—Stephen Longstreet [fr New Orleans Creole "joy house"]

make 1 *v underworld fr early 1800s* To rob; steal; = HEIST **2** *v underworld & police* To recognize or identify; make an identification: *The dealer-suspect "made" (ie, correctly identified) one of the staked-out 53 cars*—New York Times/ *He made me the minute he saw me*—John O'Hara **3** *n:* The woman gave us a make on the guy who slugged her **4** *v* To understand; grasp; = DIG: *I don't make you, kid. What did the boy do?*—H Witwer **5** *v* To bring fame, success, wealth, etc: *That one show made her* ◁**6**▷ *v* To do the sex act with; = LAY, SCREW: *Not only is the King in love with me, but the Queen tried to make me too*—Newsweek/ *in the sense of "making" handsome men*—Faubion Bowers ◁**7**▷ *n* A person regarded merely as a sex partner; = LAY: *an easy make* **8** *v* To arrive at; = HIT: *We'll never make Padanaram before dark* **9** *v* To defecate *See* EASY MAKE, ON THE MAKE, ON THE TAKE, PUT THE MAKE ON someone, RUN A MAKE

make a believer out of someone *v phr* To convince someone, esp by forceful or harsh means: *I never worried about it much, but that one wreck made a believer out of me*

make a big production (or **big deal**) *v phr* To overdo; overreact, overplan, etc; = MAKE A FEDERAL CASE OUT OF something: *All she wanted was a simple wedding, but he had to make a big production out of it*

make a Federal case out of something *v phr* To overemphasize the importance of something; exaggerate or overreact; = BLOW UP: *I merely bought a new car...so don't try to make a Federal case out of it*—S McNeil

make a hit *v phr* To succeed; be received with approval, gratitude, etc: *She made a hit with my family*

make a killing *v phr* To get a large, quick profit; win hugely

make a move on someone *See* PUT A MOVE ON someone

make (or **get**) **an offer** one **can't refuse** *v phr* To coerce or menace, esp with an ostensibly plausible offer: *"He's a businessman," the Don said blandly. "I'll make him an offer he can't refuse"*—Mario Puzo/ *The North Atlantic allies last week* *got an offer they couldn't brusquely refuse*—New York Times

make an omelet *See* YOU CAN'T MAKE AN OMELET WITHOUT BREAKING EGGS

make a pass at someone *v phr* To make a sexual advance; = PROPOSITION, PUT A MOVE ON someone: *He got high one time and made a pass at her* —Raymond Chandler [fr early 1800s in the sense of "strike at, attack"]

make a payday *v phr* To win or get money aside from regular work: *What Harry meant by "making a payday" was that he was going to win all the money from the people that had worked for it*—A Lomax

make a pitch *v phr* To make a persuasive case; advocate strongly: *He'll make a pitch for solar energy*

make a pit stop *v phr* To urinate

make a play for *v phr* To attempt to get or seduce, esp by applied attractiveness: *He's making a play for that cute millionaire*

make a scene (or **a stink**) *v phr* To exhibit anger, indignation, fiery temper, hysterics, etc, in a public outburst: *He thought the soup too hot, and made quite a little scene about it/ Why don't these pay cable services make a public stink about the Time Inc-Manhattan Cable monopoly?*—Village Voice

make a score 1 *v phr* narcotics To buy narcotics; = SCORE: *this Jewish cat looking to make a score*—New York Times **2** *v phr* gambling To win a bet: *But I make scores and they keep me going for a while*—New York Post/ *ran wild in the cabaret as soon as they made a big score*—Jimmy Cannon

make a splash *v phr* To produce a strong and usu favorable impression; be very conspicuous: *That's the book that made such a big splash a couple of years ago*

make one's (or **the**) **blood boil** *v phr* To make one very angry; infuriate one: *a devastating combination of logic, analysis, and case studies, makes the blood boil*—Fortune

make book *See* KEEP BOOK

not **make deals** *See* NOT MAKE DEALS

make feet *v phr* To run away; flee; fly: *and I made feet, kiddo, cause you just don't know how crazy these guys are*—Philadelphia Journal

make for 1 *v phr* = HEAD FOR **2** *v phr* To encourage; promote: *This will make for renewed confidence*

make one's **getaway** *v phr* To escape; flee; fly, esp from the scene of a crime: *The thugs made their getaway in a souped-up Sherman tank*

make good *v phr* To succeed; do what one set out to do in career or life

make goo-goo eyes *v phr* To look at someone longingly, lovingly, seductively, etc: *make goo-goo eyes near a tropical lagoon*—People Weekly

make hamburger (or **hash** or **mincemeat**) **out of** someone or something *v phr* To defeat definitively; trounce; = CLOBBER: *They made hamburger out of the wilting opposition*

make hay or **make hay while the sun shines** *v phr* To profit from one's chances; take full advantage

make it 1 *v phr* To succeed; = GO OVER: *The charts showed we had made it, and big* **2** *v phr* To survive; live: *He's so sick, I don't think he'll make it* **3** *v phr* To come through unscathed; succeed in enduring: *I don't see how she made it through that rotten day* **4** *v phr* To get to a particular goal or place: *He didn't quite make it to the john*

make it big *v phr* To succeed extraordinarily well

make it snappy *v phr* To hurry; go faster; act quickly; = GET THE LEAD OUT, SNAP TO IT

make it with someone *cool talk* ◁1▷ *v* To do the sex act with or to someone; = SCORE: *Man, don't think I didn't make it with her*—S Boal **2** *v phr* To succeed with someone: *Talking that way he'll never make it with the committee*

make light of *v phr* To place little importance in; deprecate: *He made light of his chances*

make like *v phr* To pretend to be; imitate: *A cop picked it up and made like a bookie*—New York Confidential/ *Brewster's gonna make like a canary* —Hannibal & Boris

make little ones out of big ones *v phr* underworld To serve a prison sentence [fr the prison work of breaking large stones into small ones]

make mincemeat out of someone or something *See* MAKE HAMBURGER OUT OF someone or something

make money hand over fist *v phr* To earn a large income; prosper hugely; = COIN MONEY

make one's **move** *v phr* To take a first and crucial action, esp one that will start a chain of reactions: *The cops are just waiting for the guy to make his move*

make my day *sentence* Go ahead and do what you appear to threaten, so that I can trounce you and have a successful day: *"Make my day" is much used in the New York subway system, where life is raw and tempers are short*—Mary McGrory/ *"Momma, if I tell you, you won't like it"..."So go ahead, make my day"*—Momma (comic strip)

make nice *v phr* To pet; cosset, caress ● The syntax simulates baby talk: *Public officials...make nice to politicians they cannot stand...because they need their good will*—New York Times

make (or **have**) **no bones about 1** *v phr* fr 1500s To be entirely candid about; to be open about; = be UP-FRONT: *They make no bones about what they're going to do*—Washington Post **2** *v phr* To show or feel no doubt or hesitation about: *This spirited Labrador...had no bones about venturing out*—Milwaukee Journal [origin unknown; the earlier form *find no bones* may indicate that the reference is to bones in soup or stew, which would hinder the eating, hence hold the matter up]

make noises 1 *v phr* To express oneself; speak, esp initially and somewhat vaguely: *The Russians began to make noises about leaving* **2** *v phr* To talk insincerely or uselessly: *Do they mean it, or are they making noises?*

make no never mind *v phr fr black* To make no difference; be insignificant: *Makes no never mind what he thinks, I'm going*

make out 1 *v phr* To succeed, esp by a slim margin; =GET BY: *Did you make out OK with that new machine?* **2** *v phr* *esp teenagers & students* To pet heavily; kiss and caress; =NECK: *holding hands, slow dancing, making out to a point*—Playboy/ *nostalgic for duck-tail haircuts, and making out in the back seat*—New York **3** *v phr* To succeed in sexual conquest

make-out artist 1 *n phr* A man known for sexual success; =COCKSMAN, STUD: *The correct description for such a fellow is "make-out artist"*—New York Times **2** *n phr* A man who tries to charm and impress his superiors

make out like a bandit *v phr* To emerge very successfully; win everything: *In an unlikely market, they made out like a bandit/ You'd make out like a bandit*—George V Higgins [probably based on Yiddish *bondit* "clever, resourceful fellow"]

maker *See* WAVE-MAKER, WIDOW-MAKER

make something out of *v phr* To interpret as a cause for combat; regard as a challenge or insult: *So you heard what I said, huh? You want to make something out of it?*—John McNulty/ *I dropped a crude insult, but he didn't make anything out of it*

make something **stick** *v phr* To cause an accusation, assertion, etc, to be believed; validate or prove something: *They accused him of rape, but they'll never make it stick*

make the cheese more binding *v phr* To make things more difficult or complicated; clutter or snarl the matter: *And just to make the cheese more binding, they're also sold through mail order*—Lawrence Sanders [a humorous pun based on the fact that cheese is thought to be *binding* "constipating," and certain elements of a situation are also *binding* "constraining"]

make the flop *v phr* *hoboes* To beg while sitting on the sidewalk

make the grade 1 *v phr* *fr late 1800s* To succeed: *He made the grade as a lawyer* **2** *v phr* To meet certain standards: *His work just didn't make the grade*

make the riffle *v phr* *hoboes fr middle 1800s* To succeed; attain one's goal [fr the sense "negotiate the rapids on a stream"]

make the rounds *v phr* To be passed from person to person; circulate: *A theory about the cause is making the rounds now*

make the scene *fr beat & cool talk* **1** *v phr* To arrive; appear: *When do you plan to make the scene?* **2** *v phr* To succeed; achieve something: *With this album they'll sure make the scene* **3** *v phr* To do; experience: *I think I'll make the political scene next*

make time *v phr fr railroad fr middle 1800s* To go fast; travel at a good speed: *They really made time after they let the passengers off*

make time with someone *v phr* To succeed sexually with someone, esp to make or approach a rapid conquest: *He was making time with Ezra's girl*

makeup *n* The composition; constituents: *What's the makeup of that club?*

make up for lost time *v phr* To work, play, travel, etc, very fast to compensate for a slow start

make waves *v phr* To cause trouble; upset things: *What he said has made waves*—Milwaukee Journal/ *John Quinn had always been a team player who didn't make waves*—San Francisco/ *The case continues to make waves in the state*—New York Times [fr the joke in which a person just arrived in hell, and hearing beautiful serene singing, finds that it is being done by inmates standing in chin-high excrement and cautiously chanting *"Don't make waves"*]

make with *v phr* To use; exercise: *The poor man's Bing Crosby is still making with the throat here in Chi*—John O'Hara [fr Yiddish *machen mit* "swing or wave something about, brandish something"]

the **makings** *n phr* The ingredients; what is necessary for: *He's young, but he's got the makings of a real pro* [fr early-20th-century Western phrase meaning the paper and tobacco, usu Bull Durham, for rolling a cigarette]

malarkey 1 *n fr 1920s* Lies and exaggerations; empty bombastic talk; =BALONEY, BULLSHIT: *Hollywood is in the business of manufacturing malarkey as well as movies*—Bob Thomas/ *That's a lot of malarkey*—Newsweek **2** *interj* =BULLSHIT [origin unknown]

male chauvinist pig 1 *n phr* A man who believes in and proclaims the superiority of men over women; =MCP: *Is it all right to call a priest a male chauvinist pig?*—New York Times **2** *modifier:* *male-chauvinist-pig-type man to the contrary notwithstanding*—New York

male member *See* MEMBER

mallie (MAW lee) *n* A person, esp a young person, who frequents shopping malls for sociability, excitement, etc: *"Mallies" always hang around the pay telephone*—Peanuts (comic strip)

mama 1 *n* Any woman **2** *n fr black* A sexually attractive or sexually available woman: *"Say, baby, you sportin' tonight?" "Yeah, Mama, if I could find somebody to sport with"*—Claude Brown **3** *n motorcyclists* A woman who belongs to a motorcycle gang: *If a girl wants to be a mama and "pull a train,"...she'll be welcome at any Angel party*—Saturday Evening Post **4** *n homosexuals* The passive, feminine partner of a lesbian couple

See RED-HOT MAMA, SWEET MAMA

mama-and-papa *See* MOM-AND-POP

mama's boy or **mammy boy** *n phr* A soft or effeminate boy or man; a male overly attached to his mother: *the stale old mama's-boy-liberated-by-looney-lovely*—Judith Crist

mammyrammer *See* MOTHERFUCKER

man *n* A dollar; =IRON MAN: *You oughta grab about 300 men*—H Witwer

See ASS MAN, BACKDOOR MAN, BLUE MAN, BOTTLE-MAN, BOX MAN, BUG MAN, BUTTER-AND-EGG MAN, CANDY MAN, CHAIN MAN, COMPANY MAN, CON MAN, DIRTY OLD MAN, FANCY MAN, FINGER MAN, FIRST MAN, G-MAN, HAMMER-MAN, HATCHET MAN, HEIST MAN, HE-MAN, HIT MAN, HONEY MAN, HOOP-MAN, IRON MAN, JIG-

GER-MAN, JUICE MAN, LADIES' MAN, LEG MAN, LOW MAN ON THE TOTEM POLE, MONDAY MAN, OUNCE MAN, PANMAN, PETE-MAN, PETERMAN, PHONY-MAN, POINT, POOR MAN'S something, ROD-MAN, SANDWICH MAN, SEAT-MAN, SEE A MAN ABOUT A DOG, SHACK MAN, STRAIGHT MAN, SWEET MAN, TAMBOURINE MAN, TIT MAN, TOMMY MAN, TRIGGER MAN, VENT MAN, WHEEL MAN

-man *combining word* A man preferring, doing, having, etc, the indicated thing: *bottle-man/ fifty-minute-man/ trigger man*

the **man** or **the Man** **1** *n phr* Any man in authority; =BOSS, HIS NIBS: *See the guy in front? That's the man* **2** *n phr* narcotics & underworld A police officer, detective, prison guard, etc; =the HEAT: *Careful, here's the man* **3** *n phr* narcotics A supplier of narcotics; =DEALER **4** *n phr* black A white man; the white establishment: *a super nigger who spends his life trying to prove he's as good as the Man*—Saturday Review/ *That's what "the man" wants you to do...to riot, so he can shoot you down*—New Yorker

a **man about a dog** *See* SEE A MAN ABOUT A DOG

man-about-town *n* A sophisticated urban man and cynosure; boulevardier

manage *v* To cope satisfactorily; survive; =GET BY: *It's a lot to pay, but we'll manage*

◁**mangoes**▷ *n* A woman's breasts: *There's the old mangoes*—Peter De Vries

mango hunter *n phr* A person, usu a drug addict, who sets fire to vacant buildings and steals the saleable items after firefighters have chopped up the floors, etc: *Then the "mango hunters," as New York cops call them...move in*—Time

mangy with *adj phr* =LOUSY WITH

Manhattan eel *n phr* A condom [fr the fact that so very many of these are seen floating amongst the offal in New York Harbor]

◁**man in the boat**▷ *n phr* fr middle 1800s British The clitoris; =CLIT: *Fortunately, the "man in the boat" did not give me any trouble*—Xaviera Hollander

mano a mano *n phr* A hand-to-hand fight or duel: *Hemingway's subject...was the mano a mano between Spain's two leading matadors*—New York Times/ *a literary mano a mano with some good books as weapons*—New York Times [fr Spanish, "hand-to-hand"]

man on the street **1** *n phr* fr early 1800s The average person; the ordinary person; =JOHN Q CITIZEN **2** *modifier*: *and some man-on-the-street TV commercials for post-convention use*—New York

man-size or **man-sized** *adj* Large; capacious; abundant: *Crump bet man-sized money*—J Lilienthal/ *a man-size meal*

◁**man with a paper ass**▷ *n phr* black A person whose ideas are not important; a trivial man; =LIGHTWEIGHT

many *See* ONE TOO MANY

mao-mao (MOU MOU) *v* To coerce with rough treatment; terrorize: *The pressure ladies half-successfully mao-maoed Communications Minister Francis Fox...to censure the offending shows*

—Toronto Life [fr the *Mau Maus*, a terrorist group in Kenya in the 1950s]

map **1** *n* fr early 1900s The face: *A funny look...spread over Kenney's crimson map*—H Witwer **2** *n* gambling A bank check

maple *See* BIRDSEYE MAPLE

map out *v phr* To plan: *Let's map out what we're gonna do tomorrow*

maps *n* jazz musicians Sheet music; written arrangements

◁**maracas**▷ *n* A woman's breasts; =BOOBS: *gams and a pair of maracas that will haunt me in my dreams*—John O'Hara

marble-dome *n* A stupid person; =BLOCKHEAD

marble orchard *n phr* A cemetery: *You'll get your names in this marble orchard soon enough*—James M Cain

marbles *See* GO FOR BROKE, HAVE ALL one's BUTTONS, HAVE SOME BUTTONS MISSING, LOSE one's MARBLES, MISSISSIPPI MARBLES

march *n* circus The circus parade

mare *See* RIDE SHANK'S MARE

marge **1** *n* homosexuals The passive, feminine partner in a lesbian couple; =MAMA **2** *n* Margarine

Mari *See* MARY

Maria *See* BLACK MARIA

◁**maricón**▷ (MAH rih kahn, MA-, -KOHN) *n* A male homosexual: *"This it is, maricón," snarled the Puerto Rican*—High Times [fr Spanish]

Marines *See* TELL IT TO THE MARINES

mark **1** *n* fr late 1800s underworld, circus, carnival, hawkers, & hoboes The target or victim of a swindle, esp one who is easily duped; =PATSY, SUCKER: *not that he's more of a mark than other horse nuts*—J Lilienthal/ *his "marks," as the gullible are called by a pitchman*—New York Times **2** *n* carnival An outsider or member of the local community; =HOME GUARD: *Marks...aren't allowed in*—F Brown **3** *n* hoboes A place where it is easy to get food, money, etc, by theft and deception **4** *v* underworld To look for or find a likely place for robbery **5** *v* teenagers To inform; =SQUEAL: *He swore he wouldn't mark if they caught him*

See EASY MARK, HASH MARK, TOE THE MARK, UP TO SCRATCH

marker **1** *n* gambling =IOU **2** *n* sports A point or score: *eight markers in the first period*

market *See* a DRUG ON THE MARKET, GRAY MARKET, MEAT MARKET, SLAVE MARKET

marks the spot *See* X MARKS THE SPOT

marmalade *n* =MALARKEY

marriage *See* SHOTGUN WEDDING

marry *v* To join; bring together: *He tries to marry the Canadian producers with the foreign buyers*—Toronto Life

marshmallow *n* black A white person: *an Oreo fronting for a "marshmallow"*—R Levine

marshmallow shoes or **marshmallows** *n phr* or *n* Shoes with very thick white platform soles

martooni *n* A martini cocktail [fr a spoonerized protestation like "I only had tee martoonis"]

Marx *See* HART, SCHAFFNER AND MARX

Mary **1** *n* A male homosexual who takes the passive, feminine role: *He passed two willowy-looking queers, Mary's who'd decided to settle for each other*—George V Higgins **2** *n* A lesbian **3** *n* (also **Mari**) *narcotics* Marijuana

Mary Ann or **Mary Jane** *n phr narcotics* Marijuana or a marijuana cigarette

Mary Warner *n phr narcotics* Marijuana

mash **1** *n esp 1920s* Love or a love affair: *just another mash*—Louis Armstrong **2** *n* A lover, of either sex: *her latest big mash* **3** *v fr middle 1800s* To make a sexual advance to; = PROPOSITION: *I wouldn't try to mash anybody like you* [apparently fr Romany, "allure, entice," and so used in mid-19th-century vaudeville by a Gypsy troupe]
See MISH-MASH

masher *n fr late 1800s* A man who habitually makes sexual approaches to women; = LADY-KILLER, WOLF

mash note *n phr* A very flattering letter, esp one proposing or offering sex: *He gets mash notes by the ton*—WR Burnett/ *showered him with embroidered pillows, mash notes, and cigars*—Reader's Digest

mask **1** *n* The face **2** *n* The large wraparound sunglasses affected by police officers, hot rodders, etc

massage **1** *v* To beat; drub; = ROUGH someone UP: *caught and massaged with rubber hoses*—HF Pringle **2** *v* To handle, process, or manipulate data, esp computer data: *The results all depend on how you massage it*

massage someone's **ego** *v phr* To soothe and flatter someone; = STROKE: *He felt all strong and confident after she massaged his ego at lunch*

massage parlor *n phr* A place that provides sexual services under the guise of legitimate body massage; = RAP CLUB

massager *See* POT-MASSAGER

master *See* RINGMASTER

mastermind **1** *n* The chief planner, decision-maker, leader, etc **2** *v*: *the fellows who mastermind prizefights, football games, hockey, baseball*—Billy Rose **3** *n railroad* A trainmaster

masters *See* SLAVES AND MASTERS

mat **1** *n black* A woman; one's wife **2** *n esp Navy* The floor; deck
See COLLISION MAT, CORKING MAT, GO TO THE MAT, HIT THE MAT, ON THE MAT

match *See* the WHOLE SHOOTING MATCH

mate *See* DATE MATE

math *n students* Mathematics

matter *See* GRAY MATTER

Mau Mau *n phr black* A black militant, esp a Black Muslim [fr the name of a terrorist group in Kenya; see *mao mao*]

mavin or **mayvin** or **maven** (MAY vən) *n* An expert; an authority; a connoisseur: *growing clientele of pizza mavins*—L Goldberg/ *A real advertising mavin must have thought that up*—Leo Rosten [fr Yiddish fr Hebrew, "understanding"]

max **1** *adv* At the most; at the highest limit: *I do three cars a week, max*—George V Higgins **2** *v*

college students To win; do the very best [fr *maximum*]
See TO THE MAX

maxed *adj narcotics* Intoxicated with a narcotic; = STONED

maxi *esp 1960s* **1** *n* A mid-calf or ankle-length skirt or coat **2** *n* The ankle-length depth of hemline: *Is the new length a midi or a maxi?*—Life **3** *adj*: *long black pants under a maxi coat*—G Emerson [fr *maximum*]

max out **1** *v phr Army* To make the best score, or one's best score **2** *v phr* To do or contribute the maximum possible amount: *go to the people with the potential of, as they say in the business, "maxing out"*—Newsweek **3** *v phr college students* To go to sleep

May *See* FIRST-OF-MAY

mayo *n fr lunch counter* Mayonnaise

mazel (MAH zəl) *n* Luck: *When a man has mazel, even his ox calves*—Leo Rosten [fr Yiddish fr Hebrew]

mazuma (mə ZŌŌ mə) *n* (Variations: **mezuma** or **mazume** or **mazoomy** or **mazoo** or **mazoola** or **mazula**) *fr early 1900s* Money: *You have to leave your mazuma behind*—George Jean Nathan [fr Yiddish fr Hebrew; perhaps fr a Chaldean word meaning "the ready necessary"]

MC or **emcee** (pronounced as separate letters) **1** *n* A master of ceremonies **2** *v*: *MC'd by Bob Hope*—New York/ *George Jessel emceed the event*—Variety

McCoy *adj* Genuine; legitimate; = KOSHER: *like every other McCoy biz*—Variety

the McCoy *See* the REAL MCCOY

McCrea *See* MOTHER MACHREE

McDucks *n college students* McDonalds (a trade name), a fast-food restaurant [reference to Disney's *Donald Duck*]

McGee *See* JERK MCGEE

MCP or **mcp** **1** *n* = MALE CHAUVINIST PIG **2** *modifier*: *a sort of anarcho-Marxist MCP*—Village Voice/ *Somehow his senior mcp act doesn't really threaten women*—Herbert Gold

MD *n lunch counter* Dr Pepper (a trade name), a soft drink

MDA *n narcotics* Methyl diamphetamine, a stimulant that is somewhat like LSD

meal *See* SQUARE

meal ticket **1** *n phr prizefight* A prizefighter in relation to his manager: *with his meal ticket, the Brown Bomber himself*—Arthur Daley **2** *n phr* Any person, skill, part of the body, instrument, etc, that provides one's sustenance: *His looks are his meal ticket*

mean *adj fr early 1900s black* Excellent; wonderful; = CLASSY, WICKED: *This...girl has already proved she can play a mean game of tennis*—Inside Sports/ *And Wheelright had a great, mean ear for dialect*—Peter Schjeldahl
See LEAN AND MEAN, SHAKE A WICKED CALF

mean bean *n phr* An expert; = MAVIN: *John, who's a mean bean at squash and horseback riding*—People Weekly

mean green *n phr fr black* Money: *Mean green won out over neighborhood purity in the end*—Village Voice

meany or **meanie** *n* A cruel, unkind person; villain; = HEAVY
See BLUE MEANY

meat ◁**1**▷ *n* A person considered merely as a sex partner or object; = ASS ◁**2**▷ *n* The vulva; = CUNT ◁**3**▷ *n fr homosexuals* The penis; = PRICK ◁**4**▷ *n fr 1700s* The sex act; copulation; = FUCKING: *He says he's hard up, needs meat* **5** *n students* A stupid person; = MEATHEAD: *to see a bunch of meats play*—Sports Illustrated **6** *n carracing* The depth of tread on a tire
See ALL THAT MEAT AND NO POTATOES, BEAT one's MEAT, COLD MEAT, DARK MEAT, EASY MEAT, JUMP ON someone's MEAT, MAKE HAMBURGER OUT OF someone or something, PIG-MEAT, WHITE MEAT

one's **meat** *fr late 1800s* **1** *n phr* An easy and favorite opponent; a chosen opponent: *He wins every time, guess I'm his meat* **2** *n phr* One's preferred work, play, effort, etc: *Tennis is his meat* [probably based on the older sense of *meat* "food, sustenance"]

the **meat** *n phr* The essential part; core: *Now we see the meat of the problem*

meat and potatoes **1** *n phr* The simple fundamentals; = the NITTY-GRITTY **2** *modifier*: *It's the meat-and-potatoes appeal, the old pull at the heartstrings*—SJ Perelman
See ALL THAT MEAT AND NO POTATOES

meat-ax *v* To assault brutally; chop down: *the jobless refugees from Doubleday's meat-axing of Dial and Delacorte*—Village Voice

meatball **1** *n esp WW2 armed forces* A stupid, tedious person; an obnoxious or disgusting person; = CREEP, JERK: *"How come?" "Because he's a meatball"*—WT Tyler **2** *n WW2 Navy* A signal flag with a black dot on a yellow field **3** *n WW2 Navy* The Japanese flag

meat card *n phr* = MEAL TICKET

meateater *n* A corrupt police officer who aggressively seeks illicit spoils: *Meat eaters...spend a good deal of their working hours aggressively seeking out situations they can exploit*—New York Times

meat-fit *n hoboes* A full meal, esp one with much meat

meathead *n* A stupid person; = MEATBALL: *The copper...was a big meathead*—JB Martin/ *Take your hand off that door, you meathead*—Tom Wolfe

meatheaded *adj* Stupid: *some meatheaded tart*—WR Burnett

meathooks *n* The hands or fists; = BISCUIT HOOKS

meat market *n phr* A place where one looks for sex partners; the milieu of the singles: *men, who are now in the meat market, just like women have always been*—New York Times/ *They go out to the meat markets, then come back and say how awful it was*—Washingtonian

meat rack *n phr esp homosexuals* A gathering place, often public like a park bench or a shopping mall, where one seeks out sex partners: *trailers parked near the river in Greenwich Village, the strip some people call "the meat rack"*—Washington Post

meat run *n phr railroad* Any fast train

meat show *n phr* A cabaret floor show featuring nude or nearly nude women: *a divertissement known in the trade as a meat-show*—Westbrook Pegler

meat wagon **1** *n phr* An ambulance: *He woke up in the meatwagon*—Forum **2** *n phr* A hearse: *They have the meat wagon following him around*—Raymond Chandler

mechanic *n gambling* An expert card player; = CARD SHARP: *No "mechanics" (sharps) were tolerated*—T Betts

med **1** *n* A medical student **2** *modifier* Medical: *med school/ a med alert*

medal *See* NO-CLAP MEDAL

media hype *n phr* Concentrated favorable publicity for a person, corporation, candidate, etc: *Most of what they say we can dismiss as media hype/ Instead of dealing in the media hype, Coplon should have...pursued the reasons*—Village Voice

medic **1** *n* A medical student **2** *n WW2 armed forces* A military medical orderly, attendant, stretcher-bearer, etc **3** *n* (also **medico**) A physician

medicine *See* GOD'S MEDICINE, TAKE one's MEDICINE

meds *n hospital* Medications

the **meemies** *See* the SCREAMING MEEMIES

meet **1** *n railroad* A point where trains are scheduled to meet **2** *n underworld* A meeting, esp for some illegal purpose: *She went out to make a "meet" to buy more bogus bills*—Fact Detective Mysteries/ *I'll call you next Friday, same time, and set up a meet*—Lawrence Sanders **3** *n bop musicians & cool musicians* = JAM SESSION
See CORNFIELD MEET

meets the road *See* WHERE THE RUBBER MEETS THE ROAD

mega **1** *adj esp students & teenagers* Much: *I got mega homework tonight* **2** *adv*: *This dude is mega gross*

mega- *prefix* A very large specimen, quantity, etc, of what is indicated: *megablitz/ mega-cost/ megagreed/ megahopes/ megatravel*

megabucks *n* Much money: *The movie should gross megabucks/ the simple faith that moves mountains and grosses megabucks*—Village Voice

the **megillah** or **the whole megillah** (mə GILL ə) *n phr* Something very long and tedious told or explained exhaustively: *Let's not have the megillah*—C McHarry/ *a whole megilla (song and dance)*—New York Times [fr Yiddish fr Hebrew, "scroll, volume," esp the Book of Esther read aloud in its entirety at Purim celebrations]

MEGO (MEE goh) *sentence chiefly news media* This is a smashingly boring affair [fr *mine eyes glaze over*]

MEGOGIGO (MEE goh GĬ goh) *sentence esp teenagers* This is totally tedious [fr *mine eyes glaze over, garbage in garbage out*]

meister *See* PERKMEISTER

mell of a hess *n phr* A dire situation; =SNAFU: *You better come over, Doc, there's a mell of a hess here/ Some mell of a hess you got us into* [spoonerism for *hell of a mess*]

mellow 1 *adj fr early 1700s* Slightly drunk; =TIDDLY **2** *adj jive talk & cool talk* Sincere and skillful ● Said of a musical performance **3** *adj* Relaxed; at ease; =LAID-BACK **4** *adj* Very friendly; intimate **5** *n* A close friend; =BUDDY **6** *v* =MELLOW OUT

mellow-back *adj black* Smartly dressed

mellow out (also **mellow**) *v phr esp musicians* To become relaxed and easy: *wondering why the family in "The Grapes of Wrath" didn't move to LA and mellow out*—Washington Post/ *He'd mellowed over the years/ Even the testiest groups and crews can be mellowed out after spending time at Alpine*—Milwaukee Journal

melo *n movie studio* A melodrama

melon ◁1▷ *n* A woman's breast **2** *n* The sum of profits, loot, etc, to be divided: *The stockholders have a meager melon to share this year*

melon-belly *n* A protuberant abdomen; a person with a big stomach

meltdown *n* A disaster: *They are...facing a credibility meltdown*—Toronto Life/ *The Glenn campaign has achieved almost total meltdown*—NBC News [fr the nuclear power-plant disaster in which the core of radioactive material *melts down* into the earth below]

melted out *adj phr gambling* Penniless, esp from gambling; =BROKE, TAPPED OUT

melt into the scenery *v phr* To disappear; become inconspicuous

Melvin *n teenagers* A disgusting and contemptible person; =CREEP, NERD

member 1 *n black* A fellow black person; =BROTHER, SISTER ◁2▷ *n* (also **male member**) The penis ● A euphemism for the even more euphemistic **membrum virile**

the men *n phr truckers* The police, esp state police; =SMOKEY BEAR

mensch or **mensh 1** *n* An admirable and substantial person; a decent and mature person: *At first I didn't like him, but then he emerged as a real mensch* **2** *n* A virile man ● Can also be used of women: *mensch, a stand-up he-man*—C McHarry/ *Trigere, almost alone, is mensch enough to candidly dismiss the misogynous midi*—Stephanie Harrington [fr Yiddish, literally "person, man"]

men's lib *n phr* Men's liberation, the counterpart, and possibly reaction, to women's liberation: *Only men's lib and women's lib can alert society*—Rosemary Park

mental *adj chiefly British* Crazy; deranged; =NUTTY: *and the son, William, went absolutely mental*—New York

mental job *n phr* A neurotic or psychotic person; =NUT

meow *See* the CAT'S MEOW

merchant *combining word* A person who esp indulges or purveys in what is indicated: *heat merchant/ speed merchant*

merge *v* To marry

merry-go-round 1 *n railroad* A turntable **2** *n* A very busy, confusing, and tiring activity, job, place, etc; =RAT RACE: *You wouldn't like it here, it's a damn merry-go-round*

the merry ha-ha *n phr* A ridiculing and dismissive laugh at someone; =the HORSELAUGH

merry hell *n phr* A severe rebuke or punishment: *He gave us merry hell for that caper*
See CATCH HELL, GIVE someone HELL

mesc *n narcotics* Mescaline, a hallucinogenic drug

meshegoss or **meshugas** *See* MISHEGOSS

meshuga (mə SHŏŏ gə, -SHIH-) *adj* (Variations: **meshigga** or **meshugah** or **meshiggah** or **mishugah** or **mishoogeh**) Crazy; =NUTTY: *Mishoogeh or mishugah...spelled either way means crazy*—C McHarry [fr Yiddish fr Hebrew; the variant pronunciations reflect major dialects of Yiddish]

meshugana or **meshiggana** or **meshiganer** (mə SHŏŏ gə nə, -SHIH-) *n* A crazy person; =NUT: *Robert, is that meshugana gone yet?* [fr Yiddish fr Hebrew]

mess 1 *n* A desperately confused situation; chaos; =FOUL-UP, FUCK-UP: *This project is turning into a mess* **2** *n* An incompetent, disorganized, and confused person: *Honey, I'm a mess* **3** *n* A disorderly or slovenly person; =SLOB: *You're always making a mess of yourself* **4** *n* Dirt, garbage, trash, etc; a dirtying: *Clean up your damn mess*

mess around *v phr* To idle about; loaf; work indolently; =GOOF OFF: *Stop messing around and get to work*

mess someone **around** (or **over**) *v phr* To victimize and exploit; maltreat; =FUCK OVER: *being messed over by Goldberg all the time*—Claude Brown/ *Here's a young black dude in a Cadillac, we'll just mess him around*—New York

mess around with or **mess with 1** *v phr fr middle 1800s* To flirt or dally with; have a sexual involvement with: *He'd waste me if I messed around with his sister/ I don't mess with married or attached women*—New York Post **2** *v phr* To defy or challenge; provoke; =FUCK WITH: *Nobody dared to mess around with Slippers*—Louis Armstrong/ *I said don't mess with me, Buster* **3** *v phr* To consort with; frequent; play with: *They go around messing with us, because we're trying to do something*—Ishmael Reed/ *What are you messing around with that crowd for?* **4** *v phr* To play or tinker with: *I caught him messing with the heating control*

mess up 1 *v phr* To disarrange; muddle: *Who messed up these figures?* **2** *v phr* To injure; damage: *The drugs and booze messed up her mind* **3** *v phr* To get into trouble; make a botch; =FUCK UP: *If you don't mess up you get an automatic promotion*

mess someone **up 1** *v phr* To thrash; beat up; =WORK someone OVER: *They sent a couple of goons to mess him up when he wouldn't pay* **2** *v phr* To damage or injure someone: *That Moony stuff* *messed him up pretty bad/ The wreck messed him up so much that he can't walk*

messy **1** *adj* Confused; chaotic; =FUCKED UP **2** *adj* Nasty; =DIRTY: *There'll be a lot of messy publicity about this*

metal *fr musicians* **1** *n* =HEAVY METAL **2** *v* To play loudly amplified rock and roll music: *Nobody can metal like Blue Oyster Cult*—B Malamut
See HEAVY METAL, PUT THE PEDAL TO THE METAL

metal head *n* A devotee of heavy-metal rock music: *the standard uniform of the metal-head: Led Zeppelin T-shirt, jeans, shoulder-length hair*—Toronto Star

metallurgist *n musicians* A heavy-metal musician

meter-reader *n aviators* The copilot of an airplane; =the KID

meth *n narcotics* Methedrine (a trade name)

meth head (or **freak**) *n phr narcotics* A habitual user of Methedrine (a trade name)

◀**Mex**▶ **1** *n* A Mexican **2** *adj* Mexican: *Ensenada is all Mex*—James M Cain

◀**Mexican breakfast**▶ *n phr* A cigarette and a glass of water

◀**Mexican infantry**▶ *n phr Army* Military intelligence

◀**Mexican promotion** (or **raise**)▶ *n phr* Advancement in rank or status with no raise of salary

Mexican red or **Mexican** *See* PANAMA RED

Mexican standoff *n phr* A stalemate; deadlock; =STANDOFF [*Mexican* seems to be used to give a sense of peril and crudeness to the situation, as if two persons faced each other directly with raised machetes or loaded guns]

mezonny (mee ZUHN ee) *n* Money, esp money spent for narcotics [fr *money* disguised by insertion of *-ez-* in the language of carnival people called "Carnese"]

mezuma *See* MAZUMA

mezz *outdated jazz musicians* **1** *n* A marijuana cigarette; =REEFER **2** *adj* Excellent; =MELLOW [fr the name of the jazz clarinetist *Mezz* Mezzrow]
See the MIGHTY MEZZ

MF or **mf** *n* A despicable person; =MOTHERFUCKER: *He used to look right at them MFs*—Pete Hamill/ *kill some of the Uncle Tomming mfs*—Eldridge Cleaver

mice *n television studio* Children

Michigan roll *n phr* A bankroll having a note of large denomination on the outside and small notes or paper making up the rest

◀**mick** or **Mick**▶ *fr middle 1800s* **1** *n* An Irishman or person of Irish descent **2** *adj: a mick politician* **3** *n* A Roman Catholic **4** *adj: my one mick friend, although he isn't Irish*—P Marks [fr the nickname of the common Irish name *Michael*]

mickey or **Mickey** ◀**1**▶ *n* =MICK **2** *n* A potato: *We stole our first mickies together from Gordon's fruit stand*—Claude Brown/ *roast mickies in the gutter fires*—Joseph Mitchell **3** *n* A stupefacient drug placed in one's drink; =MICKEY FINN: *Mickeys act so drastically that one may kill a drunk*

with a weak heart—AJ Liebling **4** *n Canadian* A half-bottle of liquor [potato sense probably by association with the common phrase *Irish potato*]
See SLIP someone A MICKEY

Mickey Ds *n phr teenagers* A McDonald's (a trade name) fast-food restaurant

Mickey Finn or **mickey finn** **1** *n phr fr late 1800s underworld* A strong hypnotic or barbiturate dose, esp of chloral hydrate, put secretly into a drink; =KNOCKOUT DROPS: *The drug, sometimes known as "knockout drops" or "Mickey Finn," is a sedative*—New York Times **2** *n phr* A purgative similarly administered [origin unknown and richly conjectured, chiefly being fathered on various characters with names like *Mickey Finn*]

Mickey Mouse or **mickey mouse** *after WW2* **1** *adj phr* (also **micky-mouse**) *musicians* Sentimental and insincere: *A "micky-mouse band" is a real corny outfit*—Stephen Longstreet/ *to the dead beat of mind-smothered Mickey Mouse music*—Eldridge Cleaver **2** *adj phr* Showy; meretricious, merely cosmetic; =GIMMICKY: *And I don't think Mickey Mouse changes are going to work*—Walter Mondale **3** *n: It's hard to get past the mickey mouse and see what the hell they're driving at* **4** *adj phr* Shoddy; inferior: *The carpentry work was just Mickey Mouse* **5** *adj phr college students* Simple; elementary; easy: *A "Mickey Mouse course" means a "snap course"*—M Crane **6** *adj phr college students* Petty; inconsequential: *A Mickey Mouse survey of popular culture/ A lot of the Mickey Mouse stuff has been eliminated from the program*—New York Times/ *got picked up on a Mickey Mouse thing in August by the State Patrol*—Ann Rule **7** *n phr: That book's pure mickey mouse* **8** *n phr esp armed forces* A blunder due to confusion and stupidity; =SCREW-UP: *The only big Mickey Mouse...was a brief shortage of...jungle boots*—Time **9** *n phr black* A stupid person, esp a white person or a police officer [apparently this pejorative trend began after the wide distribution of *Mickey Mouse* wrist watches, showing the cartoon character on the face, with his arms as the watch's hands, which were regarded as shoddy, gimmicky, etc, at that time]

Mickey Mouse around *v phr* To waste time; =FOOL AROUND: *We can't Mickey Mouse around while faced with the common technological challenges*—RG Hummerstone/ *This is ridiculous to be Mickey Mousing around on this*

Mickey Mouse ears *n phr esp students* Lights, siren, etc, on the top of a police car; =GUMBALL [members of the TV *Mickey Mouse* Club wore large black rodent *ears* on their heads]

middlebrow **1** *n* A person of average intelligence and taste **2** *adj: a middlebrow magazine/ middlebrow audience*

middle kidney *See* GRIPE one's ASS

◁**middle** (or **third**) **leg**▷ *n phr* The penis

the **middle of nowhere** *n phr* A very remote area; an isolated place; =BOONDOCKS: *They moved out of Manhattan way into Jersey, the middle of nowhere*

middy *n* A midshipman; US Naval Academy student

midnight requisition *n phr WW2 armed forces* A wrongful acquisition, esp of military property in a nonregulation manner; =CUMSHAW: *One of our sergeants was quite skillful at the midnight requisition*

miff *v fr early 1800s* To anger; offend: *His arrogance miffed all of us*

miffed *adj fr early 1800s* Angered; offended: *miffed over failure of pleas to raise his bail*—New York Daily News/ *Post-and-beam lovers may be a bit miffed too*—CoEvolution Quarterly

miffy *adj fr late 1600s* Angry; =MIFFED, PISSED OFF: *after a good bit of miffy correspondence*—A Logan

miggle 1 *n* A playing marble **2** *n narcotics* A marijuana cigarette; =JOINT

the **mighty mezz** *n phr outdated jazz musicians* Marijuana

mike 1 *n* A microphone **2** *v* To amplify with a microphone: *The club was so small they decided not to mike the show* **3** *n railroad* A Mikado engine, a type of locomotive having eight drive wheels, produced in the 1890s for the Japanese state railroad and also used in the US **4** *n* A microgram; a millionth of a gram: *I feel like I've been up on 300 mikes of acid*—Saturday Review
See BLACK MIKE

mike fright *n phr* A disabling fear felt when one tries to speak into a microphone; stage fright

mile *See* GO THE EXTRA MILE, STICK OUT

mileage *n* Advantage; profit: *Do they think there's any mileage in my idea?*
See GET MILEAGE OUT OF something

mile-high club *n phr airline* The putative association of persons who have done the sex act more than a mile high in the sky: *They had stayed behind to renew their membership in the mile-high club by sinking into one of the leather banquettes and making passionate love*—Newlook

military wedding *n phr* =SHOTGUN WEDDING

militia *See* RAGGEDY-ASS MILITIA

milk 1 *v fr show business* To exploit something to the utmost: *If I see an advantage, I milk it/ She really knows how to milk the audience for laughs* **2** *v* To get something, esp money, unfairly or fraudulently ● Originally used in the middle 1800s of manipulation in the stock market: *The agents had regularly been milking the tenants for exorbitant rents* ◁3▷ *v* To masturbate

milk cans *See* KNOCK someone FOR A LOOP

milk run 1 *n phr railroad* A train run with many stops **2** *n phr* A scheduled airline passage with many stops; *followed by a milk run to Charleston, Jacksonville, Daytona Beach, and Tampa*—Saturday Review **3** *n phr WW2 Air Forces* An easy bombing mission: *It looked like a milk run*—C Macon [fr the stopping of a train at every rural station to pick up *milk* for delivery to the cities]

milk wagon *n phr* A police van; =PADDY WAGON

mill¹ *n* A million dollars: *That'll cost the government a cool six mill*

mill² 1 *n prizefight* A prizefight: *the night of the KO Kelly mill*—Joseph Auslander **2** *n armed forces fr WW1* A military prison or guardhouse **3**

n An automobile or motorcycle engine: *Has it got the magnum mill?*—George V Higgins/ *They both chuckled and fired up their mills*—Easyriders **4** *n railroad* A locomotive **5** *n newspaper office* A typewriter
See GIN MILL, GO THROUGH THE MILL, GROG-MILL, RUMOR MILL, RUN-OF-THE-MILL, RUN someone THROUGH THE MILL, THROUGH THE MILL

million bucks *See* LIKE A MILLION BUCKS

milquetoast or **milktoast** *n* A mild, ineffectual person; a timid person; =WIMP

Milwaukee goiter (or **tumor**) *n phr* A protuberant belly; =BEERBELLY, POTBELLY [fr the fame of the *Milwaukee* breweries]

mince *n outdated teenagers* An unfashionable or tedious person; bore; =DRIP: *Anybody who still wears saddle shoes is...a "mince"*—New York Times

mincemeat *See* MAKE HAMBURGER OUT OF someone or something

mince pies *n phr underworld fr middle 1800s fr British* The eyes [fr Cockney rhyming slang]

mind *See* BEND someone's MIND, BLOW someone's MIND, DIRTY MIND, HAVE A MIND LIKE A SIEVE, a LOAD OFF someone's MIND, MAKE NO NEVER MIND, MASTERMIND, ONE-TRACK MIND, PIECE OF someone's MIND

mind-blower or **mind-bender** *esp 1960s counterculture & narcotics* **1** *n* A hallucinogenic drug **2** *n* Something exciting, beautiful, shocking, etc: *That little book's a mind-bender*

mind-blowing or **mind-bending** *esp 1960s counterculture & narcotics* **1** *adj* Hallucinogenic; psychedelic **2** *adj* Overwhelming; exciting; staggering: *The speech was mind-blowing*

minded *See* DIRTY-MINDED

◀**mind-fuck▶ 1** *v* To manipulate someone to think and act as one wishes; =BRAINWASH: *He was totally mind-fucked...but he seemed to know his stuff*—John Sayles **2** *n: such supposedly Caucasian specialties as stance and persona and pop mind-fuck*—Village Voice

◀**mind-fucker▶ 1** *n* A person who manipulates others, esp for his or her own profit: *Most gurus are magnificent and filthy-rich mind-fuckers* **2** *n* A distressful situation; =BAD SCENE

mind one's **ps and qs** *v phr fr middle 1800s fr printers* To take care of one's affairs carefully and exclusively: *What the hell are you staring at, madam, you mind your p's and q's*—H Donohue [fr the fact that the two similar letters are particularly hard to distinguish in type, where their ordinary shapes are reversed]

mind the store *v phr* To attend to routine business; carry on: *Who'll mind the store while Mr Reagan is overseas?* [fr the joke about the dying man who, finding by patient inquiry that all his children are at his deathbed, inquires testily as to who is *minding the store*]

mine *See* RUN-OF-THE-MILL

mingy (MIN jee) *adj fr early 1900s* Parsimonious; mean; tight-fisted [perhaps a blend of *mean* and *stingy*]

mini *fr 1960s* **1** *n* A very short dress, skirt, or coat ending well above the knee **2** *adj: She looked out of place in her mini dress* **3** *n* The fashion or style of wearing such short garments [probably fr *miniature*, see *mini-*, although Eric Partridge derived it fr *minimum* because it insures "the minimum of decency"]

mini- *prefix used to form nouns fr 1960s & esp fr British* Small; miniature; short: *minibus/ mininuke/ minisemester/ miniskirt* [apparently greatly stimulated by the production in 1958 of a small British car called the *Mini-Minor*]

◁**minister's face** (or **head**)▷ *n phr hoboes* A pig's head served at a meal

mink **1** *n* A sexually promiscuous person; lecher; nymphomaniac: *The...doctor was a regular mink* —WR Burnett **2** *n* A pert and attractive young woman; =DISH, FOX ◁**3**▷ *n* A woman's genitalia, pubic hair, etc; =BEAVER
See FUCK LIKE A MINK, TIGHT

Minnie *n* Minneapolis

minus *See* DOUBLE-MINUS

Mirandize *See* GIVE someone HIS RIGHTS

mishegoss (MISH ə gahs) *n* (also **mishigas** or **meshegoss** or **meshugas**) Craziness; absurdities: *a mishegoss of mixed-up crap*—Philip Roth/ *and free-lance mishigas*—Village Voice/ *Mailer's old meshugas about cancer*—Changes [fr Yiddish fr Hebrew]

mish-mash (MISH mahsh) *n* (also **mish-mosh**) *fr 1500s but chiefly fr late 1800s* A confused mixture; an indiscriminate miscellany: *regarded as a hopeless mishmash*—Brooks Atkinson [apparently originally fr German *Mischmash*, but probably in its modern use chiefly fr Yiddish]

mishugah or **mishoogeh** *See* MESHUGA

a miss *See* GIVE someone or something A MISS

missile *See* DUMB BOMB

missionary position *n phr* The sexual posture in which the male lies over the female between her spread legs: *Most of them have never gone beyond three furtive minutes in the missionary position*—Village Voice/ *enjoying sex in that reliable missionary position*—Ruth Westheimer [fr the fancied distinction between this coital configuration of Christian *missionaries* and those of the peoples among whom they labored]

missionary worker *n phr labor union* An employee hired to break a strike by nonviolent means

mission stiff *n phr hoboes* A hobo or vagrant staying at a mission run by a religious charity

Mississippi marbles *n phr* Dice

Miss Right *See* MISTER RIGHT

miss the boat *v phr* To lose an opportunity; fail; =BLOW IT: *He ignored good advice, and missed the boat*

the missus (or **the missis**) *n phr* One's wife; =the LITTLE WOMAN: *He wanted the missus to get some sleep*—E Lavine

mister *n* Man; fellow; =GUY ● Always used in direct address, usu to a stranger: *Hey, mister, where's the turn-off for Bogota?*

the mister *n phr* One's husband: *How's the mister?*

Mister Big *n phr* The chief or most important person; =BIG ENCHILADA: *I predict in three or four years he'll be Mister Big*

Mister Charlie *n phr black* A white man; =the MAN

Mister Clean *n phr* A man, esp a politician, unsullied by suspicion of corruption or bad character: *a female version of a managerial Mr Clean*—Toronto Life

Mister Ducrot or **Mister Dumbguard** (Dōō kraht) *n phr West Point* The normal insulting way of addressing first-year cadets [*Ducrot* fr French *du crotte* "(some) shit"]

Mister Fixit *n phr* A person who can and does repair, adjudicate, resolve, etc, difficulties: *has earned a reputation as an ingenious Mr Fixit* —Newsweek

Mister Hawkins *n phr black & hoboes* The cold winter wind; =the HAWK

Mister Nice Guy *n phr* A decent, fair, trustworthy, amiable, etc, man ● Often in a negative expression: *It worries me when a shark like him is suddenly Mister Nice Guy/ If I get the nomination, it'll be no more Mr Nice Guy*—Toronto Life

Mister (or **Miss** or **Ms**) **Right** *n phr* The person one would and should happily marry; one's dream mate

Mister Tom *n phr black* A black man who wishes to be or has been assimilated into the white middle-class culture; =UNCLE TOM

Mister Whiskers *See* UNCLE WHISKERS

mitt **1** *n fr late 1800s* The hand: *snatched right out of his mitt*—Charles MacArthur **2** *n prizefight* A boxing glove: *have the big mitts on*—WR Burnett **3** *v prizefight* To clasp hands above one's head as a sign of victory and acknowledgment of applause: *sitting in his corner and mitting the crowd* —WR Burnett **4** *v* To shake hands: *Mitt me, pal, I done it* **5** *v underworld* To make an arrest, esp to put handcuffs on a prisoner at an arrest **6** *n circus & carnival* =MITT-READER [fr *mitten*]
See TIP one's MITT

the mitt **1** *n phr hoboes* Any charitable source of food, lodging, etc **2** *n phr underworld* An arrest

mitt-camp or **mitt-joint** *n carnival* A fortune-teller's tent

mittens *See* IDIOT MITTENS

mitt-glommer or **mitt-glaummer** or **mitt-glahmer** *n* A handshaker; =GLAD-HANDER

mitt-reader *n circus & carnival fr early 1900s* A palmist; fortune-teller: *every confounded swamiwoman and mitt-reader in the nation*—Joseph Mitchell

mitts **1** *n underworld* A pair of handcuffs **2** *n fr late 1800s* The hands

Mitty *See* WALTER MITTY

mix **1** *n* A mixture: *most important element in an auto maker's marketing mix*—New York **2** *v* To fight; =MIX IT UP: *Them last two babies mixed...many times a month*—H Witwer

mixed up *adj phr fr late 1800s* Confused; chaotic; =MESSY: *His mind's all mixed up*

mixer **1** *n* Soda water, tonic, or any soft drink or juice to which liquor is added **2** *n fr late 1800s* A person who easily becomes acquainted and sociable with others; a gregarious person **3** *n fr 1920s* A party or other gathering intended as an occasion for people to meet and become acquainted with one another
See CEMENT MIXER

mix it up or **mix it** **1** *v phr fr early 1900s* To fight, esp with great flailing and abandon: *The principals refused to mix it up*—F Scott Fitzgerald/ *didn't seem to want to mix it*—WR Burnett **2** *v phr* To socialize; associate with: *Richards, the traditional marketing man, mixing it up with the culture gang*—Toronto Life

mixologist *n fr middle 1800s* A bartender

mix-up **1** *n fr late 1800s* Confusion; chaos; =MESS: *There's an awful mix-up over at the plant today* **2** *n fr early 1900s* A fight, esp a free-for-all

MJ *n narcotics* Marijuana

mo **1** *n* A moment: *Give me half a mo* **2** *n* =MOTHERFUCKER **3** *n* A homosexual

mob **1** *n* An underworld grouping; organized-crime family: *a narcotics mob/ the Genovese mob* **2** *modifier: mob infiltration/ a mob boss* **3** *n* Any group, gathering, class, etc; =BUNCH: *as a member of the ruling mob*—Westbrook Pegler

the **mob** *n* Organized crime; the Mafia; the syndicate: *I heard it's controlled by the mob*

mobbed up *adj phr* Controlled by or implicated with organized crime: *real hard evidence...that Schiavone or Donovan are mobbed up*—Newsweek

mobile *See* NERDMOBILE, PIMPMOBILE

mob scene *n phr* A very crowded place or occasion; =FANNYBUMPER: *The reception was a mob scene*

mobster *n* A member of a criminal grouping; a Mafioso; =GANGSTER: *nickname he got from the mobsters*—John O'Hara

moby *adj computer* Very large, complicated, and impressive [probably fr the white whale in Herman Melville's *Moby Dick*]

◄**mockie**► **1** *n* A Jew: *crashed their fists into a mockie*—James T Farrell **2** *adj: a mockie shop/ I have a mockie accent?*—Saul Bellow [origin unknown; perhaps fr *macher*; perhaps fr underworld slang "fake, phoney"; probably fr *mock*]

mock-up *n* A model; a simulation: *They made a mock-up of the building to study the traffic flow*

mocus *adj* Confused; incoherent ● An Alcoholics Anonymous term [probably fr *mokus*]

mod *adj esp 1960s* Modern; up-to-date, esp in the styles of the 1960s: *shows off her attributes in a mod wardrobe*—Bosley Crowther

mod cons *n phr chiefly British* The amenities and furnishings of a house or apartment: *The place has a good view and all mod cons* [fr *modern conveniences*]

Model-T *adj* Cheap; shabby; crude: *a real Model-T speakeasy*—Stephen Longstreet [fr the *Model T* Ford car of the early 1900s]

modoc (MOH dahk) **1** *n carnival* A dummy set up to be knocked down with a thrown baseball **2** *n carnival* A stupid person; =BOOB, KLUTZ **3** *n aviators fr 1930s* A person who becomes or pretends to be an aircraft pilot for the glamor and status of the occupation [origin unknown]

mohasky *narcotics* **1** *n* Marijuana **2** *adj* Intoxicated with marijuana; =STONED [fr *mohoska*]

mohoska *n merchant marine* Energy; strength; =MOXIE, PIZZAZZ [origin unknown]

mojo[1] *n black* A charm or amulet worn against evil; hence, power, luck, effectiveness, etc: *When you got the mojo, brother, when you're on the inside, the world is fantastic*—Robert Stone/ *gets his mojo going for conventions and elections*—Washington Post/ *The office bears a sort of superstitious, bad-mojo stamp*—Penthouse [probably fr an African language]

mojo[2] *n narcotics* Any narcotic, esp morphine [perhaps fr Spanish *mojar* "celebrate by drinking"]

moke ◄**1**► *n fr middle 1800s* A black person ◄**2**► *n fr 1930s Navy* A Filipino **3** *n* An easygoing person, esp one who solicits favors and gifts; =MOOCHER [origin unknown; perhaps fr Romany *moxio* or *moak* "donkey," with intermediate sense of "ass, fool"; perhaps related to British dialect *moke* "murk, darkness"; perhaps fr *mocha* "coffee-colored"; see *jamoke*]

the **mokers** *n phr* Sadness; =the BLUES

mokus *hoboes* **1** *n* Liquor **2** *adj* Drunk **3** *n* Loneliness [last sense perhaps related to *mokers* "despondency," of obscure origin]

moldy fig *bop talk & cool talk* **1** *n phr* A prude; pedant **2** *n phr* A person who prefers traditional jazz to the more modern styles: *Barry Ulanov and Rudi Blesh hit upon the idea of having a battle of styles, Moldy Figs vs Moderns*—Mark Gardner **3** *adj: my moldy-fig tastes*

moll *fr 1700s British* **1** *n* A woman **2** *n* A prostitute **3** *n* A criminal's woman companion, accomplice, girlfriend, etc; =GUN MOLL [fr *Molly*, nickname of Mary]

moll-buzzer **1** *n underworld fr 1920s* A thief who preys on women, esp a purse-snatcher **2** *n hoboes fr 1920s* A hobo or tramp who begs from women

molly-hogan *n lumberjacks* Anything puzzling or complicated

Molotov cocktail *n phr fr WW2* A grenade made by pouring gasoline into a bottle, adding a cloth wick and igniting [fr Vyacheslav *Molotov*, Soviet premier, because the weapon was much used by Soviet partisan guerilas]

mom-and-pop or **ma-and-pa** or **mama-and-papa** *adj* Run by a couple or a family; small-scale: *still seem wedded to the "mom and pop store," small-business approach*—Albert P Blaustein/ *All kinds of neighborhoods have them, mom-and-pop stores, laundromats*—San Francisco/ *The constitution says nothing about a mom and pop presidency*—Ms

moment *See* BIG MOMENT

momism (MAHM izm) *n* Maternal domination; matriarchalism; mother worship

momma 1 *n black* = MAMA **2** *n fr black* Any specified object, esp a large, admirable, or effective one; = MOTHER, MOTHERFUCKER: *It's time to put this momma in the oven*—Cher (TV program)

mommick up (MAHM ək) *v phr* To confuse and botch; = BOLLIX UP, FUCK UP: *She's wanting to do it all by herself, then she mommicks things up*—Gail Godwin [fr British dialect, "cut awkwardly, maul," fr the disheveled and sloppy appearance of a *mommick* "scarecrow," fr *mammet* or *maumet* "doll, puppet, grotesquely dressed figure," fr earlier "idol, figure of a pagan deity," fr *Mohamet*, the name of the Muslim prophet]

mo-mo *n* A moron

momzer or **momser** (MUHM zər, MAHM-) **1** *n* A person who expects many loans and favors; = MOOCHER, SPONGER **2** *n* A contemptible person; = BASTARD, SHITHEEL: *A very cool customer, this momzer*—Ira Levin [fr Yiddish fr Hebrew, "bastard"]

mon (MUHN) *n* Money

Monday man *n phr hoboes* A person who steals clothes from clotheslines [fr the fact that *Monday* was customarily the day for doing the laundry]

Monday morning quarterback *n phr* A person who is good at predicting things that have already happened and at pointing out the errors of quarterbacks and other leaders; = ARMCHAIR GENERAL [fr the fact that *Monday* is the first weekday or business day after the weekend, when school and college football games are played]

money *See* BLACK MONEY, CHICKEN FEED, COIN MONEY, FALL MONEY, FOLDING MONEY, FRONT MONEY, FUNNY MONEY, GREEN MONEY, HAPPY-MONEY, HARD CURRENCY, HEAVY MONEY, IN THE MONEY, a LICENSE TO PRINT MONEY, MAD MONEY, MAKE MONEY HAND OVER FIST, ON THE MONEY, PROTECTION, PUT one's MONEY WHERE one's MOUTH IS, RIGHT MONEY, the SMART MONEY, SOFT MONEY, THROW MONEY AT something, TIGHT MONEY, WHITE MONEY

moneybags 1 *n* A rich person: *some aged moneybags*—J Evans **2** *n WW2 Navy* A military paymaster

money from home *n phr* Something very welcome and useful, esp when gratis and unexpected: *but for the TV news boys...this was money from home*—Washington Post

money talks *sentence* Wealth is power: *In New York, boy, money really talks, I'm not kidding*—JD Salinger

money tree *See* SHAKE THE MONEY TREE

mongo *n* Something valuable found in the garbage, esp by a trash collector [origin unknown]

monicker *n* (Variations: **moniker** or **monniker** or **monacer** or **monica** or **monaker**) *fr middle 1800s British hoboes* A person's name, nickname, alias, etc; = HANDLE: *His "monica" was Skysail Jack*—Jack London/ *Ricord picked up a new moniker among US narcotics agents*—Time [origin unknown and very broadly speculated upon; perhaps fr transference fr earlier sense, "guinea, sovereign," when used by hoboes as an identifying mark; perhaps related to the fact that early-19th-century British

tramps referred to themselves as "in the monkery," that monks and nuns take a new name when they take their vows, and *monaco* means "monk" in Italian; perhaps, as many believe, an alteration of *monogram*]

monk 1 *n* A monkey ◀**2**▶ *n* A Chinese or Chinese-American: *known to their Occidental neighbors, the Irish especially, as monks*—RL McCardell

monkey 1 *n* A man; fellow; = GUY: *a smart monkey*—Raymond Chandler **2** *n hoboes* A person who is not a hobo, carnival worker, etc; ordinary person **3** *n carnival* A victim; = MARK **4** *n narcotics* Narcotics addiction; a drug habit: *went from monkey to nothin' in twenty-eight days*—Nelson Algren **5** *n narcotics* A kilogram of a narcotic: *and you call and you want 100 monkeys*—Washington Post **6** *v fr late 1800s* To tinker or tamper; intrude one's action: *Look, it's running fine, don't monkey with it* **7** *v* = MONKEY AROUND

See GET THE MONKEY OFF, GREASE MONKEY, HAVE A MONKEY ON one's BACK, POWDER MONKEY, ROAD MONKEY

monkey around 1 *v phr* To idle about; loaf; = GOOF AROUND: *I'm just monkeying around, nothing special* **2** *v phr* To tinker or tamper; attempt to use or repair: *Please stop monkeying around with that machine*

monkey (or **funny**) **business 1** *n phr* Frivolous pranks; japes and jests; etc: *He was full of monkey business, the clown* **2** *n phr* Dubious and dishonest stratagems; trickiness: *Show these kids that you're going to stand for no monkey business*—Time

monkey cage *n phr prison* A prison cell

monkey-chaser ◀**1**▶ *n black fr 1920s* A West Indian **2** *n* A mixed drink based on gin: *Monkey chasers are gin and ice, with a little sugar and a trace of water*—New Yorker

monkey drill *n phr armed forces fr late 1800s* Calisthenics; physical training exercises [fr the fact that the exercisers follow the movements of the instructor, as "*monkey see*, monkey do"]

monkey-house or **monkey-wagon** *n railroad* A caboose

monkey jacket 1 *n phr fr early 1800s nautical* Any tight, short jacket, esp one that is part of a uniform **2** *n phr hospital* A hospital patient's gown [fr the fact that *monkey* was a nautical term for anything small, in this case a short, informal jacket as distinct from a formal frock coat; *monkey jackets* are also the traditional garb of an organ-grinder's *monkey*]

monkey-monk *See* HIGH MUCKETY-MUCK

monkey pie *n phr lunch counter* Coconut pie

monkeyshines *n fr early 1800s* Tricks; japes and capers; pranks

monkey suit *n phr* A fancy uniform or formal suit; tight uniform: *Neither of my two hats went well with the monkey suit*—J Evans

monkey's uncle *See* I'LL BE DAMNED

Monkey Ward *n phr* The Montgomery Ward retail company

monkey with the buzz-saw *v phr* To intrude upon something perilous; court disaster: *You can go see the president about it, but you'd be monkeying with the buzz-saw*

monniker *See* MONICKER

mono (MAH noh) *n students* Mononucleosis

monokini *n* A one-piece bathing suit that leaves the breasts bare [fr *bikini*, interpreting *bi-* as "two" referring to the number of pieces]

monster 1 *n narcotics* A narcotic that acts on the central nervous system **2** *modifier: users of scag and monster drugs*—American Scholar **3** *n* A best seller, esp a recording **4** *adj* Enormous; overwhelming; = HUMONGOUS: *his monster ego/ a monster rally*
See ONE-EYED MONSTER

Montezuma's revenge *n phr* Diarrhea, esp traveler's diarrhea: *It was regarded as unfortunate that President Reagan joked about Montezuma's revenge when he introduced the president of Mexico*

moo 1 *n lunch counter* Beefsteak: *slab of moo* —Max Eastman **2** *n* Milk **3** *n* = MOOLA

moocah *n outdated narcotics* Marijuana [origin unknown; perhaps an alteration of *mooter, moota*]

mooch 1 *v fr middle 1500s British* To beg; borrow; = CADGE, SPONGE: *He went around mooching cigarettes* **2** *n* = MOOCHER **3** *v* To steal **4** *v fr middle 1500s British* To stroll; loaf along **5** *n carnival* A gullible customer; dupe; = MARK **6** *n carnival* A person who listens to the pitch, but does not buy **7** *n salespersons* A customer who painstakingly examines the merchandise before buying

moocher *n* A beggar; borrower; = DEADBEAT, SPONGER: *He heard a moocher deliver the following spiel*—Billy Rose

moogie *See* SOOGIE

moo-juice *n lunch counter & Army* Milk or cream

moola or **moolah** *n fr early 1900s* Money: *So put a little moola in your portfolio and get yourself a cash cow*—Time/ *He who rips off jazz makes mucho moolah*—Albert Goldman [origin unknown]

moon 1 *n* Cheap whiskey, esp whiskey made by unlicensed distillers; = MOONSHINE: *a couple of pints of moon*—JB Martin/ *using it to transport moon* —George V Higgins **2** *v esp teenagers & students* To exhibit one's bare buttocks as a defiant or amusing gesture, usu at a window

mooner *n police* A criminal or eccentric active during the period of the full moon
See FULL-MOONER

moonlight *v* To work at a job in addition to one's regular job: *a million guys moonlighting, holding a little back*—World
See LET MOONLIGHT INTO

moonshine 1 *n fr late 1800s* Whiskey made by unlicensed distillers; corn whiskey; = MOUNTAIN DEW: *the moonshine distilled in the mountains*—Ernie Pyle **2** *n* Any cheap, inferior whiskey; = ROTGUT **3** *n* Any liquor or whiskey **4** *n* Exaggerated talk; vain chatter; = BALONEY, BULLSHIT: *His story's plain moonshine*

Moony or **Moonie** *n* A member or disciple of the Unification Church [fr the name of the leader, Sun Myung *Moon*]

moose *n Korean War armed forces* A prostitute [fr Japanese *musume* "girl"]

moose-eye *n* A look of reproach or supplication

moose-milk *n* Whiskey

moosh *See* MUSH²

mooter *n* (also **moota** or **mootie** or **mutah** or **mu**) *fr 1920s* A marijuana cigarette; = JOINT [fr Mexican Spanish *mota* "marijuana," of uncertain origin; since the word also means "bundle of herbs" and "sheaf of hay," it may be semantically akin to *grass, hay, bale of hay*, and *herb*, all of which are disguising names for marijuana or marijuana cigarettes]

mop¹ *n hoboes* The Missouri Pacific Railroad

mop² *n black* The last item or act; the final result: *And the mop was he got caught* [probably from the notion of *mopping* or cleaning up, influenced by earlier jazz use "the last beat at the end of a jazz number"]

mope 1 *v hoboes & prison* To escape; = LAM **2** *v* To move along; walk **3** *n fr 1600s* A stupid person; fool; = BOOB: *They...weren't a bunch of mopes*—James T Farrell
See COP A HEEL

mopery 1 *n* Criminal loitering, esp with the aim of committing a sex crime: *If he'd lived long enough they'd have had him up for mopery*—Raymond Chandler **2** *n* Stupid behavior: *I'm tired of his mopery*

mop mop *adj phr outdated jazz musicians* Repetitious, loud, uninspired jazz: *"mop mop" jazz is the mechanical stuff*—Stephen Longstreet

mop-squeezer *n gambling* A queen of playing cards [fr a demeaning reference to the queen with the 18th-century term meaning "housemaid, slavey"]

mop (or **mop up**) **the floor with** someone *v phr* To defeat thoroughly; trounce; = CLOBBER

morph 1 *n narcotics* Morphine **2** *n* = MORPHADITE

morphadite *n* (also **mophrodite** or **morphrodite**) *fr 1700s* A hermaphrodite: *You morphadite*—Richard Bissell [fr a probably naive rather than humorous mispronunciation of *hermaphrodite*]

mortal lock *n phr gambling* A certainty; = CINCH, SURE THING: *Brown is what bettors would call a mortal lock to win*—Time

mortar *See* BRICKS AND MORTAR

Moses *See* HOLY CATS

mosey or **mosey along** (MOH zee) *v* or *v phr fr early 1800s* To move along, esp to walk slowly; saunter; = EASE ON: *I think I'll mosey over and see what's going on*/ *A mild river that moseyed at will*— WH Auden [perhaps fr Spanish *vamos*; see *vamoose*; perhaps fr British dialect *mose about* "walk in a stupid manner"]

mosquito *See* KNEE-HIGH TO A GRASSHOPPER

moss *n fr black fr 1940s* Hair; among black people, straightened or processed hair: *Moss is hair*—Jim Bouton
See HOUSE MOSS, RIGHTEOUS MOSS

mossback *n fr middle 1800s* A very conservative person; =FOGY: *The real mossbacks will vote for the governor* [said to have been a description of a group of poor white Carolina swamp-dwellers who had lived among the cypresses until the *moss* grew on their *backs*]

the **most** *n phr beat & cool talk* The best; =the GREATEST: *New Jetliner The Most, Reds Say*—New York Daily News

the **mostest** *n phr* =the MOST [fr Southern dialect and black normal superlative of *much*]
See FIRSTEST WITH THE MOSTEST, the HOSTESS WITH THE MOSTEST

most rickety-tick *adv phr Army* Immediately; without delay: *Please respond most rickety-tick*

mothball *See* IN MOTHBALLS

mother **1** *n homosexuals* An effeminate or homosexual male **2** *n homosexuals* The leader, usu the elder and mentor, of younger homosexuals **3** *n fr black* A despicable person; =MOTHERFUCKER: *I looked into the wallet of one of the mothers*—New York **4** *modifier: Every mother other one of 'em cried Foul*—H Norris **5** *n fr black* Any specified object, esp something large, admired, desirable, etc; =FUCKER, MOMMA, MOTHERFUCKER, SUCKER: *Grab these mothers. They'll really do the job*—Joseph N Sorrentino
See BACHELOR MOTHER, JOHN WAYNE'S SISTER

◄**motherfucker**► (Variations: **eater** or **grabber** or **jumper** or **kisser** or **lover** or **nudger** or **rammer** or some other two-syllable agent word may replace **fucker**; **mammy** or **mama** or **momma** may replace **mother**; other alliterating or rhyming terms like **motorscooter** may replace the whole form) *fr black* **1** *n* A detestable person; =BASTARD, SHITHEEL: *"You motherfucker!" she screamed, "You bastard!"*—Rolling Stone/ *blew this motherfucker's brain out*—Bobby Seale **2** *modifier: a mammyrammer blowhard fart that has no respect*—Bernard Malamud **3** *n* An admirable or prodigious person: *We will joyfully say, "Man, he's a motherfucker"*—Bobby Seale/ *You old benevolent motherjumper, I love you*—Richard Fariña **4** *n* Any specified object, esp something impressive, admirable, etc; =MOMMA, MOTHER, SUCKER: *We had a mother-jumper of a winter. Snow up the yin-yang*—George V Higgins

◄**motherfucking**► *adj* (Variations: see **motherfucker** for base forms from which **-ing** forms may be made) *fr black* Detestable; disgusting; nasty; accursed; =GOD-DAMN ● Often used for rhythmic and euphonious emphasis: *went down there with his motherfucking gun, knocked down the motherfucking door*—Bobby Seale/ *what he describes as "three hard mothergrabbin' years"*—Time

motherhood *See* APPLE-PIE-AND-MOTHERHOOD

Mother Hubbard *n phr railroad* A locomotive with the cab over the middle of the boiler; =CAMEL-BACK [fr the resemblance of such a locomotive to a woman wearing a *Mother Hubbard* hat, an old-fashioned bonnet that entirely covered the head, neck, and sides of the face, with a projecting stiffened border around the front]

mothering *adj fr black* Disgusting; accursed; =MOTHERFUCKING: *till you put them motherin' dogs on me*—R Lorning

mother-in-law apartment *n phr* A cottage or apartment where, typically, a widowed mother-in-law or other parent may live near but not actually with their children's family; =GRANNY FLAT

Mother Machree (or **McCrea**) *n phr* An alibi, esp a sad story inviting sympathy and leniency; =SOB STORY [fr the name of a sentimental Irish song]

mother-nudger *See* MOTHERFUCKER

mother's day or **Mother's Day** *n phr* The day when welfare checks come: *We had picked this day because it was Mother's Day*—R Moore

motor-mouth **1** *n* A very talkative person; a compulsive jabberer; =FLAPJAW, WINDBAG: *What else can you do with this motor-mouth but grin and bear it?*—Village Voice/ *He keeps on talking. A motor-mouth, this guy*—WT Tyler **2** *adj: I didn't know he was motor-mouth*—George V Higgins

mountain (or **Rocky Mountain**) **canary** *n phr* A donkey; burro

mountain dew *n phr* Raw and inferior whiskey, esp homemade bootleg whiskey; =MOONSHINE

mountain (or **prairie**) **oysters** *n phr* Sheep or hog testicles used as food

Mount Saint Elsewhere *n phr hospital* A place, not so prestigious, to which a patient, esp a hopelessly ill one, might be transferred

mounty *See* COUNTY MOUNTY

mouse **1** *n fr middle 1800s British* A bruise near the eye, caused by a blow; =BLACK EYE, SHINER: *One of the Kid's eyes has a little mouse under it*—H Witwer **2** *n* A young woman: *a little mouse I got to know up in Michigan*—John O'Hara/ *I'm pouring Dom Pérignon and black eggs into this little mouse*—Woody Allen **3** *n* One's wife, girlfriend, fiancée, etc **4** *n computer* A movable indicating device, usually handheld, controlling the cursor on a computer terminal screen: *The program employs a "mouse," a pointing device about the size of a pack of cigarettes*—Time/ *a mouse, a handheld device that when slid across a table top, moves the cursor on Mac's screen*—Philadelphia Inquirer

mousetrap **1** *n* A small, inferior theater or night club: *He walked out on the stage of a mousetrap called the Blue Angel*—John Crosby **2** *v sports* To trick someone into a trap, esp by various blocking moves

mouth *See* BADMOUTH, BIGMOUTH, BLOW OFF one's MOUTH, COTTON MOUTH, DIARRHEA OF THE MOUTH, FOOT-IN-MOUTH DISEASE, FOULMOUTH, FOULMOUTHED, FROM THE HORSE'S MOUTH, LOUDMOUTH, MOTOR-MOUTH, MUSHMOUTH, POOR-MOUTH, RATCHET-MOUTH, RUN OFF AT THE MOUTH, SATCHELMOUTH, SHAD-MOUTH, SHOOT OFF one's MOUTH, SMARTMOUTH, TALK POOR MOUTH, WATCH one's MOUTH, ZIP one's LIP

mouth-breather *n* A stupid person; moron: *Some mouth-breather in the office told me it would be OK* [fr the noisy *breathing* of an adenoidal idiot]

mouth-breathing *adj* Stupid; moronic: *If the dumb mouth-breathing bastards in the street only understood*—Patrick Mann

a **mouthful** *n phr* Something hard to pronounce or speak; =JAWBREAKER: *Diphosphopyridine nucleotide is a mouthful*
See someone SAID A MOUTHFUL

a **mouth full of South** *n phr* A Southern accent: *a man with a mouth full of South*—Washington Post

mouth off **1** *v phr* To talk; make comments; chat **2** *v phr* =SHOOT OFF one's MOUTH

mouth on someone *v phr* To inform on; =SQUEAL: *He got busted, and he mouthed on everybody he knew*—Claude Brown

mouthpiece **1** *n underworld fr early 1900s fr middle 1800s British* A lawyer; =LIP: *inability to hire a professional bondsman and "good front," "mouth-piece" or lawyer*—E Lavine **2** *n* A spokesperson: *Each tong has an official "mouth-piece"*—E Lavine

mouth-to-mouth resuscitation *n phr* =FRENCH KISS, SOUL KISS

move **1** *v* To steal; pilfer **2** *v* To sell merchandise; dispose of a stock: *We better move these monster Teddy Bears quick* **3** *v* To be desirable to customers; sell quickly: *Those pet rocks are not moving any more*
See MAKE one's MOVE, PUT A MOVE ON someone

move someone **back** *v phr* To cost someone; =SET someone BACK: *That ring'll move you back about 64 big ones*

move dirt *v phr railroad* To shovel coal

move into high gear **See** SHIFT INTO HIGH GEAR

moves **See** HAVE ALL THE MOVES

move up *v phr* To buy a more expensive or more cherished thing: *The smoker is exhorted to "move up" to a particular brand of cigarettes, the motorist to a new car*—Russell Baker

movie **See** BLUE MOVIE, B MOVIE, GRIND-HOUSE, SNUFF FILM, SPLAT MOVIE

moviedom *n* The motion picture industry; Hollywood

mower **See** ARMSTRONG MOWER, LAWNMOWER

moxie **1** *n fr early 1900s* Courage; =GUTS: *You're young and tough and got the moxie and can hit*—Dashiell Hammett **2** *n* Energy; assertive force; =PIZZAZZ: *We knew you had the old moxie, the old get out and get*—Max Shulman **3** *n* Skill; competence; shrewdness: *showed plenty of moxie as he scattered seven hits the rest of the way*—Associated Press [fr the advertising slogan "What this country needs is plenty of *Moxie*," used for a brand of soft drink; the name may be based on a New England Indian term found in several Maine place names]

mox nix *interj* An exclamation of dismissal, indifference, reduction, etc: *The vase? Mox nix, it was busted anyway* [fr German *macht's nichts* "it's nothing"]

Ms Right **See** MISTER RIGHT

MTA *n prison* A medical technician, orderly, etc, who might have access to drugs [fr *medical-technical assistant*]

mu **See** MOOTER

muck **1** *n* A viscous, slimy substance: *My boots were all covered with muck* **2** *n* An important person; =HIGH MUCKETY-MUCK ● Always used with **big, high,** etc: *the way some of these big mucks do*—Ellery Queen

muck about *v phr* To idle about; loaf; =GOOF AROUND ● Chiefly British

muck-a-muck **See** HIGH MUCKETY-MUCK

muck around *v phr* To tinker or tamper; interfere in; =FUCK AROUND: *I found myself mucking around my life as well as Jean's*—Philadelphia Journal [a euphemism for *fuck around*]

mucker *n fr late 1800s* A crude and unreliable man; lout: *cheap muckers with fine bodies*—P Marks [fr German, "sanctimonious bigot"]

mucket *n* =THINGAMAJIG

muckety-muck **See** HIGH MUCKETY-MUCK

muck stick *n phr hoboes* A shovel

muck up *v phr* To damage; ruin; =FUCK UP: *And let's not muck up our public spaces before we find the answers*—Philadelphia Journal [a euphemism for *fuck up*, probably influenced by mid-19th-century *mucks* "disarrange, discompose, make a muddle" fr British dialect *muxen* "make filthy"]

mucky-muck **See** HIGH MUCKETY-MUCK

mucky-muckdom *n* High circle of power: *the stratosphere of Washington mucky-muckdom*—Washington Post

mud **1** *n narcotics* Opium before it is readied for smoking **2** *n fr hoboes* Coffee **3** *n* Mortar or cement **4** *n* A mixture used to ease the heat and wear on oil-well drills **5** *n carnival* Cheap figurines, souvenirs, etc, given as prizes **6** *n* Defamatory assertions and accusations: *Watch out, they'll throw a lot of mud at you*
See someone's NAME IS MUD, SLING MUD, STICK IN THE MUD

mud-chicken *n railroad* A surveyor

mudder *n horse-racing fr early 1900s* A racehorse that runs very well on a muddy track

mud-hook *n fr early 1800s* An anchor

mud hop *n phr railroad* A yard clerk or checker who lists arriving and departing trains, box-car numbers, etc

mud (or **here's mud**) **in your eye** *interj* A toast; a health: *He raised his glass and said "Mud in your eye"*

mud opera (or **show**) *n phr circus* An old-fashioned circus that traveled in wagons

mud-slinging *n* The use of defamation, insinuation, etc, esp in politics; =SMEAR

muff **1** *v fr middle 1800s British* To fail; botch, esp by clumsiness: *If you muff this chance you won't get another* **2** *n:* *dropped the ball, "the $75,000 muff," as it was called*—Arthur Daley **3** *n* A wig; a toupee: *wasn't wearing his muff*—Raymond Chandler ◁**4**▷ *n* The vulva and pubic hair; =BEAVER [first sense fr the clumsiness of someone wearing a muff on the hands]

◁**muff-dive**▷ *v* To do cunnilingus ● Sometimes used as a plain insult: *You muff-diving, mother-fucking son of a bitch*—Philip Roth

◁**muff-diver**▷ *n* A person who does cunnilingus; = CLIT-LICKER

◁**muffins**▷ *n* A woman's breasts

mug or **mugg** **1** *n* *fr early 1700s British* The face: *She's got a handsome mug/ showing so unperturbed a face...so impudent a "mug"*—Henry James **2** *n* *prizefight* The mouth, chin, or jaw **3** *v* To photograph a person's face, esp for police records: *When crooks are photographed they are "mugged"*—H McLellan **4** *n* A photograph of the face; = MUG SHOT: *a police mug, front and profile*—Raymond Chandler **5** *v* *fr middle 1800s British* To make exaggerated faces, grimaces, etc, for humorous effect: *while Danny mugs through his program*—Time **6** *n* A man; fellow, esp a tough, rude sort or a pugilist or hoodlum: *Those mugs on the corner seem menacing* **7** *v* To assault and injure someone in the course of a robbery: *The victims were mugged in the hallways of their homes*—New York Times **8** *v* To rob someone, snatch someone's purse, etc: *I've been mugged three times, but never beaten up* [probably fr drinking mugs made to resemble grotesque human faces; the sense of violent assault comes fr mid-19th-century British specialization of the term "rob by violent strangulation," probably fr *mug-hunter* "a thief who seeks out victims who are mugs" (easy marks); the cited sense of *mug* occurs in *mug's game*]
See FLY COP

mugger **1** *n* *fr late 1800s* An actor or comedian who makes exaggerated faces, grimaces, etc, for humorous effect: *where this trivial mugger is performing*—Gene Fowler **2** *n* *fr middle 1800s* A thief who uses extreme physical violence: *apparently the victim of muggers*—New York Times/ *A knife or an armlock around the throat has been the favorite technique of muggers*—New York Post **3** *n* A portrait photographer

muggle *n* *narcotics fr early 1900s* A marijuana cigarette: *desk clerk's a muggle-smoker*—Raymond Chandler

muggles *narcotics fr early 1900s* **1** *n* Marijuana, esp dried and unshredded leaves: *Some kid was shoving muggles*—Ed McBain **2** *n* A marijuana cigarette [origin unknown]

mug joint *n phr* *circus & carnival* A tent or booth where one's photograph is taken and printed

mug's game *n phr* *fr early 1900s* A futile effort; a sure failure ● Chiefly British: *All this case-making and courtroom argument and laying out of certain facts is a mug's game, a no-win proposition*—Newsweek/ *Reliving past glory is...a mug's game*—Dick Cavett [fr British sense of *mug* "dupe, fool, sucker"]

mug shot *n phr* A photograph of a person's face, esp the front and side views made for police records; = ART: *passed around a mug shot of Willie*—J Randolph/ *She had identified a "mug shot" from the books as the man who attacked her*—New Yorker

mug up *v phr* *WW2 Navy* To have a cup of coffee

◁**muh-fuh**▷ *n esp black* A despicable person; = MOTHERFUCKER: *Them muh-fuhs are superbad*—D James

mui *n* *Gypsy* A talisman or charm

mujee *See* SOOGIE

mule **1** *n* A stubborn person: *He's a hardheaded mule* **2** *n* Crude raw whiskey; = MOONSHINE, WHITE MULE **3** *n* *outdated railroad* A train's brake operator **4** *n* *narcotics* A person who carries, delivers, or smuggles narcotics or other contraband: *The danger to the mule is that a packet may rupture*—Time/ *"Mules"...carry coke in picture frames and sealed in the sides of suitcases*—New York Times/ *American currency was spirited out of the country then, often by "mules"*—Philadelphia **5** *adj*: *otherwise law-abiding countrymen into performing muling favors*—Newsweek **6** *n* *narcotics* A condom stuffed with narcotics, carried in the vagina or rectum [narcotics senses perhaps originally suggested by the characteristic use of *mules* or donkeys in Mexico and other Latin-American countries]
See CORN JUICE, WHITE MULE

mule-skinner *n* *fr middle 1800s Western* A mule-driver; muleteer

mulligan **1** *n* *hoboes fr early 1900s* A stew, esp one made of any available meat and vegetables **2** *n* *underworld* An Irish person **3** *n* A police officer [perhaps fr the proper name *Mulligan*]

the **mulligrubs** *n* *fr 1600s* = the BLUES [origin unknown]

mullion *n* *baseball fr black* An unattractive person [origin unknown]

mum *n* A chrysanthemum

munchies **1** *n* *narcotics* Snacks, esp for the hunger that follows using marijuana **2** *n* Desire for these snacks
See HAVE THE MUNCHIES

Munchkin *See* LOW-LEVEL MUNCHKIN

munch out (or **up**) *v phr* To eat, esp to consume hungrily: *while Nancy's sipping tea and munching out on scones*—New York Post/ *You'll get together with your friends, right, and you'll be munching up or something*—San Francisco/ *She knew she shouldn't be munching out on carbos like this*—Cyra McFadden

mung **1** *n* *esp teenagers* Anything nasty; filth; = GLOP, MUCK: *Jones noticed the mung on Lydon's never-brushed teeth*—Rolling Stone/ *Fold the table down, and generations of crud and mung appear*—Scottsdale Daily Progress **2** *v* *computer* To make changes, often undesirable ones, in a file **3** *v* *computer* To destroy: *The system munged my whole day's work* [perhaps fr Latin *mungere* "blow the nose, produce nasal mucus"; perhaps fr British dialect "kneaded food for fowls"]

mung up *v phr* *esp teenagers* To make filthy: *I munged up my shoes walking across the field*

murder **1** *n* *fr jive talk* = the MOST, the GREATEST **2** *n* A very difficult or severe person or thing ● Sometimes pronounced with equal stress on each syllable: *The last two hours were murder/ Man, he's murder*—Max Shulman **3** *v* To defeat decisively;

trounce; =CLOBBER: *They murdered them all season*—G Talbot **4** *v* To make someone helpless with laughter; =FRACTURE, KILL: *This one'll murder you*

See BLOODY MURDER, GET AWAY WITH MURDER

Murder One *n phr* The criminal offense of murder in the first degree: *when he did get to trial, and they were going to go for Murder One*—Easyriders

murphy 1 *n fr early 1800s British* A potato **2** *n underworld* A confidence game in which the victim is left with a sealed envelope supposed to contain something valuable, but in fact filled with blank paper **3** *v: Mayor Smitherman was "murpheyed" by the Negro confidence man*—New York Times

muscle 1 *n* A strong-arm man; =GORILLA: *some gowed-up muscle*—J Evans **2** *n* Power; influence; =CLOUT: *DiBona will have a lot of muscle when it comes to Penn's Landing*—Philadelphia

See FLEX one's MUSCLES, LOVE-MUSCLE, ON THE MUSCLE

musclehead 1 *n* A stupid person; =KLUTZ **2** *n* A strong-arm man; =MUSCLE: *I saw three or four muscleheads gleefully beat up on a kid*—Village Voice

muscle in *v phr underworld* To force one's way in, esp into someone's criminal operation: *attempt to muscle in on some graft out of his own domain*—E Lavine/ *afraid you're muscling in on his scam*—WT Tyler

muscle out *v phr* To force out: *If she persists...she'll be muscled out of the movement*—F Sparks

museum piece *n phr* Something old or old-fashioned: *His hat's a museum piece*

mush[1] 1 *n* Empty and exaggerated talk; =BALONEY: *Don't hand me that mush, pal* **2** *n* Sentimentality; saccharinity; =CORN, SCHMALTZ: *They were all weeping over the Dickensian mush* [perhaps an alteration of *mash* "something soft and pulpy"]

See SALON MUSH, SKINNED MUSH

mush[2] or **moosh** (often M͞o͞oSH) *n fr middle 1800s* The face, esp the mouth and jaws: *He pulled his mush away from the plate and sighed*—Jerome Weidman/ *She poked him in the moosh* [origin unknown]

mush[3] 1 *n hawkers fr middle 1800s British* An umbrella **2** *v hoboes* To get money fraudulently by pretending to be engaged in a legitimate pursuit [fr *mushroom*, the shape of an umbrella, the umbrella also conceived as a concealing cover; see *mush-faker*]

mush-faker or **musher 1** *n hoboes* A faker or grafter operating in the guise of an honest worker **2** *n prison* A prisoner who produces useful items from available materials and sells them to other inmates [related to mid-19th-century British "mender of umbrellas," under which guise the criminal may have typically operated; see *mush[3]*]

mush-head *n* A stupid person

mush-headed or **mushy-headed** *adj* Stupid: *some really mushy-headed, or at least questionable, rationalizations*—Washington Post

mushmouth *n* A person who talks indistinctly and slurringly: *Say it again so I can hear it, mushmouth*

mushy 1 *adj* Sentimental; =CORNY **2** *adj* Amorous: *The kid got mushy with the broad*—Dashiell Hammett

music *See* BUBBLE-GUM MUSIC, CHIN MUSIC, ELEVATOR MUSIC, FACE THE MUSIC, FISH MUSIC, RAP SONG, SOUL

musical beds *n phr* Sexual promiscuity; =SLEEPING AROUND: *The soaps were conspicuous for their preoccupation with musical beds*—Entertainment Tonight (TV program) [modeled on the game of *musical chairs*, in which players circle a set of chairs and sit in any one available when the music stops]

muso (MYo͞o zoh) *n* A musician: *a superb band...no musos to be fooled with*—Village Voice

muss or **muss up** *v* or *v phr* To disarrange; dishevel: *He mussed his hair all up/ Who mussed the bed?*

mussy *adj* Disarranged; rumpled: *rumpled now, and mussy*—James M Cain

musta *n narcotics* Marijuana [perhaps an alteration of *moota*; see *mooter*]

mustang *n armed forces fr late 1800s* A commissioned officer who has been promoted from the enlisted ranks: *A mustang who had worked his way up from the ranks in 13 years*—Time [fr *mustang* "wild, sturdy horse of the Western US," fr Mexican Spanish *mestengo* "stray animal"]

mustard *See* NOT CUT THE MUSTARD

mutah *See* MOOTER

mutt *fr early 1900s* **1** *n* A dog, esp a hybrid; cur **2** *n* A stupid person; =KLUTZ, MUTTONHEAD: *A mutt? Yeah, he's that all right. Not too much brains*—Lawrence Sanders

muttonhead or **mutton-top** *n fr late 1700s* A stupid person

muttonheaded *adj* Stupid

muzak or **Muzak** *n* Sweet and bland background music; uninteresting taped music; =ELEVATOR MUSIC: *the theatre of media-buzz where ideas normally melt down into verbal muzak*—Toronto Life/ *a nice guy with all the charisma of Muzak in a minor key*—Time [fr the trade name of a company that provides prerecorded music to be heard in offices, elevators, etc]

muzzle-loader *n railroad* A locomotive fired by hand

muzzler 1 *n* A petty criminal **2** *n* A police officer [probably fr *muzzle* "get, take," attested from the mid-19th century]

◁**my ass**▷ *interj* An exclamation of strong denial, disbelief, defiance, etc; =IN A PIG'S ASS: *You're getting this job my ass/ My ass I'll pay you that much* [a dysphemism for *my eye*]

my boy *See* THAT'S MY BOY

my eye *interj fr late 1700s* =MY ASS, IN A PIG'S ASS [in the early and obsolete meaning "nonsense," perhaps fr a Joe Miller joke in which a Latin nonsense phrase *O mihi, beate Martine* ("O, to me, blessed Martin'') is pronounced as *all my eye and Betty Martin*]

mystery *n restaurant fr late 1800s* Hash

mystery meat *n phr students* Meat not readily identifiable, esp as served in a student dining hall, fraternity house, etc ● Sausages were called **mysteries** in the middle 1800s

N

nab **1** *v* *fr late 1600s British* To catch; seize; arrest; = COLLAR: *The officers nabbed him around the corner* **2** *n* (also **nabs**) *street gang* A police officer or detective ● The sense is recorded in British criminal slang of the early 1800s [fr dialect *nap* as in *kidnap*, perhaps related to Swedish *nappa* "catch" or Danish *nappe* "pull"; probably related to *nip*]

nabe **1** *n* A neighborhood: *The nabe is a honey, architecturally*—Village Voice **2** *n* A neighborhood movie theater: *The current films...eventually make their way to the nabes*—AD Copleman

nag *n* *fr 1400s* A horse, esp an old and worn-out racehorse: *to make dough on the nags*—New York Daily News

nail **1** *v* *fr middle 1700s* To catch; seize; = NAB: *the feared and famous Batman and Robin who'd nailed him*—New York **2** *v* To detect and expose: *She nailed them with her last question* **3** *n* *narcotics* A hypodermic needle ◁**4**▷ *v* To do the sex act to someone; = FUCK: *the publishing cupcake in the Florsheims who nailed you on the couch and then fired you*—Richard Grossbach

See EAT NAILS, HARD AS NAILS, HIT THE NAIL ON THE HEAD, SO MAD one COULD SPIT NAILS

nail something **down** **1** *v phr* To make something securely final; = CINCH: *They nailed down the arrangement and had a drink* **2** *v phr* To know thoroughly: *At least I've got Columbus Circle nailed down*—New York

nail it *v phr* To accelerate to the utmost; = FLOOR IT

nail someone or something **to the cross** (or **the wall**) *v phr* To punish severely and publicly; make an example of; crucify: *We are going to nail them to the cross*—Time/ *We would not nail an airline to the wall if it made its best effort*—New York Times

naked *See* BUCK NAKED

naked as a jaybird *adj phr* Entirely unclothed; = BARE-ASS

Nam or **'Nam** *n* *Vietnam War armed forces* Vietnam: *not like the gooks back in 'Nam who always got their goddam hands out*—M Sayle/ *I was in Nam and Nam made me like that*—New York

name **1** *n* A very important person, esp in entertainment; = HEADLINER: *I saw three or four names there/ He's a name in the carpet business* **2** *modifier* Being well-known or prestigious: *a name band/ name brand*

See BIG NAME, FRONT NAME, WHAT'S-HIS-NAME, YOU NAME IT

name-calling *n* The assigning of malicious designations in politics, debate, etc; character assassination; vilification: *They soon sank to simple name-calling*

someone's **name is mud** *sentence fr early 1800s British* One is in trouble; one is doomed: *If they catch him his name is mud* [fr earlier British dialect *mud* "fool"]

the **name of the game** **1** *n phr* What matters most; the essence: *In business, the name of the game is the bottom line*—Philadelphia/ *Good gun dogs are the name of the game*—Sports Afield **2** *n phr* The inevitable; the way things are: *Lying in politics? Hell, that's just the name of the game*

names *See* KICK ASS AND TAKE NAMES

nana *n* An affectionate name for a or one's grandmother

nance or **nancy** or **Nancy** *fr late 1800s* **1** *n* A male homosexual who takes the passive role **2** *n* An effeminate man; = LILY: *Where you need desperately a man of iron, you often get a nance*—Philip Wylie **3** *modifier: with his talk of nancy poets, his anti-intellectualism*—Esquire

nanny *See* GET someone's GOAT

-naper or **-napper** *See* DOGNAPER, PETNAPER

nappy *adj black* Kinky-haired

naps *n black* The hair, esp kinky hair: *His naps aren't together*—Ebony

narc or **narco** **1** *n narcotics* A narcotics agent or police officer; = GAZER: *another drug-scare hoax promulgated by the "narcs"*—New York Times/ *the ritual of dodging the "narcos"*—John Ciardi **2** *modifier: down to the narco police on the beat*—Esquire

nark **1** *n* *fr middle 1800s British* A police informer; = STOOL PIGEON **2** *v* (also **narc**): *He will nark on him if the first guy doesn't keep playing games*—Lawrence Sanders/ *felt the Fraynes and their youngsters had narced on them*—New York Times **3** *n* = KIBITZER, BUTTINSKY **4** *n gambling* A decoy; = SHILL: *information about known gamblers, little bookmakers, and their narks*—Fortune [fr Romany *nak* "nose"]

narrowcast *v* To plan a TV program for a special audience rather than the mass: *This "narrowcasting" approach may win NBC an unusual distinction*—Time

nash *See* NOSH

nasty 1 *n* Something unpleasant, repulsive, etc: *pathos, poverty, and other real-life nasties*—Village Voice **2** *adj black* Good; stylish; admirable

natch *fr jive talk* **1** *adv* Naturally; certainly: *will be in riding clothes (habits of the rich, natch)*—John Chapman/ *The two men, natch, are soul buddies*—Judith Crist **2** *affirmation* Of course; right: *Do I like it? Natch, what else?*

native *See* GO NATIVE

the **natives are restless** *sentence* One can expect some opposition; discontent appears to be afoot: *I told him the natives are restless, and he wondered if another speech would help* [fr a trite line in many old jungle movies]

natural 1 *n crapshooting* A first throw of the dice that yields seven or eleven **2** *n* Something or someone that is obviously and perfectly fitting; just the thing: *A novel which looks like a natural for Lassie*—New York Times **3** *n prison* A jail sentence of seven years **4** *n black fr 1960s* = AFRO

natural-born *adj black fr 1930s* Total; absolute; innate: *The man's a natural-born spazz/ a natural-born artist*

nature's call *n phr* The need to use the toilet, esp when urgent: *He's only responding to nature's call*

navigate *v fr middle 1800s* To walk, esp when drunk

Navy *n hoboes* A cigar or cigarette butt picked up from the street
See HOOLIGAN NAVY

navy chest *n phr Navy* A protuberant belly; = MIL-WAUKEE GOITER

neat 1 *adj esp teenagers fr 1920s* Excellent; wonderful **2** *adj* Without water or another mixer; = STRAIGHT UP ● Used to describe spirits: *I'll take my Scotch neat, please*

neb *n* An inconsiderable person; = NEBBISH, WIMP: *poor little nebs like Julian*—Budd Schulberg

nebbie *See* NIMBY

nebbish *n* A person without charm, interesting qualities, talent, etc; = WIMP: *"Nebbish"...is simply the one in the crowd that you always forget to introduce*—Budd Schulberg/ *Don't be a nebbish*—WT Tyler [fr Yiddish fr Czech *neboky*]

nebbishy *adj* Having the character of a nebbish: *plays a nebbishy student who...acquires telekinetic powers*—People Weekly

the **necessary** *See* the NEEDFUL

neck *v fr early 1900s* To kiss, embrace, and caress; dally amorously; = MAKE OUT, SMOOCH: *At least you'd want to neck me*—Philip Wylie/ *You "spooned," then you "petted," after that you "necked"*—E Eldridge
See CATCH IT IN THE NECK, DEAD FROM THE NECK UP, DIRTY-NECK, GET OFF someone's BACK, GIVE someone A PAIN, LEATHERNECK, NO-NECK, a PAIN IN THE ASS, REDNECK, ROUGHNECK, RUBBERNECK, STICK one's NECK OUT

necked *See* RED-NECKED

necker's knob *n phr teenagers* A knob attached to a car's steering wheel to permit easy turning with one hand

necking *n* The pleasures and procedures of those who engage in kissing, embracing, and caressing: *pupils...resort to necking*—HL Mencken/ *It was the closest we ever got to necking*—JD Salinger
See HEAVY PETTING

necktie *n* The noose used in a hanging: *They'll put a necktie on you*—WR Burnett

necktie party (or **social** or **sociable**) *n phr fr late 1800s* A hanging or lynching

the **needful** (or **necessary**) *n phr fr middle 1700s* Money

needle 1 *v fr late 1800s British* To nag at someone; criticize regularly and smartingly; = HASSLE: *He keeps needling the guy about his looks* **2** *n:* a really nasty needle **3** *v esp 1920s* To age or strengthen an alcoholic beverage artificially, esp by using an electric current passed through a needle-like rod **4** *n* A hypodermic injection; = SHOT

the **needle 1** *n phr* Injurious and provocative remarks; nagging criticism: *He's always ready with the needle* **2** *n phr* Narcotics injections; the narcotics habit: *The needle finally killed him*
See GIVE someone THE NEEDLE, OFF THE NEEDLE, ON THE NEEDLE

needle beer *n phr esp 1920s* Beer reinforced with alcohol or ether

needle candy *n phr narcotics* Any narcotic taken by injection: *Holmes has need of greater stimulants than needle candy*—WF Miksch

needle park *n phr* A public place where addicts regularly gather to deal in drugs and to take injections; = SHOOTING GALLERY

needles *See* RAIN CATS AND DOGS

need someone or something **like a hole in the head** *v phr* To have emphatically no need whatsoever for someone or something: *I needed more work like a hole in the head/ I needed Jane at that time like I needed a hole in the head* [fr Yiddish *loch in kop* "hole in head"]

Nellie or **Nelly 1** *adj homosexuals fr 1940s* Homosexual; effeminate; = GAY, SWISH: *Well, his backstroke is a little Nellie*—Armistead Maupin/ *What in the past...would have been described as a Nelly queen*—New York Times **2** *adj* Overfastidious; finicky; school-marmish: *"As follow" is Nellie usage and probably incorrect*—Red Smith
See NERVOUS NELLIE, NICE NELLIE

nemmie or **nemish** *See* NIMBY

neo-con *adj* Neo-conservative: *the neo-con idol, George Orwell*—Village Voice

nerd or **nurd** *n teenagers fr hot rodders & surfers* A tedious, contemptible person; = DORK, DWEEB, JERK [perhaps fr earlier *nert* fr *nerts* fr *nuts*]

nerdmobile *n teenagers* A large ostentatious car

nerdpack *n teenagers* A plastic shield worn to keep ink off shirt pockets

nerdy *adj teenagers* Characteristic of a nerd: *Above all, stay away from anything nerdy*—Philadelphia

nerf *v hot rodders* To bump a car out of one's way

nerts or **nertz** *See* NUTS

nerty *See* NUTTY

nerve 1 *n fr middle 1800s British students* Audacity; = CHUTZPAH **2** *n* Courage; = GUTS

See GET ON someone's NERVES, HAVE A NERVE

nervous *beat & cool talk* **1** *adj* =FAR OUT **2** *adj* =JAZZY

◁**nervous as a dog shitting razorblades**▷ (or **as a cat on a hot tin roof**) *adj phr* Very nervous; =JUMPY

nervous Nellie *n phr fr late 1930s* A timid or cautious person; a worrier: *a nervous Nellie a bit like Jeanne Dixon*—Village Voice [perhaps fr *Nervous Nellie*, the nickname of Frank B Kellogg, secretary of state 1925–29, who negotiated the Kellogg-Briand differences]

nervous pudding *n phr* Molded gelatin

nervy 1 *adj* Brave; =GUTSY **2** *adj* Brash; audacious

nest *See* FEATHER one's NEST, LOVE NEST

nest egg *n phr* Saved money, esp for use in retirement or a particular enterprise

nester *See* EMPTY NESTER

network *v* To solicit opinion and aid from associates with common interests: *I'm networking this question, but nobody had a certain answer*—CoEvolution Quarterly
See OLD BOY NETWORK

networking *n* The formation of an association of mutual interest: *Building friends and contacts is what everybody is referring to as networking these days*—New York Daily News/ *And More Jewish Networking*—Nat Hentoff

never follow a dog act *sentence fr show business* Be very careful about whom you are to be immediately compared with ● Often a rueful comment after one has been outshone

never mind *See* MAKE NO NEVER MIND

never-was *n* A person who never succeeded or captured notice; =LOSER [based on *has-been*]

new *See* WHAT ELSE IS NEW

new ball game *See* a WHOLE NEW BALL GAME

new boy *n phr* A novice; beginner: *Not a bad start for a new boy*—Time [fr the British term for a beginning school student]

Newfie *n* A Newfoundlander

new jice *n phr outdated prison* A newcomer to prison

new kid on the block *n phr* Any newcomer or recent arrival: *The Japanese are the new kid on the block in the personal computer field*

the **new look** *n phr* A new fashion; new practice, fad, etc: *Here's the new look in computer software, folks* [fr a fashion sensation of 1947, notable chiefly for the long skirts of Christian Dior dresses]

news *See* BAD NEWS, BREAK THE NEWS, NOSE FOR NEWS

newsie or **newsey** *n* A newspaper seller: *Beno, a hophead newsie*—Dashiell Hammett

newy or **newey** or **newie** *n* Something new; a novelty

New York kiss-off *See* KISS-OFF

next *See* GET NEXT TO oneself, GET NEXT TO someone

next off *adv phr* Next; at that point: *Next off, Hutch give a yell*—James M Cain

next week *See* KNOCK someone INTO THE MIDDLE OF NEXT WEEK

NG or **ng** (pronounced as separate letters) *adj* No good: *She is NG*—A Lomax/ *This gadget's ng, so give me another one*

nibs *See* HIS NIBS, TOUGH SHIT

nice *See* MAKE NICE

nice cop tough cop *See* GOOD COP BAD COP

Nice Guy *See* MISTER NICE GUY

nice guys finish last *sentence* It is foolish to be fair and decent; look out only for yourself [attributed to the baseball manager Leo Durocher]

nice Nelly 1 *n phr* A prude; =BLUENOSE **2** *adj: I've got to use "heck" because practically all my editors are...being more rabidly nice Nelly than usual*—G Dixon

nice work if you can get it *sentence fr 1930s* That would be a very pleasant thing to do; wouldn't that be fun? ● An admiring comment made when one sees something easy, pleasant, attractive, etc, used esp with sexual overtones

nicey-nice or **nicey-nicey 1** *adj* Affectedly amiable and wholesome: *This little kid here with all her nicey-nice talk*—WR Burnett/ *You flip the book over and you see all nicey, nicey things*—Bobby Seale **2** *adj* Effeminate; overly fastidious

nick 1 *v fr early 1800s British* To rob or steal ● Much more common in British than US use: *The bank is gonna be nicked*—Dashiell Hammett **2** *v* To exact something, esp by force or threat: *I think you can nick her for one fifty if you get tough*—James M Cain **3** *v* To withhold pay; =DOCK

nickel 1 *n underworld* A five-year prison sentence **2** *n narcotics* =NICKEL BAG
See BIG NICKEL, DON'T TAKE ANY WOODEN NICKELS, PLUGGED NICKEL, SMALL NICKEL

nickel and dime 1 *v phr* To drain in small increments; nibble away at: *The mack started nickel-and-diming him into the poorhouse*—George Warren/ *He said the grizzly habitat was being nickeled-and-dimed out of existence*—New York Times **2** *v phr* To quibble; niggle; bring up all sorts of trivia: *is being nickeled-and-dimed...nibbled to death by ducks*—Washington Post

nickel bag *n phr narcotics* A five-dollar packet of narcotics

nickel defense *n phr football* A defensive formation in which a fifth defensive back is added, to cover an almost certain pass receiver

nickel-nurser *n* A miser; =PENNY-PINCHER

nickels and dimes *n phr* Very small amounts of money; =PEANUTS: *We can get the improved roads for nickels and dimes*

nickel up *v phr hoboes* To offer a merchant five cents for food or other goods worth more

nifty 1 *adj fr middle 1800s* Smart; stylish; =NEAT, SLICK: *a great many niftier and hotter words*—HL Mencken/ *a nifty way to upstage the president*—Wall Street Journal **2** *n: his six blonde nifties*—Jerome Weidman/ *Another nifty is the circularization of telephone subscribers*—R Littell **3** *adv: You did that real nifty* [origin unknown; called by Bret Harte "Short for *magnificat*"; Eric Partridge thought it might be fr *magnificent*; perhaps fr *snifty* "proud, high-toned"]

◄**nig**► *n fr early 1800s* A black person

◄**nigger**► **1** *n fr early 1800s* A black person **2** *modifier: a nice nigger lady*
See BAD NIGGER

◄**nigger heaven**► *n phr* The topmost gallery or balcony of a theater

◄**nigger rich**► *adj phr* Having much money, esp suddenly; =FLUSH: *I'm either nigger rich or stone poor*—George V Higgins

◄**niggertoe**► *n* A Brazil nut

◄**niggra** or **nigra**► *n* =NIGGER

night See AMATEUR NIGHT, GOOD NIGHT, SATURDAY NIGHTS, SATURDAY NIGHT SPECIAL

nightcap 1 *n* A drink taken just before going to bed or the last drink of the evening, esp an alcoholic drink: *Let's stop at Joe's for a nightcap* **2** *n baseball* The second game of a doubleheader

nightery See NITERY

nightie *n* A nightgown: *Aphrodite in her nightie, Oh my God what a sightie*—Howard Moss

nightingale *n* An informer; =STOOL PIGEON

night-night or **nightie-night** *interj* An amiable parting salutation at night

night people (or **fighters**) *n phr* People who work at night or prefer to be up late at night: *I happen to be "night people" and I'm always up late* —Xaviera Hollander/ *Night people, the professor and his wife used to retire about 2:30 to 3 AM*—F Marja

night person *n phr* One of the night people: *She's a night person, never gets up before the afternoon*

night spot *n phr* A nightclub; cabaret; =BOITE, NITERY

-nik *suffix used to form nouns* A person involved in, described by, or doing what is indicated: *beatnik/ computernik/ peacenik/ no-goodnik* [fr Yiddish fr Russian and other Slavic languages]

nimby *n* (also **nimbie** or **nebbie** or **nemmie** or **nemish**) *narcotics* Nembutal (a trade name) or any barbiturate

nine-days' wonder *n phr fr 1500s* A marvel of rather short duration; =FLASH IN THE PAN [the notion of a wonder lasting nine days appears in Chaucer's *Troilus and Criseyde* of the late 14th century]

nine-hundred-pound gorilla See SIX-HUNDRED-POUND GORILLA

the nines See DRESSED TO THE TEETH

nineteen *n lunch counter* A banana split

the nineteenth hole *n phr golf* A drink or a spell of drinking after finishing a golf game

nine-to-five 1 *adj* Occupying the time period of a regular, salaried, probably dull office job: *a nine-to-five drag of a job* **2** *v* To be regularly employed, esp in an office job: *even when he was nine-to-fiving*—R Woodley

nine-to-fiver 1 *n* A person who is steadily employed **2** *n* A reliable, responsible person **3** *n* A regular job, esp a salaried office job

ninety-day wonder *armed forces fr WW1* **1** *n phr* An Army or Navy officer commissioned after a three-month course at an officer candidate school **2** *n phr* Any very youthful officer **3** *n phr* A reserve officer put on active status after three months of training **4** *n phr* Any person doing a job with minimal training ● Usu used sarcastically: *They sent another ninety-day wonder to run the department* [based on *nine-days' wonder*]

ninety-eight *n lunch counter* The manager of a lunch counter

ninety-five *n lunch counter* A customer who leaves without paying

ninety-nine 1 *n lunch counter* The chief fry cook or chief soda jerk **2** *n salespersons* Out-of-style or damaged goods that a salesperson is paid extra for selling

nine yards See the WHOLE NINE YARDS

◄**Nip**► **1** *n esp WW2* A Japanese or person of Japanese ancestry **2** *adj: a Nip waitress* [fr *Nippon* "Japan"]

nip and tuck *fr early 1800s* **1** *adj phr* Equally likely to win or lose; even; neck and neck: *Near the finish they're nip and tuck* **2** *adj phr* Of equal probability; equally likely: *It's nip and tuck whether I'll get there in time or not* [earlier versions included *rip and tuck*, *nip and chuck* and *nip and tack*, making the original semantics somewhat difficult to assess; the term might be from sailing or from sewing and tailoring]

nipper *n fr middle 1800s British* A small boy; lad: *warning that America's nippers are turning into microchip golem*—Washington Post [perhaps because he *nips* "moves quickly"]

nippers *n fr early 1800s British* Handcuffs: *A newly appointed policeman...has to buy...a pair of nippers* —Outlook

nips *n* The nipples: *Barb's nips are not big and dark* —Dan Jenkins

nit *n* Nothing; =ZILCH: *If you're wondering about their homosexual records, it's nit*—Lawrence Sanders [fr Yiddish or perhaps German dialect]

nitery or **nightery** *n* A nightclub; =BOITE

nit-pick *v* To quibble over trivia; niggle: *Let's not nit-pick, let's get cracking*

nit-picking 1 *n* The act and pleasure of one who quibbles over trivia **2** *adj: a highly nit-picking attitude* [from the very slow and attentive work of a person or a simian picking tiny *nits* "insect eggs" out of hair or fur]

nitro (NĪ troh) **1** *n* Nitroglycerin; =SOUP **2** *n hot rodders* Nitromethane, a fuel additive for cars

the nitty gritty or **the nitty 1** *n phr fr 1960s black* The most basic elements, esp when unwelcome or unpleasant; harsh realities: *from what they call the nitty gritty and the grass roots*—Bobby Seale/ *the awesome and awful nitty gritty of today's urban condition*—Ada Louise Huxtable/ *and shifting from ideology to the nitty*—National Review **2** *adj phr: a lot of nitty-gritty campaigning as well* —Newsweek **3** *n phr* Practical details: *I'll go over the broad outlines of the program and then Leslie will fill you in on the nitty-gritties* [fr the repellent association of *nits* "the eggs of hair lice, young hair lice" and *grit* "abrasive granules"]

nitwit *n fr 1920s* A stupid person; fool; =BOOB [apparently the equivalent of *louse-brain*, fr the sense of *nits* meaning "insect eggs"]

nix *fr late 1700s British* **1** *negation* No: *I asked her for one and she said nix* **2** *n* Nothing: *wasn't taking her out here in the park for nix*—James T Farrell **3** *n* A refusal; veto: *if the Petrillo nix stands*—Variety **4** *v* To veto; reject: *He nixed that notion right off/ had been considering marriage but have apparently nixed the idea*—Washington Post [fr German *nichts* "nothing"]

nixie *n post office fr late 1800s* A piece of mail that cannot be delivered because of damage, illegibility, etc

nix on *v phr fr early 1900s* To forbid ● Used only as an imperative: *Nix on the hurry talk*—H McHugh/ *Nix on swiping anything*—EB White

nix out *v phr* To leave; depart; =SPLIT

no-account or **no-count 1** *adj fr middle 1800s* Worthless; untrustworthy; incorrigible: *I'm a lazy no-account bum* **2** *n:* *A no-count that never did a right thing in his life*

nob *n outdated fr early 1800s British* A rich and important person; =SWELL [perhaps fr *nob* "head," with a reference to its being swelled]

no bargain *n phr* A person or thing that is not especially desirable nor good: *Well, he's OK, but no bargain*

nobbler *n gambling fr middle 1800s British* A person who drugs a racehorse or racing dog or otherwise tries to fix the outcome of a race: *the nobblers who drugged dogs*—P Jones [origin unknown; perhaps fr *hobble* "make lame," by the same interesting variation that gives *Hob* and *Nob* as nicknames for *Robert*]

nobby or **knobby** *adj fr early 1800s British* Stylish; fashionable; smart: *Polo shirts, nobby ties*—James T Farrell/ *In 1903 Larkin picked up a nobby one-cylinder Winton*—New Yorker

no better than she ought to be *adj phr* Sexually promiscuous; loose

no big deal *n phr* Nothing important; no problem: *What she did is no big deal/ Getting a passport's no big deal*

no biggie *n phr teenagers & narcotics* =NO BIG DEAL

a **nobody** *n* A person lacking fame, status, importance, etc; an uninteresting person; =NEBBISH

nobody home *sentence* This person is crazy, stupid, or feeble-minded; =OUT TO LUNCH

◁**nobody loves a wise-ass**▷ *sentence* What you just said is very offensive; you are too smart and acid for your own good: *I thought it was a pretty good pun, but she replied "Nobody loves a wise-ass, Joey"*

no bones *See* MAKE NO BONES ABOUT

no can do *sentence* I am unable or unwilling to do that ● Popularized in the 1940s by a song having the phrase as a title: *On that schedule? No can do* [a phrase in pidgin English probably adopted and disseminated by seamen]

no-clap medal *n phr WW2 Army* The Good Conduct Medal [fr the sardonic notion that not having clap "gonorrhea" is sufficient evidence of good conduct]

no-count *See* NO-ACCOUNT

nod *v narcotics* To be intoxicated with narcotics to a very drowsy or stuporous state: *with slews of rich kids nodding in the Scarsdale woods*—New York

a **nod** *n phr narcotics fr 1930s* A stuporous state following an injection of narcotics: *He goes on a "nod," his head drooping, eyelids heavy*—J Mills/ *Here was Pimp in a nod*—Claude Brown
See COLLAR A NOD

the **nod** *n phr* The affirmative decision; the signal of choosing or preference; =THUMBS UP: *Bold Ruler gets the nod over Gallant Man in today's renewal of the Carter Handicap*—The Morning Telegraph/ *We didn't know who'd end up with the nod*
See GET THE NOD

noddle *See* NOODLE

noddy or **nodding** *adj narcotics* Stupefied by a narcotic; sleepy from the effect of drugs

no dice 1 *negation* No; absolutely not; =NO SOAP, NO WAY: *A Nuevo Laredo judge said no dice*—G Spagnoli/ *Nice, but no dice*—WT Tyler **2** *adj* Worthless; =CRUMMY: *a little no-dice paper called the Rome American*—Westbrook Pegler

no flies on someone *n phr fr late 1800s* Nothing impeding one's energy, awareness, soundness, up-to-dateness, etc: *No flies on Mom, she's getting a space-age hi-tech computer/ Judging by your bankroll I'd say there's no flies on you, baby* [fr the image of an active cow, horse, etc, on which *flies* cannot settle]

no-frills *adj* Restricted to the essentials; without frivolous ornamentation or flourishes: *in keeping with his notion of a no-frills clergy*—Time/ *Imagine a no-frills warehouse crossed with an abattoir*—Toronto Life

noggin *n fr early 1800s British* The head: *the psychiatrist after diagnosing his noggin*—H Allen Smith [fr *noggin* "mug," itself used for "face"; compare *mug*]

no go *n phr fr 1830s British* An unlikely success; a sure failure; an impossibility: *We tried to save him but it was no go*

no-go *adj* Not ready to proceed; inauspicious; blocked ● Probably stimulated recently by astronauts' use: *This looks like a no-go situation*

no-good 1 *n* An unreliable or deplorable person; =BUM, NO-ACCOUNT: *A high-living no-good in a derby hat*—Hal Boyle **2** *adj:* *His father was a no-good drunk*—Life

no got *sentence* I do not have that: *We wanted 4XLBJ Mark 1 widgets, but the clerk said no got*

no great shakes *adj phr fr middle 1800s* Mediocre; not outstanding; rather ineffective; =NOTHING TO WRITE HOME ABOUT: *I'm no great shakes at serve-and-volley* [origin unknown; perhaps fr the *shaking* and rolling of dice]

no-hitter *n baseball* A game in which at least one side gets no base hits

no holds barred 1 *adv phr* Free and uninhibited; with no limits or reservations: *They went at it no holds barred* **2** *adj phr:* *The commission was* to produce a "no-holds-barred" study—Washington Post

noise *n* Empty talk; meaningless verbiage; bluster: *To hell with that noise/ That press release is plain noise*

See BIG NOISE, MAKE NOISES, RED NOISE

the **noise** *n phr* A gun: *Not the noise, bounce him* —New York Sun

noise tool *n phr outdated cowboys* A pistol: *Ammunition to be fired through a "noise tool"*—PA Rollins

no kidding *adv phr* Really; factually ● Often a question asked when one hears something astonishing or doubtful: *No kidding? They won?/ No kidding, he's a nice guy*

no-knock *adj* Providing for or including the police right of entry without a search warrant: *The cops demanded a no-knock statute so they could catch criminals*

nonbook **1** *n* A printed effort lacking literary value and normal publishing validity, usu one blatantly ghost-written and/or put out for reasons of sensation, meretricious chic, or brazen and high-pitched publicity **2** *n* A bound, published volume of blank pages

noncom (NAHN kahm) *n armed forces* A noncommissioned officer

no-neck *n* A stupid, bigoted person; a brute: *the moral and intellectual sleaziness of the media and its no-necks in residence*—Village Voice [fr the thick, neckless aspect of very muscular men, gorillas, etc]

nonevent **1** *n* An apparent event staged or produced for or by the media **2** *n* Something invalid; something that in effect did not happen: *"As a practical matter" the new rules are "a nonevent"*—Newsweek

no never mind See MAKE NO NEVER MIND

a **no-no** *n phr* Something forbidden; something very inadvisable: *The company says mustaches are a no-no*—Charlotte Observer/ *allowing members to enjoy such former no-nos as corn on the cob* —Newsweek

nonstarter *n* A failure; a total incompetent; = ALSO-RAN, LOSER: *The proposed travel book...now seemed...to be a nonstarter*—Humphrey Carpenter/ *Compromises...should be considered "nonstarters"*—New Yorker

noodge See NUDGE

noodle¹ **1** *n fr early 1900s* The head; the mind: *Most of the fellows running television today are sick in the noodle*—Philip Hamburger **2** *v* (also **noodle around**) To think, esp in a free and discursive way; indulge in mental play: *as many drafts and as much noodling as I wanted to*—Avery Corman/ *still noodling around with our...calculators and the latest census data*—Fortune/ *He noodles the lacrimae rerum note*—Time **3** *v musicians* To play idly at an instrument; improvise lazily: *I noodled a bit on it and instantly realized I could express me*—Down Beat/ *He noodled at the keys*—Studs Terkel/ *Members of an avian orchestra are already softly noodling*—WH Auden **4** *v* To play; toy: *noodling nervously with a glass of water*—Aquarian [fr earlier *noddle* "head," probably influenced by *noodle*, the food; senses of "play" perhaps derived fr "head" to "thought" to "idle thought and idle play" influenced by *doodle*]

See OFF one's NUT

noodle² *n fr middle 1700s British* A stupid person; fool; simpleton ● Still predominantly British when not entirely outdated: *Something that noodle at Interior might reflect on*—Washington Post [origin unknown; perhaps fr *noodle* the food, fr German *nudel*, because of its limp and worm-like connotations]

noodlehead *n* A stupid person; = NOODLE

noodlework *n* Mental work or effort; thinking; studying

noogie (Nŏŏ gee, Nŏŏ-) *n* = BARBERSHOP QUARTET, DUTCH RUB

See TOUGH SHIT

◁**nookie** or **nookey** or **nooky**▷ (Nŏŏ K ee) **1** *n fr late 1800s British* Sexual activity; the sex act; = ASS, COOZ: *a young kid tryin' to get his first nookey!*—Budd Schulberg/ *if you can't give her a little nooky*—People Weekly **2** *n fr 1920s* A woman regarded as a sex partner; = ASS, CUNT [origin unknown; perhaps related to 17th-century *nugging* "the sex act," and perhaps to *nudge*]

nope *negation* No [fr *no* plus an intrusive stop resulting from the closure of the lips rather than the glottis as is normal]

no picnic *n phr* A difficult or trying experience; a hard time or task: *While the ground crew didn't exactly have to carry me onto the plane kicking and screaming, it was no picnic*—Playboy/ *It's no picnic, teaching people to play*—Washington Post/ *Growing up in the Depression was no picnic*

noplaceville **1** *adj* Dull and tedious; = DEADSVILLE **2** *n* A small, unimportant town; = JERKWATER TOWN

no potatoes See ALL THAT MEAT AND NO POTATOES

no prize package or **no prize** *n phr* A person or thing of little worth, interest, charm: *He's well qualified on paper, but no prize package*

no problem *interj* An assurance that everything is under control, that no difficulties are at hand in spite of appearances

northpaw *n* A righthanded person, esp a baseball pitcher [based on *southpaw*]

nose *n outdated underworld* A police informer; = STOOL PIGEON

See BLUENOSE, BY A NOSE, DOG'S-NOSE, HARDNOSE, HAVE A BUG UP one's ASS, HAVE one's NOSE OPEN, HOOKNOSE, KEEP one's NOSE CLEAN, LOOK DOWN one's NOSE, NO SKIN OFF MY ASS, ON THE NOSE, PAY THROUGH THE NOSE, POKE one's NOSE INTO something, the POPE'S NOSE, POWDER one's NOSE, PUT someone's NOSE OUT OF JOINT, WET-NOSE

nose around *v phr fr late 1800s* To show strong inquisitiveness; investigate, esp closely and slyly: *I'll nose around and see if I can find out why he did that*

the **nosebag** **1** *n* A meal; eating; = CHOW, the FEEDBAG **2** *n hoboes* Food handed out in a paper bag **3** *n* A dinner pail; lunch box

See PUT ON THE FEEDBAG

nose candy *n phr* narcotics A narcotic, esp cocaine, taken by sniffing: *a deck of nose candy for sale*—J Evans

nosed *See* HARD-NOSED

nose dive **1** *n phr* hoboes Acceptance of religion at a mission revival: *The old hobo did a nose dive after the sermon, maybe just for the feed* **2** *n phr* A sudden and large decrease: *The price of gold took a nose dive* **3** *v:* *Our morale nose-dived yesterday* **4** *n phr* prizefight The falling of a boxer who feigns being knocked out; =DIVE: *That wasn't any knockdown, it was a nose dive*

no see *See* LONG TIME NO SEE

nose for news *n phr* fr late 1800s An ability and eagerness for learning news: *A good reporter has, first of all, a keen nose for news*

nose job (or **bob**) *n phr* Plastic surgery to beautify a nose

nose someone **out** *v phr* To defeat by a small margin; barely won over: *He nosed out the leading candidate in Iowa*

nose out of joint *See* PUT someone's NOSE OUT OF JOINT

nosey *adj* fr late 1800s Inquisitive, esp overly so; prying: *We shall not be nosey*—WH Auden

nosh or **nash** (NAHSH) **1** *v* To have a snack; nibble **2** *n:* *He always liked a little nosh between meals* [fr Yiddish]

noshery *n* A restaurant or delicatessen, esp for snacking

◁**no shit**▷ *adv phr* Really; factually; =NO KIDDING ● Often a question asked when one hears something astonishing or doubtful: *"No-o," said Gold with extravagant amazement, "shit"*—Joseph Heller/ *Uh...now, you mean? No shit*—Armistead Maupin

no-show **1** *n* fr 1930s A person who fails to keep an appointment, use a reserved seat, etc: *The airline figures about 20 percent no-shows* **2** *adj* Designating a nonexistent worker or job, usu on the public payroll: *They promised to eliminate all the no-show state jobs*

◁**no skin off my ass**▷ (or **butt** or **nose**) *adj phr* Of no concern, esp damaging concern, to me; immaterial: *Whether you make it or not, it's no skin off my ass/ and if you fall on your face, no skin off my nose*—WT Tyler

no slouch *adj phr* fr middle 1800s Very able or competent; skilled ● Most often followed by **at something**: *She's no slouch at finding good restaurants/ That guy? He's sure no slouch!* [fr British dialect *slouch* "awkward, lazy person"]

no soap *negation* fr early 1900s No; absolutely not; =NO DICE, NO WAY: *"No soap," said the assistant warden*—New York Times [origin unknown; Eric Partridge thought it was based on rhyming *no hope*]

no spring chicken *n phr* fr late 1800s An older or experienced person, esp a woman: *At forty she's no spring chicken*

no sweat *n phr* fr WW2 armed forces No problem or difficulty; an easy thing: *No sweat, though!*—New

York Times/ *It was no sweat for me*—Claude Brown

not all there **1** *adj phr* Stupid; feeble-minded; =DIM-WITTED **2** *adj phr* Crazy; eccentric; =NUTS, OUT TO LUNCH

not a one-way street *n phr* A situation, arrangement, etc, where reciprocal fairness is desired: *Remember, this negotiation is not a one-way street*

not bad for a country boy *adv phr* Better than might be expected; fairly well: *And they all said I wasn't doing bad for a country boy*

not bat an eye *v phr* To not show surprise or reluctance: *"I'm leaving," she said. He didn't bat an eye.*

not be caught dead *v phr* To be defiantly set against; be extremely reluctantly found or seen: *I wouldn't be caught dead in that dress*

not by a long shot *adv phr* fr middle 1800s Not at all; emphatically not: *It's not my best, not by a long shot*

not carved in stone *adj phr* Not having ultimate and permanent authority; able to be altered: *It's a good policy, but it's not carved in stone* [fr the *carved stone* tablets of the Decalogue]

notch **1** *v* To score; achieve: *a pacy serve that's notched a few aces in its time*—Toronto Life ◁**2**▷ *v* To do the sex act ● Use attributed to volleyball players: *Guys don't fuck, they notch*—Playboy [first sense fr use of the term in cricket, and influenced by the cowboy tradition of filing a *notch* in the handle of one's pistol for each man killed; for second sense see *notchery*]
See TOP-NOTCH

notchery or **notch-house** *n* A brothel [fr earlier *notch* "vulva"]

not count for spit *v phr* To be very insignificant; be trivial: *Aptitude for speaking...amusingly doesn't count for spit*—Fran Lebowitz [*spit* is probably a euphemism for *shit*]

not cricket *adv phr* Improper; dubious; unethical; unfair: *Something not quite cricket happened*—Washington Post [fr inadmissible actions in the game of *cricket*]

not cut the mustard **1** *v phr* fr early 1900s To be unable to achieve or finish something; not succeed: *groups who have special vested interests. And that's not gonna cut the mustard*—Philadelphia **2** *v phr* To be unimportant or unimposing: *While Clifford Irving may be a celebrity throughout the United States, he cuts little mustard here on Ibiza*—G Bocca [fr *cut* "achieve," and *the mustard* in the earlier slang sense of "the genuine thing, best thing," perhaps based on the fact that *mustard* is hot, keen, and sharp, all of which mean "excellent"]

not dry behind the ears *adj phr* (also **wet behind the ears** and **still wet behind the ears**) fr early 1900s armed forces Not mature; inexperienced; callow: *He's not dry behind the ears yet, but he's learning* [perhaps an allusion to the wet condition of newborns]

note *See* BLUE NOTE, CASE NOTE, C-NOTE, DIME-NOTE, FIVE-CASE NOTE, a HELL OF A NOTE, MASH NOTE, SWAP NOTES

not enough Indians *See* TOO MANY CHIEFS AND NOT ENOUGH INDIANS

◁**not get** one's **balls** (or one's **self**) **in an uproar**▷ *v phr* To avoid becoming excited or upset; stay calm; =COOL IT ● Often an attempt to soothe someone: *When he started hollering they told him not to get his balls in an uproar/ Come on! Don't get your feminist balls in an uproar*—Lawrence Sanders

not give a damn *v phr* (Variations: **a dang** or **a darn** or **a dern** or **a durn** or **diddly-damn** or **diddly-shit** or ◀**flying fuck**▶ or ◀**fuck**▶ or **hill of beans** or **hoot** or ◁**rat's ass**▷ or ◁**shit** ▷ or **squat** may replace **a damn**) To be indifferent to or contemptuous of; not care one whit: *I don't give a damn what they do to me/ Nobody gave a flying fuck who their influences were*—Aquarian/ *When do celebrities give a hoot about people who interview them?*—Philadelphia/ *We all busted up because George didn't give a rat's ass*—William Kennedy/ *Me, I don't give a shit, high road, low road, I go either way*—WT Tyler

◀**not give a fuck for nothing**▶ *v phr* To be absolutely indifferent and unafraid

not give spit *v phr* To be indifferent; not care; =NOT GIVE A DAMN: *I wouldn't give spit for his new concept* [a euphemism for *shit*]

not give someone **the time of day** *v phr* Not do the slightest favor for; not greet or speak to; have contempt for: *Like him? I wouldn't give that bastard the time of day*

not have a clue *v phr fr 1940s British armed forces* To be uninformed or ignorant about something: *I don't have a clue about what those people are doing/ "You know who I was?" "Haven't got a clue"*—WT Tyler

◁**not have a hair on** one's **ass**▷ *v phr Army* To lack courage, esp when dared

not have all one's **switches on** *v phr* To be retarded or demented; be mentally subnormal ● Used as a jocular insult rather than a clinical judgment: *Reasonable people come to the movies to watch the movie...the movietalker...doesn't have all his switches on*—Washington Post

not have any *v phr* To refuse to accept; reject; ignore: *Home buyers weren't having any and more than a few developers went belly-up*—Apartment Life

◁**not have a pot** (or **without a pot**) **to piss in**▷ *fr late 1800s v phr* To be very poor and deprived; be penniless: *My family didn't have a pot to piss in, but we were proud as devils/ entering their middle years without a pot to piss in*—Ed McBain

not have a prayer *See* HAVE A PRAYER

not have brain one *v phr* To be very stupid

not have brains enough to come in out of the rain (or **to walk and chew gum at the same time**) *v phr* To be lacking the most elementary intelligence

not have one dollar to rub against another *v phr* To lack money: *When we came from West Virginia we didn't have one dollar to rub against another*

not have the foggiest *v phr chiefly British fr early 1900s* To have not the slightest idea, notion, or knowledge: *When I asked him where the door might be he said he didn't have the foggiest* [fr the expression *not have the foggiest notion*]

'nother *See* A WHOLE 'NOTHER THING

nothing *adj* Inane; lacking charm, talent, interest, etc; worthless: *a nothing guy/ That was a real nothing experience*
See DANCE ON AIR, DO someone NOTHING, KNOW FROM NOTHING

a nothing *n phr* Someone or something that lacks all talent, charm, qualities, etc; =NEBBISH: *This show's a total nothing*

nothing doing 1 *negation* No; absolutely not; =NIX, NO WAY: *Buy that piece of crap? Nothing doing* **2** *n phr* A lack of activity; stasis: *Nothing doing on the job front*

nothing flat *See* IN NOTHING FLAT

nothing to write home about *n phr fr late 1800s* A very ordinary or mediocre person or thing; nothing special; =NO GREAT SHAKES: *His pitch was nothing to write home about*

not just whistling Dixie *v phr* To be saying something important or useful: *When they warned us about this they weren't just whistling Dixie*
See WHISTLING DIXIE

◁**not know** one's **ass from** one's **elbow** (or **from a hole in the ground**)▷ *v phr fr early 1900s* To be very ignorant; be hopelessly ill-informed; be stupid; =KNOW FROM NOTHING: *Opponents claim the president doesn't know his ass from his elbow when it comes to Central America/ Well, he obviously didn't know his ass from a hole in the ground*—Village Voice

not know beans *v phr* (Variations: **diddly** or **diddley** or **diddly-damn** or **diddly-poo** or **diddly-poop** or **diddly-shit** or **diddly-squat** or **diddly-squirt** or **diddly-whoop** or **shit** or **squat** or **zilch** or **zip** may replace **beans**) *fr late 1800s* To be very ignorant; not know even the fundamentals ● In each case the positive and negative idiom have the same meaning: *You don't know beans, do you?* —Russell Baker/ *may have been England's greatest mathematical puzzle inventor, but he knew beans about spiders and flies*—Games [entry form fr earlier *know how many beans make five* fr an old joke where the answer to "How many blue beans make five white beans?" is "Five, if you peel them"]

not know someone **from Ádam** *v phr* To be entirely unacquainted with or uncognizant of: *We're bigger than 90 percent of the companies on the Big Board, but nobody knows us from Adam*—Fortune

not know someone or something **from a hole in the ground** *v phr* To be totally ignorant or unacquainted with: *I was supposed to recognize her, but I didn't know her from a hole in the ground*

not know from nothing *See* KNOW FROM NOTHING

◁**not know shit from Shinola**▷ *v phr* =NOT KNOW one's ASS FROM one's ELBOW [fr *Shinola* (a trade name), a brand of shoe polish; used partly for a suggestion of brown color, mainly for alliteration]

not lay a glove (or **finger** or **hand**) on someone *v phr* To leave unscathed; fail to hurt: *To this point, they haven't laid a glove on him*—Philadelphia Inquirer

not make deals *v phr* To refuse to operate by or tolerate clandestine or unethical arrangements: *I don't make deals, especially not with crooks*

no tomorrow *See* LIKE IT'S GOING OUT OF STYLE

not on your life *negation* No; absolutely not; = NOTHING DOING, NO WAY: *Drink that? Not on your life*

not on your tintype *negation fr late 1800s* Certainly not; emphatically not

not play with a full deck *See* PLAY WITH A FULL DECK

not so hot *adj phr* Not very good; mediocre; poor: *I didn't flunk but my record isn't so hot*—P Marks

not tonight, Josephine *sentence fr late 1800s* We will not copulate tonight, my dear ● Used or said to be used by men refusing sexual favors to women [attributed to Napoleon Bonaparte as addressed to the Empress Josephine]

not touch someone or something **with a ten-foot pole** *v phr* To be loath to have anything to do with; be suspicious or apprehensive; reject: *If I were you I wouldn't touch that proposition with a ten-foot pole* [semantically akin to the proverb advising us to use a long spoon when we eat with the devil]

not to worry *sentence fr 1950s British* There is nothing to worry about ● Still chiefly British: *Not to worry, I bought plenty of food for everybody*

not worth a bucket of warm spit *See* WORTH A BUCKET OF WARM SPIT

not worth a plugged nickel *adj phr fr early 1900s* Valueless: *His word isn't worth a plugged nickel* [a *plugged* coin was counterfeit, or had an insertion of inferior metal]

nougat *n* A stupid person; = BOOB, SAP: *I told her not to be a nougat*—K Brush

Nova *n* Nova Scotia smoked salmon

Nova under snow on a sled *n phr lunch counter* Lox and cream cheese on an English muffin [fr *Nova* Scotia smoked salmon]

now *adj* Up-to-date; very much au courant; thoroughly modern: *tripping out on now words*—Newsweek/ *the Right On, Now Generation*—Gail Sheehy

no way or **no way, Jose** **1** *negation* No; absolutely not; = NO DICE: *When I asked for more he said no way/ No good. No go. No way, Jose*—Village Voice/ *No way, Jose*—Washington Post **2** *adv phr* Never; under no circumstances: *No way will I resign, you'll have to fire me*
See THERE'S NO WAY

no way to run a railroad *See* a HELL OF A WAY TO RUN A RAILROAD

nowhere or **nowheresville** *adj* Inferior; tedious; drab: *If you're not with it, you're nowhere*—L Lipton/ *rows of folding chairs, nowheresville decor*—New York
See the MIDDLE OF NOWHERE

no-win *adj* Impossible to win; hopeless ● Most often used in the phrase **no-win situation**: *Furious Volley in a No-Win Match*—Time/ *Mr. President, he has us in a no-win situation*

nozzle *n fr late 1800s prizefight* The nose; = SCHNOZZ

nudge (NŏŏJ, NŏŏD jə) (also **noodge** or **nudjh** or **nudgy** or **nudzh**) **1** *n* A chronic nagger, kibitzer, or complainer: *He's not a writer, he's a nudge*—New York Times/ *not as an assassin, but as a nudge and a nerd*—Time **2** *v*: *Usually he comes up to nudgy me while I'm writing*—Bernard Malamud/ *and oh nudjh, could he nudjh!*—Philip Roth [fr Yiddish fr Slavic "fret, dully ache"; perhaps influenced by English *nudge*]

nudge elbows *See* RUB ELBOWS

nudging *See* MOTHERFUCKING

nudie **1** *n* A movie, play, etc, in which players appear naked **2** *n* A nude or nearly nude female performer: *some of the worried little nudies*—Westbrook Pegler **3** *n* A magazine, book, etc, featuring pictures of nudes; = SKIN MAGAZINE **4** *modifier*: *I bought a couple of nudie magazines*

nudnik (NŏŏD nihk) *n* An annoying person; pest; nuisance; = NUDGE: *the story of a gang of nudniks trying to defeat the establishment*—Newsweek/ *remains an unreconstructed nudnik throughout*—Wilfred Sheed [fr Yiddish fr Slavic; see *nudge*]

nuke **1** *n* A nuclear device or facility; nuclear weapon; nuclear power plant **2** *v* To destroy with a nuclear weapon or weapons: *The global village has been nuked*—Time **3** *v* To destroy; = CLOBBER: *That English test really nuked me*—Time
See ANTINUKE

numb *adj* Stupid; unresponsive

numb-brained *adj* Stupid; dull-witted: *recruits from the numb-brained hanger-on*—E Lavine

number **1** *n fr 1920s* A person, esp one considered to be clever and resourceful or attractive; = ARTICLE, HOT NUMBER ● Always preceded by an adjective or by the locution "quite a": *some dizzy broad that must have been a snappy number*—Jerome Weidman/ *bored-looking number*—J Evans/ *Dressed up he's quite a number* **2** *n* A piece of merchandise; = ARTICLE: *I found a number I liked pretty well*—James M Cain/ *This number here's going like hotcakes* **3** *n* One's profession, avocation, favorite activity, etc; = GAME: *I don't know what his number can be* **4** *n fr show business* A theatrical act or routine; = SHTICK: *He does that number with the tablecloth* **5** *n* A tactic or trick; = ACT: *When he's pulling one of his numbers, he knows what he's doing*—H Hertzberg **6** *n homosexuals* A casual homosexual partner; = TRICK **7** *n students & narcotics* A marijuana cigarette: *smoked a couple of numbers in the room*—Richard Merkin [merchandise sense fr the model *number* that most retail items have]
See A-NUMBER-1, BACK NUMBER, BIG NUMBER, BY THE NUMBERS, DO A NUMBER ON, DO one's NUMBER, HAVE someone's NUMBER, HOT NUMBER, WRONG NUMBER

a **number** *n phr* Something noted, esp a sexual relationship; = an ITEM: *Hey, we're a number....We* have a non-casual relationship now—Leslie Hollander

number cruncher 1 *n phr* A computer or mechanical calculator **2** *n phr* (also **numbers cruncher**) One who regularly processes or works with figures, statistics, records, etc, esp with a computer: *As a veteran numbers cruncher, I find that good research often raises more questions than it answers*—Playboy/ *promote clerks rather than bring in fancy number-crunchers from outside*—Village Voice **3** *adj* Requiring mathematics, statistics, etc: *number-cruncher course*

number-crunching 1 *n computer* Using, programming, etc, a computer **2** *n teenagers* Mathematics, statistics, computer science, etc, esp in high school courses **3** *n* Calculating; doing arithmetic; figuring: *played chartered accountant for a few sessions of number crunching*—Toronto Life

Number One or **number one 1** *n phr fr early 1800s* One's own self, esp as competitive with others; = NUMERO UNO: *Always look out for Number One, he says* **2** *n phr* The chief, leader; = BOSS, HONCHO: *Who's Number One around here?* **3** *n phr* The most distinguished person in a field or endeavor: *Who's number one in lit crit these days?* **4** *n phr outdated theater* The part of a stage in front of the main drop curtain **5** *n phr* Urination **6** *v:* *The little kid had to number one real bad*

number-one boy 1 *n phr* The chief; = BOSS, HONCHO **2** *n phr* The chief lieutenant or assistant of a leader or ruler: *He's the president's number-one boy*

numbers *n sports* A player's averages, statistics, etc; = STATS: *He had 40 homers and a 325 average, the best numbers on the team*
See BY THE NUMBERS

number two 1 *n phr* Defecation **2** *v:* *He ran off in the woods, having to number two*

numbhead or **numbie** *n* A stupid person

numbheaded *adj* Stupid; = NUMB-BRAINED

◁**numb-nuts**▷ **1** *n* A despicable person; = JERK, LIMP-DICK: *You gotta get a better job, numb-nuts*—George V Higgins **2** *modifier:* *not the numbnuts chatter cornballs like Bob Hope or Yellowman peddle*—Village Voice

Numero Uno or **numero uno 1** *n phr* One's own self, esp as the object of one's best efforts; = NUMBER ONE **2** *n phr* The chief; leader; = BOSS, HONCHO: *a clear understanding between the brothers about who is Numero Uno*—Toronto Life **3** *n phr* The most distinguished person in a field or endeavor: *now an also-ran...but for many years Numero Uno*—Toronto Life [fr Italian or Spanish]
See TAKE CARE OF NUMERO UNO

nurd *See* NERD

nut 1 *n fr middle 1800s British* The head **2** *n fr late 1800s* A crazy or eccentric person; maniac; = FLAKE, SCREWBALL: *It is forbidden to call any character a nut; you have to call him a screwball*—New Yorker/ *He was acting like some kind of nut* **3** *n* A very devoted enthusiast; = BUG, FREAK: *He's a nut about double crostics* **4** *n fr late 1800s carnival & hawkers* The investment needed for a business;

capital and fixed expenses: *producing a daily income that barely met the nut*—AJ Liebling/ *Our nut is high, but our variable expenses are practically nothing*—New York **5** *n underworld* Any illegal payoff to a police officer: *what they called "the nut," payoffs to the police*—M Arnold **6** *n underworld* A share in the graft collected by police officers ◁**7**▷ *n* A testicle; = BALL: *He said it griped his left nut* [insanity sense probably fr late-19th-century *off one's nut*, that is, head; fourth and following senses based on carnival and hawkers use "rent for a stand or concession," perhaps because the rent and graft payments are a "*nut to be cracked*" before the kernel or profits are realized]
See GRIPE one's ASS, OFF one's NUT, TOUGH NUT, a TOUGH NUT TO CRACK

-nut *combining word* A devotee or energetic practitioner of what is indicated; = FREAK: *when one football nut writes a book*—Arthur Daley/ *But he's not just a word nut*—Playboy

nutball (Variations: **bar** or **cake** or **case** may replace **ball**) **1** *n* A crazy or eccentric person; = NUT: *A lot of nutballs accost you at that corner/ The Protestants in Ireland also have their share of nutcakes*—Boston Globe/ *I'm not a nut case*—Xenia Field **2** *adj: murdered by nutball moneybags Harry K Thaw*—Newsweek/ *Use the nutbar examples we've provided here*—National Lampoon/ *not such a nutcake question*—William Goldman

nut-crunching *n* The sapping or destruction of masculinity; figurative castration; = BALL-BUSTING: *Adrienne Barbeau, playing a government investigator whose best defense is nut-crunching*—Village Voice

nut house *n* (Variations: **academy** or **box** or **college** or **factory** or **farm** or **foundry** or **hatch** may replace **house**) A mental hospital; insane asylum: *goes away to the nut house*—Jim Tully/ *exceptional privacy and independence even in a nut hatch*—Earl Thompson

nuts or **nerts** or **nertz 1** *adj fr early 1900s* Crazy; very eccentric; = BUGHOUSE, MESHUGA: *Are you nuts to turn your back on a deal that could mean life or death?*—Philip Roth/ *Heir Rejected 400G, Is He Nuts?*—New York Daily News **2** *interj fr 1920s* An exclamation of disbelief, defiance, contempt, dismay, etc ● **Nerts** is a 1920s euphemization: *General McAuliffe replied "Nuts!" to the Germans at Bastogne* ◁**3**▷ *n* The testicles; = BALLS, FAMILY JEWELS: *They want to get their nuts out of the sand*—Eldridge Cleaver
See BUST one's ASS, the CAT'S MEOW, GET one's NUTS, HOT ROCKS, NUMB-NUTS, TIGHT AS KELSEY'S NUTS

the nuts or **the nerts** or **the nertz** *n phr fr 1920s* The very best; = the GREATEST: *This expanding economy is the nuts/ eulogizing anything...as "the nuts"*—English Journal [probably a shortening of *the cat's nuts*; see the *cat's meow*]

nuts about (or **over** or **on**) *adj phr* (Variations: **nutty** may replace **nuts**) *fr early 1800s British* Very enthusiastic about; devoted to; = CRAZY ABOUT: *I think I'm nuts about you*—S McNeil/ *I'd be simply* *nutty about the quadrangles at Oxford*—Sinclair Lewis [fr British slang *nutty* "piquant, fascinating," fr earlier sense "rich, tasty, desirable, like the kernel of a delicious nut," altered in slang to *nuts* and originally in the phrase *nuts upon*; the US form *nuts about* may be based on all this or on the notion *crazy about*, and probably on both]

nuts and bolts 1 *n phr* The fundamentals; the practical basics: *the nuts and bolts of wildland preservation*—CoEvolution Quarterly/ *men who are dealing with the nuts and bolts of negotiations*—Fortune/ *You've got the experience, the nuts and bolts*—WT Tyler **2** *modifier: Berger's nuts-and-bolts discussion of film-TV music*—Village Voice

nutso or **nutsy** *adj* Crazy; =NUTTY: *the nutso names of the current batch of new bands*—Village Voice/ *drove each other nutsy with crashing self-confidence*—Village Voice

nutter *n* A crazy person; =NUT, NUTBALL: *the Zodiac killer or some nutter on the loose*—Rolling Stone/ *Mick Jagger says there will always be the nutters*—Philadelphia Journal

nuttiness *n* Craziness; insanity; =GOOFINESS: *Booth's capacity for nuttiness became...a legend*—Billy Rose

nutty *adj fr late 1800s* Crazy; very eccentric; =NUTS: *I was just about nutty, I was so lonely*—Sinclair Lewis
See SLUG-NUTTY

nutty as a fruitcake *adj phr* Crazy as can be; extremely eccentric: *The old guy's nutty as a fruitcake*

nut up *v phr college students* To go crazy: *He'll just about nut up when you tell him that*

nympho *n* A nymphomaniac: *no boozing broad, no nympho, no psycho, no bitch*—Pauline Kael

O

-o 1 *suffix used to form adjectives* Having the indicated characteristics: *berserko/ luxo/ neato/ sicko/ wrongo* **2** *suffix used to form nouns: foldo/ freako/ klutzo/ muso* ● This humorous formation is increasingly current [fr a humorous imitation of Spanish or Italian words, more probably Spanish because of the similar *el -o* pattern of coinage]

O *n narcotics* Opium

See BIG O, DOUBLE-O, FIVE-O, FOUR-O, SINGLE-O

oak *See* OK

Oakley *See* ANNIE OAKLEY

oar *See* PUT one's OAR IN, ROW WITH ONE OAR

oat-burner *See* HAY BURNER

oater or **oateater** or **oat opera** *n* or *n phr movie studio* A cowboy movie; Western; =HORSE OPERA: *horse operas, also known as sagebrushers or oaters*—Bob Thomas/ *the deputy marshall in the oateater*—Paul Sann

OBE (pronounced as separate letters) *adj Army* Overcome by events

Obie¹ *n* An award given to a meritorious off-Broadway production [fr *off Broadway*]

Obie² *n narcotics* A narcotic combining four amphetamines: *The brother makes tea and they talk about Obies*—Gail Sheehy [fr *Obetrol* (a trade name), probably a portmanteau form of *obesity control*]

obit (OH bit) **1** *n* An obituary, esp in a newspaper: *getting left out of the pious obits in the The Times*—Albert Goldman **2** *modifier: This is not the obit page*—Harvey Breit

the **oblate spheroid** *n phr* A football

ochre or **ocher** *n fr middle 1800s British* Money [fr the color *ochre* which resembles gold]

OD¹ (pronounced as separate letters) *n Army* Olive drab; olive drab cloth

OD² (pronounced as separate letters) **1** *n narcotics & hospital* An overdose of narcotics: *I guess he'd taken a light OD*—Claude Brown **2** *v: met Jesus one day when I was ODing on speed in my room*—Village Voice **3** *v* To overindulge in or on anything: *Viewers may have OD'd on athletics and turned to reruns*—Time

oday (OH day) *n* Money [fr pig Latin for *dough*]

oddball 1 *n* An eccentric person; a strange one; =WEIRDO: *This little guy, opinionated, emotional, sensitive, was definitely an oddball*—Saul Bellow **2** *adj: sensible drug users and the odd-ball drug*

users—Saturday Review **3** *n* A nonconformist; outsider; odd man out: *We were generally considered to be a family of hopeless oddballs*—San Francisco **4** *adj: He had some pretty oddball ideas*

odds and ends *n phr* A miscellany of leftovers, outsizes, scraps, unmatched bits, etc

odds-on *adj fr gambling* Very promising; very convincing; sure to win: *Who's the odds-on favorite here?/ It's odds on that Thatcher will sweep*

ODs (pronounced OH DEEZ) *n Army* The former olive drab uniform of the US Army, or the trousers of that uniform

of (əV) *v* Have ● Used for humorous or dialect effect: *I must of gone crazy or something*—Joyce Carol Oates

◁**ofaginzy**▷ *n black* A white person; =OFAY: *The white visitor is...known as an "ofaginzy"*—Stephen Longstreet

◁**ofay**▷ **1** *n black* A white person; =FAY, GRAY: *Let the ofays have Wall Street to themselves*—B Brown/ *a white boy, an ofay*—Louis Armstrong **2** *adj: ofay business men and planters*—Louis Armstrong [probably fr pig Latin for *foe*]

off 1 *adj* Not working properly; =OUT OF WHACK: *The carburetor's a little off* **2** *adj* Spoiled; not fresh: *The wine's off at this joint/ The milk's a bit off* **3** *adj* Canceled; not going to happen: *The deal's off* **4** *adj* Not working; not on duty: *The cook is off today* **5** *v esp 1960s fr black* To kill or destroy; =WASTE: *ordered him to mess up a couple of guys, but instead he offed them*—John Godey/ *We'll off any pig who attacks us*—Bobby Seale ◁**6**▷ *v black* To do the sex act with or to; =SCREW: *When I off a nigger bitch, I close my eyes and concentrate real hard*—Eldridge Cleaver **7** *prep* Not using; no longer addicted to: *She's off H now/ I've been off the sauce for four years*

off artist *n phr* A thief

off at the knees *See* CUT oneself OFF AT THE KNEES

off base 1 *adj phr* Not appropriate; uncalled for: *Some of his questions were way off base* **2** *adj phr* Presumptuous; impudent; =OUT OF LINE: *When I asked for her number she said I was off base* **3** *adj phr* Incorrect; inaccurate: *These stats are a mile off base*

off one's **base** *adj phr fr late 1800s* Wrong; mistaken: *Professor McClintock is quite off his base in knocking the use of slang*—Washington Post

offbeat *adj* Unusual; unconventional; strange: *the off-beat death...in an off-Broadway hotel*—New York Daily News/ *its offbeat ad seeking 10 Renaissance-type men*—Wall Street Journal

off someone's **case** *adv phr fr black* Not meddling with someone; not nagging or pressuring someone: *I said I wanted her off my case, quick*
See GET OFF someone's CASE

off color *adj phr* Somewhat salacious; risqué; = BLUE: *a couple of off-color jokes/ Some of his observations were a bit off color*

offer *See* MAKE AN OFFER one CAN'T REFUSE, PUTTER-OFFER

off one's **feed** *adj phr fr early 1800s* Not feeling or looking well; indisposed

office 1 *n aviators* The cockpit of an airplane **2** *v outdated underworld* To signal someone: *Will you let her out when I office you?*—WR Burnett
See BOX OFFICE, FRONT OFFICE

the **office** *n phr outdated underworld* A sign or signal: *When I give you the office I want you to knock Hamilton stiff*—H Witwer

off one's **nut** *adj phr* (Variations: **bird** or **chump** or **head** or **noodle** or **onion** or **rocker** may replace **nut**) *fr middle 1800s* Crazy; deluded; = MESHUGA, NUTS: *I've been as near off my noodle as a...sane man can get*—K Brush/ *I suppose he was off his rocker*—New York Daily News [all variants mean "head," except *bird* and *rocker*; *off one's rocker* may suggest the erratic motion of a chair or cradle with a *rocker* broken or missing]

off one's **plate** *adv phr* No longer a matter of one's responsibility and concern: *Congress would like to get the abortion issue off its plate*—National Public Radio

off-putting *adj* Distressing; unsettling; discomfiting: *nor do I find pubic hair ugly or off-putting*—A Brien/ *an off-putting chip on the shoulder*—Esquire/ *Such adolescent pranks may be offputting*—Newsweek

off the air *adv phr* Out of business: *whether the authorities or the competition has ever forced him to go "off the air"*—Harper's

off the bat *See* RIGHT OFF THE BAT

off the beam *adv phr* Distant from truth or accuracy; in error: *That idea is way off the beam* [fr the radio *beam* that guides aircraft to an airport or runway]

off the charts *adj phr* Too great to be measured; off the scale: *His popularity, high before, is now way off the charts*

off the cob *adj phr 1940s teenagers* Conventional and unexciting; = CORNY: *The music was strictly off the cob*—F Brown

off the cuff 1 *adv phr* Extemporaneously; without rehearsal: *I don't speak well off the cuff* **2** *adj: a good off-the-cuff talker*

off the deep end *See* GO OFF THE DEEP END, JUMP OFF THE DEEP END

off the habit *adj phr narcotics* Cured of drug addiction; = CLEAN

off the hog *See* EAT HIGH ON THE HOG

off the hook *adj phr* Free of responsibility, blame, punishment, etc; = CLEAR: *Shagan gets Harry off the hook*—Pauline Kael/ *In brief, parents are off the hook*—Faubion Bowers
See LET someone OFF THE HOOK, RING OFF THE HOOK

off the needle *adj phr narcotics* No longer injecting or using narcotics; = CLEAN

off the pace *adv phr* Behind the leader or leaders: *The red car is about two laps off the pace*

off-the-rack *adj* Mass-produced or ready-made; not tailored or specially designed: *Buying an off-the-rack reno is expensive and not very adventurous*—Toronto Life

off the record *adv phr* Confidential; not for publication or attribution: *The mayor would only speak off the record, and very cryptically at that*

off the tit *See* LIVE OFF THE FAT OF THE LAND

off the top *adv phr* Before any deductions are made; = UP FRONT: *He demanded his percentage right off the top*

off the top of one's **head** *adv phr* Without thought or calculation; impromptu: *I can't give you the figure off the top of my head, but it's around, say, 500*

off the wagon *adj phr* Drinking liquor, after a period of abstinence: *like the bartenders, the fall off the wagon*—AJ Liebling
See FALL OFF THE WAGON

off the wall 1 *adj phr* Unusual; outrageous; = ODDBALL, OFFBEAT: *his off-the-wall sense of humor*—J Landau/ *the totally off-the-wall absurdity of existence*—Bruce Malamut **2** *adj phr* Crazy; very eccentric; = OFF one's NUT: *Mrs Morea was "very, very distraught, really incoherent, off the wall"*—New York Times/ *They're describing him as "off the wall"*—Arizona Republic [origin uncertain; perhaps fr the erratic angles at which balls bounce *off the wall* in various games, esp squash, handball, and racquetball; perhaps related to the hospital term *bounce off the walls*, referring to the behavior of a psychotic patient; perhaps fr both of these]
See BOUNCE OFF THE WALLS, PING OFF THE WALLS

offtish *See* OOFTISH

off one's **trolley** *adj phr fr early 1900s* Crazy; demented; = NUTS: *You're off your trolley*—Max Shulman [fr the helpless condition of a streetcar of which the *trolley*, a spring-loaded shaft with a wheel at the top to engage the electric wires, has come *off* the wires]

oh-dark-thirty *n Army* An early morning hour

oh fudge *interj* A very genteel exclamation of disappointment, dismay, surprise, etc: *Oh fudge, I dropped the papers*

oh yeah *interj* An exclamation of defiance or disbelief; = IZZATSO: *I told her I'd make her a star, and she said, "Oh yeah?"*

-oid 1 *suffix used to form nouns* Something resembling or imitating what is indicated: *flakoid/ fusionoid/ Grouchoid/ klutzoid* **2** *suffix used to form adjectives* Resembling or imitating what is indicated: *blitzoid/ cheesoid/ technoid/ zomboid*
● This suffix is increasingly current, probably because of the popularity of fantasy and science fic-

tion, esp among teenagers [fr the scientific suffix *-oid*, fr Greek *-oeides*, ultimately fr *eidos* "image, form"]

oil 1 *n* Flattering and unctuous talk; = BALONEY, BUNK: *Stop the oil, will you?*—Jerome Weidman/ *marinated in good old Hollywood oil*—John McCarten **2** *n* Money, esp money paid for bribery and acquired by graft **3** *v*: *We'll have to oil the mayor to get that permit*
See BANANA OIL, BOIL someone IN OIL, PALM OIL, STRIKE OIL

oil can *n phr* railroad A tank car

oiled *adj* Drunk: *choose your companions, and get properly oiled as well*—New York Times
See WELL OILED

◄**oiler**► *n* A Mexican; = GREASER

oil someone's **palm** *See* GREASE someone's PALM

oily *adj* Cunning and ingratiating; sly and unctuous

oink ◄**1**► *n esp 1960s* A police officer; = PIG **2** *v* To sound and behave like a pig: *and sends masculine outrage oinking into overdrive*—Newsweek [verb sense related to *male chauvinist pig*]

OJ or **oj** (pronounced as separate letters) *n esp lunch counter* Orange juice: *trying to persuade the public to refer to orange juice as "OJ"*—Russell Baker

OK (also **ok** or **okay** or **oka** or **okeh** or **okey** or **oak** or **oke**) **1** *affirmation* Yes; I agree; I accept that; I will do that **2** *adj* Agreeable; = COPACETIC: *He made an OK decision* **3** *adj* Acceptable but not excellent; satisfactory: *The play's okay, but I still prefer the book* **4** *adj* Good; excellent: *He's an okay guy* **5** *affirmation* & **question** Is that all right?; is that understood?; = COPPISH: *I'm going now, okay?* **6** *adv* Right; that's understood, let's get on: *So I told you about that, okay, so the next thing was he jumped the fence* [origin uncertain and the subject of essay after essay; Allen Walker Read is the great authority, and has shown that the locution began as a bumpkin-imitating game among New York and Boston writers in the early 19th century, who used *OK* for "oll korrect"]

okey-doke *affirmation* & *adj* & *question* (also **hokey-dokey** or **okie-doke** or **okey-dokey** or **okie-dokie** or **okle-dokle**) Yes, satisfactory, alright, etc; = OK: *Suppose I pick you up at seven? Okie doke*—Peter De Vries

Okie[1] **1** *n* A migratory worker, esp one in the 1930s who had to leave home because of dust storms; = ARKY **2** *n* A native or resident of Oklahoma; = SOONER

Okie[2] *n WW2 armed forces* A native or resident of Okinawa

-ola or **-olo** *suffix used to form nouns* An emphatic instance or humorous version of what is indicated: *buckola/ crapola/ schnozzola*

old 1 *adj* Familiar and despised; tired: *Don't give me that old shit/ the same old alibis* **2** *adj* Familiar and cherished; dear ● Used without regard to age or gender: *Give my best to old Fred/ Hey, you old bastard, how you doing?* **3** *adj* Accursed; wretched; = DAMNED: *That old ulcer'll get you yet*

See ANY OLD

the **old army game** *See* the ARMY GAME

◄**old bat**► *n phr* An old woman, esp a repulsive, gossipy old shrew; = BAG

old boy *See* GOOD OLD BOY

old boy network or **old boys' system** *n phr fr 1950s British* A reciprocally supportive, exclusive, and influential group of men, esp those who were friends at some prestigious school or college; = IN GROUP: *an "old-girl" network to rival the much-ballyhooed "old-boy" network*—Washingtonian/ *It's an old boys' system. Once you have a few commissions under your belt, one architect recommends you to another*—Philadelphia [fr *old boy*, the British term for public school (that is, private school) alumni]

old buddy *n phr esp Southern* Good friend ● Used chiefly in amiable direct address: *Right, old buddy, I'm coming right over*

◄**old cocker** (or **fart** or **gaffer**)► *n phr* An old man; a superannuated man; = ALTER KOCKER, POOP: *a lot of old cockers out there who wanted to hear a ball game*—New York/ *There ought to be a great advantage to prove that any old fart can do it*—Time

the **old college try** *n phr* One's utmost effort; = GIVE something one's BEST SHOT: *It's not going to be the end of the world. You give it the old college try*—Washingtonian [fr the early and innocent legends of college football]

older than God (or **than baseball**) *adj phr* Very, very old: *The famous poet is older than God, and quite nasty*

◄**old goat**► **1** *n* Any disliked elderly person, esp a man **2** *n* = DIRTY OLD MAN

old hand *n phr* An experienced person; a seasoned veteran: *She's an old hand at these diplomatic remedies*

old hat *adj phr fr 1940s British* Out of style; old-fashioned: *Isn't "old hat" pretty old hat?/ Tubular stuff is now old hat*—RM Coates

the **old heave-ho** *See* the HEAVE-HO

oldie or **oldy** *n* An old thing or person, esp an old song or story: *Our pet oldie concerns the India rubber skin man*—Walter Winchell/ *as good as a WC Fields oldie*—New York Post
See GOLDEN OLDIE

oldie but goodie *See* GOLDEN OLDIE

old Joe *n phr* Any venereal disease; syphilis; gonorrhea: *Twice I got old Joe, you know, a dose*—T Rubin

old lady 1 *n phr* One's wife; a wife: *Losin' his old lady is what crazied him*—Nelson Algren **2** *n phr* A girlfriend, mistress, woman living companion, etc: *He introduced the chick as his old lady* **3** *n phr* One's mother; a mother: *The little kid went to ask his old lady if he could come along*

old man 1 *n phr* One's husband; a husband: *She can't bear to see her old man lose his money*—J Cannon **2** *n phr* A boyfriend or lover: *Her old man was a bass guitar player in a rock group* **3** *n phr* One's father; a father: *My old man wasn't mean*—Calder Willingham **4** *n phr* A man who supports a mistress; = JOHN, SUGAR DADDY: *"Old Man," the name we used to have for a common-law*

husband—Louis Armstrong/ *She has an "old man" who "keeps" her*—New York Times **5** *n phr* prostitutes A pimp **6** *n phr* Old friend; =OLD BUDDY • Used only in direct address
See DIRTY OLD MAN, SO'S YOUR OLD MAN

the **old man** *n phr fr early 1800s* The chief, esp the captain of a ship or aircraft or the commander of a military unit; =HONCHO

the **old one-two** *See* ONE-TWO

old pro *See* PRO

old Siwash *See* SIWASH

Old Smoky (or **Sparky**) *n phr prison* The electric chair: *A half dozen men are alive today who otherwise would have ridden "Old Sparky"*—Publishers Weekly

Old Sol *n phr* The sun

old stick *n phr chiefly British* A rather stiff, perhaps aged, but pleasant and decent person: *My Aunt Sukie's not a bad old stick*

old thing *n phr fr early 1900s British* Old friend; =OLD BUDDY: *in conversation address you as "Old thing"*—Robert Lynd

old timer *n phr fr middle 1800s Western* An old man; =POP • Often used in direct address, generally affectionately: *How long have you lived here, old timer?*

old-timey *adj* Old-fashioned, esp in a pleasant and nostalgic way: *dripping with old-timey decorations*—N Winters

old turkey *n phr* A trite old story, joke, song, etc; =CHESTNUT

old woman *n phr* =OLD LADY

olive *See* SWALLOW THE APPLE

-olo *See* -OLA

omelet *See* YOU CAN'T MAKE AN OMELET WITHOUT BREAKING EGGS

on **1** *adj* Aware; informed; alerted: *I saw he was on, and quit talking*—James M Cain **2** *adj* Not canceled; scheduled to happen: *The deal's still on/ It's on for tomorrow night* **3** *adj* Accepted and confirmed as a partner, competitive bettor, etc: *He said he bet he could do it, and I told him he was on/ You want to go up there with us? You're on* **4** *adj fr show business* Performing; presenting a talk, appeal, etc, as if one were on stage: *Better review your points, since you're on next* **5** *adj* Excited, acting to get attention: *She's never relaxed, she's always on* **6** *prep* Paid for by; with the compliments of: *This was to be on him*—James M Cain **7** *prep* Taking; using; addicted to: *He had her on penicillin/ He was on acid and barbiturates at the time*

on a cloud **1** *adj phr* Very happy; euphoric; in a blissful transport: *Oh, world, I'm on a cloud today!* **2** *adj phr* Intoxicated with narcotics; =HIGH

on a dime *See* STOP ON A DIME, TURN ON A DIME

on an island *See* HOUNDS ON AN ISLAND

on a pillow *See* A PILE ON A PILLOW

on a raft *adv phr lunch counter* On toast

on a roll **1** *adj phr* Having great success; enjoying a winning impetus: *The tax cut's a smash. You're on a roll, Mr President*—Philadelphia Daily News/ *But Brad was on a roll now*—Cameron

Crowe **2** *adj phr* (also **on a kick**) Doing something enthusiastically and constantly: *She was on a philosophy roll*—Rolling Stone [fr a crapshooting term meaning "very, very lucky; unbeatable with the dice"]

on a shingle *See* SHIT ON A SHINGLE

◁**on** **one's ass**▷ (or **ear**) *adv phr* In or into a sad and helpless condition; supine; =DOWN FOR THE COUNT: *He lost three jobs, and now he's on his ass/ His hat store went kerflooie, and he's on his ear now*—James T Farrell
See FALL ON one's ASS, FLAT ON one's ASS, SIT ON one's ASS

on a tear (TAIR) *adj phr* Very angry, esp punitively so; =PISSED OFF: *Ronald Reagan is on a tear over leaks*—National Review

on someone's **back** **1** *adv phr* Persistently annoying or harassing someone; =ON someone's CASE: *The cops were on my back after that* **2** *adj phr* Heavily dependent on someone: *He was always sick and always on her back*

on book *adj phr theater* Reading one's lines from the script, before having memorized them: *Most of the actors are still "on book," clutching scripts in hand*—Toronto Life

on one's **brakes** *See* STAND ON one's BRAKES

on someone's **case** *adv phr fr black* Paying close and esp meddling or punitive attention to someone: *Maybe the world isn't on my case. Maybe the problem is me*—Garrison Keillor/ *These people got on my case heavy the first day the ol' man was dead*—Joseph Wambaugh [fr the black expression *sit on someone's case* "discuss and judge someone's problems, behavior, etc," based on a judicial analogy]

a **once-over** or **once-over lightly** *n phr* A hasty, cursory performance; =A LICK AND A PROMISE: *a razor for a hasty once-over*—Meyer Berger

the **once-over** *n phr fr early 1900s* A look or glance of inspection; scrutiny; =the DOUBLE-O: *The first thing we went to buy after giving all the pavilions the once-over was tomatoes*—Art Buchwald
See GIVE someone or something THE ONCE-OVER

oncer (WUN Sə) **1** *n* A woman who is faithful to one man all her life; a one-man woman **2** *n* (also **oner**) A rare and unique person; someone or something esp excellent: *He is, as his friend Olive Behrendt put it, a "oncer," one of a kind*—New York Times/ *That was a great joke, a oner*

on cloud nine (or **cloud seven**) *adj phr* At the very pinnacle of bliss; euphoric; =ON A CLOUD: *She came back home and he's on cloud nine*

on someone's **coattails** *adv phr* Profiting from someone else's success, esp in a decisive election: *when all these rube politicians come riding in on Reagan's coattails*—WT Tyler

on deck **1** *adv phr baseball* Waiting to be the next batter, usu in a special circle marked for the purpose **2** *adj phr*: *the on-deck hitter* **3** *adj phr* Present and ready; on hand and prepared: *If you need anybody else, I'm on deck*

on someone's **dime** *adv phr* At someone's expense other than the speaker's: *Yeah, we can* *give it a try, but it's on your dime* [fr the *dime* needed to activate a pay telephone]

one *See* BIG ONE, DEAD ONE, FAST ONE, FIFTY-ONE, FORTY-ONE, FOUR-AND-ONE, FRESH ONE, HANG ONE ON, HOT ONE, NUMBER-ONE BOY, QUICK ONE, SQUARE ONE, THIN ONE

One *See* MURDER ONE, NUMBER ONE, TRACK ONE

one-and-a-half striper *n phr Navy* A lieutenant, junior grade

one and only *n phr* One's beloved, fiancee, sweetheart, etc: *My one and only, what am I going to do if you turn me down when I'm so crazy over you*—George Gershwin

on one's **ear** *See* ON one's ASS

one-arm (or **one-armed**) **bandit** *n phr fr 1930s* A slot machine

one-arm joint or **one-arm** *n phr* or *n fr early 1900s* A cheap restaurant, esp a small one with chairs having an enlarged right arm that serves as a table: *She went with me to this one-arm where I eat*—John O'Hara

on easy street *adv phr* In a condition of solvency, ease, and tranquility

one-bagger *n baseball* A one-base hit; single

one better *See* GO something or someone ONE BETTER

on edge *See* EDGY

one dollar to rub against another *See* NOT HAVE ONE DOLLAR TO RUB AGAINST ANOTHER

one-eyed monster *n phr* A television set; television; = the BOOB TUBE

one foot in the grave *See* HAVE ONE FOOT IN THE GRAVE

one for the book (or **books**) *n phr* Something remarkable; an amazing thing, case, etc: *That storm was really one for the book*

one for the road *n phr* A last drink of the evening, party, carouse, etc; = STIRRUP CUP

one hell of a *See* a HELL OF A

one-horse *adj fr middle 1800s* Insignificant; inferior: *It's a one-horse operation he's got there*

one-horse town *n phr* A small town; = JERKWATER TOWN

one-liner *n* A quick joke or quip; a funny observation; = WISECRACK: *a new neighbor who exchanges one-liners with Lianna in the laundry room*—Toronto Life

one-lunger 1 *n* A one-cylinder engine **2** *n* A car, boat, etc, with a one-cylinder engine

one-man show *n phr* An enterprise, business, etc, controlled by one person: *The company had previously been run as a "one-man show"*—Fortune

one-night stand 1 *n phr* A performing engagement for one evening only: *Not a bad gig, but just a one-night stand* **2** *n phr* A casual sex act; a brief sexual encounter: *He never enjoyed one-night stands* **3** *n phr* A person who has a casual sexual encounter: *emerges as less the femme fatale than a one-night stand gone wrong*—Time

one oar *See* ROW WITH ONE OAR

one of the boys (or **the guys**) *n phr* An ordinary, amiable man; a man without side or lofty dignity; = ORDINARY JOE: *His Eminence was trying to be one of the boys*

one of those things *See* JUST ONE OF THOSE THINGS

one on one *adv phr* In immediate confrontation; person to person; = EYEBALL TO EYEBALL: *I go on the basketball court and have a 15-year-old guy beat me one on one*—San Francisco/ *John Rhodes was very effective, one-on-one*—Wall Street Journal

one on the house *n phr lunch counter* A glass of water

one piece *See* ALL IN ONE PIECE

oner *See* ONCER

one red cent *See* a RED CENT

one-shot 1 *n* A story or article that appears once, with no sequel **2** *n* Any transaction, event, etc, that occurs only once: *He was doing poetry readings, one-shots* **3** *modifier:* *He put her in a one-shot whodunit*—Newsweek/ *Maybe it was a one-shot shakedown*—J Ellison/ *It's a one-shot deal* **4** *n* A woman who accedes to the sex act once, then refuses repetitions

one smart apple *See* SMART APPLE

one-striper 1 *n Navy* An ensign **2** *n Army* A private first class

one thin dime *See* a THIN DIME

one too many *n phr* Enough liquor to make one drunk, and possibly more: *Its driver had obviously had one too many*—D McFerran

one-track mind *n phr* A mind limited to or obsessed with a single idea, theme, etc

one-two 1 *n* (also the **old one-two** or **one-two punch** or **one-two blow**) A combination of two blows with the fists, a short left jab plus a hard right cross, usu to the chin: *zipping "one-twos" to the jaw*—Jim Tully **2** *modifier:* *good potent one-two punches*—New Yorker

one-up 1 *adv phr* In a superior position; at an advantage: *I always try to be one-up* **2** *v* To get the advantage over: *I wasn't trying to one-up Arthur Schwartz*—M Williams **3** *adv phr* Ahead by one: *The Pinks were one-up on the Puces, 109 to 108*

one-upmanship *n* The technique and practice of having the advantage over one's opponent, esp keeping a psychological advantage by low cunning and subtle brilliance: *a wide-open but good-humored game of political one-upmanship*—Tom Wicker [coined by the late British humorist Stephen Potter]

one-way guy *n phr* An honest and decent man; = GOOD JOE, MISTER NICE GUY

one-way street *See* NOT A ONE-WAY STREET

one-with *n lunch counter* A hamburger with onions

on one's **game** *adj phr* Performing very well; = HOT: *When I was out in the water and on my game, nothing existed but the wave*—Washington Post

on one's **head** *See* STAND ON one's HEAD

on hold *adv phr* In postponement or abeyance; suspended; = IN COLD STORAGE: *All plans are on hold for a while* [fr the button on a telephone marked *hold*, used to switch temporarily from the conversation]

on ice 1 *adj phr* *fr late 1800s* Certain of being won, or of turning out well; = IN THE BAG: *The deal's on ice* **2** *adv phr* In prison, esp in solitary confinement **3** *adj phr* In reserve; ready to play a role; = IN COLD STORAGE: *If this one fails, I've got another on ice* **4** *adv phr* To the utmost; in the highest degree; = IN SPADES: *This movie stinks on ice*
See PISS ON ICE

onion 1 *n* The head **2** *n* A dollar **3** *n* *lunch counter* An inexperienced lunch counter worker
See KNOW one's ONIONS, OFF one's NUT, RED ONION

Onions *See* the BEEFSTEAK AND ONIONS

on line 1 *adj phr* *computers* Computerized: *They put the whole card catalog on line* **2** *adj phr* *fr computer* Available; ready for use; installed; = IN PLACE: *The Navy's announced plans for a new destroyer class are on line* [probably fr the connecting *lines* on a flow chart used to indicate a computer and its attached apparatus]

only *See* EYES ONLY, ONE AND ONLY

the **only game in town** *n phr* The only choice available, as undesirable as it may be: *Senator Percy called the proposal "the only game in town"/ For export industries "development bank" projects are the only game in town*—New York Times [a shortening of the expression *I know it's crooked, but it's the only game in town*]

on one's **own hook** *adv phr* *fr early 1800s* By one's own efforts; on one's own account: *I can't help, so you'll have to do it on your own hook* [origin unknown and much speculated upon; perhaps fr *fishhook*]

on one's **own time and own dime** *adv phr* Entirely at one's own expense: *She said I could go ahead if I wanted to, but strictly on my own time and own dime*

on paper *adv phr* Only by abstract report or reputation; theoretically: *I'm rich, but it's all on paper/ It works on paper but I've never actually tried it*

on sked *adv phr* On schedule: *Aside from minor setbacks…"Street Trash" has been proceeding smoothly and on sked*—New York Times

on the arm 1 *adv phr* On credit, esp when payment is not intended or expected; = ON THE CUFF **2** *adv phr* Free of charge; = FREE GRATIS: *Lots of lawyers would defend a cop on the arm/ One of those favors I do on the arm is for Nick Kenny's TV show*—Rocky Graziano [fr *on the cuff*]

on the back burner *adv phr* Not being actively considered; in reserve; = ON HOLD: *I have some good projects on the back burner right now*

on the ball *adv phr* Skillful, alert, and effective; = WITH IT: *FBI agents were very much on the ball in the Bremer snatch*—A Hynd [fr the advisability of keeping one's eyes *on the ball* when playing a ball game]
See GET ON THE BALL, KEEP one's EYE ON THE BALL, SOMETHING ON THE BALL

on the beach *adv phr* Unemployed [fr the situation of a sailor between voyages]
See PEBBLE ON THE BEACH

on the beam *adv phr* On the proper track or course; performing correctly: *It took a while, but he's on the beam now* [fr the radio *beam* used to guide aircraft]

on the bean *adj phr* Precisely right; exact; = ON THE MONEY: *Our estimates were right on the bean* [probably fr alterations of *on the beam*, and *on the head* in the phrase *hit the nail on the head*; perhaps influenced by the common contest in which one guesses the number of *beans* in a large glass jar]

on the blink *adj phr* (Variations: **bum** or **fritz** or **Fritz** may replace **blink**) *fr early 1900s* Not functioning properly; in poor condition: *His eyes are on the blink/ His pacemaker just went on the fritz*—WT Tyler/ *My heart's on the bum* [origin unknown; perhaps fr the notion that defective eyes or lights *blink*; *fritz* variant, fr the early 20th century, may be fr a comic strip called "The Katzenjammer Kids," in which two mischievous boys, Hans and *Fritz*, would regularly thwart and disable a character called the Captain]

on the brain *See* HAVE something ON THE BRAIN

on the bum *adj phr* *fr late 1800s* Leading the life of a hobo, or a similar parasitic and drifting life; = ON THE BLINK: *That year I went on the bum to California*

on the button 1 *adv phr* Precisely; exactly; = ON THE DOT, ON THE NOSE: *The meter says 35 on the button/ The plane came in at 4 on the button* **2** *adj phr* Perfectly placed; absolutely correct; = ON THE MONEY, ON THE NOSE: *Your estimate was right on the button*

on the carpet *adv phr* In the situation of being reprimanded: *Next time they caught him asleep he was on the carpet* [probably fr the early-19th-century British *walk the carpet* or *carpet* "reprimand, rebuke"]

on the cheap 1 *adv phr* *fr middle 1800s British* Very economically; as frugally as possible **2** *adj phr*: *Prices still delight the on-the-cheap set*—Toronto Life

on the cob *adj phr* = CORNY

on the cops *adv phr* On the police force: *I was on the cops once*—Raymond Chandler

on the cuff 1 *adv phr* On credit: *arranged for him to eat on the cuff*—New York Confidential **2** *adv phr* Free of charge; = FREE GRATIS, ON THE ARM: *He promised me lodging on the cuff* **3** *adj phr*: *On-the-cuff drinks are delicious* [fr the practice of noting debts on the *cuff* of the shirt, esp on a detachable *cuff*]

on the dot *adv phr* At the exact moment; punctually: *I got there on the dot*

on (or **at**) **the double** *fr Army* **1** *adv phr* At twice the rate of ordinary marching **2** *adv phr* Quickly; rapidly: *When I holler, come on the double*

on the draw *See* SLOW ON THE DRAW

on the dry *adj phr* Abstaining from liquor; = ON THE WAGON

on the Erie *hoboes & underworld* **1** *adv phr* Listening attentively **2** *adv phr* In hiding, esp for eavesdropping [fr the pun of *ear* with *Erie* Railroad]

on the fence *adv phr* Not taking a stand or making up one's mind; straddling

on the finger *adv phr* = ON THE CUFF

on the fire **1** *adj phr* Pending; in preparation; = IN THE PIPELINE: *We've got a great new model on the fire for next year* **2** *adj phr* lunch counter Being cooked; in preparation

on the fly **1** *adv phr* Hastily in passing; without preparation or forethought: *We had to make up our minds on the fly* **2** *adj phr:* *an on-the-fly decision*

on the fritz *See* ON THE BLINK

on the go **1** *adj phr* Active; energetic; indefatigable: *I'm on the go day and night*—Calder Willingham **2** *adj phr* Always moving about; restlessly in motion: *I'm on the go all the time and don't see my family*

on the gravy train (or **boat**) *adv phr* Enjoying an effortless and prosperous life; = FLUSH: *I was a couple of years on the gravy train, then the bottom fell out of things*

on the grift *adj phr* underworld Living as a confidence man, gambler, hobo, etc

on the ground floor *See* IN ON THE GROUND FLOOR

on the head *See* HIT THE NAIL ON THE HEAD

on the heavy *adv phr* underworld Engaged in and living on crime

on the hog *adj phr* hoboes Penniless; destitute; = BROKE [origin unknown; perhaps an alteration of the synonymous phrase *on the hocks*, suggesting walking on the *hock* or ankle, rather than the hoof or sole, hence beaten down]

See EAT HIGH ON THE HOG

on the hook **1** *adv phr* In trouble; liable to blame: *You're on the hook for this mess, junior* **2** *adv phr* Trapped; ensnared: *She had the old fool on the hook right soon*

on (or **in**) **the hot seat** *adv phr* In an uncomfortable situation; = IN A JAM: *The poor jerk's on the hot seat for forgetting to shut the safe*

on the house *adj phr* Free of charge; = FREE GRATIS: *Breakfasts, luncheons, and dinner....All "on the house"*—advertisement for Northwest Airlines

See ONE ON THE HOUSE

on the hustle *adj phr* Living by constant petty frauds and crimes; watchful for dupes: *sleeping till ten in the morning, on the hustle in the streets or the poolrooms*—Stewart Alsop

on the inside *adv phr* Having access to the most confidential information; near the focus of power and influence

on the lam **1** *adj phr* underworld In hiding from the police; wanted as a fugitive: *So I went on the lam*—D Purroy **2** *adj phr* Traveling about; vagrant; = ON THE ROAD

See TAKE IT ON THE LAM

on the legit *adj phr* & *adv phr* Lawful; legal; = ON THE LEVEL: *strictly on the legit*—Nelson Algren

on the level **1** *adj phr* fr early 1900s Honest; candid; = ON THE LEGIT: *to swear that I'm on the level*—H McHugh **2** *adv phr:* *and would fight on the level*—AJ Liebling

on the line *adv phr* In a risky or vulnerable position; at risk, esp deliberately; up for grabs: *The whole season's on the line this inning* [origin unknown; perhaps fr a gambling game where the bet is placed *on a line*; perhaps fr the commercial slang expression *lay* (the price or payment) *on the line* "pay, pay up"; perhaps fr the sense of *line* as separating combatants or duellists]

See someone's ASS IS ON THE LINE, LAY IT ON THE LINE, LAY something ON THE LINE, PUT one's ASS ON THE LINE

on the make **1** *adv phr* fr middle 1800s Aspiring and ambitious, esp in a ruthless and exploitive way; careeristic; = HUNGRY: *The rookies are very much on the make* **2** *adv phr* Offering and seeking sexual pleasure and conquest; openly amorous: *going on the make for the tired ones dressed like girl scout masters*—John O'Hara/ *whether they are on the make, and they all are*—Sexual Behavior

See ON THE TAKE

on the mat *adv phr* = ON THE CARPET

on the money *adj phr* Absolutely perfect; precisely as desired; accurate: *good hit, right on the money*—New York Times/ *She was right on the money with the advice*—Richard Merkin

on the muscle *adj phr* underworld fr 1920s Truculent; inclined to violence

on the needle *adj phr* narcotics Using narcotics, esp as an addict

on the nose **1** *adv phr* Precisely; exactly; = ON THE DOT: *It's six on the nose* **2** *adj phr* Perfectly placed; exactly as desired; = ON THE MONEY: *Your guess was right on the nose*

on the pad *adv phr* police Taking bribes and graft; = ON THE TAKE [fr the *pad* "notebook" listing the names of corrupt police officers]

on the pan *adj phr* Being severely criticized and deplored: *always gossiping, always with somebody on the pan*

on the peg *adj phr* Army Under arrest

on the pitch *adj phr* Ambitious; aspiring; = ON THE MAKE: *Always on the pitch, always trying to move in*—W R Burnett [fr the salesperson's or carnival barker's advertising *pitch*]

on the prowl **1** *adj phr* Actively seeking; abroad and searching, esp for victims: *Be very careful on that street for muggers on the prowl* **2** *adv phr* Seeking sexual pleasure and conquest; = ON THE MAKE

on the QT *adv phr* fr middle 1800s Secretly; quietly [fr the first and last letters of *quiet*]

◁**on the rag**▷ *adj phr* Menstruating: *Maybe I'm on the rag*—Richard Merkin/ *It seemed awkward to interrupt the moment and say, "I'm on the rag"*—Playgirl [fr *rag* used as a sanitary napkin]

on the record *See* FOR THE RECORD

on the rims *adv phr* As close as possible to insolvency [fr the image of a car with ruined tires running on its *rims*]

on the road **1** *adv phr* Traveling from place to place with a show, musical program, etc **2** *adv phr* Drifting about; = ON THE LAM: *Lots of teenagers were on the road those years*

on the rocks 1 *adv phr* In a ruined condition; hopelessly wrecked; =KAPUT: *My little enterprise is on the rocks* **2** *adv phr* Poured over ice: *Scotch on the rocks'll be fine*

on the same (or **on** one's) **wavelength** *adj phr* In agreement; in harmony; =TUNED IN: *Her door's open, but we are not on the same wavelength*—San Francisco/ *Finding a caterer "on your wavelength" is easy*—Washingtonian [fr the notion of being tuned to the same broadcast *wavelength*]

on the sauce *adj phr* Drinking liquor, esp heavily: *on the sauce in a charming school-boy way*—Stephen Longstreet

on the shake *adv phr* Practicing extortion, blackmail, etc: *You knew they was on the shake*—AJ Liebling [fr *shakedown*]

on the shelf *adv phr* Not in active use or consideration; deferred; =ON THE BACK BURNER: *We'll have to put some of those plans on the shelf for a while*

on the shikker 1 *adj phr* Drunk **2** *adj phr* =ON THE SAUCE [fr Yiddish fr Hebrew *shikor* "drunk"]

on the side *adv phr* Extra; additionally: *He moonlights as a hackie on the side/ with cole slaw on the side*

on the skids *adj phr* On a failing or declining course; deteriorating: *After that scandal his whole career was on the skids* [ultimately fr the *skids* "long pieces of timber" on which barrels, logs, and other heavy objects were rolled or slid, sometimes on a downgrade]

on the spot 1 *adj phr* Expected to cope, explain, react, etc, at once; under sharp pressure: *She can't make it, so I guess you're on the spot* **2** *adj phr* Available and ready; keen and at hand: *When I need him he's never on the spot* **3** *adv phr* Immediately; at once and at the place in question: *I was able to fix it on the spot*
See JOHNNY-ON-THE-SPOT

on the stick *adv phr* Skillful, alert, and effective; =ON THE BALL: *She said he'd better get on the stick or she'd dump him* [perhaps related to the early-19th-century British expression *be high up the stick* "be very highly placed; be successful in one's work"]

on the take (or **the make**) *adv phr* Amenable to bribery and graft; =ON THE PAD: *spent 30 years fighting everything from pigeons to cops on the make*—Time

on the thumb *adv phr fr 1920s* Soliciting rides along the highway; =HITCHHIKING

on the town *adv phr* Enjoying the pleasures of a city, esp the night life; roistering and reveling urbanly

on the up and up *See* UP AND UP

on the uptake *See* SLOW ON THE DRAW

on the wagon (or **the water wagon**) *adj phr fr late 1800s* Abstaining from liquor; teetotal, at least temporarily: *Monty didn't drink, and Clifton James went on the wagon*—This Week/ *He had all the members of the Highball Association climbing on the water wagon*—H McHugh [first attested as *on the water cart* in 1902]

on tick *adv phr fr 1600s* On credit: *getting his liquor "on tick"*—Russell Janney

on top *See* COME OUT AHEAD

on top of 1 *adv phr* Actively coping with the problem; able to guide and control the matter: *It's a nasty outlook, but I think we can get on top of it* **2** *adv phr* Fully informed about something: *Get on top of this latest development right away*

on track *See* GO ON TRACK

on one's **uppers** *adj phr fr late 1800s* Penniless; destitute; =DOWN AND OUT [fr the notion that one has worn out the soles of one's shoes and is walking *on the uppers* only]

on velvet *adv phr fr late 1700s British* In easy circumstances, such as those applying when one gambles only winnings: *in order to be able to work on "velvet"*—E Lavine

on someone's **watch** *adv phr* During someone's tenure of responsibility; while someone is in charge, esp of protection: *Jerusalem and the West Bank were lost to Jordan and the Arab world on his watch*—New Yorker [fr the nautical setting of *watches*, the designating of officers and crew members who run the ship for a specified period]

on wheels 1 *adj phr lunch counter* To be eaten elsewhere; =TO GO **2** *adj phr* To the utmost extent; of the purest sort; =IN SPADES: *We agreed she was a bitch on wheels*
See SHIT ON WHEELS

oo *v* =DOUBLE-O ● In written use only

-oo *See* -EROO, -LOO

ooch or **oonch** *See* SCRUNCH

oodles *n fr middle 1800s cowboys* A large amount; lots; =A SHITHOUSE FULL: *They have oodles of charisma* [perhaps fr *boodle, caboodle*]

oof 1 *n* Money **2** *n prizefight* Strength; power; =CLOUT

oofay *See* OFAY

ooftish or **offtish** *n gamblers fr late 1800s* Money, esp money available for gambling or investment [fr Yiddish *oyf tishe* "on the table"]

oofus[1] *n black & jive talk* A stupid person; oaf; =GOOF: *oofus, a dope*—E Horne [perhaps fr *goof, goofus*]

oofus[2] *n* Money; =OOFTISH

oogle *v* To ogle; stare at

oogley *adj jive talk* Attractive; worth ogling with admiration: *It's oogley. Also Bong*—D Willens

ooh and ah *v phr* To express wonder, amazement, etc: *How they oohed and ahhed over the new baby!*

ook *n 1940s students* A detestable, insipid person; =NERD, WIMP: *Does even an "ook" give out with a wolf whistle?*—Time

ookus or **ooks** *n fr late 1800s* Money; =OOFTISH [perhaps related to *ooftish*]

oomph 1 *n esp 1930s & 40s* Sexual attractiveness; compelling carnality; =IT **2** *n* Energy; =CLOUT, PIZZAZZ: *substance, drive, authority, emotional power, and oomph*—Frank Sullivan [an echoic coinage suggesting the gasp of someone hit hard by a blow, a transport of desire, etc]

oomph girl *n phr esp 1930s & 40s* A young woman who is notably sexually attractive; sex goddess or queen; =DISH ● A sobriquet given by press agents in 1939 to the film actress Ann Sheridan: *the oomph-girl of the Romance Language Department*—Morris Bishop

oops 1 *interj* An exclamation of surprise, dismay, apology, etc, esp when one has done something awkward: *Mr Belve, oops, I mean Webb, is ecstatic*—B Thomas/ *Oops, look at this one!* **2** *v* (also **oops up**) To vomit; =BARF: *She oopsed over the side*/ *This show'll make you want to oops up*

ooze *v* To move or walk slowly; glide or slide; saunter; =EASE: *I'd ooze across the street and into the bar*—R Starnes

ooze out *v phr* To depart inconspicuously; leave covertly

op 1 *n railroad* A telegrapher **2** *n fr 1920s underworld* A private detective: *one of your ops*—Dashiell Hammett [fr *operator* or *operative*]

OP or **op** (pronounced as separate letters) *adj* Other people's: *OP. Other people's money*—T Betts [perhaps a translation of Yiddish *yenems*; see *yenems*]

Op-Ed (or **op-ed**) **page** *n phr* A newspaper page, usu appearing across from the editorial page, made up of columns and short essays [fr *opposite editorial*]

open *adj* =WIDE OPEN

opener *See* BAG OPENER, CAN-OPENER, EYE-OPENER

openers *See* FOR OPENERS

open eyes *See* WITH EYES OPEN

open one's **face** (or **head**) *v phr* To speak; speak out; speak up: *Don't so much as open your face about this, please*

open up 1 *v phr* To commence firing, fighting, activity, etc **2** *v phr* To speak and inform candidly; =SPILL one's GUTS: *You must open up and tell us all about what happened*

open up a (or **that**) **can of worms** *v phr* To broach a very complicated and troublesome matter; set something messy in motion: *Merit pay? Let's not open up that can of worms* *See* CAN OF WORMS

open one's **yap** *v phr* To open one's mouth, esp to speak; speak up; say something: *He gets in trouble every time he opens his yap*

opera *See* CORK OPERA, HORSE OPERA, MUD OPERA, OATER, SOAP OPERA, SPACE OPERA

the opera's never over till the fat lady sings *sentence* Things are never finished until they are finished; further possibilities of action exist here: *Like they say around here, "The opera's never over till the fat lady sings." What hotel are you staying at, little lady?*—WT Tyler

operate with a full deck *See* PLAY WITH A FULL DECK

operator 1 *n* A person who busily deals and manipulates, often self-importantly; =DEALER, MACHER, WHEELER-DEALER **2** *n* =LADIES' MAN

opry *See* HORSE OPERA

oral *n college students* A spoken examination as distinct from a written one

oral days *n phr horse-racing* The times when bets were made by word of mouth, before the totalizator machines were used

oral diarrhea *See* VERBAL DIARRHEA

-orama *See* -RAMA

orange crush *n phr* A special squad of police or prison guards, clad in orange jump suits, used to deal with prison riots and other such disturbances [fr a punning reference to the soft drink *Orange Crush* (a trade name)]

Orange Sunshine *n phr narcotics* A kind of LSD: *"Orange Sunshine" began to appear in acid-starved New York City and in New England communes*—MJ Warth

orbit *See* GO INTO ORBIT, IN ORBIT

orc or **orch** *See* ORK

orchard *See* BONE-ORCHARD, EGG ORCHARD, MARBLE ORCHARD

order *See* APPLE-PIE ORDER, PECKING ORDER

orders *See* CUT someone's PAPERS

ordinary Joe *n phr* An average sort of man; =JOHN Q CITIZEN

◁**O'Reilly's balls**▷ *See* TIGHT AS KELSEY'S NUTS

or else *prep phr* Otherwise; or this unhappy thing will follow ● Used at the end of a command or warning to encourage compliance: *Get that damn thing out of here or else*

◁**Oreo**▷ *n black fr 1960s* A black person whose values, behavior, etc, are those of the white society; =AFRO-SAXON: *successful black businessmen who were regarded as "Oreos"*—AT Demaree [fr the trade name of a brand of sandwich cookies that have a white cream between round chocolate biscuits]

org[1] *n* A pipe organ or electric organ

org[2] *n* An organization: *The Joe Breen (Hays org) influence on pix*—Abel Green

organ *See* LAP ORGAN

organized *adj* Drunk [perhaps fr *hoary-eyed*]

orie-eyed or **orry-eyed** *See* HOARY-EYED

-orino *See* -ERINO

-orium *See* -ATORIUM

ork or **orc** or **orch** *n* An orchestra: *Pierre quit the New York ork*

ornament *n railroad* A station master

ornery *adj* Mean and irascible; ill-tempered: *He was confident and ornery on the mound*—Inside Sports [fr a dialect pronunciation of *ordinary*]

orphan *n* A model of a car, boat, computer, etc, which is no longer being manufactured, and for which spare parts are hard to find

orphan drug *n phr* A drug that may not be commercially feasible, though it may be very useful or necessary to a relatively small number of people: *Program to Spur "Orphan" Drugs Proves a Success*—Wall Street Journal

oryide (AWR ee īd) *n outdated late 1800s hoboes* A drunkard: *our star "oryide"*—Jack London [fr *hoary-eyed*]

oscar *n underworld* A pistol; firearm [perhaps fr *roscoe* by resemblance]

Oscar 1 *n* Any of a set of annual awards, and the statuette signifying it, from the Academy of Motion Picture Arts and Sciences **2** *n* Any award: *You won't win any Oscars for that job, you slob* [coined about 1930 by one or more of the various people, including a woman named Margaret Herrick, to whom it is attributed; *Oscar* as a quintessentially comical name was current at the time through the influence of the comic magazine *Ballyhoo*]

ossifer *n* An officer, esp a police or Army officer [presumably imitating the spoonerism of a drunken person addressing a police officer]

ossified *adj* Drunk; = STONED

other fish to fry *See* BIGGER FISH TO FRY

other half *n phr* Another large sector of society, usu the rich as distinct from the poor or the poor as distinct from the rich ● Nearly always in the expression "see how the other half lives": *Young people from West Berlin now spend their weekends "over there," trying to find out how the other half lives*—Joseph Wechsberg

other side of one's **face** *See* LAUGH ON THE OTHER SIDE OF one's FACE

ouch *n* An injury; a hurt: *A very serious injury is a "big" ouch*—David Dempsey [fr the pained interjection *ouch* fr German, probably Pennsylvania German, *autsch*, used fr the middle 19th century]

ounce *See* VIG OUNCE

ounce man *narcotics* **1** *n phr* A narcotics dealer who cuts or adulterates heroin **2** *n phr* A narcotics seller who buys from a wholesale drug seller; = CONNECTION, DEALER

out **1** *adj beat & cool talk* Attractive; au courant; = HIP, WAY OUT: *Man, that Modigliani is really out* **2** *adj* Not modern, popular, or in accord with current taste: *Those neckties are out this year* **3** *adj homosexuals* Openly avowing homosexuality **4** *adv* Away from home: *The folks are out tonight* **5** *adj* (also **out cold**) Unconscious, esp knocked unconscious: *One more drink and he'll be out* **6** *n fr 1920s* A way of escape; a plausible alibi or evasive course; = LETOUT: *You've got only one out, which is to lie like hell*
See ALL GETOUT, FAR OUT, GET OUT, WAY OUT

out-and-out *adj* Thorough; complete: *an out-and-out idiot*

outasight *See* OUT OF SIGHT

outer garden *n phr outdated baseball* The outfield

outfox *v* To outwit; outsmart; = FOX

out from under *See* GET OUT FROM UNDER

out-front *adj* Honest; candid; unevasive; = UP FRONT: *intelligent, very open, out-front people*—Tom Wolfe/ *brash, flamboyant, out-front*—Albert Goldman

out in left field *adj phr* Very unorthodox and wrong; weirdly unconventional; crazy

out like a light *adj phr* Unconscious; fast asleep

out loud *See* FOR CRYING OUT LOUD

out of one's **depth** *adv phr* In a situation where one cannot cope, esp because one is inexperienced, insufficiently skillful, etc: *I felt out of my depth in that school*

out of one's **ears** *See* HAVE something COMING OUT OF one's EARS

out of one's **head** (or **skull** or **gourd**) **1** *adj phr* Insane; crazy; = NUTS: *You're out of your head if you think I'll do that* **2** *adj phr* Dazed;

delirious; = OFF one's NUT: *He took one sniff and went right out of his gourd*

out of hell *See* TAKE OFF LIKE A BIGASS BIRD

out of it **1** *adj phr* Unable to win or succeed: *The Hawks are out of it this season* **2** *adj phr* Not a part of the trend or scene; uninitiated: *He's a nice guy, but he's out of it*—New Yorker/ *Everyone was out of it in the fifties*—New York Times **3** *adj phr* Unattending, esp because of drugs or liquor: *prefer him dreamy to guilty. We could accept him as being out of it*—John Irving/ *I had been so out of it, I hadn't heard her question*—Erich Segal

out of joint *See* PUT someone's NOSE OUT OF JOINT

out of kilter *adj phr fr early 1600s* Not in order or repair; = OUT OF WHACK [fr British dialect *kilter* or *kelter* "condition, state, frame," of obscure origin]

out of one's **league** **1** *adj phr* = OUT OF one's DEPTH **2** *adj phr* Not in one's proper province: *The matter's fortunately out of my league*

out of line **1** *adj phr* Not in accordance with what is appropriate or expected: *You was considered out of line if your coat and pants matched*—A Lomax/ *That remark was out of line* **2** *adj phr* Behaving improperly, esp presumptuously: *The little smart-ass got out of line once too often*

out of luck *adj phr* Having no chance of success; already too late for what one wants: *You're out of luck, pal, they've gone*
See SHIT OUT OF LUCK

out of pocket (or **the pocket**) *adj phr esp Southern and Southwestern* Absent or otherwise unavailable: *I'm out of the pocket for a bit, but I'll get back at ya*—Rolling Stone/ *The station chief was out of pocket*—WT Tyler

out of shape *adj phr* Very upset; angry; hysterical
See BENT OUT OF SHAPE

out of sight **1** *adj phr* (also **outasight**) *cool talk* = WAY OUT **2** *adj phr* Very high-priced; exorbitantly priced: *That hat's out of sight*

out of style *See* LIKE IT'S GOING OUT OF STYLE

out of sync *adj phr* Not coinciding or compatible; arrhythmic, esp in relation to something else, a context, etc: *his presence just self-consciously regular enough to be out of sync*—Toronto Life/ *His politics are out of sync with current conservative trends*—Time [fr the lack of *synchronism* sometimes noted between a movie or TV image and its sound track]

out of the box *adj phr* Out of contention; ruined; = FINISHED, KAPUT: *The first reviews were so bad I thought we were out of the box* [fr the condition of a baseball pitcher who has been *knocked out of the box* and hence has probably lost the game]

out of the closet **1** *adj phr* Openly avowing homosexuality **2** *adj phr* No longer secret: *The last American taboo, that of talking about indebtedness, may be out of the closet at last*—New York Times
See COME OUT OF THE CLOSET

out of the fire *See* PULL something OUT OF THE FIRE

out of the loop *adj phr* Not one of the inner and influential group; not in the network: *George Bush was out of the loop...an ineffective second in com-*

mand—Newsweek/ *an inevitable feeling of being out of the loop*—Washington Post [probably fr the military notion of radio *nets*, conceptually like *loops*, connecting various commanders]

out of the water *See* BLOW OUT OF THE WATER

out of the woodwork *See* CRAWL OUT OF THE WOODWORK

out of this world *adj phr fr early 1900s* Excellent; wonderful; superior; = the GREATEST, WAY OUT: *She had a figure which was out of this world*—H Witwer

out of town *adv phr underworld* In prison

out of one's **tree** *adj phr* Insane; crazy; = APE: *I think she's got to be out of her tree*—Washington Post

out of turn *See* TALK OUT OF TURN

out of one's **way** *See* GO OUT OF one's WAY

out of whack *fr late 1800s* **1** *adj phr* Not operating; out of order; = ON THE BLINK, OUT OF KILTER: *My car's out of whack so I'll take yours* **2** *adj phr* Not in adjustment, harmonious synchronism, etc; not in proper order: *The timer's a little out of whack is all/ Our priorities are out of whack*—Washingtonian **3** *adj phr* Strange; inexplicable; not right: *It seems out of whack to me, then, that Jakobek was the only aldermanic candidate who had a great deal of support from the young*—Toronto Life [probably fr *whack* "share, a just proportion," so called perhaps fr the blow that divides something or like the auctioneer's hammerrap signals a fair share or deal]

out on a limb *adv phr* In a very vulnerable position; exposed; in peril: *The announcement put the Mayor out on a limb*
See GO OUT ON A LIMB

◁**out on** one's **ass**▷ *adj phr* Discharged; rejected; superseded; = FINISHED: *She's the First Lady now, and I'm out on my ass*—Interview

outside *adj esp black* Born out of wedlock: *Maybe some of us is "outside" children*—A Lomax
See GET OUTSIDE OF

outside chance *n phr* A remote possibility; a slim likelihood: *He may have an outside chance to pass*

outtake *n* An excerpt; an extracted passage: *Is this an outtake from the $1.98 Beauty Show?*—Playboy/ *surprising outtakes from Brando's secret life*—Esquire

out the window/ *adj phr* Wrecked and futile; = DOWN THE TUBE, KAPUT: *All our plans are out the window now, so forget it*

out to lunch *adj phr esp students* Insane; crazy; eccentric: *On critical issues of fact and analysis he is out to lunch*—Washington Post

out to pasture *adj phr* Retired; superannuated; no longer active: *My job? I've been out to pasture the last four years*
See PUT someone or something OUT TO PASTURE

out year *n phr esp Washington bureaucracy* One of the six or so years affected by a budget or an action in question: *will rise even more sharply in the near future, or what the Pentagon calls the "out years"*—New York Times

the oval *n phr* A football; = the OBLATE SPHEROID

over **1** *adv* & *prep poker* Along with cards of lesser value: *I've got a full house, tens over sixes* **2** *adj* Turned over; flipped; fried on both sides ● Said of eggs
See the ONCE-OVER, QUICK-OVER

over a barrel *adv phr* In a helpless situation: *I knew enough about him that I had him over a barrel* [perhaps fr the tying *over a barrel* of a person about to be flogged]

overboard *adj* Very enthusiastic; strongly committed, usu in favor of something: *He's overboard for the new series*
See GO OVERBOARD

overcoat *n WW2 Air Forces* A parachute
See CHICAGO OVERCOAT, PINE OVERCOAT

over easy *adj phr* Of eggs, fried on both sides, lightly on one

over someone's **eyes** *See* PULL THE WOOL OVER someone's EYES

over one's **head** **1** *adj phr* Too difficult for one mentally; incomprehensible: *The concept's way over my head* **2** *adv phr* Better than one's usual standard; in an inspired way: *The team played over its head and by God they won*
See IN OVER one's HEAD

overkill *n* An excess, esp of needed action: *Going there twice would be overkill, don't you think?* [fr the use of the term in connection with the *killing* potential of nuclear arms and arsenals]

overseas cap *n phr Army* A garrison cap; = GO-TO-HELL CAP

overshoes *See* WIN THE PORCELAIN HAIRNET

over the coals *See* HAUL someone OVER THE COALS

over the fence *adv phr airline* On approach to the runway: *His speed over the fence was much too high* [fr the *fence* or other barrier at the end of an airport runway]

over the hill **1** *adj phr* Middle-aged or past middle age: *I turned forty yesterday, so I guess I'm over the hill/ a film for, and about, the over-the-hill gang*—Time **2** *adj phr* No longer effective; worn out; = AUSGESPIELT **3** *adj phr* (Variation: **hump** may replace **hill**) Most of the way to success or completion: *I think that you can say that we're over the hill*—Ebony **4** *adj phr Army* Absent without leave; = AWOL [first three senses fr the notion that one is no longer going upwards towards the summit, but is descending the far side of the imagined *hill*]
See DRIVE someone OVER THE HILL

over the long haul *See* FOR THE LONG HAUL

owled or **owl-eyed** or **owly-eyed** *adj* Drunk

owl show *n phr outdated show business* A performance, movie, etc, presented late at night: *an owl show in a fleabag*—SJ Perelman

the owner *n phr Navy* The captain of a naval vessel

one's **own hook** *See* ON one's OWN HOOK

one's **own horn** *See* TOOT one's OWN HORN

own time and own dime *See* ON one's OWN TIME AND OWN DIME

Owsley *See* AUGUSTUS OWSLEY

ox *See* BIG OX, DUMB OX

oyster *See* MOUNTAIN OYSTERS, the WORLD IS one's OYSTER

oyster-berry *n* A pearl

ozone or **zone** *n college students* A psychedelic condition, usu due to drugs: *He wasn't making much sense because he was way up there in a zone* [fr the notion of being as high as the *ozone* layer of the atmosphere]

P

P or **p** or **pee** *n* Any of the various units of currency whose designations begin with "p," like the Mexican peso or the Vietnamese piastre

See PEE

pace **See** OFF THE PACE

pack *v fr late 1800s* To carry, esp a weapon: *Are you packing a handgun, my friend?/ I looked and saw he was packing a badge*

See COLD PACK, NERDPACK, RAT PACK

package **1** *n* An attractive woman **2** *n* A large sum of money; =BUNDLE: *That must have cost a package* **3** *n* The collective terms of a contract or agreement: *The lefthander signed for a package including 10 million in two years, three McDonald's franchises, and the state of South Dakota* **4** *n* A particular combination or set: *That rental car is part of the vacation package* **5** *n* The manner and quality of presentation, the trappings and ornamentation, etc, of something: *It isn't what you've got, it's the package that impresses people* **6** *v:* He *never peddled his idea because he didn't know how to package it*

See NO PRIZE PACKAGE

package deal *n phr* An agreement, arrangement, purchase, etc, that comprises various separate items: *In their package deal you get hotel and breakfast but no tours*

packer **See** HEAT-PACKER

pack heat *v phr underworld* To carry a gun: *They knew all along that Elvis was packin' heat*—Albert Goldman/ *If you pack heat, you got to know what you're doing*—WR Burnett

pack in (or **up**) *v phr fr 1920s British* To cease; give up; retire from: *I intended to pack up playing all together*—Rolling Stone/ *told the FBI men he is "packing in"*—Robert M Yoder

pack it in *v phr fr 1920s British perhaps fr cockney* To stop; desist; give up what one is doing: *I decided to pack it in and move to New York*—David Standish/ *Who can fault them for not quite yet wanting to pack it in and quietly go home*—Saturday Review

a **pack of lies** *n phr* A set or series of lies; =COCK-AND-BULL STORY: *That whole eyewitness account is a damn pack of lies*

pack rat **1** *n phr* A person who cannot discard anything acquired; a compulsive keeper and storer **2** *n phr* A hotel porter; bellboy

pack the mail *v phr* =CARRY THE MAIL

packtripper *n* A person who travels with a rucksack or backpack; backpacker

pact **1** *n* An employment contract: *a settlement of his Metro pact*—Variety **2** *v:* MG *Pacts Gable* —Abel Green

pad **1** *n narcotics* A couch, bed, etc, on which one reclines while smoking opium **2** *n narcotics* A room, apartment, etc, where narcotics addicts and users gather to take drugs: *There were plenty of pads*—New York Post **3** *n 1960s counterculture fr musicians* A bed or place to sleep temporarily; =CRASH-PAD: *The girl shares her pad with other hippies*—Trans-Action/ *Longhairs found it difficult to get work and a pad*—Time **4** *n* One's home; residence: *He and I used to live in the same pad for two years*—Douglass Wallop **5** *n prostitutes* A prostitute's working room; =CRIB **6** *n* An automobile license plate: *The job was wearing California pads*—J Evans **7** *v* To increase the amount or length of: *I padded the story with some few flourishes/ He was padding his expense account*

See ACID PAD, BEAT PAD, CHINCH PAD, CRASH PAD, DAMPER PAD, KICK PAD, LAUNCHING PAD, ON THE PAD

the **pad** *police* **1** *n phr* Graft and bribe money taken and shared by police officers **2** *n phr* The list of those police officers who share graft and bribe money

See ON THE PAD

padding *n* Text added, often gratuitously and for mere bulk, to an essay, book, speech, etc

paddle **See** UP SHIT CREEK

paddlefoot *n WW2 Army* An infantry soldier; rifleman; =DOGFACE: *Murray was a paddlefoot in Europe*—Bill Mauldin

pad down **1** *v phr* To sleep; go to bed; =SACK OUT **2** *v phr* To search; =FRISK

pad duty *n phr WW2 Navy* Sleeping; reclining; =SACK DUTY

◄**paddy** or **Paddy**► **1** *n* An Irish person or person of Irish extraction **2** *n* (also **patty**) *black* A white person: *Even a drunken black shoeshine man could handle the likes of this paddy*—Joseph Wambaugh/ *called him a Technicolor Paddy* —National Review **3** *modifier: I know I can't be tight with this paddy boy*—Claude Brown **4** *n hoboes* A lazy, worthless person [fr the nickname of the given name *Patrick*]

paddy wagon *n phr* A police patrol wagon or van; =BLACK MARIA: *The cooperative family was being* *escorted into the paddy wagon*—Philadelphia Bulletin [fr *patrol wagon*]

pad out *v phr* To go to sleep; go to bed; = SACK OUT

padre (PAH dray) *n armed forces fr WW1 perhaps fr late 1800s British Navy* Any military chaplain [fr Spanish or Portuguese, "father, priest"]

pad room *n phr narcotics* A room where opium is smoked or other narcotics are used

paesan (pī ZAHN) *n* A fellow native of one's country or town; compatriot; = LANDSMAN [fr Italian dialect]

page *See* OP-ED PAGE, TAKE A PAGE FROM someone's BOOK

page turner *n phr* A book that is so absorbing that one reads it without stopping, although not necessarily for serious literary or intellectual quality: *a book that unquestionably deserves the description page turner*—New York Daily News

paid in *adj phr hoboes* Assured of a place to sleep

pail *n black* The stomach

pain *v* To annoy; irk; irritate
See FEEL NO PAIN

a **pain** **1** *n phr* Annoyance; irritation; = HEADACHE: *That clown gives me a pain/ Marvin is a real pain* **2** *n phr* = a PAIN IN THE ASS
See GIVE someone A PAIN

◁a **pain in the ass**▷ (or **neck**) *n phr* An annoying, obnoxious person or thing: *This proved a major pain in the ass as too many casual favorites fell to the wrong side*—Village Voice/ *Ain't he a pain in the neck, always bitching?*
See GIVE someone A PAIN

paint *n* Playing cards, esp picture cards
See RED PAINT, WAR PAINT

paint cards *n phr* Picture cards in a deck of playing cards; court cards

paint horse *See* PINTO

paint (or **varnish**) **remover** **1** *n phr* Raw and inferior whiskey **2** *n phr* Coffee, esp a very strong or bitter brew

paint the town or **paint the town red** *v phr fr late 1800s cowboys* To go on a wild spree; carouse: *Well, sport, let's go out and paint the town a new color*—Hal Boyle

pair *n* A woman's breasts ● Regarded as offensive by many women
See BLINDFOLD A PAIR

a **pair up** *n phr lunch counter* Two eggs fried on one side only

paisano (pī ZAHN oh) *n fr middle 1800s Western* = PAESAN [fr Spanish, "countryman"]

pajamas *See* the CAT'S MEOW

pal *n fr late 1600s British* A friend, esp a very close male friend; boon companion; = BUDDY: *has many devoted friends, but he is nobody's "pal"*—New York Times [fr Romany *phral, phal* "brother, friend," ultimately fr Sanskrit *bhratr* "brother"]

palace **1** *n railroad* A caboose **2** *n* A grand venue for something ● Always ironically used of a fairly seedy though perhaps ornate place: *porn palace/ movie palace*
See FIVE-SIDED PUZZLE PALACE

pal around *v phr* To be pals; consort as pals: *the people he palled around with*—Ira Wolfert/ *I used to see those two palling around*

pale *n black* A white person; = GRAY

paled or **paled out** *adj* or *adj phr Canadian teenagers* Completely exhausted, esp by drugs or liquor; = WASTED

paleface **1** *n black homosexuals* A white homosexual **2** *n* A circus clown

palimony **1** *n fr late 1970s* Money awarded, property shared, etc, when an unmarried couple separate **2** *modifier: a much-heralded palimony suit* [fr *pal + alimony;* coined for or at least popularized by a lawsuit against the film star Lee Marvin]

pally or **pallie** **1** *adj* Very friendly; affectionate and familiar; = PALSY-WALSY **2** *n* = PAL

palm **1** *v* To conceal a playing card against the palm in order to use it in a gambling hand: *It was five cards that he palmed, three aces and a pair of queens*—Calder Willingham **2** *v* To conceal anything from opponents or competitors
See GREASE someone's PALM

palm something **off** *v phr* To bestow something inferior as if it were of good quality; foist; fob off: *He palmed the leaky old place off like it was the Ritz*

palm oil *n phr* Money used for bribery and graft

palooka or **paluka** or **palooker** (pə LOO Kə) **1** *n fr 1920s* A mediocre or inferior boxer: *a paluka who leads with his right*—Dashiell Hammett **2** *n* A professional wrestler **3** *n* Any large and stupid man [origin unknown; perhaps fr Spanish *peluca* "wig," used as an insult]

palsy-walsy (PAL zee WAL zee) **1** *adj* Very friendly; = CHUMMY: *breezy, palsy-walsy with Baskerville, who's not a breezy type*—Nation **2** *n: Hey, palsy-walsy, what's going down?*

pan[1] **1** *n fr late 1700s* The face; = MUG: *too great for them to keep their pans shut*—Jerome Weidman **2** *v fr early 1900s* To criticize severely and adversely; derogate harshly; = ROAST: *The Daily Worker panned his first novel*—Leonard Lyons **3** *n: an out-and-out pan*—Billy Rose
See DEADPAN, FLASH IN THE PAN, ON THE PAN

pan[2] or **pam** *movie & television studio* **1** *v* To move the camera across a visual field to give a panoramic effect or follow something moving **2** *n: He used a pan to show the milieu* **3** *modifier: a pan shot* [fr *panorama*]

Panama (or **Mexican**) **red** or **Mexican** *n phr* or *n narcotics* A type, esp a choice, potent grade, of marijuana

pancake turner *n phr 1940s radio studio* A person who plays phonograph records on the radio; = DISC JOCKEY: *pancake turner on the Green web*—C Macon

panhandle *v fr early 1900s* To beg, esp by accosting people on the street: *The boys deal drugs or panhandle, even become male prostitutes*—Time [apparently because beggars held out tin *pans* in requesting alms]

panhandler *n fr late 1800s* A person who begs, esp by accosting people on the street; beggar: *This* *pan handler came up to me and braced me*—John O'Hara

panic 1 *v* To become frightened and confused, esp suddenly; =FLIP: *He panicked and dropped the ball* **2** *v* To get a strong favorable reaction, esp to get loud laughter from an audience; =FRACTURE: *Mr Todd knows how to panic the rubes*—Brooks Atkinson **3** *n* A very funny person; an effective comedian; =a STITCH

panic button *See* HIT THE PANIC BUTTON

panic rack *n phr* Air Force A pilot's ejection seat: *The jockey is in the panic rack and ready to go* —Associated Press

panky or **pank** *See* HANKY-PANKY

panman *n* A drummer in a West Indian steel band, whose players strike xylophonelike instruments made from the ends of steel containers such as oil drums

pan out *v phr fr middle 1800s* To be productive; succeed; =PAY OFF: *None of his great schemes panned out/ Ryan thought about what he'd be living with if the FBI profile panned out*—Philadelphia [fr the practice of *panning* gold in river sediments]

◁**pansified**▷ (PAN zi fīd) *adj* Effeminate; =SISSIFIED

◁**pansy**▷ *fr 1920s* **1** *n* A male homosexual; =QUEEN: *if someone had bluntly said that her friends...were pansies*—Philip Wylie/ *seen neighborhood rowdies beat up a "pansy"*—Saturday Review **2** *n* A weak or effeminate male; =LILY, SISSY **3** *adj: Stage and screen voices in recent years have become so pansy*—HW Seaman/ *You think it's a pansy drink because your faggot hairdresser goes for it?*—WT Tyler/ *Yeagley utters those pansy words with just the right amount of venom*—Washingtonian

◁**panther piss**▷ (or **sweat**) or **panther** *n phr* or *n* Raw and inferior whiskey; =ROTGUT

pantry *n prizefight fr early 1900s* The stomach; =BREADBASKET: *another real fine left to the pantry* —R Starnes

pants *See* ANTS, CATCH someone WITH someone's PANTS DOWN, CHARM THE PANTS OFF someone, CREAM one's JEANS, DUST someone's PANTS, FANCY PANTS, FLY BY THE SEAT OF one's PANTS, FUDGE one's PANTS, GET THE LEAD OUT, HAVE LEAD IN one's PANTS, HIGH WATERS, HOT PANTS, RAGGEDY-ASS, SEAT-OF-THE-PANTS, SHIT one's PANTS, SISSY PANTS, SMARTY-PANTS, SUGAR PANTS, TIN PANTS

pants-leg *n 1930s aviators* A cloth wind indicator as at an airport; windsock

the **pants off** *adv phr* To the utmost; to an extreme degree: *I'm going to sue the pants off you this time, meathead*—Washington Post [probably extended fr *charm the pants off*]

pants rabbit *n phr hoboes* A louse

pantywaist *n* A weak or effeminate male; =PANSY: *The hurt...pantywaist ran off a number of copies of his letter*—Bernard DeVoto [fr a child's garment with short *pants* buttoned to the *waist* of a shirt]

pap *n* Father; =PAPPY

papa *n esp black* A male lover; =DADDY

See SWEET MAN

paper 1 *n* A forged or worthless check **2** *v* To use or pass counterfeit money or worthless checks; =LAY PAPER: *papered Queens and Long Island with...bum checks*—New York Daily News **3** *n* theater fr late 1800s A pass or free ticket; =ANNIE OAKLEY **4** *v* theater fr late 1800s To give out free tickets in order to get a large audience: *The show was not doing well, so they papered the theater* **5** *v* police To write traffic and parking tickets: *The sergeant complained that the patrolmen were not papering enough* **6** *n* narcotics A packet of narcotics; =BAG

See BAD PAPER, LAY PAPER, ON PAPER, PEDDLE one's PAPERS, WALKING PAPERS, WALLPAPER

paper ass *See* MAN WITH A PAPER ASS

paper bag *See* CAN'T FIGHT one's WAY OUT OF A PAPER BAG

paper-belly *n* A person who cannot drink straight liquor, or who grimaces after drinking

paper chase *n phr fr British* An intense searching and collation of files, books, documents, etc, esp for the needs of bureaucratic pomp ● Popularized in the US as the title of a film and a TV series, where the **paper** was a Harvard Law School degree [fr a mid-19th-century game of hare and hounds in which the quarry would leave a trail of scraps of *paper*]

paper dolls *See* CUT OUT DOLLS

paperhanger or **paper-pusher** *n underworld* A person who passes counterfeit money or worthless checks: *The FBI's suspect was a master paperhanger, the last of a breed*—Philadelphia

paper house *n phr theater* An audience admitted mainly on free tickets

paper over *v phr* To conceal or gloss over; fail to deal with: *If the tiff were nothing but a clash of personalities...it might be quickly papered over*—Newsweek

paper profits *n phr* Monetary gains recognizable by accounting but not realized in palpable money or goods

paper-pusher or **paper-shuffler** *n* An office worker or bureaucratic functionary whose work is neither very useful nor consequential, and who also cannot be held responsible: *He said he's fired about 10,000 paper-pushers in the Navy procurement office*

papers 1 *n black* A marriage license or certificate **2** *n narcotics* Cigarette rolling papers, used to make marijuana cigarettes: *I've got the dope if you've got the papers*

See CUT someone's PAPERS, PEDDLE one's PAPERS, PUT one's PAPERS IN, WALKING PAPERS

paper tiger *n phr* A menacing person or thing that in fact lacks force; a blusterer: *doing battle with a paper tiger when he aims his wrath at the white liberal*—New York Times/ *suggested that the 23-year-old running back was a paper tiger*—New York Times [fr the Chinese expression *tsuh lao fu* "paper tiger" given currency by Mao Zedong]

paperweight *n railroad* An office or ticket clerk

pappy *n* Father; =PAP

pappy guy *n phr* An elderly man: *what we would have regarded as pappy guys, greased for the skids* —Robert Ruark

parachute *See* GOLDEN PARACHUTE

parade *See* RAIN ON someone's PARADE

paradise *See* ETHIOPIAN PARADISE

paralyzed *adj* Very drunk

parboiled *adj* Drunk

pard *n fr middle 1800s cowboys* Friend; partner; = PAL

pardon me all to hell *See* EXCUSE ME ALL TO HELL

pardon my French *interj* An exclamation of apology for the use of profane or taboo language: *That Goddamned...pardon my French*—Tennessee Williams

par for the course *n phr* What is to be expected; normal though nasty: *He had to take a little crap from the clerk, but that's par for the course/ She didn't get the answer she wanted but that's par for the course*

park **1** *v* To put or place; locate: *Where shall I park this machine?/ Park yourself anywhere, I'll be right back* **2** *v outdated teenagers* To kiss and caress; = NECK: *"parking" or "necking" in a dance* —Philadelphia Bulletin
See BALLPARK, BALLPARK FIGURE, PICKLE PARK

parking lot *See* PORTABLE PARKING LOT

park one *v phr baseball* To hit a home run: *A cheer would go up across the street, and someone who had a transistor radio would holler, "Mantle just parked one"*—New York Times

parlay **1** *v horse-racing fr late 1800s* To bet money in a series of wagers where the winnings of one are automatically placed on the next, etc **2** *n: He won a three-horse parlay* **3** *v* To build or increase something from a small initial outlay or possession: *She parlayed her dimples into movie superstardom* [fr *paralee* or *parlee*, an early-19th-century faro term fr Italian *parole* "words, promises"]

parlayed *See* LAID, RELAID, AND PARLAYED

parley-voo *v fr WW1 Army* To speak, esp a foreign language: *She wondered if he parley-vooed Chinese* [fr French *parlez-vous* "do you speak"]

parlor *n railroad* A caboose
See HORSE ROOM, MASSAGE PARLOR, RAP CLUB, RUB PARLOR, SAWDUST PARLOR

parlor pink *n phr esp 1930s & 40s* A mildly radical socialist; political liberal

parole *See* BACKGATE PAROLE, BUSH PAROLE

the **parson's nose** *See* the POPE'S NOSE

part *See* BIT

party **1** *n* A person: *the party there in the corner* **2** *n* A group of people: *We have a party of six for dinner* **3** *n* A bout of sex play or sexual activity **4** *v* To go to or give parties: *I always party a lot over the holidays* **5** *v* To enjoy oneself drinking, chatting, dancing, etc; be energetically social: *We partied all night in about eight clubs*
See BLAST PARTY, COLD-MEAT PARTY, DRAG PARTY, GI PARTY, HAVE A PARTY, HEN PARTY, KICK PARTY, NECK-TIE PARTY, POP PARTY, POT PARTY, STAG, TAILGATE PARTY

party hat *n phr* The array of lights on the roof of a police car or emergency vehicle; = GUMBALL

party-pooper or **party poop** **1** *n or n phr* The first person or couple to leave a party; a person who ends a joyous occasion **2** *n or n phr* A morose, pessimistic person; = KILLJOY, WET BLANKET: *No one can call Mr Bulganin and Mr Kruschev party poopers*—Edmund Wilson/ *What a party poop you are today, Sally*—Anne Bernays

pash *esp 1920s* **1** *n* Passion: *insisted that he get some "pash" into it*—P Marks **2** *n* One's current absorbing love object: *She's my pash this week* **3** *adj* Passionate: *That isn't as pash as some of the poems*—F Scott Fitzgerald

pass **1** *n hoboes* A passenger train **2** *v* To be thought to be something one is not, esp to be thought white when one is actually black: *the oldest daughter, so fair she could pass*—A Lomax **3** *v* To suffice or be adequate, only just barely: *It's not great pasta, but it'll pass* **4** *n phr* A sexual advance; = PROPOSITION **5** *v* To decline to do something, take something, etc: *When it comes to telling him flatly, I pass/ I'll pass on the French fries, but take the onions*
See MAKE A PASS AT someone

passion *See* WITH A PURPLE PASSION

passion pit *esp students* **1** *n phr* A drive-in movie theater: *taking his buxom daughter off to the local passion pit*—Stephen King **2** *n phr* A room used for seduction: *some minor-league Don Juan's passion pit*—Stephen King

passout **1** *n hawkers* A distribution: *When I have made a pass-out, I take the money*—JT Flynn **2** *n* A person who has passed out: *finding yourself with an 18-year-old passout on your hands*—Esquire's Handbook for Hosts

pass out **1** *v phr* To lose consciousness; faint; go to sleep, esp from drinking too much liquor **2** *v phr* To die: *He left us a lot of jack when he passed out*—P Marks

pass the buck *v phr fr early 1900s* To refer a problem or responsibility to someone else, esp to a higher authority; decline to take action: *We chickened out and passed the buck to the dean* [fr poker games where one would *pass the buck*, usu a pocketknife with a *buckhorn* handle, on to the next person, thereby passing the deal on]

pass the hat **1** *v phr* To ask for contributions of money; collect money from a group: *We passed the hat until we had her plane fare* **2** *v phr* To beg; solicit charity

pass something **up** *v phr fr late 1800s* To choose not to take, attend, etc; = GIVE someone or something A MISS: *I guess I'll pass up the concert tonight*

paste **1** *v fr middle 1800s British* To hit; strike very hard: *She grabbed the broom and pasted me* **2** *v* To defeat decisively; trounce; = CLOBBER: *The Jets got pasted* [origin unknown; perhaps an alteration of earlier *baste* "strike, trounce," of obscure origin and preserved in *lambaste*]

pasteboard 1 *n* A ticket of admission; =BOARD: *He studied the coveted pasteboard*—P Jones **2** *n* A business card or calling card **3** *n* A playing card: *Okay, shuffle the pasteboards and let's commence*

paste on *v phr* To blame or make an accusation: *two...things he could paste on them firemen*—Ira Wolfert

past post *adv phr* horse-racing After a race has ended

pasture 1 *n* The outfield of a baseball field **2** *n* A baseball park
See OUTER GARDEN, PUT SOMEONE OR SOMETHING OUT TO PASTURE

pasty or **pastie** (PAY stee) *n* A small circular bit of cloth, often sparkling, covering the nipple of a woman dancer in a burlesque show or other lewd display

patch *See* STRAWBERRY PATCH, TEARING UP THE PEA PATCH

◁**pato**▷ (PAH toh) *n* A male homosexual [fr Spanish]

patoot or **patootie** (pə To͞oT) *n* The buttocks; fundament; =ASS: *You hear with your patoot, curlylocks*—Earl Thompson/ *You can bet your patootie I'm going to stay/ tutelage in the honorable art of not making a horse's patoot of yourself*—Toronto Star [origin unknown; perhaps fr dialect *tout* "buttocks," fr Middle English, pronounced *toot*, and altered to conform with *sweet patootie* by folk etymology]

patootie or **sweet patootie 1** *n* or *n phr* One's girlfriend or boyfriend; sweetheart: *tell their patooties how pretty they are*—New York Confidential **2** *n* or *n phr* A young woman: *a batch of pretty-panned patooties*—G Dixon [perhaps fr a play on *sweet patootie* suggested by *sweetheart* and *potato* as used, like *tomato*, to mean a person]

patrol *See* YARD PATROL

patsy *fr early 1900s* **1** *n* A victim; dupe; =SUCKER: *a patsy, a quick push, a big softie*—WR Burnett/ *But to retain lawyers is clear proof that you're a patsy*—Saul Bellow **2** *n* A person who takes the blame for a crime, who is put up against a superior opponent in order to lose, etc; =FALL GUY [origin unknown; perhaps fr *Pasqualino*, the Italian diminutive for *Pasquale* just as *Patsy* is the American English diminutive. *Pasqualino* is used to designate a vulnerable, weak, and small boy or man, and is probably based in this sense at least partly on the relation between *Pasqua* "Easter," the derivative names *Pasquale* and *Pasqualino*, and the notion of the Pascal sacrifice or Pascal lamb as an innocent victim]

pattern *See* IN A HOLDING PATTERN

◁**patty**▷ *n* Hispanics A white person; =ANGLO [probably fr black *paddy*]
See PADDY

patzer or **potzer** (PAHT zər) *n* A mediocre but often enthusiastic chess player [probably fr Yiddish; see *potsky*]

the **pavement** *See* POUND THE PAVEMENT

paw 1 *n* A hand: *You let me get my paws on the money*—Raymond Chandler **2** *v* To touch and handle, esp in a crude sexual way
See NORTHPAW, SOUTHPAW

pax *n* A passenger: *There were twenty pax listed for the trip*—John Ball [apparently derived fr *passenger* as *prexy* is fr *president*]

pay *See* BAD PAY, GOOD PAY, HELL TO PAY

payday *See* MAKE A PAYDAY

pay dirt *n phr* Profit and success: *I'll try a fast-food franchise, where there's sure to be paydirt*
See HIT PAY DIRT

pay one's **dues** *v phr* To serve and suffer such that one deserves what good comes to one; =GO THROUGH THE MILL: *I hate it when a guy who hasn't paid his dues gets it all*

payoff 1 *n* underworld Payment, esp of bribery, graft, etc: *The rogues hung around waiting for their payoff* **2** *n* fr 1920s The final outcome or bit of information, esp when it is surprising or amusing: *OK, here's the payoff, she's the Albanian consul!*

pay off 1 *v phr* underworld To give someone bribe money, blackmail money, or the like: *We'll have to pay them off handsomely to keep them quiet* **2** *v phr* To bring in profit; succeed; pay **3** *v phr* To discharge; =CAN, FIRE: *Any more of this and I'll pay off the whole bunch of you*

payola *n* fr 1930s Graft; extortion money; bribery, esp that paid by recording companies to disc jockeys for playing their records on the radio [coined probably fr *payoff* and the ending of *Pianola*, trade name of an automatic piano-playing device, or *Victrola*, trade name of a gramophone]

pay the freight *v phr* To pay for; compensate for; bear the expense of; =PICK UP THE TAB: *We may have to "pay the freight for well-meant efforts at improvement"*—New Yorker

pay through the nose *v phr* To pay exorbitantly; give too much in recompense

pay up *v phr* To pay; settle one's account: *Pay up and be done with it*

pay-wing *n* baseball A pitcher's throwing arm

pazzazza (pə ZAZ ə) *n* A piazza: *young woman is sitting on the pazzazza*—H Witwer

PC *n* airline A pilot check flight or ride, where a pilot's continued qualification to fly is periodically tested

PCP *n* narcotics Phencyclidine, an animal tranquilizer smoked as a narcotic; =ANGEL DUST

p'd *See* PISSED OFF

pdq *adv* Pretty damn quick

pea *See* SWEET PEA

peabrain or **peahead** *n* A stupid person

peacenik *n* esp 1960s & 70s A member of a peace movement; pacifist; antiwar demonstrator

peach[1] *v* fr 1400s British To inform; =SQUEAL [fr *appeach* "lodge an accusation"]

peach[2] *fr middle 1800s* **1** *n* An attractive young woman: *She really was a "peach"*—SA Clark **2** *n* Any remarkable, admirable, amiable, or attractive person: *You're a peach*—Dorothy Parker **3** *n* Anything superior or admirable: *The hotel was a peach*

peacherino *n fr early 1900s* =PEACH[2]

peachy or **peachy-keen** *adj* Excellent; wonderful; =GREAT, NEAT: *this president's political health, which Wirthlin thinks is peachy*—George Will

peanut 1 *n fr early 1800s* A small or trivial person; something insignificant **2** *adj: a peanut operation/ his peanut mind*

peanut gallery *n phr fr late 1800s* The topmost rows of a theater

peanut roaster *n phr railroad* A small locomotive

peanuts *n* A small amount of money; a trivial sum; =NICKELS AND DIMES: *They got you working for peanuts*—Budd Schulberg/ *a ten-grand fix? That's gotta be peanuts*—WT Tyler
See THAT AIN'T HAY

pea patch *See* TEARING UP THE PEA PATCH

pearl-diver *n* A person who washes dishes, esp in a restaurant

pea-shooter 1 *n* A firearm, esp one so-called by a person who scorns its small caliber **2** *n WW2 Army Air Force* A fighter pilot or plane

pea soup (or **souper**) *n phr* A thick fog

peat *See* PETE

pebble on the beach *n phr fr late 1800s* A person, esp as reduced in significance by being of a numerous sort

pec *n* A pectoral muscle: *All the male weight lifters love her a bushel and a pec*—Playboy/ *dirt cheap and pecs that won't quit*—Armistead Maupin

peck ◁**1**▷ *n black* =PECKERWOOD **2** *n railroad* A very short period for a meal **3** *v* To eat, esp to eat very little and choosily **4** *n teenagers* Food **5** *n* A perfunctory kiss: *She gave him a friendly peck and got back to work*

◁**pecker**▷ *n* The penis

◁**peckerhead**▷ *n* A despicable person; =ASSHOLE, JERK: *Do you hear me, peckerhead?*—Andrew Coburn

◁**pecker tracks**▷ *n phr* Traces on a man's pants showing that he has had an orgasm or near orgasm

◁**peckerwood**▷ *black* **1** *n* A poor Southern white, esp a farmer; =CRACKER, REDNECK **2** *n* Any white Southern man: *Any white man from the South is a "Peckerwood"*—Stephen Longstreet [fr rural black use of the red-headed *woodpecker*, with dialect inversion of the word elements as a symbol for white persons in contrast with the blackbird as a symbol for themselves; the red head may be the symbolic base, suggesting *redneck*]

pecking order *n phr* In any organization or society, the hierarchy of status requiring that those below show respect for those above, etc [fr the behavior of chickens that shows such a stratification of privilege]

peckings (or **pecks**) *n fr black* Food

peckish *adj fr late 1700s British* Hungry

pedal *See* PUT THE PEDAL TO THE METAL, SOFT-PEDAL

peddle out *v phr* To sell one's personal belongings, esp to a second-hand store

peddle one's **papers** *v phr* To go about one's business ● Often an irritated command that one leave the speaker alone: *I told him to go peddle his papers*—Hal Boyle/ *He had been told to peddle his papers elsewhere*—Billy Rose

peddler *n hoboes* A local or slow freight train
See ASS PEDDLER, FLESH-PEDDLER, PILL-PUSHER

pee 1 *v* To urinate; =PISS, WHIZZ **2** *n* Urine
See P

peed off *See* PISSED OFF

pee-eye *n* A pimp [fr pronouncing the first two letters of *pimp*]

peejays *n* Pajamas; =PJS

peek *v horse-racing* To win third place in a horse race; =SHOW: *He bet on Clammy Crumpet to peek*

peekaboo *adj* Made of a sheer fabric; transparent; =SEE-THROUGH: *Peekaboo blouses are not the most calming of garments*

peek freak *n phr* A voyeur; Peeping Tom

peel 1 *v* To undress; strip **2** *v* =PEEL OUT

peeler *n* A striptease dancer; =STRIPPER: *grinders, peelers, and bumpers*—Louis Sobol
See BRONCO BUSTER

peel out *v phr fr hot rodders* To leave quickly; =SPLIT [probably fr the Air Force term *peel off* "break away fr a formation, esp fr one end and in a dive," fr 1920s British Royal Air Force use]

◁**peenie**▷ *n* The penis
See POUND one's PEENIE

peep *n* A word; a sound; the least utterance: *If I hear a peep out of you, you've had it*

peeper *n* A private detective; =PRIVATE EYE: *and don't bother to call your house peeper*—Raymond Chandler
See HEADSHRINKER

peepers 1 *n fr middle 1800s underworld* The eyes: *If anything was wrong with my peepers the army wouldn't of took me*—Nelson Algren/ *staring into the distance with those big, wet peepers*—Village Voice **2** *n* A pair of sunglasses; =SHADES: *I'd come through the employee door with one of my peepers on*—D James

peep show 1 *n phr* A supposedly private view, usu through a hole in the wall, of some forbidden sexual activity **2** *n phr* =LEG SHOW

peet *See* PETE

peeties *n gamblers fr late 1800s* Loaded dice [fr *repeaters*]

peeve 1 *n fr early 1900s* A cause of annoyance: *You probably have a long list of peeves* **2** *v: That crap really peeves me* **3** *n* A grudge; continued hostility: *having a peeve on a poor kid*—Budd Schulberg [by back formation fr *peeved*, which in turn derives by back formation fr *peevish*, fr Middle English *peivish*, "perverse, wayward, capricious," perhaps fr Latin *perversus*]
See PET PEEVE

peeved or **peeved off** *adj* or *adj phr fr early 1900s* Annoyed; irritated; irked: *He got peeved*—Billy Rose

pee-warmer *n* Something pleasant and agreeable: *The last issue...is a pee-warmer. I sure got a kick out of it*—Nevada

peewee *n* A short or small person, animal, etc: *That peewee doesn't scare me*

Peewee *n* Nickname for a short or small person

peezy *See* JEEZ

peg 1 *v* To identify; classify; pick out; = BUTTON DOWN: *I could peg a joint like that from two miles away*—John O'Hara **2** *v* To taper or bind a pair of trousers at the lower end: *Pants must be pegged to fit snugly around the ankle*—Max Shulman **3** *n* baseball A throw, esp a hard one: *His peg missed and the runner scored* **4** *v*: *He pegged it sharply to first*
See ON THE PEG, SQUARE PEG, TAKE someone DOWN A PEG

◁**peg boy**▷ **1** *n phr* outdated merchant marine A boy used as a catamite by a man, esp a sailor **2** *n phr* A male homosexual who takes the passive role in anal sex [fr the notion that sailors' young catamites were forced to sit on *pegs* to dilate their anuses]

Peggy *n* hoboes A one-legged man

peg leg 1 *n phr* A person who wears a wooden leg **2** *modifier: Watch me pass that peg-leg gimp*—Nelson Algren

peg legs *n phr* Pants which are tapered at the ankle

peg out *v phr* fr middle 1800s To die: *Harrison...actually pegged out in 1841*—HL Mencken [fr the ending of play in cribbage by *pegging*]

pegs *n* Legs; = PINS: *He was wobbly on his pegs*

Pelican *n* fr middle 1800s A native or resident of Louisiana [the flag of Louisiana shows a *pelican* feeding her young]

pellet *n* The ball used in a ball game: *Berra...searched the premises for the pellet*—Asociated Press

pelter *fr middle 1800s* **1** *n* An inferior horse; = HAY-BURNER **2** *n* A fast horse

pen *n* A prison of any sort, esp a penitentiary
See BULLPEN, HEN-PEN, PIGPEN, POISON-PEN LETTER, PUSH A PEN

pencil *See* HAVE LEAD IN one's PENCIL

pencil-pusher (or **-driver** or **-shover**) *n* An office worker, esp a clerk, bookkeeper, or the like; = DESK JOCKEY: *The number of pencil pushers and typists has increased*—S Dawson

penguin 1 *n* Air Force fr 1920s A nonflying member of an air force; = KIWI **2** *n* movie studio An actor who wears a full-dress suit as part of a crowd scene **3** *n* A nun ● Used esp by Catholic parochial school students

penicillin *See* JEWISH PENICILLIN

penman 1 *n* underworld A forger **2** *n* teenagers A student who signs his or her parents' names to made-up excuses

pennant *See* IRISH PENNANT

Pennsy *n* The Pennsylvania Railroad

Pennsylvania salve *n phr* hoboes Apple butter

penny *n* teenagers A police officer [fr a play on *copper*]

penny ante 1 *n phr* A trivial transaction; a cheap offer, arrangement, etc **2** *adj: I despised his penny-ante ideas*

penny-pincher *n* A stingy person; miser; = TIGHTWAD

penny pool *n phr* A paltry game or affair; = PENNY ANTE: *I told him to shove his deal, it was penny pool*

See PLAY PENNY POOL

pennyweight *n* outdated underworld Jewelry, esp diamonds

pennyweighter *n* outdated underworld A jewel thief or shoplifter

pen-pusher *n* = PENCIL-PUSHER

pen yen *n phr* narcotics Opium [probably a shortening of Cantonese Chinese *nga pun-yin* "opium"; see *hop²*]

peola *n* black A very light-skinned black person, esp a young woman

people *n* A person: *She's very nice people*
See the BEAUTIFUL PEOPLE, BOAT PEOPLE, FLOWER CHILDREN, FREE PEOPLE, HARE KRISHNA KIDS, JESUS PEOPLE, NIGHT PEOPLE, ROAD PEOPLE, STREET PEOPLE

the **people** *n phr* narcotics Narcotics dealers on a large or wholesale scale; = KILO CONNECTION

Peoria *n* hoboes Soup, esp a very thin and meager soup [fr humorous mispronunciation of *puree*]
See PLAY IN PEORIA

pep 1 *n* fr early 1900s Energy; vitality; = PISS AND VINEGAR, PIZZAZZ **2** *modifier: pep talk/ pep pill* [fr *pepper*]

pepped out *adj phr* Exhausted; sapped: *I'm tired and pepped out*—F Scott Fitzgerald

pepper 1 *n* fr early 1900s Energy; vitality; = PEP: *The old moral support is what gives we players the old pepper*—Westbrook Pegler **2** *v* baseball To throw a baseball very hard; = BURN **3** *n* baseball A fast and hard session of pitch-and-catch; = BURNOUT **4** *v* To hit a baseball, golf ball, etc, hard: *She peppered it about 80 yards* ◀**5**▶ *n* A Mexican or person of Mexican extraction
See SALT AND PEPPER

pepper-upper *n* A thing, food, drink, person, etc, that imparts pep; stimulant: *"Say fellows," said a uniformed pepper-upper to a bunch of GI assault troops*—M Mayer

pep pill *n phr* Any amphetamine pill; = UPPER

peppy *adj* Energetic; vital; = ZINGY

pep rally *n phr* A meeting where the participants are stimulated to some activity, harder effort, etc: *a Republican pep rally in downtown Grosse Pointe*

pep talk *n phr* A hortatory speech, usu given by a team coach or other leader: *I always had to give myself a pep talk before I went out to sing*—Peggy Lee

pep up *v phr* To stimulate; excite; energize; = JAZZ something UP

perambulator *n* railroad A caboose

perc *See* PERK

percentage *n* Profit or advantage: *I don't see any percentage in doing it that way*

percenter *See* FIVE-PERCENTER, TEN-PERCENTER

perch *v* To kiss and caress; = NECK: *Now you may "smooch" or "perch"*—E Eldridge [fr the activity of lovebirds]
See COME OFF one's PERCH

percolate 1 *v* fr 1920s To run smoothly and well: *The little engine was percolating nicely* **2** *v* To penetrate; permeate: *It was percolating through my mind that maybe I should leave* **3** *v* 1930s jive talk To saunter; stroll; = EASE, OOZE: *I'll percolate* *over and ask the cop* [all senses fr the coffee-making device; sense of "run well," for example, fr the steady cheery bubbling of the coffee-maker]

percolator *n black* A party where one sells drinks and food to friends in order to pay one's rent; = RENT PARTY: *You could always get together and charge a few coins and have a percolator*—Stephen Longstreet

Percy or **Percy boy** or **Percy-pants** *n* or *n phr* An effeminate male; = LILY, PANSY: *He never prated about his Oedipus complex like the Percy boys*—SJ Perelman

per each *adv phr* For each; apiece; = a THROW: *Those are $8 per each, to you* [fr a humorous substitution of Latin *per* for *for* in imitation of pretentious business use]

perform *v* To do the sex act; function sexually: *She didn't love him, but liked the way he performed*

perk¹ or **perc 1** *n cowboys & hoboes* Percolated coffee **2** *v fr 1920s* To run smoothly and well; = PERCOLATE: *The project's perking now*

perk² or **perc** *n fr early 1800s British* Extra money, privileges, fringe benefits, etc, pertaining to a job or assignment: *His men were delighted to be in Afghanistan, he said, mostly because of the perks* —Time/ *Some perks belong, though, to all unwilling celibates*—WH Auden [fr *perquisite*]

perk (or **perc**) **along 1** *v phr fr 1920s* To run smoothly and easily: *The outboard's perking along sweetly* **2** *v phr 1930s jive talk* To move at a relaxed pace; = EASE, MOSEY: *I'm not hurrying, just perking along* [fr the persistent and even sound of a coffee *percolator*]

perker-upper *n* = PEPPER-UPPER

Perkmeister *n* An official in charge of favors, jobs, patronage, etc, in a political organization: *after two years as executive aide to "Perkmeister" John FW Rogers, who administers all agencies in the executive office of the president*—Washingtonian [fr *perk* + German *Meister* "master"]

perk (or **perc**) **over** *v phr fr 1920s* To run slowly; idle; = TICK OVER [see *perk along*]

perk up 1 *v phr* To stimulate; invigorate: *Gotta perk up this class* **2** *v phr fr middle 1600s* To recuperate; recover; gain energy: *He's perking up after a two-week illness/ Perk up. We're almost done* [origin uncertain; perhaps related to *perch*, and semantically to the notion of being placed high]

perky *adj fr middle 1800s* Energetic and jaunty; lively; = CHIPPER

perp *n police* A criminal engaged in a specific crime: *The perp stood up, stepped back, took out a handgun and fired at least two shots*—New York Daily News [shortened form of *perpetrator*]

persnickety or **pernickety** *adj fr early 1800s British* Overfastidious; finical; fussy [fr Scots dialect, perhaps fr *particular*]

persuader *n fr middle 1800s British* Any weapon, esp a gun; = HEAT

per usual *See* AS PER USUAL

pesky *adj fr middle 1700s* Vexatious; annoying; pesty

peso (PAY soh) *n* A dollar [fr Mexican Spanish]

pet 1 *v fr early 1900s* To kiss and caress: *Pet? My God!*—P Marks/ *torrid hugging, smooching, and petting*—Calder Willingham **2** *n* Darling; sweetheart; = DOLL: *It's you, pet! How frightfully tickety-boo!*
See HEAVY PETTING

pete *n* (also **pete-box** or **peet** or **peat**) *underworld fr early 1900s fr British* A safe; = CRIB [fr *peter¹*]

Pete *See* FOR THE LOVE OF PETE, PISTOL PETE, SNEAKY PETE

pete-man *n underworld* A criminal who specializes in opening safes; = BOX MAN

peter¹ *n outdated underworld* A safe; strongbox; vault [fr 17th-century British criminal slang, origin unknown]

peter² *n narcotics* = KNOCKOUT DROPS

◁**peter³**▷ *n* The penis [fr the association with *pee* "urine"]

◁**peter-eater**▷ *n* A person who does fellatio, esp homosexually; = COCKSUCKER

Peter Funk *n phr fr early 1800s* An auctioneer's covert accomplice, who bids up the prices; = SHILL [perhaps fr early sense of *funk* "smoke," and the notion that these persons were "blowing smoke" into the eyes of honest bidders, to confuse and deceive them]

peterman *n outdated underworld* A safe-cracker; = PETE-MAN: *the petermen of half a century ago*—E DeBaun

peter out *v phr fr middle 1800s* To become exhausted; dwindle away in strength, amount, etc: *They ran well the first mile or so, then petered out* [origin unknown; fr mining jargon, and perhaps fr French *peter* "flatulate, explode weakly"; compare *fizzle*]

petnapper *n* A person who steals pets, esp valuable creatures for sale or ransom; = DOGNAPPER

pet peeve *n phr esp 1920s & 30s* One's particular and most cherished dislike or annoyance: *long been one of my pet peeves*—Word Study

petrified *adj* Drunk; = OSSIFIED, STONED

petting *n* The activity of those who pet: *Petting is necking with territorial concessions*—Frederick Morton
See HEAVY PETTING

petting party *n phr* A spell or session of fondling and caressing: *great American phenomenon, the "petting party"*—F Scott Fitzgerald

pez *n bop musicians* A head of hair; mustache or goatee

pfft (FəT) *adj* Finished; dissolved: *Their seemingly happy marriage is pfft*

pfui *See* PHOOEY

PG (pronounced as separate letters) *n narcotics* Paregoric, an opium product

phenagle *See* FINAGLE

phenom (FEE nahm) *n fr baseball fr late 1800s* A phenomenally skilled or impressive person; performing wonder, esp in sports: *Sawyer's two other 24-year-old phenoms*—F Eck/ *Veeck was a phenom, too*—Sports Illustrated

Phi Bete (FĪ BAYT) **1** *n phr* The academic honor society Phi Beta Kappa **2** *n phr* A member of Phi Beta Kappa

Philadelphia bankroll *n phr* A roll of $1 bills with a larger bill wrapped around it; = MICHIGAN ROLL

a **Philadelphia lawyer** *n phr* One who makes things unnecessarily complicated and obfuscates matters: *He was talking like a Philadelphia lawyer, trying to cover up* [fr a traditional reputation for the shrewdness of such attorneys, perhaps ultimately based on that of Andrew Hamilton, a *Philadelphia lawyer*, who successfully defended the New York newspaper publisher John Peter Zenger against charges of criminal libel in 1710, a defense crucial to the doctrine of the freedom of the press]

Philly or **Phillie** *n* Philadelphia

phiz or **phizog** (FIZ, FIZ ahwg) *n fr middle 1800s* The face; = MUG [fr *physiognomy*]

Phoebe or **little Phoebe** (or **fever**) *n* or *n phr* crapshooting Five or the point of five

phone *See* HOLD THE PHONE, TALK TO THE BIG WHITE PHONE

phoniness *n* Falseness: *fed up on the phoniness of Hollywood films*—Bob Thomas

phono 1 *n* A phonograph **2** *modifier: a phono album/ phono cartridge*

phonus bolonus (or **balonus**) **1** *n phr* Something false and meretricious: *Phonus bolonus, he said*—Irwin Shaw **2** *adj: What a phonus-balonus smile he's got on*

phony or **phoney** *fr late 1800s* **1** *adj* Not real or genuine; false; fake: *You phony little fake*—Arthur Miller **2** *n* A fake thing: *That window's a phony, it don't open* **3** *v: I ain't phoneying them woids*—Jimmy Durante **4** *n* A person who affects some identity, role, nature, etc; poseur: *some phony calling himself a writer*—James M Cain [fr late-18th-century British underworld slang *fawney* fr Irish *fáinne* "ring," referring to a swindle in which the *fawney-dropper* drops a cheap ring before the victim, then is persuaded to sell it as if it were valuable; as the sequence of spellings, *phoney* and later *phony*, indicates, the US spelling is probably based on an attested folk etymology revealing the notion that one's feelings or even identity could be readily falsified on the *telephone*]

phony as a three-dollar bill *adj phr* Very false indeed; not remotely genuine

phonyman *n circus* A peddler of cheap imitation jewelry [fr late-18th-century British underworld slang *fawney-man*]

phooey *interj* (also **phoo** or **pfui** or **fooey** or **fooy** or **fuie**) *fr 1930s* An exclamation of disbelief, rejection, contempt, etc [fr Yiddish fr German; popularized by the newspaper columnist Walter Winchell]

phooey on that *interj* An exclamation of strong rejection: *A give-back? Phooey on that!*

photog or **fotog** (FOH tahg) *n* A photographer: *The Swedish fotogs were actually saving film*—R Montgomery

phreaking (FREE king) *n* The imitation of telephone touch-tone signals by whistling or by using mechanical devices, so that free calls may be readily made: *The entire range of tandems became known and "phreaking," the art of using the telephone for fun but no profit for the company, came into being*—Toronto Life

physical *adj* Using the body, esp roughly or intimately: *Vanderbilt is a lot better than last year and more physical*—Birmingham News/ *I had to ask her to keep her distance when she tried to be physical with me*
See GET PHYSICAL

piano *n black* Spareribs, esp a single section of broiled spareribs: *cornbread with a piano on a platter*—Zora Neale Hurston
See HORSE PIANO

pic *n* A movie; = FLICK: *Raft's next pic*—Abel Green

Piccadilly commando *n phr WW2 Army* A London prostitute

◁**piccolo player**▷ *n phr* A person who likes and does fellatio [fr a double reference to the *picklelike* shape of a penis, and the fact that fellatio is referred to as "playing the skin flute"]

pick *See* NIT-PICK

pick a berry *v phr hoboes* To steal clothing off a clothesline; = GOOSEBERRY

pick someone's brain 1 *v phr* To question someone closely for one's own profit; exploit someone's creativity by imitation; be an intellectual parasite **2** *v phr* To inquire of someone; ask someone for information, advice, etc

pick 'em *sentence gamblers* The opponents are about equal; it's a toss-up: *pick 'em, when two opponents in sports are rated even for betting, ie, no point spread*—New York Times
See one CAN REALLY PICK 'EM

pick 'em up and lay 'em down 1 *v phr* To run, esp to run fast **2** *v phr* To dance

picker *See* BRAIN-PICKER, CHERRY-PICKER, FRUIT-PICKER, PRUNE-PICKER

picker-upper 1 *n* A person or thing that picks up: *A hitchhiker caught a ride....The picker-upper was soon arrested*—Associated Press **2** *n* = PEPPER-UPPER, PICK-ME-UP

picking *See* COTTON-PICKING

pickings *See* SLIM PICKINGS

pickle 1 *n* (also **picklement**) A parlous situation; predicament; dilemma: *I was in a sad pickle when I lost my job* **2** *n WW2 Navy* A torpedo **3** *n* A bullet: *He fired six pickles at the knob*—Westbrook Pegler **4** *v* To ruin; wreck: *This will promptly pickle her college chances*—F Sparks [first sense fr 16th-century British slang *in a pickle*, and may refer to the situation of a mouse fallen into a pickling vat; *picklement* is a handy echo of *predicament*]

pickled *adj* Drunk; = SOUSED

pickle park *n phr truckers* A roadside rest area

picklepuss *n* A frowning and pessimistic person; = SOURPUSS

pick-me-up *fr middle 1800s* **1** *n* A drink or snack that invigorates; = PEPPER-UPPER, PERKER-UPPER **2** *n* A drink of liquor taken to restore tone and morale

pickup 1 *n* A person accosted and made a companion, esp in a bar, on the street, etc, for sexual purposes: *His next girlfriend was a pickup he made at Rod's* **2** *n* An arrest **3** *n* (also **pickup truck**) A small truck having a cab, and cargo space with low sidewalls **4** *n* The ability of a car to accelerate rapidly, esp from a halt **5** *n* The act of getting or acquiring something: *He made the pickup at the post office* **6** *adj* Impromptu; unceremonious: *We'll have a pickup lunch in the kitchen* **7** *adj* For one occasion; temporary; ad hoc: *a pickup band/ a pickup corps of waiters*

pick up 1 *v phr* To resume; begin again: *We'll pick up the story where George had the nervous crisis* **2** *v phr* To increase; raise: *Let's pick up the pace a little, okay?* **3** *v phr* To get; acquire: *He picked up a few thou hustling* **4** *v phr fr middle 1800s* To make things clean and neat; tidy up: *You'd better pick up in your room, it's a godawful mess* **5** *v phr* To answer the telephone

pick someone **up 1** *v phr* To arrest someone: *The cops picked up six muggers and hauled their asses in* **2** *v phr* To make someone's acquaintance boldly, esp in a bar, on the street, etc, for sexual purposes: *She lets the [soldiers] pick her up* —Associated Press **3** *v phr* To stimulate or invigorate someone: *A book like this really picks you up*

pick something **up** *v phr* To notice; discover: *Did you pick that wink up?*

pick up on something **1** *v phr* To notice; become aware of: *I pick up on people's pain, Alexander* —New Yorker/ *after word...got around, and other entrepreneurs picked up on it* —Time **2** *v phr* To refer to and add to; bring back to notice, esp in order to query: *Your readers can pick up on the fact* —Rolling Stone/ *I want to pick up on what you just said about Philadelphia*

pick someone **up on** something *v phr fr middle 1800s* To object or call special attention to; correct: *I want to pick you up on that reference*

pick up the tab (or **check**) *v phr* To pay; assume the expense; =PAY THE FREIGHT: *Who's gonna pick up the tab for this mess?/ also somebody to pick up the tab. She admitted that this was important* —Saul Bellow

picnic 1 *n* Something very easy; =CINCH, PIECE OF CAKE: *That job's a picnic* **2** *n* An enjoyable time; =a BALL, BLAST: *The last week we had a picnic* See NO PICNIC

picture See DRAW A PICTURE

the **picture** *n phr* The situation; present shape of things: *After he explained he asked me if I had the picture/ I don't like the picture, it stinks* See the BIG PICTURE, GET THE PICTURE, PUT someone IN THE PICTURE

picture gallery 1 *n phr circus* The tattooed man in a sideshow **2** *n phr* =ROGUES' GALLERY

pictures *n cardplayers* Picture cards See IN PICTURES, TAKE PICTURES

piddle 1 *v* To urinate; =PEE: *So you piddled on the floor. But you don't have to have your face wiped in it* —Time **2** *v* To waste; idle: *You just piddle the day away* —Washington Post [a euphemism for *piss*]

piddle around *v phr fr middle 1500s* =FART AROUND, FIDDLE AROUND

piddling *adj* Meager; trivial; paltry: *It was an effort, though a piddling one*

pie 1 *n* An easy task or job; =GRAVY: *The climb is pie for a character like Joan* ◁**2**▷ *n* The vulva: *found their way into her hot, wet pie* —Earl Thompson

See APPLE-PIE ORDER, CUTESY-POO, CUTIE-PIE, EASY AS PIE, FLY PIE, FUR PIE, HAIR PIE, MINCE PIES, MONKEY PIE, SWEETIE-PIE

pie card 1 *n phr hoboes* A union card, esp used to borrow money, get food, etc **2** *n phr labor union* A corrupt or self-serving union official: *Among 'em were some good organizers, but among 'em was also pie cards* —Studs Terkel

piece 1 *n* A share; portion; financial interest; =a PIECE OF THE ACTION, SLICE: *a piece of the racket* —American Mercury/ *offered to let me buy a small piece of "As You Like It"* —Billy Rose **2** *n* A gun; pistol: *They step up to the driver's side and shove a piece in his ear* —Time ◁**3**▷ *n* =PIECE OF ASS **4** *n narcotics* An ounce of heroin or other narcotic: *He buys heroin in "pieces"* —J Mills **5** *n* A graffito on a subway car: *A train rumbles in...and we all pause to view its pieces* —M Blaine

See ALL IN ONE PIECE, COME UP SMELLING LIKE A ROSE, CONVERSATION PIECE, KNOCK OFF A PIECE, MOUTH-PIECE, MUSEUM PIECE, TEAR OFF A PIECE, THINK-PIECE

◁**piece of ass** (or **tail**)▷ **1** *n phr* The sex act; a completed sex act **2** *n phr* A person regarded as a sex object, organ, or partner
See TEAR OFF A PIECE

piece of cake *n phr* Anything very easy; anything easily or pleasantly done; =BREEZE, DUCK SOUP ● Originally and chiefly British: *The interview was a piece of cake/ It's a piece of cake because you don't have the fear that they are going to pitch out on you* —Inside Sports

piece of calico (or **goods**) *n phr* A woman ● **Piece** meant "woman" as long ago as the 1400s

piece of change *n phr* (Variations: **hunk** may replace **piece**; **jack** may replace **change**) Money, esp a large amount: *a handsome piece of change* —James T Farrell/ *which would come to quite a piece of change* —Village Voice

piece someone **off** *underworld & merchant marine* **1** *v phr* To pay a part of one's wages in return for a job **2** *v phr* To pay a bribe; =GREASE someone's PALM **3** *v phr* To lend money to a friend

piece of fluff See BIT OF FLUFF

piece of meat *n phr* A person regarded as merely a physical body; unaccommodated man: *I'm just a piece of meat...but I know I'm a good piece of meat* —Sports Illustrated

piece of someone's **mind** *n phr* A strong rebuke; severe criticism and correction

◁**piece of shit**▷ **1** *n phr* Something inferior or worthless; a wretched effort: *This show's a piece of* shit **2** *n phr* A lie; hypocrisy; =A PACK OF LIES: *Everything she said is a big piece of shit*

◁**piece of tail**▷ *See* PIECE OF ASS

a **piece of the action** *n phr* A share of something, esp in profits, a business, or speculation, etc: *a piece of the "Gunsmoke" action*—L Raddatz/ *see that everybody, regardless of party, gets a piece of the action*—Ben Wattenberg [fr *action* "gamble, gambling"]

piece of trade *n phr* A prostitute; a promiscuous woman: *with some good-natured piece of trade*—Nelson Algren

piece something **out** *v phr* To make more complete or acceptable by additions; eke out: *We'll piece the salary out with perks*

piece up *v phr* underworld To divide loot; =DIVVY

pie-eyed 1 *adj* *fr early 1900s* Drunk: *the pie-eyed brothers*—P Marks **2** *adj* Astonished; wide-eyed: *Randall was pie-eyed. His mouth moved, but nothing came out of it*—Raymond Chandler

pieface *n* *esp 1920s* A stupid or foolish person

pie-faced *adj* Stupid; foolish: *a pie-faced boy from Minnesota*—Pulpsmith

pie in the sky *n phr* *fr early 1900s* The reward one will get for compliant behavior, later; hence, wishful thinking or utopian fantasies [fr a Wobbly expression of contempt for those who maintained that suffering and penury on earth would be compensated for by bliss and luxury in heaven; the *locus classicus* is a parody of the hymn "In the Sweet By and By," ascribed to the Wobbly martyr Joe Hill]

pies *See* MINCE PIES

pie wagon *n phr* *fr late 1800s* underworld =PADDY WAGON

piffed or **piffled** *adj* Drunk

piffle *fr late 1800s British* **1** *n* Nonsense; =BALONEY, BUNK: *the kind of piffle actors have to go up against*—H McHugh **2** *interj* A mild exclamation of disbelief, contradiction, rejection, etc

pifflicated *adj* Drunk

pig ◁**1**▷ *n* *esp 1960s* counterculture *fr middle 1800s* underworld A police officer: *The innocent kids all hollered "Off the pigs!"* ◁**2**▷ *n* A bigot, racist, or fascist; a person who contributes to the oppression of a people ◁**3**▷ *n* Any fat, sloppy, obnoxious person ◁**4**▷ *n* A glutton **5** *v*: *When you eat too much, you can say "I pigged"*—Milwaukee Journal ◁**6**▷ *n* A promiscuous woman, esp one who is blowsy and unattractive: *spoke of a pig he had recently picked up*—James T Farrell **7** *n* horse-racing A racehorse, esp an inferior one; =BEETLE: *why the hell that pig didn't win*—Fortune **8** *n* railroad A locomotive, esp a switch engine or yard engine **9** *n* (also **Pig**) A large and powerful motorcycle, esp a Harley-Davidson (a trade name)

See BLIND PIG, IS A FROG'S ASS WATERPROOF, LIKE PIGS IN CLOVER, LONG PIG, MALE CHAUVINIST PIG, RENT-A-PIG, YARD GOAT

pigboat *n* *esp WW1 Navy* A submarine: *the archaic "pigboat" of the First World War*—JL Riordan

pigeon 1 *n* underworld An informer; =STOOL PIGEON: *I don't like pigeons*—Raymond Chandler **2**

n fr late 1500s British underworld The victim of a swindle; dupe; =MARK, SUCKER: *You've got a couple of guys who have been up all night, real pigeons*—Washingtonian/ *I'm your pigeon now and you guys are gonna rip me off*—WT Tyler **3** *n* A young woman; =CHICK **4** *n* underworld A used or void ticket passed as valid, esp a losing lottery ticket sold as a winning one ● This sense is derived from a late-18th-century British underworld term **5** *n* A former alcoholic in the care of a helpful sponsor or guardian [for first sense see *stool pigeon*; the second sense probably derives fr the expression *pluck a pigeon* and may be based on a notion that *pigeons* are easy to catch; the sense "young woman" is probably fr or related to *quail* and again suggests an easy victim]

See CLAY PIGEON, DEAD DUCK, STOOL PIGEON

pigeonhole 1 *v* To classify; identify; =BUTTON DOWN, PEG: *I pigeonhole this clown as a total bigmouth* **2** *v* To put away or aside; =FILE AND FORGET [fr the separate compartments of a desk or sorting system, likened to the orifices in a *pigeon cote*]

◀**pig-fucker**▶ *n* A despicable person; =BASTARD, FUCKER, SHITHEEL

piggyback 1 *n* The transport of loaded containers or semitrailers on railroad flatcars **2** *v* To originate or prosper with the help of something else: *Aerobic dancing piggybacked on the jogging craze* [fr the term for carrying someone, esp a child, on one's back derived by folk etymology fr *pick-a-back*, of unknown origin]

pighead *n* A stubborn person

pigheaded *adj* Stubborn; stupidly obstinate

pig in a poke *See* BUY A PIG IN A POKE

pig-iron *n* Raw and inferior liquor

◁**pig-meat**▷ **1** *n* esp black A woman, esp a sexually promiscuous one **2** *n fr prizefight* A defeated or moribund person; =LOSER

◁**pigmobile**▷ *n* *esp 1960s counterculture* A police car; squad car: *that took one pigmobile off patrol*—Niven and Bournelle

pig out 1 *v phr* *fr teenagers* To overeat: *I pigged out on a runny Brie* **2** *v phr* To overindulge in anything: *It was time to pig out on rock and roll*—Village Voice

pigpen 1 *n* railroad A roundhouse **2** *n* (also **pigsty**) Any filthy, littered place: *His room's a pigpen*

◁**pig's ass** (or **ear** or **eye**)▷ *See* IN A PIG'S ASS

◁**pig shit**▷ *See* STRONGER THAN PIG SHIT

pigskin 1 *n* A football; =the OBLATE SPHEROID **2** *modifier*: *the pigskin parade*/ *a pigskin superstar*

pig-sticker 1 *n* *fr WW1 Army* A bayonet, lance, etc **2** *n* railroad A cowcatcher

pig sweat 1 *n phr* Beer **2** *n phr* Inferior whiskey; =PANTHER PISS

pike *See* COME DOWN THE PIKE

piker 1 *n* *fr late 1800s* A mean and stingy person; miser; =TIGHTWAD **2** *n* A shirker; loafer [originally a vagrant, esp a gambler, who wandered along the *pike*; hence a poor sport, a cheapskate]

pile 1 *n fr middle 1700s* All one's wealth, esp if it is fairly much: *He made his pile flim-flamming little old ladies* **2** *v* To dash; run; thrust oneself: *I piled after her hell to split*—James M Cain
See GRUB-PILE, WOODPILE

a **pile** *n phr fr late 1800s* A large amount of money; a fortune; =a BUNDLE

◁**pile of shit**▷ **1** *n phr* =CROCK OF SHIT **2** *n phr* Something inferior or worthless; a shabby performance or product; =PIECE OF SHIT: *The whole project's a pile of shit*

a **pile on a pillow** *n phr lunch counter* A ham sandwich on a roll

piles *n* A large amount of money; =a PILE: *She'll inherit piles*

pileup *n* A wreck, esp one involving a number of cars: *6-car, end-to-end pile-up on the New Jersey Turnpike*—Associated Press

pile up 1 *v phr* To wreck; =RACK UP, TOTAL: *after he piled up his car*—J Evans **2** *v phr fr late 1800s* To go aground: *We piled up at Wood's Hole*

pile up Zs *See* COP ZS

pill 1 *n fr late 1800s* A boring, disagreeable person; =a PAIN IN THE ASS: *Oh, don't be a pill, Valerie*—SJ Perelman **2** *n* A baseball or golf ball **3** *n narcotics* An opium pellet for smoking **4** *n narcotics* A Nembutal (a trade name) capsule; =NIMBY **5** *n fr late 1600s* A bomb, cannonball, bullet, etc: *He was drinking coffee when the big pill came down*—New York Daily News
See COOK UP A PILL, PEP PILL

the **pill** or **the Pill** *n phr* Any oral contraceptive for women: *now that the joint and the pill are with us*—Society/ *can obtain "the pill" or diaphragms there*—US News & World Report

pillhead *n narcotics* A person who habitually takes tranquilizers, amphetamines, barbiturates, etc, in pill or capsule form: *Papoose and me were a bunch of pillheads*—Rolling Stone

pillow 1 *n prizefight* A boxing glove **2** *n baseball* A base; =BAG
See a PILE ON A PILLOW

pillow-puncher *n* A chambermaid

pillow talk *n phr* Intimate talk, like that between a couple in bed

pill pad *narcotics* **1** *n phr* A place where addicts gather to smoke opium; opium den **2** *n phr* A place where narcotics users gather to take drugs of any sort; =PAD

pill-popper *n narcotics* =PILLHEAD

pill-popping *narcotics* **1** *adj* Addicted to or using narcotics in pill or capsule form: *The prostitute is now a suicidal, pill-popping Newsweek reporter*—Saturday Review **2** *n phr* The use of narcotics in pill form: *They don't do so much pill-popping any more*

pill-pusher or **pill-roller** or **pill-peddler** **1** *n* A physician: *gynecological phenomena you pill-peddlers are always talking about*—Ellery Queen **2** *n* A pharmacist or student of pharmacy

pilot 1 *n* The manager of a sports team **2** *n* A jockey
See COW PILOT, HOT PILOT, SKY-PILOT

pimp *n lumberjacks* A boy who does menial jobs at a logging camp [probably related to *pimp* "procurer," perhaps influenced by *imp* "mischievous child"]

pimpish *adj teenagers* Stylishly dressed

pimple *n* The head

pimpmobile 1 *n* A fancy car used by a prostitute's procurer and manager: *used the car to deliver his "girls" to their street-walking posts. Police called it a "pimpmobile"*—New York Times/ *There's a red Cadillac pimpmobile parked outside*—New York **2** *n* Any very fancy and overlavish car **3** *modifier:* *The pimpmobile mantle will be donned by the 1983 Cougar*—Car and Driver

pimp stick *n phr lumberjacks* A ready-made cigarette; =TAILOR-MADE

pin 1 *n* A leg **2** *v* To classify and understand someone; =PEG, PIGEONHOLE: *I got this guy pinned as a turkey* **3** *v* To look over; survey; =DIG: *just pinning the queer scene*—John Rechy **4** *v students* To declare a serious commitment to someone by giving or taking a fraternity pin
See HAIRPIN, KING, PIN someone DOWN, PIN something DOWN, PIN someone's EARS BACK, PIN ON, PINS, PIN-SHOT

pin a rose on it *v phr lunch counter* To add onion to an order

pincers *n teenagers fr 1960s* The eyes

pinch 1 *v fr 1600s* To steal; =SWIPE: *Who pinched the script?*—L Ford **2** *v fr middle 1800s British* To arrest; =BUST: *The stores will invite ill will if they pinch indiscriminately*—Fortune **3** *n:* *make a respectable number of pinches to stay off the transfer list*—Rolling Stone
See IN A PINCH

pincher *See* PENNY-PINCHER

pinchers *n* Shoes

pinch-gut *n fr middle 1600s* A miser; =TIGHTWAD

pinch hit *n phr baseball fr early 1900s* A hit made by a player who bats in place of another

pinch-hit 1 *v baseball* To bat for a player who has been removed from the lineup, usu at a critical point in the game **2** *v* To substitute for someone else: *I had to pinch-hit for her when she got sick and make that fund-raising pitch myself*

pinchpenny 1 *n fr middle 1600s* A miser; =PINCH-GUT, TIGHTWAD **2** *adj:* *your pinchpenny budgets*

pin someone **down 1** *v phr* To get a definite answer, commitment, piece of information, etc, from someone: *He wouldn't say just when, I couldn't pin him down* **2** *v phr* To make someone immobile, esp to keep soldiers in place with constant or accurate fire **3** *v phr* To identify or classify someone definitely; =PEG, PIN: *I can't pin her down, but I've seen her before*

pin something **down** *v phr* To recognize, identify, or single out something definitely; make explicit: *I can't quite pin my feeling down*

pineapple *n fr WW1 Army* A hand grenade or small bomb; =CHICAGO PINEAPPLE, ITALIAN FOOTBALL: *Nobody tried to throw a pineapple in my lap*—Raymond Chandler [fr the resemblance of a fragmentation grenade, with its deeply segmented ovoid surface, to a *pineapple*]

pin someone's **ears back** *v phr fr 1930s* To punish someone, either by words or blows; chasten: *a flip-lipped bastard who should have had his ears pinned back long ago*—J Evans

pine (or **wooden**) **overcoat** *n phr fr middle 1800s* A coffin, esp a cheap one: *what they call in the army a pine overcoat*—RH Thornton

◁**pinga**▷ (PEEN gah) *n* The penis; =BICHO [fr Spanish]

ping jockey *See* BLIP JOCKEY

ping off the walls *v phr Army* To be very nervous; be tense and excited: *Better stop pinging off the walls and start making some plans*

ping-pong *v hospital* To refer a patient, esp a Medicaid recipient, to other doctors, in order to maximize fees: *"Medicaid mills" or clinics…reap enormous profits by such practices as "Ping Ponging"*—Time [fr Ping-Pong, trade name for a manufacturer's table tennis set and game]

ping-wing *n narcotics* A narcotics injection, esp in the arm

pinhead *n* A stupid person

pinheaded *adj* Stupid

pink **1** *n black* A white person; =GRAY **2** *n* A political liberal or mild socialist radical; =PARLOR PINK **3** *adj: pink perspective on Palestine* **4** *n hot rodders* A legal certificate of car ownership **5** *adj* Redheaded ● Often used as a nickname **6** *adj homosexuals* Homosexual
See IN THE PINK, PARLOR PINK, TICKLED PINK

pink chord *n phr esp 1930s musicians* A mistake in reading or improvising music

pink collar **1** *adj phr* Traditionally held by women of the middle class: *Mature women tended to gravitate toward pink collar jobs as secretaries, teachers, nurses, and saleswomen*—New York Times **2** *adj phr* Working in a job traditionally held by women of the middle class: *the TV character to whom real-life blue- and pink-collar working women most relate*—Time [modeled on *blue collar* and *white collar*]

pinked *adj* Slightly drunk; =TIDDLY

pink elephants *See* SEE PINK ELEPHANTS

Pinkerton or **Pink** or **Pinkie** *n fr middle 1800s* An operative or agent of the Pinkerton detective agency: *how you suppose Pinkies get trainin'*—Nelson Algren

pink ink *n phr* Romance novels; =BODICE-RIPPERS

pinko **1** *n* A person of liberal or mildly radical socialist political opinions; =PINK: *pinko James J Matles and pinko Julius Emspak*—Time **2** *adj: How come those Niggers and those creepy pinko hippies call us names like "pigs"?*—Ebony

pink puffer *n phr hospital* A thin emphysema patient

pink slip **1** *n phr fr 1920s* A discharge notice; =WALKING PAPERS: *All 1,300 employees got pink slips today*—Associated Press **2** *v: They had pink-slipped Hartz one brutal afternoon*—Washingtonian
See GET THE PINK SLIP, GIVE someone THE PINK SLIP

pink tea *n phr* A very exclusive party or event

pink-toes *n black* A light-skinned black woman

pinky[1] or **pinkie** **1** *n fr middle or early 1800s* The little finger: *He paused and ran his pinkie along his lower lip*—Raymond Chandler/ *Pardon my lifted pinky*—Hy Gardner **2** *modifier: pinky ring* [fr an earlier adjective sense, "small, tiny"]
See PLAY STINKY-PINKY

pinky[2] or **pinkie** **1** *n black* =PINK-TOES **2** *n* A redheaded person ● Often used as a nickname [fr the color]

pinky-crooker *n* A person of affectedly refined tastes and manners: *You'll find only the pinky-crookers at the concerts*—Time

pinned **1** *adj narcotics* Contracted: *his pupils are "pinned"*—J Mills **2** *adj students* Seriously involved, by the act of taking or giving a fraternity pin

pinnings *See* UNDERPINNINGS

pinochle season *n phr* The off-season in the garment industry

pin on *v phr* To make an accusation; inculpate; =HANG ON: *Police indicated they had little to pin on them*—Associated Press

pin one on *See* HANG ONE ON

pins *n fr 1500s* The legs: *knocked clean off his pins*—O Johnson

pin-shot *n narcotics* A narcotics injection made with a safety pin and an eyedropper

pint *See* HALF-PINT

pinto or **paint** *n cowboys* A piebald or mottled horse: *Tex galloped off in their direction on his eager pinto* [fr Spanish, "painted"]

pin-up **1** *n esp 1940s* A picture, usu a provocative photograph, esp of a pretty young woman **2** *modifier: pin-up collections and books*—Playboy **3** *n* A young woman shown in a pin-up: *Betty Grable was the services' favorite pin-up*

pin-up girl *See* SWEATER GIRL

pip *n* A minor skin lesion, esp of teenagers: *whiteheads, blackheads, goopheads, goobers, pips, acne trenches*—New York Times

a pip (or **a pipperoo** or **a pippin**) **1** *n phr fr early 1900s* A person or thing that is remarkable, wonderful, superior, etc; =BEAUT, HUMDINGER: *a pip of a shiner*—J McNulty/ *His wildest dreams have to be pips*—Washington Post **2** *modifier: a pipperoo flick* [fr *pippin*, a prized kind of apple; the shift was probably fr *peach* as one kind of excellent fruit to *pippin* as another]

the pip *n phr* A severe case of being annoyed: *People gave him the pip*—P Marks [fr a disease of fowl]

pipe[1] *n fr early 1900s students* Anything easily done; =CINCH: *Getting in is a pipe* [apparently fr *pipe dream*, suggesting something as easily or magically done as in a wishful dream]

pipe[2] **1** *n circus* A letter or note **2** *v: Bill Johnson pipes from Frisco that times are hard*—DW Maurer **3** *n* A telephone **4** *v* To speak up; say something; =PIPE UP: *But I am not suppose to know that and do not pipe*—John O'Hara **5** *v fr late 1800s* To look at; see; notice: *Did you pipe her hands?*—Eugene O'Neill **6** *n* (also **pipeline**) *surfers* The tubular inner section of a breaking wave **7** *v underworld* To hit someone on the head, esp with a metal pipe: *Someone was gonna pipe me* —Prison [all senses probably derived fr *pipe* as a conduit or a musical instrument; the sense "look at" is related to criminal slang "follow, keep under surveillance," of obscure origin and difficult to relate to any sense of *pipe*]

See BIG PIPE, DOWN THE TUBE, HIT THE PIPE, LAY PIPE, LEAD-PIPE CINCH, SMALL PIPE

pipe course *n phr college students* An easy course; = GUT COURSE: *You are all freshmen and you may not be familiar with the term "pipe course"* —Max Shulman

pipe down *v phr fr late 1800s* To stop talking; speak more quietly: *The others got sore at him and told him to pipe down*—John O'Hara [fr naval jargon, probably related to the use of the boatswain's *pipe* for giving commands, or to its shrill noise]

pipe dream *n phr* An improbable and visionary hope, ideal, scheme, etc, such as an opium smoker might have: *He has some ambitious plans, mostly pipe dreams*

pipe-jockey *n Air Force* A jet fighter pilot

pipeline 1 *n* A channel of communication, esp a direct and special one: *You'd think he has a pipeline to Jesus* **2** *n* A channel or course for routine production, processing, etc: *We'll have fewer men in what we call the "pipeline" who are moving*—US News and World Report **3** *modifier: a pipeline review*

See IN THE PIPELINE, PIPE

pipe someone **off** *v phr merchant marine* To blacklist someone [fr the nautical practice of blowing the boatswain's *pipe* to welcome someone aboard or usher someone off a ship]

pipes or **set of pipes** *n* or *n phr* The voice, esp the singing voice: *He was trying out his pipes on a new speech/ to bring that great set of pipes into your very own living room*—Changes

See BANG PIPES, CUT UP THE TOUCHES

pipe up *v phr* To speak up; raise one's voice; = SING OUT: *He piped up with a couple of smart-ass cracks* [perhaps fr a play on the nautical *pipe down*; perhaps fr the playing of the *pipe* or *pipes*]

pippy-poo *adj* Small; teeny: *That's just a pippy-poo minuscule example of what I mean*—Washington Post

◁**piss¹**▷ **1** *n* Urine **2** *v: He had to piss* **3** *v* (also **piss and moan**) To complain; grumble; = BITCH, KVETCH: *Find out what he is pissing about now/ Angie's mother pissed and moaned about it for months*—Easyriders/ *whatever agency they are pissing over at the moment*—New Jersey **4** *adj* Of wretched quality; = PISS POOR: *Europe is a piss place for music*—Rolling Stone

See EYES LIKE PISSHOLES IN THE SNOW, FULL OF PISS AND VINEGAR, NOT HAVE A POT TO PISS IN, PANTHER PISS, TICKLE THE SHIT OUT OF someone

◁**piss²**▷ *combining word* A term placed before an adjective to intensify its meaning: *piss-awkward/ piss-elegant/ piss-ugly*

◁**piss and vinegar**▷ *n phr* Energy; vitality; = PEP, PIZZAZZ

See FULL OF PISS AND VINEGAR

◁**piss and wind**▷ *n phr fr late 1900s* Pretentious but feeble show; gaudy display: *They strut with the piss and wind traditional among victors in political intrigues*—Village Voice [fr the situation of a person who can urinate and flatulate, but not achieve a substantial defecation]

◁**pissant**▷ (PIHS ant) **1** *n* A despicable person; an insignificant wretch: *That sorry damn pissant* —Pat Conroy **2** *adj* Insignificant; paltry: *this little pissant country*—New York Times [fr *piss* and *ant*, based on earlier *pissmire* "ant" because ants were thought to have an unpleasant smell]

◁**piss** something **away**▷ *v phr* To waste and dissipate something foolishly; squander: *There was a part of him that wanted to piss it away and be a loser*—Washingtonian

◁**piss call**▷ *n phr fr Navy* Reveille, the military signal to get out of bed in the morning

◁**piss-cutter**▷ *n* A person or thing that is remarkable, wonderful, superior, etc; = BEAUT, HUMDINGER, PIP: *Isn't our new colleague a piss-cutter?*

◁**pissed off**▷ *adj phr* (Variations: **pissed** or **p'd** or **peed off** or **p o'd**) *fr WW2 armed forces* Angry; profoundly annoyed; indignant: *His face got all red-colored whenever he was pissed off*—Rolling Stone/ *He gets a little pissed like I'm making fun of him*—Rex Burns

◁**piss-elegant**▷ (Variations: ◁**piss-ass** or **pissy** or **pissy-ass**▷) *adj* Ostentatiously elegant; affecting great refinement; = HOITY-TOITY: *whose piss-elegant members include an amnesiac, a narcoleptic, and a morphine addict*—Village Voice/ *a piss-elegant new wave Chinese restaurant and bar*—Rolling Stone/ *He was a jerk for needing to hang around with pissy queens*—Armistead Maupin/ *a place with a pissy-ass little fountain in the courtyard*

◁**pisser**▷ **1** *n* A very difficult job or task; = BALL-BUSTER, BITCH: *That climb was a pisser* **2** *n* A person or thing that is remarkable, wonderful, superior, etc; = PISS-CUTTER: *You're a pisser, you are* —Lawrence Sanders **3** *n* A very funny person or thing: *What a pisser when he opened the wrong door by mistake* **4** *n* A toilet: *windowless with a pisser and no benches*—Rolling Stone [third sense fr the notion that one laughs hard enough to *piss* in one's pants]

◁**pisshead**▷ *n* A despicable person; a stupid bore; = ASSHOLE: *that made such a pisshead of herself* —Stephen King

◁**pissholes in the snow**▷ *See* EYES LIKE PISSHOLES IN THE SNOW

◁**pissing contest** (or **match**)▷ *n phr* An argument; disagreement; confrontational debate: *warned him against getting into a pissing contest with Bittman*—Washingtonian/ *I'm not going to sit here and get in a pissin' match about petty problems like work shoes*—Philadelphia Journal [fr actual vying among boys as to who can project the urinary stream farthest]

◁**piss in the wind**▷ *v phr* To waste one's time and effort: *If you think that'll work you're pissing in the wind*

◁**piss-off**▷ *n* Anger; indignation: *in a state of high piss-off*—Stephen King/ *There's a basic, well-justified piss-off all over the country*—Newsweek

◁**piss** someone **off**▷ *v phr* To make angry; arouse indignation

◁**piss on** someone or something▷ *v phr* To dismiss or treat contemptuously; defile or violate ● Often used as an angry and defiant dismissal: *I won't take it, piss on it*/ *As the old dog says, if you can't eat it and you can't fuck it, piss on it*

◁**piss on ice**▷ *v phr* To live well; = EAT HIGH ON THE HOG, SHIT IN HIGH COTTON [fr the practice of putting cakes of *ice* in the urinals of expensive restaurants and clubs]

◁**piss poor**▷ **1** *adj phr* Of wretched quality; inferior; bad: *dat a pisspoor excuse fo' a apology*—Esquire/ *outgrow its status as one of the many piss-poor modern dance groups playing college campuses*—Village Voice **2** *adj phr* *fr 1920s* Penniless; in pauperdom: *They're all born piss-poor*—Lawrence Sanders

◁**piss-ugly**▷ *adj* Very ugly; nasty and menacing: *Beer-bellied brutes...peered at the world through piss-ugly eyes*—Village Voice

◁**piss up a rope**▷ *See* GO PISS UP A ROPE

◁**piss up a storm**▷ *v phr* (Variations: **blow** or **kick** may replace **piss**) To make a great noisy fuss about something, esp in complaint: *When I came in she was pissing up a storm because they didn't have what she wanted*

◁**piss-warm**▷ *adj* As warm as fresh urine: *I can't drink piss-warm beer*

◁**pissy** or **pissy-ass**▷ *See* PISS-ELEGANT

pistol 1 *n* A person or thing that is remarkable, wonderful, superior, etc; = BEAUT, PIP, PISS-CUTTER: *That Ruby Jean, she's a pistol*—New York Times/ *A colleague described Curley as a pistol*—Washingtonian **2** *n* *lunch counter* Hot pastrami [lunch counter sense because the eater feels as if shot in the stomach soon after eating hot pastrami] *See* HOT AS A THREE-DOLLAR PISTOL

pistol Pete *n phr* A zealous and effective lover; = COCKSMAN [fr the usual jocular analogue between *pistol* and "penis," "shooting" and having an orgasm, etc, reinforced by alliteration and the fact that *Peter* means "penis"]

pistol, shoot it all the way *sentence lunch counter* Serve up an order of hot pastrami with french fries and cole slaw

piston *n* A slide trombone

pit *v* To take a racing car into the pit: *He pitted for fresh rubber and thus lost a lap*—Sports Illustrated *See* CONVERSATION PIT, GREASE TROUGH, PASSION PIT

pitch *fr middle 1800s British* **1** *n* *hawkers* A hawker's or street vendor's place of business; = HIGH PITCH, LOW PITCH **2** *n* *hawkers* The sales talk or spiel of a hawker: *He recited a part of his pitch*—New Yorker **3** *n* *hawkers* A hawker **4** *v:* *Louie...pitches kitchen gadgets*—M Zolotow/ *He*

pitches household items like the Magic Towel—New Yorker **5** *n* *fr hawkers* Any sales talk or persuasional plea: *other gifts to prospective brides, along with a pitch to honeymoon at Holiday Inns*—Time/ *a legitimate pitch for help*—World **6** *n* A sexual approach, esp a tentative one; = PASS: *I never made a pitch with Herta*—John O'Hara **7** *v:* *I wouldn't try to pitch to that Ice Maiden* **8** *v homosexuals* To penetrate the anus in anal sex [all senses are fr the notion of *pitching* or establishing a place of trade] *See* BUTTERFLY BALL, HIGH PITCH, IN THERE PITCHING, LOW PITCH, MAKE A PITCH, ON THE PITCH, PURPOSE PITCH, SUNDAY PITCH, THROW

the pitch *n phr* The situation; the matter; the point: *I think I get the pitch*

pitchforks *See* RAIN CATS AND DOGS

pitching *See* IN THERE PITCHING

pitchman 1 *n* A person who sells novelties, household items, clever toys and tricks, etc, on the streets or at a fair or carnival **2** *n* Any advocate, promoter, persuader, spokesman, etc: *chief pitchman for Big Oil*

pitchout 1 *n* *baseball* A pitch thrown wide of the plate so that the catcher can more easily throw to one of the bases to forestall an attempted steal **2** *n* *football* A lateral pass from one back to another

pitch out *v phr baseball* To make a pitch-out

pitch (or **fling**) **woo** *v phr esp 1930s & 40s* To kiss and caress; = NECK: *And she pitches some more woo with Dr Jan*—SJ Perelman

the pits *n phr* The most loathsome place or situation imaginable: *This school is the pits* [fr armpits]

pit stop *n phr* A stop so that people may go to the toilet: *Pit stop. Head run*—Pat Conroy [fr the *pit stops* made by racing cars for service, repair, rest, etc]

Pittsburgh feathers *n phr hoboes* Coal, when regarded as something to lie on in a railroad car

pivot *n Army* A soldier with the rank of private [fr the abbreviation *pvt*]

pix¹ 1 *n* Movies; the movies; = the FLICKS: *You ought to be in pix* **2** *n* Photographs, esp the artwork of a newspaper, magazine, book, etc; graphics **3** *modifier:* *pix credit*

**pix² ** *n* A male homosexual [fr *pixie*, suggested by *fairy*]

pixilated 1 *adj* Crazy; eccentric; confused **2** *adj* Drunk [fr enchantment by *pixies*]

pizzazz 1 *n* Energy; power; = PEP, PISS AND VINEGAR: *The J-57 has more pizzazz*—Time/ *What's missing is overall pizzazz and pace*—Judith Crist **2** *n* A feature designed mainly for a gaudy and flashy appeal; = GIMMICK: *However it stacks up...in panoply and pizzazz, this year's Inauguration will be the most expensive*—Newsweek [origin unknown; perhaps echoically suggested by *piss, ass,* and *piss and vinegar*]

PJs or **pjs** *n* Pajamas; = PEEJAYS: *New arrivals like me still flapped about in pj's and robes*—New York/ *as though I were running around in my PJs*—Sports Afield

place 1 *v* *horseracing* To come in second in a race **2** *v* To be among the winners of a race or competition: *I didn't even place*

See COFFEE-AND-CAKE PLACE, IN PLACE, NOPLACEVILLE

place out *v phr* *students* To be exempted: *He placed out of calculus* [fr doing so well in a *placement* test that the student is judged qualified in the subject]

places *See* GO PLACES

plain vanilla *adj phr* Unadorned; simple; basic: *more lushly appointed variants of plain vanilla family cars are due to arrive*—New York Times/ *Plain Vanilla, but Very Good*—Newsweek

plain white wrapper *n phr* *citizens band* An unmarked police car

◁**plank¹**▷ *v* To do the sex act with or to; = SCREW: *had witless good fun with his children while his wife was out getting planked*—John Irving

plank² *See* WALK THE PLANK

plank down (Variations: **plunk down** or **plump down** or **clunk down** or **plank out** or **plank**) *fr early 1800s* **1** *v phr* To put down with a thud or crash; place decisively: *an overstuffed chair some admirer had planked down next to the booth*—AJ Liebling **2** *v phr* To pay money; put down or put up money; offer or bet money: *planked down a cool $8,000,000*—RH Fetridge/ *plunked down...$65,000* —Bob Thomas [fr the hard striking of the *plank* of a table]

planker *n* A steak [fr the technique of broiling or baking and serving meat or fish on a plank]

plant 1 *v* *fr middle 1800s* To bury; hide **2** *v* To place evidence secretly so that someone will be incriminated: *Someone is planting evidence*—Erle Stanley Gardner **3** *v* To place a blow: *He planted a left on my poor snoot* **4** *n* = SHILL **5** *n* *hoboes* A hideout **6** *n* *fr early 1800s British* A cache, esp of stolen goods **7** *n* A false and falsely based accusation; = FRAME-UP: *They were planning to disgrace the mayor, using a plant* **8** *n* A spy, esp a police spy: *The new guy turned out to be a plant*

See CAT PLANT

planting *n* A funeral: *I get in on a lot of these plantings*—J Evans

plaster 1 *n* A banknote, esp a one-dollar bill: *If you need a couple of plasters until Ed gets out, tell me*—Lawrence Sanders **2** *v* To disseminate or spread widely: *They plastered the city with leaflets* **3** *n* A person who surreptitiously follows another; shadow; = TAIL: *He probably knew he had a plaster by this time*—J Evans **4** *n* A subpoena or summons; arrest warrant [money sense fr *shinplaster*, an early-19th-century term for "currency of little value or very small denomination"]

plastered *adj* Drunk

plastic 1 *adj* *esp 1960s counterculture* False and superficial; meretricious; = HOKED-UP, SLICK, PHONY: *in California...a plastic society*—BW Dipple/ *a license for contempt of their plastic souls*—New York Times **2** *n* A credit card; monetary credit afforded by the use of credit cards

plate 1 *n* = FASHION PLATE **2** *n* = DISH **3** *n* = PLATTER

See HAVE one's HANDS FULL, HOME PLATE, OFF one's PLATE, READ one's PLATE

plater *n* *horse-racing* A race horse, esp an inferior one; = BEETLE, PIG

See SELLING PLATER

platforms or **pyramids** *n* Shoes with extremely thick soles and heels

platter *n* A phonograph record; = DISC

the platter *n* *baseball* Home plate

play 1 *v* To acquiesce; cooperate; = PLAY BALL: *They'd come back and get her, if I didn't play with them*—Raymond Chandler **2** *v* To go very well; succeed: *The O'Connor appointment's playing...you're on a roll, Mr President*—Philadelphia Daily News/ *I know these guys like it, but how will it play in Iowa?*

See BONEHEAD PLAY, DRAW PLAY, GRANDSTAND PLAY, MAKE A PLAY FOR

play along *v phr* = PLAY BALL

play around 1 *v phr* To do something, esp one's job, casually or frivolously; = HORSE AROUND: *Quit playing around and start playing hardball* **2** *v phr* To be sexually promiscuous; = SLEEP AROUND: *I guess I'd never given much thought to the idea of Dad playing around*—Claude Brown/ *She plays around*—Raymond Chandler

play around with someone **1** *v phr* To flirt or dally with; have a sexual involvement with **2** *v phr* To treat lightly or insultingly; challenge or provoke: *I wouldn't play around with that gorilla if I were you*

play ball 1 *v phr* *fr middle 1800s* To begin; get started: *Let's play ball now, it's time* **2** *v phr* To cooperate; collaborate; acquiesce: *I might have played ball just a little, but I scorned to*—Agnes DeMille **3** *v phr* To deal honestly and fairly: *He was playing ball with Artrim*—Erle Stanley Gardner [fr baseball]

◁**play bouncy-bouncy**▷ *v phr* To do the sex act, esp in the superior position; copulate: *He keeps cool...while she plays bouncy-bouncy on him*—Herbert Gold

playboy *n* *fr 1920s* A man devoted to glossy and luxurious self-indulgence; bon vivant; = GOOD-TIME CHARLIE, MAN-ABOUT-TOWN

play catch-up (or **catch-up ball**) **1** *v phr* To play a game determinedly and desperately when one is losing: *when college wishbone teams go to the air to play catchup*—Sports Illustrated **2** *v phr* To work to recover from a disadvantage, defeat, etc: *After the quarterly profits disaster we had to play catch-up/ For the last two years it's been a matter of playing catch-up ball with the budget*—Washington Post

play checkers *v phr* *homosexuals* To move about from seat to seat in a movie theater, soliciting possible sex partners

play close to the chest (or **the vest**) *v phr* To be secretive and uncommunicative; keep one's counsel [fr the practice of a careful card player]

play dirty *v phr* To use unethical, illegal, or injurious means; be deceptive and tricky; chicane: *When he started in politics he didn't mean to play dirty*

play-doctor *n theater* A writer who specializes in altering and improving other writers' plays

played out **1** *adj phr* *fr late 1800s* Exhausted; worn out; =AUSGESPIELT, FRAZZLED: *I was played out, and quit at once* **2** *adj phr* No longer useful, viable, fashionable, etc: *I think the alienation theme is about played out*

player **1** *n* *gamblers* A bettor: *A lot of players are avoiding OTB* **2** *n* =SWINGER **3** *n* A pimp: *some of his fellow "players" (as pimps refer to themselves)*—F Ianni

See BUTTON MAN, CHALK-EATER, HORSEPLAYER, PICCOLO PLAYER

play footsie *See* FOOTSIE

play for keeps (or **rough**) *v phr* To be intent and serious to the point of callousness; =PLAY HARDBALL: *We're out here man for man and playin' for keeps*—Claude Brown/ *I thought, well, if they can play rough, we can too* [fr the game of marbles and other childrens' games where the tokens may be either returned or *kept* by the winner]

play games *v phr* To maneuver and manipulate cunningly; toy and gamble: *Don't play games with me, Linda*—National Lampoon/ *the temptation to "play games" with the companies' stock prices*—Fortune

playgirl *n* A woman devoted to glossy and luxurious self-indulgence

◁**play grab-ass**▷ *v phr* To indulge in sexual clutching and touching; to feel and fondle; =GROPE ● Sometimes used metaphorically: *were currently inside a doughnut shop, playing grabass with the counter girl*—Easyriders/ *His reluctance to play what he called grab-ass with Congress*—Newsweek

play handies *v phr* To indulge in the mutual fondling of hands: *Beneath the counter they were playing handies*—Christopher Morley

play hardball *v phr* To be intent and serious to the point of callousness; =PLAY FOR KEEPS: *You want to play hardball, here we go*—George Warren/ *Helms Plays Hardball*—Newsweek [fr the presumed distinction in difficulty, severity, and manliness between baseball, that is, *hardball*, and softball]

play hell with something *v phr* To damage or destroy: *The rain had played hell with business*—Armistead Maupin [fr *play hell and Tommy*, attested in the mid-19th century and said to be fr earlier *play Hal and Tommy*, in reference to the behavior of Henry VIII and his minister Thomas Cromwell]

◁**play hide the weenie**▷ *v phr* To do the sex act; copulate; =SCREW

play hooky (or **hookey**) *v phr* *fr middle 1800s students* To stay away from work and duty, or esp from school without an excuse; be truant [probably fr *hook it*]

play in Peoria *v phr* To succeed in areas distinct from such focuses of power as Washington and New York or the Northeast in general: *When you're under a deadline, it's hard to judge what will play in Peoria*—Art Buchwald [fr the theater sense of *play*, to succeed on the stage]

play in the family *See* PLAY THE DOZENS

play it by ear *v phr* To handle a situation instinctively and extemporaneously, rather than by informed planning; improvise: *We didn't have much to go on, so we just had to play it by ear* [fr the playing of music imitatively, without training and notation]

play it cool *v phr* To behave in a calm, controlled, uncommitted way; be watchful and impassive: *We asked for a price and the agent "played it cool"*—Publishers Weekly

play it (or **play**) **safe** *v phr* To choose a cautious line of behavior; avoid much risk: *Now we're ahead, let's play it safe*

play kissie (Variations: **kissy-face** or **kissy-facey** or **kissie-kissie** or **kissy-poo** or **lickey-face** or **smacky lips** may replace **kissie**) **1** *v phr* To kiss and caress; =MAKE OUT, NECK: *Salesmen got them to buy an awful lot of perfume when they weren't busy playing lickey-face*—New York Post/ *Newlyweds play kissy-poo in a resort hotel*—People Weekly **2** *v phr* To be friendly and flattering; =PLAY UP TO someone: *We have to play kissie with him*—New Yorker

playmate *n* One's companion in the pursuit of pleasure, esp of sexual delight

play (or **play Man**) **on** someone *v phr esp black* To treat roughly; intimidate physically: *If Tony stole your woman...you'll get your chance to play on him*—Donald Goines/ *Dreamer can't play Man on Shake...Shake'll dust his ass*—Dan Jenkins

play penny pool *v phr* To deal in paltry matters; be concerned with childish trivia: *This isn't penny pool these guys are playing*—George Warren

play rough *See* PLAY FOR KEEPS

plays *See* the WAY IT PLAYS

play second fiddle *v phr fr middle 1700s or earlier* To be in an inferior position; lack power or will to lead: *They won't play second fiddle to their spouses any more*

play snuggle-bunnies *v phr* To kiss and caress; cuddle amorously; =PLAY KISSIE: *Mr. De Varennes is playing snuggle-bunnies with Mrs. Martin*—Washington Post

◁**play stinky-pinky** (or **stink-finger**)▷ *v phr* =FINGERFUCK

play the dozens (or **the dirty dozens**) *black fr early 1900s* **1** *v phr* To play an elaborate word-game of reciprocal insult, esp against the opponent's mother: *Great God from Zion!...Y'all really playing de dozens tuhnight!*—Zora Neale Hurston **2** *v phr* To take advantage of; deceive; =DO A NUMBER ON: *He burst into tears, crying, "You all played the dozens on me"*—Joseph Wambaugh [origin unknown]

play the field *v phr* To have a number of sex or love partners, rather than settling on one: *I thought I'd play the field, until Joan came along* [fr gamblers who bet on other horses than the favorites]

◁**play the skin flute**▷ *v phr* To do fellatio

play up to someone *v phr fr early 1800s British theater* To flatter; be compliant: *If you play up to him he'll think you're brilliant* [fr the behavior of an actor who gives featuring support to another]

play who shot John *v phr Army* To bandy excuses, recriminations, accusations, etc

play whupass (WHUHP as) *v phr* To have a rough sort of game, fight, etc: *Our Frogs are gonna play some whupass with the Rice Owls today* [fr a dialect pronunciation of *whip ass*]

◁**play with** oneself▷ *v phr* To masturbate; =JACK OFF: *I was going with girls...and I didn't feel the urge to play with myself*—HK Fink

play (or **deal** or **operate**) **with a full deck** **1** *v phr* To be sane and reasonable; have normal intelligence ● Usu in the negative: *Neither of the poor things was playing with a full deck*—Saul Bellow/ *but she is dealing with a full deck, as it were* —Philadelphia Journal/ *He wasn't playing with a full deck of cards*—John Irving **2** *v phr* To be honest and straightforward; avoid deception: *He has bluffed you into thinking he was playing with a full deck* —Playboy

plea *See* COP A PLEA

plead the fifth (or **a five**) *v phr cool musicians* To refuse to do something; opt out: *Pleading a five, when one cat refuses to get up on the bandstand and play with another*—E Horne [fr the legal *plea* to the *Fifth* Amendment of the US Constitution, against self-incrimination]

pleat *See* REET PLEAT

plebe *n service academy* A first-year student at a service academy [fr *plebeian* "lower-class person," fr Latin]

pledge **1** *n students fr late 1800s* A student who has agreed to join a certain college fraternity or sorority **2** *v: Without a second thought MacCrimmon pledged Xi Phi*

plenty *adv* Very; very much; extraordinarily: *I was plenty cautious*—Erle Stanley Gardner

pling *v hoboes* To beg; beg from

plonk **1** *n fr 1930s British fr Australian* Inferior wine; cheap wine: *It's a humble plonk, but you'll like it* **2** *n* A boring and obnoxious person; =PILL

plonked *adj* Drunk

plotzed *adj* Drunk: *even smashed as you were, friend, plotzed out of your wits*—John D MacDonald [probably fr Yiddish *plotzen*, German *platzen* "burst, split," reflecting the same notion of violent destruction as *smashed, bombed, etc*]

◁**plow** or **plough**▷ *v fr time immemorial* To do the sex act with or to a woman; =SCREW

plow (or **plough**) **into** **1** *v phr* To collide with very hard; ram: *so long as they don't fry in the sun or plow into an atmosphere*—CoEvolution Quarterly **2** *v phr* To attack heartily; assault: *We ploughed into the scumbags and made quick work of them/ They plowed into the job and finished it that day*

ploy *n fr 1700s British fr dialect* A device or stratagem; a move, esp one designed to disconcert an opponent while keeping one's position; a shrewd maneuver ● Popularized by the late British humorist Stephen Potter

PLU (pronounced as separate letters) *adj* Admirable and fitting; discriminating: *The wife admires their living room ("Very PLU, people like us")*—Judith Crist [fr *people like us*]

pluck[1] *v* To rob or cheat; fleece: *These bimbos once helped pluck a bank*—Dashiell Hammett [fr the image of *plucking* a chicken]

◁**pluck**[2]▷ *v* To do the sex act with or to; =SCREW [a rhyming euphemism for *fuck*]

plug[1] **1** *n fr middle 1800s* An inferior old horse; =NAG **2** *n fr early 1900s* An average or inferior prizefighter [perhaps fr Dutch *plug* "a sorry nag," related to Swiss-German *pflag* and to Danish *plag* "foal"]

plug[2] **1** *n fr late 1800s* A silver dollar **2** *n* A counterfeit coin or one tampered with by the insertion of a plug of inferior metal **3** *adj* (also **plugged**) Worthless; =PHONY ● This sense may be influenced by the notion of inferiority in **plug**[1]: *and furthermore the author does not give a plug damn*—Pauline Kael **4** *v fr middle 1800s* To shoot, esp shoot to death: *The mugger got plugged by an indignant on-looker* **5** *n railroad* A locomotive's throttle [all senses fr the notion of *plug* as hole-filler]

See CUT-PLUG, PULL THE PLUG, SPARK PLUG

plug[3] **1** *v* (also **plug along** or **plug away**) *fr middle 1800s British students* To work steadily and fairly hard; keep busy but not excitingly so: *I plugged away at the required subjects* **2** *v* To give a flattering appraisal, esp with a view to selling something; advocate and support; cry up: *Cosmetic manufacturers plugged products to give women ersatz tan*—R Adler/ *If you'll plug my book I'll plug yours* **3** *n: I certainly would appreciate him giving me a plug with the owners*—John O'Hara [fr Oxford University slang, apparently in imitation of heavy plodding steps, or perhaps the steps of an old and tired horse; sense of selling or advocating fr the fact that such commendation was originally constant and repetitive]

plug for *v phr* To support actively; cheer for; =ROOT FOR: *She was plugging for the coalition candidate*

plugged in (or **into**) **1** *adj phr* In direct touch with; sensitive to and aware of: *Teachers simply aren't plugged into the world*—Richard Yates/ *You have to be very careful that you stay plugged in* —Newsweek **2** *adj phr* =TURNED ON [fr the metaphor of a person as an electrical or electronic device]

plugged nickel *See* NOT WORTH A PLUGGED NICKEL

plugger **1** *n fr late 1800s* A diligent but not brilliant worker or student; dependable drudge **2** *n* A hired killer; =HIT MAN

plug hat *n phr fr middle 1800s* A top hat

plug in (or **into**) **1** *v phr* To become a part of; participate in; gain access to: *Parents were beginning to be plugged directly into the decision-making process*—Toronto Life/ *Wilson initially plugged in to what he terms "an old-boy network of 26-year-olds"* —GQ **2** *v phr* To discover and exploit to one's advantage; tap: *Nixon...has plugged into a great* *national yearning*—Hugh Sidey [fr the notion of the electrical *plug* and socket]

plugola 1 *n* Illicit payment, often not in money, given to media people for mentioning commercial products in noncommercial contexts **2** *n* Such a mention; =PLUG [based on *payola*]

plug puller *n phr* railroad A locomotive engineer, that is, one who pulls the throttle

plug-ugly *fr middle 1800s* **1** *n* A rowdy; tough; =GORILLA, HOOD **2** *n* A prizefighter; =PUG [origin unknown; perhaps fr the fact that such persons are *ugly* from being *plugged* "hit" in the face; perhaps fr competing Baltimore volunteer fire companies who became combative around *fireplugs*; a Baltimore origin is strongly suggested by the early occurrences]

plum *n fr late 1800s* Something highly prized, esp an easy job with high pay and prestige, usu given for political favors [probably influenced by Little Jack Horner's feat of reaching in his thumb and pulling out a *plum* (in fact a raisin); compare early-19th-century British *plummy* "good, desirable"]

plumb *adv fr late 1500s* Completely; entirely; =STONE: *What he said was plumb silly* [fr notions of exact extent and precision associated with the *plumb bob* or sailor's *plumb line* (for measuring depth of water), ultimately fr Latin *plumbum* "lead"]

plumber 1 *v* To botch; ruin: *I tho't I plumbered it* —John O'Hara **2** *n* esp 1970s A member of a White House group under President Richard M Nixon which exerted itself to stop various leaks of confidential information: *One of the jobs carried out by the plumbers was burglarizing the office of Dr Daniel Ellsberg's former psychiatrist*—New York Times

plumbing 1 *n* jive musicians A trumpet **2** *n* The digestive, excretory, and reproductive systems and organs: *Something is really wrong with my plumbing; I haven't been able to eat or make love in weeks*

plummy *adj* Rich and sonorous; orotund and fruity; unctuous; =SMARMY: *the rich, plummy voice of Edward Arnold*—K Harris/ *He is a master of the plummy compliment*

plump or **plunk** *adv* Precisely; exactly; =SMACK: *It came down plump on his head*/ *She stood plunk on the line* [fr *plumb*]

plump down *See* PLANK DOWN

plumpie or **plumpy** *n* An overweight person; a chubby person: *A studio of plumpies!*—Esquire

plunk *fr late 1800s* **1** *n* A dollar: *my five thousand plunks*—H McHugh **2** *v* To shoot: *I saw him and plunked him* [echoic]

plunk down *See* PLANK DOWN

plunkie *n* circus A cookhouse waiter

plush or **plushy 1** *adj* Luxurious; stylish; costly: *a swank, plush, exclusive cabaret club*—Westbrook Pegler/ *singer Ella Logan at the plushy Casablanca* —Budd Schulberg **2** *n*: *All the plush in the world won't tidy up his vulgar soul* [fr the soft and costly fabric]

plushery *n* A plush hotel, nightclub, restaurant, etc

plute *n fr late 1800s* A rich person; plutocrat: *The tutoring sections were only for "plutes"*—P Marks

po *See* PISSED OFF

pocket *n* A constricted place; cul de sac: *He was afraid they had him in a pocket* *See* DEEP POCKET, HIGHPOCKETS, IN someone's POCKET, IN THE POCKET, OUT OF POCKET

pocket cabbage (or **lettuce**) *n phr* Money

pocket litter *n phr* The usual miscellany in a person's pocket: *just a driver's license and some pocket litter*—H Hunt

◁**pocket pool**▷ *n phr* The fondling of one's own genitals with a pocketed hand

po'd *See* PISSED OFF

pod *n* narcotics Marijuana; =POT: *Diane smoked jive, pod, and tea*—Orville Prescott [origin unknown; perhaps fr the *pod*, or seed container, the flowering and fruiting head of the female cannabis plant]

pod people *n phr* Stupid, unfeeling, machinelike people; =ZOMBIES: *Have body snatchers invaded America's airwaves? Is this pure pop for pod people?*—Newsweek [fr the extraterrestrial creatures depicted in the movie *Invasion of the Body Snatchers*, who spawn in *pods* and take over the bodies of human beings]

podspeak *n* Automatic, meaningless, ritual talk, the idiom of pod people; tedious bromides: *Clerks utter such podspeak as the inescapable "Have a nice day"*—Washington Post

Podunk (POH dunk) *n fr early 1900s* The legendary small country town; =EAST JESUS, JERKWATER TOWN [originally an Algonquian place name, meaning "a neck or corner of land," used for several places in New England]

pogey or **pogie** or **pogy** (POH gee) **1** *n* hoboes fr late 1800s A poorhouse, workhouse, or old folks' home **2** *n* A jail; =POKEY **3** *n* Free food, as distributed by charity, sent to soldiers, prisoners, etc, esp candy and cake; =POGEY BAIT **4** *n* =POGUE [origin unknown; perhaps fr the common name of the trash fish menhaden, as suggesting something cheap, common, and to be caught with bait; perhaps fr the Southern pronunciation of *porgy*, another fish of a similar quality; both fish names are of obscure origin]

pogey bait *n phr* (Variations: **pogie** or **pogy** or **poggie** or **poggy** may replace **pogey**) *fr WW1 armed forces* Candy and cake, etc; sweets; nonmilitary food and delicacies carried on field exercises [so called because they could be used in the seduction of boys and young men, *pogues*, into homosexual acts]

poggie (PAW gee) *n* Army A recruit; =DUMBJOHN, ROOKIE

pogue (POHG) **1** *n* A youthful homosexual male, or either willing or unwilling partner of a homosexual male; =PUNK: *The kid was a pogue*—Robert Stone **2** *n* esp Vietnam War armed forces Any despicable boy or young man; =PUNK: *I was just a pogue, humpin' connex containers at a depot in Long Binh*—Doonesbury (comic strip)/ *Yeah, that's the pogue's name*—Pat Conroy [shortened form of *pogey*]

point **1** *n* *prizefight fr 1920s* The jaw **2** *n* *narcotics* A hypodermic needle; = SPIKE **3** *n* (also **point man**) *fr armed forces & underworld* A forward reconnaissance man; lookout man; scout who warns his associates of danger, and may get the first shock of attack: *He is the point man for organized labor*—Philadelphia Journal
See BROWNIE POINTS

pointed head **1** *n phr* A stupid, duncelike mind; a brainless cranium: *I hope you got that idea into your pointed head, creep* **2** *n phr* An intellectual; = BIGDOME, EGGHEAD: *the guys who think we're all a bunch of pointed heads and all we want is poetry*—Washington Post

pointer *n* An item of advice or instruction: *She gave me a few pointers about how to say it*
See FOUR-POINTER

pointhead or **pointy-head** **1** *n* A stupid person; = TURKEY **2** *n* An intellectual; = EGGHEAD: *The "pointy heads" are impractical as politicians*—Newsweek

point-shaving *n sports & gambling* The illegal practice, esp on the part of athletes, of controlling the score of a game, match, series, etc, so that professional gamblers will have to pay less to the bettors or will win for themselves

point-spread *n gambling* The difference between the handicapping points added or subtracted for various teams in football and basketball betting

pointy-headed **1** *adj* Intellectual; cultured: *uninterested in...any of the pointy-headed criticism generated in the last two decades*—Village Voice/ *considered scientists like Wald pointy-headed intellectuals out to decommission the whole industry*—Philadelphia **2** *adj* Stupid; idiotic

poison **1** *n* A situation, person, event, etc, that portends harm and evil; = MURDER: *Don't try that route, it's poison* **2** *n fr early 1800s* Liquor, esp cheap whiskey
See SNAKE POISON

poisoning *See* LEAD-POISONING

poison-pen letter *n phr* A malicious anonymous letter; an obscene crank letter

poke[1] **1** *v fr late 1800s cowboys* To herd cattle **2** *n fr late 1800s* A cowboy: *Each poke pays his own transportation to the Rodeo*—Ithaca Journal **3** *n* = SLOWPOKE **4** *v baseball* To hit the ball, esp to hit fairly lightly with precise aim: *He just poked it into the hole* ◁**5**▷ *v fr late 1800s* To do the sex act with or to; = SCREW
See BUY A PIG IN A POKE, COWPOKE, GUNPOKE, SLOWPOKE

poke[2] *fr hoboes, underworld & carnival* **1** *n* A wallet, pocket, or purse: *with only about $85 in my poke*—John O'Hara/ *bumped into me and helped himself to my "poke"*—New York **2** *n* Money; one's bankroll [fr Southern dialect, "pocket, bag," fr Middle English, ultimately fr Old Norman French]

poke a tip *v phr hawkers* To give a free show or free gifts to attract a crowd

poke fun *v phr* To tease; jape; mock

poke one's **nose into** something *v phr* To pry and meddle; examine: *and to poke your nose into all the most interesting places*—Philadelphia

poke-out *n hoboes fr late 1800s* Food, esp that handed out in a package from a back door: *He returned with a "poke-out"*—J Flynt

poker face **1** *n phr* An expressionless face; neutral mask; = DEADPAN **2** *n phr* A person whose face is usually expressionless

poker-faced *adj* Without expression; showing a neutral mask; = DEADPAN, STRAIGHT-FACED: *She's great at poker-faced zingers*

pokerino **1** *n* A poker game with very small stakes **2** *n* Any paltry game, transaction, business, etc

pokery *See* JIGGERY-POKERY

pokey[1] or **poky** *n* A jail; = CLINK, SLAMMER: *My thoughts centered around the prospect of the "Pokey"*—James Simon Kunen [origin unknown]

pokey[2] or **poky** **1** *adj* Slow; dawdling; sluggish: *What a pokey waiter* **2** *adj* Insignificant; paltry: *a pokey little town* [fr poke[1], apparently as a contrast between merely *about* and an action of more vigor]
See HOKEY-POKEY

pol (PAHL) *n* A politician: *only another pol on the take*—Newsweek

◁**polack**▷ (POH lahk) (also **pollack** or **Pollack** or **pollock** or **Pollock**) **1** *n* A Pole or a person of Polish extraction **2** *adj*: *a polack miner* ● It is curious that this word is pejorative in English even though it is the Polish word for "Pole"

pole *See* BEANPOLE, NOT TOUCH someone or something WITH A TEN-FOOT POLE

poler *n early 1900s college students* An overstudious student; = GREASY GRIND: [Edmund Wilson] *was a withdrawn..."poler" or grind*—A Turnbull [perhaps fr late-19th-century sense "a horse or other draught animal harnessed to the shaft (pole) of a wagon," hence a workhorse as distinguished fr a showier beast]

police or **police up** *v* or *v phr esp armed forces fr middle 1800s* To clean up a camp, barracks, parade ground, etc; make neat and orderly

Polish *See* IS THE POPE POLISH

polish apples *v phr* = APPLE-POLISH

polisher *See* APPLE-POLISHER, BONE-POLISHER

polish off *fr early 1800s British* **1** *v phr* To eat; consume, esp quickly and heartily: *I had polished off a platter of beans*—Boston Post **2** *v phr* To finish; accomplish: *He polished off the week's quota in four days* **3** *v phr* To put out of action; defeat; kill: *polish him off by crowning him with a Coca-Cola bottle*—Life

politician *n* A person who succeeds through charm, diplomacy, mutual favors, etc: *If you called him an asshole to his face you're no politician*

politico (pə LI ti koh) *n* A politician, esp a spectacular or unscrupulous one: *the heavy-duty Bay State politicoes* [fr Spanish or Italian]

pollack or **pollock** or **Pollock** *See* POLACK

polloi *See* POP POLLOI

polluted *adj* Drunk

polly *n movie studio* An unwanted echo in a recording or tape

◁**pom-pom**▷ *n* The sex act; = SCREWING [perhaps fr the echoic name *pom-pom* of various rapid-fire automatic guns]

ponce 1 *n chiefly British fr late 1800s British* A pimp, or any man supported by a woman **2** *v: He quit work and took to poncing* [origin unknown; perhaps fr French *pensionnaire* "boarder, lodger, person living without working"]

the **pond** *n* The ocean

  See the BIG POND, the HERRING POND

◀**pong**[1]▶ *n fr Australian* A Chinese or a person of Chinese extraction

pong[2] *n fr middle 1800s British* A smell; a stink: *when I catch that pong in the air*—Robert Stone [perhaps fr Romany *pan* "stink"]

pony 1 *n students fr early 1800s* A literal translation of a foreign-language school text, used as a cheating aid; = TROT **2** *n* Any cheating aid as used by a student **3** *n fr late 1800s* A small, bell-shaped liquor glass, used esp for brandy and liqueurs **4** *n* A racehorse: *Do you follow the ponies?* **5** *n* A chorus girl or burlesque dancer: *The ponies...slumped into place*—F Scott Fitzgerald/ *pony in a burlecue*—F Brown [in all senses fr the thing being small like a *pony*; the student senses, which have or have had *horse* and *trot* as synonyms, may also suggest something that carries one, gives one a free ride]

pony act *See* DOG AND PONY ACT

pony up *v phr fr early 1800s* To pay; = FORK OVER: *He had ponied up a silver quarter*—Jack London/ *got tired of ponying up $100 for my connection* —San Francisco/ *The Faulkners ponied up a cool million*—People Weekly [fr earlier British *post the pony* "pay," fr 16th century *legem pone* "money," fr the title of the Psalm for quarter day, March 25, the first payday of the year]

poo or **pooh 1** *interj* A mild exclamation of disbelief, dismay, disappointment, etc: *Oh poo, I dropped it* **2** *n* Excrement; = DO, POO-POO ● Along with **pooh**, this is a euphemism used by and to children: *Zoo Poo garden fertilizer is made from the waste of all manner of exotic creatures* —Toronto Life/ *and just about any old pooh that dribbles from McLaren's mouth*—Village Voice

  See CUTESY-POO, HOT POO, ICKY

-poo *combining word* Little; silly little ● A nonsense word used after diminutive forms to give an arch baby-talk effect: *A little kissy-poo?*/ *settled down for a well-bred nappy-poo*—Village Voice

pooch *n* A dog: *a card for...your pooch*—Associated Press

  See SCREW THE POOCH

pooched out *adj phr* Protruding: *round shoulders, pooched out stomach*—Glamor

poochy 1 *n* = POOCH **2** *adj* Doggy; doglike: *a poochy smell*

poodle-faker 1 *n WW1 Army fr British* A self-important newly commissioned officer **2** *n* = LADIES' MAN [second sense fr the notion that such

a man would emulate a *poodle* or other lapdog to ingratiate himself with women]

◁**poof**▷ *n* (also **poofter** or **poove** or **pouffe**) *chiefly British fr early 1900s Australian* A male homosexual; = FAGGOT, QUEER [origin unknown; perhaps echoic of a male homosexual's more or less feminine interjections *poof!* or *poo!*; perhaps fr French *pouf* "cushioned ottoman chair," with its suggestions of effete luxury; perhaps fr *puff*, attested in mid-19th-century British hobo slang as "homosexual," and semantically akin to *blow* "do fellatio"; perhaps fr *puff* in the sense of something soft and unmanly, as seen in *powderpuff* or *creampuff*]

pooh-bah *n fr late 1800s* An important person; = BIG SHOT, HONCHO, VIP: *where presidents and pooh-bahs commune*—Westworld [fr the character in Gilbert and Sullivan's *The Mikado*, the name probably coined fr two exclamations of contempt and derision]

poohed or **poohed out** *adj* or *adj phr* = POOPED

pool *See* DIRTY POOL, PENNY POOL, PLAY PENNY POOL, POCKET POOL

poolroom *n horse-racing & gambling fr late 1800s* An illegal bookmaker's establishment: *a poolroom...from auction-pool betting*—T Betts

◀**poon tang** or **poon**▶ *n phr* or *n* A black woman regarded as a sex object or partner: *Eye that poon tang there*—Calder Willingham/ *just about to get a little poon*—Village Voice/ *watching all that young poon*—Joseph Wambaugh [probably fr French *putain* "prostitute," by way of New Orleans Creole; though perhaps fr Chinese, since variants *poong tai* and *poong kai* have been recorded, according to Eric Partridge]

poop[1] *n fr 1930s Army & students* Information; data; = SCOOP: *The girl's given us the complete poop*—G Cotler [see *poop sheet*]

poop[2] **1** *n fr early 1900s* Excrement; = POO ● Along with **poo**, this is a euphemism for use to and by children **2** *v: The dog pooped on the rug* **3** *n* A contemptible, trifling person; = PILL ● Often used ironically and affectionately, esp of an old person: *a sweet old poop who was seventy-six* —Kurt Vonnegut, Jr/ *a poop like Belfont*—Sinclair Lewis **4** *v* To tire; fatigue; = BUSH: *Being with him poops me exceedingly* [probably fr a merging of 14th-century *poupen* "to toot," with 15th-century *poop* "the rear part of a ship," fr Latin *puppis* of the same meaning; the fatigue sense may be related to the condition of a ship which is *pooped* "has taken a wave over the stern"]

◁**poop chute**▷ *n phr* The anus: *I fingered her pussy and poop chute*—Penthouse

pooped or **pooped out** *adj* or *adj phr fr late 1800s* Exhausted; deeply fatigued; = BEAT, BUSHED: *starting to get pooped out*—James T Farrell/ *deflated derrieres and pooped out pecs*—San Francisco [fr a British nautical term describing a ship that has been swept by a wave at the stern]

pooper *See* PARTY-POOPER

pooper (or **poop**) **scooper** *n phr* A shovel and container set designed for cleaning one's dog's feces off the sidewalk, and, by extension, anything so used: *to buy a pooper scooper or something like it*—Village Voice/ *bearing a paper bag and a poop-scooper*—Newsweek

poo-poo or **pooh-pooh** **1** *v* To dismiss lightly and contemptuously; airily deprecate; deride: *I don't poo-poo his talent, just his character* **2** *n* Excrement; = POO ● A euphemism used to and by children: *He reverts to that childishness of poo-poo ca-ca*—Time/ *hit in the head with a potty full of poo-poo*—High Times

poop (or **poo**) **out** *v phr* To fail; lose energy and impetus; stop striving: *They would have won, but they suddenly just pooped out*

poop sheet *n phr fr 1930s Army & students* Any set of data, instructions, official notices, etc: *Here's the poop sheet from the comptroller* [origin unknown; perhaps fr *poop* "excrement"; improbably but possibly an unaccounted shortening of *liripoop* "lore, tricks of the trade" as found in the 16th-century phrases *to know one's liripoop, to teach someone his liripoop*, perhaps related to *lerrie* "something learned or spoken by rote"]

poop someone **up** *v phr* Army To inform; brief; = FILL someone IN

◁**poor-ass**▷ *adj* Wretched; nasty; = LOUSY: *a poor-ass place to live*—Earl Thompson

poor boy *n phr* A very large sandwich; = DAGWOOD, HERO SANDWICH [perhaps so called because the ingredients are not elegant or costly, and the sandwich is large]

poor-boy it *v phr* To be forced to impoverished extremities; be severely deprived: *We're poor-boying it in Criminal Court*—New York Times

poor deck *See* DEAL someone A POOR DECK

poor fish *n phr* An ordinary person, esp regarded as a victim of existential perversity: *The poor fish is damned if he does and damned if he doesn't*

poor John (or **john**) *n phr* An average man, whose fortunes are notably more meager than his merits

poor man's something or someone *n phr fr late 1700s* A thing or person less glamorous, desirable, famous, etc, than the top grade: *the Poor Man's Palm Beach*—Ring Lardner/ *Burton, "Poor Man's Olivier"*—The Morning Telegraph

poor-mouth **1** *v* To deny one's wealth and advantages; emphasize one's deficiencies; = TALK POOR MOUTH: *Richard Nixon often poor-mouthed his chances*—J Rekkanen **2** *v* To deprecate severely; = BAD-MOUTH: *I'm not going around poor-mouthing the war*—A Shuster

◁**poot**▷ **1** *n fr black* Excrement; = CRAP, SHIT: *Did she think I usually walked around festooned in pigeon poot?*—Village Voice/ *Which one of you has got the most poot stains on your underwear?*—Dan Jenkins **2** *n* A contemptible person; = PILL, POOP: *some old poots patrolling with a dog or two*—John Farris **3** *v* To flatulate; = FART **4** *n: The dog laid a loud poot* [probably a variant of *poo* or *poop*]

poot around *v phr* To waste time; behave frivolously: *There's been a lot of pootin' around but very little maximum effort*—Pat Conroy

pootbutt *n black* A callow and ignorant person; a stupid and unfledged youth, esp one lacking the cunning of the ghetto: *show Chester that he wasn't a poot-butt*—Donald Goines

poove *See* POOF

pop¹ or **pops** **1** *n* Father: *My pop's the champ/ Your pops is an interesting guy* **2** *n* An older or elderly man ● Used in informal, yet respectful, direct address: *Hey, pop, slow down a bit*

pop² **1** *n* Flavored carbonated water; soda; soda pop **2** *n* Ice cream or flavored ice on a stick; Popsicle (a trade name) **3** *n car-racing & hot rodders* Nitromethane or any other fuel additive for cars: *fuel additives...called pop*—Fort Worth Star-Telegram **4** *v narcotics* To take narcotics by injection; = SHOOT UP **5** *v narcotics* To take pills, esp barbiturates, amphetamines, etc, and esp habitually **6** *n narcotics* A quantity of narcotics; = BAG: *Each of them had a couple of pops on 'em*—New York ◁**7**▷ *v* To do the sex act with or to; = JAZZ, SCREW: *Well, did you pop her?*—Claude Brown ◁**8**▷ *n* The sex act; sexual activity; = SCREWING **9** *v* To give birth: *She expects to pop in November* **10** *v* To hit; smack: *popped him on the snoot* **11** *v* To achieve spectacularly; hit: *I knew if I had a good day, I could really pop one*—Newsweek **12** *v student* To catch: *The guard popped us as we tried to sneak in the back door* [all senses related to *pop* as an echoic term for a sharp noise or a sharp blow]

pop³ *adj* Popular; having a very broad audience: *Tom Wolfe, the pop journalist*—New York Times/ *well thought of nowadays by pop ecologists*—Sports Illustrated

a **pop** *n phr* A time; each occasion; = CRACK: *stay up...for hours at a pop*—New Jersey/ *Steinem gets $3000 a pop for talking*—New York Times [fr *pop* "blow, stroke, crack," and according to Eric Partridge used by the Australians in the 1920s] *See* DOUGH-POP

pop a drum *v phr* To rupture an eardrum

pop a wheelie *v phr motorcyclists & bicyclists* To raise the front wheel of a motorcycle or bicycle off the ground and ride on the rear wheel only

pop bottle *n phr photography* An inferior lens in a camera or photo-enlarger

pop car *n phr railroad* A small, motor-driven open car used by track workers [fr the *pop-pop* sound of the one-cylinder engine]

◁**pop** someone's **cherry**▷ *v phr* To terminate someone's virginity: *I would definitely pop his cherry*—Xaviera Hollander

◁**pop** one's **cookies**▷ *v phr* To have an orgasm; climax; = COME: *The knot comes away, and he pops his cookies*—Xaviera Hollander/ *Madam Gray, who couldn't ever pop her cookies enough*—Paul Sann

pop one's **cork** *v phr* To become furious; explode angrily; = BLOW one's TOP: *I didn't expect her to pop her cork either*—Dennis Day

Pope *See* IS THE POPE POLISH

the **pope's** (or **the parson's**) **nose** *n phr* The triangular tailpiece of a cooked fowl

Popeye *n* Spinach

popeyed 1 *adj* Having protuberant eyes; exophthalmic; = BUGEYED **2** *adj* Regrettable; nasty; = COCKEYED: *Ain't it a popeyed shame?*

pop for *v phr* To pay for, esp as a treat to others; = PICK UP THE TAB: *I'll pop for the drinks*

popoff 1 *n* A death or killing **2** *n* A bragging, blatant, brash, and/or stupid declaration: *It was a typical senatorial popoff*—Ithaca Journal **3** *n* = BIGMOUTH

pop off 1 *v phr* *fr middle 1700s* To die: *If he had popped off sooner, less trouble for all* **2** *v phr* To talk loudly and perhaps prematurely; = SHOOT OFF one's MOUTH: *I'm not popping off about the pennant until we get it*—Casey Stengel **3** *v phr* To leave; depart; = TODDLE OFF

pop someone **off** *v phr* *fr early 1800s* To kill someone, esp by shooting: *The police never found who popped off the informer off*

popout *n surfers* A mass-produced surfboard

pop out *v phr baseball* To make an out by hitting a short but often high fly ball

poppa 1 *n* One's father **2** *n* Any older man **3** *n* = DADDY, SUGAR DADDY

pop party *n phr narcotics* A gathering or party for the purpose of taking narcotics

popper 1 *n black* A pistol **2** *n narcotics* A pill or capsule of amyl or butyl nitrite: *I'm just giving you a harmless popper*—Xaviera Hollander/ *use poppers and speed*—New York Times

See EYEPOPPER, FINGER-POPPER, JOY-POPPER, PILL-POPPER

pop polloi *n phr* The common people; hoi polloi

poppycock *n fr middle 1800s* Nonsense; foolishness [apparently fr Dutch *pappekak* "soft dung"]

pop quiz or **shotgun quiz** or **pop test** *n phr college students* A surprise test; an unexpected examination

pops *See* POP

the **pops** *n phr* Popular records, songs, etc: *the best of the pops*

popskull *n* Raw inferior whiskey; = MOONSHINE

pop-top 1 *n* A small sailboat, camper, etc, whose top rises to provide headroom and sleeping room **2** *n* (also **flip-top**) A beverage can with a preperforated opening and a ring-like lever on the top for access to the liquid

pop up *v phr baseball* To hit a high fly ball in the infield, either fair or foul

pop-up *n baseball* A high fly ball in the infield

pop wine *n phr* Any very sweet wine of low alcoholic content: *"pop" wines, low-alcohol, fruit-flavored wines specially designed for the soda- and fruit-punch palate*—New York [because they are bought by drinkers of soda *pop*]

porcelain god *See* PRAY TO THE PORCELAIN GOD

porcelain hairnet *See* WIN THE PORCELAIN HAIRNET

porcupine *n WW2 Navy* A frayed wire rope

◁**pork**▷ *v* To do the sex act; copulate; = SCREW: *I decided to lay some groundwork for porking her brains out*—National Lampoon

pork and *n phr lunch counter* Pork and beans

pork-chopper *n labor union* A person, like a venal officer or friend or relative of an officer, on a union's payroll with a sinecure

pork out *v phr* To eat over-heartily; overeat; = PIG OUT: *We were porking out on three sweet rolls*—Clark County Press

porky *adj* Obese; porcine: *a porky, middle-aged waitress with a mustache and bad feet*—Lawrence Sanders

porn or **porno 1** *n* Pornography: *the merry world of pimps and porno*—Judith Crist/ *or witness the amount of porn around*—Saturday Review **2** *adj:* *The very best porn film ever made*—New York Times/ *little prospect of pay-TV turning our homes into porno palaces*—David Lachenbruch

porny *adj* Pornographic

portable parking lot *n phr truckers* A car-hauler truck

portsider 1 *n* A lefthanded person; = SOUTHPAW: *We despair that portsiders will ever get their rights*—Philadelphia Record **2** *n* A lefthanded baseball pitcher

posh *adj fr early 1900s British* Luxurious; fancy; chic; = CUSHY, SWANKY: *The apartment...is now rather posh*—A Logan/ *have made a regular practice of roughing up the kids in the more posh Ashkenazic sections*—New Yorker [origin uncertain; perhaps fr the mid-19th-century term *posh* "money" fr Romany *pash* "a half," referring to a half-penny; perhaps fr mid-19th-century *posh* "a dandy," of unknown origin; perhaps fr early-20th-century Cambridge University slang *push* or *poosh* "stylish"; perhaps a mispronunciation of *polish*; perhaps an acronym for *port out starboard home*, said to be the formula for choosing the side of the ship with the most comfortable cabins on the steamer route from England to India or return; perhaps none of the above]

posse *See* PUSSY POSSE

possum belly *n phr hoboes* An extra storage compartment under a railroad car

post *See* PAST POST

postcard *See* FRENCH POSTCARD

post-deb *n* A young woman who has made her formal social debut some while ago or is of such an age

post holes *See* A LOAD OF VW RADIATORS

pot¹ 1 *n gambling fr early 1800s* The total amount bet on a hand of poker or some other gambling matter; = KITTY: *The goulashes' takeout was 5 percent of the pot*—T Betts **2** *n* A rather obnoxious person, esp an unattractive woman; = PILL: *one of the pots that sat at the table*—Jerome Weidman **3** *n fr early 1900s* = BEER BELLY, POTBELLY **4** *n hot rodders* A carburetor **5** *n hot rodders* A car engine **6** *n railroad* A locomotive **7** *v fr middle 1800s* To shoot: *He potted a woodchuck* **8** *v* To hit; strike: *pots him in the puss/ He potted it right out of the park* [all senses fr cooking *pot*, as something containing a *pot*-luck mess of food, something sooty and unattractive, something fat-looking, something to be filled by hitting the hunt's prey, etc, hence hitting in general]

See COFFEE POT, GO TO POT, NOT HAVE A POT TO PISS IN, RUMPOT, SEXPOT, a SHITLOAD, STEEL POT, TALLOW-POT, TINPOT

pot² *narcotics* **1** *n* Marijuana; =GRASS, TEA: *Most of the parties I had been invited to recently, pot had been passed around freely*—New York Times **2** *modifier:* pot smokers/ a pot party [origin unknown; perhaps by folk etymology fr *pod*, occurrences of which are generally earlier; perhaps fr the association between *tea* "marijuana" and *pot*]

pot³ *n* A potentiometer

the pot *n phr* The toilet; =CRAPPER: *closed the stall door, and sat down on the pot*—Richard Fariña
See SHIT OR GET OFF THE POT

potassium *n students* A banana [because bananas are a valued dietary source of *potassium*]

potato **1** *n* The head: *stick their potato in every office*—AJ Liebling **2** *n* A dollar: *You can get this wonderful coat for 497 potatoes*—Time **3** *n* A ball, esp a baseball
See ALL THAT MEAT AND NO POTATOES, COUCH POTATO, HOT POTATO, MEAT AND POTATOES, SMALL POTATOES, SWEET POTATO

potato-head *n* A stupid person

potato patch *See* FRUIT SALAD

potato-trap *n fr early 1800s* The mouth

potbelly or **potgut** **1** *n* A protuberant belly; =BEER BELLY, POT **2** *n* A person with a potbelly, esp a man

potbelly (or **belly**) **stove** *n phr* An old-fashioned stove, esp a rotund one: *rickety armchairs around the big belly stove*—Joseph Mitchell

potboiler *n* A book, play, etc, written just to get money, esp something done rather badly by a writer who can do very well [fr the notion that one does such work only to keep the food *pot boiling* in the domicile]

potch **1** *n* A slap, esp to a child **2** *v* To slap or spank a child **3** *v* To slap; bump: *potching against the waves in a plastic foam Sunflower*—Philadelphia Journal [fr Yiddish fr German *patsch* "smack, splash"]

potchkie or **potchky** or **potsky** (PAHCH kee) *v* (Variation: **around** may be added) To putter; tinker; =MESS: *Louie's down potchkying in the shop/ The dentist potchkied around in Stanley's mouth*—Esquire/ *how you could potsky around with such superstitions*—Billy Rose [fr Yiddish fr German *patschen* "splash, slap"]

pothead *n narcotics* A user of marijuana, esp a heavy user: *a few potheads who don't move up from marijuana*—New York Times

pothooks **1** *n* One's handwriting; scribble; =HEN TRACKS **2** *n cowboys* Spurs

pothunter *n* A person who scavenges in abandoned buildings, towns, etc: *Cemeteries are also considered fair game for pothunters*—Wall Street Journal [probably an informal term for "archeologist," since *pots* and *pot* fragments are so crucial to their work]

pot liquor *n* The residue left in a pot after cooking: *rubbed him...with pot liquor to give him strength*—Carson McCullers

pot luck **1** *n phr* A meal composed of odds and ends of leftovers, or of whatever turns up **2** *adv phr:* Come on and dine pot luck **3** *modifier:* pot-luck supper

pot-massager *n* A pot and pan washer; =POT-WAL-LOPER

pot out *v phr hot rodders* To stop running; fail; =CONK OUT

pot party *n phr narcotics* A gathering or party for the purpose of smoking marijuana in company; =BLAST PARTY

potshot *See* TAKE A POTSHOT

pot-slinger *n* A cook

potsy **1** *n police* A police badge: *Ernie goes in the lobby and flashes his potsy*—Lawrence Sanders **2** *n New York City* The game of hop-scotch [perhaps a variant of the nickname *Patsy*]

potted or **potted up** **1** *adj* or *adj phr* Drunk **2** *adj* or *adj phr narcotics* Intoxicated by marijuana or another narcotic: *all potted up on something*—E Trujillo

◁**a pot to piss in**▷ *See* NOT HAVE A POT TO PISS IN

pottrie (PAH tree) *n* A type of usu opaque white playing marble [probably a pronunciation of *pottery*, because the marbles resembled porcelain or other china]

potty **1** *n* A young child's toilet seat and chamber pot **2** *n: failure to perform potty at the proper hour*—Time **3** *n* Any toilet **4** *modifier: time out for a potty break*—Playboy **5** *adj fr early 1900s British* Slightly crazy; eccentric; =DOTTY, GOOFY

pot-walloper **1** *n* A pot and pan washer; =POT-MASSAGER **2** *n lumberjacks* A cook

potzer *See* PATZER

pouffe *See* POOF

◁**pound**▷ *v* To do the sex act to or with; =SCREW

pound brass *v phr telegraphers & radio operators* To transmit telegraph or radio-telegraph signals with a key

◁**poundcake**▷ *n* An attractive young woman [fr the vulgar sense of *pound*]

pound one's **ear** *v phr hoboes* To sleep, esp heavily

pounder *n* A police officer, esp one who walks a beat
See BRASS-POUNDER, HAIR-POUNDER, SAND-POUNDER

◁**pound** one's **meat**▷ *See* BEAT one's MEAT

◁**pound** one's **peenie**▷ *v phr* To masturbate; =BEAT one's MEAT: *Who is he mooning over as he pounds his peenie?*—John Farris

pound salt (or **sand**) *See* GO POUND SALT

pound the books *v phr college students* To study hard; =HIT THE BOOKS

pound the pavement (Variations: **pavements** or **the sidewalks** or **the streets** may replace **the pavement**) **1** *v phr* To walk a police beat **2** *v phr* To trudge about the streets, esp looking for work: *the liberal arts graduates...pounding the Park Avenue pavements*—New York

poured into one's **garment** *adj phr* Wearing very tight and revealing clothing: *She's in those TV commercials, poured into her jeans*

pour it on 1 *v phr* To make an intense effort; maximize striving: *I was pouring it on, looking for a promotion* **2** *v phr* To exert all one's charm and persuasiveness; =COME ON STRONG: *He was really pouring it on to that judge* **3** *v phr* To speed; =POUR ON THE COAL: *The driver was pouring it on to close the gap*—J Evans

pour money down the drain (or **the rathole**) *v phr* To waste money utterly; spend hugely for nothing: *The Legislature is not going to pour more money down that rathole*—Philadelphia Journal

pour on the coal *v phr fr* railroad To travel very fast; speed up; =STEP ON IT: *The pilot apparently decided to go around again and poured on the coal*—Associated Press

pout-out *n hot rodders* Engine failure in a hot rod

pow 1 *interj* An imitation of a blow, collision, explosion, etc, used for sudden emphasis or to show sudden understanding: *Suddenly bells went off and I knew that was it! Pow!*—New York Post/ *Pow, dig this*—Ramparts **2** *n* Power; influence; =CLOUT: *only be apprehended by government action, that is, by political "pow"*—G Tyler [second sense reinforced by *power*]

powder 1 *v underworld* To leave; depart hastily, esp in escaping: *The crooks powdered like scared rabbits* **2** *n: Bonnie murdered a constable during the powder*—A Hynd **3** *v* To hit very hard; =PULVERIZE: *after he had powdered the second pitch*—Associated Press [sense of running away probably fr similar *dust* fr the notion of raising dust as one runs; perhaps, in view of *take a powder* and *run-out powder*, the basic notion is reinforced by that of taking a medicinal *powder*, esp a laxative, so that one has to leave in a hurry, or perhaps a magical *powder* that would cause one to disappear]
See FLEA POWDER, FOOLISH POWDER, JOY-POWDER, RUN-OUT POWDER, TAKE A POWDER

powder-bag *n Navy* A gunner's mate

powder city *adj phr* baseball Pitching very fast: *The big lefthander's really powder city today!*

powder monkey *n phr lumberjacks & miners* A person who works with explosives in mining, construction, etc

powder one's **nose** (or one's **puff**) *v phr* Of a woman, to go to the toilet or powder room

powderpuff 1 *n prizefight* A cautious, agile fighter as distinct from a slugger **2** *v: He just powderpuffed his opponent until he tired* **3** *adj* For or involving women; women's: *the pampered, powderpuff existence of the Ultra-feminine*—Eldridge Cleaver/ *the Powderpuff Derby air race for women*

power *v baseball* To hit the ball very hard: *He powered that one to the wall*
See FLOWER POWER

powerhouse 1 *n* A formidable team, organization, etc: *Georgia Tech, another powerhouse*—Associated Press/ *Texas Instruments, a powerhouse in electronics* **2** *n* An energetic and effective person **3** *n* A vigorous, muscular person, esp an athlete **4** *n* Anything that constitutes win-

ning force: *If you control six votes that's a powerhouse*

power tool *n phr teenagers* A person who studies hard

power trip *n phr* A show of personal power, esp of a blatant sort: *the classic Latin American dictator's power trip*—Toronto Life

pow-wow *n* A meeting; discussion: *The directors are having a crucial pow-wow* [ultimately fr an American Indian word for "medicine man," meaning "he dreams," extended to mean counsel and a council]

PR or **pr** (pronounced as separate letters) **1** *n* Public relations **2** *modifier: the PR department/ pr hype*

practice *See* SKULL PRACTICE

prairie oysters *See* MOUNTAIN OYSTERS

prat or **pratt 1** *n fr late 1500s* The buttocks; =ASS: *He does not fall on his prat*—Time **2** *v underworld* To observe or menace someone from behind [origin unknown]

pratfall *fr theater* **1** *n* A fall on one's rump, esp by a clown or comedian: *a perfect pratfall*—Edmund Wilson **2** *n* A humiliating defeat; an embarrassing humiliation: *Losing the election was a resounding pratfall* **3** *n* A danger; pitfall: *the pratfalls of the rhyming racket*—Billy Rose/ *is shorter of pratfalls and trapdoors*—Saturday Review

prat kick *n phr pickpockets* A hip pocket

prayer *See* HAVE A PRAYER

prayer bones *n phr* The knees

prayer book *See* CALIFORNIA PRAYER BOOK

pray to the porcelain god *v phr college students* To vomit in the toilet

preem 1 *n theater* A first showing or performance; premiere: *set for an Oct 4 preem*—Variety **2** *v: show which preems via ABC*—New York Daily News [fr *premiere*]

preemie or **preemy** or **premie** *n fr 1920s* A premature baby: *the tiny, three-pound premie*—Good Housekeeping/ *like a human preemie, it was placed in an Isolette*—Time

preggers *adj fr 1920s British universities* Pregnant: *Meredith gets preggers by Jos*—Playboy/ *Heather Young is preggers*—TV Guide

preggy 1 *adj* Pregnant **2** *n: Six preggies were waiting to see the doctor*

pregnant duck *See* RUPTURED DUCK

prego 1 *n* A pregnant teenager **2** *adj* Pregnant: *as if one-half the female population is...prego*—Ebony

prelim (PREE lim) **1** *n prizefight* A professional boxing match coming before the main match in a given program **2** *n college students* One of the comprehensive examinations required for the PhD degree

premed (PREE med) *college students* **1** *n* A premedical student **2** *n* A premedical course of study or major **3** *modifier: a required premed course*

prep 1 *n* =PREPPIE **2** *v students* To go to preparatory school: *Where'd you prep?*—F Scott Fitzgerald/ *The poorer person did not prep with your* *brother*—Fran Lebowitz **3** *n* Preparation; preliminary steps: *The nurses did the prep for the operation* **4** *v*: *a pitcher who has prepped earnestly for many years*—Arthur Daley

preppie or **preppy 1** *n* A student or graduate of a preparatory school: *Wouldja please watch your profanity, Preppie?*—Erich Segal **2** *adj* Typical of the manners, attitudes, folkways, etc, of preppies: *The handshake is firm and preppy*—J Cameron/ *George Bush predicted with characteristic preppie self-confidence*—Time

prep school 1 *n phr* A preparatory school, usu rather expensive and aristocratic **2** *adj*: *prep school grad*

pres (PREZ) *n* (Variations: **Pres** or **prez** or **Prez** or **prexy** or **Prexy** or **prexie** or **Prexie**) A president

press *See* FULL COURT PRESS

press roll *n phr musicians* A drum roll that intensifies in volume

press the bricks 1 *v phr lumberjacks* To loaf in town **2** *v phr* To walk a police beat; = POUND THE PAVEMENT: *Go press the bricks*—WR Burnett

press the flesh (or the **skin**) **1** *v phr* To shake hands ● Used chiefly of politicians and others who ingratiate themselves with the public **2** *adj*: *Williams conducted a press-the-flesh campaign*—Newsweek

pressure cooker 1 *n phr* A place or situation of great personal stress: *the pressure cooker on the Hudson*—Gore Vidal **2** *modifier*: *flung into the pressure-cooker existence of live TV*—Pauline Kael

pretty *adv fr 1500s* Quite; more than a little: *The weather's pretty rotten*
See SITTING PRETTY

pretty-boy 1 *n* A man who is good-looking in an epicene way; an effeminate dandy **2** *modifier*: *their "pretty boy" young preacher*—Malcolm X **3** *n circus* A bouncer or professional strong man

pretty ear *n phr prizefight* An ear deformed from blows; = CAULIFLOWER EAR: *busted bones and pretty ear*—WR Burnett

pretty face *See* JUST ANOTHER PRETTY FACE

pretzel *n musicians* A French horn

pretzel-bender 1 *n musicians* A French horn player **2** *n* A wrestler

prevert (PREE vert) *n* A pervert

previous *adj esp 1920s & 30s* Tight; snug; = QUICK: *Aren't those pants sort of previous on you?*
See QUICK, SNEAK

prexy or **Prexy** or **prexie** or **Prexie** *See* PRES

prez or **Prez** *See* PRES

pricey or **pricy** *adj fr 1940s British fr Australian* Expensive; dear: *Godiva chocolates and other pricey goodies*—Philadelphia Journal/ *Its glittery fast-lane image later included pricy real estate*—Time

◁**prick**▷ **1** *n fr late 1500s* The penis; = COCK **2** *n* A detestable person, esp a man; obnoxious wretch; = ASSHOLE, BASTARD: *He's an antagonistic prick*—Rolling Stone/ *Alex the little prick*—Philip Roth

pricklies *See* COLD PRICKLIES

◁**prick-teaser**▷ *See* COCK-TEASER

◁**pricky** or **prickish**▷ *adj* Obnoxious; detestable: *What a pricky kid*—Philip Roth/ *a prickish man*—Changes

prima donna *n phr* A person of great and touchy self-esteem; a person who requires to be the sole focus of adulatory attention and who indulges in temperamental displays [fr Italian, literally "first lady," a title for superstar opera singers and the like]

primed *adj* Prepared; readied; = PREPPED: *The place is primed for the prima donna's visit*

prince *n* A very decent and admirable person; = ACE ● Often used ironically: *He told me he thinks you're a goddam prince*—JD Salinger

Prince *See* JEWISH AMERICAN PRINCE

Princess *See* JEWISH AMERICAN PRINCESS

print 1 *n* A fingerprint: *My prints ain't on that gun*—Erle Stanley Gardner **2** *v*: *They printed me*—Erle Stanley Gardner
See FINGERPRINT, the SMALL PRINT

print money *See* a LICENSE TO PRINT MONEY

prissy 1 *adj fr late 1800s chiefly Southern* Overfastidious; primly censorious: *He has a prissy distaste for heavy shoes* **2** *n*: *these do-gooding prissies*—Newsweek [origin uncertain; perhaps a blend of *prim* or *precise* with *sissy*; perhaps the nickname for *Priscilla*, thought of as conveying the priggish and effeminate essence]

private *See* BUCK PRIVATE

private eye *n phr* A private detective; a private investigator

privates *n* The genitals; private parts

privy *n* An outdoor toilet without plumbing; = BACKHOUSE, CHIC SALE

no **prize package** *See* NO PRIZE PACKAGE

pro^1 **1** *n* A professional in any field, as distinct from an amateur, and mainly distinguished by superior and dependable performance: *hear his song played and sung by pros*—C Lowry **2** *modifier*: *pro golf tour/ pro ranks* **3** *n* (also **old pro** or **real pro**) A seasoned and dependable performer; expert; model of excellence **4** *n* A prostitute: *He treats all women like pros and all men like enemies*—Budd Schulberg [the last sense perhaps fr *professional* reinforced by *prostitute*, or vice versa]

pro^2 *n esp WW2 armed forces* A prophylactic for preventing venereal disease; condom; = RUBBER

pro^3 **1** *n* Probation, as a judicial sentence **2** *n* A person on probation

pro-am *adj* Admitting or including both professional and amateur performers, esp athletes; open: *a pro-am golf tournament*

problems *See* HAVE PROBLEMS WITH something

process *n black* = CONK

production *See* MAKE A BIG PRODUCTION

prof *n college students* Professor

professor 1 *n* An orchestra leader **2** *n* The piano player in a saloon, brothel, etc: *the job of regular professor*—A Lomax

profile *See* KEEP A LOW PROFILE, LOW PROFILE

prog *n* Food [origin unknown; perhaps fr obsolete *prog* "poke and forage about," of obscure origin]

program *v fr computer* To train; predispose by rigorous teaching, condition: *He's programmed to be polite to old ladies and all*
See CRASH PROGRAM

project *See* CRASH PROGRAM

projo or **pro Joe** *n* or *n phr Army* An artillery projectile

pro-kit or **pro-pack** *n WW2 armed forces* A kit for preventing venereal disease [fr *prophylactic kit*]

prole (PROHL) *n fr British perhaps fr 1920s Australian* A member of the lower or working class: *Chez Tom Wolfe proles, for example, wear new down coats*—Atlantic/ *ignored by the gawkers and proles at the fence*—Esquire [fr *proletarian* "member of the working class," ultimately fr Latin; popularized by George Orwell's 1949 novel *Nineteen Eighty-Four*]

prom **1** *n students fr late 1800s* A dance, esp a formal ball in celebration of graduation from high school: *neither the fraternity dance nor the Prom*—P Marks **2** *modifier: prom night/ prom queen* [fr *promenade*]

promise *See* a LICK AND A PROMISE

promo (PROH moh) **1** *n* Advertising and promotion: *Who's handling the promo for this show?* **2** *n* A film, tape, printed piece, etc, for promotion: *He shot some promos for his syndicated TV show*—New Yorker

promote **1** *v fr early 1900s underworld & hoboes* To get, esp by theft, hard persuasion, or begging: *He promoted a couple of new tires from the neighbors* **2** *v* To accost in an acquisitive spirit; = HIT: *begun promoting him for something to drink*—James M Cain

promotion *See* MEXICAN PROMOTION

prom-trotter *n college students* A person who leads an active campus social life

◁**prong**▷ **1** *n* The penis; = PRICK **2** *v* To do the sex act to or with; = SCREW: *every guy who had ever pronged her*—Earl Thompson/ *And Mr Sheldon must be pronging the maid*—Lawrence Sanders

◁**prong on**▷ *n phr* A penile erection; = HARD ON: *I got this huge prong on*—George V Higgins

pronto *adv fr middle 1800s Southwest* Immediately; quickly [fr Spanish]

prop[1] **1** *n theater* An article used on stage or in a film; property **2** *n circus* The stage crew, property supervisor, and tent-crew supervisor

prop[2] *n* A propeller

property *See* HOT PROPERTY

proposition **1** *n* An invitation or request for sexual favors; = a PASS: *He made a rude proposition and got his ears pinned back* **2** *v: He propositioned every woman at the party*

props **1** *n theater* The property manager at a theater or movie studio **2** *n* = FALSIES
See KNOCK THE PROPS FROM UNDER

prosty *n* (Variations: **prostie** or **pross** or **prossy** or **prossie**) A prostitute: *a retired prosty*—Playboy/ *Fighting the Prostie Problem*—New York Post/ *the dedicated pross with a meter ticking under her skirt*—New York

protection or **protection money** *n* or *n phr* Bribe or extortion money paid to the police or to gangsters to forestall harassment, arrest, mayhem, etc

prowl *v* To search by running the hands over the person; = FRISK: *prowled me over carefully with his left hand*—Raymond Chandler
See ON THE PROWL

prowl car *n phr fr 1930s* A police squad car

prune **1** *n* A foolish person who is easily duped; = MARK, PATSY **2** *n* A pedantic, stiff, and prudish person; = PRISSY **3** *v hot rodders* To accelerate faster than another car in a race

pruneface *n* A homely or sad-looking person: *Pruneface wants ya*—D Brooks

prune-picker *n early 1900s hoboes & Navy* A Californian

prunes *See* FULL OF BEANS

pruno *n* Any fermented fruit juice, esp prune juice

prushon or **prushun** *hoboes fr late 1800s* **1** *n* A boy tramp who begs for an adult tramp: *a prushon, who averaged...$3 a day*—J Flynt **2** *n* A young homosexual who lives with tramps [origin unknown]

prut *n* Dirt; filth

ps and qs *See* MIND one's PS AND QS

pseud (So͞oD) **1** *n* Something false; a fraud; = FAKE, PHONY **2** *adj: That guy is really pseud, with all his big talk* [fr *pseudo*]

psych **1** *n college students* Psychology, esp as an academic study **2** *modifier* Psychiatry; psychiatric: *makes it down from the psych ward on the 15th floor*—Maclean's **3** *v* (also **psych out**) To outsmart another person: *The bastards psyched me* **4** *v* (also **psych out**) To sense or infer the motives, behavior, etc, of others; feel out a situation: *an uncanny ability to "psych out" audiences and make them love her*—Saturday Review/ *They're very difficult to psyche out*—Sexual Behavior **5** *interj chiefly teenagers* An exclamation uttered when one has fooled or deceived another, meaning "I'm only kidding" **6** *v* (also **psych out**) To unnerve someone; cause someone to lose composure, will, skill, etc: *He won't psych me as he did her*—New York Post/ *He's never tried to psych us out*—New Yorker/ *the pre-interrogation bravado that I had employed to psych them*—Playboy

psych oneself or **psych** oneself **up** *v phr* To arouse oneself emotionally, spiritually, mentally, etc, to a maximum effort; raise oneself to a state of keen readiness and capability; = PUMP oneself UP: *That's almost a whole year of psyching yourself up as high as you can go*—Esquire/ *I tried to psyche myself for this new challenge*—Anne Bernays/ *Diana Nyad would psyche herself up for grueling aquatic bouts*—New York Post

psyched or **psyched up** *adj* or *adj phr* In a state of excited preparedness and heightened keenness; = PUMPED UP: *They were all psyched up to carry the blue and white banner of Catawba College*—Charlotte Observer/ *are generally so psyched that elation becomes their bottom line*—S Shapiro
See GET PSYCHED

psych-jockey *n* The host and consultant of a radio or television call-in program on personal, emotional, sexual, and generally speaking psychological subjects [fr blend of *psychology* and *disc jockey*]

psycho 1 *n* A crazy person; maniac; psychopath; =NUT: *You can always tell psychos, they have dirty hands*—New York/ *no buzzing broad, no nympho, no psycho, no bitch*—Pauline Kael **2** *adj*: *a special psycho channel that I know nothing about*—New York [probably fr *psychotic*]

psychobabble 1 *n* Talk about oneself, one's feelings, motives, etc, esp in psychological jargon: *Let's call it psychobabble, this spirit which now tyrannizes conversation*—RD Rosen/ *His characters have absorbed the attitudes of post-1960s psychobabble, and tend to say things like "Viet Nam is a reality warp..."*—New York Times **2** *v*: *"If you want space," she tells a psychobabbling boyfriend, "go to Utah"*—Village Voice

psych up *v phr* To bring to a state of keen attention; excite and incite; =PUMP UP

psywar (SĪ wawr) **1** *n* Psychological warfare **2** *modifier*: *an impressively orchestrated psywar operation*—New Republic

◁**pt** or **PT**▷ (pronounced as separate letters) *n* =PRICK-TEASER

pu or **PU** (pronounced as separate letters) *interj* An exclamation of displeasure upon smelling something fetid or encountering something disgusting or botched

pub *n fr middle 1800s British* A saloon; bar; tavern: *a round of Long Island pubs*—New York Daily News [fr British *public house*]

pub crawl 1 *v fr early 1900s British* To carouse about from one saloon to another **2** *n*: *They went on a memorable pub crawl afterwards* *See* BARHOP

pubes (PYŌŌ beez) *n* The pubic region, esp the pubic hair; crotch ● Even though this is the medical, Latin anatomical term, it somehow takes on a slang aura by association in contexts: *stretching the satin front of her hot pants over her pubes*—Rolling Stone/ *shaved pubes, infantile fantasies, sodomy*—San Francisco

pucker *n fr middle 1700s* Fear; state of fright: *Don't get in such a pucker*

◁**pucker-assed**▷ *adj* Timid; fearful; =CHICKEN [fr *pucker*]

◁**pud**▷ (PUHD, PŎŎD) *n* The penis [fr slang sense of *pudding*] *See* PULL one's PUD

◁**pudding**▷ *n* The penis: *You can't even come off unless you pull your own pudding*—Philip Roth

puddinghead *n fr middle 1800s* A stupid person, esp one who is also amiable: *a natural nitwit, a puddinghead, a stand-up comedian*—WT Tyler

puddle-jumper 1 *n* A small or rickety vehicle: *I wouldn't ride in that puddle-jumper* **2** *n* An aircraft that makes several stops along a cross-country route

◁**pud-pulling**▷ **1** *n* Masturbation: *a frenzied bout of pud-pulling*—Village Voice **2** *modifier*: *a stupid pud-pulling jerk*

puff 1 *n* (also **puff job**) A specimen of extravagant praise, esp for commercial or political purposes; =PLUG **2** *v*: *There is little need for us to puff this book*—Saturday Review *See* CREAM PUFF, POWDER one's NOSE, POWDER-PUFF

puff artist *n phr* A person who praises something extravagantly, esp for commercial reasons; =FLACK: *That dealer's a real puff artist, calls everything a masterpiece*

puffer *See* PINK PUFFER

puff piece *n phr* Something written in extravagant praise, esp for sales purposes; =HYPE

puffy *adj* Very favorable; adulatory; drum-beating: *Even the stern People's Daily ran extraordinarily puffy coverage of Reagan*—Time

pug 1 *n fr middle 1800s British* A prizefighter or boxer; pugilist **2** *n* =PLUG-UGLY [fr *pugilist*]

◁**puke**▷ **1** *v* To vomit **2** *n* Vomit; spew **3** *n* Something so disgusting that it might be vomit and the cause of vomit: *Who wrote this puke?*

◁**puke-in**▷ *n* A public occasion where participants vomit together in order to make some point or other

◁**puker**▷ *n Pacific Northwest* A charter fishing boat

◁**puky** or **pukey**▷ *adj* Nasty; inferior; disgusting: *It's a pukey sort of ballad*

pull 1 *n fr late 1800s* Influence; special power or favor; =CLOUT: *irregularities and instances of political pull*—Associated Press/ *officials in the low echelon bracket did not have much pull*—American Scholar **2** *n* A sip or gulp of a drink, a puff on a cigarette, etc: *I took a big pull at my drink and looked up* **3** *v* To earn; receive; =PULL DOWN: *I pulled an A on the quiz* ◁**4**▷ *v prison* To masturbate *See* LEG-PULL

pull a boner (or **a bonehead play**) *v phr* To blunder; commit an error, esp an egregious one: *I'm afraid you've pulled a boner this time, the thing sank*

pull a fast one *v phr* To execute or attempt a deception; achieve a clever fraud or swindle; =PULL something ON someone: *You're accusing me of trying to pull a fast one?*—Saul Bellow [probably fr *fast shuffle*]

pull a line *v phr* To try to persuade or deceive someone with a false, overelaborate story, appeal, etc: *She's honest, never pulls a line*

pull an all-nighter *v phr teenagers* To study all night

pull an el foldo *v phr* To lose energy; wilt; fade; =FOLD: *The Saints chose that time to pull an el foldo*—Sports Illustrated

◁**pull a train** (or **the train** or **the choo-choo**)▷ *v phr fr motorcyclists* Of a woman, to do the sex act with several men serially: *taking some dame in the woods and making her pull a train*—Rockford Files (TV program)/ *The brothers brought an apolitical but dynamic hooker into the house and she pulled the train*—Rolling Stone

pull someone's chain (Variations: **jerk** or **rattle** may replace **pull**; **string** may replace **chain**) **1** *v phr* To deceive; fool; =PULL A FAST ONE: *too busy*

trying to figure out if I had been pulling his chain
—Richard Price **2** *v phr* To upset someone;
anger someone: *She got real mad and I wondered
what had pulled her chain/ I did not know you can
rattle his chain with marvelous results*—Washington
Post/ *He was insecure and sensitive. It was easy to
pull his string*—New York Times [probably fr the
image of a person who upsets a captive animal by
pulling or *jerking* at the *chain*; perhaps influenced
by the notion of *pulling* a *chain* or string to turn on
an electric light]

pull down 1 *v phr* (also **pull in**) To earn;
receive: *I pull down about 300 a week* **2** *v phr*
To disassemble; take apart: *I am going to pull the
engine down again*—Popular Science

puller 1 *n* A smuggler **2** *n narcotics* A person
who smokes marijuana; = POTHEAD
See WIRE-PULLER

pulleys *n* Suspenders

pull (or **drag**) one's **freight** *v phr esp early
1900s* To leave; depart: *This bird's gonna pull his
freight*—WR Burnett

pull in 1 *v phr* To arrive: *She pulled in about
noon* **2** *v phr* = PULL DOWN

pull someone **in** *v phr* To arrest someone

pull in one's **belt** *See* TIGHTEN one's BELT

pull in one's **ears 1** *v phr* To be cautious;
watch out for oneself **2** *v phr* To be less aggressive; moderate oneself: *You better pull in your ears
a little or you'll scare them away* [origin uncertain;
perhaps in some cases an alteration of *pull in* one's
horns]

pull in one's **horns** *v phr fr late 1500s British* To
moderate or retract one's behavior; = BACK OFF:
The USFL Pulled In Its Financial Horns—Inside
Sports [fr the way an anxious snail behaves]

pull it off *v phr fr late 1800s gambling & horseracing* To accomplish something; succeed; = MAKE IT:
*pull it off and keep the patients coming back for
more*—San Francisco

pull someone's **leg** *v phr fr late 1800s British* To
deceive in fun; fool; = KID: *I suspected that he was
pulling my leg*—F Scott Fitzgerald/ *I think she's pulling my leg*—Games [fr the act of playfully tripping
someone]

Pullman *See* SIDE-DOOR PULLMAN

pull off 1 *v phr fr middle 1800s* To succeed in or
at; achieve: *Fegley managed to pull off a hat trick
for this issue*—Playboy ◁**2**▷ *v phr* To masturbate: *At Smolka's signal, each begins to pull off*
—Philip Roth

◁**pull** oneself **off**▷ *v phr* To masturbate; = JACK OFF

◁**pull** someone **off**▷ *v phr fr early 1900s* To cause
someone to ejaculate semen by manipulating the
penis

pull on *v phr* To take a sip of a drink, a puff of a
cigarette, etc: *a 17-year-old kid pulling on a beer*
—Toronto Life/ *The boss kept pulling on his big fat
cigar*

pull something **on** someone *v phr* To deceive or
cheat; take advantage of; = PULL A FAST ONE: *At first
she thought I was trying to pull a slick scam on her*

pull out 1 *v phr* To leave; depart: *He pulled out
after 45 minutes and disappeared*—Associated
Press **2** *v phr* To withdraw; terminate one's
association: *He threatened to pull out if we didn't
raise the ante*

◁**pull** something **out of** one's **ass**▷ *v phr Army*
To produce something, esp information or an idea,
unexpectedly

pull something **out of the fire** *v phr* To salvage
something; rescue: *We got hot and pulled the game
out of the fire*

◁**pull** one's **pud**▷ (PUHD, PŌŌD) *v phr* (Variations:
dong or **joint** or **wang** or any other word for
"penis" may replace **pud**) To masturbate; = JACK
OFF

pull one's **punches** *v phr fr prizefight* To soften
one's blows; be lenient and moderate: *Ouch...You
don't pull your punches*—Xaviera Hollander/ *He
pulled no punches because the reigning official was
both a woman and a black*—Joseph Heller

pull rank *v phr fr WW1 armed forces* To over-
whelm with one's authority; be officiously arrogant:
Each was frightened that the other would pull rank
—Eldridge Cleaver

pull strings (or **wires**) *v phr* To exert influence;
use one's power, esp clandestinely: *If she pulls a
few wires I think I might get the job* [probably fr the
use of *strings* or *wires* to control marionettes]

pull teeth through the armpit *v phr armed
forces* To do something in the most difficult way; do
something the hard way

pull the plug[1] **1** *v phr* To terminate something;
end support or cooperation: *if the affiliates...rise up
in rebellion and pull the plug*—New Yorker/ *The
project's pretty shaky, but I won't pull the plug quite
yet* **2** *v phr* To terminate various mechanical
and electronic efforts being used to keep life in a
moribund patient [fr the disconnecting of an electrical *plug*]

pull the plug[2] *v phr Navy* To dive in a submarine;
submerge [fr the withdrawing of a bathtub *plug*]

pull the rug from under (or **out from under**)
v phr To undermine or disable; put opponents at a
great and often sudden disadvantage: *They were
intended to pull the rug out from under left-wing
critics*—Nation

pull the string 1 *v phr baseball* To pitch a
change-of-pace ball, a very slow ball after the
motion for a fast one **2** *v phr* To rudely reveal
the truth, previously kept hidden; unveil true intentions; reveal the catch: *They doubled their efforts,
showering her with affection, then they pulled the
string*—Playboy [perhaps fr the use of a *string* to
fasten and release a concealing sheet on something
about to be unveiled; perhaps fr *pull the lanyard* "to
fire a cannon"]

pull the wool over someone's **eyes** *v phr fr
middle 1800s* To deceive; mislead: *The whole indignant act was an attempt to pull the wool over the
voters' eyes*

pull up one's **socks** *fr early 1900s British* **1** *v
phr* To correct one's behavior; look to one's performance; = GET ON THE BALL: *Whittingham was ter-*

minated after having failed to pull up his socks enough during six months on probation—Toronto Life **2** *v phr* To prepare; ready oneself: *He said we'd pull up our socks and get the damn job done*

pulp 1 *n* A magazine printed on rough paper and devoted to adventure, science fiction, cowboy stories, rude erotica, etc **2** *modifier: pulp fiction/ a pulp romance*

the **pulps** *n phr* Pulp magazines collectively: *He used to write sci-fi for the pulps*

pulverize 1 *v* To hit hard; =CLOBBER, POWDER **2** *v* To defeat thoroughly; =CLOBBER

pump ◁**1**▷ *v fr 1700s* To do the sex act; =FUCK, HUMP: *They were pumping away on the floor* **2** *v* To question someone long and closely; extract information: *The cops pumped him for three days straight* **3** *n* (also **pumper**) The heart; =TICKER: *He had a hole through his pump*—Asphalt Jungle (movie)

See SLUSH PUMP, TOWN PUMP

pump bilge (or **ship**) *v phr fr late 1700s nautical* To urinate: *The Duke of Wellington's most cogent advice was "Never lose an opportunity to pump ship"*

pumped up 1 *adj phr* In a state of excited preparedness and heightened keenness; =PSYCHED UP ● Used most often of athletes in or before competition: *The girls were really pumped up*—Playboy/ *I was very pumped up*—Aquarian/ *The mayor has got me so pumped up on DC in general*—Washingtonian **2** *adj phr* Exaggerated; artificial; =PHONY: *a pumped-up conviviality. Concannon didn't like it*—Barry Reed

pump iron *v phr* To lift weights

pumpkin or **pumkin** or **punkin** *n* The head

pumpkinhead or **punkinhead** *n* A stupid person

◁**pumpkin** (or **punkin**) **roller**▷ *n phr* A rural person; farmer: *Like as not the feller is a punkin roller*—Time

the **pumpkins** *n phr circus & carnival* A small town; a rural site: *I never worked the pumpkins*—New Yorker

pump up 1 *v phr* To exaggerate; assign too much importance to; =BLOW UP: *His job wasn't much, but he pumped it up into a key assignment* **2** *v phr* To persuade to keen excitement; =HYPE: *Experts like Dr Edward Teller...have steadily "pumped up" Reagan...about the potential of such defensive-weapons systems*—Newsweek

pump oneself **up** *v phr* To arouse oneself emotionally, spiritually, mentally, etc, to a maximum effort; =PSYCH oneself ● Much used by sports commentators, esp by baseball announcers of pitchers: *The big lefthander's really pumped himself up for this crucial encounter*

punch *n* Power; force; impact; =CLOUT: *This article has no punch*

See BEAT someone TO THE DRAW, CAN'T FIGHT one's WAY OUT OF A PAPER BAG, ONE-TWO, SUCKERPUNCH, SUNDAY PUNCH

punchboard *n* A very promiscuous woman; =ROUNDHEELS [fr a gambling or lottery device where one paid to *punch* a round scroll of paper out of a hole in a *board* for a possible prize; related to 18th-century *punch* "deflower"]

punch cows (or **cattle**) *v phr cowboys fr late 1800s* To herd or drive cattle

punch-drunk 1 *adj* Exhibiting brain damage from repeated blows to the head; slow in movement, slurring in speech, disoriented and shambling; =PUNCHY, SLAP-HAPPY **2** *adj* Dazed from overwork, excessive stress, etc: *He was punch-drunk after the annual meeting*

punched *See* GET one's CARD PUNCHED, HAVE one's TICKET PUNCHED

punched-up *adj* Improved; increased in energy, impressiveness, impact, etc: *no more than a punched-up form of the sentiment that the prose style of most social scientists "is Greek to me"*—New York Times

puncher 1 *n cowboys fr late 1800s* A cowboy **2** *n railroad* A telegraph operator

See COWPUNCHER, DONKEY-PUNCHER, DOUGH-PUNCHER, PILLOW-PUNCHER

punches *See* PULL one's PUNCHES, ROLL WITH THE PUNCHES, TELEGRAPH one's PUNCHES

punch in (or **out**) *v phr* To come or go at a certain time, esp to or from a job; =CLOCK IN or OUT [fr the stamping of one's work-card at a time-clock]

punch someone's **lights out** *v phr* To beat or defeat someone severely; trounce; =CLOBBER: *Sugar Ray Leonard punched Thomas Hearns's lights out*—Sports Illustrated/ *If he'd been a truck driver I would have punched his lights out a long time ago*—Washingtonian [fr the earlier *beat out someone's liver and lights*, where *lights* reflects a Middle English word for "lungs, esp of a slaughtered animal or game animal," now certainly interpreted as "eyes" and as "electric lights"]

punch line *n phr* The last line or part of a joke, which makes it funny; =KICKER, ZINGER: *I remember the jokes, but not the punch lines*

punch out 1 *v phr* To beat, esp with the fists; =BEAT UP, CLOBBER: *Oh...I punched out this guy*—Armistead Maupin/ *You've escaped 14th and Third without getting taken-off, frisked-down, or punched-out*—New York Times **2** *v phr Air Force* To use the ejection seat for escape from a aircraft

punch-out *n* A fist fight; brawl; fisticuffs

punch up 1 *v phr* To improve; increase the energy, impressiveness, etc, of; =JAZZ something UP: *The TV-movie version will punch it up*—Village Voice/ *this sort of "punching up" of the text in the name of being colloquial*—New Yorker/ *I guess they hired me because their material needed punching up*—National Lampoon **2** *v phr television studio & recording industry* To bring a specified part of a recording tape into view, into place at the playing head, etc **3** *v phr computers* To call up a software program

punchy 1 *adj fr 1930s* Exhibiting brain damage from repeated blows to the head; =PUNCH-DRUNK: *Sailor Bob a punchy stumble-bum*—John O'Hara **2** *adj* Feeling somewhat confused and battered, as if punch-drunk: *I feel a little punchy after that session with the committee* **3** *adj fr* 1920s Having force, impact, energy, etc; potent; =JAZZY, ZINGY: *The English language may some day be as colorful and punchy as it was in Elizabethan times*—Literary Digest/ *the right educational background and a gift for punchy phrases*—Joseph Heller

punish 1 *v* To attack forcefully: *I had a bottle along and he punished it*—Raymond Chandler/ *He sat down at the Steinway and began punishing the ivories* **2** *v* To have sex with; =FUCK: *Time to go home, have a brew, and punish the old lady*

punk¹ 1 *n prison, merchant marine & hoboes* A catamite; young companion of a sodomite; =GUN-SEL ◁**2**▷ *v* To sodomize; do anal sex to; =BUG-GER, CORNHOLE: *The guy peeled off Tate's pants and punked him*—Tom Aldibrandi **3** *n* Any young or inexperienced person; boy; =KID: *Sparky was always a fresh punk*—John O'Hara **4** *n* A petty hoodlum; meager minor tough or criminal: *to emphasize just how tough a Division Street punk could be*—Nelson Algren **5** *n* Any inferior, insignificant person, like an ineffective fighter, jockey, pool player, waiter, porter, etc **6** *n circus* Any young circus animal [ultimately fr 16th-century British, "prostitute, harlot," of unknown origin]

punk² 1 *adj fr late* 1800s Inferior; poor; bad: *The idea strikes me as punk*—Westbrook Pegler **2** *n esp lunch counter fr late* 1800s Bread **3** *n* hawkers A patent medicine **4** *modifier: the punk workers who sell corn removers*—M Zolotow [probably early-18th-century, "rotting wood, touchwood," of unknown origin, usu taken to be fr *spunk*, of the same meaning, fr Gaelic *spong* "tinder"]

punk³ 1 *n* (also **punker**) An adherent to a style of dress and behavior marked by seemingly threatening, dangerous, and aggressive attributes, such as safety pins worn through ear lobes, razor blades around the neck, and torn clothes ● Originally meant to be reminiscent of the hoodlums called punks in the 1950s, but soon an independent style **2** *adj: The atmosphere in north London's pubs is really punk*

punk day *n phr* A day when children are admitted free

punked out *adj phr* Having the style of dress and behavior marked by seemingly threatening, dangerous, and aggressive attributes

punkette *n* A young woman who adopts the manners and appearance of the punk milieu: *a scruffy, androgynous punkette with close-cropped hair and dressed all in black except for a pair of electric-red socks*—New York

punkin *See* PUMPKIN

punkoid 1 *n* =PUNK³, PUNK ROCKER **2** *adj: his punkoid slouch and sneer*

punk out 1 *v phr fr early* 1900s, now esp street gang & teenagers To quit, esp from fear; =CHICKEN OUT, FOLD: *The Soho News punked out*—Philadelphia **2** *v phr* To adopt the style of a punk rocker

punk-pusher *n circus* The supervisor of boy workers

punk rock *n phr* Loud and crude rock and roll music played by persons who purport, in their dress, vile behavior and language, repellent names, and ugly appearance, to be loathsome louts: *The bad equivalent of "bubble-gum," it was called punk-rock, and it was totally utilitarian music*—Changes

punk rocker 1 *n phr* A player of loud and crude rock and roll music who purports to be a loathsome lout **2** *n phr* A person who adheres to a style of dress and behavior marked by seemingly threatening, dangerous, and aggressive attributes; =PUNK

punt¹ *v fr* 1700s To gamble; bet [fr French *ponte*, Spanish *punta* "point," used for playing against the banker in faro and other games]

punt² 1 *v college students* To drop a course in order not to fail it **2** *v college students* To give up; withdraw; =COP OUT: *I hate to punt, but I just don't have time to finish this job* [fr the kick out of danger in football, fr middle-19th-century Rugby football, "kick the ball before it hits the ground," of unknown origin; perhaps echoic]

punter *n fr early* 1700s A gambler; a bettor: *Inside the clubhouse, the punters sit enraged on their slatted benches*—Village Voice [fr French *punter* "place a bet against the bank in a card game," of uncertain origin]

punt someone or something **off** *v phr college students* To deliberately forget; ignore and evade: *He decided to punt the whole problem off*

pup 1 *n* A young, inexperienced person; =KID, PUNK **2** *n* =HOT DOG **3** *n truckers* A small four-wheeled truck trailer

See GUTTERSNIPE, SNUGGLE-PUP

puppy-dog feet *n cardplayers* The suit of clubs

puppy love *n phr fr early* 1800s Love or infatuation of very young persons; =CALF LOVE

pups *n* The feet; =DOGS

pup (or **dog**) **tent** *n phr fr middle* 1800s A small tent; an Army shelter tent: *The crew loaded pup tents and cooking equipment into motorcycle sidecars*—King Vidor

pup tents *n phr circus* Overshoes

purp *n* A dog; pup: *after the purp solved a few simple problems*—Billy Rose

purple *See* TURN PURPLE

purple heart *n phr narcotics* Any barbiturate, or a mixture of a barbiturate and morphine; =NIMBY, GOOFBALL

purple passion *See* WITH A PURPLE PASSION

purpose pitch *n phr baseball* A pitch thrown purposely intimidatingly close to a batter

◁**pus bag**▷ *n phr* A despicable person; a filthy wretch; =SCUMBAG: *like Tina. The pusbag he was married to*—Patrick Mann/ *He hissed that I was "a goddam scum-sucking pus bag"*—Peter Gent

pus-gut or **pustle-gut 1** *n* A protuberant belly **2** *n* A person with a pus-gut: *You'd better call old pus-gut*—Richard Starnes/ *some pus-gut in an American Legion cap*—Time [origin unknown; perhaps from *purse*, suggesting a full, baggy gut; perhaps fr dialect *puscle* or *puskile* "pustule," suggesting a swollen gut]

push 1 *n* *outdated street gang* A fight between street gangs; =RUMBLE **2** *n* *lumberjacks* A supervisor: *Jigger's first season as a camp push* —Stewart Holbrook **3** *n* *Army* A radio frequency, such as is tuned by pressing a push-button **4** *n* =PUSHOVER **5** *n* An intense sustained effort: *They made a big push to get the damn thing done* **6** *v* *esp cabdrivers* To drive a taxi, truck, etc: *pushing a hack all day*—F Dickenson **7** *v* To kill someone: *when one of our boys gets pushed*—J Evans **8** *v* To approach a specified age: *You're pushing 50*—Earl Wilson **9** *v* To advertise; publicize; promote: *They don't have to push reference books too much* **10** *v* (also **push for**) To recommend; boost; =GET BEHIND: *He decided to push my idea, and push for two new labs* **11** *v* To sell, esp in an aggressive way; hawk: *Push the specials today, okay?* **12** *v* To press or importune too often and too hard: *I'll probably do what you want, just stop pushing* **13** *v* *narcotics* To sell narcotics; peddle; =DEAL: *Funny cigarettes ain't all that one pushes*—Nelson Algren **14** *v* *underworld* To distribute and pass counterfeit money **15** *v* *underworld* To smuggle
See QUICK PUSH, STABLE PUSH

push across *v phr* *underworld* To kill; murder: *He might have pushed Foster across*—The Sleeping City (movie)

push a pen *v phr* To do office work: *Why should I want to push a pen in an office?*—New Yorker

push one's **button** *v phr* To annoy or provoke one; =NEEDLE: *Don't push my button. I haven't exactly been behind him, pushing and clapping* —Washington Post

push comes to shove *sentence* A touchy situation becomes actively hostile; a quarrel becomes a fight; =the CHIPS ARE DOWN: *If push comes to shove can you count on him?*

pusher 1 *n* *lumberjacks* A supervisor; =PUSH **2** *n* *narcotics* A narcotics peddler or distributor; =CANDY MAN, CONNECTION: *queen of the Broadway narcotics pushers*—Associated Press **3** *n* *underworld* A distributor or passer of counterfeit money; =PAPERHANGER
See COOKIE-PUSHER, DIAMOND-CRACKER, GOSPEL-PUSHER, GREASE-PUSHER, PAPERHANGER, PAPER-PUSHER, PENCIL-PUSHER, PEN-PUSHER, PILL-PUSHER, PUNK-PUSHER, WOOD-PUSHER

pushmi-pullyu *n* A case or situation of neat symmetry in function: *It's the pushmi-pullyu of the business world, an organization that's a corporation at one end and a partnership at the other*—Jane Bryant Quinn [fr the name of an imaginary creature with two front ends, described in Hugh Lofting's Dr Doolittle books]

push off 1 *v phr* To leave; =SHOVE OFF **2** *v phr* *underworld* To kill; murder; =PUSH

pushover 1 *n* *fr late 1800s* A person who is easily defeated, imposed upon, convinced, etc: *whisper to him that she thought he was sexy. After that he was a pushover*—Joseph Heller/ *an eight-round preliminary with some pushover*—H Witwer/ *I'm a pushover for flattery* **2** *modifier*: *He wasn't a*

pushover kind of cat—Claude Brown **3** *n* =PUNCHBOARD, ROUNDHEELS **4** *n* An easy job or task; =CINCH, DUCK SOUP: *two ways to do it. One was a pushover*—Jerome Weidman [coined by Jack Conway in the late 19th century]

◁**push-push**▷ *n* The sex act: *If they don't go where she wants, it's no push-push for him that night* —Lawrence Sanders

push the panic button *See* HIT THE PANIC BUTTON

push up daisies *v phr fr middle 1800s* To be dead; be buried

pushy *adj* Assertive in a repellent way; aggressive: *Pushy people alarmed him*—Ira Wolfert

puss *n fr early 1900s* The face: *one sock in the puss* —American Mercury/ *a beer-breath in the puss* —Bob Salmaggi [fr Irish *pus*]
See GLAMOR-PUSS, PICKLEPUSS, SOURPUSS

pussy ◁**1**▷ *n fr late 1800s* The vulva or vagina ◁**2**▷ *n* A woman as a sex object or partner; =ASS, TAIL: *Where I come from we call that kind of stuff table pussy*—Calder Willingham/ *some-a the best pussy in New York*—Claude Brown **3** *n* A harmless person, either gentle or timid or both; =PUSSYCAT: *Space Invaders are pussies compared to the marketing aggression of the major producers* —Toronto Life **4** *adj* Harmless and undemanding; fit for the timid: *The bumper cars are pussy* —Cameron Crowe
See EATIN' STUFF, WOOD-PUSSY

◁**pussy butterfly**▷ *n phr* An intrauterine contraceptive device; IUD

pussycat 1 *n* A harmless, gentle, or timid person: *Iacocca is no closet pussycat masquerading as a tiger*—Washington Post **2** *n* A pleasant and amiable person; =DOLL, HONEY

pussyfoot or **pussyfoot around** *v or v phr fr early 1900s* To be careful and hesitant; be evasive; tergiversate; =BEAT AROUND THE BUSH: *Please stop pussyfooting and get to the point* [fr the nickname of WE Johnson, given because of his catlike stealth as a law-enforcement officer in the Indian Territory (Oklahoma); Johnson became a famous advocate of Prohibition, and the term briefly meant "prohibitionist"]

◁**pussy posse** (or **squad**)▷ *n phr* A police morals or vice squad

◁**pussy-whipped**▷ *adj* Dominated by one's wife or female lover; obsequiously uxorious; henpecked: *Francie...had had it with bore-ass "pussy-whipped" men*—Village Voice/ *My husband would have called you pussy-whipped*—John Irving

pustle-gut *See* PUS-GUT

◁**put**▷ *v* To proffer or do the sex act; =LAY: *With men buyers, you get them put and you can sell them the Brooklyn Bridge*—Jerome Weidman [a shortening of *put out*]
See KNOW WHAT one CAN DO WITH something, TELL someone WHAT TO DO WITH something

◁**puta**▷ (Pōō tah) **1** *n* A prostitute: *A white puta like you got to have more money than that*—High Times **2** *n* =PUNCHBOARD [fr Spanish]

put a bug in someone's **ear** *v phr* To give someone a special and private piece of information, esp in the hope of favorable action

put something **across** (or **over**) **1** *v phr* = GET something ACROSS **2** *v phr* To succeed; = PULL IT OFF: *Ask her, she knows how to put it across*

put a damper on *v phr* To cool and reduce enthusiasm; discourage and depress: *His words of wisdom put a damper on our plan*

put a hat on it *sentence lunch counter* Top the order with ice cream

put a lid on someone or something *v phr* To suppress; quiet; quell: *Putting A Lid on The Kid* —Washington Post

put a move on someone *v phr* (Variations: **make** can replace **put**; **the move** or **the moves** can replace **a move**) To make a sexual advance to someone: *Why don't you put a move on that Tuck girl?*—John Irving/ *We talked about a woman whose boss put a move on her*—Sally Forth (comic strip)/ *Remember that time down at Malibu...and this guy put the move on you?*—WT Tyler/ *when he makes a move on Diane*—Washington Post

◁**put** one's **ass in a sling**▷ *See* HAVE one's ASS IN A SLING

◁**put** one's **ass on the line**▷ *v phr* To assume risk and responsibility; put oneself in peril: *I agreed with him, but I wasn't going to put my ass on the line to prove the point*

put away *v phr* To eat or drink, esp heartily or excessively: *They were able to put away a lot of noodles, turkey hash, corn, Jell-O, bread, peanut butter, jelly, and water*—Playboy

put someone or something **away** **1** *v phr* To commit to an asylum or send to jail, an old age home, nursing home, etc **2** *v phr* To kill someone **3** *v phr* To knock someone unconscious: *The Champ put him away in the second round* **4** *v phr* To defeat an opponent, esp in sports: *McEnroe put Connors away in the finals/ The Rangers put the Devils away handily* **5** *v phr* To assure victory; = PUT something ON ICE, CLINCH: *They put it away in the first period, really, with nine goals* **6** *v phr* To please someone enormously; = KNOCK someone's SOCKS OFF: *His voice really puts me away*—Rolling Stone/ *It put me away. It destroyed me*—Washington Post **7** *v phr* To classify; categorize

◁**put balls** (or **hair**) **on**▷ *v phr* To make more emphatic, effective, etc; add impact to: *Rewrite that paragraph and put balls on it*

put daylight between *v phr* To separate things, esp to separate oneself from someone or something disadvantageous: *The President is trying hard to put daylight between himself and the National Rifle Association*

put-down *n* Something disparaging, humiliating, or deflating; a reducing insult; = KNOCK: *since it is such a neat put-down of the arrogant administrator*—Fortune/ *This is a typical Reynolds self-put-down*—L Smith

put someone or something **down** *v phr* To criticize adversely and severely; denigrate; = DUMP ON, KNOCK: *Not that I mean to put down the Old Masters*—D Gillespie

put someone or something **down for** something *v phr* To identify or classify; recognize; = PEG: *When I see a guy with a pull-over sweater under a double-breasted suit, I put him down for an Englishman*—Joe Cannon

put one's **finger on** something *v phr* To recall or specify a desired matter with precision; define exactly: *I remember it, but can't quite put my finger on the outcome*

put one's **foot in it** *v phr* To get into difficulties, esp by blundering: *Trying to be delicate, I put my foot right in it*

put one's **foot in** one's **mouth** *v phr* To make an embarrassing comment; say something stupid: *part of the same hysterical syndrome that caused me to put my foot in my mouth*—Saul Bellow

put someone **in the picture** *v phr fr 1930s British armed forces* To give necessary orienting data; brief; = BRING someone UP TO SPEED: *Nobody put me in the picture, and I was confused for weeks*

put in one's **two cents worth** *See* PUT one's TWO CENTS IN

put it away *v phr* To eat or drink large quantities with urgent appetite

put it in your ear or **take it in the ear** *v phr* To insert something figuratively into one's ear as a means of contemptuous disposal; = STICK IT ● Mild euphemistic forms of **stick it up your ass**, used for reduced effect and among friends: *It was easy to say things like "take it in the ear" to them...they didn't get it*—John Irving

put it on the line *See* LAY IT ON THE LINE

put it on the street *v phr* To disclose something, esp rather publicly: *So we put it on the street that she was leaving*

put it over on someone *v phr fr early 1900s* To deceive; fool: *Be careful, nobody puts it over on her*

◁**put it to** someone▷ *v phr* To do the sex act with or to; = SCREW

put one's **money where** one's **mouth is** *sentence* Support your statements, brags, opinions, etc, with something tangible: *I won't believe he's leaving until he puts his money where his mouth is and goes away*

put someone's **nose out of joint** *v phr* To make someone envious or jealous

put one's **oar in** *v phr* = PUT one's TWO CENTS IN

put something **off** (or **over**) *v phr* To postpone; delay: *We'll put it off to next week*

put on *v phr* = PUT ON AIRS

put-on *fr middle 1800s* **1** *n* An act, remark, etc, intended to fool someone; a more or less amiable deception: *a master of the "put-on," a mildly cruel art*—Time/ *They nudge us that what they're doing is just a "put-on"*—Pauline Kael **2** *n* (also **put-on artist**) A pretender; = PHONY: *to equate an original talent like Kenneth Anger with a put-on like Andy Warhol*—Jack Newfield/ *He's the biggest put-on since Murph the Surf*—Harper's Bazaar **3** *adj* Feigned; affected: *his put-on machismo*

put someone **on** *v phr fr late 1800s* To fool someone, esp by pretending; tease: *Are you putting me on? Or pulling my leg?*—New York Times/ *The Countess who adores the poet pities him and puts him "on"*—Wallace Stevens

put on airs **1** *v phr* To affect a refinement and hauteur one is not born to: *Now that I have the Rolls Royce I'll put on airs* **2** *v phr* To be snobbish and aloof

put someone **on ice** *v phr* To kill; = ICE, OFF

put on the chill *v phr* To assume a cold, unfriendly manner; become distant and hostile

put on the feedbag (or **the nosebag**) *v phr* To eat; have a meal

put someone **on the floor** *v phr* To please someone enormously; = PUT someone AWAY, KNOCK someone OUT: *Schaefer said the strip "put me on the floor"*—Washington Post

put something **on the line** *See* LAY something ON THE LINE

put on the ritz (or **the dog**) **1** *v phr* To make a display of wealth and luxury: *everything they could...to put on the ritz*—Car and Driver/ *put on the dog and give him the ritz like this*—Ira Wolfert **2** *v phr* To dress stylishly and flashily **3** *v phr* = PUT ON AIRS [fr the name of the Swiss César *Ritz* and the various luxurious European hotels he built; *put on the dog* fr a late-19th-century college, esp Yale, expression; see *doggy*]

put someone **on the spot** **1** *v phr* To require action, a solution, etc, at once: *It had to be ready tomorrow, which put our department on the spot* **2** *v phr* To embarrass; put in a difficult position: *I felt he was always trying to put me on the spot with the clients/ I don't want her to put us on the spot again*—New Yorker

put someone **on the stake** *v phr underworld* To blackmail; victimize by extortion; = SHAKE DOWN

put someone **on to** someone or something *v phr* To introduce someone; get someone access to: *that little Andronica you put me onto*—Lawrence Sanders

putout *n baseball* An out, other than a strikeout

◁**put** (or **give**) **out**▷ *v phr* To proffer sexual favors, esp to do so readily; be promiscuous: *A guy gives a dame a string of beads...and she puts out*—Lawrence Sanders/ *As a Yale woman I am resented because I will not "put out" for Yale men*—Yale Alumni Magazine/ *A guy buys a gift for his wife because he knows she won't give out if he don't*—Lawrence Sanders

put-out *adj* Angry; upset; offended: *I couldn't talk to him because he was quite put-out*

put someone **out** *v phr* To impose upon; cause inconvenience

put someone or something **out to pasture** *v phr* To retire; take out of active use, practice, etc, usu after long service: *That old machine's about shot, and we should put it out to pasture/ The university put six of us out to pasture last year* [fr the farm practice of letting an old horse graze at will, and work no longer]

put over *See* PUT something OFF

put one's **papers in** **1** *v phr teenagers* To apply for admission, enlistment, etc **2** *v phr police* To retire or resign

putter-offer *n* A procrastinator: *No, admitted Franklin Roosevelt, as weakly as any putter-offer*—Time

put the arm (or **the sleeve**) **on** someone **1** *v phr* To detain or arrest, esp by force: *It was a signal for the waiter to hustle over and put the arm on the customer who was trying to stiff him*—M Zolotow **2** *v phr* To hit; beat up **3** *v phr* To ask for a loan; = PUT THE BITE ON someone: *writing a letter to my friend Ted without putting the arm on him for a couple of bucks*—John O'Hara

put the bite (or **the bee**) **on** someone or something **1** *v phr fr early 1900s* To ask for money, esp for a loan: *I'll put the bite on my rich cousin* **2** *v phr* To make a request; solicit: *Sullivan continues putting the bee on other Government agencies*—Variety

◁**put the blocks to** someone▷ *v phr fr late 1800s lumberjacks* To do the sex act with or to; = SCREW: *putting the blocks to the Winnipeg whore*—Canadian folk song [fr the logging practice of placing *blocks* on a tree that is to be felled, perhaps with the reinforcing sense that *blocks* suggests "testicles"]

put the chill on someone **1** *v phr* To treat coldly; snub; cut; = COLD SHOULDER **2** *v phr* To kill

put the clamps on *v phr* To seize, esp to steal

put the claw on someone *underworld* **1** *v phr* To arrest **2** *v phr* To inform on or implicate; = PUT THE FINGER ON someone **3** *v phr* = PUT THE BITE ON someone

put the clip on someone *v phr* To overcharge; = CLIP

put the cuff on someone *underworld v phr* To arrest

put the eye on someone **1** *v phr* To look at invitingly or seductively; = GIVE someone THE EYE: *I was having the eye put on me*—Raymond Chandler **2** *v phr* To look at; look over; examine; = SCOPE OUT

put the finger on someone *underworld* **1** *v phr* To locate and identify a victim; = FINGER **2** *v phr* To provide evidence leading to the arrest of a criminal; betray a criminal to the police: *He put the finger on my husband*—New York Daily News

put the freeze on someone *v phr* To reject; treat very coldly: *Women are quick to put the freeze on free loaders*—Hal Boyle

put the heat on someone *v phr* To use coercive pressure; = LEAN ON someone: *He put the heat on me to vote that way*

put the icing on the cake *See* ICE THE CAKE

put the kibosh on someone or something (KĪ bahsh) *v phr fr early 1800s British* To quash or stifle; put the quietus to: *I was praying that the kid wouldn't...put the "kibosh" on me*—Jack London/ *and quietly put the "kibosh" on Donald Nixon, Inc*—Jack Anderson [origin unknown and richly speculated upon; many regard it as probably fr Yiddish because it sounds as if it ought to be; Padraic

Colum, however, attributed it to Irish *cie bais* "cap of death," presumably the black cap donned by a judge before pronouncing the death sentence, which is a semantically appealing suggestion; the phrase was used by Dickens in his first published book, in 1836, and put into the mouth of a London urchin]

put the make on someone *v phr* To make sexual advances; = MAKE A PASS AT someone: *The codger was horny and put the make on the lady cop* —Playboy

put them in the aisles *See* LAY THEM IN THE AISLES

put the moves on someone *v phr* To make sexual advances; = PUT THE MAKE ON someone: *Steve Antin put the moves on Gerri Idol*—People Weekly/ *tryin' to put the moves on every girl in the place* —John Sayles

put the pedal to the metal *v phr* To drive a car at full speed: *Bolan...settled back on creaky springs, and put the pedal to the metal*—Don Pendleton

put the screws to someone *v phr* To use extreme coercive pressure; harass; = PUT THE HEAT ON someone: *The only reason Fidel agreed...was to put the screws to Reagan*—Art Buchwald [fr a torturer's use of *thumbscrews*]

put the skids under someone or something *v phr* To cause to fail, be defeated, be rejected, etc: *They put the skids under him when they found out he had cheated*

put the slug on someone **1** *v phr* To hit or attack: *fined for putting the slug on a heckling fan* —Arthur Daley **2** *v phr* To criticize harshly; = KNOCK: *needn't think he can get away with putting the slug on rummies*—Red Smith

put the snatch on someone or something *v phr* To take or commandeer; seize; kidnap: *showed their true gangster coloration by putting the snatch on a South Korean DC-3 airliner*—New York Daily News/ *The Treasury Department is going to put the snatch on virtually the entire 40 grand*—Billy Rose

put the squeeze on someone *v phr* To put under heavy pressure or exigency; = LEAN ON someone, PUT THE HEAT ON someone: *She hired me to put the squeeze on Linda for a divorce*—Raymond Chandler

put the wood to someone *v phr* To punish; coerce by threat of punishment: *Why can't Mayor Barry put the wood to school administrators and demand more caring than this?*—Washingtonian

put someone **through the mill** *See* RUN someone THROUGH THE MILL

put someone **through the wringer** *v phr* To subject to harsh treatment, esp by severe interrogation [fr the image of squeezing something out by passing it through a clothing *wringer*]

putting *See* OFF-PUTTING

putt-putt **1** *n* A small marine engine **2** *n* A motorboat, esp a slow one **3** *v*: *We'll putt-putt over to the island* **4** *n* Any small motor vehicle

put (or **add**) one's **two cents** (or **two cents worth**) **in** *v phr* To volunteer one's advice, esp when it is not solicited; = KIBITZ: *If I may put my two cents in, I think we should shut up*

putty-head *n* A stupid person; = PUDDINGHEAD

put up *v phr* To contribute or pay money, esp money bet or promised

put someone **up** *v phr* To provide lodging for

put-up job *n phr fr middle 1800s underworld* A prearranged matter; a contrived affair: *The surprise award was a put-up job*

put up or shut up *sentence* = PUT one's MONEY WHERE one's MOUTH IS

put up with someone or something *v phr* To tolerate or accept: *I'll put up with it if you think I should/ How can you put up with him?*

put someone **wise** *v phr fr early 1900s* To make aware; inform, esp of something shrewd and elementary or covert: *The kindly old clerk put me wise to how things were done around there*

◁**putz**▷ **1** *n* A detestable person; obnoxious wretch; = PRICK, SCHMUCK: *Here comes the Moravian putz*—Joseph Heller **2** *n* An ineffectual person; = NEBBISH: *The poor little putz didn't realize what they were after* **3** *n* The penis [fr Yiddish, literally "ornament"]

putz around *v phr* To behave idly; putter around; = FOOL AROUND, FUTZ AROUND [fr *putz* and semantically related to *dick around*, *fuck around*, though less coarse than these to any but, probably, Jewish ears]

puzzle palace **1** *n phr Army* Any higher headquarters, including the Pentagon **2** *n phr* A place, like the White House, where vital decisions are made in great and pompous secrecy: *some kind of puzzle palace on the Potomac*—Ronald Reagan *See* FIVE-SIDED PUZZLE PALACE

pyramids *See* PLATFORMS

Q

the **Q** *n phr hoboes* The Chicago, Burlington, and Quincy Railroad

Q and A *modifier* Questions and answers: *get the police into our Q and A contest*—W & F Simpson

the **QT** *See* ON THE QT

quad **1** *n* Any architectural quadrangle, esp one at a college or university **2** *n* =QUOD **3** *n hot rodders* A car having four headlights

quads *n hot rodders* A set of four headlights on a car

quail ◁**1**▷ *n fr middle 1800s college students* An attractive young woman; =CHICK: *a lovely little quail from Arkansas*—Arthur Godfrey/ *lotsa native Hoosier quail for the wayfaring birdwatcher to ogle*—Easyriders **2** *n jazz musicians* A cornet or trumpet: *listen to that kid blow that quail*—Louis Armstrong

See SAN QUENTIN QUAIL

◁**quail-roost**▷ *n early 1900s college students* A women's dormitory

quarterback *v* To lead or direct; control; manage: *and quarterbacking the rise of Action News at Channel 6*—Philadelphia

See MONDAY MORNING QUARTERBACK

quartet *See* BARBERSHOP QUARTET

queen **1** *n* A woman, esp a wealthy and gracious one: *Wouldn't it be luck if some ritzy queen fell for him!*—James T Farrell/ *What a lady...a queen*—JD Salinger **2** *v* (also **queen it**) To behave in a refined and haughty way **3** *n homosexuals* A male homosexual, esp one who ostentatiously takes a feminine role: *The queens look great strutting along the boardwalk*—Albert Goldman [homosexual sense probably a late-19th-century alteration of *quean* "harlot, prostitute," influenced by connotations of *queen* "aged, dignified, tawdry, and overadorned"]

See BUBBLE QUEEN, CLOSET QUEEN, DRAG QUEEN, MAIN QUEEN, SIZE QUEEN, TEAROOM QUEEN, TOE-JAM QUEEN

queer **1** *adj fr 1500s perhaps fr Scots* Counterfeit **2** *n* (also **the queer**) *underworld fr early 1900s* Counterfeit money: *eagle-eyed concessionaires always on the lookout for the queer*—W & F Simpson ◁**3**▷ *adj fr 1920s* Homosexual; =CAMP, GAY: *Some girls said that I was queer*—New York Post/ *The other guy...isn't queer or a drinker, either*—Herbert Gold ◁**4**▷ *n* (also **queerie**): *a closet queer/ a lot of queeries in the State Department*

—Westbrook Pegler **5** *v fr late 1700s British* To spoil; ruin; =GOOF UP: *Food is what queered the party*—F Scott Fitzgerald

queer fish *n phr* A strange or weird person; =WACK, WEIRDO

quetor *See* CUTER

quick *adj esp 1920s & 30s* Tight; snug: *That sweater seems a little quick*

quick-and-dirty *n* =GREASY SPOON

quick buck *See* FAST BUCK

be **quick-draw** *v phr* To act or respond impulsively and aggressively; =SHOOT FROM THE HIP

quick fix *n phr* A hasty repair or relief job: *He called my idea a quick fix at best, but he'd do it* [fr *fix* as "repair" influenced by *fix* as "dose of narcotics"]

quickie **1** *n* Anything taken or done very hastily; something rushed: *a "quickie," one of those overnight film concoctions*—Picture Play/ *has written his slightly sounder quickies*—Robert Shaplen **2** *modifier: the new "quickie divorce" law*—Selden Rodman/ *the "quickie" increases, if approved by Congress*—Associated Press **3** *n* The sex act done very hastily: *Do you have time for a quickie?* **4** *n labor union* An unauthorized strike; =WILDCAT

quick like a bunny *adv phr esp 1940s* Very quickly

quick one *n phr* Something taken or done hastily, esp an unleisurely drink or sex act; =QUICKIE, a SHORT ONE

quick on the draw (or **the trigger** or **the uptake**) *adj phr fr middle 1800s* Quick to respond or react; touchy; sensitive

quick-over *n* A quick glance or inspection; =the ONCE-OVER

quick push *n phr* =PUSHOVER

quiet *See* ALL QUIET ON THE WESTERN FRONT

quiff *n underworld* A prostitute or promiscuous woman; =ROUNDHEEL: *because some quiff is going to give you head*—Lawrence Sanders/ *There would be a lot of loose quiff we could meet*—Philadelphia [perhaps related to late-19th-century British, "vulva," which may be fr earlier verb sense "copulate"; perhaps related to late-19th-century British armed forces slang, "a small flat curl or lock of hair on the temple or forehead," perhaps fr Italian *cuffia* "coif" or fr *coif* with sense transferred to pubic hair]

quill *n narcotics* A folded matchbook cover used to hold heroin or cocaine for sniffing

◁**quim**▷ *n fr 1600s* The vulva or vagina; =CUNT [origin unknown; perhaps fr Middle English *queme* "pleasure, satisfaction," cognate with Latin *convenire*, hence with *convenient*, *convenience*, etc, and perhaps influenced by Middle English *queint* "cunt"]

quits *See* CALL IT QUITS

quiz *n students fr middle 1800s* A brief examination in college
See POP QUIZ

quod (KWAHD) *n outdated underworld fr late 1600s British* A prison [perhaps fr *quadrangle*; perhaps fr Romany *quaid* "prison"]

R

R *See* R AND R

RA (pronounced as separate letters) **1** *n* Anger **2** *n college students* Supervisor of a floor in a dormitory [first sense fr the *Red Ass*; see *get the red ass*; second sense fr *Resident Advisor*]

rabbi *n politics fr police & underworld* An influential sponsor; a high-placed patron: *I see you got the gold tin, who's your rabbi?*—New York Times/ *Moretti recognized the voice of his rabbi, a Tammany hack*—Patrick Mann/ *described by a Reagan transition official: "To get a job, you gotta have a rabbi"*—Washingtonian

rabbit **1** *n sports* The pacesetter in the early laps of a mile race **2** *v* To run away fast; escape in a hurry; =LAM: *The man who had rabbited was later identified*—Ann Rule [first sense fr the mechanical *rabbit* used to lure dogs in a race]

See PANTS RABBIT

rabbit ears *n phr* A V-shaped television antenna

rabbit food *See* BUNNY FOOD

rabbit-foot **1** *n prison* A convict who escapes from prison **2** *v* =RABBIT, LAM

race *See* BOAT RACE, DRAG RACE, DRUGSTORE RACE, HORSERACE, RAT RACE

rack *v* (also **rack out**) *teenagers* To sleep; nap; =COP ZS: *I'll rack out for awhile on the grass till I get it together*—Perception & Persuasion

See MEAT RACK, OFF-THE-RACK, PANIC RACK, RIM-ROCK

the rack *n fr Navy* Bed; =SACK: *who gets some Greek broad in the rack and tries some funny business*—WT Tyler/ *Jeanne is pretty good in the rack* —George V Higgins

rack duty (or **time**) *n phr Navy* Sleep; time spent in one's bunk; =SACK TIME

racked *adv* For certain; under control; =TAPED [probably fr the *racking* of the balls before a pool game, putting them in a precise pattern]

racked out *adj phr teenagers* Asleep; in bed

racket **1** *n fr middle 1800s British* Any illegal concern or enterprise; a criminal business; =DODGE, GRIFT: *the narcotics racket/ loan-shark racket* **2** *n circus & carnival* Any concession, stand, etc **3** *n* One's legitimate occupation or concern: *Lexicography's my racket* **4** *n* An easy and pleasant situation, esp a sinecure: *That's no job, it's a racket* [fr early-19th-century British underworld fr *racket* "noise, confusion," etc]

racketeer *n fr 1920s* A person who works in an illegal racket; a member of the rackets; =GANGSTER, MOBSTER

racket-jacket *n* =ZOOT SUIT

the rackets *n phr* Organized crime; the syndicate; the Mafia

rack up[1] *v phr* To register or post; accumulate; achieve: *more representative of actual consumer use than 60,000 miles would have been if racked up in short order*—Popular Science/ *with the years of hackdom racked up in his face*—New York [fr the *racking up* of pool balls in a triangular frame before a game]

rack up[2] *v phr* To wreck; ruin; damage severely; =TOTAL: *got caught raping a nine-year-old Japanese girl. He got racked up*—Lawrence Sanders/ *The fall really racked up his leg* [probably related to *rack* "junk, rubbish," as found in the mid-19th-century term *rack heap*; perhaps influenced by *wreck* and *wrack and ruin*]

rad[1] **1** *n* A radical **2** *adj teenagers* Extraordinary; wonderful

rad[2] *n Army* A German [fr German *Kamerad* "comrade, friend"]

radiclib or **rad-lib** **1** *n* A political left-winger: *impartially Agnewthematized as a "radiclib"*—B Brower **2** *adj: my rad-lib line*

radio *n lunch counter* A tuna-fish sandwich [fr the synonymy of *radio* with *tuner*]

See THUNDERBOX RADIO

raft **1** *n fr early 1800s* A large number; =OODLES, SLEW: *I have rafts of reasons for not doing that/ She gave me a raft of excuses* **2** *n lunch counter* A slice of toast [first sense fr earlier uses of *raft* to mean a dense flight of waterfowl and a mass of driftwood in a river]

See ON A RAFT

rag **1** *n* An article of clothing, esp a dress **2** *n circus* A tent **3** *n Navy* A signal flag **4** *n baseball* The pennant awarded to the annual winner of a league championship **5** *n* A newspaper or magazine, esp one that the speaker does not like: *This so-called revolutionary organ is a horrible rag*—O Chubb **6** *n cardplayers* A playing card, esp one that does not improve the hand; =PASTEBOARD **7** *n railroad* A switch operator **8** *n fr early 1900s* =RAGTIME **9** *n fr early 1900s* A piece of ragtime music **10** *v fr early 1900s* To play in a ragtime style: *The street bands ragged a tune by taking one*

351

note and putting two or three in its place—Stephen Longstreet **11** *v fr early 1900s* To dance to ragtime music **12** *v fr late 1800s college students* To tease; banter disparagingly with; =NEEDLE, RIDE: *Sometimes we'd rag one another in the rough manner that is safe only for friends*—FG Patton

See BEAN RAG, the BIG RAG, BULLY RAG, DAMP RAG, GLAD RAGS

◁the **rag**▷ **1** *n* A sanitary napkin; a vaginal tampon: *She told him she was wearing the rag, which cooled his ardor some* **2** *n* Menstruation; =the CURSE

See CHEW THE FAT, HAVE THE RAG ON, ON THE RAG, TAKE THE RAG OFF THE BUSH

rag bag 1 *n phr* Any miscellany, esp a very random and confusing one: *What he calls his philosophy is a rag bag of trite trivialities* **2** *modifier:* a *rag-bag collection, but an interesting one*

rag-chewing *n fr late 1800s* Talking, esp of an amiable and idle sort

ragged *See* RUN someone RAGGED

◁**raggedy-ass**▷ or **raggedy-pants** *adj fr WW1 armed forces* Inferior; sloppy; =HALF-ASSED: *some kinda raggedy-ass agreement she thinks is a legal will*—Joseph Wambaugh/ *picked up from some raggedy-pants US trackside*—Sports Illustrated

◁**raggedy-ass militia**▷ *n phr Army* A sloppy or inept military unit

raggle-taggle *See* TAKE THE RAG OFF THE BUSH

◀**raghead**▶ **1** *n* A Hindu or other Eastern or Middle Eastern person: *speaks Arab like a raghead*—WT Tyler **2** *n* A gypsy: *You let that raghead touch your hand*—Harry Crews

rag out (or **up**) *v phr fr middle 1800s* To dress in one's best clothes; =DOLL UP

rags *n* Clothing; =THREADS: *She got into her rags*—John O'Hara

See GLAD RAGS

ragtime 1 *n fr late 1800s* A highly syncopated style of music, esp for the piano, having a heavily accented tempo and a melody consisting of many short rapid notes **2** *modifier:* a *ragtime classic*

ragtop or **rag-roof 1** *n* A convertible car: *It's been a while since the ragtops rolled off the assembly line*—Aquarian/ *Return of the rag roofs*—Time/ *Ragtops Are the Rage Once Again*—New York Times **2** *modifier:* I *sure wouldn't sleep in that rag-top car*—Earl Thompson

the **rag trade** *n phr fr middle 1800s* The clothing and fashion industry; the garment industry; =SEVENTH AVENUE: *the enormously canny middle-aged men of the rag trade*—New Yorker

rah-rah 1 *adj fr 1920s* Naively enthusiastic and hortatory, esp in a partisan collegiate context **2** *n:* I *just couldn't see myself spending four years of my life with rah-rahs like them*

rail *n narcotics* A thin row of powdered narcotic to be sniffed; =LINE: I *snorted the rails that Hondo offered*—Peter Gent

railbird *n fr late 1800s* An ardent horse-racing devotee: *another three-year-old...that set the railbirds agog*—Audax Minor/ *Rail birds come in all shapes and sizes but, at least the way the term is commonly applied, never with feathers*—New York Times

railroad 1 *v fr late 1800s* To convict and imprison someone very rapidly, perhaps unjustly or illegally: *The prisoner is railroaded to jail*—E Lavine **2** *v* To force a resolution of something quickly, perhaps without due process: *if all cases were railroaded through that quick*—James M Cain

See a HELL OF A WAY TO RUN A RAILROAD

railroad stiff *n phr hoboes* A hobo traveling free by rail; esp in freight cars

railroad tracks 1 *n phr WW2 Army* An Army captain's two silver bars, the insignia of rank **2** *n phr* Braces on teeth: a *chubbette with "railroad tracks" across her teeth*—New York

rain *v black* To complain; =BITCH

rain cats and dogs *v phr* (Variations: **chicken coops** or **darning needles** or **pitchforks** may replace **cats and dogs**) *fr middle 1700s British* To rain very hard [origin unknown, although many improbable derivations have been proposed, from classical Greek to pagan Scandinavian]

rain check *n phr* A postponement or delay, with promise of renewal, of a sports event, dinner, party, date, receipt of a sale item at a store, etc [fr the ticket stub that permits one to see another baseball game if the game one has a ticket for is not played on account of rain]

See TAKE A RAIN CHECK

rain dance *n phr* An impressive political reception or banquet

rainmaker *n* A powerful and successful representative or agent, esp for a law firm: *to a six-figure "rainmaker" generating fees for one of the most politically connected law firms in the state*—Village Voice/ *All such well-connected persons are "rainmakers" capable of making their employer's cause prosper*—Newsweek

rain on someone's **parade** *v phr* To spoil someone's day, performance, special occasion, etc

raise *See* MEXICAN PROMOTION

raise Cain (or **a ruckus**) *v phr fr middle 1800s* To make a disturbance; complain loudly and bitterly; =KICK UP A FUSS

raise hell 1 *v phr* =RAISE CAIN **2** *v phr* To carouse and celebrate boisterously **3** *v phr* To rebuke strongly; castigate: *He raised hell with me when he found out*

raiser *See* DUST-RAISER, HELL-RAISER

raise sand *v phr* =RAISE CAIN

raise the decibel level *v phr* To make something more conspicuous; increase the intensity of something: *They decided it was time to raise the decibel level of her mayoral campaign*

raise the roof 1 *v phr* To complain angrily and bitterly; issue a strong rebuke: *When the president sees this fuck-up she'll raise the roof* **2** *v phr* To make a boisterous noise; carouse raucously

raked *adj hot rodders* Of a customized car, having the front end lower than the rear

rake-off *fr late 1800s* **1** *n* A gambling house's percentage of each pot or stake **2** *n* An illegal or unethical share or payment [fr the *rake* used by casino croupiers]

rake someone **over the coals** *See* HAUL someone OVER THE COALS

rally *See* PEP RALLY

ralph *v* (Variations: **Ralph** or **ralph up** or **rolf**)
teenagers To vomit; = BARF: *He ralphs up the
downers and the quarts of beer*—J Gallick [probably
echoic]

-rama or **-arama** or **-orama** *suffix used to form
nouns* A spectacular display or instance of what is
indicated: *boatarama/ videorama* [fr *panorama*,
ultimately fr Greek *horama* "sight"]

ram-bam thank you ma'am *See* WHAM-BAM
THANK YOU MA'AM

rambling *adj hoboes* Fast: *a rambling freight*

rambunctious *adj fr early 1800s* Boisterous;
obstreperous; wild [perhaps fr Irish *rambunkshus*; a
US contribution to a mock inkhorn series with British variants *robustious, rumbumptious,* etc]

◁**ram it**▷ *v phr* = STICK IT

rammer *See* MOTHERFUCKER

rammy *adj* Sexually aroused; = HORNY

ranch *See* BUY THE FARM, HENCOOP

R and R¹ *n phr* A several-days' carouse [fr military
phrase *Rest and Recreation*]

R and R² *n phr* Rock and roll

randy 1 *adj fr late 1700s fr British dialect* Sexually aroused; = HORNY: *a desperately randy brain
surgeon*—Time **2** *adj* Desirous; yearning: *randy
for the smell of setting cement*—Washingtonian [ori-
gin unknown; various dialect senses suggest a possible derivation fr "wild movement," "boisterousness," "wantonness"]

rank 1 *v underworld* To say or do something that
reveals another's guilt: *She ranked him by busting
out with that new fur so soon after the robbery*—E
Booth **2** *v fr 1920s* To harass; annoy; = NEEDLE
● Used by 1960s teenagers in the preferred variant
rank out, both as a verb phrase and a noun
phrase: *He will rank you for what happened*—Wash-
ingtonian/ *the fine, foul art of "ranking." Light
insults were his way of making friends*—Time
See PULL RANK

rap¹ 1 *n fr late 1700s* A rebuke; = KNOCK **2** *n
fr 1920s underworld* Arrest, indictment, or arraign-
ment for a crime: *Gangs with influence can beat
about 90 percent of their "raps"*—E Lavine **3** *n*
An official complaint or reprimand: *Honest cops will
often take a "rap" or complaint rather than testify
against a fellow cop*—E Lavine
See BEAT THE RAP

rap² 1 *v esp 1960s counterculture & black* To
converse; chat and exchange views, esp in a very
candid way: *drugs, youth cult, ecstasy questing, rapping*—New York Times **2** *n* Informal talk; candid
conversation and communion **3** *v* To sympathize; be of chiming views **4** *v fr late 1970s* To
chant a rap song **5** *n* = RAP SONG [origin
unknown; perhaps related to *repartee*, perhaps to
rapport, perhaps to *rapid*]

the **rap** *n phr fr middle 1800s* The blame; an accusation: *He wouldn't accept the rap for that particular screw-up*
See TAKE THE RAP

rap club (or **parlor** or **studio**) **1** *n phr* A
place that offers sexual services in the guise of conversation and companionship: *"rap clubs," which
have replaced massage parlors*—New York Post/
The rap studios began springing up earlier this year
—New York Post **2** *n phr* A nightclub, discotheque, etc, featuring rap music

rape wagon *n phr* = PIMPMOBILE

rap group *n phr esp 1960s counterculture* A discussion group

rap someone's **knuckles** *v phr* To give a light
and insufficient punishment; = GIVE someone A SLAP
ON THE WRIST: *Tokyo had been rapped over the
knuckles*—New York Review

rapper¹ 1 *n outdated underworld* A person who
charges or identifies another as a criminal **2** *n
outdated underworld* A judge or prosecutor **3** *n*
A crime for which someone not guilty has been punished: *a couple of gang murders solved, but they
were just rappers*—Raymond Chandler [first senses
fr early-18th-century *rap* "charge with a crime"]

rapper² 1 *n esp 1960s counterculture* A person
who converses and chats, esp a member of a rap
(discussion) group **2** *n fr late 1970s* The chanter
of a rap song **3** *n fr late 1970s* A devotee of rap
music and its attendant styles of dressing, dancing,
etc: *as rappers pick up on a little new wave
style...and make their moves*—Time/ *among the
rappers and breakers joining an organization called
We Care About New York*—New York Daily News
4 *modifier: rapper talk, which pulls in language
from...40s hipsters, 60s hippies, and even cockney
rhyming slang*—Time

rap session 1 *n phr* A conversation; a bout of
candid chat: *talk shows featuring rap sessions
between hosts and listeners*—Newsweek **2** *n phr*
A meeting of a discussion group: *I was asked to
lead a rap session*—Betty Friedan

rap sheet *n phr* A person's record of arrests and
convictions: *The last one is called a rap sheet*
—Bobby Seale/ *Their rap sheets listed convictions
for the possession or sale of controlled substances*
—Village Voice [see *rapper¹*]

rap song (or **music**) *n phr* A song that is rapidly
spoken rather than actually sung, usu with an electronic rhythm accompaniment

rare back *v phr* To gather one's strength; poise
oneself for action: *She rared back and let him have
it* [fr the verb *rear*, and the image of a horse *rearing*
on its hind legs]

be **raring to go** *v phr* To be very eager and keen
to begin; = LEAN FORWARD IN THE SADDLE [fr the
image of a *rearing*, mettlesome horse]

raspberries or **razzberries** (RAZ behr eez)
interj esp 1920s An exclamation of disbelief, defiance, disgust, etc; = NUTS

raspberry *n* An instance of the raspberry, a rude
labial flatulation: *You should expect an occasional
heathen to utter a raspberry*—Washington Post
See FLIP one's LID

the **raspberry** (or **razzberry**) (RAZ beh ree) *n
phr fr late 1800s British* A rude and contemptuous
expulsion of breath through vibrating lips; = the

BIRD: *that staccato sputter of derision known as the Bronx cheer, or raspberry*—Newsweek [fr Cockney rhyming slang *raspberry tart* "fart"]

rat 1 *n* A treacherous and disgusting person: *He's acting like a prime rat on this* **2** *n fr late 1800s* An informer; = STOOL PIGEON: *In most cases they were "rats" and the best tools the keepers had*—PL Quinlan **3** *v*: *an inmate, rankled by Angelo's attempts to woo his daughter, ratted on them* —Time **4 combining word** A frequenter and devotee of the place indicated: *arcade rat/ gym rat* *See* BRIG RAT, DESERT RAT, DOCK RAT, LOOK LIKE A DROWNED RAT, PACK RAT, RUG APE, SACK RAT, SHACK MAN, SMELL A RAT, WINTER RAT

rat around *v phr* To idle about; loaf; = BAT AROUND: *Oh, I don't know. Ratting around*—John O'Hara

rat (or **rat-trap** or **store**) **cheese** *n phr* An undistinguished yellow cheddar-like American cheese

ratchet *v* To change by increments in one direction: *Gold...had ratcheted down to 385*—New York Times/ *We have ratcheted up the violence in Lebanon*—Cable News Network [fr the *ratchet* action of a winch or of a wrench, where an increasing pressure, torque, pull, etc, is registered by the clicking of a cog on a gear wheel]

ratchet-mouth or **ratchet-jaw** *n* A person who is constantly talking; = MOTOR-MOUTH [perhaps because a *ratchet* wrench can be operated without pause, and makes a constant rapid rasping, clacking noise]

rate 1 *v* To merit; deserve: *He rates a big cheer, folks* **2** *v* To be highly esteemed: *What stunt did he ever pull that makes him rate?*—Billy Rose *See* CUT-RATE, FIRST-RATE

rated *See* X-RATED

rate with someone *v phr* To be highly regarded, cherished, trusted, etc, by someone: *That sort of persuasion doesn't rate a damn with me*

rat-face *n* A cunning and treacherous person

rat fink 1 *n phr esp 1960s* A treacherous and disgusting person; = BASTARD, SHITHEEL: *that rat-fink Danny's kid*—TV Guide **2 modifier:** *the rat-fink Eastern press*—New Yorker [perhaps originally fr labor union use, since both terms mean "scab"]

◁**rat fuck**▷ *college students* **1** *adj phr* Unacceptable to conventional moral traditions **2** *adj phr* = FAR OUT **3** *v phr* To have a good time; = JAM **4** *v phr* To loaf and idle about; = RAT AROUND **5** *n phr* A despicable person; = RAT-FINK: *You lousy bastard rat-fuck*—Barry Reed

rathole 1 *n* A wretched, messy place; a filthy hovel; = DUMP: *Those days we lived in a rathole* **2** *v* To store up food and supplies; stockpile; = STASH *See* POUR MONEY DOWN THE DRAIN

rations *See* GROUND RATIONS

rat on someone *v phr* To inform on someone; give evidence against someone; = SQUEAL: *No power on earth can keep her from ratting on you*—James M Cain

rat out *v phr* To abandon or desert; withdraw; = FINK OUT: *I wouldn't feel you were ratting out* —Budd Schulberg [fr the *rats* that desert a sinking ship]

rat pack *n phr* A teenage street gang: *juvenile gangs, sometimes called rat packs*—RS Prather

rat race *n phr* A job, situation, milieu, etc, marked by confusion and stress; futile and enervating hyperactivity: *She found the internship a 24-hour rat race/ the rat-race of ordinary social gatherings*—E Wilder

the **rat race** *n phr* The everyday world of toil and struggle; the routine workaday world: *Will Heacock ever renounce the freelance life and rejoin the rat race?*

rats *interj* An exclamation of disgust, disappointment, dismay, etc

◁a **rat's ass**▷ *n phr* Nothing; very little; = DIDDLY, ZILCH ● **Not** is used to intensify rather than to negate this phrase: *That thing's not worth a rat's ass* *See* NOT GIVE A DAMN

◁**rat's asshole**▷ *n phr* A despicable person; = BASTARD, RAT-FINK: *You rat's asshole*—John Irving

ratter *n* An informer; = RAT, STOOL PIGEON

rattle 1 *v* (also **rattle on**) To talk on and on, esp foolishly or pointlessly; babble **2** *v* To confuse; upset; disturb concentration: *I rattled him with veiled menaces*

rattlebrain *n* A silly or stupid person; = SCATTER-BRAIN: *Mother would like to travel around but not with an old rattlebrain like you driving*—Ring Lardner

rattle someone's **cage 1** *v phr* To stir into action: *Something rattling your cage?*—Easyriders/ *Reiner and friends affectionately rattle the cage of rock music and its every pretension*—Washingtonian **2** *v phr* To make a scene or disturbance; = RAISE CAIN: *I'm going into his office and rattle his cage*

rattle cages *v phr* To cause excitement; shake things up: *"You like to rattle cages," the saleswoman observed, explaining that it was a California expression*—Village Voice

rattle someone's **chain** *See* PULL someone's CHAIN

rattler 1 *n fr middle 1800s British* A railroad train: *a very luxurious rattler*—W Davenport **2** *n* hoboes A fast freight train or a freight car **3** *n* A rattlesnake *See* CAGE RATTLER

rattlesnakes *See* UP TO one's ASS IN something

rattling 1 *adv* Very; extremely: *a rattling good story*—A Hays **2** *adj* Good; = GREAT: *a rattling party*

ratty or ◁**rat-ass**▷ *adj* Shabby; slovenly; = SCRUFFY, TACKY: *a fairly ratty bar*—T Robinson/ *the rat-ass rags he's always wearing*—National Lampoon

raunch 1 *n* Vulgarity; smut; = PORN: *no obscenities in Glen's Bar....Too tired for raunch*—Herbert Kastle/ *the latest batch of 8mm raunch*—Playboy **2** *v* To do the sex act with or to; = SCREW: *just because she's raunched a few law students* —National Lampoon [back formation fr raunchy]

raunchy or **ronchie 1** *adj* *WW2 Air Forces* Sloppy; slovenly; careless: *depending on how good or how "raunchy" we were*—R Hubler **2** *adj* *teenagers* Inferior; cheap; =CRUMMY, GRUNGY: *my raunchy old jeans* **3** *adj* *esp students* Vulgar; salacious; =DIRTY: *I'm gonna do some raunchy blues this time*—Rolling Stone/ *In the beginning there was* Playboy, *then came raunchy* Penthouse —Time/ *But then things got a little raunchy*—Lawrence Sanders **4** *adj* *esp students* Ill; indisposed; =BLAH, YUCKY: *I feel raunchy as hell today* **5** *adj* Drunk [probably fr Italian *rancio* "rancid, stale, rank"]

rave 1 *v* *fr late 1800s* To commend or applaud enthusiastically: *He's raving over this new book* **2** *n*: *The critics gave it a rave* **3** *modifier*: *a rave review/ rave notices*
See FAVE

rave-up 1 *n* *chiefly British teenagers* A wild party **2** *n* Something loud and exciting: *in "Take Me Back," a lively rave-up*—Time

raw 1 *adj* Inexperienced; unfledged; callow: *a raw young actress* **2** *adj* Harsh; inhospitable: *a raw reception* **3** *adj* Nude; naked; =IN THE RAW: *You can't go raw on this beach, ma'am* **4** *adj* Vulgar; salacious; dirty; raunchy: *He offended us all with a very raw story*
See IN THE RAW

raw deal *n phr* A case of harsh, unfair, or injurious treatment; =a ROYAL FUCKING: *The Academy officers were heaping raw deal after raw deal on him*—Sloan Wilson

rays *n* Sunshine: *soaking up some rays*
See BAG SOME RAYS

razor *v* *outdated underworld* To divide loot into shares; =DIVVY UP: *When loot is divided...it is "razored"*—H McLellan

razorback *n* *circus & hoboes* A manual laborer; roustabout

razz *v* *fr early 1900s* To insult and ridicule; =NEEDLE, RIDE: *The fellows razzed the life out of me*—P Marks/ *Is there ever any razzing about the fact that you report to your wife?*—Washington Post [fr *raspberry*]

the **razz** *n phr* Mocking insults; rude splatting sounds; =the RASPBERRY: *They begin to give him the razz*—H Witwer

the **razzberry** *See* the RASPBERRY

razzle-dazzle *fr late 1800s* **1** *n* Adroit deception; slick dodging and feinting; =DOUBLE SHUFFLE, RAZZMATAZZ: *suspecting some sort of razzle-dazzle* —New Yorker **2** *modifier*: *a razzle-dazzle quarterback/ razzle-dazzle salesmanship* **3** *n* Excitement; gaudiness; spectacular show: *put razzle-dazzle into the grocery business*—This Week/ *You don't spend an estimated $25 million without getting some razzle-dazzle for your money*—Washington Post **4** *adj*: *A great many people are reading Mr Wakeman's razzle-dazzle novel*—CV Terry/ *its razzle-dazzle weapons and command and control systems*—Newsweek **5** *n* *carnival* An exciting carnival ride **6** *n* *carnival* A prostitute [probably a reduplication of *dazzle*]

razzmatazz or **razzamatazz 1** *n* *outdated jazz talk* Anything outdated, esp old and sentimental; =CORN: *"Razzmatazz" is corny jazz*—Stephen Longstreet **2** *n* Swift and adroit deception; slick jugglery; =RAZZLE-DAZZLE: *The sales rep will lay a lot of razzmatazz on you/ more glitter, more razzmatazz, more false human interest*—Washington Post **3** *adj* Spectacular; showy; dazzling; =RAZZLE-DAZZLE: *a razzmatazz New Year's Eve bash* —Philadelphia/ *one of the most interesting razzmatazz careers of our time*—Billy Rose **4** *adj* =GEEWHIZ, RAH-RAH

reach-me-down 1 *adj* *fr late 1800s* Inferior; shoddy: *the nice and the reach-me-down manners* —Raymond Chandler **2** *n* =HAND-ME-DOWN

reach-me-downs *n* Cheap, ready-made clothing

reaction *See* GUT REACTION

read 1 *v* *WW1 Army* To inspect clothing for lice **2** *v* To lip-read **3** *v* *fr radio operators* To receive and interpret a radio signal; understand: *He's breaking up and I can't read him* **4** *v* *cool talk fr radio operators* To understand; =DIG: *I read you, baby, and I flatly agree* **5** *v* =READ someone LIKE A BOOK

read 'em and weep *sentence* Here is some probably unwelcome information for you; here is the truth [fr the crapshooter's or poker player's injunction that his opponents look carefully at a winning roll or hand]

reader 1 *n* *hawkers* A license to do business **2** *n* *carnival* Money paid for a license: *We couldn't play St. Louis because we couldn't raise the reader* **3** *n* *narcotics* A prescription for narcotics **4** *n* *fr underworld fr middle 1800s British* A poster or notice describing a wanted criminal: *They got readers out on him and there was quite a hunt*—J Evans
See METER-READER, MITT-READER

readers *n* *gambling fr late 1800s* Marked playing cards: *The cards and dice were crooked, the cards being readers*—W & F Simpson

read someone **his rights** *See* GIVE someone HIS RIGHTS

read someone **like a book** *v phr* To know and understand someone thoroughly, including deep motives and likely actions: *She thinks she's pretty clever, but I read her like a book*

read someone **loud and clear** *v phr* *fr radio operators* To understand someone very well; comprehend perfectly: *Do you read me loud and clear, mister?*—Pat Conroy

read my lips or **can you read lips 1** *sentence* I am thinking but not uttering something obscene, insulting, or otherwise not for the public ear: *Psst. Hey, parents! Read my lips*—Erma Bombeck **2** *v phr* You seem to be too stupid to understand what I'm saying, so look at me very attentively and try

read one's **plate 1** *v phr* To say grace before a meal **2** *v phr* To keep one's head down and eat in silence

read the riot act *v phr fr middle 1800s* To rebuke firmly; reprove severely, esp in the vein of a stern warning

the ready *n phr fr early 1700s British* Money: *Take the ready and send it along*—John Kieran [fr *ready money*]

real *adv* Really; truly
See FOR REAL, IT'S BEEN REAL

the real cheese *See* the CHEESE

real estate **1** *n phr railroad* Low-grade coal **2** *n phr* Dirt, such as smirches on the hands and face

the real George *n phr outdated bop talk & teenagers* Anything superb and genuine; the best or greatest

really pick 'em *See* one CAN REALLY PICK 'EM

the real McCoy (or **the McCoy**) *n phr* Any genuine and worthy person or thing; the genuine article: *egg bagels, a sweeter variety of the real McCoy*—New York Times/ *You can trust her, she's the McCoy* [probably fr a Scottish phrase *the real Mackay* (mə KĪ), of uncertain origin, attested fr the late 19th century]

real money *See* HEAVY MONEY

real pro *See* PRO

ream **1** *v* (also **rim**) To cheat; swindle, esp by unfair business practice; = SCREW: *A new technique for reaming the customers*—AJ Liebling **2** *v* (also **ream out**) To rebuke harshly; = BAWL OUT, CHEW OUT: *I've seen him just ream guys out for not getting the job done*—Time ◁**3**▷ *v* (also **rim**) *fr homosexuals* To stimulate the anus, either orally or with the penis

rear end *n phr* (also **rear**) The buttocks; = ASS: *He got a shrewd boot in the rear/ She's a pain in the rear end*—Jerome Weidman

reat *See* ALL REET, REET

Rebel or **Reb** *n* A white Southerner

rebop *n* = BOP

recap (REE kap) **1** *v* To repeat, esp in a summary form; recapitulate; = REHASH **2** *n: I gave her a quick recap of the incident*

record *See* BROKEN RECORD, FOR THE RECORD, OFF THE RECORD, TRACK RECORD

red *See* IN THE RED, MEXICAN RED, PAINT THE TOWN RED, SEE RED

Red or **Red Devil** *n* or *n phr narcotics* Seconal (a trade name), a barbiturate capsule: *dropping Reds and busting heads*—Eldridge Cleaver

the red ass *See* GET THE RED ASS

◁**red-assed**▷ *adj* Very angry; livid; = PISSED OFF

red ball **1** *n phr railroad* A fast freight train **2** *n phr* Any train, bus, or truck running fast and given priority [fr the pole-mounted *red ball* used as a controlling signal on early railroads]

red carpet **1** *n phr* A sumptuous welcome: *He was sort of expecting the red carpet and not the fish-eye* **2** *adj phr* Luxurious; plush; = RITZY, SWANKY: *Jewelry gives you a red carpet elegance*—Life [fr an ancient custom, at least as old as Aeschylus's *Agamemnon*, of putting down a *red carpet* over which a welcomed dignitary would walk]
See ROLL OUT THE RED CARPET

a (or **one**) **red cent** (Variation: a (or one) **red**) **1** *n phr* The least amount of money; = a THIN DIME: *The poor man claimed he didn't have a red cent* **2** *n phr* A cent; penny; a trivial amount; = BEANS,

DIDDLY: *It didn't cost her a red cent* [fr the fact that a copper *cent* is *red*]

red dog *n phr football* A defensive assault in which the linebacker goes directly for the quarterback

redeye **1** *n fr early 1800s* Raw and inferior whiskey; = PANTHER PISS, ROTGUT: *Barrow put down a slug of redeye*—A Hynd **2** *n* Ham gravy **3** *n armed forces* Ketchup

the red-eye or **the red-eye special** *n phr* An airline flight from coast to coast, esp from west to east, that leaves one coast late at night and arrives early in the morning: *I just flew in on the red-eye*—Vincent Canby/ *boards what he calls the red-eye special for Los Angeles*—New York Times [fr the bleary sleepless look of overnight passengers]

red face *n phr* An embarrassed and guilty countenance: *You should've seen his red face when they caught him sneaking out*
See HAVE A RED FACE

red-faced *adj* Embarrassed; abashed; guilty-looking

redhanded *adv* In a situation of inescapable guilt; = DEAD TO RIGHTS, WITH A SMOKING GUN: *They got me redhanded, so I confessed*
See CATCH someone REDHANDED

red horse *n phr* Corned beef

red hot **1** *adj phr* Very hot; sizzling ● In all slang senses of **hot**: *This guy's just busted out of jail and he's red hot/ That little lady's a red hot fox* **2** *n phr* A frankfurter; = HOT DOG

red-hot mama **1** *n phr* An especially lively, amorous, and attractive woman **2** *n phr* A type of heavy, loud, and somewhat vulgar woman singer of the 1920s

red ink **1** *n phr* Red wine, esp of an inferior sort: *A pint of red ink still sells for two bits*—NY Confidential **2** *n phr* Financial loss or losses: *a flood of red ink totaling close to $80 billion*—Fortune

red lead **1** *n phr* Jelly **2** *n phr* Ketchup

redleg *n Army* An artillery soldier [fr the artillery uniform of pre-Civil War times]

red-letter day *n phr* A very important or consequential day, esp for an individual person [fr the typographical practice of printing the words of Jesus or the dates of certain holidays in *red*]

redlight **1** *v circus & carnival* To push someone off a moving train; kill by pushing off a train: *Who'd you red-light, Ferris?*—Dashiell Hammett **2** *v* To eject someone from a car

redline **1** *v Army* To cross a soldier's name off the payroll for some wrongdoing **2** *v* To designate neighborhoods, usu minority neighborhoods, as ineligible for housing loans and mortgages; discriminate in lending: *The same with the big six banks. Show that they're still redlining the city*—Neal Travis

redneck **1** *n* = CRACKER **2** *modifier: This is a redneck rural county*—Newsweek **3** *n* A bigoted and conventional person; a loutish ultraconservative: *Fred is a crude redneck, and Carol is his latest bimbo*—Time [perhaps fr the characteristic ruddy neck of an angry person, and influenced by the image of a bigoted rural Southern white person;

perhaps fr the fact that pellagra, a deficiency disease associated with poor Southern whites, produces a dermatitis that turns the neck red]

red-necked *adj* Angry; = RED-ASSED

red noise *n phr* lunch counter Tomato soup

red onion *n phr* lunch counter An experienced counter worker

red paint *n phr* Ketchup

redshirt 1 *v* sports To extend a college student's period of athletic eligibility, usu for football **2** *n* A student whose period of athletic eligibility has been extended [fr the *red shirts* worn by such athletes in contrast with varsity players]

red tape *n phr* fr early 1800s British Delay and complication; bureaucratic routine; petty officious procedure [fr the tape used for tying up official documents]

red totem poles *See* KNOCK someone FOR A LOOP

reef *See* TAKE A REEF IN IT

reefer[1] *n* hoboes, railroad, Navy & truckers A refrigerated railroad car, truck, ship, etc; = FREEZE: *A malfunction in a refrigerated trailer, or reefer, raises the temperature*—Smithsonian [fr *refrigerated*]

reefer[2] **1** *n* fr 1920s prison, black & narcotics A marijuana cigarette; = JOINT **2** *n* narcotics A person who smokes marijuana; = POTHEAD [origin unknown; perhaps originally *rifa* fr Mexican Spanish *grifa* "marijuana," the *g-* lost because it is not aspirated or exploded in Spanish pronunciation and hence not readily heard by English speakers]

reefer weed *n phr* narcotics Marijuana; = POT

reeler *n* A spree; drunken carouse: *before he realizes he is off on a reeler*—J Alexander

reenter *v* narcotics To cease feeling the effects of a narcotic; descend from a narcotic ecstasy [fr the *reentry* of a space vehicle into the Earth's atmosphere]

reentry *n* narcotics The act of descent from a narcotic ecstasy

reet or **reat** *adj* (also **reet and compleat**) *jive talk* Good; proper; excellent; right: *With her good looks, she was still "reet" with me*—Louis Armstrong/ *looking extremely reet and compleat*—Stephen King *See* ALL REET

reet pleat *n phr* jive talk A long, narrow pleat in a zoot suit

register *v* fr 1920s To express with the face and body: *I jumped up and registered horror* [fr the imprinting or *registering* of something on movie film]

regs *n* Regulations; rules: *All regs say you can't*

regular 1 *adj* Real; genuine: *He thinks he's a regular Casanova* **2** *n* fr lunch counter A cup of coffee with the usual moderate amount of cream and sugar ● In New York City no sugar is included **3** *adj*: *regular coffee*

regular fellow (or **guy**) *n phr* An honest, pleasant, convivial person, esp of the moral bourgeoisie: *I know I'm not a regular fellow, yet I loathe anybody else that isn't*—F Scott Fitzgerald/ *She's like Wallace....A real fighter. A regular guy*—New York

rehab (REE hab) **1** *n* Rehabilitation, esp of a drug addict, alcoholic, etc: *After a few weeks' rehab*

they sent him back home **2** *modifier*: *more work-release and rehab centers*—LJ Berry **3** *v* To rehabilitate, esp a building, factory, etc: *Williams has worked for minimum wage, rehabbing houses* —Philadelphia/ *had to give up a sublease because the building was rehabbed*—Village Voice

rehash 1 *v* To review; discuss again; repeat; = RECAP: *the things...they had hashed and rehashed for many a frugal conversational meal*—F Scott Fitzgerald **2** *n*: *a rehash of stale political charges* —Associated Press

◁**Reilly's balls**▷ *See* TIGHT AS KELSEY'S NUTS

reinvent the wheel *v phr* To go laboriously and unnecessarily through elementary stages in some process or enterprise; waste time on tediously obvious fundamentals

rejigger *v* To alter or readjust; tinker with: *sought to raise output this year by rejiggering its agricultural policies*—Time/ *Rejiggering assignments because of pregnancy is a fact of life*—Time [fr mid-19th-century *jigger* "shake or jerk rapidly," related to *jig* as a rapid movement, dance, etc, hence "rearrange or readjust by shaking," semantically similar to *shake up*]

relaid *See* LAID, RELAID, AND PARLAYED

religion *See* GET RELIGION

◁**reltney**▷ *n* The penis: *My reltney was ready for action*—Playboy [origin unknown]

remover *See* PAINT REMOVER

reno (REH noh) **1** *n* A renovated house: *Buying an off-the-rack reno is expensive and not very adventurous*—Toronto Life **2** *modifier*: *Today a boarded-up construction site, tomorrow a reno Parthenon*—Toronto Life

rent *See* BET THE RENT, HIGH-RENT

◁**rent-a-pig**▷ or **rent-a-cop** *n* A uniformed security guard [coined on the model of *rent-a-car*, on which model depends also the coinage *Rent-a-Kvetch* and probably others]

rent party *n phr* esp 1930s black A party where one's friends and neighbors buy drinks, food, etc, and help one pay the rent; = PERCOLATOR, SHAKE

rents *n* teenagers Parents

rep[1] *n* fr late 1800s Reputation: *gettin' the rep a not havin' a big schnozz*—Jimmy Durante *See* DEMI-REP

rep[2] *n* A representative: *The sales rep from Kokomo*

rep[3] **1** *n* theater Repertory: *She played in rep a couple years* **2** *modifier*: *a rep company*

repeaters *n* gambling Loaded dice

repeat on someone *v phr* To cause eructation or belching: *I never eat that stuff because it always repeats on me*

repellent *See* CESSNA REPELLENT

replay *See* INSTANT REPLAY

repo[1] (REE poh) **1** *n* A car repossessed for nonpayment of installments **2** *v*: *when the best times are to repo or rip off cars*—Time

repo[2] (REE poh) *n* A type of investment: *investments known as retail repurchase agreements, or repos for short*—Newsweek

report *See* SUGAR REPORT

repple-depple or **rep-dep** or **reppo-depot** *n* WW2 *Army* A military replacement center or depot where soldiers await assignment, processing, etc: *the Naples "repple depple"*—J McKnight

resin *See* KISS THE CANVAS

rest *See* GIVE IT A REST

rest one's **jaw** *v phr* To stop talking; = SHUT UP: *Aw, rest your jaw*—WR Burnett

restless *See* the NATIVES ARE RESTLESS

resuscitation *See* MOUTH-TO-MOUTH RESUSCITATION

◁**retard**▷ (REE tard) *n* A stupid person; = AIRHEAD, SPASTIC: *the stereotype of the crazy retard*—Philadelphia [fr mentally *retarded*]

retool *v* To make improving changes, esp of one's attitudes, capabilities, etc: *if you plan for the future, and retool if necessary*—Pauline Kael

retread (REE tred) **1** *n* A used tire with new tread **2** *n* WW2 *armed forces* A former military person recalled or accepted for additional service

retro 1 *n* A retrospective art exhibit, movie festival, etc: *the Bleecker's current Godard retro*—Village Voice **2** *adj* Nostalgic; historically resurrectional: *retro fashion, American clothes from the fifties*—Philadelphia/ *a sense of what is called "retro" elegance has taken hold of many men*—Time

Reuben *n fr carnival & circus* = HAYSEED, HICK, RUBE

re-up 1 *v* Army *fr early 1900s* To reenlist: *Are you really going to re-up and go to that chopper school?*—Earl Thompson/ *You can't re-up to get out of the field any more*—New York Times **2** *v* To obligate or engage oneself again: *I had re-upped for two more classes with him*—Richard Price/ *paying him $6,000,000 to re-up with the Cubs*—KYW radio news

rev or **rev up 1** *v* or *v phr* To speed up a motor; increase the rpm's **2** *v* or *v phr* To stir up; stimulate; or enliven; = JAZZ something UP: *seems to think he has to really rev his prose every now and again*—Washington Post/ *try to rev up this deadass bunch*

revolving-door *modifier* Rapid and of short duration; helter-skelter: *revolving-door justice in the courts*/ *revolving-door presidents and prime ministers, that's what's happening*—WT Tyler

RF (pronounced as separate letters) *college students* **1** *n* = RAT FINK **2** *n* = RAT FUCK **3** *n* = a ROYAL FUCKING

RHIP (pronounced as separate letters) *sentence* Army Rank hath its privileges

rhubarb[1] *n fr late 1900s or earlier theater* A loud quarrel or squabble; a controversy of riotous potential, esp among baseball players on the field: *beanball throwing, rhubarbs, and umpire baiting*—J Durant/ *Willie Gets Frisco Home After a Racial Rhubarb*—New York Daily News [fr the theatrical practice of having people say and shout *rhubarb* repeatedly to give the effect of an angry crowd]

rhubarb[2] **1** *n fr WW2 Air Forces* A low-level aerial strafing mission **2** *v: flying for rhubarbing*—C Macon [said to be fr the resemblance between bullet-spatters and luxuriant *rhubarb* plants]

the **rhubarbs** *n phr fr early 1900s* Small towns; rural venues; the provinces: *what the game meant as it's played out in the rhubarbs*—G Patten [fr a humorous alteration of *suburbs*]

rib 1 *v fr 1920s* To tease; make fun of; = KID, RAG, RIDE: *His trick is gently ribbing the audience* **2** *n: Carson sensed that he was the victim of a rib*—Russell Baker [probably fr the tickling of the *ribs* to provoke laughter]

ribbie or **ribby** *n baseball* A run batted in; RBI: *had two other big ribbies*—Sports Illustrated

rib joint *n phr* A brothel: *fracas in a Minneapolis rib joint*—Max Shulman [probably fr earlier *rib* "woman," fr Adam's rib, influenced by the designation of a restaurant specializing in barbecued spare ribs]

ribs *n bop & cool talk* Food; a meal [extension of barbecued spare *ribs*, semantically similar to the extension of *grits*]

rib-tickler *n* Something amusing, esp a joke

◀**rice-belly**▶ *n* A Chinese or a person of Chinese extraction

rice-burner *n motorcyclists* A motorcycle of Japanese manufacture

rich *See* STRIKE IT RICH, TOO RICH FOR someone's BLOOD

Richard Roe *See* JOHN DOE

◁**rich bitch**▷ **1** *n phr* A wealthy woman **2** *adj phr: his rich-bitch mother-in-law*—Newsweek

rickety-tick *See* MOST RICKETY-TICK

ricky-tick (Variations: **ricky-ticky** or **rinky-dink** or **rinky-tink**) *fr jazz musicians* **1** *n* Bouncy ragtime music of the 1920s **2** *adj* Old-fashioned; outworn; = CORNY: *the accompaniment of a rickyticky orchestra*—Richard Schickel/ *a brassy, rickyticky big band sound*—Life **3** *adj* Cheap and showy; shabbily inferior: *the rickytick, ingroup details sprinkled through the text*—New York Review/ *its deserted beaches, summer houses, and ricky-tick towns*—Denison Hatch [probably echoic fr the clicking mechanical percussion sounds of an uninspired musical group]

ride 1 *v* To tease; make fun of; = NEEDLE, RIB: *thinking how the critics would ride me*—Margaret Mitchell/ *I can remember riding Pete Rose to death from the bench*—Inside Sports ◁**2**▷ *v* To do the sex act with or to a woman; mount; = SCREW **3** *n: He asked her for a ride and she slapped him* **4** *n jazz musicians* An improvised passage; = BREAK, RIFF **5** *n* A race horse **6** *n narcotics* A psychedelic narcotic experience; = TRIP **7** *n black & student* A car; esp one that travels with body very close to the street or road: *The car a lowrider drives...is also called a lowrider or ride*—Calvin Trillin

See FULL-RIDE, GO ALONG FOR THE RIDE, GRAVY RIDE, HITCH A RIDE, JOY RIDE, LET something RIDE, SLEIGHRIDE, TAKE someone FOR A RIDE, THUMB

ride cymbal or **ride** *n phr* or *n musicians* A drummer's cymbal used for keeping up a constant tintinnabulation, as distinct from a crash

ride herd on someone or something *v phr fr late 1800s* To keep someone or something under control; monitor and correct; manage: *He was riding herd on a bunch of juveniles*

rideout *v jazz musicians* To play the last chorus of a jazz number in a free and lively way

rider **1** *n cowboys* A cowboy **2** *n* A jockey
See BAREBACK RIDER, BUG BOY, FREE-RIDER, JOYRIDER, LOW RIDER, SLEIGHRIDER

ride (or **go**) **shank's mare** *v phr* To walk

ride shotgun **1** *v phr* To act as a guard, esp on a vehicle; keep a vigilant eye peeled; insure safety: *beefing up security and changing the pattern of deliveries, although nobody will start to ride shotgun* —Time/ *Several wives have gotten wise and are riding shotgun on who checks in and out*—Amsterdam News **2** *v phr teenagers* To ride in the front passenger seat of a car [fr the Old West practice of having an armed guard with a *shotgun riding* beside the driver on the stage coaches]

ride the arm *v phr cabdrivers* To collect a fare without using the meter; = ARM IT, HIGHFLAG

ride the blinds *v phr hoboes* To ride a train in the spaces at the locked or doorless ends of baggage cars

ride the gravy train (or **gravy boat**) *v phr fr early 1900s sports* To enjoy a good and effortless life; bask in prosperous ease

ride the lightning *v phr prison* To be executed in the electric chair; = BURN, FRY

ride (or **hit**) **the rods** *v phr hoboes* To ride trains as a hobo, esp to ride perilously in the steel reinforcing struts beneath a freight car

ride with someone *v phr prison* To be a friend of someone

ridge-runner *n* A southern Appalachian mountain dweller; = HILLBILLY

rif (pronounced as separate letters or as an acronym RIF) **1** *v* To notify an employee of dismissal or layoff: *when he receives his Reduction in Force letter, and he will say, "I've been riffed"*—New York Times **2** *n* A dismissal; layoff **3** *v* To demote: *had been "rif'd" back to sergeants*—C Bryan **4** *n* A demotion [fr *reduction in force*]

riff¹ **1** *n jazz musicians* An improvised passage, esp a solo; = BREAK, LICK: *an initially funky bass riff* —Rolling Stone **2** *n* A solo passage of any sort: *He never inflates a movement, never accelerates into showy riffs of excess energy*—Time [origin unknown; perhaps echoic; perhaps fr *refrain*; perhaps fr *riffle* or *ripple* in the sense of "try, shot, crack"]

riff² *n railroad* A refrigerator car; = REEFER¹

riffle¹ *n baseball* A hard swing at the ball; = RIPPLE: *gives it a really good solid riffle*—H Lobert [probably fr *ripple* fr *rip*]

riffle² **1** *v* To shuffle playing cards **2** *n: Give that deck a good riffle* [probably echoic]

riffle³ *See* MAKE THE RIFFLE

rig **1** *v* To prearrange or tamper with a result or process; = FIX: *Prizefights or horse-races have been rigged*—Literary Digest **2** *n* Clothing; outfit: *How come you're wearing that rig?* **3** *n truckers* A truck; bus

right **1** *adj chiefly underworld* Reliable; safe: *He assured them his partner was a right guy* **2** *affirmation* Yes; correct: *Did you say left? Right!* **3** *question* Am I not right?; = COPPISH, OK: *He's in charge, right?*
See ALL RIGHT, ALL RIGHT ALREADY, DEAD TO RIGHTS, FLY RIGHT, HANG A RIGHT

Right *See* MISTER RIGHT

righteous *black fr 1930s jazz musicians* **1** *adj* Excellent; genuine; = the GREATEST: *what we used to call the righteous jazz*—National Review **2** *adj* Typical of white persons or white society

righteous moss *n phr black* Hair of a Caucasian sort; nonkinky hair

right guy **1** *n phr fr underworld* A reliable and helpful person: *You was a right guy*—J Lilienthal/ *With us you are a right guy*—John O'Hara **2** *n phr* A person who can be trusted, esp not to inform to the police

right-handed *adj* Heterosexual; = STRAIGHT: *He was about 60 percent right-handed and he ended up as a male go-go dancer*—George V Higgins

right joint **1** *n phr underworld* A trustworthy gambling place, criminal haunt, etc **2** *n phr prison* A prison, reformatory, etc, where prisoners are treated fairly: *Great Meadow...a "right joint"* —John Lardner

right money *n phr* = the SMART MONEY

right-o *affirmation* (Variations: **righto** or **right-ho** or **rightho**) *fr early 1900s British* Yes; correct; all right

right off the bat *adv phr* Immediately; without delay: *I normally get four cars right off the bat*—Philadelphia

right on **1** *interj fr 1960s black* An exclamation of approval, encouragement, agreement, etc: *Oh mercy, baaabeh, riiight onnnn!*—Time/ *Right on, Billie Jean!*—Sports Illustrated **2** *adj phr* Precisely right; very effective: *Michael Caine...is right on as the medic*—Judith Crist

rights *See* BANG TO RIGHTS, DEAD TO RIGHTS, GIVE someone HIS RIGHTS

right there *See* IN THERE PITCHING, THERE

right up there *adv phr* Among the leaders, the most distinguished, etc; in contention: *Two weeks to go and the Mets are still right up there*

righty *n* A righthanded person, esp a baseball pitcher; = NORTHPAW
See ALL RIGHTY

rigmatick *n* A complicated procedure; rigmarole: *We went through the whole rigmatick*—Xaviera Hollander

rigor *n theater* Stiffness; coolness, esp in a performer or audience [fr *rigor mortis*]

rig-out *n fr late 1800s* Clothing; garb; outfit: *a waiter's or a chef's rig-out*—Niven Busch

◁**rim**▷ *v homosexuals* To lick or suck the anus
See REAM

rim-rock or **rim-rack** **1** *v outdated cowboys* To kill animals by stampeding them over a precipice **2** *v* To ruin someone's chances; cause someone's failure, esp by deception

rims *See* ON THE RIMS

rinctum *n black* The rectum
See SPIZZERINCTUM
ring 1 *v horse-racing* To substitute one horse illegally for another in a race: *to attempt ringing*—A Hynd **2** *v* (also **ring up**) To call on the telephone; =GIVE someone A RING: *I rang him next day but he was out*
See GIVE someone A RING, THROW one's HAT IN THE RING
ring a bell *v phr* To remind one of something; sound familiar: *Doesn't that name ring a bell?*
ring-a-ding-ding or **ring-a-ding 1** *n* Glamor and show; spectacular impressiveness; =RAZZLE-DAZZLE: *an aura of breathless showbiz ring-a-ding-ding*—Albert Goldman **2** *adj:* Our new stack addition is a huge brick building full of metal, a ring-a-ding book box*—American Libraries
ring someone's **bell** *v phr* To be sexually attractive to someone; =TURN someone ON
ring changes *v phr* To make or try out variations, esp ingeniously: *Berle could do the same mugging bits...and ring many more changes on them*—Pauline Kael [fr *change-ringing*, the elaborate esp British ringing of sets of church bells]
ring-dang-do (RING DANG Do͞O) *n* A complicated process, scene, affair, etc; rigmarole: *the whole ring-dang-do of moral Darwinism*—Village Voice
ring-ding *n* A stupid person; =DING-A-LING: *that South American ring-ding with his sequined rodeo shirt*—Richard Fariña
ringer 1 *n fr late 1800s horse-racing* A person or animal substituted for another, esp a racehorse put in to run in place of an inferior beast: *"ringers," good horses masquerading as poor ones*—Fortune **2** *n horse-racing* A person who arranges the illegal substitution of a horse: *the master horse ringer of them all*—A Hynd **3** *n fr late 1800s* A person or thing that closely resembles another; =DEAD RINGER: *With the mustache and glasses, Blackmer is a ringer for Teddy*—Associated Press [fr the expression *ring someone in* "announce or herald someone"]
See DEAD RINGER
ringmaster *n railroad* A yardmaster
ring off 1 *v phr* To end a telephone conversation; hang up **2** *v phr* To stop talking; =SHUT UP
ring off the hook *v phr* To ring constantly and often: *Says the director of the hotline: "The phones have been ringing off the hook"*—Time
ringtail 1 *n hoboes* A grouch **2** *n underworld* An offensive person; =BASTARD, JERK ◄**3**► *n dockworkers* An Italian dockworker or one of Italian extraction ◄**4**► *n WW2 Navy* A Japanese [origin unknown]
ringtailed snorter *n phr fr early 1800s* A vigorous, impressive person; =HUMDINGER: *He's a ringtailed snorter*—Ithaca Journal [*ringtailed* was an early-19th-century US superlative, perhaps fr the *ringtailed painter*, a fierce wild cat of the Western US, or perhaps fr the coonskin caps, with *ringed tails* appended, worn by frontiersmen]
ring the bell 1 *v phr* To succeed; be a winner: *That last contribution rang the bell* **2** *v phr football*

ball To be hit so hard in play that one feels as if an enormous bell had been rung in one's head [first sense fr the carnival machine where one wins, esp a cigar, by *ringing a bell* with a hard hammer stroke]
rinktum See SPIZZERINKTUM
rinky-dink 1 *n carnival* Cheap and gaudy merchandise; =DRECK, JUNK **2** *n* Used merchandise; secondhand articles: *Let's go see what sort of rinky-dink the Salvation Army has this week* **3** *n* A small, cheap nightclub, cabaret, etc; =HONKY-TONK: *as she was called when she played the Rinky-dinks*—Edward Weeks **4** *adj* Inferior; cheap; =CRUMMY: *described by federal attorneys as rinky dink and a very strange document*—Wall Street Journal **5** *n* A deception; swindle; =RUN-AROUND: *Don't give me the rinkydink*—Sherman Billingsley
See RICKY-TICK
rinky-tink See RICKY-TICK
a riot *n phr* A very amusing person or thing, joke, occasion, etc; =a HOOT, a SCREAM: *The show's a genuine laff riot!/ Carlin can be a riot*
See LAFF RIOT
the riot act See READ THE RIOT ACT
rip[1] *n fr late 1700s British* A debauched and dissolute person; libertine: *the proper way to treat a rip*—J Stephens [a variant of *rep* fr *reprobate*]
rip[2] 1 *n police* An official demerit or fine **2** *n esp baseball* An insult; =KNOCK: *master of the off-field rip*—Milwaukee Journal **3** *v: I was not a good enough player to rip anybody*—Milwaukee Journal **4** *n* A joy; a pleasure: *What a rip it is to know there are still people...who feel for the cars they put together*—Car and Driver **5** *n* A try; attempt; =CRACK, RIPPLE, SHOT: *I'll have a rip at that old record* [all, one way or another, fr *rip* "tear"]
See GIVE something A SHOT, HAVE A CRACK AT something
◄**rip-ass**► *v* To speed; tear; =BARREL: *cars rip-assing up and down the street*—Stephen King
ripe 1 *adj* Rotten; spoiled; gamy; =FUNKY **2** *adj* Drunk
ripoff *fr 1960s fr black* **1** *n* A theft; an act of stealing **2** *n* A fraud; swindle; =SCAM: *The whole arms-reduction policy is a big ripoff* **3** *n* (also **ripoff artist**) A person or company that steals or swindles: *He was the biggest ripoff ever seen, even in Congress*
rip off *fr 1960s fr black* **1** *v phr* To steal: *Somebody ripped off my bike* **2** *v phr* To swindle; defraud; =GYP: *I don't know who rips us off more, business or government*
rip on someone *v phr fr black* To harass and insult: *Kids sit there and rip on you, tell you what you're doing wrong*
ripped *adj fr black* Intoxicated, either from narcotics or alcohol; =HIGH: *I'm ripped to the tits as it is*—Armistead Maupin
ripping *adj fr late 1800s British* Excellent; =SWELL
ripple *n* A try; an attempt; =CRACK, RIP, SHOT: *I'll never figure out how these pieces fit, so why don't you have a ripple?* [perhaps fr *rip* in the sense of a strong action or attempt; perhaps fr 19th-century

make a riffle "succeed, make it," based on crossing or getting through dangerous rapids in a river]
See GIVE something A SHOT, HAVE A CRACK AT something

ripsnorter *n fr middle 1800s* A person or thing that is remarkable, wonderful, superior, etc; =BEAUT, HUMDINGER: *The villain is a real ripsnorter*—SJ Perelman

a **rise** *See* GET A RISE OUT OF someone

the **ritz** *n phr* Luxury; plush showiness; =SWANK: *Just a simple feed, folks, none of the ritz* [fr the name of the Swiss César *Ritz* and the various luxurious European hotels he built]
See PUT ON THE RITZ

ritzy 1 *adj fr 1920s* Elegant; luxurious; =CLASSY, POSH, SWANKY: *The ritziest dance hall was the Haymarket*—E Lavine **2** *adj* Wealthy; affluent: *a ritzy neighborhood* **3** *adj* Haughty; supercilious; =STUCK-UP

river *See* SELL someone DOWN THE RIVER, SEND UP, UP THE RIVER

rivethead *n Army* A member of a tank crew

rivets *n* Money

roach 1 *n prison & black* A police officer **2** *n horse-racing* A racehorse, esp an inferior one; =BEETLE **3** *n narcotics fr 1930s* The stub or butt of a marijuana cigarette: *He lighted the toke again, a roach now that he impaled on a thin wire*—Lawrence Sanders/ *how to roll joints, how to hold roaches*—American Scholar **4** *n students* An unattractive woman [narcotics sense perhaps fr earlier *roach mane*, a horse's mane clipped very short and tied; perhaps fr the insect]

roach clip (or **holder**) *n phr narcotics* Any tweezerlike device for holding a marijuana cigarette stub too short to be held in the fingers; =AIRPLANE, CRUTCH: *necessitating the invention of the "roach clip," which holds roaches*—New York Times

road *modifier theater* Traveling; itinerant: *a road show/ the road company*
See BURN THE ROAD, GO THE HANG-PUT ROAD, HARD-ROAD FREAK, HIT THE ROAD, LET'S GET THE SHOW ON THE ROAD, ONE FOR THE ROAD, ON THE ROAD, SKID ROAD, WHERE THE RUBBER MEETS THE ROAD, WIDE PLACE IN THE ROAD

road apple *See* ALLEY APPLE

road dog *n phr Philadelphia black* A good friend; =ACE BOON COON

road hog *n phr* A driver who takes more than his or her share of the road

roadie 1 *n* (also **roadster**) A person who travels with a musical, political, theatrical, or other group to handle booking, business arrangements, equipment, etc: *"...the stage wouldn't support the drums," a roadie exclaimed proudly*—J Sims/ *Microphones tossed by Chapman land in unlikely places, one on a roadie, another in the lap of the audience*—Changes/ *"I'm a roadie," said Bob Kholos, who has the title of deputy press secretary*—New York Times **2** *adj* Eager to travel; touched with wanderlust: *I get a little roadie on Fridays*

road monkey *n phr lumberjacks* A roadmender or worker

road people *n phr fr 1960s* Persons, esp young, who travel about in vans or with backpacks; itinerants: *Some road people tend to display a continual inability to adjust*—A Miller

road-stake *n hoboes* Money for traveling

roast 1 *v fr early 1700s* To make fun of; ridicule; insult, often in an affectionate way: *had been roasted often by the critics as a ham*—Russell Baker **2** *n*: *this national love for a good "roast," this spirit of mockery*—H Spencer

robber *See* BELLY-ROBBER, CRADLE-ROBBER, DOG-ROBBER, STOMACH-ROBBER

Robin Hood's barn *See* GO AROUND ROBIN HOOD'S BARN

rob the cradle 1 *v phr* To marry or date someone much younger than oneself **2** *v phr* To recruit, use, or exploit young persons

robuck *v prison* To instigate something; get something going [fr a mispronunciation of *robot*, with the notion that one performs certain provocative actions as one would push a button or throw a switch to activate a robot]

rock 1 *n esp 1920s* A dollar; =BUCK: *I want to see you make twenty rocks*—R Starnes **2** *n underworld* Any precious stone, esp a diamond **3** *n* A rock and roll devotee: *teenagers called "rocks"*—Herbert Mitgang **4** *n* Rock and roll music: *punk rock/ hard rock* **5** *v* To move, dance, writhe, etc, to rock and roll music; =BOOGIE, BOP: *Soon just one couple was rocking in the middle of the floor* **6** *v* To be resonant with and physically responsive to rock and roll music; =JUMP: *Soon the whole room was rocking* **7** *n narcotics* A small cube of very pure cocaine, intended for smoking rather than inhalation: *Dealers sell pellet-size "rocks"...in small plastic vials*—Time **8** *n prison* A cellblock: *When is the wagon due back on this rock, Pops?*—Donald Goines
See ACID ROCK, EIGHT-ROCK, GLITTER ROCK, HARD ROCK, HOT ROCK, PUNK ROCK, RIM-ROCK

the **Rock 1** *n phr* Alcatraz Island and its (former) federal penitentiary **2** *n fr middle 1800s* Gibraltar

rockabilly 1 *n* A blend of black rhythm and blues with white hillbilly music **2** *modifier: showing up at rockabilly dances and clubs in full '50s regalia*—Newsweek

rock and roll or **rock 'n' roll 1** *n phr fr 1950s* A style of heavily accented music evolved from blues, folk, and country music, usu having sung lyrics, and played on very highly amplified electronic instruments **2** *modifier: a rock and roll group/ rock 'n' roll concert* **3** *n phr* Dancing done to such music

rock candy *n phr* A diamond; diamonds; =ICE

rock crusher *n phr* A convict or former convict

rock 'em, sock 'em *adj phr* Violent and energetic; concussive: *the rock 'em, sock 'em action that goes on inside a full-sized truck*—Car and Driver

rocker¹ 1 *n fr 1950s* A rock and roll musician, singer, radio station, etc: *general manager of*

rhythm-and-blues rocker WOL in Washington, DC
—National Observer **2** *n* A rock and roll song: *classic country rockers, sometimes with an old-timey flavor*—Playboy

See PUNK ROCKER, TEENYBOPPER

rocker² *See* OFF one's NUT

rocket *n fr 1930s British Army* A complaint or rebuke; = BEEF, DING: *you get a rocket from one of the parties*—Time

rockhead 1 *n* A stupid person **2** *modifier: some rockhead hoodlums*—I, Mobster

rocks 1 *n* Ice cubes ◁**2**▷ *n* The testicles; = FAMILY JEWELS, NUTS

See GET one's ROCKS, HAVE ROCKS IN one's HEAD, HOT ROCKS, ON THE ROCKS, TOUGH SHIT

rocks in one's (or **the**) **head** *n phr* Stupidity; foolishness; mental incapacity: *dedicated to whiny losers with rocks in their heads*—Village Voice

See HAVE ROCKS IN one's HEAD

rock the boat *v phr* To cause trouble; create inconveniences; disrupt things: *Fritz Mondale doesn't want to rock the boat*—Associated Press

rocky 1 *adj* Drunk **2** *adj* Weak and unsteady; groggy; = WOOZY: *came back to work, looking pale and rocky*—Hal Boyle

Rocky Mountain canary *See* MOUNTAIN CANARY

rod 1 *n underworld fr early 1900s* A pistol: *Here's a rod, blow your brains out*—Ernest Boyd **2** *n hot rodders* A car, esp a specially prepared car; = HOT ROD: *A restless youth buys a broken-down rod*—New York Times ◁**3**▷ *n* The penis; = SHAFT

See GRAB A HANDFUL OF RODS, HAVE A ROD ON, JOHNSON ROD, WRINKLE-ROD

rod-man *n underworld* A gunman; = TORPEDO

rod up *v phr underworld* To arm; provide with a pistol: *They do not rod up or arm themselves*—E DeBaun

Roe *See* JOHN DOE

Roger or **Roge** or **Rodger-dodger** *affirmation fr WW2 armed forces* Yes; I understand; = OK: *Get your asses over there...Roge*—New York Times [fr the military phonetic alphabet word designating *R* for "received," apparently first used by the British Royal Air Force in the 1930s]

rogues' gallery 1 *n phr* A collection of photographs of criminals; = MUG SHOTS **2** *n phr* Any group or collection of unsavory persons; den of thieves: *The new building commission is a plain rogues' gallery*

Rok (RAHK) *n* A South Korean, esp a soldier [fr *Republic of Korea*]

rolf *See* RALPH

roll 1 *v* To rob, esp a stuporous or helpless drunkard who is literally rolled over for access to pockets: *rolling a stiff*—Jack London/ *the less perilous profession of rolling lushes*—Wolcott Gibbs **2** *v* To rob any relatively helpless person **3** *v railroad* To displace another worker: *Negro firemen on the good runs should be "rolled" by whites*—Survey Graphic **4** *v movie studio* To run or start a movie camera: *Quiet, and roll 'em*—King Vidor **5** *v* To get started; to commence; get under way:

The leader hollered "Let's roll!" and we all began the exercises/ *We'd better roll now, it looks like rain* **6** *n* Money; funds; = BANKROLL **7** *n* The sex act; = a ROLL IN THE HAY **8** *v prison* To start a fight; assault someone

See CRUMB-ROLL, JACKROLL, JELLY-ROLL, LOG ROLL, MICHIGAN ROLL, ON A ROLL, PHILADELPHIA BANKROLL, PRESS ROLL, ROCK AND ROLL

rollback *n* A reduction, esp of wages or production

roller 1 *n prison* A prison guard **2** *n black* A police officer **3** *n* A thief who robs drunks [first two senses fr late-18th-century British *rollers* "horse and foot patrols of police," perhaps so called because the second syllable of *patrol* suggested rolling along at a fast pace]

See DOUGH-ROLLER, DOWN THE GOODYEARS, HIGH ROLLER, LUSH ROLLER, PILL-PUSHER, PUMPKIN ROLLER, STEAMROLLER

roll in 1 *v phr* To arrive; = SHOW UP: *What time did you finally roll in?* **2** *v phr* To go to bed; = HIT THE SACK

rolling doughnut *See* TAKE A FLYING FUCK

rolling (or **swimming**) **in** *prep phr* Very well supplied with: *We weren't rolling in dough at the time*/ *We've been swimming in chicken pot pies since we won that frozen food contest*

rolling off a log *See* EASY AS PIE

a roll in the hay *n phr* The sex act, esp when regarded as casual and joyous: *A roll in the hay with Seattle Slew cost $710,000*—Philadelphia

roll out *v phr* To get out of bed ● Often a command

roll out the red carpet *v phr* To give someone a very sumptuous and/or ceremonious welcome

rollover *n prison* The last night of a prison sentence

roll over *v phr* To reinvest bonds, certificates of deposit, or other monetary instruments upon maturity, rather than liquidating them

roll with the punches *v phr* To behave so as to defend oneself against damage and surprise; absorb punishment and survive: *"You roll with the punches....My experience was, I was going to lose her....But I'm thankful for what I've gotten so far"*—Washington Post [fr the evasive action of a boxer who does not avoid a *punch* but reduces its effect by moving in the direction of the blow]

romp 1 *n street gang* A fight, esp between street gangs **2** *v: The gangs romped on Thursday*

ronchie *See* RAUNCHY

-roo *See* -EROO

roof *See* FALL OFF THE ROOF, RAISE THE ROOF

the roof falls (or **caves**) **in** *v phr* A sudden and total catastrophe occurs; one's joy and world collapses: *long before the roof fell in on Gossage*—Village Voice/ *They were happy for about three months, then the roof caved in*

rook 1 *v fr late 1500s* To cheat; defraud; = GYP: *who would rook them for two dollars*—Abel Green **2** *n:* Balcony seats for 40 bucks are a real rook [probably fr the thieving habits of the *rook*, which it shares with other corvine birds like the crow and magpie]

rookie or **rookey** or **rooky** **1** *n fr late 1800s* British armed forces A newcomer; novice; tyro: *the rookies and substitutes*—Babe Ruth/ *some rookie receiving small pay*—E Lavine **2** *modifier: The shooting of "rookie" patrolman James A Broderick* —E Lavine [probably fr shortening of *recruit*; perhaps fr the black, *rook*-colored coat worn by some British army recruits]

room *n show business* A nightclub; =BOITE, NITERY
   See BALLOON ROOM, BUCKET SHOP, CRYING ROOM, ELBOW ROOM, HORSE ROOM, LIVING-ROOM GIG, PAD ROOM, RUMPUS ROOM, TEAROOM

roost *n* One's home; =PAD
   See QUAIL-ROOST

root[1] *v fr late 1800s* To cheer; applaud; urge on: *We rooted and rooted, but they folded*

root[2] **1** *n* A cigarette **2** *n narcotics* A marijuana cigarette [perhaps fr *cheroot* or *cigaroot*]

◁**root**[3]▷ *n* The penis [fr something that is or can be planted]

rooter *n* A supporter or fan, esp of a team, fighter, school, etc

root for **1** *v phr fr late 1800s* To be a regular supporter of; be a fan of: *He rooted for the Giants* **2** *v phr* To urge hopefully: *I'm rooting for the tax bill* [perhaps fr British dialect *route* "roar, bellow"]

root-hog-or-die *sentence fr early 1800s* Work extremely hard, or fail; =the CHIPS ARE DOWN: *A red-faced rookie tackle from the University of Michigan...screamed, "Root hog or die!"*—Peter Gent

rootin'-tootin' *adj* Boisterous; noisy; vigorous: *a rootin'-tootin' romance*—H Birney

rootle out *v phr fr middle 1800s British* To root out: *rootle out Government fraud and waste*—Village Voice

rooty *adj* Sexually aroused; =HORNY [fr *root* "penis"]

rooty-toot *n musicians* Old-fashioned music; =CORN, RICKY-TICK

rope **1** *n* A cigar; =HEMP **2** *v* To ensnare someone with amity and concern, as a means of swindling; =ROPE IN
   See FROZEN ROPE, GOAT FUCK, GO PISS UP A ROPE, KNOW THE ROPES, SUCK

rope in *fr early 1800s* **1** *v phr* =ROPE **2** *v phr* To swindle; cheat

Roscoe or **roscoe** *n fr late 1800s underworld* A pistol; =HEAT [a pet name, used for dissimulation]
   See JOHN ROSCOE

rose *n hospital* A comatose and dying patient [fr the color and the perilous frailty of such a patient]
   See COME UP SMELLING LIKE A ROSE, PIN A ROSE ON IT, SMELL LIKE A ROSE

◁**rosebud**▷ *n esp homosexuals* The anus

rose garden *See* FRUIT SALAD

rose room *n phr hospital* A room where comatose and dying patients are treated

rosewood *n black fr underworld* A police officer's nightstick; =BILLY CLUB [origin unknown]

rosy **1** *adj* Slightly drunk; =TIDDLY **2** *adj* Promising; favorable; =COPACETIC: *Things look rosy now*

rot **1** *n fr middle 1800s British* Nonsense; =BALONEY, BULLSHIT **2** *v esp teenagers fr 1960s* To be deplorable, nasty, inept, or bungled, etc; =STINK, SUCK: *This idea of yours rots*

Rotacy (ROH tə see, RAH-) *n* (Variations: **rot-see** or **rotasie** or **Rot-corps**) *college students* The Reserve Officers Training Corps

rotgut *n fr late 1500s* Inferior liquor; =PANTHER PISS: *pure Prohibition rotgut*—H Allen Smith

rotorhead *n Army* A helicopter pilot or crew member

rotten *adj fr late 1800s* Deplorable; nasty; inept and bungled: *This is a rotten situation altogether*

rough **1** *adj* Lewd; salacious; =DIRTY: *Some of the jokes were pretty rough* **2** *adj* Difficult; dangerous; =TOUGH **3** *n salespersons* A used car that has been in a wreck
   See PLAY FOR KEEPS

rough around the edges *adj phr* Somewhat crude; unpolished: *a slightly rough-around-the-edges New York manner*—Toronto Life

rough as a cob *adj phr* Very rough [fr the rural use of *corncobs* as toilet paper]

◁**rough-ass**▷ *adj* Harsh; crude; =KICK-ASS: *She liked his rough-ass ways for a while*

roughhouse **1** *n fr late 1800s* Boisterous and rowdy behavior; more or less harmless scuffling **2** *v fr early 1900s: The kids roughhoused half the night* **3** *n* Physical violence; mayhem **4** *adj: rough-house work for the political boss*—E Lavine **5** *v: Gun-toting bodyguards roughhoused Swedish citizens*—Associated Press

roughneck **1** *n fr early 1900s* A thug and brawler; =PLUG-UGLY, TOUGH: *The so-called roughneck is hit with everything*—E Lavine **2** *n* A worker or laborer, esp in a circus or on an oil-drilling rig

rough stuff **1** *n phr* Physical violence; mayhem: *have graduated from the "rough stuff" class*—E Lavine **2** *n phr* Obscenity; profanity; =PORN

rough trade *n phr homosexuals* A sadistic or violent sex partner, often heterosexual; ruffianly partner of a homosexual: *The gay boys call us "rough trade"*—S Silverstein/ *I hope the next time he meets some rough trade from uptown*—Lawrence Sanders

rough someone **up** **1** *v phr* To hit or pummel, esp as intimidation: *He told it like a good citizen, and got roughed up for his pains* **2** *v phr* To injure someone: *The wreck roughed me up some*

roulette *See* VATICAN ROULETTE

round *See* MERRY-GO-ROUND

rounder *n fr middle 1800s* A debauchee; habitual carouser: *some rich "rounders" of the town*—Theodore Dreiser/ *He's a rounder*—Playboy

round-eye **1** *n esp Korean War armed forces* A Caucasian as distinct from an Asian **2** *modifier: a round-eye woman/ inscrutable round-eye expression*

roundheel or **roundheels** **1** *n fr 1920s* An inferior prizefighter; =PALOOKA **2** *n* A promiscuous woman; =PUNCHBOARD: *little roundheels over there*—Raymond Chandler

roundheeled 1 *adj* Easily defeated or knocked down **2** *adj* Easily induced to the sex act; =CHEAP

roundhouse 1 *n fr early 1900s* A long, looping punch to the head **2** *modifier: He swung a roundhouse left*—H Witwer **3** *n baseball fr early 1900s* An extreme curveball **4** *modifier: a roundhouse pitch*

round the bend *adv phr* =AROUND THE BEND

round the horn *See* AROUND THE HORN

round-tripper *n baseball* A home run: *a round-tripper in the ninth*—D Parker

round up *v phr* To find and bring together, esp to a police station or lockup: *rounded up in a raid*—Louis Armstrong/ *Round up all the votes you can find*

roust 1 *v black* Esp of police officers, to harass someone; =CHIVVY: *always being rousted by cops*—The Gauntlet (movie) **2** *v* To arrest **3** *v* To raid: *They're rousting all the gay bars*—Lawrence Sanders **4** *n: What's the roust? You gonna close this place?*—Herbert Kastle [fr *rouster* or *rooster* "a deckhand or waterfront laborer," attested fr the mid-19th century, hence with connotations of roughness; related to *roustabout* fr British dialect *rous-about* "unwieldy," *rousing* "rough, shaggy," and *rousy* "filthy"; the semantic core seems to combine roughness with laziness, in the old heroic mold, and to be associated with the behavior of the *rooster*, who combines rough vigor with long periods on the perch]

routine 1 *n fr show business* A passage of behavior; act; =BIT, SHTICK: *He goes into his God-save-us routine* **2** *n cool talk fr show business* An evasive or contrived response: *I look for revelation and get routine*

row *n narcotics* An elongated pile of narcotic, esp cocaine, for sniffing; =LINE: *and snorted a row of coke*—Harry Crews
See BALD-HEADED ROW, a HARD ROW TO HOE, HAVE one's DUCKS IN A ROW, a HILL OF BEANS, KNOCK someone FOR A LOOP, SKID ROW

row-dow (ROU dou) **1** *n* =ROWDY-DOW **2** *n 1920s jazz musicians* Exaggerated syncopation; ragtime

rowdy-dow (Variations: **rowdy-dowdy** or **row-de-dow** or **row-de-dowdy**) *fr early 1800s* **1** *n* Boisterousness; excitement; =RUMPUS, WHOOP-DE-DO: *the old rowdy-dow of burlesque*—Brooks Atkinson **2** *adj: this rowdy-dow round-up*—Time **3** *n* A brawl; fight

row with one oar *v phr* (Variation: **in the water** may be added) To behave irrationally; be crazy or stupid: *Ellis sounds as if he is rowing with one oar*—Ann Landers

royal *adj* Thorough; definitive: *gives me a royal pain in the ass*—JD Salinger

◀**a royal fucking**▶ *n phr* Very rough and unfair treatment; =RAW DEAL

rub 1 *n 1920s students* A dancing party **2** *n 1930s students* A session of hugging and kissing **3** *v* =RUB OUT
See CHIEF ITCH AND RUB

rubber[1] 1 *n fr late 1800s* To gaze; gape: *Don't be rubbering at McCorn*—P Dunning & G Abbott ◀**2**▶ *n* A condom: *"Rubbers,"* Cushie told him—John Irving **3** *n* Automobile tires: *The thing's a wreck but has good rubber*
See BURN RUBBER, LAY RUBBER

rubber[2] *n underworld* A professional killer; =HIT MAN

rubber boots *n phr* Condoms: *My husband don't like rubber boots*—George V Higgins

rubber check *n phr fr 1920s* A check that cannot be cashed, because not enough money is on deposit [because it "bounces"]

rubber-chicken *modifier* Featuring the unappetizing usual sort of banquet food occupationally eaten by politicians, lecturers, etc: *She's on the rubber-chicken circuit/ one of those rubber-chicken banquets for the visiting dignitaries*

rubber drink *n phr* A drink that causes one to vomit

rubber duck *See* TAKE A FLYING FUCK

rubber heel *n phr* A detective; =GUMSHOE

rubber meets the road *See* WHERE THE RUBBER MEETS THE ROAD

rubberneck 1 *n fr late 1800s fr cowboys* A person who stares and gapes; gawker **2** *v: They all slowed down and rubbernecked at the wreck*

rubberneck wagon (or **bus**) *n phr fr early 1900s* A sightseeing bus

rubber sock 1 *n phr hoboes* A timid or delicate person **2** *n phr WW2 Navy* A naval recruit; =BOOT

rube or **Rube 1** *n fr late 1800s* A rustic; farmer; =HAYSEED **2** *n* An unsophisticated person, esp a newcomer; =GREENHORN **3** *n circus* A member of the audience or public; =CITIZEN: *Mr Todd knows how to panic the rubes*—Brooks Atkinson **4** *adj: a rube police force*—R Starnes [short for *Reuben*]
See HEY RUBE

Rube Goldberg *n phr* A much overcomplicated machine or arrangement: *The public's got the idea that this is a boondoggle, a Rube Goldberg*—Time [fr the fancifully articulated machines depicted by the cartoonist *Rube Goldberg*]

rub (or **nudge**) **elbows** *v phr* To meet and consort; spend time together; mingle: *Here we rub elbows with saints and scholars*

rub it in *v phr* To increase the pain or embarrassment of something; exacerbate something: *always trying to rub it in*—WT Tyler/ *I goofed and he never let me forget it, kept rubbing it in*

rub joint *n phr* A cheap dance hall or nightclub with hostesses: *Rub joints where the girls danced with whoever stood them a snort*—Stephen Longstreet

◀**rub off**▷ *v phr* To masturbate, as a female

rub out *v phr fr underworld* To murder; kill; =HIT: *whose husband you rubbed out*—Samuel Liebowitz

rub-out *n fr underworld* A murder; gangster-style killing: *the hombre she blamed for Paddy's rub-out*—Dashiell Hammett

rub parlor *n phr* A massage parlor: *the rub parlors, kiddy porn*—Neal Travis

rub someone **the wrong way** *v phr fr middle 1800s* To be distasteful or obnoxious to someone's sensibilities; regularly displease: *I don't quite know why, but that woman rubs me the wrong way*

ruckus *n fr late 1800s* A disturbance; uproar; brawl; = RUMPUS [perhaps fr *ruction* + *rumpus*]

ructious *adj fr early 1800s* Vexed and violent; turbulent: *the long and ructious road that is life*

rug *n fr theater* A toupee; hair piece: *I even wear a little rug up front*—John O'Hara
See CUT THE RUG, PULL THE RUG OUT FROM UNDER, SKY RUG

rug ape or **rug rat** or **carpet rat** *n phr* (Variations: **yard** may replace **rug** or **carpet**) An infant or small child; = CRUMB CATCHER: *He lived with his wife and their two rug apes*

rug-cut 1 *v black* To dance at rent parties and other fairly cheap occasions **2** *v jive talk* To dance to swing music; = JITTERBUG

rug-cutter *n jive talk* A person who dances to swing music: *the rug-cutter's way of saying "all right"*—New Yorker

rugged *adj fr WW2 Army* Very trying; dangerous; = ROUGH: *They had a real rugged time getting away*

rug joint *n phr* An elegant club, hotel, etc: *not a rug joint* (*a lavishly decorated casino*)—J Scarne

rule *See* SQUEAL RULE

rum bag *n phr* A drunkard; = LUSH: *a lot of cowardly rum bags*—Joe Cannon

rumble 1 *n underworld* Information or notification given to the police: *The cops had gotten a rumble that gangsters were holed up*—A Hynd **2** *n police* A police search or raid; = ROUST **3** *n street gang* A fight between street gangs: *Teenagers Injured in Brooklyn Rumble*—New York World-Telegram **4** *v airline* To steal; loot: *ending a run by rumbling...everything from airline glasses to grub*—Philadelphia Journal

rum-dum 1 *n* A stupid person, esp one slow-witted from habitual drunkenness: *The murmuring rum-dums were being let out to wash*—Nelson Algren **2** *adj*: *a sleazy rum-dum hangout*

rummy or **rummie** *n fr middle 1800s* A drunkard; = LUSH

rumor *See* LATRINE RUMOR

rumor mill *n phr* The source of rumors, esp those that seem to be deliberately passed along: *There has been a rumor mill on him for years*—New York Times

rumpot *n* A heavy drinker; drunkard; = LUSH

rumpus *n fr late 1700s* A disturbance; uproar; = RUCKUS [origin unknown]

rumpus room *n phr* A family room used for games, parties, etc

run 1 *n* A route followed by a vehicle, esp regularly: *In the middle of her run, the bus driver was attacked by a gang of thugs* **2** *n* A ride **3** *n* A race, esp a car race **4** *v* To drive, or chauffeur someone, by car
See CUT AND RUN, DRY RUN, IN THE LONG RUN, MEAT RUN, MILK RUN, TAKE A RUN AT someone

run a book *v phr* To have credit at a store

run a game on *v phr fr black* = DO A NUMBER ON [fr *running* a whole *game* of pool without yielding the cue]

run a make *v phr police & prison* To perform a checking procedure for identifying someone, that is, for "making" an identification

run-and-gun 1 *v basketball* To play in an aggressive single-handed way, for high scoring: *as a big city ball player looking to run-and-gun*—Philadelphia **2** *adj*: *the Lakers' run-and-gun offense*—Newsweek

run a number on *See* DO A NUMBER ON

runaround *n fr theater* Deceptive, evasive, and diversionary treatment, esp in response to a request: *I asked for an explanation and what I got was a runaround/ I'm tired of you giving me the runaround*—WT Tyler

run something **by again** *v phr* To repeat; = COME AGAIN: *Just run that name and address by again, will you?*

rundown *n* A summary or account: *a brief rundown of what happened*—Associated Press

run something **down 1** *v phr fr black* To tell or explain completely: *Maybe one day I'll run it down to you*—Donald Goines **2** *v phr* To denigrate; = BAD-MOUTH: *I'm not running down his sincerity, but he sounds a bit slick*

rung up *adj phr* Emotionally disturbed

run hog-wild *See* GO HOG-WILD

run hot *v police* To drive a police car with siren, lights, etc, turned on: *Wager didn't bother with running hot*—Rex Burns

run in *v phr* To run an engine at a special rate, with special fuel, etc, to prepare it for full operation; = BREAK IN

run-in 1 *n* A quarrel; an unpleasant confrontation: *sorry we had the run-in*—H McHugh **2** *n* An arrest

run someone **in** *v phr fr early or middle 1800s* To arrest; = PULL someone IN: *Am I going to have to run you in?*—Nathaniel Benchley

run (or **work**) something **into the ground** *v phr fr late 1800s fr cowboys* To overdo; carry too far: *You already warned us, now don't run it into the ground*

runner *See* FRONT RUNNER, RIDGE-RUNNER, TENNIES

running dog *n phr Army* A subordinate with little authority; = FLUNKY [fr abusive Chinese and North Korean Communist phrases like "a *running dog* of Western imperialism," fr Mandarin *zou gou* "running dog," a dog that runs at its master's command]

running shoes *See* GIVE someone HIS WALKING PAPERS

run off at the mouth *v phr* To talk too much; = SHOOT OFF one's MOUTH

run-of-the-mill (or **-of-the-mine**) *adj* Ordinary; average; = GARDEN-VARIETY

run-out *n* A fleeing; desertion; escape: *has taken a run-out with the bankroll*—E Booth

run out of gas *v phr* To lose impetus, effect, etc; fail; stall: *He ran out of gas a lot slower*—Village Voice

run-out powder *See* TAKE A POWDER

run over someone *v phr* To treat arrogantly, slightingly, or flippantly

run someone **ragged** *v phr* To exhaust; wear out

the **runs** *n phr* Diarrhea; = the GIS

run scared *v phr* To show signs of panic and fear; try to escape: *Members...aren't exactly running scared*—New York Times

runt 1 *n* A small, short person **2** *n* A contemptible person; = JERK

run through *v phr* To rehearse; = DRY RUN: *I ran through my story once more, to polish it*

run-through *n* A rehearsal; = DRY RUN: *After the first run-through, Mr Berlin casually tossed out three songs*—New York Times

run (or **put**) someone **through the mill** *v phr* To subject to an arduous experience; be rough on someone: *She's quite eager to try again, although they really ran her through the mill See* GO THROUGH THE MILL, THROUGH THE MILL

run something **up the flagpole** *v phr* (Variation: **and see if anybody salutes** may be added) *fr 1960s* To test the reaction to; to try out an idea, concept, etc ● An expression attributed to the Madison Avenue advertising milieu, along with others like "Put it on a train and see if it gets off at Westport": *Television runs these vapidities up the flagpole and we salute as though we had been programmed to do so*—Washington Post

ruptured (or **pregnant**) **duck** *n phr* WW2 armed forces A lapel pin, featuring an eagle rather than a duck, given to veterans honorably discharged after World War 2

rush 1 *v fr middle 1800s* To court a woman ardently: *He had "rushed" her, she said, for several months*—Ellery Queen **2** *n: appears to want to give her a big rush*—F Blake **3** *v college students* To entertain and cultivate a student wanted as a fraternity or sorority member **4** *n movie studio* A motion picture print made immediately after the scene is shot **5** *n narcotics* An intense flood of pleasure, with quickened heart rate, felt soon after ingestion of a narcotic: *He didn't have to wait long for the rush* **6** *n fr narcotics* A surge of pleasure; an ecstasy: *To Friend, it's a kind of a rush...the last big high*—Chicago Tribune/ *gives her a unique rush*—Time

the **rush act** *n phr* A case of rushing, esp an intense courtship of a woman

rushee *n* A person being rushed, esp by a college fraternity or sorority

rush-in *n hoboes* A meal in a restaurant paid for by money begged on the street

rushing *See* GROWLER-RUSHING

rush (or **work**) **the growler** *fr late 1800s* **1** *v phr* To buy and take home a container of beer from a bar: *see who rushes a growler of beer*—Sinclair Lewis **2** *v phr hoboes* To drink liquor or beer, esp in large quantities

Russian *n black* A Southern black in the North: *One of them Russians, eh? Rushed up North here to get away*—Zora Neale Hurston

rust bowl (or **belt**) **1** *n phr* The beleaguered and declining industrial areas, esp of the Middle West: *in the midwestern middle, the "rust bowl"*—Time **2** *modifier: The subjects: Wall Street, Chrysler, high-tech enterprises vs "rust bowl" basic industries* [modeled on the 1930s term *dust bowl* and the 1970s term *sun belt*]

rust bucket or **rustpot** *WW2 Navy* **1** *n phr* or *n* An old worn naval destroyer **2** *n phr* or *n* Any ship

rustle 1 *n* A robbery; = HEIST: *the $300,000 rustle that he got away with*—Westbrook Pegler **2** *v* (also **rustle up**) To find and produce; prepare: *two bachelors rustlin' up some grub*—Pulpsmith/ *I can rustle up some if you need it*—William Kennedy [origin unknown; perhaps fr *rush* + *hustle*]

rustle one's **bustle** *v phr* To get active; hurry; = GET THE LEAD OUT

rusty-dusty 1 *n esp black fr 1930s* The buttocks; rump; = ASS ● Nearly always with the suggestion of torpor or laziness: *sitting around on his rusty-dusty doing nothing*—WV Shannon **2** *n theater* A property pistol [fr the notion that something not in frequent use or active motion will become *rusty* and *dusty*]

rusty gate *See* SWING LIKE A RUSTY GATE

rutabaga *n* A dollar: *We've spent 60,000 rutabagas*—SJ Perelman

S

-s *suffix used to form nouns* A diminutive or affectionate version of what is indicated, used as a term of address: *babes/ ducks/ moms/ sweets*

SA (pronounced as separate letters) *n fr 1920s* Sex appeal

sack[1] **1** *v fr middle 1800s British* To discharge; dismiss; =CAN, FIRE: *by refusing to sack his aide* —Philadelphia Bulletin/ *I've been sacked*—Time **2** *n fr armed forces* A bed, bunk, sleeping bag, etc; sleeping place; =RACK: *Let me stay in the sack all day*—Hal Boyle **3** *n* Sleep; =SACK TIME: *He needed some sack* **4** *modifier: sack duty/ sack artist* **5** *n* A dress that fits loosely over the shoulders, waist, and hips, and is gathered at the hem line **6** *n* *baseball* A base: *He slid into the sack* [first sense probably fr the notion of giving a discharged person a traveling bag or *sack*, since the earliest expression was *get the sack*]
See FART SACK, HIT THE HAY, the KEYSTONE, SAD SACK

sack[2] *v football* To tackle the quarterback behind the line of scrimmage [fr *sack* "assault and pillage"]

the sack *n phr fr middle 1800s* Discharge from a job; dismissal; =the BOOT: *He was late once too often and got the sack* [apparently fr an old practice of giving someone a *sack* when sending him away; corresponding expressions are found in French: *donner son sac à quelqu'un*]

sack artist *n phr WW2 armed forces* A chronic loafer; =GOLDBRICK, GOOF-OFF

sack duty (or **drill** or **time**) *n phr WW2 armed forces* Sleeping time; sleep; loafing: *get in some sack drill*—JL Riordan

sacker *See* FIRST SACKER, SECOND SACKER, THIRD SACKER

sack out (or **in** or **up**) *v phr WW2 armed forces* To go to bed; sleep; =HIT THE SACK: *Well, it's time to sack out*—Hal Boyle

sack rat *n phr* =SACK ARTIST

sack time *fr WW2 armed forces* **1** *n phr* =SACK DUTY **2** *n phr* Bedtime; time to retire

sad *adj* Inferior; botched or bungled; =CRUMMY: *It's a sad dump*

sad apple **1** *n phr* An obnoxious individual; a contemptible person; =DRIP, JERK, A PAIN IN THE ASS **2** *n phr* A gloomy or pessimistic individual

saddle *See* BOOT AND SADDLE, LEAN FORWARD IN THE SADDLE

saddle shoes *n phr* Low-cut, laced white shoes with a brown or black instep

sadie-maisie *See* S AND M

sad sack *n phr students fr 1920s & esp WW2 armed forces* An awkward, unfortunate, harried, and maladjusted person; =EIGHTBALL, SCHLEMAZEL: *nevertheless stuck with an inexplicable sad sack of a leading man*—Washington Post [fr the unflattering image of a human being as primarily a container for feces]

safecracker *n* A person who blows or breaks open safes; =BOX MAN, PETE-MAN

safety or **safe** *n* A condom; =RUBBER

sagebrusher *n* =HORSE OPERA

someone said a mouthful *sentence* Someone spoke accurately and cogently; someone said something very important ● Often an expression of vehement agreement: *Daisy sure said a mouthful*

said it *See* YOU SAID IT

sail in *v phr fr middle 1800s* To go boldly to the attack or to the rescue

sailing *See* CLEAR SAILING

sail into *v phr* To attack; criticize severely; =LAMBASTE: *He quickly sails into anyone that complains*

sail through *v phr* To do easily and smoothly: *We'll sail right through this little jobbie*

Saint Elsewhere *See* MOUNT SAINT ELSEWHERE

Sal or **Sally** or **Sally Ann** *n or n phr hoboes* The Salvation Army, or any other mission or place that gives food and shelter

salad *See* FRUIT SALAD

salary wing *n phr baseball* A pitcher's throwing arm

Sale *See* CHIC SALE

salon mush *n phr musicians* Bland and pleasant music played quietly in a bar

saloon *n railroad* A caboose

salt **1** *n fr early 1800s* A sailor, esp an old and seasoned one **2** *n narcotics* Heroin in powder form
See GO POUND SALT

salt and pepper **1** *n phr narcotics* Impure or low-grade marijuana **2** *adj phr* Interracial; =BLACK AND TAN: *a salt and pepper neighborhood in Detroit* **3** *adj phr* Referring to hair that is turning gray

salt horse *n phr fr middle 1800s nautical* Corned beef; dried or chipped beef, salted [*horse* used as a derogatory term for the unappetizing meat]

the salt mines *See* BACK TO THE SALT MINES

salts *See* LIKE SHIT THROUGH A TIN HORN

salty 1 *adj* *Navy fr early 1900s* Audacious; daring; aggressive **2** *adj* *teenagers fr jive talk* Terrible; nasty; unpalatable **3** *adj* *esp black* Angry; hostile **4** *adj* Crude; uncouth; earthy: *His language is often quite salty*
See JUMP SALTY

salute *See* RUN something UP THE FLAGPOLE

salvage *v* *WW1 Army* To steal; loot; =LIBERATE

salve 1 *n* *hoboes* Butter **2** *n* *fr early 1900s* Cajolement; flattery; =SOFT SOAP: *I handed him a little salve*—Erle Stanley Gardner **3** *n* A bribe; =PALM OIL **4** *n* Money, esp as a remedy or reward for something unpleasant **5** *v* To pay, esp to pay a bribe
See PENNSYLVANIA SALVE

Sam or **sam** *n* *narcotics* A federal narcotics agent; =NARC

the **same difference** *n phr* *fr early 1900s* The same thing; something exactly equal: *So they fire him or he quits, it's the same difference*

the **same wavelength** *See* ON THE SAME WAVELENGTH

Sam Hill *n phr* *fr early 1800s* Hell: *Where in Sam Hill do you think you're going?/ What the Sam Hill's that?* [an echoic euphemism]

sand *esp late 1800s* **1** *n* Courage; stamina; =GRIT **2** *n* *Navy* Sugar
See CRATE OF SAND, GO POUND SALT

sandbag 1 *v* To attack someone viciously, esp with a blackjack or similar bludgeon; =BUSHWHACK: *I was sandbagged from behind*—Life **2** *v* To intimidate; cow; =BULLDOZE: *Persuasion didn't work, so they tried to sandbag her* **3** *v* *gambling* To check and then to raise the bet **4** *v* *fr gambling* To pretend weakness or ineptitude; mislead an opponent by apparent inferiority: *He charged that the Aussies were "sand bagging" (deliberately losing) to take the limelight off their disputed keel*—Time **5** *v* *hot rodders* To drive a hot rod very fast **6** *n* *WW2 Navy* A type of life preserver

sandlot 1 *n* A rough or improvised baseball field; =HOGAN'S BRICKYARD **2** *modifier:* *sandlot ball*

S and M or **S/M** or **sadie-maisie 1** *n phr* or *n* Sado-masochism; perverse sexual practices featuring whips, chains, etc **2** *n phr* or *n* The dominant person in a sado-masochistic sexual relation; slave master

sand-pounder *n* *Navy* A sailor on shore duty

sandwich *See* HERO SANDWICH

sandwich board *n phr* A board bearing advertising messages, and worn one in front and one behind by a sandwich man

sandwich man *n phr* A person paid to walk about bearing sandwich boards

San Quentin quail *n phr* A girl below the legal age of sexual consent; =JAIL BAIT [fr the name of a California state penitentiary]

Santa Claus 1 *n phr* *airline* A check pilot who is very lenient and agreeable on a pilot check flight **2** *n phr* A male donor or benefactor; a very generous man: *What the orphanage needed was a Santa Claus to pay the debts*

sao (SOU) *n* *Vietnam War armed forces* A repulsive, obnoxious, or dishonorable person; =BASTARD [fr Vietnamese]

sap[1] *n* *fr early 1900s fr early 1800s British* A stupid person; fool, esp a gullible one: *Quit acting like a sap* [fr British dialect, short for *sapskull* "person with a head full of soft material"; probably influenced by early-19th-century British schoolboy slang, "compulsive studier, grind," which is probably fr *sap* as an ironic abbreviation of Latin *sapiens* "wise," and is hence semantically akin to *sophomore*]

sap[2] **1** *n* A blackjack; bludgeon: *the sap...a nice little tool about five inches long, covered with woven brown leather*—Raymond Chandler **2** *v:* *One of the others sapped him from behind with the blackjack*—Life [probably fr Middle English *sape* "shovel," the shovel being for ages a popular club]

sapfu (SAP foo) **1** *adj* *WW2 armed forces* Surpassingly and incredibly botched **2** *n:* *a stupefying sapfu we had* [fr *surpassing all previous fuck-ups*]

sap-happy *adj* Drunk

saphead *n* *fr late 1700s* A stupid person; =BLOCKHEAD, SAP: *one young woman who just seems to be a saphead*—Wolcott Gibbs

◁**sapphire**▷ *n* *black* An unattractive, unpopular black woman [fr the name of a character on the Amos 'n' Andy radio program popular fr the late 1920s until the 1950s; *Sapphire* was the shrewish wife of a character called "The Kingfish"]

sappy 1 *adj* Stupid; foolish; =GOOFY: *lay off them sappy songs*—WR Burnett **2** *adj* Sentimental; mawkish; =SCHMALTZY

sarge *n* *fr middle 1800s armed forces* A sergeant

sashay *v* *fr early 1800s* To go; walk; flounce: *after a great deal of extravagantly publicized sashaying about*—Washington Post [fr the square-dance gait, fr French *chasser* "chase"]

sass 1 *n* *fr middle 1800s* Impudence; impertinent backtalk: *if this reporter was going to give her any sass*—Washington Post **2** *v:* *He kept sassing his mama till she decked him* [fr *sauce* "rude and impudent language or action"]

satch *fr black* **1** *n* A man with a large mouth; =SATCHELMOUTH **2** *n* An overly talkative man; =WINDBAG: *in the days when I was fearlessly denouncing old satch*—Westbrook Pegler

satchel 1 *n* The buttocks; rump; =KEISTER: *a chance to rest my satchel*—G Moore **2** *n* =SATCH **3** *n* *jazz musicians* A jazz musician who plays a horn **4** *v* To prearrange the outcome of a fight, race, etc; =FIX, RIG: *It was satcheled against him*—D Egan [verb sense fr *in the bag*]

satchelmouth *n* =SATCH

saturated *adj* Drunk: *to keep them saturated indefinitely*—American Mercury

Saturday nights *n phr* *lunch counter* Baked beans

Saturday night special 1 *n phr* A cheap, small-caliber revolver quite easy to obtain: *Detroit lawmen began to refer to the weapons as "Saturday night specials"*—B Kaiser **2** *n phr* *hospital* A person, often an alcoholic, who comes to a hospital on weekends seeking a bed and board

sauce *See* APPLESAUCE

the **sauce** *n* Liquor; whiskey; = BOOZE: *It made him sad and he almost began hitting the sauce*—John O'Hara
See HIT THE BOTTLE, ON THE SAUCE

saucered and blowed *adj phr* Processed and prepared; ready for completion: *Take this job over, please, it's all saucered and blowed* [fr a dialect expression referring to the process of getting a cup of coffee or tea cooled and ready to drink]

sausage 1 *n* A prize fighter, esp one with a swollen and battered face **2** *n* A stupid person; = MEATHEAD

savage *n police* A young police officer eager to make arrests

saved by the bell *adj phr fr prizefighting* Rescued, relieved, or preserved at the last minute [fr the plight of a boxer who is being severely punished when the *bell* rings to end the round]

savvy or **savvey** *fr early 1800s* **1** *v* To understand; know; grasp: *I'm the honcho here, savvy?* **2** *n* Comprehension; intelligence; = BRAINS, SMARTS: *He's a guy with much savvy* **3** *adj*: *a very savvy lady* [fr West Indian pidgin fr Spanish *sabe usted* "do you know?"]

saw 1 *n* = SAWBUCK **2** *n black* The landlord of a rooming house
See DOUBLE SAWBUCK

sawbones *n fr early 1800s British* A surgeon; a physician: *without being able to rouse a sawbones*—R Ruark

sawbuck *n fr middle 1800s* A ten-dollar bill; ten dollars [fr the resemblance of the Roman numeral X to the ends of a *sawhorse*]
See DOUBLE SAWBUCK

sawdust 1 *n underworld* Dynamite **2** *n students* Sugar

sawdust eater *n phr lumberjacks* A sawmill worker or lumberjack

sawdust parlor *n phr* A cheap nightclub, restaurant, etc: *not a rug joint...but rather a sawdust parlor*—J Scarne [fr the former use of *sawdust* as a floor covering]

sawed-off *adj fr late 1800s* Short of stature: *sawed-off fight manager from Newark*—J Cuddy

saw wood 1 *v phr fr early 1900s* To sleep, esp very soundly **2** *v phr* To snore [fr the sound of snoring]

sawyer *n 1920s underworld* A sawed-off shotgun

sax 1 *n* A saxophone **2** *modifier: a sax virtuoso*

say *See* WHAT DO YOU SAY

say a mouthful *See* someone SAID A MOUTHFUL

say-so *n fr late 1700s* One's word, report, recommendation, etc: *No jury'll convict Manny on your say-so alone*—Raymond Chandler

says which *interrogation* What did you say?: *Says which? I don't believe what I heard*

says you or **says who** *interj* (Variations: **sez** or **sezz** may replace **says**) *fr early 1900s & esp fr WW1 armed forces* An exclamation of defiance, dis-

belief, mere pugnacity, etc; = IZZATSO: *I'm in the wrong seat? Says who?*

say that again *See* YOU CAN SAY THAT AGAIN

say uncle *v phr* To surrender; give up: *Despite your exquisite Byzantine torture, I will never say uncle*

say what *interj esp teenagers fr black* A request for more information; excuse me?

scab *n labor union fr early 1800s* A nonunion worker, esp one who attempts to break a strike; = FINK

scads 1 *n fr middle 1800s* A large quantity of money **2** *n* A large quantity of anything; = BAGS, OODLES: *I have scads of study to do*—Philadelphia Bulletin [origin unknown; perhaps fr British dialect, "shed," and hence semantically akin to *a shithouse full*]

scag *See* SKAG

scag jones *n phr narcotics* A heroin addiction: *sell them to janitors for a quarter to support their "scag jones"*—Claude Brown

scairdy cat *See* SCAREDY CAT

scale 1 *n prison & Army fr early 1900s* A louse **2** *n labor union* The basic wage guaranteed by a union
See FISH SCALE

scalp *v fr middle 1800s* To sell tickets at a higher than normal or legal price

scalper 1 *n fr middle 1800s* A person who scalps tickets **2** *n gambling* A person who places bets and backs bets in such a way that he will win whether the horse wins or loses

scam 1 *n fr carnival* A swindle; confidence game; fraud; = CON: *It was a full scam*—Time/ *when I made the bust on the scam*—Joseph Wambaugh **2** *v* (also **scam on**): *You guys are scamming me/ good place to scam on the rich tourists*—Joseph Wambaugh **3** *n* The information; = LOWDOWN, the SCOOP: *Here's the scam....We're holing in for the night*—Patrick Mann [origin unknown; perhaps related to early-19th-century British *scamp* "cheater, swindler"]
See WHAT'S THE SCAM

◄**Scandahoovian** or **Scandanoovian**► **1** *n* A Scandinavian or person of Scandinavian extraction **2** *adj*: *the Scandahoovian language/ murky Scandanoovian movies*

scandal sheet *n phr* A sensationalistic and vulgar newspaper, magazine, etc; cheap tabloid; = RAG
See SWINDLE SHEET

Scandinavian dynamite *n phr* (Variations: **Scandahoovian** or **Scandanoovian** may replace **Scandinavian**) *lumberjacks* Snuff, esp strong snuff

◁**scank**▷ *n black teenagers* An unattractive girl

scankie *adj black teenagers* Disheveled; sloppy

the **scare** *n phr 1930s underworld* Extortion based on menaces: *We build the sap for the scare*—American Mercury/ *They tried the scare on him, but he didn't back down*

scare badge *n phr Army* A badge given in recognition of paratroop or other rigorous and prestigious training

◁**scared shitless**▷ *adj phr* Very frightened; terrified: *And the producer is scared shitless of the sponsor*—Sterling Hayden/ *Behind the Yale, they're scared shitless*—Sexual Behavior [based on the expression *scare the shit out of* someone]

scared spitless (or **witless**) *adj phr* Very frightened; terrified; =SCARED SHITLESS: *They were scared spitless at the prospect of appearing in a play*—Richard Wright [two plausible euphemisms for *scared shitless*]

scared stiff *adj phr* Very frightened; paralyzed by terror [fr the notion of being *scared to death*]

scaredy (or **scairdy**) **cat** *n phr* =FRAIDY CAT

scarehead *n newspaper office* A very large and conspicuous headline; =SCREAMER

◁**scare** someone **shitless**▷ (or **spitless** or **witless**) *v phr* To frighten very much; terrify: *It scared me shitless, but that didn't stop me from watching it again and again*—Edward Koch

scare (or **scared**) **strap** *n line repairers* A safety belt

◁**scare the shit** (or **living shit**) **out of** someone▷ *v phr* To frighten very much; terrify: *It scares the living shit out of them*—National Lampoon

scare up *v phr fr middle 1800s* To find and produce; =RUSTLE: *was among the goodies scared up at a flea market*—Casper Star-Tribune [fr the rising of birds frightened by hunters]

scarf *esp teenagers fr black* **1** *n* Food; a meal; =CHOW, SCOFF **2** *v* (also **scarf up**) To eat or drink; consume: *puffing on his morning joint, eating cereal, and scarfing up a beer*—Easyriders **3** *v* (also **scarf up**) *esp students* To pilfer; =SWIPE: *People scarf up food after truck overturns*—Casper Star-Tribune **4** *v students* To throw away; discard; =DEEP-SIX

scarf out *v phr* To eat very heartily; overeat; =PIG OUT: *I took the band there and we scarfed out*—Vegetarian Times

scat[1] **1** *n jazz musicians* Pattering staccato gibberish sung to songs, esp jazz songs: *using scat for novelty back in 1906*—Alan Lomax **2** *modifier:* precise *"scat" singing*—F Grunfeld **3** *v:* Scatting *has almost always been used by jazz singers as an interlude*—San Francisco [attributed to Louis Armstrong, fr the 1920s, echoic of the nonsense sounds he used when he forgot song lyrics or was imitating instruments in an interlude]

scat[2] *v* To drive or otherwise move very fast [fr early-19th-century *s'cat*, a hissing address designed to drive away a cat; the earliest occurrence is in the expression *quicker than s'cat*]

scatback *n football* A very fast and agile backfield runner

scatter *underworld* **1** *n* A saloon or speakeasy; =HANGOUT **2** *n* =HIDEOUT **3** *n* A room; lodging: *send him up to the scatter*—Raymond Chandler [perhaps a place to which or from which one may *scat*]

scatterbrain *n fr middle 1800s* A silly or stupid person, esp one who cannot attend properly to a

subject or get simple things done; =DITZ, RATTLE-BRAIN

scattergun **1** *n fr cowboys* A shotgun **2** *n WW2 Army* A machine gun, submachine gun, or machine pistol; =BURP GUN **3** *modifier* Broadly and imprecisely directed; crudely comprehensive: *the scattergun memo*—New York Daily News

scatter-joint *n esp 1930s fr underworld* A nightclub

scatty *adj fr British* Irrational; crazy; =GOOFY, SCATTERBRAINED: *the ferociously ambitious, slightly scatty Louise Bryant*—Vincent Canby/ *Images are very dense, only the connections between them look scatty*—Time

scenario *n* A reasoned or imagined pattern of events in the future; a possible plan: *According to one scenario we only kill 80 percent of them* **See** WORST-CASE SCENARIO

scene *esp 1960s counterculture fr black* **1** *n* The setting or milieu of a specific activity or group; specialized venue: *the rock "scene"*—E Willis/ *It is really quite difficult...to understand their scene*—Trans-Action **2** *n* One's particular preference, activity, etc; =BAG, THING: *I mean that's not my own scene or anything*—Changes **See** ALL-ORIGINALS SCENE, BAD SCENE, LAY A TRIP ON someone, MAKE A SCENE, MAKE THE SCENE, MOB SCENE, SPLIT THE SCENE

scenery **See** CHEW UP THE SCENERY, MELT INTO THE SCENERY

Schaffner **See** HART, SCHAFFNER AND MARX

schizo (SKITSO, SKIH zoh) **1** *n* (also **schiz**) A schizophrenic: *Docs find he's a schizo*—New York Daily News **2** *adj:* a schizo *drug addict* **3** *adj* (also **schizy** or **schizzy** or **schizie** or **schizoid**) Crazy; demented, esp in a self-contradictory way; psychotic; =NUTTY: *People in democracies...are a little schizzy about authority*—Newsweek/ *with dramatically schizoid effect*—Rolling Stone/ *this same schizy little brain*—Esquire/ *new, schizzy heights*—Village Voice/ *I was in fact extremely schizie*—Ms

schiz out *v phr* To go crazy; become schizophrenic; =FLIP: *She thought he'd schizzed out completely*—Cyra McFadden/ *on the perpetual verge of schizing out*—Richard Merkin

schlang **See** SCHLONG

schlemazel or **schlemasel** or **shlemozzle** (shlə MAH zəl) *n* An awkward, unfortunate, maladjusted person; =SAD SACK [fr Yiddish *shlimazel* fr *shlim mazel* "rotten luck"]

schlemiel or **schlemihl** or **shlemiel** (shlə MEEL) *n* A stupid person; fool; oaf; esp, a naive person often victimized: *Don't talk like a schlemiel, you schlemiel*—Budd Schulberg/ *playing the lovable schlemiel to Brooklyn Jews*—Esquire [fr Yiddish *shlemiel*, probably fr the name of the main character in A von Chamisso's German fable *The Wonderful History of Peter Schlemihl*, 1813]

schlep or **schlepp** or **shlep** **1** *v* To carry; drag along: *We have Mercedeses for you and your purchases, Ma'am, so why shlep?*/ *go through a contortionist's routine to schlepp your packages*—Village Voice **2** *v* To move or advance with difficulty; drag: *then I'd have to schlep around to the Quarter Note*—Nashville **3** *n: even with the four-flight schlep to the editorial office*—New York **4** *n* A stupid person; oaf; = KLUTZ: *dead schleps playing behind him*—Rolling Stone/ *a real drudging, seat-of-pants schlepp*—Earl Thompson **5** *n* = SCHLEPPER [fr Yiddish *shleppen*]

schlepper or **shlepper** *n* A person who is always looking for a bargain, expects little favors, is selling something, etc; = A PAIN IN THE ASS: *Schleppers the world over recognize me*—GQ

schleppy or **shleppy** *adj* Awkward; stupid; = KLUTZY

schlock 1 *n* (also **schlack** or **schlag** or **shlock**) Inferior merchandise; an inferior product; = CRAP, JUNK: *that "Macbird" is a piece of schlock*—Russell Baker/ *They are bringing out schlock so they can pay for the books they care about*—Pauline Kael **2** *adj: unlike all those schlock films*—CL Westerbeck, Jr [fr Yiddish *shlak* "a curse"]

schlockmeister *n* A successful maker or seller of schlock: *Low-budget, high-profit exploitation has solidified their position as Hollywood's premier schlockmeisters*—Newsweek [fr *schlock* + German *Meister* "master"]

schlock shop (or **joint**) *n phr* A store that sells inferior merchandise, esp a junk shop, thrift store, etc

schlocky or **shlocky** *adj* Inferior; shoddy; cheap and gaudy; = JUNKY

◁**schlong**▷ *n* (Variations: **schlang** or **shlang** or **shlong**) The penis; = PRICK: *you know with his schlong hanging out there*—Rolling Stone/ *Don's big schlong was staring at me*—Xaviera Hollander [fr Yiddish *shlang* "snake"]

◁**schlontz** or **shlontz**▷ *n* The penis [perhaps a blend of Yiddish *shlong* and *shwants*]

schloomp (SHLo͞oMP) (Variations: **schlump** or **shloomp** or **shlump**) **1** *n* A stupid person; = KLUTZ: *For openers, he looks like a shlump*—Phil-adelphia Journal/ *calling George Shultz a dumb shlump*—Washingtonian **2** *v* (also **shalump** or **schloomp around**) To loaf; idle about; = GOOF OFF: *She shalumps around the Ritz in her loose clothes and sneakers*—Washington Post [fr Yiddish *shlump*, related to German *Schlumpe* "a slovenly woman"]

schlub *See* ZHLUB

schmaltz or **shmaltz** (SHMAWLTS) **1** *n fr 1930s swing musicians* Blatant sentimentality, esp musical or theatrical material of a cloyingly sweet and maudlin sort; = CORN: *happy combination of good theater and good pathos known as schmaltz*—New Yorker **2** *n* A viscid substance; = GLOP, GOO [fr Yiddish *shmalts*, literally "rendered fat"]

schmaltzy or **schmalzy** or **shmaltzy** *adj* Sentimental; sweetly melancholy; = CORNY, ICKY: *It is not always the schmalzy moment that dissolves me*—New Yorker/ *this schmaltzy king of schlock & roll*—Rolling Stone

schmancy *See* FANCY-SCHMANCY

schmatte (SHMAH tə) *n* (Variations: **schmattah** or **schmatteh** or **shmatte** or **shmotte**) A shabby

or unstylish garment: *She had on a tired old schmattah*—Xaviera Hollander [fr Yiddish *shmatte*, literally "rag"]

schmear[1] or **shmear** or **shmeer 1** *v* To bribe; = GREASE someone's PALM **2** *n: The prime minister took a big schmear from the airplane company* **3** *v* To flatter and cajole someone; = BUT-TER UP, SOFT SOAP **4** *v* To spread a large dab of something such as butter or cream cheese: *Just schmear it on real thick* **5** *n: I'll have a bagel with a schmear* [fr Yiddish *shmeer*, literally "grease"]

schmear[2] **1** *v* To treat someone very roughly; = CLOBBER, CREAM, SMEAR **2** *n* An accusation or innuendo meant to harm someone's reputation; a slander [fr a humorous mispronunciation of *smear*]

the schmear *n phr* = the WHOLE SCHMEAR [fr Yiddish *shmeer*]

schmeck or **shmeck 1** *n* A taste; a bite: *How about a little schmeck?*—Esquire **2** *n narcotics* Heroin; = SMACK: *She's hustling right now, schmeck, tail, abortion, the whole bit*—Lawrence Sanders [fr Yiddish *shmek* "a smell, sniff," related to German *schmecken*]

Schmedlap *n Army* An inept soldier

schmegeggy or **shmegeggy** or **schmegegge** (shmə GEG gee) **1** *n* A stupid person; oaf; = SCHLEMIEL: *the shmegeggy she lives with*—Philip Roth/ *a new story...about some gringo schmegegge exchanging his dollars for a worthless mess of Batista money*—Village Voice **2** *n* Nonsense; foolishness; = BALONEY [fr Yiddish *shmegegi* of unknown origin, perhaps coined in American Yiddish]

schmendrick or **shmendrick** *n* A stupid person, esp an awkward and inept nonentity; = SCHLEMIEL: *a schmendrick with a noodle for a brain*—A Hirschfield [fr Yiddish *shmendrik*, fr the name of a character in an operetta by A Goldfaden]

schmo (Variations: **schmoe** or **shmo** or **shmoe**) **1** *n* A naive and hapless person; fool; = GOOF: *I've been standing here like a schmoe for 20 min-utes*—Fred Allen/ *How does a schmoe acquire a look?*—Village Voice **2** *n* A person; man; = GUY: *Them big-time schmoes was stockholders*—Satur-day Evening Post [perhaps a euphemistic alteration of Yiddish *shmok* "penis"; perhaps a quasi-Yiddish coinage for amusing effect; the term has been adopted into American Yiddish]

See JOE SCHMO

schmooz (Variations: **schmoo** or **schmooze** or **schmoos** or **schmoose** or **schmoozl** or **schmoozle** or **schmoosl** or **schmoosle** or any of these spelled with **sh-**) **1** *v* To converse, esp lengthily and cozily: *The three of us started schmoosing for a few minutes*—John McNulty/ *We would schmoose all afternoon*—Calvin Tomkins/ *lawyers schmoozing in the halls*—Village Voice/ *It's very hard for me to just sit around and schmoo*—Washington Post **2** *n: Two buddies enjoying a quiet schmooz* [fr Yiddish fr Hebrew *schmuos* "things heard"]

schmoozer *n* A person who schmoozes, esp as an aspect of personality: *He has none of the small coin of politics. He's not a schmoozer*—Washington Post

schmuck or **shmuck** *n* A detestable person; an obnoxious man; = BASTARD, PRICK: *You must be a real schmuck*—Nora Ephron/ *It's happened to bigger schmucks than me*—Joseph Heller [fr Yiddish *shmok* "penis," literally "ornament"]

schneider **1** *v* *fr 1940s* To win before one's opponent has scored; = SHUT OUT **2** *n*: *The Yanks took four straight, a schneider* **3** *v* To defeat decisively; trounce; = CLOBBER [fr German, literally "tailor," probably by way of Yiddish; the term is used in various card games for a clean sweep]

schnockered *See* SNOCKERED

schnook or **shnook** (SHNo͝oK) *n* An ineffectual person; a naive person often victimized; = PATSY • A more affectionate and compassionate way of designating a **schlemiel**: *Don't be such an apologetic schnook*—Jack Benny/ *a post-adolescent Brooklyn schnook*—New Times [fr American-Yiddish *shnook*, said to be fr German *Schnucke* "small sheep"; probably related to the pet names *snooks, snookums,* etc]

schnorrer or **shnorrer** **1** *n* A beggar, esp one who counts parasitically on a family or community; = MOOCHER, SPONGER: *The room has generally been ignored by serious schnorrers*—Toronto Life/ *"Hooray for Captain Spaulding, the African explorer!" "Did someone call me schnorrer?"* —Animal Crackers (movie) **2** *n* A person who habitually haggles; niggard [fr Yiddish *shnorrer*]

schnozz *n* (Variations: **schnoz** or **schnozzle** or **schnozzola** or any of these spelled with **sh-** or **snozzle**) The nose, esp a large one; = BUGLE: *the rep of not havin' a big schnozz*—Jimmy Durante/ *Five players broke their schnozzolas*—Associated Press [fr Yiddish *shnoz* fr *shnoitsl* fr German *Schnauze* "snout"]

school *n underworld* A state penitentiary; = the BIG HOUSE

See BIG SCHOOL, LITTLE SCHOOL, PREP SCHOOL

schpilkes *See* SHPILKES

schpritz *See* SHPRITZ

schtarker *See* SHTARKER

schtick *See* SHTICK

schtoonk (SHTo͝oNK) *n* (Variations: **schtunk** or **shtoonk** or **shtunk**) A person one detests or despises; = JERK, STINKER [fr Yiddish *shtunk*]

schtup *See* SHTUP

schussboom (SHo͝oS bo͞om) *v* To ski very fast downhill [fr German *Schuss*, literally "shot" + American English *boom* "speed"]

schvantz or **schvontz** *See* SHVANTZ

◄**schvartze**► (SHVAHR tsə) *n* (Variations: **shvartzeh** or **shvartze** or **schwartze** or **schvartzer** or **shvartzer** or **schwartzer**) A black person: *irons even better than the schvartze*—Philip Roth [fr Yiddish fr *shvartz* "black"]

science *See* HARD SCIENCE

sci-fi (SĪ FĪ) **1** *n* Science fiction **2** *adj: sci-fi fans...secretly crave*—Rolling Stone/ *standard sci-fi feelings of speculative wonder*—Village Voice

scillion *See* SKILLION

scissorbill or **scissorsbill** **1** *n* *esp early 1900s labor union* A person whose income is not from wages; a wealthy or privileged person **2** *n labor union* A worker who will not join a union; = SCAB **3** *n hoboes* A railroad detective or police officer: *Paoli is a dirty scissorbill!* [origin unknown; first attested fr late-19th-century lumberjacks as a generalized term of contempt, perhaps alluding to the bird; attested in early-20th-century hobo use with gloss "a farmer who can clip coupons," hence perhaps contemptuously to designate bondholders and others inimical to workers and labor unions]

scissors bull *n phr hoboes* A railroad police officer or detective; = SCISSORBILL

scoff **1** *v* *fr hoboes & merchant marine fr middle 1800s British merchant marine* To eat or drink; = SCARF: *I'll take you over...so you can scoff*—Jim Tully/ *Truman scoffed a bowl*—Westbrook Pegler **2** *n* Food: *Beef heart is their favorite scoff* **3** *v teenagers* To steal; pilfer; = SWIPE: *Who scoffed my butts?* [origin uncertain; perhaps fr Afrikaans *schoft*, defined in a 17th-century dictionary as "eating time for labourers or workmen foure times a day"; perhaps fr British dialect *scaff*; South African use in current senses is attested in late 18th century]

scoffings *n hoboes fr late 1800s* Food; meals: *A hard town for "scoffings"*—Jack London

scooch *See* SCRUNCH

scoop **1** *v newspaper office fr late 1800s* To publish or file a news story before another newspaper or another reporter: *I was afraid of being scooped because I knew a lot of reporters were on the same story*—New York Post **2** *n*: *The paper scored a major scoop with that revelation* **3** *n lunch counter* A standard hemispherical portion of ice cream, mashed potatoes, etc; = DIP **4** *v fr early 1900s* In singing, to attain a desired note by beginning lower and sliding up to pitch

the **scoop** *n phr fr 1940s students & armed forces* News or data, esp when anxiously awaited, heretofore secret, etc; = POOP: *We all gathered around when he said he had the scoop*

scooper *See* POOPER SCOOPER

scoot **1** *v fr middle 1700s* To move rapidly, esp in fleeing or escaping: *When they saw the cops they scooted right out of there* **2** *v fr middle 1800s* To slide, esp suddenly as on a slippery surface: *Let's scoot this thing into the corner* **3** *n* A dollar: *Greg could have the sixty scoots, the guns, everything*—Joseph Wambaugh [origin unknown; perhaps ultimately fr a Scandinavian cognate of *shoot*, by way of Scottish dialect; the third sense may have an entirely different derivation than the first two]

scope a vic *See* VIC³

scope on (or **out**) *v phr esp teenagers fr black* To look at; examine; = CHECK OUT, DIG: *scoping on the foxy sisters*—New York Times/ *I'd scoped him out pretty well*—Richard Merkin

scorch 1 *v* *esp early 1900s* To travel very fast; =BARREL: *I proceed to scorch to make up for lost time*—Jack London **2** *v* *baseball* To throw the ball very fast and hard; =BURN

score 1 *n* *fr underworld* A success or coup in theft, swindling, gambling, etc: *He was always hoping for a big score* **2** *n* *fr underworld* The loot or proceeds from a robbery, swindle, gamble, etc; also, the amount of such loot; =HAUL **3** *n* *fr 1930s underworld* A share of loot; =CUT **4** *v* To succeed, esp to please an audience, interviewer, or others who judge; =RATE: *The show didn't score with the TV critics* **5** *v* To do the sex act with or to someone; =MAKE IT WITH someone **6** *n: He was always looking for an easy score* **7** *v* *prostitutes* To find a client for prostitution **8** *n: The little hooker got only five scores all evening* **9** *n* *underworld* A planned murder; =HIT **10** *v* *narcotics* To buy or get narcotics: *you'll score from him*—D Haburd/ *Want to score, Blackie?*—New Yorker **11** *n: He's out looking for a score* **12** *v* *students* To get: *Where'd you score that Frisbee?/ Most of them score their clothes as gifts from parents*—Time

See EVEN THE SCORE, MAKE A SCORE

the score *n* *fr 1940s students* The main point; crux; =BOTTOM LINE: *I heard the facts, now what's the score?*

See KNOW THE SCORE

scosh *See* SKOSH

scouse *n* *esp early 1900s* Any cheap, tasteless dish, esp a thin stew: *What's scouse? Beef stew without beef*—Sinclair Lewis [fr *lobscouse*, of unknown origin, a sailor's stew containing hardtack]

scow *n* *truckers* A large truck

scrag[1] **1** *v* To kill; murder: *overshoot or undershoot and scrag some scared civilian*—Robert Ruark **2** *v* To destroy or severely damage; ruin: *The beet sugar people...try to scrag the cane sugar people*—R Starnes ◁**3**▷ *v* To do the sex act with or to; =SCREW, SCROG: *the middle-American hobby of scragging the random housewife at any opportunity*—John D McDonald [fr earlier slang, "hang by the neck"]

◁**scrag**[2]▷ *n* *esp 1940s students* An unattractive woman; =DOG [probably fr *hag* reinforced by the name of the ugly *Scraggs* family in the comic strip "Li'l Abner" and possibly by earlier slang, "a rawbones; a skinny person"]

scraggy *adj* Disheveled; unkempt-looking; gaunt and wasted: *snapshot of a scraggy Sindona as an apparent captive*—Time

scram 1 *v* *fr early 1900s underworld & circus* To leave quickly; flee; =BEAT IT: *Customers scrammed screaming when the trailer went on*—Village Voice/ *Scram, you kids* **2** *n: I got ready for a sudden scram* **3** *n* *underworld & circus* Money, clothing, etc, ready for a quick departure [fr *scramble*]

scram-bag *n* *underworld & circus* A suitcase packed and ready for a quick departure

scrambled eggs *armed forces* **1** *n* Gold braid, embroidery, etc, on the uniform of a senior officer, esp on the bill of a cap **2** *n* Senior officers; =BRASS, the TOP BRASS

scrambler *n* *motorcyclists* A motorcycle used for mountain or hill riding

scram money *n phr* *underworld & circus* Money kept in reserve for a hasty departure

scrap 1 *n* *fr late 1800s British* A fight; quarrel; =DUSTUP **2** *v: They scrapped for days over the appointment* [origin uncertain; perhaps fr *scrape*]

scrape along (or **by**) *v phr* To survive; carry on; =GET BY: *I'm not flourishing, but I'm scraping along, barely*

scrape the bottom of the barrel *v phr* To use one's last and worst resources; be forced to desperate measures: *He scraped the bottom of the barrel when he proposed that topic for his paper*

scrape (or **scratch**) **up** *v phr* To get, esp laboriously and bit by bit: *Where'll I scrape up some support?/ even if you can't scratch up all of that cash now*—Sports Afield

scrape up (or **together**) *v phr* To find and acquire with difficulty; exploit meager resources: *They scraped up all the talent they had, which wasn't much*

scrap iron *n phr* Inferior whiskey; =ROTGUT

scratch 1 *n* *fr early 1900s* Money; =BREAD, DOUGH: *If the mayor doesn't come up with the scratch*—Saturday Review/ *She also had plenty of scratch*—John O'Hara **2** *n* A loan; an act of borrowing money: *They gave him a scratch for the tuition* **3** *v* *horse-racing* To cancel a horse from a race **4** *n:* two scratches in the third race **5** *n* *horse-racing* A betting ticket on a horse canceled from a race: *She had found one "scratch," a ticket...bet on a horse that had not started*—New York Times **6** *v* To cancel a plan, an entrant, someone on a list, etc; =SCRUB: *Looks like our tête-à-tête will be scratched* **7** *v* (also **itch**): *pool fr late 1800s* To put the cue ball into a pocket inadvertently **8** *n* (also **itch**): *He made a scratch at a crucial juncture/ And when the cue ball goes into the pocket, you call that an itch*—Max Shulman **9** *modifier* *sports fr middle 1800s* Competing without an assigned handicap: *a scratch boat in the race/ a scratch golfer* **10** *adj* Hastily arranged; impromptu; spur of the moment; =PICKUP: *a scratch jazz ensemble/ scratch ball team* **11** *n* *fr late 1930s* A mention of one's name in the news media, esp when this is useful publicity

See FROM SCRATCH, START FROM SCRATCH, UP TO SCRATCH, YOU SCRATCH MY BACK I SCRATCH YOURS

scratch someone's **back** *v phr* To please someone, esp by flattery; be very accommodating to someone

scratcher *n* *underworld fr middle 1800s* A forger

scratch (or **scratch around**) **for** something *v phr* To search for something, esp something hard to find or get: *I was scratching around for whatever work I could get* [fr the food-seeking action of chickens]

scratch hit *n phr* *baseball* A lucky base hit that is nearly an out: *scratch single/ scratch double*

scratch house *n phr esp early 1900s merchant marine & hoboes* A cheap lodging house; = FLEABAG, FLOPHOUSE

scratch sheet *n phr horse-racing* A daily publication giving betting data, including the cancellations, on races to be run that day: *the first scratch sheet that ever appeared*—T Betts

scraunched or **scronched** *adj* Drunk

a **scream** *n phr fr early 1900s* Someone or something that is hilariously funny; = a HOOT, a RIOT: *Isn't this decor a scream?*

screamer 1 *n print shop fr early 1900s* An exclamation point **2** *n show business fr 1920s* A murder mystery, horror show, or thriller **3** *n* A very conspicuous advertising plaque or banner **4** *n newspaper office* = SCAREHEAD

screaming *See* DRAG someone KICKING AND SCREAMING INTO THE TWENTIETH CENTURY

screaming meemie 1 *modifier* Resembling or causing a state of nervous hysteria: *rather than endure another minute of screaming-meemie loneliness*—New York Times **2** *n phr WW2 Army* A small rocket launched from a jeep or truck

the **screaming meemies** or **the meemies** *n phr fr WW1 Army* A state of nervous hysteria; = the HEEBIE-JEEBIES: *a town that would give the ordinary thrill-seeker the screaming meemies*—GS Perry/ *Knowing (a chimpanzee) was on the loose gave him the meemies*—F Brown [apparently fr the soldier's echoic name for a very loud and terrifying German artillery shell, and then the battle fatigue caused by exposure to such materiel; the name may reflect a soldier's pattern of giving feminine names, here the French *Mimi*, to projectiles and weapons, such as *Betsy, Big Bertha, Moaning Minnie,* etc]

screech *n* Inferior whiskey; = PANTHER PISS

◁**screw**[1]▷ **1** *v fr 1700s* To do the sex act with or to someone; = FUCK ● Felt by many to be excusable when **fuck** is the term really intended, and used as an attenuated form in nearly the whole range of **fuck** senses and compounds: *At last people are screwing like minks*—Saturday Review/ *women they don't really want to screw*—Playboy **2** *n: She loves a good screw* **3** *n* A person regarded merely as a sex object: *She's only a medium screw* **4** *v* To take advantage of; swindle; maltreat; = FUCK ● Rapidly losing all offensive impact: *The city's taxpayers get screwed*—Village Voice/ *We can use the available Federal machinery to screw our political enemies*—New York Times *See* GOAT FUCK, PUT THE SCREWS TO someone, THROW A FUCK INTO someone

screw[2] **1** *n underworld fr 1700s* A prison guard or warden; turnkey: *a hard-boiled screw*—E Lavine **2** *n underworld* Any law officer; = COP [fr 18th-century underworld, "a skeleton key," then turnkey, the bearer of such a key]

screw[3] *v* To leave hastily; flee; = SCRAM: *Now go on. Screw*—Nathaniel Benchley [perhaps imitative of *scram*; perhaps semantically derived fr *fuck off* "leave, depart," by way of less taboo *screw off*]

screw around 1 *v phr* To pass one's time idly and pleasantly; potter about; = GOOF AROUND **2** *v*

phr To joke and play when one should be serious; = FUCK AROUND: *Quit screwing around and take this call* **3** *v phr* To flirt or dally, esp promiscuously; = be a SWINGER: *After he met Janet, he stopped screwing around*

screw around with someone **1** *v phr* To flirt or dally with someone; have a sexual involvement with someone; = PLAY AROUND WITH someone: *Anyhow he never screwed around with anybody's wife* **2** *v phr* To treat someone lightly or insultingly; provoke someone; = MESS AROUND WITH someone: *I wouldn't screw around with her, she's got a terrible temper*

screw around with something *v phr* To play or tinker with; = MESS WITH: *I told her to stop screwing around with the TV dial*

screwball[1] **1** *n fr 1930s* An eccentric person; = FREAK, ODDBALL: *a catchall for screwballs and semi-screwballs from all over*—Saturday Evening Post/ *It is forbidden to call any character a nut; you have to call him a screwball*—New Yorker **2** *adj: screwball antics*—Time/ *my screwball consciousness* **3** *n 1930s jazz musicians* Inferior, commercial jazz played for indifferent faddists [fr *screwy* and probably based on *screwball*[2]; the *-ball* of this term is the source of the very productive combining word that yields *oddball, nutball,* etc]

screwball[2] *n baseball fr 1930s* A pitched ball that moves to the right from a righthanded pitcher and the left from a lefthanded pitcher, unlike a curve ball [said to have been coined by the pitcher Carl Hubbell around 1930]

screwed *adj chiefly British* Drunk *See* HALF-STEWED

screwed, blued, and tattooed *adj phr* Thoroughly cheated; victimized; maltreated [*blued* is probably fr earlier *blewed* "robbed"; *tattooed* has the standard sense "struck rapidly and repeatedly"]

screwed up 1 *adj phr esp WW2 armed forces* Confused; tangled; spoiled, esp by bungling; = BALLED UP, FUCKED UP: *He screwed up the punch line/ Our plans got all screwed up* **2** *adj phr* Mentally and emotionally disturbed; neurotic; = FUCKED UP: *Hamlet was a sad, screwed-up type guy*—JD Salinger/ *screwed-up Washington wives*—Playboy/ *We weren't as screwed up with sexist attitudes*—Esquire

◁**screwee**▷ *n* A sex partner; a person being screwed: *My screwee was so angry that nothing would distract her*—Playboy

screw-loose *n* An eccentric person; = NUT, SCREWBALL

a **screw loose** *n phr fr late 1800s* A mental disorder; extreme eccentricity; craziness: *Or was he a man with a screw loose*—WR Burnett

◁**screw off**▷ **1** *v phr* To masturbate; = JACK OFF **2** *v phr esp WW2 Army* = FUCK OFF

screw-off *n esp WW2 Army* A person who evades work; idler; loafer; = FUCK-OFF

screw someone **over** *v phr* To take advantage of; swindle and victimize; = FUCK OVER: *don't trust the Government. They feel it screwed them over*—Time

screws *See* PUT THE SCREWS TO someone

◁**screw the pooch**▷ *v phr* = FUCK THE DOG

screw up 1 *v phr fr WW2 Army* To fail by blundering; ruin one's prospects, life, etc; = FUCK UP: *I screwed up and got canned* **2** *v phr* To confuse; tangle; spoil by bungling; = BALL UP, FUCK UP: *It really screws up my sex life*—JD Salinger/ *One man screwing up the whole world is inconceivable*—New York Times

screw-up 1 *n fr WW2 Army* A chronic bungler; a consistently inept person; = FUCK-UP **2** *n* A confused situation; a botch; = FUCK-UP: *The program's a total screw-up*

screwy 1 *adj* outdated fr early 1800s British Drunk **2** *adj fr 1920s* Very eccentric; crazy; = NUTTY, SCREWBALL: *Newspaper guys are mostly screwy* [semantically the gait of a drunk person suggested by the twistiness of a *screw* thread, whence the various senses of deviation; influenced by the notion of having a *screw loose* in one's head]

◁**screw you**▷ *interj* An exclamation of strong defiance and contempt; = FUCK YOU: *Screw you all* —New York/ *After all the promotions and raises and encouragement, she turned around and said, "Screw you"*

scrip *underworld fr late 1920s* **1** *n* A dollar; a dollar bill **2** *n* A forger; = SCRATCHER

script[1] *n narcotics* A doctor's prescription, often a forged or stolen one

script[2] *n publishing* A manuscript

◁**scrog**▷ **1** *v* To do the sex act with or to; = SCRAG, SCREW: *You guys gotta scrog the sociable cervix* —Samuel Shem **2** *modifier*: *All that scroggin' material out there*—Calvin Trillin [probably fr *scrag*]

scronched *See* SCRAUNCHED

scrooch or **scrooge** or **scrouge** (SKRŌŌCH, SKRŌŌJ) *See* SCRUNCH

scrooched *adj esp 1920s* Drunk

Scrooge *n* A miser; = PINCHPENNY, TIGHTWAD [fr the Dickens character in *A Christmas Carol*]

scrooge up *v phr* To tense and narrow one's eyelids: *I find myself scrooging up my eyes*—Sports Afield

scroogie or **scroogy** (SKRŌŌ jee) *n baseball* An unconventional pitch, esp a screwball thrown with a change of pace: *It was some sort of a scroogie...a changeup screwball*—Associated Press [said to have been coined by Mickey Mantle, probably fr *screwball* and *screwy*]

scrounge or **scrounge up 1** *v* (also **scrounge up**) *fr WW1 British Army* To acquire by such dubious ways as habitual borrowing, begging, foraging, scavenging, pilfering, etc; = CADGE, MOOCH: *eating what little he could scrounge*—Louis Armstrong **2** *v* (also **scrounge up**) To seek and collect; = SCRAPE UP: *Let's see what we can scrounge up for supper* **3** *n* (also **scrounger**) A person who acquires by begging, borrowing, or pilfering; = CADGER, MOOCHER, SCHNORRER [probably fr British dialect *scrunge* "squeeze," hence "steal," semantically parallel with *pinch*]

scroungy or **scrounging** or **scrungy** *adj* Inferior; wretched; = CRUMMY, GRUNGY: *I'd tell my own children to wear something scroungy*—Time/ *The musical has a scroungy book*—New York/ *could*

have bundled all this scrungy stuff into my car —John D McDonald [probably fr the notion of inferior things *scavenged* and *scrounged*, with the form now influenced by *grungy*]

scrub[1] *v* To cancel or eliminate: *They were forced to scrub the whole plan* [ultimately fr the British naval practice of writing signals or orders on a slate, and *scrubbing* or *washing* them out if they were cancelled]

scrub[2] *n fr late 1800s* An athlete who is not on the first or varsity team; a lowly substitute [ultimately fr 16th-century British slang, "a contemptible person, shabby fellow," related to another sense, "an inferior or mongrel animal," the basic notion being stuntedness]

scrub club *n phr* A uniformly ineffectual group, business, project, etc

scrub the slate clean *v phr* To cancel or ignore what has gone before; begin anew: *Let's just scrub the slate clean and pretend it never happened* [perhaps fr the same naval source as *scrub*[1]]

scrud or **double scrud** *fr 1930s Army* **1** *n or n phr* Any disease, esp something quite serious and painful; = CRUD **2** *n or n phr* Any venereal disease; = CRUD

scruff[1] or **scruff along** *v or v phr carnival* To make a bare living; = SCRAPE ALONG

scruff[2] *adj teenagers* = SCRUFFY [fr *scruffy*]

scruffy *adj* Dirty and unkempt; shabby; slovenly: *The scruffy little city, Knoxville, did it*—Wall Street Journal/ *one bearded, sad-eyed, scruffy-looking lad* —Albert Goldman [fr obsolete British *scruff* "valueless, contemptible," probably an alteration of *scurf* "scabbiness of the skin," hence related to *scurvy*]

scrumptious *adj fr early 1800s* Excellent; superior; luxurious [perhaps a humorous alteration of *sumptuous*]

scrunch (Variations: **ooch** or **oonch** or **scooch** or **scrooch** or **scrooge** or **scrouge**) **1** *v* To squeeze oneself into a tighter space: *I scrunched into the corner and covered my ears*/ *She scrooged over and patted the sofa beside her*/ *Ooch over* —WR Burnett **2** *v* To squeeze, esp so as to make small changes: *If what chiefly interests him is literary stunts...the writer can oonch...just a little* —John Gardner/ *He kept tuning the engine to ooch every bit of speed from the boat* [ultimately fr late-16th-century *scruze* "squeeze," perhaps a blend of *screw* and *squeeze*]

scrunge *n student* Dirt; filth; a nasty substance; = GRUNGE: *Wipe the scrunge off your shoe*

scuffle or **scuffle along 1** *v or v phr* To make one's modest living the best one can; struggle along; = GET BY, SCRAPE ALONG **2** *v or v phr jive talk* To dance

◁**scum**▷ *n* Semen; = COME

◁**scumbag**▷ **1** *n fr 1920s* A condom; = RUBBER **2** *n* A despicable person; = ASSHOLE, BASTARD: *calls...Charlton Heston a scumbag*—National Review/ *The scumbag dunno what the fuck she is* —Xaviera Hollander **3** *modifier*: *accused us of practicing scumbag journalism*—Village Voice [fr *scum* "semen"]

◁**scumsucker**▷ **1** *n* A person who does fellatio; = COCKSUCKER: *strumpet called Tony a scumsucker* —San Francisco **2** *n* A despicable person; = SCUMBAG

◁**scumsucking**▷ *adj* Despicable; disgusting: *He's a miserable scumsucking bastard*

a **scunner** *n fr late 1800s* Extreme dislike; hostility: *had taken a scunner against the main competitor* —Atlantic Monthly [fr Scots dialect]

scunnion *See* BRING SCUNNION

scupper *n WW2 Navy* A prostitute [probably fr the sewerish connotations of *scupper* "deck drain on a ship"]

scurve *n* A despicable person; = CRUMB, SCUMBAG, DIRTBAG: *A beer-bottle-in-pocket, fast-talking scurve pushes through the crowd*—Village Voice/ *The scurves are on the street again tonight*—Harpers [fr *scurvy*; see *scruffy*]

scut 1 *n* A detestable or contemptible person; = CRUMB, LOUSE: *You bloody scut!*—Lawrence Sanders **2** *n* A novice; recruit; neophyte: *The fraternity was famous for treating scuts very roughly* **3** *n* (also **scud** or **scut work**) Menial work such as would be given to a novice: *a detention company doing scut work around the fort*—Newsweek **4** *n* (also **scut work**) *hospital* Routine and tedious medical procedures usually relegated to the least senior members of the staff **5** *n hospital* A patient held in very low regard [the 16th-century slang use, "vulva, cunt," and the standard use "tail of a hare or deer," suggest a core sense "tail, buttocks, ass," reinforced by British dialect *skut* "crouch down," and perhaps related to Old Norse *skutr* "stern of a ship"]

scuttle ◀**1**▶ *n cabdrivers* A black person, esp a black taxi passenger; = HOD **2** *n hotel staff* A pitcher or other container filled with ice and delivered to a room [because a *scuttle* is a container for coal, which, as the taboo sense recalls, is black]

scuttlebutt *n Navy fr 1930s* Rumors; gossip; presumed confidential information: *worry about a slump, according to business scuttlebutt*—Associated Press [fr the chit-chat around the *scuttlebutt* "drinking fountain, water cask," on naval vessels]

scuzz *teenagers* **1** *n* (also **scuzzo**) Dirt; filth; a nasty substance; = GRUNGE, MUNG, SCRUNGE: *He has scuzz all over his pants and in his mind* ◁**2**▷ *n* An unattractive young woman; = SCANK, SKAG

scuzzbag or **scuzzo** *n* A despicable person; = CRUMB, SCURVE, SLEAZEBAG: *He calls a minister a "scuzzbag"*—Time

scuzz-food *n* Food like potato chips, popcorn, sugar-coated cereal, etc; = JUNK FOOD: *I will take a back seat to no one as a scuzz-food fanatic*—Car and Driver

scuzz someone **out** *v phr esp teenagers* To disgust mightily; nauseate; = GROSS someone OUT: *With-it slanguists are scuzzed out at the squared-out weirdos who still use grossed out*—William Safire

scuzzy or **scuz** *adj teenagers* Dirty; filthy; repellent; = GRUNGY: *a bunch of scuzzy Moroccan A-rabs* —Village Voice [perhaps fr *disgusting*; perhaps a blend of or influenced by *scum* and *fuzz*]

seaboard *n lunch counter* An order to be taken out [fr *c board*, that is, *cardboard*, referring to the container]

sea cow *n phr WW2 Navy* Milk, esp canned milk

seafood 1 *n esp 1920s underworld* Whiskey **2** *n homosexuals* A sailor regarded as a homosexual sex partner **3** *n* Cunnilingus; = HAIR PIE: *Want some seafood, mama*—Hold Tight (song) **4** *n* A woman regarded as a sex organ for cunnilingus; = EATIN' STUFF [fr various aspects of seafaring, trade, and the taste of *seafood*; the last two senses perhaps a pun, *c food* "cuntfood"]

seagoing bellhop *n phr Navy* A US Marine [fr the colorful and elaborate dress uniform]

seagull *v WW2 Navy* To travel by airplane; fly

sea gull 1 *n phr WW2 Navy & Marine Corps fr Annapolis* Chicken, esp canned or frozen chicken **2** *n phr WW2 Navy* A woman, wife, sweetheart, etc, who follows the fleet **3** *n phr WW2 Navy* A very hearty or gluttonous eater

sea lawyer *See* FORECASTLE LAWYER

seams *See* COME APART AT THE SEAMS

seam squirrel *n phr hoboes & WW2 Army* A body louse; = COOTIE

search me *interj* An exclamation or acknowledgment of ignorance; = BEATS ME: *Who said it? Search me, I couldn't say*

season *See* PINOCHLE SEASON, SILLY SEASON

seas over *See* HALF SEAS OVER

seat *n* The buttocks; = ASS

See BUDDY SEAT, CATBIRD SEAT, DEACON SEAT, DRIVER'S SEAT, the HOT SEAT, SMOKY SEAT, TAKE A BACK SEAT

seat-man 1 *n 1920s circus* A person in the audience who is a confederate of the hawker, barker, etc; = SHILL **2** *n gambling* A professional card dealer

seat-of-the-pants *adj* Inclined to work by instinct, feel, impulse, etc, rather than by precise rules; practical: *The news had seat-of-the-pants editors who knew their audience*—Washingtonian [see *fly by the seat of one's pants*]

seaweed *n Navy* Spinach

sec[1] *n* A second of time: *Come here a sec, Billy* —Sinclair Lewis

sec[2] *n* A secretary: *His femme secs open the mail* —Variety

second *n* A somewhat flawed, soiled, or otherwise not perfect new article for sale

second fiddle 1 *n* A person or thing that is not the most favored, the best, the leader, etc: *definitely second fiddle before the Convention started*—Pete Martin **2** *adj: a sort of second-fiddle appointment*

See PLAY SECOND FIDDLE

second john *n phr WW2 Army* A second lieutenant

second line *v phr early 1900s* To follow the leader or first rank, esp in hope of advancement: *I was "second lining"...following the brass bands in parades*—Louis Armstrong

second off *adv phr* Second in order; secondly: *and, second off, readers and authors both*—New York Times

seconds 1 *n* A second portion of food or drink **2** *n* A pot of coffee brewed from used grounds

second sacker *n phr baseball* A second baseman

second thought *See* DON'T GIVE IT A SECOND THOUGHT

secret *See* DIRTY LITTLE SECRET

section eight or **section 8** *esp WW2 Army* **1** *n phr* A military discharge given for emotional or psychological disability, defective character, or military inaptitude **2** *n phr* A crazy or eccentric person; a neurotic; = NUT [fr *Section VIII*, Army Regulation 615-360]

security blanket *n phr* A thing or person that provides someone with a sense of safety and emotional comfort: *Zeigler instead is...Mr Nixon's "security blanket"*—Newsweek [fr the *blanket* or token fragment of blanket that some small children carry about as a source of comforting familiarity; Charles M Schulz, creator of the comic strip "Peanuts," has claimed coinage of the term]

see 1 *n police* Recognition; complimentary notice by a superior: *He was a good cop ten years, but never got a see* **2** *n police* A visit of inspection: *numerous "sees" or visits from the sergeant*—E Lavine **3** *v underworld* To pay protection money or graft: *doing business without "seeing the cops"*—E Lavine **4** *v poker* To equal a bet or a raise rather than dropping out of the game [first sense perhaps an abbreviation of *commendation*] *See* LONG TIME NO SEE, LOOK SEE, LOOK-SEE

see a man about a dog *v phr fr late 1800s* To take one's leave for some urgent purpose, esp to go to the bathroom or in earlier times to go have a drink or to meet one's bootlegger ● Usu a smiling apology for one's departure; a bland euphemism to conceal one's true purpose

seed *n narcotics* = ROACH *See* BIRDSEED, HAYSEED, SWALLOW A WATERMELON SEED

see pink elephants *v phr* To have hallucinations from alcoholism

see red *v phr* To become very angry: *Politics make him see red*

see the chaplain *sentence WW2 Army* Stop complaining; I can't help you with your problems ● Often part of the advice that one **get a TS ticket and take it to the chaplain**

see the light *v phr* To grasp something finally; understand something one had been ignoring or disbelieving: *She's seen the light and gone to another job*

see the light at the end of the tunnel *v phr esp Vietnam War period* To see at last the beginning of the end of a difficult struggle, period, etc: *The Flower People of Saigon...invite you to see the light at the end of the tunnel*—New York Times

see-through *adj* Transparent; made of a very sheer fabric; = PEEKABOO: *a see-through blouse*

see you *interj* A casual farewell; = SO LONG: *the careless "see you's" that people say*—Life

see-you *n salespersons fr late 1920s* A customer who always asks to be waited on by a certain person

segue or **seg** (SEHG way or SEHG) **1** *v musicians* To go from one piece of music, record, etc, to the next without an obvious break; make a smooth transition **2** *v* To go smoothly from one thing to another: *His features seg rapidly from fascination to fear*—Playgirl/ *So we'll segue from wooing them to screwing them, somehow* **3** *n college students* A sequel; something that follows or follows up [fr Italian, "now follows," an instruction on musical scores]

sell 1 *v outdated fr early 1600s* To cheat; swindle; hoax **2** *n fr middle 1800s:* A hoax or swindle; a deception: *The Cardiff Giant was a "sell"*—AT Vance **3** *v* To convince someone of the value of something; = SELL someone ON something: *I tried to sell him the idea of stopping off in Chicago on our way/ After his spiel I was sold See* HARD SELL, SOFT SELL, be SOLD ON

sell oneself *v phr fr 1920s* To make oneself appealing and successful with an audience, a potential employer, etc

sell someone **down the river** *v phr* To betray; take victimizing advantage of [perhaps fr slavery days, when a black person or escaped slave *sold down the river* was sent to or returned to the South]

selling plater *n phr horse-racing* An inferior race horse: *these selling platers with a shot of dope in them*—Ernest Hemingway

sell someone **on** something *v phr fr early 1900s* To convince someone of the value of something; successfully extol: *She sold me on the new wage policy*

sell out[1] *v phr fr middle 1800s* To become a traitor, esp to prostitute one's ideals, talents, etc, for money or other comforts: *are often labeled Toms and mammies who sold out*—Saturday Review

sell out[2] *v phr* To dispose of entirely by sale: *He sold out all copies of the book the first day/ You can't get that here, we sold out*

sell-out 1 *n* An act or instance of selling out, in either sense: *He disappointed us, but he was honest enough and it was no sell-out/ The new bathing suits should be a quick sell-out* **2** *n* A person who sells out, in the sense of betrayal or pecuniary self-serving: *In spite of his early protestations of loyalty, he was a contemptible sell-out*

sell someone or something **out** *v phr* To betray; sacrifice or desert for one's own advantage: *accuse them of selling out Chiang Kai-shek*—David Halberstam

semolia *n black* A stupid person; fool

send *v esp 1940s jive talk fr jazz talk* To arouse keen admiration, esp as an ecstatic response; excite; = TURN someone ON: *Bessie Smith really sent him*—Stephen Longstreet

sender *See* SOLID SENDER

send-off *n* A funeral: *give a man a classy send-off*—Billy Rose

send someone **to the showers 1** *v phr baseball* To remove or eject a player from a game **2** *v phr* To dismiss or reject someone

send up 1 *v phr* (also **send up the river**) *fr middle 1800s* To send someone to prison: *He got sent up for grand theft* **2** *v phr fr 1930s British* To ridicule, esp by parody; mock; lampoon; = SPOOF: *cracking jokes, sending up everyone and everything in sight*—Rolling Stone [first sense fr or influenced by the course from New York City *up the Hudson River* to Sing Sing Prison at Ossining; second sense fr British public school *sending* of a delinquent boy *up* to the headmaster for punishment]

send-up *n fr British* A mocking, teasing parody; lampoon; = SPOOF: *just another stupid soap send-up*—People Weekly/ *a relentless send-up of attitudes and gestures*—Vincent Canby

sensaysh (sen SAYSH) *adj* Sensational: *I had a sensaysh time*—Max Shulman

sergeant *See* BUCK SERGEANT

serious 1 *adj black fr 1940s bop talk* Very commendable; excellent; superb **2** *adj* Intended to make a good and sober impression; overtly conformistic; = SINCERE: *in a serious suit and striped tie*—Dan Jenkins

See FOR SERIOUS

session 1 *n esp 1930s teenagers* A dance or party; = HOP **2** *n narcotics* The period of intoxication from a dose of narcotics, esp of LSD; = TRIP **3** *n musicians* An occasion at which a recording is made in a studio; a studio rehearsal or performance: *They never let anybody in for their sessions, not even their families* **4** *modifier: He used to do a lot of session playing but hardly ever worked for an audience*

See BITCH SESSION, BULL SESSION, GRIPE SESSION, HASH SESSION, JAM SESSION, RAP SESSION, SKULL SESSION

set 1 *n musicians* The group of pieces musicians perform during about a 45-minute period at a club, show, etc: *clarinetist Scott opened his set*—Metronome **2** *n jazz musicians* An improvisatory musical interchange of about half an hour **3** *n black & jazz talk* A small party or friendly conversational gathering; = SCENE: *Don't stop belly rubbing just because we showed on the set*—Donald Goines **4** *n chiefly black* A discussion; = RAP: *He never said get those Panthers out...all through the whole set*—Bobby Seale **5** *n narcotics* A narcotic dose of two Seconals (a trade name) and one amphetamine

See the BUBBLE-GUM SET, the JET SET

set someone **back** *v phr fr late 1800s* To cost: *How much will it set me back if I order a plain steak?*—H McHugh/ *set us back what was then an astonishing $18 a person*—San Francisco

set of pipes *See* PIPES

set of threads (or **drapes**) *n phr jazz & bop talk fr 1940s* A suit of clothing, esp a new and stylish one: *the smart set of threads*—Stephen Longstreet

set of wheels *n phr* A car: *if you're feverish for a great set of wheels*—Playboy

set someone **over** *v phr 1920s underworld* To kill; murder; = RUB OUT: *They have to set a guy over*—WR Burnett

settle *n early 1900s underworld* To imprison, esp for a life sentence: *Foley was "pinched" and "settled" in San Quentin*—Literary Digest

settle (or **fix**) someone's **hash** *fr late 1700s* **1** *v phr* To injure or ruin someone definitively; = FINISH, COOK someone's GOOSE: *I'll check you out after I settle his hash*—Pulpsmith **2** *v phr* To deflate; humiliate; defeat; = FIX someone's WAGON [origin unknown; semantically related to such similar and ironic expressions as *clean someone's clock, cook someone's goose,* and *fix someone's wagon*]

setup 1 *n* A person who is easily duped, tricked, etc; = PATSY, SUCKER: *a set-up, a tout's dream come true*—J Lilienthal **2** *n 1920s underworld* A one-day jail sentence **3** *n fr 1920s* A glass, ice, soda, etc, to be mixed with liquor: *They supplied the setups*—NY Confidential **4** *n lunch counter & restaurant fr 1920s* Dishes, utensils, etc, constituting a place setting for a meal **5** *n* Arrangement; organization; situation; mode of operation: *except its size and its co-op set-up*—New York Times/ *She strode in, looked around, and asked what was the setup* **6** *n* A house, office, apartment, etc: *He has a very comfy setup in a rehabbed brownstone* [most senses apparently fr the *setting up* of billiard or pool balls to insure a special or a trick shot]

set up *adj* Gratified; elated; braced: *He looks real set up now that they've published his book*

set someone **up 1** *v phr* To prepare and maneuver someone for swindling, tricking, etc; = BUILD **2** *v phr* To gratify and encourage; brace: *Finishing first for a change really set me up* **3** *v phr fr middle 1800s* To treat someone; provide food or drink

seventeen *See* FILE SEVENTEEN

seventeener *n underworld fr early 1900s Australian* A corpse [origin unknown]

Seventh Avenue *n phr* The garment and fashion industry; = the RAG TRADE [fr the fact that New York City's *Seventh Avenue* is the traditional center of the garment industry]

seventy-'leven 1 *n* An indefinite large number; = FORTY-'LEVEN **2** *modifier: about seventy-'leven years*

sewer *n narcotics* A vein or artery: *if I had put it right in the sewer instead of skin popping*—RV Winslow

sewer hog *n phr construction workers* A ditch digger

sew something **up 1** *v phr* To finish; put the finishing touches on: *They sewed up the contract today* **2** *v phr* To insure a victory; make a conclusive score, stroke, etc; = CLINCH, ICE: *The last-period goal sewed it up for the Drew Rangers*

sex *See* UNISEX

sex goddess *n phr* A woman, usu a movie star, who is a provocative and famous sexual object

sex job *n phr* A sexually attractive, provocative, or available person

sex kitten (or **bunny**) *n phr* A young woman who is highly attractive, provocative, and seemingly available sexually

sexpert *n* A sex expert, esp a therapist who treats persons complaining of sexual dysfunction: *The behavioristic sexpert would call this situation homosexuality*—Playboy

sexploitation 1 *n* Commercial exploitation of sex: *Female chauvinist sexploitation will reach a new level*—Time **2 modifier:** *a camp sexploitation horror musical*—Esquire

sexpot *n* A person, esp a woman, who is especially attractive and provocative sexually: *How pitiful the American who cannot command the smile of a sexpot*—Frederic Morton

sex wagon *n phr* =PIMPMOBILE

sexy *adj* Very appealing; exciting; desirable; stimulating: *hyping the sexy "career education" schools* —Village Voice/ *Acid rain is politically sexy but it hasn't half the allure of jobs*—Toronto Life

-sey *See* -IE

sez (or **sezz**) **you** *See* SAYS YOU

shack 1 *n* railroad The caboose of a freight train **2** *n* railroad, hoboes & circus A railroad brake operator, who rode in the caboose **3** *n* hoboes Any place where hoboes meet **4** *n* radio operators & ham radio A radio office or radio room **5** *n* =SHACK JOB **6** *v* =SHACK UP [fr late-19th-century *shack* "hut, shanty," probably fr earlier *shackle* fr American Spanish *jacal* fr Aztec *xacalli*]

shack fever hoboes **1** *n phr* Fatigue; drowsiness **2** *n phr* Fear, fatigue, etc, which keeps a hobo from traveling [perhaps fr the notion that anything keeping a hobo off the road and sequestered in a *shack* is a sort of disease]

◁**shack job**▷ *n phr* esp WW2 Army A woman one lives with adulterously; common-law wife; mistress: *This was an early shack-job, not the girl mentioned above*—New Yorker

shackles *n* fr early 1900s British Stew or soup [probably fr British dialect *shacklebone* "knucklebone," suggesting that the stew or soup is made of scant and inferior meat]

shack man (or **rat**) *n phr* esp WW2 Army A man who lives with or does the sex act with a woman who is not his wife; a man who keeps a mistress

shack up 1 *v phr* esp WW2 Army fr 1920s truckers & traveling salespersons To live with, do the sex act with, and support a woman who is not one's wife; keep a mistress: *The medicine man had shacked up with a halfbreed cook*—Time/ *When I was 13 I shacked up with a Puerto Rican chick of 38* —New York **2** *v phr* To do the sex act; esp, to lead a promiscuous sex life; =SLEEP AROUND: *If you drink and shack up with strangers you get old at thirty*—Tennessee Williams **3** *v phr* To live; reside, esp in a nonpermanent place: *got rid of his home and shacked up in a hotel*—Westbrook Pegler

shade ◁1▶ *n* fr middle 1800s A black person **2** *n* esp 1920s underworld A receiver of stolen goods; =FENCE: *It is sold to a "fence" or "shade"* —Collier's **3** *v* sports To defeat by a narrow margin: *Michigan shaded Iowa. The final score was 98 to 96*

shades *n* fr 1940s bop musicians Sunglasses

◁**shad-mouth**▷ **1** *n* A person with a prominent upper lip **2** *n* black A black person

shadow ◁1▶ *n* A black person **2** *v* fr late 1800s To follow a person secretly; do physical surveillance; =TAIL **3** *n:* *They put a shadow on the suspect*

shadow gazer *n phr* hospital A radiologist

◁**shaft**▷ *v* To treat unfairly or cruelly; victimize: *The good guys always get shafted/ When do you shaft a pal, when do you hand him the poison cup?*—Saul Bellow/ *The oil companies you leased the land to shafted you out of an estimated $650 million*—Art Buchwald [fr the notion of sodomizing a victim]

◁**the shaft** or **a shafting**▷ *n phr* Unfair or cruel treatment: *Jamaicans have learned from past experience to expect the shaft from foreign journalists* —Newsweek/ *He was hoping for a raise and got a shafting*
See GET THE SHAFT, GIVE someone THE SHAFT

shag 1 *v* fr middle 1800s To depart; leave, esp quickly; =SHAG ASS: *You'd best shag now*—W Henry **2** *v* fr late 1800s To chase: *I was allowed to "shag" foul balls*—CH Claudy/ *shagging rabbits* —E Kasser **3** *v* 1930s teenagers To tease and harass; =HASSLE, HOUND **4** *n* teenagers fr 1930s A party or session where boys and girls experiment sexually: *The kids were fondling each other, having a shag* **5** *n* A person's date or escort; =DRAG: *He didn't have a shag for the prom* **6** *adj* With a date or escort: *Did you go to the party stag or shag?* **7** *adj* esp 1950s teenagers Excellent; wonderful [all senses probably ultimately fr *shake* by way of *shack*; the sexual senses are attested in late-18th-century British slang]
See GANG BANG

◁**shag ass**▷ *v phr* To depart; leave, esp hurriedly; =HAUL ASS, SCRAM

shagger *n* A person who follows another secretly; =SHADOW, TAIL [fr *shag* "chase"]

shake 1 *n* fr middle 1800s A dance: *charge a few coins and have a shake*—Louis Armstrong **2** *n* A moment; =SEC: *Be ready in two shakes* **3** *n* fr 1920s Blackmail or extortion; =SHAKEDOWN: *This isn't any kind of a shake*—Raymond Chandler **4** *v:* *tried to shake one of the big boys*—Raymond Chandler **5** *v* To search a person or place thoroughly; =SHAKE DOWN **6** *n:* *We'd better give the entire house a shake; I know it's here somewhere* **7** *v* =GIVE someone THE SHAKE
See a FAIR SHAKE, HALF A SHAKE, ON THE SHAKE, SKINSEARCH, TWO SHAKES

shake a leg *v phr* fr late 1800s To hurry; speed up

shake a wicked calf *v phr* (Variations: **mean** may replace **wicked**; **hoof** or **leg** may replace **calf**) esp 1920s To dance well, impressively, or joyfully: *Phoebe and I are going to shake a wicked calf* —F Scott Fitzgerald

shakedown 1 *n* fr early 1700s A night's lodging; an impromptu bed **2** *n* Sleep: *I'll get a shakedown on the couch*—The Thirty-Nine Steps (movie) **3** *n* fr underworld An instance of or a demand for blackmail, extortion, etc; victimization by the protection racket: *Listen, I know this is a shakedown*—New

York **4** *n* A thorough search of a person or place; =SHAKE: *We gave the room a first-class shakedown*—R Starnes **5** *n* A trying-out or first tentative use, esp of a machine, ship, process, etc: *Let's give this new idea a shakedown and see if it works* [final sense fr *shakedown cruise*]

shake down 1 *v phr* To blackmail or extort; demand protection money: *shaking down poor peddlers, newsboys*—E Lavine/ *The cat who was shaking you down heard some change jingling*—Claude Brown **2** *v phr* To search a person or place thoroughly; =SHAKE: *a couple of policemen to shake down the neighborhood*—R Starnes

shakedown cruise *n phr* Navy fr early 1900s A cruise or sea trial for a new or a newly repaired ship

shake it or **shake it up** *v phr* To hurry; =SHAKE A LEG: *We've got to shake it*—Dashiell Hammett

shake one *v phr* lunch counter To make a milk shake

shakeout *n* A business upheaval, esp a reduction in the number of competitors in a field; a spate of failures and bankruptcies: *The central event was a major shakeout and contraction of the Eurodollar market*—Fortune/ *There will be thousands of "locals," then a big shakeout*—Saturday Review/ *The recorded-music business is going through a significant shakeout*—New York

shaker *See* BONE-SHAKER

the **shakes** *n phr* An attack of trembling, esp one due to alcoholism or drug abuse; =the CLANKS

shake the money tree *v phr* To produce profit, esp in great amounts: *It took two to shake the money tree*—Village Voice

shake-up 1 *n* fr late 1800s The reorganization of a working group, its methods, etc, usu including some dismissals: *The remedy is a shake-up in the Bureau of the Budget*—Ithaca Journal **2** *n* A mixture of several liquors shaken and drunk

shaking *See* WHAT'S SHAKING

shalump *See* SCHLOOMP

shame *See* DIRTY SHAME

shamrock or **shambro** or **shambrogue** *n* Any of several mixed drinks, esp a mixture of whiskey and stout

shamus (SHAH məs, SHAY-) (also **shammus** or **shamos** or **shommus**) **1** *n* A police officer, private detective, security guard, etc; =COP: *a British-accented burlesque of the tough American shamus*—New York Times/ *scores of hoodlums, gunsels, informers, shyster lawyers, and crooked shamuses*—SJ Perelman **2** *n* A police informer; =STOOL PIGEON [fr Yiddish, "sexton of a synagogue," fr Hebrew *shamash* "servant"; probably influenced by the Celtic name *Seamus* "James," as a typical name of an Irish police officer]

Shangri La *n phr* esp 1930s & 40s An ideal place of leisure and secure remoteness; an earthly paradise [fr the fictional Himalayan country in James Hilton's novel *Lost Horizon*]

shank 1 *n* prison & street gang fr 1950s A stiletto-like weapon: *We'd yoke him with a shank*—New York Post/ *looks like a large screwdriver and is known in prison parlance as a shank*—Philadel-phia Journal **2** *v: that dude the dicks want for shanking his old lady*—Joseph Wambaugh **3** *v* sports To kick: *is shanking punts all over the lot*—Philadelphia **4** *n* fr early 1800s The end or last part of a period of time, esp of the evening ● Also interpreted as the early or chief part of a period of time: *Let's have one for the road, my friends, it's the shank of the evening/ Leaving already? It's only the shank of the evening* [all senses reflect the basic notion of something long and thin] *See* CHANK

shank it *v phr* early 1900s To walk; hike

shank's mare *See* RIDE SHANK'S MARE

shanty 1 *n* fr early 1800s A rickety hut; a hovel; a shack **2** *n* railroad A caboose [probably fr Irish *sean-tig*; perhaps fr Canadian French *chantier*, although this is more probably a borrowing of *shanty*]

◁**shanty Irish**▷ *n phr* Poor or disreputable Irish people: *oh, not shanty Irish*—Stephen Longstreet

shantytown fr late 1800s **1** *n* A poor, dilapidated neighborhood **2** *n* A cluster of makeshift dwellings, often on the edge of a town and inhabited by the vagrant or the very poor; =HOOVERVILLE

shape *See* BENT OUT OF SHAPE, DRAPE SHAPE

shape up 1 *v phr* (also **shape up or ship out**) esp WW2 armed forces fr cowboys To correct one's behavior; conform and perform ● Often a firm command or admonition: *From this day on you're going to shape up or ship out. Is that understood?* —Art Buchwald/ *a message to Martin S Feldstein....The message was: Shape up, or ship out* —Washington Post **2** *v phr* To progress; go along: *How are your plans shaping up?*

shape someone **up** *v phr* esp WW2 armed forces To cause someone to conform and perform; correct someone's behavior: *praying for a good depression that could shape these kids up*—World

shark 1 *n* fr 1500s A confidence man or swindler; =HUSTLER, SHARP **2** *n* early 1900s college students A very able student, esp one who does not seem to work hard **3** *n* esp 1920s & 30s An expert, esp a somewhat exploitive or unscrupulous one ● Usually preceded by a modifier showing the field of skill: *He was a real pool-shark, a hustler/ I got to be a computer shark/ the gun-shark's report* —Raymond Chandler **4** *n* hoboes An employment agent; a hiring boss [all senses fr the predaceous fish, except that the oldest sense may originally have been fr German *schurke* "rascal"]

See CARD SHARK, LOAN SHARK

sharp 1 *n* fr middle 1800s An expert, esp at card games; =PRO: *Hurstwood's a regular sharp*—Theodore Dreiser **2** *n* (also **sharper**) fr late 1700s A confidence trickster; a swindler, esp a dishonest card player; =CARD SHARP **3** *adj* fr jive talk Stylish; of the latest and most sophisticated sort: *He wore bow ties and sharp suits*—Truman Capote **4** *adj* fr jive talk Good; excellent; admirable; =COOL: *I sound like everything was sharp*—John O'Hara *See* CARD SHARP

sharpie 1 *n* jive talk A devotee of swing music, esp one who dances well to swing **2** *n* fr jive talk

A stylish dresser in the flashy modes: *and not just among the sharpies*—Associated Press **3** *modifier:* *an incredible sharpie opulence of leather pockets and hand-wrought belt loops*—New York **4** *n* A shrewd person watchful of his or her profit: *an open invitation for a sharpie to have the free use of a new car for 30 days*—Time **5** *n* A confidence trickster; a swindler; = SHARP, SHARK: *They were outwitted...by three "sharpies"*—Associated Press/ *been beset by hustlers, sharpies, hangers-on, bad-advice artists*—Playboy

◁**shat on**▷ *v phr* Maltreated; victimized; = SHAFTED: *Because women have been shat on for centuries*—Off Our Backs [fr the humorous past tense form of *shit*]

◁**shatting on** one's **uppers**▷ *adj phr fr late 1800s* hoboes Entirely out of money; = BROKE: *She has to blow and she's shatting on her uppers*—Raymond Chandler [fr *shat*, humorous past tense of *shit*, and uppers "shoes so worn they have no soles"]

shaved 1 *adj* Drunk **2** *adj* hot rodders Having the ornamental and other nonfunctional parts removed; = STRIPPED DOWN

See HALF-SHAVED

shave points or **shave** *v phr* or *v sports & gambling* To get a gambling or money advantage by failing to score as much as one could; fraudulently lose a game

shaver *See* LITTLE SHAVER

shavetail *n* Army *fr late 1800s* A second lieutenant, esp a newly commissioned one [perhaps fr an early-19th-century sense, "unbroken Army mule"; perhaps also fr the fact that a newly commissioned officer might have shoulder straps made with material cut off the shirttail]

shaving *See* POINT-SHAVING

shay *See* GANG BANG

shazam (shə ZAM) *interj* An exclamation of triumphant and delighted announcement, emphasis, etc: *SHAZAM! He was up on the table*—Richard Fariña/ *Go ahead and say it, Shazam!, juice it up*—Tom Wolfe [fr the operative or command word of a magician, similar to *presto change-o*]

the **shebang** (shə BANG, shee-) *n* Everything; = the WHOLE SHEBANG: *You can have the shebang* [fr a mid-19th-century sense, "shanty, hut," of obscure origin; perhaps fr an approximate pronunciation of French *char-à-banc*, "bus-like wagon with many seats," in which case the semantics of *the whole shebang* would depend upon the hiring of the whole vehicle rather than one or two seats]

she can sit on my face any time *sentence* She attracts me very powerfully in a basic sexual way

shed *See* WOODSHED

shee *See* YEN-SHEE

◁**shee-it**▷ (SHEE ət) *interj* = SHIT [a humorous imitation of a drawled Southern pronunciation]

◀**sheeny** or **sheenie**▶ **1** *n fr early 1800s* British A Jew **2** *adj:* *one of those Sheeny employment bureaus*—Sinclair Lewis **3** *n* A pawnbroker, tailor, junkman, or member of another traditionally Jewish occupation [origin unknown]

sheep-dip 1 *n* Inferior whiskey; = ROTGUT **2** *v* espionage To cause a military officer to become a civilian, at least purportedly, before undertaking a nonmilitary mission

sheepskin *n fr 1700s* A college or university diploma [fr the fact that diplomas used to be made of *sheepskin*]

sheesh[1] *interj* An exclamation of disgust, frustration, etc: *Pronounce this...sheesh! and it gives you some idea of what you'll say living with a cheap bastard*—Village Voice [a euphemism for *shit*]

sheesh[2] *n narcotics* Hashish

sheet 1 *n* A newspaper: *Both morning sheets have written it up*—J Evans **2** *n* police = RAP SHEET

See DOPE SHEET, POOP SHEET, RAP SHEET, SCRATCH SHEET, SOUND SHEET, SWINDLE SHEET, THREE SHEETS TO THE WIND

the **sheets** *n fr hoboes* Money: *You ain't got any clothes or anything when you ain't got the sheets*—James T Farrell

sheik (SHEEK) *esp 1920s* **1** *n* A handsome, sleek, romantic male lover; a ladies' man **2** *v* To attempt to captivate; charm; seduce: *Are you sheiking me, Ralph?*—New York Times [fr the 1922 movie *The Sheik*, starring Rudolph Valentino]

sheive *See* SHIV

shekels (SHEK əls) *n fr middle 1800s* Money; wealth [fr the Hebrew name of a unit of weight and money]

shelf *See* ON THE SHELF

shell 1 *n outdated underworld* A safe; a vault **2** *v* To pay; = SHELL OUT: *to shell at least a buck*—NY Confidential

See HARD-SHELL

shellac *v sports* To defeat decisively; trounce; = CLOBBER: *The Giants got shellacked again Monday* [perhaps fr the use of *shellac* as a finish]

shellacked *adj* Drunk: *One of the boys got beautifully shellacked*—Philadelphia Bulletin

shellacking 1 *n* A beating: *"Shellacking"...and numerous other phrases are employed by the police as euphemisms*—E Lavine **2** *n* sports A decisive defeat; a drubbing; an utter rout: *Should Black take a shellacking, the National Leaguers are in bad trouble*—Associated Press

shell out *v phr fr early 1800s* To pay; put out; contribute; = FORK OVER: *get ready to shell out again*—Associated Press/ *Several companies shelled out upwards of $150,000 for the weekend's fun and games*—Rolling Stone

shells *See* CLAM SHELLS

shemale 1 *n* A female **2** *n* A male transvestite

shemozzle (also **shimozzle** or **shlamozzle** or **shlemozzle**) *chiefly British & Canadian fr late 1800s* **1** *n* A difficult and confused situation; an uproar; melee; = MESS, RHUBARB: *His quiet announcement touched off a dreadful shemozzle/ It became clear that the whole shlamozzle, introns and exons, are transcribed into RNA*—Gordon Rattray Taylor **2** *v* To depart; = POWDER, SCRAM [ultimately probably fr Yiddish *shlim mazel* "rotten luck," hence "a difficulty or misfortune," and related to *shlemazel*]

shenanigan or **shenanigans** *n fr middle 1800s Western* A trick or bit of foolery; a mild cheat or deception [origin unknown; perhaps fr Irish *sion-nachuighim* "play tricks, be foxy"]

Sherpa or **sherpa** *n* A high-ranking assistant of a head of state, esp one who makes the arrangements for a summit meeting: *high-level civil servants known in the diplomatic community as Sherpas* —New York Times [fr the Himalayan tribe that specializes in guiding and assisting mountain climbers to summits]

she-she *n WW2 armed forces* A young woman; =CHICK [based on Pidgin English; the term originated in the Pacific area]

shiever (SHEEVER) *n 1920s underworld* A traitor or informer: *The worst thing you can call a crook is a "shiever"*—H McLellan [probably fr the notion of being stabbed in the back with a *shieve* or *shiv*]

shift *See* GRAVEYARD SHIFT, LOBSTER SHIFT, SWING SHIFT

shifter *underworld* **1** *n early 1900s* A grafter **2** *n* A receiver of stolen goods; =FENCE **3** *n* An agent who mediates between a thief and a receiver of stolen goods

shift (or **move**) **into high gear** *v phr* To begin to work at top speed; become serious: *although the Senate hearings are just shifting into high gear* —George Will

shikker or **shicker** *adj* Drunk: *We'll eat good, then we'll get shikker*—AJ Liebling/ *Doyle, The Shicker Goy*—Philip Roth [fr Yiddish fr Hebrew *shikkur*]

See ON THE SHIKKER

shikkered *adj esp Australian* Drunk

◁**shikse** or **shiksa** or **shikseh**▷ (SHIK sə) *n* A non-Jewish woman, esp a young woman ● Usually at least somewhat derogatory: *That Alice was so blatantly a shikse caused no end of grief*—Philip Roth [fr Yiddish fr Hebrew *sheques*, literally "blemish"]

shill[1] **1** *n* (also **shillaber**) *fr circus* An associate of an auctioneer, gambler, hawker, etc, who pretends to be a member of the audience and stimulates it to desired action: *The shill is innocuous-looking*—New York Times **2** *v: That summer he shilled for a sidewalk hawker* **3** *n fr 1940s* A barker, hawker, advertising or public relations person, or anyone else whose job is to stimulate business; =FLACK [origin unknown; perhaps, since it is a shortening of *shillaber*, ultimately fr *Shillibeer*, the name of an early-19th-century British owner of a large bus company, the reference being to persons hired as decoys to sit in buses and attract passengers]

shill[2] *n* A police officer's nightstick [fr Irish *shillelagh* "cudgel," fr the name of a town famous for oak trees]

shim *n esp 1950s rock and roll* A person not appreciative of rock and roll; = CLYDE

shimmy[1] *n* (also **shimmy shirt**) *esp early 1900s fr middle 1800s* A woman's chemise: *to persuade the young matron to doff her wet shimmy*—SJ Perelman [fr *chemise*]

shimmy[2] **1** *n* A very energetic vibrational dance and dancing style **2** *v: I wish that I could shimmy like my sister Kate* **3** *n* A flick or flirting of the buttocks: *She calls to the owner, with a little shimmy* —New York **4** *n* (also **shimmy pudding**) *lunch counter* Gelatin desserts and other foods that shake when moved

shimmy[3] *n gambling* Chemin de fer: *a "shimmy" (chemin de fer) table*—J Scarne

shimmy in the hay *n phr lunch counter* Strawberry gelatin

shimozzle *See* SHEMOZZLE

shindig *n fr middle 1800s* A party, reception, festival, etc, esp a noisy dancing party; =CLAMBAKE [probably fr *shin dig* "a blow on the shin incurred while dancing"; perhaps by folk etymology fr the older *shindy*]

shindy *n fr early 1800s British nautical* An uproar; a confused struggle; =DONNYBROOK [origin unknown; perhaps fr Irish *sinteag* "skip, caper"; perhaps fr *shinny*, the name of a rough hockey-like schoolboy game; perhaps fr Romany *chindi* "a cut, a cutting up"]

shine ◀**1**▶ *n fr early 1900s* A black person ◀**2**▶ *modifier: another shine killing*—Raymond Chandler **3** *n* Bootleg whiskey; =MOONSHINE: *non-blinding shine sold in fruit jars*—Robert Ruark **4** *v teenagers fr black* To ignore; disregard; avoid; =SKIP **5** *v students* To abandon; fail; =PUNT [the racial sense may have originated among blacks, may refer to the glossiness of a very black skin, and hence may reflect the caste system based upon color; among white speakers, this sense was surely influenced by the fact that most *shoeshine* persons were black; the teenager sense has a black parallel, *shine on*, and the origin may be the poetic notion that when one turns one's back on something one is letting his "moon (that is, buttocks) *shine on*" it]

See MONKEYSHINES, STICK IT, TAKE A SHINE TO someone or something, WHERE THE SUN DOESN'T SHINE

◀**shine box**▶ *n phr* A black bar, nightclub, etc

shiner **1** *n fr early 1900s* A bruise near the eye; =BLACK EYE, MOUSE: *a pip of a shiner*—John McNulty **2** *n gambling* A shiny table top or other mirror-like surface a dealer can use to see the faces of the cards he deals **3** *n railroad* A train crew's lantern

shines *See* MAKE HAY

shine up to someone *v phr fr late 1800s* To court and flatter someone; curry favor; =SUCK UP TO someone

shingle *n fr middle 1800s* A signboard, esp one designating professional services: *He got him a shingle and started practice last year*

See HANG UP one's SHINGLE, SHIT ON A SHINGLE

shinny or **shinny up** *v fr middle 1800s* To climb a rope, pole, wall, etc [fr the use of *shins* and ankles in climbing a rope or pole]

Shinola *See* NOT KNOW SHIT FROM SHINOLA

ship *See* PUMP BILGE, SHAPE UP OR SHIP OUT

shirt *See* BET YOUR BOOTS, BOILED SHIRT, GIVE someone THE SHIRT OFF one's BACK, KEEP one's SHIRT ON, SHIMMY, SKIVVY, STUFFED SHIRT

shirttail 1 *adj* Impoverished; mean; paltry: *My brother and I had a pretty shirttail existence as kids* —Playboy **2** *n newspaper office* An editorial column: *The boss blurbed the story in his shirttail* —Collier's [both senses depend on the *shirttail* being a short appendage to a shirt; the first sense derives fr the shortness, hence meagerness, the second fr the appendedness, the editor's personal addition]

shirttail kin *n phr Southern & Midwestern* Distant relations; third and fourth cousins, etc

shirty *adj fr middle 1800s British* Angry; very upset; = HUFFY, PISSED OFF: *He was a little ashamed of himself for getting shirty with Ivar*—Lawrence Sanders [said to be fr the dishevelment resulting when one is actively angry, since a mid-19th-century verb variant was *get someone's shirt out*]

◁**shit**▷ **1** *n fr 800s or earlier* Feces; excrement; = CRAP, POO **2** *v*: *They diurnally shit, shave, and shower* **3** *interj* An exclamation of disbelief, disgust, disappointment, emphasis, etc: *Oh, shit, I missed the bus!/ Shit, I never had it so good!* **4** *n* Nonsense; pretentious talk; bold and deceitful absurdities; = BULLSHIT: *The judge was talking a lot of shit* **5** *v* To lie; exaggerate; try to deceive: *"Don't shit me," said Dina*—Joseph Heller/ *"You're shitting me, baby," he said*—Lawrence Sanders/ *The sky's the limit, Wilson, I shit you not* —WR Tyler **6** *n* Offensive and contemptuous treatment; disrespect; insults: *I took a lot of shit from her before I left* **7** *n* Anything of shoddy and inferior quality; pretentious and meretricious trash; = CRAP, DRECK: *a costly flop, gilded shit/ What kind of shit are they selling here?* **8** *modifier*: *as well as shit loans to companies like Massey-Ferguson and Turbo Resources*—Toronto Life **9** *n* One's possessions; one's personal effects: *Get your shit, both of you are moving*—Donald Goines **10** *n* An obnoxious, disgusting, or contemptible person; a despicable wretch; = PRICK, SHITHEEL **11** *v* To respond powerfully, esp with alarm, anger, or panic: *He'll shit when we tell him about this* **12** *n* narcotics Heroin; = HORSE: *insisted on retaining the word "shit" as junkie slang for heroin*—Dwight MacDonald **13** *n* Nothing; the least quantity; = DIDDLY: *of whom I hadn't seen shit*—R Grossbach/ *He doesn't know shit about his own subject/ The millionaires gave him shit*—Joseph Heller/ *Engine's froze up, frame's out of line, not worth shit*—WT Tyler

See ACT LIKE one's SHIT DOESN'T STINK, ALL THAT KIND OF CRAP, BAD SHIT, BEAT THE SHIT OUT OF someone or something, as BLAZES, BULLSHIT, CHICKEN SHIT, CLEAN UP one's ACT, CROCK, the DAY THE EAGLE SHITS, DEEP TROUBLE, DIDDLY, DOES A BEAR SHIT IN THE WOODS, DOODLE-SHIT, EAT SHIT, FULL OF SHIT, GOOD SHIT, HAVE SHIT FOR BRAINS, HOLY COW, HOLY SHIT, HORSESHIT, HOT SHIT, I'LL BE DAMNED, LIKE HELL, LIKE PIGS IN CLOVER, LIKE SHIT THROUGH A TIN HORN, LOOK LIKE TEN POUNDS OF SHIT IN A FIVE-POUND

BAG, NO SHIT, NOT GIVE A DAMN, NOT KNOW BEANS, NOT KNOW SHIT FROM SHINOLA, PIECE OF SHIT, PILE OF SHIT, SCARE THE SHIT OUT OF someone, SHOOT THE BULL, SHOVEL THE SHIT, STRONGER THAN PIG SHIT, SURE AS SHIT, TAKE A DUMP, TAKE SHIT, THINK one IS KING SHIT, THINK one's SHIT DOESN'T STINK, TICKLE THE SHIT OUT OF someone, TOUGH SHIT, TREAT someone LIKE A DOORMAT, WORTH A DAMN

◁**shit a brick** (or **bricks**)▷ *v phr* To be very upset and angry; have an emotional crisis; = SWEAT BULLETS: *At Cheri's, Mott was shitting a brick*—Richard Price/ *Swarthmore College would shit a brick*—Off Our Backs/ *I had a few scenes where I was really shittin' bricks*—Rolling Stone

◁**shit-all**▷ *adj* Not any; none at all: *Monica, we have shit-all evidence of what the killer looks like*—Lawrence Sanders [related to and perhaps derived fr British *bugger-all* and *fuck-all* in the same sense, used as intensives and based on *not at all*; Dylan Thomas's mythical Welsh village *Llareggub* has a pseudo-Welsh name which is *bugger-all* spelled backwards]

◁**shit-ass**▷ **1** *n* An insignificant, contemptible person; = JERK **2** *n* = SHITHEEL **3** *v* To behave like a despicable or contemptible person, esp by betrayal of a duty or promise: *I don't want anybody shitassing out of it*—Jackie Collins

◁**shit bullets**▷ *See* SWEAT BULLETS

◁**shitcan**▷ *v* To discard; throw away; abandon: *If it rained before he entered the tunnel, he would have to shitcan his plans*—Easyriders/ *I'd already kind of shitcanned the idea*—Stephen King [fr *shitcan* "refuse can"]

shit creek *See* UP SHIT CREEK

◁one's **shit doesn't stink**▷ *See* THINK one's SHIT DOESN'T STINK

◁**shit-eating grin**▷ *n phr* An expression of satisfaction; a gloating look: *Go ahead, sit there with that shit-eating grin on your face*—Earl Thompson/ *stood there with a smug, shiteating grin on his face* —Fingered City

◁**shit-faced**▷ *adj esp students* Drunk

◁**shit fit**▷ *See* HAVE A SHIT FIT

◁**shit-for-brains**▷ *n* A very stupid person: *What's old Shit-for-brains trying to say?*
See HAVE SHIT FOR BRAINS

◁**shit for the birds**▷ *n phr esp WW2 armed forces* Nonsense; lies and exaggerations; = BULLSHIT [probably an alteration of *birdshit* akin to *chickenshit*]
See FOR THE BIRDS

◁**shit green**▷ *v phr* To be alarmed, shocked, or enraged; = SHIT A BRICK: *The second the going gets jumpy, you shit green*—Patrick Mann

◁**shithead** or **shitface**▷ **1** *n* A stupid, confused, and blundering person; = FUCK-UP: *and this shithead comes sneaking around, asking questions*—WT Tyler **2** *n* = SHITHEEL

◁**shitheel**▷ *n* A despicable person; a scoundrel and blackguard; = BASTARD, PRICK [probably an intensive form of *heel*]

◁the **shit hits the fan**▷ *sentence fr 1930s* Trouble breaks out; a fearful crisis ensues; things turn nasty

● Often part of a time clause beginning with **when** or **then**: *The shit is going to hit the fan, buddy* —Philip Roth/ *The shit didn't hit the fan till this guy, Eddie Jaffe, takes the pad*—Rocky Graziano/ *"When the shit hit the fan," says a local wholesaler* —Philadelphia [apparently fr and certainly related to the classical joke about the man who, finding no toilet, defecated into a hole in the floor; back downstairs, finding the barroom emptied of its celebrants, he inquired why, and was asked, "Where were you when the shit hit the fan?"]

◁**shithook**▷ *n* = SHITHEEL

◁**shithouse**▷ **1** *n* A toilet: *This ain't no shithouse, man*—John R Powers **2** *n* A filthy, sloppy place; a shambles: *How can you live in this shithouse?/ The kid's room was always a shithouse*
See BUILT LIKE A BRICK SHITHOUSE

◁a **shithouse full**▷ *n phr* A very large number or amount; = OODLES: *He had to wade through a shithouse full of people to get here*

◁**shit in high cotton**▷ *v phr* To live well and opulently; enjoy prosperity, esp newly; = EAT HIGH OFF THE HOG, PISS ON ICE [fr the notion that well-grown *cotton* means wealth]

◁**shit** (or **go shit**) **in your hat**▷ *sentence* = GO TO HELL, GO FUCK oneself: *It's unfair, but say so and people tell you to go shit in your hat*—Village Voice

◁**shitkicker**▷ **1** *n* A farmer or other rural person; = HICK, RUBE: *looked like he'd just come off the farm and was nothing but a Midwest shitkicker* —Washingtonian/ *raise the shitkicker however high the gods may*—Murray Kempton **2** *adj* Rural; country; country and western: *the old shitkicker country guitarist*—George Warren **3** *n* A cowboy movie; = HORSE OPERA

◁**shitkickers** or **shit stompers**▷ *n* or *n phr* Heavy boots such as farm, cowboy, or hiking boots: *I never see you in anything but those old shitkickers* —Stephen King

◁**shit-kicking**▷ *adj* Rough and rural; crude: *It's down-home, shit-kickin', ball-scratchin' country* —Aquarian/ *Shit-kicking cops and blood-letting cowboys are waning*—Penthouse

◁**shitless**▷ *See* SCARED SHITLESS, SCARE someone SHITLESS

◁**shit** (or **crap**) **list**▷ *n phr* One's fancied or real list of persons who are hated, not trusted, to be avoided, etc: *I wondered how I got on her shit list*

◁a **shitload** (or **shitpot**)▷ *n* A very large number or amount; = a SHITHOUSE FULL: *They sure sell a shitload of them*—San Francisco/ *make a shitload of noise*—Richard Merkin/ *a whole shitpot of that stuff*—George Warren

◁**shit on** someone or something▷ *interj* An exclamation of powerful disgust, contempt, rejection, etc: *Shit on his suggestions!*

◁**shit on a shingle**▷ *n phr* WW2 Army Creamed chipped beef on toast, or some similar delicacy

◁**shit on wheels**▷ *n phr* = HOT SHIT

◁**shit or get off the pot**▷ **1** *sentence* (Variation: **piss** may replace **shit**) = FISH OR CUT BAIT **2** *modifier*: *It's shit-or-get-off-the-pot time*—Armistead Maupin

◁the **shit out of** someone▷ *See* BEAT THE SHIT OUT OF someone

◁**shit out of luck**▷ *adv phr fr early 1900s* Having no chance of success; already too late for what one wants; very ill-starred; = OUT OF LUCK: *I guess I'm shit out of luck on this one*

◁**shit** one's **pants** (or **in** one's **pants**)▷ *v phr* (Variations: **drawers** may replace **pants**) To become frightened; be scared; panic: *Michael was shitting in his drawers*—Richard Merkin

◁the **shits**▷ *n phr* Diarrhea; = the TROTS
See the GIS

◁**shitstick**▷ *n* A contemptible, stupid person; = SHIT-ASS

◁**shitstorm**▷ *n* A very confused situation or affair; a crazy jumble: *an artist trying to turn the shitstorm of his life into music*—Village Voice

◁**shitsure**▷ *adv* Very certainly; definitely: *Shitsure it's gonna be a rough winter*—Village Voice

◁**shitter**▷ *n* A toilet: *Know where the movie of the week went? Right in the old shitter*—Dan Jenkins

◁**shit through a tin horn**▷ *See* LIKE SHIT THROUGH A TIN HORN

◁**shitty**▷ **1** *adj* Mean; malicious; nasty: *That's a shitty thing to say/ accepted what he characterized as his "shitty offer"*—Inside Sports **2** *adj* Tedious and unpleasant; futile; wearing: *a real shitty day* **3** *adj* Unwell; ill: *He felt real shitty and went home/ Ralph, I feel shitty tonight*—Joseph Heller

◁the **shitty** (or **shit**) **end of the stick**▷ *See* SHORT END OF THE STICK

◁**shitwork**▷ **1** *n* Menial and tedious work; degrading routine work; = SCUT WORK: *the boredom, the shitwork, the perpetual deadlines*—Armistead Maupin **2** *modifier*: *something better than shitwork jobs*—Ms

shiv (Variations: **chev** or **chib** or **chiv** or **chive** or **sheive** or **shive**) **1** *n fr 1600s British* A knife, esp a clasp-knife or similar weapon: *She gets this anonymous letter sticking the shiv in my back*—John O'Hara/ *The big knife called the chib*—Louis Armstrong **2** *v fr 1700s British*: *being shivved by Johnny Mizzoo*—Damon Runyon **3** *n esp hoboes* A razor; anything with a sharp cutting edge [fr Romany *chiv* "blade," by way of British underworld slang]

shlamozzle *See* SHEMOZZLE

shlang or **shlong** *See* SCHLONG

shlemiel *See* SCHLEMIEL

shlemozzle *See* SCHLEMAZEL, SHEMOZZLE

shlep *See* SCHLEP

shlepper *See* SCHLEPPER

shleppy *See* SCHLEPPY

shlock *See* SCHLOCK

shlocky *See* SCHLOCKY

shlontz *See* SCHLONTZ

shloomp or **shlump** *See* SCHLOOMP

shlub or **shlubbo** *See* ZHLUB

shlunk *v* To cover in a viscid and repellent way: *He dumped the bucket of slime and let it shlunk all over me*—Time [apparently a quasi-Yiddish echoism]

shmaltz *See* SCHMALTZ

shmaltzy *See* SCHMALTZY

shmatte *See* SCHMATTE

shmear or **shmeer** *See* SCHMEAR[1], the WHOLE SCHMEAR

shmeck or **shmack** *See* SCHMECK, SMACK

shmee *n narcotics* Heroin [perhaps a shortening of *shmeck*]

shmegeggy *See* SCHMEGEGGY

shmendrick *See* SCHMENDRICK

shmo or **shmoe** *See* SCHMO

shmooz *See* SCHMOOZ

shmotte *See* SCHMATTE

shmuck *See* SCHMUCK

shnook *See* SCHNOOK

shnorrer *See* SCHNORRER

shnozz *See* SCHNOZZ

shoe 1 *n esp underworld* A plainclothes police officer; = GUMSHOE **2** *n underworld & espionage* A forged passport **3** *n car-racing* An automobile tire **4** *n gambling* A box from which cards are dealt in casinos: *granted a request by Mr Sinatra that the blackjack dealer deal from her hand. The state requires dealing from a box called a "shoe"*—New York Times **5** *n 1950s bop musicians* A person who is well dressed, esp in the latest fashion **6** *n* = WHITE SHOE

See GUMSHOE, MARSHMALLOW SHOES, SADDLE SHOES

shoehorn *v* To insinuate by effort; force or fit in: *Attorney General Griffin Bell managed to shoehorn an energy pitch into a speech*—Time/ *Cannon manages to shoehorn all that into its new ad campaign*—Wall Street Journal

shoestring catch *n phr baseball* A catch made near the ground, usu by an outfielder while running, stooping, and lunging

shommus *See* SHAMUS

shoobies *n* Excursion passengers for a day trip, on a bus or train [fr the *shoe* box they typically carry their lunch in]

shoo-fly or **shoo-fly 1** *n police fr early 1900s* A police officer in disguise set to watch other police officers: *Fuck the shooflies...I never took a nickel from anybody*—Ed McBain **2** *n railroad* A stretch of temporary track **3** *n miners* A transverse passage in a mine [perhaps the police sense is spelled *shoo* only because it rhymes with *shoe*, since *shoe* and *fly* both mean detective, and the sense may be "a detective of detectives"]

shoo in *v phr horse-racing* To arrange for a particular horse, esp an inferior one, to win a race [fr the notion that the beast, not caring to run and not needing to, can be shooed over the finish line, and win]

shoo-in or **shoe-in 1** *n horse-racing* A horse who wins a race by prearrangement **2** *n* A person, team, candidate, etc, who will or did win easily: *The big, powerful Trojans were the shoo-ins*—Associated Press/ *Harvey Fierstein and Kate Nelligan are shoo-ins*—Village Voice **3** *modifier: to be a shoe-in candidate*—Ms ● This spelling may simply be a misspelling, but it is probably based on a misunderstanding of the origin of the term; it is a sort of folk etymology

shook up (Variations: **shook** or **all shook** or **all shook up**) **1** *adj phr* or *adj fr late 1800s but esp teenagers fr 1950s* In a state of high excitement or extreme disturbance; very much upset: *So Woody kept his voice down, but he was all shook up*—Saul Bellow **2** *adj phr* or *adj teenagers & rock and roll fr 1950s* Very happy; exhilarated; = HIGH: *I expected years in prison...they let me go free, boy was I shook up*—New York Post

shooper *See* SHUPER

shoot 1 *v fr early 1900s* To photograph, esp to make a movie: *They were shooting over in Jersey* **2** *n* a photographic or movie-making session: *That one shoot took six hours* **3** *interj fr 1920s* An invitation to speak, explain, etc: *He asked if I wanted to know, and I said shoot* **4** *interj fr late 1800s* A mild exclamation of disgust, disappointment, distress, etc ● A euphemism for **shit**: *Shoot, the guy forgot to pay me* **5** *n* = SHOOT THE BREEZE **6** *v narcotics* = SHOOT UP ◁**7**▷ *v* (also **shoot off**) To ejaculate semen; = COME **8** *v* To play certain games: *Shall we shoot some pool?/ watch the flamingos, shoot a little golf, grow a little garden*—WT Tyler

See TURKEY-SHOOT

shoot someone **a line** *v phr* To flatter and cajole; overwhelm with glib plausibility

◁**shoot** (or **fire**) **blanks**▷ *v phr* To do the sex act without causing pregnancy

shoot one's **cookies** *v phr* (Variations: **breakfast** or **dinner** or **lunch** or **supper** may replace **cookies**; **toss** or **lose** may replace **shoot**) To vomit; = BARF, RALPH: *If I'm any judge of color, you're going to shoot your cookies*—Raymond Chandler/ *smelled like someone just tossed his cookies*—JD Salinger

shoot someone **down** (or **down in flames**) *v phr esp students* To defeat someone; thwart or ruin somone's efforts; = BLOW someone OUT OF THE WATER: *Woody, who had been flying along, level and smooth, was shot down in flames*—Saul Bellow

shoot-'em-up 1 *n* A movie or TV program with much gunplay and violence: *gambled for cigarettes, slurped Tang or watched shoot-'em-ups on TV*—New York Times **2** *modifier: an exaggerated reaction to the male-oriented "shoot-'em-up games"*—Washington Post

shooter *See* BEAVER-SHOOTER, HIP SHOOTER, PEASHOOTER, SIX-SHOOTER, SQUARE SHOOTER

shoot from the hip *v phr* To act or respond impulsively and aggressively; be recklessly impetuous; = be QUICK-DRAW

shooting gallery *narcotics* **1** *n phr* A place where a narcotics user can get a dose or injection **2** *n phr* A party or gathering where narcotics users take injections: *in a fellow musician's hotel room during a "shooting gallery" (dope party)*—New York Daily News

shooting iron *n phr fr late 1700s* A pistol

shooting match *See* the WHOLE SHOOTING MATCH

shooting war *n phr* = HOT WAR

shoot oneself **in the foot** *v phr* To wound or injure oneself by ineptness; attack wildly and hurt oneself: *Ted Turner has taken to shooting himself in the foot*—Village Voice/ *a situation, Vance writes, "where we were shooting ourselves in the foot"*—Newsweek

◁**shoot** one's **load**▷ *v phr* To ejaculate semen; have an orgasm; = COME

shoot off one's **mouth** *v phr* (Variations: **bazoo** or **face** or **gab** or **yap** may replace **mouth**) *fr middle 1800s* To talk irresponsibly and inappropriately, esp to bluster and brag; = TALK BIG: *You come busting in here and shoot off your bazoo at me*—J Evans

shoot one *v phr* lunch counter To draw and serve a glass of Coca-Cola (a trade name)

shoot-out 1 *n* (also **shoot-up**) *fr early 1900s* A gunfight: *the justly famous shoot-out between the Earps and the Clantons in the O-K Corral*—New York Times/ *The shoot-up may have been a skirmish between Mafia factions*—New York Times **2** *n* Any fight or violent confrontation; a hotly contested game or issue: *the simple corporate shoot-out reported by the newspapers*—New York/ *another sociological shoot-out, with men as the heroes this time*—New Yorker **3** *n* soccer A form of tie-breaker used in the North American Soccer League, in which five players from each team have five seconds each to attempt goals one-on-one against the goalkeeper

shoot the agate *v phr* black & jive talk To walk jauntily with hands at sides and thumbs extended [fr the extension of the thumb when playing marbles]

shoot the breeze (or **the fat**) *v phr* To chat amiably and casually; = CHEW THE FAT: *making transatlantic calls just to shoot the breeze*—Village Voice/ *enjoying ourselves and shooting the breeze*—Billy Rose/ *sit down on a bench and shoot the fat*—Village Voice

◁**shoot the bull** (or **crap** or **shit**)▷ **1** *v phr* To lie and exaggerate; talk grandly but emptily; = BULL-SHIT: *And they weren't just shooting the crap*—JD Salinger **2** *v phr* To chat amiably; = SHOOT THE BREEZE: *stand on a corner, shoot the bull*—Langston Hughes/ *The basketball guys shoot the shit during timeouts*—Village Voice

shoot the lights out *v phr* esp sports To excel; perform superbly: *These kids will jump right up and shoot the lights out on you*—Sports Illustrated/ *He shoots the lights out in physics, calculus, biology*—Sports Illustrated [perhaps fr the accuracy of marksmanship implied if one is to hit a small target like a *lightbulb*; certainly influenced by the notion of knocking the *daylights*, or earlier the *liver and lights*, "liver and lungs, innards," out of someone or something]

shoot the works *v phr* To act, give, spend, etc, without limit; = GO FOR BROKE: *In whatever pertains to comfort, shoot the works*—James M Cain [fr the *shooting* of dice in craps, with its extended sense of betting or gambling all one has]

shoot up *v phr* narcotics To take an injection of narcotics; = JAB A VEIN, MAINLINE

shoot-up *n* narcotics A narcotics injection
See SHOOT-OUT

shoot one's **wad** *fr 1920s* **1** *v phr* To commit or bet everything one has; = GO FOR BROKE, SHOOT THE WORKS **2** *v phr* To say everything one can on a subject; have one's say **3** *v phr* To exhaust one's resources; be unable to persist ◁**4**▷ *v phr* = SHOOT one's LOAD

shop *See* BUCKET SHOP, BUTCHER SHOP, CHOP SHOP, GUZZLE SHOP, HEAD SHOP, HOCKSHOP, HOOKSHOP, JUNK SHOP, SCHLOCK SHOP, SMOKE SHOP

-shop *combining word* Place where the indicated thing is carried on, used, etc; = FACTORY: *brain shop/ love-shop/ talk shop*

shop around 1 *v phr* *fr 1920s* To search for something or someone: *I heard he was shopping around for a new Secretary of the Interior* **2** *v phr* To compare prices, services, etc of items: *I really wish I had more time to shop around before buying that yacht*

shopping-bag lady *See* BAG LADY

shopping list *See* LAUNDRY LIST

short 1 *n* 1920s prison & underworld A prisoner near the end of his term **2** *n* hot rodders & black fr 1920s underworld A car; = WHEELS **3** *v* narcotics To inhale a narcotic in crystal or powder form; = SNORT [origin of automobile sense unknown; perhaps a back formation fr *hot short* with its reference to electrically *shorting* the ignition to by-pass the key, an operation later called *hot-wiring*]
See HOT SHORT

◁**short-arm inspection**▷ *n phr* (also **short-arm drill** or **short-arm**) armed forces fr early 1900s Medical inspection of the squeezed, milked penis for a discharge symptomatic of gonorrhea [fr the notion that the penis is a limb, combined with the notion that it is a weapon]

short-change artist *n phr* circus & carnival A ticket-seller skillful at returning less change than is due

short dog *n phr* A derelict's bottle of wine or liquor: *staggering down Broadway sucking on a short dog*—Joseph Wambaugh

◁**short** (or **shitty** or **shit**) **end of the stick**▷ *n phr fr late 1930s* The worst of a transaction, encounter, etc; very bad treatment; = the SHAFT: *Pastorini got the shit end of the stick, as usual*—Rolling Stone

short eyes *n phr* prison A sexual molester of children: *end up in the punk tank with the free-world queers and the short eyes*—Ezra Hannon

short fuse *See* HAVE A SHORT FUSE

short hairs *See* HAVE someone BY THE SHORT HAIRS

short heist *n phr* underworld Petty theft, shoplifting, purse-snatching, etc

a **short one** *n phr* A single shot of whiskey, often drunk quickly; a small drink

the **shorts** *n phr* Lack of money; a shortage of funds: *I told him I had the shorts*—Lionel Stander/ *This partnership...still has a severe case of the shorts*—Village Voice

short-sheet *v* To play a nasty trick; maltreat: *headed for big things until the Reagan crowd short-*

sheeted you—WT Tyler [fr a student and barracks practical joke in which a *bedsheet* is folded in half and made to appear as an upper and lower sheet, so that when the victim gets into bed the stretching legs and toes are painfully arrested]

shortstop **1** *v* To take food being passed to someone else at table **2** *n: I avoided that table where the shortstop always sat* **3** *v* salespersons To wait on another salesperson's customer

shorty or **shortie** **1** *n* A very short person; = DUSTY BUTT **2** *n* A woman's short garment, esp a nightgown

Shorty George *n phr* A 1930s jazz dance: *all the famous dances of the jitterbugging thirties: the Big Apple, the Shag, the Boogie, the Shorty George, Truckin', Peckin',...the Lindy Hop*—Albert Goldman

shot **1** *n* A drink of straight liquor **2** *n esp Southern & Western lunch counter* A glass or other serving of Coca-Cola (a trade name) **3** *n narcotics fr late 1920s* An injection of narcotics; = FIX ◁**4**▷ *n* An ejaculation of semen; a male orgasm **5** *n* An atomic explosion, a rocket or missile launching, or some other complex sort of military and technological blasting **6** *n* = BIG SHOT **7** *n fr 1960s* A person's particular preference, style, etc; = BAG, THING: *That's our shot. That's who we are* —Rolling Stone **8** *n* A try; an attempt, esp at something rather difficult: *He didn't make it, but he gave it a hell of a shot* **9** *adj fr middle 1800s* Drunk **10** *adj fr late 1920s* Worn out or out of repair: *This old machine is shot* **11** *adj fr 1930s* Exhausted; ill; in bad shape: *Say, am I shot?*—James T Farrell [the drinking senses are shortenings of an early-19th-century expression *shot in the neck* meaning both "a drink" and "drunk"]
See BEAVER SHOT, CALL THE SHOTS, CHEAP SHOT, DROP CASE, GIVE something A SHOT, GIVE something one's BEST SHOT, GRAB SHOT, HALF-SHOT, HAVE A CRACK AT something, HOT SHOT, LONG SHOT, MUG SHOT, NOT BY A LONG SHOT, ONE-SHOT, UNGODLY SHOT

shot glass *n phr* = JIGGER

shotgun[1] **1** *n WW2 Army* A machine gun or other rapid-fire gun **2** *n narcotics* A type of pipe used for smoking marijuana **3** *n football* An offensive formation in which the quarterback lines up well behind instead of immediately behind the center **4** *adj* Very diffuse and general; indiscriminate: *I hate it when the administrators make shotgun accusations*
See RIDE SHOTGUN, SIT SHOTGUN

shotgun[2] *n* A matchmaker; a marriage broker [fr Yiddish *shadchen*, which is pronounced something like *shotgun;* perhaps reinforced by the notion of a *shotgun wedding*]

shotgun quiz *See* POP QUIZ

shotgun wedding (or **marriage**) *n phr fr 1920s* A wedding under duress, esp when the bride is pregnant; a forced marriage; = MILITARY WEDDING

a **shot in the arm** *n phr fr 1900s* Something that stimulates and enlivens; an invigorating influence or event: *has given his campaign for the Democratic*

presidential nomination a shot in the arm—Washington Post

◁a **shot in the ass**▷ **1** *n phr* = a SHOT IN THE ARM **2** *n phr* = a KICK IN THE ASS

shot John *See* PLAY WHO SHOT JOHN

shoulder *See* COLD SHOULDER, STRAIGHT FROM THE SHOULDER

one **should have stood in bed** *sentence* This has been a complete disaster or a waste of time, and one should not have bothered to get up in the morning

shouldn't happen to a dog *See* IT SHOULDN'T HAPPEN TO A DOG

shout **1** *n jazz musicians* A hymn or traditional blues song, esp when sung with a heavily accented beat **2** *n print shop* An exclamation point

shouter *n 1920s underworld* A criminal's girlfriend; = MOLL

shove **1** *v fr middle 1800s* To pass counterfeit money **2** *v railroad* To shovel **3** *v underworld* To kill; = HIT: *Who shoved her?*—J Evans **4** *v fr middle 1800s* = SHOVE OFF
See KNOW WHAT one CAN DO WITH something, PUSH COMES TO SHOVE, TELL someone WHAT TO DO WITH something

shove it *See* STICK IT

shovelhead *n* A fool; an idiot: *I replied, playing the shovelhead*—Rolling Stone

◁**shovel shit** (or **the shit**)▷ *v phr fr 1930s* To lie and exaggerate; = BULLSHIT, SHOOT THE BULL: *I was just fooling, shoveling the shit a little/ no varsity letters for shoveling shit*—John Irving

shove off **1** *v phr fr late 1800s* To leave; depart; = SCRAM: *when we shoved off*—James M Cain **2** *v phr underworld* To kill; murder: *People got shoved off for their money*—Agatha Christie [fr the boating term]

shover *See* PENCIL-PUSHER

show *v fr early 1800s* To arrive; appear; = SHOW UP: *You suppose he'll show?*—WR Burnett
See BALLY SHOW, CATTLE SHOW, DOG SHOW, GRIND SHOW, KID SHOW, LEG SHOW, LET'S GET THE SHOW ON THE ROAD, MEAT SHOW, MUD OPERA, NO-SHOW, ONE-MAN SHOW, PEEP SHOW

show a leg *v phr* = SHAKE A LEG

show-and-tell *n* An elaborate display, usu for selling or other persuasion; = DOG AND PONY ACT: *There just hasn't been time to arrange the kind of show-and-tell that attracts media attention*—Village Voice/ *No one seems to have been impressed by the show-and-tell*—New Yorker [fr the name of an elementary-school teaching technique where pupils exhibit and explain things]

show biz *n phr* The entertainment industry; show business

showboat **1** *v* To behave in a showy, flamboyant way; = GRANDSTAND, HOT DOG: *And, please, no showboating, fist-pounding, breast-beating, or blame-casting*—Washingtonian/ *I don't believe in showboating or playing the martyr* —Arizona Republic **2** *n* (also **showboater**): *Jesse is a showboater, privately*—Amsterdam News/ *a couple of South Carolina showboaters who like and under-*

stand each other—Washington Post **3** *v* = PULL RANK

show business *See* THAT'S SHOW BUSINESS

showcase 1 *n theater* A theater, performance, etc, where a major aim is to exhibit relatively unknown performers and work **2** *v* To feature or exhibit a relatively unknown player, performer, work, etc: *We'll showcase her play next year/ You don't showcase a guy by sending him smack into the middle of the line*—Sports Illustrated

showdown 1 *n poker* A hand where the cards are dealt face up and the best hand wins at once **2** *n fr late 1800s* A confrontation, esp a last one **3** *modifier: the opening game of the showdown Yankee-Red Sox series*—Associated Press

shower *See* GOLDEN SHOWER, SEND someone TO THE SHOWERS

show off *v phr* To behave in an ostentatiously skilled and assured way in order to impress others; = GRANDSTAND, HOT DOG: *He ran a quick eight miles, just showing off*

show-off *n* A person who habitually shows off; = HOT DOG, SHOWBOAT

show someone **the door** *v phr* To dismiss someone summarily; eject someone

showup 1 *n police* = LINEUP **2** *modifier: a group about to be shoved into the show-up line*—WR Burnett

show up *v phr fr late 1800s* To arrive; be present: *I had to show up to make a touch*—Erle Stanley Gardner

show someone or something **up** *v phr* To reveal; expose: *That slip showed him up for a fraud*

shpilkes (SHPIL kəs) *n* Apprehensiveness; nervousness; = the JITTERS: *The night before the exam I had a bad case of shpilkes* [fr Yiddish]

shpos (SHPAHS) *n hospital* An obnoxious patient [fr *subhuman piece of shit*]

shpritz *n* A bit or touch; a dose: *each a free-associational shpritz of surreal hi-de-ho*—Village Voice [fr Yiddish, literally, "a squirt"]

shriek *n print shop fr middle 1800s* An exclamation point

shrimp *n* A very short or small person; = PEANUT

shrink *n fr 1960s* A psychiatrist, psychoanalyst, or other psychotherapist; = HEADSHRINKER
See HEADSHRINKER

shtarker or **schtarker** or **starker** (SHTAHR kə, -kər or STAHR kər) *n* A strong person; = TOUGH GUY: *I went from dealing with shtarkers to intellectual bullies*—Playboy/ *an agent who's a shtarker, a monster, half-man, half-rhino*—National Lampoon [fr Yiddish]

shtick or **schtick** or **shtik** *fr show business* **1** *n* A small theatrical role or part of a role; a piece of theatrical "business"; = BIT: *It turned out to be a nice little "shtick"*—New York Post **2** *n* A characteristic trait of performance or behavior; a typical personal feature: *To each his own schtick. Chapman performs his with gusto*—Changes/ *But shtick, even first-class shtick, goes only so far*—New York Times **3** *n* A clever device; = GADGET, GIMMICK: *The "shtick" is that the taped remarks of a number*

of political figures are tacked onto questions dreamed up by writers—Playboy [fr Yiddish, literally, "piece, bit"]

shtoonk or **shtunk** *See* SCHTOONK

◁**shtup** or **schtup** or **stup**▷ (SHTo͞oP) **1** *v* To do the sex act with or to; = FUCK: *Why of course he was shtupping her*—Philip Roth/ *liked to get shtupped by bald-headed men wearing deerstalker hats*—Ed McBain **2** *modifier: take a big video plunge, coming closer than any outfit yet to breaking the shtup barrier*—Village Voice **3** *n* A person regarded merely as a sex partner; = ASS **4** *n* The sex act; copulation [fr Yiddish, literally, "push, shove"]

shuck 1 *v fr middle 1800s* To undress; strip oneself **2** *v* (also **shuck and jive**) *esp black* To joke; tease; = FOOL AROUND: *22 percent of each trash-truck crew's workday is spent shucking and jiving and shadowboxing*—Philadelphia/ *We ain't got no time for shuckin'*—Joseph Wambaugh **3** *v* (also **shuck and jive**) *black & student fr black* To swindle; cheat; deceive; esp to bluff verbally and counterfeit total sincerity **4** *v cool musicians fr black* To improvise chords, esp to a piece of music one does not know; = FAKE IT, VAMP **5** *n esp black* A theft or fraud; = RIP OFF: *Linear thinking was a total shuck*—Cyra McFadden **6** *v black* To lie; exaggerate; = BULLSHIT [black senses probably fr the fact that black slaves sang and shouted gleefully during *corn-shucking* season, and this behavior, along with lying and teasing, became a part of the protective and evasive behavior normally adopted towards white people in "traditional" race relations; the sense of "swindle" is perhaps related to the mid-19th-century term *to be shucked out* "be defeated, be denied victory," which suggests that the notion of stripping someone as an ear of corn is stripped may be basic in the semantics]

shucks *See* AW SHUCKS, CORN SHUCKS

shuffle 1 *v street gang* To have a gang fight; = RUMBLE **2** *v black* To behave in the stereotypical obsequious way of a black person in "traditional" race relations; = TOM: *A lot of brothers and sisters died. So...are we just going to shuffle and jive?*—Ebony
See DOUBLE SHUFFLE

shuffler *n underworld* A confidence trickster, hawker, etc; = GRIFTER [fr older *shuffle* "deceive, defraud," probably fr the shuffling of cards cheatingly by a professional gambler]
See PAPER-PUSHER

shuffle them up *v phr railroad* To switch railroad cars

shunt *n car-racing* An accident; a collision

shuper or **shooper** or **shupper** (SHo͞o pər) *n fr early 1900s* A large glass or stein for beer: *spent for "shupers" of beer*—Jack London [perhaps fr German *Schüppe* "scoop"]

shure or **shurr** *See* FOR SURE

shush *v* To tell someone to be quiet and stop talking ● Very often a command: *He kept shushing his wife/ "Shush!" he shouted, uselessly, to the large noisy hound*

shut *See* EYE-SHUT

shutdown *n* A complete cessation; a stoppage: *assembly line shutdowns*—Associated Press

shut-eye *n fr early 1900s* Sleep; = some ZS: *I've got to get some shut-eye before the exam*

shut one's **face** *v phr fr early 1900s* To stop talking; = SHUT UP ● Often an irritated command

shutout *n sports* A game in which one side is held scoreless

shut out *v phr sports fr late 1800s* To hold an opponent scoreless; = BLANK, SCHNEIDER, SKUNK: *The Lakers shut them out 95 zip*

shutterbug *n* A photographer, esp an enthusiastic amateur: *Two of the more prominent Senate-shutterbugs are Sens Patrick J Leahy...and John C Danforth*—Washington Post

shutters *n* The eyelids

shut one's **trap** *v phr fr 1600s* = SHUT one's FACE

shut up *v phr* To be quiet; stop talking ● Very often a stern or angry command

◁**shvantz**▷ (SHVAHNTS) *n* (Variations: **schvantz** or **schvanz** or **schwantz** or **schwanz** or **schvontz** or **shvonce** or **shvuntz**) The penis; = SCHLONG [fr Yiddish, literally, "tail"; hence semantically analogous with *penis*, literally, "tail"] *See* STEP ON IT

◀**shvartze** or **shvartzer**▶ *See* SCHVARTZE

shy *n* A usu criminal usurer; = LOAN SHARK, SHYLOCK: *a shy on East Houston who lent money*—Fran Lebowitz/ *I don't know who's got the markers....It's some shy*—George V Higgins

shylock or **Shylock 1** *n* A usurer; = LOAN SHARK: *In Toronto and Hamilton both, loan sharks ("shylocks") appeared in the gambling clubs*—Maclean's **2** *v:* *the shylocking that went with it as hot dogs go with baseball*—Mario Puzo/ *numbers games, shylocking, and other illegal operations*—Gay Talese [fr the character in Shakespeare's *The Merchant of Venice*]

shy of a load *See* THREE BRICKS SHY OF A LOAD

shyster 1 *n fr middle 1800s* A dishonest and contemptible lawyer or politician: *You lousy little shyster bastard*—Ira Wolfert **2** *n* Any lawyer [origin unknown and hotly disputed; perhaps fr the name of a Mr Sheuster, a New York City lawyer of the early 1800s; perhaps fr German *Scheisse* "shit" or *Scheisser* "shitter" by way of anglicized forms *shice* and *shicer* attested fr the mid-19th century; perhaps because prisoners were said and advised to *fight shy of* "avoid," lawyers who frequented jails, esp the Tombs in New York City; perhaps fr earlier sense of *shy* "disreputable, not quite honest"]

sick 1 *adj* (also **sicko** or **sicksicksick**) *fr 1950s* Mentally twisted; psychopathic, esp in a sadistic vein: *some sick vandal/ a rapist or a sicko father who abuses his teenage daughters*—Philadelphia Journal **2** *adj* (also **sicko** or **sicksicksick**) *fr 1950s* Gruesome; morbid; mentally and spiritually unhealthy: *a sick sense of humor/ Label it S for Sicko*—Philadelphia/ *He is even better at establishing a sicksicksick atmosphere*—New York Times **3** *adj narcotics* Needing a dose of narcotics **4** *n*

narcotics The craving and misery of an addict in need of a narcotic dose

sickie or **sicky** *n* A mentally unhealthy person; a psychopath: *It was not considered very kosher to toss out the sickies once they had taken their final vows*—John R Powers/ *Only sickies get involved with married women*—New York

sick joke *n phr fr 1950s* A joke with a grimly morbid tone or point; a nasty sort of jape

the **sick lame and lazy** *n phr Army* Persons, esp troops, who generally or particularly are not available for duty

sickroom *adj* Unhealthy; repellent; = SICK: *I have something to tell you....It's kind of sickroom*—Armistead Maupin

side 1 *n theater fr 1920s* A line of dialogue for one performer; also, a sheet containing the lines and cues for one performer **2** *n fr black fr 1930s* A phonograph record **3** *n* The music on one side of a phonograph record, one band of a long-playing record, one segment of a cassette or other tape, etc ● Usu used in the plural: *He had never heard these classic sides until recently*—San Francisco *See* ON THE SIDE, STATESIDE, SUNNY SIDE UP, TOPSIDE, the WRONG SIDE OF THE TRACKS

sidearms *n armed forces fr 1920s* Salt and pepper, cream and sugar, or other regular adjuncts to a meal

sidebar 1 *n news media* A news or feature story serving as a supplement or background to a main story: *Banner headlines and sidebar after sidebar flashed in front of our eyes*—New York Times/ *the wandering sidebars and frivolous frolicking of the Post*—Washingtonian **2** *adj* Auxiliary; supplementary: *Now he has a side-bar job, hustling beer or sports equipment*—Robert Ruark [perhaps fr the late-19th-century use of *sidebar buggy* or *wagon* for a vehicle having longitudinal reinforcements along the *sides*; perhaps fr *side-bar* "an auxiliary toll-gate on a road leading into a main toll-road"]

side-door Pullman *n phr railroad & hoboes* A railroad freight car: *I rode into Niagara Falls in a "side-door Pullman"*—Jack London

sidekick 1 *n fr early 1900s* A close friend, partner, associate, etc: *Wayne and his side-kick James Arness*—New York Herald-Tribune **2** *n fr early 1900s fr pickpockets* A side pocket [first sense fr earlier *sidekicker*, perhaps fr the cardplaying sense of *kicker* as a reserve of dependable strength, perhaps fr the notion that a companion can *kick* to the *side* while the principal kicks to the front in fighting]

the **side of a barn** *See* CAN'T HIT THE SIDE OF A BARN

side of one's **face** *See* LAUGH ON THE OTHER SIDE OF one's FACE

sider *See* PORTSIDER

sides of the street *See* WORK BOTH SIDES OF THE STREET

sideswipe *n* A critical observation, esp an oblique one: *took a sideswipe at "restrictive court decisions"*—New York Times

sidetrack *v underworld* To arrest

sidetracked *See* GET SIDETRACKED

sidewalks *See* HIT THE SIDEWALKS, POUND THE PAVEMENTS

sidewalk superintendent 1 *n phr* A person who watches excavation or other construction work, usu through a hole in the surrounding fence **2** *n phr* Any amateur critic or observer

side-wheeler 1 *n* A lefthanded person **2** *n baseball* A lefthanded pitcher; =SOUTHPAW **3** *n horse-racing* A pacing horse; a pacer [fr the *side-wheel* steamboat]

sidewinder¹ 1 *n fr middle 1800s* A wide, looping blow with the fist; =ROUNDHOUSE **2** *n lumber-jacks* A tree that does not fall where it was intended to [both senses literally from a *winding* at or to a *side*, and the second sense probably influenced by *sidewinder²*]

sidewinder² 1 *n* A dangerous and pugnacious man **2** *n underworld* A gangster's bodyguard; =GORILLA: *Eddy Prue, Morny's sidewinder* [fr the dangerous *sidewinder* rattlesnake, so called fr its lateral locomotion, and presumed to be treacherous]

-sie *See* -IE

sieve *n* A leaky boat or ship

See HAVE A MIND LIKE A SIEVE

◁**siff** or **the siff**▷ *See* SYPH

sight gag *n phr* A joke or comic turn that depends entirely on what is seen

sightseer handle *n phr horse-racing* A small total amount of money bet on a horse race: *The handle...much less than $100 per capita, was described as a "sightseer" handle by an employee of the calculating room*—New York Times

sign *See* HIGH SIGN, INDIAN SIGN

signify *black* **1** *v* To boast; =SHOW OFF **2** *v* To insult and derogate someone, esp in a formal and game-like way; =PLAY THE DOZENS: *signifying back and forth between themselves*—Donald Goines

sign off *v phr fr late 1920s fr radio studio* To stop talking; =HANG UP, SHUT UP [fr the legal requirement that a radio station cite its legal call *sign* as it ended broadcasting for the day]

sign-off 1 *n fr 1920s radio studio* The formal ending of a broadcast day **2** *n* A parting comment; a final note or gesture: *Jimmy Durante's sign-off to Mrs Calabash*

sign off on something *v phr* To agree to or approve of a proposal, a legislative bill, etc, esp without actual formal endorsement: *When enough Senators had signed off on the treaty, the President announced it*

sign up *v phr* To join; enroll; enlist: *They signed up for a course in hands-on interpersonal relations*

sigoggling *See* SKYGODLIN

Silicon Valley *n phr* The Santa Clara Valley south of San Francisco in California: *smack in the middle of Silicon Valley*—San Francisco [fr the concentration of manufacturers of *silicon* chips for computers, watches, etc in the Santa Clara *Valley*]

silk *n black* A white person

See HIT THE SILK

silk-stocking *adj fr late 1700s* Wealthy; affluent: *a silk-stocking neighborhood*

silly season *n phr fr middle 1800s British* Any period when people do silly things, esp when these are reported in the news media [fr a term designating the months of August and September, when Parliament was not sitting and valid and useful news was scarce, and the newspapers resorted to reporting frivol and trivialities]

silver Jeff *n phr rock and roll fr 1950s* A quarter or a nickel [fr the image of Thomas Jefferson on the nickel coin, apparently transferred to the quarter by confusion with George Washington]

silver wing *n phr rock & roll fr 1950s* A fifty-cent piece [fr the image of an eagle with spread *wings* on the coin]

simmer down *v phr* To become calm and quiet, esp after anger; =COOL IT ● Often a command or a bit of advice

simoleon (sih MOH lee ən) *n fr late 1800s* A dollar [origin unknown; perhaps fr an earlier slang term *Simon* "dollar," influenced by the French *napoleon* "twenty-franc coin"]

Simon Legree *n phr* A cruel, unsympathetic person, esp a tyrannical superior; a slave-driver [fr the character in *Uncle Tom's Cabin*, somewhat unfairly]

simp *n fr early 1900s* A simpleton; a stupid person; =KLUTZ: *Simps with mustaches are a menace to society*—Playboy/ *I really thought it would be till death do us part. I was such a simp*—Lawrence Sanders

simpatico *adj* Nice; pleasant; sympathetic and congenial [fr Italian or Spanish]

simple *See* COW-SIMPLE, STIR-CRAZY

sincere *adj* Intended to make a good and sober impression; overtly conformistic; =SERIOUS: *packaged in a sincere apothecary-type bottle*—New York Times

sing *v underworld* To inform; incriminate oneself and others; =SQUEAL: *Vice Prisoners Ready To Sing*—New York Daily News [perhaps related to the expression *a little bird told me*]

See HEAR THE BIRDIES SING, the OPERA'S NEVER OVER TILL THE FAT LADY SINGS

singer *n underworld* =CANARY, STOOL PIGEON

single 1 *n* A dollar bill **2** *n fr underworld* A person, esp a criminal, who works alone: *Dillinger now becomes a single*—A Hynd **3** *n show business* A solo performer; a one-person act **4** *n* An unmarried person: *The place tried to attract singles*

See SWINGING SINGLE

single-jack *n hoboes* A one-legged, one-armed, or one-eyed beggar: *the detested single-jacks*—Atlantic Monthly

single-o 1 *adj* Unmarried; single **2** *adj underworld* Working alone; unpartnered: *There are "single-o" heist-men*—E DeBaun **3** *n underworld* A person, esp a criminal, who works alone; =SINGLE **4** *adv* Alone; solo: *instead of working single-o as was the custom*—Billy Rose

singles *modifier* For unmarried persons: *a singles bar/ a singles party*

sing out 1 *v phr* To speak up; make oneself known and heard; =PIPE UP: *If anybody doesn't like it, just sing out* **2** *v phr fr early 1800s* To inform; =SQUEAL: *and get him to sing out*—J Roeburt

sinker[1] *n fr late 1800s* A biscuit or doughnut [fr the lead weight used by fishermen to *sink* line and bait, probably an ironic reference to the weight of the biscuit or doughnut]

sinker[2] *baseball* **1** *n* A pitch that dips downward as it nears home plate **2** *n* A line drive or other batted ball that sinks suddenly toward the ground

sinkers and suds *n phr lunch counter* Doughnuts and coffee

sis 1 *n* A sister: *That's his sis with him* **2** *n* Woman; girl ● Used in direct address: *What's up, sis?* **3** *n late 1800s* A weak, effeminate boy; =SISSY **4** *n cool talk* A young woman or girl; =CHICK [a shortening of *sister*]

sissified *adj* Timorous; weak and effeminate; =CHICKENHEARTED, PANSIFIED

sissy *fr late 1800s* **1** *n* A timorous, weak, and effeminate male; =DAISY, LILY, PANSY **2** *adj: his sissy ways/ wearing sissy clothes* **3** *n* A male homosexual; =PANSY [fr *sis* fr *sister*]

sissy bar *n phr* A high metal projection at the back of a bicycle to prevent it from rolling over backwards [fr the fact that someone adopting such a device is timorous]

sissy pants *n phr* =SISSY

sister 1 *n* Woman; girl ● Used in direct address: *Hey, sister, you'd better leave* **2** *n black* A fellow black woman **3** *n* A fellow feminist
See JOHN WAYNE'S SISTER, SOB SISTER, WEAK SISTER

sister act *n phr homosexuals* Sexual relations between a homosexual man and a heterosexual woman

sit *v* To take care of; attend and watch over: *Who'll sit your house while you're gone?*
See BABY-SIT, HOUSE-SIT

sitcom *n* A situation comedy series on television: *the new family of sitcoms*—Newsweek

sit-down 1 *n hoboes* A meal, usu a free one, eaten at a table **2** *n* (also **sit-down strike**) A strike in which the workers occupy their job sites but do not work

sit fat *v phr* To be in a commanding and successful state; =be a FAT CAT, be in FAT CITY

sit in 1 *v phr musicians* To join and play with other musicians, esp on one occasion or temporarily: *had the very good fortune of sitting in with him*—Metronome **2** *v phr fr 1960s* To occupy a place as a participant in a sit-in

sit-in *n fr 1960s* An illegal occupation of a place, in order to make a political or philosophical statement ● The term was popularized during the movement for black civil rights and has many offspring: **be-in, love-in, puke-in**, etc

sit in the catbird seat *v phr* To be in the position of advantage; =be SITTING PRETTY, SIT FAT: *willing to give us a hundred seventy million in preferred notes. We're sitting in the catbird seat*—Art Buchwald [fr a term used by a poker opponent of the superb sportscaster Red Barber to explain his situa-

tion with an ace in the hole at stud poker; Mr Barber adopted the term, which was afterwards used by James Thurber in a story called "The Catbird Seat" with attribution to Red Barber; probably a Southern dialect term based on a folk notion of the cleverness and masterfulness of *catbirds* and/or their high and superior perch]

sit on one's **ass** *v phr* To remain inactive; esp, to fail to cope or deal with a responsibility: *The congressman sat on his ass while the neighborhood hospital deteriorated*

sit on one's **hands 1** *v phr* To refrain from applauding; be an unresponsive or adverse audience: *They sat on their hands until he started waving the flag* **2** *v phr* To do nothing; be passive; =SIT ON one's ASS: *Even when the thing fell down they just sat on their hands*

sit on my face *See* SHE CAN SIT ON MY FACE ANY TIME

sit shotgun *v phr* To sit in the passenger seat of a car; =RIDE SHOTGUN: *I sat shotgun in my pop's flower truck*—Philadelphia

sit still for something *v phr* To accept or condone; tolerate something provocative: *The nation will simply not sit still for...the years of slow growth*—Time

sitter *n* A person who baby-sits, house-sits, etc

◁**sit there with** one's **finger** (or **thumb**) **up** one's **ass**▷ *v phr* To be passive and unresponsive; fail to cope; be useless: *I suppose you think I'm just sitting around every day with my thumb up my ass*—Village Voice

sit tight 1 *v phr* To keep one's present position, stance, convictions, etc; refuse to be moved; =STAND PAT **2** *v phr* To wait patiently: *Just sit tight, she'll be here in a minute*

sitting duck *n phr* An easy target; a totally defenseless person

be **sitting pretty** *v phr fr early 1900s* To be in a superior and very pleasant position; =SIT FAT: *He's just the same genial idiot whether he is out of luck or sitting pretty*—WW Rose

situash (sit yoo AYSH) *n* Situation

situation *See* ON TOP OF

sitzfleish *See* ZITSFLAISH

Siwash or **old Siwash** (SĪ wahsh) *n* or *n phr* Any small college; the archetypical small college; =EAST JESUS STATE: *collegians (from Harvard to Siwash) and their professors*—Time [fr Chinook jargon "north Pacific Coast Indian," fr French *sauvage* "savage, native," adopted as a term of contempt by cowboys; used in short stories by George Fitch, probably because some provincial colleges have similar Indian names]

six *See* DEEP SIX, EIGHTY-SIX, FIFTY-SIX, HIT ON ALL SIX

six-bit *modifier* Worth or costing seventy-five cents: *a six-bit sandwich*

six bits *n phr fr middle 1800s* Seventy-five cents

six-by *n truckers* A truck, esp a large one [fr *six-by-six*, the designation of a truck with six wheels and a six-speed transmission]

sixer *n underworld* A six-month prison sentence

six-hundred-pound gorilla *n phr* (also **eight-hundred-pound gorilla** or **nine-hundred-pound gorilla**) A powerful force; a virtually irresistible influence: *She is a 600-pound gorilla....She can intimidate anybody*—Time / *likens Spielberg to an "800-pound gorilla," which can be defined as a high-priced Hollywood species that makes its own decisions*—Los Angeles Times [fr a joke in which the question "Where does a *six-hundred-pound gorilla* sleep?" is answered "Anywhere it wants"]

six-pack *n circus* Three performances a day for two days: *Fridays and Saturdays...he has three [shows], the two days' stint known as a "six-pack"*—New Yorker

See JOE SIX-PACK

six-shooter or **six-gun** **1** *n fr middle 1800s cowboys* A revolver with a cylinder holding six cartridges **2** *n* Any revolver

sixty *See* LIKE SIXTY

◁**sixty-nine** or **69**▷ *n* Simultaneous oral sex between two persons, whose reciprocally inverse positions suggest the numeral 69

six ways to Sunday *See* FORTY WAYS TO SUNDAY

size *See* KING-SIZE, WHITTLE someone or something DOWN TO SIZE

size queen *n phr homosexuals* A homosexual who is particularly and nearly exclusively concerned with the length of penises

size up *v phr fr middle 1800s* To estimate or assess: *How do you size up his chances?*

sizzle *v* = FRY

sizzler **1** *n* A person or thing that is hot in any sense of the word **2** *n lumberjacks* A cook

sizzling *adj* Hot, in any sense: *sell some of the sizzling green at a discount*—Abel Green

sizz-water *See* FIZZ-WATER

ska (SKAH) *n* An early form of reggae music: *various musical trends, punk, New Wave, power-pop, ska*—Aquarian [origin unknown]

skag or **scag** **1** *n armed forces fr early 1900s* A cigarette or cigarette butt **2** *n 1960s teenagers fr black* A despicable person or thing; = JERK **3** *adj: a very skaggy guy* **4** *n black fr 1920s* An unattractive woman; = BAT, SKANK **5** *n narcotics* Cheap, low-quality heroin

skank **1** *n black* An unattractive woman; a malodorous woman; = SKAG **2** *n* A prostitute; = HOOKER: *How long would it take for them to find them f— skanks [the hookers] again?*—New York Times **3** *v* To move rhythmically in place like a rock and roll performer: *They move in sympathetic response to the music, skankin' from side to side*—Village Voice **4** *n:* *then back to that gentle skank*—Village Voice

skanky *adj teenagers fr black* Nasty; repellent; = GROTTY, SCUZZY: *The girls were somewhat skanky, with lank hair and rotten posture*—Richard Price

skate **1** *v fr 1930s black* To default a debt; avoid paying **2** *v black teenagers* To leave; = SPLIT **3** *v armed forces* To evade duty; = GOLDBRICK, GOOF OFF: *The gunny...accuses you of trying to skate*—New York Times **4** *n fr late 1800s* An inferior horse: *They'd kill that bunch of skates for their hides*—Ernest Hemingway

skate on thin ice *v phr* To take risks; behave perilously

sked *See* ON SKED

skedaddle *v fr middle 1800s* To run away; flee; fly; depart hastily [origin unknown; perhaps fr an attested Scots dialect sense, "spill," which could suggest "scatter, disperse"]

skeeter *n fr middle 1800s* A mosquito

sketch *See* HOT SKETCH, THUMBNAIL SKETCH

skewgee (SKOO jee) **1** *adj* Rattled and confused **2** *adj* Disorderly; = MESSY

◁**skibby**▷ **1** *n fr 1920s* A Japanese or person of Japanese descent **2** *n WW2 armed forces fr Pacific Northwest* An Asian prostitute [origin unknown]

ski (or **snow**) **bunny** *n phr* A young woman who frequents skiing resorts and skiers, and who may or may not ski herself

skid grease *n phr fr 1920s* Butter

skid lid *n phr motorcyclists* A motorcyclist's helmet: *suffered severe brain damage while wearing one of the company's skid lids*—Easyriders

skidoo or **skiddoo** *v* To depart hastily; = SCRAM ● Often a command or a bit of advice: *We heard the shooting and we skiddooed quick / Skidoo, skidoo, and quit me*—H McHugh [fr *skedaddle*]

skidoodle *v* = SKEDADDLE

skid road or **skidroad** **1** *n phr* or *n fr lumberjacks fr late 1800s* A forest track over which logs are dragged **2** *n phr* or *n* (also **Skid Road** or **Skidroad**) *fr lumberjacks, hoboes & underworld* A street or district of cheap shops and resorts; a relatively disreputable district: *I headed towards the Skidroad and its cheap eating joints*—Atlantic Monthly / *no skid road for the professor*—Westworld **3** *modifier: a tightwad with latent skid-road tendencies*—Washington Post [fr the *skidding* of logs]

skid row or **Skid Row** *n fr 1920s* A street or district frequented by derelicts, hoboes, drifters, etc, such as the Bowery in New York City [fr *skid road*]

Skid Row bum *n phr* A usu alcoholic derelict or drifter who frequents a street or district frequented by many such types and who lives by begging and pilfering; = BOWERY BUM, STUMBLEBUM, WINO

the **skids** *See* GREASE THE SKIDS, HIT THE SKIDS, ON THE SKIDS, PUT THE SKIDS UNDER someone or something

skillet *n outdated black* A black person: *You skillets is trying to promote a meal on me*—Zora Neale Hurston

skillion or **scillion** *n* An indefinite very large number: *I have a scillion things to say*—Philadelphia Bulletin

See JILLION

skim **1** *n gambling* Income not reported for tax purposes, esp from the gross earnings of a gambling casino or other such enterprise; = BLACK MONEY: *allegedly "cleansed" in the neighborhood of $2-million in "skim," untaxed gambling profits*—New York Times / *Caltronics is in on the skim*

—WT Tyler **2** *v:* *"appropriate, conceal, and skim" part of the winnings*—New York Times

skin 1 *n esp black* The hand as used in handshaking or hand-slapping as a salutation ● Nearly always in the expression **some skin**: *My man!...Gimme some skin!*—Malcolm X/ *Slip me some skin*—Ray Noble **2** *n fr earlier armed forces and rural* An inferior racehorse; =BEETLE: *They take the first bunch of skins out to gallop*—Ernest Hemingway **3** *n fr 1920s fr early 1800s British* A pocketbook, wallet, etc **4** *n* One dollar; a dollar bill: *One laid out 190 skins*—New Yorker ◁**5**▷ *n* A condom; =RUBBER **6** *modifier* Featuring nudity; indecently exposing; =GIRLIE: *a skin flick/ skin mag* **7** *n fr jazz musicians* A drum **8** *n* Life and health: *If he doesn't like you your skin isn't worth shit* **9** *v* To defeat decisively; trounce; =SKUNK: *They skinned the Wolverines 20 zip* **10** *v* To cheat or swindle; victimize: *You got skinned in that deal*—C Kuhn **11** *v* To slip through; squeeze hurriedly out: *and then skin out the window*—Harold Robbins

See FROGSKIN, GET UNDER someone's SKIN, GIVE SOME SKIN, NO SKIN OFF MY ASS, PIGSKIN, PRESS THE FLESH, SHEEPSKIN

skin-beater *n fr 1930s* A drummer: *the reefer-smitten skin beater*—New York Times

skin (or **flesh**) **flick** *n phr* A movie featuring nudity and more or less patent sexual activity; =BLUE MOVIE

◁**skin flute**▷ *n phr* The penis

See PLAY THE SKIN FLUTE

a **skinful** *n phr* One's intoxicating fill of liquor; =a SNOOT FULL: *Dey bot' got a skinful*—Eugene O'Neill

skin game *n phr fr late 1800s* A confidence game; =SCAM

skinhead 1 *n* A bald person or person with a shaved head **2** *n Marine Corps* A Marine recruit

skin house *n phr* A theater featuring nude shows, sex movies, etc

skin magazine *n phr* A magazine featuring nudity, more or less explicit sexual activity, etc; =NUDIE

skinned mush *n phr hawkers* A cane [fr the hawker term *mush* "umbrella," fr *mushroom* as describing the shape of an opened umbrella]

skinner **See** HACK-SKINNER, MULE-SKINNER

skinny *n phr* Information; facts: *claims to be the true, accurate, inside skinny on the David Begelman scandal*—GQ [probably fr *skinny* "naked, bare" as in *skinny dipping*]

the **skinny** *n phr fr WW2 armed forces* The truth; =the LOWDOWN, the SCOOP: *Are you giving me the straight skinny?*—Rex Burn/ *Here's the skinny: the show's an old-fashioned formula musical*—Village Voice [origin unknown; perhaps an alteration of *the naked truth*]

See the STRAIGHT SKINNY

skinny-dip *v phr* To swim naked: *Andrew went skinny-dipping in rocky pools*—Newsweek

skinny something **down** *v phr* To reduce something, esp to a minimum: *We were told to skinny the budget down still more*

skin pop *v phr narcotics* To inject narcotics into the skin or muscles, rather than into the circulatory system: *I'll have to skin pop*—H Braddy

skins 1 *n jazz musicians* A set of drums **2** *n fr hot rodders & truckers* Automotive tires: *Protect your present skins*—Playboy

skin-search or **body-shake** *police* **1** *n* A thorough scrutiny of a naked person, esp for hypodermic needle marks, concealed narcotics, etc **2** *v:* *They skin-searched both couples*

skint *adj fr late 1800s British* Lacking money; =BROKE ● Still chiefly British [fr *skinned*]

skip 1 *v esp students* To fail to attend; absent oneself; =SHINE: *if I let you skip school this afternoon*—JD Salinger **2** *v* (also **skip out**) *fr middle 1800s* To depart hastily, escape, abscond, esp to avoid paying a bill, being arrested, etc: *They skipped out of the motel at 2 AM* **3** *n* A person who absconds, esp to avoid paying a bill: *The skip took off...with a girl friend*—John D McDonald **4** *n esp armed forces* =SKIPPER

skipper 1 *n nautical* The captain of a ship or boat **2** *n Army* Any commanding officer; =the OLD MAN

◀**skippy**▶ *n fr WW2 Army* A Japanese woman, esp a prostitute [fr *skibby*]

skirt *n fr late 1800s* A woman, esp a young woman; =BROAD, CHICK ● Regarded by some women as offensive: *a real skirt*—Eugene O'Neill/ *never give any skirt a tumble*—Sinclair Lewis

skirt-chaser *n* A ladies' man; =LOVER-BOY

ski-trip *n narcotics* The taking of cocaine; a dose of cocaine [by extension fr *snow* "cocaine"]

skiv *n* =SHIV

skivvies 1 *n fr Navy* Underwear; underpants and undershirt: *stripped down to his skivvies and played his harmonica*—Playboy **2** *n* A pair of sandal-like slippers

skivvy *fr Navy* **1** *n* (also **skivvy shirt**) A man's undershirt, esp a T-shirt: *pants, sneakers, some skivvy shirts*—Harper's **2** *n* A pair of mens' underpants, esp of the boxer type

skivvy-waver *n WW2 Navy* A naval signal operator

skookum *adj lumberjacks fr middle 1800s* Effective; powerful [fr Chinook jargon, "powerful evil spirit," fr Chehalis *skukum*]

skosh or **scosh** (SKOHSH) *n fr Korean War armed forces* A little bit; =SMIDGEN: *You need a skosh more room here for your desk* [fr Japanese *sukoshi*]

skull **See** GO OUT OF one's SKULL, OUT OF one's HEAD, POPSKULL

skull-buster 1 *n black fr 1930s* A police officer **2** *n students fr 1920s* A very difficult course

skullduggery or **skulduggery** *n fr middle 1800s* Shady behavior; =DIRTY WORK, HANKY-PANKY [a US alteration of Scots *sculduddery* "bawdry, obscenity," which is attested from the early 18th century]

skull practice *n phr sports* The learning of plays, patterns, etc, esp in football by blackboard demonstrations

skull session *n phr* An intensive learning and teaching period, esp a briefing session: *two separate "skull sessions" with six members of the US negotiating team*—Newsweek

skunk *v fr middle 1800s* To defeat utterly, esp to hold the opponent scoreless in sports; trounce; =CLOBBER: *They're saying I'm going to get skunked in the black community*—Time [perhaps fr the definitive way in which a spraying *skunk* routs all present] *See* DRUNK AS A SKUNK

skunk someone **out of** something *v phr fr middle 1800s college students* To cheat someone out of something

sky *v sports* To hit or kick or throw a ball very high: *Winfield skied one into the bleachers/ This time he skied the punt right over the end zone See* PIE IN THE SKY

skycap *n* A porter at an air terminal [modeled on *red cap* "a railroad terminal porter"]

skygodlin or **sigoggling** (SKĬ gahd lən, SĬ gahg ling) *adj fr middle 1800s* Slantwise; askew; =COCKEYED, SLONCHWAYS [origin unknown; perhaps the original form was *skygoggling* or *sidegoggling*, where *goggle* means "eye," and the term would be an exact synonym of *cockeyed*]

skyhook *n* An imaginary hook in the sky which explains why some things stay up, which solves the problems of keeping some things up, etc: *How will I hold up the roof when I fix the wall? On a skyhook, of course*

skyhoot *v* To rise: *Jigger's reputation as a "rugged" man skyhooted from this point*—Stewart Holbrook

skyjack **1** *v* To take control of an aircraft illegally, usu by claiming to have a weapon or a bomb; commit air piracy **2** *n: the week's third skyjack to Cuba*

skypiece *n teenagers* A hat

sky-pilot *n fr late 1800s nautical* A member of the clergy

sky rug *n phr* A toupee

skyscraper *n baseball* A very high fly ball

sky up (or **out**) *v phr Army* To leave, esp to avoid work or trouble; leave work early

skywest *See* KNOCK someone or something GALLEY WEST

slab **1** *n 1930s jive talk* A bed **2** *n* One dollar; a dollar bill: *Ten slabs for two days' work!*—Merrill Blosser **3** *n baseball* Home plate **4** *n truckers* A highway *See* SUPER SLAB

slag *v* To denigrate; =BAD-MOUTH, PUT DOWN: *Everybody was getting slagged*—Rolling Stone/ *I don't mean to slag the girls at Douglas*—Aquarian [origin unknown; perhaps fr German *schlagen* "beat, whip"]

slag someone **off** *v phr apparently fr rock & roll* To denigrate severely; =SLAG: *This time I can't give it to you, can't totally slag you off*—Village Voice

slam **1** *n fr late 1800s* An uncomplimentary comment; a jibe; =KNOCK: *took a slam at the male stars who dress like "ranch hands"*—Associated Press **2** *v: Stop slamming the place and maybe they'll like*

you better **3** *v* (also **slam-dance**) To do a physically colliding and athletic sort of rock-and-roll dancing, esp in the vein of punk rock: *The music is hardcore, the dance is slamming*—Village Voice *See* GRAND SLAM

the **slam** *n phr* = the SLAMMER

slam-bang **1** *n prizefight fr 1920s* A wild and vicious fight **2** *adv* Violently: *They went at it slam-bang* **3** *adj* Raucous, violent, vigorous, etc: *in climaxes as slam-bang as a four-horse stretch drive*—Heywood Hale Broun/ *a couple of slam-bang musical numbers*—Playboy *See* SLAP

slam dunk *v phr basketball* To score a field goal by leaping up and thrusting the ball violently down through the hoop: *the first to slam-dunk a football over the crossbar after a touchdown*—Philadelphia Journal

slammer *n basketball* = SLAM DUNK *See* GRAND SLAMMER

the **slammer** **1** *n phr fr 1930s jive talk* A door: *twister to the slammer*—Variety **2** *n phr* (also the **slams**) *fr black* A jail, prison, etc: *Drunk drivers go to the slammer in this town*

slang *n fr middle 1700s British* A style or register of language consisting of terms that can be substituted for standard terms of the same conceptual meaning but having stronger emotive impact than the standard terms, in order to express an attitude of self-assertion towards conventional order and moral authority and often an affinity with or membership in occupational, ethnic, or other social groups, and ranging in acceptability from sexual and scatological crudity to audacious wittiness (see Preface) [origin unknown; probably related to *sling*, which has cognates in Norwegian that suggest the abusive nature of slang; the British dialect original term *slang* meant both "a kind of projectile-hurling weapon," and "the language of thieves and vagabonds," reinforcing the connection with "sling"]

slant **1** *n* A look; an ocular inspection: *Take a slant at dat*—Eugene O'Neill/ *The prowl car takes a slant down now and then*—Raymond Chandler **2** *n* One's opinion or point of view; =ANGLE: *something about his tone or his "slant" that irritated his contemporaries*—Joseph Wood Krutch/ *The editor suggested I give it a human-interest slant*

◄**slant-eye**► *n* An Asian person or person of Asian descent

slap or **slap-bang** or **slam-bang** *adv* Precisely; directly: *Streets that ended slap in a courtyard*—Sinclair Lewis/ *The storm was pointed slam-bang at Tampa*—Associated Press

slap and tickle *n phr* Amorous dalliance; playful fondling: *a spot of slap and tickle*—Peter De Vries

slapdash *adj* Hasty and careless; heedless of the fine details; =SLOPPY

slap someone **five** *See* GIVE someone FIVE

slap-happy **1** *adj* Disoriented and stuporous, esp from being hit too often about the head: *a slap-happy bum*—Jim Tully **2** *adj* Vertiginous; off balance: *designed to knock philologists slap-happy*—Newsweek **3** *adj* Euphoric; intoxicated;

=HIGH: *He was slap-happy a whole week after the baby came*

a **slap in the face** *n phr* An insult or rebuke, esp when unexpected; a rebuff: *His not saying anything is a slap in the face*

slapman *n 1920s underworld* A plainclothes police officer

a **slap on the wrist** *See* GIVE someone A SLAP ON THE WRIST

slapper *See* KNEE-SLAPPER

slap someone's **wrist** *v phr* To punish very lightly ● Usu said when the punishment is felt to be unjustly lenient

slat *n* A ski

slate *See* SCRUB THE SLATE CLEAN

slathers *n fr middle 1800s* A large quantity; =OODLES: *It cost the railroads slathers of money* —Jack London [ultimately fr Irish *sliotar*]

slats *n fr early 1900s* The ribs: *pokes him in the slats* —Ben Hecht

slave *n black fr 1930s* A job: *You got a job, man. You got a slave*—New York

slave market *n phr* An employment office or a place or occasion where jobs are sought and candidates present themselves

slaves and masters *n phr* Sadists and masochists, in sexual taste: *referred to by the cognoscenti as "S and M," or "slaves and masters,"...the most prevalent of the freak syndrome*—Xaviera Hollander

slay *v fr 1930s* To impress someone powerfully, esp to provoke violent and often derisive laughter: *Pardon me, this will slay you*—Heywood Broun/ *The boys who slay me are the ones who have set pieces to recite when they answer the phone*—H Allen Smith

sleaze **1** *n* Anything shabby and disgusting; particularly revolting trash; =CRAP, SCHLOCK, SHIT: *a paragon of Dorothy Malone low-fashion sleaze*—Village Voice **2** *n esp teenagers & students* =SLEAZEBAG **3** *v esp teenagers & students* To be sexually promiscuous and disreputable **4** *v students* To scrounge; =MOOCH [a back-formation from *sleazy*]

sleazebag or **sleazeball** *n* A despicable person; =DIRTBAG, SCUZZBAG: *Tartikoff calls the character "a total sleazebag"*—Time/ *If you're a sleaze-ball, you deserve a recall*—Newsweek

sleaze-bucket *adj* Nasty; degradingly repellent: *sleaze-bucket movies*

sleazemonger *n* A producer or seller of nasty entertainment: *one of Hollywood's lowlier sleazemongers*—Washington Post

sleazy or **sleazo** or **sleazoid** *adj* Disgusting; filthy; nasty; =GRUNGY, SCUZZY: *dirty buildings in sleazy sections*—New York Daily News/ *a tremendous evocation of the sleazoid speed-freak scene* —Rolling Stone/ *who makes sleazo blood films* —Pauline Kael [fr late-17th-century British *sleasie* "thin, flimsy, threadbare," of uncertain origin, whence it came to mean "of inferior workmanship, shoddy"; perhaps fr *Sleasie* "Silesian," used of linen cloth from that part of Germany]

sled *See* NOVA UNDER SNOW ON A SLED

sleep around *v phr* To be sexually promiscuous; =PLAY AROUND

sleeper *fr 1930s* **1** *n* Anything, esp a low-budget movie, a show, or a book, which achieves or probably will achieve success after a time of obscurity: *"My Name is Julia Ross" is the first "sleeper" to come to Philadelphia in months*—Philadelphia Bulletin/ *whose "Return of the Secaucus Seven" ranked among the more astute sleepers of 1980* —Playboy **2** *modifier: a sleeper play* **3** *n football* A player who unexpectedly and cunningly gets the ball and runs **4** *n narcotics* A sleeping pill or a sedative [the first sense may be fr the mid-19th-century gambling term *sleeper* meaning both "an unexpected winning card," and "a pot whose owner has ignored it, and hence is free to anyone who takes it"]

sleepville or **Sleepville** *adj cool talk* Sleepy; comatose

sleep with someone *v phr* To do the sex act with someone; =GO TO BED WITH someone ● Perhaps not so much slang as merely a much-needed euphemism: *No girl could love a man unless she had slept with the man over a period of time*—Calder Willingham

sleeve *See* ACE UP one's SLEEVE, PUT THE ARM ON someone

sleighride **1** *n narcotics fr early 1900s* Intoxication from cocaine **2** *v narcotics* To use cocaine [fr the association of *sleighrides* with *snow* "cocaine"]

sleighrider *n narcotics fr early 1900s* A cocaine addict; also, a user of cocaine; =COKEHEAD

slew *n fr middle 1800s* A large quantity; =OODLES, SLATHERS: *a slew of cops*—G Homes [origin uncertain; perhaps fr Irish *sluagh*]

slewed *adj fr middle 1800s British* Drunk [fr *slew* "veer, swing around"]

slewfoot **1** *n fr late 1800s* A clumsy, stumbling person; a person who moves awkwardly **2** *v* (also **sloughfoot**) To walk with the feet turned away from the straight direction: *The Airedale slough-footed away*—Richard Starnes **3** *n* A police officer or detective [fr the awkwardness of a person whose feet *slew* outwards overmuch or are otherwise ill-controlled]

slice *n fr 1920s* A portion or share; =PIECE: *Five grand wouldn't get you a slice of her*—Fredric Brown

slice and dice film *n phr* A horror movie, esp one featuring bloody mutilation: *Mr De Palma's movies are distinguished from "slice and dice films"* —New York Times

sliced bread *See* the BEST (or GREATEST) THING SINCE SLICED BREAD

slick **1** *adj fr early 1600s* Smooth and clever; smart: *She's a very slick talker* **2** *adj* Cunning; crafty: *more than a match for any slick city lawyer* —Erle Stanley Gardner **3** *adj fr early 1800s* Excellent; =NIFTY: *The soup was "simply slick"* —Sinclair Lewis **4** *adj fr 1940s* Glib and superficial; without real substance: *They turn out people with slick plastic personalities* **5** *n* A magazine printed on glossy paper and usu having some artistic or intellectual pretensions: *magazines...from top slicks to minor pulps*—New York Times **6** *n hot rodders* An automobile tire with a very smooth tread [earlier 19th-century uses were in comparative phrases like *slick as bear's grease* and *slick as molasses*]

slick chick *n phr fr 1930s jive talk* An attractive young woman, esp one who is notably up-to-date and au courant: *the "slick chicks" at Sequoia Union High*—Life/ *a slick chick, a pretty girl*—Meyer Berger

slicker 1 *n fr early 1900s* A clever and crafty person, esp a confidence trickster, a dishonest business executive, a shrewd and predatory lawyer, etc; =CROOK: *I don't admire slickers who peddle get-rich-quick bubbles*—Major Hoople (comic strip) **2** *n esp 1920s* A socially smooth and superficially attractive person; =SMOOTHIE: *The slicker was good-looking and clean-looking*—F Scott Fitzgerald **3** *v* To cheat; =CON, SCAM: *outsmarted and slickered by Moscow*—CV Jackson/ *A fox tried to slicker him out of the cheese*—Bing Crosby
See CITY SLICKER

the **slicks** *n phr* Glossy, expensive, and high- or middle-brow magazines, as distinguished from pulp magazines: *She finally sold a story to the slicks*

slickum *n* Hair oil; pomade

slick someone or something **up** *v phr* To make neat and more attractive; furbish; =GUSSY UP: *We'd better slick this place up before the President arrives/ What are they all slicked up for?*

slide *v fr middle 1800s & now esp black* To depart; =SPLIT

slim *n jazz musicians* A cigarette

Slim *See* JERUSALEM SLIM

slimebag or **slimeball** or **slimebucket** *n* A despicable person; a repugnant wretch; =GEEK, SCUMBAG, SLEAZEBAG: *I'm a disgusting slime bag, but I don't grovel*—Washington Post/ *I remember when the slime-balls used to be packed in there so solid*—Joseph Wambaugh

slim pickings *n phr* Very little to be had or earned; extremely unprofitable returns: *You'll find it's slim pickings there, if you're looking for a fast buck*

sling *See* HAVE one's ASS IN A SLING, PUT someone's ASS IN A SLING

sling beer *v phr* To be a bartender or waiter: *would look at home slinging beer at any tavern*—Toronto Life

slinger *n* A waiter or waitress; a food server: *Anybody but a California Bar-B-Q slinger would know that*—James M Cain [fr the mid-19th-century phrase *sling hash*]
See GRUB-SLINGER, GUN-SLINGER, HASH-SLINGER, INK-SLINGER, LIGHTNING-SLINGER, POT-SLINGER

sling hash *v phr fr middle 1800s* To work as a waiter or waitress: *I used to sling their hash*—Joseph Auslander/ *She slung hash for a couple of weeks*—Life

slinging *See* MUD-SLINGING

sling ink *v phr fr middle 1800s* To write, esp as a newspaper reporter or otherwise professionally

sling it or **sling the bull** *v phr* To exaggerate and lie; talk smoothly and persuasively; =BULLSHIT, SHOOT THE BULL: *The chief reason for the conversational effectiveness of many individuals is their inherent ability to sling it*—AH Marckwardt and FG Cassidy

sling mud *v phr* To defame; malign one's character: *They've got no real case, so all they can do is sling mud at her*

sling Ss *v phr prison* To stare

slinky *adj* Sinuous and sexy: *one of those slinky glittering females*—Raymond Chandler

slip 1 *v fr 1930s* To give; hand: *So I slip him a double Z*—Lawrence Sanders **2** *v fr 1920s* To lose one's competence or touch; decline: *Only six pages today? I must be slipping*
See BUCK SLIP, PINK SLIP

slip someone **a mickey** (or **a Mickey**) *v phr* To give knockout drops, esp chloral hydrate, secretly in a drink: *He passed out as if someone had slipped him a Mickey*

slip between the cracks *See* FALL BETWEEN THE CRACKS

slip-horn *n jazz musicians* A trombone

slip in between the lily whites *v phr* To go to bed; go to sleep

slip (or **give**) **me five** *sentence fr early 1900s* Shake hands with me: *Slip me five so I know you're alive*

slipper *v fr 1920s underworld* To renounce a life of crime; reform; =GO STRAIGHT: *When a crook is reformed he is "slippered"*—Collier's [fr the image of retirement: putting on one's *slippers* and sitting in an easy chair before the fire]

slippy *adj* Quick; fast

slipstick *n students fr 1920s* A slide rule

slip one's **trolley** *v phr* To lose one's rational composure; =FLIP OUT, FREAK OUT: *She was going around babbling as if she had slipped her trolley*

slip-up *n fr middle 1800s* A miscalculation; an accident; =GLITCH: *There must have been a hell of a slip-up somewhere along the line*

◁**slit**▷ *n* The vulva; =CUNT

slob 1 *n fr late 1800s British* A pudgy, generally unattractive, and untidy person: *You great, fat slob!*—Owen Johnson/ *a big slob with a chin that stuck out like a shelf*—Raymond Chandler **2** *n* A slovenly and disorderly person; a sloppy and disheveled person: *What a slob! You'd think his room was the town dump* **3** *n* A mediocre person, esp one who is likely to fail or be victimized: *just another poor slob*—Jerome Weidman [fr Anglo-Irish, used affectionately of a quiet, fat, slow child]

slo-mo *adv* Slowly; in slow-motion: *A man named Ahmed skated slo-mo*—Village Voice

slonchways *adj* =SKYGODLIN

slope¹ 1 *v* (also **slope out**) *fr early 1800s* To run away; depart; =LAM **2** *v underworld & hoboes* To escape from jail [perhaps fr Dutch *sloop* "sneaked away"]

◄**slope²** ► *n Vietnam War armed forces* An Asian; = DINK, GOOK [fr the apparent slanting of eyes caused by the typical epicanthic fold of Asian peoples]

slopped *adj* Drunk

sloppy 1 *adj fr 1920s* Slovenly; disorderly; = MESSY **2** *adj* Careless; = SLAPDASH

sloppy Joe 1 *n phr esp 1940s students* A long, loose pullover sweater worn by women **2** *n phr* A dish made from ground meat cooked in a barbecue sauce and spread on an open bun **3** *n phr* A multi-decked sandwich served in small thick triangles and filled with meats, cheeses, and mayonnaise, such that it is difficult to eat while keeping the fingers and face clean

sloppy Joe's *n phr fr 1940s* A cheap restaurant or lunch counter; = GREASY SPOON

slops *n hoboes fr early 1900s* Beer

sloshed *adj* Drunk: *a youngish man in a bar, a little sloshed and pouring out his troubles to the bartender*—New Yorker/ *You'll spend the night...getting sloshed on 3.2 salmon piss*—Village Voice

slot *n* A slot machine; = ONE-ARM BANDIT: *The slots are going day and night*—Richard Bissell

slouch *See* NO SLOUCH

sloughfoot *See* SLEWFOOT

slough in (or **up**) (SLŌŌ) *v phr fr late 1800s hoboes* To arrest; imprison: *I've boozed around this town for seven years, and I've not been sloughed up yet*—J Flynt

slow *See* TAKE IT SLOW

slow burn *See* DO A SLOW BURN

slow coach *n phr fr middle 1800s students* A dull fellow; a stupid person

slowly in the wind *See* TWIST SLOWLY IN THE WIND

slow on the draw (or **the uptake**) *adj phr* Dull and dilatory; mentally sluggish [fr the action of drawing one's pistol, in the classical cowboy context]

slowpoke *n fr late 1800s Australian* A slow, sluggish, slothful person: *an old slowpoke*—Philip Wylie [fr *slow* used for vowel rhyme with the early-19th-century *poke* "behave dilatorily, potter, saunter," perhaps influenced by 16th-century *slowback* "sluggard"]

sludgeball *n* A slovenly person; = DIRTBALL, SLOB: *I saw her drink beer out of a paper cup....I thought she was a sludgeball*—Washington Post [probably based in part on the increased currency of *sludge* as the product of sewer treatment plants]

sluff *v* To avoid work and responsibility; shirk: *No one accused Bo of sluffing*—People Weekly

slug¹ 1 *n fr middle 1800s* A bullet: *Doctors said they're still unable to remove the slug*—New York Post **2** *n fr late 1800s hoboes & circus* A dollar: *do the job at 125 slugs a week*—Associated Press **3** *n* A drink of liquid, esp of whiskey; = SNORT: *ordering a slug of old stepmother*—Westbrook Pegler **4** *v* (also **slug down:**) *We were happily slugging our martinis/ in between slugging down at least ten Dr Peppers a day and puffing on as many*

fat cigars—Time [origin uncertain; perhaps fr the resemblance of a lump of metal to the snail-like creature the *slug*; the earliest attested US senses are "gold nugget, lump of crude metal"; the drink and drinking senses appear to be derived fr phrases like *fire a slug* and *cast a slug* "take a drink of liquor," found as metaphors in late-18th-century British sources]

slug² 1 *v fr middle 1800s* To hit hard, esp with the fist; = CLOBBER: *He tried to make peace, but he got slugged* **2** *v baseball* To make or try for long base hits, esp regularly; = GO FOR THE FENCES [fr British dialect *slog*, probably ultimately fr Old English *slagan*, cognate with German *schlagen*]

See PUT THE SLUG ON someone

slugfest 1 *n fr early 1900s* A hard and vicious fight, esp a prizefight more marked by powerful blows than by skillful boxing **2** *n fr 1930s* A baseball game in which many base hits are made

slugged *adj* Drunk: *I want you really slugged when we shoot the scene*—SJ Perelman

slugger 1 *n baseball fr late 1800s* A consistent long-ball hitter: *He's no slugger, he likes to place his hits* **2** *n* A boxer more notable for hard hitting than for artistic finesse

See CIRCUIT SLUGGER

slug it out *v phr* To fight with powerful blows; try to smash one another; = GO TOE TO TOE: *The principals were slugging it out in the alley*

slug-nutty *adj fr 1930s* Stuporous or uncoordinated mentally and physically from taking too many blows on the head; = PUNCH-DRUNK: *"Slug-nutty" fighters are often very talkative*—Literary Digest

slum¹ or **go slumming** *v* or *v phr fr middle 1800s* To visit places or consort with persons below one's place or dignity; mix with one's inferiors: *So we went slumming over in Philadelphia* [fr *slum* "wretched poor area," origin unknown]

slum² or **slumgullion** or **slumgudgeon** *n esp hoboes & armed forces fr late 1800s* Any inferior and esp unidentifiable food or drink; a nasty nameless stew; slop [origin unknown; perhaps a vaguely echoic denigratory coinage related to *slum¹*]

slurb *n* A suburb of cheap mass-produced houses, ugly business places, etc: *The towns all merged in one faceless, undifferentiated slurb*—George Warren [probably a blend of *slum* and *suburb*]

slurp or **slup 1** *v fr 1920s* To eat or drink with noisy sucking sounds: *slurping porridge from a wooden spoon*—Ogden Nash/ *The cat slupped up the milk in no time*—Christian Science Monitor **2** *n:* *Take a slurp of this soup, it's great!* **3** *n jazz musicians* A glissando passage [echoic]

slush *n fr late 1800s* Blatant sentimentality; = GOO, SCHMALTZ: *I sort of wept and uttered a lot of slush*

slush fund *n phr fr late 1800s* In politics, money used for shady enterprises like buying votes, bribing officials, etc: *the use of slush funds to defeat selected victims*—Westbrook Pegler [fr the armed forces and especially nautical practice of selling grease and other garbage to accumulate a *fund* to buy little luxuries for the troops or crew]

slush pump *n phr jazz musicians fr 1930s* A trombone; = SLIP-HORN

slut lamp *n phr esp hoboes* An improvised lamp; = BITCH LAMP: *Byron called it a "slut lamp"*—Nelson Algren [fr *slut* "piece of rag dipped in fat and used as a light," attested fr the early 17th century; perhaps so-called because of its use by *sluts* "kitchen maids"; the version *bitch lamp* represents a synonymous substitution]

smack¹ **1** *n* A blow; a slap: *He gave her a smack on the kisser* **2** *v:* *She smacked him hard* **3** *n* A kiss; = SMACKER **4** *v:* *She smacked him square on the lips* **5** *n* A try; = CRACK: *Let's have a smack at it, shall we?* **6** *adv* (also **smack dab**) *fr late 1800s* Exactly; precisely: *What he said was smack on the mark* [probably ultimately echoic]

smack² or **shmack** or **shmeck** *n narcotics* Heroin; = HORSE: *The cocaine pulled from the front while the smack pushed from the back. It was an incredibly intense high*—High Times [fr Yiddish *shmek* "a smell, sniff"; an earlier sense was "a small packet of drugs," hence merely a sniff or whiff]

smacker **1** *n fr early 1900s* A dollar; = BUCK: *having to cough up a thousand smackers*—Lowell Thomas/ *That car's not worth a smacker* **2** *n* A kiss; = SMACK: *Slip me a smacker, sister*—Jimmy Durante [the money sense, attested also of pesos and pounds sterling, may echo the slapping down of a bill on a counter, gambling table, etc, and hence be semantically related to *plank* and *plunk* for coins] See BELLY-SMACKER

smacko *n* A sound suggesting a blow or a kiss: *He went up to the bully and smacko, he let him have it*

smacky lips See PLAY KISSIE

smadge *n Army* A sergeant major [fr *sergeant major*]

small-bore *adj fr late 1800s* Trivial; insignificant; petty: *No more of your small-bore notions, please* [fr the *bore* or caliber of a gun, which indicates its size and importance]

small fry **1** *n phr* Children or a child • Often used as a term of address, either affectionate or derogatory **2** *n phr* An insignificant person or persons; nonentities: *conveniences not enjoyed by the small fry overhead*—Theodore Dreiser **3** *adj:* *small-fry writers like me*—Budd Schulberg [fr *fry* "small or immature fish"]

small nickel *n phr gambling* Five hundred dollars, esp as a bet

small pipe *n phr cool talk* An alto saxophone

small potatoes (Variations: **beer** or **bread** or **change** may replace **potatoes**) *fr middle 1800s* **1** *n phr* A trivial amount of money; = CHICKEN FEED, PEANUTS: *I received $120,000, which is no small potatoes*—Danny Thomas **2** *n phr* An insignificant person, enterprise, etc: *His highest ambition is pretty small potatoes/ Those plans look like small beer to me*

the small (or **fine**) **print** *n phr* Unsuspected and injurious conditions or requirements, esp when part of a contract, an insurance policy, etc: *Be sure you look at the small print if you make any deals with that guy/ Does the mayor read the fine print?*—Philadelphia

the small time *n phr fr show business fr early 1900s* Mediocre or inferior businesses, enterprises, entertainment or sports circuits, etc; = the BUSH LEAGUES: *After six years in the small time she finally had a big hit and went to Broadway*

small-time *adj fr show business fr early 1900s* Characteristic of the small time; inferior; petty; second-rate; = BUSH LEAGUE: *I was a small-time gun-runner/ a small-time political power*—E Lavine

smarmy **1** *adj fr early 1900s British* Smooth and flattering; unctuously ingratiating; fulsome: *a rather smarmy doctor and a highly officious nurse*—Time **2** *adj* Rich and sonorous; orotund and fruity; = PLUMMY: *an announcer with a smarmy voice* **3** *adj* Smug and self-righteous: *Uncle Sam's Smarmy Look Into Employee Sex Lives*—Nashville [origin unknown; since the earliest attested uses have to do with hair oil, it may be a vague blend of *smooth, smear, palm oil, cream,* etc]

smart *adj armed forces esp fr Vietnam War* Guided toward a target by laser beams, television signals, etc, rather than simply aimed: *The subs are equipped with smart torpedoes*—New York Times/ *the potential accuracy of "smart" bombs and missiles*—Foreign Affairs See GET WISE, STREET-SMART

smart (or **one smart**) **apple** *n phr* An intelligent person; a sagacious person: *I told you....You're up against a smart apple*—Lawrence Sanders

◁**smart-ass** or **wise-ass**▷ **1** *n* A person who is quick to offer often abrasive opinion or comment from a posture of superior intelligence and learning; smart aleck; = BIGMOUTH, KNOW-IT-ALL, WISE GUY: *Only a real smart-ass would try to tell the general what to do/ You're a real wiseass sometimes, Mary Anne*—Pat Conroy/ *a born wiseass*—John Irving **2** *adj:* *That's a smart-ass question*—Newsweek/ *a smart-ass tone of voice*—Mother Jones

smart guy *n* A smart aleck; = SMART-ASS: *Well, I've got news for you, smart guy*—Joseph Heller

the smart money *n phr* The predictions, expectations, and bets of those who know best: *The smart money says you better stock lots of prunes/ Try to stick where the smart money is*

smartmouth *n* An annoyingly impudent, assertive, and critical person; = SMART-ASS: *keeps getting beaten up because he's a smartmouth at school*—Philadelphia

smarts *n* Intelligence; = BRAINS, SAVVY: *If they had any smarts, they would have put a silencer on a gun and pumped a bullet in his head*—Playboy [probably on analogy with *brains* and *wits*] See STREET SMARTS

smarty *n fr middle 1800s* A smart aleck; = SMART-ASS • Most often used in address: *I will bid seven on hearts, smarty*—Sinclair Lewis

smarty-pants *n* A smart aleck; = SMART-ASS, SMARTY: *That smarty-pants always gives a flip answer*

smash **1** *n fr middle 1800s* A total failure; a disaster **2** *n* (also **smash hit**) *fr show business fr*

1920s A great success; =HIT: *"Key Largo" is an unqualified smash*—Variety **3** *n* black Wine

smashed *adj* Drunk

smasher *n fr late 1700s British* Something remarkably impressive and successful: *I thought the book was a smasher*—AJ Liebling

See BAGGAGE SMASHER

smashing 1 *adj fr late 1800s British* Excellent; wonderful ● Still chiefly British: *I told her she looked smashing* **2** *n* outdated teenagers Kissing; =NECKING

smear[1] **1** *v* prizefight *fr 1920s* To knock unconscious; =KAYO **2** *v* To defeat decisively; trounce; =CLOBBER, SKUNK: *The Rangers got smeared 12 zilch* **3** *v* To attack someone's reputation, esp with false or vague charges of the ad hominem sort; defame: *His technique was always to smear his opponent and avoid talking about issues of substance* **4** *n:* *His whole campaign was a vile smear of the other party's man* **5** *modifier:* *They never stoop to smear tactics*

smear[2] *v* To bribe or otherwise make an illegal payment to someone; =SCHMEAR

smell 1 *v* To be nasty and contemptible; =STINK, SUCK: *The whole damn situation smells* **2** *v* To take narcotics by inhaling; =SNIFF: *You must be smelling the stuff*—John Roeburt

smell a rat *v phr* To be suspicious: *impossible for Schwartz not to have smelled a rat if he had day-to-day contact*—Village Voice

smell blood *v phr* To be aroused and exhilarated by the imminent destruction of one's prey or opponent: *The Democrats "smelled blood" over the trade issue*—New York Times [fr the behavior of predators who attack prey, esp wounded prey]

smeller *n* The nose: *a sock on his smeller*—Charles MacArthur

smelling *See* GOAT-SMELLING

smell like a rose *v phr* To be pure and innocent; be in good odor: *Some of the President's associates don't quite smell like a rose/ Just make sure you smell like a rose*

See COME UP SMELLING LIKE A ROSE

smidgen *n fr middle 1800s* A little bit; =CUNT-HAIR, SKOSH: *The deck may be stacked a smidgen against Lianna's husband*—Playboy

smile *See* CRACK A SMILE

-smith *combining word* A person who makes or skillfully uses what is indicated; =ARTIST: *tunesmith/ wordsmith/ wafflesmith*

smoke 1 *n* A cigarette: *I mooched a couple of smokes* **2** *n* narcotics Marijuana; =POT: *something called smoke or snow*—Carson McCullers **3** *n* hoboes Inferior liquor, esp denatured alcohol: *drink that smoke, then pass out petrified*—Harper's **4** *n* Artful lies; talk meant to deceive; =BULLSHIT: *Those sections of the article are pure smoke*—New York Times ◄**5**► *n* A black person **6** *v* underworld *fr 1940s* To shoot someone; =PLUG **7** *v* police & underworld To be executed in a gas chamber: *still faced death and might one day be smoked*—Joseph Wambaugh **8** *n* baseball A very fast fastball: *Has Joe lost his smoke?*—Newsweek/ the

Yankees' smoke-throwing reliever—Aquarian **9** *v:* pitchers are supposed to be cranked up and smoking—Sports Illustrated **10** *v* To be very angry; =BURN: *He was smoking for about an hour after she called him that* **11** *n* college students A dollar: *He paid six smokes for that shirt*

See BLOW SMOKE, BRING SCUNNION, GO UP IN SMOKE, HOLY CATS, J, JOY SMOKE

a **smoke** *n* Tobacco and a smoking of tobacco

the **smoke** *n phr* narcotics Opium: *He went for the smoke himself*—Stephen Longstreet

smoke and joke *v phr* Army To relax; idle and be casual

smokeball *n* baseball A very fast fastball

smoke-eater *n fr 1930s* A firefighter

smoke factory *n phr fr early 1900s* An opium den: *a No 9 pill in Hop Lee's smoke factory*—H McHugh

smoke out *v phr* To find out: *I'll try to smoke out where the bodies are hidden* [fr the use of smoke in order to get bees out of the hive and take the honey]

smoke someone **out 1** *v phr* To get information from someone: *He isn't saying now, but she'll smoke him out* **2** *v phr* To cause someone to emerge, esp from hiding: *The offer of clemency smoked out the whole gang*

smoker 1 *n* Something thrown, moving, played, etc, very fast: *a number which is a quartet smoker*—Down Beat **2** *n* railroad A locomotive

smoke (or **chiba**) **shop** *n phr* narcotics A place where one may buy marijuana, esp a shop where it is sold rather openly: *Smoke shops are taking over our streets*—New York Times/ *Thousands of clerks operate more than 800 smoke shops around the city*—New York

Smokey Bear or **Smokey the Bear** or **Smoky** *n phr* or *n* citizens band & truckers A police officer, esp a state highway patrol officer: *Keep Don advised for the location of "Smokies"*—Rolling Stone [fr the fact that many state highway patrol police wear a broad-brimmed ranger's hat like that worn by the US Forest Service's ursine symbol]

smoking gun *n phr esp fr early 1970s* Incontestable evidence; =the GOODS: *They had discovered the "smoking gun" that would destroy the general's case*—New York Times/ *In fact, there may be no "smoking gun," no incontrovertible, black-and-white evidence of wrongdoing*—Time [fr the image of a murderer caught with the fatal firearm still in hand, smoking]

◄**smoky**► *adj* Black; Negroid: *The spades are moving in and it's getting smokier every day*—Nelson Algren

Smoky *See* OLD SMOKY

smoky seat *n phr* The electric chair; =OLD SMOKY

smooch or **smooge** or **smouge 1** *v* To steal; pilfer; =MOOCH: *Then she went over to the cash box and smooched four $20 bills*—James M Cain **2** *v* fr late 1500s fr British dialect To kiss and caress; =NECK, PET ● Even though quite old, the term was reestablished in US use in the 1930s: *College kids are still smooching*—Max Shulman/ *a few* *minutes of torrid hugging and smooching*—Calder Willingham **3** *n: I'd rather have hooch, and a bit of a smooch*—Hal Boyle [the pilfering sense probably derives from the kissing sense by way of *mooch*; the kissing sense is perhaps echoic, imitating a noisy smacking osculation]

smooching *n* The act or practice of one who kisses and caresses

smooth *adj fr late 1800s* Excellent; pleasing; attractive: *Boy, she was smooth*—Jerome Weidman
See JUMP SMOOTH

smoothie or **smooth article** or **smooth operator** *n* or *n phr* A person who is attractive, pleasant, and full of finesse ● **Smoothie** is like **slicker**, but today lacks the connotations of dishonesty and trickiness: *thought of Dr Hugo Barker as a smooth article*—AR Hilliard/ *You think you're such a smoothie*—Sinclair Lewis

snafu (SNA Foo) *fr WW2 armed forces* **1** *n* A very confused situation; = FUCK-UP, MESS: *The snafu occurred at Markwood Road*—New York Daily News **2** *adj: It's a very snafu set-up here* **3** *n* A blunder; an egregious mistake; = BLOOPER: *My attempt to set things right was a total snafu* **4** *v: He gave it a good shot, but snafued horribly* [fr *situation normal, all fucked up*]

snake 1 *n WW1 Navy* A young woman **2** *n railroad* A switch engine **3** *n* (also **Snake**) A native or resident of West Virginia **4** *v* To depart, esp unobtrusively; sneak: *He snakes out of here without an overcoat*—Leslie Ford
See BLACK SNAKE

snake-bitten *adj* Helplessly incapacitated; ineffective: *O'Neal seems particularly snake-bitten these days*—Playboy

snake eater *n phr Army* A soldier trained in survival and commando tactics, the initiates of which actually kill and eat snakes

snake eyes *n phr crapshooting* The point or the roll of two

snake-hips or **swivel-hips** *n* A person whose hips move smoothly and effectively, such as a clever runner in football, a hula dancer, etc

snake poison *n phr fr late 1800s* Whiskey

snap 1 *n fr middle 1800s* Energy; vim; dash; = PIZZAZZ **2** *n fr late 1800s* A photograph; snapshot **3** *v: The photographer snapped him making a rude gesture* **4** *v esp college students* To go crazy; = FREAK OUT: *that Richard Herrin should have snapped*—Ms [the last sense is fr the cliché "something *snapped* in his mind"]

a **snap** *n phr fr late 1800s* Something easily done; = BREEZE, CINCH: *Winning next time will be a snap* [fr mid-19th-century *a soft snap* "something *snapped* up easily, a bargain"]

snap course *n phr college students fr late 1800s* An easy course; = CRIP: *His heavily attended snap course is good for a laugh*—Atlantic Monthly

snap it up *v phr* To hurry; act faster; = SNAP TO IT: *Drop over to the main drag and snap it up*—Raymond Chandler

snap out of it *v phr fr early 1900s* To recover, esp from gloom or sluggardness; become energetic

snapper *n* The point or risible climax of a story or joke; = PUNCH LINE, ZINGER: *With Neil Simon's vaudeville snappers what matters is that they come on schedule*—Pauline Kael/ *The final snapper was that Lubben never got his income tax paid by his ex-partners, either*—Fargo Forum
See BRONCO BUSTER, MACKEREL-SNAPPER

snappers *n* Teeth

snappy 1 *adj* Quick; energetic: *Be snappy about it* **2** *adj fr late 1800s British* Trim and attractive; fashionable; smart: *wearing a snappy light gray suit*—Associated Press
See MAKE IT SNAPPY

snap to *v phr* To become sharply attentive and responsive: *His soldiers snapped to and did what they were told*—New York Times [fr the quick way a military person *snaps to attention* on command]

snap to (or **into**) **it** *v phr fr early 1900s* To hurry; go faster; = MAKE IT SNAPPY: *Get that floor clean and snap to it*

snarky *adj fr early 1900s* Irritable; touchy: *She's just in a snarky mood, that's all*—Noel B Gerson/ *a snarky, no-illusions, but far-from-hopeless comedy*—Ms [fr British dialect *snark* "find fault, complain," fr the basic sense "snort, snore"; of echoic origin, with cognates in many Germanic languages]

snatch 1 *v fr 1920s* To kidnap: *The kid was snatched as he left school* **2** *n: a $50,000 ransom to get him back from a snatch*—Westbrook Pegler **3** *v* To steal, esp by shoplifting **4** *n: A piece of paper covering the slit was rolled aside in the course of a snatch*—Forum ◁**5**▷ *n* The vulva; = CUNT
See PUT THE SNATCH ON someone or something

snatcher *n* A kidnapper
See CRADLE-ROBBER, DUCAT-SNATCHER

snazz *n* Elegance; smartness; = CLASS: *parading his tricks with skill and snazz*—Time

snazz something **up** *v phr* To make something smarter and more elegant; enhance; = GUSSY UP: *and snazzes them up with appliqués*—Philadelphia/ *Install a new loo, or snazz up your current water closet*—Philadelphia

snazzy 1 *adj* Elegant; smart and fashionable; clever and desirable; = NIFTY, RITZY: *mounted on snazzy mag-type wheels*—New Yorker/ *While they may appear snazzy now...time will take its toll*—Sports Afield **2** *adj* Gaudy and meretricious; = HOKEY, JAZZY: *TVs wittiest, toughest, least snazzy news strip*—Time [perhaps a blend of *snappy* and *jazzy*]

sneak 1 *v movie studio* To show a movie unexpectedly to an audience in order to assess its appeal: *We sneaked it in several cities*—Psychology Today **2** *n* (also **sneak preview**): *After a sneak in Chicago they decided to shelve it*

sneakers or **sneaks** *n fr late 1800s* Rubber-soled sports shoes: *wearing a sweater, a shirt, short socks, and sneakers*—EB White/ *Anybody see my old sneaks?* [because one can move noiselessly in such footwear]

sneaky pete (or **Pete**) **1** *n phr* Inferior liquor, often homemade or bootleg; = PANTHER PISS: *dis-*

cussing the effects of "sneaky-pete"—Collier's/ piled into the Ritz bar and polished off a whole row of "sneaky pete"—Life **2** *n phr* hoboes A cheap fortified wine sold in pint bottles called "jugs": *full of that cheap wine they call "sneaky pete"*—A Lomax **3** *n phr* Any cheap and inferior wine **4** *n phr* Marijuana mixed in wine [perhaps all senses fr Navy use "medicinal or other ship's alcohol drunk as liquor," *sneaky* because it had to be taken by stealth and because its effects were sudden and powerful, it would *sneak up on* the drinker; *Pete* simply gives a vowel rhyme]

snide *adj fr late 1800s* Contemptible; mean; nasty, esp in an insinuating way ● Now used nearly exclusively in reference to remarks and persons who make them: *A woman gets nothing but snide remarks about her driving skills*—Associated Press/ *The critics on that paper tend to be very snide* [origin unknown]

sniff *v* narcotics To inhale a narcotic powder; = SNORT

sniffer *n* narcotics A cocaine user or addict: *The Baron was "a sniffer" himself*—American Mercury

sniffy or **snifty** *adj fr late 1800s* Disdainful; haughtily fastidious; fault-finding: *even the sniffiest of lexicographers*—HL Mencken [fr the mien of a person who often seems to be smelling something nasty]

snifter 1 *n fr middle 1800s* A drink of liquor; dram; = SLUG, SNORT: *plastered on a couple of snifters*—New Yorker **2** *n fr 1930s* A large, bulbous, stemmed glass used for drinking brandy **3** *n* narcotics = SNIFFER [origin uncertain; perhaps fr the common upper-respiratory reaction to taking a strong swallow of liquor, also noted in the earlier term *sneezer* and in *snorter*; *snifter*, *sneezer*, and *snorter* were all three used to mean "a strong breeze, gale," and all three came to mean "something large and impressive, something very strong," apparently after the drinking senses were established; before the drinking senses, the terms applied to snuff-taking, with its even more pronounced nasal spasms]

snipe 1 *n fr late 1800s* hoboes A cigarette or cigar butt **2** *n* Navy fr early 1900s An engine-room hand, aircraft mechanic, or other below-decks crew member: *"Snipes"...service and maintain their flying crews' birds*—New York Times [origin obscure, although apparently these, along with several other slang uses, both British and US, all refer somehow to the long-billed bird and its habits]
See KING SNIPE

sniptious *adj fr early 1800s* Neat; elegant; spruce

snit *n* A fit of angry agitation; = SWIVET: *He goes into such a snit that he ploughs the car into a wall*—Saturday Review/ *He has a reputation for throwing considerable snits*—Car and Driver

snitch 1 *v* early 1800s To inform; = SING, SQUEAL **2** *n* An informer; = RAT, STOOL PIGEON: *Maybe some of my old snitches have run across something new*—Rex Burns **3** *v fr 1920s* To steal; pilfer; = SWIPE: *He snitched a couple of cookies* [first senses probably fr underworld slang *snitch* "nose"]

snitzy *adj* Elegant; = POSH, RITZY: *who becomes a cabana boy at a snitzy beach club*—Rolling Stone [perhaps a blend of *snooty* or *snazzy* and *ritzy*]

snockered or **schnockered** *adj* Drunk: *while all the male guests got snockered*—Philadelphia/ *He looks snockered. Are you snockered, Ed?*—WT Tyler [perhaps fr British dialect *snock* "a blow"]

snog *v esp 1960s counterculture fr 1930s British RAF* To flirt; court; make love [origin unknown]

snooker (SNŏŏ kər, SNŏŏ-) *v fr early 1900s* To cheat; swindle; = SCAM: *The Chinese clearly believe that they snookered Nixon*—National Review/ *I've been snookered before, and it'll happen again*—Book World/ *The simple arithmetic shows that Koch and the city were snookered*—Village Voice [fr the pool game called *snooker*, apparently because a novice at the game can easily be tricked and cheated by an expert; compare *euchre*]

snookums *n* Precious one; sweet and dear one ● Used to address small dogs, babies, etc: *Yes, you are. You're my little snookums*—New Yorker

snoop *n* A detective: *Private snoop, hunh?*—J Evans [ultimately fr Dutch *snoepen* "pry"]

snoose (SNŏŏS) *n* lumberjacks Snuff, esp a strong moist kind [fr Swedish *snus*]

snoot 1 *n fr late 1800s* The nose; snout; = SCHNOZZ: *Pokin' him one in the snoot*—Arthur Kober **2** *v* To behave haughtily toward; disdain: *people who snoot goat milk*—R Starnes

a **snoot full 1** *n phr* One's intoxicating fill of liquor; = a SKINFUL: *I met a lot of other reporters and I got a snoot full*—Jim Tully/ *You've had a snoot full*—Robert Ready **2** *n phr* More than enough of something; a great quantity: *Ask him what's so good about it and you'll get a snoot full/ By that time I'd had a snoot full of good advice*

snooty *adj fr 1930s* Snobbish; haughty and disdainful; supercilious; = HOITY-TOITY, SNIFFY: *the snootiest madame in America*—H Asbury/ *a generally vain and snooty class of men*—HL Mencken/ *not snooty with her, no enemy*—Saul Bellow [fr the mien of a person who smells something nasty and holds the nose high]

snooze 1 *v fr late 1700s* To sleep; = COP ZS, SACK OUT **2** *n: not comfortable enough to suit me for a snooze*—Jack London **3** *n* Something that induces sleep; a soporific event, person, etc: *The concert was a snooze*—William Goldman [origin unknown; perhaps echoic of a snore]

snop *n* narcotics Marijuana [origin unknown]

snort 1 *n fr early 1900s* A drink of liquor, esp of plain whiskey; = HOOKER: *Who's ready for another short snort?*—K Brush/ *All hands had another snort*—H Allen Smith **2** *v* narcotics To inhale narcotics, esp cocaine; = SNIFF: *since ma was a viper, and daddy would snort*—H Braddy [drinking sense fr earlier *snorter* of same purport; see *snifter*]

snorter *See* RINGTAILED SNORTER, RIPSNORTER

◁**snot**▷ **1** *n fr 1400s* Nasal mucus **2** *n* A despicable person, esp a self-important nonentity: *Tell that little snot to get lost* **3** *v* To treat someone disdainfully; be haughty: *I should not be "snotted" by an owner, maitre d', or waiter*—Time [ultimately fr a common Germanic term for "nose," also represented by *schnozle, snout, snoot,* etc; the last two senses probably influenced by *snooty*]

◁**snotnose** or **snottynose**▷ **1** *n* An importunate upstart; a neophyte, esp a knowing one: *I won't be instructed by any snotnose* **2** *modifier: He's just a snotnose kid/ some snot-nose in New York*—Washington Post

◁**snotty**▷ *adj* Disagreeable; nasty, esp in the sense of supercilious and disdainful: *I won't give that snotty bastard the time of day* [fr *snot* and influenced by *snooty*]

snow **1** *n* narcotics fr early 1900s Cocaine: *And he was also snorting snow* **2** *v* To persuade in a dubious cause, esp by exaggeration, appeals to common sentiment, etc; = BLOW SMOKE: *The electorate will not be snowed into supporting that silly measure* **3** *n: I thought his rationale was pure snow* [second sense fr the idea of *snowing* someone *under* with articulate reasons]
See DEATH SNOW, EYES LIKE PISS-HOLES IN THE SNOW, NOVA UNDER SNOW ON A SLED

snowball **1** *v* To increase rapidly: *Soon the racket began to snowball*—Time **2** *v* To dominate and crush; = STEAMROLLER: *He's less sensitive to people's feelings. He runs over them, snowballs them*—Time [first sense fr the fact that a *snowball* rolled downhill becomes larger and larger]

a **snowball's chance in hell** *n phr* No possibility whatever; = CHINAMAN'S CHANCE: *He doesn't have a snowball's chance in hell of getting that degree in time*

snowbird **1** *n* fr early 1900s hoboes A person, esp a migratory worker or a hobo, who goes south in the winter to escape the cold **2** *n* narcotics A cocaine user or addict; = COKEHEAD: *Nelly's eyes had a glassy, faraway look. Snowbird, he thought to himself*—William Weeks **3** *n* narcotics Any narcotics addict

snow bunny *See* SKI BUNNY

snowed in (or **up**) *adj phr* narcotics fr 1920s Intoxicated with narcotics; = HIGH

snow job **1** *n phr* esp fr WW2 armed forces Strong and persistent persuasion, esp in a dubious cause; an overwhelming advocacy: *This is no snow job, either. I wish I had 25 Jerry Koosmans*—Inside Sports/ *Don't let Slattery give you a snow job and get you into trouble*—Halls of Montezuma (movie) **2** *v: I was snow-jobbed into giving the maximum* [fr the idea of *snowing under* with insistent reasons; now probably reinforced by the narcotics sense of *snow*]

snow someone or something **under** *v phr* fr late 1800s To burden or assail with excessive demands, work, etc; overwhelm: *until a frailer man than he would have been snowed under*—F Scott Fitzgerald

snozzle *See* SCHNOZZ

snozzled *adj* Drunk

snubby or **snubbie** *n* A cheap, short-barreled revolver; = SATURDAY NIGHT SPECIAL: *cheap, concealable guns with short barrels called "snubbies"*—Atlantic/ *the short-barreled handguns known as "snubbies"*—New York Times

snuff **1** *v* To kill: *more chillingly, STRESS snuffed at least 20 civilians*—Ramparts/ *Garlic never snuffed me*—Cyra McFadden **2** *modifier* Showing or doing murder, esp the killing of women in sadistic shows or orgies: *the snuff murder of an abused and homeless teenaged girl*—Penthouse/ *the vogue of the snuff film* [latterly fr black English, ultimately fr the idea of *snuffing out* a flame]
See UP TO SNUFF

snuff film *n phr* A movie in which the actual killing of a person is shown: *Year Zero has the shock value of a snuff film*—Village Voice/ *If he'd told them he was making a snuff movie he would have been treated better*—New York Review

snuffing *n* A killing, esp a murder: *too eager to put together two unconnected snuffings*—Lawrence Sanders

snuffy *adj* Drunk

snug *n* underworld A small, concealable revolver [probably fr earlier sense, "conceal"]

snuggle-bunnies *See* PLAY SNUGGLE-BUNNIES

snuggle-pup *n* esp 1920s teenagers A boyfriend or girlfriend

snuggy *n* A sexually interesting and interested woman: *It's a snuggy. No, too young, a snugette. Fourteen years old and hot to trot*—Flare

snurge *v* To avoid work; shirk, esp by sneaking away [fr early-20th-century British nautical, probably fr British dialect *snudge* "sneak about"]

so *See* SAY-SO

soak **1** *v* fr late 1800s To hit; = SOCK: *to soak you in the midriff*—J McHugh/ *Why don't you soak him?*—Sinclair Lewis **2** *v* fr late 1800s To overcharge; make someone pay exorbitantly: *a good case of how soak-the-rich corporation taxes wind up right in the pocketbooks of all of us*—Associated Press **3** *n* fr late 1800s A drunkard; = LUSH, SOUSE

soaked *adj* fr middle 1700s Drunk

soak yourself *See* GO SOAK YOURSELF

so-and-so *n* A despicable person; = BASTARD, JERK: *I think I'll sue the so-and-so*—Heywood Broun
See SON OF A BITCH

soap **1** *v* To flatter and cajole; = SWEET-TALK: *one of those Republicans who soaped Vivien*—Westbrook Pegler **2** *n* = SOFT SOAP **3** *n* = SOAP OPERA
See NO SOAP, SOFT SOAP

soapbox *n* The attitude from which one orates, pontificates, counsels urgently, etc: *Be careful or she'll get on the old soapbox and preach about fiscal iniquity*

soaper or **soper** or **sopor** *n* narcotics A sedative drug, methaqualone; Quaalude (a trade name): *an apparently insatiable market for the "sopers"*—Newsweek [fr *Sopor* the trade name of a brand of the drug, fr the Latin root for "sleep"]

soap freak *n phr* A devotee of radio or television daily dramatic series, esp a college student with such tastes

soap opera **1** *n phr* A radio or television daily dramatic series typically showing the painful, passionate, and riveting amours and disasters of more or less ordinary people: *a new soap opera which* *threatens to out-misery all the others*—John Crosby **2** *modifier: The average man and woman in this country live a soap-opera existence*—Robert Ruark **3** *n phr* A life or incidents in life which resembles such shows: *You want to hear the latest in my never-ending soap opera?* [fr the fact that in radio days such shows were typically sponsored by *soap* manufacturers]

the **soaps** *n phr* Radio or television daily dramatic series collectively

◁**sob** or **SOB**▷ (pronounced as separate letters) *n* = SON OF A BITCH

so bad one **can taste it** *adv phr* Very urgently; very keenly: *She wanted the book so bad she could taste it* [fr the earlier expression *I have to piss so bad I can taste it,* implying that the urine had risen in one to the level of the throat and tongue]

sober *See* COLD SOBER, STONE COLD SOBER

sob sister *n phr fr 1920s* A woman news reporter or writer who specializes in sentimental or human interest material

sob story *n phr* A very affecting tale, esp an account of one's disabling troubles; a story that disingenuously appeals to one's charitable nature

sob stuff *n phr* Affecting stories collectively, or the material of which they are made: *Eppingham had prepared to lay on the sob stuff*—William Weeks

soch or **soc** or **sosh** (SOHSH) **1** *n teenagers* A social climber; a person who does the things required to be socially acceptable ● **Sosh** form attested fr early 1900s: *the true sign of a high school social climber known as the "sosh"*—Cameron Crowe **2** *adj: The entire sosh face detonated into a grin*—Cameron Crowe

social disease *n phr* A venereal disease

sock¹ **1** *v fr late 1600s British* To strike; hit hard; = CLOBBER, PASTE: *bein' socked to dreamland*—H Witwer **2** *n: To land another sock on Mr Renault's nose*—Ben Hecht **3** *n baseball* A base hit **4** *n musicians* A set of mounted cymbals sounded by tramping on a foot-pedal; = HIGH-HAT [probably echoic]

sock² **1** *n* A place where money is kept, esp saved; also, savings collectively: *Every dollar which he will receive for the current four-year term will go into the family sock*—Westbrook Pegler **2** *n underworld fr 1930s* A box, bag, safe, etc, where money is kept

sock away *v phr* To save or horde; put away as savings: *Last year that group socked away $128 billion in savings bonds*—Time/ *The American people socked away $3,200,000 in the year's second quarter*—B Garrett [perhaps fr the notion of concealing money in a *sock*; but *sock* "sew up and conceal" is attested fr the alteration of 19th-century *sock* or *sock down* "pay, dispose of money"]

sockdollager or **socdollager** **1** *n fr early 1800s* A decisive blow **2** *n fr early 1800s* A person or thing that is remarkable, wonderful, superior, etc; = HUMDINGER: *This book is a genuine sockdollager!/ his Dauntless Quest to lay his Sockdollager of a Product at the feet of the Public*—Washington Post [fr a metathesis of *doxology* "the finish or fin-

ishing part of a religious service," as suggesting something that terminates, like a heavy blow; influenced by *sock¹*]

socked in *adj phr* Plagued by adverse weather, esp by fog, heavy rain or snow, etc: *You may find yourself partly socked in if you're coming down the Jersey Turnpike this morning/ The captain told us the Boston field was socked in and we would have to land at Bridgeport* [probably fr the adverse weather indications given by the *wind sock* at early or small airports; perhaps influenced by the notion of being closed up in a *sock* as money is when it is *socked away*]

sock 'em *See* ROCK 'EM SOCK 'EM

socker *See* BOBBY-SOXER

sockeroo **1** *n* A great success; something with extraordinary power and impact; esp, a lavish and popular film, show, etc; = BLOCKBUSTER: *an old-fashioned Hippodrome sockeroo*—Time/ *with Paramount's "Dear Ruth"...the only sockeroo*—Variety **2** *modifier: putting some sockeroo catches in the president's plan*—Drew Pearson

sock hop **1** *n phr esp 1950s teenagers* An easy and intimate party where young people typically dance in their stockinged feet: *I feel like a kid at a sock hop, sneaking in here*—Philadelphia Journal/ *many side forays to the drive-in burger stand, the sock hop, lover's lane*—Village Voice **2** *modifier: a kind of sock-hop benefit for Approaching Middle Age*—Time

sock it to someone *v phr fr late 1800s* To attack someone vigorously and effectively; = LET someone HAVE IT: *Some congressional liberals would like to sock it to business by taking away the tax reductions*—Fortune/ *Thanks for socking it to Barbie, that all-American plastic tart*—Rolling Stone

socko **1** *n prizefight fr 1920s* A hard punch **2** *interj* An exclamation imitating the impact of a hard blow, and expressing abrupt force: *Socko!...he punches the villain in the jaw*—Waverly Root **3** *adj fr show business* Very powerful; explosively impressive; terrific: *Okay, now a socko surprise*—Xaviera Hollander/ *the socko effect, recorded here by...camera*—New York **4** *adv: find they do socko in their native heath*—Variety

socks *See* BOBBY SOCKS, DROP YOUR COCKS AND GRAB YOUR SOCKS, KNOCK someone's SOCKS OFF

the **socks off** *adv phr* Very thoroughly ● Always used, like the semantically similar **the brains out** and **the pants off**, to intensify a verb: *undressed her and screwed the socks off her*—George V Higgins/ *a theoretical homily on the true meaning of Eros that, I am forced to admit, absolutely bored the socks off me*—Washington Post

See BEAT THE SOCKS OFF someone

soda jerk (or **jerker**) *n phr fr early 1900s* A person who makes ice cream sodas and other treats at a soda fountain: *She worked for a while as a soda jerk*—Life/ *the champion soda jerker of the United States*—Ernie Pyle [fr earlier *beer jerk* "tapster," perhaps fr the action of drawing back on the vertical handle that controlled the flow of beer; perhaps also related to *jerkwater*]

See JERK SODA

soft *See* WALK SOFT

◁**soft-ass**▷ *adj* Slack and feeble; ineffectual; =WIMPY: *basic economic psychology, not the soft-ass welfarism of Down East*—Toronto Life

softball *adj* Trivial and contemptible; nonserious; =PISS ELEGANT: *a softball question if ever there was one*—New York [based on *hardball*]

soft-clothes *modifier police* Wearing civilian clothes on duty; nonuniformed; plainclothes: *We're all plainclothes ("soft-clothes") men armed to the teeth*—Saul Bellow

soft-core 1 *adj* Somewhat less than extreme; moderated; slightly ameliorated: *He's a soft-core radical, really/ The fashion magazine is soft-core pornography/ a softcore picture of a bare-chested woman*—All Things Considered (radio program) **2** *n* Something that is not extreme, esp a sexually arousing but not carnally explicit movie, magazine, etc: *She doesn't care for X-rated, but enjoys a little soft-core now and then* [based on *hard-core*]

soft drug *n phr* A narcotic like marijuana and some hallucinogens, thought of as nonaddictive and only slightly damaging to health [based on *hard drug*]

soft hands *n phr baseball* The particular ability to field ground balls, esp those hit very hard: *He has "soft hands," baseball slang for an uncanny ability to field ground balls*—Washingtonian

softie or **softy** *n* A person who is amiably and quickly compliant; someone easy to cajole and victimize: *You are a patsy, a quick push, a big softie*—WR Burnett

soft in the head *adj phr* Stupid; dim-witted; =LAMEBRAINED

soft money (or **currency**) **1** *n phr fr middle 1800s* Currency that is highly inflated or likely to become less and less valuable **2** *n phr politics* Campaign donations that are not regulated by the Federal Election Commission: *raising millions of dollars of what is known in election-financing language as "soft money"*—Washington Post National Weekly Edition [based on *hard money*]

soft-pedal *v* To make less prominent; de-emphasize: *Even my friends advised me to soft-pedal my criticisms*—New York Daily News [fr the *pedal* on a piano that *softens* the notes played]

soft sell *n phr* Selling or advertising in a nonstrident, noninsistent tone [based on *hard sell*]

soft soap 1 *n phr fr early 1800s* Flattery; cajolement; =SWEET-TALK: *I won her over finally with a lot of soft soap* **2** *v*: *We had to soft-soap the electorate pretty shabbily*

soft touch 1 *n phr* A person from whom it is easy to borrow or wheedle something: *You get the reputation of being a soft touch*—John O'Hara **2** *n phr* =SOFTIE **3** *n phr* An easy job; a sinecure: *He spent his life seeking the ultimate soft touch*

SoHo *n* The area in New York City that is located south of Houston Street

so hot *See* NOT SO HOT

sol (SAHL) *n* Solitary confinement in prison: *He draws sol till he's crazy*—American Mercury

Sol *See* OLD SOL

◁**SOL**▷ (pronounced as separate letters) *adv esp fr WW1 armed forces* Ruined; =KAPUT: *If the press gets ahold of this we're SOL* [fr *shit out of luck*]

soldier 1 *n* =DEAD SOLDIER **2** *v fr early 1800s Army* To avoid work; shirk; =GOLDBRICK: *He soldiered on the job and the place was deserted*—Carson McCullers **3** *n underworld* A low-ranking member of the Mafia; an ordinary thug or gangster; =BUTTON MAN

See FIRST MAN, SUNDAY SOLDIER

soldier on *v phr* To persist doggedly: *The odds were against us, but we decided to soldier on anyway*

be **sold on** *v phr* To be convinced of the value of something or someone; strongly favor or accept: *It took me a half hour to get sold on the job*—James M Cain

solid *adj jive talk fr 1930s* Wonderful; remarkable; =GREAT, GROOVY: *Man, what solid jive*—Max Shulman/ *That's solid, Willie, let's get together and blow*—Slim Gaillard

solid gold chamber pot *See* WIN THE PORCELAIN HAIRNET

solid sender *n phr 1930s jive talk* An admirable and effective person, esp a swing or jazz musician: *a drag one minute and a solid sender the next*—Louis Armstrong

so long *interj fr middle 1800s* A parting salutation [origin unknown; perhaps fr German *adieu so lange*; perhaps fr Hebrew *shalom* and related Arabic *salaam*, both greetings meaning "peace"; perhaps fr Irish *slan* "health," used as a toast and a salutation]

so mad one **could spit nails** *adj phr* Very angry; furious

some *adj fr middle 1800s* Very good; very effective; real ● Often used ironically: *That is some idea you got!*

somebody *n* A consequential person: *Leroy was a somebody*—New York Post/ *I could have been somebody, Charley. I could have been a contender*—On the Waterfront (movie)

some jeans *See* STRETCH SOME JEANS

some kind of *adj phr* Very good; very effective; =SOME: *God, isn't she some kind of a singer?*

some pumpkins *n phr fr middle 1800s* Something or someone very effective, impressive, etc: *He is some pumpkins*—FK Secrist/ *My new car is some pumpkins, I tell you*

some skin *See* GIVE SOME SKIN, SKIN

something *n fr late 1500s* A remarkable person or thing: *Did you see his shirt? It's something!*

See MAKE SOMETHING OUT OF

something else *n phr jive talk* =SOMETHING [an intensive of *something*]

something fierce (or **awful**) *adv phr* In a harsh and pronounced way; severely ● Slang or dialect relics of the adverbial use of **something** attested from the early 1500s: *He cusses her out something fierce*—Sinclair Lewis/ *She came at me something awful*

something on the ball *n phr fr early 1900s* Talent; skill; ability: *a guy with something on the ball* —Budd Schulberg [fr the curve, speed, etc, that a baseball pitcher puts *on the ball*]

something's got to give *sentence* A resolution is necessary and imminent now; the situation is tense and perilous: *The negotiators are deadlocked and something's got to give*

something the cat draggged in *See* WHAT THE CAT DRAGGED IN

some Zs *See* COP SOME ZS, some ZS

song *See* RAP SONG, TORCH SONG

song and dance or **song** *n phr* or *n* A prepared account or speech aimed at persuasion, apology, advocacy, wheedling, etc: *I got this song and dance about how his car wouldn't start/ Some bum will brace you with a long song of utter inconsequence* —Robert Ruark

See GO INTO one's DANCE

◁**son of a bitch** or **sumbitch**▷ (also **son of a b** or **son of a gun** or **son of a so-and-so**, all euphemistic) **1** *n phr* or *n* A despicable person; =BASTARD, SHITHEEL: *I told the son of a bitch what I thought of him* **2** *n phr* or *n* Something very difficult or vexatious, esp a hard task: *Getting that thing fitted was a son of a bitch/ What a sumbitch of a job it was!* **3** *n phr* or *n* A person or thing that is remarkable, wonderful, superior, etc; =BITCH: *Their new album is a son of a bitch, I tell you* **4** *interj* An exclamation of anger, annoyance, amazement, disappointment, etc: *Son of a bitch! The thing's busted again!* [the *son of a gun* variant is said to refer to a time when women could accompany men to sea, and when children could be born and cradled under a gun or gun carriage, hence have no proper legitimate parentage]

◁**son-of-a-bitching** or **sumbitching**▷ *adj* Wretched; accursed; =DAMNED: *Get that son-of-a-bitching thing out of here right now*

soogie (Sōō jee) (also **sujee** or **soujge** or **soogie moogie** or **sujee-mujee**) **1** *n fr late 1800s British Navy* A soap and caustic mixture used for washing painted surfaces, esp on ships: *a bucket of "soujge"*—Time **2** *v: I was sooging down the walls*—Richard Bissell/ *loading cargo and doing soogie moogie (scrubbing paint work) with the crew* —Time [origin unknown; perhaps fr Scots dialect *sooch* "the sound of something splashing in water or mud"; perhaps an alteration of *squeegee*; perhaps fr Hindi *suji* "mixture of granulated wheat and liquid"]

Sooner **1** *n* A native or resident of Oklahoma **2** *modifier: the Sooner football team* [fr the fact that some settlers entered the public land and staked their claims *sooner* than the legal date and hour in 1889]

SOP or **sop** (pronounced as separate letters) *n fr WW2 armed forces* The way things are properly and usually done: *The SOP here is that you ask the chairman first* [fr *standard operating procedure*]

soper or **sopor** *See* SOAPER

soph (SAHF) *n* A sophomore

soppy *adj* Sentimental; maudlin; =MUSHY, SCHMALTZY: *the soppy story of a rich-boy drop-out* —Judith Crist

sore *adj fr late 1800s* Angry; irritated; =PISSED OFF: *I was sore*—Eugene O'Neill

sorehead *n fr middle 1800s* An irritable person; a constant complainer; a grouch

sore thumb *See* STICK OUT

sorrow *See* DROWN one's SORROWS

sorry about that *sentence* I am sorry; please forgive me ● Most often an ironic understatement, as when one has been responsible for making a big mistake; popularized in the 1960s TV program Get Smart

◁**sorry-ass**▷ *adj* Wretched; sorry; inferior; =HALFASSED: *The reputation of the Barclay...has been one of sorry-ass service*—Philadelphia

sort of *See* KIND OF

sort something **out** *v phr chiefly British* To clarify or put something to rights; straighten something out

sorts *n gambling* Marked cards; a marked deck

SOS[1] (pronounced as separate letters) *n fr WW2 armed forces* The usual tedious exaggerations, pieties, wretched food, etc [fr *same old shit*]

SOS[2] (pronounced as separate letters) *n esp WW2 armed forces* Chipped beef on toast or some similar food; =SHIT ON A SHINGLE: *It was commonly referred to in the service as SOS*—Prison [fr *shit on a shingle*]

sosh *See* SOCH

so-so *adj* Average; ordinary: *It's a so-so movie*

so's your old man *interj fr early 1900s* An exclamation of contempt and defiance, usu reciprocal: *the most desperate exercise of so's-your-old-man since polemics began*—National Review

soujge *See* SOOGIE

soul *fr black, esp fr musicians* **1** *n* An instinctive, sensitive, humorous, and sympathetic quality felt by black persons to be inherent and to constitute their essential and valuable attribute: *He's got soul when he dances! I mean SUPER SOUL!*—New York Post **2** *adj: program content on soul radio stations* —Black Week/ *That's what the Soul scene taught everybody*—Albert Goldman **3** *n* (also **soul music**) This quality in music, and music having this quality: *When Aretha Franklin pours forth a thousand cups of soul*—S Leaks/ *For a few years the group specialized in soul* **4** *adj: a soul ballad* —Playboy/ *a soul-jazz-blues quintet*—Saturday Review

See BLUE-EYED SOUL, BODY AND SOUL, GRIPE one's ASS

soul brother *n phr esp black* A male black person; =BLOOD, BROTHER

Soul City or **Soulville** *n phr black* Harlem

soul food *n phr black* Food characteristic of and preferred by black persons, esp of Southern culture

soul kiss **1** *n phr* An intraoral and interlingual osculation, usu of a steamy sort; =FRENCH KISS, MOUTH-TO-MOUTH RESUSCITATION **2** *v phr: The blissful pair soul-kissed the evening away*

soul sister *n phr esp black* A female black person; =SISTER

sound 1 *v* *street gang fr 1950s* To taunt or provoke; goad; = RAZZ **2** *v* *black* = SIGNIFY

sound off 1 *v phr* *fr WW1 Army* To talk, esp to complain, loud and long; bluster: *Its leaders have sounded off on various issues*—Philadelphia Bulletin **2** *v phr* *fr WW2 Army* To boast; brag: *always sounding off about what a big shot he is*

sound sheet *n phr* A phonograph record pressed on a sheet of thin plastic, esp as used in an advertising or promotional mailing

soup 1 *n* *fr late 1800s oilfield & underworld* Nitroglycerine; = NITRO **2** *n* *railroad* Water taken aboard a moving locomotive **3** *n* Fuel, esp that used in fast cars, airplanes, etc **4** *v* = SOUP UP **5** *n* *surfers* The foamy part of a wave: *a big wave with lots of soup, or white water*—Houston Chronicle
See DUCK SOUP, IN THE SOUP, JERKWATER, LAUGHING SOUP, PEA SOUP

soup-and-fish *n* *fr early 1900s* A man's formal evening dress: *getting into the soup-and-fish*—Sinclair Lewis [fr the formality of a dinner that commences with the *soup* and then the *fish* course]

soupbone *n* *baseball fr early 1900s* A pitcher's pitching arm [probably fr the notion that *soup* represents one's sustenance]

souped up 1 *adj phr* Producing a higher power or acceleration than the normal: *a Ford with a souped-up motor*—A Hynd/ *teen-age infatuation with souped-up cars in which speed-crazy kids raced*—Life **2** *adj phr* Increased or heightened in value, attraction, production, etc: *the souped-up Premium Bonds are also designed to this end*—N Ridley [fr *supercharged*, referring to a pump that forces additional air into the cylinders of an engine to increase its power; perhaps reinforced by *soup* "fuel for a powerful engine," and "material injected into a horse with a view to changing its speed or temperament," the latter attested fr 1911 and earlier]

souper *n* *baseball* = SOUPBONE

soup job *n phr* *teenagers* A car that has been altered mechanically for increased power and speed

soup jockey *n phr* A waiter or waitress

soup-strainer *n* A mustache, esp a luxuriant one

soup up *v phr* To increase power and speed above the normal: *He souped up the motors*—A Hynd

soupy *adj* = SOPPY

sour *See* GO SOUR

sourball or **sourbelly** *n* = SOREHEAD

sourpuss or **sourpan** *n* A morose person; a chronic complainer and moaner; = PICKLEPUSS: *the regular assortment of first-night sourpusses and professional runners down*—Philadelphia Bulletin/ *He has a serious face and never smiles. People think he's a sour puss/ He'd change into a sour-pan*—American Mercury

souse 1 *n* *fr early 1900s* A drunkard; = LUSH: *A wonderful thyroid substance...sobered up the souse in 30 minutes*—New York Post **2** *n* Drunkenness; intoxication: *Economic and religious saviors give a new kind of emotional souse*—American Mercury [fr an extension of *souse* "pickle brine, something pickled," hence semantically akin to *soak* "drunkard" and *pickled* "drunk"]

soused *adj* (Variation: **to the gills** may be added) *fr early 1900s* Drunk [probably fr the image of a pickled herring or other pickled fish]

south *See* GO SOUTH WITH something

South *See* a MOUTH FULL OF SOUTH

south of the border *adj phr* Failed and ineffective; rejected; = NG ● The phrase is similar to and enacted by the thumbs-down sign: *As performances go, yours was somewhat south of the border* [see *go south*; apparently a blend of the general notion of *down* as the direction of failure and rejection, with the legendary significance of the Mexican *border* as the demarcation *south* of which a hunted or rejected person may disappear]

southpaw 1 *n* *baseball fr late 1800s* A left-handed player, esp a pitcher; = FORKHANDER: *Southpaw Warren Spahn pitched his 17th victory*—Associated Press **2** *n* Any lefthanded person: *Many brilliant persons are southpaws, although perhaps only coincidentally* **3** *modifier: switched to a southpaw stance for his 11th round*—Associated Press [apparently coined by the humorist Finley Peter Dunne in 1887 when he was a Chicago sports journalist and baseball diamonds were regularly oriented with home plate to the west]

sow-belly *n* Fat salt pork, or bacon

so what 1 *interj* An exclamation of specified indifference; = BIG DEAL: *When she heard the president was outside, she said, "So what?"* **2** *interj* An exclamation of defiance, reciprocal challenge, etc: *He told me I had screwed the affair up, and I said, "So what?"*

so what else is new or **what else is new** *sentence* Do you have any other startling information? ● Always used with heavy irony: *The Mayor's a crook? So what else is new?*

soxer *See* BOBBY-SOXER

sozzled *adj fr late 1800s* Drunk

space or **space out** *v* or *v phr* *teenagers* To daydream; wool-gather; not attend to what one is doing: *He didn't get much work done because he kept spacing*

space bandit *n phr* *fr 1940s show business* A press agent [fr the fact that the press agent would strive, even unscrupulously, to have newspaper column *space* devoted to his or her clients]

space cadet or **space-out** *n phr* or *n* A mad or eccentric person, esp one who seems stuporous or out of touch with reality as if intoxicated by narcotics; = NUT, SPACED-OUT: *Alda presents her as such a space cadet that the agony of divorce is tempered*—Kings Courier/ *meant to convince the jury that he is an unreliable space-out, that perhaps he was hallucinating*—Washington Post [probably fr the 1950s TV program Tom Corbett, Space Cadet which followed the adventures of a group of teenage cadets at a 24th-century space academy, thought of humorously as being *far out, way out*, etc]

spaced-out 1 *adj* (also **spaced** or **spacey** or **spacy**) Stuporous from narcotic intoxication; in a daze; = BOMBED OUT, HIGH, STONED: *queerly bashful,* *shy, respectful, or spaced-out*—New York/ *with very spaced-out movements, examines the parts of her body*—New York Times/ *You get into a trance, spaced, makin' plans*—Esquire **2** *adj* Crazy or eccentric; = NUTTY: *the teacher, a spacey and sweetly strange spinster*—Richard Peck/ *He is not spaced-out, a point he makes clear in his new book*—TG Harris [probably fr black *space* or *space out* "go, depart," reinforced by the notion of distance and remoteness in *outer space* and by the notion of blanks, gaps, and *spaces* in an otherwise sane and reasonable train of thought, speech, etc]

space opera *n phr* A movie or show about interplanetary exploration, warfare, sex, etc

◄**spade►** *n fr early 1900s* A black person: *The spades inhabited Harlem and let the ofays have Wall Street to themselves*—American Mercury [fr the color of the playing-card symbol and fr the phrase *black as the ace of spades*]

spades *See* ACE OF SPADES, IN SPADES

spaghetti ◄1► *n* An Italian or person of Italian descent **2** *n firefighters* Fire hose: *A foreman will always "Lay Spaghetti" when running out the hose*—New Yorker **3** *n* Tubular insulation that may be cut and fitted over a wire conductor in radio or other electronic work [the taboo sense is semantically similar to Yiddish *luksh* "an Italian," fr *lukshen* "noodle"]

spaghetti Western *n phr fr early 1970s* A cowboy movie usu made by Italian directors and producers, often in Europe: *reacquaint yourself with films that made the spaghetti Western a grindhouse phenomenon*—Village Voice/ *The best turkeys, he went on, were spaghetti Westerns, because they earned a lot of bread*—Russell Baker

spaldeen or **Spaldeen** (spawl DEEN) *n New York City* A small pink rubber ball used in various street games, esp stickball: *Only New York kids call it "Spaldeen"*—New York [fr a mispronunciation of *Spalding*, the name of the manufacturer, perhaps influenced by *balleen* fr Italian *pallino* "little ball," the target ball used in the game of bocce]

spang 1 *adv fr middle 1800s* Precisely; exactly; = SMACK: *Abilene was spang on a new westering railroad line*—advertisement for Time-Life books **2** *adv* Entirely; totally: *I had got spang through the job before they interrupted me* [fr British dialect, "spring, leap," and so semantically similar to an expression like *jump on the hour he got there*, because of the sharp precipitousness of a leap]

Spanish walk *See* FRENCH WALK

spanking *adv fr middle 1600s British* Very; extremely, esp in an admirable sense: *a spanking big bonus/ The car is brand spanking new* [fr British dialect *spank* "move rapidly and smartly," probably echoic of the sharp slapping sounds made by a horse's hooves]

spare tire 1 *n phr fr 1920s* Flab about the waist; a certain embonpoint; = BULGE: *At forty, many men have a definite spare tire and must undertake the Battle of the Bulge* **2** *n phr fr 1940s* A superfluous and unwelcome person: *I didn't come because I knew I'd be a spare tire in that crowd* **3** *n phr* A tedious person; a bore

spark *v* To initiate and stimulate; trigger: *Willy Mays sparked an eighth inning Giant drive by stealing second*—Associated Press

sparkler *n* A gem, esp a diamond

sparkler one *v phr lunch counter* To prepare a dose of Bromo-Seltzer (a trade name) for a customer [fr the appearance of the bubbles in the glass]

spark plug *n phr* The most stimulating and energetic member of a group, team, etc; = LIVE WIRE: *Mr Fadiman himself is a splendid spark-plug*—H Allen Smith

Sparks 1 *n merchant marine fr early 1900s* A ship's radio officer or operator **2** *n movie studio* A studio electrician

Sparky *See* OLD SMOKY

sparrow cop *n phr* A police officer in disfavor, and assigned to the park to guard the grass

spas-out (SPAZ-) *n* A showing or experiencing of strong emotional spasms, esp by children: *Every time we mentioned homework the kid would have a spas-out* [fr spastic]

◄**spastic** (also **spas** or **spaz**)► **1** *n esp teenagers fr 1960s* A strange and stupid person; = WEIRDO: *Her brother's a spastic/ The man's a spaz, a total spaz*—Joseph Wambaugh **2** *adj*: *only the spastic twits in competition*—Village Voice **3** *n students* A nonathletic person, esp an awkward one [cruelly, fr the plight of cerebral palsy patients exhibiting constant body *spasms*]

◄**spazzy** or **spassy**► *adj esp teenagers fr 1960s* Stupid; = WEIRD: *You gotta be spassy if you think that, just because kids aren't admitted to the casinos, they can't have a groovy...time in Atlantic City*—Philadelphia Inquirer [fr spastic]

speakeasy or **speak** or **speako** *n fr late 1800s* A cheap saloon, esp an illegal or after-hours place: *It had been a speakeasy once*—L Ford/ *All they give you in these speaks is smoke*—James M Cain/ *one thing that puts a speako over*—Joel Sayre [Samuel Hudson, a journalist, says in a 1909 book that he used the term in Philadelphia in 1889 after having heard it used in Pittsburgh by an old Irish woman who sold liquor clandestinely to her neighbors and enjoined them to "speake asy"; hence related to early-19th-century Irish and British dialect *spake-aisy* or *speak softly* shop "smugglers' den"]

spec *n circus* The spectacular opening procession of a circus: *Mrs Webster rode an elephant in the "spec"*—Hamilton Basso

special *See* the RED-EYE, SATURDAY NIGHT SPECIAL

speck bum *n phr hoboes* A helpless and alcoholic bum; = STUMBLEBUM [apparently fr earlier slang *speck* "contemptible person," fr the notion of smallness and unimportance]

specs¹ *n fr late 1800s* Spectacles: *Oh Lord, I broke my new specs*

specs² *n fr WW2* The specifications of a blueprint, architectural plan, printing order, etc

speechify *v* To talk, esp in a pompous, pontifical way

speed 1 *n* A usu affectionate nickname or term of address for a man: *Hi, Speed, what's up?* **2** *n narcotics* An amphetamine, esp Methedrine (a trade name)

See BRING someone UP TO SPEED

speedball *n narcotics* A dose of a stimulant and a depressant mixed, esp of heroin and cocaine: *smack, coke, reefers, acid, speedballs (snorting cocaine and heroin together), a "luxury"*—New York

speedfreak or **speedo** *n narcotics* A habituated user of amphetamines and other such stimulants

speed merchant 1 *n phr* A very fast runner: *The little guy could really scoot, a speed merchant* **2** *n phr* A very good fastball pitcher: *He had a glass arm and he certainly was no speed merchant* —Ithaca Journal

Speedy Gonzalez *n phr* A man or woman who is very fast; a very rapid worker, operator, etc [fr the classical joke about a very quick and eager fornicator named *Speedy Gonzalez*]

spell out 1 *v phr* To explain very patiently in great detail: *Are you a schoolboy I have to spell out everything for you?*—Ira Wolfert **2** *v phr* To explain; define: *a commission of distinguished citizens to spell out the difference between right and wrong*—Associated Press

spender *See* BIG-TIME SPENDER

sphere *n* A baseball, golfball, etc

spheroid *n* A baseball: *Hitting the ball is just as important as slugging the spheroid*—Associated Press

See the OBLATE SPHEROID

◄**spick** or **spic**► *n* A Latino or person of such descent: *female spick, short fat*—Ira Wolfert [fr the presumed protestation "*No spick English*"]

spiel *fr late 1800s circus* **1** *n* A barker's or hawker's persuasive talk **2** *n* A speech meant to persuade by force and eloquence; a sales patter; = LINE: *I'll give his honor a spiel*—Jack London **3** *n fr 1940s* An advertising monologue on radio or television [fr German *spielen* "play"]

spieler *n* A person who makes a persuasively eloquent speech: *a real accomplished spieler*—Outlook

spiffed *adj* Drunk

spiffed out *adj phr* Fancily and formally dressed; = DOLLED UP

spifflicated *adj fr early 1900s* Drunk: *a slightly spifflicated gent*—Hy Gardner/ *a spifflicated patient entangling himself in a revolving door*—Time [fr an 18th-century British dialect *spifflicate* "confound, dumbfound," of obscure origin]

spiff someone or something **up** *v phr* To spruce up; smarten; groom handsomely and neatly; = GUSSY UP: *You are really attractive when you spiff yourself up* [fr British dialect *spiff* "dandified, bedizened"]

spiffy 1 *adj fr middle 1800s British* Elegant; smart and fashionable; = SNAZZY: *They wear spiffy red-and-gold scarves*—Time/ *New Model Buggy for Amish Is Spiffy*—Cleveland Plain Dealer **2** *adv* Well: *They don't translate so spiffy*—Arthur Baer

spike 1 *v fr early 1900s* To strengthen a drink by adding alcohol or liquor: *He spiked his coffee with brandy* **2** *adj: This drink is spiked!* **3** *n narcotics* A hypodermic needle **4** *v* To rise to a high level, esp rapidly: *He also...spikes into the upper registers*—Down Beat/ *push fluids when the patient has spiked a temp*—American Speech **5** *v* To reject; quash: *confident the man's disbelieving New York editors will spike the story*—People Weekly **6** *v volleyball* To punch a volleyball powerfully and unreturnably down **7** *v football* To slam the ball down, usu done by a player who has just scored a touchdown [all senses fr *spike* "large nail," hence "sharp point"; the sense "to reject" may be fr the earlier phrase *spike a gun* "render a cannon useless by driving a spike into the touchhole," or fr the notion of dealing with a paper, bill, manuscript, etc, by impaling it on a spindle or spindle file]

spike someone's **gun** *v phr* To prevent someone's action; thwart or circumvent someone's intention; spoil someone's chance for success; deny someone pleasure [fr the disabling practice of driving a *spike* into the touchhole of a cannon to prevent ignition]

spike up *v phr narcotics* To inject narcotics; = SHOOT UP: *if he came home and found her spiking up*—Richard Merkin

spill 1 *v fr late 1800s* To upset; down; dump: *I'll spill you in the drink*—Atlantic Monthly **2** *v* To confess or admit something, esp to inform on associates

spill one's **guts** *v phr fr hoboes* To tell everything one knows; be totally and lengthily candid: *"Can I be perfectly frank with you?" "Good. Spill your guts"*—Armistead Maupin

spill the beans *v phr fr early 1900s* To tell something inadvertently; blurt out a secret

spinach 1 *n fr late 1800s* A beard **2** *n esp 1930s* Nonsense; worthless matter; = JUNK: *You could put up with this spinach*—Richard Bissell/ *"I say it's spinach and I say to hell with it"*—a Carl Rose New Yorker cartoon

spin doctor *n phr* An advisor or agent, esp of a politician, who imparts a partisan analysis or slant to a story for the news media: *Just after the debate, Johnson took his place with the other "spin doctors"*—Washington Post [fr the notion of *spin* on a baseball or pool ball, which gives a deviant rather than a straight track; semantically related to throwing someone a curve]

spinner *n truckers* A truck driver

spin off 1 *v phr* To produce as an entity separated from the whole: *The conglomerate spun off five new companies* **2** *n: This store is a spin-off from the big one downtown* **3** *v phr* To dispose of; rid oneself of; = DITCH: *Why didn't he spin off this stupid cunt?*—Saul Bellow

spin one's **wheels** *v phr* To waste time; work fruitlessly: *Nobody spun his wheels. I'm proud of them* —Washington Post/ *Stop spinning your wheels, get yourself in gear*—WT Tyler

spit *See* HOT SPIT, NOT COUNT FOR SPIT, NOT GIVE SPIT, SO MAD one COULD SPIT NAILS, SWAP SPIT, WORTH A BUCKET OF WARM SPIT

spitball 1 *v* To make harmless jibes or attacks; make weak accusations: *Well, I'm just spit-balling*—Paul Theroux/ *You're just spitballing*—Lawrence Sanders **2** *n* A nasty but feeble attack: *despite the spitballs he keeps getting from the critical liberal media*—Philadelphia Journal [fr the mischievous schoolboy's vice of throwing bits of paper soaked in saliva]

spitless *See* SCARED SPITLESS, SCARE someone SHITLESS

spit tacks *v phr* To become very upset and angry; = SHIT A BRICK: *I expected Eartha to spit tacks over the injustice*—Village Voice

spitter *n baseball* A pitched ball that has been wet with saliva or some other substance, illegally; a spitball

spizzerinktum or **spizzerrinctum** *n outdated fr middle 1800s* Vigor; pep; = PIZZAZZ: *the fellow who put foresight, science, and spizzerinktum into their business*—American Mercury [origin unknown; since the earliest meaning is "money," perhaps a coinage fr Latin *species rectum* "the right sort"]

splash *See* MAKE A SPLASH

splat movie or **splatter film** *n phr* A movie that features a major catastrophe or other event where things and people are severely damaged [fr echoic *splat*, indicating a smashing and jellying blow]

◀**splib**▶ *n esp black* A black person who opposes discrimination, etc, but will not challenge the status quo; a liberal black: *Don't nobody want no nice nigger anymore....They want an angry splib*—Al Young [fr *spade* + *liberal*]

splice *v fr middle 1700s* To marry • Most often in the passive: *crying to be spliced*—Joseph Auslander

splice the main brace *v phr nautical* To have a drink of liquor

spliff *n narcotics* A marijuana cigarette *See* ENGLISH SPLIFF

splinter *See* KNEE-HIGH TO A GRASSHOPPER

split *v fr 1950s black musicians* To leave; depart; = CUT OUT: *This party is dullsville, let's split* *See* HELL TO SPLIT, LICKETY-SPLIT

split a gut *v phr* To try very, very hard; make a maximum effort; = BUST one's ASS: *We may not make it, but we'll split a gut trying*/ *She laughed till I thought she'd split a gut*

◁**split beaver**▷ *n phr* A photograph or view of a woman's vulva between spread legs; = SPREAD BEAVER: *I can toss off phrases like "split beaver" with almost devil-may-care abandon*—Esquire

splitter *See* LIP-SPLITTER

split the scene *v phr fr 1950s black musicians* To leave; depart; = CUT OUT, SPLIT: *just as I was about to split the scene*—Tennessee Williams

split-up 1 *n* A separation, esp an angry one: *Me and the old man had a split-up*—WR Burnett **2** *n* A divorce or legal separation of a married couple

split week *n phr poker* A potential straight with the middle card missing [fr show business use, where a

split week is one in which a performer works in two towns, theaters, etc, serially]

spoil *v* To kill; = WASTE: *You wanted to hate his guts so it would be easier to spoil him?*—Lawrence Sanders

Spokane (SPOH kan) *n outdated fr hoboes* Pork and beans [fr the pronunciation, which resembles *po'k and*]

spondulics or **spondulix** (spahn Dᴏᴏ liks) *n fr middle 1800s* Money [origin unknown]

sponge 1 *n* (also **sponger**) *fr 1500s* A parasite; = FREELOADER, MOOCHER, SCHNORRER: *You avoided college boys, sponges*—F Scott Fitzgerald **2** *v*: *We were able to sponge lots of meals off his parents* **3** *n* A drunkard; = SOAK *See* THROW IN THE SPONGE

spoof 1 *v fr late 1800s British* To fool; hoax; tease: *He was just spoofing*—Sinclair Lewis **2** *n*: *Don't take it seriously, it was just a spoof* **3** *n* A parody or pastiche; = SEND-UP, TAKEOFF: *The show was a spoof of a TV sit-com* [coined by the British comedian Arthur Roberts as the name of a nonsense game that he invented]

spook ◀**1**▶ *n* A black person: *Some are just spooks by the door, used to give the organization a little color*—Amsterdam News **2** *n espionage* A spy; secret agent: *Mr Wolfson isn't a spook for the CIA*—Wall Street Journal **3** *v fr middle 1800s* To put on edge; make apprehensive; frighten: *"It's the first time in my life I've ever been spooked,"* says a Byrd staffer*—Washington Post

spoon *v outdated fr late 1800s* = NECK, PET *See* EAT someone UP, GREASY SPOON

spoon up *v phr West Point* To clean up and make neat

spoony or **spooney 1** *adj fr middle 1800s* Amorous; romantic: *I guess we got kind of spoony*—Ring Lardner **2** *n fr late 1700s British* A foolish or silly person: *I don't believe a cock-and-bull story like that. Quiz was no spooney*—Stanley Elkin **3** *adj West Point* Neat and clean

sport 1 *n* A stylish and rakish man • Often used as a term of address, sometimes with an ironical tinge: *What did she tell you, sport?* **2** *n* = GOOD SPORT

sporting house *n phr fr late 1800s* A place for gambling and dissipation, esp a brothel

spot 1 *v sports & gambling* To give odds or a handicap: *They spotted Pittsburgh five runs before getting down to serious business*—New York Times/ *I spotted him a rook and two pawns* **2** *v* To give, but with the suggestion of a loan: *I spotted her a couple drinks* **3** *v fr early 1700s British* To recognize or identify: *I spotted her as a phony long ago* **4** *n* A short commercial or paid political announcement on radio or television: *How do you like the spots, Senator?*—New York **5** *n* A night club, restaurant, or other such venue of pleasure: *They were seen in a fashionable spot uptown* *See* BING SPOT, DEUCE SPOT, FIVE-SPOT, HIT THE SPOT, HOT SPOT, JOHNNY-ON-THE-SPOT, NIGHT SPOT, ON THE SPOT, PUT someone ON THE SPOT, SWEET SPOT, TWO-SPOT, X MARKS THE SPOT

spotlight *v* To single out prominently; focus on for emphasis: *He was trying to spotlight the danger of high deficits*

spot market *n phr* The free market in petroleum, outside the price scales set by the producers' organization

spout *See* UP THE SPOUT

spread **1** *n* Coverage in a newspaper or magazine, esp the full use of facing pages: *Do you know how much a two-page spread in the New York Times costs these days?* **2** *n fr early 1800s British* A copious meal; a feast

spread oneself *v phr fr middle 1800s* To make a great effort; do one's utmost: *You may be sure the staff will spread itself to accommodate you*

◁**spread beaver**▷ *n phr* = SPLIT BEAVER

◁**spread for** someone▷ *v phr* For a woman, to do or offer to do the sex act with someone

spread it thick *v phr fr middle 1800s* To exaggerate; overstate; = BULLSHIT ● Very often used with **on**: *To say it was for the good of humanity is spreading it a bit thick/ She spread it on very thick with those compliments*

spring **1** *v underworld fr early 1900s* To get out of or be released or escape from prison: *The proprietor knew how to "spring" them, that is, get them out of jail*—Louis Armstrong/ *When's he springing?*—Lawrence Sanders **2** *v* To reveal or do something as a surprise ● Very often used with **on**: *John L Lewis is preparing to spring a dramatic move*—Lowell Thomas/ *If we spring it on them suddenly they won't know how to react*

springbutt *n* A very eager person; = EAGER BEAVER

no **spring chicken** *See* NO SPRING CHICKEN

spring for something *v phr* To pay for, esp a treat of food or drink; = POP: *always more than glad to guzzle the pitchers of Michelob you sprung for on payday*—Philadelphia

spritz **1** *v* To spray or sprinkle: *the fixative with which he spritzed it so it would not smear*—Earl Thompson/ *She spritzed a little scent behind her ear and was ready* **2** *n* A serving of carbonated water, esp an addition of carbonated water to a glass of wine: *She asked for white wine with a spritz* **3** *n* A slight rain or shower: *We may get just a wee spritz this afternoon* [fr Yiddish, "spray"]

spritzer *n* A glass of wine mixed with carbonated water

spritzy *adj* Light and volatile; airy; frothy: *She now does a string of spritzy little jetés that barely get her off the ground*—New Yorker/ *the hair-trigger switch between Nathan's spritzy charm and the scary violence of his anger*—Newsweek

sprout *n* A child, esp an infant: *A girl out your way has married...and is coming home with a sprout*—Harper's

sproutsy *adj* Unconventional, unorthodox in habits and opinions: *I joined a sorority, now I'm seen as a sister, not as a sproutsy type*—MS [fr the eating of bean-sprouts as symbolizing radical or nonconformist behavior]

sprout wings **1** *v phr fr late 1800s* To become very chaste and upright: *Noticed how he's sprouted*

wings since he got married? **2** *v phr* To die [fr the *winged* nature of angels]

sprung *adj fr early 1800s* Drunk

spud *n fr middle 1800s British* A potato [origin unknown; perhaps related to the fact that in British dialect use *spud* means "a weeding instrument" and in US dialect it means "a spade," hence potatoes would be something *spudded* or dug; a relation has been seen between the fact that potatoes are also the nickname of men named Murphy, or indeed of any Irishman]

spudge around *v phr fr early 1900s* To exert oneself; apply oneself: *If she would only spudge around, get her work done*—Scribner's [origin unknown; perhaps related to British dialect *spuddle* "move about busily"; perhaps fr *spud* in the sense "dig"]

spunk **1** *n fr late 1700s* Energetic courage; mettle; = BALLS, GUTS: *little girl's got a lot of spunk* ◁**2**▷ *n fr late 1800s* Semen: *rushing with their hot spunk in their hands to the microscope*—John Irving ◁**3**▷ *v* To ejaculate semen; = COME: *the filthy pigs spunking into women*—Herbert Kastle [apparently fr Celtic *spong* "tinder, touchwood, punk" fr Latin *spongia* "sponge"; apparently semantically fr a resemblance between semen and a spongy excrescence found on trees, in which sense the word is found in British dialect]

spurs *See* WIN one's SPURS

Sputnik *n 1950s* An artificial earth satellite [fr Russian "companion, fellow-traveler"]

squab *n fr 1920s* A young woman; = CHICK ● Considered offensive by some women

squad *See* BEEF SQUAD, GOON SQUAD, PUSSY POSSE, TAXI SQUAD

square **1** *n* (also **square meal**) *fr late 1800s* A copious meal: *I've had my three squares every day*—J Flynt **2** *n fr black jazz musicians* A conventional person, esp one with musical tastes not extending to jazz, swing, bop, etc; = CLYDE, UNCOOL: *That GL...strictly a square*—Max Shulman/ *I do a little vocal number for the squares*—Mary Lou Williams **3** *adj:* *His tastes were very corny, very square/ You do not try to convert the square world*—Eugene Burdick **4** *n* (also **square joint**) *narcotics* A tobacco cigarette; = SLIM, STRAIGHT **5** *adj* Fair; even-handed; just: *I'll be square with you* **6** *v fr late 1800s* To make things right, just, proper, etc: *He could never square himself with the police after that/ I know I was wrong, and now I'll square it* [the sense "conventional person, etc," is said to come fr a jazz musician's and standard conductor's hand gesture that beats out regular and unsyncopated four-beat rhythm, the hand doing so describing a *square* figure in the air]

square broad *n phr* A woman who is not a prostitute: *He takes a "square broad" (a nonprostitute) and "turns her out"*—Time

◀**squarehead**▶ *n fr early 1900s* A Scandinavian or person of Scandinavian descent; = SCANDAHOOVIAN

square John (or **john**) *n phr fr underworld fr 1920s* An ordinary honest person; a good citizen; a noncriminal person who can be victimized by, and is contemptuously regarded by, criminals

square off *v phr fr early 1800s* To put oneself in a fighting posture: *The two biggest companies are squaring off over the microchip market*

square one *n phr* The place where some process begins or has begun; the original configuration: *So after all this fuss we are at square one again* [fr board games where a token is moved off the *first square* after the shake of a die, drawing of a card, etc]

See GO BACK TO SQUARE ONE

square peg *n phr* A misfit; an inconvenient and intractable person: *They were square pegs who weren't succeeding*—E Lavine [fr the earlier expression *put* or *drive a square peg in a round hole*, fr carpentry or joinery]

squares *See* THREE SQUARES

square shooter *n phr fr early 1900s* An honest and candid person; = STRAIGHT ARROW ● Now used nearly always with the conscious irony of archaic sincerity

Squaresville or **squaresville 1** *n fr 1960s bop talk* A putative city inhabited entirely by dull, conventional people: *The Innocent Nihilists Adrift in Squaresville*—The Reporter/ *intimidated by being in the squaresville which is also the power center of the free world*—Hugh Sidey **2** *adj: on campus, where it once was squaresville to flip for the rock scene*—Time

square the beef *v phr fr underworld* To repair a grievous situation; resolve a complaint

squat 1 *v* To sit: *Hey, squat there a minute and I'll be right with you* ◁**2**▷ *v* To defecate; = SHIT, TAKE A DUMP ◁**3**▷ *n: Don't step in the squat* **4** *n* Nothing; zero; = DIDDLY, ZILCH, ZIP: *She's got squat to do with that kind of shit*—Richard Fariña/ *You can't do squat anyway these days*—George V Higgins/ *I didn't hear squat*—WT Tyler

See the HOT SQUAT, NOT GIVE A DAMN, NOT KNOW BEANS, TAKE A DUMP

squat hot *v phr* To be executed in the electric chair; = FRY: *If the crook ever squatted hot, that would be doing something for the country*—James M Cain

◁**squaw**▷ *n* A woman, esp one's wife

squawk 1 *v fr late 1800s* To complain; = BEEF, BITCH: *Will you stop squawking about the food, please?* **2** *n: Okay, what's your squawk this morning?* **3** *v underworld* To inform; = SQUEAL: *Joe squawked*—WR Burnett [echoic of an unpleasant sound, esp the grating screech of a bird]

squawk box *n phr esp WW2 Navy* A military public address system; = BITCH BOX

squeak by (or **through**) *v phr* To pass, succeed, achieve a goal, etc, by the narrowest of margins: *He just barely squeaked through his medical boards*

squeaker 1 *n* A very closely contested and uncertain game, contest, etc: *They met in a squeaker that year, 23 to 24* **2** *n* Something poised on the edge of one result or another, esp a success versus a disaster: *"It'll be a squeaker," Bar-*

tow said. "This is a nervous time for us"—Washington Post

squeaky-clean *adj phr* Perfectly clean; white, sanitary, and untarnished ● Sometimes used ironically to emphasize conventionality and unimaginativeness: *this English band, made up of six squeaky-clean men in their early twenties*—Westworld/ *one of the most squeaky-clean and buttoned-down of US corporations*—Wall Street Journal [fr the *squeaky* sound produced by rubbing a finger across chinaware free of grease or dirt]

squeal 1 *v fr late 1800s underworld fr British dialect* To inform; = RAT, SING, SQUAWK **2** *n fr early 1800s* An informer; = RAT, SNITCH, STOOL PIGEON: *He was working on a case with a squeal, and he knifed him*—New York Post **3** *n* (also **squeak**) A complaint to the police: *cop at stationhouse took the squeal*—Ed McBain/ *The young cops who had caught the squeal didn't know what to do*—Lawrence Sanders

squealer *n fr middle 1800s* An informer; = RAT, SNITCH

squeal rule (or **law**) *n phr* A law requiring that her parents be notified when a woman under 18 applies for a prescription for contraceptives

squeeze *n* A situation of great pressure or peril; = CRUNCH: *I'm afraid we're in something of a squeeze just now*

See MAIN SQUEEZE, PUT THE SQUEEZE ON someone

squeeze-box *n* An accordion

squeeze one *sentence lunch counter fr 1930s* Prepare a glass of orange juice

squeezer *See* DUCK SQUEEZER, MOP-SQUEEZER

squib *n* A brief, sometimes witty piece of material in a newspaper or magazine, usu a space-filler: *A friend of mine, he writes those witty "squibs"*—Westbrook Pegler [fr *squib* "a small firecracker," of unknown origin]

squiffed or **squiffy** or **squiffy-eyed** *adj fr late 1800s British* Drunk: *so-and-so's getting "squiffy" at a dance*—Robert Lynd/ *one of Frenise's squiffy-eyed nieces*—Paul Theroux

squiggle *n computer* The tilde, a sinuous diacritical mark

squirrel 1 *v* (also **squirrel away**) To hoard or cache something; hide and save something for later **2** *n* A crazy or eccentric person; = NUT, WEIRDO: *I seen some squirrels in my life, but you got 'em all beat*—H Allen Smith **3** *n hot rodders* A hesitant or confused hot rod driver **4** *v hot rodders* To weave about the road while driving, esp a hot rod **5** *n* An internal combustion cylinder; = BANG: *That car boasts six mighty squirrels* ◁**6**▷ *n college students* The vulva; = PUSSY ◁**7**▷ *n college students* A young woman

See SEAM SQUIRREL

squirrel-food *n* A crazy or eccentric person; = NUT, SQUIRREL: *I'm afraid the old mentor is squirrel food by now* [fr the fact that *squirrels* eat nuts]

squirrely *adj* Crazy; eccentric; = NUTTY: *I tell you, working out alone can make you squirrely*—Erma Bombeck

squirt 1 *n fr middle 1800s British* A short or small person, esp an insignificant, contemptible little male; = PEANUT: *Out of my way, you little squirt/ Ah, what a little squirt is there*—WH Auden **2** *n* (also **young squirt**) *fr late 1800s students* A young man, esp a presumptuous or foppish youth

squishy *adj* Sentimental; = SCHMALTZY, SOPPY: *The sentiment may sound squishy to those who have never been close to him*—Washington Post/ *the squishy sentimentality attributed to him by most critics*—Village Voice [fr late-19th-century *squishy* "soft and yielding," fr earlier echoic *sqush*]

squooshy (SKWŏŏ shee) *adj* Soft; yielding and insubstantial: *Support for Reagan is "all very squooshy"*—Newsweek

SRO (pronounced as separate letters) **1** *n theater* Standing room only, usu indicating a full house and a successful production **2** *n* Single room occupancy residence hotel: *They're planning to demolish the SROs on this street*

ss (pronounced as separate letters) *n underworld & narcotics* A suspended sentence

Ss *See* SLING SS

stab *n* A try; = CRACK, SHOT, WHACK: *Well, I'll have a stab at it*

stable *n* The group of people performing similar work, managed by one person: *She's part of his stable of writers*

stable push *n phr horse-racing* Inside information on a horse's condition, eagerness, etc

stache *See* STASH

stack 1 *n lunch counter* A serving of pancakes, usu three **2** *n* A car's tail pipe or exhaust pipe: *It was a twin-stack Bugatti* *See* BLOW one's TOP

◁**stack asses**▷ *v phr* To play or behave violently; knock and throw people to the ground: *Let the other side know you've come to stack asses*—Dan Jenkins

stacked *adj* Very well-built in the sexual sense; having an attractive body: *She's well-stacked and sort of young*—Lionel Stander

stack of Bibles *See* SWEAR ON A STACK OF BIBLES

stack the deck (or **the cards**) *v phr* To prearrange something dishonestly; assure one's advantage fraudulently; = COLD DECK: *I should have had the job, but they stacked the deck against me/ He'll win if he stacks the cards*

stack up 1 *v phr fr late 1800s* To transpire; go along; succeed: *How are things stacking up for you this year?* **2** *v phr* To compare; measure against: *I'd like for somebody to begin stacking up Native Son with some of Frank Norris's stuff* —American Scholar **3** *v 1950s teenagers* To wreck a car; = RACK UP **4** *n* A multiple car wreck [first two senses fr the *stacking up* of one's poker chips to show winnings or for comparison]

stack Zs *See* COP ZS

staff *See* CHIEF OF STAFF

stag 1 *n fr early 1900s* A man who goes to a party alone, without a woman partner **2** *adj* For men only; without women: *a stag function* **3** *adv: Several of the brothers were going to the dance*

stag—P Marks **4** *n* (also **stag party**) A party for men only: *as broad as the jokes at a Legion stag*—J Evans

stage *See* UPSTAGE

stagflation *n* A simultaneous stagnation and inflation in the economy

the staggers *n phr fr late 1800s* A faltering and unsteady physical state, esp from liquor or narcotics intoxication: *The next day you've got the staggers and your fine coordination is destroyed for 72 hours* —Albert Goldman

stag line *n phr esp 1920s* The group of unescorting males at a dance, thought of as a line beside the floor, studying the women as possible dance partners

stairs *See* UPSTAIRS

stake *See* GRUBSTAKE, ROAD-STAKE, WOODEN-STAKE

stake out *v phr police* To put someone or something under constant police surveillance: *He's been staked out often enough*—Mickey Spillane/ *The sergeant told them to stake out the suspected warehouse* [fr earlier senses, as old as the 17th century, where *stake out* meant "mark off a territory, a line, a track, etc, with stakes"]

stake-out *n police* A police surveillance: *as silently as only a cop on a stake-out knows how to stand* —Raymond Chandler/ *The stake-outs continued* —Dragnet (radio program)

stakes *See* UP STAKES

stake someone **to** something *v phr fr late 1800s* To give or provide something to someone, inferentially as a loan: *Could you stake me to a new suit so I can get a job?* [fr the earlier senses where *stake* meant someone's basic provisions for farming, prospecting, etc]

stall[1] **1** *v fr late 1800s* To delay; temporize; consume time and delay action; = BUY TIME: *I told him to quit stalling and give us a decision* **2** *v* To be halted or delayed; stagnate; bog down ● Usually in the passive: *The negotiations are hopelessly stalled* **3** *v* (also **stall off**) To subject someone to delay; make excuses for inaction: *You stall her while I try to find her original letter/ He kept stalling the women off with one excuse or another*—A Hynd **4** *n* A pretext or excuse for delaying; a reason for inaction: *His claim of illness is only a stall* **5** *n fr middle 1800s* A pretense or false indication, esp as part of a criminal alibi: *"I'd take meals up to him. I think that was just a stall" "You mean the meals were for someone else?"*—Erle Stanley Gardner [fr Old English *steall* "standing, state, place, animal stall," whence the notion of stubbornly holding one's place]

stall[2] **1** *n underworld fr late 1600s* A pickpocket's accomplice who in one way or another maneuvers the victim **2** *n underworld* A criminal's accomplice who primarily diverts attention, obstructs pursuit, keeps watch, etc: *an excellent lookout or "stall" for her male companions*—A Lavine [fr earlier *stale* or *stall* "decoy bird," probably fr Anglo-French *estale* or *estal* "a pigeon used to lure a hawk into a nest"; since delaying and misleading are involved in both, this derivation and that of *stall*[1] have probably intermingled over the centuries, as illustrated by the fact that *stand* meant "a thief's assistant" in the late 16th century]

stallion 1 *n* =STUD **2** *n* *black* A sexually attractive and/or active woman; =FOX

stamping ground (or **grounds**) *n phr* One's particular domain or territory; one's native heath: *Ann Arbor used to be my stamping ground* [fr 18th-century sense, "a place frequented by animals"]

stand 1 *v* *fr early 1800s* To give or pay for as a treat: *She stood him tea and muffins*—Sinclair Lewis/ *Who'll stand the next round?* **2** *v* To cost; =SET someone BACK: *The suit I got on stood me ten cents*—AJ Liebling **3** *n* A shop or store; a place of business: *You can get it at the Brooks Brothers stand on Fifth Avenue*

See BALLY STAND, ONE-NIGHT STAND

◁ **stand around with** one's **finger up** one's **ass**▷ (or **in** one's **ear**) *v phr* To be idle and helpless; fail to cope; be useless: *If you're just standing around with your finger up your ass you might as well lend a hand here*

standee *n fr middle 1800s* A person forced to stand because all seats are sold or occupied: *long lines of standees waiting their turns*—Philadelphia Inquirer

stand for something *v phr fr late 1800s* To tolerate or abide something; swallow something • Usu in the negative: *He said he wouldn't stand for being replaced*

stand in *v phr fr show business* To substitute; act as a proxy: *I'll have to stand in for her and run the meeting*

stand-in 1 *n* *show business fr early 1900s* A performer who takes the place of another, and is often hired to be prepared to do so at any time **2** *n* A substitute or proxy; a deputy: *Naïve Stingo, as stand-in for us*—Philadelphia [perhaps fr the use of a substitute to replace a performer during such tedious procedures as adjusting lights, arranging the stage or set, etc; perhaps also fr the earlier notion of a deputy or place-holder, literally a lieutenant, in French "place-holder"]

standing on one's **head** *See* DO something ON TOP OF one's HEAD

standing up *See* DIE STANDING UP

standoff *n fr middle 1800s* A balanced and static conflict; a stalemate; a deadlock: *The union and the company are locked in a standoff*

See MEXICAN STANDOFF

standoffish *adj* Haughty; aloof; reserved and snobbish: *He gave us all a standoffish look* [fr late-19th-century *stand-off* "aloof, proud"]

stand on one's **brakes** *v phr* To apply the brakes of a car very hard: *The guy on my right stood on his brakes*—Philadelphia Journal

stand on one's **head** *v phr* To make a very great effort; =BUST one's ASS: *I may not make it, but I'll sure stand on my head trying*

stand-out *n* A person or thing that is extraordinary, usu uncommonly good or talented; an outstanding person or thing: *Her performance of Amanda is the stand-out of the season*

stand pat 1 *v phr* *poker fr late 1800s* To keep one's original five cards in draw poker, without drawing new ones **2** *v phr* *fr late 1800s* To retain one's position; refuse to shift; carry on as one is; =SIT TIGHT: *The President stood pat on his decision to cut taxes* [fr the adverb *pat* "exactly, precisely to the purpose," and ultimately perhaps fr the echoic noun *pat*, analogously with expressions like *smack on the mark* and *smack-dab*, where precision and aptness are equated with a sharp blow or sound]

stand tall *v phr fr Army* To be proud and ready; have an imposing and confident stance

stand the gaff *v phr* To persist and endure against rigors; =TAKE IT: *I've had...at least seven lifetimes on Seventh Avenue, mainly because I've learned to stand the gaff*—New York Times [fr *gaff*, the steel spur attached to the leg of a fighting cock]

stand the heat *See* IF YOU CAN'T STAND THE HEAT STAY OUT OF THE KITCHEN

stand there with one's **bare face hanging out** *v phr* To speak openly and brazenly; behave without shame or reticence: *Do you mean to stand there with your bare face hanging out and tell me such a weird story?/ My boss, his bare face hanging out, suggested it would be a nice idea*—Modern Maturity

stand-up *adj* Courageous and personally accountable; =GUTSY • Most often in the expression **stand-up guy**: *He handled the humiliating defeat like a stand-up guy*—Philadelphia/ *And he's very, very stand-up*—George V Higgins [probably fr *stand up and be counted*]

stand someone **up** *v phr fr late 1800s* To fail to keep an appointment, esp a date, with someone: *You won't stand me up, now will you?*—Jerome Weidman [perhaps related to *stand up* in the sense of "go through a wedding ceremony," the image being the forsaken bride or groom left standing alone at the altar]

stand up and be counted *v phr fr early 1900s* To announce and be accountable for one's convictions, opinions, etc; not be afraid to speak up: *Maybe a lot agree with you, but they won't stand up and be counted*

stand-up comic (or **comedian**) *n phr* A performer who typically stands alone before the audience in a nightclub, telling jokes, engaging in patter, etc: *We saw Woody Allen way back when he was a rather obscure stand-up comic*

stand up for someone *v phr* To defend and support someone; =GO TO BAT FOR someone: *Nobody stood up for her so she had to back off*

stanza *n sports* A period, an inning, a round, a chukker, or some other division of a game or contest; =CANTO: *The Jets did an el foldo in the third stanza*

star *See* TIN STAR

starboarder *n baseball* A righthanded pitcher

◀ **starfucker**▶ **1** *n* A person, esp a young woman, who spends time with star performers and relishes the sex act with them; =GROUPIE **2** *modifier:*

Mellencamp appears to revel in the starfucker mentality he pokes fun at—Village Voice

starker *See* SHTARKER

starkers *adj fr early 1900s British students* Naked; stark naked; =BARE-ASS: *sitting there at the bar starkers from the waist up*—Ed McBain/ *You jog about, absolutely starkers, and then dive straight into a swimming pool*—Vogue [fr *stark* + the British slang suffix *-ers*]

starter *See* ARMSTRONG STARTER

starters *See* FOR OPENERS

start from scratch 1 *v phr* To begin on an even footing, with no advantage or handicap: *We started from scratch, but he got rich and I went broke*/ *We're gonna have a good life together starting from scratch*—Inside Sports **2** *v phr* To begin with the very first and simplest steps; build from the ground up: *Starting from scratch she got it finished in just two years* [fr the *scratch-line*, the starting line for races, often scratched in the earth]

Star Wars defense *n phr* A system of defense against guided missiles that depends on orbiting laser-beam weapons: *to spend between $22 billion to $29 billion over the next four years to build a "Star Wars" defense*—Scripps-Howard News Service [fr the name of a very popular science fiction movie of the 1970s]

stash[1] or **stache 1** *v* (also **stash away**) *fr early 1900s* To hide; hoard; save up: *I had not stashed any dough away*—John O'Hara/ *I'd stash that jug*—James T Farrell **2** *v* To put or place; deposit; dispose of: *Just stash your coat on the chair* **3** *n* A hoard or cache: *She had a little stash of money in her bureau drawer* **4** *n* A hiding place: *if he wasn't home or in his stash, people would say*—Claude Brown/ *I have some here, in a stash downstairs* **5** *n narcotics* A supply of narcotics, esp one's personal supply: *meeting him at the airport with samples of their "special stash"*—New York Times **6** *n narcotics* A place where narcotics and associated paraphernalia are hidden, esp by a dealer [origin unknown; perhaps a blend of *stow* or *store* with *cache*]

stash[2] *n* A mustache: *He had a little red stash*—David W Maurer

stash bag *n phr fr narcotics* A small bag for carrying personal possessions, esp one used for marijuana

state *See* EAST JESUS STATE, IN A STATE

state-o *n prison* A convict's prison uniform: *It griped me to have to put on "state-o" or official clothes*—Life [perhaps fr *state* official]

state of the art *adj phr fr 1970s* The latest; the very newest and most advanced: *Our magic machine uses state-of-the-art circuitry*/ *Many of the escort services are so state-of-the-art that they make Toner's look primitive*—Philadelphia [the phrase has specialized fr the 1960s sense, "the present condition of knowledge, technique, etc, in a given field"]

Stateside or **stateside 1** *n esp fr WW2 armed forces* The United States itself as distinct from foreign places, overseas possessions, etc **2** *adj: a genuine Stateside flavor to the celebration*—Yank

static *n* Complaints, backtalk, trivial objections, etc: *Here's the policy, and let's not have any static about it*

station *See* FILLING STATION

stats *n* Figures or statistics, esp relating to sports; =NUMBERS: *They are the kind of stats that a college powerhouse...might covet*—Time/ *An extraordinary cornucopia of mathematical data....Still, the line had to be drawn. No stats*—Philadelphia

◁**stay**▷ *v* To maintain a penile erection

stay loose *See* HANG LOOSE

stay out of the kitchen *See* IF YOU CAN'T STAND THE HEAT STAY OUT OF THE KITCHEN

steady *n fr late 1800s* One's constant and only boyfriend or girlfriend
See GO STEADY

steak *See* AUSSIE STEAK, TUBE STEAK

steal *n* A great bargain: *I got that for half price, a real steal*

steal someone **blind** *v phr* To rob someone absolutely thoroughly; strip someone [fr the notion that the person being robbed must or might as well be *blind*]

steam 1 *v* To anger; make furious: *I steam easily*—Richard Starnes/ *It steams me to hear that our fair burg is the Crime Capital of the World*—Washington Post **2** *v* To make someone hotly amorous: *Be thrilled by...chilled by...and steamed by Gilbert and Garbo*—San Francisco
See LET OFF STEAM

steamed *adj* Angry; =PISSED OFF: *I'm too steamed to sleep, Lacey*—Doonesbury (comic strip)/ *O'Neill wasn't the only member of Congress to be steamed*—CBS News

steamed up 1 *adj phr* Angry; =HOT AND BOTHERED, PISSED OFF: *The first thing she does is get all steamed up about it*—Hal Boyle **2** *adj phr* Eager; excited: *He's really steamed up about the new initiative*

steam fiddle *n phr circus* A steam calliope

steamroller *n* To dominate and crush; achieve by sheer force; =SNOWBALL: *They almost literally steamrollered the opposition*/ *The governor tried to steamroller the bill through*

steam someone **up** *v phr* To excite and stimulate; incite enthusiasm

steam was (or **is**) **coming out of** someone's **ears** *sentence* He or she was or is very angry: *Houk...was red-faced with anger....Steam was coming out of his ears*—Inside Sports

steamy *adj* Excitingly carnal; sexually arousing; =HOT, SEXY: *a couple of steamy bedroom scenes*/ *Hollywood's steamiest starlet*—Esquire

steel pot *n phr Army* A military helmet

steer 1 *v underworld* To take or inveigle someone to a place or person where gamblers or confidence men might victimize him: *I been steerin' for Schwiefka all day*—Nelson Algren **2** *n* (also **steerer**) A person who steers patrons and victims: *He is nothing but a steer for a bust-out joint*—Damon Runyon **3** *n* Advice or information; a bit of useful data
See BUM STEER

steerer *See* BUNCO-STEERER

Steinway *See* STOMACH STEINWAY

stem 1 *n esp hoboes* A street, often the main street of a town or city **2** *v hoboes* To beg; =PANHANDLE **3** *n narcotics* An opium pipe *See* MAIN DRAG, WORK THE STEM

stems *n* The legs, esp the attractive legs of a woman

stem-winding 1 *n* Strong persuasion; powerful rhetoric: *Any arguments are exercises in stem-winding*—Car and Driver **2** *modifier:* *Reagan delighted the crowd with a stem-winding speech* —Washington Journal [probably an extension of the 19th-century term *stem-winder* "something excellent," in turn related to the *stem-winding watch*, very advanced and first-rate when introduced]

stephen *See* EVEN-STEVEN

step on it 1 *v phr* (also **step on the gas**) *fr 1920s* To accelerate; hurry; speed up: *We better step on it, there's only five minutes left* **2** *v phr* (Variations: one's **dick** or one's **shvantz** may replace **it**) *Army* To blunder; make a serious mistake

step out 1 *v phr fr late 1800s* To go out socially, esp to a dance or a party: *I haven't stepped out much lately, too busy* **2** *v phr* To escort someone socially; =DATE: *Who is she stepping out with these days?*

step out on someone *v phr* To be romantically or sexually unfaithful to someone; =CHEAT, TWO-TIME

-ster *suffix used to form nouns* A person involved with, doing, or described by what is indicated: *clubster/ gridster/ mobster/ oldster*

Stetson *n* A man's hat [fr the name *John B Stetson*, whose company made hats]

steven *See* EVEN-STEVEN

stew[1] 1 *n* A drunkard **2** *n* A drunken carouse; =BINGE **3** *n* Confusion; chaos; =MESS *See* IN A STEW

stew[2] or **stewie** *n* An airline cabin attendant, esp a female one: *Aeroflot personnel, beefy pilots and no-nonsense stewies*—Village Voice

stew-builder *n hoboes & lumberjacks* A cook

stewbum *n* A drunken derelict; =SKID ROW BUM: *about the kid, as, say, compared to an old stewbum* —Earl Thompson/ *Get up and go home, you stewbum*—William Kennedy

stewed or **stewed to the gills** *adj* or *adj phr fr 1700s* Drunk: *He knew where the colonel lived from the time he'd taken him home stewed*—Peter De Vries/ *He came in stewed to the gills*—Nelson Algren *See* HALF-STEWED

stick 1 *n fr late 1800s* A baseball bat **2** *n* A baton, esp a conductor's baton **3** *n fr early 1900s* A golf club: *The golf dudes had their bag of sticks*—Sinclair Lewis **4** *n* A billiard cue: *I lived off the stick three months*—Nelson Algren **5** *n* The mast of a ship or boat: *The gale blew the sticks right out of her* **6** *n* A control lever or handle; =JOY-STICK **7** *n* (also **stick shift**) A manual gearshift lever, esp one mounted on the floor **8** *n* A slide rule; =SLIPSTICK **9** *n* A ski pole **10** *n* A clarinet; =LICORICE STICK **11** *n hawkers* A

fountain pen; =INKSTICK **12** *n narcotics* A marijuana cigarette; =JOINT, STICK OF GAGE, STICK OF TEA: *Marijuana was easy to get, 25 cents a "stick"* —New York Post **13** *n* A tall, thin person; =BEANPOLE **14** *n* A stiff, awkward person; an over-formal person **15** *n* A dull person; =STICK IN THE MUD **16** *n gambling* A casino croupier **17** *n carnival & underworld fr 1920s* An assistant who poses as an ordinary innocent person; =SHILL: *The man who won the $246 was a shill, sometimes referred to as a "stick"*—John Scarne/ *One operator, known as a "stall" or "stick," distracts or frames the sucker in some way*—New York/ *the highly visible "stick," or carnival worker pretending to be a townsperson*—Society **18** *v fr late 1600s* To cheat; swindle; esp, to overcharge: *runs the Bowie garage, routinely sticking what customers come his way*—Washington Post *See* BANANA STICK, BIG STICK, BOOM STICK, CARRY THE STICK, CHEAT STICK, DIPSHIT, DOPE STICK, DREAMSTICK, FIRE STICK, GET ON THE STICK, GOB-STICK, GUESS-STICK, HAVE A BROOM UP one's ASS, HOP-STICK, INKSTICK, JIVE STICK, JOY-STICK, KICK STICK, KNOW WHAT one CAN DO WITH, LICORICE STICK, MAKE something STICK, MUCK STICK, OLD STICK, ON THE STICK, PIMP STICK, SHITSTICK, the SHORT END OF THE STICK, SLIPSTICK, SWIZZLE-STICK, TEA-STICK, TELL someone WHAT TO DO WITH something, WORK BEHIND THE STICK

stick around *v phr* To stay at or near a place; =HANG AROUND: *I asked the cops to stick around for a few minutes*

sticker *See* FROG-STICKER, PIG-STICKER

sticker shock *n phr* The nasty impact of a price-sticker in inflationary times, esp one on a new car

stick in the mud *n phr fr early 1700s* A dull, conservative person; =FOGY: *Be cautious, but don't be a stick in the mud*

stick it ◁1▷ *v phr* (Variations: **cram** or **ram** or **shove** or **stuff** may replace **stick**; **up** one's **ass** or **in** one's **ear** or **where the sun doesn't shine** may be added) To dispose of or deal with something one vehemently rejects; take back something offered and scorned ● Very often used as a rude interjection conveying both rejection and insult: *Take that token raise and stick it/ Take the job and shove it*—Pietro di Donato/ *Cram it, will you?*—John Irving/ *He told them to take the money and ram it* —Interview/ *You can send them to President Carter or stick them in your ear*—Atlantic **2** *v phr* (also **stick it out**) To endure; =HANG IN: *It's rough as hell, but I'll stick it*

stick it to someone or something *v phr* To assault violently and definitively; =SOCK IT TO someone or something: *If he finds out he'll really stick it to you*

stick one's **neck out** *v phr fr 1930s* To put oneself at risk; invite trouble: *Don't stick your neck out too far*—Budd Schulberg

stick of gage *n phr outdated fr narcotics* A cigarette, either of marijuana or of tobacco

stick of tea *n phr outdated narcotics* A marijuana cigarette; =JOINT

stick something **on** someone *v phr* To subject someone to something; force something on someone: *He's nervous and he sticks shtick à la Don Rickles on everyone*—Village Voice

stick out *v phr* (Variations: **like a sore thumb** or **a mile** may be added) To be very conspicuous; stand out starkly: *She really sticks out in that bunch/ Low profile? He sticks out like a sore thumb/ His humility doesn't exactly stick out a mile*

sticks 1 *n* jazz musicians Drumsticks: *the snare drummer throwing his sticks up*—A Lomax **2** *n fr early 1900s* A drummer ● A standard nickname **3** *n fr middle 1800s* Legs; =GAMS: *a shapely pair of sticks*

See BOOM STICKS

the **sticks** *n phr fr early 1900s fr lumberjacks* Rural or suburban places; the provinces; =the BOON-DOCKS, the RHUBARBS: *A cop was transferred to the "sticks"*—A Lavine/ *a revue being tried out in the sticks*—HI Phillips [fr *sticks* "trees," representing the backwoods]

See the BIG STICKS

stick shift *See* STICK

stick to one's **knitting** *v phr* To attend strictly to one's own affairs; not interfere with others; be single-minded: *I'm not a personal confidant. I stick to my knitting*—Washington Post

stickum 1 *n* Glue; paste; cement **2** *n* Any viscous fluid; =GLOP, GUNK

stickup 1 *n* An armed robbery; =HOLDUP: *a robbery or a "stick-up"*—John Gunther **2** *n* An armed robber: *Mallory looked at the dark stick-up*—Raymond Chandler

stick up *v phr fr early 1900s* To rob, esp at gunpoint; =HOLD UP: *being "stuck up" by highwaymen*—Nation/ *They're liable to go out and stick up a bank if they owe you*—Jimmy Cannon [apparently fr the command *stick 'em up* "hold up your hands"]

stick up for someone or something *v phr* To defend and support: *If his own family won't, who will stick up for him?/ Don't be a jerk! Stick up for your rights!*

sticky 1 *adj fr early 1900s British* Difficult; tricky; nasty: *We all had a very sticky half hour until the firefighters came along* **2** *adj* Sentimental; =SCHMALTZY, SOPPY: *a sticky little song about a crippled puppy* [first sense apparently fr the notion of a *stick* as being unbending and unyielding, represented in *stick* "a stiff, awkward person," perhaps reinforced by the notion of something that is hard to move or disengage because it is *stuck* or more or less glued; the second sense fr the viscousness of a *sticky* substance]

See ICKY

sticky-fingered *adj fr middle 1800s* Prone to steal or pilfer; larcenous; =LIGHT-FINGERED: *What are you, sticky-fingered?*—James Thurber

sticky wicket *n phr fr 1940s British* A very difficult or awkward situation; a nasty affair: *"It's a sticky wicket," he said, but he left open the possibility that it could be orchestrated in a few cases*—Philadelphia Journal/ *It's the original sticky wicket*—Car and Driver [fr the British phrase *bat on* (or *at*) a *sticky*

wicket "contend with great difficulties," fr the game of cricket; *sticky* probably means simply "tricky, nasty," rather than having to do with the case where the bails or small horizontal pieces of wood are not readily dislodged from the three vertical ones of the wicket; in any event, cricket is a rather mysterious game]

stiff 1 *adj fr middle 1700s* Drunk: *when the regular piano player got stiff and fell from the stool*—Westbook Pegler **2** *n* A drunken person: *Robbing a drunken man they call "rolling a stiff"*—Jack London **3** *n fr middle 1800s* A corpse: *They found a couple of stiffs in the millpond* **4** *n* hoboes *fr late 1800s* A hobo; tramp; vagabond: *He bore none of the earmarks of the professional "stiff"*—Jack London **5** *n fr early 1900s* A migratory worker; =OKIE **6** *n fr early 1900s* A working man or woman; a nonclerical and nonprofessional employee; =WORKING STIFF: *Coolidge always seemed unreal to the ordinary stiff*—Robert Ruark **7** *n* underworld *fr late 1800s* A clandestine letter, esp one passed around among prisoners **8** *n* underworld *fr late 1800s* A forged check, banknote, etc **9** *adj* underworld Forged; =PHONY: *"I put over a couple of stiff ones," is the way a paperhanger describes an operation*—Saturday Evening Post **10** *n fr late 1800s British horse-racing* A team, fighter, contestant, etc, that is bound to lose; esp, a race horse that will not, cannot, or is not permitted to win: *There is also a rumor that Follow You is a stiff in the race*—Damon Runyon **11** *n* Any failure; =FLOP, TURKEY: *gets a million dollars worth of hype, and I hear it's a stiff*—Aquarian **12** *v fr horse-racing* To cause a horse to lose a race: *He admitted that he himself had stiffed horses for a fee*—Sports Illustrated **13** *v* To fail to tip a waiter or other employee: *But he was slow about getting our orders, so we stiffed him*—National Lampoon/ *who not only stiffs waiters and cab drivers, but golf caddies as well*—Art Buchwald **14** *v* To cheat, esp out of money, fair wages, etc: *It was a signal for the waiter to hustle over and put the arm on the customer who was trying to stiff him*—Saturday Evening Post/ *The company defends its plan as a business decision and denies it was trying to stiff the women*—Newsweek/ *which creditors he could stiff, which he could stall, which had to be paid at once*—Lawrence Sanders **15** *v* To swindle; defraud; =SCAM: *Some of the lessons were not as palatable, though, such as the one about a young woman who stiffed him*—Morris County Daily Record/ *In other words, New York City got stiffed*—Village Voice **16** *v* To maltreat; mislead and trick: *I was stiffed*—Ronald Reagan/ *Nobody was supposed to stiff a member of the family the way Vinnie had stiffed his niece's boy*—Patrick Mann **17** *v* (also **stiff-arm**) To treat unfairly and harshly; snub or push aside brutally: *one of the nearly 5,000 travel agencies that stiffed the Air Traffic Conference*—Philadelphia/ *He had stiffed a Philadelphia charity golf tournament without explanation*—Sports Illustrated/ *understandable for President Reagan to stiff-arm the issue as "much ado about nothing"*

—New York Times/ *I'll just stiff-arm them*—James Watt [the underworld senses having to do with forged and clandestine papers, cheating, etc, are derived fr an early-19th-century British sense, "paper, a document," probably based on the *stiffness* of official documents and document paper; the senses having to do with failure, etc, are related to the *stiffness* of a corpse; the sense of harsh snubbing, etc, is fr the *stiff-arm* in football, where a player, usu a runner, straightens out his arm and pushes it directly into the face or body of an intending tackler]
See BIG STIFF, BINDLESTIFF, BLANKET STIFF, BORED STIFF, JUNGLE STIFF, KNOCK someone OUT, MISSION STIFF, RAILROAD STIFF, SCARED STIFF, TUNNEL STIFF, WORKING STIFF

stiffener *n prizefight* A blow that renders one unconscious

still wet behind the ears *See* NOT DRY BEHIND THE EARS

sting 1 *v fr early 1800s* To cheat; swindle; defraud; = SCAM **2** *v* To overcharge; = STICK: *He got stung in the corner hockshop* **3** *n esp fr early 1970s* A tricking or entrapment, either in a confidence scheme or as part of a law enforcement operation: *have used sting to describe undercover operations that use a bogus business operation as a front*—New York Times/ *Let's contrast Abscam with traditional law-enforcement stings*—Village Voice/ *It is the rare Bay Area driver who has managed to entirely escape the parking sting*—San Francisco

stinger *n* An unpleasant or adverse element; = CATCH: *Seems like a good proposition, but there's a stinger in it*

stink 1 *v* (also **stink on ice**) To be deplorable, nasty, totally inept or bungling, disgusting, etc; = ROT: *The whole idea stinks, if you ask me/ The group and its main man stunk on ice*—Rolling Stone **2** *n* A complaint; a noisy fuss or row: *He decided to make a stink about it*
See ACT LIKE one's SHIT DOESN'T STINK, BIG STINK, THINK one's SHIT DOESN'T STINK

stink bomb *n phr* Something disgusting, inept, deplorable, etc: *the stink bomb of a film, Flashdance*—Village Voice

stinker 1 *n* A despicable person; = BASTARD: *Stop acting like a stinker* **2** *n* (also **stinkeroo**) Something disgusting, nasty, badly done, etc: *Few of Hitchcock's films were genuine stinkers/ If it proves to be a "stinkeroo" leave the theater quietly or suffer in silence*—Coronet

◁**stink-finger**▷ *See* PLAY STINKY-PINKY

stinking 1 *adj* Despicable; wretched; = LOUSY: *Ain't it a stinking shame?/ It was a stinking way to treat her* **2** *adj* (also **stinking rich**) Very wealthy; = FILTHY RICH, LOADED: *The family, in those years, was stinking* **3** *adj* (also **stinko**) Drunk: *and he got pretty stinking*—Max Shulman

stinkpot *n sailors* A motorboat, esp a cabin cruiser

stink to high heaven *v phr* To be very disgusting, inept, nasty, etc: *filler items that definitely stunk to high heaven*—Village Voice

stink with *v phr* To have much of; be oversupplied with: *He stinks with confidence, certainly*

stinky *adj* Despicable; nasty

stinky-pinky *See* PLAY STINKY-PINKY

stir 1 *n fr middle 1800s British underworld* A jail or prison: *John went to stir*—E DeBaun **2** *modifier:* *with the stir haircuts*—Damon Runyon [perhaps fr Romany *steriben*; the mid-19th-century *sturbin* "state prison" may represent a transitional sense]

stir-crazy *adj* (Variations: **bugs** or **daffy** or **simple** may replace **crazy**) *prison* Insane, stuporous, hysterical, or otherwise affected mentally by imprisonment: *Any number of others were what we call "stir-crazy," going about their routine like punch-drunk boxers*—American Mercury

stir-wise *adj prison* Having the sort of cunning, patience, etc, instilled by imprisonment: *Johnson was stir-wise, a tough man to question*—Fact Detective Mysteries

a stitch *n phr* An amusing or hilarious person or thing; = a HOOT: *The Gossages were a stitch, playing it very loose*—Sports Illustrated/ *What a stitch*—Paul Theroux/ *Calling this tarty turn an "interpretation" really is a stitch*—Washington Post [fr the expression *in stitches* "laughing uncontrollably," perhaps fr the notion of laughing so much that it gives one *stitches* "sudden sharp pains"]

stitched *adj* Drunk

St Louis (or **Chicago**) **flats** *n phr* Shoes made of a piece of leather shaped to the sole, without heels, and worn like a moccasin

stocking *See* SILK-STOCKING

stocking stuffer *n phr* A small, usu cheap present to be put into the Christmas stocking

stoked *adj esp teenagers* Enthusiastic; happily surprised: *Everyone's stoked that he's here and...would he do a couple of tunes*—Playboy

stoked on *adj phr* Enthusiastic over; very much pleased with: *Stoked on cats? If you like catamarans*—Yachting/ *I was really stoked on that chick, man*—Dan Jenkins [fr the notion of being fueled and hot like a furnace]

stomach-robber *n lumberjacks* A logging-camp cook

stomach Steinway *n phr* A piano accordion

stomp 1 *n fr early 1900s* A jazz number with a heavy rhythmic accent **2** *v* To assault viciously; savage; = CLOBBER: *These chaps went about stomping everyone they thought might be homosexual* **3** *n teenagers* A person who habitually wears cowboy boots [fr a dialect pronunciation of *stamp*]

◁**stomp-ass**▷ *adj* Violent and pugilistic; rough and vicious: *I never even touched the slut and now there's gonna be some sort of stompass scene*—Easyriders

stompers *n students* Boots, esp cowboy boots
See SHITKICKERS, WAFFLE-STOMPERS

stone 1 *adj fr black* Thorough; perfect; total: *Reba's a stone psycho, I tell you*—Joseph Wambaugh/ *People think it's a stone groove being a superstar*—Esquire **2** *adv* Totally; genuinely: *He is a stone crazy dude* [fr earlier adverbial sense "like or as a stone," in phrases like *stone* blind or *stone* deaf]

See NOT CARVED IN STONE

stone blind *adj phr* Very drunk

stone broke *adj phr fr late 1800s* Penniless; impoverished: *the money that is made out of stone-broke tramps*—Jack London

stone cold sober *adj phr* Totally unintoxicated; = COLD SOBER

stoned or **stoned-out** *adj fr 1940s cool talk* Intoxicated with narcotics or liquor; = BOMBED OUT, ZONKED: *They get themselves stoned on beer*—Dorothy Parker/ *The old man was stoned mad*—Robert Stone/ *giggling in that mutually exclusive stoned-out way*—San Francisco

stone dead *adj phr* As dead as can be

stoned to the eyes *adj phr* Completely intoxicated; = HIGH: *Under that tree, stoned to the eyes, I wolf down Daybreak, Joan Baez's autobiography*—Village Voice

stoner *adj* An intoxicated or stuporous person: *mumbles a stoner performance that's sidesplittingly funny*—Village Voice

stonewall 1 *v fr British fr late 1800s Australian* To delay and obstruct, esp by stubbornly keeping silent • The term became prominent during the early 1970s Watergate scandal: *I want you all to stonewall it*—Richard M Nixon **2** *n: A sustained stonewall, no one's been willing to answer questions for a week*—Village Voice [fr a cricket term used of a determined batsman who blocked everything as if he were a *stone wall*; in the US probably influenced by the stolid reputation of the Confederate general Thomas J "*Stonewall*" Jackson]

stonies *n phr* Urgent sexual desire: *They passed a local law prohibiting a dude with stonies from soliciting a woman-of-the-night for a piece of ass*—Easyriders [semantically similar to *hard up*, with its suggestion of penile erection; probably transferred because of the hardness of *stone* and the sense of *stones* as "testicles"]

stony cold broke *adj phr fr late 1800s* Absolutely penniless; pauperized; destitute

stood in bed *See* one SHOULD HAVE STOOD IN BED

stooge 1 *n fr late 1800s show business* A servile assistant; a mere flunky or tool: *Whenever Gulliver is not acting as a stooge there is a sort of continuity in his character*—George Orwell/ *his bail-bond stooges*—Erle Stanley Gardner **2** *v: We're glad to stooge for him*—Raymond Chandler [origin unknown; perhaps an alteration of *student*, humorously mispronounced as STŌŌ jənt, in the sense of an apprentice, especially one unskilled at or learning a theatrical turn of some sort while serving as the underling of a master]

stool 1 *n underworld* A police informer; = STOOL PIGEON: *He's nothing but a cop's stool*—James M Cain **2** *v: to make me stool on a friend*—J Evans [back formation fr *stool pigeon*]

stoolie *n underworld* A police informer; = STOOL PIGEON: *There was stoolies and wire tappers working all over town* [back formation fr *stool pigeon*]

stool pigeon *n phr underworld fr early 1800s* A police informer; = SNITCH, SQUEALER: *In New York he is also called a stool-pigeon*—J Flynt [fr earlier sense "decoy," fr the early-19th-century practice of fastening *pigeons* and other birds to *stools* or stands as decoys; this term was applied to the decoy or "hustler" for a faro bank]

stoop *See* STUPE

stooper *n* A person who looks on the ground at betting parlors and race tracks for betting tickets that may be valuable: *The girl said she had become a stooper*—New York Times

stop *n underworld* A receiver of stolen goods; = FENCE

See PIT STOP, WHISTLE STOP

stop someone or something **dead in** someone's or something's **tracks** *v phr* To stop someone or something very definitely and abruptly: *She said the magic words that stopped me dead in my tracks*/ *The economy could be stopped dead in its tracks*—Art Buchwald [fr the image of a person or animal dropping straight down on being struck]

stop on a dime *v phr* To stop quickly and neatly: *The car corners smoothly and stops on a dime*

storage *See* IN COLD STORAGE

storch 1 *n* An easy victim; dupe; = MARK, PATSY **2** *n* An ordinary person; = GUY, JOE

Storch *See* JOE BLOW[1]

store *n circus & carnival* A concession

See BUDDY STORE, MIND THE STORE

store cheese *See* RAT CHEESE

storm *v hot rodders fr 1950s* To speed; drive very fast

See BARNSTORM, BLOW UP A STORM, BRAINSTORM, SHITSTORM, UP A STORM

stormer *See* BARNSTORMER

story *See* FISH STORY, LOOSE IN THE BEAN, SOB STORY, TOP STORY, UPPER STORY

stove *See* HOT STOVE LEAGUE, POTBELLY STOVE

stow it *Navy* **1** *v* To stop doing something • Often an irritated command **2** *v* = STICK IT

stow the gab *v phr Navy* To hold one's peace; = SHUT UP

STP (pronounced as separate letters) *n narcotics* A powerful hallucinogen: *a strictly contemporary folk drug, called STP by its Haight-Ashbury discoverers*—Scientific American [fr *Serenity Tranquility Peace*, named in imitation of the oil additive STP (a trade name)]

strack *adj Army* Very strict in one's military appearance and grooming [origin unknown]

straddler *See* FENCE-STRADDLER

straddle the fence *v phr* To avoid taking a public position on one or another side of an issue; remain neutral or ambiguous: *The candidate kept straddling the fence about abortion*

straight 1 *adj fr middle 1800s* Unmixed; undiluted: *He takes his liquor straight* **2** *adj narcotics fr 1960s* Not using narcotics; not addicted **3** *adj narcotics since 1960s* Having had a narcotics dose, esp the first one of the day: *Once the addict has had his shot and is "straight" he may become...industrious*—Reader's Digest **4** *n esp* musicians & students A tobacco cigarette; =SQUARE **5** *adj* *fr homosexuals* Heterosexual; not sexually deviant **6** *adj* True; honest and direct: *from straight-poop tough to moral*—Village Voice/ *straight talk/ straight goods/ just a straight kind of guy* **7** *adv* Truthfully and directly: *I'll tell it to you straight*

See GO STRAIGHT

straight-ahead *adj* Unflinching; undeviating: *Bill was a straight-ahead guy*—Philadelphia

straight arrow 1 *n phr* A person who observes the social norms of decency, honesty, legality, heterosexuality, etc; a nondeviant: *It turns out the boy is a straight arrow underneath his finery*—Richard Schickel/ *This is a supervisory job that ordinarily is won by the group Straight Arrow, the Eagle Scout type*—Harper's **2** *adj*: *For marches you have to be straight arrow because what if they interview us for TV?*—Ms/ *The distraught heroine murmured...to the straight-arrow hero*—Studs Terkel [fr an archetypical upright Native American brave named *Straight Arrow*, mythically associated with a similar Caucasian who is a *straight shooter*]

straighten someone *v phr* narcotics To get or administer a narcotic for someone

straighten someone **out** *v phr* To give the correct information, explanation, etc: *First let me straighten you out about where we were when it happened*

straighten up and fly right *v phr* =CLEAN UP one's ACT

straight face *n phr* A face revealing no ironic amusement or disbelief: *He couldn't tell me that story with a straight face*

straight-faced *adj* Maintaining a straight face; =POKER-FACED: *It was a big lie, straight-faced, but a lie*

straight from the horse's mouth *See* FROM THE HORSE'S MOUTH

straight from the shoulder *adv phr* Honestly and directly; unflinchingly; =STRAIGHT: *He gave it to us straight from the shoulder* [perhaps from the notion of an honest blow delivered *straight from the shoulder* rather than deviously, from the side, etc]

straight goods *n phr* The truth: *Is all dat straight goods?*—Eugene O'Neill

straight job *n phr* truckers An ordinary truck as distinct from a semitrailer

straight lane *See* IN THE STRAIGHT LANE

straight man *n* show business A comedian's interlocutor and companion, who acts as the foil

the **straight skinny** *n phr* The truth; =STRAIGHT GOODS: *lame enough to have told me the straight skinny about that*—Richard Merkin [see the skinny]

straight talk *n phr* Direct and honest discourse; =STRAIGHT GOODS

straight-up 1 *adj* Honest; upright; =STRAIGHT ARROW: *They were straight-up, nice people*—Claude Brown **2** *adj* Of cocktails, served without ice cubes; =NEAT

strain *n* Gonorrhea; =the CLAP

strainer *See* SOUP-STRAINER

strangioso *adj* Very strange; weird: *a strangioso publication like Raw*—Village Voice [fr the Italian or Spanish intensive form of *strange*]

strap *n* esp students A student interested primarily in sports; =JOCK [fr *jock strap* "athletic supporter"] *See* SCARE STRAP

strapped *adj* fr middle 1800s Short of money; penniless; =BROKE: *He happens to be strapped financially*—Ellery Queen [origin unknown; perhaps related to the idea of tightening one's belt when it becomes necessary, perhaps related to British dialect *strap* "credit," so that a *strapped* person would be one forced to buy on credit]

strapper *See* BOOT STRAPPER

strategist *See* ARMCHAIR GENERAL

strawberries *See* ARMY STRAWBERRIES, BOSTON STRAWBERRIES

strawberry patch *n phr* railroad The rear end of a caboose with its red lights seen at night

straw boss hoboes fr late 1800s **1** *n phr* The foreman of a work crew **2** *n phr* Any assistant chief or subordinate director [said to be fr the arrangement of a threshing crew, where the chief would superintend the grain itself, and the second the *straw*; perhaps fr Dutch *stroodekkerbaas*]

straw-cat *n* A harvest worker, esp a migratory one

straw hat *n phr* show business A summer theater: *a new play that's...at a straw hat*—Abel Green

straw-hat circuit *n phr* show business Summer theaters collectively

streak 1 *v* esp early 1970s To run naked in public **2** *n*: *The students did a streak across the square* *See* a BLUE STREAK

streaker *n* A person who streaks: *She complained that several streakers marred her view of the campus*

street *modifier* Having to do with the streets and the street life of a city, esp of a ghetto: *Curtis Sliwa, founder of the street-tough Guardian Angels*—Philadelphia Journal/ *The defendant was not some street punk with a long criminal record*—Playboy *See* EASY STREET, NOT A ONE-WAY STREET, TWO-WAY STREET

the **street** *n phr* prison fr early 1900s The world outside of prison *See* PUT IT ON THE STREET, TAKE IT TO THE STREET, WORK BOTH SIDES OF THE STREET

street (or **garbage**) **furniture** *n phr* Furniture put in the street for the trash collectors, and sometimes taken for use

street people fr 1960s **1** *n phr* Ghetto dwellers **2** *n phr* Homeless people like transient hippies, bag ladies, and the like; drifters

the **streets** *See* POUND THE PAVEMENT

street-smart or **street-bright** or **street-wise** *adj* Cunning and clever in various practical ways, esp in the street culture of the urban ghetto: *a place for very sophisticated, street-bright people*—Toronto Life/ *supplanting preppie glamour with what's euphemistically called a "streetwise" look. Supertramp is more like it*—Us

street smarts *n phr* Cunning and cleverness of a very practical sort, esp that useful in the urban ghetto: *that raging philosophical conflict between street smarts and pinstripes*—Philadelphia

street time *prison* **1** *n phr* The period when a convict is not imprisoned, but is on parole or probation **2** *n phr* The time between prison terms

stretch 1 *v fr 1600s* To hang or be hanged **2** *n prison* A prison term: *a stretch in the Big House*—A Lavine **3** *n lunch counter* Coca-Cola (a trade name) [prison sense originally "a one-year prison sentence"; lunch counter sense fr the phrase *shoot one and stretch it* "put syrup in a glass and add soda water"]

stretch limo *n phr* A limousine that has been lengthened to provide more seating and more luxurious surrounds: *certified designer fashions, eye-popping jewelry, stretch limos*—Philadelphia/ *a bar the length of a few stretch limos*—Washingtonian [probably modeled on the earlier term *stretch* or *stretched* applied to a jetliner with a lengthened fuselage providing more seating]

stretch one *v phr lunch counter* Provide a large Coca-Cola (a trade name)

stretch out *v phr jazz musicians* To play uninhibitedly: *When a cat stretches out, he can make the moon*—E Horne

stretch some jeans *n phr prison* To do the sex act, esp homosexually

strib *n underworld* A prison warden [origin unknown]

strictly *adv* Totally; entirely: *Everything about it is strictly from yuck*—Washington Post

stride 1 *n jazz musicians* A jazz piano style of alternating bass with treble notes in particular patterns **2** *modifier: stride piano, Harlem's version of ragtime*—Albert Goldman/ *stride bass*

strike *See* SIT-DOWN, WILDCAT

strike it rich *v phr fr middle 1800s* To have a sudden financial success

strike oil *v phr fr middle 1800s* To succeed: *I worked at the problem eight days before I struck oil*

striker 1 *n Army fr early 1800s* An officer's servant or orderly; = DOG-ROBBER **2** *n WW2 Navy* An assistant; a helper **3** *n WW2 Navy* A sailor on the lookout for his own advancement, even by flattering means; = EAGER BEAVER

string *v fr middle 1800s* To deceive; fool; hoax: *Who are you trying to string, anyhow?*—Elmer Rice *See* PULL someone's CHAIN, PULL THE STRING

string along *v phr* To agree; follow; join in: *As long as you string along with me, your cafeteria days are over*—Jerome Weidman

string someone **along** *v phr fr late 1800s* To deceive; fool, esp into a continuing adherence, cooperation, etc; = STRING: *I'm afraid that he's just stringing me along, trying to encourage me*—P Marks [probably fr early-19th-century British *string on*, in the same sense]

stringbean *n* A tall, thin person; = BEANPOLE

string someone **out 1** *v phr* To intoxicate someone: *I couldn't figure what she had done in there to string him out so bad*—Harry Crews **2** *v phr* To disturb someone; upset someone: *The one thing that strings me out...is punks who travel in packs*—Noel Gerson

strings *See* PULL STRINGS

string someone **up** *v phr* To hang someone

strip *See* DRAG STRIP, LEAVE A STRIP

Strip *See* SUNSET STRIP

the Strip *n phr* Any of various main streets in US cities, esp the street in Las Vegas where most of the gambling casinos are found

stripe *See* HASH MARK

striper *See* BROKEN-STRIPER, CANDY STRIPER, FOUR-STRIPER, ONE-AND-A-HALF-STRIPER, ONE-STRIPER, THREE-STRIPER, TWO-AND-A-HALF-STRIPER

stripes 1 *n circus* A tiger **2** *n Army* Chevrons worn as insignias of noncommissioned rank; = CROW TRACKS

stripped down 1 *adj phr* Of a car, divested of ornaments and other unnecessary parts; = SHAVED **2** *adj phr* Reduced to the essentials; disencumbered: *a stripped-down version of the Oedipus myth*

stripper *n* A striptease dancer: *Norma Vincent Peel, the noted stripper*

strippers *n gamblers* A deck of fraudulent playing cards from which narrow strips have been trimmed off certain cards; a marked deck *See* LOW-BELLY STRIPPERS

strip-search *n* = SKIN-SEARCH

stroke 1 *v fr black* To praise and please; caress the ego of; flatter; cosset: *Mr Hoover should be called in privately for a stroking session*—Cal McCrystal/ *and ads in Rolling Stone were more for the purpose of stroking recording artists*—Wall Street Journal **2** *n: Everybody needs a stroke or two every once in a while* ◁**3**▷ *v* To masturbate [*stroker* "flatterer" is attested in the early 17th century]

stroke book *n phr* A lewd or suggestive publication; a pornographic book or magazine; = FUCK BOOK: *It took a stroke book for me to break the ice*—Richard Price [fr *stroke* "masturbate"]

stroke house *n phr* A pornographic movie theater [fr *stroke* "masturbate"]

strong *See* COME ON STRONG

strong-arm *fr late 1800s* **1** *modifier* Using threats of violence; physically brutal: *strong-arm work around election time*—E Lavine/ *We reprehended his strong-arm tactics* **2** *v* To use force and intimidation: *We can't strong-arm them into voting our way*

strong-arm man *n phr* A man who uses physical force, usu as a hired agent; a thug; = ENFORCER, GOON

◁**stronger than pig shit**▷ *adj phr* Very strong: *beautiful and a genius...stronger than pig shit*—Dan Jenkins

struggle 1 *n outdated college students & Army* A party or dance; = FIGHT **2** *v sports* To have difficulty winning or holding the pace; be in athletic travail: *Mets Struggling; Cardinals soaring*—New York Times/ *Lendl Struggles to Win*—New York Times *See* BUN-STRUGGLE

struggle-buggy *n esp 1920s & 30s students* A car [fr the use of cars as sites for sexual endeavor]

strung out **1** *adj phr* *narcotics fr 1950s* Using or addicted to narcotics; intoxicated with narcotics: *The entire college population is "strung out" thrice weekly*—New York Post/ *got fairly well strung out, fairly well addicted*—Esquire **2** *adj phr* *narcotics & students fr 1960s* Emotionally disturbed; psychologically tense, brittle, and vulnerable; =UPTIGHT: *She got herself strung way out...just one more little push and she was a dead duck*—Changes/ *or slung low and strung-out on drugs or inner tensions*—Ramparts **3** *adj* *black* Infatuated; in love: *He's strung out on her* [apparently fr extension fr the black term *on a tight leash* "in love; addicted," stressing the tethered helplessness of each condition]

strut one's **stuff** *See* DO one's STUFF

stuck on someone or something *part phr fr late 1800s* In love with; infatuated: *That feller was stuck on yuh, Bess*—H Witwer/ *She looks real stuck on herself*

stuck-up *adj fr early 1800s* Haughty and conceited; snobbish; =HINCTY: *We didn't like her at first because we thought she acted stuck-up*

stuck with *past part phr* Burdened with; endowed with: *Imagine being stuck with a moniker like that all your life*—Leslie Ford/ *That's my story and I'm stuck with it*/ *She always gets stuck with the bill*

stud **1** *n* *fr 1930s jive talk* A man, esp one who is stylish, au courant, etc; =DUDE **2** *n* A sexually prodigious man; =COCKSMAN **3** *n* An attractive man: *Her boyfriend's such a stud!* [fr early-19th-century US *stud* or *studhorse* "stallion, esp one kept for breeding"]

student *n narcotics fr 1930s* A newly addicted and still lightly addicted drug user: *On a quarter grain a week a man was still a student*—Nelson Algren

studio *See* RAP CLUB

stuff **1** *n* *1920s prohibition era* Liquor, esp bootleg liquor: *The stuff is here and it's mellow* **2** *n* *narcotics* Any narcotic: *Where's the stuff?*—Saturday Evening Post/ *He came out and seemed to be off the stuff*—New York Post ◁**3**▷ *n* A woman regarded as a sex object; =ASS, COOZ, PUSSY: *classiest stuff this side of Denver*—Stephen Longstreet ◁**4**▷ *v* To do the sex act; =FUCK ● Chiefly British and most often heard in the passive imperative form **get stuffed**, a rude insult; used in any sense of **fuck**: *No women, no children, no fun. Stuff this*—John Leonard

See ALL THAT KIND OF CRAP, BLACK STUFF, EATIN' STUFF, the GREEN STUFF, HARD STUFF, HOT STUFF, KID STUFF, KNOW one's ONIONS, KNOW WHAT one CAN DO WITH something, ROUGH STUFF, SOB STUFF, TELL someone WHAT TO DO WITH something, WHITE STUFF

stuff cuff *n phr jive talk* A padded cuff on the pants of a zoot suit: *zoot suit, reet pleat, stuff cuff*—Leonard Feather

stuffed *See* GET STUFFED

stuffed shirt *n phr fr early 1900s* A pompous person; a stiff, self-important bore

stuffer *See* STOCKING STUFFER

the **stuffing** *See* BEAT THE SHIT OUT OF

stuff it *See* STICK IT

stuff the ballot box *v phr fr middle 1800s* To cast or record fraudulent votes in an election

stuffy **1** *adj fr early 1800s* Angry; sulky; obstinate **2** *adj fr 1920s* Tediously conventional; pompous and self-righteous: *He was inclined to be a bit stuffy in sexual matters* [later sense fr *stuffy* "stale, lacking freshness," influenced by *stuffed shirt*]

stumble *v underworld* To be arrested; =FALL

stumblebum *n* An alcoholic derelict; a drunken drifter; =SKID ROW BUM, SPECK BUM: *to bemoan the lack of charisma and to paint the candidates as a wrangling collection of stumblebums*—Washington Post

stump **1** *v fr early 1800s* To baffle; perplex; nonplus: *The whole problem's got me stumped* **2** *v fr middle 1800s* To make speeches, esp on a political tour: *The candidate is stumping today in Illinois* **3** *v line repairers* A telephone or other wire-carrying pole [first sense fr the notion of being blocked by *stumps* in one's way; second sense fr standing up on a *stump* to make a speech]

stump for someone or something *v phr* To advocate or support, esp very actively [fr the notion of giving speeches from *stumps*]

◁**stump-jumper**▷ *n* A rural person; farmer; =SHITKICKER

stumps *n* The legs: *Everybody stir your stumps when Pa calls*

stunned *adj* Drunk

stunner *n* Something very attractive or impressive, esp a good-looking woman

stunning *adj* Attractive; impressive: *Isn't that a stunning little dress?*

stunt *n* Act; bit of behavior; thing to do: *That was a stupid stunt, my dear*

◁**stup**▷ *See* SHTUP

stupe or **stoop** *n fr middle 1700s* A stupid person: *"Don't call me stupe," Humphrey said*—G Homes

stutter-stepping *n football* To run with rapid short steps: *Never mind all that stutter-stepping and looking for daylight*—Sports Illustrated

style **1** *v fr black* To act or play in a showy, flamboyant way; =HOT DOG, SHOWBOAT **2** *pres part:* *The proper reward for a styling player is a fast ball in the ribs*—Philadelphia Journal

See CRAMP someone's STYLE, DOG FASHION, LIKE IT'S GOING OUT OF STYLE

stymie *v fr early 1900s fr golf* To block or thwart; frustrate: *We have to figure a way to stymie that guy* [fr British dialect *stimey* "dim-sighted person," fr *stime* "ray or bit of light"; adopted in golf for situations where the player or, as it were, the ball, cannot "see" a clear path ahead]

suave or **swave** (SWAYV) *n teenagers* Smooth skill; polished adroitness: *He has plenty of suave when it comes to girls*

sub[1] **1** *n* A substitute of any sort, esp an athlete who replaces another or an athlete not on the first team **2** *v:* *Who'll sub for me when I go on leave?*

sub[2] **1** *n* A submarine: *Saw sub, sank same* **2** *n* =HERO SANDWICH

submarine sandwich or **sub** or **submarine** *n phr* or *n* = HERO SANDWICH [fr the shape of the bread cut lengthwise for the sandwich]

◁**suck**▷ **1** *v* To do fellatio; = EAT **2** *v* (also **suck rope**) To be disgusting or extremely reprehensible; be of wretched quality; = ROT, STINK: *a failure as an album. It sucks*—Rolling Stone/ *Life irretrievably sucks, and what's the use*—Village Voice/ *Your decision sucks rope*—Bob Newhart (TV program) **3** *v* = SUCK ASS **4** *n* = SUCTION

suck air *v phr* To be afraid, so as to pant: *Were you afraid? I was sucking air a couple of times*—Bernard Arkules

suck around *v phr* To loiter about; frequent a place, esp with a view to currying favor: *What's the kid sucking around the clubhouse for?*

◁**suck ass**▷ *v phr* To curry favor; flatter and cajole; = BROWN-NOSE, POLISH APPLES: *He sucks ass with everybody in the front office*

suck canal water *v phr Army* To be in trouble; be in a bad situation: *If you keep this up you'll be sucking canal water next week*

suck eggs 1 *v phr esp Southern* To be mean and irritable: *We've sucked on these eggs long enough*—Peter Gent **2** *v phr* To be disgusting or reprehensible; be of wretched quality; = SUCK ● A euphemism for the same sense of **suck**: *his own pet phrase, "That sucks eggs," for expressing disdain*—Washington Post **3** *v phr* To do something very nasty, esp when invited to; = GO FUCK oneself ● A euphemism: *Tell your husband to suck huge eggs*—Village Voice

sucker 1 *n fr early 1800s* An easy victim; dupe; = MARK, PATSY: *I'm no sucker*—Theodore Dreiser/ *I'm a sucker for a beautiful blonde*—George Sanders **2** *v* To victimize or dupe someone: *if I can sucker him into drawing first*—Mickey Spillane **3** *n* Any specified object, esp one that is prodigious, troublesome, effective, etc; = MOMMA, MOTHERFUCKER ● A euphemism for **cocksucker**: *It took me 90 days to get that sucker straightened out*—New York/ *Careful, that sucker's heavy* [origin uncertain; perhaps fr the *sucker*, a fish supposed to be easily caught; perhaps fr the notion of an unweaned and relatively helpless creature, as suggested by an earlier sense, "greenhorn, simpleton"]
See COCKSUCKER, EGG-SUCKER

Sucker *n* A native or resident of Illinois [origin uncertain]

sucker list *n phr* A list of prospective customers, victims, etc: *The directory is not intended to be a sucker list*—Philadelphia Bulletin

suckerpunch 1 *n* A blow that fools and surprises the recipient, who ought to have dodged or parried it **2** *v*: *He suckerpunched me*—Peter Gent/ *I'll sucker punch a man in a second to get what I want*—Rolling Stone

suck face *v phr* To kiss and caress; = NECK, PET: *You know, kiss. Suck face, kiss*—Ernest Thompson

suck hind tit *v phr* To be in a disadvantageous situation; get the worst and least of things: *They all collected a fortune and I was left sucking hind tit*

again [fr the presumed disadvantage of a *suckling* at the *nethermost teat*]

suck someone **in** *v phr fr middle 1800s* To deceive; befool or dupe; esp with false promises [said to be fr the action of quicksand]

sucking *See* COCKSUCKING

suck it up *v phr* To become serious; stop dallying or loafing: *forced the 76ers to suck it up for game four, which they did to beat LA*—Sports Illustrated [fr the military expression *suck up* or *suck in your guts* "pull in your stomach and look trim, as a soldier should"]

◁**suck off**▷ *v phr* To do fellatio or cunnilingus; = BLOW, GO DOWN ON someone

◁**suck-off**▷ **1** *n* A despicable person, esp a flatterer; = BROWN-NOSE **2** *adj* Despicable; nasty; = SCUZZY: *We did a suck-off thing*—Stephen King

suck up *v phr* To defeat in a speed race; pass in a drag race: *I have also sucked up plenty of cherry red Vettes*—Car and Driver [fr the notion of drawing the passed car along in one's turbulence behind]

suck up to someone *v phr fr middle 1800s British* To flatter and cajole someone; curry favor with someone; = BROWN-NOSE, SUCK ASS: *He gets ahead by sucking up to the mayor*

suction *n* Influence; = DRAG, PULL

sudden death 1 *n phr sports* Any of several arrangements for breaking a tie by playing an extra period during which the first team to score wins the game: *They were tied, so went into sudden death* **2** *modifier*: *It's like playing a sudden death inning at the beginning of a game*—Walter Mondale

suds *n fr early 1900s* Beer
See SINKERS AND SUDS

sudser *n* A soap opera; = SOAP: *Harvey Fierstein's savvy sudser about a not-so-gay drag queen*—Time

sudsing *n* Beer-drinking

sugar 1 *n fr middle 1800s* Money; = BREAD: *I'd take a trip if I had the requisite sugar* **2** *n* Dear one; sweetheart ● Most often a term of address: *I hear you, sugar* **3** *n narcotics* LSD; = ACID [narcotics sense fr the taking of LSD soaked in a *sugar cube*]
See HEAVY MONEY

Sugar *See* UNCLE SUGAR

sugar-coat something *v phr* To make something more acceptable or palatable: *He did not have to sugar-coat the facts for us*

sugar daddy *n phr* A man who provides money, esp one who supports a clandestine sweetheart or a gold-digger: *Mrs Shawsky must have had a sugar daddy on the side*—Fact Detective Mysteries/ *The Pentagon seems to be playing sugar daddy to a lot of American workers*—Newsweek
See DADDY

Sugar Hill *black* **1** *n phr* A black brothel or brothel district **2** *n phr* A wealthy neighborhood overlooking Harlem in New York City

sugar pants *n phr* A mild person; = PUSSYCAT: *You'd have thought he was a bad, scary guy, but he was just a little sugar pants*—San Francisco

sugar report *n phr students & WW2 armed forces* A letter from one's sweetheart

◁**sugar tit**▷ *n phr* Something that gives comfort and security; = SECURITY BLANKET [fr the use of a cloth soaked in *sugar* water to appease a suckling infant]

suit *n* A serious business or professional person: *They thought it was time he got out of jeans and became a suit* [fr the wearing of a *suit*, shirt, tie, etc, at work]
See BIRTHDAY SUIT, JUMP SUIT, MONKEY SUIT, ZOOT SUIT

suitcase *n jazz musicians* A drum

suiter *See* ZOOT SUITER

suit up *v phr fr astronautics* To get into the appropriate clothing; prepare for action by donning proper gear or uniform

sujee or **sujee-mujee** *See* SOOGIE

◁**sumbitch**▷ *See* SON OF A BITCH

◁**sumbitching**▷ *See* SON-OF-A-BITCHING

sun *See* MAKE HAY, STICK IT

Sunday **1** *modifier* The best; one's best: *Sunday punch/ Sunday clothes* **2** *modifier* Amateur; occasional: *For a Sunday painter he's not bad*
See FORTY WAYS TO SUNDAY

Sunday clothes *n phr* One's best clothes; = BEST BIB AND TUCKER [fr the earlier *Sunday-go-to-meeting clothes*]

Sunday driver *n phr* A slow and careless driver, like one out for a leisurely Sunday drive

Sunday punch **1** *n phr prizefight* A very hard and effective blow or assault, with the fist or otherwise: *and lay his Sunday punch on your snoot* —Damon Runyon **2** *modifier: rockets, the "Sunday punch" weapon of the war*—Associated Press **3** *n phr baseball* A strong and effective pitch, esp an overpowering fastball

Sunday soldier or **weekend warrior** *n phr* A military reservist or member of the National Guard, who typically goes on uniformed duty at the weekend

sunlight *See* LET DAYLIGHT INTO

sunny side up *adj phr* Of eggs, fried on one side only with the yolk showing yellow

sunset *v* To subject a government agency, a legislative provision, etc, to automatic termination after a specified period: *Many senior members of the CAB favor legislative proposals to "sunset" the agency earlier*—New York Times [fr *sunset law*]

sunset law *n phr* A law requiring a government agency to be reviewed periodically, or to be automatically terminated after a specified period

Sunset Strip *n phr* A section of Los Angeles, along Sunset Boulevard, frequented by alienated teenagers, drug users, derelicts, and other sub- and counterculture persons

sunshades *n* Sunglasses; = SHADES

sunshine *n narcotics* LSD, esp taken as an orange tablet; = ACID, ORANGE SUNSHINE: *powerful as a tab of "sunshine" dropped before you step in the cab* —Albert Goldman [fr the yellow-orange color]
See YELLOW SUNSHINE

Sunshine *See* ORANGE SUNSHINE

sunshine law *n phr* A law requiring that meetings of legislative bodies be opened to the public: *After the sunshine law the city council had to open its doors*

super[1] *n* A superintendent, esp one who is custodian of an apartment building

super[2] *adj esp teenagers fr 1940s* Wonderful; excellent; very superior ● Also British fr 1920s and still very common in Great Britain among a larger group than teenagers: *America's Teenage Girls Speak Language of Their Own That Is Too Divinely Super* —Life [perhaps fr *superior* or *superfine*]

super[3] *n outdated underworld fr middle 1800s British* A watch [a misspelling of *souper*, probably fr *soup-plate*, referring to the size and shape of watches]

super- **1** *prefix used to form nouns* A superbly qualified and prodigious specimen of what is indicated: *superjerk/ superjock/ superchick/ Supermom* **2** *prefix used to form adjectives* Having the indicated quality to an extraordinary degree: *superhappy/ superwonky*

super-duper or **sooper-dooper** *adj esp 1940s* Excellent; wonderful; splendid; superb: *this new MGM sooper-dooper musical smash*—New York Times/ *Bloomingdale's sells a super-duper pooper-scooper* [rhyming]

superfly *adj black* Superior; wonderful; = SUPER: *He really thinks he's superfly when he gets into his thing*—Richard Woolley

superintendent *See* SIDEWALK SUPERINTENDENT

superpatriot *n* A person given to conspicuous patriotism; a nationalist; = HARD HAT

super slab *n phr truckers* A superhighway; an Interstate highway

Superwoman *n* A woman who successfully undertakes marriage, motherhood, and a full working life all at the same time

supper *See* SHOOT one's COOKIES

sure *affirmation fr early 1700s British* Yes; certainly: *Sure, I'll support you*
See SHITSURE

sure as God made little green apples *adj phr* Certain; definite: *It's sure as God made little green apples that they'll never get here*

◁**sure as shit**▷ (or **as shooting**) **1** *affirmation* Yes; certainly **2** *adj phr* Certain; definite: *It's sure as shit that she doesn't want to go* **3** *adv phr: He'll sure as shit do it if you ask him/ Thousands of them are sent by civic leaders...and, sure as shooting, by other federal judges*—Saul Bellow [alliterating, perhaps fr *shitsure*]

sure-fire *adj fr early 1900s* Unfailing; certain to succeed, happen, etc: *His election is a sure-fire thing*

one **sure knows how to pick 'em** *See* one CAN REALLY PICK 'EM

sure thing *affirmation fr middle 1800s* Yes; certainly; willingly: *Sure thing I'll go with you*

a **sure thing** *n phr fr early 1800s* A certainty, esp a bet which one cannot lose: *His election is a sure thing, right?*

surf bunny *n phr* = BEACH BUNNY

suss out *v phr* To discover by intuition or inquiry; find out; learn: *I sussed out Whoosh was the chief my first time...here*—Richard Price/ *I've got to start* sussing out nonscuzzy places to pee all along our most-traveled routes—Village Voice [fr *suspect* or *suspicion*, attested as *sus* in British sources fr about 1925; perhaps popularized and brought to the US by British rock-and-roll groups]

Suzy *n* A one-dollar coin bearing the portrait of the pioneer feminist Susan B. Anthony: *The "Suzy" was enjoying a certain vogue in San Francisco's sex parlors*—Newsday

-sville or **-ville** **1** *suffix used to form adjectives* Characterized by what is indicated: *dragsville/ squaresville* **2** *suffix used to form nouns* Place characterized by what is indicated: *Derbyville/ Motorsville*

swab *n* A merchant sailor

swabby or **swabbie** *n* A sailor, esp a Navy seaman [probably fr the characteristic activity of using *swabs* for cleaning the decks and other features of a ship]

swab-downs *n Navy fr late 1700s British* An officer's epaulets [fr their resemblance to a cleaning mop]

swacked *adj* Drunk: *Besides, you're swacked all the time*—Saul Bellow

swag *n fr early 1800s British underworld* Stolen goods, moneys, etc; loot [probably fr the *swag* "sack" in which loot might be carried]

swagging *n* Getting money or property illegally, esp by pilfering government property or by taking illegal payoffs or tips: *a lack of hard evidence that "swagging" or tipping had actually taken place*—Philadelphia

swak or **SWAK** (pronounced as separate letters) *sentence* Sealed with a kiss

swallow something *v* To affirm or endure reluctantly; stomach: *What I can't swallow is that he was then promoted*

swallow a watermelon seed *v phr* To become pregnant: *Did you hear that Pamela Wall swallowed a watermelon seed?*—Pat Conroy

swallow the anchor *v phr nautical fr late 1900s* To leave the sea and settle down ashore

swallow the apple (or **the olive**) *v phr sports* To become tense and ineffective; =CHOKE UP: *I flatout swallowed the apple and blew it*—Philadelphia Journal

swallow (or **eat**) **the Bible** *v phr* To lie; forswear oneself: *The police will..."swallow the Bible"...to protect some grafter*—E Lavine

swamper *n truckers fr late 1800s teamsters* A trucker's helper or loader: *The cops want to know if any of the wives knew which swampers their husbands were using*—George Warren

swank **1** *adj* (also **swanky**) *fr early 1900s* Elegant; stylish; =RITZY: *Carroll's swank office*—Associated Press **2** *n: the...swank of his riding clothes*—F Scott Fitzgerald **3** *v: I saw her swanking up the avenue in furs* [origin unknown; perhaps fr Middle English *swanken* "to sway," cognate with German *schwenken* "to flourish"; perhaps fr Efik *swanga buckra* "well-dressed white man"]

swap notes *v phr* To exchange information: *I thought we might be swapping notes on that by now*—Armistead Maupin

swap spit *v phr college students* To kiss

swat *v fr early 1900s* To strike; hit: *He spoke up and got swatted for it*

swat flies *v phr hoboes* To beg from people at curbs or store fronts

swat (or **SWAT**) **team** *n phr fr 1960s* A police unit wearing military-like uniforms and using military assault weapons on assignments requiring extraordinary coordination and force: *When the terrorists took over the whole building, the commissioner sent in the swat team* [fr *special weapons and tactics* used as a modifier]

swave *See* SUAVE

swear off *v phr* To cease something, with or as if with an abstemious vow: *He swore off cheese and crackers for a whole week*

swear (or **swear to**) **on a stack of Bibles** *v phr* To affirm with absolute confidence and considerable vehemence: *Don called all those short-term signals for Joe. I'd swear to that on a stack of Bibles*—New York/ *She swore on a stack of Bibles that she'd never seen him before*

sweat **1** *v* To suffer; stew; =COOK: *Let 'em sweat for a while before you tell them* **2** *v* To work very hard and meticulously: *I do the main job and let my partner sweat the details*
See FLOP SWEAT, IN A SWEAT, KITCHEN SWEAT, NO SWEAT, PANTHER PISS, PIG SWEAT, TIGER SWEAT

sweat bullets **1** *v phr* To be very worried; be apprehensive; =SHIT A BRICK: *They've been sweating bullets since they heard he was looking for them* **2** *v phr* To work very hard: *Their father has to sweat bullets to make a living*—People Weekly

sweater (or **pin-up**) **girl** *n phr esp 1940s* A young woman, esp a movie actress or a model, with a notably attractive body which she features by wearing tight and short clothing

◁**sweat hog**▷ **1** *n phr college students* A heavy and unattractive woman **2** *n phr* A sexually promiscuous woman

sweat it *v phr fr rock and roll fr 1950s* To be apprehensive; =be UPTIGHT ● Most often used in the negative: *Well, don't sweat it. Look, is a buck and a quarter okay?*—New York

sweat out *v phr* To endure or suffer, esp with nervous anticipation: *a young writer sweating out the creation of his first short stories*—Village Voice/ *We're sweating out the week or so before the announcements are made*

sweat something **out of** someone *v phr* To discover by intimidation or harsh questioning: *The cops finally sweated his name out of Duke*

Swedish fiddle *n phr lumberjacks* A crosscut saw

Sweeney *See* TELL IT TO SWEENEY

sweep **1** *n sports* The winning of a tournament, series, etc, without losing a single game: *He took the match in a sweep, straight sets* **2** *v: The Giants swept the World Series that year*

sweet *See* BLONDE AND SWEET, FRESH AND SWEET

sweet ass *See* BUST one's ASS

sweeten *v* To make something more attractive, esp more remunerative: *Then they sweetened the offer by several thousand dollars/ If he sweetens the deal with a few more fringe benefits, I'll sign*

sweeten someone **up** **1** *v phr* To bribe or otherwise recompense someone in exchange for something: *He had to sweeten the cops up even after he had the license* **2** *v phr* To flatter and cajole someone; =SUCK UP TO someone: *He sweetened up the audience a little by praising the town*

sweetheart **1** *n* Something excellent; a cherished and valuable object; =HONEY: *See that sweetheart of a car?* **2** *n* A pleasant person; =DOLL: *Wait'll you meet her father, he's a sweetheart*

sweetheart contract (or **agreement**) *n phr* labor union A labor contract that particularly favors the employer, and is usually negotiated by a corrupt union official

sweetheart deal *n phr* A mutually profitable and either unethical or illegal arrangement, usu involving a public agency: *what the cable companies now term a "sweetheart deal." The Port Authority just turned over the whole thing to Merrill Lynch*—Village Voice

sweetie *n* A sweetheart, in all senses ● Often a term of endearment in address: *And Tom's the first sweetie she ever had*—F Scott Fitzgerald/ *Are you calling me, sweetie?/ Ain't my new computer a sweetie?*

sweetie-pie *n* A sweetheart, in all senses: *His sweetie pie came home in the early hours*—Associated Press/ *He showed us a sweetie-pie of a little boat*

sweet mama *n phr esp black* A female lover

sweet man (or **papa**) *n phr esp black* A male lover

sweet on someone *adj phr fr 1700s* Enamored of someone; in love with someone: *He was never really sweet on Miss Carlisle*—Agatha Christie/ *very sweet on a handsome young man*—Frederic Morton

sweet patootie *See* PATOOTIE

sweet pea *n phr* A sweetheart [perhaps a shortening of *sweet patootie*, influenced by the name of the garden plant]

sweet potato *n phr* An ocarina

sweets *n* =SWEETHEART, SWEETIE ● A term of endearment: *I'll get it for you, sweets*

sweet spot *n phr* The best area on a tennis racket, hockey stick, or baseball bat for contact with the ball or puck

sweet-talk **1** *v phr* To seek to persuade or soften someone, esp by flattery and endearments; =FAT-MOUTH **2** *n*: *He listened to her sweet-talk very receptively*

sweet-tooth *n narcotics* Narcotic addiction or craving

swell **1** *n fr early 1800s British* A stylish and well-groomed person; =DUDE **2** *n fr early 1800s British* A wealthy, elegant person; a socialite; =NOB: *up on the hill where the swells live* **3** *adj fr middle 1800s* Excellent; wonderful; superb: *The hotels are swell*—Theodore Dreiser/ *He was a hell of a swell fellow*—Charles MacArthur **4** *adv: The new owners have treated me swell*—Associated Press [perhaps fr the late-18th-century phrase *cut a swell* "swagger," describing the behavior of a person who *swells* with arrogance]

swellelegant *adj* =SWELL

swellhead **1** *n* A conceited person; a person whose head is swollen with pride: *She acted like a swellhead after she got the prize* **2** *n* Conceit: *I was afraid you'd get the swellhead*—WR Burnett

swig *n fr early 1600s* A swallow of liquor; =PULL [origin unknown]

swill *n* Nasty and inferior food or drink; =BELLY-WASH: *What is this swill they've placed before us?*

swim *v* To perform well; succeed; =FLY: *I didn't think the Harptones quite swam last time I saw them*—Village Voice

swimming in *See* ROLLING IN

swindle (or **scandal**) **sheet** *n phr* An expense account: *Only one goes on the swindle sheet*—AR Hilliard

swindle stick *See* CHEAT STICK

swing **1** *n* A style of white jazz music of the 1930s and 40s, developed from hot jazz and usu played by big bands: *That pastime was called Swing, and its king, Benny Goodman, and most of its greatest exponents and exploiters were quartered here in New York*—Albert Goldman **2** *v musicians* To have a strong but easy and pleasant impetus: *Chaucer and Jazz are quite similar; they both swing, they both have the same punch, vitality, and guts*—Jazz World **3** *v* To perform very well, as a good jazz musician does: *It is appropriate that gifted, gravel-voiced Herschel Bernardi should swing eight times a week in this particular hit*—Walter Wager **4** *v black fr musicians* To have a good time; enjoy oneself hugely, as at a good party **5** *v fr late 1960s* To do the sex act, esp promiscuously with various partners either seriatim or at once: *The sexual revolution is not new, people have been swinging as long as they are on this earth*—Rona Jaffe **6** *v fr 1960s* To be stylish, au courant, sophisticated, etc; =be HIP: *"Songs for Swingin' Lovers"*—Frank Sinatra album title **7** *v street gang* To be a member of a teenage street gang **8** *n* An interval between work periods: *with two hours' swing in the afternoon for lunch*—Ira Wolfert

swing both ways *v phr fr late 1960s* To be bisexual; =be AC-DC

swinger *n* A person who swings, esp in the mode of sexual promiscuity: *Kissinger, who enjoyed a reputation as a swinger, was asked to explain his oft-quoted remark*—Joseph Heller/ *Many swingers even pride themselves on preserving their marriages through these arrangements*—S Rudikoff

swinging single *n phr* A merry and celebratory unmarried person, esp one who is sexually promiscuous as well as au courant: *entertaining other couples every weekend and making jokes about the "swinging singles" all around them*—Albert Goldman

swingle *n* =SWINGING SINGLE

swing like a rusty gate **1** *v phr* To swing at a baseball awkwardly or wildly **2** *v phr* *fr 1930s* To play swing music well

swingman *n* narcotics A narcotics dealer; = CONNECTION

swing shift *n phr* A work shift between the regular day and night shift, typically from four to midnight

swipe[1] **1** *v* *fr middle 1800s* To steal, esp something small or trivial; pilfer: *nix on swiping anything* —EB White **2** *n* *fr late 1800s* A stroke or blow, esp a strong one ● Most often in the phrase **take a swipe at**: *Let somebody...take a swipe at him* —Bennett Cerf **3** *n* *fr early 1900s* A stable groom who rubs down horses [all senses perhaps fr alterations of *sweep* or *swoop* and the actions of sweeping or swooping up, or of hitting a sweeping blow; second sense perhaps fr dialect preservation of Old English *swippan* "beat, scourge"; final sense may in addition be a blend with *wipe*]
See SIDESWIPE, TAKE A SWIPE AT someone or something

swipe[2] *n* Inferior liquor, esp of the homemade sort: *the homemade bootleg mess made by the natives out of fruit and called "swipe"* —James Jones [probably related to several late-18th-century and early-19th-century British senses of *swipe* "to gulp liquor quickly and deeply," of *swipes* "small beer," and of *swipey* "tipsy," all of which may be related to the British nautical *swipes* "rinsings of the beer barrel," and hence to a sibilation of *wipe*]

swish[1] **1** *adj* *fr homosexuals fr 1930s* Showing the traits of an effeminate male homosexual; mincing; limp-wristed; = NELLIE: *His walk was quite swish* **2** *n* *fr homosexuals* An effeminate male homosexual; = QUEEN: *that fat swish* —Budd Schulberg **3** *v* *fr homosexuals* To move, walk, speak, etc, in the manner or presumed manner of effeminate male homosexuals [fr the swinging movements of the hips in a mincing walk, and perhaps the *swishing* sound of a gown]

swish[2] *adj* *fr late 1800s British* Elegant; fancy; = POSH, RITZY, SWANKY: *You can get a very swish version...or a very basic version* —New York Times [fr British dialect, an apparent variant of *swash* "a swaggerer," hence semantically related to *swank*]

switch **1** *v* *underworld* To inform; = SNITCH **2** *n* A knife; = SHIV
See ASLEEP AT THE SWITCH, CHICKEN SWITCH, NOT HAVE ALL one's SWITCHES ON

switchblade *n* *fr 1940s* A knife with a blade that springs out when a switch is pressed

switched *See* I'LL BE DAMNED

switched-off *adj* Not in the current fashion; unconventional; = OUT OF SYNC: *responding...to his unconventional* (at that time), *bohemian, "switched-off" quality* —Garry O'Conor

switched on **1** *adj phr* *fr 1960s British* Fashionable and admirable; au courant; up-to-date; = GEAR: *A larger number of the women were in short, switched-on dresses* —New Yorker/ *They are among the current drop of switched-on young matrons* —Enid Nemy **2** *adj phr* Exhilarated; stimulated; = HIGH, PLUGGED IN, TURNED ON: *In his moments of happiness the person with machine envy will declare himself "plugged in" or "switched on"* —Russell Baker/ *He has powerful friends and you don't, switched-on in-crowd celebrity friends, high-all-the-time-and-getting-away-with-it friends* —TG Harris

switcheroo *n* A switch or shift; a reversal: *For people in search of titillating diversion from their daily lives, switcheroos may seem exciting* —American Scholar/ *We'll pull a switcheroo. We'll use olives instead of cherries* —HT Webster

switch-hitter **1** *n* *baseball* A player who bats both righthanded and lefthanded **2** *n* A versatile person **3** *n* A bisexual person

switch hog *n phr* *railroad* A yardmaster

switch on **1** *v phr* *fr 1960s British* To join the current trends, tastes, etc; become up-to-date **2** *v phr* To excite and exhilarate; arouse sexually; = TURN ON: *He didn't see any girls that switched him on much* **3** *v phr* To become intoxicated with narcotics; = TURN ON

swivel-hips *See* SNAKE-HIPS

swivet *n* *fr late 1800s* A fit of angry agitation; = SNIT: *You can't get yourself in a swivet over some isolated instances* —Robert Ruark

swizzled or **swozzled** *adj* *fr middle 1800s* Drunk; tipsy

swizzle-stick *n* *fr late 1800s* A stick for stirring a mixed drink [fr earlier *swizzle* "stir a drink," fr *swizzle* "a drink, to drink," perhaps related to *switchel* "drink of molasses and water, often mixed with rum"]

swoopy *See* ULTRASWOOPY

-sy *See* -IE

sync **1** *v* To synchronize: *Let's sync our plans, okay?* **2** *n* Synchronism; synchronization
See IN SYNC, LIP-SYNC, OUT OF SYNC

◁ **syph** or **the syff** ▷ *n* or *n phr* (Variations: **siff** or **the siff**) *fr early 1900s* Syphilis: *syphilis, not siff* —Calder Willingham/ *They found out he had the syph while he was doin' time* —Rocky Graziano

syrup *See* COUGH SYRUP

sysop (SISS ahp) *n* *computer* The computer operator who manages a computer bulletin board, a computer display where those with access may get or convey information: *People look up to the sysop* —New York Times [fr *system operator*]

system *See* OLD BOY NETWORK

T

T *narcotics* **1** *n* Marijuana; =TEA **2** *n* A gram of methamphetamine

◁**TA** or **T and A**▷ (TA pronounced as separate letters) **1** *n phr* *fr show business* A display of female bosoms and bottoms; a show featuring such display; =CHEESECAKE: *the realm of feminine esthetics or, as it is known in the profession, TA*—Playboy/ *to enliven their product they call for T and A*—Toronto Life **2** *adj phr:* *They turned it into a T and A show*—Philadelphia Journal [fr *tits* + *ass*]

tab¹ **1** *n phr* *fr late 1800s* The bill or check for something, esp for food or drink: *three- or four-hundred-dollar tabs for unpaid liquor*—Stephen Longstreet/ *Everybody wondered who would get the tab for all that extravagance* **2** *n* A written acknowledgment of debt; =IOU: *They're liable to go out and stick up a bank if they owe you a tab*—Jimmy Cannon [origin unknown; perhaps a shortening of *tabulation*]

See PICK UP THE TAB

tab² *v fr early 1900s* To identify or designate; label: *I tabbed him immediately as a crook* [fr *tab* "a tied-on baggage label," of unknown origin; perhaps an alteration of *tag*]

tab³ *narcotics* **1** *n* A tablet **2** *n* A dose of LSD; =HIT

table *See* UNDER THE TABLE

table finisher *n phr* A glutton; =PIG

table grade *See* EATIN' STUFF

table-hop *v* To go from table to table in a restaurant, night club, etc, visiting and chatting: *Linda goes to Elaine's to table-hop, not to eat*

tablet *See* BRAIN TABLET

tabs *See* KEEP TABS ON

tach *n* A tachometer

tack *n horse-racing* A jockey's equipment for riding

tackhead **1** *n* A stupid person **2** *n* A troublemaker **3** *n* An overstylish person

tacks *See* BRASS TACKS, SPIT TACKS

tacky *adj fr late 1800s Southern* Inferior; shabby; vulgar; =ICKY, RATTY: *She talked in a manner that would be considered a bit countrified, if not slightly tacky*—Calder Willingham/ *That would be tacky...I'm not here promoting myself*—Washington Post [apparently fr *tacky* "small, useless horse," and later "hillbilly, cracker"]

See TICKY-TACKY

◀**taco**▶ *n* A Mexican or person of Mexican descent

◁**Taco**▷ *See* TIO TACO

tad **1** *n fr late 1800s* A small boy; a child: *I've liked reading since I was just a tad* **2** *n* A small amount; =CUNT-HAIR, SKOSH, SMIDGEN: *may be taking his new series...just a tad too seriously*—People Weekly [origin uncertain; perhaps a shortening of *tadpole*; perhaps fr British dialect *tadde* "toad"]

tag **1** *n* A person's name **2** *n underworld* An arrest warrant: *Is there a tag out for me?*—Raymond Chandler **3** *n* An automobile license plate: *The Seminoles get special tags*—Associated Press

See DOG TAGS

tah-dah or **ta-daaa** **1** *interjection* A vocal imitation of a stage or circus fanfare, used to call attention to one's entrance, to something dramatically revealed, etc: *and tah-dah, a whole section of the model flipped over to show the change*—Philadelphia **2** *adj:* *a big tah-dah promotion*

tail **1** *n fr 1300s* The buttocks; =ASS: *if all of us parked ourselves on our tails*—P Marks/ *I hadn't tossed him out on his tail*—Jerome Weidman ◁**2**▷ *n* A person regarded solely as a sex partner, object, or organ; =ASS: *a nice piece of tail* ◁**3**▷ *n* Sexual activity or gratification; =ASS, FUCKING: *It was said that the freshmen up at Yale got no tail* **4** *n* A person who follows another for surveillance; =SHADOW: *The security officer was even going to put a tail on the children*—John McCarten **5** *v:* *tailing a jewelry salesman*—American Mercury

See one's ASS OFF, BROOM TAIL, DRAG-TAIL, DRAG one's TAIL, GET one's TAIL IN A GATE, HAVE A BROOM UP one's ASS, HAVE A TIGER BY THE TAIL, HAVE someone or something BY THE TAIL, PIECE OF ASS, PONY TAIL, RINGTAIL, SHAVETAIL, WORK one's ASS OFF

tail bone *n phr* The buttocks; =ASS

tailed *See* RINGTAILED SNORTER

tailgate **1** *v* To follow another car, truck, etc, dangerously closely; =HIGHTAIL: *drove her car behind him, tailgating him between red walls of dead brick*—Saul Bellow **2** *v college students* To watch girls go by **3** *v Army* To join what one says closely to what has just been said; =DOVETAIL

tailgate party **1** *n phr* An outdoor party or picnic, typically in the parking lot of a sports stadium, and served on the tailgates of station wagons **2** *n phr jazz musicians* A style of jazz said to resemble the early New Orleans sort [final sense fr the fact that the *tailgate* of the band's wagon was left down to give slide-room for the trombone]

tailor-made 1 *adj* Exactly fitting or appropriate: *a situation tailor-made for that sort of intervention* **2** *adj* Made especially for someone or something; custom-made: *He had his own tailor-made piano stool* **3** *n* A ready-made cigarette, as distinct from a hand-rolled one; = PIMP STICK

tailpipe *See* BLOW IT OUT

tails *n* Men's formal dress

take 1 *n* The money taken in for a sporting event, at a gambling casino, etc; = GROSS: *Nevada's take has been hit by a recession*—New York Post **2** *v fr early 1900s* To cheat or defraud someone; swindle; = SCAM: *The old couple got taken for their life savings* **3** *v* (also **take** someone **into camp** or **take** someone **downtown**) *fr middle 1800s* To defeat someone utterly; trounce; = CLOBBER: *UCLA took Illinois in the Rose Bowl/ Last year Tanner took Borg downtown in the same round*—Sports Illustrated **4** *n* An acceptable portion of movie or TV recording, musical recording, taping, etc: *The director said okay, it was a take* **5** *n* A portion; extract; bit; = OUTTAKE: *fast takes from the latest research that may change your life*—Working Woman

See CUT A TAKE, DOUBLE-TAKE, ON THE TAKE

take a back seat *v phr fr middle 1800s* To assume or accept a subordinate position; demote or degrade oneself: *He said he wouldn't take a back seat to anybody but the president himself*

take a bath *v phr* To suffer a financial loss; esp, to go into bankruptcy; = GO TO THE CLEANERS, TAKE A BEATING: *Is it possible to take a bath on items previously thought to be incapable of depreciation?*—Toronto Life/ *So the bank stands to take a bath of one and three-quarter million dollars*—John D MacDonald [fr Yiddish, where *er haut mikh gefirt in bod arayn*, literally "he led me to the bath," means "he tricked me"; the sense is derived fr the deception of persons reluctant to take a steam bath and have their clothing decontaminated who hence had to be tricked; probably reinforced by *cleaned out* and *taken to the cleaners* as terms for loss of money in gambling or business]

take a beating 1 *v phr* = TAKE A BATH **2** *v phr* To be bested in a transaction; pay too much: *You really took a beating if you paid $2 a pound*

take a brace *v phr fr late 1800s* To improve or reform oneself; pull oneself together

take a break *v phr* To rest or cease temporarily from working; = CAULK OFF, KNOCK OFF: *Why don't you guys take a break while I figure this out?*

take a bye *v phr fr sports* To decline; choose not to take; = PASS something UP: *The kid took a bye on breakfast*—Tom Aldibrandi [fr the term *bye* used when a participant in a tournament passes to the next level without playing, since he or she has drawn no opponent]

take a chance *See* the GENTLEMAN WILL TAKE A CHANCE

take a crack at something *See* HAVE A CRACK AT something

take a D *v phr movie studio* To commit suicide [fr the dramatic mythical sort of suicide where the

unhappy person, usu a disappointed movie actor, leaped off the letter *D* in the HOLLYWOOD sign on Mount Lee]

take a dig at someone *v phr* To make an irritating or contemptuous comment; = BAD-MOUTH: *When he took a dig at his mother his brother decked him*

take a dim view of something or someone *v phr fr 1930s British armed forces* To regard as not especially hopeful, delightful, etc; greet with less than buoyant enthusiasm: *Her parents take a decidedly dim view of me*

take a dive *v phr fr sports* To fall in a feigned knockdown or knockout; lose a fight, game, etc, dishonestly; = TANK: *He refused to take a dive, so they took him out*

take a douche *v phr teenagers* To leave hurriedly; = BEAT IT, GET LOST ● Usually an irritated command

take a drink *v phr baseball* To strike out [fr fact that the player can then go to the *drinking fountain* in the dugout]

◁**take a dump**▷ *v phr* (Variations: **crap** or **shit** or **squat** may replace **dump**) To defecate; = SHIT: *two dogs taking a dump in a restaurant*—Village Voice/ *like taking a dump on Mom's apple pie*—National Lampoon

take a fall *v phr underworld* To be arrested; = FALL: *He took a fall, Duke*—Lawrence Sanders/ *who had already taken two falls for burglary*—Ed McBain

take a flyer (or **flier**) *v phr fr late 1800s* To take an ambitious gamble; take a risky chance or chancy risk, esp financially: *I don't believe you, but what the hell, I'll take a flyer* [fr *flyer* "jump, leap"]

◀**take a flying fuck**▶ *v phr* (Variations: **frig** may replace **fuck**; **at a rubber duck** or **at a rolling doughnut** may be added) May you be accursed, confounded, humiliated, rejected, etc; = GO FUCK oneself, GO TO HELL: *about four guys who could really tell me to go take a flying frig and make it stick*—Larry Niven & Jerry Bournelle/ *They told me as gently as possible to take a flying fuck*

take a gander *v phr* To have a look; scrutinize; inspect: *I go over and take a gander into it*—Raymond Chandler

take a hike *sentence* Leave me alone; go away; = GET LOST

take a hinge at *See* GET A HINGE AT

take a hosing *v phr* To be cheated or duped; be unfairly used: *The average worker and his family think they're taking a hosing*—Walter Mondale

◁**take a leak**▷ *v phr* To urinate; = PISS, WHIZ: *fella has to take a leak*—Tom Wolfe/ *You worry you'd miss it if you took a leak and went to the refrigerator*—Village Voice

take a load off one's **feet** *v phr* To sit down; rest; relax

take a page from someone's **book** *v phr* To imitate or emulate someone: *I think I'll take a page from Castro's book and grow a beard and cigar*

take a potshot at someone *v phr fr middle 1800s* To criticize harshly; assault critically: *I don't* *want to take potshots at Frank*—Changes [fr the notion of a *shot* taken merely to put game in the cooking *pot*, hence not sportsmanlike or punctilious but crudely practical]

take a powder (or **a run-out powder**) *v phr* To leave; depart hastily, esp to avoid arrest or detection; = POWDER: *and take a powder out of here that day*—John O'Hara/ *that goddamned Matthews, who took a powder to Florida*—WT Tyler

take a rain check *v phr* fr sports To arrange postponement or delay of some occasion which one cannot attend at the invited time: *Thanks awfully, Syl, but we're booked that night and will have to take a rain check* [see rain check]

take a reef (or **bight**) **in it** *v phr* fr nautical To stop; cease; = CUT IT ● Often an irritated command [fr the nautical way of shortening a sail with a *reef*, a tucking and tying, or a line with a *bight*, a loop]

take a run at someone *v phr* To approach or assault with a view to capture or seduction: *I wouldn't take a client of mine...into the place, unless he was such a close associate that nobody was going to take a run at him*—Toronto Life

take a shine to someone or something *v phr* fr early 1800s To incur a liking for; like: *She really took a shine to the new recording/ May Venus...take such a shine to you both*—WH Auden

◁**take a shit** (or **a squat**)▷ *See* TAKE A DUMP

take a swipe at someone or something *v phr* To strike or aim a blow at; esp, to criticize very harshly: *The Council couldn't adjourn before taking a swipe at the Mayor*

take a walk 1 *v phr* fr middle 1800s To leave; absent oneself, esp fr labor negotiations, etc; go out on strike; = WALKOUT: *If they don't at least look at our terms we'll have to take a walk* **2** *n phr* lunch counter An order prepared to be taken out; an order to go

take care *v phr* To be wary; pay attention ● Nearly always a parting salutation

take care of business *v phr* black fr 1950s To perform stylishly and effectively; deal well with what one needs to: *I got up and took care of business*—Time

take care of Numero Uno *v phr* To devote oneself to one's own profit and well-being; see to oneself; = FEATHER one's NEST: *The Lord helps them that take care of Numero Uno* [see Numero Uno]

take someone **down a peg** *v phr* To deflate or reduce someone; esp, to humiliate someone pompous or vainglorious; = CUT someone OFF AT THE KNEES: *Somebody ought to take that cocky bastard down a peg* [perhaps fr the notion of wall *pegs* for hanging clothing, arranged hierarchically fr higher to lower]

take someone **downtown** *See* TAKE

take fire *v phr* To have a sudden spurt of enthusiasm, activity, success, etc; become meteoric; = TAKE OFF: *When the show takes fire we'll all get rich*

take five *v phr* To take a short respite from work; = TAKE A BREAK

take someone **for a ride 1** *v phr* esp 1920s & 30s To murder by kidnapping and disposing of the body in a remote place, in gangster fashion **2** *v phr* To cheat or swindle someone

take gas or **catch a rail** *v phr* surfers To lose control of one's surfboard and fall off: *To "take gas"...is to lose a board in the curl of a wave*—Time

take heat *v phr* To endure punishment, complaints, etc: *I took a lot of heat and I stayed in the kitchen*—New York Post/ *They think they're taking the heat for being unaware and not doing anything*—New York Times [fr *if you can't stand the heat stay out of the kitchen*]

take in *v phr* To perceive and understand: *I can't quite take in what he's saying*

take someone **into camp** *See* TAKE

take it *v phr* fr prizefight To endure pain, violent attack, the buffets of fate, etc; = HANG TOUGH, TOUGH IT OUT: *Valley Forge proved the Continentals could take it*

take it easy 1 *v phr* To keep one's anger and excitement under check; be calm: *Take it easy, Mac, nobody's hurt* **2** *v phr* To work slowly and smoothly: *Hurry and you're dead, take it easy and you survive* **3** *v phr* To stop working; relax; loaf: *I got to take it easy for a few minutes* ● **Take it easy** is most often used as a parting salutation or a bit of advice for living, in each case intending all senses at once

take it hard (or **big**) *v phr* To react very strongly to something: *I thought she'd ignore it, but she took it big/ We were surprised he took the news so hard*

take it in the ear *See* PUT IT IN YOUR EAR

take it on the chin 1 *v phr* = TAKE IT **2** *v phr* To be soundly defeated; be trounced: *They took it on the chin badly in the last period*

take it on the lam *v phr* underworld To leave, esp hastily; escape; = LIGHT OUT: *The girl..."took it on the lam"*—Atlantic Monthly

take it out of someone's **hide** *v phr* To exact the harshest kind of compensation, even physical punishment, usu in place of a gentler or a monetary one: *He'll pay up, by God, or I'll take it out of his hide!*

take it out on someone or something *v phr* To punish or mistreat an innocent subject for wrongs one has suffered: *Whenever his boss yells at him, he takes it out on his secretary* [perhaps fr *take it out of someone's hide*]

take it slow *v phr* To go very carefully; be cautious: *I've never done this before, so I'm going to take it real slow*

take it to the street *v phr* To continue and broaden a more or less private conflict in a public arena: *The debate was quiet for a time, then they took it to the street* [from the tradition of finishing a quarrel in the outdoors, after the invitation "Let's step outside and settle this"]

take one's **lumps** *v phr* To accept and endure severe treatment; = TAKE IT: *The boys were taking their lumps trying to stay on wild Brahma bulls*—New York Daily News/ *Taking your lumps is living*

take one's **medicine** *v phr* To accept and endure what one has deserved; = FACE THE MUSIC

taken *See* be HAD

take names *See* KICK ASS AND TAKE NAMES

take no shit *See* TAKE SHIT

be **taken to the cleaners** *See* GO TO THE CLEANERS

takeoff 1 *n* An imitation, esp of a famous person, actor, etc; an impression: *You should hear her take-off of Liz Taylor* **2** *n* A robbery, esp an armed street robbery or mugging: *He always uses the mugger's jargon for a street robbery: "take-off"*—New York Post **3** *modifier*: *and if it comes to a take-off thing in the street*—New York

take off 1 *v phr esp fr WW2 armed forces* To leave; depart; = SPLIT: *He had to take off early/ They all took off for Houston* **2** *v phr* To have a sudden success, spurt of activity, etc; = TAKE FIRE: *but nonsense that doesn't take off can be a trial*—Edith Oliver **3** *v phr police & underworld* To rob; commit burglary; = HOLD UP, RIP OFF: *We took off a bar*—Clarence Cooper/ *They want to keep dealing, not just take off two dudes for a little cash*—New York **4** *v phr black* To kill; = WASTE, ZAP **5** *v phr narcotics* To give oneself a narcotic injection; = SHOOT UP **6** *v phr* To leave work for a time: *I'm going to take off without pay for a week or so* **7** *v phr fr middle 1700s* To imitate; mimic; parody: *She takes off a drunk hilariously* [first sense based on the rising and departure of an airplane]

takeoff artist *See* RIPOFF

◁**take off like a bigass bird** (or **like a bat out of hell**)▷ *v phr esp WW2 armed forces* To depart hastily; leave in a hurry; = CUT OUT

take on 1 *v phr* To behave angrily; make a fuss: *How you do take on!* **2** *v phr police* To stop and search someone, demand identification, question harshly, etc; = JACK UP, ROUST: *We were also taught that good cops take on a lot of people*—Rolling Stone

take someone or something **on 1** *v phr* To accept an assignment, job, role, etc: *I'm a bit diffident about my qualifications, but I'll take the chairmanship on* **2** *v phr* To accept combat or confrontation with someone or something: *The Knights took over the Philadelphia Inquirer...and later took on the Morning Journal head-to-head*—San Francisco

takeout 1 *n* A percentage of profit or receipts; = CUT **2** *modifier* Having to do with food bought to be eaten away from the place where it is prepared: *pies she hoped to sell to the "take-out" trade*—James M Cain

take someone or something **out** *v phr* To kill; destroy; totally disable: *asked Col Beckwith what he intended to do with the Iranian guards. "Take them out," said Col Beckwith...they would each get two 45 caliber rounds between the eyes*—Wall Street Journal/ *The Brits were just seeking to reassure themselves that we were not planning to take out a country*—Time [probably fr the football term *take out* "block an opponent decisively"]

takeover *n* The buying of the control of one company by another, usu by the wooing and rewarding of stockholders and often against the wishes of the acquired company's management: *a popular means of conducting corporate takeovers*—New York Times

take pictures *v phr citizens band* To use a radar speed-indicating device along the highway

taker *n* A person who accepts a bet, challenge, offer, etc: *I dared them all but got no takers*

◁**take** (or **eat**) **shit**▷ *v phr* To accept or endure humiliation, victimization, bullying, etc; = EAT DIRT
● Often in the negative: *She told us she took no shit from nobody/ They thought I would eat shit, so I just quit*

take some doing *v phr* To be very difficult; be arduous: *It took some doing, but they got there inside an hour*

it **takes two to tango** *See* IT TAKES TWO TO TANGO

take ten *v phr* To take a short respite from work, specifically ten minutes; = TAKE A BREAK, TAKE FIVE

take the cake 1 *v phr fr late 1800s* To win or deserve the highest award and admiration: *His new sonnets quite take the cake* **2** *v phr* To be improbable; be incredible: *That excuse really takes the cake* [fr the prize awarded in a *cakewalk* dancing contest]

take the cure *v phr* To cease from doing something one enjoys; = SWEAR OFF: *I used to see a lot of movies before I took the cure* [fr the usual expression for *curing* one of alcoholism]

take the heat off *v phr* To reduce or remove harassing pressure; = COOL IT: *She won't say yes or no till you take the heat off*

take the long count *v phr fr prizefight* To die

take the pipe *v phr esp sports* To become ineffective under pressure; = CHOKE UP, SWALLOW THE APPLE: *He could have taken the pipe after that horrendous first half, but he didn't*—Sports Illustrated

take the rag off the bush *v phr outdated fr early 1800s* To surprise one; be a wonder; = BEAT ALL [said to be fr shooting competitions in the western US, where the target was a *rag* to be shot off a *bush*]

take the rap (or **the fall**) *v phr fr underworld* To accept or suffer the punishment for something, esp for something one did not do: *If she gets caught, I'll take the rap for her/ Make sure Brewster doesn't come unglued. He has to take the fall right along with Beck*—Hannibal & Boris

take things easy *v phr* To cease being upset or excited over things; relax; = COOL IT: *I'm gonna buy a boat and take things easy*

take someone **to the cleaners** *v phr* To win or otherwise acquire all or very much of someone's money, esp at gambling, in a lawsuit or business deal, etc; = CLEAN someone OUT: *Smarten up, Chrystie, take him to the cleaners*—People Weekly/ *Ephron did not take him to the cleaners in the divorce*—Washingtonian

take to the streets *v phr* To make a public and conspicuous demonstration of opinion, political demands, etc: *The antiwar sentiment became a serious concern when activists took to the streets in their hundreds of thousands*

tale *See* FISH STORY

tale of woe *n phr* A distressing story ● Most often used ironically: *Well, let's hear your current tale of woe, Mr Kvetch*

talk 1 *v somewhat outdated underworld* To inform; confess and implicate others; =SQUEAL: *Socks would never never talk* **2** *v* To mean something; have something particular in mind ● Always in the progressive tenses: *Okay, we're talking three or four million, right?/ Are you talking a strike?*
See BACK TALK, BAD TALK, BIG TALK, FAST TALK, HAPPY TALK, LOUD-TALK, PEP TALK, PILLOW TALK, STRAIGHT TALK, SWEET-TALK

talk big *v phr* To boast and exaggerate; be self-aggrandizing; =SHOOT OFF one's MOUTH: *He was talking pretty big about how they treated him*

talk someone's **ear off** *v phr* To talk incessantly; prate; =GAS: *Donna talked his ear off*—New York Daily News

talker *n circus & carnival* =BARKER

talkie *n esp 1920s & 30s* A talking movie
See WALKIE-TALKIE

talking head (or **hairdo**) *n phr television studio* A person, esp a news reporter, an interviewer, an expert, etc, who appears on television in a close-up, hence essentially as a bodiless head: *using the medium as something more than a static platform for talking heads*—John J O'Connor/ *what the TV experts term a talking head, just Ronnie in an easy chair*—Time/ *one of those plays for which talking hairdos go to the videotape*—Sports Illustrated

talk out of turn *v phr* To speak too candidly; be too bold verbally; =SHOOT OFF one's MOUTH: *I may be talking out of turn, but I think you ought to make the decision right now, and live with it*

talk poor mouth *v phr* To deny one's wealth, advantages, etc; depreciate one's assets; =POOR-MOUTH: *And it is hard to talk poor mouth just after the papers have written of your daughter's coming-out party for 2,000 guests*—New York Times

talk-talk or **talky-talk** *n* Mere talk, esp bombast or idle chatter

talk through one's **hat** *v phr fr late 1800s* To lie and exaggerate; talk nonsense; =BULLSHIT [said to be fr the deceptive demeanor of men who hold their hats over their faces on entering church, and are supposed to be praying]

talk to the big white phone *v phr college students* To vomit into the toilet bowl; =DRIVE THE BIG BUS

talk-trap *n* The mouth; =TRAP, YAP: *Dodo won't ever open her talk-trap*—H McHugh

talk turkey *v phr fr early 1800s* To speak candidly and cogently; =LAY IT ON THE LINE, LEVEL: *Do you want to talk turkey, or just bullshit?* [fr a story attested in 1830, of the white man who said to the Native American, Wampum, that in dividing the game he would give him the choice: "You take the crow and I'll take the turkey, or I'll take the turkey

and you take the crow," whereupon Wampum declared that the white man was not *talking turkey* to him]

talk up a storm *v phr* To talk loud, long, impressively, incessantly, etc; =CHEW someone's EAR OFF: *City Teen-Agers Talking Up a "Say What?" Storm*—New York Times

tall *See* STAND TALL, WALK TALL

tall can of corn *See* CAN OF CORN

tall cotton *See* IN TALL COTTON

tallow-pot *n railroad* A locomotive fire stoker

tall red totem poles *See* KNOCK someone FOR A LOOP

the **tall timbers** *n phr fr show business* Rural areas; =the BOONDOCKS, the RHUBARBS

tambourine man *n phr narcotics* A narcotics dealer; =CONNECTION [either the origin of or originating from the Bob Dylan song *Mr Tambourine Man*]

tan or **tan** someone's **hide** *v or v phr fr middle 1800s* To beat someone severely; thrash [fr the making of a hide into leather by *tanning*]
See BLACK AND TAN

◁**T and A**▷ *See* TA

tang *See* POON TANG

tangle *v* To fight; =MIX IT UP

◁**tangle assholes**▷ *v phr* To come into conflict; disagree; quarrel; fight

tangle-foot or **tangle-leg 1** *n fr middle 1800s Western* Liquor, esp cheap whiskey **2** *modifier: a Western writer describing the effects of tangle-foot whiskey*—Brander Matthews

tangle-footed or **tangle-legged** *adj fr middle 1800s* Drunk

tango *See* IT TAKES TWO TO TANGO

tank 1 *n* A detention cell; a jail cell: *when he goes into the tank as a prisoner*—Erle Stanley Gardner/ *A police reporter had to pick him out of the collection in the drunk tank*—AR Bosworth **2** *v* (also **tank up**) *fr late 1800s* To drink liquor, esp heavily: *I think he'd tanked up a good deal at luncheon*—F Scott Fitzgerald **3** *v sports* To lose a game, match, etc, deliberately; =THROW: *He lost so implausibly they were sure he had tanked* **4** *pres part: the "tanking" of unlucrative doubles matches merely to catch a plane*—Time [for sports senses, see go in the tank]
See DRUNK TANK, FISH TANK, GO IN THE TANK, THINK TANK

tanked or **tanked up** *adj or adj phr fr late 1800s* Drunk

tank fight *n phr fr prizefight* A fight, game, contest, etc, that is deliberately lost, esp one lost for a gambling or monetary advantage; a prearranged loss

tank top *n phr* A style of sleeveless woman's blouse resembling the top of the swimming suit called a "tank suit"

tank town *n phr fr early 1900s show business* A small town, such as one featuring mainly a water tank for locomotives; =JERKWATER TOWN

tanky 1 *adj* Drunk: *Behind me sat four tanky guys*—Richard Price **2** *n WW2 Navy* A butcher

tap 1 *v* To attack; =MUG: *Only chicks this guy taps?*—Ed McBain **2** *adj* Lacking money; =BROKE, TAPPED OUT

See HEEL-TAP

Tap City *adj* Lacking money; penniless; =BROKE, TAP: *You're Tap City? No problem*—Philadelphia Journal

tap dance *v phr* Army To improvise, tergiversate, etc, in order to hide one's ignorance: *I didn't read the poop sheet, so I had to tap dance when the question came*

tape *See* RED TAPE

taped *adv* For certain; under control; =IN THE BAG, RACKED: *By the third round he had the fight taped*

See HAVE something CINCHED

tap someone for something *v phr* To solicit money from; beg or borrow from; =HIT someone, TOUCH: *I tapped my brother for another two hundred*

tap out *v phr* gambling To lose all one's money, esp in a gambling game; =be CLEANED OUT: *"It's tapping me out," he says*—Philadelphia Journal [perhaps fr the gesture of *tapping* the table when one cannot or does not wish to bet in his turn; perhaps fr having *tapped* everyone available for a loan and found none]

tapped out 1 *adj phr* Penniless; =BROKE, TAP CITY: *Tapped out, a...bank goes under*—Time/ *the tapped-out underdog he is supposed to be*—Sports Illustrated **2** *adj phr* Exhausted; =FRAZZLED, POOPED: *thought he looked terrible, haggard, pale, tapped out*—Time

tar¹ *n fr 1700s* A sailor [fr the *tarpaulin* garments they made and wore]

tar² *See* BEAT THE SHIT OUT OF

tar bucket *n phr* West Point A military full-dress hat

◁**tard**▷ *n* =RETARD

tarfu (TAR Fōō) *adj WW2 armed forces* Totally botched and confused; =SNAFU [fr *things are really fucked up*]

Tarheel *n fr middle 1800s* A native or resident of North Carolina [origin uncertain; perhaps fr the gummy resins of the pine barrens, which would cling to their feet; perhaps because a North Carolina unit which lost a hilltop position in the Civil War were jestingly told they had not *tarred their heels* to make them stick]

tarp *n* A tarpaulin, esp a weatherproof cover for a car, boat, etc

tart *n fr late 1800s* A promiscuous woman, esp a prostitute; harlot; =HOOKER: *nothing cheap for us like the grimy tarts on Mercury Street*—Stephen Longstreet [fr *tart* the pastry confection, esp the English *jam-tart*; in original early-19th-century use it meant any pleasant or attractive woman, and only specialized at the end of the century]

tart up *v phr fr 1920s British* To decorate; prettify; bedizen; =GUSSY UP: *go the glam route or tart it up or punk it down*—Village Voice/ *American directors feel obliged to tart up Shakespeare*—San Francisco/ *They tarted them up with fanciful decor*—Time

taste 1 *n* theater A share or percentage of profits; =a PIECE OF THE ACTION **2** *n* narcotics A dose of a narcotic; =HIT **3** *n* black Liquor in general; a drink of liquor

See SO BAD one CAN TASTE IT

ta-ta *interj fr early 1800s British* A parting salutation; a farewell

tater *baseball* **1** *n* A base hit: *the man who hit all those taters in the American League*—Sports Illustrated **2** *n* A home run [fr a dialect term for *potato*, and perhaps related to the admiring term *some potatoes* that would describe a base hit or home run]

tattooed *See* SCREWED, BLUED, AND TATTOOED

tatty *adj fr early 1900s Australian* Inferior; cheap; shoddy; =TACKY: *have met over lunch in tatty banquet halls to press the flesh*—Village Voice

tawny *adj teenagers* Excellent; wonderful; =NEAT

taxi *See* TIJUANA TAXI

taxi squad *n phr football* A group of professional football players who are not officially members of a team, although they may be paid to be available as a reserve [fr the fact that a former owner of the Cleveland Browns would give such players jobs with his *taxicab* company to support them and keep them available]

TCB (pronounced as separate letters) *v black* To perform very well what one needs to do: *where he is always to be found TCBing*—New Times [fr *take care of business*]

tchotchke (CHACH kə, TSAHTS kə) (Variations: **tchatchka** or **tchotzke** or **tsatske**) **1** *n* Something trivial, esp a gew-gaw or decorative trifle; bagatelle; plaything: *little rainbows and neon tchatchkas found in California neon boutiques*—New Times/ *you know, the tchotzkes, the jewelry*—Boston Globe/ *Kafka Tchotchke*—Village Voice **2** *n* A precious or adorable person, usu a child: *The baby is a tchotchke* **3** *n* A woman considered as a plaything: *She's Harry's tsatske* [fr Yiddish *tsatske* fr Slavic *shaleh* "play pranks"]

TD (pronounced as separate letters) *n football* A touchdown

t'd off *See* TEE'D OFF

tea 1 *n* (also **T**) narcotics fr 1920s black Marijuana **2** *n* narcotics fr 1920s black A marijuana cigarette; =JOINT, TEA-STICK **3** *n* horse-racing A stimulant, often cocaine or strychnine, given to a racehorse to increase its speed [the narcotics senses probably fr use of *tea* as winking and ironic concealment]

See CUP OF TEA, PINK TEA, STICK OF TEA, WEED TEA

teacups *See* ASS OVER TINCUPS

tea'd up *adj narcotics* Intoxicated with marijuana; =GOWED UP, HIGH

teakettle *n railroad* An old locomotive

See ASS OVER TINCUPS

team *See* SWAT TEAM

team up *v phr* To join together in some effort; =BUDDY UP

tea pad *n phr outdated narcotics* A place where marijuana smokers gather

tea party 1 *n phr outdated narcotics* A gathering where marijuana is smoked: *Marijuana "tea parties" are little things*—Eugene Burdick **2** *n phr* An easy, pleasant, safe occasion ● Most often used in the negative: *It wasn't exactly a brawl, but the meeting was no tea party either*

tear[1] (TAIR) *n fr middle 1800s* A drinking spree; = BENDER, BINGE: *Fred wanted to go on a little tear in the big town*—Fact Detective Mysteries

See ON A TEAR

tear[2] (TEER) *n* A pearl [fr the *tear* shape of some pearls]

tearing up the pea patch *adj phr* Very energetic; hyperactive; = FULL OF PISS AND VINEGAR

tear-jerker 1 *n* A sentimental story, movie, song, etc: *see the old tear-jerker*—HR Hoyt **2** *n* A person who appeals to sentimentality; a fomenter of pathos: *a magniloquent tear-jerker named Delmas*—American Mercury

tear off *v phr* To play or perform: *The musicians began to tear off a La Conga*—Richard Starnes

◁**tear off a piece** (or **a piece of ass**)▷ *v phr* To do the sex act; = FUCK

tearoom or **t-room** *n homosexuals* A public toilet

tearoom queen *n phr homosexuals* A male homosexual who frequents public toilets seeking sexual encounters

tears *See* THAT KILLS IT

teaser 1 *n* A woman who invites or offers sexual activity but refuses to do the sex act; = COCK-TEASER: *Maybe Bella was right in calling his "uptown lady" a "teaser"*—Stephen Longstreet **2** *n* Anything offered as a sample and intended to increase appetite or desire: *He showed them one chapter as a teaser*

See COCK-TEASER

tea-stick *n outdated narcotics* A marijuana cigarette: *There isn't much record that he went for tea-sticks himself*—Stephen Longstreet

teat *See* ANGEL TEAT

tea (or **tearoom**) **trade** *homosexuals* **1** *n phr* Male homosexuals who seek encounters in public toilets **2** *n phr* Sexual encounters in public toilets

tec or **teck 1** *n fr late 1800s British* A detective; = DICK **2** *n* A detective story [a shortening of *detective*]

See TOUGH-TEC

tech[1] *n* An engineering or technology college [fr *technology*]

See HIGH TECH

tech[2] *n* A technician, esp an electronics or wire-tapping expert: *I got a guy to do it, a tech named Ernie Mann*—Lawrence Sanders

techie *n* A computer enthusiast, expert, etc: *You don't have to be a "techie" or a "computer nut" to join*

Technicolor yawn *n phr teenagers* The act and product of vomiting [fr *Technicolor*, trade name for a color-film process]

techno- *prefix used to form nouns* Having the indicated knowledge of, involvement with, or attitude towards technology, esp advanced and computer technology: *technofreak/ technopeasant*

teddy *n fr early 1900s* A one-piece women's undergarment serving as both chemise and panties

tee'd (or **teed** or **t'd**) **off** *adj phr* Angry; = PISSED OFF: *When people get teed off they want to march*—Time [perhaps fr *ticked off*; perhaps a euphemism for *pee'd off* "pissed off"]

Tee Dee *n phr* = TD

teed up *adj phr* Drunk [probably fr 1920s black *teed* "drunk," probably related to marijuana or *tea* intoxication, and to *tea* "whiskey," a use attested fr the 17th century]

teen 1 *n* (also **teener** or **teenie** or **teeny**) A teenage person; teenager: *a really interesting biz for a teen who loves being busy*—Deseret News/ *a robust health that would be remarkable on a teener*—Robert Ruark/ *"You only pass this way once," he tells a teenie in persuading her to come along for a ride*—Terry Southern **2** *modifier:* *teen flicks/ the teen scene*

teensy-weensy *adj* Very small; tiny: *the teensy-weensy kind that small-town dailies like*—Philadelphia

teenybopper *n* (also **teenie bopper** or **teenybop** or **teeny-rocker**) *fr 1960s counterculture & rock and roll* A teenager or preteenager, esp one who undertakes the hippie or rock-and-roll culture and way of life: *Teenyboppers opt for zodiac signs*—Village Voice/ *attract shady record promoters like rock stars attract teeny-boppers*—National Observer/ *Behind me, teenie boppers pop gum and make pubescent wisecracks*—Playgirl

teenzine *n* A magazine for teenagers: *this teen-zine cover boy*—Rolling Stone

tee off *v phr* To hit someone or something very hard: *He hit a homer, really teed off* [fr the opening shot of each hole in golf, off the *tee*]

tee someone **off** *v phr* To make angry; = PISS someone OFF: *and this moping is teeing me off*—Hannibal and Boris [probably a euphemism for *pee* or *piss* someone *off*, influenced by *tee off on* someone, fr golf]

tee off on someone or something **1** *v phr* To verbally assault someone, esp to reprimand: *The critic really teed off on my book, alas* **2** *v phr baseball* To make many hits against a particular pitcher: *They teed off on Gossage in the twelfth* **3** *v phr baseball* To hit the ball very hard: *He teed off on it and it went right over the wall*

teeth *See* DRESSED TO THE TEETH, DROP one's TEETH, PULL TEETH THROUGH THE ARMPIT

telegraph *v* To signal one's intentions, often inadvertently: *The tone of her voice telegraphed it*—J Evans

telegraph one's **punches** *v phr fr prizefight* To let an opponent know one's intentions inadvertently: *never get to the top, he telegraphs his punches*—Jim Tully

tell *See* SHOW-AND-TELL

tell it like it is *v phr esp 1960s fr black* To be candid and cogent; tell the truth, even though it be unpleasant; = GIVE IT TO someone: *by Negro psychi-*

atrists *William H Grier* and *Price M Cobbs, who tell it like it is*—McCall's [perhaps fr an exhortation used in black church services]

tell it to Sweeney *sentence* =TELL IT TO THE MARINES [*Sweeney* is one of a group of surely mythical Irishmen, like *Riley, Kelsey,* and *Kilroy*, whose names are used apparently for some humorous effect]

tell it to the Marines *sentence fr early 1800s British Navy* I do not believe what you have just told me; what you say is false and futile [the usage reflects the contempt in which *marines* were held by naval seamen, leading to the assertion that they would believe nonsense that sailors would never believe]

tell someone **off** *v phr fr early 1900s British armed forces* To reprimand; =CHEW someone OUT: *The man had just been told off, and told off plenty* —G Homes

tell the world *See* I'LL TELL THE WORLD

tell someone **what to do with** something *v phr* (Variations: **where to put** (or **shove** or **stick** or **stuff**) may replace **what to do with**) To reject something vehemently and defiantly ● A euphemism for **stick it up your ass**: *She told me rudely what to do with my proffered assistance/ The first thing I did when I got home was to tell my old boss where to stick my old job*—Max Shulman

tell someone **where to get off** (or **to go**) *v phr* To rebuke, rebuff, or deflate firmly; =LET someone HAVE IT ● A euphemism for **go to hell**: *I advised Alice to tell him where to get off when he tries that big-shot stuff*

telly *See* BELLY TELLY

ten *See* FIVE-AND-TEN, HANG TEN, KEN-TEN LAMP, TAKE TEN

a **ten** *n phr* A young woman who is maximally sexually attractive; a perfect female specimen [perhaps fr *ten-carat*; perhaps fr the conventional question "Where would you put her (him, it) on a scale of one to *ten*?"]

ten-carat *adj* Excellent; wonderful; superior

ten cents *n phr narcotics* A ten-dollar packet of narcotics; =DIME BAG

tenderfoot *n fr middle 1800s Western* A newcomer; neophyte; callow person

tenderloin or **Tenderloin** *n outdated fr late 1800s* The disreputable section of a city; the redlight district, gambling district, etc [said to be fr the remark of a New York City police captain who, when assigned to the original *Tenderloin* in Manhattan, observed that he had always eaten chuck steak but would now eat *tenderloin*]

ten-foot pole *See* NOT TOUCH someone or something WITH A TEN-FOOT POLE

ten four 1 *n phr citizens band* The signal that a message has been received, the equivalent of the earlier and military "roger" **2** *affirmation fr citizens band* That is correct: *That's a ten four, you have it just right* [fr a code of conventional procedure signals used esp by the police, where *ten* was a sort of prefix, and the numeral following bore the

message; *ten seven*, for example, meant "transmissions finished"]

tenner 1 *n fr late 1800s* A ten-dollar bill: *spent the tenner on Jersey applejack*—Billy Rose **2** *n prison* A ten-year prison sentence

tennies or **tenny runners** *n* or *n phr* Tennis shoes, running shoes, or other such rubber-soled footwear: *He came on late in the program in his tennies*—Washington Post/ *a plain black T-shirt and beige tennies*—Rolling Stone

tenor *See* WHISKEY TENOR

tenpercenter *n fr show business & underworld* A person who receives ten percent of someone's earning, loot, etc, esp an actor's or athlete's agent

ten pounds of shit in a five-pound bag *See* BLIVIT

tense up *v phr* To become stiff, ineffective, and semiparalyzed from nervous tension; =CHOKE UP, CLUTCH UP

ten-spot 1 *n fr late 1800s* A ten-dollar bill; ten dollars; =DIME-NOTE: *A ten-spot can't get you past two counters in a grocery store without limping* —Hal Boyle **2** *n prison* A ten-year prison sentence: *after having served a ten-spot*—D Purroy

tent *See* PUP TENT

-teria *See* -ATERIA

tern *n hospital* An intern

terps *n narcotics* Elixir of terpin hydrate with codeine, a cough syrup prized as a narcotic

terrific *fr early 1900s* **1** *adj* Excellent; wonderful; =GREAT: *The script is apt to be terrific*—Time **2** *adj* Prodigious; extreme; amazing: *Times Square hotel biz is on the terrific fritz*—Variety

territory *See* GO WITH THE TERRITORY

terror *See* HOLY TERROR

test *See* BUG TEST, POP QUIZ

tetchy *adj* Crazy; eccentric; wild: *the days when tetchy film crews invaded the center of soporific conferences*—Washington Post [fr dialect *tetched* "crazy, touched in the head"]

Texas leaguer *n phr baseball fr late 1800s* A hit that falls out of reach between the infielders and the outfielders: =BANJO HIT [fr the fact that such hits were used in minor-league baseball's *Texas League* as trick plays]

Tex-Mex 1 *adj* Texan-Mexican **2** *n* A native of the Texas-Mexico border region: *Fender...who calls himself a Tex-Mex, was born in the south Texas valley border town of San Benito*—Washington Post **3** *n* A style of cooking characteristic of the Texas-Mexico border region: *exemplars of Tex-Mex, the mongrel cuisine that has grown up along America's southern border*—Newsweek

TGIF (pronounced as separate letters) *sentence* Thank God it's Friday

thank you ma'am *n phr fr middle 1800s* A bump or hole in the road [because riders bounce up and down as if they were bowing thanks]
See WHAM-BAM THANK YOU MA'AM

that ain't (or **isn't**) **hay** *sentence* (Variations: **peanuts** or **chopped liver** may replace **hay**) That is a large sum; that is not insignificant: *And what they pay me in addition ain't hay*—John O'Hara/

We have spent $25 million to adapt. And that isn't chopped liver—New York Times/ *He asked for a million, which ain't peanuts*

that kills (or **does** or **tears**) **it** *sentence* That ruins things; that's the last straw

that's all someone **needs** *sentence fr 1930s or earlier* That is precisely what someone does not need; that is excessive, fatal, very ill-timed, etc: *Another tax increase is all I need right now/ A speeding ticket? Brother, that's all you needed* [perhaps fr a translation of the ironical Yiddish lament *Dos felt mir nokh* "I still lack that"]

that's all she wrote *sentence* That is the sum and end of it; that is the bitter end: *Tell him that's it, brother, that's all she wrote*—Hannibal & Boris [fr the sad case of someone, esp a World War 2 soldier, who got a Dear John letter from his sweetheart, ending the affair]

that's my boy (or **girl**) *sentence* You have done very well; I'm proud of you; = WAY TO GO

that's show business (or **show biz**) *sentence* Such is the unpredictable or grim nature of things; = THAT'S THE WAY THE BALL BOUNCES: *We didn't get invited, but that's show business*

that's the ball game *sentence* That's the end of the affair ● Usu spoken by the loser

that's the way the ball bounces (or **the cookie crumbles**) *sentence fr 1950s* Such is life; such are the buffetings of fate; c'est la vie: *guess that's the way the ball bounces*—Sidney Skolsky

that way *adj phr fr 1930s* In love; enamored: *He decided he was that way about her* [perhaps coined by Walter Winchell, and at any rate characteristic of the arch gossip-column style]

them apples *See* HOW DO YOU LIKE THEM APPLES

therapy *See* GREYHOUND THERAPY

there or **right there** *adj* or *adj phr fr 1920s* Very competent; very well informed; = WITH IT: *When it comes to piano-playing he's right there/ She's there, if you want to know about feminist criticism*

there's no (or **no such thing as a**) **free lunch** *sentence* The world is a hard place and one must work for what one gets (and even then one may not get it) [fr the memory of old-time saloons, where one could eat from a copious *free lunch* on the bar, even with a minimal liquor purchase]

there's no way *adv phr* Under no conceivable circumstances: *There's no way I'll ever see it your way*

there you go or **there you are 1** *sentence* That is, unfortunately, the way things happen; = THAT'S THE WAY THE BALL BOUNCES: *She ran out on him? Well, there you go* **2** *sentence* Things happen as expected; results follow actions: *You push this one, see? There you go, it turned on* **3** *sentence* You have done something wrong again, of your habitual sort: *There you go, meddling again*

thick 1 *adj* Stupid; dull-witted **2** *adj* (also **thick as thieves**) Intimate; very well acquainted: *The two of them are very thick*
See SPREAD IT THICK

thicko *n* A stupid person; = DIM-WIT: *Charlie doesn't know anything. He's a thicko*—Paul Theroux

thighs *See* THUNDER THIGHS

thin 1 *adj hoboes & carnival* Lacking money; penniless; = BROKE **2** *n* = A THIN DIME

a (or **one**) **thin dime 1** *n phr fr 1920s* The least amount of money; = a RED CENT *He was stony broke, not a thin dime could he produce* **2** *n phr* A dime; ten cents: *which sells old-fashioned ice cream sundaes for one thin dime*—Associated Press [fr the fact that the *dime* is the *thinnest* and smallest of US coins]

thing *n esp 1960s counterculture* One's particular predilection, skill, way of living or perceiving, etc: *He ignored the world and stuck to his thing*
See the BEST (or GREATEST) THING SINCE SLICED BREAD, DO one's THING, HAVE A THING ABOUT, JUST ONE OF THOSE THINGS, OLD THING, SURE THING, a SURE THING, a WHOLE 'NOTHER THING

thingamajig *n most forms fr middle 1700s British* (also **thingumabob** or **thingumadoodle** or **thingummy** or **thingamadoger** or **thingamadudgeon** or **thingumbob** or **thingamananny**) An unspecified or unspecifiable object; something one does not know the name of or does not wish to name; = DINGUS, DOODAD, GADGET: *When you want to go down you push this thingamajig up as high as it will go/ a thingummy so addicted to lethal violence*—WH Auden

thingy *n* A thing; = GIZMO, THINGAMAJIG: *one of those thingies on the roofs of churches that the water spouts through*—Patrick Mann

thin in the upper crust *adj phr* Stupid; = DIM-WITTED

think *See* DEEP-THINK

think-box *n* The brain

◁**think** one **is King Shit**▷ *v phr* To have an elevated notion of one's importance, power, charm, etc; = THINK one's SHIT DOESN'T STINK: *The new dean thinks she's King Shit*

think-piece *n* A newspaper or magazine article of intellectual virtue or pretension; a thoughtful essay: *The Knightly Quest drifts off into a think-piece on the nature of romantics and the state of the nation*—Partisan Review

◁**think** one's **shit doesn't stink**▷ *v phr fr middle 1800s British* To be very conceited; be stuck up and self-impressed: *The way she looks down her nose you know she thinks her shit doesn't stink*

think tank *n phr* An institute or institution that specializes in the custody of interpretive intellectuals, esp in the social sciences, and usu caters to and is financed by a government in return for studies, prognostications, etc: *A peace academy would be part graduate school, part think tank*—George F Will

thin one *n phr jive talk fr hoboes* A dime; = THIN DIME: *He "drops the lug" on you for "a thin one"*—Charles Carson

third base *See* GET TO FIRST BASE

third degree or **third** *n phr* or *n fr late 1800s* Long and harsh, even brutal, questioning, esp by the police: *The Third Degree, A Detailed and Appalling Exposé of Police Brutality*—A Lavine/

He's giving me a third about some gun he says I had—Raymond Chandler

third leg *See* MIDDLE LEG

third lieutenant *n phr WW2 armed forces* A commissioned officer, such as a warrant officer or a flight officer, ranking below a second lieutenant

third sacker *n phr baseball* A third baseman

the **third sex** *n phr* Homosexuals

third wheel *n phr* An unwanted or superfluous person; =EXCESS BAGGAGE: *I'm afraid I was a sort of third wheel there, they wanted to be alone*

thirteen *interj lunch counter* A signal that the manager is nearby [fr the unluckiness of the number *thirteen*]

See FILE SEVENTEEN

thirty or **30** *sentence fr newspaper office, telegraphers & broadcasting* That's all; that's the end of the story or message [fr the use by early telegraphers of the symbol *XXX* to designate the end of a story filed by a newspaper correspondent]

See OH-DARK-THIRTY

this is it *sentence* The final crisis is here; the unavoidable has come; prepare for the worst: *He held her hand fast and said, "This is it, kid"*—Saul Bellow

thou (THOU) *n fr middle 1800s* A thousand, esp a thousand dollars; =GRAND: *A hundred and fifty thou is business*—Dashiell Hammett

thought *See* DON'T GIVE IT A SECOND THOUGHT

threads *n fr 1930s jive talk* Clothes, esp a suit of clothes; =DUDS

See SET OF THREADS

the **Three** *n phr airline* The Douglas DC-3 airplane; =the GOONEY BIRD: *The airlines call it simply, "the Three"*—New York Post

three-bagger *n baseball* A three-base hit; a triple

three bricks shy of a load *adj phr* Stupid; =NOT ALL THERE

three D or **3-D** or **3D 1** *n phr* or *n* The technique of making or showing stereoscopic, three-dimensional movies: *They started making a lot of dreadful splat movies in three D* **2** *adj* Three-dimensional: *a three-D turkey of a movie*

three-dollar bill *See* PHONY AS A THREE-DOLLAR BILL

three-dollar pistol *See* HOT AS A THREE-DOLLAR PISTOL

three-letter man *n phr college students fr 1930s* A homosexual [fr the fact that *fag* has three letters, and based on the custom of gauging athletic distinction by the number of varsity letters]

three-point landing *See* CHINESE THREE-POINT LANDING

three-sheet *n print shop* A large advertising poster of the sort used in railroad stations, subways, etc: *Did you ever hear of an actor or a manager getting out a three-sheet which held a newspaper up to ridicule?*—H McHugh [fr the fact that they were originally printed in *three sheets* because of limitations in press size]

three (or **four**) **sheets to the wind** *adj phr fr early 1800s British* Drunk [fr the fact that a drunken person is as helpless and disorganized as a sailboat

with its *sheets*, that is, with its sails flying, and hence its course and movement entirely out of control]

three squares *n phr* Enough to eat; an acceptable standard of living: *He isn't rich, but he gets his three squares every day*

three-striper 1 *n Navy* A commander **2** *n Army* A sergeant

three- (or **four-**) **time loser** *n phr* A criminal who has been convicted several times, and is in jeopardy of an automatic life sentence if convicted again; hence, a hardened and perhaps dangerous criminal

thriller *n* An exciting movie, play, etc, esp a horror show; =CHILLER

thriller-diller *n* A very effective thriller; =CHILLER-DILLER

throat *n college students* A very intense and competitive student, esp a premedical student [fr *cutthroat*]

See CUT one's OWN THROAT, JUMP DOWN someone's THROAT

throb *See* HEART-THROB

throttle *See* BEND THE THROTTLE

through a tin horn *See* LIKE SHIT THROUGH A TIN HORN

through one's **hat** *See* TALK THROUGH one's HAT

through the mill *adv phr fr early 1800s* By the course of hard experience; where the most difficult and practical experience is to be had: *He knows just where it's at, he's been through the mill*

See GO THROUGH THE MILL, RUN someone THROUGH THE MILL

throw 1 *v esp sports & gambling fr middle 1800s* To lose a game, race, etc, deliberately; =TANK: *Basketball players confess that they have accepted bribes to "throw" games*—Arthur Daley **2** *v* (also **pitch** or **toss**) *fr early 1900s* To be host or hostess at; arrange for: *The president has to throw him a luncheon*—P Edson/ *One of his assistants actually pitched a party for me*—Robert Ruark/ *Kendall tossed a cocktail party for a group of us visiting writers*—New York Daily News

a **throw** *adv phr fr early 1900s* For each; apiece; =PER EACH: *The meetings were a dollar "a throw"*—P Marks [probably fr carnival games where the customer pays so much for several *throws* of a ball, a ring, etc, trying to win a prize]

throw someone **a curve** *v phr* To do something quite unexpected; deceive by the unpredicted; =CURVE someone: *But Spicoli threw him a curve*—Cameron Crowe

throw a fit (or **a hyper**) *v phr fr late 1800s* To behave or react very angrily; =HAVE KITTENS: *She just about threw a fit when I told her we weren't going*/ *My teacher threw a hyper at that dumb remark*

◀**throw a fuck into** someone▶ *v phr* (Variations: **bop** or **boff** or **screw** may replace **fuck**) To do the sex act with someone; =FUCK: *It's inevitable that someone is going to want to throw a bop into someone else's wife*—Esquire

throw something **at** something *v phr* To cover or pelt a problem with some usu futile remedy: *Experi-*

ence with throwing bureaucrats at such problems does not presage success—New York Times/ The University will now throw lots of paper at this demographic muddle

throwaway 1 *n* *fr show business* A line, joke, etc, deliberately spoken unemphatically, thus increasing its effect **2** *modifier:* He had a sort of throwaway casualness about him **3** *modifier* Designed to be thrown away; disposable: It came in throwaway bottles **4** *modifier* Useless; superfluous: a three-times convicted killer, a throwaway man now—Ann Rule

throw away *v phr* *show business* To deliver a throwaway line, joke, etc: I love the way he threw away that misquotation from Plato

throw back *v phr* To drink or eat: He will announce that he must stop to "throw back a hamburger"—Westworld

throw bouquets at someone or something *v phr* To praise; give kudos to: I don't make a practice of throwing bouquets at any politician

throw down 1 *v phr* To threaten or challenge; start trouble: irate macho mesomorphs about to throw down—Village Voice **2** *v phr* *esp teenagers* To challenge a rival break dancer by performing a particularly difficult feat or gyration [perhaps fr late-19th-century throw down on "aim one's pistol at"; perhaps fr throw down the gauntlet "issue a challenge"]

thrower *See* DIAMOND-CRACKER, HATCHET-THROWER

throw someone or something **for a loop** *See* KNOCK someone or something FOR A LOOP

throw one's **hat in the ring** *v phr* *fr early 1800s* To issue a challenge, esp to announce one's candidacy in an election, for an appointment, etc

throw in the sponge (or **the towel**) *v phr* *fr middle 1800s British* To concede defeat; give up; =FOLD [fr the signal of surrender given by a defeated boxer's manager or associate when he tosses a sponge or a towel in the air or into the ring]

throw lead *v phr* To shoot a firearm

throw leather *v phr* To box; fight, esp with gloves: I was throwin' leather before you could crawl—Jim Tully

throw money at something *v phr* To spend extravagant amounts of money, in the hope of solving some problem: The answer to the quality of schools is not just to throw money at the problem

◁**throw** someone **out on** someone's **ass**▷ (or **ear**) *v phr* To eject someone, esp violently; =BUM-RUSH: I just raised a little question and they threw me out on my ass

throw the book at someone *v phr* To give a severe punishment, esp to assign a maximum sentence to a criminal; treat mercilessly [fr the image of a judge throwing the whole lawbook full of punishment indiscriminately at the convicted person]

throw the bull *v phr* =SHOOT THE BULL

throw the hooks into someone *v phr* To cheat; defraud; swindle: It takes...work to throw the hooks into a life insurance company—Erle Stanley Gardner [a strong variant of earlier hook "cheat, deceive, rook"]

throw together *See* KNOCK TOGETHER

throw one's **weight around** *v phr* To use one's influence, esp in a crude way; exploit one's authority: You'll never get picked if you start throwing your weight around

thrush *n* A female singer; =CANARY

thumb 1 *v* (also **thumb a ride**) To solicit rides along a highway by pointing with one's thumb in the direction one wishes to travel; =HITCHHIKE **2** *n* *narcotics* A marijuana cigarette; =JOINT [narcotics sense fr the fact that one sucks the cigarette as a baby does its *thumb*]

See DOWN-THUMB, a GREEN THUMB, ON THE THUMB, STICK OUT

thumb down *v phr* To veto; reject; refuse; =NIX: He tends to thumb down all my best ideas

a **thumb in** one's **eye** *n phr* An annoyance; a constant irritant: Yeah, he's been a thumb in my eye for a long time—Rolling Stone

thumbnail sketch *n phr* A very brief account; esp, a quick biography [so brief, that is, as to be written on a *thumbnail*]

thumbprint *n* *theater* What is characteristic and individual about one's personality, work, etc; one's seal: The director has achieved what is known in the theater as his thumbprint—Al Hirschfeld

thumbs *See* ALL THUMBS, TWIDDLE one's THUMBS

thumbs down *n phr* A negative response; a negation: It's thumbs down on his promotion this year [fr the *pollice verso* gesture of the audience at a Roman gladiatorial show, indicating that a defeated gladiator was to be killed rather than spared]

See TURN THUMBS DOWN

thumbs up *n phr* *fr early 1900s* A positive response; an affirmation; =the NOD: We go, the answer is thumbs up [the opposite of *thumbs down*; see thumbs down]

thumper *See* IVORY-THUMPER

thunderbox radio *n phr* A large stereo radio, esp one played very loud in public places; =GHETTO BOX: the thunderbox radios blaring trumpet fanfares —Village Voice

thunder thighs *n phr* Heavy thighs, esp when regarded as ugly and undesirable: Bye-bye thunder thighs. You can have slimmer legs in 30 days—People Weekly/ the sinewy thunder thighs of marathoner Gayle Olinekova—Time

thusly *adv* *fr middle 1800s* Thus: content to sum up his contribution thusly: "It was the toughest thing I ever attempted"—New York Times

tick[1] *n* *fr 1600s* Credit: plenty of canned goods and plenty of tick at the store—Westbrook Pegler [fr ticket]

See ON TICK

tick[2] **1** *n* A degree, esp of upward motion or increase; a discrete amount: if the price would have stayed where it was or skipped up a few more ticks —Nicholas von Hoffman **2** *n* A second; =a JIFFY: I'll be there in a couple of ticks

See RICKY-TICK, UPTICK, WHAT MAKES someone TICK

tick[3] *See* FULL AS AN EGG, LEAP-TICK, TIGHT

ticked off or **ticked** *adj phr* or *adj* Angry; =PISSED OFF, TEE'D OFF: Steve Kemp is ticked off

—Village Voice/ *a ticked future cop*—Car and Driver

ticker *n fr late 1800s* The heart: *tapped the left side of his chest. "Ticker," he said*—JD Salinger

ticket *n fr late 1800s* An official license or certificate, esp one for a ship's officer, a radio operator, etc

See BIG TICKET, BLUE TICKET, HAVE one's TICKET PUNCHED, MEAL TICKET, TS TICKET, WALKING PAPERS

the **ticket** *n phr fr middle 1800s British* Exactly what is wanted: *That's the ticket, my dear, exactly what we needed* [perhaps fr *the winning ticket* in a lottery, a race, etc]

tickety-boo 1 *adv fr WW2 British armed forces fr 1920s British Navy* Very well; splendidly: *Weitz's report just after liftoff that "everything's going tickety-boo so far"*—Newsweek **2** *adj: The sergeant reported that all was tickety-boo* [origin uncertain; perhaps fr *the ticket*; more likely fr the slightly earlier Royal Air Force *tiggerty boo* in the same sense, fr Hindi *teega* plus unexplained but euphonious *boo*]

tickle *See* SLAP AND TICKLE

tickled pink *adj phr* Very much pleased; happy as can be: *I am tickled pink to have been asked*

tickler *See* FRENCH TICKLER, RIB-TICKLER

tickle the ivories *v phr* To play the piano, esp to play it well

◁**tickle the shit** (or **piss**) **out of** someone▷ *v phr* To please someone very much; overjoy someone

tick someone **off** *v phr* To anger someone; = PISS someone OFF: *Her tone of voice ticked him off/ Just the slightest thing could tick off Harold*—Philadelphia

tick over *v phr* To idle; barely run; operate very slowly *The motor was just ticking over*

ticky-tacky 1 *n* Shabby materials; insubstantial and inferior goods: *little houses made of ticky-tacky* **2** *adj* (also **ticky-tack**) Inferior; shabbily made or done; = TACKY: *oil rigs and ticky-tack motels*—Advertisement for Time-Life Books/ *ticky-tacky direction by Allan Arkush*—Newsweek/ *draw their energy from the ticky-tacky-taco style of curio shops*—Newsweek [coined by Malvina Reynolds and used in "Little Boxes," a 1960s satirical song about California housing tracts where the houses are described as little boxes made of *ticky-tacky*]

tiddly *adj late 1800s British* Drunk, esp slightly drunk: *a little tiddly, which is to say, shot or blind*—Philip Wylie [probably related to the mid-19th-century British term *tiddlywink* "an unlicensed saloon or tavern," and to the early-20th-century British *tiddlywink*, rhyming slang for "drink"]

◁**tiddy**▷ *See* TOUGH SHIT

tie (or **get**) **a bag on** *v phr* To go on a drinking spree; get drunk: *You still tie a bag on now and again*—Westbrook Pegler

tie a can to (or **on**) someone *v phr* To dismiss; discharge; = CAN, FIRE: *First it was the Braves who tied a can to Tommy Hughes*—Raymond Johnson [probably fr *can* "discharge"]

tied up 1 *adj phr* Very busy; totally occupied **2** *adj phr* Snarled; blocked; knotted: *Traffic was tied up for miles this side of the tunnel*

tie-in 1 *n* A business arrangement usu contingent on one's accepting something less desirable in order to get something more desirable **2** *n* An item sold because of the existence of another item: *The book is a movie tie-in*

tie into *v phr fr early 1900s* To assault; attack or deal with vigorously: *She put her head back and tied into her drink*—J Evans/ *No sooner had I said it but both of them tied into me*

tie it up *v phr* = WRAP something UP

tie one on *See* HANG ONE ON

ties *See* COUNT TIES, HIT THE TIES

tie one's **shoes** *v phr* To improve or correct one's behavior; = GET WITH IT, PULL UP one's SOCKS, SHAPE UP: *He'll never get promoted if he doesn't tie his shoes*

tie up *v phr narcotics* To inject narcotics into a vein, or put a rubber tubing around one's arm in order to find a vein; = SHOOT UP: *pop a handful of bennies, then tie up, smoking a joint at the same time*—Harper's

tiger *n* A strong, virile man; a dangerous man: *He's switched from being a pussycat to being a regular tiger*

See BLIND PIG, BLIND TIGER, HAVE A TIGER BY THE TAIL

tiger sweat *n phr* Cheap, raw liquor; = PANTHER PISS, ROTGUT: *cheap alcohol, also known as tiger-sweat*—Stephen Longstreet

tight 1 *adj fr early 1800s* Parsimonious; tight-fisted; stingy: *He is tight in his dealings*—A Lavine **2** *adj* (Variations: **as a drum** (or **a lord** or **a mink**) may be added) *fr middle 1800s* Drunk: *Little tight, honey?*—Dorothy Parker/ *I wasn't especially tight*—Gene Fowler **3** *adj* Close, sympathetic: *John and Mary are very tight*

See SIT TIGHT, WRAPPED TIGHT

◁**tight as Kelsey's nuts** (or **Reilly's balls** or **O'Reilly's balls**)▷ *adj phr* Very parsimonious; stingy; close; = TIGHT

◁**tight-ass**▷ **1** *n* A tense and morally rigid person: *I know that one...a real tight-ass*—Erich Segal **2** *adj: a very tightass sort of guy*

tightassed 1 *adj* Tense; overly formal: *tight-assed British film critic*—Changes **2** *adj fr late 1800s* Not disposed to sexual promiscuity; chaste: *Washington, I saw, was full of tight-assed women*—Irwin Shaw

tighten (or **pull in**) one's **belt** *v phr* To prepare for an end of ease and plenty; become austere and earnest: *The economic predictors say we have to tighten our belts*

tightly wrapped *adj phr* Sane and normal; mentally and otherwise trim: *You gotta be fucking crackers. I mean, you aren't too tightly wrapped*—Tom Aldibrandi

tight money *n phr* Money when the supply is scarce, esp during a period of high interest rates

the **tights** *n phr* A penniless or financially grim condition; = the SHORTS: *No go. Everyone's got the tights*—Herbert Kastle

tight spot *n phr fr middle 1800s* A difficult situation; = JAM: *I'm in a tight spot and would appreciate your help*

tightwad 1 *n fr late 1800s* A parsimonious person; a stingy person; a miser: *the "tightwads" who have saved money*—New Republic **2** *adj: Don't be so tightwad with that hootch*—Sinclair Lewis

Tijuana Bible *n phr* A pornographic book of the most revolting sort

Tijuana taxi *n phr citizens band* A police car [probably because of the relatively colorful decoration of such cars]

till *See* WITH one's HAND IN THE TILL

till (or until) one is blue in the face *adv phr* Until one is able to do no more; to the point of helpless exhaustion: *I told you till I was blue in the face you should quit smoking/ Hail and beware the dead who will talk life until you are blue in the face* —Charles Olson [fr the *facial blueness* or darkening symptomatic of choking]

till the fat lady sings *See* the OPERA'S NEVER OVER TILL THE FAT LADY SINGS

timber *interj* An exclamation of triumph, achievement, etc [fr the cry of lumberjacks as a tree begins to fall]
See the TALL TIMBERS

time *See* BACK TIME, BAD TIME, BEAT someone's TIME, the BIG TIME, DOUBLE-TIME, FLYING TIME, GIVE someone A HARD TIME, GOOD TIME, HAVE oneself A TIME, MAKE TIME, MAKE TIME WITH someone, ON one's OWN TIME AND OWN DIME, RACK DUTY, SACK TIME, the SMALL TIME, STREET TIME

the time of day *See* NOT GIVE someone THE TIME OF DAY

timer *See* OLD TIMER

times *See* HARD TIMES

time's a'wasting *sentence* Hurry, please; it's late

time warp *n phr* A blank, an inordinate rapidity or slowness, a seeming anachronism, or some other anomaly of time: *The case of five people indicted more than four years ago...has been "lost in a time warp" of delays, state prosecutors say*—Arizona Republic [fr science fiction notions of instantaneous eons and the like, devised to legitimize travel over enormous distances within conceivable and dramatically useful periods of time, and based on Albert Einstein's concept of "curved space"]

timey *See* OLD-TIMEY

tin 1 *n police* A police officer's badge; = POTSY: *Boone had to flash his tin*—Lawrence Sanders **2** *n narcotics* A few grains of cocaine **3** *n* A trifling amount of money; = SMALL POTATOES

tin can 1 *n phr Navy* A depth charge **2** *n phr esp WW2 Navy* A naval warship, esp a destroyer **3** *n phr 1920s* A car, esp a Model T Ford

tin (or tinned) cow *n phr fr hoboes* Canned milk

tin ear *n phr* Unselective and unmusical hearing; auditory tastelessness: *He sometimes has a tin ear for dialogue*—Village Voice/ *I have a tin ear*—Studs Terkel

tin fish *n phr Navy fr early 1900s* A torpedo

tinfoil doorknob *See* WIN THE PORCELAIN HAIRNET

tin hat *n phr WW1 Army* A soldier's helmet

tinhorn or **tinhorn gambler** *n* or *n phr fr late 1800s* A petty but flashy gambler, or any person with those characteristics: *denunciations of punks, tin-horns, and gyps*—Westbrook Pegler [fr the horn-shaped metal can used by chuck-a-luck operators for shaking the dice; the notion of inferiority comes fr the presumed superiority of other, more sophisticated, kinds of gambling, and fr the generalized inferiority of *tin* to other metals]

tin horn *See* LIKE SHIT THROUGH A TIN HORN

tinkle 1 *n fr early 1900s British* A telephone call ● Chiefly in the expression **give** someone **a tinkle 2** *v fr early 1900s* To urinate; = PEE ● Child's and humorous euphemistic use

tin Lizzie (or lizzie) 1 *n phr fr early 1900s* An early Ford car, esp a Model T: *It is as simple and homely as an old tin Lizzie*—Reader's Digest **2** *n phr* Any old, ramshackle car or truck [probably because such vehicles were sturdy, dependable, and black, like the traditional ideal Southern servant, called *Elizabeth*]

Tin Pan Alley *n phr fr early 1900s* The site where popular music was composed, arranged, published, recorded, etc, designating the neighborhood on Seventh Avenue between 48th and 52d Streets in New York City; also, the realm of popular music composition, publishing, etc [fr the late-19th-century musicians' term *tin pan* "cheap, tinny piano"]

tin pants *n phr lumberjacks* Waterproof canvas trousers treated with paraffin

tinpot *adj fr late 1800s* Inferior; petty; = TINHORN: *tinpot Napoleons*—Richard Starnes/ *individual liberty from coercive tin-pot bigots*—Toronto Life [apparently in part fr the image of a ludicrous military figure wearing a grandiose *tin* helmet, a sort of *tin* soldier]

Tinseltown 1 *n* Hollywood; the Los Angeles-Hollywood movie and TV area and culture: *if he couldn't nab a ride to Tinsel Town in an hour's time* —George Warren/ *It sometimes seems that the whole society has spiritually decamped for Tinseltown*—Richard Schickel **2** *modifier: With familiar Tinseltown inventiveness, the new film has been entitled Grease 2*—Time [fr *tinsel* "gaudy, glittering decoration" + *town*]

tin star *n phr* A private detective; = PRIVATE EYE: *You cheap tin star*—J Evans

tintype *See* NOT ON YOUR TINTYPE

tin wife *n phr police* A police officer's wife [fr *tin* "police badge"]

◁**Tio Taco**▷ *n phr* A Chicano who emulates or truckles to the values of the non-Hispanic majority [fr Spanish, literally "Uncle Taco," using the name of the Mexican fried tortilla; modeled on *Uncle Tom*]

tip 1 *v* (also **tip off**) *fr middle 1700s British* To give useful information or advice, esp advance information that gives an advantage of some sort: *The room clerk tipped him*—Scene of the Crime (movie)/ *Who tipped Larkin off?*—Erle Stanley Gardner **2** *n: our tip to Doc Jansen would be* —New York Daily News/ *Any hot tips on the election?* [origin uncertain; perhaps fr the notion of *tip*-

ping, that is, tilting something in someone's direction]

See COPPER A TIP, POKE A TIP

tip one's **mitt** (or **hand**) *v phr fr early 1900s* To disclose one's plans, secrets, etc, esp inadvertently: *That would be tipping her mitt too much*—Heywood Broun [fr the revealing of one's *hand*, that is, *mitt* in a card game]

tip-off *n fr early 1900s* A revealing, esp a warning; a particularly useful clue: *the tip-off on what's ahead* —Associated Press

tip over *v phr underworld* To rob; =HEIST, KNOCK OVER

tipster *n fr late 1800s* A person who gives tips, esp on horse races

tip the elbow *See* BEND THE ELBOW

tip-top *adj* Excellent; first-rate: *He assured me his health was tip-top*

tire *See* FLAT TIRE, SPARE TIRE

◁**tired-ass**▷ *adj* Tedious; overused; tired: *thinking in tired-ass racial cliches*—Philadelphia Journal

tired blood *n phr fr 1950s* A condition and presumed cause of listlessness, enervation, etc: *With Clark out, Meese and Deaver going, and Baker having tired blood, something had to give*—Time/ *a battle against tired blood by shuffling the lineup* —New York Times [fr an advertising slogan used by a nonprescription brand of tonic]

tish *v fr carnival* To pad or enhance something to make it seem larger or more valuable [fr *tissue* paper, which is used for padding]

◁**tit**▷ *n fr 1600s* A woman's breast: *She couldn't make it out there....No tits*—Calder Willingham [a respelling of *teat*]

See COLD AS HELL, GET one's TAIL IN A GATE, LIVE OFF THE FAT OF THE LAND, SUCK HIND TIT, SUGAR TIT

◁**tit art**▷ *n phr newspaper office* Appealing photographs of young women; =CHEESECAKE

◁**tit cap**▷ *n phr Army* The Army garrison cap, esp when worn with front and back sticking up

◁**tit man**▷ *n phr* A man whose favorite part of the female body is the breasts

◁**tits**▷ **1** *adj* Excellent; wonderful; =GREAT, NEAT: *What a tits car she's got!* **2** *adj college students* Easy; simple: *a real tits quiz*

See WITH BELLS ON

◁**tits and ass**▷ **1** *n phr* A display of female bosoms and bottoms; also, a show, dance, etc, featuring such a display; =CHEESECAKE, TA: *Tits and ass, that's what the attraction is....An Apache team and tits and ass*—Lenny Bruce **2** *modifier: The magazine had a tits-and-ass section purporting to be a review of bathing-suit styles*

◁**tits-and-zits**▷ *modifier* Dealing with teenage love and sex: *yet another entry in the lamentable tits-and-zits genre of teenage sex comedies*—Time [modeled on *tits-and-ass*]

◁**titty**▷ *n* A woman's breast; =TIT: *His dipping titties touched the floor before his chin did*—Saul Bellow

See TOUGH SHIT

tizzy *See* IN A TIZZY

TKO (pronounced as separate letters) **1** *n prizefight* A technical knockout, declared when one

fighter is judged unfit to continue, although still conscious **2** *v: He was TKO'd in the fourth round*

TL[1] *n* =TRADE-LAST

TL[2] *n* A person who curries favor; toady; sycophant; =ASS-KISSER [fr *tokus licker* fr Yiddish *toches lecher* "ass-licker"; see *trade-last*]

TO (toh) *n* Toronto, Ontario: *What makes you so sure Holden Caulfield is in TO?*—Toronto Life

toad *See* CAR TOAD, HOP TOAD, KNEE-HIGH TO A GRASSHOPPER

to a fare-thee-well (or **a fare-you-well**) *adv phr* Thoroughly; completely; =TO THE MAX: *That new hairdo suits you to a fare-thee-well*

to a frazzle *adv phr fr middle 1800s* Completely; totally; to a ruined condition: *After the marathon I was beat to a frazzle* [fr dialect *frazzle* "frayed end of a rope"]

toast 1 *v musicians* A kind of talking or chanting done in the reggae music mode: *not exactly toasting, it was a kind of primitive rapping, consisting mainly of new slang words and an occasional joke* —Village Voice **2** *adj teenagers fr black* Excellent; wonderful; =COOL, TITS, TUBULAR: *She told me my clothes were real toast*

toaster *n musicians* A person who toasts: *an albino reggae rapper or "toaster"*—Rolling Stone/ *the song, though funny in a glib toaster's way*—Village Voice

to beat the band (or **the Dutch**) *adv phr fr late 1900s* In an unrestrained way; to the highest pitch; very much; =ALL OUT: *I hollered to beat the band/ We ran to beat the Dutch* [fr the notion that such extreme effort could even drown out *the band*; or, in the mid-18th-century version *this beats the Dutch*, could convince even a stolid, phlegmatic *Dutch*man]

to boot *adv phr fr 1000s* In addition; in extra measure: *She has lots of talent and more to boot* [fr Old English, "as profit"]

to'd (TEE OHD) *adj* =TEED OFF

toddle off *v phr* To leave; =BUZZ OFF, POP OFF

toe *See* GO TOE TO TOE, NIGGERTOE, PINK-TOES, TURN UP one's TOES

toehold *See* GET A TOEHOLD

◁**toe jam**▷ *n phr* Malodorous matter and filth under and around the toenails

◁**toe-jam queen**▷ *n phr homosexuals* A male homosexual foot-fetishist

toe the mark (or **the line**) *v phr* To behave properly; =KEEP one's NOSE CLEAN: *If he doesn't toe the mark, fire him* [fr the *mark* or *line* indicating the starting point of a race]

toe to toe *See* GO TOE TO TOE

together 1 *adj fr 1960s counterculture fr black* Composed and effective; free of tension and anxiety: *Now they're together, unless they're strung out* —William Zinsser/ *I know you don't look it, but you're coming on together*—Rolling Stone **2** *adj black* Stylish and au courant; socially adept

See GET IT TOGETHER, GO TOGETHER, HAVE IT ALL TOGETHER

to go *modifier lunch counter* Ordered and packaged to be consumed elsewhere; =TAKEOUT: *She asked for a chef's salad to go*

togs *n fr early 1800s British* Clothing, esp that worn for a specific purpose: *riding togs* [fr *tog* "coat," ultimately fr Latin *toga*]

to hell 1 *adv phr* (also **to hell and gone**) Thoroughly; irretrievably: *This thing's busted to hell/ The plan's wrecked to hell and gone* **2** *adv phr* (also **to heaven** or **to high heaven**) Very strongly; fervently; sincerely: *He swore to hell he'd never do it again/ I wish to heaven she'd leave*

toity *See* HOITY-TOITY

toke[1] **1** *n* A puff or drag at a cigarette, cigar, etc, esp a marijuana cigarette: *He still took a toke of marijuana from time to time*—Norman Mailer **2** *v*: *to toke vigorously on an oversize cigar*—Rocky Mountain Magazine **3** *n* A cigarette, esp a marijuana cigarette: *Elaborately, I lit a toke*—Easyriders [probably fr Spanish *tocar* in its sense "touch," or "tap, hit," or "get a shave or part," or a combination of these]

toke[2] **1** *n gambling* A gambling chip or token, esp one given to a dealer as a tip **2** *n* A gratuity given by a gambling casino, brothel, or other business to cab drivers for bringing in clients: *Cab drivers have long been paid "tokes"...when they deliver customers to a long list of varied business establishments*—Toronto Globe and Mail

tokus (TOH kəs, Tŏŏ kəs) *n* (also **tokis** or **tuchis** or **tuckus** or **tush** or **tushie** or **tushy**) The buttocks; =ASS, BOTTOM ● A frequent euphemism for **ass**: *knocked him right square on his tokus/ He shakes his tushie with elegant languor*—New York Post/ *bumps her tush gently along*—Village Voice [fr Yiddish; *tush* forms are affectionate, used esp with children]

tokus licker *n phr* (Variations: **tokis** or **tuckus** may replace **tokus**) =ASS-KISSER, TL

told *See* FUCKING WELL TOLD

◁**Tom** or **tom**▷ **1** *n black* A black person who emulates or truckles to the white majority taste and culture; =OREO, UNCLE TOM **2** *v*: *sleeping, resisting, tomming, killing the enemy*—Amiri Baraka/ *You too young to be Tomming*—John Godey
See AUNT TOM, BLIND TOM, MISTER TOM, UNCLE TOM

Tomahawk *See* UNCLE TOMAHAWK

tomato *n fr early 1900s* An attractive young woman; =CHICK: *the idea that such a luscious tomato might be mixed up in murder*—RS Prather/ *I was telling you about this kraut and the English tomato*—Russell Baker [fr the connotations of lusciousness, tautness, full color, etc]

tomato can 1 *n phr hoboes* A small-town police officer's or constable's badge **2** *n phr prizefight* A boxer picked because he is unlikely to win: *uncomplicated opponents the boxing trade calls tomato cans*—New York

tomboy or **tomgirl** *n* A young girl who prefers boyish pursuits, looks, etc, to the presumed feminine ones

tomcat 1 *v* To pursue male sexual activity avidly **2** *n*: *In his younger days he was a notorious tomcat*

Tom, Dick, and Harry *See* EVERY TOM, DICK, AND HARRY

tomfool *adj* Stupid; foolish; =NUTTY: *some tomfool scientist*—Newsweek

tommy 1 *n* =TOMBOY: *The red-haired tommy...she'd put him over the jumps*—WR Burnett **2** *n lunch counter* A slice of tomato

Tommy *n fr late 1800s* A private in the British army; =TOMMY ATKINS: *He met three Tommys in a bar*

Tommy Atkins *n phr fr late 1800s* A private in the British army; =TOMMY [fr the name *Mr Thomas Atkins* used on sample forms of the British army]

Tommy (or **tommy**) **gun** *n phr fr underworld* A handheld automatic repeating firearm; a submachine gun; =BURP GUN, CHOPPER [fr the name of the .45-caliber *Thompson* submachine gun, the earliest well-known weapon of this sort, and a favorite arm of the gangster era]

Tommy man *n phr fr 1930s* A gangster armed with a Tommy gun

tommyrot *n fr late 1800s British* Nonsense; balderdash; =BALONEY, BULLSHIT [origin unknown; perhaps fr British *tommy* "goods, esp food, supplied to workers in lieu of wages"]

ton *n teenagers & car-racing fr 1960s* A speed of 100 miles an hour; a high speed

a ton *adv phr* Very powerfully; with great impact: *He hit that ball a ton, and it's a home run*

toned *See* HIGH-TONED

tongue *n* A lawyer; =MOUTHPIECE

tonk *n* =HONKY-TONK

ton of bricks *See* HIT someone LIKE A TON OF BRICKS

tony or **toney 1** *adj fr late 1800s* Stylish; very elegant; =SWANKY **2** *n*: *St Michael's alley, still inhabited by the tony*—HL Mencken [probably fr French *bon ton* "high fashion, chic"]
See HIGH-TONED

toodle-oo *interj fr early 1900s British* A parting salutation ● Thought of as a humorous affectation, like **cheerio** [perhaps an alteration of French *à tout à l'heure* "see you soon, so long"]

took *See* be HAD

tool ◁**1**▷ *n fr middle 1500s* The penis **2** *n underworld fr early 1900s* A pickpocket **3** *n* A stupid and gullible person; =PATSY, SUCKER **4** *n college students* A diligent student; =GREASY GRIND **5** *v* (also **tool along**) To speed: *They were tooling down the freeway/ Look at them tool along* **6** *v* To drive a car very fast; tear; =BARREL: *I climbed into the Buick and tooled it down the ramp*—Raymond Chandler [underworld sense perhaps fr the practice of using a small boy as a sort of *tool* in pickpocketing, or perhaps fr Romany *tool* "handle, take"; driving senses fr early-19th-century British *tool* "drive," apparently fr the notion of handling a coach and team as skillfully as one handled a *tool*]
See NOISE TOOL, POWER TOOL

toolie *n college students* An engineering student: *My friends are engineers, or, as they call themselves, toolies*—New York Times

tools *n fr late 1800s* Eating utensils; knife, fork, and spoon

See FIGHTIN' TOOLS

too many *See* ONE TOO MANY

too many chiefs and not enough Indians *sentence* Nobody wants to work around here, though everybody wants to be a boss; the project suffers from a surplus of directors and advisers

too much 1 *adj phr* jazz musicians Wonderful; superb; = the MOST: *The way she blows that horn is too much* **2** *adj phr* fr 1930s jive talk Excessively good, bad, wonderful, incredible, etc; prodigious; overwhelming: *You ate 23 hot dogs in one sitting? Man, you're too much* **3** *n* = FAR OUT

toon *See* LOONY-TUNE

too rich for someone's **blood** *adj phr fr middle 1800s* Exceeding someone's capabilities, purse, desires, etc; too much: *I don't go out with them anymore, it's too rich for my blood*

toot 1 *n fr middle 1800s* A spree, esp of drinking; = BENDER, BINGE, KICK: *It gave me an excuse to go off on a four-day toot*—Humphrey Bogart/ *He got a bonus and went on a shopping toot* **2** *n* narcotics Cocaine: *Am I witnessing mere incompetence or too much toot?*—Playboy/ *made it easier for the press to imagine him doing a little toot in the basement of...Studio 54*—Washingtonian **3** *n* narcotics A whiff of cocaine into the nose; = SNORT **4** *v:* *He was himself tooting cocaine on a daily basis*—New York [the drinking sense is probably fr the image of someone *tooting* on a drinking horn, that is, holding a glass up as if it were a horn one were blowing; *toot* or *tout* "drink deeply, quaff" are attested fr the 17th century; narcotics sense probably related to *honker* "horn, nose" as something to be *tooted*]

tooth *See* CLEAN AS A HOUND'S TOOTH, LONG IN THE TOOTH, SWEET-TOOTH

toothpick *n fr middle 1800s* A pocket knife, esp a switchblade: *Any of her roomers handy with a toothpick?*—J Evans

tootie fruitie *n phr* A weak and ineffective male; = SISSY, WIMP: *We're all a bunch of Goddamned tootie fruities*—Dan Jenkins [fr *tutti-frutti* "ice cream containing candied fruit," fr Italian, literally "all fruits," with the major sense a punning on *fruity* "homosexual, gay"]

tootin' *See* ROOTIN'-TOOTIN', YOU'RE DAMN TOOTIN'

too too *adj phr fr late 1800s* British Excessive, esp in social elegance, fastidiousness, affectation, etc: *Well, isn't his caring just too too!*

toot (or **blow**) one's **own horn** *v phr* To praise and flatter oneself; advertise one's virtues; boast: *I am not ashamed of the text, but of being thought to "toot my own horn"*—Washington Post

toots (TŌŌTS) **1** *n* (also **tootsie** or **tootsy** or **tootsie-wootsie** or **tootsy-wootsy**) A woman; = DOLL ● Often used in address, often disparagingly, and as a nickname: *Not any more, toots, not any more, my precious darling angel*—Raymond Chandler/ *How about one of those tootsie-wootsies?*—Saturday Evening Post/ *He was also paying for a penthouse apartment on Park Avenue for his tootsie*—Art Buchwald **2** *n fr middle 1800s* A foot, esp a child's or baby's foot [the second and

earlier sense is a childish pronunciation of *foot*; the woman-designating sense perhaps developed from the fact that one plays affectionately with a baby's foot, eg, "This little piggie went to market," and that this cozy toying led by semantic association to notions of *tootsie* or *toots* as a baby, a doll, a cherished woman, etc; perhaps fr Yiddish *zees tushele* "sweet bottom," used affectionately of babies and euphemized to *toots* and *tootsie*, under the influence of English *tootsie*, for older children, adults, women, etc; see *tushie*]

tootsies *n fr middle 1800s* The feet: *Pull up a chair and warm your tootsies*

top 1 *v fr 1700s* To hang someone: *A colleague sent to the gallows has been topped*—HL Mencken **2** *v* underworld To kill; = BUMP OFF, HIT **3** *v* To surpass; better; = CAP: *I'll top that story with one of my own* **4** *n fr WW1* Army = TOP SERGEANT **5** *n* circus & carnival A tent: *The cook tent is the cookhouse. All others are called tops*—American Mercury **6** *adj* Best; most superior: *He got the top recommendation*

See BIG TOP, BLOW one's TOP, BONE-TOP, CHOPPED TOP, COME OUT AHEAD, FROM THE TOP, GO someone or something ONE BETTER, KID TOP, MUTTONHEAD, OFF THE TOP, ON TOP OF, POP-TOP, RAG-TOP, TANK TOP, TIP-TOP

Top *See* BROWN TOP

top banana 1 *n phr* show business The leading or featured comedian in a burlesque show; the chief comic **2** *n phr* The leader, president, manager, etc; = BOSS, BIG ENCHILADA: *refuses its members...opportunity to become top banana*—Fran Lebowitz [said to have originated fr a burlesque routine having to do with a bunch of *bananas*]

the **top brass 1** *n phr fr 1930s* The highest of military officers: *They went to the top brass at the Pentagon* **2** *n phr* The highest of executives, managers, etc: *The top brass at Xerox liked the idea*

top dog 1 *n phr* The most important person; the chief; = BOSS: *Who's top dog around this place?* **2** *adj phr* Most important; most superior; = TOPS: *The small strong bands were not top dog anymore*—Stephen Longstreet

top dollar *n phr* The highest sum of money offered or given: *They pay top dollar over there*

top-drawer *adj fr early 1900s* British Of the highest quality; most superior; = TOPS: *The drinks they serve are absolutely top-drawer* [fr a British expression *out of the top drawer* "upper-class, well-bred"]

top-kick *n fr WW1* Army A first sergeant; = FIRST MAN: *The Top Kick was caught shorthanded*—American Legion Magazine

topless 1 *modifier* Not wearing anything on the upper body; with breasts exposed: *walking about the square topless/ a topless dancer* **2** *modifier* Having to do with entertainment, bars and clubs, etc, featuring women bare from the waist up: *only at bars and only if they were topless*—Rolling Stone

top-notch *adj phr fr early 1800s* Superior; of the highest quality; = TOP-DRAWER: *She's a top-notch racquetball player* [fr *notch* as representing position, rank, etc]

top of one's **head** *See* OFF THE TOP OF one's HEAD

topper 1 *n fr early 1800s* A top hat **2** *n* Something that surpasses something else, usu a joke, comments, etc; esp, a remark that both surpasses and perfects something already said: *I have a topper for that dirty crack* **3** *n* = TOPSIDER *See* BLOW one's TOP

tops *adj fr 1930s* Best; most superior; absolutely first rate; = the TOPS: *I wish you could print Mencken every month, he's tops*—American Mercury/ *Sanitation Service Is Tops*—New York Times

the **tops** *n phr* The best; the acme: *The English department is the tops here*

top sergeant 1 *n phr Army fr late 1800s* A first sergeant; = TOP-KICK **2** *n phr* homosexuals A lesbian who takes the dominant, masculine role; = BUTCH, DYKE

topside *adv* nautical Upstairs; above

topsider *n* A high executive, officer, manager, etc: *sighed one Pentagon topsider last week*—Newsweek/ *and also "delightfully puzzled," as one topsider put it*—Newsweek [related to late-19th-century British *topside* "in control, commanding," in turn related to the nautical term *topside*, by the suggestion that the master of a ship works on the bridge, which is the highest deck of the ship]

top story *n phr* The head: *He's not quite right in the top story/ This guy's got a very canny top story*

torch 1 *v* To set a fire deliberately; burn a building: *The lumberyard at 12th and C was torched, for the insurance*—Village Voice **2** *n* An arsonist; an incendiary; = FIREBUG: *If your suspicions are right, the torch will be close by*—L Turner *See* BUG TORCH, CARRY THE TORCH

torch job *n phr* An instance of arson: *mob-linked torch jobs for a 10 percent cut of insurance proceeds*—New York Times

torch song *n phr* A popular song bemoaning one's unrequited love: *If it is unrequited, the song is a torch song*—Haskin News Service [see *carry the torch*]

torchy *adj* In love with someone who does not reciprocate; hopelessly enamored: *Junie still torchy for the Ragtime Kid*—SJ Perelman [fr *carry the torch*]

-torium *See* -ATORIUM

torp *n fr WW1 Navy* A torpedo; = TIN FISH

torpedo 1 *n fr underworld* A gunman, esp a hired killer; = HIT MAN: *the torpedoes who worked for Ciro Terranova*—Time **2** *n* = HERO SANDWICH

torpedo (or **torp**) **juice** *n phr fr WW2 armed forces* Liquor made from whatever ingredients were available; improvised alcoholic military drink [fr the fact that *torpedoes* were fueled with very pure grain alcohol and *juice* commonly means "fuel"]

torqued *adj Air Force* Angry; upset; = PISSED OFF [probably somehow fr the sense "twisted," and so semantically akin to *bent out of shape*]

toss *v underworld* To search, esp a person for weapons, drugs, etc; = SHAKE DOWN: *The cops regularly toss anybody they stop on the street* [fr the sometimes violent way such searches are made]

See THROW

toss one's **cookies** (or **lunch**) *See* SHOOT one's COOKIES

toss in the sponge *v phr* = THROW IN THE SPONGE

toss it in *v phr* To surrender; stop fighting; quit

toss off 1 *v phr* To do something easily and casually: *They sat down and tossed off a couple of limericks* **2** *v phr* To drink, esp at one gulp; = KNOCK BACK: *She tossed off three double Scotches*

a **toss-up** *n fr early 1800s* An even matter; a case of even probabilities, values, etc: *It's a toss-up between those two candidates/ I don't know which way to bet, it's a toss-up* [fr the fact that the choice might as well be made by *tossing up* a coin]

total 1 *v* To destroy; totally wreck, esp a car: *It didn't look like much of a wreck, but his car was totaled/ The paratroopers got mad and totaled the place* **2** *v* To maim or kill; grievously injure; = WASTE: *Mightn't a tile have fallen off a roof and totaled us by dinnertime?*—National Lampoon/ *I'm gonna total that bastard*—Erich Segal [fr the phrase *a total loss*, having to do with something insured]

totaled 1 *adj* Destroyed; wrecked completely: *The totaled car made you wonder how they survived the wreck* **2** *adj* Stuporous from narcotics, liquor, etc; = STONED, WASTED

a **total loss** *n phr* A person or thing that is hopelessly futile; = a DISASTER, LOSER: *Don't tell me about that guy, he's been a total loss since he got divorced*

totally clueless *adj phr* teenagers Uninformed; ignorant; in the dark ● **Clueless** is a late-1930s Royal Air Force term

tote[1] *n* = TOTE BAG [fr Southern dialect, "carry," perhaps fr Gullah *tot* "carry"; cognates are found in several African languages]

tote[2] *v* Total; add up to: *How much does it tote?* —James M Cain

tote[3] *n* (also **tote board**) A totalizator, a machine that displays odds at a race track

tote bag *n phr* A carrying sack or shoulder bag, usu strongly made and decorated with some attractive label or symbol: *He was carrying a canvas tote bag bearing the portrait of Geoffrey Chaucer* [fr *tote*[1]]

totem poles *See* KNOCK someone FOR A LOOP

to the eyes *See* STONED TO THE EYES

to the gills *See* SOUSED, STEWED

to the ground *See* BEAT TO THE GROUND, DOWN TO THE GROUND

to the mark *See* UP TO SCRATCH

to the max *adv phr* teenagers & Army To the highest degree; utterly; totally: *Many of these were obscure to the max*—Philadelphia [fr a shortening of *to the maximum*] *See* GROTTY

to the nines *See* DRESSED TO THE TEETH

to the salt mines *See* BACK TO THE SALT MINES

to the teeth *See* DRESSED TO THE TEETH

to the tune of *adv phr* In the amount of; to the extent of: *It'll cost him a bundle, to the tune of sixty grand or so*

to the wall *See* BALLS TO THE WALL

totsie *See* HOTSIE-TOTSIE

touch 1 *v* (also **touch up**) *fr middle 1700s* To solicit money, a loan, etc; = HIT: *He touched his sister for a couple of bucks/ Who better to touch up than the richest guys in town?*—Philadelphia **2** *n*: *a quick ten- or twenty-dollar touch*—E Lavine [*touch up* variant may be influenced by British *touch up* "caress in order to excite"]

See SOFT TOUCH

touch all bases 1 *v phr* To be thorough; leave nothing undone, esp in matters of consultation, communication, etc: *The plan flopped because you didn't touch all bases on the way* **2** *v phr* To be very versatile; be apt for various experiences: *Humphrey is a man to touch all bases*—Toronto Life [fr the necessity of *touching all bases* in baseball when one makes a home run]

touch base with someone *v phr* To consult with or inform as to an impending matter: *Before you sign it you'd better touch base with your lawyer* [fr *touch all bases*]

touch dancing *n phr* Kinds of dancing in which partners hold one another

touches *See* CUT UP THE TOUCHES

touchie-feelie *adj esp 1970s* Having to do with sensitivity training and other such goings-on where people touch and feel each other: *They're all part of the touchie-feelie movement*—National Review

not **touch** someone or something **with a ten-foot pole** *See* NOT TOUCH someone or something WITH A TEN-FOOT POLE

tough 1 *adj fr early 1900s* Physically menacing; vicious: *Don't act tough with me, you little jerk* **2** *n fr early 1900s* A hard and menacing person **3** *adj cool talk & students fr 1960s* Excellent; superb; = the MOST ● Sometimes spelled **tuff**: *That's a really tough set of wheels*

See TOUGH IT OUT

tough cat *n phr black* A man successful with women; = COCKSMAN

tough cookie *n phr* A durable person; a survivor ● Usually said in admiration: *You gotta respect the old guy, he's a real tough cookie*

tough cop *See* GOOD COP BAD COP

tough guy *n phr* A menacing man; a hoodlum; = BIMBO, ROUGHNECK, TOUGHIE: *Bogart used to play tough guys a lot*

toughie or **toughy 1** *n* A menacing person, esp a man; = TOUGH, TOUGH GUY: *getting the toughies off the streets*—New Republic/ *That servant will talk her out of it. She's a toughie*—Saul Bellow **2** *n* Something difficult; a severe test: *This is a toughie*—Max Shulman/ *has 3 toughies barring its way to a perfect season*—Associated Press

tough it out *v phr fr early 1800s* To endure something doggedly and bravely; persist and survive against rigors; = HANG TOUGH: *He's never really had to tough it out in this world of ours*—J Bell/ *He is toughing out a feeling that since Mom divorced he is essentially homeless*—Richard Schickel

tough nut *n phr* An obstinate, difficult person [fr the phrase *a tough nut to crack*]

a **tough nut to crack** *n phr* A difficult problem; = BITCH, TOUGHIE: *Getting them all here on time will be a tough nut to crack*

a **tough row to hoe** *See* a HARD ROW TO HOE

◁**tough shit**▷ *sentence* (Variations: **nibs** or **noogies** or **rocks** or **tiddy** or **titty** may replace **shit**) That's too bad; that's a terrible shame ● Always ironical and mocking: *"Tough tiddy," the Boss said*—Robert Penn Warren/ *Well, my friend, that's just tough shit about your lost plane ticket/ to which one has to say, with whatever empathy...tough nibs*—Village Voice/ *That's tough shit, man, my heart really bleeds*—WT Tyler/ *Well...tough titty*—Armistead Maupin [most forms probably fr black or Southern; the mammary forms seem based on a black folk-saying, "It's tough titty, but the milk is good"]

tough-tec *modifier* Having to do with the "hard-boiled school" and style of crime fiction: *a darn good tough-tec mystery*—New York

tour *n* A period of duty; an enlistment period; a working shift

See COOK'S TOUR

tour guide *n phr narcotics* A person who aids and supports someone having a psychedelic drug experience or "trip"; = GURU

tourist trap 1 *n phr* A museum, pageant, shop, etc, of minimal significance established to attract transient visitors **2** *n phr* A restaurant, nightclub, etc, in a tourist resort, that charges exorbitant prices for often inferior goods or services: *We had to eat in a shabby tourist trap, and it cost far too much money*

tout 1 *n fr middle 1800s* A person who sells betting advice at a race track; = TIPSTER **2** *n*: *He makes a slender living with his touting at Belmont* **3** *v* To advocate aggressively; publicize; = BALLYHOO, FLACK: *He's now touting acupuncture* [ultimately fr Middle English *tuten* "look around, peer," by way of *tout* "be on the lookout"]

towel *See* CRYING TOWEL, THROW IN THE SPONGE

town *See* GO TO TOWN, HICK TOWN, MAN-ABOUT-TOWN, ONE-HORSE TOWN, the ONLY GAME IN TOWN, ON THE TOWN, OUT OF TOWN, PAINT THE TOWN, SHANTY-TOWN, TANK TOWN, TINSELTOWN

Town *See* BEAN TOWN

townie or **towney 1** *n college students fr middle 1800s* A nonacademic resident of a college or university town **2** *n circus or carnival* A resident of a town where a show is performing: *a fight with the townies*—New York Times

town pump (or **bike**) *n phr* A very promiscuous woman; = PUNCHBOARD: *whose reputation as a town pump makes Stony doubt her worth as a human being*—Richard Price [a pun on the commonness and availability of the *town pump* and the coital sense of *pump*; *bike* variant based on the phrase *common carrier*]

track 1 *v Army* To agree with other information; chime: *What you say doesn't track with what I know* **2** *v* To make sense; be plausible; = FIGURE: *It does not necessarily track that because Son of Sam sells papers in New York he will sell books in Seattle*

—California Magazine/ *She's practically out of her mind. Like, she isn't even tracking*—Cyra McFadden [probably fr *track* "the groove of a phonograph record, a continuous line or passage of a tape recording," influenced by earlier *track* "follow, come closely and directly behind"]

See FAST LANE, GO ON TRACK, HAVE THE INSIDE TRACK, ONE-TRACK MIND

the track *See* the TURF

Track One *n phr Canadian police* The brothel district of a city; the red-light district

track record *n phr* Any record of performance, esp of success; = CHART, FORM: *I have a lot of relevant experience and a good track record*—New York Times/ *Voluntary organizations have a much better track record in the third world*—New York Times [fr the *record* of performance of a racehorse on the race*track*]

tracks **1** *n WW2 Army* = RAILROAD TRACKS **2** *n narcotics* The scars or puncture-marks caused by narcotics injections: *wear long sleeves (to cover their "tracks," needle marks)*—Reader's Digest

See CROW TRACKS, HEN TRACKS, PECKER TRACKS, RAILROAD TRACKS, STOP someone DEAD IN someone's or something's TRACKS, the WRONG SIDE OF THE TRACKS

Track Two *n phr Canadian police* The homosexual quarter of a city; the gay ghetto

trad *adj* Traditional

trade **1** *n prostitutes & homosexuals* A person regarded merely as a sex partner; = ASS, PIECE OF ASS **2** *n homosexuals* A man, usu heterosexual, who takes gratification from homosexuals without reciprocation, identification, etc; a man of masculine build attractive to homosexuals: *is flashy, precise, and humpy as decidedly sexy trade in a Czardas with six girls*—Village Voice **3** *v homosexuals* To look for sexual encounters; = CRUISE

See PIECE OF TRADE, the RAG TRADE, ROUGH TRADE, TEA TRADE

trade-last *n (also TL) fr late 1800s* A compliment, esp one conveyed to someone in the hope that the conveyer will win a compliment in return: *some "trade-lasts" gleaned at dancing school*—F Scott Fitzgerald [may be a folk etymology of *trade-me-lassie*, suggesting the end of a chain of compliments; the term in its abbreviated form has been mingled with the basically Yiddish *TL²* "ass-licker, sycophant, toady," by both formal and semantic resemblance]

trade up *v phr* To achieve higher status, esp by expenditure; climb socially: *If you're trading up you'll avoid this unchic resort* [fr an advertising term of the car industry, advising one to *trade up* "trade in one's present car for a more expensive one laden with prestige"]

tragic magic *n phr narcotics* Heroin: *you know, duji, scag, tragic magic*—Richard Woolley

trailer *n fr movie studio* A preview of a coming movie, a brief travelogue, or another short film shown before or after a feature movie

train **1** *v underworld* To do the sex act on a woman serially, man after man, in a gang; = GANG-

BANG: *announced that they were going to train her*—Philadelphia Journal **2** *n:* popularly known as *gang bangs* or *trains*—Ms [related to *pull a train;* perhaps influenced by earlier *train* "romp, carry on wildly"]

See CATTLE TRAIN, GRAVY TRAIN, ON THE GRAVY TRAIN, PULL A TRAIN, RIDE THE GRAVY TRAIN

train with *v phr fr late 1800s* To associate with; consort with; = HANG OUT: *the money it required to train with such*—Theodore Dreiser/ *and I don't train with lawyers*—Leslie Ford [probably fr the notion of linking up with or even riding on the *train with;* perhaps influenced by the prizefighter's close association with those he *trains with*]

tramp *n* A promiscuous woman; a harlot; = PUNCH-BOARD, TOWN PUMP

trank *n* A tranquilizer; a tranquilizer tablet or capsule

tranquilizer *See* ELEPHANT TRANQUILIZER

trans *n black teenager* A car; = TRANSPORTATION

transportation *n* An old or decrepit car; an unappealing car: *It ain't pretty, but it's transportation*

trap **1** *n fr late 1700s* The mouth; = YAP: *When she opens her trap she has an accent that is British*—John O'Hara **2** *n* A nightclub: *a pretty good East Side trap*—Gilbert Milstein **3** *n (also trap money) black* An amount of money earned by a prostitute, and usu given to her pimp: *Ray's woman got in the car. Her trap was fat*—Donald Goines **4** *modifier: to figure out why my trap money was shitty*—Donald Goines

See BEAR TRAP, BLOW OFF one's MOUTH, BOOB TRAP, BOOBY TRAP, CLAM SHELLS, FISH TRAP, FLEABAG, FLY TRAP, KISSING TRAP, POTATO-TRAP, SHUT one's TRAP, TALK-TRAP, TOURIST TRAP

trash **1** *n* A despicable, ill-bred person or group: *Don't mind them, they're just trash* **2** *v fr late 1960s* To vandalize; mutilate or destroy, sometimes as an act of political protest; = WASTE: *They have also made it a practice to "trash" (wreck) restaurants, publishing houses, and other businesses that discriminate against the third world of sex*—Saturday Review/ *One year we were trashed three times*—Time **3** *v fr late 1960s* To vilify; excoriate; = DUMP ON: *the other mayoralty that Koch likes to trash whenever he gets the chance*—New York/ *Much given to the rave-pan approach to her craft, she can trash in a flash*—Toronto Life **4** *v* To hit someone repeatedly; trounce; = CLOBBER **5** *v* To scavenge discarded furniture and other items that have been thrown away [first sense fr *white trash,* a black term of opprobrium]

See WHITE TRASH

trashing *n fr late 1960s* The act or an act of those who trash in the senses of wrecking and vilification: *the Weathermen favoring of trashing was a ridiculous concept*—New York Times/ *In my experience the public contributes every bit as much to the trashing of our presidents as we grimy ones do*—Newsweek

trashy *adj* Despicable; inferior; ill-bred; = LOW-RENT, LOW-RIDE

traveler *See* FELLOW TRAVELER

treadhead *n Army* A member of a tank crew

treat someone **like a doormat** (or ◁**like shit**▷) *v phr* To deal with in a humiliating, haughty, or oppressive manner: *We treated poor old Uncle Bob like a doormat/ and is also a fucking nitwit imbecile who treats me like shit and makes me talk about vultures*—Joseph Heller

tree *See* CHRISTMAS TREE, LIT UP, OUT OF one's TREE, SHAKE THE MONEY TREE, UP A TREE

tree jumper *n phr prison* A sexual molester: *He was, in prison parlance, a tree jumper*—Milwaukee Journal

tref *n* (also **treff** or **trif** or **triff**) A clandestine underworld meeting [fr German *Treffen* "meeting," perhaps borrowed fr the Central Intelligence Agency after World War 2]

Trekkie or **Trekker** *n* A devotee of the television science-fiction series "Star Trek": *Star Trek II. The Wrath of Khan. Come, all ye Trekkers*—Playboy

trembler *n prison* A convict, usu not an experienced criminal, who is very much afraid of his fellow inmates

trenches *See* IN THE TRENCHES

trendy 1 *adj fr 1960s British* Following new trends in fashion, art, literature, etc; anxiously au courant: *Fetch a tumbril for these fellows, or at least a trendy tailor*—Saturday Review/ *It is led by trendy bisexual types*—New York **2** *n: That will undoubtedly have great appeal to all you trendies out there*—East Side Express

trey *n narcotics* A three-dollar packet of a narcotic, esp of cocaine

trial balloon *n phr* Something done or said in order to test the reaction: *Those provocative comments were a sort of trial balloon*

Tribeca or **TriBeCa** (trī BEK ə) *n early 1980s New York City* An area in Manhattan being developed as an artist's and residential neighborhood: *They've traipsed all over Lower Manhattan, from Greenwich Village to Tribeca*—Playboy [fr *triangle below Canal Street*]

trick 1 *n fr early 1900s prostitutes* A prostitute's client or sexual transaction: *woman walking the streets for tricks to take to her room*—Louis Armstrong **2** *v prostitutes* To serve a customer: *She had tricked a john from Macon*—Playboy **3** *n homosexuals* A casual homosexual partner; =NUMBER **4** *v* (also **trick out**) To do the sex act, either hetero- or homosexually; =FUCK: *They can go "tricking out" with other gay people*—Deviant Reality **5** *v underworld* To inform; =RAT, SQUEAL: *I wasn't going to trick on him* **6** *n fr nautical fr late 1900s* A shift: *a trick at the wheel/ She doesn't require any breaks at her eight-hour trick*—New York Daily News
See CHAMPAGNE TRICK, HAT TRICK, LOBSTER SHIFT, TURN A TRICK

trickledown 1 *n* The stimulation of a whole economic system by the enrichment and encouragement of those in the upper reaches **2** *modifier: The planners counted on a trickledown effect when they relieved the rich of all taxation*

tricks *See* DIRTY TRICKS, GO DOWN AND DO TRICKS, HOW'S TRICKS

trif or **triff** *See* TREF

trifecta 1 *n gambling* A bet in which the gambler must pick the first three finishers in a horse-race, in the proper order **2** *n* A chance situation involving three: *Though having look-alike covers is an editor's nightmare...the science magazines' trifecta was an interplanetary long shot*—Time

trigger 1 *n underworld fr 1930s* A gunman; =HIT MAN, TRIGGER MAN: *He's a trigger*—Scene of the Crime (movie) **2** *v* To commit a robbery: *Police said Sims has triggered dozens of holdups*—Associated Press **3** *v* To initiate something; provoke something: *What triggered the feud in the first place?/ My remark triggered a strange reaction*
See QUICK ON THE DRAW

trigger man *n phr underworld fr 1920s* A gunman; =HIT MAN, TRIGGER

trikini *n* A woman's bathing suit with two top parts [fr *bikini*, based on the amusing assumption that *bi-* is Greek for "two," to be replaced with *tri-* "three"]

trim 1 *v* To defeat utterly; trounce; =CLOBBER: *They got trimmed 8 zip* ◁**2**▷ *n fr black* The vulva; =CUNT ◁**3**▷ *n fr black* The sex act with a woman; =ASS, CUNT, GASH: *you looking for some trim*—Ed McBain/ *I know what you need..a little trim*—Joseph Wambaugh

trip[1] *n underworld fr 1920s* An arrest; a prison sentence; =FALL [fr *trip* "stumble, fall"]

trip[2] **1** *n narcotics & students fr 1960s* A psychedelic narcotics experience: *users like beat poet Allen Ginsberg (30 trips)*—New York Post **2** *v* (also **trip out**): *Are you still tripping on LSD?/ They were stoned, as if they were tripping out* **3** *n* Any experience comparable with a psychedelic experience: *The park is an ikon. A nostalgia trip back into a youth*—Boston Magazine/ *His lecture was a pure trip* [fr *trip* "journey"]
See BAD TRIP, EGO TRIP, HEAD TRIP, LAY A TRIP ON someone, POWER TRIP, SKI-TRIP

tripe[1] **1** *n fr late 1800s* Nonsense; exaggerations; =BULLSHIT: *Stop peddling that tripe* **2** *n fr late 1800s* Contemptible material; worthless stuff; =CRAP, JUNK: *What the hell do they have to give us that tripe for?*—P Marks/ *anyone who could make money on "such tripe"*—Time [fr *tripe* "animal stomach used as food," because it is held in low regard]

tripe[2] *n* A tripod used by a street peddler: *the typical tripe of the street hawker*—Collier & Westrate

tripes *n fr middle 1400s* The intestines; =GUTS, INNARDS, KISHKES: *He doesn't put their tripes in an uproar*—Westbrook Pegler

triple whammy *n phr* A three-part attack, difficulty, threat, etc: *Triple Whammy on the Farm*—Newsweek

tripped out *adj phr* Having or symptomatic of a psychedelic narcotics experience: *a tripped-out laughing jag*—Crawdaddy/ *a couple of tripped-out teenagers in the corner*

tripper 1 *n fr late 1800s* An excursionist; a tourist: *the tripper class*—Sinclair Lewis **2** *n narcotics*

& students fr 1960s A person who takes psychedelic narcotics
See PACKTRIPPER, ROUND-TRIPPER

trippy *teenagers* **1** *adj* Intoxicated with narcotics; dazed; = SPACED-OUT, STONED **2** *adj* Bizarre; phantasmal; surreal: *a trippy fantasy, the Harvard University Press version of Instant Wingo*—Village Voice

troll[1] *n Army* A stupid person; a dullard [probably fr the dwarf or demon of Norse mythology]

troll[2] *v* To go about looking for sexual encounters; = CRUISE: *Women who are out trolling bars do not deserve the protection of the law*—Ms [fr the action of fishing by *trolling*]

trolley *See* OFF one's TROLLEY, SLIP one's TROLLEY

trot *n students fr late 1800s* A literal translation; = PONY: *I'm trying to get into Dante, with a trot*—Sinclair Lewis [a development fr *pony*]

the trots *n phr fr early 1900s* Diarrhea; = the SHITS

trotter *See* BOG-TROTTER

trouble *See* the BIG TROUBLE, DOUBLE-TROUBLE, DROWN one's SORROWS, HAND TROUBLE

trough *See* GREASE TROUGH

troupe *n police* A team of cooperating pickpockets

trouser *See* DUST someone's PANTS

truck **1** *v* To carry; haul; lug: *Why are you trucking all that weight around?* **2** *v 1930s jive talk fr early 1900s black* To leave; go along **3** *v 1930s jive talk* To dance the jitterbug; esp, to do a jitterbug dance called "Truckin'"
See MACK TRUCK

truck driver **1** *n phr narcotics* An amphetamine capsule or pill **2** *n phr homosexuals* A very masculine homosexual [narcotics sense fr the fact that *truck drivers* use stimulants to stay awake while driving]

trucking *See* KEEP ON TRUCKING

trust *See* BEEF TRUST

try *See* the OLD COLLEGE TRY

try out *v phr fr early 1900s* To apply for something; become a candidate: *I think I may try out for the choir this year*

try-out *n fr early 1900s* A trial, esp of someone's skill, acting or singing ability, etc

TS *n* = TOUGH SHIT

tsatske *See* TCHOTCHKE

TS ticket *n phr WW2 Army* A putative ticket which a soldier could take to the chaplain, who, upon hearing the soldier's tale of woe, would punch the ticket [fr *tough shit*]

tsuris or **tsoris** or **tzuris** (TSŏŏR əs, TSAWR əs) *n* Troubles; tribulations; anxieties; sufferings: *if Samuels, with all his tsuris, wins the Democratic nomination*—New York/ *There is a tsoris, which is a kind of trouble spot*—New York Times/ *during a long streak of tzuris*—T Betts [fr Yiddish fr Hebrew *tsarah* "trouble"]

tub *See* IN THE TUB

tubby *n* A fat person ● Used as a nickname, and nearly always affectionately and sympathetically: *the ex-tubbies trying to live on lettuce leaves*—Hal Boyle

the tube *n phr* Television, as an industry, a medium, a television set, etc: *making a name for*

herself as a singer on the tube—New York Sunday News/ *not a chance, unless you were back at the hotel watching on the tube*—Time/ *Occasionally one of them returns to the tube in midafternoon on reruns*—Erma Bombeck [shortening of *cathode ray tube* or *picture tube*]
See the BOOB TUBE, DOWN THE TUBE

tube it *v phr students* To fail an examination, course, etc

tube steak *n phr* A frankfurter; = HOT DOG

tub of guts (or **of lard**) *n phr* A fat person, esp a repulsive one: *that tub-o'-guts*—G Holmes

tubular *adj teenagers* Wonderful; excellent; = AWESOME, GREAT [fr surfing term describing a wave with a *tube*, that is, a cylindrical space around which the crest is curling as the wave breaks, and inside which the surfer happily rides]

tuchis or **tuckus** *See* TOKUS

tuck *See* NIP AND TUCK

tucker *See* BEST BIB AND TUCKER

tude *n teenagers fr black* Attitude; view of things; typical reaction ● Usually negative, sour, or surly [fr *attitude*]

tuff *See* TOUGH

tuifu (Tŏŏ EE Fŏŏ) *n WW2 armed forces* A totally botched situation; an incredible blunder [fr *the ultimate in fuckups*]

tumble *v underworld* To be arrested; = FALL, TRIP
See GIVE someone A TUMBLE

tumble to something *v phr fr middle 1800s* To discover; suddenly understand: *I tumbled to what she was really up to*—James M Cain [fr the notion of falling upon something, perhaps by stumbling over it]

tummy or **tum-tum** *n fr middle 1800s* The stomach: *eliminating the protruding tummy*—Syracuse Post-Standard [fr a childish pronunciation of *stomach*]
See GYPPY TUMMY

tummyache *n* A stomachache: *An elephant died of an outsize tummyache at London Airport*—Associated Press

tumor *See* MILWAUKEE GOITER

◁**tuna** or **tuna fish**▷ *fr black* **1** *n* or *n phr* The vulva; = CUNT **2** *n* or *n phr* A woman; a female [fr the similarity, recognized esp in black slang, between the odor of the vulva and that of fish or other seafood; see *seafood*; perhaps somehow influenced by *Tiny Tuna*, homosexual slang for a sailor as a sex object]

tuna wagon *n phr* An old, decrepit car; = HEAP, JUNKER: *the title of an article...in Vermont Life, "Junkers, Beaters, and Tuna Wagons"*—New York Times

tune *See* FINE-TUNE, LOONY-TUNE, TO THE TUNE OF

tuned **1** *adj 1920s* Drunk **2** *past part Canadian teenagers* Possessed or practiced upon sexually; = be HAD [Canadian sense perhaps related to earlier British and Australian *tune* "beat, hit," hence semantically to *bang*]

tune in *v phr esp 1960s counterculture* To become aware, au courant, involved, etc: *Tune in, turn on, drop out*—Timothy Leary

tune out *v phr esp 1960s counterculture* To cease being aware, au courant, etc; the opposite of "tune in"

tune someone or something **out** *v phr* To ignore deliberately; withdraw attention: *If he annoys you, just tune him out*

tune up *v phr* To bring something, esp a car motor, to its best state of effectiveness; tinker with to improve: *tuning up for the race at Santa Ana*—Life [fr the process of *tuning* a musical instrument, suggested by the fact that the performance of motors can be gauged by their sound]

tunk **1** *n college students* An informal eating or drinking party, esp one with coffee and doughnuts • Colgate University use fr early 1900s **2** *v* =DUNK [fr German *tunken* "dip," but more probably a variant pronunciation of Pennsylvania German *dunken*; see *dunk*]

tunnel *v underworld* To go into hiding
See SEE THE LIGHT AT THE END OF THE TUNNEL

tunnel stiff *n phr* A tunnel worker: *"Sandhogs" or "tunnel stiffs" are blasting a new water-supply tunnel*—New York Times

tunnel vision *n phr* Very narrow and restricted vision or perception; the inability to see anything except what is directly in front: *He's an idiot afflicted with tunnel vision*

◁**turd**▷ **1** *n fr 1000s* A piece of excrement **2** *n* A despicable person; =PRICK, SHIT
See GHOST TURDS

turd in the punchbowl *See* GO OVER LIKE A LEAD BALLOON

turf **1** *n 1930s jive talk* The sidewalk; the street **2** *n street gang* The territory claimed or controlled by a street gang: *I tried to imagine my Deacons pacing the turf or talking about me*—Life **3** *n fr street gang* A particular specialized concern; =THING: *Counterterrorism is not their exclusive turf*—Newsweek/ *I never thought of myself as pretty, that was my sister's turf*—Village Voice **4** *v hospital* To transfer a patient to another ward or service in order to evade responsibility, decisions, irritations, etc

the **turf** (or **track**) *n phr* The work and venue of a prostitute; the street: *During early years "on the turf," as the saying went, she was...thrifty and ambitious*—H Asbury/ *I didn't want to lose her, now that she was ready for the track*—Donald Goines [fr an analogy between the prostitute's work and that of a racehorse]

turista *n* Diarrhea; =AZTEC TWO-STEP, MONTEZUMA'S REVENGE [fr Spanish, "tourist"]

turk *n* =TURKEY

Turk *n football* An employee of a professional football team, generally not a highly placed one, who tells players they are to be dismissed [fr the image of a *Turk* with a scimitar sword, who "cuts" the player]
See YOUNG TURK

turkey **1** *n show business fr 1920s* An inferior show, esp a failure; =BOMB, FLOP: *Management prudently kept the turkey out of town*—Gene Fowler/ *Stars generally attract an audience no mat-*

ter what picture they are in (*unless it's a turkey*)—Bob Thomas **2** *n* Anything inferior, stupid, or futile; =LEMON, LOSER: *For all ordinary purposes it was simply a turkey*—James M Cain/ *calling the bill a turkey...said it would send the wrong signal*—New York Times **3** *n* A stupid, ineffectual person; =JERK: *You'd be stuck with that turkey practically until he died*—D Larsen/ *They may be hawks (or turkeys), but when it comes to self-interest they're no fools*—Village Voice **4** *n underworld & teenagers* The victim of a mugging or street robbery: *On an average night, they...attacked eight victims or "turkeys," taking a total of about $300*—Time [fr the common and perhaps accurate perception of the *turkey* as a stupid creature, an avian loser]
See CAPE COD TURKEY, COLD TURKEY, DEEPSEA TURKEY, FULL OF SHIT, IRISH TURKEY, OLD TURKEY, TALK TURKEY

turkey-shoot *n phr* Something very easy; =CINCH, PIECE OF CAKE: *Getting a job is no turkey-shoot any more* [fr the marksmanship contests where *turkeys* are tied behind a log with their heads showing]

turn *See* TALK OUT OF TURN

turn someone **around** *v phr* To change someone's attitude, behavior, etc: *You fuck it up, that's turning me around*—Robert Stone

turn a trick *v phr* To do the sex act for profit; do one piece of work as a prostitute; =TRICK: *A chick might say she turned a trick with a cat who was too big*—Claude Brown/ *Many of the prostitutes were students, models, or would-be actresses who turned tricks part-time*—Washington Post

turn someone's **damper down** *v phr* To relieve someone's immediate sexual need; cause someone to cool: *I'm Sweet Papa Stovepipe, I'll turn your damper down*—blues song

turned off **1** *adj phr narcotics* No longer using narcotics; =CLEAN **2** *adj phr* Indifferent; bored **3** *adj phr* Tired; =FED UP

turned on **1** *adj phr esp narcotics fr late 1950s* Intoxicated, esp from narcotics; =HIGH: *I'm really turned on, man....I'm higher than a giraffe's toupee*—Stephen Longstreet **2** *adj phr* Stimulated; aroused; excited; switched on: *You are so sexualized, and so turned on*—Sexual Behavior **3** *adj phr* Aware and up-to-date; au courant; =HIP, PLUGGED IN: *flower children who flock to New York's turned-on Macdougal Street*—Trans-Action/ *an outlaw lobbyist, a turned-on Nader*—New York Times

turner *See* PAGE TURNER

turn in *v phr fr late 1600s* To go to bed; =HIT THE SACK

turnip *n fr early 1800s* A watch [fr the fact that an old-fashioned watch resembled a *turnip* in shape]

turnkey job *n phr* A good job that will not need to be done again; a definitive treatment: *Scott has given us something less than a turnkey job*—Chronicle of Higher Education [fr the phrase that *locks it up* "that ends it and achieves it definitively"]

turn off *v phr* To become indifferent; lose concern: *When he found he couldn't hack it, he just turned off*

turn-off *n* Something that damps one's spirits; a sexual or emotional depressant; = WET BLANKET: *The film is in fact a sexual turnoff*—Saturday Review/ *and when it happened it was some turn-off*—Xaviera Hollander

turn someone **off** *v phr fr 1950s beat talk* To depress someone; be a deterrent to someone's spirits: *It seems like everybody turns you off*—New York Times/ *Policies and practices that are not "relevant," to use his language, "turn him off"*—US News & World Report

turn off someone's **water** *See* CUT OFF someone's WATER

turn on *fr 1960s counterculture & narcotics* **1** *v phr* To use narcotics, esp to begin to do so: *Tune in, turn on, drop out*—Timothy Leary **2** *v phr* To take or inject narcotics: *Do you turn on with any of the local heads?*—Trans-Action

turn-on **1** Something that arouses and excites; a sexual or emotional stimulant: *which physical attributes of men are a turn-on for women*—Saturday Review/ *Reluctance is often a turn-on*—New York Times **2** *n* Excitement; ecstasy; elation: *He'd never felt a turn-on like that*

turn someone **on** **1** *v phr fr musicians & 1950s beat talk* To excite or stimulate someone; arouse someone: *The professor was trying to find out what turns women on* **2** *v phr fr beat talk* To introduce someone to something; pique someone's curiosity: *He turned me on to Zen*—Lawrence Lipton

turn on a dime *v phr* To be able to turn around in a very short radius: *That car corners very sweetly, and turns on a dime*

turn on the heat *v phr* To increase effort, pressure, activity, etc; = COME ON STRONG

turn on the waterworks *v phr fr middle 1800s* To weep; begin to cry; = BLUBBER: *I turned on the waterworks*—Paul Theroux

turnout **1** *n* An audience, the participants at a meeting, etc: *We always get a good turnout for the council sessions* **2** *n* Clothing; dress; = GET-UP, TOGS

turn someone **out** *v phr esp black* To introduce someone to something; initiate someone, esp to narcotics, sex, prostitution, etc

turnover **1** *n* Change or rate of change; replacement or rate of replacement: *There's not much turnover in higher education these days* **2** *n prison* The eve of one's release from prison: *He told me next Sunday was his turnover and I should meet him at the gate*

turn purple *v phr* To become very angry; become livid

turn thumbs down *v phr* To refuse, reject, or negate; = NIX: *The voters turned thumbs down to the change in zoning*

turn turtle *v phr* To turn upside down; capsize: *The big truck turned turtle right on the highway* [fr an equivocation on *turn*, with the sense of "rotate" and the sense of "become" both present; the thing that capsizes becomes like an unhappy *turtle* on its back]

turn someone **up** *v phr underworld* To inform; in effect, to turn someone over to the police: *Maybe you better turn me up*—WR Burnett/ *Somebody turned him up*—Raymond Chandler

turn up one's **toes** *v phr* To die

turpentine *See* UP THINE WITH TURPENTINE

turtle *n underworld* An armored car *See* TURN TURTLE

turtle doves *n phr* A pair of sweethearts

tush or **tushie** or **tushy** *See* TOKUS

tux *n* A tuxedo

TV *n* A transvestite: *TVs are not as feminine as they themselves think they are*—The Realist

◁**twat**▷ (TWAHT) **1** *n fr middle 1600s* The vulva; = CUNT **2** *n* A woman considered merely as a sex object or organ; = ASS, PIECE OF ASS

tweak *v computer* To adjust a computer program slightly; refine

twee *adj fr late 1800s British* Tiny; dainty; miniature; cute ● Chiefly British; the term is used especially to describe villages, thatched cottages, and other aspects of ye olde England as preserved: *no tiny, twee money to dole out*—Village Voice [fr *tweet*, a childish pronunciation of *sweet*]

tweeter *n fr 1950s* A small loudspeaker for the higher tones

twenty-five *n narcotics* LSD [fr the fact that 25 is part of its chemical designation]

twenty-one *lunch counter* **1** *n fr 1930s* An order of lemon- or limeade **2** *n* Two of an item for the same person or the same table

twenty-twenty (or **20-20**) **hindsight** *n phr* Perfect foresight of what has already been seen: *observers empowered with 20-20 hindsight wanted to know*—New York Times

twerp or **twirp** *n esp 1930s & 40s teenagers* A contemptible person; = JERK, NERD: *ill-mannered, foul-mouthed little twirp*—Westbrook Pegler/ *Wrangel may have been a pretentious twerp*—Saul Bellow

twiddle **1** *v computer* To change something in a small way; = TWEAK **2** *n* The tilde, a diacritical mark

twiddle one's **thumbs** *v phr* To waste time; be forced to sit idly: *I was anxious to help, but all I could do was twiddle my thumbs while they debated*

twink or **twinkie** or **twinky** **1** *n esp teenagers & homosexuals* A young, sexually attractive person; tempting teenager: *You know, the twink who used to be Fielding's lover*—Armistead Maupin/ *The Weemawee twinkies troop out to the kickoff line*—New York **2** *modifier: I found this gorgeous twink carpenter in the Mission*—Armistead Maupin **3** *n* A weird or deviant person, esp a homosexual; a social outcast: *They think "twinky" or sissy or something like that*—Washington Post **4** *adj: Quentin Crisp...croaks in a nasal monotone like a twinkie Mr Magoo*—Village Voice [origin, and indeed semantics, uncertain; perhaps related to *Twinkies* (a trade name), a sort of cupcake with a soft center, a favorite confection esp of young persons; the trade name may in turn be related to the rather nubile *Tinkerbelle* of *Peter Pan*, and to the *twinkling* of little stars; perhaps all senses are fr *twinkle-toes*, an arch name for a dainty, mincing person or ironically for an awkward dancer]

twin pots *hot rodders* **1** *n phr* Dual carburetors **2** *n phr* A car with dual carburetors

twirl *n underworld* A skeleton key or duplicate key

twist *n fr underworld* A young woman: *sexy little twist...but a kook*—Joseph Wambaugh/ *a tough, smart twist who got away with murder*—Lawrence Sanders [fr rhyming slang, US and not British, *twist and twirl* "girl," attested in a poem of EE Cummings]

the **twist** *n phr fr 1950s* A social or ballroom dance in which the pelvis and upper body are vigorously counterrotated

twist someone's **arm** *v phr* To induce or persuade someone very strongly; importune someone powerfully, as if by physical force: *You grab this opportunity to twist my arm*—Saul Bellow

twisted *adj narcotics* Very much intoxicated with narcotics; = HIGH: *twisted...that's when he's so high he doesn't know where the hell he is*—Clarence L Cooper

twister **1** *n fr late 1800s* A tornado **2** *n esp 1930s jive talk fr underworld* A key **3** *n* A spree; = BENDER: *their periods of sobriety between twisters*—Saturday Evening Post

See BRONCO BUSTER

twist slowly (or **twist**) **in the wind** *v phr* To suffer protracted humiliation, obloquy, regret, etc: *The second mistake was to let Sherrill twist slowly in the wind*—Washington Post/ *just letting you twist slowly, slowly in the wind*—New York Times [fr the gruesome image of a hanging body]

twisty *adj* Attractively feminine; = SEXY: *Most female doctors aren't as, uh...young. No, ah, say twisty might be more like it*—William Brashler

twit *n fr 1920s British* A contemptible and insignificant person; a trivial idiot ● Being very rapidly adopted, perhaps because of the popularity of the British comedy series "Monty Python's Flying Circus," on which the term is often employed: *Craig Stevens as her twit of a husband*—Village Voice/ *but tell me, you officious twit*—Leslie Hollander/ *I've got the authorization, you fucking twit*—Stephen King [origin unknown; perhaps a blend of *twat* with *twirp*; perhaps a shortening of *nitwit*]

two *See* FIFTY-TWO, NUMBER TWO, ONE-TWO

Two *See* TRACK TWO

two and a half *n phr lunch counter fr 1930s* A small glass of milk

two-and-a-half-striper *n Navy* A lieutenant commander

two-bagger **1** *n baseball* A two-base hit; a double **2** *n* A very ugly person; = DOUBLE-BAGGER: *two-bagger, a girl who needs exactly that to cover her ugliness*—Time

two-bit *adj fr middle 1800s* Cheap; tawdry; trivial; = TACKY: *the two-bit bureaucrats*—Billy Rose/ *Congressmen were panic-stricken, running around like two-bit whores*—Washingtonian [literally, worth only two bits]

two bits *n phr fr early 1700s* A quarter; twenty-five cents [fr the quarter part of a Mexican *real*, which had eight *bits*]

two-blink *adj* Very small, insignificant: *a two-blink town in soybean, cotton, and Elvis country*—Washington Post [something that has gone by, that is, before one can wink twice]

two-by-four *adj fr late 1800s* Small; insignificant; inferior; = TWO-BIT: *We stopped at a two-by-four hotel near the tracks*

two cents *See* PUT one's TWO CENTS IN

two cents' worth *n phr* A little; a trivial amount: *I'll give you two cents' worth of advice about that*

twofer (Tŏŏ fər) **1** *n* A cheap cigar **2** *n* A theater ticket sold at half the normal price [fr the phrase *two for*, in these cases *two for a nickel* and *two for the price of one*]

two hats *See* WEAR TWO HATS

two shakes or **two shakes of a lamb's tail** *n phr* A moment; a wink; = JIFFY: *Hold it, I'll just be two shakes*

two-spot *n* A two-dollar bill

two-step *See* AZTEC TWO-STEP

two-striper **1** *n Navy* A lieutenant, junior grade **2** *n Army* A corporal

two-time *v* To deceive and betray someone; esp, to betray one's proper sweetheart by consorting with someone else: *Two-Timing Boy Wrecks Girl's Dream*—New York Daily News [perhaps fr *two at a time*; perhaps fr *making time with two at once*]

two-time loser **1** *n phr underworld* A person who has been convicted twice, and therefore risks a higher sentence another time **2** *n phr* A person who has been divorced twice: *It does sound odd coming from a two-time loser*—Bob Thomas/ *Nora Ephron: funny two-time loser*—Time

two to tango *See* IT TAKES TWO TO TANGO

two ways *See* WORK BOTH WAYS

two-way street *n phr* A situation that cannot or should not be handled by only one person: *After all, Sam, keeping a marriage happy is a two-way street*

typewriter *n underworld fr WW1 armed forces* A machine gun, esp a submachine gun; = TOMMY GUN

tzuris *See* TSURIS

U

ugly *See* PLUG-UGLY

ultraswoopy *adj* Very spectacular; glamorously styled: *a down-sized, hitech, ultraswoopy model next year*—Car and Driver

umlaut *n* Half of a bottle of Löwenbräu (a trade name) beer: *Slick ordered four more umlauts for himself*—Dan Jenkins [two *umlauts* is a bottle, since the name has two diereses]

umpteen *modifier fr WW1* Of any large unspecified number: *exhausted all the encomia in your vocabulary on umpteen reviews*—Anthony Boucher [said to have been first used by British military signalers during World War 1 to disguise the number designations of units]

umpteenth *modifier fr WW1* The ordinal form of umpteen: *Here's the umpteenth development in the battle*—Associated Press

umpty *modifier fr WW1* Of an unspecified number of the decimal order: *the umpty-fifth regiment*—Bill Mauldin

umpty-umpth *modifier fr WW1* Of a large and unspecified ordinal number: *making the same speech for the umpty-umpth time*—Eleanor Roosevelt/ *the umpty-umpth revision*—Bennett Cerf

unc *n* Uncle

uncle 1 *n fr 1700s British* A pawnbroker **2** *n underworld* A receiver of stolen goods; = FENCE **3** *n underworld & narcotics* A federal narcotics agent; = NARC
See SAY UNCLE

Uncle Dudley *See* YOUR UNCLE DUDLEY

Uncle Sam 1 *n phr fr early 1800s* The US Government; the US as a nation **2** *n phr underworld* A federal agent or agency [said to have originated during the War of 1812 when Samuel Wilson of Troy, New York, locally known as *Uncle Sam*, stamped US on supplies he provided for the Government, and this was jocularly taken to be his own initials]

Uncle Sugar *n phr WW2 armed forces* The United States government; = UNCLE SAM [fr the military phonetic alphabet words for *U* and *S*]

Uncle Tom *n phr fr black* A black man who emulates or adopts the behavior of the white majority; a servile black man; = AFRO-SAXON, OREO [fr the title character of Harriet Beecher Stowe's novel *Uncle Tom's Cabin*, who was stigmatized as a dishonorably submissive black]

Uncle Tomahawk *n phr Native American* A Native American who emulates or adopts the behavior of the majority culture; a servile Native American

Uncle (or **Mister**) **Whiskers** *n phr esp underworld fr late 1920s* The federal government or one of its agents or agencies: *do we get our percent of the gross, but Charley said not with Mr Whiskers at the gate*—John O'Hara/ *You can't do business with Uncle Whiskers*—NY Confidential [fr the *bewhiskered* image of *Uncle Sam*]

uncool *adj fr cool talk* Not cool; wrong, excited, rude, etc

under *See* GET OUT FROM UNDER, HALF UNDER

under a cloud *adj phr* Suspect; dubious: *He has been somewhat under a cloud since they found the corpse in his closet*

under one's **belt** *adj phr* Successfully achieved or survived: *Get a couple more months' experience under your belt and we'll talk about a promotion*

underground 1 *adj fr 1960s counterculture* Apart from and opposed to conventional society; esp, advocating and representing the hippie and narcotics subculture: *The Voice started as a sort of underground newspaper* **2** *adj* In hiding; concealing one's identity and whereabouts, esp to escape arrest: *He escaped, and had to live underground for the next ten years*/ *Mengele was underground in Brazil a long while*
See GO UNDERGROUND

the underground *n phr esp WW2 & 1960s counterculture* Political or cultural dissenters collectively who lead a partly or wholly clandestine life and resist the dominant regime; also, their arena of life and operations ● This term first applied to the various resistance movements against German occupation in World War 2, and then was adopted by the 1960s counterculture, which saw the US government and culture as analogous with the Hitlerian: *Marc Bloch fought in the underground for several years, then was betrayed to the Gestapo*/ *Her daughter dropped out of college in 1964 and joined the Haight-Ashbury underground*

underground comic *See* HEAD COMIC

under one's **hat** *adj phr fr early 1900s* Secret; in confidence: *Here it is, but it's strictly under the hat, see?*—Joel Sayre

underpinnings *n fr middle 1800s* The legs; = GAMS, STEMS

under snow *See* NOVA UNDER SNOW ON A SLED

under the collar *See* HOT UNDER THE COLLAR

under the table 1 *adj phr* Very drunk: *After six vodka martinis I was under the table* **2** *adv phr* Illegal; secret and illicit; unethical: *He would never make any deals under the table* **3** *adj phr:* *What was the best under-the-table offer you got?*—Playboy

under the weather 1 *adj phr fr middle 1800s nautical* Not feeling well; ill **2** *adj phr* Drunk: *I'm a little under the weather*—Gene Fowler [probably fr the seasickness or lesser malaise felt at sea when the *weather* roughens]

underwear *See* LONG-HANDLE UNDERWEAR, LONG UNDERWEAR

underwhelm *v* To impress very little; be quite insignificant; be less than overwhelming: *Her performance rather underwhelmed the audience*

under wraps *adv phr* In secrecy; in obscurity: *We had better keep this under wraps for a while*

undies *n fr early 1900s* Underwear, esp women's panties: *a glimpse of her undies*—Morris Bishop *See* FUDGE one's PANTS

unflappable *adj fr WW2 Army Air Forces* Calm; imperturbable; cool: *They admired Mrs Thatcher's unflappable quality*

unglued *See* COME UNGLUED

ungodly shot *n phr baseball* A hard line drive: *A hard line drive is a blue darter, frozen rope, or an ungodly shot*—Jim Bouton

unhep or **unhipped** *adj fr 1930s jive talk* Conventional; unstylish; unimaginative: *faith, devotion, and other such unhep subjects*—Billy Rose

unisex *adj fr 1960s* Intended for or fitting for both sexes: *The unisex trend was launched by the era's pacesetters, the teenagers*—Life

unkjay *n narcotics* A narcotics addict; =JUNKIE: *He'd seen them coming in the rain, the unkjays*—Nelson Algren [pig Latin for *junk*]

unlax *v esp 1920s & 30s* To relax ● Often a piece of advice: *Just unlax for a while, and I'll find out* [a humorous version of *relax*, popularized by characters of the Amos and Andy radio program of the 1930s and 40s]

unmentionables *n fr early 1900s* Underwear; undergarments: *required to don upper and lower unmentionables*—Owen Johnson

uno *See* NUMERO UNO, TAKE CARE OF NUMERO UNO

un poco (ŌŌN POH KOH) *n phr* or *adv phr* A little; a small amount [fr Spanish or Italian]

unreal *adj fr beat talk & cool talk* Excellent; wonderful; =GREAT: *Like great. She's real unreal*—Harper's Bazaar

unstuck *See* COME UNGLUED

until one **is blue in the face** *See* TILL one IS BLUE IN THE FACE

untogether *fr black* **1** *adj* Ineffectual; confused; =SCREWED UP: *leading us to think you are so untogether that you want other blacks to go through the same thing*—Ebony **2** *adj* Not fashionable or stylish **3** *adj* Not smooth and effective socially

unzip 1 *v* To solve a problem in a methodical way; define and resolve **2** *v* To open: *Hey, unzip your mouth and say something*

up 1 *adj* Exhilarated; happy; hopeful: *I was feeling up. I thought it had been a very successful evening*—Lawrence Sanders **2** *adj* Encouraging; hopeful; =UPBEAT: *I don't like down movies, I like up movies*—New Yorker **3** *n* A source of excitement; a pleasurable thrill; =LIFT: *Her words gave me a huge up* **4** *v* To raise; increase: *My confidence has upped itself*—New York Post **5** *adj* Ready and effective; keyed up; in one's best form: *Obviously, Kennedy wanted to be "up" for the meeting*—Village Voice **6** *adj narcotics* Intoxicated by narcotics, esp amphetamines; =HIGH: *as it does when you're up on bennie*—Hubert Selby, Jr **7** *n narcotics* An amphetamine dose, capsule, etc; =UPPER: *Let's do some ups tonight* **8** *n* A blunder; =GOOF, FUCK-UP: *Joining that company was the biggest up of my life*

up against it *adj phr fr late 1800s* In a difficult situation; in serious trouble: *When they saw the gap they knew they were really up against it*

up against the wall *sentence esp 1960s counterculture fr black* Prepare to be humiliated, attacked, robbed, despised, etc; =GO FUCK oneself: *our commune motto, "Up against the wall, motherfuckers"*—James Simon Kunen/ *Up against the wall, IBM and General Electric and Xerox and Procter & Gamble and American Express*—Wall Street Journal [fr a line in a poem by Leroi Jones (Amiri Baraka), "Up against the wall, motherfuckers," fr the command of a holdup man to his victim, or of the police to a person being arrested, forcing him to immobilize himself by leaning forward arched with hands against a wall; probably influenced by the fact that people are executed by being shot against a wall]

up one's **alley** *See* DOWN one's ALLEY

up-and-coming *adj fr middle 1800s* Promising and energetic: *I gathered a few up-and-coming young writers for my staff*

up-and-down *n* A look; scrutiny: *The tray-toter gave me the slow up-and-down*—Billy Rose

up and up or **on the up and up** *adj phr fr middle 1800s* Honest; reliable; =STRAIGHT-UP: *It's an up and up place*—WR Burnett/ *I almost wonder if the whole bunch of 'em are on the up and up*—Sinclair Lewis

up a rope *See* GO PISS UP A ROPE

◁**up** one's **ass**▷ *See* SIT THERE WITH one's FINGER UP one's ASS, STICK IT

up a storm *adv phr* Very intensively; very diligently; very competently: *and they're really dancing up a storm*—Washingtonian/ *She spent the morning writing up a storm*

up a tree *adj phr fr early 1800s* In a predicament; faced with a dilemma; helpless

upbeat *adj* Optimistic; encouraging; positive: *They use catchy, upbeat phrases*—Saturday Review/ *A triumph of upbeat pictures over the downbeat*—Associated Press [apparently fr the musical term *upbeat* "a beat on which a conductor raises his baton," but since such beats have no emotional connotations, the coiner must have seized on the general positive notion of *up* and taken *beat* to mean "stroke, movement"]

upchuck *v fr 1920s* To vomit; throw up; =BARF, RALPH [fr *up* + *chuck* "throw"]

update 1 *v* To give, add, record, etc, the latest information: *He updated me on a couple of gimmicks*—John Crosby **2** *n*: *I'll give you a quick update* **3** *modifier*: *Is this the update material?*

up for grabs *fr black* **1** *adj phr* Available, esp newly available: *"High Haven," Luke repeated sonorously, "is up for grabs"*—John Le Carré/ *I got two doozies up for grabs*—Esquire **2** *adj phr* Problematical or undecided, esp newly so: *The whole question of one-man-one-vote is up for grabs again*

up front 1 *adv phr* (also **in front**) In advance; before any deductions: *His twin wasn't getting enough cash (something like $1,000) up front*—Pulpsmith/ *Don't pay your money up front*—Consumers Digest/ *Our firm would be glad to explain...but we first like to have ...a little something in front*—Newsweek **2** *adj phr* In the beginning; first; at once: *we knew right up front that if I did the film*—Rolling Stone **3** *adj phr* Honest; open; truthful: *very up-front about who she is and what she thinks*—J Nolan/ *"These people are not being up-front and honest," the Mayor said*—New York Times **4** *adj phr* In the forefront; on the firing line

up in the air *adj phr* Unsettled; undecided; uncertain: *When he left, the whole project was up in the air for a while*

up in the clouds *adj phr* Not alert and attentive; preoccupied with idealism, romance, etc: *can't keep his mind on business, always up in the clouds somewhere*

upmanship *See* ONE-UPMANSHIP

upmarket *adj* Appealing to or created for people to whom price is not important: *upmarket book/ upmarket store*

upper 1 *n narcotics* An amphetamine; a stimulant narcotic; =UP: *the effect of mixing "uppers" and "downers"*—New Republic/ *the frenzied accompaniment of bourbon, women, and uppers*—Terry Southern **2** *n* A source of excitement; a pleasurable thrill; =UP: *It may not be the same kind of thrill as winning a hand of poker at a casino, but it's definitely an upper*—Games

See PEPPER-UPPER, PICKER-UPPER, WARMER-UPPER, WINDER-UPPER

upper crust *See* THIN IN THE UPPER CRUST

the upper crust *n phr fr early 1800s* The social aristocracy; the elite

uppers *See* ON one's UPPERS, SHATTING ON one's UPPERS

upper story *n phr fr late 1700s* The brain; the mind: *definite shortcomings in the upper story*—D Nowinson

See LOOSE IN THE BEAN

uppity *adj fr late 1800s black* Conceited; arrogant; snobbish; =HINCTY ● Once used almost exclu-

sively of black people felt to be too self-assertive by the white speaker: *the most uppity colored fellow I ever ran into in my life*—Calder Willingham/ *to estimate if this reporter was going to give her any sass or put on any uppity airs*—Washington Post

See GET one's BALLS IN AN UPROAR

upscale *adj* Having to do with upper social and economic reaches; wealthy; aristocratic; =RITZY: *The killing...by Jean Harris was...an upscale crime*—Time

◁**up shit** (or **shit's**) **creek**▷ or **up the creek** *adj phr* (Variation: **without a paddle** may be added) In serious difficulty; very unfortunate; ruined: *If the cops see you you'll be up shit creek for sure/ Then you guys'll be up the creek for good*—Jerome Weidman [perhaps related to the early-19th-century term *up Salt River*, of much the same meaning, and which may refer to the Salt River in Kentucky, a legendary abode of violent and brutal people; but the term is attested in British armed forces use without US attribution fr the early 20th century]

upside or **upside of** *prep esp black* On the side of; in: *He got whacked upside the head with a board*—William Brashler

upside one's **face** *See* GO UPSIDE one's FACE

up one's **sleeve** *See* ACE UP one's SLEEVE

up-South *n black* The North, esp with respect to its racism

upstage 1 *v theater* To attract attention to oneself and away from other performers, esp by standing upstage so that they must look at you and turn their backs to the audience **2** *v* To demand and receive inordinate attention at the cost of others: *The secretary was trying to upstage the president on this, so he had to act at once* **3** *adj* Haughty; aloof; snobbish: *"Upstage" has taken on the additional meaning of "ritzy," that is, arrogantly proud and vain*—B Sobel

upstairs *adv* In the brain; mentally: *became a little balmy upstairs*—Hal Boyle

See KICK someone UPSTAIRS

up stakes *v phr fr middle 1800s* To leave, esp hurriedly; depart; =SCRAM

uptake *See* QUICK ON THE DRAW, SLOW ON THE DRAW

up the ante *v phr* To raise the price, offer, sum in question, etc; increase; make a higher demand: *I think I may up the ante to a cool fifty*—Pat Conroy/ *The trader decides to up the ante*—Philadelphia

◁**up the ass**▷ *adv phr* Thoroughly; perfectly well: *I know country music up the ass on the guitar*—Rolling Stone

up the flagpole *See* RUN something UP THE FLAGPOLE

up the kazoo (or **gazoo** or **gazool**) *adv phr* To a very great extent; in excess; =UP TO HERE: *I've got lawsuits up the gazool, which is one thing that disillusions me about writing*—Billy Joel/ *We're up the kazoo in leaflets here*

See KAZOO

up there *adv phr* In heaven

up the river *adv phr underworld fr 1930s* In prison [fr the fact that Ossining Correctional Facility, for-

merly called Sing Sing, is *up the Hudson River* from New York City]
See SEND UP

up the spout *adv phr* To waste; fruitlessly gone; = DOWN THE TUBE: *Fifty dollars tuition, all our plans...just gone up the spout*—Tennessee Williams/ *I'm afraid the project's up the spout*

up the wall *adj phr fr 1930s or earlier* Crazy; wild; = NUTTY: *It doesn't drive us crazy. At least, I don't know anybody who is up the wall about it*—Washingtonian [fr the image of insane persons, frantic and deprived drug addicts, wild animals, etc, trying to climb a wall, to escape]
See DRIVE someone UP THE WALL

◁**up thine with turpentine**▷ *interj* An exclamation of very strong defiance and rejection; = FUCK YOU, STICK IT

uptick 1 *n* A rise, esp in stock prices; an increase of value: *the strongest and broadest uptick in the history of the company*—Time/ *Another 10 percent uptick and you double up again*—Forbes **2** *n* Improvement; raising: *His apparent uptick in spirit was contagious*—Newsweek [fr the use, on boards above stock-market stations, of a plus sign (compare British *tick* "check mark") beside a stock of which the last sale represented a rise in price; a minus sign represents a *down tick*; probably influenced by the *tick*, like *click*, or *notch*, representing one degree of change; compare *ratchet up*]

uptight *adj fr 1960s counterculture fr black* Tense; anxious: *He was all uptight about student plagiarism*

up to one's **ass** *See* one HAS HAD IT

◁**up to** one's **ass in** something▷ *adj phr* (Variations: **in alligators** or **in rattlesnakes** may be added for emphasis; **asshole deep** may replace **up to** one's **ass**) Deeply involved; overwhelmed: *Every time I turn around we're up to our asses in something*—Leslie Hollander/ *Coldiron was up to his ass in cotton*—Tom Aldibrandi/ *Suddenly we were asshole deep in candidates for the deanship*/ *Call me later, I'm up to my ass in alligators here now*

up to one's **eyeballs** (or **eyebrows**) *adv phr* To a very great extent; totally; = UP TO HERE: *one smaller outfit...which is in farm equipment smack up to its corporate eyeballs*—Barron's

up to one's **eyebrows** *See* one HAS HAD IT

up to here 1 *adv phr* To the utmost; excessively ● Most often in the expression "I've had it up to here": *Look, my friend, I've had it up to here with your bitching* **2** *adj phr* Surfeited; disgusted; = FED UP: *I'm so up-to-here with the primaries and the TV news interviews*—Washington Post [fr the

notion of being fed to excess, fed up, and with the implicit gesture of indicating one's throat as the place up to which one has had it]
See one HAS HAD IT

up to scratch (or **the mark**) *adj phr fr prizefight* Satisfactory; acceptable; qualified: *I'm afraid this story isn't quite up to scratch* [fr the early custom of drawing a line across a boxing ring and requiring that the able and willing fighter stand with his toe touching the *mark* or *scratch-line*]

up to snuff 1 *adj phr fr early 1800s British* Satisfactory; acceptable; = UP TO SCRATCH: *His work doesn't come anywhere near up to snuff* **2** *adj phr* In good health; feeling well: *I don't feel quite up to snuff this morning* [origin uncertain; the original British sense was "shrewd, not gullible," apparently referring to the fact that one could be blinded with *snuff* in the eyes, and victimized; the early-19th-century US phrases *in high* (or *great*) *snuff* "in good form, high fettle, etc," perhaps having to do with *snuff* as an aristocratic commodity and symbol, may also be related]

up to speed *See* BRING someone UP TO SPEED

up to the wire *See* COME UP TO THE WIRE

uptown *n narcotics* Cocaine; = the LADY [fr the aristocratic and wealthy overtones of cocaine as compared with other narcotics, fr the earlier sense of *uptown* "affluent, swanky," as distinct fr *downtown*; the topography and demography of Manhattan Island underlies these senses]
See the BOYS UPTOWN

◁**up yours**▷ *interj* (Variations: **you** or **your ass** or **your butt** or **your gig** or **your giggy** or any other synonym of **ass** may replace **yours**) *fr late 1800s* An exclamation of strong defiance, contempt, rejection, etc: *Up yours, sister, he thought tardily as the barbs quivered home*—WT Tyler ● A shortening of **stick it up your ass**

use *v narcotics* To use narcotics; take a dose or injection of a narcotic: *I used this morning and I'm still nice*—Clarence Cooper

use one's **head** (or one's **bean**) *v phr* To think; reason out one's actions: *teaches a man to use his head and to do the best he can*—Hal Boyle/ *You certainly used the old bean*—P Marks

user *n narcotics* A person who uses narcotics, esp an addict

ush *v* To be an usher: *the rancid troglodytes who ush at the Knicks' games*—Playboy

usual *See* AS PER USUAL

UVs (Yoō VEEZ) *n teenagers* Sunshine; ultraviolet light or rays; = RAYS [fr *ultraviolet*]

V

vacation *n underworld* A prison sentence: *who won a 20 years' vacation in the Big House*—E Lavine

vag (VAYG) **1** *n fr 1600s* A drifter; derelict; vagrant; vagabond; =BAG LADY: *America can almost compete with England in the number of her "city vags"*—J Flynt **2** *n police fr late 1800s* Vagrancy, as a legal offense: *We'll book him on vag*—Asphalt Jungle (movie)

vamoose or **vamose** (va M⁻OS) *v fr middle 1800s Southwestern* To leave; depart, esp hastily; =LAM, SCRAM, SPLIT: *We better vamoose, Moose* [fr Spanish *vamos* "let us depart"]

vamp¹ *v musicians fr middle 1800s* To improvise, esp an accompaniment; play casually and extemporaneously; =FAKE, SHUCK [probably fr 16th-century *vamp* "provide with a new (shoe) vamp, renovate," ultimately fr conjectured Anglo-French *vampé* fr Old French *avant-pié* "foot-sock"; a refooted sock or a *revamped* shoe were felt to be in a way false, or improvised, hence the sense of "fake"]

vamp² **1** *n fr early 1900s* A seductive, sexually aggressive woman; a temptress: *The flirt had become the "baby vamp"*—F Scott Fitzgerald **2** *v: She's vamping you, Harold*—P Marks/ *I haven't tried to vamp Sam*—Elmer Rice [fr *vampire*, and esp fr the 1914 movie *A Fool There Was*, in which Theda Bara played a seductive woman, the title and concept coming fr Rudyard Kipling's poem "The Vampire"]

vamp³ *n esp Long Island, New York, fr middle 1800s* A volunteer firefighter [origin unknown; said to be fr *Voluntary Association of Master Pumpers*]

vamp⁴ or **vamp on** **1** *v or v phr esp black* To assault; trounce; =BEAT UP, CLOBBER: *They knew that he'd vamp on them if they got wrong*—Bobby Seale/ *So we went for them and vamped on them*—New York Times/ *Chairman, chairman wake up, the Pigs are vampin'*—New York Times **2** *v or v phr fr black* To arrest; =BUST [perhaps related to black English *vamp* someone "come at someone suddenly and aggressively"; probably fr *vamp²* reinforced by the murderous aggression of Count Dracula, a genuine and popular *vampire* in Bram Stoker's novel and the movies made from it]

van **1** *n railroad* A caboose **2** *n lunch counter* Vanilla ice cream

vanilla **1** *n black* A white person, esp a white woman **2** *n* A person of ordinary and normal sexual preferences; a usual heterosexual; =STRAIGHT: *They called women who did not proclaim joy at being chained to the bedposts or chaining someone else "vanilla"*—Village Voice **3** *adj: As a self-confessed vanilla-sexual*—Village Voice [fr the white color and the perhaps unimaginative choice of *vanilla* ice cream]
See PLAIN VANILLA

vanner *n* A person who drives a van, esp as a symbol of a somewhat alienated and independent social attitude: *A vanner is tough to put your finger on...some are former bikers*—US News & World Report

varnish *See* COFFIN VARNISH

varnish remover *n phr* Raw and inferior whiskey; =PANTHER PISS
See PAINT REMOVER

varoom *See* VROOM

Vatican roulette *n phr* The rhythm method of birth control

va-voom or **va-va-voom** **1** *interj* An exclamation of delight, esp of excited sexual interest **2** *adj* (also **voomy**): *fressing the tits of this va-va-voom sophomore and shtupping her pussy*—National Lampoon/ *Under that icky mask, I think you're the voomiest*—Spiderman (comic strip) [probably fr *vroom* and *varoom*]

VC *n fr Vietnam War armed forces* The Vietcong or a member of the Vietcong; =VICTOR CHARLIE [fr *Vietcong*]

veeno *See* VINO

veep *n fr 1940s* A vice president: *Veep Fresco Thomas, Coach Jake Pitler, and Dressen*—Associated Press [fr pronunciation of *vp*]

veg¹ (VEJ) **1** *n fr late 1800s British* A vegetable **2** *n* =VEGETABLE

veg² (VEJ) *v* (also **vedge** or **veg out**) *college students* To relax luxuriously and do nothing; vegetate; =GOOF OFF, MELLOW OUT [fr *vegetate*]

vegetable *n* A person lacking normal senses, responses, intelligence, etc; =BASKET CASE, RETARD: *He was fine the first couple of years of marriage, but then he turned into a vegetable*

vegetable patch *See* FRUIT SALAD

veggies or **vegies** *n* Vegetables

veggy **1** *n* A vegetarian **2** *adj: a veggy pal of ours*

vein *See* JAB A VEIN

velvet *n fr late 1800s* Profit, esp an easy and unexpected profit; gambler's winnings; money in general: *There are substantial money returns, "velvet,"...for those who secure places*—Oskar von Engeln

See BEGGAR'S VELVET, BLUE VELVET, ON VELVET

vent *n show business* A ventriloquist

vent man *n phr* A homeless drifter who typically sleeps on the warm sidewalk air-vents from subways and other underground places: *There are the bag ladies and the vent men*—Philadelphia

verbal (or **oral**) **diarrhea** *n phr* (also **diarrhea of the mouth**) Logorrhea; uncontrollable loquaciousness: *You've got verbal diarrhea*—Calder Willingham

Vermont charity *n phr hoboes fr early 1900s* Sympathy, only

verse *n sports* = STANZA

See CHAPTER AND VERSE

vest **See** PLAY CLOSE TO THE VEST

vet¹ **1** *n* A veteran, esp a former member of the armed forces: *I'm a combat vet*—Nelson Algren **2** *modifier:* *the vet producer of scouting plays*—Esquire

vet² **1** *n* A veterinarian **2** *modifier* Veterinary: *the vet school* **3** *v fr early 1900s British* To examine closely; scrutinize critically: *Random House plans a review of its procedures for "vetting" or checking a book prior to publication*—Washington Post/ *The hosts are a carefully vetted collection of bubble brains*—Time [third sense fr the close examination of an animal by a *veterinarian*]

vette or **'vette** *n* A Corvette (a trade name) car

V-girl *n WW2* A woman who more or less freely made love to soldiers, sailors, etc, from patriotic motives [fr Victory *girl*]

vibes¹ *n jazz musicians* A vibraphone or vibraharp

vibes² or **vibrations** *n esp 1960s counterculture* What emanates from or inheres in a person, situation, place, etc, and is sensed; = CHEMISTRY, KARMA: *The vibes were good that morning for our reunion*—Saturday Review

vic¹ *n underworld* A convict

vic² *n* A phonograph; Victrola (a trade name)

vic³ **1** *n New York City teenagers* A victim; = MARK, PATSY **2** *v* (also **scope a vic**) To look for someone to rob, mug, etc

vicious *adj teenager* Excellent; superb; wonderfully attractive

Victor Charlie *n phr Vietnam War armed forces* Vietcong; = VC [fr the military phonetic alphabet words for *V* and *C*]

vidaholic *n* An addict of television: *a lifelong vidaholic, the 33-year-old Simmons*—Newsweek [fr video + -aholic]

video jock or **VJ** *n phr* A television performer who plays and comments on music videos

Vietnik **1** *n 1960s & 70s* A person who actively protested US military involvement in Vietnam **2** *modifier:* *the latest Vietnik demonstration*—Time

vig or **vigorish** or **viggerish** *n fr gambling* Profits of a bookmaker, a usurer, a criminal conspirator, a casino, etc: *I'm not nailing you no vig for last week*—George V Higgins/ *About 180 percent a year in interest, known in the trade as vigorish, vig, or juice*

—Wall Street Journal/ *The Vig? Seventy-five percent plus my fourteen-year-old sister*—Richard Price [probably fr Yiddish fr Russian *vyigrysh* "profit, winnings"]

vig ounce *n phr narcotics* An ounce of narcotics

-ville **See** -SVILLE

vin (or **vinegar**) **blink** *n phr fr WW1 armed forces & hoboes* White wine [fr a mispronunciation of French *vin blanc* "white wine"]

vinegar **See** FULL OF PISS AND VINEGAR

vines *n fr 1930s jive talk* Clothing; a suit, esp a stylish one; = THREADS [fr earlier prison *vine* "civilian clothes, nonprison clothes"; perhaps fr a semantic extension of *weeds* "clothing"]

vino or **veeno** (VEE noh) *n* Wine, esp red jug wine [fr Italian, "wine"]

vinyl **1** *n* Phonograph records; recording: *Now this disco graffiti has found its way to vinyl and created quite a bit of excitement*—Variety **2** *modifier:* *woman who rides the vinyl grooves*—New York Daily News **3** *modifier* Having to do with discotheques, the dancing done there, etc: *The only vinyl junkies were the nattily-suited variety*—Circus [fr the chemical material used for phonograph records, semantically analogous with earlier *wax*]

VIP (pronounced as separate letters) *n fr WW2* A very important person; = BIG SHOT

viper *n narcotics fr 1930s* A marijuana dealer or user

vis (VIZ) *n Army* Visibility: *It's a job with big vis*

vision **See** TUNNEL VISION

visiting fireman *n phr* An out-of-town visitor, esp a dignitary: *He meets a good many distinguished visiting firemen*—New Yorker [fr the earlier sense *fireman* or *fire maker* "a Native American ceremonial dignitary who was responsible for lighting the fires"]

vita (VEE də) *n* (also **vita sheet**) A curriculum vitae or brief biography, esp of education and work; resumé [fr *curriculum vitae*]

VJ **See** VIDEO JOCK

volume¹ *n* A dose or capsule of Valium (a trade name), a tranquilizer: *I'd take maybe five volumes in the morning*—New York Times

volume² **See** DECREASE THE VOLUME

vomity or **vomitrocious** *adj* So nasty as to cause one to vomit: *Gross and even grossening are out. Vomitrocious is in*—George F Will [longer form fr vomit + (a)trocious]

voomy **See** VA-VOOM

vote with one's **feet** *v phr* To escape; become a refugee or emigrant: *Nearly three million people voted with their feet*—New York Times

vroom or **varoom** **1** *n* The noise of a powerful car **2** *modifier* (also **vroom-vroom**): *if you drive a sporty, vroom-vroom model*—Washingtonian **3** *v* To speed, esp in a roaring car: *as we vroomed up and down the Watchung Mountains*—Esquire/ *He would presumably be vrooming a Porsche through the streets of Bel-Air*—Richard Schickel

VW radiators **See** A LOAD OF VW RADIATORS

W

wack or **whack** *n fr 1940s* A crazy or eccentric person; =NUT, SCREWBALL, WEIRDO: *two wacks if I ever saw one*—John O'Hara/ *a father who was so abrasive and married now to such a wack*—Joseph Heller [see *wacky*]

wack off *See* WHACK OFF

wacky or **whacky** *adj* (also **wacked-out** or **wacko**) Crazy; eccentric; =NUTTY, WEIRD: *You think I'm going wacky?*—John O'Hara/ *annually collects whacky accidents*—NEA Service/ *the most wacked-out cop game anybody had ever seen any cops play*—Tom Wolfe/ *the wacked-out hustler who talks Winkler into running a call-girl service out of the morgue*—People [fr British dialect *whacky* "fool," attested fr the early 20th century; *whacky* "a person who fools around," is attested in British tailors' talk fr the late 19th century; perhaps fr being *whacked* over the head too often; perhaps influenced by *whack off* "masturbate," and semantically akin to *jerk*]

-wacky *combining word* =CRAZY, NUTTY: *car-wacky/ chick-wacky*

wad *n fr early 1800s* A roll of money: *My grandmother'd just sent me this wad about a week before*—JD Salinger

See SHOOT one's LOAD, SHOOT one's WAD

wader *See* HIGH WATERS

waffle¹ **1** *v* *fr British fr late 1800s* To speak or behave evasively; tergiversate; equivocate: *When asked for specifics, I demur, I waffle*—New York/ *unlike the windy, waffling, anonymous editorial writers*—Philadelphia **2** *n*: *I was tired of all the candidates' waffle* [fr northern British dialect, "fluctuate," probably by way of late-19th-century British printers' talk, "incessant and copious chat"; perhaps influenced by US *whiffling* "using shifts and evasions, wavering," attested from 1865]

waffle² *v* To trample viciously; =STOMP: *No player called out at second threatened to waffle an umpire*—Philadelphia Daily News

waffle-iron *n* A sidewalk grating

waffle-stompers *n* Heavy hiking boots; =SHITKICKERS [fr the pattern of the soles, which make a *wafflelike* print]

wag *See* CHIN-WAG

wag one's **chin** *v phr* To talk: *to be seen waggin' your chin with a sleuth*—Dashiell Hammett

wagon *n Navy fr WW1* A naval vessel

See BEAN WAGON, BUTCHER WAGON, BUZZ-BUGGY, CHUCK WAGON, CLOWN WAGON, COVERED WAGON, DEAD WAGON, DOG-WAGON, FALL OFF THE WAGON, FIX someone's WAGON, FRUIT WAGON, GLORY WAGON, HONEY WAGON, MEAT WAGON, MILK WAGON, MONKEY-HOUSE, OFF THE WAGON, ON THE WAGON, PADDY WAGON, PIE WAGON, RAPE WAGON, RUBBERNECK WAGON, SEX WAGON, TUNA WAGON

Wahoo *n Navy* Hawaii [fr *Oahu*, the principal island]

wah-wah **1** *n musicians* A pronounced wavering, scooping sound from an instrument, the voice, etc: *imitations of animal sounds...such as wah-wahs on trumpets and trombones*—A Lomax/ *Then Wah-Wah Waddy breaks into his best funkadelic solo*—Village Voice **2** *n* A pedal-operated electronic device for producing wah-wahs, esp on electric guitars: *the same kind of highly-perfected control over use of the wah-wah, distortion, and amplifier*—Peter Occhiogrosso **3** *modifier*: *By passing his vocal sounds through an amplifier with the aid of a wah-wah pedal, he has achieved spectacular effects*—Ebony [echoic; interestingly similar to Chinook jargon *wawa* "speech, talk," and to Cree *wawa*, an echoic name for the snow goose, Canada goose, and gray goose]

wail **1** *v jazz musicians fr 1930s* To play jazz well and feelingly: *We were wailing but nobody had a tape machine*—Nat Hentoff **2** *v college students fr cool talk fr jazz musicians* To do very well; perform well **3** *v black* To sing [fr the notion of a well-performed blues number, with its melodious lamentations]

wailing or **whaling** *adj esp black students* Excellent; wonderful; =GREAT

waist *See* PANTYWAIST

wait up *v phr* To pause, when well ahead, for someone to overtake one ● Often a panting request

walk *underworld & prison* **1** *v* To be released from prison **2** *v* To be acquitted of or otherwise freed from a criminal indictment: *Actually, I'm gonna cop a plea. A $15 fine and I'll walk*—New York Times

See FRENCH WALK, LET IT WALK, TAKE A WALK, WIN IN A WALK

walk and chew gum at the same time *See* NOT HAVE BRAINS ENOUGH TO COME IN OUT OF THE RAIN

walkaway *See* WALKOVER

walkboy *n black* A good male friend; =HOME BOY: *to groove on emotional intersubjectivication with a woman more than you groove on hanging with your walkboys*—Village Voice

walker *See* HOT WALKER

walk heavy *v phr fr black* To be important and influential; =have CLOUT

walkie-talkie *n fr WW2 Army* A small and portable radio transmitter and receiver

the **walk-in** *n phr theater* The half hour before a Broadway theater curtain goes up

walking papers (or **ticket**) *n phr fr early 1800s* A dismissal or discharge; esp, a rejection; =PINK SLIP: *Two baseball veterans got their walking papers today*—Associated Press *See* GIVE someone HIS WALKING PAPERS

walking wounded *n phr* Persons who are injured, esp in a psychological or spiritual way, but still functional; depressed people [fr a military medical term for a *wounded* person who is ambulatory]

walk-on *n fr theater* A very minor, usu nonspeaking, role; an insignificant or minimal sort of participation

walk on eggs *v phr* To proceed very carefully; go gingerly and warily: *I always feel as if I'm walking on eggs around her*

walkout *n* A strike: *There's a walkout at the supermarkets right now*

walk out on someone or something *v phr* To abandon; =TAKE A WALK: *She was fed up, and just walked out on the whole deal*

walkover or **walkaway** *n* An easy victory; =CINCH, PUSHOVER: *It looked like a walkover for Clarence*—H McHugh/ *The odds were on the Redskins in a walkaway*

walk soft *v phr black* To behave quietly and peacefully; be modest: *I told him he was acting like an ass, and he walks a lot softer now*—Eugene E Landy

walk Spanish *See* FRENCH WALK

walk tall *v phr* To be brave and honest; be upright and proud: *Take the 89G. Run....Walk tall, turn it in*—New York Daily News

walk the plank *v phr* To be dismissed; =be FIRED: *Rostow's Deputy Walks the Plank; Rostow Hangs In*—New York Times [fr the pirate practice of forcing unwanted persons to *walk* out on a *plank* and plunge into the sea]

walk-up *n* A room, apartment, building, etc, without an elevator: *second-floor walk-ups above stores*—Raymond Chandler

wall *See* BALLS TO THE WALL, BOUNCE OFF THE WALLS, CLIMB THE WALL, DRIVE someone UP THE WALL, GO TO THE WALL, HOLE IN THE WALL, NAIL someone TO THE CROSS, OFF THE WALL, PING OFF THE WALLS, UP AGAINST THE WALL, UP THE WALL

wall banger *n phr teenagers & narcotics* A dose or capsule of Quaalude (a trade name) or methaqualone; =LUDE: *called wall bangers by the kids*—Albert Goldman

wall-eyed *adj* Drunk

wallflower *n fr early 1900s* A person, esp a woman, who is peripheral and uncourted at a dance, party, etc: *the homely and ugly girls who were called wall-flowers*—James T Farrell

wallop 1 *n* A hard blow; a severe and resounding stroke: *She gave him a wallop on the chin* **2** *v*: *He walloped the ball right over the wall* **3** *n fr early 1800s British* Power; =CLOUT, MOXIE: *She'd be good if she had a little more wallop* [fr British dialect, "beat, thrash," apparently fr *gallop*] *See* CIRCUIT BLOW

walloper *See* DOCK-WALLOPER, POT-WALLOPER

wallpaper *n* Worthless monetary paper such as counterfeit bills, invalid securities, and the like

wall-to-wall *adj* Total; all-encompassing: *a wall-to-wall nightmare in which society dissolves*—S Kanfer/ *wall-to-wall hookers, niggers, and junkies*—WT Tyler/ *It was wall-to-wall people*—Time [fr the phrase *wall-to-wall carpeting*]

walrus *n fr 1920s* A short, fat person

walsy *See* PALSY-WALSY

Walter Mitty *n phr* An unimpressive person who regularly has daydreams of glory: *Walter Cronkite is a Walter Mitty in reverse*—Playboy [fr the title character in "The Secret Life of Walter Mitty," a story by James Thurber]

waltz 1 *n prizefight* A single round of a fight; =CANTO, STANZA **2** *v prizefight* To box and spar lightly and unseriously **3** *n* Something easily accomplished; =CINCH, PIECE OF CAKE

waltz someone **around** *v phr* To evade or deceive: *He kept waltzing me around but he never gave me a direct answer*

walyo or **Wally-O** (WAHL yoh) **1** *n* A young man; =GUY ● Like **goombah**, used in affectionate address, often by an older man to a younger: *how the walyo had kept his muscles so finely tuned on health food*—Paul Sann **2** *n* An Italian or a male of Italian descent: *Did you hear how the Wally-Os stole a ballot box in the Fifth Ward?*—William Kennedy [fr Italian dialect *uaglio* or *uaiu* pronounced wah Yōō, meaning something like "young squirt," but nearly always used affectionately; perhaps cognate with French *voyou* "street bum, urchin," fr *voie* "street, road"; perhaps related to mid-19th-century *Whyo* "member of a New York criminal gang"; possibly the source of earlier *wally* "dude, fop, novice at gambling"]

wampum *n* Money; cash; =BREAD [short for Algonquin *wampumpeag* "beads made from quahog shells and used as money"]

◁ **wang** or **whang** or **whanger** ▷ *n fr early 1900s* The penis; =COCK, PRICK: *I can see your whang. Your dong is visible*—William Goldman/ *a trigger that was bigger than an elephant's proboscis or the whanger of a whale*—John Steinbeck [origin uncertain; perhaps fr late-19th-century British *whanger* "something extraordinarily large and admirable," fr dialect *whang* "beat, hit," in the same semantic pattern as terms like *whacking, socko* and others where the power to hit is equated with impressive merit; the penis as the sexual instrument is of course thought of as *banging* a woman, or *socking it to her*] *See* PULL one's PUD

wangdoodle *See* WHANGDOODLE

wangle 1 *v fr late 1800s British* To get or arrange by shrewd maneuvering; contrive cunningly: *President Truman has given Ching a free hand in trying to wangle agreements*—Associated Press **2** *n: made a precise science out of the wangle*--H Allen Smith [origin unknown; perhaps a form of *waggle* "overcome, get the better of"]

wanker *n chiefly British fr late 1800s* A masturbator, either literally or figuratively; = JERK-OFF: *There I was, this clubfooted wanker sitting on the organ seat*—Playboy/ *all manner of artsy bubbleheads and academic wankers*—Village Voice [perhaps fr British dialect *wank* "a violent blow," and semantically analogous with *beat one's meat, whack off,* etc]

wank off *v phr chiefly British fr late 1800s* To masturbate

want list *See* WISH LIST

war *See* HOT WAR, PSYWAR, SHOOTING WAR

war club *n phr* A baseball bat

ward heeler *n phr fr late 1800s* A low-ranking associate or flunky of a political boss; a menial crony [fr *heeler* "one who follows obediently at the heels of another"]

warhorse *n fr late 1800s* A seasoned and reliable veteran; a grizzled doyen

warm body *n phr* A person regarded as merely such, without individual qualities, virtues, vices, etc; an animate person who occupies space; = CHAIR-WARMER: *Why come to these lectures if you're only going to be a warm body to sit at this desk*

warm someone's **ear** *v phr* To talk insistently and passionately to someone, esp about scandals and the like

warmed over *adj phr fr late 1800s* Derivative and only slightly changed; revived unimaginatively: *The president, he wrote, had "offered the poor the Protestant Ethic warmed over"*—Daniel Patrick Moynihan/ *out of the mouths of bunnies and gulls, some warmed-over Gibran*—Irving Kolodin

See LOOK LIKE DEATH WARMED OVER

warmer *See* BENCH WARMER, CHAIR-WARMER

warmer-upper *n* Something that warms: *wonderful warmer-upper, four-button coat sweater*—New York Herald Tribune/ *Now try it as a warmer-upper*—Saturday Evening Post

warm fuzzy *n phr* A compliment; a word of praise; also, such praise collectively; = STROKE: *You need some warm fuzzy*—Time [probably fr the notion of a snuggling small animal, like Charles Schulz's *warm puppy*]

warm spit *See* WORTH A BUCKET OF WARM SPIT

warm up *v phr* To do exercises and preparatory maneuvers before some activity, esp some sports effort

warm someone **up** *v phr* To induce a receptive and approving attitude in someone, esp by joking and cajoling: *The second banana warmed the audience up before the star appeared*

Warner *See* MARY WARNER

warp *See* TIME WARP

war paint *n phr fr middle 1800s* Cosmetics

warp factor *n phr* A very large factor of multiplication; a high exponent: *We feel it won't increase by warp factor five, either*—Toronto Life [fr the notion of *warp speed*, a velocity greater than the speed of light, popularized in science fiction and especially by the TV series Star Trek; it is necessary to imagine such enormous speeds in order to keep fictional cosmic travel more or less in the realm of the humanly compassable; see *time warp*]

warp out *v phr* To move, esp to leave, very rapidly; = CUT OUT

warrant *See* the DEATH WARRANT

warrior *See* SUNDAY SOLDIER

wart *n* A flaw; an imperfection: *The new format has some warts, but no integrity warts*—Philadelphia Journal

See WORRY WART

warts and all *n phr* The accurate totality of someone or something, including the imperfections: *Audiences hearing the local orchestra week after week hear it with warts and all*—Village Voice/ *Your friends see Doherty, warts and all*—George V Higgins/ *I think it showed Lyndon Johnson, warts and all*—Washington Post [fr the putative remark of Oliver Cromwell to his portraitist Peter Lely: "Remark all these roughnesses, pimples, warts, and everything as you see me"]

was *See* NEVER-WAS

wash 1 *n* A drink to follow another, to wash it down; = CHASER: *what for a wash?*—Richard Bissell **2** *v fr middle 1800s British* To prove valid; bear testing ● Usually in the negative: *Well, it just won't wash*—Atlantic/ *The stereotype of gay males as child molesters just doesn't wash any more*—Village Voice/ *That washes. I'll buy it*—Lawrence Sanders **3** *n* An elaborate justification; = WHITEWASH: *It looked like a wash to me*—George V Higgins **4** *n* A balance between opposing values, cases, effects, etc; a moot situation; = STANDOFF, a TOSS-UP: *The net effect of the medical testimony was a wash*—Legal Times/ *I'd have to go to bed at the same time as my 6-year-old. So it's pretty much a wash*—Philadelphia Journal/ *the Ferraro factor. Was it a political plus, a minus, a wash?*—Washington Post [final sense perhaps fr the notion that equal opposing elements *wash* each other out or away, or *scrub the slate clean*]

See HANG OUT THE WASH, WHITEWASH

wash (or **air**) one's **dirty linen** *v phr* (Variation: **in public** may be added) To talk or argue about intimate matters in public

washed up or **all washed up** *adj phr* No longer valid or active as a performer, competitor, worker, etc; = AUSGESPIELT, FINISHED: *I'm all washed up*—Ben Hecht & Charles MacArthur/ *Borden is all washed up*—G Homes [fr the notion of *washing up* one's hands at the finish of a job or a day's work]

washout 1 *n fr early 1900s British* A failure; a total fiasco; = FLOP: *I'm afraid our big birthday bash was a washout* **2** *n aviators* A crash landing **3** *n fr WW1* A student pilot or aviation cadet who fails to complete the course and become a qualified pilot: *the major cause for the large number of "washouts"*—New York Times [origin unknown; perhaps fr the damage done by strong erosion; perhaps fr the 19th-century British military practice of indicating a marksman's hits on iron targets with a paint or *wash*, so that a *wash out* would be nowhere near the bullseye; perhaps fr the notion of a party or picnic ruined, *washed out*, by a storm]

wash out 1 *v phr fr WW1* To fail, esp to fail to finish a pilot-training course and be qualified: *Then I was washed out on a slight technicality*—Max Shulman **2** *v phr* To eliminate or cancel; = SCRATCH, SCRUB **3** *v phr fr early 1900s* To lose all one's money; = TAP OUT: *hustlers who really knew how to gamble. I always got washed out*—Louis Armstrong

WASP or **wasp 1** *n fr black* A person of nonminority or nonethnic background, ancestry, etc, as conceived in the United States; a White Anglo-Saxon Protestant: *The Republican Party is run largely by "wasps"*—Stewart Alsop **2** *adj: Westchester and Darien and places like that, WASP country*—New York Herald Tribune [said to have been coined by the Philadelphia author E Digby Baltzell]

waspish *adj* Dominated by and characteristic of WASPs: *This town is naughty and waspish and expensive*—Village Voice

waste 1 *v teenagers fr 1950s street gang* To defeat utterly; trounce; = CLOBBER **2** *v fr 1960s counterculture* To wreck; destroy; mutilate; = TRASH **3** *v fr black* To kill; = BLOW someone AWAY, TAKE someone or something OUT

wasted 1 *adj fr 1950s cool talk* Penniless; = BROKE **2** *adj narcotics & cool talk* Intoxicated by narcotics; = STRUNG OUT: *Everybody was getting kind of high on acid, wasted, in fact*—Tom Wolfe **3** *adj* Wrecked; ruined; destroyed: *Like, I'm wasted...I can't lose no more*—Claude Brown

wasting *See* TIME'S A'WASTING

watch *See* GRAVEYARD WATCH, ON someone's WATCH

watcher *See* CLOCK-WATCHER

watch one's **mouth** *v phr* To be careful of what one says, esp to stop being provocative, obscene, presumptuous, etc ● Often an irritated command: *Just watch your mouth, Buster*

watch my lips 1 *sentence Army* Listen very carefully to me **2** *sentence* Do you read lips? ● Second sense is a euphemism for a silently-spoken obscenity or insult

water *See* BLOW OUT OF THE WATER, COME HELL or HIGH WATER, CUT OFF someone's WATER, DEAD IN THE WATER, FIREWATER, FIZZ-WATER, HIGH WATERS, HOLD one's WATER, HOT WATER, IN DEEP WATER, IN HOT WATER, JERKWATER, LONG DRINK OF WATER, ON THE WAGON, SUCK CANAL WATER

waterfront *See* COVER THE WATERFRONT

Watergate 1 *n* A scandal usu involving corruption **2** *v* To find and publicize, or at least to publicize, instances of corruption: *The news media have been Watergating the Department pretty good*—CBS Television [fr the name of the Washington building complex where Democratic headquarters were burglarized in 1972, an act that led finally to the resignation of Richard M. Nixon as President of the US]

waterhole or **watering hole** *n* or *n phr* A bar; a saloon; a drinking place: *That place is the waterhole of choice for aspiring actors/ a posh watering hole on Madison Avenue*

watermelon seed *See* SWALLOW A WATERMELON SEED

water wagon *See* ON THE WAGON

waterworks *See* TURN ON THE WATERWORKS

wavelength *See* ON THE SAME WAVELENGTH

wave-maker *n* A person who raises questions, imposes difficulties and objections, etc: *said that he is a wave-maker whose troubles arose from his insistence on injecting moral values*—Philadelphia Journal

waver *See* FLAG-WAVER, SKIVVY-WAVER

wax 1 *v fr late 1800s* To defeat; outdo; = BEAT, CLOBBER, ZAP **2** *v* To assault and maul; injure or kill: *I've always got a few bucks to wax Red Gs*—Soldier of Fortune **3** *v fr 1920s* (also **put on wax**) To make a phonograph recording; record: *Louis Armstrong waxed "Beale Street Blues"/ put the Stone Age stuff of jazz on wax*—Stephen Longstreet **4** *n: play the tune and cut a wax of it*—John O'Hara [the origin of the violent senses is unknown; perhaps semantically analogous with *polish off*, referring to *wax* as a polish; recording senses fr the material used, as *vinyl* was used later]

See the WHOLE BALL OF WAX

waxed *adj* Drunk

way *See* BEAT one's WAY, the FRENCH WAY, GO OUT OF one's WAY, GO THE LIMIT, the GREEK WAY, the HARD WAY, IN A BIG WAY, the IRISH WAY, KNOW one's WAY AROUND, NOT A ONE-WAY STREET, NO WAY, ONE-WAY GUY, RUB someone THE WRONG WAY, THERE'S NO WAY

way car *n phr railroad* The caboose of a freight train

the **way it plays 1** *adv phr* According to the usual pattern: *The way it plays in there, you can't plead the Fifth*—Paul Sann **2** *n phr* The usual pattern; what is to be expected: *Well, I guess that's the way it plays when you get old*

way out 1 *adj phr 1930s jazz musicians* Imaginative; original and bold, esp successfully and admirably so **2** *adj phr fr 1950s cool talk fr jazz musicians* Excellent; wonderful; = FAR OUT, GREAT, OUT OF SIGHT **3** *adj phr narcotics* Intoxicated with narcotics; = HIGH, OUT OF IT

ways *See* FORTY WAYS TO SUNDAY, HAVE IT BOTH WAYS, SWING BOTH WAYS, WORK BOTH WAYS

way the ball bounces (or **the cookie crumbles**) *See* THAT'S THE WAY THE BALL BOUNCES

way to go *sentence* You are doing extremely well; that is splendid ● An exclamation of praise and encouragement: *Ron, stick that old hand out....Way to go, Prez*—Washingtonian [a shortening of *that's the way to go*]

wazoo *n* The buttocks; anus; = ASS [perhaps a variant of *kazoo*]

weak sister *n phr fr middle 1800s* An unreliable and timid man

the **wearies** *n phr* Fatigue and depression; ennui: *I'm getting the evening wearies*—Nelson Algren

wear two hats *v phr* To have two separate jobs or functions ● The phrase may specify more than two hats: *Each of these men wears two hats: one as top-braid officer...the other as a member of the Joint Chiefs*—Time/ *Rockefeller to Wear Two Hats*—New York Post/ *Busy women may complain that they wear three hats, wife, mother, worker*

Weary Willie *n phr fr early 1900s* A hobo, a migrant worker, or other itinerant man; tramp; vagabond [fr a cartoon tramp character of the British artist Tom Browne]

weasel **1** *v fr late 1800s* To evade and equivocate; use deceptive language; = WAFFLE: *They told the candidate to stop weaseling and get to the substance* **2** *v underworld fr 1920s* To inform; = SING, SQUEAL **3** *n: Little Joe turned weasel* [the first sense is said to be based on the *weasel's* habit of sucking the meat or substance from an egg, leaving only the shell; the other senses reflect the more general nasty reputation of the *weasel*]

weasel out *v phr* To withdraw from or evade, esp a promise or obligation, in a sneaky, underhanded way: *We made an open agreement, and you cannot weasel out of it*

weasel words *n phr* Language designed to deceive; empty talk; self-serving verbiage

weather *See* UNDER THE WEATHER

web *n radio studio* A broadcast network

web-foot *modifier* Devoted to and advocating preservation of the environment: *Anyone favoring the bottle bill must be web-foot conservationist* —Boston Globe [presumably fr the notion that lovers of wild life are thus adapted to walking about in swamps; similar to *web-foot* "a native of the wet state of Oregon," and British "a dweller in the fens of East Anglia"]

wedding *See* MILITARY WEDDING, SHOTGUN WEDDING

weed **1** *n* (also **the weed**) *fr 1500s* Tobacco **2** *n fr middle 1800s* A cigar, esp an inferior one: *Throw that weed away and have a good one*—Earl Wilson **3** *n fr early 1900s* A cigarette; = BUTT, COFFIN NAIL **4** *n* (also **the weed**) *narcotics fr 1920s* A marijuana cigarette; = JOINT

See GRASS WEED, REEFER WEED

weedhead *n narcotics* A user of marijuana; = POTHEAD

weeds *n jive talk* Clothes; = THREADS, VINES [a survival or revival of *weeds* "clothing," fr Old English *wæd*, fr earlier forms meaning "to weave"]

the **weeds** *n phr hoboes* A hobo camp; = JUNGLE

weed tea *n phr narcotics* Marijuana

weejuns *n teenagers* Mocassins; loafers [fr *Weejuns*, trade name of a brand of such shoes]

week *See* KNOCK someone INTO THE MIDDLE OF NEXT WEEK, SPLIT WEEK

weekend warrior *See* SUNDAY SOLDIER

weenchy *adj fr late 1800s* Very small; tiny: *just a weenchy...little dash of perfume*—Ira Wolfert [fr *wee*]

weenie (also **weeny** or **weeney** or **weinie** or **wienie**) **1** *n* (also **wiener** or **weener**) A frankfurter; = HOT DOG: *this wienie and kraut combination*—New York Daily News ◁**2**▷ *n* (also **wiener** or **weener**) The penis; esp, the relaxed penis **3** *n* An ineffectual, despised person; = JERK: *She plans to be a weenie, is a weenie, asks to be loved anyway, and is loved anyway*—Village Voice **4** *n* (also **ween**) *college students* A very serious student; = GREASY GRIND, THROAT: *premeds...known to their less pressurized campus colleagues as throats and weenies*—Newsweek/ *Weens are strange creatures with pallid faces, glassy eyes, and calculators strapped to their belts*—Dirk Johnson [fr German *Wienerwurst* "Vienna sausage," with pejorative senses developing fr its penile shape]

See PLAY HIDE THE WEENIE

weenie bin *n phr college students* An academic library carrell, where a serious student spends time studying

weensy *See* TEENSY-WEENSY

weep *See* READ 'EM AND WEEP

weeper or **weepie** *n* A sentimental or otherwise tearful movie, play, etc; = TEAR-JERKER: *It was the weepers that established her as a top Hollywood star*—Bob Thomas/ *The day-time weepies have been greatly enriched by a new soap opera*—John Crosby

Weepers *interj teenagers* A mild, euphemistic exclamation of surprise, distress, etc [fr *Jeepers Creepers*, a euphemism for *Jesus Christ*]

the **weeps** *n phr* Weeping; crying

weevil *See* BOLL WEEVIL

wee-wee **1** *v* To urinate **2** *n: specimen of wee-wee*—Carson McCullers [perhaps a euphemism for the euphemism *pee-pee* for *piss*]

weigh in *v phr* To make a contribution to something, esp to a debate, quarrel, etc: *John weighed in with the suggestion that we adjourn* [fr the formal *weighing* or *weighing in* of a prizefighter before a match]

weight *n narcotics* The amount of narcotics an addict needs for a week: *I'm going up there to give her her weight for the week, you know*—Claude Brown

See CARRY A LOT OF WEIGHT, CARRYING WEIGHT, PAPERWEIGHT, PENNYWEIGHT, THROW one's WEIGHT AROUND

weighter *See* PENNYWEIGHTER

weird *adj 1940s bop talk & cool talk* Excellent; wonderful; = COOL ● Also attested as 1920s British upper-class use

weirdo or **weirdie** or **weirdy** *n fr 1940s* A very strange, eccentric, repellent person; = BIRD, CREEP, GEEK: *He's a weirdy, all right*—WR Burnett

weird out *v phr* To become intoxicated by narcotics; suffer hallucinations, loss of sense of reality, etc: *Talk to me. I'm weirding out*—Armistead Maupin

welcome to the club *sentence* Now you have joined me in adversity; now you see how badly things turn out: *So you've been fired? Welcome to the club, old buddy*

◁**welldigger's ass**▷ *See* COLD AS HELL

well-heeled 1 *adj fr late 1800s* Having much money; rich: *the average, fairly well-heeled, middle-aged American male*—New Yorker **2** *adj fr middle 1800s* Well armed: *He's always well-heeled*—Gangbusters (radio program)

◁**well-hung**▷ *adj fr early 1800s British* Having large genitals: *Death takes the innocent young. And those who are very well hung*—WH Auden/ *A guy with 640K of RAM is the electronic equivalent of well-hung*—New Republic

well-met *See* HAIL-FELLOW

well-oiled *adj fr early 1900s* Drunk: *He happened to be well-oiled, as was usually the case*—Stewart Holbrook

well told *See* FUCKING WELL TOLD

welsh or **welch 1** *v fr middle 1800s British gambling* To default on or evade an obligation, esp paying a gambling debt: *Say, are you going to welsh on me?*—H McHugh/ *Some American officials feel that the Syrians welshed on their promise*—New York Times **2** *n: Link can't take a welsh so he looks around for a way to get his dough*—Mickey Spillane [apparently fr the same bigoted stereotype of the *Welsh* reflected in the English nursery rhyme "Taffy was a Welshman, Taffy was a thief," although perhaps a borrowing of German *Welsch* "foreigner"]

wench *n teenagers* A woman ● A revived usage, not necessarily reflecting the pejorative sense of the old and standard senses [fr Middle English *wenche*, fr Old English *wencel*, pronounced WEN chel, "child"]

west *See* GALLEY-WEST

West *See* MAE WEST

western or **Western** *n* A book, movie, etc, about the Old West

See EASTERN WESTERN, SPAGHETTI WESTERN

Western front *See* ALL QUIET ON THE WESTERN FRONT

wet 1 *adj fr late 1800s* Permitting or advocating the sale of liquor: *This is a wet county* **2** *adj fr early 1900s* Inferior; stupid and unappealing ● Nearly obsolete in the US but still in occasional British use: *A man is "wet" if he isn't a regular guy*—P Marks

See ALL WET, GET one's FEET WET

◁**wetback**▷ *n fr 1940s* A Mexican who enters the US illegally, esp as a migratory worker ● The term may be generalizing to include all illegal immigrants: *An American's as good as a wetback, who is a Mexican that we don't know how he got here*—James M Cain [fr the fact that they get their *backs wet* in wading across the Rio Grande; the terms *wet pony, wet cow,* etc, were used earlier for animals brought illegally across the border]

wet behind the ears *See* NOT DRY BEHIND THE EARS

wet blanket *n phr* A person who dampens and smothers all enthusiasm; a person who prevents fun; a pessimist; = KILLJOY

◁**wet deck**▷ *n phr fr late 1800s nautical* A woman, often a prostitute, who does serial sex acts

◁**wet dream**▷ *n phr* A male's erotic dream during which he has an orgasm

wet one's **goozle** *v phr* To have a drink

wet hen *See* MAD AS A WET HEN

wet-nose *n* = SNOTNOSE

wet one's **whistle** *v phr* To have a drink, esp of liquor

whack 1 *v fr early 1700s* To strike; hit **2** *n: He took a whack at the ball and missed* **3** *v* To cut; chop: *He whacked off a big slice for me* **4** *n fr late 1800s* A try; = BASH, CRACK, SHOT: *He was given a whack at drama reviewing*—Bennett Cerf **5** *v narcotics* To dilute a narcotic; cut a narcotic **6** *n* = WACK [probably echoic]

See HAVE A CRACK AT something, OUT OF WHACK, WACK

◁**whack** (or **wack**) **off**▷ *v phr* To masturbate; = JERK OFF

whack out *v phr gambling* To lose all one's money; = TAP OUT

whack up *v phr fr early 1800s* To divide and distribute something, esp loot, gambling gains, etc, into shares

whacky *See* WACKY

whale[1] *n fr late 1800s* A large or fat person; = WALRUS

whale[2] *v fr early 1800s* To hit; thrash; trounce: *They whaled us six zip/ She hauled off and whaled him a shrewd blow* [fr British dialect spelling of *wale* "strike, beat," perhaps related to Old English *wæl* "slaughter, carnage, death"]

whale away *v phr* To attack or do something vigorously and joyfully: *I was whaling away at the cleaning job/ He's best when he's whaling away at the other candidates*

whale into someone or something *v phr* To attack vigorously: *He'd barely met me when he whaled into me for not answering his letter*

a **whale of a** someone or something *n phr fr early 1900s* An excellent or large example; a very superior specimen: *That woman is a whale of a politician* [fr the prodigious size of the *whale*]

whaling *See* WAILING

wham 1 *v* To hit; strike; = SOCK: *And the whamming continues*—E Lavine **2** *interj* (also **whammo**) An exclamation signalling the suddenness, violence, surprise, etc, of a quick, sharp blow: *And then when I was off guard, whammo!*—Fibber McGee and Molly (radio program)/ *I turned my back and, wham, they were gone* [echoic, and related in sound symbolism to *whip, whale, whack* and other *wh-* words denoting blows]

wham-bam (or **ram-bam**) **thank you ma'am** *n phr esp WW2 armed forces fr Southwestern US* A very quick sex act, esp a casual coupling: *And short it was: a regular "wham, bam, thank you, Ma'am"*—CoEvolution Quarterly

whambang *adj* Huge; loud and vigorous; = WHOPPING: *a demonstration, a whambang, half-million strong demonstration*

whammy *n* A crushing blow or threat, esp one that literally or figuratively disables: *with a whammy of ordinary indebtedness over his head*—Robert Ruark [fr *wham;* see the *whammy*]
See DOUBLE WHAMMY, TRIPLE WHAMMY

the **whammy** *n phr* The evil eye; a crippling curse; =HEX, the INDIAN SIGN: *When threatened with the whammy they quickly agreed/ That pitcher tried to put the whammy on me, but I hit a home run anyway* [fr and perhaps coined in the comic strip "Li'l Abner" by Al Capp, where one character can paralyze with a stare]

whams *See* the WHIM-WHAMS

whang *v* To hit; =WHAM: *She whanged him a shrewd one*
See WANG

whangdoodle or **wangdoodle** or **wingdoodle** *n fr early 1900s* An unspecified or unspecifiable object; something one does not know the name of or does not wish to name; =GIZMO, THINGAMAJIG: *Push in this dingus, step on this wingdoodle*—Billy Rose [fr mid-19th-century sense, "a mythical beast of strange but indefinite traits"]

whanger *See* WANG

what *See* SAY WHAT

whatchamacallit or **what-you-may-call-it** (WHUT chǝ mǝ CAWL it) *n fr middle 1800s* An unspecified or unspecifiable object; something one does not know the name of or does not wish to name; =GIZMO, THINGAMAJIG: *Bring me that whatchamacallit over there, it's leaking*

what do you say *sentence fr early 1900s* How are you?; how have things been?: *What do you say, Ed? Long time no see*

what else is new *See* SO WHAT ELSE IS NEW

what for *n phr fr late 1800s* A drubbing, either physical or verbal; a thrashing; severe punishment: *a sadistic desire to watch the big shots get what for*—John Crosby [fr the startled question *what for? why?* asked by someone being assaulted]
See GIVE someone WHAT FOR

what gives 1 *sentence* What is going on?; =WHAT'S UP: *What gives, I asked her*—John O'Hara **2** *sentence* How are you?; how have things been with you?; =WHAT DO YOU SAY **3** *sentence* What is wrong?; I do not understand: *"What gives?" he croaked in an annoyed tone*—Raymond Chandler [a translation of Yiddish or German *was gibt* "what's going on"]

what goes around comes around *sentence esp black* Things will happen as they will; what will be will be, and fate has its ironies: *"What goes around comes around," Young said*—Philadelphia/ *Always remember this, what goes around comes around*—Donald Goines

what one **is driving at** *n phr* What one means; what one is trying to say: *The persons may know what you are driving at*—CoEvolution Quarterly

what it takes *n phr* The desirable strength, character, appeal, etc: *I wonder if he has what it takes to get this job done*

what makes someone **tick** *n phr* Someone's motives, inner psychology, system of principles, etc: *It's the gambling instinct that makes me tick*—Esquire/ *more realistic and understandable to those who grasp what makes him tick*—Washingtonian [fr the analogy of human motivation with the mechanism of a clock]

what say *sentence* =WHAT DO YOU SAY

what's been shaking *See* WHAT'S SHAKING

what's buzzin', cousin *sentence fr 1930s jive talk* What is happening?; =WHAT'S COOKING

what's cooking or **what cooks 1** *sentence fr 1930s jive talk* What is happening?; =WHAT'S GOING DOWN: *What cooks, Jimmy?*—Lionel Stander **2** *sentence* How have you been?; =WHAT DO YOU SAY

what's going down *sentence fr black* What is happening?; =WHAT'S COOKING

what she wrote *See* THAT'S ALL SHE WROTE

what's-his- (or **-her-** or **-its-**) **name** (or **-face** or ◁**-ass**▷) *n* An unspecified or unspecifiable person or thing; someone or something one does not know or remember the name of or does not wish to name; =WHOOZIS: *What did old what's-his-face have to tell you?*

what's-it or **whatsis** or **whatzis** (WHUT sit, -sǝs) *n* An unspecified or unspecifiable object; something one does not know the name of or does not wish to name; =DINGUS, THINGAMAJIG: *the world's tallest free-standing what's-it*—Toronto Life/ *What's that whatsis he's playing with?*

what's shaking or **what's been shaking** *sentence* What is happening?; =WHAT'S GOING DOWN: *Hello, what's shakin'?*—Buffalo Bill (TV program)

what's the big idea *sentence* Why are you being so presumptuous, aggressive, etc?; account for your behavior at once

what's the good word *sentence* How are things going with you?; what have you to tell me about yourself? ● A cordial greeting

what's the scam *sentence* What is happening?; =WHAT'S GOING DOWN, WHAT'S UP

what's up *sentence* What is happening?; what is the matter, question, problem, etc?; =WHAT'S THE SCAM

what's with someone or something **1** *sentence* What is the problem, difficulty, etc?: *What's with this guy? All I did was say hello* **2** *sentence* What is the explanation?; why is this?: *What's with the free food? Explain*—John O'Hara [fr Yiddish *vos iz mit* "what is with"]

what (or **something**) **the cat dragged in** *n phr* Someone or something very nasty and disreputable; an inferior or messy thing or person: *It is for the disheveled, what the cat dragged in, the rumpled in spirit*—Stanley Elkin

what the hell 1 *interj* An exclamation of surprise, puzzlement, resentment, etc: *What the hell! Who does this clown think he is, anyhow?* **2** *interj* An exclamation of resignation, acceptance, etc: *What the hell, it isn't the greatest, but it'll do*

what the Sam Hill *interj fr early 1800s* =WHAT THE HELL ● A euphemistic form

what-you-may-call-it *See* WHATCHAMACALLIT

what you see is what you get *sentence* The situation, thing, person, etc, is precisely as it appears to be; no trickery, decoration, glowing promises, etc, are involved here [probably fr the supposed statement of a salesperson both assuring and warning a customer about the wares]

whatzis *See* WHAT'S-IT

wheats *n* Pancakes; wheatcakes: *lighter than a stack of wheats*—Damon Runyon

whee *n* Urine; = PISS, WHIZZ: *that will scare the whee out of you*—Car and Driver [probably fr *wee-wee*]

wheel *See* BIG WHEEL, INVENT THE WHEEL, REINVENT THE WHEEL, THIRD WHEEL

wheel and deal *v phr* To make many and frequent arrangements and agreements, esp in business and aggressively

wheeler *See* EIGHTEEN WHEELER, FOUR-WHEELER, SIDE-WHEELER

wheeler-dealer *n* A person who wheels and deals; = BIG-TIME OPERATOR, GANZE MACHER

wheelhouse *n baseball* A batter's preferred hitting zone over the plate; = KITCHEN [probably fr the controlling prominence of the *wheelhouse* on a river boat or a ship]

wheelie *n motorcyclists & bicyclists* A riding on the rear wheel only, with the front wheel raised off the ground
See POP A WHEELIE

wheeling *See* FREE-WHEELING

wheel man *n phr underworld* The driver of the escape car for criminals

wheels 1 *n* The legs: *even the veiny old wheels*—Joseph Wambaugh **2** *n fr 1950s hot rodders* A car
See SET OF WHEELS, SHIT ON WHEELS

wheeze *n fr middle 1800s British* An old joke; = CHESTNUT: *even remembered a wheeze I pulled*—Groucho Marx/ *this tired little wheeze*—Billy Rose [origin unknown; perhaps fr a *wheezing* delivery used by clowns in telling jokes; the earliest attested use refers to a circus clown's joke]

when the balloon goes up *adv phr Army fr WW1 British Army* When war, action, etc, begins [fr a *balloon* released to signal the beginning of a barrage]

when the eagle flies *n phr black* Pay-day; = EAGLE DAY [fr the *eagle* symbol on money]

where someone's **head is at** *adv phr* One's mental condition; one's attitudes, thoughts, aberrations, etc: *They have the maturity to understand where a freak's head is at*—Xaviera Hollander

where he lives *See* HIT someone WHERE HE LIVES

where someone **is at** *n phr fr black* Someone's essential nature, current value system, attitudes, etc: *might make sense in evaluating where you are all at*—New York Times/ *everything from Woody Guthrie to the country blues. That's where I was at*—Rolling Stone

where someone **is coming from 1** *n phr fr black* What someone means; what someone is saying: *Where I'm coming from, what I'm getting at*—New York Times/ *He doesn't know where this guy is coming from*—WT Tyler **2** *n phr* = WHERE someone IS AT

where it's at 1 *n phr* The essential locus of the truth; the core of things: *A lot of cats are finding out where it's at in the joint*—Claude Brown **2** *adv phr: Why should only book writers write books?...They're not where it's at*—James Simon Kunen/ *TV is where it's at*—Village Voice **3** *adv phr* At the site of stimulating and modish events, trends, etc; = WHERE THE ACTION IS: *Where the important stuff is going on. This is where it's at*—New York Times
See KNOW WHERE IT'S AT

where someone **lives** *adv phr* In one's most essential nature, feelings, etc; profoundly: *an ability to capture the moment and zap you where you live*—Playgirl/ *Her appeal hit me where I live*

where's the beef *interj* An interrogatory exclamation of disbelief or defiance, esp as to the firm substance of something promised or proposed: *Fritz Mondale's ludicrous Sunday punch of the 1984 campaign: "Where's the beef?"*—Washingtonian [fr a television commercial for Wendy's (a trade name) hamburgers, in which a little old lady peers into the bun of a competing delicacy and, finding no or little meat, inquires "Where's the beef?"]

where the action is 1 *n phr* The site of stimulating and modish events, trends, etc; a place of excitement; = WHERE IT'S AT: *Don't come here if you're looking for where the action is* **2** *adv phr: Do you want to live where the action is?*

where the bodies are buried *See* KNOW WHERE THE BODIES ARE BURIED

where the rubber meets the road *n phr Army* The lower echelons; those in the trenches; = the GRASSROOTS

where the sun doesn't shine 1 *n phr* One's anus; = ASS, ASSHOLE **2** *adv phr: Put it and all his other contributions where the sun doesn't shine*—Car and Driver/ *Give you a hickey where the sun doesn't shine*—National Lampoon
See STICK IT

where to get off (or **to go**) *See* TELL someone WHERE TO GET OFF

where to put (or **shove** or **stick** or **stuff**) something *See* KNOW WHAT one CAN DO WITH something, TELL someone WHAT TO DO WITH something

the **wherewithal** *n phr fr early 1800s* Money; = the NEEDFUL

which *See* SAYS WHICH

whiff 1 *v sports* To strike at a ball and miss **2** *v baseball* To strike out: *surpassed Sandy Koufax's single-season strikeout record, whiffing 383 batters*—Inside Sports **3** *n narcotics* Cocaine; = SNOW: *Hey, man, know where I can score some whiff?*—Dan Jenkins **4** *v narcotics* To inhale cocaine into the nose; = SNORT, TOOT

while the sun shines *See* MAKE HAY

whimp *See* WIMP

the **whim-whams** (or **wim-wams**) *n phr* Nervousness; = the JIM-JAMS, the JITTERS: *gives Pavarotti* *the whim-whams before every performance*—Time/ *Kittenish dames give us the wim-wams*—Time

whingding *See* WINGDING

whings *See* WINGS

whip *See* BUGGY WHIP

whip out *v phr* To shake hands or give some other gesture of greeting

whip-out *n* Money, esp a first payment, investment, etc: *a whole lot of what you call your up-front whip-out*—Dan Jenkins

whipped *See* PUSSY-WHIPPED

whipped up *adj phr fr 1950s cool talk* Exhausted; =BEAT: *found the controllers dangerously whipped up*—Time

whipsaw 1 *v* To attack or operate by letting rival parties attack one another, to the benefit of the more or less passive manipulator: *pit one plant against another, using interplant rivalries to spur production, a tactic called "whipsawing"*—Time **2** *v* To assault; =CLOBBER: *I'm not trying to sandbag anybody, and I'm not trying to whipsaw anybody* —George V Higgins [first sense perhaps fr the reciprocal action of the *whipsaw*, a pit saw operated by one person above and one in the pit below; in an earlier slang use *whipsaw* meant "to take bribes from two political sources at once"; second sense probably fr the cutting efficiency of this two-person saw]

whip the dog *v phr merchant marine* =FUCK THE DOG

whip up *v phr* To make hurriedly: *Let's whip up a new policy on this/ Just relax while I whip up dinner*

whirlybird *n* A helicopter; =CHOPPER

whiskers *n* An old man: *I had those whiskers by the short hairs*—Paul Sann
See BET YOUR BOOTS, the CAT'S MEOW, UNCLE WHISKERS

whiskey *n lunch counter* Rye bread [because *rye* is also a kind of *whiskey*]

whiskey down *n phr lunch counter* Rye bread toasted

whiskey tenor *n phr fr early 1900s* A strained and husky tenor voice: *unsure baritones and "whisky" tenors*—P Marks

whispering campaign *n phr* An effort at discrediting someone or something, esp by starting false rumors: *start a whispering campaign against your product*—SJ Perelman

whistle *See* BELLS AND WHISTLES, BLOW THE WHISTLE, DOODAD, NOT JUST WHISTLING DIXIE, WET one's WHISTLE, WHISTLING DIXIE, WOLF WHISTLE

whistle-blower 1 *n underworld* =STOOL PIGEON **2** *n* A person who makes an accusation of wrongdoing, illegality, etc: *Thanks to yet another whistle blower, it is now known that even the cost of the one-inch square plastic caps...has flown as high as the planes*—Time/ *trading inside information with whistle-blowers and publicity seekers*—Washingtonian

whistler *n underworld* An informer; =STOOL PIGEON

whistle stop *n phr fr railroad* A small town [perhaps fr the fact that the train does not regularly stop

at such a town, or stops only when signalled to stop, and announces itself by blowing the *whistle* when it does *stop*]

whistling Dixie 1 *v phr* To say something of no consequence for the purpose of making a positive impression **2** *v phr* To engage in wishful thinking

white *n narcotics fr 1940s* Cocaine
See BLACK AND WHITE, BLEED someone WHITE, CHINA WHITE, LILY WHITE

white bready or **white-bread** *adj phr* or *adj* Conventional; bourgeois; =PLASTIC, SQUARE: *Some of the sequences are Middle American. Evans calls them white bready*—Time/ *He taught them to give up the safe, white-bread types*—Playboy

white buck *See* WHITE SHOE

white-collar 1 *modifier* Employed as clerks, office workers, etc: *The white collar workers don't strike very often* **2** *modifier* Performed by people who work in offices: *White-collar crime is becoming a serious problem*

white cow 1 *n phr fr 1920s* A vanilla milk shake **2** *n phr fr 1940s* A vanilla ice cream soda

white elephant *n phr* Something putatively valuable, often a gift, that one does not want; an embarrassing piece of bric-a-brac: *a wonderful collection of white elephants, trash, treasures*—Washington Post [fr a consideration of the *white elephant* of Thailand which, although it is sacred and royal, is also a clumsy sort of possession for one's house]

white-face *n circus* A clown

white flight *n phr* The moving by white persons into the suburbs to avoid the hazards of urban life and esp to avoid living among various ethnic minorities

white-haired boy *See* FAIRHAIRED BOY

white hat 1 *n phr* A law-abiding, morally upright, and heroic person, as distinct from the villainous black hat **2** *modifier: I told them they were the white-hat guys*—Larry Hagman

white knuckle *n phr* Something tense, uncertain, frightening, very suspenseful, etc; =CLIFFHANGER: *It was a white knuckle*—CBS News

white-knuckle *adj* Marked by tension, suspense, fear, etc: *Invocations of a Soviet threat have become so common....He calls it "the white-knuckle show"*—Washingtonian/ *It's going to be a white-knuckle time Thursday*—New York Times

white-knuckled *adj phr* Tense; anxious; frightened: *Are you as white knuckled as I am when traveling as an airline passenger?*—Newsweek/ *Metro's countless thousands of white-knuckled motorists* —Toronto Life [fr the *whiteness* of knuckles when the hands are clenched in anxiety and suspense]

white knuckler 1 *n phr* An airplane flight, esp an anxious one: *You take a white-knuckler. Smilin' Jack at the controls*—Paul Theroux **2** *n phr* A tense and anxious person; someone or something frightened: *A list of companies in trouble: The white knucklers*—New Jersey Monthly

white lightning 1 *n phr* Inferior whiskey; =PANTHER PISS, ROTGUT: *He had a pint of bootleg* *white lightning*—Carson McCullers **2** *n phr* narcotics LSD; =ACID

◁ **white meat** ▷ *n phr* A white person, esp a woman, regarded solely as a sex partner

white money *n phr* Money, esp an illegal political contribution, that has been provided with a legitimate history and provenience; =LAUNDERED MONEY

white mule *n phr fr early 1900s* Strong bootleg liquor, esp nearly pure grain alcohol

white phone *See* TALK TO THE BIG WHITE PHONE

the **whites** *n phr* Gonorrhea; =the CLAP [fr the color of the characteristic genital discharge]

white shoe (or **buck**) **1** *n phr* college students *fr early 1900s* A typical Ivy League student **2** *adj phr* Having the attitudes, appearance, etc, of the Ivy League [fr the *white buckskin shoes* that were part of that student's dress]

white stuff 1 *n phr fr 1920s* Grain alcohol used for making bootleg liquor **2** *n phr* narcotics Cocaine or morphine; =SNOW

◁ **white trash** ▷ *n phr fr middle 1800s black* =PECKERWOOD, REDNECK

whitewash 1 *v fr middle 1800s* To win decisively, esp not permitting the opponent to score; =SKUNK **2** *v* To make something unsavory, damaging, etc, seem to be legitimate and acceptable, usu by falsification or concealment; decontaminate someone's actions or reputation **3** *n: Several Republican senators reported that the report was a "whitewash" of McCarthy's charges*—Associated Press

white wrapper *See* PLAIN WHITE WRAPPER

Whitey or **whitey** *n black* A white person; =MISTER CHARLIE, OFAY

whittle (or **cut**) someone or something **down to size** *v phr* To counter and neutralize; deflate: *That remark sure whittled him down to size*

whiz[1] *n fr early 1900s* A very successful performer; an outstanding expert; =HUMDINGER: *the town's most promising high school football whiz*—Associated Press/ *a whiz at exterior (as opposed to psychological) characterization*—New York Times [shortened form of *wizard*]

whiz[2] or **whizz 1** *v* To urinate; =PISS: *exactly twenty-five minutes after whizzing in his pants for the last time*—Stephen King/ *I gotta whiz, will you just cover me at the register for a minute?*—Cameron Crowe **2** *n: I just came down for a whizz*—Paul Theroux [perhaps echoic; perhaps related to late-19th-century British *hold your whiz* "be quiet, shut up," similar to *hold your water*]

whiz[3] *v underworld fr early 1900s* To pick pockets [apparently fr the *whizzing* speed with which an expert pickpocket works]

whiz[4] *See* GEE WHIZ[2]

whizbang 1 *n* A person or thing that is remarkable, wonderful, superior, etc; =BEAUT, HUMDINGER: *It's a whiz-bang of an idea* **2** *modifier: definitely has been a whiz-bang franchise-winning tool*—Village Voice **3** *n* A very successful performer; an outstanding expert; =WHIZ: *In time we'll all be varsity whizbangs*—Arthur Daley/ *The TV whizbangs were sweating through their pancake makeup*

—Washington Post **4** *n* narcotics *fr 1920s* A mixture of cocaine and morphine; an injection of this mixture [fr an intensification of *whiz* either due to or influenced by the echoic use of *whizbang* to designate an artillery shell in World War 1]

whiz kid 1 *n phr fr 1960s* A very clever young person; a youthful prodigy: *the physics whiz kid*—WT Tyler **2** *modifier: Then the whiz-kid lawyers collided with a tougher adversary*—Village Voice [fr *whiz*[1] blended with *quiz kid* "very bright child or young person," used of participants in a 1930s radio quiz program]

whizzer *n underworld* A pickpocket; =WHIZ

who *See* SAYS YOU

whodunit *n fr 1930s* A mystery or detective story, play, movie, etc, esp a novel: *a conventional whodunit*—Anthony Boucher [fr *who done it*, "who committed the crime?"; claimed as a coinage by and of various persons]

the **whole ball of wax** *n phr fr 1950s* The totality; everything; the whole thing; =the WHOLE SHEBANG: *For that price you get the whole ball of wax* [origin unknown; perhaps fr a manner of distributing the land of an estate to heirs, described in the early 17th century, in which the amount of each portion is concealed in a *ball of wax* which is drawn out of a hat in a sort of lottery]

the **whole enchilada** *n phr* The totality; everything; the whole thing

whole famn damily *n phr* The whole family
● An amusing euphemism: *I hate him and his whole famn damily*
See CHUCK YOU, FARLEY

whole hog *adv phr* Utterly; without reservation: *He believed me whole hog* [fr the early-19th-century *go the whole hog* "act, give, etc, without reservation"; perhaps fr the fact that Muslims were said to have been denied the eating of pork because one unspecified part of the swine was unclean, and, as the poet William Cowper wrote in 1779, "thought it hard from the *whole hog* to be debarred"]

the **whole megillah** *See* the MEGILLAH

a **whole new ball game** *n phr* A totally new situation; something completely different from what has been the case; =a WHOLE 'NOTHER THING: *Since the government got into it this has been a whole new ball game*

the **whole nine yards** *n phr fr Army & Air Force* The totality; everything; the whole thing; =the WHOLE SHEBANG: *went with the odd-looking ship, built a press platform in front of it, had power brought in for press lights, "the whole nine yards"*—Washingtonian/ *guys in black tie passing champagne and the whole nine yards*—Washington Post/ *Floods. Fires. The whole nine yards*—New Yorker [origin unknown; perhaps fr or related to the mid-19th-century British term *to the nines* or *up to the nines* "perfectly, thoroughly," still heard in *dressed to the nines* and apparently based on *nine* as a perfect number in numerology; perhaps based on the load of a concrete mixing and hauling truck, which normally comes in a *nine-yard* and a ten-yard size;

perhaps based on *yard* "one hundred dollars," rather than on the linear or cubic measure]

a **whole 'nother thing** *n phr* A completely different or new affair, process, question, etc: *Now whether you get to go along, that's a whole 'nother thing*

the **whole schmear** *n phr* (Variations: **schmier** or **schmeer** or **shmear** or **shmeer** or **shmier** may replace **schmear**) The totality; everything; the whole thing; =the WHOLE SHEBANG: *names, ages, business they're in, daily schedules, the whole schmear*—Lawrence Sanders/ *the whole fucking schmeer*—George Warren [fr Yiddish *shmeer* fr *shmeeren* "spread"; probably immediately fr the spreading out of the hand in a pinochle or rummy game]

the **whole shebang** *n phr* The totality; everything; the whole thing; =the WHOLE SCHMEAR: *We could move the whole shebang*—Washington Post/ *The whole shebang is festive, pleasantly show-offy and communal*—Village Voice [fr earlier *shebang* "hut, hovel," perhaps fr Irish *shebeen* "cheap saloon," hence, "the house and everything in it"]

the **whole shooting match** *n phr fr late 1800s* The totality; everything; the whole thing; =the WHOLE SCHMEAR [probably fr the crowd that would gather at a frontier *shooting match*, hence, "the whole crowd"; perhaps influenced by earlier British *the whole shoot* of the same meaning, fr *the whole shot* "the whole cost or price"]

the **whole works** *See* the WORKS

whomp or **whump** **1** *v* To defeat utterly; =CLOBBER: *The Tigers got badly whomped* **2** *v* To hit; =BASH: *sturdily whumped at the New Deal's "insane deficit policy"*—Life [fr dialect *whup* "whip"]

whomp up *v phr* To make; devise or build: *I whomped me up one heck of a nightmare*—Billy Rose/ *I better whomp up an explanation for this black eye*

whoop-de-do (HōōP dee dōō) (Variations: **hoopty-doo** or **hoopty-do** or **hoop-de-doo** or **hoop-a-doop** or **hoop-de-doop** or **whoop-de-doo** or **whoop-de-doodle**) **1** *n* Raucous confusion; noisy celebration; jolly fuss: *a gay sense of flossy whoop-de-doo*—Esquire/ *but, in spite of this whoop-de-doo*—Time/ *Cowboys and soldiers created a deafening hoop-a-doop*—New York Times **2** *adj*: *The racketeering, gossiping, whoop-de-doodle thing, it is a piece of stinking fish*—Thomas Wolfe [echoic]

whoopee (WHōō pee) **1** *n fr middle 1800s* Exuberant merriment; wild celebration; =WHOOP-DE-DO **2** *interj* An exclamation of joy and approval; hurrah

whoopee (or **whoopie**) **cushion** *n phr* A bladder that makes a loud flatulating sound when sat upon: *It's Grandma's whoopie cushion. I thought you'd like that, you little fart*—National Lampoon

whooper-dooper *n fr 1920s* A carouse; a wild party: *He finds himself off on a rousing whooper-dooper*—Saturday Evening Post

whoop it up *v phr fr late 1800s* To celebrate; carouse; have raucous fun: *It's natural the Boys should whoop it up for so huge a phallic triumph*—WH Auden

whoopla *See* HOOPLA

whoops (HōōPS) *v* To vomit; =OOPS: *A man...had whoopsed into his National Observer*—Stephen King

whoosh *See* IN A WHOOSH

whoozis or **whozis** (Hōō zəs) *n* An unspecified or unspecifiable object; something one does not know the name of or does not wish to name; =THINGAMAJIG: *Is impotence in the whoozis?*—San Francisco/ *There should be a whozis over the first n*—AH Holt/ *What do you call this whoozis on top here?*

whoozit (Hōō zət) *n* A person whose name one does not know; =WHAT'S-HIS-FACE: *Hello to Fred and Whoozit*—Village Voice

whop **1** *v fr 1700s* To hit; =WHACK **2** *n*: *Give a good whop this time* **3** *n* A try or chance; =CRACK, SHOT: *politicians, judges, people from out of town, $50 to $100 a whop*—Milwaukee Journal [echoic]

whopper **1** *n fr 1700s British* Something huge: *the Mauritius tortoise must have been a whopper*—J Williams/ *That blister's a whopper* **2** *n* A very bold lie: *He told a whopper and got away with it* [fr *whop*]
See BELLY-WHOPPER

whopping *adj* Huge; very impressive: *It was a whopping idea she had*

◁**whore-hopper**▷ *n* A sexually voracious man, esp one who goes often to prostitutes: *This kid wasn't any whore-hopper*—Calder Willingham

◁**whorehouse**▷ *adj* Of a gaudiness or bad taste befitting a cheap brothel; =HONKY-TONK: *The room is painted a sort of whorehouse pink*

who shot John *See* PLAY WHO SHOT JOHN

whump *See* WHOMP

whupass *See* PLAY WHUPASS

Wichita *n prison* A betrayal; =DOUBLE CROSS

wicked **1** *adj fr early 1900s* Impressive; prodigious; =MEAN: *He can shake a wicked spatula*—AL Bass/ *Look at the wicked bat he swings!* **2** *adj teenagers* Excellent; wonderful; =BAD, GREAT
See SHAKE A WICKED CALF

wicket *See* STICKY WICKET

wickey *See* ICKY

wide *See* HIGH, WIDE, AND HANDSOME

wide ones *See* FOUR WIDE ONES

wide open **1** *adj phr* Free of police hindrance; hospitable to profitable vice: *Phoenix City was a famous wide-open town* **2** *adj phr* Going at full speed; =FLAT OUT, LIKE SIXTY **3** *adv phr*: *He always drove his bike wide open*

wide place in the road *n phr fr truckers fr Western* A small town; =JERKWATER TOWN: *A Wide Place in the Road*—Look

widget or **widgit** **1** *n fr early 1920s* A mechanical, electrical, or electronic device; =GADGET, GIZMO: *It's three floors of sights, sounds, illusions, movements, gadgets, widgets, and gizmos*—Westworld/

not an activity I would recommend to anyone daunted by a widgit more complicated than a stapler—Village Voice **2 modifier:** *as though it were read aloud from the press release of a widget manufacturer*—Time [an alteration of *gadget*, perhaps based on hypothetical *which it* on the model of *whatzit*]

widow 1 *n print shop & publishing fr late 1800s* A short line of type, esp an isolated one at the top of a column or page **2** *n* A spare hand dealt in certain card games
See GOLF WIDOW, GRASS WIDOW

widow-maker *n esp lumberjacks* Anything that is lethally dangerous, esp a falling bough or a dead tree

wiener *See* WEENIE

wife 1 *n prostitutes* A member of a pimp's group of prostitutes: *She is his favorite "wife" at the moment*—New York Times **2** *n homosexuals* The more passive of a homosexual couple
See TIN WIFE

wiff or **wif** (WIF) **1** *n* A wife **2** *n* = WHIFF

wig 1 *n fr 1930s jive talk* One's head; one's mind **2** *v fr 1930s jive talk* To talk, esp casually and freely; = RAP: *We stood around wigging* **3** *v fr 1930s jive talk* To annoy someone; = BUG: *She ordered me to stop wigging her* **4** *n fr 1950s jazz musicians* A cool jazz musician **5** *v fr 1950s jazz musicians* To play cool or progressive jazz **6** *v fr cool talk* To behave more or less hysterically; = FLIP, FREAK OUT, WIG OUT: *I realized my goddamn father wasn't there, again, and I wigged*—Richard Price **7** *v fr cool talk* To be happy and in harmony; = DIG **8** *adj esp 1960s teenagers* Excellent; wonderful; = GREAT, NEAT: *a real wig rock trio*
See BLOW one's TOP, FLIP one's LID, a HOLE IN THE HEAD, LOOSE WIG

wigged out 1 *adj phr* Out of touch with reality; deluded; = OUT OF IT: *one of whom is comically wigged out on cleanliness and ecology*—Richard Schickel **2** *adj phr narcotics* Intoxicated with narcotics; = HIGH

wiggle *See* GET A MOVE ON

wiggy 1 *adj fr cool talk* Exciting and up-to-date; = COOL, FAR OUT: *But I have some really wiggy experiences*—Dayton Daily News **2** *adj* Intoxicated on or using narcotics; = OUT OF IT, SPACED-OUT, WIGGED OUT: *one of whom is so wiggy that she got fired from her job*—Newsweek **3** *adj* Crazy; weird; strange: *Things were wiggy*—Robert Stone/ *the wiggy Playboy bunny, remember*—WT Tyler

wig out *1950s cool talk fr jazz musicians* **1** *v phr* To become ecstatic; = FLIP, FREAK OUT, WIG: *The first time I read The Collected Stories I wigged out*—Saturday Review **2** *n phr* To become mentally unbalanced; lose one's sanity: *whose guiding genius, Brian Wilson, spent years wigging out in a sandbox*—Rolling Stone

wild *adj fr cool talk* Excellent; exciting; wonderful; = COOL

wild about (or **over**) **1** *adj phr fr early 1900s* Enthusiastically approbatory of; = CRAZY ABOUT: *the*

new lemon flavored cough drop everyone's wild about—New York Post **2** *adj phr* In love with

wild and woolly *adj phr fr late 1800s* Crude and raucous; untamed; uncouth: *a couple of good old country boys having a wild and woolly time* [fr an alliterating phrase *wild and woolly West*, the *woolly* perhaps referring to range steers, to range horses, or to the unkempt heads of cowboys and frontiersmen]

◁**wild-ass** or **wild-assed**▷ *adj* Madly exuberant; untamed; = CRAZY: *Shepard tops himself as a wild-ass country boy*—Playboy/ *and for goddamned sure a wild-assed warrior*—Don Pendleton/ *Ijah was a kind of wild-ass type*—Saul Bellow

wild card 1 *n phr* Something outside of the normal rules, category, etc; an unpredictable thing, event, etc: *Being from Princeton wasn't like being from Jersey, it was a wild card*—Philadelphia **2** *n phr sports* A team picked for a playoff by some more or less arbitrary method, not having won its championship during the season: *We can always hope the Lions will be the wild card* **3** *modifier:* *the wild-card slot/ last year's wild-card team* [fr poker, where in some games one or more *wild cards*, having any value the player desires, may be designated]

wildcat 1 *v fr late 1800s* To drill for oil, esp without strong corporate and financial backing **2** *modifier fr 1920s* Done or ventured individually, apart from ordinary corporate structures: *a wildcat well/ a wildcat cab* **3** *n* (also **wildcat strike**) *labor union* A strike not authorized by the union authorities

wild horses couldn't drag it out of someone *sentence* That person will never betray a secret
● A humorous melodramatic intensive

willie *n* = CORN WILLIE
See DOODAD

Willie *See* WEARY WILLIE

Willie Fudd *n phr Navy fr Vietnam War* A WF-2 propeller-driven naval radar aircraft [fr the name of a cartoon character, whose initials are *WF* like the designation of the aircraft]

the **willies** *n phr fr late 1800s* Acute nervousness; a spell of uneasiness; = the JITTERS: *all soft and womanish from the willies*—Ira Wolfert/ *For years her friends' shoptalk gave him the willies*—Geoffrey T Hellman [origin unknown]

willikers *See* GEE²

wimp or **whimp** *n* An ineffectual person; a soft, silly person; a weakling; = DRIP, NEBBISH: *unmacho. Short hair, glasses, awkward, uncertain. WIMP* —New York Sunday News/ *his unfortunate and unfounded charge that Thompson portrayed him as a "wimp"*—Newsweek/ *Apparently whimps complained it was too hot*—Nashville [origin unknown; perhaps fr J Wellington *Wimpy*, a relatively unaggressive character in the comic strip "Popeye"; perhaps fr the early-20th-century Cambridge University *wimp* "young woman," perhaps fr *whimper*]

wimpy or **wimpo** or **wimpoid** *adj* Having the traits of a wimp; soft; weak: *less wimpy version of the husband she leaves*—Ms/ *seats that go wimpo* during cornering—Car and Driver/ *a wimpoid MOR ballad with the refrain "the doggone girl is mine"* —Rolling Stone

Wimpy *n* A hamburger sandwich [fr J Wellington *Wimpy*, an obsessive lover and seeker of such sandwiches; see *wimp*]

win *n* A victory: *a win in the Kentucky Derby*—AJ Liebling

win a few lose a few *sentence* One cannot always be victorious or successful; =YOU CAN'T WIN 'EM ALL

wind *See* BAG OF WIND, BAKED WIND, BREAK WIND, a LOAD OF VW RADIATORS, PISS AND WIND, TWIST SLOWLY IN THE WIND

windage *See* KENTUCKY WINDAGE

windbag *n* A person who talks too much, esp a pompous prater; =BAG OF WIND, GASBAG: *a windbag who shoots the gab*—JR Williams

wind-box *n* An accordion; =SQUEEZE-BOX: *a small vogue for the "Letter Edged in Black" on the old wind box*—Robert Ruark

wind down **1** *v phr* To come or bring to a gradual halt or conclusion: *The campaign has begun to wind down/ Shall we wind down our collection drive?* **2** *v phr* To relax gradually; =UNLAX: *Let me sit here for a few minutes, to wind down* [modeled on the *winding down* of a clock or other machine]

winder *See* CLUB-WINDER, SIDEWINDER, STEMWINDING

winder-upper *n* The final song, musical number, joke, speech, etc: *That's the winder-upper, listeners*

window *n fr astronautics* A time period when something may be accomplished; a critical period: *We now have a window of opportunity to try for peace in Lebanon again/ They're worried about a window of vulnerability* [originally fr the exact time and directional limits governing the launching of a rocket to achieve a certain orbit or destination, which were pictured as a *window* through which the rocket must be shot]

See BAY WINDOW, OUT THE WINDOW

windows *n* Eyeglasses; =SPECS

wind up *v phr* To have as an end result; finish with: *We wind up learning less*—Philadelphia Journal/ *How much did he wind up with, after taxes?*

wind something **up** *v phr* To finish; bring to a conclusion: *I suggest we wind this discussion up and go home*

windy *adj* Given to talking too much; overly garrulous, esp pompously so: *It's another one of his windy orations*

wine *See* HIGH-WINE, JUG WINE, POP WINE

win for losing *See* someone CAN'T WIN FOR LOSING

wing **1** *n fr early 1800s* An arm, esp a baseball pitcher's throwing arm **2** *v fr middle 1800s* To shoot, esp to wound with a shot, not necessarily in the arm: *You were winged by something big, 45 maybe*—R Starnes **3** *v* =WING IT **4** *n* teenagers A raucous party; =WINGDING

See PAY-WING, PING-WING, SALARY WING, SILVER WING

wingding or **whingding** **1** *n* hoboes, prison & narcotics fr early 1900s A drug-induced or epileptic fit; also, such a fit counterfeited in order to attract sympathy **2** *n* fr 1930s A fit of anger; a violent outburst of feeling: *going to throw a wingding they'll hear in Detroit*—J Evans **3** *n* (also **wingdinger**) fr 1940s An energetic celebration or commotion; a noisy party; =RUCKUS: *Then they did their wingding out in front of the West Wing*—Washington Post

wingdoodle *See* WHANGDOODLE

wing it or **wing** *v phr* or *v* To extemporize; improvise; =FAKE IT: *Winging It, Coping Without Controllers*—Time/ *one of those people...who never wings a speaking engagement though she averages two or three a week*—Philadelphia/ *Forget it. I'll wing it* —Armistead Maupin

wings or **whings** *n* narcotics fr early 1900s Cocaine; =SNOW [fr the sensations of flight, of being "high"]

See EARN one's WINGS, SPROUT WINGS

wingy *adj* Intoxicated with narcotics; =HIGH: *I've never been wingy or suffered a psychotic episode* —New York Daily News

◁**Wingy**▷ *n* Nickname for a one-armed man

win in a walk *v phr fr late 1800s* To win easily; be a confident victor

winkie *n* The penis; =COCK: *Had Kaufman discovered a bump on his winkie, he probably would have shared that with us too*—Village Voice

winks *See* FORTY WINKS

winner *n* A very promising and successful person or thing; =HOT SHOT: *Your new poem is a winner/ Hire this guy, he looks like a winner*

wino **1** *n fr early 1900s hoboes* A habitual drunkard, esp a derelict who drinks cheap wine; =STUMBLEBUM: *a couple of "winos" who had been drinking cheap sherry in the bar*—G Homes/ *patronized largely by vagrants, winos, dehorns, grifters*—Max Shulman **2** *n* A person who drinks wine in preference to liquor; a wine drinker

win out *v phr fr late 1800s* To win; prevail: *De Bird of Time will win out in a walk*—L Coley

win one's **spurs** *v phr fr cowboys* To be fully accepted as competent: *After a few months on the job he had won his spurs*

winter rat *n phr* An old car; =JALOPY: *old cars known as clunkers, lunkers, winter rats*—New York Times

win the porcelain hairnet *v phr* (Variations: **barbwire garter** or **cast-iron overcoat** or **fur-lined bathtub** or **hand-painted doormat** or **solid gold chamber pot** may replace **porcelain hairnet**) To deserve a spectacularly useless reward; merit nothing more than something absurd ● Said ironically either about something stupid and ineffective or something guardedly admirable

wipe *n* A killing; a murder: *I don't know a goddam thing about this goddam Covino wipe*—Rex Burns

wiped out **1** *adj phr* Drunk: *Everybody had been too wiped out to watch*—Washington Post **2** *adj phr* Tired; exhausted: *At the end of that hearing she felt wiped out* be **wiped out** *v phr* To be wrecked, ruined, finished; = GET IT IN THE NECK, SHOOT someone DOWN

wipe it off *v phr esp WW2 armed forces* To force oneself to stop smirking or joking; stop larking ● Very often a stern command: *Wipe it off, Mister, this is no comic routine*

wipe out 1 *v phr surfers* To lose control of the surfboard during a ride and be thrown off into the water: *About six of them wiped out on one big wave* **2** *n phr* A failure; = LOSER: *The guy's a total wipe out*—Washington Post **3** *v phr*: *The strike wiped out after only two days*

wipe someone **out 1** *v phr fr 1920s* To kill; = ICE, OFF: *In the St Valentine's Day massacre, Capone wiped out his whole opposition* **2** *v phr* To defeat utterly; trounce; = CLOBBER, CREAM: *Unexpectedly, Baylor wiped Syracuse out that year*

wipe (or **mop**) **up the floor with** someone *v phr* To defeat utterly and abjectly; trounce easily; = CLOBBER: *That bum? The Champ'll wipe up the floor with him*

wire 1 *n underworld fr early 1900s* A pickpocket, esp the one of a team that actually steals the loot: *the wire who abstracts the objective from the victim's kick*—American Mercury **2** *v fr middle 1800s* To send a telegram: *Wire me when you get there* **3** *n*: *Send me a wire if you get the job* **4** *n* Information; news; a message: *He had heard the wire through the grapevine that the man was a paid informer*—Donald Goines **5** *v* To place eavesdropping devices in a room, office, etc; = BUG: *She quietly checked to see if her bedroom was wired* **6** *n* An overstimulated person; an anxious, excitable person: *You know I'm a natural wire....What I need is a drink to calm me down*—Harry Crews [the first sense derives fr the use of *wire* as a lifting line; the second, third, fourth, and fifth senses from *wire* as the conductor of electric messages; the sixth sense fr *wire* as the conductor of stimulating impulses]

See COME UP TO THE WIRE, DOWN TO THE WIRE, GO TO THE WIRE, HAYWIRE, HOT-WIRE

wired 1 *adj* (also **wired up**) *narcotics* Intoxicated by narcotics; = HIGH, SPACED-OUT: *"If you're wired, you're fired," is how Willie Nelson warns band members about cocaine usage*—Chicago Tribune/ *That night Elvis was wired for speed*—Albert Goldman **2** *adj* (also **wired up**) Eagerly excited; overstimulated; = HIGH, JACKED UP: *Keeping the people wired with a mix of sixties vines and eighties technology*—Rolling Stone/ *Yes, I was definitely wired...I was so wired I couldn't concentrate*—Richard Price/ *They have him wired up tight with the slogans of TV and the World Series*—Eldridge Cleaver **3** *adj* Anxious; nervous; = UPTIGHT: *I got wired when Myrt was sneaking a break and Jerry showed up*—Ms **4** *adj* Securely in the proper circles, esp those of political or business power; = IN THE LOOP: *Bob Gray was wired. There wasn't a political celebrity there who wouldn't return his phone calls*—Washingtonian **5** *adj* (also **wired up**) Certain and secure; totally under control; assured; = RACKED, TAPED: *Mention of all those*

other top contenders is just a smokescreen and Brown's got it wired—Washington Post/ *This deal has already been, er, wired*—Village Voice/ *Then I get this wired up and I think, well*—George V Higgins [the first three senses derive fr *wire* as the conductor of stimulating electricity; the fourth sense probably fr *wire* as a conductor of messages and as a connector; the fifth sense fr *wire* as used for tying and binding; *wired up* is recorded as a US term for "irritated, provoked" in the late 19th century, and may be related to the sense "anxious, nervous"]

See COOL AS A CHRISTIAN WITH ACES WIRED, HAVE something CINCHED

wired into *adj* Intimately involved in; closely and sympathetically connected with; = INTO: *"I'm wired into Marin Transit right now." "That's cool...if you get off on buses"*—Cyra McFadden/ *for the first time, I really felt wired into that poem*—Adrienne Rich

wire-puller *n fr early 1800s* A person who exerts influence, esp in a covert way; = OPERATOR: *Grunewald, bigtime wire-puller in the tangled Washington bureaucracy*—New York Daily News

wires **See** PULL STRINGS

wisdom box *n phr railroad* A yardmaster's office

wise 1 *adj fr late 1800s* Aware; cunningly knowing; = HEP: *Get wise, son!*—Sinclair Lewis/ *He's close-mouthed and wise, stir-wise*—Erle Stanley Gardner **2** *v* To make aware; inform, esp in shrewd particulars; = WISE someone UP: *She wised me about how to get promoted*

See CRACK WISE, GET WISE, PUT someone WISE, STREET-SMART

◁ **wise-ass** ▷ **See** NOBODY LOVES A WISE-ASS, SMART-ASS

wisecrack *n fr early 1900s* a witty remark, esp one with a knowing, sarcastic edge; a joke; = GAG, ONE-LINER: *at least two wisecracks in the first paragraph*—Nation/ *makers of wars and wise-cracks, a rum creature*—WH Auden [said to have been coined by the early-20th-century American humorist Chic Sale; probably related to *crack* "brag, boast" attested fr the middle 15th century and basically echoic]

wise guy 1 *n phr* (also **wise apple**) *fr early 1900s* A person who is ostentatiously and smugly knowing; a smart aleck; = SMART-ASS: *My little brother is an irrepressible wise guy* **2** *n phr* (also **wise hombre**) *fr early 1900s* A shrewd and knowing person; a person who is "wised up": *The wise guys said Frank didn't stand a chance*—Philadelphia Bulletin

wisenheimer (WĪ zən hī mər) *n fr early 1900s* A person who is ostentatiously and smugly knowing; a smart aleck; = SMART-ASS: *the way an old-time carny handles a tough wisenheimer with the aid of a hammer*—New York Times [fr *wise* plus the German or Yiddish element *-enheimer* found in surnames based on German place names ending in *-heim*; the coinage may be motivated by the humorous attempt to add weight to the term, and is perhaps tinged with anti-Semitism]

wise up *v phr* To become shrewdly aware; =GET SMART ● Often an exhortation: *Wise up or you'll lose this opportunity*

wise someone **up** *v phr* To give useful and usu covert particulars; =PUT someone WISE: *My adviser was a good scout and wised me up*—P Marks

wishbone *n football* A football formation in which the quarterback and three other backs line up in a Y pattern with the quarterback at the base and directly behind the center

wish book *n phr fr 1920s* A mail order catalogue

wish (or **want**) **list** *n phr* A presumed list of things one wants: *intent on buying every weapon the generals and admirals put on their wish lists*—Time

wishy-washy *adj fr 1700s* Marked by imprecision and vacillation; inconstant; uncertain: *The wishy-washy player keeps putting off the evil day*—Oswald Jacoby/ *It's not overpowering like Opium and not wishy-washy*—Washington Post [fr a rhythmic reduplication of *washy* "weak, diluted, watered-down," probably influenced by *wishy* as suggesting vacillating desires]

wit *See* NITWIT

witch *n* A vicious woman ● A euphemism for bitch: *She's being very nasty about it, a real witch*

witch's tit *See* COLD AS HELL

with *adj phr lunch counter fr 1930s* Having the usual accompaniment, that is, onions with hamburger, cream with coffee, etc: *We ordered two coffees with, to go*
See GIVE WITH, ONE-WITH

with a bang *adv phr* Very impressively; very successfully: *The thing succeeded with a bang*
See GO OVER WITH A BANG

with a full deck *See* PLAY WITH A FULL DECK

with a purple passion *adv phr* Very ardently; very enthusiastically: *They greeted the notion with a purple passion*

with a ten-foot pole *See* NOT TOUCH someone or something WITH A TEN-FOOT POLE

with bells on *adv phr* (Variations: **on** may be dropped; **knobs** or **tits** may replace **bells**) *fr 1930s* Very definitely; without any doubt; emphatically ● Used especially in affirming that one will be present at a certain time and place: *Don't worry, I'll be there with bells on/ I'll be here Thursday. With bells*—James M Cain [perhaps the suggestion is that one will be very conspicuous, like a train or a fire engine *with bells*]

with eyes open or **with open eyes** *adv phr* Fully understanding; quite aware of the possibilities and dangers: *Well, she went into the thing with eyes open, so we can't pity her all that much/ He undertook it with open eyes*

with one's **feet** *See* VOTE WITH one's FEET

◁**with** one's **finger up** one's **ass**▷ *See* SIT THERE WITH one's FINGER UP one's ASS

with flying colors *adv phr* In a bold and assured way; grandly; =HIGH, WIDE, AND HANDSOME: *She won nicely, in fact with flying colors* [probably fr the image of a naval vessel with the national flag bravely flying]

with one's **hand in the till** (or **the cookie jar**) *adv phr* With no possibility of escape or evasion; in flagrante delicto; =DEAD TO RIGHTS: *She can hardly deny it, because we caught her with her hand in the till/ Sure enough, there he was with his hand in the till* [fr the situation of a thief caught *with his hand in the money-box* or *cash register*]

within an ace *See* COME WITHIN AN ACE

with it 1 *adj phr fr 1950s beat talk & cool talk fr black* Coolly cognizant; absolutely in touch; stylish and au courant; =HEP: *He affects clothes that carefully cultivate the "with-it" image*—New York Times/ *to spend less time attempting to be "with it" and to exert greater effort to communicate with our deprived and our outcast*—New York Times/ *Shadows of course there are, Porn-Ads, with-it clergy*—WH Auden **2** *adj phr carnival & circus fr 1920s* Working in a carnival as a full-time professional: *had previous short experiences traveling with carnivals ...before becoming fully "with it" (as carnival workers describe the fully-initiated member)*—Society
See GET WITH IT

with one hand tied behind one's **back** (or **behind** one) *adv phr* Very easily; readily and neatly: *I can do that job with one hand tied behind my back*

◁**without a pot to piss in**▷ *See* NOT HAVE A POT TO PISS IN

with one's **pants down** *See* CATCH someone WITH one's PANTS DOWN

with the punches *See* ROLL WITH THE PUNCHES

with the territory *See* GO WITH THE TERRITORY

witless *See* SCARED SPITLESS, SCARE someone SHITLESS

wobble *n narcotics* =ANGEL DUST

wobbly or **Wobbly** *n esp 1920s* A member of the Industrial Workers of the World or IWW, a radical labor organization [said to be fr a Chinese-American pronunciation of *w* as "wobble", in IWW]

wobbly one *n phr Army* A warrant officer, first class

woe *See* TALE OF WOE

◀**wog** or **Wog**▶ *n WW2 armed forces fr British* A native of India, esp a laborer [the British usage, "any native of an Eastern country," is said to derive fr an arch acronym for *Worthy Oriental Gentleman* or *Westernized Oriental Gentleman*; some think it is more likely to be a shortening of *golliwog* "a black doll with wild frizzy hair and staring eyes," fr the name of such a doll in late-19th-century childrens' stories by Bertha Upton, and a popular toy in British nurseries]

wolf 1 *n fr early 1900s prison & hoboes* An aggressive male homosexual; a homosexual rapist: *the sodomist, the degenerate, the homosexual "wolf"*—New Republic **2** *n fr 1930s* A sexually aggressive man; an ardent womanizer; =COCKSMAN: *Mary considered him quite a wolf* **3** *v: I give with the vocals and wolf around in a nite club*—John O'Hara
See LONER

wolf whistle *n phr* A two-note whistled expression, esp of male appreciation for the sexual attributes of a woman

woman *See* BAG LADY, BOTTOM WOMAN, the LITTLE WOMAN, OLD WOMAN

woman-chaser *n* A womanizer; =LADIES' MAN, SKIRT-CHASER, WOLF

wombat *n teenagers* An eccentric person; =FREAK, NUT [probably fr the inherently amusing name of the *wombat*, a pudgy Australian marsupial, and the occurrence of *bat* "crazy person, nut," as an element of the name]

womp *n television studio* =BLOOM

wonder *See* NINE-DAYS' WONDER, NINETY-DAY WONDER

wonk *n esp college students* An overstudious student; an intellectual; =GREASY GRIND: *I had a real wonk of a roommate. The guy drove me bats*—National Lampoon/ *Along come these wonks with slide rules sewn into their sports jackets*—John Leonard [perhaps fr *wanker* "masturbator"]

wonky¹ *adj esp Canadian fr middle 1800s British printers* Badly done or made; ineffective; weird; =COCKEYED: *As the race in the riding narrowed...the vision began to get wonky*—Toronto Life/ *the wonky clutter of a Victorian parlor*—Toronto Life/ *Only the steering feels wonky to me*—Car and Driver [fr British dialect *wanky* or *wankle* "weak, unsteady"]

wonky² *adj esp Harvard students* Tedious and serious, esp anxious and overstudious in an academic situation: *"Jenny Cavilleri," answered Ray. "Wonky music type"*—Erich Segal/ *a class which I have long dismissed as hopelessly wonky*—Illinois Times [fr *wonk*]

woo *See* PITCH WOO

◁**wood**▷ *n black* A white person; =PECKERWOOD, REDNECK: *just because they find some cum in that wood's ass*—Donald Goines [fr a shortening of *peckerwood*]
See SAW WOOD

wood butcher **1** *n phr fr late 1800s* A carpenter, esp an incompetent one **2** *n phr Navy fr WW1* A carpenter's mate

woodenhead *n* A stupid person; =BLOCKHEAD, KLUTZ

wooden Indian *See* LIKE A WOODEN INDIAN

wooden kimono *n phr fr 1930s* =PINE OVERCOAT

wooden nickels *See* DON'T TAKE ANY WOODEN NICKELS

wooden overcoat *See* PINE OVERCOAT

wooden-stake *v* To postpone permanently; file and forget: *Let's wooden-stake that bright little idea of his* [fr the use of a *wooden stake* driven through the heart as the means of killing a vampire, esp Count Dracula]

woodhead *n hoboes* A lumberjack

woodhick *n* A rural person; =HAYSEED, HICK, SHITKICKER

woodpecker *n* =PECKERWOOD

woodpile *n jazz musicians* A xylophone

wood-pusher *n* A chess player, esp an unskilled one; =PATZER: *enough to make any parlor wood-*

pusher loosen his collar and roll up his sleeves—Time

wood-pussy *n* A skunk; a polecat

the woods are full of someones or somethings *sentence* The named things or persons are in plentiful supply; these things are cheap and available: *Look, the woods are full of computer programmers, I want one that's a real whiz*

woodshed **1** *v fr jazz musicians fr 1930s* To rehearse; practice one's part, role, etc, esp to do so alone and rigorously: *Bix did plenty of woodshedding, playing alone*—Stephen Longstreet/ *If that speech sounded good it was only because I woodshedded so hard* **2** *v* To work out the harmonies of a barbershop quartet number, esp by ear [fr the *woodshed* as the traditional place where one could be alone to work, think, smoke, etc]

woodshedder **1** *n* A person who woodsheds: *I've always been a "woodshedder." What I do is go off alone and think things out and practice*—Good Housekeeping **2** *n* A barbershop quartet singer who prefers to improvise rather than to sing arranged parts

woodwork *See* CRAWL OUT OF THE WOODWORK

woody *n surfers* A station wagon with wooden outside trim: *Get your woody working*—Rocky Mountain Magazine

woof **1** *v fr 1930s jive talk* To talk idly; chatter; =BAT one's GUMS: *I ain't woofin'. I'm not fooling*—Life **2** *v esp black* To boast, esp menacingly; bluff: *The extreme of arguing is "woofing," like Ali and Frazier*—Washington Post [echoic fr the idle or menacing barking of a dog]

woofer **1** *n* A person who woofs **2** *n fr 1950s* A loudspeaker designed to reproduce bass notes faithfully

◁**wool**▷ *n* A woman: *She's deep down a pretty good wool*—Dan Jenkins [perhaps like *pussy*, a metonymic reference to pubic hair, in this case stressing its curliness]
See PULL THE WOOL OVER someone's EYES

◁**wool hat**▷ *n phr fr early 1800s* A rural person; a bumpkin; =REDNECK

woolies *n* Long woolen underwear; =LONG JOHNS

woolly *See* WILD AND WOOLLY

woolly-headed *adj* Inclined to idealism and hopeful fantasy; impractical: *She dismissed it as another woolly-headed scheme of mine*

wootsie or **wootsy** *See* TOOTS

woozily *adv* In a woozy manner: *I balanced myself woozily on the flats of my hands*—Raymond Chandler/ *tottered woozily off a plane from Tripoli*—Associated Press

woozy **1** *adj fr late 1800s* Not fully alert and conscious; half-asleep; befuddled: *You'll just get woozy if you stay up any longer*—P Marks/ *some woozy tourist*—Gene Fowler **2** *adj* Dizzy; faint; unwell [origin unknown; perhaps fr *oozy*, suggesting the insolidity and limpness of mud]

◀**wop** or **Wop**▶ **1** *n fr early 1900s* An Italian or a person of Italian extraction; =DAGO **2** *adj*: *big wop tenor*—James M Cain [apparently fr southern

Italian dialect *guappo* "dandy, dude, stud," used as a greeting by male Neapolitans]

word *interj* New York City teenagers An exclamation of agreement and appreciation, used when someone has said something important or profound: *If it's really meaningful, "Word, man, word," should be used*—New York Times

See EAT one's WORDS, FIGHTIN' WORDS, FROM THE WORD GO, WEASEL WORDS, WHAT'S THE GOOD WORD

work **1** *v* *fr early 1800s British* To go about a place begging, selling, stealing, etc; ply one's often dishonest trade: *He worked the bus terminal for a few days until they chased him* **2** *v* To exert one's charm, power, persuasiveness, etc, esp on an audience: *We watched in admiration as the candidate skillfully worked the huge crowd*

See BULLWORK, DIRTY WORK, DONKEYWORK, GRUNT WORK, NICE WORK IF YOU CAN GET IT, NOODLEWORK, RUSH THE GROWLER, SCUT

workaholic **1** *n* A person whose primary and obsessive interest is work; a compulsive worker: *This type of person is a work freak, a workaholic* —National Observer **2** *modifier*: *I made a hardy attempt to suppress my workaholic tendency*

◁**work** one's **ass**▷ (or **buns** or **tail**) **off** *v phr* To work very hard; =BUST one's ASS: *I worked my sweet ass off trying to convince her/ The dead acoustics of the room force the quartet's ensemble students to work their tails off*—Esquire/ *Complains one Apple staffer: "People are working their buns off"*—Time

work behind the stick *v phr* To be an active police officer, esp a patrolling officer: *I used to work behind the stick in the afternoons*—Lawrence Sanders [fr the patrolling officer's *nightstick*]

work both sides of the street *v phr* To take two contrary positions at once; =HAVE IT BOTH WAYS: *Most politicians have a good instinct for working both sides of the street* [probably fr the notion of a hoboes' or beggars' agreement to parcel out the territory]

work both ways or **cut two ways** *v phr* To suggest or entail a necessary contrary; have double and opposite application: *Most often the claim of mental cruelty works both ways in a marriage/ I see your point, but don't you see it cuts two ways?*

worker **See** GLIM WORKER, LUSH ROLLER, MISSIONARY WORKER

working **See** HAVE something GOING FOR someone or something

working girl *n phr* *prostitutes* A prostitute; =HOOKER: *an old white pimp named Tony Roland who was known to handle the best-looking "working" girls in New York*—Xaviera Hollander

working stiff *n phr* *fr early 1900s* A common working man; an ordinary worker: *made good cars cheap and paid working stiffs $5 a day*—Stewart Holbrook/ *The author has been a novelist...he has also been a movie and TV working stiff*—Time

work it into the ground **See** RUN something INTO THE GROUND

workout **1** *n* *fr early 1900s* A session of strenuous physical exercises, practice athletic efforts, etc:

He came in sweating after his morning workout **2** *n* A hard job; an exhausting effort: *She told us that handling that kid all day is one hell of a workout*

work out **1** *v phr* To do strenuous exercises; have a hard session of physical conditioning: *The president works out every day in the palace gym* **2** *v phr* To amend, finish, repair, etc, by careful effort; =IRON OUT: *They agreed to work out the flaws and snags before trying the idea on the public*

work something **out** *v phr* To achieve an agreement, esp by compromise: *We'll just stay at it until we work something out*

work someone **over** *v phr* To beat someone, esp cruelly and systematically; =MESS someone UP: *The secret police worked him over brutally until he confessed*

works *n narcotics* The devices used for injecting narcotics; drug paraphernalia; =FIT: *When he awakes in the morning he reaches instantly for his "works," eyedropper, needle,...and bottle top* —Reader's Digest

the **works** or **the whole works** *n phr fr early 1900s* Everything; the totality of resources; =the WHOLE SCHMEAR, the WHOLE NINE YARDS: *I want it all, the whole works/ the works, shave, haircut, massage, and tonic*—Hal Boyle [perhaps like *kit and caboodle* in referring to an entire outfit of equipment, conceived as a *works* "factory, workplace and equipment"; perhaps referring to the entirety of a mechanism like that in *gum up the works*]

See GIVE someone THE WORKS, GUM UP, IN THE PIPELINE, SHOOT THE WORKS

work the growler **See** RUSH THE GROWLER

work the stem *v phr* *hoboes* To beg on the streets

work up *v phr* To devise; =WHOMP UP: *We'll have to work up a good story to explain this one*

world **See** FREEWORLD, OUT OF THIS WORLD

the **world** *n phr Army* The territorial US

See DEAD TO THE WORLD, GO AROUND THE WORLD, HAVE THE WORLD BY THE BALLS, I'LL TELL THE WORLD

world-beater *n fr late 1800s* A very effective person; a winner; a champion: *Sometimes I think you're a world-beater*—Raymond Chandler

world-class *adj* Very superior; outstanding; superexcellent: *This guy's a world-class bullshit artist* [fr the superiority of an athlete who competes successfully in the Olympic Games or other world-wide events]

the **world is** one's **oyster** *sentence* The person referred to is doing very well, is prosperous, is happy, has great prospects, etc: *Before the crash his rich grandfather figured the world was his oyster*

worm *n* A despicable person; =BASTARD, JERK: *Cut that out, you little worm*

See CAN OF WORMS

worm out of something *v phr* To evade or avoid an unpleasant situation, esp by ignominious means: *This time we have him dead to rights, and he won't worm out of it*

worry **See** NOT TO WORRY

worry wart *n phr fr 1930s* A person who worries excessively; a constantly apprehensive person [fr the designation of such a person in the comic strip "Out Our Way" by JR Williams]

worst-case scenario *n phr fr armed forces fr 1960s* A speculation or prediction as to what would happen if everything turned out as badly as possible: *our worst-case scenario in Western Europe* —Time

worth *See* TWO CENTS' WORTH

worth a bucket of warm spit *adj phr* Of very little value; worthless ● Often used in the negative: *The new telephones are not worth a bucket of warm spit/ a cable TV contract for the Bronx, Brooklyn, Queens, and Staten Island that's worth about as much as a bucket of warm spit*—Village Voice

worth a damn (or **a shit**) **1** *adv phr* At all; in the least degree ● Most often in the negative: *This guy doesn't sing worth a damn/ She doesn't like me worth a shit* **2** *adj phr: Those promises aren't worth a damn*

not **worth a plugged nickel** *See* NOT WORTH A PLUGGED NICKEL

wounded *See* WALKING WOUNDED

wow[1] **1** *interj* An exclamation of pleasure, wonder, admiration, etc ● This interjection, which probably dates to the early 1900s, had a new popularity and currency during the 1960s and later: *Wow, what a nice voice you have!/ Oh, wow, far out!* **2** *n fr early 1900s* Something very exciting and successful; a sensation: *It would be a wow of a scrap*—H Witwer/ *a wow of a line!*—Katharine Brush **3** *v fr 1920s* To impress someone powerfully and favorably; = KNOCK someone DEAD, LAY THEM IN THE AISLES: *wondering whether he'll make a fraternity and whether or not he'll wow the girls*—Saturday Evening Post/ *all self-proclaimed poets who, to wow an audience, utter some resonant lie*—WH Auden [origin unknown; perhaps echoic of a bark or howl of approval; perhaps fr *pow-wow* by sound alone, the associations of *pow* "sound of a blow, power of impact," carrying to *wow*]

See POW-WOW

wow[2] *n fr 1950s* An intrusive wavering sound from a record player, usu caused by uneven running of the turntable [echoic]

wowser[1] *n* Something very successful and impressive; a sensation; = WOW[1]: *It would make a wowser of a movie*—Pittsburgh Press/ *The four-beat peroration is a wowser*—National Review [fr *wow*, perhaps influenced by *rouser*]

wowser[2] *n esp 1920s fr British fr early 1900s Australian* A stiff and puritanical person; a prude and prig ● Probably imported by HL Mencken: *men of letters, who would swoon at the sight of a split infinitive, such wowsers they are in regard to pure English*—Robert Lynd [origin unknown; perhaps echoic of a bark of disapproval; perhaps related to British dialect *wowsy* "an exclamation of surprise"; said to be, surely ex post facto, an acronym for the name of a reform organization *We Only Want Social Evils Righted*]

wrap **1** *v esp show business* To complete; finish; = WRAP UP: *Filming, based on Bob Randall's 1977*

thriller, wrapped last summer*—People Weekly/ *Because when it wraps, they strike the sets and you're stuck*—GQ **2** *n: Well, it's a wrap on the squash*—Dan Jenkins

wrapped around the axle *adj phr Army* Tangled in complex and trivial matters; involved in pointless discussion [fr the plight of a person whose vehicle *axle* has become ensnarled in a tangle of rope or some other material]

wrapped tight *adj phr* Sane; of sound mind ● Often used in the negative: *I told him he wasn't wrapped too tight himself* [fr the image of something *wrapped* neatly without loose ends, spillage, etc]

wrapper *See* PLAIN WHITE WRAPPER

wraps *See* UNDER WRAPS

wrap up *v phr* To complete; finish: *Let's wrap up the negotiations and get to the next stage*

wrap-up *n* A completion; a final treatment, summary, etc: *This is the 11:30 pm wrap-up of the news*

wrap something **up** **1** *v phr* To complete, esp successfully; be the final touch, act, event, etc: *Well, folks, that about wraps it up for this time/ They wrapped the job up ahead of schedule* **2** *v phr* To be the winning or conclusive score, stroke, element, etc; = ICE: *They wrapped the game up in the third period with a power-play goal*

wreck **1** *n* An old car or other vehicle; = HEAP, JALOPY **2** *n fr 1920s* An exhausted or dissipated person; a human ruin: *He's pretty smart, but physically a wreck* **3** *v lunch counter* To scramble, as eggs

wrecked *adj narcotics* Intoxicated with or addicted to narcotics

wreck 'em *n phr lunch counter* An order of or for scrambled eggs served on toast

wringer *See* FINGER-WRINGER, GET one's TAIL IN A GATE, PUT someone THROUGH THE WRINGER

wrinkle **1** *n fr middle 1500s* An idea, device, trick, notion, style, etc, esp a new one: *She tried a couple of new wrinkles in writing that script/ Wearing the thing sideways is a nice wrinkle* **2** *n* A defect or problem, esp a minor one; = BUG: *The plan's still got a few wrinkles, nothing we can't handle* [origin of first sense unknown; perhaps fr the same semantic impulse as *twist* in a similar sense, referring to a quick shift in course; perhaps a reference to a lack of plain simplicity in dress or decoration, and the prevalence of stylish pleats, folds, etc, since the earliest form is *without all wrinkles*; second sense fr the notion of *ironing the wrinkles out* of something; see *iron out the kinks*]

Wrinkle City **1** *n phr* Wrinkled or lined skin, as a sign of age: *Women live with an unspoken fear of Wrinkle City*—Time **2** *n phr* A place inhabited or frequented by old people

wrinkle-rod *n esp hot rodders* A car's crankshaft

wrist *See* GIVE someone A SLAP ON THE WRIST, LIMP WRIST, SLAP someone's WRIST

write someone **a blank check** *See* GIVE someone A BLANK CHECK

write home about *See* NOTHING TO WRITE HOME ABOUT

write the book *v phr* To be very authoritative or seasoned; be an expert ● Usu in the past tense: *Can she sing? Hell, she wrote the book*

write-up *n fr late 1800s* A written article, news story, etc: *I figure you have seen the write-ups* —John O'Hara/ *The papers gave his book a good write-up*

wrong *adj* Dubious and suspect; illegal; criminal: *You're guilty the second that spotlight hits you 'cause you're a wrong guy*—Nelson Algren

See GO WRONG, IN THE WRONG, IN WRONG

wrong gee *n phr esp underworld* A man who cannot be trusted; a devious and corrupt man

wrong number 1 *n phr* A mistaken notion; an erroneous concept **2** *n phr* = WRONGO

wrongo 1 *n* A wicked or criminal person; a villain **2** *n* An undesirable person; a person of the wrong sort: *a "closet for wrongos" on the second floor that "looks like an attic decorated by a cross-eyed paper hanger in a hurry"*—Playboy **3** *n* Something wrong or improper; an error, lie, mis-statement, etc: *They haven't hit me with a wrongo*

yet, *although they did miss a whopper this morning* —Paul Sann **4** *adj* Prone to error; inept: *an almost endearingly wrong-o, sloppily managed outfit*—Washington Post

wrong side of the bed *See* GOT UP ON THE WRONG SIDE OF THE BED

the wrong side of the tracks *adv phr* A socially and economically inferior neighborhood; the slums: *He did very well for a boy from the wrong side of the tracks/ I was born on the wrong side of the tracks* [fr the fact that poor and industrial areas were often located on one side of the railroad tracks, partly because prevailing wind patterns would carry smoke into them and away from the better-off neighborhoods]

the wrong way *See* RUB someone THE WRONG WAY

wrote *See* THAT'S ALL SHE WROTE

wussy or **wuss** (Wŏŏ see) *n teenagers* A weak person; = PUSSYCAT, WIMP: *"Wussy" was a particularly expressive word...the handy combination of wimp and pussy*—Cameron Crowe [perhaps a shortening of hypothetical *pussy-wussy*]

X

X *n* A person's signature: *Just put your X on this and we're in business* [fr the custom of an illiterate person to make an *X* in place of a written signature]

X-double-minus *adj* Very much inferior; wretched

X marks the spot *sentence* This is the place; here is the exact location: *I pointed to the map and told her "X marks the spot"* [fr the graphic convention of designating a precise location on a picture, map, etc, with an *X*]

x out 1 *v phr* To delete something from a written text, esp by covering it with xs **2** *v phr* To annul or cancel something

X-rated *adj* Lewd; obscene; pornographic; =BLUE, DIRTY: *He uttered a few well-chosen X-rated words* [fr the system of rating movies according to the amount of sex, verbal obscenity, violence, etc, they contain, *X* being the most censorious rating]

XX (duh bəl EKS) *n* A betrayal; =DOUBLE CROSS: *I know you gave me the XX*—John O'Hara

Y

-y *See* -IE

the **Y** *n phr* One of the recreational, social and athletic organizations or facilities for young persons, such as the YMCA, the YMHA, the YWCA, etc: *He lives in a room at the Y*

yak (Variations: **yack** or **yack-yack** or **yack-yack-yack** or **yackety-yack** or **yackety-yak** or **yak-yak** or **yak-yak-yak** or **yakitty-yack** or **yakkity-yak** or **yock** or **yock-yock** or **yock-yock-yock** or **yok** or **yok-yok** or **yok-yok-yok** or **yuck** or **yuck-yuck** or **yuck-yuck-yuck** or **yuk** or **yuk-yuk** or **yuk-yuk-yuk**) **1** *n* Talk, esp idle or empty chatter; mere babbling: *All they can talk about...yack-yack-yack is their own specialty*—Associated Press/ *I don't care how owlish you look, how convincing you sound, this is just yak yak yak until you do it*—John McPhee/ *in the midst of all the political yuk-yuk that dins around us*—New York Times/ *if the State Department would stop its incessant yakitty-yak*—Associated Press **2** *v* (Variations: **yack it up** or **yak it up** or **yock it up** or **yuk it up**): *Everybody is yakking out an opinion on whether he should now reconsider his candidacy*—Life/ *sparing the rod and yak-yakking and explaining all the time*—Associated Press/ *The students were seated on the floor, still yocking away*—Max Shulman/ *I'll be 75 and hanging around bars yocking it up*—Newsweek **3** *n* A laugh; a guffaw: *"Take off your clothes." Pause for audience yuks*—Judith Crist/ *It makes me furious when I have a corny line and it gets a yock*—New York Times **4** *v* (Variations: **yack it up** or **yak it up** or **yock it up** or **yuk it up**): *Ken Gaul is yukking, tugging at his pointy satyr's beard*—Changes/ *There'd be Don, yockin' it up like crazy...he's so hysterical with laughter*—Arthur Kober/ *former senator George McGovern, yukking it up with...Paul Volcker*—Washington Post [echoic]

yakky *adj* Talkative; garrulous; noisy

Yale *See* JOE YALE

yammer **1** *v* To talk loudly; = YAK: *They were yammering away about taxes* **2** *n*: *He kept up his tedious yammer* **3** *v* To complain; whine and nag; = BITCH: *They are always yammering about mere details* [fr German *Jammer* "lamentation, misery"]

yang *n* The penis; = JANG, WANG: *A macho... machine...a celebration of the yang, bang...whang*—Penthouse

See YING-YANG

yank *v* To victimize or harass; dupe; mislead: *The detective uses expressions like "You gotta be yankin' me"*—Washington Post [an alteration and shortening of *yank someone's chain* or *jerk someone around* or *jack someone around*]

Yank **1** *n* *fr middle 1800s* A US citizen; an American: *inquiring after the "Yank" and swearing to have his life*—Life **2** *n* *fr WW1 British* A US soldier: *Some Tommies resented the Yanks for being overpaid* [a shortening fr *Yankee* for both senses]

yank someone's **chain** *See* JERK someone's CHAIN

yantsy *adj* Excited; nervous; aroused; = ANTSY [probably an alteration of *antsy*]

yap¹ **1** *n* *fr late 1800s* A stupid person; a half-wit; = BOOB: *just a no-account yap*—WR Burnett **2** *n* hoboes *fr late 1800s* A rural person; = HICK, YOKEL **3** *n* underworld *fr early 1900s* A criminal's victim; = MARK, PATSY [probably fr British dialect, "half-wit"]

yap² **1** *n* *fr late 1800s* The mouth; = BAZOO: *every time you open your yap to say something*—Jerome Weidman **2** *v* To talk, esp idly or naggingly; = YAMMER: *You've been yapping away*—Jerome Weidman/ *come home with a little jag on, yapping in a phony cheerful way*—Harper's [probably echoic, and similar to the sense "yelp," esp as a small dog does]

See BLOW OFF one's MOUTH, OPEN one's YAP

YAP (pronounced as separate letters) *n* A young person in one of the learned and well-paid professions [fr *Young American Professional*]

Yarborough *n* cardplayers A hand in bridge or whist containing no card higher than a nine [fr the Earl of *Yarborough*, late-19th-century British sportsman, who is said to have offered a standing bet of 1000 to 1 that it would not occur in any game he played in]

yard¹ *n* *fr early 1900s* hawkers A hundred dollars; a $100 bill: *How much? Five yards. He wanted a grand at first*—Philip Dunning & George Abbott/ *"Mac, what you payin' for this?" Stony looked around the room. "A yard and a half"*—Richard Price [fr the unit of measure]

See GO THE FULL YARD, HALF A YARD

yard² *v* *fr black* To be sexually unfaithful; = CHEAT: *She told him she didn't like to yard on her man*

479

—Clarence L Cooper [said to be fr the phrase *backyard woman* "mistress, illicit sex partner"]
See the BACK YARD

yard ape *See* RUG APE

yardbird 1 *n* A convict **2** *n* armed forces A recruit; a basic trainee **3** *n* armed forces A soldier who because of ineptitude or misdemeanor is confined to a certain area, and often ordered to keep it clean and neat [fr the fact that convicts exercise in the *yard* of the prison, and that neophyte soldiers are confined to the grounds of the training post during their first weeks; the basic metaphor is probably based on the behavior of urban pigeons]

yard bull 1 *n phr* A railroad police officer, guard, or detective **2** *n phr* (also **yard hack**) A prison guard; = SCREW

yard goat or **yardpig** *n phr* or *n* railroad A switching engine: *a short, heavy work train, with what they called a yardpig for an engine*—Stephen Longstreet

yard goose *n phr* railroad A railroad switch operator

yard patrol prison **1** *n phr* The convicts in a prison or jail **2** *n phr* The guards at a prison or jail

yards *See* the WHOLE NINE YARDS

yatata (YA tə tə) **1** *n* Talk, esp idle talk and chatter; = YAK **2** *v*: *mustn't yatata yatata yatata in the public library*—William Saroyan [echoic]

yatter *n* Talk, esp loud talk; chatter; = YAK, YAMMER: *the yatter against a military man in the White House*—Time [echoic, and perhaps also a blend of *yak* and *chatter*]

yawn *See* TECHNICOLOR YAWN

yea (YAY) **1** *adv* fr 1950s & esp black To this extent; this; so ● A sort of demonstrative adverb used with adjectives of size, height, extent, etc, and often accompanied by a hand gesture indicating size: *Dorsey almost did him in yea years ago*—WT Tyler/ *The thing was about yea big and sort of green*/ *I'd say the fence is about yea high* **2** *interj* An expression of support, accolade, triumph, encouragement, etc; harrah: *Yea for our side!/ Yea, hurray, we made it!* [first sense perhaps fr *yea* "yes," specialized fr an earlier sense "even, truly, verily" to something like "even so, truly so, verily so"; second sense probably a vehement affirmation, conveniently rhyming with *hurray*!]

yeah (YE, YE ə) *affirmation* Yes; certainly; right: *Don't say "yeah." It's common*—Raymond Chandler
See OH YEAH

year *n* fr underworld One dollar; a dollar bill
See OUT YEAR

yearling *n* West Point A second-year cadet; a sophomore: *His femme fell for a yearling*—Collier's

yecch or **yech** *See* YUCK

yegg *n* fr underworld fr late 1800s hoboes A thief or burglar, esp an itinerant thief or safecracker [origin unknown; said to be fr the name of John *Yegg*, an early hobo safecracker; perhaps fr German *Jäger* "huntsman," applied to a safecracker's advance scouts, but originally *yeggman*]

yell one's **head off** *v phr* To complain loudly and persistently; express oneself forcefully

yellow 1 *adj* fr middle 1800s Cowardly; fainthearted; = CHICKEN: *Don't get into this race if you're yellow* **2** *n* Cowardice; poltroonery; excessive timidity ● Most often in the expression "yellow streak" or "streak of yellow": *I'm afraid he has a streak of yellow in him* ◀**3**▶ *adj* fr early 1800s Having light skin for a black person: *You know that baker we hired. The yellow boy*—Calder Willingham [the origin of the coward sense is unknown; perhaps it is derived fr the traditional symbolic meanings of *yellow*, among which were "deceitfulness, treachery, degradation, the light of hell"]
See HIGH YELLOW

yellow-bellied *adj* fr early 1900s Cowardly; = YELLOW: *you yellow-bellied jerk*—Joseph Mitchell

yellow-belly *n* A coward; a poltroon: *He is a contemptible yellow-belly, scared of his own shadow* [probably a rhyming expansion of *yellow*; influenced by the early-19th-century sense, "a Mexican, esp a Mexican soldier," perhaps fr the color of their uniforms]

yellow dog contract *n phr* labor union fr early 1900s An employee's work contract that forbids membership in a union [*yellow dog* was a common term for a contemptible person or thing fr the early 19th century]

◀**yellowfish**▶ *n* esp Pacific Coast An illegal Chinese immigrant: *a thoughtful man for whom yellowfish begin as a commodity to be hauled for pay and end as tragic figures*—Time

yellow jacket *n phr* narcotics A capsule of Nembutal (a trade name), a barbiturate narcotic

yellow sunshine *n phr* narcotics LSD; = ACID

yelper *n* The screaming and wavering warning signal used on police cars, ambulances, and other emergency vehicles: *two police cars going north...with yelpers wide open*—John Farris

yen 1 *n* fr early 1900s West Coast & hoboes A strong craving; a keen desire; a passion: *He's got a yen for faro*—WR Burnett/ *a yen to put on paper what I was saying in class*—AAUP Bulletin **2** *v*: *I yenned to own a Rolls Royce*—Billy Rose [fr a Peking dialect Chinese word, "smoke," hence opium, perhaps reinforced by *yearn*]
See PEN YEN

yenems (YE nəmz) Someone else's property, cigarettes, liquor, etc: *What's my favorite smoke? Yenems* [fr Yiddish, "those, that one's, hence, not my own"]

yen-shee *n* narcotics Opium

yenta (YEN tə) *n* A garrulous and gossipy person, usu a woman; = BLABBERMOUTH: *Terrible Tom and Rampaging Rona stopped talking to each other, which is something small-screen yentas should never do*—Us/ *The people in Washington think we're a bunch of screaming yentas here*—New York [fr a Jewish woman's given name perhaps derived fr Italian *Gentile* or French *Gentille*, degraded by its association with a humorous character *Yente*

Telebende in a regular column of the New York Yiddish newspaper the *Jewish Daily Forward*]

yep *affirmation fr early 1800s* Yes; certainly; sure; = YEAH [the *p* is produced by closing the mouth to finish the pronunciation of *yeah*, and thereby producing the voiceless bilabial stop; see *nope*]

yesca *n narcotics* Marijuana; = POT

yes-man *n fr early 1900s* An obsequious and flattering subordinate; = ASS-KISSER: *Joe Davies, Roosevelt's yes-man at the Kremlin*—Westbrook Pegler/ *This president doesn't want yes-men* —Joseph Heller [said to have appeared first in a 1913 drawing by the sports cartoonist TA Dorgan, showing a group of newspaper assistants, each labeled *yes-man*, all firmly agreeing with their chief]

◀**Yid** or **yid**▶ (YID) *n* A Jew ● Not felt to be offensive if pronounced (YEED) by Jews themselves: *Some boy was not admitted to a secret society...because he was a "Yid"*—Stephen Longstreet [fr Yiddish, ultimately fr Hebrew *Yehuda* "Judea"]

ying-yang or **yin-yang** **1** *n* The anus; = ASS, ASSHOLE, WHERE THE SUN DOESN'T SHINE: *A motherjumper of a winter. Snow up the yin-yang*—George V Higgins **2** *n* The penis; = PRICK: *a peek at one of my troopers with tubes up his ying-yang*—Richard Merkin **3** *n Army* A stupid or foolish person [perhaps coined because of the increasing currency of the Chinese term *yin and yang* "the female and male principles in nature," influenced by *wang* "penis"]

yip *v fr early 1900s* To talk in an insistent, petulant, and annoying way: *Will you please stop yipping about your rights?* [echoic of the high-pitched bark of a small dog]

yipe or **yipes** or **yikes** *interj esp teenagers* An exclamation of dismay, alarm, emphatic response, etc: *Yipes, it's a rattlesnake!/ Yipe, that hurt!* [probably fr the spontaneous interjection *yi*, a cry of pain or dismay, with the *p* or *k* stop intruding after lip closure, as it does in *nope* and *yep*]

yippee (yip EE) *interj* An exclamation of pleasure, approval, triumph, etc: *Yippee, all my candidates won!*

yippie *n esp late 1960s* A member of the Youth International Party, a left-wing group espousing values of the counterculture movement of the 1960s and early 70s [fr the acronym of the name of the group, reinforced by the rhyme with *hippie*]

yock *See* HON-YOCK, YAK

yok *See* YAK

yoke *v middle Atlantic Coast fr early 1900s* To rob with violence; rob and mutilate; = MUG: *They decided to "yoke" the old man with the hearing aid* —New York Post [said to be fr the seizing of the *yoke* of a sailor's collar from behind in order to subdue and rob him]

yokel *n fr British dialect* A rural person; a bumpkin; = HAYSEED, HICK [perhaps fr a dialect name for a woodpecker, hence semantically similar to British dialect *gowk* "cuckoo, simpleton"] *See* LOCAL YOKEL

yoker *n* A person who yokes: *In Washington, muggers are called "yokers"*—New York Post

yold *n* An easy victim; = SUCKER, PATSY: *Yold, which rhymes with cold...means a chump*—New York Daily News [fr Yiddish "simpleton, fool," fr Hebrew *yeled* "boy"]

yonder *See* DOWN YONDER

you *See* SAYS YOU

you bet (or **betcha**) *affirmation fr middle 1800s Southwest* Yes; certainly; surely; = BET YOUR BOOTS: *You bet I'll be there!/ Am I happy? You betcha!* [*betcha* form fr *you bet you* or *you bet your life*]

you (or **you'd**) **better believe** something *sentence fr middle 1800s* Something is absolutely certain; something is assured; you are absolutely right: *Am I ready to fight? You better believe it/ You'd better believe she's the best*

you can say that again *sentence* That is absolutely right; I totally agree with you

you can't fight city hall *sentence* It is futile to pit yourself against the political or other chiefs and their establishment; it is foolish to take on a battle you cannot possibly win

you can't get there from here **1** *sentence* The place referred to is very remote and the route hard to describe **2** *sentence* The problem described is insoluble

you can't make an omelet without breaking eggs *sentence* One must sometimes do evil or cause damage and inconvenience to accomplish good; the end justifies the means [attributed to VI Lenin, the Russian Bolshevik leader]

you can't win 'em all *sentence* One cannot always be successful; = WIN A FEW LOSE A FEW ● Often said ruefully after one has failed, or comfortingly to someone else who has failed

you go *See* THERE YOU GO

you-know-what *n* Something one does not wish to name, usu because it is both obvious and indelicate or taboo; = WHATSIS: *They were knocked on their you-know-what/ So he and she had a pleasant bout of you-know-what*

you name it *sentence* You cannot designate anything not included here; = the WHOLE SCHMEAR: *She got looks, talent, ontological authenticity, you name it* [fr the retailing locution *you name it, we got it*]

youngblood *n* A young black man; = BLOOD, BROTHER: *youngbloods from Bed-Stuy looking for a reputation*—Village Voice

young squirt *See* SQUIRT

youngster *n Annapolis* A second-year naval officer trainee

Young Turk *n phr* A person, usu a young one, who threatens to overthrow an established system or order; an active rebel or reformer: *He scrutinizes the new staff very carefully, and is dreadfully fearful of potential Young Turks* [originally, a member of *Young Turkey*, a revolutionary party of late-19th-century Turkey which finally established constitutional government in 1908]

your ear *See* PUT IT IN YOUR EAR

you're damn (or **darn**) **tootin'** *affirmation* That is emphatically true; you are absolutely right: *Did I run? You're damn tootin' I did*

you're on drugs or **you must be high** *sentence* *teenagers* You are crazy

yours truly *pron phr fr middle 1800s* I; me; myself; = YOUR UNCLE DUDLEY: *If nobody else wants that, just ask yours truly* [fr the conventional parting salutation of a letter]

your Uncle Dudley *n phr* Oneself; I or me; = YOURS TRULY: *If you want to know about that, just ask your uncle Dudley*

you said it *affirmation* You are absolutely right; that is correct

you scratch my back, I scratch yours *sentence* Let us cooperate; let us be reciprocally and mutually helpful: *I'd love the whole country to get a good gander at how a labor union's supposed to run! You scratch my back, I'll scratch yours!*—Hannibal & Boris

yo-yo 1 *n* A vacillating person; one who has no firm convictions: *Feldstein's sudden turnaround...makes the president look like a yo-yo*—Newsweek **2** *n fr teenagers* A stupid and obnoxious person; = JERK, NERD: *Some yo-yo yells "What happened, you bum..."*—Inside Sports

yuck (also **ech** or **yecch** or **yech**) **1** *interj* An exclamation of disgust: *"Those women on the PBS specials seem to love it." "Yuck,"* Connie mugged—Armistead Maupin/ *Then there is this little item entitled YECH*—Village Voice **2** *n* A disgusting substance, person, or thing; someone or something nasty: *precipitation in the form of rain, snow, and assorted other atmospheric yuck*—Washington Post/ *clean all the yecch out of her system*—Cyra McFadden/ *Mario is an intellectually dishonest person. He's just yecch*—New York [perhaps echoic of gagging or vomiting]
See YAK

Yucko City *adj phr* Disgusting; nasty; = YUCKY: *Have you ever tried any popular American beer warm?...Yucko City*—Illinois Times

yucky or **yecchy** *adj* Disgusting, esp in a filthy and viscous way; thoroughly nasty: *Some of it is awful yucky*—Philadelphia Daily News/ *What's that yucky blob on your collar?/ He looked at me like I was something yecchy*

yuk *See* YAK

yummy *adj* Pleasant, esp sensually; delicious; delightful: *What a yummy cake!/ a yummy prospect*

Yumpie *n* = YUPPIE: *the highly desirable "Yumpies," young, upwardly mobile professionals*—Washingtonian [fr *young upwardly mobile professional*]

yum-yum 1 *interj fr late 1800s* An exclamation of pleasure, esp of sensual delight **2** *n* Something sweet or pleasant, esp to eat [perhaps fr a locution used with children, hence contextually as well as phonetically related to *tummy* or *tum-tum*]

yup *affirmation fr early 1900s* = YEP

Yuppie *n* (also **Yup**) An affluent, usu city-dwelling, professional in his or her 20s and 30s; a prosperous and ambitious young professional: *Yuppies are dedicated to the twin goals of making piles of money and achieving perfection through physical fitness and therapy*—Time/ *The narrow dance floor is soon crammed with "Yuppies," young urban professionals taking time out from social climbing*—Washingtonian/ *The Yups discover that the locals have been putting up with this...for years*—Philadelphia [fr *young urban professional*, and modeled on *yippie*; perhaps coined for a 1983 book called *The Yuppie Handbook*, which was modeled on the earlier book *The Official Preppy Handbook*]

Z

Z¹ *See* FROM A TO Z

Z² or **Zee** **1** *v* *teenagers* To sleep; snooze; =COP ZS: *Gotta Z a little while* **2** *n* Some sleep; a nap: *If he wants a few zees we can go on automatic*—Robert Stone [fr the conventional sibilant or buzzing sound attributed to a sleeping person]

Z³ *n narcotics* An ounce of a narcotic: *trips to the rundown neighborhood to purchase Zs (ounces) and even Ks (kilograms) of cocaine*—New York Times [fr the conventional abbreviation of *ounces* "oz"]

za (ZAH) *n teenagers* Pizza [a shortening of *pizza*]

zaftig *See* ZOFTIG

zap **1** *v fr underworld, street gang & Vietnam War armed forces* To kill or disable; strike violently; =CLOBBER, WASTE: *Sitcom Zaps Boardroom Bozos*—Time **2** *v hospital* To administer electroshock therapy **3** *interj* An exclamation imitating sudden impact; =WHAM: *It's a gradual thing. It ain't zap, you're healed*—Philadelphia Journal **4** *n* Vitality; force; =PIZZAZZ, ZIP [fr the echoic word used to convey the sound of a ray gun in the comic strip "Buck Rogers in the Twenty-Fifth Century"]

zappy *adj* Having force, impact, energy, etc; =PUNCHY, ZINGY: *black outlines, comicbook blonde, and zappy words*—Village Voice

zazz *modifier* Having to do with the world of high or jaunty fashion: *everything very haut couture, of course, the whole zazz world*—Ray Smith [perhaps fr unattested *zazzy* fr *jazzy* influenced by *pizzazz*]

zazz something **up** *v phr* To make more decorative and impressive; =GUSSY UP, JAZZ UP: *relied heavily on somewhat musty shadings, zazzing them up, however, with bursts of dusty mauve*—Cosmopolitan [perhaps fr *jazz* something *up*, influenced by *pizzazz*]

zebra **1** *n sports* A referee or other sports official, who wears a striped shirt on the playing field: *Pro football zebras point immediately toward the offending team*—New York Daily News/ *a crooked Zebra (also known as an umpire)*—Washington Post **2** *n hospital* An unlikely, arcane, or obscure diagnosis [the medical sense is fr the saying "If you hear horse's hoofbeats going by outside, don't look for zebras"]

Zelda *n teenagers fr 1950s cool talk* An uninteresting woman; a female square: *If you don't know the girl's name, she's a Zelda*—Philadelphia Inquirer

zerking *adj teenagers* Behaving in a strange way; =GOOFY, WACKY

zero cool *adj phr college students fr cool talk* Extremely aware, alert, up-to-date, relaxed, etc; =COOL [probably fr the concept of *absolute zero*]

zero hour *n phr fr WW1 armed forces* The exact time appointed for some event, such as an attack, an embarkation, etc [fr the last unit of a countdown, when the hours of preparation for the event have passed]

zero in *v phr* To aim at or concentrate on a specific person, thing, etc; single out: *We're trying to zero in on the problem* [fr the *zeroing* of the sights of a rifle, that is, adjusting the sights so that the round hits the exact point aimed at and the shooter needs to make no, or *zero*, estimated correction in aiming]

zetz *n* A blow; a punch: *I'd love to give that guy such a zetz*—National Lampoon/ *Although Mifune gives the proceedings a zetz, everyone else seems tired*—Village Voice [fr Yiddish, related to German *Zurücksetzung* "a setting back"]

zhlub *n* (also **schlub** or **shlub** or **shlubbo** or **zhlob** or **zshlub**) A coarse person; a boorish man; =JERK, SLOB: *the presence of fine wines and the absence of shlubs*—Philadelphia/ *replied Angela as she glided off to cut the poor schlub out of her will*—Newsweek/ *Lieberman was the worst. Lieberman was a real zshlub*—Joseph Heller [fr Yiddish fr Slavic, "coarse fellow"]

zhlubby *adj* Having the qualities of a zhlub; coarse; boorish: *booze station for the zhlubby middle-aged boat owners from the other side*—New York

◄ **zig** or **zigabo** or **zigaboo** ► *See* JIGABOO

ziggety *See* HOT DIGGETY

zig-zig *See* JIG-JIG

zilch **1** *n fr late 1960s* Nothing; zero; =ZIP: *The city...has turned its smaller islands into zilch*—New York/ *got the jeep for practically zilch*—George V Higgins **2** *modifier*: *York has close to zilch industry*—Toronto Life **3** *n esp teenagers* =STORCH **4** *n teenagers* A minor skin lesion; =ZIT [probably fr *zero*, and like *zip¹*, primarily a variant coined from a familiar word beginning with z; notice, in this regard, how *zilch* has become a variant of *zit*; in British use, but not US, *zilch* might be reinforced by *nil* "zero"; all senses may derive fr the early-20th-century US college use *Joe Zilsch* "any insignificant person," popularized during the 1930s by ubiquitous use in the humor magazine

Ballyhoo with the spelling *Zilch,* an actual German surname of Slavic origin; see *Joe Blow[1]*; Eric Partridge's suggestion that *zilch* is a three-element blend of *zero* with *nil* and Yiddish *nich* is extremely unlikely and unnecessary]

See JOE BLOW, NOT KNOW BEANS

zillion *See* JILLION

zillionaire *n* An enormously rich person; a supertycoon: *and Larry Dunlap will become an instant zillionaire*—Village Voice/ *his earlier piece about how the Hong Kong zillionaires are buying up San Francisco*—San Francisco

-zine (ZEEN) *suffix used to form nouns* Magazine: *teenzine/ fanzine*

zing 1 *n fr early 1900s* Energetic vitality; power; vigor; =OOMPH, PEP, PIZZAZZ, ZIP: *Rock...adds zing*—Toronto Star/ *with plenty of zing in both the...V-8 engine and the powerful Six*—Philadelphia Bulletin **2** *v* also **zing along** To move rapidly and strongly; =ZIP: *The movie zings right along*—Playboy **3** *v* To throw; inject, esp rapidly and strongly: *like the Beatles every once in a while can zing it in there*—Rolling Stone **4** *v* To insult; assault verbally, esp with bitter humor: *King Caen, who zings everyone, gets a taste of his own medicine*—California/ *A woman on the editorial board merrily zinged the winking minister*—Village Voice [probably echoic of the whishing sound of rapid movement, like *zip* and *zoom*]

zinger 1 *n* A quip, esp one that is somewhat cruel and aggressive; a funny crack or punch line: *Watt's off-the-cuff zingers have been a frequent source of pain for the Reagan Administration*—Time/ *The plump little actor is polished and funny; his zingers stay zung*—Washington Post **2** *n* A quick and sharp response; a sturdy retort: *get right in there with Williams, stand eyeball to eyeball, and plant the zinger on him, bang, or else you would be dismissed*—Harper's

zingy *adj* Full of energy and vigor; =PEPPY, ZIPPY: *written by no less than the zingy Nora Ephron*—Philadelphia/ *Zingy Zeroes, Wall Street's hot bonds*—Time

zip[1] or **zippo 1** *n students fr late 1800s* A mark or grade of zero **2** *n* Zero; nothing; a score of zero; =ZILCH: *The Tigers won 12-zip/ People aren't exactly beating down the doors to buy California port. "The market...is zip, zero, and not too much"*—San Francisco/ *dipped into your moneybag and found zippo*—Washington Post [like *zilch,* probably coined from a familiar word beginning with z; see *zilch*]

See NOT GIVE A DAMN, NOT KNOW BEANS

zip[2] or **zippo** *n fr early 1900s* Energy; vitality; vim; =PIZZAZZ, ZING: *There is a zip and a zing here*—NY Confidential/ *bounced back with the real zippo*—Joseph Wambaugh [echoic of the sound of something swishing rapidly through the air, giving an impression of force, and also of the tearing of cloth; such a use is attested fr 1875]

◀**zip[3]**▶ *n Vietnam War* A Vietnamese; =DINK [said to be fr *zero intelligence*]

zip gun *n phr esp 1950s street gang* A homemade pistol: *a zip gun, the kind kids make themselves*—Pageant

zip one's lip (or **one's mouth**) *v phr* To stop talking, esp abruptly and completely; =SHUT UP: *She ordered me to zip my lip/ I just had to zip my mouth and do what I could*—Toronto Life [fr the notion that one has a *zipper* fastener *on one's mouth*]

zippo *v Army* To set something on fire; ignite something [fr *Zippo,* trade name of a cigarette lighter, probably fr the sound made as one turns the sparking wheel, and the speed with which the lighter ignites]

zippy *adj fr early 1900s* Energetic; =PEPPY, ZINGY [fr *zip[2]*]

zit *esp teenagers* **1** *n* A minor skin lesion; a pimple; a blackhead: *First Arnie's zits mysteriously clear up*—Newsweek **2** *n* A mark left by a love-bite, a strong kiss, etc; =HICKEY: *She tried to conceal the big zit on her neck* [origin unknown; perhaps echoic of the squishy pop made when the pus is squeezed from a blackhead]

zit doctor *n phr* A dermatologist

zits *See* TITS-AND-ZITS

zitsflaish *n* Patience; the ability to be inactive
● Often in the negative: *She's got no zitsflaish* [fr Yiddish, literally, "flesh that is sat upon, buttocks"]

zizz 1 *v fr 1920s British armed forces* To sleep; snooze; nap; =COP ZS: **2** *n: She stretched out for a short zizz* [echoic of the sibilance or buzzing of one who sleeps, hence semantically akin to the notion of *sawing wood*]

zizzy[1] *n fr WW2 armed forces fr British* A sleep; a nap; a snooze [fr *zizz*]

zizzy[2] *adj* Showy and frivolous; light; frothy [perhaps a thinning of *zazzy*; perhaps an alteration of *fizzy*]

zod 1 *n teenagers* An eccentric and obnoxious person; =CREEP, NERD **2** *adj: Yuck, what a weird and zod idea* [origin unknown; perhaps related to the alligator represented on *Izod* (a trade name) apparel]

zoftig or **zaftig** (ZAWF tik,ZAHF-) *adj* Sexually appealing or arousing to males, esp in a plump and well-rounded way; curvaceous; =BUILT LIKE A BRICK SHITHOUSE: *zoftig...pleasantly plump and pretty*—New York Daily News/ *Parton's film debut...was clearly just a warm-up for this zaftig after-hours diversion*—People Weekly [fr Yiddish, literally "juicy"]

zoid *n* A nonconforming person; a misfit: *Andie doesn't "fit in," she's an outsider, a "zoid"*—Washington Post

zombie (ZAHM bee) **1** *n fr 1930s students* A very strange person, esp one with a vacant corpselike manner; =WEIRDO **2** *n* An unresponsive person; a mentally numb or dead person: *My students are all zombies this term* [origin uncertain; perhaps fr an African word akin to *nzambi* "god"; perhaps fr Louisiana Creole, "phantom, ghost," fr Spanish *sombra* "shade, ghost"; popularized by horror stories and movies featuring the walking dead persons of voodoo belief]

zone[1] *See* IN A ZONE, OZONE

zone[2] or **zoner** *n narcotics* A person intoxicated with narcotics, esp habitually so; =SPACE CADET [fr *ozone* "a very high level of the atmosphere"]

zoned or **zoned out** *adj* or *adj phr* Intoxicated with narcotics; =HIGH [fr *zone*; influenced by *spaced out*]

zone something **out** or **zone out** *v phr* To omit from consciousness; shut out of the mind: *I can just zone everything out and keep going*—New York Sunday News/ *If she'd just zone out for a while, we could plan her surprise party*

zonk or **zonk out 1** *v* or *v phr* To lose consciousness, esp from alcohol or narcotics; fall asleep; become stuporous: *He suddenly zonked and went rigid* **2** *v* or *v phr* To strike a stupefying blow; =CLOBBER: *"We've been zonked," said Jim Robbins, head of the huge sportswear manufacturing business called Crazy Horse...shut out since Wednesday morning*—Washington Post [fr *zonked*]

zonked or **zonked out** or **zonkers 1** *adj* or *adj phr* *students & narcotics* Intoxicated by narcotics or alcohol; =HIGH, STONED: *zonked, one step past being stoned*—E Horne/ *I guess you weren't as zonked as I thought*—Easyriders **2** *adj* or *adj phr* Very enthusiastic; excited; =HIGH: *Rene Carpenter remembers Gilruth as "a kindly, wonderful man who was zonked on this project"*—Washingtonian [probably echoic, like *bonk*, of a dull and stupefying blow; the variant *zonkers* is like the phonetically and semantically similar *bonkers*, from which it probably derives; see *bonkers*]

zoo *n railroad* The caboose of a freight train

zoo daddy *n phr* A divorced or separated father who sees his children rarely; =DISNEYLAND DADDY

zooey *adj* Like a zoo; nasty; barbaric: *It's been zooey down here...it's been hectic*—Philadelphia Daily News

zoom *v esp black fr 1940s* To get something without paying for it, esp to go somewhere without paying admission

zoom buggy *n phr outdated teenagers* A car, esp a fast one

zoom someone **out** *v phr black* To impress strongly; overwhelm; =BLOW someone's MIND

zoomy *adj* Fast and stylish; high-flying; showy and flaunting: *and it isn't just a matter of zoomy looks, either*—Car and Driver/ *jet-setters, sort of really zoomy people*—George V Higgins [fr *zoom* "fly up spectacularly"]

zoot suit *n phr esp 1930s & 40s* A man's suit with a jacket having very wide lapels, heavily padded shoulders, and many-buttoned sleeves, with very high-waisted trousers full in the leg and tapering to narrow cuffs ● Such garments were worn as symbols of status and defiance, esp by urban black hipsters and Los Angeles Chicanos: *Some were garbed in short sleeve shirts, others in zoot suits*—Associated Press/ *Jelly got into his zoot suit with the reet pleats*—Zora Neale Hurston [origin unknown; probably in essence a rhyming phrase of the sort common in black English and slang; perhaps related to other jive and cool talk terms like *vootie*]

zoot suiter *n phr esp 1930s & 40s* A man, esp a young black hipster or a Chicano, who wears a zoot suit and/or exemplifies the values symbolized by such a garment

zot or **zotz** *n esp students* Nothing; zero; =ZILCH, ZIP: *Zero. Nothing. Absolutely zotz*—Psychology Today [like *zip* and *zilch* based mainly on the initial *z* suggesting *zero*; perhaps influenced by *squat* in the same sense]

zowie 1 *interj* An exclamation imitating sudden impact; =POW, WHAM: *I ducked, but zowie, it caught me on the nose* **2** *n* Energy; vitality; vim; =ZING, ZIP: *full of zing, full of zest, full of zowie*—Mad Wednesday (movie)

some Zs *n phr* Sleep; =SHUT-EYE: *He was bleary and needed some Zs* [fr the traditional likening of snoring with sawing wood, and its representation in comic strips by a series of *Zs*]

See COP ZS

zshlub *See* ZHLUB

zuch (Z⊙CH) *n underworld* An informer; =STOOL PIGEON [perhaps related to 18th-century British underworld *zouch* or *sycher* "despicable person," which is perhaps fr Devonshire dialect *sich* "bad man"]